Tort Law Desk Reference

2002 Edition

TORT LAW DESK REFERENCE
A Fifty-State Compendium

2002 Edition

MORTON F. DALLER

Editor-in-Chief

ASPEN LAW & BUSINESS
A Division of Aspen Publishers, Inc.
New York   Gaithersburg

This publication is designed to provide accurate and authoritative information in regard to the subject matter covered. It is sold with the understanding that the publisher is not engaged in rendering legal, accounting, or other professional services. If legal advice or other professional assistance is required, the services of a competent professional person should be sought.

> —From a *Declaration of Principles* jointly adopted by a Committee of the American Bar Association and a Committee of Publishers and Associations

Copyright © 2002 by Aspen Law & Business
A Division of Aspen Publishers, Inc.
A Wolters Kluwer Company
www.aspenpublishers.com

All rights reserved. No part of this publication may be reproduced or transmitted in any form or by any means, electronic or mechanical, including photocopying, recording, or any information storage and retrieval system, without permission in writing from the publisher. Requests for permission to make copies of any part of the work should be mailed to:

> Permissions
> Aspen Law & Business
> 1185 Avenue of the Americas
> New York, NY 10036

Printed in the United States of America

1 2 3 4 5 6 7 8 9 0

ISBN 0-7355-2947-7

ISSN 1529-2525

About Aspen Law & Business

Aspen Law & Business is a leading publisher of authoritative treatises, practice manuals, services, and journals for attorneys, corporate and bank directors, accountants, auditors, environmental compliance professionals, financial and tax advisors, and other business professionals. Our mission is to provide practical solution-based how-to information keyed to the latest original pronouncements, as well as the latest legislative, judicial, and regulatory developments.

We offer publications in the areas of accounting and auditing; antitrust; banking and finance; bankruptcy; business and commercial law; construction law; corporate law; criminal law; environmental compliance; government and administrative law; health law; insurance law; intellectual property; international law; legal practice and litigation; matrimonial and family law; pensions, benefits, and labor; real estate law; securities; and taxation.

Other Aspen Law & Business products treating product liability and tort law include:

Law of Torts
Preparation of a Product Liability Case
Product Liability Case Digest
Product Liability Desk Reference
Psychological Experts in Personal Injury Actions
2002 Expert Witness Update

ASPEN LAW & BUSINESS
A Division of Aspen Publishers, Inc.
A Wolters Kluwer Company
www.aspenpublishers.com

SUBSCRIPTION NOTICE

This Aspen Law & Business product is updated on a periodic basis with supplements to reflect important changes in the subject matter. If you purchased this product directly from Aspen Law & Business, we have already recorded your subscription for the update service.

If, however, you purchased this product from a bookstore and wish to receive future updates and revised or related volumes billed separately with a 30-day examination review, please contact our Customer Service Department at 1-800-234-1660 or send your name, company name (if applicable), address, and the title of the product to:

Aspen Law & Business
A Division of Aspen Publishers, Inc.
7201 McKinney Circle
Frederick, MD 21704

Contents

Introduction ix
Contributing Editors xi

Alabama 1
Alaska 15
Arizona 27
Arkansas 53
California 65
Colorado 83
Connecticut 99
Delaware 115
District of Columbia 127
Florida 145
Georgia 197
Hawaii 209
Idaho 231
Illinois 249
Indiana 265
Iowa 289
Kansas 307
Kentucky 321
Louisiana 335
Maine 347
Maryland 363
Massachusetts 381
Michigan 401
Minnesota 417
Mississippi 445
Missouri 457
Montana 471
Nebraska 501
Nevada 515
New Hampshire 533
New Jersey 543
New Mexico 561
New York 579
North Carolina 599
North Dakota 625
Ohio 639
Oklahoma 657
Oregon 673

Pennsylvania	691
Rhode Island	709
South Carolina	725
South Dakota	737
Tennessee	749
Texas	771
Utah	787
Vermont	801
Virginia	825
Washington	843
West Virginia	861
Wisconsin	881
Wyoming	897

INTRODUCTION

The *Tort Law Desk Reference — A Fifty-State Compendium*, 2002 edition, provides a succinct survey of the tort laws of the 50 states and the District of Columbia. It is designed to serve as a handy initial reference for:

- the corporate in-house counsel or the litigation management professional who is overseeing tort cases in more than one state;

- the in-house professional at the liability, casualty, or property insurance company concerned with claims and litigation management;

- the attorney handling tort cases in more than one state.

This book is designed to complement the *Product Liability Desk Reference*, also published by Aspen Law & Business. With both books available, the user should have ready reference to helpful summaries of the laws pertinent to a great many of the lawsuits or claims that cross his or her desk.

Tort law differs widely from state to state. Statutes of limitation differ. Employer immunity under workers' compensation law differs. The "economic loss" doctrine is applied differently in many states. Premises liability laws differ widely and in Colorado premises liability is governed entirely by statute. The application of joint and several liability differ from state to state. Punitive damages differ widely. Most importantly, many states have passed tort reform statutes and many courts are finding those statutes to be unconstitutional.

Each summary is designed to provide an overview. To be useful each summary must therefore be brief, which is, of course, very difficult. The summaries are not designed as full-scale research tools, but rather as starting points for assessing the merits or pitfalls of litigation in a particular jurisdiction.

On behalf of all the contributing editors, I hope that each user of the *Tort Law Desk Reference—A Fifty-State Compendium* will find the book a useful and practical tool.

Morton F. Daller
Editor-in-Chief
Daller Greenberg & Dietrich, LLP
Valley Green Corporate Center
7111 Valley Green Road
Fort Washington, PA 19034
(215) 836-1100 / (215) 836-2845 (fax)
E-mail: mdaller@dallergreenberg.com

February 2002

CONTRIBUTING EDITORS

ALABAMA

John E. Goodman, Esquire
Bradley Arant Rose & White L.L.P.
2001 Park Place, Suite 1400
Birmingham, Alabama 35203
(205) 521-8000 / (205) 521-8800 (fax)
jgoodman@barw.com
www.barw.com

ALASKA

John B. Thorsness, Esquire
Lisa C. Hamby, Esquire
Hughes Thorsness Powell Huddleston
   & Bauman, L.L.C.
550 West Seventh Avenue, Suite 1100
Anchorage, Alaska 99501-3563
(907) 274-7522 / (907) 263-8320 (fax)
lch@htlaw.com

ARIZONA

Graeme Hancock, Esquire
Thomas D. Ulreich-Power, Esquire
Fennemore Craig
3003 North Central Avenue, Suite 2600
Phoenix, Arizona 85012-2913
(602) 916-5448 / (602) 916-5648 (fax)
ghancock@fclaw.com
tulreich@fclaw.com

ARKANSAS

Patricia A. Sievers Harris, Esquire
Justin T. Allen, Esquire
Wright, Lindsey & Jennings, L.L.P.
200 West Capitol Avenue, Suite 2200
Little Rock, Arkansas 72201-3699
(501) 371-0808 / (501) 376-9442 (fax)
pharris@wlj.com
jallen@wlj.com
www.wlj.com

CALIFORNIA	Arnold D. Larson, Esquire Melissa A. Immel, Esquire Iverson, Yoakum, Papiano & Hatch One Wilshire Building 624 South Grand Avenue, 27th Floor Los Angeles, California 90017-3328 (213) 624-7444 / (213) 629-3358 (fax) mimmel@iyph.com alarson@iyph.com www.iyph.com
COLORADO	John P. Craver, Esquire Todd Clarke, Esquire Franz Hardy, Esquire White & Steele, P.C. 950 Seventeenth Street Suite 2100 Denver, Colorado 80202 (303) 296-2828 / (303) 296-3131 (fax) law@wsteele.com
CONNECTICUT	Philip J. O'Connor, Esquire Gordon, Muir & Foley, L.L.P. Hartford Square North Ten Columbus Boulevard Hartford, Connecticut 06106-5123 (860) 525-5361 / (860) 525-4849 (fax) poconnor@gmflaw.com www.gmflaw.com
DELAWARE	James W. Semple, Esquire Morris, James, Hitchens & Williams, L.L.P. 222 Delaware Avenue, Tenth floor P.O. Box 2306 Wilmington, Delaware 18998-2306 (302) 888-6800 / (302) 571-1750 (fax) jsemple@morrisjames.com www.morrisjames.com
DISTRICT OF COLUMBIA	Robert N. Kelly, Esquire Jackson & Campbell, P.C. 1120 20th Street N.W. Suite 300-South Washington, D.C. 20036 (202) 457-1647 / (202) 457-1678 (fax) rkelly@jackscamp.com www.jackscamp.com

FLORIDA	G. William Bissett, Esquire Hardy & Bissett, P.A. 13205 S.W. 137th Avenue, Suite 127 Miami, Florida 33186 (305) 969-3990 / (305) 969-3558 (fax) hardybissettpa@aol.com
GEORGIA	Alfred B. Adams III, Esquire Donna L. Johnson, Esquire Holland & Knight, L.L.P. 2000 One Atlantic Center 1201 West Peachtree Street, N.E. Atlanta, Georgia 30309-3400 (404) 817-8500 / (404) 881-0470 (fax) aadams@hklaw.com www.hklaw.com
HAWAII	William C. McCorriston, Esquire Darolyn H. Lendio Lisa M. Ginoza McCorriston Miller Mukai MacKinnon Five Waterfront Plaza, Suite 400 500 Ala Moana Boulevard Honolulu, Hawaii 96813 (808) 529-7300 / (808) 524-8293 (fax) mccorriston@m4law.com www.m4law.com
IDAHO	Ronald E. Bush, Esquire Jason D. Scott, Esquire Hawley Troxell Ennis & Hawley L.L.P. 333 South Main Street P.O. Box 100 Pocatello, Idaho 83204-0100 (208) 233-0845 / (208) 233-1304 (fax) reb@hteh.com jds@hteh.com www.hteh.com
ILLINOIS	Frances E. Prell Thomas R. Woodrow Holland & Knight 55 West Monroe Street Suite 800 Chicago, IL 60603 (312) 263-3600 / (312) 578-6666 (fax) fprell@hklaw.com www.hklaw.com

INDIANA

Pamela J. Hermes, Esquire
Gambs Mucker & Bauman
10 North Fourth Street
P.O. Box 1608
Lafayette, Indiana 47902
(765) 423-1001 / (765) 742-4535 (fax)
PamH@gmbslaw.com

IOWA

Brent B. Green, Esquire
Bradley C. Obermeier, Esquire
Duncan, Green, Brown, Langeness & Eckley, P.C.
400 Locust Street, Suite 380
Des Moines, Iowa 50309
(515) 288-6440 / (515) 288-6448 (fax)
bgreen@duncangreenlaw.com
bobermeier@duncangreenlaw.com

KANSAS

Darrell L. Warta, Esquire
Stephen M. Kerwick, Esquire
Foulston & Siefkin, L.L.P
Bank of America Center
100 North Broadway, Suite 700
Wichita, Kansas 67202
(316) 267-6371 / (316) 267-6345 (fax)
skerwick@foulston.com
www.foulston.com

KENTUCKY

Charles M. Pritchett, Jr., Esquire
Steven M. Crawford, Esquire
Frost Brown & Todd, LLC
400 Market Street, 32nd floor
Louisville, Kentucky 40202-3363
(502) 589-5400 / (502) 581-1087 (fax)
cpritchett@ftblaw.com
scrawford@ftblaw.com
www.frostbrowntodd.com

LOUISIANA

William J. Hamlin, Esquire
William C. Ellison, Esquire
Bordelon, Hamlin & Theriot
701 South Peters Street, Suite 100
New Orleans, Louisiana 70130
(504) 524-5328 / (504) 523-1071 (fax)
whamlin@bh-t.com
wellison@bh-t.com

MAINE	Peter W. Culley, Esquire Teresa A. Curtin, Esquire Pierce Atwood One Monument Square Portland, Maine 04101 (207) 791-1100 / (207) 791-1350 (fax) www.pierceatwood.com
MARYLAND	Sidney G. Leech, Esquire Carlos A. Braxton, Esquire Goodell, DeVries, Leech & Dann, L.L.P. One South Street, 20th floor Baltimore, Maryland 21202 (410) 783-4000 / (410) 783-4040 (fax) sgl@gdldlaw.com cab@gdldlaw.com
MASSACHUSETTS	Francis H. Fox, Esquire Paul M. Robertson, Esquire James P. Lucking, Esquire Bingham Dana L.L.P. 150 Federal Street Boston, Massachusetts 02215 (617) 951-8000 / (617) 951-8736 (fax) www.bingham.com
MICHIGAN	Butzel Long 150 W. Jefferson Avenue, Suite 900 Detroit, Michigan 48226 (313) 225-7000 / (313) 225-7080 (fax) www.butzel.com
MINNESOTA	William L. Killion, Esquire Erik T. Salveson, Esquire Kacy F. Kleinhans, Esquire Gray, Plant, Mooty, Mooty & Bennett, P.A. 3400 City Center 33 South Sixth Street Minneapolis, Minnesota 55402 (612) 343-2800 / (612) 333-0066 (fax) www.gpmlaw.com
MISSISSIPPI	George E. Abdo, III, Esquire Daniel Coker Horton & Bell, P.A. 4400 Old Canton Road, Fourth floor Jackson, Mississippi 39211 (601) 969-7607 / (601) 969-1116 (fax) gabdo@danielcoker.com

MISSOURI

Robert A. Horn, Esquire
K. Christopher Jayaram, Esquire
Horn Aylward & Bandy, L.L.C.
2600 Grand Boulevard, Suite 500
Kansas City, Missouri 64108
(816) 421-0700 / (816) 421-0899 (fax)
cjayaram@hab-law.com
rhorn@hab-law.com

MONTANA

Kristi Blazer, Esquire
Gregory G. Gould, Esquire
Luxan & Murfitt, P.L.L.P.
24 West 6th Avenue
Montana Club Building, Fourth Floor
Helena, Montana 59601
(406) 442-7450 / (406) 442-7361 (fax)
kristib@luxanmurfitt.com
gregg@luxanmurfitt.com
www.luxanmurfitt.com

NEBRASKA

Mark A. Christensen, Esquire
Cline, Williams, Wright, Johnson & Oldfather
1900 U.S. Bank Building
233 South 13th Street
Lincoln, Nebraska 68508-2095
(402) 474-6900 / (402) 474-5393 (fax)
mchristensen@cline-law.com
www.cline-law.com

NEVADA

Albert F. Pagni, Esquire
Molly D. Malone, Esquire
Jones Vargas
100 West Liberty Street
P.O. Box 281
Reno, Nevada 89504-0281
(775) 786-5000 / (775) 786-1177 (fax)

Douglas M. Cohen, Esquire
Jones Vargas
3773 Howard Hughes Parkway
Las Vegas, Nevada 89109
(702) 734-2220 / (702) 737-7705 (fax)
www.jonesvargas.com

NEW HAMPSHIRE	John E. Friberg, Esquire Todd J. Hathaway, Esquire Wadleigh, Starr & Peters, P.L.L.C. 95 Market Street Manchester, New Hampshire 03101 (603) 669-4140 / (603) 669-6018 (fax) thathaway@wadleighlaw.com www.wadleighlaw.com
NEW JERSEY	Edward A. Greenberg, Esquire Daniel M. Young, Esquire Daller Greenberg & Dietrich, L.L.P. 457 Haddonfield Road, Suite 120 Cherry Hill, New Jersey 08002 (856) 488-0173 / (856) 488-5645 (fax) egreenberg@dallergreenberg.com www.dallergreenberg.com
NEW MEXICO	W. Robert Lasater, Jr., Esquire Deborah E. Mann, Esquire Rodey, Dickason, Sloan, Akin & Robb, P.A. P.O. Box 1888 201 3rd Street N.W., Suite 2200 Albuquerque, New Mexico 87103 (505) 765-5900 / (505) 768-7395 (fax) rlasater@rodey.com demann@rodey.com www.rodey.com
NEW YORK	Susan T. Dwyer, Esquire Stacy Kellner Rosenberg, Esquire Herrick, Feinstein LLP 2 Park Avenue New York, New York 10016 (212) 592-1400 / (212) 889-7577 (fax) sdwye@herrick.com www.herrick.com
NORTH CAROLINA	William F. Womble, Jr., Esquire Jack M. Strauch, Esquire Womble Carlyle Sandridge & Rice, P.L.L.C. P.O. Drawer 84 Winston-Salem, North Carolina 27102 (336) 721-3600 / (336) 733-8318 (fax) bwomble@wcsr.com jstrauch@wcsr.com www.wcsr.com

NORTH DAKOTA   H. Patrick Weir, Esquire
                        Vogel Law Firm
                        502 First Avenue North
                        P.O. Box 1389
                        Fargo, North Dakota 58107-1389
                        (701) 237-6983 / (701) 237-0847 (fax)
                        vogellaw@vogellaw.com

OHIO   Mark A. Belasic, Esquire
                        Dennis L. Murphy, Esquire
                        Jones Day Reavis & Pogue
                        North Point
                        901 Lakeside Avenue
                        Cleveland, Ohio 44114
                        (216) 586-3939 / (216) 579-0212 (fax)
                        mabelasic@jonesday.com
                        www.jonesday.com

OKLAHOMA   John C. Niemeyer, Esquire
                        Linda G. Alexander, Esquire
                        Niemeyer, Alexander, Austin & Phillips, P.C.
                        300 North Walker
                        Oklahoma City, Oklahoma 73102-1822
                        (405) 232-2725 / (405) 239-7185 (fax)
                        johnniemeyer@niemeyerfirm.com
                        lindaalexander@niemeyerfirm.com

OREGON   Bruce C. Hamlin, Esquire
                        Lane Powell Spears Lubersky L.L.P.
                        601 S.W. Second Avenue, Suite 2100
                        Portland, Oregon 97204
                        (503) 778-2100 / (503) 778-2200 (fax)
                        hamlinb@lanepowell.com
                        www.lanepowell.com

PENNSYLVANIA   Morton F. Daller, Esquire
                        Brendan P. Burke, Esquire
                        Daller Greenberg & Dietrich, L.L.P.
                        Valley Green Corporate Center
                        7111 Valley Green Road
                        Fort Washington, Pennsylvania 19034
                        (215) 836-1100 / (215) 836-2845 (fax)
                        mdaller@dallergreenberg.com
                        www.dallergreenberg.com

RHODE ISLAND	Mark O. Denehy, Esquire Linda A. Mayer, Esquire Adler Pollock & Sheehan P.C. 2300 Financial Plaza Providence, Rhode Island 02903 (401) 274-7200 / (401) 751-0604 (fax) www.apslaw.com
SOUTH CAROLINA	Val H. Stieglitz Nexsen Pruet Jacobs & Pollard, L.L.P. 1441 Main Street, Suite 1500 Columbia, South Carolina 29201 (803) 771-8900 / (803) 253-8277 (fax) vstieglitz@npjp.com www.npjp.com
SOUTH DAKOTA	J. Crisman Palmer, Esquire David E. Lust, Esquire Gunderson, Palmer, Goodsell & Nelson, L.L.P. 440 Mount Rushmore Road P.O. Box 8045 Rapid City, South Dakota 57709-8045 (605) 342-1078 / (605) 342-9503 (fax) cpalmer@gpgnlaw.com dlust@gpgnlaw.com
TENNESSEE	Robert L. Crawford, Esquire Scott B. Ostrow, Esquire Wyatt, Tarrant & Combs, L.L.P. 1715 Aaron Brenner Drive, Suite 800 Memphis, Tennessee 38120-4367 (901) 537-1000 / (901) 537-1010 (fax) lcrawford@wyattfirm.com sostrow@wyattfirm.com www.wyattfirm.com
TEXAS	C. Vernon Hartline, Jr., Esquire Scott G. Edwards, Esquire Hartline, Dacus, Dreyer & Kern, L.L.P. 6688 North Central Expressway, Suite 1000 Dallas, Texas 75206 (214) 369-2100 / (214) 369-2118 (fax) hartline@flash.net sedwards@hddk.com www.hddk.com

UTAH

Rick L. Rose, Esquire
Melissa H. Bailey, Esquire
Cheri K. Gochberg, Esquire
Kristine M. Larsen, Esquire
Ray, Quinney & Nebeker
36 South State Street
Suite 1400
P.O. Box 45385
Salt Lake City, Utah 84111
(801) 532-1500 / (801) 532-7543 (fax)
www.rqn.com

VERMONT

Allan R. Keyes, Esquire
Ryan Smith & Carbine, Ltd.
P.O. Box 310
Rutland, Vermont 05702-0310
(802) 786-1035 / (802) 786-1100 (fax)
ark@rsclaw.com

VIRGINIA

William R. Rakes, Esquire
J. Scott Sexton, Esquire
Gentry Locke Rakes & Moore
P.O. Box 40013
Roanoke, Virginia 24022-0013
(540) 983-9300 / (540) 983-9468 (fax)
www.gentrylocke.com

WASHINGTON

Douglas A. Hofmann, Esquire
S. Jay Terry, Esquire
Mary R. Knack, Esquire
W. K. & G., P.L.L.C.
Two Union Square
601 Union Street, Suite 4100
P.O. Box 21926
Seattle, Washington 98111-3926
(206) 628-6600 / (206) 628-6611(fax)
dhofmann@wkg.com
jterry@wkg.com
mknack@wkg.com

WEST VIRGINIA	Stephen R. Crislip, Esquire Amber L. Hoback, Esquire Jackson & Kelly P.L.L.C. 1600 Laidley Tower P.O. Box 553 Charleston, West Virginia 25322 (304) 340-1000 / (304) 340-1050 (fax) scrislip@jacksonkelly.com ahoback@jacksonkelly.com www.jacksonkelly.com
WISCONSIN	J. Ric Gass, Esquire Thomas Gonzalez, Esquire Kravit, Gass, Hovel & Leitner, S.C. 825 North Jefferson, Suite 500 Milwaukee, Wisconsin 53202 (414) 271-7100 / (414) 271-8135 (fax) jrg@kravit-gass.com tg@kravit-gass.com
WYOMING	Scott P. Klosterman, Esquire Brown, Drew & Massey, L.L.P. 123 West First Street, Suite 800 Casper, Wyoming 82601 (307) 234-1000 / (307) 265-8025 (fax) spk@browndrew.com

ALABAMA

A. STATUTES OF LIMITATION

Most tort claims in Alabama, including fraud, are governed by a two-year statute of limitations,[1] though trespass to person or property,[2] assault and battery,[3] false imprisonment,[4] and conversion[5] are subject to a six-year statute of limitations. Tort claims based on *respondeat superior* or vicarious liability theories also are subject to a two-year statute.[6]

Tort claims generally accrue, and the limitations period begins to run, when injury is sustained (not when injury is discovered).[7] Claims of fraud accrue when the facts constituting the fraud are discovered, or reasonably should have been discovered.[8]

Medical and legal malpractice actions are subject to two-year limitations periods; each statute has distinctive accrual and other provisions.[9] Tort claims under the Alabama Deceptive Trade Practices Act must be brought within one year of discovery of the act or practice that is the subject of the action.[10]

Claims for breach of warranty are governed by a four-year statute of limitations.[11] In cases of personal injury caused by consumer goods, the statute begins to run when plaintiff first suffers injury.[12] In the case of nonconsumer goods, the statute of limitations begins to run from the date of sale, unless the warranty sued upon expressly extends to future performance of the goods.[13]

B. TORT REFORM

The Alabama legislature in 1999 passed legislation capping punitive damage awards (*see* Section Q, *infra*), as well as addressing venue in civil actions,[14] and procedures in class actions.[15]

C. "NO FAULT" LIMITATIONS

Alabama is not a "no fault" jurisdiction with regard to any aspect of tort law.

D. THE STANDARD FOR NEGLIGENCE

A claim of negligence under Alabama law requires (1) existence of a duty on the part of the defendant; (2) breach of that duty by the defendant; (3) existence of a causal relationship between the defendant's conduct and the plaintiff's injury; and (4) injury to the plaintiff.[16] The existence of a duty depends on the facts presented, but ultimately rests on whether the defendant could reasonably foresee that harm might result if due care were not exercised.[17] Evidence of customary practices is typically admissible as bearing on the existence and extent of defendant's duty.[18]

A person who owes certain duties to another imposed by law or statute is not permitted to delegate them by hiring an independent contractor to perform them.[19] Examples of such nondelegable duties are the duty to avoid a breach of the peace when performing a repossession,[20] and the duty to avoid injuring others in the course of engaging in inherently or intrinsically dangerous activities (such as, for example, the aerial spraying of pesticides).[21]

A physician or person in a similar professional calling is held to the standard of care attendant to the professional level to which he holds himself out.[22]

A child under seven years of age cannot be guilty of negligence.[23] Children between the ages of seven and fourteen are *prima facie* incapable of negligence, but may be shown by evidence to possess sufficient discretion, intelligence, and sensitivity to danger so as to be capable of negligence.[24]

E. CAUSATION

A negligence plaintiff must prove that defendant's act was the cause-in-fact of the injury, as well as the proximate cause (defined as the primary moving cause without which the injury would not have been inflicted, and without the intervention of any new or independent cause).[25] It must appear that the harm inflicted was foreseeable from the act.[26] Where the acts of two or more tortfeasors combine or concur to produce an injury, each tortfeasor's act is considered the proximate cause of the injury.[27]

F. CONTRIBUTORY NEGLIGENCE AND ASSUMPTION OF THE RISK

In Alabama, negligence on the part of the plaintiff that proximately contributes to plaintiff's injury is a complete defense to a claim of negligence.[28] Contributory negligence is not a defense, however, to claims of wantonness or willfulness.[29] Additionally, in the ordinary case the negligence of a parent cannot be imputed to its child so as to bar the child's action.[30] The burden of establishing contributory negligence lies with the defendant asserting it.[31]

The rules governing the ability of individuals to be capable of negligence due to their youth are also applicable to contributory negligence.[32]

Alabama does not recognize comparative negligence or fault.

A plaintiff's assumption of the risk is also a complete defense to a claim of negligence in Alabama. A defendant asserting the defense must show that plaintiff (1) had knowledge of the existence of the dangerous condition; (2) had an appreciation of the danger; and (3) yet failed to exercise reasonable care by putting himself in the way of the known danger.[33]

G. *RES IPSA LOQUITUR* AND INHERENTLY DANGEROUS ACTIVITIES

The elements of *res ipsa loquitur* under Alabama law are: (1) the defendant must have had full management and control of the instrumentality that caused plaintiff's injury; (2) the circumstances must be such that, according to the common knowledge of the experience of mankind, the accident could not have happened without negligence on the part of those having control of the instrumentality; and (3) the injury of plaintiff must have resulted from the accident.[34] *Res ipsa loquitur* cannot be used to prove willful or wanton misconduct,[35] and does not serve to prove proximate cause.[36]

Alabama, following the Restatement (Second) of Torts, recognizes a form of strict liability for injuries caused by defendant's engaging in abnormally dangerous activities.[37] Among the factors to be considered in whether an activity is abnormally dangerous are: whether the activity creates a high risk of serious harm to others; whether the activity or instrumentality is one of common usage; whether the place in which the activity is carried on is appropriate to the activity; and whether the dangerous attributes of the activity outweigh the activity's value to the community.[38]

H. **NEGLIGENCE *PER SE***

Negligence *per se* is based on the breach by a party of a statutory or regulatory duty; under certain circumstances breach of that duty can be found to be negligence as a matter of law. The requirements to make out negligence *per se* are (1) that the statute or regulation on which plaintiff relies was enacted or promulgated to protect a class of persons including plaintiff; (2) the injury sustained must be of a type contemplated by the statute or regulation; (3) the party charged with negligence must have violated the statute or regulation; and (4) the statutory or regulatory violation must have proximately caused plaintiff's injury.[39]

Violation of Alabama's "rules of the road" can be negligence *per se*, if the rule in question does not require a judgment to be made by the driver. If judgment on the part of the driver is required, then a "reasonable man" negligence standard applies.[40]

I. **JOINT AND SEVERAL LIABILITY**

Liability of joint tortfeasors is joint and several in Alabama, in that either tortfeasor may be held liable for the entire resulting loss, without apportionment of damages (though plaintiff is entitled to only one recovery).[41] Persons may be deemed joint tortfeasors either where their separate acts combine and concur to produce a single harmful result[42] or where they stand in certain relation to one another (such as principal and agent or joint venturers).[43] Because the right of action against joint tortfeasors is one and indivisible, the jury is not permitted to assess separate amounts against joint tortfeasors.[44]

J. **INDEMNITY AND CONTRIBUTION**

Joint and several liability (*see* Section I, *supra*) has the further consequence that joint tortfeasors may not obtain contribution or indemnity from other joint tortfeasors, except when an indemnification agreement exists between the liable parties, clearly indicating indemnity of the type of conduct in question.[45] A further, very limited exception to the no-contribution rule exists (though its applicability is not entirely clear) when the party seeking contribution is totally without fault but is held liable solely because of an absolute nondelegable duty to the injured plaintiff.[46]

K. **BAR OF WORKERS' COMPENSATION STATUTE**

Under Alabama's worker's compensation statute, neither an employee nor his personal representative, next of kin, or surviving spouse may sue for damages for injuries or death caused by an accident in the performance of the employee's employment, except as provided by the statute.[47] Thus, all actions for personal injuries against the employer based on any negligence theory are barred; the rights and remedies provided by the statute are exclusive.[48] However, claims based on intentional tort theories, such as intentional fraud,[49] intentional infliction of emotional distress,[50] and invasion of privacy (in the sexual harassment context)[51] are not barred.

Under certain circumstances injured employees may avoid the exclusivity bar and bring tort actions for damages against their fellow employees, when such claims are based on statutorily defined instances of willful misconduct.[52]

L. PREMISES LIABILITY

A landowner's liability for injuries sustained on the premises — insofar as the claim is based on the condition of the premises, rather than the conduct of the landowner — depends on the plaintiff's legal status as invitee, trespasser, or licensee.[53] A landowner owes an invitee the duty to warn of dangers of which the landowner knows, or ought to know, and of which the invitee is ignorant, and the duty to have the premises in a reasonably safe condition for use within the contemplated invitation.[54] A landowner owes to a licensee the duty not to wantonly or willfully injure him, or negligently injure him after discovering his peril, and the duty not to expose the licensee to new, hidden dangers.[55] A landowner owes a trespasser only the following duties (which are similar to, though somewhat lesser than, the duties owed to a licensee): not to wantonly or intentionally injure the trespasser; not to place traps or pitfalls in his way; to warn of dangers actually known by the landowner after the landowner has knowledge of the trespasser's presence; and a duty not to negligently injure the trespasser after discovering his peril.[56] A trespasser may not seek damages based on injuries that were the direct result of the injured party's intentional participation in a crime involving moral turpitude.[57]

The above classification system does not apply where the affirmative conduct of the landowner causes the injury; standards of ordinary and reasonable care apply to the landowner's duties in such situations.[58]

M. DRAM SHOP LIABILITY

Alabama has a statutory cause of action for any person injured "in consequence of" another's intoxication, against the seller or provider who has provided liquor or other beverages to the intoxicated person "contrary to the provisions of law."[59] A person who is injured by reason of his own intoxication cannot recover.[60] A plaintiff proceeding under this statutory claim is not held to the usual standards of proof of causal connection between the illegal sale of beverages and the injury; plaintiff need only prove that the injury was "in consequence of" the intoxication brought about by the illegal sale.[61] The Alabama Supreme Court has generally declined to apply the statute to cover social hosts, and has stated that in the usual case the sale of alcohol by a licensed vendor is an element of the claim.[62] By judicial interpretation, the statutory prohibition on provision of alcohol "contrary to the provisions of law" can include provision to visibly intoxicated persons;[63] the sale of liquor by a private bar to a nonmember or nonguest;[64] and the provision of alcohol to minors.[65] The direct sale or provision of alcohol to the person causing the injury is a requirement for liability under the statute.[66] Both compensatory and punitive damages are recoverable.[67]

A separate statute creates a cause of action in favor of the parent or guardian of a minor (under the age of 21) against anyone who sells or furnishes alcohol to a minor, provided the seller or provider had knowledge of or was chargeable with notice of the minor's minority.[68]

N. ECONOMIC LOSS

Alabama follows the rule that a plaintiff making a claim for a defective product, where plaintiff has suffered no personal injury or property damage or where the sole damage is to the product itself, cannot recover in tort.[69]

O. FRAUD AND MISREPRESENTATION

In order to make out a claim for fraudulent misrepresentation, plaintiff must show that the defendant made (either innocently, negligently, recklessly, or intentionally) a misrepresentation of existing material fact, on which plaintiff reasonably relied, which proximately resulted in injury.[70] Punitive damages are recoverable in cases of reckless or intentional fraud.

To make out a claim of promissory fraud, the plaintiff must show that the defendant made a promise, or false representation about future performance, that plaintiff justifiably relied thereon, that plaintiff was damaged as a proximate result, that the defendant made the promise or representation with no intent to keep it at the time it was made, and that the defendant had a present intention to deceive.[71]

To make out a claim for fraudulent suppression, the plaintiff must demonstrate a duty on the defendant to disclose a material fact, the defendant's concealment or nondisclosure of that fact, inducement of the plaintiff to act, and action by the plaintiff to his injury.[72] Silence on the part of the defendant regarding a material fact is not considered suppression unless the defendant has an obligation to communicate that fact. By statute, the obligation to communicate a fact may arise from the confidential relations of the parties or from the particular circumstances of the case.[73] The "particular circumstances" that impose on a party a duty to speak may arise from the relationship of the parties, the relative knowledge of the parties, the value of the particular fact, and other factors.[74]

P. CONSUMER FRAUD STATUTES

Alabama's principal consumer fraud statute is the Alabama Deceptive Trade Practices Act (ADTPA).[75] The ADTPA designates 23 acts and practices as unlawful,[76] most relating to misrepresentation in connection with product sale or advertising. A "catch-all" provision prohibits "any other unconscionable, false, misleading or deceptive act or practice in the conduct of trade or commerce."[77] The ADTPA authorizes the state's Attorney General or any district attorney to investigate complaints and to bring actions for both injunctive relief and civil penalties.[78] The ADTPA also creates a private right of action on behalf of consumers.[79] They may recover actual damages or $100 (whichever is greater); in the court's discretion, up to three times actual damages; and reasonable attorney's fees.[80] Significantly, class actions by consumers are not permitted under the ADTPA, though the Attorney General or district attorney may file a *parens patriae*-type representative action.[81] No consumer may simultaneously maintain an ADTPA claim and a common law fraud claim.[82]

Other consumer fraud-related statutes address telemarketing,[83] lemon-law rights for motor vehicle consumers[84] and securities violations.[85]

Q. PUNITIVE DAMAGES

Except in wrongful death actions[86] (where all damages are punitive, *see* Section R, *infra*), punitive damages are awardable only in tort actions where plaintiff proves by clear and convincing evidence that defendant consciously or deliberately engaged in statutorily defined "oppression, fraud, wantonness or malice" with regard to plaintiff.[87] A principal or employer cannot be liable for punitive damages for the acts or omissions of its servant or employee unless it is shown that the employer (1) knew or should have known of the employee's unfitness; (2) authorized the wrongful conduct; (3) ratified the wrongful conduct; or (4) the wrongful conduct was calculated to or did benefit the employer.[88]

In 1999, Alabama enacted certain statutory caps on punitive damage awards.[89] The caps do not apply to actions for wrongful death or intentional infliction of physical injury, or in class actions.[90] In cases involving small business defendants (defined as a business with a net worth of $2 million or less at the time of the occurrence made the basis of the suit), punitive damages may not exceed $50,000 or 10 percent of the business's net worth, whichever is greater.[91] In cases involving other defendants, punitive damages may not exceed three times compensatory damages or $500,000, whichever is greater,[92] except in cases of physical injury, where the caps are three times compensatory damages or $1.5 million, whichever is greater.[93] For purposes of the statutory cap, physical injury does not include mental anguish or emotional distress.[94]

R. WRONGFUL DEATH ACTIONS

Under Alabama's wrongful death statute, as interpreted, the *only* damages recoverable by plaintiff are punitive damages, the amount depending on the nature of the defendant's act, his degree of culpability, and the need for deterring the defendant and others from committing similar wrongful conduct.[95] Evidence of loss of earnings, loss of enjoyment of life, and contributions to family are inadmissible because they are irrelevant. A wrongful death plaintiff can also bring a claim (or a separate action), where appropriate, under a breach of warranty theory, for compensatory damages incurred during the period of time between the accident and death.[96]

The decedent's "personal representative" is the proper party plaintiff in a wrongful death action.[97] In the usual case this is the administrator or executor of the decedent's estate.[98] However, if the dependents of a decedent, as defined in

Alabama's workers' compensation act, have a statutory right to bring suit for workers' compensation benefits against the decedent's employer, such dependents (rather than the "personal representative") also have a right to bring a wrongful death action against a third party potentially liable for the decedent's death.[99] In the case of the death of a minor, either parent (or the custodial parent in the event the parents are divorced) has the right to bring the action.[100] If the father and mother are both dead or if they fail to commence the action within six months from the death of the minor, the personal representative of the minor may commence the action.[101]

Damages recovered in a wrongful death action are not subject to the payment of debts or liabilities of the testator or intestate, but must be distributed according to the statute of distributions.[102]

The wrongful death statute requires that all actions arising under it be brought in Alabama courts; courts in other states have, however, applied the statute to actions brought in those states.[103] The statute cannot be used to support an action brought in Alabama where the wrongful act was committed in another state.[104]

S. CHOICE OF LAW

Alabama, following the First Restatement of Conflicts of Law, applies *lex loci delicti*, or law of the place of the wrong in tort actions.[105] In practice, this means that the substantive law of the state of the place of plaintiff's injury will govern.[106] In contract cases, the law of the state wherein the contract was entered (*lex loci contractus*) ordinarily governs,[107] though Alabama will enforce contractual choice-of-law provisions.[108] Alabama courts will refuse to apply the substantive law of another state when to do so would violate Alabama public policy.[109]

John E. Goodman
BRADLEY ARANT ROSE & WHITE L.L.P.
2001 Park Place, Suite 1400
Birmingham, Alabama 35203
(205) 521-8000
Fax (205) 521-8800
jgoodman@barw.com
www.barw.com

ENDNOTES - ALABAMA

1. *See* Ala. Code § 6-2-38 (1975). Certain torts (for example, defamation, wrongful death, and malicious prosecution) are covered by separate subsections; a "catch-all" provision, addressing "[a]ll actions for any injury to the person or rights of another not arising from contract and not specifically enumerated in this section" governs most other tort claims. *Id.*, § 6-2-38(l).

2. Ala. Code § 6-2-34(1), (2) (1975).

3. Ala. Code § 6-2-34(1) (1975).

4. *Id.*

5. Ala. Code § 6-2-34(3) (1975).

6. Ala. Code § 6-2-38(n) (1975).

7. *Stephens v. Creel*, 429 So. 2d 278 (Ala. 1989). *Cf.* Ala. Code § 6-2-30(b) (actions for injuries based on exposure to asbestos accrue from when the injury was, or reasonably should have been, discovered).

8. Ala. Code § 6-2-3 (1975); *Liberty Nat'l Life Ins. Co. v. McAllister*, 675 So. 2d 1292 (Ala. 1995).

9. Ala. Code § 6-5-482 (1975) (medical malpractice); § 6-5-574 (legal malpractice).

10. Ala. Code § 8-19-14 (1975).

11. Ala. Code § 7-2-725(1) (1975).

12. Ala. Code § 7-2-725(2) (1975); *Moon v. Harco Drugs, Inc.*, 435 So. 2d 218 (Ala. 1983).

13. *Simmons v. Clemco Indus.*, 368 So. 2d 509 (Ala. 1979).

14. Ala. Code § 6-3-7 (1975).

15. Ala. Code § 6-5-641 (1975).

16. *See, e.g., Ford Motor Co. v. Burdeshaw*, 661 So. 2d 236 (Ala. 1995).

17. *See, e.g., Keeton v. Fayette County*, 558 So. 2d 884 (Ala. 1989).

18. *See, e.g., Collins Co. v. City of Decatur*, 533 So. 2d 1127 (Ala. 1988).

19. *See, e.g., Wheeler v. Wright*, 668 So. 2d 779 (Ala. 1995).

20. *General Finance Corp. v. Smith*, 505 So. 2d 1045 (Ala. 1987).

21. *Boroughs v. Joiner*, 337 So. 2d 340 (Ala. 1976).

22. *See* Ala. Code § 6-5-484(a) (1975) (defining standard of care in medical liability actions); Ala. Code §§ 6-5-572(3)a (1975), 6-5-580(1) (1975) (defining standard of care in legal liability actions).

23. *See generally* 2 Alabama Pattern Jury Instructions: Civil Nos. 30.06–30.08 (2d ed. 1993).

24. *Id.*

25. *See, e.g., City of Mobile v. Havard*, 268 So. 2d 805 (1972).

26. *See, e.g., Peters v. Calhoun County Comm'n*, 669 So. 2d 847 (Ala. 1995).

27. *See, e.g., General Motors Corp. v. Edwards*, 482 So. 2d 1176 (Ala. 1985).

28. *See, e.g., Brown v. Piggly-Wiggly Stores*, 454 So. 2d 1370 (Ala. 1984); 2 Alabama Pattern Jury Instructions: Civil No. 30.02 (2d ed. 1993).

29. *See, e.g., Watkins v. Central Contracting, Inc.*, 603 So. 2d 899 (Ala. 1992).

30. *See, e.g., Nunn v. Whitworth*, 545 So. 2d 766 (Ala. 1989).

31. *See, e.g., Robertson v. Travelers Inn*, 613 So. 2d 376 (Ala. 1993).

32. *See, e.g., Superskate, Inc. v. Nolen*, 641 So. 2d 231 (Ala. 1994).

33. *See, e.g., Central Ala. Elec. Co-op v. Tapley*, 546 So. 2d 371 (Ala. 1989).

34. *Ward v. Forrester Day Care, Inc.*, 547 So. 2d 410 (Ala. 1989).

35. *Smith v. Kennedy*, 195 So. 2d 820 (Ala. Civ. App. 1966).

36. *Daniels v. Twin Oaks Nursing Home*, 692 F.2d 1321 (11th Cir. 1982).

37. *Harper v. Regency Development Co.*, 399 So. 2d 248 (Ala. 1981) (citing Restatement (Second) of Torts, § 519-20 (1977)).

38. *Id.*

39. *See, e.g., Fox v. Bartholf*, 374 So. 2d 294 (Ala. 1979); *Alabama Power Co. v. Dunaway*, 502 So. 2d 726 (Ala. 1987).

40. *See, e.g., Consolidated Freightways, Inc. v. Pacheco-Rivera,* 524 So. 2d 346 (Ala. 1988).

41. *See, e.g., Tatum v. Schering Corp.,* 523 So. 2d 1048 (Ala. 1988); 2 Alabama Pattern Jury Instructions: Civil No. 28.08 (2d ed. 1993).

42. *See, e.g., Beloit Corp. v. Harrell,* 339 So. 2d 992 (Ala. 1976).

43. *See, e.g., Larry Terry Contrs., Inc. v. Bogle,* 404 So. 2d 613 (Ala. 1981); *Underwood v. Holy Name of Jesus Hosp.,* 266 So. 2d 773 (Ala. 1972).

44. *See, e.g., Vanguard Indus. Corp. v. Alabama Power Co.,* 455 So. 2d 837 (Ala. 1984).

45. *Crigler v. Salac,* 438 So. 2d 1375 (Ala. 1983).

46. *Consolidated Pipe & Supply Co., Inc. v. Stockham Valves & Fittings, Inc.,* 365 So. 2d 968, 970 (Ala. 1978).

47. Ala. Code § 5-5-52 (1975).

48. Ala. Code § 25-5-53 (1975).

49. *Lowman v. Piedmont Executive Shirt Mfg. Co.,* 547 So. 2d 90 (Ala. 1989).

50. *Garvin v. Shewbart,* 564 So. 2d 428 (Ala. 1990).

51. *Busby v. Truswal Sys. Corp.,* 551 So. 2d 322 (Ala. 1989).

52. Ala. Code §§ 25-5-11(b)-(c) (1975).

53. *See, e.g., Orr v. Turney,* 535 So. 2d 150 (Ala. 1988); *Baldwin v. Gartman,* 604 So. 2d 347 (Ala. 1992).

54. *Mills v. Bruno's, Inc.,* 641 So. 2d 777 (Ala. 1994).

55. *Johnson v. Harris,* 585 So. 2d 1349 (Ala. 1991).

56. *Ryals v. United States Steel Corp.,* 562 So. 2d 192 (Ala. 1990).

57. *Oden v. Pepsi-Cola Bottling Co.,* 621 So. 2d 953 (Ala. 1993).

58. *See, e.g., Orr v. Turney,* 535 So. 2d 150 (Ala. 1988).

59. Ala. Code § 6-5-71 (1975).

60. *Maples v. Chinese Palace, Inc.,* 389 So. 2d 120 (Ala. 1980).

61. Ala. Code § 6-5-71(a) (1975); *Duckett v. Wilson Hotel Management Co.*, 669 So. 2d 977 (Ala. Civ. App. 1995).

62. *Hatter v. Nations*, 480 So. 2d 1209 (Ala. 1985); *Beeson v. Scoles Cadillac Corp.*, 506 So. 2d 999 (Ala. 1987).

63. *Buchanan v. Merger Enterprises*, 463 So. 2d 121 (Ala. 1984).

64. *Attalla Golf & Country Club, Inc. v. Harris*, 601 So. 2d 965 (Ala. 1992).

65. *Martin v. Watts*, 513 So. 2d 958 (Ala. 1987).

66. *Jones v. B.P. Oil*, 632 So. 2d 435 (Ala. 1993).

67. Ala. Code § 6-5-71(a) (1975).

68. Ala. Code § 6-5-70 (1975).

69. *Lloyd Wood Coal Co. v. Clark Equipment Co.*, 543 So. 2d 671 (Ala. 1989) (agreeing with *East River S.S. Corp. v. Transamerica Delaval, Inc.*, 476 U.S. 858 (1986)). The applicability in Alabama of the economic loss rule beyond the products liability context is uncertain.

70. *See* Ala. Code §§ 6-5-100-104 (1975).

71. *Howard v. Wolff Broadcasting Corp.*, 611 So. 2d 307 (Ala. 1992).

72. *Foremost Insurance Co. v. Parham*, 693 So. 2d 409 (Ala. 1997).

73. Ala. Code § 6-5-102 (1975).

74. *Lowder Realty, Inc. v. Odom*, 495 So. 2d 23 (Ala. 1986).

75. Ala. Code § 8-19-1 *et seq.* (1975 and 2000 Supp.).

76. Ala. Code § 8-19-5 (1975 and 2000 Supp.).

77. Ala. Code § 8-19-5(23) (1975 and 2000 Supp.).

78. Ala. Code §§ 8-19-4, -8, -10, -11 (1975).

79. Ala. Code § 8-19-10 (1975). Persons other than consumers are permitted to sue under the ADTPA only under certain limited circumstances. *Id.*

80. *Id.*

81. Ala. Code § 8-19-10(f) (1975).

82. Ala. Code § 8-19-15(b) (1975).

83. Ala. Code §§ 8-19-A-1 *et seq.* (1975 and 2000 Supp.).

84. Ala. Code §§ 8-20A-1 *et seq.* (1975).

85. Ala. Code §§ 8-6-1 *et seq.* (1975 and 2000 Supp.).

86. Ala. Code § 6-11-29 (1975).

87. Ala. Code § 6-11-20(a) (1975 and 2000 Supp.).

88. Ala. Code § 6-11-27(a) (1975 and 2000 Supp.). Dram shop claims (*see* section M) are expressly exempted from this statute. § 6-11-27(b) (1975 and 2000 Supp.).

89. Earlier-enacted punitive damage caps were invalidated on constitutional grounds. *See Henderson v. Alabama Power Co.*, 627 So. 2d 878 (Ala. 1993).

90. Ala. Code §§ 6-11-21(j), -(h) (1975 and 2000 Supp.).

91. Ala. Code §§ 6-11-21(b), -(c) (1975 and 2000 Supp.).

92. Ala. Code § 6-11-21(a) (1975 and 2000 Supp.).

93. Ala. Code § 6-11-21(d) (1975 and 2000 Supp.).

94. Ala. Code § 6-11-21(k) (1975 and 2000 Supp.).

95. *See, e.g., Deaton v. Burroughs*, 456 So. 2d 771 (Ala. 1984).

96. *Benefield v. Aquaslide 'N' Dive Corp.*, 406 So. 2d 873 (Ala. 1981).

97. Ala. Code § 6-5-410 (1975).

98. *See, e.g., Downtown Nursing Home v. Pool*, 375 So. 2d 465 (Ala. 1979), *cert. denied*, 445 U.S. 930 (1980).

99. Ala. Code § 25-5-11 (1975); *Baggett v. Webb*, 248 So. 2d 275 (Ala. Civ. App), *cert. denied*, 248 So. 2d 284 (1971).

100. Ala. Code §§ 6-5-390–391 (1975); *see also Coleman v. Stitt*, 514 So. 2d 1007 (Ala. 1987).

101. Ala. Code § 6-5-391 (1975).

102. *See, e.g., Baggett v. Sellers,* 210 So. 2d 796 (Ala. 1968). The provisions for distribution under intestate succession are governed by Ala. Code §§ 43-8-40 *et seq.* (1975).

103. *See, e.g., Stevens v. Pullman, Inc.* 388 So. 2d 580 (Fla. App. 1980); *Spriggs v. Dredge,* 140 N.E. 2d 45 (Ohio App. 1955).

104. *See, e.g., Spencer v. Malone Freight Lines, Inc.,* 298 So. 2d 20 (Ala. 1974).

105. *See, e.g., Fitts v. Minnesota Mining & Mfg. Co.,* 581 So. 2d 819 (Ala. 1991).

106. *See, e.g., Norris v. Taylor,* 460 So. 2d 151 (Ala. 1984).

107. *See, e.g., Cincinnati Ins. Co. v. Girod,* 570 So. 2d 595 (Ala. 1990).

108. *See, e.g., Chazen v. Parton,* 739 So. 2d 1104 (Ala. 1999).

109. *See, e.g., Cherry, Bekaert & Holland v. Brown,* 582 So. 2d 502 (Ala. 1991).

ALASKA

A. STATUTES OF LIMITATIONS

Claims for relief (accruing on or after August 7, 1997) sounding in tort for personal injury or death, or for damage to personal property, must be commenced within two years from the date the cause of action accrues.[1] The two years "does not begin to run until the claimant discovers, or reasonably should have discovered, the existence of all elements essential to the cause of action."[2]

Strict liability and negligence claims asserting only damage to personal property and accruing prior to August 7, 1997, are governed by the six-year limitation period.[3]

A "catch-all" provision for actions not subject to another statute of limitations requires commencement within ten years from the date of accrual.[4]

There is a ten-year statute of repose for personal injury, death, or property damage, but it has a multitude of exceptions.[5]

If a person who is entitled to bring an action is, at the time the action accrues, a minor or mentally incompetent, the statute of limitations is tolled.[6] However, if the claim involves a personal injury to a child under eight years of age, and if it accrued on or after August 7, 1997, the action may have to be brought before the child's tenth birthday. To date, the Alaska Supreme Court has not decided if it will interpret Alaska Stat. § 09.10.140(c) in such a manner as to limit the timeframe in which claims can be filed on behalf of children who were injured when they were less than eight years old.[7]

Under most circumstances, a sexual abuse victim must commence an action against the perpetrator, for damages from an injury or condition suffered as a result of the sexual abuse, within three years.[8] The statute of limitations for claims for sexual abuse is tolled during any period of minority and incompetency and may extend beyond three years after the plaintiff reaches majority if certain conditions can be shown.[9]

B. TORT REFORM

The several significant limitations on noneconomic and punitive damages that have been accomplished legislatively are currently being challenged on constitutional due process grounds.

C. "NO FAULT" LIMITATIONS

Not applicable in Alaska.

D. **THE STANDARD FOR NEGLIGENCE**

In order to prevail on a negligence claim, a party must prove "a duty, a breach of that duty, and an injury which was proximately caused by the breach."[10]

The following factors are considered in determining whether a duty exists: (1) foreseeability of harm to plaintiff; (2) degree of certainty that plaintiff suffered injury; (3) closeness of connection between defendant's conduct and injury suffered; (4) moral blame attached to defendant's conduct; (5) policy for preventing future harm; (6) extent of burden to defendant and consequences to community by imposing a duty to exercise care, with resulting liability for breach; and (7) availability, cost, and prevalence of insurance for the risk involved.[11]

Under common law, there is no duty to safeguard others from foreseeable harm, by controlling or warning of the conduct of third parties.[12] There is an exception to this rule when a special relationship with either the victim or third party exists.[13] A special relationship has been found to exist where a person voluntarily renders services, or aids another.[14]

E. **CAUSATION**

The two prongs to legal cause in negligence are: (1) actual causation; and (2) a more intangible legal policy element.[15] In most cases, the "but for" test is the appropriate test for actual causation.[16] As for the legal policy prong, the question is "whether the conduct has been so significant and important a cause that the defendant should be legally responsible."[17] A valid instruction on legal causation must include both of these elements.[18]

In Alaska, the doctrine of superseding cause will relieve a negligent actor of liability only in exceptional cases. An act will not constitute a superseding cause where, though unforeseeable by the original negligent actor, it does not appear in retrospect to have been highly extraordinary.[19]

F. **COMPARATIVE NEGLIGENCE AND ASSUMPTION OF RISK**

In 1975, the Alaska Supreme Court adopted the "pure" comparative negligence model.[20] The legislature has since codified it.[21] Accordingly, the plaintiff's contributory fault does not bar recovery, but merely diminishes proportionately the amount awarded as compensatory damages.[22] Similarly, assumption of risk is not a complete defense to a tort action either.[23] It is just another factor that may reduce the plaintiff's recovery under the principles of comparative fault.

The Alaska Supreme Court recently held that the definition of "comparative negligence" in a products liability action is no longer limited to product misuse and unreasonable assumption of risk, but also includes other types of comparative fault including the plaintiff's ordinary negligence.[24]

For actions accruing before August 7, 1997, a jury may only allocate fault to parties to the action, including third-party defendants and released parties.[25] For actions accruing after August 7, 1997, a jury may allocate fault to every claimant, defendant, third-party defendant, and person who has been released from liability, and in addition, any person "responsible for the damages" unless the parties to the action had a "sufficient opportunity" to join them and failed to do so.[26] Although not an express requirement of the statute, it is suggested that notice of intent to seek allocation of fault to such a person is advisable if not required.[27]

A third-party defendant can be sued for apportionment of fault under Alaska Stat. § 09.17.080 after the statute of limitations has run on the plaintiff's claim and can be held liable to the plaintiff for any money damages allocated to the third-party defendant.[28]

G. *RES IPSA LOQUITUR* AND ULTRAHAZARDOUS ACTIVITIES

1. *Res Ipsa Loquitur*

The doctrine of *res ipsa loquitur* "'dispens[es] with the requirement that a plaintiff specifically prove breach of duty, once that duty and proximate cause have been established,' and applies only when an accident ordinarily does not occur in the absence of negligence."[29]

The plaintiff is entitled to a "res ipsa loquitur instruction if the trial court determines that the evidence introduced at trial, viewed in a light most favorable to the plaintiff, could lead the jury reasonably to conclude that the doctrine's elements were established."[30]

2. Ultrahazardous Activities

Alaska has adopted the "ultrahazardous activities" test as formulated in the First Restatement.[31] "An activity is ultrahazardous if it (a) necessarily involves a risk of serious harm to the person, land or chattels of others which cannot be eliminated by the exercise of the utmost care; and (b) is not a matter of common usage."[32] The court, not the jury, decides whether or not an activity is ultrahazardous.[33]

H. NEGLIGENCE *PER SE*

Alaska has adopted the Second Restatement for the determination of negligence *per se*.[34] The trial court makes the determination on whether or not the conduct implicates the statute, regulation, or ordinance in question before giving an instruction to the jury on negligence *per se*.[35] If the court so finds, it is obligated to give the instruction unless it determines the law is obscure, outdated, or amounts essentially to the common law duty to act reasonably under the circumstances.[36]

I. SEVERAL LIABILITY

Joint and several liability has been abolished.[37] Multiple tortfeasors are individually financially responsible only to the extent of their proportional fault, as allocated by the jury.[38] There is no contribution between joint tortfeasors.[39]

J. INDEMNITY

"The obligation of indemnity is the obligation resting on one party to make good a loss or damage another has incurred."[40] However, an indemnitee is not able to recover from indemnitor if the indemnitee "actively participated in the wrongful acts that caused the damage."[41] As provided by statute, each tortfeasor must pay their respective portion of plaintiff's damages.[42] Further, Alaska law "voids indemnity clauses in construction-related contracts when they purport to indemnify the promisee against liability from the sole negligence 'of the promisee or the promisee's agents, servants or independent contractors who are directly responsible to the promisee.'"[43]

K. BAR OF WORKERS' COMPENSATION STATUTE

Under the Alaska Worker's Compensation Act, the employee is barred from suing the employer who has paid workers' compensation benefits for the employee's work-related injuries.[44] Workers' compensation is the exclusive remedy.[45] The employee is compensated irrespective of fault.[46] Receiving benefits does not preclude an employee from seeking damages from a third party who was at fault or otherwise negligent.[47] Nor does it affect the ability of the employer to seek recovery from the third party in order to recover any amounts paid by the employer.[48] An exception to the exclusivity doctrine exists in cases of intentional torts committed by the employer or fellow employee.[49]

However, evidence of an employer's negligence may be admitted in an employee's action against third-party tortfeasors to allow the jury to allocate fault to the employer, even though the employer is not answerable in damages to the employee/plaintiff.[50]

L. PREMISES LIABILITY

The Alaska Supreme Court abolished the distinctions of trespasser, invitee, and licensee for purposes of premises liability.[51] Instead, "a landowner or owner of other property must act as a reasonable person in maintaining his property in a reasonably safe condition in view of all the circumstances, including the likelihood of injury to others, the seriousness of the injury, and the burden on the respective parties of avoiding the risk."[52]

Alaska does have a recreational use/landowner immunity statute.[53] This statute provides tort immunity for personal injury or death occurring on unimproved land if: (1) the injury or death resulted from a natural condition *or* the person entered the land purely for recreation; (2) the person was not obligated to compensate the landowner for this use or occupancy of the land; and (3) the landowner did not engage in any act or omission that was grossly negligent, reckless, or intentional misconduct.[54]

M. DRAM SHOP LIABILITY

A licensed vendor and/or his agents or employees may be held civilly liable for damages if, with criminal negligence, they sell alcoholic beverages, and the customer's intoxication was a proximate cause in bringing about the harm.[55] Social hosts are immune from civil liability, even if serving minors.[56]

N. ECONOMIC LOSS

"For the purpose of strict liability, recovery for economic loss is limited to contractual remedies."[57] Recovery for purely economic loss for a negligence claim requires a plaintiff to establish that "the defendant[ ] knew or reasonably should have foreseen both that particular plaintiffs or an identifiable class of plaintiffs were at risk and that ascertainable economic damages would ensue from the conduct."[58]

O. FRAUD AND MISREPRESENTATION

The Alaska Civil Rules require that a cause of action for fraud be pleaded with particularity.[59]

An action for fraud requires proof of the five elements of the tort action for deceit: (1) false representation; (2) defendant knows representation to be false; (3) defendant intends to induce plaintiff to take action or refrain from taking action; (4) plaintiff justifiably relies on the false statement in taking action or refraining from taking action; and (5) plaintiff suffers damages.[60]

Further, the law permits recovery for emotional distress damages under a fraud theory, but only when such damages are severe.[61]

The elements of negligent misrepresentation include: (1) knowledge, or its equivalent, by defendant, that the information is desired for a serious purpose and plaintiff intended to rely on it; (2) foreseeability of harm to plaintiff; (3) degree of certainty that plaintiff would be harmed; (4) directness of cause; and (5) policy of preventing future harm.[62]

P. CONSUMER FRAUD STATUTES

Alaska's Unfair Trade Practices and Consumer Protection Laws (UTPCPL) protects consumers from unfair or deceptive methods of trade.[63] The attorney general may pursue civil penalties and/or injunctive relief for violations.[64] Private actions may also be brought under the UTPCPL.[65] A private or class action must be brought within two years.[66]

Q. PUNITIVE DAMAGES

Punitive damages are determined in a bifurcated manner for all actions accruing on or after August 7, 1997.[67] First, the jury, concurrent with its decision on all other issues presented to it, must decide if the plaintiff proved, by "clear and convincing evidence," that the defendant's conduct was outrageous, or evidenced reckless indifference to the interests of others.[68] If shown, the amount of punitive damages to be awarded is then determined at a separate proceeding.[69]

Factors considered at the subsequent proceeding include, in part: (1) financial condition of defendant; (2) duration of conduct and intent in concealment; (3) presence of financial gain as motive; (4) defendant's awareness of likelihood of serious harm; and (5) total deterrence of other damages and punishments imposed on defendant, including criminal.[70]

The 1997 Tort Reform placed several caps on punitive damages for actions accruing on or after August 7, 1997.[71] Under the new caps, in most cases, a punitive damage award cannot exceed the greater of three times the amount of compensatory damages awarded, or $500,000.[72]

R. WRONGFUL DEATH

An action for wrongful death is statutory, but treated similarly to common law tort actions.[73] The amount recovered by the decedent's personal representative is for the exclusive benefit of the decedent's spouse, children, and/or other dependents.[74] If none exists, the amount recovered shall be distributed as personal property, but is limited to pecuniary loss.[75]

Alaska's wrongful death statute does not provide the parents of a minor child who is killed with a loss of society claim, but Alaska Stat. § 09.15.010 creates a separate, independent parental cause of action under which such a claim may be made.[76]

S. ATTORNEY'S FEES

Alaska Civil Rules provide for a prevailing party to be awarded a portion of its attorney's fees.[77] The rule provides for a sliding scale amount, dependent on the stage of litigation and the judgment awarded (including prejudgment interest).[78] In the case where the prevailing party recovers no money judgment (e.g., a defendant), it is entitled to a sliding scale amount of its reasonable actual attorney's fees, which are necessarily incurred.[79] The rule also allows the court to vary the amount, up or down, depending on the application of several listed factors.[80]

John B. Thorsness
Lisa C. Hamby
HUGHES THORSNESS POWELL HUDDLESTON
& BAUMAN L.L.C.
550 West Seventh Avenue, Suite 1100
Anchorage, Alaska 99501-3563
(907) 274-7522
Fax (907) 263-8320
lch@htlaw.com

ENDNOTES - ALASKA

1. *See* Alaska Stat. § 09.10.070 which lists the following actions as having a two-year statute of limitations:

    (1) libel, slander, assault, battery, seduction, or false imprisonment;
    (2) personal injury or death, or injury to the rights of another not arising on contract and not specifically provided otherwise;
    (3) taking, detaining, or injuring personal property, including an action for its specific recovery;
    (4) upon a statute for a forfeiture or penalty to the state;
    (5) upon a liability created by statute, other than a penalty or forfeiture; or
    (6) against a peace officer or coroner upon a liability incurred by the doing of an act in an official capacity or by the omission of an official duty, including the nonpayment of money collected upon an execution.

2. *Russell v. Municipality of Anchorage*, 743 P.2d 372, 375 (Alaska 1987) (citing *Hanebuth v. Bell Helicopter Int'l*, 694 P.2d 143, 144 (Alaska 1984)).

3. *See Kodiak Elec. Assn. v. Delaval Turbine, Inc.*, 694 P.2d 150 (Alaska 1984); ch. 26, S.L.A. 1997.

4. *See* Alaska Stat. § 09.10.100.

5. *See* Alaska Stat. § 09.10.055. The section does not apply if:

    (1) the personal injury, death, or property damage resulted from:
       (a) prolonged exposure to hazardous waste;
       (b) an intentional act or gross negligence;
       (c) fraud or misrepresentation;
       (d) breach of an express warranty or guarantee;
       (e) a defective product; in this subparagraph, "product" means an object that has intrinsic value, is capable of delivery as an assembled whole or as a component part, and is introduced into trade or commerce; or
       (f) breach of trust or fiduciary duty;
    (2) the facts that would give notice of a potential cause of action are intentionally concealed;
    (3) a shorter period of time for bringing the action is imposed under another provision of law;
    (4) the provisions of this section are waived by contract; or

(5) the facts that would constitute accrual of a cause of action of a minor are not discoverable in the exercise of reasonable care by the minor's parent or guardian.

Further, the statute of repose is tolled during any period in which there exists the undiscovered presence of a foreign body that has no therapeutic or diagnostic purpose or effect in the body of the injured person and the action is based on the presence of the foreign body.

6. *See* Alaska Stat. § 09.10.140.

7. See Alaska Stat. § 09.17.040(c).

8. *See* Alaska Stat. § 09.10.060.

9. *See* Alaska Stat. § 09.10.140(b).

10. *Richey v. Oen*, 824 P.2d 1371, 1374 (Alaska 1992) (citation omitted).

11. *R.E. v. State*, 878 P.2d 1341, 1346 (Alaska 1994) (citing *D.S.W. v. Fairbanks N. Star Borough Sch. Dist.*, 628 P.2d 554, 555–56 (Alaska 1981)).

12. *See id.* at 1348; *see also Division of Corrections, Dept. of Health & Social Services v. Neakok*, 721 P.2d 1121, 1126 (Alaska 1986).

13. *See R.E.*, 878 P.2d at 1348.

14. *See id.*

15. *See Vincent by Staton v. Fairbanks Memorial Hosp.*, 862 P.2d 847, 851 (Alaska 1993) (footnotes omitted).

16. *See id.*

17. *Id.* at 851 (quoting W. Page Keeton et al., Prosser and Keeton on Torts § 42, at 273 (5th ed. 1984)).

18. *See id.*

19. *Griffith v. Taylor*, 12 P.3d 1163, 1168 (Alaska 2000); *Chenega Corp. v. Exxon Corp.*, 991 P.2d 769, 798 (Alaska 1999).

20. *See Kaatz v. State*, 540 P.2d 1037, 1049 (Alaska 1975).

21. *See* Alaska Stat. §§ 09.17.060 & .080.

22. *See* Alaska Stat. § 09.17.060.

23. *See Hiibschman ex rel. Welch v. City of Valdez*, 821 P.2d 1354 (Alaska 1991).

24. *Smith v. Ingersoll-Rand Co.*, 14 P.3d 990, 996 (Alaska 2000).

25. *See Benner v. Wichman*, 874 P.2d 949, 958 (Alaska 1994).

26. *See* Alaska Stat. § 09.17.080(a)(2).

27. *See Fancyboy v. Alaska Village Elect. Coop., Inc.*, 984 P.2d 1128 (Alaska 1999).

28. *See Alaska General Alarm, Inc. v. Grinnell*, 1 P.3d 98 (Alaska 2000).

29. *Falconer v. Adams*, 974 P.2d 406, 417 n.12 (Alaska 1999) (quoting *State Farm Fire & Cas. Co. v. Municipality of Anchorage*, 788 P.2d 726, 730 (Alaska 1990) (quoting *Widmyer v. Southeast Skyways, Inc.*, 584 P.2d 1, 10 (Alaska 1978))).

30. *State Farm*, 788 P.2d at 730 (citation omitted).

31. *See Matomco Oil Co., Inc. v. Arctic Mechanical, Inc.*, 796 P.2d 1336, 1344 (Alaska 1990); *State Farm*, 788 P.2d 726.

32. Restatement (First) of Torts § 520 (1938).

33. *See Yukon Equipment v. Fireman's Fund*, 585 P.2d 1206, 1210 (Alaska 1978).

34. *See Ferrell v. Baxter*, 484 P.2d 250, 263 (Alaska 1971); Restatement (Second) of Torts §§ 286, 288A & 288B (1965).

35. *See Shanks v. Upjohn*, 835 P.2d 1189 (Alaska 1992).

36. *See id.*

37. *See* Alaska Stat. § 09.17.080(d); *Robinson v. Alaska Properties & Inv., Inc.*, 878 F. Supp. 1318 (D. Alaska 1995).

38. *See Robinson*, 878 F. Supp. 1318.

39. *See Carriere v. Cominco Alaska, Inc.*, 823 F. Supp. 680 (D. Alaska 1993).

40. *Fairbanks North Star Borough v. Kandik Const., Inc. and Associates*, 823 P.2d 632, 637 (Alaska 1991) (citation omitted).

41. *Id.* at 638 (citations omitted).

42. *See* Alaska Stat. §§ 09.17.060 & .080.

43. *Aetna Cas. & Sur. Co. v. Marion Equipment Co.*, 894 P.2d 664, 671 (Alaska 1995) (quoting Alaska Stat. § 45.45.900)).

44. *See* Alaska Stat. § 23.30.055.

45. *See id.*

46. *See* Alaska Stat. § 23.30.045.

47. *See* Alaska Stat. § 23.30.015(a).

48. *See* Alaska Stat. § 23.30.050.

49. *Van Biene v. ERA Helicopters, Inc.*, 779 P.2d 315, 318 (Alaska 1989).

50. *See* Alaska Stat. 09.17.080; § 1, ch. 26, S.L.A. 1997.

51. *See Webb v. City and Borough of Sitka*, 561 P.2d 731, 733 (Alaska 1977).

52. *Id.*

53. *See* Alaska Stat. § 09.65.200.

54. *See id.; see also, Alaska v. Shanti*, 835 P.2d 1225 (Alaska 1992).

55. *See Kavorkian v. Tommy's Elbow Room, Inc.*, 711 P.2d 521 (Alaska 1985); Alaska Stat. § 04.16.030.

56. *See* Alaska Stat. § 04.21.020; *Chokwak v. Worley*, 912 P.2d 1248 (Alaska 1996).

57. *Smith v. Tyonek Timber, Inc.*, 680 P.2d 1148, 1152 (Alaska 1984).

58. *See Mattingly v. Sheldon Jackson College*, 743 P.2d 356, 360 (Alaska 1987).

59. *See* Alaska Rule of Civil Procedure 9(b).

60. *See Palmer v. Borg-Warner Corp.*, 838 P.2d 1243, 1252 n.16 (Alaska 1992) (citing W. Page Keeton et al., Prosser and Keeton on the Law of Torts, § 105 at 728 (5th ed. 1984)).

61. *See Nelson v. Progressive Corp.*, 976 P.2d 859, 868 (Alaska 1999).

62. *See Howarth v. Pfeifer*, 443 P.2d 39, 42 (Alaska 1968).

63. *See* Alaska Stat. §§ 45.50.471, *et seq.*

64. *See* Alaska Stat. §§ 45.50.501 & 551.

65. *See* Alaska Stat. §§ 45.50.531 & 535.

66. *See* Alaska Stat. § 45.50.531.

67. *See* Alaska Stat. § 09.17.020.

68. *See* Alaska Stat. § 09.17.020(b).

69. *See* Alaska Stat. § 09.17.020(a).

70. *See* Alaska Stat. § 09.17.020(b).

71. *See* § 55, ch. 26, S.L.A. 1997.

72. *See* Alaska Stat. § 09.17.020.

73. *See Tommy's Elbow Room, Inc. v. Kavorkian*, 727 P.2d 1038 (Alaska 1986) (citing *Haakanson v. Wakefield Seafoods*, 600 P.2d 1087, 1092 (Alaska 1979)); Alaska Stat. § 09.55.580.

74. *See* Alaska Stat. § 09.55.580.

75. *See id.*

76. *See Gillispie v. Beta Const. Co.*, 842 P.2d 1272, 1273 (Alaska 1992).

77. *See* Alaska Rule of Civil Procedure 82.

78. *See id.*

79. *See id.*

80. *See id.*

ARIZONA

Arizona's tort law is an amalgam of common law, constitutional law, and statutory law. In the absence of an Arizona case, statute, or other authority on point, Arizona generally follows the Restatements of the Law.[1]

A. STATUTES OF LIMITATION

Actions for malicious prosecution, false imprisonment, libel, slander, seduction or breach of promise of marriage, breach of an oral or written employment contract (including actions based on employee handbooks or policy manuals that do not specify a time period in which to bring an action), and wrongful termination must be brought within one year.[2] Actions created by statute must also be brought within one year (absent an overriding provision in the liability-creating statute).[3] Actions against a public entity or public employee also must be brought within one year,[4] and a notice of the claim must be filed within 180 days after the cause of action accrues.[5]

Actions for personal injuries, medical malpractice, death, or property damage must be brought within two years.[6] The "discovery" rule applies.[7] Negligence and product liability actions are subject to the two-year statute of limitation.[8]

Actions on oral contracts, stated or open accounts, and for fraud or mistake must be brought within three years.[9] State civil RICO actions also must be brought within three years.[10]

An action for specific performance of a contract to convey realty must be brought within four years.[11]

Actions on written contracts must be brought within six years.[12]

The "catch-all" provision provides a four-year limitation period for all actions that are not subject to another limitation section.[13]

An eight-year statute of repose applies to contract claims arising out of improvements to real property.[14] In the case of injury to real property or improvements to real property, actions based on injuries that occurred in the eighth year following substantial completion, or on a latent defect discovered during the eighth year, may be brought within one year of the injury or discovery, but no more than nine years following substantial completion of the improvement.[15]

A "saving statute" provides a six-month refiling period following termination for actions filed within the statutory time period but terminated in any manner other than abatement, voluntary dismissal, dismissal for lack of prosecution, or a final judgment on the merits.[16]

B. TORT REFORM

Before August 31, 1984: (1) joint and several liability applied in Arizona; (2) the plaintiff's contributory negligence was an absolute bar to recovery (unless the defendant's conduct was wanton or reckless); and (3) joint tortfeasors had no right to contribution. Effective August 31, 1984, Arizona enacted the Uniform Contribution Among Tortfeasors Act (UCATA), Arizona Revised Statutes (A.R.S.) §§ 12-2501–2509. The Act created: (1) a right of contribution among tortfeasors; and (2) comparative negligence, which allowed the plaintiff's recovery to be reduced proportionally based on his or her negligence, but removed the absolute bar of contributory negligence.

Effective January 1, 1988, the Arizona Legislature enacted A.R.S. § 12-2506, which abolished joint and several liability, except in very limited circumstances. In situations where joint and several liability still exists (currently, where the parties are acting in concert or where one party was acting as the agent or servant of another party), the UCATA contribution provisions still apply. Accordingly, Arizona is now a "pure" comparative fault state, and fault for an injury can be allocated among those responsible for an injury, whether their fault arises from negligence in all of its degrees, contributory negligence, assumption of the risk, strict liability, breach of express or implied warranty of a product, products liability and misuse, or modification or abuse of a product.[17]

In the last several years, the legislature has made other efforts at major substantive tort reform, but such efforts have been defeated by the voting public through the referendum process.

C. "NO FAULT" LIMITATIONS

In general, Arizona requires motor vehicles operated on an Arizona highway to be covered by an automobile liability policy that covers certain "financial responsibility requirements." A.R.S. § 28-4135. There is no statute, however, legislating mandatory insurance compensation for injuries resulting from motor vehicles.

D. THE STANDARD FOR NEGLIGENCE

Actionable negligence is "the existence of a duty owed by the defendant to the plaintiff, a breach of that duty and an injury proximately caused by that breach."[18] To recover, a plaintiff must prove: (1) the defendant owed the plaintiff a duty of care; (2) the standard defining the nature and extent of the duty; (3) the defendant breached that duty by falling below the standard of care; (4) damages; (5) the damages would not have occurred "but for" the defendant's conduct; and (6) the defendant's conduct proximately or legally caused the damages.[19]

The basic standard of conduct is simple: A person must act with "reasonable care under the circumstances."[20] Arizona recognizes a special standard of care for professionals. Professionals are required to possess a minimum level of special knowledge and ability associated with their field of expertise.[21] Expert testimony may be necessary to establish the applicable standard and whether a breach of the standard has occurred.[22] Typically, the question of duty is a question of law for the courts.[23] Arizona recognizes the general rule that a defendant has no duty to control the conduct of third persons.[24] However, a duty to control the conduct of third persons may arise if there is a special relationship between the parties.[25]

A child is not held to the same objective standard of care as that of an adult. In Arizona, children must conform to the behavior of a "reasonable person of like age, intelligence, and experience under the circumstances."[26] Early Arizona decisions suggest that children under the age of five and one-half are incapable of negligence.[27]

E. CAUSATION

In order to establish a *prima facie* case in negligence, the plaintiff must demonstrate that the defendant's negligence was a legal "cause" of plaintiff's injury. Legal causation consists of two parts: cause-in-fact and proximate cause.[28]

The defendant's negligence is a "cause-in-fact" of the plaintiff's injury if it helped produce the injury.[29] Because Arizona does not follow the "substantial factor" test,[30] the plaintiff need only show a "reasonable connection" between the defendant's negligence and the plaintiff's injury.[31] "Cause-in-fact" can be found even where the defendant's negligence contributed only slightly to the plaintiff's injury.[32]

The defendant's negligence is a "proximate cause" of the plaintiff's injury if in the natural and continuous sequence of events, the plaintiff's injury would not have resulted without the defendant's negligence.[33]

When an act in addition to the defendant's negligence intervenes to cause the plaintiff's injury, a court must ask whether the "intervening act" is legally responsible for the plaintiff's injury as a "superseding cause."[34] A "superseding cause" is an event that, with the benefit of hindsight, was both unforeseeable and abnormal or extraordinary from the point of view of the party who caused the first event to occur.[35] Generally, a "superseding cause" is not found where the defendant's negligence was a substantial factor in bringing about the plaintiff's injuries.[36] The defendant is not liable to the plaintiff for the injuries that resulted from a "superseding cause."[37]

In Arizona, causation ordinarily is a question of fact reserved for the jury.[38]

F. CONTRIBUTORY NEGLIGENCE, COMPARATIVE NEGLIGENCE, ASSUMPTION OF RISK, AND PROSPECTIVE RELEASE

1. Contributory Negligence

With the adoption of the Uniform Contribution Among Tortfeasors Act (UCATA),[39] Arizona abolished the common law notion of contributory negligence as an absolute defense.[40] Nevertheless, in any civil action, the finder of fact may find the defendant not liable if the defendant proves that the claimant was under the influence of alcohol or drugs and, as a result, the claimant was at least 50 percent responsible for the event causing harm.[41] Likewise, in any civil action, a defendant is not liable for damages to the plaintiff that stem from the negligence or gross negligence of any defendant while the plaintiff is attempting to commit, committing, or fleeing from a felony criminal act.[42] In the case of a misdemeanor, the defendant is not liable to the plaintiff for negligence or gross negligence if the plaintiff was attempting to commit or committing a misdemeanor criminal act that directly relates to the defendant or the defendant's property.[43]

Arizona recognizes the "seat belt defense."[44]

2. **Comparative Negligence**

Comparative negligence is a form of contributory negligence.[45] The defense of contributory/comparative negligence is always a question of fact that must be left to the jury (the Arizona Constitution allows the jury to disregard a plaintiff's contributory negligence as it sees fit under the facts of each case).[46] The jury is permitted to determine, first, whether contributory negligence exists from the facts, and then whether to apply the law of contributory negligence as a defense.[47]

The UCATA provides for the application of comparative negligence in Arizona.[48] With comparative negligence, instead of barring a claimant's action, the damages are reduced in proportion to the relative degree of the claimant's fault that is the proximate cause of the injury or death.[49] Thus, although Arizona still uses the term "contributory negligence," it is applying comparative negligence principles rather than the absolute bar of common law contributory negligence.[50]

A person who has intentionally, willfully, or wantonly caused or contributed to an injury or death does not have a right to the benefit of comparative negligence.[51] Thus, if the jury finds that a person willfully or wantonly contributed to his own injury, the jury should not determine relative degrees of fault, but may find for the defendant or plaintiff as the jury sees fit.[52] A willful and wanton defendant, however, still has a right to benefit from the principles of comparative negligence.[53]

Although the common law defense of contributory negligence is not a defense in a strict product liability action, Arizona applies comparative fault to product misuse in a strict liability case.[54] Employers who fail to secure workers' compensation for their employees cannot assert the defense of contributory negligence.[55]

3. **Assumption of Risk**

In Arizona, assumption of risk is a comparative defense.[56] Thus, if the jury applies assumption of risk, the plaintiff's claim is not barred, but the damages will be reduced in proportion to the relative degree of the plaintiff's fault that is the proximate cause of the injury.[57]

The elements of assumption of risk are: (1) a risk of harm to plaintiff caused by defendant's conduct or property, (2) plaintiff's actual knowledge of the particular risk and appreciation of its magnitude, and (3) plaintiff's voluntary choice to accept the risk given the circumstances.[58] The distinct difference between assumption of risk and contributory negligence is that contributory negligence arises when the plaintiff fails to exercise due care, but assumption of risk arises regardless of the due care used and is fundamentally based on consent.[59] The defense of assumption of risk is always a question of fact that must be left to the jury.[60] The jury is permitted to determine, first, whether assumption of risk exists from the facts, and then whether to apply the law of assumption of risk as a defense.[61] The defense is not available to employers that fail to secure workers' compensation for their employees.[62]

4. **Prospective Release**

Under certain circumstances, Arizona recognizes that a party may agree in advance that one party shall not be liable to the other for negligence. In general, the release should be specific, explicit, and conspicuous, and should clearly indicate that the party is being released from its own negligence. The language of the release will be strictly construed against the party relying upon it.[63]

G. *RES IPSA LOQUITUR* AND INHERENTLY DANGEROUS ACTIVITIES

1. *Res Ipsa Loquitur*

Arizona recognizes the circumstantial evidence doctrine of res ipsa loquitur ("the thing speaks for itself"), which deals with situations where the fact that a particular injury occurred may itself establish or tend to establish a breach of duty owed.[64] The doctrine applies if: (1) the event is of a kind that ordinarily does not occur in the absence of someone's negligence;[65] (2) the event is caused by an agency or instrumentality within the exclusive control of the defendant; and (3) plaintiff is not in a position to show the cause of the particular circumstances that caused the offending agency or instrumentality to operate to his injury.[66]

The first requirement of the doctrine requires the plaintiff to establish that it is more likely than not that negligence was the cause of the injury.[67] Negligence must be established by a preponderance of the evidence.[68] However, the plaintiff is not required to rule out every conceivable explanation other than negligence.[69] The mere fact that an injury occurred is not sufficient. Thus, plaintiff must produce some evidence to support an inference of negligence on the part of the defendant.[70]

The second requirement, exclusive control of the instrumentality by defendant, is liberally construed.[71] Accordingly, the doctrine has been applied to multiple defendants so long as all defendants had exclusive control of the instrumentality.[72] Similarly, a third party entrusted with the object may meet this requirement.[73]

Under the last requirement of *res ipsa loquitur*, the plaintiff must establish that he or she is not able to prove the defendant's negligence. Significantly, however, it is only where the existence of negligence is a more reasonable deduction from the facts shown that a plaintiff is permitted to call this rule to his aid.[74] Plaintiff should not be allowed to prevail where, on proof of the occurrence, without more, the matter still rests on conjecture alone.[75] If the plaintiff alleges specific acts of negligence, the doctrine is inapplicable.[76]

The doctrine, where applicable, does not change the burden of proof, nor does it create a presumption of negligence; it merely permits an inference of negligence to be drawn.[77]

2. Inherently Dangerous Activities

An actor may be liable, regardless of his use of due care, when he injures someone while engaged in an inherently dangerous activity, such as blasting. An activity may be characterized as inherently dangerous if: (1) the risk of harm cannot be eliminated through the exercise of reasonable care; and (2) the risk is to person, land, or chattels of another.[78] However, no bright line exists for classifying work that is inherently dangerous and that which is not.[79] The determination is made on a case-by-case basis depending on the facts.[80]

H. NEGLIGENCE *PER SE*

"A person who violates a statute enacted for the protection and safety of the public is guilty of negligence per se."[81] Negligence *per se* establishes both duty and the required breach of duty elements of a negligence action.[82] To recover, a plaintiff also must prove that the defendant proximately caused the plaintiff's injury.[83]

I. JOINT AND SEVERAL LIABILITY

Pursuant to the Uniform Contribution Among Tortfeasors Act,[84] joint and several liability has been abolished in Arizona except in very limited circumstances.[85] In general, liability is several only and not joint.[86] Liability is assessed in direct proportion to the defendant's percentage of fault.[87] The judgment against each defendant is determined by multiplying the total amount of damages recoverable by the plaintiff by each defendant's percentage of fault, and that amount is the maximum the plaintiff can recover against that defendant, regardless of plaintiff's ability (or lack thereof) to recover damages from other parties.[88]

Exceptions: When Joint and Several Liability Is Still Available

Joint and several liability still exists when parties are found to be acting in concert, where one party acts as an agent or servant of the other party, or where liability arises under the Federal Employers' Liability Act (45 U.S.C. § 51).[89] Arizona recognizes the distinction between employees and independent contractors for purposes of respondeat superior liability.[90] Arizona's statute defines "acting in concert" as:

> entering into a conscious agreement to pursue a common plan or design to commit an intentional tort and actively taking part in that intentional tort. Acting in concert does not apply to any person whose conduct was negligent in any of its degrees rather than intentional. A person's conduct which provides substantial assistance to one committing an intentional tort does not constitute acting in concert if the person has not consciously agreed with the other to commit the intentional tort.[91]

If a defendant is found jointly and severally liable to the plaintiff, the defendant has a right to contribution from other defendants to the extent that the defendant satisfies more than its proportionate share of the award.[92]

J. INDEMNITY

Indemnity shifts the entire loss of the plaintiff from one defendant to another based on an implied contract for indemnity or when justice demands there be the right.[93] In other words, a person who, in whole or in part, has discharged a duty that is owed by him but which, between himself and another, should have been discharged by the other, is entitled to indemnity from the other.[94] The cornerstone of implied indemnity is the relationship of the parties.[95] Indemnity exists, however, only where the whole of the fault was in the one against whom indemnity is sought.[96]

Indemnity may be provided by contract. When the parties expressly agree on indemnity provisions in their contract, the extent of the duty is defined by the contract itself rather than common law principles.[97] An agreement for indemnity will not be interpreted to indemnify against the indemnitee's own negligence or wrongdoing unless the indemnification agreement so provides in clear and unambiguous terms.[98]

K. WORKERS' COMPENSATION

The Arizona Workers' Compensation Act[99] provides that an injured worker cannot sue his or her employer for work-related injuries if the employer has provided the appropriate workers' compensation benefits.[100] Similarly, an injured worker is barred from suing a coworker if the coworker was acting within the scope of his or her employment at the time of the injury-causing event.[101] There are limited exceptions to this exclusive remedy rule.[102] The primary exception concerns injuries resulting from "willful misconduct." If injury results from willful misconduct, the employee must opt either to accept compensation benefits or institute an action at law for damages.[103]

The exclusive remedy doctrine does not prevent an injured employee from suing a third person wholly or partially responsible for his or her injuries.[104] There is no requirement that an injured worker elect between workers' compensation benefits and the institution of a lawsuit against a third party. However, the payor of workers' compensation benefits is awarded a lien on the employee's third-party recovery.[105] The lien extends to all compensation, medical, surgical, and hospital benefits paid,[106] and the injured employee cannot compromise the third-party claim for less than the amount of benefits paid without the written approval of the workers' compensation insurance carrier.[107] The exclusive remedy doctrine does not prevent a third-party defendant from allocating fault to the employer or its employees for purposes of contributory negligence or other theories of fault, even though the employee is barred from bringing an action against the employer or coemployees.[108] To the extent that the employer is ultimately found to be partially at fault in a lawsuit against a third party, its lien is reduced in proportion to its fault.[109] If the injured worker obtains a settlement without approval, he or she will be precluded from reopening the claim, thus forfeiting the right to future benefits.[110]

If the injured employee fails to institute a suit against the third party within one year after that cause of action accrues, the claim is automatically assigned to the insurance carrier or person/entity liable for the payment of workers' compensation benefits.[111] The Act permits the payor of benefits to "reassign" the claim back to the injured employee, but reassignment is permissive and the payor may opt to retain a claim that has passed to it through the operation of the statute.[112] Thus, the injured employee should be careful to institute suit against the third party within one year even though the statute of limitations for the relevant cause of action may be longer.

L. **PREMISES LIABILITY**

The particular duty owed by landowners to entrants on land is defined by the entrant's status.[113] Arizona follows the Restatement's categories of entrants to land: trespassers, licensees, and invitees.[114] Landowners have a duty to invitees to maintain their property in a reasonably safe manner.[115] Owners owe a duty to licensees to warn of hidden perils and to refrain from willfully causing a licensee harm.[116] Finally, a landowner owes a duty to trespassers to refrain from willfully or wantonly injuring the trespasser.[117] Arizona, however, has adopted the "attractive nuisance" doctrine set forth by the Restatement.[118] Under the attractive nuisance doctrine, a landowner is liable to a child trespasser for injuries caused by artificial conditions on the land if "the children because of their youth do not discover the condition or realize the risk involved in intermeddling with it or in coming within the area made dangerous by it. . . ."[119]

Arizona's Recreational Use Statute limits landowner liability to recreational or educational users of land.[120] The Recreational Use Statute provides that a landowner is not liable to a recreational or educational user "except upon a showing that the owner . . . was guilty of willful, malicious or grossly negligent conduct which was a direct cause of the injury to the recreational or educational user."[121]

M. DRAM SHOP LIABILITY

Arizona's Dram Shop Act[122] assigns liability to licensees who serve alcohol to obviously intoxicated persons where such persons actually consume the alcohol and the alcohol is the proximate cause of a subsequent injury, death, or property damage.[123] Under the statute, "obviously intoxicated" is defined as a person "inebriated to such an extent that a person's physical faculties are substantially impaired and the impairment is shown by significantly uncoordinated physical action or significant physical dysfunction, that would have been obvious to a reasonable person."[124]

Liability is also assigned to licensees who serve alcohol to persons under the legal drinking age without requesting identification containing proof of age or with knowledge that the person was under the legal drinking age when the underage person consumes the alcohol and the alcohol is a proximate cause of an injury, death, or property damage.[125] If the fact finder determines that an underage person purchased alcohol from a licensee and the injury, death, or property damage occurs within a reasonable time after the sale, a rebuttable presumption that the alcohol was consumed by the underage person is established.[126]

The legislature's attempt to codify assumption of risk and contributory negligence principles by disallowing liability to a licensee for injury, death, or property damage suffered by the person to whom the alcohol was sold or an accompanying person who knew of the impaired condition of the person served was ruled unconstitutional.[127]

Social hosts are generally immune from liability for injuries caused or suffered by their guests.[128] Social hosts, however, are not immune from liability for injuries caused or suffered by underage guests to whom they serve alcohol.[129]

N. ECONOMIC LOSS

Arizona follows an "economic loss" rule, which bars tort recovery if the plaintiff suffers only economic injury due to the failure of a defective product.[130] The rationale is that contract law is the appropriate remedy for failed commercial expectations.[131] Arizona does not, however, endorse a blanket application of the rule.[132] Instead, to determine whether a plaintiff is entitled to tort as opposed to contract damages in a case involving economic loss resulting from product failure, Arizona analyzes three interrelated factors: (1) the nature of the defect, (2) the manner in which the loss occurred, and (3) the type of loss for which the plaintiff seeks redress.[133] Under this analysis, if the plaintiff suffers economic losses such as repair costs, diminished value, or lost profits, the plaintiff typically is restricted to contract remedies.[134] On the other hand, tort recovery is appropriate if physical damage to property other than the defective product results.[135]

Under certain limited circumstances, Arizona has permitted tort recovery when the loss is strictly economic and the physical damage is restricted to the defective product itself.[136]

Some jurisdictions bar tort claims where a defendant's duty would not exist "but for" the existence of a contract. Arizona has not addressed this subject. The extent to which Arizona courts will extend the economic loss rule to areas outside the product liability arena is still undetermined.

O. FRAUD AND MISREPRESENTATION

The elements of fraud under Arizona law are: (1) a representation; (2) its falsity; (3) its materiality; (4) the speaker's knowledge of its falsity or ignorance of its truth; (5) his intent that it should be acted on by and in the manner reasonably contemplated; (6) the hearer's ignorance of its falsity; (7) his reliance on its truth; (8) his right to rely thereon; and (9) his consequent and proximate injury.[137] Actionable fraud cannot exist without a concurrence of all essential elements.[138] Under Rule 9, Arizona's Rules of Civil Procedure, fraud must be pled with specificity.

P. NEGLIGENT MISREPRESENTATION

In Arizona, the tort of negligent misrepresentation is governed by Section 552 of the Restatement (Second) of Torts. In order to prevail on a claim of negligent misrepresentation, the plaintiff must prove that: (1) defendant, in the course of its business, gave incorrect information for the guidance of others in their business transactions; (2) defendant intended that plaintiff rely on that information or could reasonably foresee that plaintiff would rely on that information; (3) defendant failed to exercise reasonable care in obtaining or communicating that information; (4) plaintiff relied on that incorrect information; (5) plaintiff's reliance was justified; and (6) plaintiff's reliance was a cause of damage to plaintiff.[139]

Liability for negligent misrepresentation does not extend to every person "who might reasonably be expected sooner or later to have access to the information and foreseeably to take some action in reliance upon it."[140] Liability is not that far-reaching. This does not mean, however, that the defendant's liability is confined to the individual or entity that actually received the information from the defendant or the individuals or entities that the defendant knows will ultimately receive the information.[141] Instead, it is sufficient that the defendant know that the recipient intended to supply the information for the benefit of a limited group or class of persons and that the plaintiff be a member of that limited group or class.[142]

Q. CONSUMER FRAUD STATUTES

The Arizona Consumer Fraud Act (ACFA)[143] was designed to eliminate unlawful practices in merchant-consumer transactions.[144] In construing the ACFA, courts are guided by federal agency and court interpretations of the Federal Trade Commission Act.[145]

In order for a transaction to fall within the ambit of the AFCA, it is not necessary for a merchant to be involved, but rather, only merchandise.[146] The term "merchandise" is broadly defined to include "any objects, wares, goods, commodities, intangibles, real estate, or services."[147]

A "sale" is defined under the foregoing statute as "any sale, offer for sale, or attempt to sell any merchandise for any consideration, including sales, leases and rentals of any real estate subject to any form of deed restriction imposed as part of a previous sale."[148] A consumer loan is also subject to the provisions of the ACFA to the extent it is a sale of present use of money for a promise to repay.[149]

The attorney general is granted various powers to accomplish the objectives of the ACFA.[150] Private causes of action may also be brought by injured consumers under the ACFA.[151] The elements of a private cause of action under this statute are a false promise or misrepresentation made in connection with the sale or advertisement of merchandise, and injury consequently and proximately caused by such false promise or misrepresentation.[152] The consumer must establish reliance on the false promise or misrepresentation, but does not need to demonstrate the reliance was reasonable.[153]

A private individual may recover under the ACFA for actual damages suffered as a result of the unlawful act or practice, including the consideration paid in the contract and out-of-pocket expenses.[154] In addition, where the conduct that violates the ACFA is deemed to be wanton or reckless, shows spite or ill will, or demonstrates a reckless indifference to others, punitive damages may be recovered for violations of the ACFA.[155]

In an action under the ACFA, a private individual is required to prove the claim by a preponderance of the evidence.[156] An action under the ACFA is subject to a one-year statute of limitations,[157] and the statute commences to run when the fraud was or could have been discovered.[158]

R. PUNITIVE DAMAGES

To recover punitive damages in Arizona, a plaintiff must prove by clear and convincing evidence that the defendant engaged in aggravated and outrageous conduct with an "evil mind."[159] An "evil mind" may be shown by evidence that the defendant intended to injure the plaintiff or consciously pursued a course of conduct knowing that it created a substantial risk of significant harm to others.[160] A defendant's gross negligence or mere reckless disregard of the circumstances, however, will not support an award of punitive damages.[161] The act on which punitive damages are based must be a proximate cause of the injury.[162]

A jury may consider several factors when deciding whether a defendant acted with an evil mind, including: (1) the reprehensibility of the defendant's conduct and the severity of the harm likely to result; (2) any harm that actually occurred; (3) the duration of the misconduct; (4) the degree of the defendant's awareness of the harm or risk of harm, and the defendant's deliberate continuation of the offending conduct; (5) attempts to conceal the misconduct; (6) defiance of law or prior orders; and (7) the defendant's failure to remedy the misconduct.[163]

A plaintiff may meet the clear and convincing standard by either direct or circumstantial evidence that persuades the jury of the high probability of the defendant's evil mind.[164] Arizona's appellate courts must affirm a jury's award of punitive damages if any reasonable view of the evidence would satisfy the clear and convincing standard.[165]

The amount of punitive damages rests in the jury's discretion and will not be disturbed on appeal unless it is so unreasonable that it is the product of passion or prejudice.[166] When assessing punitive damages, the defendant's wealth is a relevant factor to consider, but evidence of wealth is not determinative or required.[167]

A plaintiff can recover punitive damages for any tort the defendant committed with the requisite level of culpability.[168] Punitive damages cannot be awarded for breach of contract unless the defendant's conduct independently constitutes a tort.[169] A plaintiff must be awarded compensatory damages before being entitled to punitive damages.[170] Punitive damages may be awarded against the estate of a dead tortfeasor, and against an employer based on the employee's conduct under the doctrine of respondeat superior.[171]

S. WRONGFUL DEATH AND SURVIVORSHIP ACTIONS

In Arizona, wrongful death actions are based on statute.[172] A wrongful death action is one action with one plaintiff and one judgment for damages.[173] The beneficiaries are defined by statute to be the spouse, parents, and children of the decedent, or where none of them survive, the decedent's estate.[174]

In wrongful death actions, the jury shall award such damages as it deems "fair and just" to the surviving parties who are entitled to recover.[175] While the purpose of the statute is to compensate survivors for lost financial support, "the measure of damages is no longer limited to pecuniary damages, but also includes allowance for such things as loss of companionship, comfort, and guidance."[176] A plaintiff may also recover for "anguish, sorrow, mental suffering, pain and shock," even though these items are not specifically mentioned in the wrongful death act.[177] The decedent's character and relationship to the surviving parties is a matter in issue in a wrongful death action.[178] Evidence of decedent's capacity and disposition to earn money is also pertinent to the damage issue.[179]

Pursuant to Arizona's survival statute, every cause of action, with certain limited statutory exceptions, survives the death of the person entitled thereto or liable therefor, and may be asserted by or against the personal representative of such person, provided that damages for the decedent's pain and suffering are not allowed.[180]

T. LOSS OF CONSORTIUM

Arizona law allows spouses, parents, and children to sue for losses of consortium, but not siblings, grandparents, other relatives, or friends.[181] Not all injuries to a parent will result in a child's claim for loss of consortium; instead, such a claim exists where the parent suffers a serious, permanent, disabling injury rendering the parent unable to provide love, care, companionship, and guidance to the child.[182] A claim for loss of consortium is derivative, and defenses against a parent will reduce a child's recovery under the principles of comparative negligence.[183] A defendant may request that all loss of consortium claims be joined with the personal injury claim brought by the injured party.[184]

U. EXPERT TESTIMONY

In *Logerquist v. McVey*,[185] the Arizona Supreme Court held that Arizona courts will continue to evaluate expert testimony under the *Frye* test, rather than the *Daubert/Kumho Tire* test established by the United States Supreme Court and adopted by a number of other states. *Logerquist* also observed that *Frye* does not apply to certain types of expert testimony, stating, "[E]xpert evidence based on a qualified witness' own experience, observation, and study is treated differently from opinion evidence based on novel scientific principles advanced by others. As in the past, *Frye* continues to apply only to the latter."[186]

V. REPRESENTATION OF INSUREDS

Although a comprehensive discussion of an attorney's duties is outside the scope of this desk reference, in *Paradigm Ins. Co. v. The Langerman Law Offices,* the Arizona Supreme Court ruled that when an insurer assigns an attorney to represent an insured, the attorney has certain duties to the insurer even though the insurer is not the client.[187] Attorneys in that position should be aware of *Paradigm*.

Graeme Hancock
Thomas D. Ulreich-Power
FENNEMORE CRAIG
3003 North Central Avenue, Suite 2600
Phoenix, Arizona 85012-2913
(602) 916-5448
Fax (602) 916-5648
ghancock@fclaw.com
tulreich@fclaw.com

ENDNOTES - ARIZONA

1. *Dorman v. Swift & Co.*, 162 Ariz. 228, 782 P.2d 704 (1989).

2. Ariz. Rev. Stat. § 12-541 (1994 and Supp. 2001).

3. *Alaface v. National Investment Co.*, 181 Ariz. 586, 591, 892 P.2d 1375, 1379 (App. 1994) (consumer fraud action subject to one-year statute of limitation).

4. Ariz. Rev. Stat. § 12-821 (1994 and Supp. 2001).

5. Ariz. Rev. Stat. § 12-821.01 (1994 and Supp. 2001).

6. Ariz. Rev. Stat. § 12-542 (1994 and Supp. 2001).

7. *See, e.g., Logerquist v. Danforth*, 188 Ariz. 16, 19–20, 932 P.2d 281, 284–85 (App. 1996).

8. Ariz. Rev. Stat. § 12-551 (1994 and Supp. 2001). Section 12-551's statute of repose for product liability actions has been declared an unconstitutional abrogation of a plaintiff's right to recover damages for injuries. *See Hazine v. Montgomery Elevator Co.*, 176 Ariz. 340, 861 P.2d 625 (1993).

9. Ariz. Rev. Stat. § 12-543 (1994 and Supp. 2001).

10. Ariz. Rev. Stat. § 13-2314.04(F) (2001 and Supp. 2001).

11. Ariz. Rev. Stat. § 12-546 (1994 and Supp. 2001).

12. Ariz. Rev. Stat. § 12-548 (1994 and Supp. 2001).

13. Ariz. Rev. Stat. § 12-550 (1994 and Supp. 2001).

14. Ariz. Rev. Stat. § 12-552 (A) (1994 and Supp. 2001).

15. Ariz. Rev. Stat. § 12-552 (B) (1994 and Supp. 2001). The courts have held that this statute of repose is constitutional when applied to actions based in contract. However, the statute does not preclude actions for negligence between contracting parties. To do so would be an unconstitutional abrogation of the right to recover for injuries. *See Fry's Food Stores of Arizona, Inc. v. Mather & Associates, Inc.*, 183 Ariz. 89, 900 P.2d 1225 (App. 1995). *See also Hazine*, 176 Ariz. 340, 861 P.2d 625.

16. Ariz. Rev. Stat. § 12-504 (A) (1994 and Supp. 2001). If a timely filed action is terminated by abatement, voluntary dismissal by order of the court or dismissal for lack of prosecution, the court in its discretion may provide a period of commencement for a new action of the same cause although the time limit has expired.

17. Ariz. Rev. Stat. § 12-2506(F)(2) (1994 and Supp. 2001).

18. *Flowers v. K-Mart Corp.*, 126 Ariz. 495, 497, 616 P.2d 955, 957 (App. 1980).

19. *Markowitz v. Arizona Parks Bd.*, 146 Ariz. 352, 354–59, 706 P.2d 364, 366–71 (1985); *Ontiveros v. Borak*, 136 Ariz. 500, 505, 667 P.2d 200, 205 (1983).

20. *Markowitz*, 146 Ariz. 352, 356, 706 P.2d 364, 368 (1985).

21. *See, e.g., Easter v. Percy*, 168 Ariz. 46, 49–50, 810 P.2d 1053, 1056–57 (App. 1991); *Kriesman v. Thomas*, 12 Ariz. App. 215, 221, 469 P.2d 107, 113 (App. 1970).

22. *Easter*, 168 Ariz. at 49–50, 810 P.2d at 1056–57. Where a claim is brought against a licensed professional, Ariz. Rev. Stat. § 12-2602 (1994 & Supp. 2001) may require plaintiff to disclose expert testimony supporting that claim early in the litigation.

23. *Flowers*, 126 Ariz. at 497, 616 P.2d at 957.

24. *Davis v. Mangelsdorf*, 138 Ariz. 207, 208, 673 P.2d 951, 952 (App. 1983).

25. *Davis*, 138 Ariz. at 208, 673 P.2d at 952.

26. *First Nat. Bank of Arizona v. Dupree*, 136 Ariz. 296, 298, 665 P.2d 1018, 1020 (App. 1983).

27. *Beliak v. Plants*, 84 Ariz. 211, 216, 326 P.2d 36, 41 (1958).

28. *Ontiveros v. Borak*, 136 Ariz. 500, 505, 667 P.2d 200, 205 (1983); *Porterie v. Peters*, 111 Ariz. 452, 456, 532 P.2d 514, 518 (1975); *McDowell v. Davis*, 104 Ariz. 69, 71, 448 P.2d 869, 871 (1968).

29. *Ontiveros*, 136 Ariz. at 505, 667 P.2d at 205; *McDowell*, 104 Ariz. at 71–72, 448 P.2d at 870–71.

30. *See McDowell*, 104 Ariz. at 71–72, 448 P.2d at 870–71.

31. *See, e.g., Smith v. Johnson*, 183 Ariz. 38, 41, 899 P.2d 199, 202 (App. 1995); *Robertson v. Sixpence Inns of America, Inc.*, 163 Ariz. 539, 546, 789 P.2d 1040, 1047 (1990).

32. *Ontiveros*, 136 Ariz. at 505, 667 P.2d at 205; *McDowell*, 104 Ariz. at 71–72, 448 P.2d at 870–71.

33. *Porterie*, 111 Ariz. at 456, 532 P.2d at 518; *McDowell*, 104 Ariz. at 71–72, 448 P.2d at 870–71.

34. *Robertson*, 163 Ariz. at 546, 789 P.2d at 1047; *Rossell v. Volkswagen of America*, 147 Ariz. 160, 168–69, 709 P.2d 517, 525–26 (1985); *Ontiveros*, 136 Ariz. at 505-06, 667 P.2d at 205–06.

35. *Robertson*, 163 Ariz. at 546, 789 P.2d at 1047; *Rossell v. Volkswagen of America*, 147 Ariz. 160, 168–69, 709 P.2d 517, 525–26 (1985); *Ontiveros*, 136 Ariz. at 505–06, 667 P.2d at 205–06; *see also Tellez v. Saban*, 188 Ariz. 165, 171–72, 933 P.2d 1233, 1239–40 (App. 1996); *Smith*, 183 Ariz. at 41, 899 P.2d at 202; Restatement (Second) of Torts §§ 440–52 (1965).

36. *Rossell*, 147 Ariz. at 169, 709 P.2d at 526; *Serrano v. Kenneth A. Ethridge Contracting Co.*, 2 Ariz. App. 473, 474–76, 409 P.2d 757, 758–60 (1966); Restatement §§ 435, 442(B) & 447.

37. *Rossell*, 147 Ariz. at 169, 709 P.2d at 526.

38. *Robertson*, 163 Ariz. at 546, 789 P.2d at 1047.

39. Ariz. Rev. Stat. §§ 12-2501 (1994 and Supp. 2001) *et seq.*

40. *See Wareing v. Falk*, 182 Ariz. 495, 498, 897 P.2d 1381, 1384 (App. 1995).

41. *See* Ariz. Rev. Stat. § 12-711 (1994 and Supp. 2001).

42. *See* Ariz. Rev. Stat. § 12-712 (A) (1994 and Supp. 2001).

43. Ariz. Rev. Stat. § 12-712 (B) (1994 and Supp. 2001).

44. *Law v. Superior Court*, 157 Ariz. 147, 755 P.2d 1135 (1988).

45. *Williams v. Thude*, 188 Ariz. 257, 260, 934 P.2d 1349, 1352 (1997).

46. Ariz. Const. art. 18, § 5.

47. *Galindo v. TMT Transp. Inc.*, 152 Ariz. 434, 437, 733 P.2d 631, 634 (App. 1986).

48. Ariz. Rev. Stat. § 12-2505 (A) (1994 and Supp. 2001).

49. *Id.*

50. Ariz. Rev. Stat. § 23-806 (1995 and Supp. 2001) (if an employee is guilty of contributory negligence, the jury shall reduce damages in proportion to the employee's negligence, rather than bar recovery).

51. Ariz. Rev. Stat. § 12-2505(A) (1994 and Supp. 2001).

52. *Williams*, 188 Ariz. at 260, 934 P.2d at 1352.

53. *Lerma v. Keck*, 186 Ariz. 228, 231, 921 P.2d 28, 31 (App. 1996).

54. *See Jimenez v. Sears, Roebuck and Co.*, 183 Ariz. 399, 408, 904 P.2d 861, 870 (1994); *see also* Ariz. Rev. Stat. § 12-2509 (B) (1994 and Supp. 2001).

55. *See* Ariz. Rev. Stat. § 23-907 (A) (1995 and Supp. 2001).

56. *See Jimenez*, 183 Ariz. at 404, 904 P.2d at 866.

57. *See* Ariz. Rev. Stat. § 12-2505 (A) (1994 and Supp. 2001).

58. *See Gonzales v. Arizona Pub. Serv. Co.*, 161 Ariz. 84, 89, 775 P.2d 1148, 1153 (App. 1989).

59. *See Galindo*, 152 Ariz. at 437, 733 P.2d at 634.

60. *See* Ariz. Const. art. 18, § 5.

61. *See Galindo*, 152 Ariz. at 437, 733 P.2d at 634.

62. *See* Ariz. Rev. Stat. § 23-907 (A) (1995 and Supp. 2001).

63. *Benjamin v. Gear Roller Hockey Equipment*, 198 Ariz. 462, 11 P.3d 421 (App. 2000).

64. *Ward v. Mount Calvary Lutheran Church*, 178 Ariz. 350, 354, 873 P.2d 688, 692 (App. 1994); *McDonald v. Smitty's Super Valu, Inc.*, 157 Ariz. 316, 318, 757 P.2d 120, 122 (App. 1988); *Faris v. Doctors Hospital*, 18 Ariz. App. 264, 267, 501 P.2d 440 (1972).

65. *Ward*, 178 Ariz. at 355, 873 P.2d at 693; *Tucson Gas & Elec. Co. v. Larsen*, 19 Ariz. App. 266, 267, 506 P.2d 657, 658 (1973); *Ruiz v. Otis Elevator*, 146 Ariz. 98, 101, 703 P.2d 1247, 1250 (App. 1985).

66. *Ward*, 178 Ariz. at 355, 873 P.2d at 693. Traditionally, Arizona required the plaintiff to establish that he or she was not negligent because, at common law, a plaintiff was barred from recovery if he or she negligently caused the damage at issue. This requirement has been eliminated by the adop-

tion of comparative fault principles. *Cox v. The May Department Store Co.*, 183 Ariz. 361, 366, 903 P.2d 1119 (App. 1995).

67. *Ward*, 178 Ariz. 350, 354, 873 P.2d 688, 692 (App. 1994).

68. *Stewart v. Crystal Coca-Cola Bottling Co.*, 50 Ariz. 60, 64, 68 P.2d 952, 954 (1937).

69. *McDonald v. Smitty's Super Valu, Inc.*, 157 Ariz. 316, 321, 757 P.2d 120, 125 (App. 1988).

70. *Ward*, 178 Ariz. 350, 355, 873 P.2d 688, 693 (App. 1994).

71. *Byars v. Arizona Public Service Co.*, 24 Ariz. App. 420, 426, 539 P.2d 534, 540 (1975).

72. *Jackson v. H.H. Robertson Co., Inc.*, 118 Ariz. 29, 32, 574 P.2d 822, 825 (1978).

73. *McDonald*, 157 Ariz. 316, 321, 757 P.2d 120, 125 (App. 1988).

74. *Byars* at 426, 539 P.2d at 540; *Stewart v. Crystal Coca-Cola Bottling Co.*, 50 Ariz. 60, 68 P.2d 952, 956 (1937).

75. *Stewart*, 50 Ariz. 60, 68, 68 P.2d 952, 956 (1937) (*res ipsa loquitur* inapplicable when it was just as probable that the explosion was due to the action on glass of sudden changes in temperature as that it was caused by an overcharge of gas or a defective bottle).

76. *Pickwick Stages Corp. v. Messinger*, 44 Ariz. 174, 182, 36 P.2d 168, 171 (1934).

77. *McDonald*, 157 Ariz. 316, 321, 757 P.2d 120, 125 (App. 1988).

78. *Miller v. Westcor Ltd. Partnership*, 171 Ariz. 387, 392, 831 P.2d 386, 391 (App. 1991).

79. *Miller*, 171 Ariz. at 392, 831 P.2d at 391; *E.L. Jones Construction Co. v. Noland*, 105 Ariz. 446, 456, 466 P.2d 740, 750 (1970).

80. *Miller*, 171 Ariz. at 392, 831 P.2d at 391; *Bible v. First Nat'l Bank of Rawlins*, 21 Ariz. App. 54, 57, 515 P.2d 351, 354 (1973).

81. *Good v. City of Glendale*, 150 Ariz. 218, 221, 722 P.2d 386, 389 (App. 1986).

82. *Orlando v. Northcutt*, 103 Ariz. 298, 300, 441 P.2d 58, 60 (1968).

83. *Orlando*, 103 Ariz. at 300, 441 P.2d at 60.

84. Ariz. Rev. Stat. §§ 12-2501 (1994 and Supp. 2001) *et seq.*

85. Ariz. Rev. Stat. § 12-2506 (1994 and Supp. 2001); *see also Hutcherson v. City of Phoenix*, 192 Ariz. 51, 54, 961 P.2d 449, 452 (1998).

86. Ariz. Rev. Stat. § 12-2506(A) (1994 and Supp. 2001); *see also Piner v. Superior Court*, 192 Ariz. 182, 188, 962 P.2d 909, 915 (1998).

87. Ariz. Rev. Stat. § 12-2506(A) (1994 and Supp. 2001). *See also Natseway v. City of Tempe*, 184 Ariz. 374, 376, 909 P.2d 441, 443 (App. 1995). Ariz. Rev. Stat. § 12-2506(F)(2) defines "fault" as:

> an actionable breach of legal duty, act or omission proximately causing or contributing to injury or damages sustained by a person seeking recovery, including negligence in all of its degrees, contributory negligence, assumption of risk, strict liability, breach of express or implied warranty of a product, products liability and misuse, modification or abuse of a product.

88. Ariz. Rev. Stat. § 12-2506(A) (1994 and Supp. 2001); *see also Piner*, 192 Ariz. at 189, 962 P.2d at 916.

89. Ariz. Rev. Stat. § 12-2506(D) (1994 and Supp. 2001); *see also Bishop v. Pecanic*, 193 Ariz. 524, 528–29, 975 P.2d 114, 118–19 (App. 1998).

90. *Ruelas v. Staff Builders Personnel Services, Inc.*, 199 Ariz. 344, 18 P.3d 138 (App. 2001).

91. Ariz. Rev. Stat. § 12-2506(F)(1) (1994 and Supp. 2001).

92. Ariz. Rev. Stat. § 12-2506(E) (1994 and Supp. 2001), and Ariz. Rev. Stat. §§ 12-2501(A), (B) (1994 & Supp. 2001); *see also Herstam v. Deloitte & Touche, LLP*, 186 Ariz. 110, 113, 919 P.2d 1381, 1384 (App. 1996).

93. *Herstam*, 186 Ariz. 110, 117–18, 919 P.2d 1381, 1388–89 (App. 1996); *Schweber Elecs. v. National Semiconductor Corp.*, 174 Ariz. 406, 410, 850 P.2d 119, 123 (App. 1992).

94. *Schweber Elecs.*, 174 Ariz. at 410, 850 P.2d at 123 (*citing* Restatement of Restitution, § 76 (1937)).

95. *Schweber Elecs.*, 174 Ariz. at 410, 850 P.2d at 123.

96. *Herstam v. Deloitte & Touche, LLP*, 186 Ariz. 110, 118, 919 P.2d 1381, 1389 (App. 1996).

97. *Schweber Elecs.*, 174 Ariz. at 410, 850 P.2d at 123.

98. *Hauskins v. McGillicuddy*, 175 Ariz. 42, 50, 852 P.2d 1226, 1234 (App. 1992).

99. Ariz. Rev. Stat. §§ 23-101 (1995 and Supp. 2001) *et seq.*

100. Ariz. Rev. Stat. § 23-1022(A) (1995 and Supp. 2001). Prior to a work-related accident, an Arizona employee has the option of rejecting coverage and retaining the right to sue the employer at common law. Ariz. Rev. Stat. § 23-906 (1995 and Supp. 2001). Moreover, the exclusive remedy doctrine will not relieve an employer from a contractual obligation to indemnify a third party from liability arising from its employee's work-related injuries. *Superior Cos. v. Kaiser Cement Corp.*, 152 Ariz. 575, 580, 733 P.2d 1158, 1163 (App. 1986).

101. Ariz. Rev. Stat. § 23-1022(A) (1995 and Supp. 2001).

102. *See* Ariz. Rev. Stat. §§ 23-1022(A), (C) (1995 and Supp. 2001).

103. Ariz. Rev. Stat. § 23-1022(A) (1995 and Supp. 2001). The willful act must be "personal" and must indicate a disregard for the life, limb, or bodily safety of an employee. *Id.* "Willful misconduct" means an act done knowingly and purposefully with the direct object of injuring another. Ariz. Rev. Stat. § 23-1022(B) (1995 and Supp. 2001). Even gross negligence or wantonness amounting to gross negligence does not constitute "willful misconduct" unless accompanied by intent to inflict injury. *Diaz v. Magma Cooper Co.*, 190 Ariz. 544, 551, 950 P.2d 1165, 1172 (App. 1997).

104. Ariz. Rev. Stat. § 23-1023(A) (1995 and Supp. 2001).

105. Ariz. Rev. Stat. § 23-1023(C) (1995 and Supp. 2001).

106. Ariz. Rev. Stat. § 23-1023(C) (1995 and Supp. 2001). The lien shall be satisfied only from the amount "actually collectable" from the third party. The amount "actually collectable" is the total recovery less the reasonable and necessary expenses, including attorneys' fees, actually expended in securing such recovery.

107. Ariz. Rev. Stat. § 23-1023(C) (1995 and Supp. 2001).

108. *Dietz v. General Electric Co.*, 169 Ariz. 505, 821 P.2d 166 (1991).

109. *Aitken v. Industrial Comm'n of Arizona*, 183 Ariz. 387, 904 P.2d 456 (1995).

110. *See, e.g., Grinnell v. Industrial Comm'n*, 139 Ariz. 124, 677 P.2d 287 (App. 1983).

111. Ariz. Rev. Stat. § 23-1023(B) (1995 and Supp. 2001).

112. *Id.*

113. *Nicoletti v. Westcor, Inc.*, 131 Ariz. 140, 142, 639 P.2d 330, 332 (1982).

114. *Nicoletti* at 142, 639 P.2d at 332; Restatement (Second) of Torts §§ 329–32.

115. *Nicoletti* at 142, 639 P.2d at 332.

116. *Shaw v. Petersen*, 169 Ariz. 559, 561, 821 P.2d 220, 222 (App. 1991).

117. *Barnhizer v. Paradise Valley Unified School District #6*, 123 Ariz. 253, 254, 599 P.2d 209, 210 (1979).

118. *Barnhizer*, 123 Ariz. at 255, 599 P.2d at 211; Restatement (Second) of Torts § 339.

119. Restatement (Second) of Torts § 339(c).

120. Ariz. Rev. Stat. § 33-1551 (2000 and Supp. 2001).

121. *Id.*

122. Ariz. Rev. Stat. §§ 4-311 & 4-312 (1995 and Supp. 2001).

123. Ariz. Rev. Stat. §§ 4-311(A)(1)–(3) (1995 and Supp. 2001).

124. Ariz. Rev. Stat. § 4-311(C) (1995 and Supp. 2001).

125. Ariz. Rev. Stat. §§ 4-311(A)(1)–(3) (1995 and Supp. 2001).

126. Ariz. Rev. Stat. § 4-311(B) (1995 and Supp. 2001).

127. *Schwab v. Matley*, 164 Ariz. 421, 793 P.2d 1088 (1990) (ruling that Ariz. Rev. Stat. § 4-312(A) is unconstitutional pursuant to Article 18, § 5 of the Arizona Constitution).

128. Ariz. Rev. Stat. § 4-301 (1995 and Supp. 2001); *Hernandez v. Arizona Board of Regents*, 177 Ariz. 244, 866 P.2d 1330 (1994).

129. *Hernandez*, 177 Ariz. at 256, 866 P.2d at 1342.

130. *See, e.g., Arrow Leasing Corp. v. Cummins Arizona Diesel, Inc.*, 136 Ariz. 444, 446–47, 666 P.2d 544, 546–47 (App. 1983). Arizona has applied the "economic loss" rule in cases dealing with defective construction. *Nastri v. Wood Bros. Homes*, 142 Ariz. 439, 690 P.2d 158 (App. 1984) (rejecting pure economic loss damages in negligence and strict liability claims arising out of the defective construction of a residence because there was no claim for damage to personal property or personal injury).

131. *Salt River Project Agric. Improvement and Power Dist. v. Westinghouse Electric Corp.*, 143 Ariz. 368, 376, 694 P.2d 98, 106 (1984).

132. *Id.* at 379, 694 P.2d at 109.

133. *Id.* at 376, 694 P.2d at 106.

134. *Id.*

135. *Id.* Of course, tort recovery is available whenever personal injuries exist.

136. *Id.* at 381, 694 P.2d at 111.

137. *Services Holding Co. v. Transamerica Occidental Life Ins. Co.*, 180 Ariz. 198, 208, 883 P.2d 435, 445 (App. 1994); *Echols v. Beauty Built Homes, Inc.*, 132 Ariz. 498, 500, 647 P.2d, 629, 631 (1982); *Spudnuts, Inc. v. Lane*, 131 Ariz. 424, 426, 641 P.2d. 912, 914 (App. 1982).

138. *Page v. Sagebrush Sales Co.*, 114 Ariz. 271, 275, 560 P.2d 789, 793 (1977); *Lininger v. Sonenblick*, 23 Ariz. App. 266, 267, 532 P.2d 538, 539 (1975).

139. *Standard Chartered PLC v. Price Waterhouse*, 190 Ariz. 6, 29, 945 P.2d 317, 340 (App. 1996); *Hoffman v. Greenberg*, 159 Ariz. 377, 767 P.2d 725 (App. 1988).

140. *Standard Chartered*, 190 Ariz. at 31, 945 P.2d at 342.

141. *Standard Chartered*, 190 Ariz. at 31–32, 945 P.2d at 342–43.

142. *Standard Chartered*, 190 Ariz. at 32, 945 P.2d at 343.

143. Ariz. Rev. Stat. §§ 44-1521 (1994 and Supp. 2001) *et seq.*

144. *Enyart v. Transamerica Ins. Co.*, 195 Ariz. 71, 78, 985 P.2d 556, 563 (App. 1998); *Holeman v. Neils*, 803 F. Supp. 237, 242 (D. Ariz. 1992).

145. Ariz. Rev. Stat. § 44-1522(D) (1994 and Supp. 2001).

146. *Holeman*, 803 F. Supp. at 243.

147. Ariz. Rev. Stat. § 44-1521(5) (1994 and Supp. 2001).

148. Ariz. Rev. Stat. § 44-1521(7) (1994 and Supp. 2001).

149. *Villegas v. Transamerica Financial Services, Inc.*, 147 Ariz. 100, 102, 708 P.2d 781, 783 (App. 1985).

150. Ariz. Rev. Stat. §§ 44-1524 to 44-1534 (1994 and Supp. 2001).

151. *Holeman*, 803 F. Supp. at 242; *Dunlap v. Jimmy GMC of Tucson, Inc.*, 136 Ariz. 338, 342, 666 P.2d 83, 87 (App. 1983).

152. *Dunlap*, 136 Ariz. at 342, 666 P.2d at 87 (App. 1983).

153. *Correa v. Pecos Valley Dev. Corp.*, 126 Ariz. 601, 605, 617 P.2d 767, 771 (App. 1980).

154. *Holeman*, 803 F. Supp. at 242; *Parks v. Macro-Dynamics, Inc.*, 121 Ariz. 517, 521, 591 P.2d 1005, 1009 (App. 1979).

155. *Holeman*, 803 F. Supp. at 242–43; *Dunlap*, 136 Ariz. at 342–43, 666 P.2d at 87–88.

156. *Dunlap*, 136 Ariz. at 343–44, 666 P.2d at 88–89.

157. *Teran v. Citicorp Person-to-Person Financial Center*, 146 Ariz. 370, 377, 706 P.2d 382, 389 (App. 1985).

158. *Id.*

159. *Thompson v. Better-Bilt Aluminum Prod. Co.*, 171 Ariz. 550, 556–57, 832 P.2d 203, 209–10 (1992); *Volz v. Coleman Co., Inc.*, 155 Ariz. 567, 570, 748 P.2d 1191, 1194 (1987); *Hyatt Regency Phoenix Hotel Co. v. Winston & Strawn*, 184 Ariz. 120, 132, 907 P.2d 506, 518 (App. 1995), *cert. denied*, 517 U.S. 1234 (1996).

160. *Volz*, 155 Ariz. at 570, 748 P.2d at 1194; *Hyatt Regency*, 184 Ariz. at 132, 907 P.2d at 518 (proof that defendant consciously disregarded an unjustifiable and substantial risk of significant harm to others or intended to injure or defraud will establish requisite evil mind to support punitive damage award); *Piper v. Bear Med. Sys., Inc.*, 180 Ariz. 170, 180, 883 P.2d 407, 417 (App. 1994) ("A jury may infer an evil mind if defendant deliberately continued his actions despite the inevitable or highly probable harm that would follow.").

161. *Volz*, 155 Ariz. at 570, 748 P.2d at 1194. In *Volz*, a child was burned when gasoline sprayed on her from a camp stove manufactured by Coleman. Coleman had long known that the stove could spray gas, but continued to market the stove. The court held that this evidence did not even justify a jury instruction on punitive damages, and reversed the punitive damage award. *Accord Piper*, 180 Ariz. at 180, 883 P.2d at 417 (reversing punitive damage award in product liability case where manufacturer's conduct amounted to mere negligence).

162. *Saucedo v. Salvation Army*, 200 Ariz. 179, 24 P.3d 1274 (App. 2001).

163. *Thompson*, 171 Ariz. at 556, 832 P.2d at 209; *Hyatt Regency*, 184 Ariz. at 132, 907 P.2d at 518 (affirming punitive damage award where attorney concealed conflict of interest from first client and acted to benefit second client throughout lengthy litigation); *Hooper v. Truly Nolen of America, Inc.*, 171 Ariz. 692, 694, 832 P.2d 709, 711 (App. 1992) (affirming award of punitive damages where exterminator persisted in improperly spraying homes with carcinogenic chemical for several years after manufacturer issued warning and exterminator concealed potential harm in response to consumer concerns).

164. *Thompson*, 171 Ariz. at 557, 832 P.2d at 210; *Hyatt Regency*, 184 Ariz. at 132, 907 P.2d at 518.

165. *Thompson*, 171 Ariz. at 557–58, 832 P.2d at 210–11; *Hyatt Regency*, 184 Ariz. at 132, 907 P.2d at 518.

166. *Olson v. Walker*, 162 Ariz. 174, 179, 781 P.2d 1015, 1020 (App. 1989). *But see Cooper Industries, Inc. v. Leathermantool Group, Inc.*, 532 U.S. 424 (2001) (applying a de novo standard of review to the question of whether an award of punitive damages is constitutionally excessive).

167. *White v. Mitchell*, 157 Ariz. 523, 529, 759 P.2d 1327, 1333 (App. 1987) (plaintiff need only introduce evidence sufficient to allow trier of fact to calculate reasonable award; defendant's financial position is relevant proof, but is not required); *cf. Rhue v. Dawson*, 173 Ariz. 220, 234, 841 P.2d 215, 229 (App. 1992) (amount of punitive damages should be based in part on defendant's wealth to achieve appropriate level of punitive effect).

168. *See Thompson*, 171 Ariz. at 556, 832 P.2d at 209.

169. *Rhue*, 173 Ariz. at 232, 841 at 227.

170. *Wyatt v. Wehmueller*, 167 Ariz. 281, 285, 806 P.2d 870, 874 (1991); *Hyatt Regency*, 184 Ariz. at 131, 907 P.2d at 517.

171. *Haralson v. Fisher Surveying, Inc.*, 201 Ariz. 1, 31 P.3d 114 (2001).

172. Ariz. Rev. Stat. §§ 12-611 (1994 and Supp. 2001) *et seq.*

173. *Begay v. City of Tucson*, 148 Ariz. 505, 715 P.2d 758 (1986).

174. Ariz. Rev. Stat. § 12-612 (1994 and Supp. 2001) provides the parties who may recover under the wrongful death act: "An action for wrongful death shall be brought by and in the name of the surviving husband or wife or personal representative of the deceased person for and on behalf of the

surviving husband or wife, children or parents, or if none of these survive, on behalf of the decedent's estate." If the decedent's spouse, child, or parent survives, "brothers, sisters, cousins, aunts ... and others should not recover any amount or ... have their loss be a measure of the damages for the wrongful death." *Solomon v. Harman*, 107 Ariz. 426, 430, 489 P.2d 236, 240 (1971).

175. Ariz. Rev. Stat. § 12-613 (1994 and Supp. 2001).

176. *City of Tucson v. Wondergem*, 105 Ariz. 429, 433, 466 P.2d 383, 387 (1970), citing *Boies v. Cole*, 99 Ariz. 198, 203, 407 P.2d 917, 920 (1965).

177. *Wondergem*, 105 Ariz. at 434, 407 P.2d at 388.

178. *Kemp v. Pinal County*, 8 Ariz. App. 41, 45, 442 P.2d 864, 868 (1968).

179. *Kemp*, 8 Ariz. App. at 45, 442 P.2d at 868.

180. Ariz. Rev. Stat. § 14-3110 (1995 and Supp. 2001).

181. *Barnes v. Outlaw*, 192 Ariz. 283, 964 P.2d 484 (1998); *Villareal v. Arizona Dept. of Transp.*, 160 Ariz. 474, 744 P.2d 213 (1989).

182. *Villareal* at 480, 744 P.2d at 219.

183. *Id.* at 481, 744 P.2d at 220.

184. *Id.*

185. *Logerquist v. McVey*, 196 Ariz. 470, 1 P.3d 113 (2000).

186. *Logerquist*, 196 Ariz. at 480, 1 P.3d at 123.

187. *Paradigm Ins. Co. v. The Langerman Law Offices*, 200 Ariz. 146, 24 P.3d 593 (2001).

ARKANSAS

A. STATUTES OF LIMITATION

Any cause of action founded on assault, battery, false imprisonment and slander must be brought within one year.[1] The Arkansas Code also provides a three-year statute of limitations for causes of action based on trespass, libel and conversion.[2] The very same three-year statute is also applied to actions based on negligence,[3] fraud and deceit,[4] nuisance,[5] tortious interference with contract,[6] invasion of privacy,[7] legal malpractice[8] and accounting malpractice.[9] An action for wrongful death is governed by a separate three-year statute of limitations.[10]

A cause of action for negligence is said to accrue when there is a complete and present cause of action, and, in the absence of concealment of the wrong, when the injury occurs, not when it is discovered.[11]

A cause of action for medical malpractice must be brought within two years.[12] It is clear that the statute begins to run on the date of the negligent act, not when the harm is discovered.[13] One exception to this rule arises where a foreign object is negligently left in the body.[14] The other exception, created by the courts, arises under the continuous treatment doctrine.[15] Additionally, medical malpractice which results in death is governed by the two-year statute, not the three-year wrongful death statute.[16]

The statute of limitations for an action based on products liability is three years.[17] The discovery rule does apply in the products liability context.[18] Although the statute of limitations for breach of warranty under the Uniform Commercial Code is four years,[19] when damages are sought for personal injury the three-year statute applies.[20]

All causes of action where no statute of limitations is specifically provided for must be brought within five years.[21]

B. TORT REFORM

To date, the Arkansas legislature has yet to pass any tort reform legislation.

C. "NO FAULT" LIMITATIONS

Drivers of automobiles must maintain minimum insurance limits pursuant to the Arkansas Motor Vehicle Safety Responsibility Act[22] (AMVSRA). The minimum coverage required to satisfy the AMVSRA is not less than $25,000 for the bodily injury or death of one person in any one accident.[23] If two or more persons are injured or killed in an accident, the coverage must not be less than $50,000.[24] The minimum coverage for property damage is $25,000.[25]

D. **THE STANDARD FOR NEGLIGENCE**

In order to succeed on a claim of negligence, a plaintiff must prove the four common law elements. The specific elements are: (1) the existence of a duty on the part of the defendant; (2) a breach of that duty; (3) injury to the plaintiff that was actually and proximately caused by the breach; and (4) damage to the plaintiff or his property.[26]

Under the Arkansas Model Instructions, one breaches his duty, hence he is negligent, when he fails to exercise ordinary care.[27] Ordinary care is that which would be exercised by a reasonably careful person under circumstances similar to those present in the case at hand.[28]

A minor must exercise that degree of care that a reasonably careful minor of his age and intelligence would exercise under similar circumstances.[29] However, a minor engaged in an adult activity is held to the adult standard of care.[30]

A physician, surgeon, dentist, or other medical care provider must possess and apply with reasonable care that degree of skill and learning ordinarily possessed and used by members of his profession in good standing, engaged in the same type of service and the locality in which he practices, or in a similar locality.[31] Generally, a plaintiff must produce expert testimony in order to prevail on an action for medical malpractice.[32]

An attorney must possess and use with reasonable diligence that degree of skill ordinarily used by attorneys acting in the same or similar circumstances.[33] Unless the issue is within the common knowledge of a lay juror, the plaintiff must produce expert testimony in order to prevail.[34]

E. **CAUSATION**

In order to prevail on a claim for negligence, a plaintiff must show that the defendant's negligent acts were both the cause in fact and the proximate cause of his injury.[35] Proximate cause is "that which in a natural and continuous sequence, unbroken by any sufficient intervening cause, produces the injury, and without which the result would not have occurred."[36] That an injury resulted from the defendant's negligence must be established by a reasonable probability; a mere possibility will not suffice.[37]

F. **CONTRIBUTORY NEGLIGENCE, COMPARATIVE NEGLIGENCE, AND ASSUMPTION OF RISK**

1. **Contributory Negligence**

   Arkansas does not recognize the doctrine of contributory negligence as it is known at common law. That is, negligence on the part of the plaintiff will not act as an absolute bar to his claim. Instead, Arkansas has adopted a comparative fault statute, which is discussed below. However, one dealing in this area should be aware that practitioners and courts in Arkansas often use the terms "contributory" and "comparative" interchangeably. Nevertheless, both refer to application of the Arkansas comparative fault statute.[38]

2. Comparative Negligence

Arkansas follows the doctrine of comparative negligence, which allows the defendant to assert the plaintiff's negligence as a bar to, or a reduction of, the plaintiff's claim.[39] Arkansas is a "modified" comparative fault state. If a jury apportions fault to both the defendant and the plaintiff, the percentages are compared. In the event the plaintiff's fault is equal to or greater than the fault of the defendant (50 percent or higher), the plaintiff is completely barred from recovering.[40] If the plaintiff's fault is less than that of the defendant (49 percent or lower), he may recover, but only after his damages are reduced in proportion to his degree of fault.[41]

3. Assumption of the Risk

The common law doctrine of assumption of the risk is no longer applicable as a separate theory in Arkansas.[42] It is, however, referred to in the definition of fault contained in the comparative fault statute.[43] Consequently, the definition of assumption of the risk remains as a model jury instruction in Arkansas.[44]

G. *RES IPSA LOQUITUR* AND INHERENTLY DANGEROUS ACTIVITIES

1. *Res Ipsa Loquitur*

The doctrine of *res ipsa loquitur* is available if: (1) the defendant owes a duty to the plaintiff to use due care; (2) the accident is caused by the thing or instrumentality under the control of the defendant; (3) the accident that caused the injury is one that, in the ordinary course of things, would not occur if those having control and management of the instrumentality used proper care; and (4) there is an absence of evidence to the contrary.[45]

If all of these elements are present, then the accident from which the injury results is *prima facie* evidence of negligence.[46] The burden will then shift to the defendant to prove that the accident did not result from his lack of care.[47]

2. Inherently Dangerous Activities

Arkansas imposes "absolute" or "strict" liability for injuries resulting from the exercise of "ultrahazardous" activity.[48]

H. NEGLIGENCE *PER SE*

In Arkansas, the violation of a statute, or any other law or regulation, is simply evidence of negligence to be considered by the jury.[49] A violation is not negligence *per se*.[50]

I. JOINT AND SEVERAL LIABILITY

In assessing the liability of joint tortfeasors, Arkansas has adopted the Uniform Contribution Among Tortfeasors Act.[51] The Act defines joint tortfeasors as "two (2) or more persons jointly or severally liable in tort for the same injury to person or property...."[52]

In order to impose joint liability, both parties must be responsible for the same injury.[53] "Even if the parties' tortious acts are temporally separate, if they cause the same injury or loss, the parties are jointly liable."[54] Joint and several liability is not measured by impact, and where there is a single injury, it does not matter whether the individual acts alone would not have caused the entire result.[55]

A judgment against one tortfeasor does not discharge the liability of another joint tortfeasor.[56] Furthermore, a release by the plaintiff of one joint tortfeasor does not discharge the other tortfeasors unless the release so provides. However, the release does reduce the claim against the other tortfeasors in the amount of the consideration paid for the release.[57]

A joint tortfeasor is entitled to contribution from another tortfeasor when he has either discharged the common liability or paid more than his *pro rata* share.[58] A defendant tortfeasor is entitled to request that the finder of fact apportion the degree of fault respective to each tortfeasor in order to ascertain the amount of each one's liability.[59]

J. INDEMNITY

Indemnity shifts the entire loss from a tortfeasor who has been forced to pay over to the one who contracted to bear it or who more properly should bear it.[60] Arkansas recognizes a contractual and an equitable right of indemnity.[61] The equitable right of indemnity arises where there is a special relationship.[62]

K. BAR OF WORKERS' COMPENSATION STATUTE

Under the Arkansas Workers' Compensation Act,[63] an injured employee is precluded from suing his employer in tort for an injury incurred on the job.[64] This remedy is an exclusive remedy so long as the employer has secured the proper workers' compensation insurance.[65] An employee still retains the right, regardless of the receipt of compensation benefits from his employer, to pursue an action against a negligent third party.[66]

Arkansas does recognize an exception to the exclusive remedy provision of the Act for the commission of intentional torts by the employer.[67] However, the employer's acts must go beyond willful and wanton; there must be a deliberate act by the employer or the desire to bring about the consequences of the act.[68]

The Arkansas Act also provides an employer who has secured workers' compensation benefits a right of subrogation against negligent third parties.[69] An employer or carrier is also entitled to a lien on any recovery had by the employee in a suit against a third party.[70]

L. **PREMISES LIABILITY**

Arkansas follows the traditional common law distinction between trespassers, licensees, and invitees. A trespasser is defined as a person who goes on the premises of another without permission and without express or implied invitation.[71] No duty is owed by the owner or occupier to a trespasser until the trespasser's presence is known. The duty then is to avoid injury to the trespasser by willful or wanton conduct.[72]

A licensee is a person who goes on the premises of another with the consent of the owner or the occupier of the premises for the licensee's own purposes.[73] The owner or occupier then owes a duty not to cause injury to the licensee by willful or wanton conduct.[74] However, if the owner or occupier knows or reasonably should know that a licensee is in a position of danger, the owner or occupier has a duty to use ordinary care to avoid injury to the licensee.[75]

An invitee is a person who, by express or implied invitation, goes on the premises of another for a purpose connected with the owner's business or for a purpose connected with the activity that the owner conducts on the premises, or for a purpose mutually beneficial to himself and the owner.[76] The owner and occupier must use ordinary care to maintain the premises in a reasonably safe condition, which includes a duty to protect invitees not only from dangers that the business owner knows about, but also any dangers that he reasonably should discover.[77]

M. **DRAM SHOP LIABILITY**

Recently, the Arkansas Supreme Court recognized that the sale of alcohol to a minor[78] or an intoxicated person[79] can be the proximate cause of an injury to a third party. Acting on those decisions, the Arkansas General Assembly passed a "dram shop" act.[80] Specifically, an alcoholic beverage retailer can be liable for damages proximately caused by selling alcohol to a minor[81] or any clearly intoxicated person.[82]

N. **ECONOMIC LOSS**

It is unclear under Arkansas law whether one can recover solely economic damages in an action based on tort. However, Arkansas does allow an action based on strict products liability where the only damages incurred were economic.[83]

O. **FRAUD AND DECEIT**

In order to prevail upon a claim of fraud and deceit, the plaintiff must affirmatively establish the following elements by a preponderance of the evidence: (1) a false representation, usually of a material fact; (2) knowledge or belief by the defendant that the representation is false or that the defendant lacks a sufficient basis or information to make the statement, that is, the *scienter* requirement; (3) intent to induce the plaintiff to act or to refrain from acting in reliance on the representation; (4) justifiable reliance by the plaintiff on the representation; and (5) resulting damage to the plaintiff.[84]

Under the Arkansas Rules of Civil Procedure, the circumstances of fraud must be alleged with particularity.[85]

P. CONSUMER FRAUD STATUTES

Arkansas' Deceptive Trade Practices Act[86] protects consumers from deceptive and unconscionable trade practices.[87] Under the Act, the Attorney General has standing to bring a civil action on behalf of injured consumers.[88] The statute of limitations for such an action is five years.[89]

Q. PUNITIVE DAMAGES

Arkansas has no statutory scheme for punitive damages; rather, the law of punitive damages has developed through decisions of the Arkansas Supreme Court.[90] Under Arkansas law, punitive damages may be imposed, in addition to compensatory damages, to punish a wrong-doer and to deter others from similar conduct.[91]

The degree of proof required to support a punitive damages instruction so that the jury may consider the issue is substantial evidence of actual or inferred malice.[92] Malice can be inferred from a conscious indifference to, or from a reckless disregard of, the consequences of one's actions.[93] The standard of proof for the actual punitive damages is a preponderance of the evidence.[94]

Negligence alone, even gross negligence, is not enough to support punitive damages.[95] In vehicle accident cases, the Arkansas Supreme Court has held that the operation of a motor vehicle while intoxicated will support an award for punitive damages.[96] Similarly, punitive damages have been upheld where the defendant was racing.[97]

Arkansas has enacted no specific caps or limits on punitive damages. However, the Arkansas Supreme Court has held that punitive damages cannot be awarded unless compensatory damages are first awarded by the jury.[98]

R. WRONGFUL DEATH AND SURVIVORSHIP ACTIONS

A statutory cause of action for wrongful death and survivorship exists under Arkansas law.[99] These are distinct claims and the remedies under each of them are cumulative.[100]

Under the wrongful death statute, recovery can be had by a defined group of beneficiaries.[101] Recovery under the survival statute passes to the decedent's estate and is to be prosecuted by the executor or administrator of the estate.[102]

Patricia A. Sievers Harris
Justin T. Allen
WRIGHT, LINDSEY & JENNINGS, L.L.P.
200 West Capitol Avenue, Suite 2200
Little Rock, Arkansas 72201-3699
(501) 371-0808
Fax (501) 376-9442
pharris@wlj.com
jallen@wlj.com
www.wlj.com

ENDNOTES - ARKANSAS

1. Ark. Code Ann. § 16-56-104 (Michie Supp. 1999).

2. Ark. Code Ann. § 16-56-105 (Michie 1987).

3. *Faulkner v. Huie*, 205 Ark. 332, 168 S.W.2d 839 (1943).

4. *Beam v. Monsanto Co.*, 259 Ark. 253, 532 S.W.2d 175 (1976); *Hughes v. McCann*, 13 Ark. App. 28, 678 S.W.2d 784 (1984).

5. *Consolidated Chem. Indus. Inc. v. White*, 227 Ark. 177, 297 S.W.2d 101 (1957).

6. *Bankston v. Davis*, 262 Ark. 635, 559 S.W.2d 714 (1978).

7. *Norris v. Bakker*, 320 Ark. 629, 899 S.W.2d 70 (1995).

8. *Wright v. Compton, Pruitt, Thomas & Hickey, P.A.*, 315 Ark. 213, 866 S.W.2d 387 (1993); *Chapman v. Alexander*, 307 Ark. 87, 817 S.W.2d 425 (1991).

9. *Swink v. Ernst & Young*, 322 Ark. 417, 908 S.W.2d 660 (1995).

10. Ark. Code Ann. § 16-62-102(c) (Michie Supp. 1999).

11. *Chalmers v. Toyota Motor Sales, USA, Inc.*, 326 Ark. 895, 935 S.W.2d 285 (1996).

12. Ark. Code Ann. § 16-114-203(a) (Michie Supp. 1999).

13. Ark. Code Ann. § 16-114-203(b) (Michie Supp. 1999).

14. *Id.*

15. *Lane v. Lane*, 295 Ark. 671, 752 S.W.2d 25 (1988).

16. *Hertlein v. St. Paul Fire & Marine Ins. Co.*, 323 Ark. 283, 914 S.W.2d 303 (1996).

17. Ark. Code Ann. § 16-116-103 (Michie 1987).

18. *Martin v. Arthur*, 339 Ark. 149, 3 S.W.3d 684 (1999).

19. Ark. Code Ann. § 4-2-725 (Michie 1987).

20. *Follette v. Wal-Mart Stores, Inc.*, 41 F.3d 1234 (8th Cir. 1994).

21. Ark. Code Ann. § 16-56-115 (Michie 1987).

22. Ark. Code Ann. § 27-19-101 (Michie 1987).

23. Ark. Code Ann. § 27-19-605 (Michie Supp. 1999).

24. Id.

25. Id.

26. *Young v. Paxton*, 316 Ark. 655, 873 S.W.2d 546 (1994); *Hall v. Arthur*, 141 F.3d 844 (1998).

27. AMI Civil 4th, 303; *Shannon v. Wilson*, 329 Ark. 143, 947 S.W.2d 349 (1997).

28. AMI Civil 4th, 303; *Newberry v. Scruggs*, 336 Ark. 570, 986 S.W.2d 853 (1999).

29. AMI Civil 4th, 304.

30. *Newman v. Crawford Constr. Co.*, 303 Ark. 641, 799 S.W.2d 531 (1990). A child hunting with a high-powered rifle was held not to be engaged in an adult activity. *Purtle v. Shelton*, 251 Ark. 519, 474 S.W.2d 123 (1971).

31. AMI Civil 4th, 1501 (Supp. 2001-2002).

32. *Robson v. Tinnin*, 322 Ark. 605, 911 S.W.2d 246 (1995).

33. AMI Civil 4th, 1512 (Supp. 2001-2002).

34. *Callahan v. Clark*, 321 Ark. 376, 901 S.W.2d 842 (1995).

35. *Dodson v. Charter Behavioral Health Sys., Inc.*, 335 Ark. 96, 983 S.W.2d 98 (1998).

36. *Union Pacific R.R. v. Sharp*, 330 Ark. 174, 952 S.W.2d 658 (1997).

37. *Arthur v. Zearley*, 337 Ark. 125, 992 S.W.2d 67 (1999).

38. Ark. Code Ann. § 16-64-122 (Michie Supp. 1999).

39. Id.

40. Id.

41. Id.

42. *Ouachita Wilderness Inst. Inc. v. Mergen,* 329 Ark. 405, 947 S.W.2d 780 (1997); *Dawson v. Fulton,* 294 Ark. 624, 745 S.W.2d 617 (1998).

43. Ark. Code Ann. § 16-64-122 (Michie Supp. 1999).

44. AMI Civil 4th, 306.

45. *Eisener v. Fields,* 67 Ark. App. 238, 998 S.W.2d 421 (1999); *Schmidt v. Gibbs,* 305 Ark. 383, 807 S.W.2d 928 (1991).

46. *Id.*

47. *Id.*

48. *Tri-B Adver. Co. v. Thomas,* 278 Ark. 58, 643 S.W.2d 547 (1982).

49. *Berkley Pump Co. v. Reed-Joseph Land Co.,* 279 Ark. 384, 653 S.W.2d 128 (1983).

50. *Id.*

51. Ark. Code Ann. §§ 16-61-201 to 212 (Michie 1987 & Michie Supp. 1999).

52. Ark. Code Ann. § 16-61-201 (Michie 1987).

53. *Arthur Young & Co. v. Reeves,* 937 F.2d 1310 (8th Cir. 1991).

54. *Id.* at 1337.

55. *Woodard v. Blythe,* 249 Ark. 793, 462 S.W.2d 205 (1971).

56. Ark. Code Ann. § 16-61-203 (Michie 1987).

57. Ark. Code Ann. § 16-61-204 (Michie 1987).

58. Ark. Code Ann. § 16-61-202 (Michie 1987).

59. Ark. Code Ann. § 16-61-202(4) (Michie 1987).

60. *Missouri Pacific R.R. Co. v. Star City Gravel Co.,* 452 F. Supp. 480 (1978).

61. *Mosley Mach. Co. v. Gray Supply Co.,* 310 Ark. 214, 833 S.W.2d 772 (1992).

62. *Id.* A special relationship can arise by statute or contract. *Id.*

63. Ark. Code Ann. §§ 11-9-101 to 1001 (Michie 1987 & Michie Supp. 1999).

64. Ark. Code Ann. § 11-9-105 (Michie 1987).

65. *Id.*

66. Ark. Code Ann. § 11-9-410 (Michie 1987).

67. *Hill v. Patterson*, 313 Ark. 322, 855 S.W.2d 297 (1993).

68. *Id.*

69. Ark. Code Ann. § 11-9-410(b) (Michie 1987).

70. Ark. Code Ann. § 11-9-410(a) (Michie 1987).

71. *Coleman v. United Fence Co.*, 282 Ark. 344, 668 S.W.2d 536 (1984).

72. AMI Civil 4th, 1102.

73. AMI Civil 4th, 1107.

74. AMI Civil 4th, 1103.

75. AMI Civil 4th, 1103.

76. AMI Civil 4th, 1106 & 1107.

77. *DeVazier vs. Whit-Davis Lumber Co.*, 257 Ark. 371, 516 S.W.2d 610 (1974).

78. *Shannon v. Wilson*, 329 Ark. 143, 947 S.W.2d 349 (1997).

79. *Jackson v. Cadillac Cowboy*, 337 Ark. 24, 986 S.W.2d 410 (1999).

80. Ark. Code Ann. §§ 16-126-101 to 106 (Michie Supp. 2001).

81. Ark. Code Ann. § 16-126-103 (Michie Supp. 2001).

82. Ark. Code Ann. § 16-126-104 (Michie Supp. 2001).

83. *Farm Bureau Ins. Co. v. Case Corp.*, 317 Ark. 467, 878 S.W.2d 741 (1994).

84. *Mick Williams v. Zedlitz*, 294 Ark. 336, 742 S.W.2d 929 (1988); AMI Civil 4th, 402.

85. Ark. R. Civ. P. 9(b).

86. Ark. Code Ann. §§ 4-88-101 to 115 (Michie 1987 & Michie Supp. 1999).

87. Ark. Code Ann. § 4-88-107 (Michie 1987).

88. Ark. Code Ann. § 4-88-113 (Michie Supp. 1999).

89. Ark. Code Ann. § 4-88-115 (Michie 1987).

90. *Stin v. Lukas*, 308 Ark. 74, 823 S.W.2d 832 (1992).

91. AMI Civil 4th, 2218.

92. *Stin v. Lukas*, 308 Ark. 74, 823 S.W.2d 832 (1992).

93. *Id.*

94. *Nashville Bank of Commerce v. McNeil Trucking Co., Inc.*, 309 Ark. 80, 828 S.W.2d 584 (1992).

95. *Dongary Holstein Leasing Inc. v. Covington*, 293 Ark. 112, 732 S.W.2d 465 (1987).

96. *Honeycutt v. Walden*, 294 Ark. 440, 743 S.W.2d 809 (1988).

97. *Turner v. Rose Warren*, 250 Ark. 119, 464 S.W.2d 569 (1971).

98. *Lake v. Lake*, 262 Ark. 852, 562 S.W.2d 68 (1978).

99. Ark. Code Ann. §§ 16-62-101 to 102 (Michie 1987 & Michie Supp. 1999).

100. *Murrell v. Springdale Mem'l Hosp.*, 330 Ark. 121, 952 S.W.2d 153 (1997).

101. Ark. Code Ann. § 16-62-102 (d) (Michie Supp. 1999).

102. Ark. Code Ann. § 16-62-101 (Michie 1987).

CALIFORNIA

A. STATUTES OF LIMITATION

Personal injury and wrongful death actions founded on negligent, intentional, or tortious conduct generally must be brought within one year in California.[1] Under the discovery rule, the statute begins to run when a plaintiff has knowledge of injury, and knowledge of facts creating, or which in any reasonable person would create, a suspicion of wrongdoing on the part of someone, even if plaintiff is unable to identify the wrongdoer.[2]

The time for commencement of actions against healthcare providers is within three years after the date of injury or one year after the plaintiff discovers or reasonably should have discovered the injury, whichever occurs first. The time within which an action for professional medical negligence may be brought may in no event exceed three years, unless tolled by one of the following: (1) proof of fraud, (2) intentional concealment, or (3) the presence of a foreign body, which has no therapeutic or diagnostic purpose or effect, in the injured person.[3] Likewise, actions for professional negligence against an attorney, other than for actual fraud, must be brought within one year after the plaintiff discovers or reasonably should have discovered the facts constituting the wrongful act or omission on the part of the attorney, or four years from the date of the wrongful act or omission, whichever occurs first. In no event shall the time for commencement of legal action against an attorney for professional negligence exceed four years except that the period shall be tolled during certain periods of time.[4]

Causes of action for property damage have a three-year statute of limitations. An action upon a liability created by statute, other than a penalty or forfeiture also must be brought within three years.[5] A four-year statute of limitations exists for actions for damages from persons performing or furnishing design, specifications, surveying, planning, supervision or observation of construction, or construction of improvement to realty for patent deficiencies.[6] For latent deficiencies, however, there is a ten-year statute of limitations.[7]

Subject to certain limitations, actions for recovery of damages suffered as a result of childhood sexual abuse must be brought within eight years of the date the plaintiff attains the age of majority or within three years of the date the plaintiff discovers or reasonably should have discovered that psychological injury or illness occurring after the age of majority was caused by the sexual abuse, whichever period expires later.[8] A civil action for damages suffered as a result of domestic violence must be brought by the later of the following: (1) within three years from the date of the last act of domestic violence by the defendant, or (2) within three years from the date the plaintiff discovers or reasonably should have discovered the injury was a result of an act of domestic violence by defendant.[9]

Claims for relief on the ground of fraud or mistake must be brought within three years of the discovery of the facts constituting the fraud or mistake.[10]

Claims against a public entity for death or injury to person or property must be presented in writing to the public entity not later than six months after the accrual of the cause of action.[11] Thereafter, a lawsuit must be brought within six months of written rejection of the claim.[12] If no written rejection of the claim is given, the lawsuit must be brought within two years of the accrual of the cause of action.[13]

For any action not otherwise provided for either by the specific statute pertaining to the cause of action, or the code sections pertaining to limitations generally, there is a catch-all limitation of four years after the cause of action accrues.[14]

B. TORT REFORM

In 1996, California voters passed Proposition 213 which has now been codified in the Civil Code, and limits the recoverable damages by uninsured motorists and drunk drivers in an action arising out of the operation or use of a motor vehicle to economic damages only.[15]

Also, in any action based on negligence, a plaintiff who is injured during a commission of a felony or immediate flight therefrom and has been convicted, may not recover any damages.[16]

In 1999, AB169 was introduced in the California legislature. The bill sought to require that judges, not juries, would determine the amount of punitive damages according to specific criteria and explain their decision in writing. The bill died in committee.[16.1]

C. "NO FAULT" LIMITATIONS

Attempts to institute no fault limitations in California have been largely unsuccessful. Most recently, Proposition 200, which proposed a no fault vehicle insurance system for personal injuries resulting from vehicle accidents, was voted down by California voters in 1996.

D. THE STANDARD FOR NEGLIGENCE

A plaintiff establishes a prima facie case of negligence by showing that the defendant had a legal duty to exercise due care, a breach of that duty, and that the breach was the proximate cause of plaintiff's injury.[17] Subject to certain public policy limitations, the general rule in California is that every person is liable for injuries caused by his or her failure to exercise reasonable care under the circumstances.[18] The care required is that of an ordinary prudent or reasonable person.[19] Once a legal duty is established, a breach may be shown by establishing that the defendant did not act as a reasonable person should have under the circumstances.[20]

If the individual alleged to have been negligent is a child, the standard of care required will be examined by comparing the child's behavior to that of other children of like maturity, intelligence, and capacity under similar circumstances.[21]

E. CAUSATION

In California, the plaintiff must establish that the breach of a legal duty is the proximate, or legal, cause of the plaintiff's injuries. Proximate cause is shown by establishing that the defendant's conduct was a substantial factor in the production of plaintiff's injuries.[22]

F. CONTRIBUTORY NEGLIGENCE, COMPARATIVE NEGLIGENCE, AND ASSUMPTION OF RISK

1. Contributory Negligence

In California, the all-or-nothing rule of contributory negligence has been superceded by a system of pure comparative negligence.[23]

2. Comparative Negligence

The California Supreme Court has adopted a system of "pure" comparative negligence under which the assessment of liability in proportion to fault proceeds in spite of the fact that the plaintiff is equally at fault or more at fault than the defendant.[24] This system compares the fault of the plaintiff with the fault of all other persons whose conduct contributed to the injury.[25]

It is unsettled whether plaintiff's own willful misconduct that causes his or her injuries should act as a bar to recovery or whether his or her recovery should be reduced by his or her proportionate responsibility for the accident.[26]

3. Assumption of Risk

Generally, assumption of risk requires that the person undertaking the risk has knowledge of the particular risk and appreciation of its magnitude.[27] Assumption of risk can be implied or express. California distinguishes between two kinds of implied assumption of risk: primary and secondary.[28] Primary assumption of risk applies in instances where the assumption of risk doctrine embodies a legal conclusion that there is no duty on the part of the defendant to protect the plaintiff from a particular risk. In such cases, plaintiff is barred from recovery. Secondary assumption of risk applies in instances where the defendant does owe a duty of care to the plaintiff, but the plaintiff knowingly encounters a risk of injury caused by the defendant's breach of that duty.[29] When secondary assumption of risk is established, it is merged into the comparative fault scheme, and the trier of fact may consider the relative responsibilities of the parties.[30] Whether primary or secondary assumption of risk applies turns on whether, in light of the activity in which the plaintiff and defendant were engaged, the defendant's conduct breached a legal duty of care to the plaintiff.[31] The test is objective; it depends on the nature of the sport or activity in question and on the parties' general relationship to the activity rather than the particular plaintiff's subjective knowledge and awareness.[32]

Express assumption of risk may operate as a complete defense if a release from liability clearly notifies the releasor, in clear and unambiguous language understandable to any layperson, of the effect of signing the agreement, unless the release is against public policy.[33] If the release is too broad, it will violate public policy since this would include a release from liability for fraud and intentional acts.[34]

G. *RES IPSA LOQUITUR*

Res ipsa loquitur may be applied if the following conditions exist: (1) the accident must be of a kind that ordinarily does not occur in the absence of someone's negligence; (2) it must be caused by an agency or instrumentality within the exclusive control of the defendant; (3) it must not have been due to any voluntary action or contribution on the part of the plaintiff.[35] The existence of one or more of these conditions is usually a question of fact for the jury.[36] In a proper case, however, they all may exist as a matter of law.[37]

If the evidence satisfies all three conditions, a presumption affecting the burden of proof is created.[38] Therefore, when the plaintiff has established the three conditions that give rise to the doctrine, the jury is required to find that the accident resulted from the defendant's negligence unless the defendant comes forward with evidence that would support a contrary finding.[39] If evidence is produced that would support a finding that the defendant was not negligent or that any negligence on his part was not a proximate cause of the accident, the presumptive effect of the doctrine vanishes.[40] However, the jury may still be able to draw an inference that the accident was caused by the defendant's lack of due care from the facts that gave rise to the presumption.[41]

H. NEGLIGENCE *PER SE*

In California, the failure of a person to exercise due care is presumed if: (1) he or she violated a statute, ordinance, or regulation of a public entity; (2) the violation proximately caused death or injury to person or property; (3) the death or injury resulted from an occurrence of the nature that the statute, ordinance, or regulation was designed to prevent; (4) the person suffering the death or injury to his or her person or property was one of the class of persons for whose protection the statute, ordinance, or regulation was adopted.[42]

Once established, the presumption of negligence may be rebutted by proof that: (1) the person violating the statute, ordinance, or regulation did what might reasonably be expected of a person of ordinary prudence, acting under similar circumstances, who desired to comply with the law; or (2) the person violating the statute, ordinance, or regulation was a child and exercised the degree of care ordinarily exercised by persons of his maturity, intelligence, and capacity under similar circumstances, but the presumption may not be rebutted by such proof if the violation occurred in the course of an activity normally engaged in only by adults and requiring adult qualifications.[43]

I. JOINT AND SEVERAL LIABILITY

The Fair Responsibility Act of 1986 ("Proposition 51") modified the established rule of joint and several liability.[44]

The statute distinguishes economic damages from noneconomic damages. Liability for economic damages is joint and several.[45] Liability for noneconomic damages is limited to a proportion of such damages equal to the tortfeasor's percentage of fault, and a separate judgment is rendered against that tortfeasor for that amount.[46] Damages must be apportioned among the "universe of tortfeasors" including nonjoined defendants.[47]

Although the statute states that Proposition 51 only applies to actions based on comparative fault, it limits a tortfeasor's liability whether the joint tortfeasor is negligent or acts intentionally.[48] Proposition 51 does not apply to actions based on vicarious tort liability of persons for the acts of others that are not based on principles of comparative fault.[49] Since an injured consumer may sue any business entity in the chain of production and distribution under the principles of strict liability, Proposition 51 will not apply to these particular product liability actions unless plaintiff proves defendants' negligence.[50]

Under Proposition 51, when a tortfeasor settles before trial with the plaintiff, a nonsettling joint tortfeasor who sustains a money judgment is entitled to a setoff only for the economic portion of the settlement.[51] The nonsettling tortfeasor has the burden of showing which percentage of the jury award is attributable to economic damages.[52] Failure to meet this burden waives any right to setoff.[53]

J. INDEMNITY

Indemnity operates either to effect a complete shift of loss from the indemnitee to the indemnitor or to effect a partial shifting of loss according to the respective shares of comparative fault of the various tortfeasors.[54] Of course, indemnity may be provided for expressly by contract.[55]

In California, however, a defendant who enters into a settlement deemed to be in "good faith" pursuant to certain criteria is discharged from any further liability on all equitable indemnity claims.[56]

K. BAR OF WORKERS' COMPENSATION STATUTE

Under the California Workers' Compensation Act, the right to recover such compensation is the exclusive remedy for injury or death of an employee against the employer or any other employee of the employer acting within the scope of his or her employment.[57]

An employee, or his or her dependents in the event of death, can maintain an action for damages against the employer outside of the Workers' Compensation Act in the following instances: (1) the employee's injury or death is proximately caused by a willful physical assault by the employer;[58] (2) the employee's injury is aggravated by the employer's fraudulent concealment of the existence of the injury and its connection with the employment;[59] (3) the employee's injury or death is proximately caused by a defective product manufactured by the employer and sold, leased, or otherwise transferred for valuable consideration to an independent third person, and that product is thereafter provided for the employee's use by a third person.[60] This third exception also provides a basis for asserting a tort action against an employer based on the "dual capacity doctrine" which has otherwise been eliminated in California.[61]

Another exception to California's rule that worker's compensation is the exclusive remedy for claims against the employer provides that an action may be brought against an employer if injury or death is caused by the employer's knowing removal of, or failure to provide a guard on, a power press.[62] An employer who designs, manufactures, and installs its own power presses for employee use is subject to potential liability as a third-party tortfeasor.[63]

L. PREMISES LIABILITY

California has eliminated the common law principles of premises liability based on classifying the plaintiff as a trespasser, licensee, or invitee.[64] Instead, premises liability is governed by the statute that defines California's ordinary negligence standard. The statute states that everyone is responsible for an injury occasioned to another by his want of ordinary care or skill in the management of his property or person, except so far as the latter has brought the injury upon himself.[65]

The proper test to be applied to the liability of the possessor of land is whether in the management of his property he has acted as a reasonable man in view of the probability of injury to others.[66] The plaintiff's status as a trespasser, licensee, or invitee may still have some relevance since the facts giving rise to such status have some bearing on the question of liability, but the status is not determinative.[67]

Since the injured party's status is no longer determinative of his right to recover, the attractive nuisance doctrine is no longer applicable.[68] This doctrine was an exception to the rule that a trespasser could not recover from a landowner and provided that a child could recover for injuries caused by a dangerous condition on the land if certain elements were proven.[69]

Although premises liability is generally based on the law of negligence, in 1985, the California Supreme Court, analogizing to products liability decisions, imposed a rule of strict liability on residential landlords for harm caused by defects that existed at the time the premises were leased.[70] In 1995, the Supreme Court overruled its decision in that case and held that strict liability should not be imposed in premises liability actions.[71] The court, however, left open the possibility that a landowner who participated in the construction of the building may be held strictly liable.[72]

An injured party may have a nuisance cause of action against the owner or possessor of land for injuries occurring on or near the premises.[73]

M. DRAM SHOP LIABILITY

In California, it is a misdemeanor to serve alcoholic beverages to any habitual or common drunkard or to any obviously intoxicated person.[74] However, under California statute, no person who supplies alcoholic beverages or permits consumption of alcoholic beverages on their premises is civilly liable to an injured person or to an injured person's estate for injuries inflicted as a result of intoxication by the consumer of the alcoholic beverage.[75] It is the consumption of alcoholic beverages rather than the serving of alcoholic beverages that is the proximate cause of injuries inflicted upon another by an intoxicated person.[76]

Liability attaches if the alcoholic beverage is sold or supplied to an obviously intoxicated minor.[77] Liability for injury or death from a vehicle accident attaches when the bartender serves alcohol to an obviously intoxicated person *and* the bartender knew or should have known that the customer was going to drive a motor vehicle on a public highway.[78]

N. ECONOMIC LOSS

Recovery in negligence and strict liability tort actions is limited to damages for personal injuries and to physical damages to plaintiff's property.[79] There is no recovery for economic losses alone.[80] However, economic damages have been awarded in cases involving malpractice liability of professionals for negligence in the rendition of services[81] and in actions for negligent interference with prospective economic business advantage where a special relationship exists between the parties.[82] In the latter action, recovery is limited to instances where the risk of harm is foreseeable and is closely connected with the defendant's conduct, and where damages are not wholly speculative and the injury is not part of plaintiff's ordinary business risk.[83]

O. FRAUD AND DECEIT

Under California law, one who willfully deceives another with intent to induce him to alter his position, to his injury or risk, is liable for any damages which he thereby suffers.[84] The elements of fraud that give rise to a tort action of deceit are: (1) false representation, concealment, or nondisclosure; (2) knowledge of falsity or scienter; (3) intent to defraud or induce reliance; (4) justifiable reliance; and (5) resulting damages.[85] Plaintiff must plead all elements with specificity; general and conclusory claims of fraud are not sufficient.[86] The standard of proof is by a preponderance of the evidence.[87]

The California statute defines deceit in four categories that are generally known as:[88] (1) intentional misrepresentation;[89] (2) negligent misrepresentation;[90] (3) concealment;[91] (4) false promise.[92]

Liability for negligent misrepresentation attaches where the defendant makes false statements, honestly believing that they are true, but without reasonable ground for such belief.[93] Elements of negligent misrepresentation include justifiable reliance on the misrepresentation and resulting damages.[94] Neither scienter nor intent to deceive is necessary for negligent misrepresentation.[95] If the belief is both reasonable and honest, the misrepresentation is innocent and no tort liability attaches.[96]

P. CONSUMER FRAUD STATUTES

The Consumers Legal Remedies Act[97] (CLRA) allows a consumer to bring an individual action[98] or a class action on behalf of himself and other consumers in similar situations[99] if he has suffered any damage from the use or employment of unfair methods of competition and unfair or deceptive acts or practices deemed unlawful by the act.[100] The purpose of the act is to protect consumers against unfair and deceptive business practices and to provide efficient and economical procedures to secure such protection.[101]

The remedies provided by the CLRA are not exclusive but are in addition to any other procedures or remedies for any violation or conduct provided for in any other law.[102] The consumer may recover or obtain actual damages, an injunction against unfair methods or practices, restitution of property, and punitive damages.[103] Damages will not be awarded if defendant proves that: (a) violation of the act was not intentional and resulted from a bona fide error, and (b) the defendant made an appropriate and timely correction, repair, or replacement, or other remedy.[104]

Any action brought under CLRA must commence within three years from the date of the commission of the unfair method, act, or practice.[105]

Q. PUNITIVE (EXEMPLARY) DAMAGES

California allows recovery of punitive (exemplary) damages, in addition to compensatory damages,[106] in tort actions where it is proven by clear and convincing evidence[107] that the defendant is guilty of oppression, fraud, or malice[108] and must have acted with intent to vex, injure or annoy, or with a conscious disregard of plaintiff's rights.[109] Punitive damages are incidental to the cause of action; they do not constitute a basis for a separate cause of action.[110] The purpose of punitive damages is to punish and deter the defendant and others from such conduct in the future.[111]

Plaintiff must have suffered actual damages from defendant's wrongful act to recover an award of punitive damages.[112] Nominal damages are sufficient to justify an award of punitive damages.[113] Although punitive damages may be awarded for unintentional torts,[114] an award for punitive damages may not be based on mere negligence.[115]

Punitive damages must bear a reasonable relation to the amount of actual or compensatory damages sustained.[116] There are three factors considered in determining the amount of punitive damages:[117] (1) the wealth or net worth of the defendant;[118] (2) the amount of compensatory damages;[119] and (3) the reprehensibility of the defendant's conduct.[120]

Punitive damages are not recoverable in wrongful death actions,[121] but may be recoverable in wrongful life actions.[122] Punitive damages that the decedent would have been entitled to recover if he had lived may be recovered in a survival action brought on behalf of the decedent's estate.[123]

R. WRONGFUL DEATH AND SURVIVORSHIP ACTIONS

Wrongful death actions have statutory rather than common-law origin.[124] The purpose of the wrongful death statute is to provide compensation for loss of companionship and other losses resulting from decedent's death.[125] The right to bring an action for wrongful death is limited only to those persons described in the statute.[126] The statute of limitations runs from the date of death, not the date of the accident causing death.[127]

The action is considered "joint" so that all heirs should join in the action and a single verdict should be rendered for all recoverable damages.[128] A lump-sum verdict is required even though total recovery is the aggregate of the pecuniary loss of each of the heirs.[129] Recoverable damages are limited to "pecuniary losses" which include amounts that compensate plaintiffs for loss of decedent's society, comfort, protection, love, companionship, affection, sexual relations, and solace.[130] There is no recovery for the suffering or grief of the plaintiffs or of the deceased.[131]

California has statutory provisions governing survival and continuance of actions belonging to decedent.[132] An action or proceeding may be commenced by the decedent's successor in interest if there is no personal representative.[133] The personal representative or successor in interest has an absolute right to be substituted for the decedent.[134] Damages recoverable are limited to the loss or damage that the decedent sustained or incurred before death, including any penalties or punitive or exemplary damages that the decedent would have been entitled to recover had the decedent lived.[135] Damages for pain, suffering, or disfigurement are not recoverable in survival actions following the legislature's reasoning that once deceased, the decedent cannot be compensated for injuries, pain and suffering, or be made whole.[136]

Arnold D. Larson
Melissa A. Immel
IVERSON, YOAKUM, PAPIANO & HATCH
One Wilshire Building
624 South Grand Avenue, 27th Floor
Los Angeles, California 90017-3328
(213) 624-7444
Fax (213) 629-3358

ENDNOTES - CALIFORNIA

1. Cal. Civ. Proc. Code § 340(3) (West Supp. 2002).

2. *Jolly v. Eli Lilly & Co.*, 44 Cal. 3d 1103, 245 Cal. Rptr. 658 (1988); *Bernson v. Browning-Ferris Industries*, 7 Cal. 4th 926, 931, 30 Cal. Rptr. 2d 440 (1994); *Frederick v. Calbio Pharmaceuticals*, 89 Cal. App. 3d 49, 53-58, 152 Cal. Rptr. 292 (1979).

3. Cal. Civ. Proc. Code § 340.5 (West 1982); *Williamson v. Prida*, 75 Cal. App. 4th 1417, 1424, 89 Cal. Rptr. 2d 868 (1999) (veterinary malpractice cases are treated like medical malpractice cases for purposes of the statute of limitations).

4. Cal. Civ. Proc. Code § 340.6 (West 1982).

5. Cal. Civ. Proc. Code § 338 (West Supp. 2002).

6. Cal. Civ. Proc. Code § 337.1 (West 1982).

7. Cal. Civ. Proc. Code § 337.15 (West 1982).

8. Cal. Civ. Proc. Code § 340.1 (West Supp. 2002).

9. Cal. Civ. Proc. Code § 340.15 (West Supp. 2002).

10. Cal. Civ. Proc. § 338(d) (West Supp. 2002).

11. Gov. Code § 911.2 (West 1995).

12. Gov. Code § 945.6 (West 1995).

13. *Id.*

14. Cal. Civ. Proc. Code § 343 (West 1982).

15. Cal. Civ. Code § 3333.4. (West 1997) (§ 3333.4, which was created by the Personal Responsibility Act of 1996, a voter initiative designated as Proposition 213, has been declared constitutional in two lower appellate court reviews; *Yoshioka v. Superior Court*, 58 Cal. App. 4th 972, 68 Cal. Rptr. 2d 553 (1997); *Quakenbush v. Superior Court*, 60 Cal. App. 4th 454, 70 Cal. Rptr. 2d 271 (1997), *cert. denied*, 67 U.S.L.W. (U.S. Cal. Oct. 5, 1998) (No. 97-2058). *But see, Horwich v. Superior Court*, 21 Cal. 4th 272, 275, 87 Cal. Rptr. 2d. 222 (1999) wherein the California Supreme Court held that Civil Code Section 3333.4 does not preclude a wrongful death plaintiff whose decedent was the uninsured operator of a motor vehicle involved in an accident from recovering damages for loss of

care, comfort, and society; and, *Montes v. Gibbens,* 71 Cal. App. 4th 982, 987, 84 Cal. Rptr. 2d 324 (1999) where it was held that Civil Code Section 3333.4 does not prohibit recovery of noneconomic damages by an employee for injuries he received while driving his employer's uninsured motor vehicle.)

16. Cal. Civ. Code § 3333.3 (West 1997).

16.1. Assem. Bill No. 169, 1999–2000 Regular Session.

17. 6 Witkin, Summary of Cal. Law (9th ed. 1988), Torts § 732, pp. 60-61.

18. *Rowland v. Christian,* 69 Cal. 2d 108, 119, 70 Cal. Rptr. 97 (1968); Cal. Civ. Code § 1714 (West 1998).

19. *Fouch v. Werner,* 99 Cal. App. 557, 565, 279 P. 183 (1929); *Phoenix Assur. Co. v. Texas Holding Co.,* 81 Cal. App. 61, 73, 252 P. 1082 (1927); *Beck v. Sirota,* 42 Cal. App. 2d 551, 557, 109 P.2d 419 (1941).

20. *Rowland, supra,* 69 Cal. 2d at 119; Cal. Civ. Code § 1714 (West 1998); 6 Witkin, Summary of Cal. Law (9th ed. 1988), Torts § 732.

21. 6 Witkin, Summary of Cal. Law (9th ed. 1988), Torts §§ 806-08, pp. 160-163.

22. *Mitchell v. Gonzales,* 54 Cal. 3d 1041, 1 Cal. Rptr. 2d 913 (1991).

23. *Li v. Yellow Cab Co.,* 13 Cal. 3d 804, 829, 119 Cal. Rptr. 858 (1975).

24. *Id.*

25. *American Motorcycle Assn. v. Superior Court,* 20 Cal. 3d 578, 589, 146 Cal. Rptr. 182 (1978).

26. *Zavala v. Regents of University of California,* 125 Cal. App. 3d 646, 647, 178 Cal. Rptr. 185 (1981) (plaintiff's willful misconduct should be compared with negligent misconduct); *Sissle v. Stefenoni,* 88 Cal. App. 3d 633, 152 Cal. Rptr. 56 (1979) (survivors of a decedent guilty of willful misconduct could not recover despite defendant's negligence).

27. *Allabach v. Santa Clara County Fair Assn.,* 46 Cal. App. 4th 1007, 1012, 54 Cal. Rptr. 2d 330 (1996).

28. *Knight v. Jewett,* 3 Cal. 4th 296, 308, 11 Cal. Rptr. 2d 2 (1992); *Cheong v. Antablin,* 16 Cal. 4th 1063, 1067, 68 Cal. Rptr. 2d 859 (1997).

29. *Id.*

30. *Knight, supra,* 3 Cal. 4th at 315; *Cheong v. Antablin,* 16 Cal. 4th at 1068.

31. *Id.*

32. *Knight, supra,* 3 Cal. 4th at 313; *Cheong, supra,* 6 Cal. 4th at 1068.

33. *McAtee v. Newhall Land & Farming Co.,* 169 Cal. App. 3d 1031, 1033, 216 Cal. Rptr. 465 (1985); *Paralift, Inc. v. Superior Court,* 23 Cal. App. 4th 748, 755, 29 Cal. Rptr. 2d 177 (1993).

34. *Baker Pacific Corp. v. Suttles,* 220 Cal. App. 3d 1148, 1154, 269 Cal. Rptr. 709 (1990); Cal. Civ. Code § 1668 (West 1985).

35. *Newing v. Cheatham,* 15 Cal. 3d 351, 359, 124 Cal. Rptr. 193 (1975); *Blackwell v. Hurst,* 46 Cal. App. 4th 939, 54 Cal. Rptr. 2d 209 (1996).

36. *Newing, supra,* 15 Cal. 3d at 359.

37. *Id.*

38. Cal. Evid. Code § 646 (West 1995); *Newing, supra,* 15 Cal. 3d at 359.

39. Cal. Evid. Code § 604 (West 1995); Cal. Law Revision Comm'n. Comment to Evid. Code § 646 (West 1995).

40. *Id.*

41. Cal. Evid. Code § 604 (West 1995); Cal. Evid. Code § 646(c) (West 1995); Cal. Law Revision Com. comment to Evid. Code § 646 (West 1995).

42. Cal. Evid. Code § 669(a) (West 1995); *California Service Station and Automobile Repair Assn. v. American Home Assurance Co.,* 62 Cal. App. 4th 1166, 1177, 73 Cal. Rptr. 2d 182 (1998).

43. Cal. Evid. Code § 669(b) (West 1995).

44. Cal. Civ. Code § 1431 *et seq.* (West Supp. 2002).

45. Cal. Civ. Code § 1431.2(a) (West Supp. 2002).

46. *Id.*

47. *Roslan v. Permea, Inc.,* 17 Cal. App. 4th 110, 21 Cal. Rptr. 2d 66 (1993).

48. *Weidenfeller v. Star & Garter,* 1 Cal. App. 4th 1, 2 Cal. Rptr. 2d 14 (1991); *Baird v. Jones,* 21 Cal. App. 4th 684, 27 Cal. Rptr. 2d 232 (1993); *Scott v. County of Los Angeles,* 27 Cal. App. 4th 125, 32 Cal. Rptr. 2d 643 (1994).

49. *Srithong v. Total Investment Co.,* 23 Cal. App. 4th 721, 28 Cal. Rptr. 2d 672 (1994).

50. *Wimberly v. Derby Cycle Corp.*, 56 Cal. App. 4th 618, 65 Cal. Rptr. 2d 532 (1997); *Springmeyer v. Ford Motor Co.*, 60 Cal. App. 4th 1541, 71 Cal. Rptr. 2d 190 (1998).

51. *Conrad v. Ball*, 24 Cal. App. 4th 439, 29 Cal. Rptr. 2d 441 (1994).

52. *Id.*

53. *Id.*

54. *American Motorcycle Assn., supra*, 20 Cal. 3d at 589; *Far West Financial Corp. v. D&S Co.*, 46 Cal. 3d 796, 808, 251 Cal. Rptr. 202 (1988).

55. Cal. Civ. Code § 2772 (West 1993).

56. Cal. Civ. Proc. Code § 877(b) (West Supp. 2002); *Far West Financial Corp., supra*, 46 Cal. 3d at 808.

57. Cal. Labor Code §§ 3601(a), 3602(a) (West Supp. 2002).

58. Cal. Labor Code § 3602(b)(1) (West 1989).

59. Cal. Labor Code § 3602(b)(2) (West 1989).

60. Cal. Labor Code § 3602(b)(3) (West 1989).

61. Cal. Labor Code § 3602(a) (West 1989); *Perry v. Heavenly Valley*, 163 Cal. App. 3d 495, 501, 209 Cal. Rptr. 771 (1985).

62. Cal. Labor Code § 4558 (West 1989).

63. *Flowmaster, Inc. v. Superior Court*, 16 Cal. App. 4th 1019, 1030, 20 Cal. Rptr. 2d 666 (1993).

64. *Rowland, supra*, 69 Cal. 2d at 119.

65. Cal. Civ. Code § 1714(a) (West 1998).

66. *Rowland, supra*, 69 Cal. 2d at 119.

67. *Id.*

68. *Smith v. Americania Motor Lodge*, 39 Cal. App. 3d 1, 7, 113 Cal. Rptr. 771 (1974).

69. *O'Keefe v. South End Rowing Club*, 64 Cal. 2d 729, 741, 51 Cal. Rptr. 534 (1966).

70. *Becker v. IRM Corporation*, 38 Cal. 3d 454, 464, 213 Cal. Rptr. 213 (1985).

71. *Peterson v. Superior Court*, 10 Cal. 4th 1185, 43 Cal. Rptr. 2d 836 (1995).

72. *Id*. at 1200.

73. Cal. Civ. Code § 3479 (West 1997); *Carson v. Facilities Development Co.*, 36 Cal. 3d 830, 846-48, 206 Cal. Rptr. 136 (1984).

74. Cal. B & P Code § 25602(a) (West 1997).

75. Cal. B & P Code § 25602(b) (West 1997); *Leong v. San Francisco Parking, Inc.*, 235 Cal. App. 3d 827, 833-34, 1 Cal. Rptr. 2d 41, 45 (1991); *Cantwell v. Peppermill, Inc.*, 25 Cal. App. 4th. 1797, 1802, 31 Cal. Rptr. 2d 246, 248 (1994).

76. Cal. B & P Code § 25502(c) (West 1997); *Cory v. Shierloh*, 29 Cal. 3d 430, 434, 174 Cal. Rptr. 500, 502 (1981); *Cantwell, supra*, 25 Cal. App. 4th. at 1802.

77. Cal. B & P Code § 25602.1 (West 1997) (Note: This statute applies only to licensed alcoholic beverage dealers, not social hosts. *Zieff v. Weinstein*, 191 Cal. App. 3d 243, 245, 236 Cal. Rptr. 536, 537 (1987). Where alcoholic beverages are supplied to sober minors, such dealers are immune from claims by third parties injured as a result of the intoxication of those minors. *Rogers v. Alvas*, 160 Cal. App. 3d 997, 1003-04, 207 Cal. Rptr. 60, 64 (1984)]; *Cardinal v. Santee Pita, Inc.*, 234 Cal. App. 3d 1676, 1680, 286 Cal. Rptr. 275, 277 (1991).

78. *Paula v. Gagnon*, 81 Cal. App. 3d 680, 686, 146 Cal. Rptr. 702, 705 (1978).

79. *Seely v. White Motor Co.*, 63 Cal. 2d 9, 45 Cal. Rptr. 17 (1965); *Anthony v. Kelsey-Hayes Co.*, 25 Cal. App. 3d 442, 102 Cal. Rptr. 113 (1992); *Pisano v. American Leasing*, 146 Cal. App. 3d 194, 194 Cal. Rptr. 77 (1983).

80. *Id.*

81. *Cooper v. Jevne*, 56 Cal. App. 3d 860, 128 Cal. Rptr. 724 (1976); *Biakanja v. Irving*, 49 Cal. 2d 647, 320 P.2d 16 (1958).

82. *J'Aire Corp. v. Gregory*, 24 Cal. 3d 799, 157 Cal. Rptr. 407 (1979); *Biakanja, supra*, 49 Cal. 2d 647; *Chameleon Engineering Corp. v. Air Dynamics, Inc.*, 101 Cal. App. 3d 418, 161 Cal. Rptr. 463 (1980).

83. *J'Aire Corp., supra*, 24 Cal. 3d at 799; *Pisano, supra*, 146 Cal. App. 3d at 194.

84. Cal. Civ. Code § 1709 (West 1998).

85. *Engalla v. Permanente Medical Group, Inc.*, 15 Cal. 4th 951, 974, 64 Cal. Rptr. 2d 843, 857 (1997).

86. *Lazar v. Superior Court*, 12 Cal. 4th 631, 645, 49 Cal. Rptr. 2d 377, 385 (1996).

87. Cal. Evid. Code § 115 (West 1995); *Liodas v. Sahadi*, 19 Cal. 3d 278, 286-87, 137 Cal. Rptr. 635, 640 (1977).

88. Cal. Civ. Code § 1710 (West 1998).

89. Cal. Civ. Code § 1710 (1) (West 1998) ("The suggestion, as a fact, of that which is not true, by one who does not believe it to be true.").

90. Cal. Civ. Code § 1710 (2) (West 1998) ("The assertion, as a fact, of that which is not true, by one who has no reasonable ground for believing it to be true.").

91. Cal. Civ. Code § 1710 (3) (West 1998). ("The suppression of a fact, by one who is bound to disclose it, or who gives information of other facts which are likely to mislead for want of communication of that fact.").

92. Cal. Civ. Code § 1710 (4) (West 1998). ("A promise made without any intention of performing it.").

93. *Gagne v. Bertran*, 43 Cal. 2d 481, 275 P.2d 15 (1954); *Walters v. Marler*, 83 Cal. App. 3d 1, 147 Cal. Rptr. 655 (1978).

94. *B.L.M. v. Sabo & Deitsch*, 55 Cal. App. 4th 823, 64 Cal. Rptr. 2d 335 (1997).

95. *Gagne, supra*, 43 Cal. 2d 481 (1954).

96. *Graham v. Ellmore*, 135 Cal. App. 129, 132, 26 P. 2d 696, 699 (1933).

97. Cal. Civ. Code § 1750 *et seq.* (West 1998).

98. Cal. Civ. Code § 1780(a) (West Supp. 2002).

99. Cal. Civ. Code § 1781(a) (West 1998).

100. Cal. Civ. Code § 1780 (West Supp. 2002); California Civil Code § 1781 (West 1998).

101. Cal. Civ. Code § 1760 (West 1998).

102. Cal. Civ. Code § 1752 (West 1998).

103. Cal. Civ. Code § 1780(a)(1) (West Supp. 2002).

104. Cal. Civ. Code § 1784 (West 1998).

105. Cal. Civ. Code § 1783 (West 1998).

106. *Sterling Drug, Inc. v. Benatar*, 99 Cal. App. 2d 393, 221 P.2d 965 (1950); *Neal v. Farmers Ins. Exchange*, 21 Cal. 3d 910, 148 Cal. Rptr. 389 (1978).

107. *Stewart v. Truck Ins. Exchange*, 17 Cal. App. 4th 468, 481, 21 Cal. Rptr. 2d 338, 347, (1993); *Waits v. Frito-Lay, Inc.*, 978 F.2d 1093 (9th Cir. 1992).

108. Cal. Civ. Code § 3294 (West 1997); *Campbell v. Cal-Gard Surety Services, Inc.*, 62 Cal. App. 4th 563, 570, 73 Cal. Rptr. 2d 64, 67 (1998); *Wetherbee v. United Ins. Co. of America*, 18 Cal. App. 3d 266, 95 Cal. Rptr. 678 (1971).

109. *Silberg v. California Life Ins. Co.*, 11 Cal. 3d 452, 113 Cal. Rptr. 711 (1974); *Beck v. State Farm Mut. Auto Ins. Co.*, 54 Cal. App. 3d 347, 126 Cal. Rptr. 602 (1976).

110. *Hilliard v. A.H. Robbins Co.*, 148 Cal. App. 3d 374, 391, 196 Cal. Rptr. 117, 128 (1983); *James v. Public Finance Corp.*, 47 Cal. App. 3d 995, 1000, 121 Cal. Rptr. 670, 673 (1975).

111. *Ferraro v. Pacific Fin. Corp.*, 8 Cal. App. 3d 339, 87 Cal. Rptr. 226 (1970); *Fletcher v. Western Nat. Life Ins. Co.*, 10 Cal. App. 3d 376, 89 Cal. Rptr. 78 (1970); *Stevens v. Owens-Corning Fiberglass Corp.*, 49 Cal. App. 4th 1645, 1652, 57 Cal. Rptr. 2d 525, 532 (1996).

112. *Jackson v. Johnson*, 5 Cal. App. 4th 1350, 7 Cal. Rptr. 2d 482 (1992); *Esparza v. Specht*, 55 Cal. App. 3d 1, 127 Cal. Rptr. 493 (1976).

113. *Werschkull v. United California Bank*, 85 Cal. App. 3d 981, 1001-04, 149 Cal. Rptr. 829, 842-44 (1978); *Civic Western Corp. v. Zila Industries, Inc.*, 66 Cal. App. 3d 1, 135 Cal. Rptr. 915 (1977); *Sterling Drug, Inc., supra*, 99 Cal. App. 2d 393 (1950).

114. *Potter v. Firestone Tire & Rubber Co.*, 6 Cal. 4th 965, 1004, 25 Cal. Rptr. 2d 550, 576 (1993).

115. *Moody v. Moody*, 4 Cal. 297 (1854); *Roth v. Shell Oil Co.*, 185 Cal. App. 2d 676, 8 Cal. Rptr. 514 (1960); *Ebaugh v. Rabkin*, 22 Cal. App. 3d 891, 99 Cal. Rptr. 706 (1972).

116. *Vallbona v. Springer*, 43 Cal. App. 4th 1525, 1536, 51 Cal. Rptr. 2d 311, 318 (1996).

117. *Stevens, supra*, 49 Cal. App. 4th at 1658.

118. *Bertero v. National General Corp.*, 13 Cal. 3d 43, 65, 118 Cal. Rptr. 184 (1974); *Adams v. Murakami*, 54 Cal. 3d 105, 110, 284 Cal. Rptr. 318 (1991); *Richmond v. Allstate Ins. Co.*, 897 F.Supp. 447 (S.D. Cal. 1995); *Kenly v. Ukegawa*, 16 Cal. App. 4th 49, 56, 19 Cal. Rptr. 2d 771, 775 (1993); *Chodos v. Insurance Co. of North America*, 126 Cal. App. 3d 86, 103, 178 Cal. Rptr. 831 (1981).

119. *Little v. Stuyvesant Life Ins. Co.*, 67 Cal. App. 3d 451, 469, 136 Cal. Rptr. 653, 663 (1977).

120. *Walker v. Signal Companies, Inc.*, 84 Cal. App. 3d 982, 997-98, 149 Cal. Rptr. 119, 126-28 (1978).

121. Cal. Civ. Proc. Code § 377.61 (West Supp. 2002); *Grimshaw v. Ford Motor Co.*, 119 Cal. App. 3d 757, 807, 174 Cal. Rptr. 348, 381 (1981).

122. *Curlender v. Bio-Science Laboratories*, 106 Cal. App. 3d 811, 831, 165 Cal. Rptr. 477, 490 (1980).

123. Cal. Civ. Code § 377.34 (West 1992); *Grimshaw, supra*, 119 Cal. App. 3d 757.

124. *Ruttenberg v. Ruttenberg*, 53 Cal. App. 4th 801, 62 Cal. Rptr. 2d 78 (1997).

125. *Phraner v. Cote Mark, Inc.*, 55 Cal. App. 4th 166, 170, 63 Cal. Rptr. 2d 740, 742 (1997).

126. Cal. Civ. Proc. Code § 377.60 (West Supp. 2002); *Phraner, supra*, 55 Cal. App. 4th at 170.

127. Cal. Civ. Proc. Code § 340(3) (West Supp. 2002); *Norgart v. Upjohn Co.*, 21 Cal. 4th 383, 404, 87 Cal. Rptr. 2d 453 (1999).

128. *Ruttenberg v. Ruttenberg*, 53 Cal. App. 4th 801, 62 Cal. Rptr. 2d 78 (1977); *Smith v. Premier Alliance Ins. Co.*, 41 Cal. App. 4th 691, 697, 48 Cal. Rptr. 2d 461, 464 (1995).

129. *Morales v. Superior Court of Kern County*, 99 Cal. App. 3d 283, 160 Cal. Rptr. 194 (1979).

130. *Krouse v. Graham*, 19 Cal. 3d 59, 67-70, 137 Cal. Rptr. 863, 866-69 (1977).

131. Cal. Civ. Proc. Code § 377.61 (West Supp. 2002); *Canavin v. Pacific Southwest Airlines*, 148 Cal. App. 3d 512, 525, 196 Cal. Rptr. 82, 90 (1983).

132. Cal. Civ. Proc. Code §§ 377.10–377.35 (West Supp. 2002).

133. *Id.*

134. Cal. Civ. Proc. Code § 377.30 and § 377.31 (West Supp. 2002); *Pepper v. Superior Court*, 76 Cal. App. 3d 252, 260-63, 142 Cal. Rptr. 759, 765-66 (1977).

135. Cal. Civ. Proc. Code § 377.34 (West Supp. 1992).

136. Cal. Civ. Proc. Code § 377.34 (West Supp. 1992); *Garcia v. Superior Court*, 42 Cal. App. 4th 177, 183, 49 Cal. Rptr. 2d 580, 584 (1996).

COLORADO

A. STATUTES OF LIMITATION

The following are some of the actions that must be brought within three years after the cause of action accrues: (1) contract actions, including personal contracts and actions under the Uniform Commercial Code; (2) all actions for fraud, misrepresentation, concealment, or deceit; (3) all actions for breach of trust or breach of fiduciary duty; (4) all claims under the Uniform Consumer Credit Code; (5) all actions of replevin or for taking, detaining, or converting goods or chattels; (6) all actions under the Motor Vehicle Financial Responsibility Act; (7) all actions under the Colorado Auto Accident Reparations Act; (8) all actions accruing outside Colorado if the limitation of actions of the place where the cause of action accrued is greater than that of Colorado; and (9) all tort actions for bodily injury or property damage arising out of the use or operation of a motor vehicle except for actions based upon strict liability, absolute liability, or failure to instruct or warn.[1]

The following are some of the actions that must be brought within two years after the cause of action accrues: (1) tort actions, including but not limited to actions for negligence, trespass, malicious abuse of process, malicious prosecution, outrageous conduct, interference with relationships, and tortious breach of contract; except for torts arising out of the use or operation of a motor vehicle; (2) all actions for strict liability, absolute liability, or failure to instruct or warn; (3) all actions against any veterinarian; (4) all actions for wrongful death; (5) all actions against any public or governmental entity; and (6) all other actions of every kind for which no other period of limitation is provided.[2]

The following are some of the actions that must be brought within one year after the cause of action accrues: (1) the following tort actions: assault, battery, false imprisonment, false arrest, libel, and slander; (2) all actions for escape of prisoners; (3) all actions against sheriffs, coroners, police officers, firefighters, national guardsmen, or any other law enforcement authority; (4) all actions for any penalty or forfeiture of any penal statutes; and (5) all actions against a person alleging liability for a penalty for commission of a class A or a class B traffic infraction.[3]

Colorado also recognizes special limitations on actions against certain classes of individuals. For example, most tort or contract actions against hospitals or health care providers must be brought within two years after the cause of action accrues, and in no instance shall an action be brought more than three years after the act or omission that gave rise to the action.[4] Actions against contractors, architects, and others who furnish construction-related services must also be brought within two years after the cause of action accrues, and in no instance can such an action be brought more than six years after the services were provided.[5] Manufacturers of products are also generally afforded a two-year statute of limitations regardless of the claim.[6] There are other more narrow classifications that receive special treatment by the Colorado Legislature and the practitioner should review Colo. Rev. Stat. §§ 13-80-101 *et seq.* prior to offering an opinion on a statute of limitations question.

B. "NO-FAULT" LIMITATIONS

Colorado generally requires minimum automobile third-party liability coverage of $15,000 for property damage in any one accident, $25,000 for bodily injury or death to any one person, with a total of $50,000 for bodily injury or death in any one accident.[7] Colorado generally requires minimum insurance for personal injury protection, or "PIP" coverage, which provides compensation to the policy holder without regard to fault, in the amount of $50,000 for medical expenses, $50,000 for rehabilitation expenses, payment for up to 52 weeks of wage loss (calculated according to a set formula), and an insured can receive reimbursement of up to $25 per day for 52 weeks for lost essential services.[8]

C. THE STANDARD FOR NEGLIGENCE

The standard for negligent conduct is well established in Colorado.[9] In order to recover in a negligence action the plaintiff must prove:

1. the plaintiff incurred damage;
2. the defendant was negligent, which means a failure to do an act that a reasonably careful person would do, or the doing of an act that a reasonably careful person would not do, under the same or similar circumstances to protect others from harm (reasonable care is defined as that degree of care that a reasonably careful person would use under the same or similar circumstances); and
3. the defendant's negligence was a cause of the plaintiff's injuries.

D. CAUSATION

1. Proximate Cause

In order to be held liable for negligence, a defendant must be the cause of the plaintiff's injury.[10] In Colorado, the "but for" test is followed when analyzing the proximate cause issue. Thus, but for the defendant's negligence, the plaintiff's injury would not have occurred.[11] Likewise, the proximate cause of a plaintiff's injury occurs when in the natural and continued sequence, unbroken by any efficient intervening cause, the defendant causes the plaintiff's claimed injury, and had it not been for the defendant's actions the injury would not have occurred.[12] Under Colorado law, an act is a proximate cause when it substantially contributes to the plaintiff's injury.[13]

2. **Foreseeability**

Foreseeability is the touchstone of proximate cause.[14] "The duty to exercise reasonable care extends only to foreseeable damage and injuries that occur to foreseeable plaintiffs."[15] Thus, remote damages and injuries to unexpected persons will not constitute proximate cause.

3. **Concurrent Causes**

When several events may have brought harm to the plaintiff and if the defendant's negligence is the predominate cause of the plaintiff's injuries, then the defendant will be held liable.[16] However, if it appears that another event was the predominate cause of a plaintiff's injuries, then the defendant cannot be considered the substantial factor of that plaintiff's injuries.[17] Additionally, the defendant will be held liable for the plaintiff's entire harm if the defendant cannot prove to what extent the other concurrent causes contributed to the plaintiff's injuries.[18]

4. **Intervening and Superseding Causes**

An intervening act is an act by a third person that relieves the defendant from liability.[19] A defendant can be relieved of liability for negligence if an intervening cause was not reasonably foreseeable.[20] On the other hand, foreseeable negligent acts of third persons do not relieve the defendant of liability for his or her own negligence.[21] Reasonably foreseeable intentional torts or criminal acts by third persons are not considered superseding causes that shield the defendant from liability.[22]

5. **Unavoidable Accident**

An "unavoidable act" is one that happens unexpectedly and suddenly.[23] A defendant is not considered liable for injuries that result from an unavoidable accident.

6. **Act of God**

The "act of God" defense is available only to defendants that can prove a plaintiff's injury resulted entirely from an act of God; thus, the defendant must be free from contributory negligence.[24]

E. **COMPARATIVE NEGLIGENCE**

Like virtually every other state, Colorado has abolished contributory negligence as a complete defense and adopted a rule of modified comparative negligence.[25] Plaintiffs cannot recover if their negligence is greater than that of the defendants.[26] This means that a 50/50 verdict is a defense verdict and the plaintiff does not recover.

F. **ASSUMPTION OF THE RISK**

In adopting a rule of modified comparative negligence, the Colorado Legislature eliminated the doctrine of assumption of the risk, as it was applied in the traditional contributory negligence setting.[27] Today, a knowing and voluntary assumption of a known risk is most routinely considered as an element of a plaintiff's comparative negligence.

G. RES IPSA LOQUITUR

Res ipsa loquitur is typically used to show a lack of proof as to negligence and operates to allow an inference of negligence when the evidence does not help define how the injury occurred.[28] Thus, the doctrine of *res ipsa loquitur* is not a cause of action, but rather it is a rule of evidence.[29] This rule of evidence defines situations under which the presumption of negligence will arise.[30] This presumption occurs when an unexplained event creates a *prima facie* case of negligence without proof as to specific conduct resulting in malfeasance.[31] This doctrine applies only when the accident is so unusual such that the accident itself is considered evidence of negligence.[32] Additionally, no other probable cause could be established to explain the cause of the injury.[33]

In order to establish a *prima facie* case of *res ipsa loquitur*, the plaintiff must present evidence of the following:

1. the event causing the injury is the kind that ordinarily does not occur in the absence of negligence;
2. the evidence sufficiently eliminates responsible causes other than defendant's negligence; and
3. the presumed negligence is within the scope of the defendant's duty to the plaintiff.[34]

In order to establish a *prima facie* case of *res ipsa loquitur*, "the plaintiff must produce evidence that, in the light most favorable to the plaintiff, established that the existence of each element of that doctrine is more probable than not."[35] However, the plaintiff is not required to eliminate every possible cause other than the defendant's negligence in order to successfully establish a *prima facie* case.[36]

H. NEGLIGENCE *PER SE*

Colorado recognizes negligence *per se* as a viable cause of action.[37] Negligence *per se* may be established where the defendant's actions are in violation of a statute enacted for the public's safety, and where it is established that the violation of the statute proximately caused the plaintiff's injury.[38] The plaintiff "must also show that he or she is a member of the class of persons whom the statute was intended to protect and that the injuries suffered were of a kind that the statute was enacted to prevent."[39]

I. WRONGFUL DEATH

Causes of action for wrongful death in Colorado are a creature of statute.[40] A wrongful death action may be brought by the spouse of the deceased, the heirs of the deceased, or both.[41] The statute of limitations on wrongful death actions is two years.[42] Damages are generally limited to $250,000, unless the court finds justification by clear and convincing evidence therefore. In no case shall the amount of such damages exceed $500,000.[43] There is no limitation on damages in the case of felonious killings.[44] In order to recover damages under a wrongful death action, plaintiff must prove the nature and extent of damages by a preponderance of the evidence. Damages can include noneconomic losses, including grief, loss of companionship, impairment of the quality of life, inconvenience, pain and suffering, and emotional stress to the plaintiff, both present and future. Damages can also include economic losses, including reasonable funeral, burial, internment, or cremation expenses, and any net financial loss, which the plaintiff incurred as a result of the death. The net financial loss is the same as the financial benefit the plaintiff might reasonably have expected to receive from the decedent had he or she lived.[45]

J. JOINT AND SEVERAL LIABILITY

Colorado has an abolished joint and several liability, except for cases in which defendants conspire or work jointly to commit an injury.[46] In a normal tort action, each defendant will only be liable for his or her own *pro rata* liability. In order to allow a defendant every opportunity for the fact finder to consider the culpable conduct of all applicable parties, defendants may designate nonparties who may be at fault in causing plaintiff's damages within 90 days of the commencement of an action.[47] If properly designated, the applicable jury instruction will contain spaces for the jury to assign a percentage of negligent conduct to each plaintiff, defendant, and designated nonparty.

K. INDEMNITY

In Colorado, the common law doctrine of indemnity has been abolished when one tortfeasor is required to reimburse a second joint tortfeasor for the entire amount paid in damages to an injured plaintiff due to the negligence of both joint tortfeasors.[48] Further, there has been no Colorado case law interpreting the area of indemnification in strict product liability cases.[49] However, § 3-21-111.5 should be applicable to both negligence and strict liability cases.[50]

L. WORKERS' COMPENSATION BAR TO EMPLOYEE ACTIONS AGAINST EMPLOYERS

Generally, Colorado's Workers' Compensation Act provides the exclusive remedy through which an employee may recover against an employer for work-related injuries.[51] This prohibition against civil actions extends not only to actual employees of the employer, but to statutory employees as well.[52] Colorado courts have held that a statutory employee is anyone who performs the regular business of the employer, even if the employee is technically employed by a subcontractor hired by the employer.[53] The Act ensures that employers meet their obligations under the Act by expressly stating that employers cannot use contracts or leases to avoid liability under the Act when the "subcontractor" or "lessee" is performing work typically performed by an employee.

M. PREMISES LIABILITY

In Colorado, the law of premises liability is governed entirely by statute.[54] The premises liability statute clearly defines the duties of landowners.[55] The classification of a person who enters real property determines what duty a landowner owes to that person. Colorado classifies persons who enter real property in three different ways, as follows:

1. Trespasser—A trespasser is a person who enters or remains on the land of another without the landowner's consent. A trespasser may recover only for damages willfully or deliberately caused by the landowner.
2. Licensee—A licensee is a person who enters or remains on the land of another for the licensee's own convenience or to advance his own interests pursuant to the landowner's permission or consent. A social guest is a licensee. A licensee may recover against a landowner in two situations:
   (a) A landowner has a duty to exercise reasonable care with respect to known dangers on the land created by the landowner.
   (b) A landowner has a duty to reasonably warn a person of dangers on the property when there is a condition on the land that was not created by the landowner, that is not ordinarily present on the property of the type involved, and that the landowner actually knew of.
3. Invitee—An invitee is a person who enters or remains on the land of another to transact business in which the parties are mutually interested, or one who enters or remains on the land at the express or implied request or invitation of the landowner. A business customer is typically an invitee. A landowner owes different duties to invitees depending on what type of land is in question.
   (a) Farmland or Vacant Land—An invitee may recover against the landowner for damages caused by the landowner's unreasonable failure to exercise reasonable care to protect against dangers of which the landowner actually knew.
   (b) All Other Types of Land—An invitee may recover against a landowner for damages caused by the landowner's unreasonable failure to exercise reasonable care to protect against dangers of which he actually or should have known.

N. SKI SAFETY ACT

Colorado has adopted a Ski Safety Act to establish reasonable safety standards for skiers and ski areas.[56] The Act prescribes duties for ski area operators and skiers during recreational and competitive ski conditions.[57] The statute specifically states that a violation of the Act, which leads to injury and damages, is negligence.[58] The Act also states, however, that injuries occurring as a result of the inherent dangers and risks of skiing are not subject to recovery.[59] In the case of an injury subject to recovery, a civil action must be brought within two years.[60] There are also limits on the amount of damages recoverable from a liable ski area operator.[61] The duties of operators prescribed by the Act include posting specified signs for lifts and trails, use of maintenance equipment around skiers, and specific language regarding liability to be printed on lift tickets.[62] Regulations regarding skiers include a duty of skiers to know their ability and maintain control, follow instructions and heed warnings, and respond to accidents with other skiers.[63]

O. **DRAM SHOP LIABILITY**

In Colorado, no common law remedy was provided against one who furnished alcoholic beverages to a person who became inebriated and consequently injured himself or another.[64] In 1986 the Colorado Legislature rejected the common law rule of nonliability and permitted actions against alcohol vendors and social hosts.[65] From that point forward, the civil liability of a state licensee who sells alcoholic beverages is strictly a creature of statute in Colorado.[66]

The Dram Shop expresses the Colorado Legislature's recognition that, in certain cases, it is the consumption and not the sale of alcohol that is the proximate cause of injury.[67] A vendor of alcoholic beverages is not liable for injury or property damage caused by the intoxication of any person except when:

> [i]t is proven that the licensee willfully and knowingly sold or served any alcohol beverage to such person who was under the age of twenty-one years or who was visibly intoxicated. . . .

See Colo. Rev. Stat. § 12-47-801(3). Thus, the only way a vendor of alcoholic beverages can be held liable for injuries caused by the intoxication of any person is if the vendor willfully and knowingly sold alcohol to an individual[68] who was (1) under 21 years old, or (2) visibly intoxicated at the time of the sale.

P. **ECONOMIC LOSS**

A party suffering only economic loss from the breach of an express or implied contractual duty may not assert a tort claim for such a breach absent an independent duty of care under tort law.[69] Economic loss is defined generally as damages other than physical harm to persons or property.[70]

In Colorado, in order to recover for economic loss in tort, there must be physical injury to persons or property.[71] It is necessary to have actual loss or damage in order to bring forth a tort action.[72] The economic loss rule does not prevent asserting a claim to recover for physical injury to property or persons because in this situation the duty that is breached usually arises independent of the contract.[73]

The economic loss rule cannot be used as a roadblock to recover on a contractual theory by translating a claim for economic loss on a contract into a claim sounding in tort.[74] The economic loss rule disallows recovering in tort when only a contractual duty has been breached and the harm that resulted was due to failing to abide by the purpose of the contract.[75] "The rule prohibits parties who deal with each other at arms length through contractual arrangements from circumventing their bargained-for contractual remedies by attempting to recover purely pecuniary losses in tort."[76]

The tort of negligent misrepresentation is an exception to the economic loss rule.[77] However, there are a limited number of situations that would allow a defendant to be liable under both contract and negligent theories.[78] "Professionals, such as attorneys and accountants, who communicate representations with the knowledge that the information is to be relied on by others may be subject to both tort and contract liability for economic loss if third parties rely on their negligent misrepresentations made in the course of rendering a service pursuant to a contract.[79]

Q. FRAUD

The elements of a fraud claim are well established in Colorado. In order to recover on a claim of fraud, a plaintiff must prove:

1. the defendant made a false representation of a past or present fact;
2. the fact was material;
3. the defendant made the representation knowing it to be false or they were aware that they did not know whether it was true or false;
4. the defendant made the representation with the intent that the plaintiff act or decide not to act in reliance on the representation;
5. the plaintiff relied on the representation;
6. the plaintiff's reliance was justified; and
7. the reliance caused damage to the plaintiff.[80]

R. NEGLIGENT MISREPRESENTATION

The Colorado Supreme Court has defined "negligent misrepresentation" according to Section 552 of the Restatement(Second) of Torts (1977).[81] Section 552 of the Restatement (Second) of Torts provides, in relevant part:

(1) One who, in the course of his business profession or employment, or in any other transaction in which he has a pecuniary interest, supplies false information for the guidance of others in their business transactions, is subject to liability for pecuniary loss caused to them by their justifiable reliance upon the information, if he fails to exercise reasonable care or competence in obtaining or communicating the information.
(2) Except as stated in subsection (3), the liability stated in subsection (1) is limited to loss suffered:
  (a) by the person or one of a limited group of persons for whose benefit and guidance he intends to supply the information or knows that the recipient intends to supply it; and

(b) through reliance upon it in a transaction that he intends the information to influence or knows that the recipient so intends or in a substantially similar transaction.[82]

The tort of negligent misrepresentation provides a remedy when money is lost due to misrepresentation in a business transaction.[83] To establish a claim for negligent misrepresentation, it must be shown that the defendant supplied false information to others in a business transaction, and failed to exercise reasonable care or competence in obtaining or communicating information on which other parties justifiably relied.[84]

S. LIMITATIONS ON NONECONOMIC DAMAGES

Colorado limits the amount a plaintiff may recover in various situations. In cases where the basis of the complaint is a felonious killing, there is no cap on noneconomic recovery.[85] The legislature has enacted a statutory cap on noneconomic damages. Per statute, in any given case, the total recovery for noneconomic losses may not exceed $250,000, unless the court finds justification for increasing the amount by clear and convincing evidence.[86] If the court allows higher noneconomic damages, the amount may not exceed $500,000.[87] No damages may be awarded for derivative noneconomic losses, unless the court finds justification for an award by clear and convincing evidence.[88] If the court does allow derivative noneconomic damages, the amount may not exceed $250,000. These limits do not apply to compensatory damages for physical impairment or disfigurement.[89] Caps apply to each defendant rather than to the plaintiff.[90] Thus, if a plaintiff proves the liability of multiple defendants, he will be allowed to max out the caps against each defendant. Under the damages statute, the $250,000/$500,000 cap rises each year to reflect inflation; thus, the current cap may be greater than the number stated in the statute.

In wrongful death actions, noneconomic losses are absolutely capped at $250,000, unless the act causing death constituted a felonious killing.[91] Subject to the cap, surviving plaintiffs are expressly allowed to recover for grief, loss of companionship, pain and suffering, and emotional stress.[92] This cap on noneconomic damages is applied to the plaintiff and not to the defendant, meaning that a defendant is liable on a per plaintiff basis.

T. PUNITIVE OR EXEMPLARY DAMAGES

Exemplary damages are available in Colorado pursuant to statute.[93] The amount of exemplary damages shall not exceed an amount that is equal to the amount of the actual damages awarded to the injured party.[94] The statute provides that the court may increase the award of exemplary damages to a sum not to exceed three times the amount of actual damages. The appropriateness of exemplary damages must be proved beyond a reasonable doubt, rather than by the usual civil standard of preponderance of the evidence.

The Colorado General Assembly has recently allowed for exemplary damages in wrongful death actions.[95] If the death complained of is attended by circumstances of fraud, malice, or willful and wanton conduct, the trier of fact, in addition to the actual damages, may award reasonable exemplary damages not to exceed an amount equal to the amount of the actual damages awarded to the injured party.[96] Exemplary damages in wrongful death actions may not be included in any initial claim for relief, but the original complaint may be amended after the passage of 60 days following the exchange of initial disclosures pursuant to C.R.C.P. 26, and the establishment of *prima facie* proof of a triable issue.[97]

U. **CONSUMER FRAUD STATUTES**

Colorado has an extensive Consumer Protection Act.[98] The act defines "deceptive trade practices" and establishes rules regarding enforcement of the act, reporting of consumer fraud, hearings, remedies, restraining orders, civil penalties, damages, criminal penalties, and limitations on actions.[99] The list of deceptive trade practices punishable under the statute is also extensive. The statute regulates practices in the course of a person's business, vocation, or occupation in every aspect of trade from labeling of products to marketing.[100] Tort damages are available to actual or potential consumers, successors in interest of actual consumers, or persons injured as a result of deceptive trade practices in the course of their business or occupation.[101] The standard limitation on actions involving consumer fraud is three years.[102] Violators of the Consumer Protection Act are liable for damages in the amount of actual damages or $500, whichever is greater.[103] Evidence of bad faith on the part of the violator can increase damages to three times the actual damages. Bad faith is defined as fraudulent, willful, knowing, or intentional conduct.[104]

John P. Craver
Todd Clarke
Franz Hardy
WHITE & STEELE, P.C.
950 17th Street, Suite 2100
Denver, Colorado 80202
(303) 296-2828
Fax (303) 296-3131
law@wsteele.com

ENDNOTES - COLORADO

1. Colo. Rev. Stat. § 13-80-101.

2. Colo. Rev. Stat. § 13-80-102.

3. Colo. Rev. Stat. § 13-80-103.

4. Colo. Rev. Stat. § 13-80-102.5

5. Colo. Rev. Stat. § 13-80-104.

6. Colo. Rev. Stat. § 13-80-106.

7. Colo. Rev. Stat. §§ 10-4-701 *et seq.*

8. *Id.*

9. *See* Colo. Pattern Jury Instructions, §§ 9:1, 9:4 & 9:6.

10. *Rodriguez v. Morgan County R.E.A., Inc.*, 878 P.2d 77, 82 (Colo. App. 1994).

11. *Smith v. State Compensation Ins. Fund*, 749 P.2d 462, 464 (Colo. App. 1987).

12. *In re (Swine Flu Immunization) Products Liability Litigation v. United States of America*, 495 F. Supp. 1188, 1206 (D. Colo. 1980).

13. *FDIC v. Refco Group Ltd.*, 989 F. Supp. 1052, 1068 (D. Colo. 1997).

14. *Walcott v. Total Petroleum, Inc.*, 964 P.2d 609, 611 (Colo. App. 1998).

15. *Leppke v. Segura*, 632 P.2d 1057, 1059 (Colo. App. 1981).

16. *Ayala v. United States*, 846 F. Supp. 1431, 1441 (D. Colo. 1993).

17. *Id.*

18. *Northington v. Marin*, 102 F.3d 1564, 1569 (10th Cir. 1996).

19. *Ayala* at 1441.

20. *White v. Caterpillar, Inc.*, 867 P.2d 100, 109 (Colo. App. 1993).

21. *Chartier v. Winslow Crane Serv. Co.*, 350 P.2d 1044, 1050 (Colo. 1960).

22. *Ekberg v. Greene*, 588 P.2d 375, 496 (Colo. 1978).

23. *Dugan v. Kuner-Empson Co.*, 369 P.2d 82, 84 (Colo. 1962).

24. *Moore v. Standard Paint & Glass Co.*, 358 P.2d 33, 36 (Colo. 1960).

25. Colo. Rev. Stat. § 13-21-111.

26. *Id.*

27. *Id.*

28. *Trigg v. City and County of Denver*, 784 F.2d 1058, 1060 (10th Cir. 1986).

29. *Kaplan v. C Lazy U Ranch*, 615 F. Supp. 234, 236 (D. Colo. 1984).

30. *Bilawsky v. Faseehudin*, 916 P.2d 586, 589 (Colo. App. 1995).

31. *Id.*

32. *E.I. Du Pont de Nemours & Co. v. Cudd*, 176 F.2d 855, 858 (10th Cir. 1949).

33. *Id.*

34. *Ravin v. Gambrell*, 788 P.2d 817, 822 (Colo. 1990).

35. *Id.*

36. *Id.*

37. *See Canape v. Peterson*, 897 P.2d 762 (Colo. 1995).

38. *Id.*

39. *Lyons v. Nasby*, 770 P.2d 1250, 1257 (Colo. 1989).

40. Colo. Rev. Stat. §§ 13-21-201 and 13-21-202.

41. Colo. Rev. Stat. § 13-21-201.

42. Colo. Rev. Stat. § 13-80-102(1)(d).

43. Colo. Rev. Stat. § 13-21-102.5(3)(a).

44. Colo. Rev. Stat. § 13-21-203(1).

45. Colorado Jury Instruction, 10:3.

46. Colo. Rev. Stat. § 13-21-111.5.

47. *Id.*

48. *Brochner v. Western Ins. Co.*, 724 P.2d 1293, 1299 (Colo. 1986).

49. *Shirely O'quinn and Fidelity & Casualty Co. v. Wedco Technology, Inc.*, 746 F. Supp. 38, 39 (D. Colo. 1990), *aff'd*, 955 F.2d 49 (10th Cir. 1992).

50. *Id.; Barton v. Adams Rental, Inc., d/b/a Adams Rental and Sales*, 938 P.2d 532, 535 (Colo. 1997); *see also Miller v. Byrne*, 916 P.2d 566, 578 (Colo. App. 1995).

51. Colo. Rev. Stat. §§ 8-41-401 *et seq.*

52. Colo. Rev. Stat. § 8-41-401.

53. *Finlay v. Storage Technology Corp.*, 764 P.2d 62 (Colo. 1988).

54. Colo. Rev. Stat. § 13-21-115.

55. Under the statute, a landowner includes an authorized agent or a person in possession of real property and persons legally responsible for the condition of the real property.

56. Colo. Rev. Stat. § 33-44-102.

57. Colo. Rev. Stat. §§ 33-44-102 *et seq.*

58. Colo. Rev. Stat. § 33-44-104.

59. Colo. Rev. Stat. § 33-44-112.

60. Colo. Rev. Stat. § 33-44-111.

61. Colo. Rev. Stat. § 33-44-113.

62. Colo. Rev. Stat. §§ 33-44-106, 33-44-107, and 33-44-108.

63. Colo. Rev. Stat. §§ 33-44-105 and 33-44-109.

64. *See Sigman v. Sea Food Ltd.*, 817 P.2d 527 (Colo. 1991).

65. Colo. Rev. Stat. § 12-47-128.5 (1991 Repl. Vol. V).

66. *See Charlton v. Kimata*, 815 P.2d 946 (Colo. 1991).

67. Colo. Rev. Stat. § 12-47-801(1).

68. The Dram Shop Act prohibits a plaintiff from bringing an action in relation to his own intoxication. *See* Colo. Rev. Stat. § 12-47-801(3)(b).

69. *Town of Alma v. Shanks*, 10 P.3d 1256, 1264 (Colo. 2000); *Grynberg v. Agri Tech, Inc.*, 10 P.3d 1267, 1269 (Colo. 2000). Footnote 4 in *Grynberg* lists insurance brokers and architects as examples of persons who have an independent duty of care under tort law.

70. *Id.*

71. *Jardel Enters., Inc. v. Triconsultants, Inc.*, 770 P.2d 1301, 1304 (Colo. App. 1988).

72. *Perlmutter v. U.S. Gypsum Co.*, 4 F.3d 864, 868 (10th Cir. 1993) (citing *Bayly, Martin & Fay, Inc. v. Pete's Satire, Inc.*, 739 P.2d 239, 242 (Colo. 1987)).

73. *Commercial Union Ins. Co. v. Roxborough Village Joint Venture*, 944 F. Supp. 827, 831 (1966) (citing *Jardel*, 770 P.2d at 1304).

74. *Id.*

75. *Id.*

76. *Id.* (citing *Jardel*, 770 P.2d at 1304 (to hold otherwise permits the non-breaching party to avoid the contractual limitation of remedy); *see Colorado Nat'l Bank v. Adventura Assocs., L.P.*, 757 F. Supp. 1167, 1172-73 (D. Colo. 1991) (permitting parties to recover economic losses under a tort theory "would frustrate" the ability of contracting parties to allocate the risk of loss and, therefore, "would undermine" certainty in commercial practices).

77. *Colorado Nat'l Bank of Denver* at 1172.

78. *Id.*

79. *Id.* at 1172-73 (citing *Jardel*, 770 P.2d at 1304-05).

80. *See Concord Realty Co. v. Continental Funding Corp.*, 776 P.2d 1114, 1117-18 (Colo. 1989), *Southeastern Colorado Water Conservancy Dist. v. Cache Creek Mining Trust*, 854 P.2d 167 (Colo. 1993) & Colorado Jury Instruction, 19:1.

81. *See Keller v. A.O. Smith Harverstore Prods.*, 819 P.2d 69, 71 n.2 (Colo. 1991).

82. Quoted in *Mehaffy, Rider, Windoholz & Wilson v. Central Bank of Denver*, 892 P.2d 230 (Colo. 1995).

83. *See Western Cities Broadcasting, Inc. v. Schueller*, 849 P.2d 44, 49 (Colo. 1993).

84. *See Burman v. Richmond Homes Ltd.*, 821 P.2d 913, 919 (Colo. App. 1991).

85. Colo. Rev. Stat. § 13-21-102.5.

86. Colo. Rev. Stat. § 13-21-102.5(3)(a).

87. *Id.*

88. Colo. Rev. Stat. § 13-21-102.5(3)(b).

89. Colo. Rev. Stat. § 13-21-102.5(5).

90. *General Elec. Co. v. Neimer*, 866 P.2d 1361 (Colo. 1994).

91. Colo. Rev. Stat. § 13-21-203.

92. *Id.*

93. Colo. Rev. Stat. § 13-21-102.

94. Colo. Rev. Stat. § 13-21-102(1).

95. H.B. 01-1167, 63rd General Assembly, 1st Reg. Sess. (Colo. 2001). Changes to be incorporated into Colo. Rev. Stat. § 13-21-203 as section (3)(a).

96. H.B. 01-1167, 63rd General Assembly, 1st Reg. Sess. (Colo. 2001). Changes to be incorporated into Colo. Rev. Stat. § 13-21-203 as section (3)(a).

97. *Id.* at section (3)(c).

98. Colo. Rev. Stat. §§ 6-1-101 *et seq.*

99. *Id.*

100. Colo. Rev. Stat. § 6-1-105.

101. Colo. Rev. Stat. § 6-1-113(1).

102. Colo. Rev. Stat. § 6-1-115.

103. Colo. Rev. Stat. § 6-1-113.

104. *Id.*

CONNECTICUT

A. STATUTES OF LIMITATION

Causes of action founded on negligence or reckless misconduct for personal injury, or property damage must be brought within two years of the injury and no more than three years from the act or omission complained of.[1] Death[2] and minority[3] do not toll the running of the statute of limitations. The defendant's absence from the state may toll it under some circumstances.[4]

Causes of action founded on other tortious conduct or intentional misconduct must be brought within three years of the conduct in question.[5]

Causes of action predicated on a breach of an oral contract must be brought within three years of the breach.[6] Causes of action based on a breach of a written contract must be brought within six years of the breach.[7]

Actions under the Connecticut Unfair Trade Practices Act are subject to a three-year statute of limitations.[8]

Dram Shop actions must be brought within one year of the service of alcohol.[9]

Actions alleging defamation and invasion of privacy must be brought within two years of the date of the act complained of.[10]

Actions against the state and municipalities based on negligence are generally subject to a two-year statute of limitations; notice requirements having been earlier satisfied.[11]

Claims against architects or professional engineers are generally subject to a seven-year statute of limitations.[12]

Products liability actions, suits that embrace claims negligence, breach of warranty, and strict tort liability, must be brought within three years of the date of injury or the date when the injury should have reasonably been discovered, except that no action can be brought within ten years from the date when the defendant last parted with possession or control of the product, subject to exceptions for fraudulent concealment and express warranty and for useful safe life of the product in consumer plaintiff cases.[13]

Personal injury claims against manufacturers and distributors of asbestos are subject to a 60-year statute of limitations.[14]

Connecticut's "catch all" tort provision sets forth a three-years' limitations period.[15]

An insurance carrier may provide in its policy a provision limiting the commencement of a UM or UIM claim to three years from the date of the accident. If the policy does not so provide, then the six-year contractual statute of limitations is applicable.[16]

B. **TORT REFORM**

Connecticut has enacted tort reform.[17] The changes have addressed a broad range of issues including the imposition of limitations on attorney's contingency fees,[18] the classification and calculation of damages,[19] the application of collateral source payments,[20] and the installment payment of judgments.[21]

Tort reform has mandated the need for the filing of "good faith certificates"[22] and for designated experts in medical malpractice cases.[23] The doctrines of last clear chance and assumption of risk were abolished;[24] limited immunity for designated volunteers of nonprofit organizations was enacted.[25] The scope of potential municipal liability was defined.[26] The law now provides for a finding by the court of lack of "good faith" in the bringing of an underlying action preparatory to the filing of a vexatious litigation suit.[27]

C. **"NO FAULT" LIMITATIONS**

Connecticut's "No Fault" Law was repealed effective January 1, 1994.[28] Connecticut's motor vehicle insurance law requires minimum coverage of $20,000/$40,000 per accident, $5,000 property damages, and requires minimum uninsured/underinsured motorist coverage of $20,000/$40,000 per accident.[29]

D. **THE STANDARD FOR NEGLIGENCE**

The plaintiff must show that the defendant owed the plaintiff a duty of care cognizable at law.[30] The existence of a duty is predicated on the relationship between the plaintiff and the defendant.[31] The plaintiff must show that the defendant breached that duty.[32] Breach is shown when the plaintiff demonstrates that the defendant engaged in conduct that deviated from the general standard of care expected under the circumstances.[33]

Connecticut recognizes a "professional" standard of care.[34]

Civil cases require a showing of a fair preponderance of evidence, more probable than not. Allegations of fraud invoke the need for clear and convincing evidence.[35]

The standard of care expected of a minor requires a comparison of the individual child to minors of like age, experience, capacity, and development under similar circumstances.[36] A cut-off age below which a child will not be held negligent has not been fixed.[37]

Although a parent is not ordinarily liable for the torts of an unemancipated child, the parent may be liable for the negligence of the child in driving a family automobile.[38] Statutory liability up to $5,000 may be imposed on a parent whose child willfully or maliciously causes injury to another party.[39]

E. CAUSATION

Connecticut follows the general rule that, to establish a *prima facie* case in negligence, the plaintiff must demonstrate that the defendant's negligence was a substantial factor in producing the damage complained of.[40] The act of efficient cause that sets in motion a train of events that brings about a result without the intervention of any force started and working actively from an independent source is the proximate cause.[41]

F. CONTRIBUTORY NEGLIGENCE, COMPARATIVE NEGLIGENCE, AND ASSUMPTION OF RISK

1. Contributory Negligence

Connecticut has abolished contributory negligence as an absolute defense in actions based in negligence seeking recovery for personal injury, death, or damage to property.[42] The burden of establishing comparative negligence lies with the defendant unless freedom from comparative negligence is pled by the plaintiff.[43] The failure of the plaintiff to wear a seat belt is not admissible.[44]

2. Comparative Responsibility

A plaintiff can recover damages if the plaintiff's negligence is not greater than the combined negligence of the parties against whom recovery is sought.[45] Damages are diminished by the proportion of the percentage of negligence attributed to the plaintiff. If the plaintiff's negligence is greater than the combined negligence of the defendants, there is no recovery. Product liability actions are governed by a "pure" comparative responsibility rule.[46]

3. Assumption of Risk

The doctrines of assumption of risk and last clear chance have been abolished.[47] The defenses of unavoidable accident, sudden emergency, and sudden physical illness remain viable.[48]

In general, parent-child immunity continues to exist. There is no immunity between parent and child for actions based on the negligent operation of a motor vehicle.[49] There is no spousal immunity to negligence actions.[50]

G. *RES IPSA LOQUITUR* AND INHERENTLY DANGEROUS ACTIVITIES

1. *Res Ipsa Loquitur*

Res ipsa loquitur permits an inference that the defendant caused the plaintiff's harm if: (1) the situation is such that in the ordinary instance no injury would result unless from a careless construction, inspection, or user; (2) both inspection and use at the time of the injury must have been in control of the party charged with negligence; and (3) the injurious event must have happened irrespective of any voluntary action at the time by the injured party.[51]

The jury may draw an inference of negligence on the part of the defendants; it is not compelled to find negligence.[52]

2. Inherently Dangerous Activities

A party who uses an intrinsically dangerous means in such a way as necessarily or obviously to expose another party to the danger of probable injury is liable if such injury results even though all proper care is exercised.[53] Contributory negligence generally will not bar a recovery for an injury as a result of an inherently dangerous activity.[54]

H. NEGLIGENCE *PER SE*

Negligence *per se* is based on the breach by a party of a statutory duty and establishes both duty and the required breach of duty elements of a negligence action.[55] A statutory violation is negligence *per se* if the plaintiff is within the class of persons whom the statute was intended to protect and if the harm was of the type that the statute's enactment was intended to protect.[56] The issue of negligence is generally a question of fact for determination by the jury.[57]

I. INDEMNITY

Indemnity shifts the entire loss of the plaintiff from one defendant to another party by reason of some legal obligation to pay damages occasioned by the negligence of another.[58] Indemnity may be provided by contract.[59] Common law indemnity is generally available to those who are secondarily liable from those who are primarily liable.[60] If the party seeking indemnification is actively negligent and its negligence is a proximate cause of underlying injuries, common law indemnity is not available as a matter of law.[61] There is no requirement of an independent legal relationship between the parties.[62] There is no common law indemnity in products liability.[63]

J. JOINT AND SEVERAL LIABILITY

Under Connecticut common law, joint tortfeasors are jointly and severally liable when their conduct concurs in proximately causing a single injury.[64] Concert of action between the two tortfeasors is not required.[65] Joint and several liability means that the plaintiff can sue either or both of the joint tortfeasors and can recover the full amount of damages, or any part thereof, from either tortfeasor.[66] Moreover, there is no general right of contribution among joint tortfeasors.

The common law rules have been legislatively modified in cases involving negligent joint tortfeasors.[67] Under the statute, the trier of fact apportions percentages of negligence to the defendants (and to settled or released persons) and makes separate awards for economic and noneconomic damages. Ideally, each defendant pays its share of the combined award, in which case there is no need for contribution. If one defendant is unable to pay its share, the other defendants can be compelled to pay a portion of the uncollectable amount. In the case of economic damages, the other defendants must pay all of the uncollectable amount. Those defendants' reallocated liability is based on their respective percentages of negligence as compared with the other nondefaulting defendants (not the defaulting defendant). In the case of noneconomic damages, a similar reallocation procedure is followed, except that each nondefaulting defendant pays only its original percentage of negligence times the uncollectable amount. The nondefaulting defendants retain a right of contribution against any defendants who do not pay their determined share.

There is no general right of contribution, because the comparative negligence procedure obviates the need for it. When a plaintiff fails to sue a negligent joint tortfeasor, the tortfeasors who were sued can bring the other tortfeasor into the case as an "apportionment defendant," which means that it will share in the allocation of negligence.[68]

In product liability cases there is a similar apportionment of responsibility among the parties—with a right of contribution against defendants who fail to pay their share—but each defendant remains fully liable to the plaintiff for the entire award.[69]

A release of one joint tortfeasor will not release other joint tortfeasors unless the release so provides.[70]

K. BAR OF WORKERS' COMPENSATION STATUTE

Under the Connecticut Workers' Compensation Act, an employee is barred from suing an employer who has complied with the Act's insurance requirements for the employee's work-related injury.[71] Workers' compensation is an exclusive remedy.[72] The employer assumes responsibility regardless of fault.[73] The receipt of benefits does not bar an employee from seeking damages from a third party.[74]

When an injury for which workers' compensation benefits are payable is sustained by an employee under circumstances creating liability in a person other than an employer who has complied with the requirements of the Workers' Compensation Act, either the employee or the employer may bring an action for damages against that person.[75] When either initiates an action against a third party, the initiator must provide statutory notice to the other of the action for the purposes of allowing the other to intervene. If proper notice is sent, and the other party fails to intervene within 30 days, that party's right of action shall abate.[76]

Notwithstanding the provisions of this statute, the employer or its insurance carrier may secure lien rights to the extent of benefits already paid, if a proper lien notice is sent prior to the settlement or judgment of the matter.[77]

Connecticut recognizes a common law exception to the exclusive remedy provision of the Workers' Compensation Act for injuries sustained as a result of an intentional tort if the tort is committed by the employer or its alter ego.[78] Minor plaintiffs unlawfully employed in hazardous occupations who are injured during the course of employment may sue their employers.[79]

L. PREMISES LIABILITY

Possession or control of premises, rather than the ownership of premises, imposes liability.[80] The duty owed depends on an individual's common law status as a trespasser, licensee, or invitee.[81] The possessor may not intentionally injure a trespasser or lay a trap and owes the trespasser the duty of due care once the trespasser's presence is actually known.[82] The possessor must warn licensees of dangerous hidden hazards actually known to the possessor; there is no duty to warn of the obvious condition of the premises.[83] The possessor must exercise reasonable care to protect invitees from any actually or constructively known dangerous conditions that the invitee will not realize or against which the invitee will fail to protect him- or herself.[84]

M. DRAM SHOP LIABILITY

Connecticut's Dram Shop Act governs the sale of alcoholic liquor to intoxicated persons.[85] Persons who serve alcohol to minors,[86] or who provide alcohol in a reckless, indifferent fashion may be subject to common law liability.[87]

To establish violation of the Dram Shop Act, the plaintiff must prove that alcohol was sold to an intoxicated person, who, in consequence of such intoxication, proximately caused injury to the plaintiff.[88] Contributory negligence is generally not a defense.[89]

Recovery under the Dram Shop Act is limited to $20,000 per person.[90] The plaintiff must provide notice to the seller within 60 days of the occurrence of injury and must bring suit within one year of the date of the sale.[91]

N. ECONOMIC LOSS

Recovery under actions alleging negligence is generally permitted only for personal injury, death, or property damage.[92] Claims seeking recovery of economic loss may be sustained under such theories as tortious interference with a business relationship,[93] defamation,[94] and noncommercial products liability claims.[95]

Damages, including claims of economic loss, that are derivative of harm suffered by third parties may be deemed to be too remote to be recoverable under common law tort principles.[96] Generally speaking, courts have declined to find that the economic loss doctrine is a bar to tort actions where the relationship between the parties is contractual and the losses alleged are economic.[97]

O. FRAUD AND MISREPRESENTATION

The Connecticut Practice Book requires each pleading to contain a plain and concise statement of the material facts on which the plaintiff relies.[98] Fraud is a fact to be specially pled.[99]

Each of the following elements for fraud, deceit, or intentional misrepresentation must be proved by clear and convincing evidence:[100] (1) a representation; (2) which is material to the transaction; (3) made falsely; (4) with the intent of misleading another relying on it; (5) the recipient's justifiable reliance in the misrepresentation; and (6) the resulting injury was proximately caused by the reliance.[101]

The elements of negligent misrepresentation are (1) a misrepresentation of a material fact; (2) made under circumstances in which the misrepresenter ought to have known of its falsity; (3) with intent to induce another to act on it; and (4) which results in a party acting in justifiable reliance on the misrepresentation.[102] These elements differ from intentional misrepresentation in that the declarant need not know that his or her words are untrue, but has the means of knowing, ought to know, or the duty of knowing the truth.[103]

P. CONSUMER FRAUD STATUTES

Connecticut's Unfair Trade Practices Act[104] (CUTPA) protects consumers from unfair methods of competition and unfair or deceptive acts or practices in the conduct of any trade or commerce.[105] CUTPA provides that the Attorney General may seek to recover civil penalties.[106] Private actions may also be brought under CUTPA; in which case, the plaintiff must establish a causal connection between the unlawful practice and the plaintiff's loss.[107]

The "catch-all" section of CUTPA is designed to cover generally all unfair and deceptive acts or practices in the conduct of trade or commerce.[108] Under the catch-all section, the plaintiff must move that an act had a tendency or capacity to deceive.[109]

CUTPA does not apply to mere claims of negligence or malpractice against physicians or lawyers.[110]

As previously noted, CUTPA actions are subject to a three-year statute of limitations.[111]

Q. PUNITIVE DAMAGES

Punitive damages may be awarded in negligence actions when the defendant acts with a reckless indifference to the rights of others, or with an intentional and wanton violation of those rights.[112] The purpose of punitive damages is to compensate the plaintiff for his or her injuries.[113]

Punitive damages include plaintiff's attorney's fees and nontaxable costs.[114]

Punitive damages are not ordinarily recoverable in breach of contract actions.[115] They are not awarded for misconduct constituting ordinary negligence.[116] They may be recovered in wrongful death actions.[117]

In motor vehicle accident cases where the plaintiff proves violations of specified statutes, punitive damages of either two or three times the compensatory damages may be awarded.[118] Punitive damages may also be awarded in CUTPA actions.[119]

R. **WRONGFUL DEATH**

Under common law, there is no recovery for wrongful death or right of action for a decedent's personal injuries.[120] However, recovery is allowed under Connecticut's Wrongful Death Statute.[121]

Discovery under the Wrongful Death Statute may be obtained by the executor or administrator of the decedent's estate.[122] The cause of action must be one that the decedent could have asserted if he or she had lived.[123] Recovery may include compensation for conscious pain and suffering, compensation for loss of earnings or earning capacity less living expenses, and reasonable necessary medical and funeral expenses.[124]

The spouse of the decedent also has a cause of action for postmortem loss of consortium.[125]

Peter C. Schwartz
Philip J. O'Connor
GORDON, MUIR & FOLEY, L.L.P.
Hartford Square North
Ten Columbus Boulevard
Hartford, Connecticut 06106-5123
(860) 525-5361
Fax (860) 525-4849
po'connor@gmflaw.com
www.gmflaw.com

ENDNOTES - CONNECTICUT

1. Conn. General Statutes § 52-584. An action may be barred before a cause of action arises. *Vilcinskas v. Sears Roebuck & Co.*, 144 Conn. 170, 127 A.2d 814 (1956). Fraudulent concealment will toll the running of a statute of limitations, Conn. General Statutes § 52-595, as will a continuing course of negligence. *See Handler v. Remington Arms Co.*, 144 Conn. 316, 130 A.2d 793 (1957). A statute of limitations defense will be waived unless specifically pled. Conn. Practice Book § 164. Conn. General Statutes § 52-593 allows an additional year in the event of an accidental failure of suit. In wrongful death cases, the "act or omission" limit is five years. Conn. General Statutes § 52-555.

2. Conn. General Statutes § 52-594. If the statute has not run by the time of death, an additional year is allowed to the fiduciary.

3. *Lametta v. Connecticut Light & Power Co.*, 139 Conn. 218, 92 A.2d (1952).

4. *Coombs v. Darling*, 116 Conn. 643, 166 A.70 (1933); service may be made on the Commissioner of Motor Vehicles in the case of a nonresident motor vehicle operator who is involved in an accident in Connecticut pursuant to Conn. General Statutes § 52-62. In non–motor vehicle cases, the statute of limitations may be tolled for that period not to exceed seven years the defendant is outside Connecticut. Conn. General Statutes § 52-590.

5. Conn. General Statutes § 52-577.

6. *Id.*

7. Conn. General Statutes § 52-576 (except for those contracts that may be governed by the U.C.C. or other case-specific statute).

8. Conn. General Statutes § 42-110g(f).

9. Conn. General Statutes § 30-102. Written notice must be served within 60 days of injury.

10. *Id.*

11. The state is immune from suit unless it has consented to be sued. Conn. General Statutes Const. Art. II, § 4; Conn. General Statutes § 4-141–4-166. As to municipalities: defective road or bridge, Conn. General Statutes § 13a–149, written notice must be given within six months. As to state of Connecticut: defective highway or bridge, Conn. General Statutes § 13a–144, written notice must be given within 90 days of injury. Claims pre-

Endnotes - Connecticut

sented to Claims Commissioner are governed by a one-year-from-injury or damage-sustained-or-discovered, no more than three years from date of act omission complained of, rule. Conn. General Statutes § 4-148(a).

12. Conn. General Statutes § 52-584a. Actions against attorneys for erroneous title opinions must be brought within two years of damage or discovery and not more than ten years of delivery of the title. Conn. General Statutes § 52-593.

13. Conn. General Statutes § 52-577a.

14. Conn. General Statutes § 52-577a(e). Property damage claims based on asbestos exposure are subject to a 30-year statute of limitations.

15. Conn. General Statutes § 52-577. Actions on public works bonds are governed by Conn. General Statutes § 49-41; Conn. General Statutes § 38a-290 applies to actions on private bonds.

16. Conn. General Statutes § 38a-336(g). *See* Berk & Jainchill, Atlantic Law Book, Connecticut Law of Uninsured and Underinsured Motorist (second edition, 1999), for a comprehensive discussion of U.M. and U.I.M.

17. P.A. 86-338 and P.A. 87-227.

18. Conn. General Statutes § 52-251c.

19. Conn. General Statutes § 52-225d.

20. Conn. General Statutes § 52-225a.

21. Conn. General Statutes § 52-225d.

22. Conn. General Statutes § 52-190a.

23. Conn. General Statutes § 52-184c.

24. Conn. General Statutes § 52-572h(l).

25. Conn. General Statutes § 52-557m. Connecticut does not recognize the common law defense of charitable immunity. Conn. General Statutes § 52-557d.

26. Conn. General Statutes § 52-557n.

27. Conn. General Statutes § 52-226a.

28. P.A. 93-297, § 28.

29. Conn. General Statutes § 14-122; *see* Regs. Conn. State Agencies § 38a-334-8. *Also see* Berk & Jainchill, Atlantic Law Book, Connecticut Law of Uninsured and Underinsured Motorist (*second edition*, 1999), for a comprehensive discussion of U.M. and U.I.M. The minimum requirements for taxis, buses, and livery vehicles vary depending on seating capacity. Conn. General Statutes § 14-29.

30. *Frankovitch v. Burton,* 1185 Conn. 14, 440 A.2d 254 (1981); *Sheiman v. Lafaette Bank & Trust Co.,* 4 Conn. App. 39, 492 A.2d 219 (1985). A nuisance can be negligently created. *Zatlein v. Katz,* 126 Conn. 445, A.2d 843 (1940).

31. *Dean v. Herskowitz* (contract), 119 Conn. 398, 117 A. 262 (1935); *Bartone v. Mahr* (statute), 147 Conn. 187, 158 A.2d 173 (1960); *Borso v. Sparice* (circumstance relationship), 141 Conn. 366, 106 A.2d 170 (1954).

32. *Barrett v. Central Vermont Railway, Inc.,* 2 Conn. App. 530, 480 A.2d 589 (1984).

33. *Catz v. Rubenstein,* 201 Conn. 39, 513 A.2d 98 (1986).

34. Conn. General Statutes § 52-184 imposes a standard for health care practitioners. *Logan v. Greenwich Hospital Assoc.* (health care providers), 191 Conn. 282, 299, 465 A.2d 294 (1983); *Grayson v. Wolsey, Rosen, Kweskin & Kuriansky* (lawyers), 231 Conn. 168, 646 A.2d 195 (1994); *Rivera v. Pat's Medical Pharmacy, Inc.* (pharmacist), 3 CSCR 710 (1988); *Madden v. Price Waterhouse,* 3 CSCR 776 (1988).

35. *Alaimo v. Boyer,* 188 Conn. 36, 39, 448 A.2d 207 (1982).

36. *Grenier v. Glastonbury,* 118 Conn. 477, 173 A. 160 (1934).

37. *Illedge v. The Standard Mattress Co.,* 27 Conn. Sup. 358, 238 A.2d 602 (1968); *but see Simon v. Nelson,* 118 Conn. 154, 170 A. 796 (1934), where a two-year-old child was not chargeable with a duty of due care.

38. Conn. General Statutes § 52-182.

39. Conn. General Statutes § 52-572.

40. *Mahoney v. Beatman,* 110 Conn. 184, 147 A. 762 (1929).

41. *Edgerton and Sons, Inc. v. Minneapolis Fire and Marine Insurance Co.,* 142 Conn. 669, 116 A.2d 514 (1955); see *Wagner v. Clark Equipment Co.,* 243 Conn. 168, 700 A.2d 38 (1997).

42. Conn. General Statutes, § 52-572h.

43. *Greki v. New Britain*, 174 Conn. 200, 384 A.2d 372 (1978).

44. Conn. General Statutes § 14-100a.

45. Conn. General Statutes § 52-572h.

46. Conn. General Statutes § 52-572o.

47. Conn. General Statutes § 52-572h.

48. *See Miller v. Porter*, 156 Conn. 466, 242 A.2d 744 (1968); *Mei v. Alterman Transport Lines, Inc.*, 59 Conn. 387, 268 A.2d 639 (1970).

49. Conn. General Statutes § 52-572c.

50. *Silverman v. Silverman*, 145 Conn. 663, 145 A.2d 826 (1958).

51. *Lowman v. Housing Authority*, 150 Conn. 665, 192 A.2d 883 (1963).

52. *Sliwoski v. New York, N.H. & H. R.R. Co.*, 94 Conn. 303, 108 A. 805 (1920).

53. *Worth v. Dunn*, 98 Conn. 51, 116 A. 467 (1922).

54. *Welz v. Manzello*, 113 Conn. 674, 155 A. 841 (1931).

55. *Staudinger v. Barrett*, 208 Conn. 94, 544 A.2d 164 (1988). Negligence *per se* is not applicable to a minor under 16 years old. Conn. General Statutes § 52-217.

56. *Small v. South Norwalk Savings Bank*, 205 Conn. 751, 535 A.2d 12922 (1988).

57. *Weinstein v. Hallas*, 140 Conn. 387, 100 A.2d 733 (1953).

58. *Reilly v. DeBianco*, 6 Conn. App. 556, 507 A.2d 106 (1986); *cert. denied*, 200 Conn. 804, 510 A.2d 192 (1986). A claim for indemnification may be brought within three years of the judgment or settlement of the underlying action. Conn. General Statutes § 52-598a.

59. *Laudano v. General Motors Corp.*, 34 Conn. Supp. 684, A. (1977).

60. *Preferred Accident Insurance Co. v. Musante, Berman & Steinberg Co.*, 133 Conn. 536, 52 A.2d 862 (1947).

61. *Kaplan v. Merberg Wrecking Corp.*, 152 Conn. 405, 207 A.2d 732 (1965).

62. *Skuzinski v. Bouchard Fuels, Inc.*, 240 Conn. 694, 694 A.2d 788 (1997).

63. *Krystatas v. Stop & Shop, Inc.*, 205 Conn. 694, 535 A.2d 357 (1988).

64. *Donner v. Kearse*, 234 Conn. 660, 662 A.2d 1269 (1995).

65. *Cartesen v. Town of Stratford*, 67 Conn. 428 (1896).

66. *Rose v. Heisler*, 118 Conn. 632, 174 A. 66 (1934).

67. Conn. General Statutes § 52-572h.

68. Conn. General Statutes § 52-572o. A defendant may move to cite in an apportionment defendant, a person not already a party to the action, within 120 days after the return date of the plaintiff's complaint.

69. Conn. General Statutes § 52-102b.

70. Conn. General Statutes § 52-572e. Vicariously liable parties are not considered to be joint tortfeasors for purposes of the rule. Thus, e.g., releasing a negligent employee will automatically release the vicariously liable employer. *Alvarez v. New Haven Register, Inc.*, 249 Conn. 709, 735 A.2d 306 (1999).

71. Conn. General Statutes § 311-284.

72. *Id.*

73. *Klapproth v. Turner*, 156 Conn. 276, 240 A.2d 886 (1968).

74. Conn. General Statutes § 31-293. Generally speaking, an employee cannot sue a fellow employee in negligence for injuries suffered during the course of employment. An employee, however, can sue a fellow employee for injuries caused by the negligent operation of a motor vehicle during the course of employment. Conn. General Statutes § 31-293a.

75. *Id.*

76. *Id.*

77. *Id.*

78. *Jett v. Dunlap*, 179 Conn. 215, 425 A.2d 1263 (1979); *Buckman v. J.P. Carroll*, 2000 Conn. Ct. Sup. 4135, — C.L.R. — (Apr. 6, 2000).

79. *Blancato v. Feldspar*, 203 Conn. 34, 522 A.2d 1233 (1987).

80. *Mack v. Clinch*, 166 Conn. 295, 348 A.2d 669 (1974).

81. *Corcoran v. Jacovino*, 161 Conn. 462, 290 A.2d 225 (1971).

82. *Kalmich v. White*, 95 Conn. 568, 111 A. 845 (1920).

83. *Deacy v. McDonnell*, 131 Conn. 101, 38 A.2d 101 (1944). Although Connecticut does not recognize the attractive nuisance doctrine, a land possessor may be liable to minors for a condition likely to be dangerous to children. *Zaremaski v. Three Lakes Park*, 177 Conn. 603, 419 A.2d 339 (1979).

84. *Warren v. Stancliff*, 157 Conn. 216, 251 A.2d 74 (1968).

85. Conn. General Statutes § 30-102.

86. *Ely v. Murphy*, 207 Conn. 88, 540 A.2d 54 (1988).

87. *Kowal v. Hofer*, 181 Conn. 355, 436 A.2d 1 (1980).

88. *Kelehear v. Larcon, Inc.*, 22 Conn. App. 384, 577 A.2d 740 (1990); *Coble v. Maloney*, 34 Conn. App. 655, 643 A.2d 277 (1994).

89. *Belanger v. Village Pub I, Inc.*, 26 Conn. App. 509, 603 A.2d 1173 (1992).

90. Conn. General Statutes § 30-102.

91. *Id.*

92. *Dellott v. Roraback*, 179 Conn. 406, 426 A.2d 791 (1980); *see generally* Conn. General Statutes §§ 52-236 *et seq.*

93. *Feen v. Benefit Plan Administrators*, 28 C.L.R. 137 (2000); 1999 WL 33972 (Conn. Super. 1999).

94. *Proto v. Bridgeport Herald Corp.*, 130 Conn. 557, 72 A.2d 820 (1950); *Abdelsayd v. Narumanchi*, 39 Conn. App. 775, *cert. denied*, 237 Conn. 915, 676 A.2d 397, *cert. denied*, 117 S. Ct. 180, 136 L. Ed. 120 (1995).

95. Conn. General Statutes § 52-572n; *Chiang v. Pyro Chemical, Inc.*, — C.L.R. — (1997); 1997 WL 330622.

96. *Mayor Joseph P. Ganim v. Smith & Wesson Corp., et al.*, Docket X06-CV-99-0153198, Complex Litigation Docket, Superior Court at Waterbury, Memorandum of Decision on Defendants, Motions to Dismiss, December 10, 1999.

97. *Connecticut Mutual Life Insurance Co. v. N.Y. & N.H. R.R. Co.*, 25 Conn. 265 (1856); *Darien Asphalt Paving v. Town of Newington*, 23 C.L.R. 495 (1998).

98. Conn. Practice Book § 10-1.

99. *Kelduff v. Adams, Inc.*, 219 Conn. 314, 593 A.2d 478 (1991); *DeLucia v. Valente*, 83 Conn. 107, 75 A. 150 (1910). Fraud must be specifically raised as a defense.

100. *Connell v. Colwell*, 214 Conn. 242, 571 A.2d 116 (1990).

101. *Bradley v. Oviatt*, 86 Conn. 84 A. 321 (1912); *Maturo v. Gerard*, 196 Conn. 584, 494 A.2d 1199 (1985).

102. *Clark v. Haggard*, 141 Conn. 668, 109 A.2d 358 (1954); *Warman v. Delaney*, 148 Conn. 469, 172 A.2d 188 (1961).

103. *Gibson v. Caponi*, 41 Conn. App. 548, 676 A.2d 896; *cert. granted in part*, 239 Conn. 902, 682 A.2d 1000; *aff'd*, 241 Conn. 725, 699 A.2d 68 (1997).

104. Conn. General Statutes § 42-110b. *See also* Connecticut Unfair Insurance Practices Act. Conn. General Statutes § 38a-815.

105. Conn. General Statutes § 42-110b.

106. Conn. General Statutes § 42-110o.

107. Conn. General Statutes § 42-110g.

108. *Thames River Recycling, Inc. v. Gallo*, 50 Conn. App. 767, 720 A.2d 242 (1998).

109. *Gebbie v. Cadle Co.*, 49 Conn. App. 265, 714 A.2d 678 (1998); *Brandew v. Emory Worldwide*, 890 F. Supp. 79, *aff'd*, 66 F.3d 308 (D. Conn. 1994).

110. *Beverly Hills Concepts, Inc. v. Shatz and Schatz, Ribicoff and Kotkin*, 247 Conn. 48, 717 A.2d 724 (1998); *Haynes v. Yale–New Haven Hospital*, 243 Conn. 17, 699 A.2d 1964 (1997).

111. *Fictora v. Mine Hill Corp.*, 207 Conn. 204, 541 A.2d 472 (1988).

112. *Sorrentino v. All Seasons Services, Inc.*, 245 Conn. 756, 717 A.2d 150 (1995); *Venturi v. Savitt, Inc.*, 191 Conn. 588, 468 A.2d 933 (1983).

113. *Santis v. Picadilly Land Corp.*, 3 Conn. App. 310, 487 A.2d 1110 (1985); *but see Lewis v. Cowenn*, 979 F. Supp. 99 (D. Conn. 1997); *Champagne v. Baybestos Manhattan*, 212 Conn. 519, 562 A.2d 110 (1989) (purpose to punish and/or deter similar conduct).

114. *Larsen Chelsey Realty Co. v. Larsen*, 232 Conn. 480, 656 A.2d 1009 (1995).

115. *Barry v. Posi-Seal Intern, Inc.*, 40 Conn. App. 577, 672 A.2d 514, *cert. denied*, 237 Conn. 917, 676 A.2d 1373 (1996).

116. *Lanese v. Carlson,* 32 Conn. Supp. 163, 344 A.2d 361 (1975).

117. *Murphy v. N.Y. & N.H. R.R. Co.,* 29 Conn. 496 (1961).

118. Conn. General Statutes § 14-295.

119. *Stahle v. Michael's Garage, Inc.,* 35 Conn. App. 455, 646 A.2d 888 (1994).

120. *Shattuck v. Gulliver,* 40 Conn. Supp. 95, 481 A.2d 1110 (1984).

121. Conn. General Statutes § 52-555.

122. *Id.*

123. *Foran v. Carangelo,* 153 Conn. 356, 216 A.2d 638 (1966).

124. *Floyd v. Fruit Industries, Inc.,* 144 Conn. 659, 136 A.2d 918 (1957).

125. Conn. General Statutes § 52-555a-c.

Delaware

A. STATUTES OF LIMITATION

1. Two Years

A two-year limitations period applies to claims for wrongful death or injury to personal property;[1] for personal injury,[2] for medical malpractice—two years from the date of injury except that if the injury is inherently unknowable within two years, then within three years of the date the injury occurred "and not thereafter." A minor under the age of six shall have until his sixth birthday or the two-to-three year time period whichever is longer.[3]

2. Three Years

A three-year limitations period applies to claims for tortuous injury to real property,[4] fraud,[5] breach of contract,[6] legal malpractice (tort or contract).[7] For Person Injury Protection (PIP), the period is three (3) years from the date of the accident.[8]

3. Four Years

A four-year limitations period applies to claims for breach of warranty under the Uniform Commercial Code. It is four years from date of sale.[9]

4. Six Years

A six-year limitations period applies to claims for death or injury arising out of construction on real property.[10] This Statute provides that the statute of limitations runs from the date of various events, such as substantial completion and/or acceptance by the owner. It also provides that to the extent that the previous statutes provide for a shorter time period, they shall control. It does not apply to someone in actual control such as an owner or a tenant at the time when the improvement constitutes the proximate cause of injury or death.

5. Minors

The statute of limitation runs on a minor's personal injury claim under 10 Del. C. § 8119. However, the savings statute, 10 Del. C. § 8116, applies to a minor's contract claim under 10 Del. C. § 8106. That is why court approval is necessary for most minor's settlements.[11]

6. Indemnity and Contribution

A claim for indemnity does not run from the date of event or accident, but from when the indemnitee's liability is fixed.[12] For contribution claims, the statute begins to run when the defendant has a judgment against him or has paid more than his share. The statute does not begin to run at the time of the accident.[13] The ordinary statute of limitations runs on a counterclaim. This is true even where the plaintiff waits until the last possible moment to file his initial lawsuit.[14]

7. **Tolling**

Fraud tolls the statute of limitations.[15]

8. **Time of Discovery**

Ordinarily, a statute of limitations runs mechanically on claims and ignorance of the cause of action, absent fraud, does not toll the statute.[16] However, in certain cases of professional negligence, where: (1) the injury is not ascertainable by reasonable care and diligence; (2) the injury is inherently unknowable in that (a) there is no physical manifestation, (b) the injury is triggered by a third-party action such as an IRS deficiency notice or the assertion of a mechanics lien; and (3) the plaintiff is blamelessly ignorant. The statute of limitations does not begin to run until the plaintiff knew or should have known of his cause of action.[17]

B. TORT REFORM

There has been no meaningful tort reform in Delaware since the adoption of special legislation for health care providers.[18]

C. "NO FAULT" LIMITATIONS

A plaintiff who has received no-fault insurance benefits cannot recover such benefits from a defendant. The insurer who paid the benefits has a separate claim against the defendant in a separate action.[19]

D. THE STANDARD FOR NEGLIGENCE

Negligence is the lack of ordinary care; that is, the absence of the kind of care a reasonably prudent and careful person would exercise in similar circumstances. That standard is your guide. If a person's conduct in a given circumstance doesn't measure up to the conduct of an ordinarily prudent and careful person, then that person was negligent. On the other hand, if the person's conduct does measure up to the conduct of a reasonably prudent and careful person, the person wasn't negligent. The mere fact that an accident occurred isn't enough to establish negligence.[20]

A child's negligence has to be determined by a standard of care which is based upon an individualized assessment of the child's age, intelligence, maturity and other factors relevant to conduct involved.[21]

E. CAUSATION

Delaware has long recognized that there may be more than one proximate cause of an injury.[22] Nevertheless, Delaware's "time honored definition of proximate cause" has been the "but for" rule. "Most simply stated, proximate cause is [defined in Delaware as] that direct cause without which the accident would not have occurred."[23] It has rejected the "substantial factor" formulation.[24]

The issue of proximate cause is ordinarily a question of fact to be submitted to the jury in a negligence action.[25] It is permissible for a plaintiff to make a *prima facie* case that a defendant's conduct was a proximate cause of the plaintiff's injuries, based upon an inference from the plaintiff's competent evidence, that such a finding relates to a matter which is within a lay person's scope of knowledge.[26] However, if the matter in issue is one within the knowledge of experts only, and not within the common knowledge of laymen, it is necessary for the plaintiff to introduce expert testimony in order to establish a *prima facie* case.[27]

F. CONTRIBUTORY NEGLIGENCE, COMPARATIVE NEGLIGENCE, AND ASSUMPTION OF RISK

1. Contributory Negligence

Contributory negligence has been abrogated by the comparative negligence statute.[28]

2. Comparative Negligence

Plaintiff is barred from recovery if plaintiff's negligence is greater than the combined negligence of all defendants against whom recovery is sought [i.e., 51 percent or more].[29] Based upon the court's jury instructions, comparative negligence may be permitted as a defense.[30] Comparative negligence is an affirmative defense to a claim for enhanced injuries in a crashworthiness case.[31]

3. Assumption of Risk

Assumption of risk is a defense in all Delaware cases where strict liability is not permitted. It is unclear whether this defense would be permitted in strict liability actions.[32]

Delaware common law distinguishes between primary and secondary assumption of risk in the context of comparative negligence.[33] Secondary assumption of risk as a complete defense is inconsistent with comparative negligence.[34]

G. *RES IPSA LOQUITUR* AND INHERENTLY DANGEROUS ACTIVITIES

1. *Res Ipsa Loquitur*

Res ipsa loquitur may only be used where the plaintiff establishes that the likelihood of other causes is so reduced by the plaintiff's proof that the greater probability of negligence lies with the defendant.[35]

2. Inherently Dangerous Activities

The history of the doctrine in Delaware is found in *Handy v. Uniroyal, Inc.*[36] It is far from clear that the doctrine has ever been adopted in Delaware.

H. NEGLIGENCE *PER SE*

Delaware has recognized "negligence per se" as a "long settled" principle in cases that involved negligence claims predicated upon specific legislative enactments.[37] The effect of the principle is a less onerous burden of proof for the plaintiff.[38]

I. JOINT AND SEVERAL LIABILITY

In all tort actions in which no fault is assessed to the plaintiff, the liable defendants are jointly and severally liable for the entire judgment. The plaintiffs can select that defendant or those defendants from which to collect the judgment.[39]

J. INDEMNITY

With the exception of indemnification against the indemnitee's own negligence in certain construction related contracts, contractual indemnification is available in Delaware. "Generally, a right to indemnity arises by contract, although equitable grounds have been recognized."[40] An indemnification contract "is construed to give effect to the parties' intent; in other words, only losses which reasonably appear to have been intended by the parties are compensable under such contract."[41]

Agreements under which the indemnitee is indemnified against the indemnitor's own negligence are valid under Delaware law. At common law, there was no duty placed upon a contract to make restitution or to make indemnification to the principal as to a claim for damages arising out of the principal's own negligence.[42] In general, the Delaware Supreme Court looks with disfavor upon causes which exonerate a party from the consequences of his own negligence or that of his agent. The contract must clearly and unequivocally spell out the intent to grant such immunity. If the language used can be construed as not conferring immunity, it will be so interpreted.[43] This policy was enunciated as the law in Delaware.[44] The general rule is that an indemnification contract provision must be crystal clear and unequivocal in requiring the contractor to assume all liability for damage claims, whichever party may have been guilty of the negligence which actually caused the injury.[45] However, 6 Del. C. § 2704(a) makes void and unenforceable clauses in a broad range of construction and construction related contracts in which the indemnitee is indemnified against its own negligence.[46] Section 2704(a) applies to all contracts or agreements entered into after July 14, 1988.

Contractual indemnification can arise by an express contract, as described above, or by an implied contract. There is strong authority, however, for the proposition where the parties have a specific indemnification agreement, the court will not examine their relationship to determine if an implied duty to indemnify exists.[47] If it is established that there is an express promise of indemnification in the contract, even one which proves unenforceable as to the indemnities' own negligence, the implied duty doctrine does not apply.

K. BAR OF WORKERS' COMPENSATION STATUTE

In situations where the Delaware Workers' Compensation law is applicable, workers' compensation is the exclusive remedy of an employee or other party for tort damages against the employer. 19 Del. C. § 2304.[48] An employer, however, is not immune from a suit based on breach of contract. "The employer is not only not liable to the employee for negligence, but the employer is not liable for joint and concurrent negligence with another party;" however, "[a] breach of contractual obligation, either express or implied, would be a proper basis" for holding the employer liable.[49] Insurers who provide workers' compensation insurance have the same protection as the insured employer against tort litigation. "Insurers who provided workers' compensation insurance are protected from tort suits brought by employees who worked for that employer during the period of that coverage."[50]

L. **PREMISES LIABILITY**

The extent of the landowner's duty, and the standard of care to which the landowner must conform, is measured in terms of the foreseeability of injury from the situation created by the landowner.[51] One who conducts business owes a duty to those who come to his place to do business to exercise due care to keep the property in a reasonably safe condition as to any condition which is known to the business operator or which should have been known in the exercise of reasonable care or diligence.[52] In addition, if the injured party knows or should know of the danger, the landowner has no duty to warn.[53] Moreover, "the landowner is not liable for the torts of an independent contractor hired by the owner unless the owner retains the power to control the methods and manner of doing the work."[54] A landowner not only has a duty to protect business invitees from unsafe conditions on the property, but also has "a residual obligation of reasonable care to protect business invitees from the acts of third persons."[55]

M. **DRAM SHOP LIABILITY**

There is none.

N. **ECONOMIC LOSS**

Under Delaware law, the economic loss doctrine bars plaintiff's claim of strict liability in tort. The economic loss doctrine "prohibits recovery in tort where a product has damaged only itself (*i.e.*, has not caused personal injury or damage to other property) and, the only losses suffered are economic in nature."[56] Economic loss is defined as "'damages for inadequate value, costs of repair and replacement of the defective product, or consequent loss of profits—without any claim of personal injury or damage to other property,' as well as 'the diminution in value of the product because it is inferior in quality and does not work for the general purposes for which it is manufactured and sold.'"[57]

O. **FRAUD AND MISREPRESENTATION**

The elements of fraud in Delaware are clearly established: (1) False representation of material facts; (2) The knowledge or belief that the representation was false, or made with reckless indifference for the truth; (3) The intent to induce another party to act or refrain from acting; (4) The action or inaction taken was in justifiable reliance on the representation; and (5) Damage to the other party as a result of the representation. Equity may find fraud even if the representation was made negligently or innocently.[58]

The rescission of an insurance policy is addressed in 18 Del. C. § 2711. It disfavors rescission unless the misstatements were fraudulent; or material either to the acceptance of the risk or to the hazard assumed by the insurer; or the insurer in good faith would either not have issued the policy or contract, or would not have issued at the same premium rate, or would not have issued a policy or contract in as large an amount or would not have provided coverage with respect to the hazard resulting in the loss if the true facts had been made known to the insurer as required either by the application for the policy or contract or otherwise. The threshold issue in interpreting this statute is whether a misrepresentation has, in fact, been made.[59] When a person is required to fill out an insurance application, the prospective insured may assume that information not requested on the application is immaterial.[60] Delaware also recognizes the fundamental principal in insurance law that both the insured and insurer have a duty to deal with each other with utmost fairness, one seeking such insurance coverage must disclose information concerning material physical diseases known to the application in order for there to be an enforceable contract.[61]

P. CONSUMER FRAUD STATUTES

The Insurer Unfair Trade Practices Act was promulgated to regulate trade practices, not to provide a private cause of action.[62] Although a private cause of actions for treble damages under the Deceptive Trade Practices Act[63] might be permitted, it is restricted to one who has standing to seek injunctive relief under § 2533(a).[64] Under the Consumer Fraud Act,[65] a consumer who has been damaged by a violation of § 2513 may assert a private cause of action.[66]

Q. PUNITIVE DAMAGES

Punitive damages are imposed in situations where the defendant's conduct, although unintentional, has been particularly reprehensible, *i.e.*, reckless, or motivated by malice or fraud.[67] In actions arising in contract, punitive damages may be assessed only if the breach of contract is characterized by willfulness or malice.[68] Punitive damages may be recovered against the estate of a deceased tortfeasor.[69] There is no statutory cap on punitive damages. However, Delaware case law imposes a limitation of reasonable relation between the amount of punitive damages awarded in the amount of compensatory damages. Bifurcation is available under Superior Court Rule 42; Federal Rule of Civil Procedure 42.

R. WRONGFUL DEATH AND SURVIVORSHIP ACTIVITIES

Delaware law provides that when a person dies as a result of another's wrongful act, certain immediate family members may recover fair compensation for their losses resulting from the death.[70] There is a priority among those eligible to recover benefits. The surviving spouse and children, if any, are the primary beneficiaries. If there is no surviving spouse or children, surviving parents may recover. If there are no surviving parents, a recent amendment permits surviving siblings to recover.[71]

In determining a fair compensation, the jury may consider the following:

(1) the loss of the expectation of monetary benefits that would have resulted from the continued life of the decedent; that is, the expectation of inheritance that the beneficiaries have lost;

(2) the loss of the portion of decedent's earnings and income that probably would have been used for the support of the beneficiaries;

(3) the loss of decedent's parental, marital, and household services, including the reasonable cost of providing for the care of minor children;

(4) the reasonable cost of funeral expenses, not to exceed $2000; and

(5) the mental anguish suffered by family members as a result of decedent's death.[72]

The term "mental anguish" encompasses the grieving process associated with the loss of a loved one, accompanied by its physical and emotional upheaval, that will be experienced differently by different people, both in its intensity and in its duration. The ability to cope with the loss may be different for each person. There is no fixed standard or measurement. The jury determines a fair and adequate award through its judgment and experience after considering all the facts and circumstances presented during the trial.[73]

The plaintiff has the burden of proving damages by a preponderance of the evidence, but is not required to claim and prove with mathematical precision the exact sums of money representing their damages for mental anguish. It is required only that the plaintiffs furnish enough evidence so that the jury can make a reasonable determination of those damages.[74]

James W. Semple
MORRIS JAMES HITCHENS & WILLIAMS, L.L.P.
222 Delaware Avenue, Tenth Floor
P.O. Box 2306
Wilmington, Delaware 18998-2306
(302) 888-6800
Fax (302) 571-1750
jsemple@morrisjames.com
www.morrisjames.com

ENDNOTES - DELAWARE

1. 10 Del. C. § 8107.

2. 10 Del. C. § 8119.

3. 18 Del. C. § 6856.

4. 10 Del. C. § 8106.

5. 10 Del. C. § 8106.

6. 10 Del. C. § 8106.

7. 10 Del. C. § 8106; *Hood v. McConemy*, 53 F.R.D 435 (D. Del. 1971).

8. *Harper v. State Farm Mutual Insurance Co.*, 703 A.2d 136 (Del. Supr. 1997), overruling *Nationwide Insurance Co. v. Rothermel*, 385 A.2d 691 (Del. Supr. 1978); uninsured and underinsured motorist coverage, from the date the insurer denies coverage and/or notifies insured of rejection of any claim for such benefits. *Allstate Insurance Company v. Spinelli*, 443 A.2d 1286 (Del. Supr. 1982).

9. 6 Del. C. § 2-725. *Johnson v. Hockessin Tractor, Inc.*, 420 A.2d 154 (Del. Supr. 1980). But see *Alaska Bulk Carriers, Inc. v. Goodall Rubber Co., et al.*, No. 87-573-CMW, Wright, J. (June 14, 1990); 1990 WL 82361 (D. Del.).

10. 10 Del. C. § 8127.

11. *Tilden v. Anstreicher*, 367 A.2d 632 (Del. Supr. 1976).

12. *Chesapeake Utilities v. Chesapeake and Potomac Telephone Company of Maryland*, 401 A.2d 101 (Del. Super. 1979).

13. *Royal Car Wash v. Mayor & Council of Wilmington*, 240 A.2d 144 (Del. Super. 1968). *Goldsberry v. Frank Clendaniel, Inc.*, 109 A.2d 405 (Del. Super. 1954).

14. *Floyd v. Ballenger*, 258 A.2d 911 (Del. Super. 1969).

15. *Walls v. Abdel-Malik*, 440 A.2d 992 (Del. Super. 1982).

16. *Mastellone v. Argo Oil Corp.*, 82 A.2d 379 (Del. Supr. 1951).

17. *Layton v. Allen*, 246 A.2d 794 (Del. Supr. 1968). *Isaacson Stolper & Co. v. Artisans Savings Bank*, 330 A.2d 130 (Del. Supr. 1974).

18. 18 Del. C. § 6801-6871.

19. 21 Del. C. § 2118.

20. *Duphily v. Delaware Elec. Coop., Inc.*, 662 A.2d 821, 828 (Del. Supr. 1995); *Culver v. Bennett*, 588 A.2d 1094, 1096-97 (Del. Supr. 1991); *Robelen Piano Co. v. DiFonzo*, 169 A.2d 240 (Del. Supr. 1961); *Rabar v. E.I. duPont de Nemours & Co., Inc.*, 415 A.2d 499, 506 (Del. Super. 1980); *DeAngelis v. U.S.A.C. Transport*, 105 A.2d 458 (Del. Super. 1954); *Kane v. Reed*, 101 A.2d 800 (Del. Super. 1954).

21. *Moffitt v. Carroll*, 640 A.2d 169 (Del. Supr. 1994).

22. *McKeon v. Goldstein*, 164 A.2d 260, 262 (Del. Supr. 1960).

23. *Chudnofsky v. Edwards*, 208 A.2d at 518 (Del. Supr. 1965).

24. *Culver v. Bennett*, 588 A.2d 1094 (Del. Supr. 1991).

25. *Id.*; *Money v. Manville Corp. Asbestos Disease Comp. Trust Fund*, 596 A.2d 1372, at 1375 (Del. Supr. 1991).

26. Compare *Chudnofsky v. Edwards*, 208 A.2d 516, 518 (Del. Supr. 1965); *Money v. Manville Corp. Asbestos Disease Comp. Trust Fund*, 596 A.2d 1372, at 1375 (Del. Supr. 1991).

27. *Money v. Manville Corp. Asbestos Disease Comp. Trust Fund*, at 1375. *Mountaire of Delmarva, Inc. v. Glacken*, 487 A.2d 1137, 1141 (Del. Supr. 1984); *Weiner v. Wisniewski*, 213 A.2d 857, 858 (Del. Supr. 1965); *Laskowski v. Wallis*, 205 A.2d 825, 826 (Del. Supr. 1964).

28. 10 Del. C. § 8132.

29. 10 Del. C. § 8132; *Garrison v. Mollers N.A., Inc.*, 820 F. Supp. 814 (D. Del. 1993).

30. *Elmer v. Tenneco Resins, Inc.*, 698 F. Supp. 535 (D. Del. 1988).

31. *Meekins v. Ford Motor Co.*, 699 A.2d 339 (Del. Super.1997).

32. *Baynard v. General Motors Corp.*, C.A. No. 974, 1974 (Del. Super. 1979).

33. *Delmarva Power & Light v. King*, 608 A.2d 726 (Del. 1992).

34. *Koutoufaris v. Dick*, 604 A.2d 390, 398 (Del. 1992); *Laws v. Webb*, 658 A.2d 1000, 1006 (Del. 1995).

35. *Phillips v. Delmarva Power & Light*, 202 A.2d 131 (Del. Super. 1964); see also *DiIenno v. Libbey Glass Division, Owens-Illinois, Inc.*, 668 F. Supp. 373 (D. Del. 1987).

36. *Handy v. Uniroyal, Inc.*, 327 F. Supp. 596, 603-605 (D. Del. 1971).

37. *Nance v. Rees*, 161 A.2d 795, 797 (Del. Supr. 1960); (violation of motor vehicle statute); *Wealth v. Renai*, 114 A.2d 809, 810 (Del. Super. 1955) (violation of motor vehicle statute); *Lynch v. Lynch*, 195 A. 799, 801 (Del. Super. 1937) (violation of motor vehicle statute); *Wollaston v. Stiltz*, 114 A. 198, 200 (Del. Super. 1921) (violation of motor vehicle law); *Farrow v. Hoffecker*, 79 A. 920, 921 (Del. Super. 1906) (violation of town ordinance).

38. *Toll Bros., Inc. v. Considine*, 706 A.2d 493 (Del. Supr. 1998); Delaware law provides that before a violation of a motor vehicle statute can be established, it must be demonstrated that the driver was aware or reasonably should have been aware of the situation requiring compliance with the statute. *Green v. Millsboro Fire Co.*, 403 A.2d 286 (Del. Supr. 1979); *Wilmington Country Club v. Cowee*, 747 A.2d 1087 (Del. Supr. 2000).

39. 10 Del. C., chapter 63.

40. *Insurance Co. of North America v. Waterhouse*, 424 A.2d 675, 678 (Del. Super. 1980).

41. *Oliver B. Cannon and Son, Inc. v. Dorr-Oliver, Inc.*, 394 A.2d 1160, 1165 (Del. Supr. 1978).

42. *Hollingsworth v. Chrysler Corporation*, 208 A.2d 61 (Del. Super. 1965); *Bar Steel Construction Corp. v. Read*, 277 A.2d 678 (Del. Supr. 1971).

43. *Pan American World Airways, Inc. v. United Aircraft Corp.*, 163 A.2d 582 (Del. Supr. 1960); *Wilmington Housing Authority v. Williamson*, 228 A.2d 782 (Del. Supr. 1967).

44. *Marshall, et al. v. Maryland, D. and V. Ry. Co.*, 112 A. 526 (Del. Super. 1921).

45. *State v. Interstate Amiesite Corporation*, 297 A.2d 41, at 44 (Del. Supr. 1972). Cf. *Blum v. Kauffman*, 297 A.2d 48 (Del. Supr. 1972).

46. Subsection (b) of Section 2704 makes clear that "[n]othing in subsection (a) of this section shall be construed to void or render unenforceable policies of insurance issued by duly authorized insurance companies and insuring against losses or damages from any causes whatsoever." 6 Del. C. § 2704(b).

47. *Waller v. J.C. Brenneman Company*, 307 A.2d 550 (Del. Super 1973); *Slover v. Fabtek, Inc.*, C.A. No. 82C-DE-108, Gebelein, J. (Mar. 4, 1985) (Del. Super).

48. Section 2304 provides that "Every employer and employee, adult and minor, except as expressly excluded in this chapter, shall be bound by this chapter respectively to pay and to accept compensation for personal injury or death by accident arising out of and in the course of employment, regardless of the question of negligence and to the exclusion of all other rights and remedies."

19 Del. C. § 2304. *Diamond State Tel. Co. v. Univ. of Delaware*, 269 A.2d 52, 56 (Del. Supr. 1970).

49. *Powell v. Interstate Vendaway, Inc.*, 300 A.2d 241, 244 (Del. Super. 1972).

50. *Mergenthaler v. Asbestos Corp. of Am., Inc.*, 534 A.2d 281, 283-84 (Del. Super. 1987).

51. *Hercules Powder Co. v. DiSabatino*, 188 A.2d 529, 534 (Del. Supr. 1963).

52. *Vorous v. Cochran*, 249 A.2d 746, 747 (Del. Super. 1969). *See also Woods v. Prices Corner Shopping Center Merchants Assoc.*, 541 A.2d 574, 575 (Del Super. 1988).

53. *DiSabatino Bros., Inc. v. Baio*, 366 A.2d 508, 510 (Del. Supr. 1976).

54. *Rabar v. E. I. duPont de Nemours & Co.*, 415 A.2d 499, 506 (Del. Super. 1980).

55. *Jardel Co., Inc. v. Hughes*, 523 A.2d 518, 525 (Del. Supr. 1987).

56. *Danforth v. Acorn Structures, Inc.*, 608 A.2d 1194, 1195 (Del. Supr. 1992). The General Assembly, however, abolished this doctrine in the residential construction setting by passing the Home Owner's Protection Act. *See* 6 Del. C. §§ 3651-52.

57. *Id.* at n.3 (quoting *Moorman Mfg. Co. v. Nat'l Tank Co.*, 435 N.E.2d 443, 449 (1982)).

58. *In re Brandywine Volkswagon, Ltd.*, 306 A.2d 24 (Del. Super. 1973), *aff'd.*, 312 A.2d 632; *Wilmington Sixth District Community Committee v. Pettinaro Enterprises*, C.A. No. 8668, Hartnett, V.C., (October 27, 1988) (Del. Ch.) 1988 WL 116496; *In the Matter of Enstar Corp.*, 593 A.2d 543, 549 (Del. Ch. 1991).

59. *Diana Dickson-Witmer v. Union Bankers Insurance Co.*, C.A. No. 92C-07-107, Barron, J. (April 27, 1994) (Del. Super) [major medical health insurance policy].

60. *New Castle County v. Hartford Accident and Indemnity Company*, 685 F. Supp. 1321, 1327 (D. Del. 1988).

61. *American Casualty Company of Reading, Pa. v. Ford*, 187 A.2d 425, 427 (Del. Ch. 1963); *Dickson-Witmer v. Union Bankers Insurance Co., supra.*

62. *Moses v. State Farm Fire & Casualty Insurance Co.*, No. Civ. A. 90C-10-020 (Del. Super., Nov. 20, 1991) 1991 W.L. 269886; *National Union v. Rhone-Poulenc*, No. Civ. A. 87C-SE-11, (Del. Super. April 30, 1992) 1992 WL 111201 [*only* the Insurance Commissioner can prosecute for violations of the Act].

63. 6 Del. C. §§ 2531-2536.

64. *Grand Ventures, Inc. v. Whaley*, 622 A.2d 655 (Del. Super. 1992); *aff'd*, 632 A.2d 63 (Del. Supr., 1993).

65. 6 Del. C. § 2511-2527.

66. *Young v. Joyce*, 351 A.2d 857 (Del. Supr. 1975).

67. *Jardel Co., Inc. v. Hughes*, 523 A.2d 518 (Del. Supr. 1987).

68. *Casson v. Nationwide Insurance Co.*, 455 A.2d 361 (Del. Super. 1982).

69. *Estate of Farrell ex rel. Bennett v. Gordon*, 770 A.2d 517(Del. Supr. 2001).

70. 10 Del. C. § 3724 (Wrongful Death Statute).

71. *Id.*

72. 10 Del. C. § 3724.

73. *Bennett v. Andree*, 252 A.2d 100, 101-03 (Del. Supr. 1969); *Gill v. Celotex Corp.*, 565 A.2d 21, 23-24 (Del. Super. 1989) (mental anguish); *Saxton v. Harvey & Harvey*, C.A. No. 85C-JL-3, Poppiti, J. (Del. Super. April 14, 1987); *Sach v. Kent Gen. Hosp.*, 518 A.2d 695, 696-97 (Del. Super. 1986) (claim by surviving parents); *Okie v. Owens*, C.A. No. 83C-AP-15, Poppiti, J. (Oct. 16, 1985) (Del. Super.); 1985 WL 189292.

74. *See also Frantz v. United States*, 791 F. Supp. 445, 448 (D. Del. 1992) (proper beneficiaries of claim for wrongful death); *Johnson v. Physicians Anesthesia Serv.*, 621 F. Supp. 908, 915-16 (D. Del. 1985) (action and potential damages arise only after time of death).

DISTRICT OF COLUMBIA

A. STATUTES OF LIMITATION

Causes of action on the following claims must be commenced within one year: libel, slander, assault, battery, mayhem, wounding, malicious prosecution, false arrest or false imprisonment, statutory penalty or forfeiture. Suits against a common carrier for injury or death of an employee also must be commenced within one year, as must suits for death or injury caused by exposure to asbestos. By statute, the cause of action for death or injury caused by asbestos must be brought within one year from the later of (1) when plaintiff first suffered disability; or (2) when plaintiff knew or should have known that disability was caused by asbestos exposure.[1]

The following forms of action must be commenced within three years: real or personal property damages, including claims for personal injury based on negligent manufacturing, products liability, breach of warranty (other than actions for breach of contracts for sale) and misrepresentation; simple contract; negligence; abuse of process; medical malpractice; intentional infliction of emotional distress (when not associated with any other cause of action for which another period of limitation is specifically provided); actions brought under the D.C. Survival Act; and all other actions for which a limit is not specifically prescribed.[2]

An action for breach of contract for sale, including breach of warranty, must be brought within four years.[3] The cause of action accrues when the breach occurs, regardless of the defendant's lack of knowledge. A breach of warranty occurs when the tender of delivery is made.

Recovery of damages for an injury to real property from toxic substances including products containing asbestos must be commenced within five years from the date the injury is discovered or with reasonable diligence should have been discovered.[4]

Recovery of damages for personal injury, injury to real or personal property or wrongful death resulting from defective or unsafe conditions of improvements to real property must be commenced within ten years. This limitation does not apply to any action brought against the owner or person in actual possession or control of such real property or any manufacturer or supplier of equipment or machinery installed upon real property.[5]

At common law, a cause of action accrues at the time the injury occurs.[6] In cases where, at the time the injury occurs, the relationship between the fact of injury and the alleged tortious conduct is obscure, the courts in the District of Columbia apply a discovery rule to determine when the statute of limitations commences to run.[7] For a cause of action to accrue under the discovery rule, one must know or by the exercise of reasonable diligence should know (1) of the injury, (2) its cause in fact, and (3) of some evidence of wrongdoing.[8] The discovery rule, however, does not give a plaintiff license to defer institution of suit and wait and see whether additional injuries come to light; a cause of action will accrue once a plaintiff has knowledge of *some* injury and *some* wrongdoing.[9] The District of Columbia courts have refused to adopt the rule that a cause of action does not accrue until a plaintiff has a reasonable opportunity to discovery *all* the essential elements of a possible cause of action. On the other hand, also considered and rejected was a rule by which a cause of action accrues with knowledge of the existence of injury and its causes, but without any evidence of wrongdoing.[10]

B. TORT REFORM

There has been no tort reform legislation in the District of Columbia.

C. "NO FAULT" LIMITATIONS

The District of Columbia's statute governing Compulsory/No-Fault Motor Vehicle Insurance[11] legislates certain aspects of insurance coverage and negligence suits arising out of motor vehicle accidents. The statute compels insurers to offer optional personal injury protection (PIP) coverage to cover medical and rehabilitation, work loss, and funeral expenses of an insured (or an occupant of a vehicle which the insured is driving) arising from a motor vehicle accident.[12] PIP payments are provided without regard to the negligence or fault of any person.[13]

An accident victim shall notify the PIP insurer within 60 days of an accident of the victim's election to receive PIP benefits. Once that election is made, a victim may maintain a civil action based on the liability of another person only if the victim suffers substantial permanent impairment or the medical and rehabilitation expenses exceed the victim's PIP benefits.[14] These standards are exacting ones, designed to filter out undeserving cases.[15]

D. THE STANDARD FOR NEGLIGENCE

To establish a *prima facie* case for negligence the following elements must be proved: (1) the existence of a duty of care on the part of the defendant to the plaintiff; (2) a breach of that duty by the defendant; and (3) that the breach of duty by the defendant proximately caused damage to the plaintiff.[16]

The plaintiff bears the burden of proof on the applicable standard of care, a deviation from that standard by the defendant, and a causal relationship between that deviation and the plaintiff's injury.[17] If the subject in question is so distinctly related to some science, profession, or occupation as to be beyond the ken of the average layperson, expert testimony as to the standard of care will be required.[18]

In civil negligence cases, a child is not necessarily held to the same standard of conduct as an adult, but rather is required to exercise that degree of care which is ordinarily exercised by children of like age, education, knowledge and experience.[19] In the District of Columbia there are no "degrees" of care; instead, the care required is always reasonable care, and what is reasonable depends on all the circumstances, including the dangerousness of the activity involved.[20]

E. CAUSATION

Proximate cause has been defined as "that which, in natural and continual sequence, unbroken by any efficient intervening cause, produces the injury, and without which the result would not have occurred."[21] An intervening negligent or criminal act breaks the chain of causation if it is not reasonably foreseeable.[22] Similarly, there is no proximate causation when the sequence of events leading to an injury is "highly extraordinary in retrospect."[23]

When an intervening act is criminal, the District of Columbia courts demand a heightened showing of foreseeability than if it were merely negligent, because of the extraordinary nature of criminal conduct.[24] The defendant will be liable only if the criminal act is so foreseeable that a duty arises to guard against it.[25]

Proximate cause is divided into cause in fact and policy considerations that limit the liability of persons who have, in fact, caused the injury where the chain of events is highly extraordinary in retrospect.[26] In determining whether there has been cause in fact, the plaintiff is not required to prove causation to a certainty. The proper test is whether the plaintiff can prove, by a preponderance of the evidence, that the asserted negligence was a "substantial factor" in causing the injury.[27]

F. CONTRIBUTORY NEGLIGENCE, COMPARATIVE NEGLIGENCE, AND ASSUMPTION OF RISK

1. Contributory Negligence

Contributory negligence is an absolute bar to recovery for negligence under District of Columbia law.[28] The District of Columbia defines contributory negligence in terms of unreasonable conduct; that is, conduct "which falls below the standard to which a plaintiff should conform for his own protection and contributes to the plaintiff's injury."[29]

A plaintiff may recover despite his or her contributory negligence under the "last clear chance" doctrine.[30] In order to prevail under this doctrine, a plaintiff must establish the following elements: (1) that the plaintiff was placed in danger because of the negligence of both the plaintiff and defendant; (2) that the plaintiff was either oblivious to the danger or unable to move from the position of danger; (3) that the defendant was aware or should have been aware of the plaintiff's danger and inability to move from the position of danger; and (4) that the defendant could have avoided injuring the plaintiff but failed to do so.[31] The last clear chance doctrine does not apply to emergencies where there is no time to avoid the injury,[32] nor may the last clear chance doctrine be employed to restore liability of another for a plaintiff's intentional intervening act.[33]

Contributory negligence is not a defense in strict liability cases.[34] While a plaintiff may proceed in a failure to warn case on a negligence or strict liability theory, "the principal benefit to a plaintiff proceeding under a strict liability theory . . . is that a defendant cannot claim contributory negligence as a defense."[35]

2. Comparative Negligence

The District of Columbia does not recognize apportionment of damages based on degrees of fault,[36] and the liability of joint tortfeasors will not be affected by the relative degree of negligence.[37] Thus, in the District of Columbia compensatory damages may not be apportioned among joint tortfeasors.[38] The courts would favor the apportionment of punitive damages among joint tortfeasors, however, reasoning that punitive damages relate to the degree of culpability and the defendant's ability to pay.[39]

3. Assumption of Risk

It is settled in the District of Columbia that the doctrine of assumption of risk is a valid defense which bars a plaintiff's claim of negligence, provided two conditions are met. First, the plaintiff must engage in an activity with knowledge of the risk and full appreciation of its dangers. Second, the plaintiff's decision to incur the known risk must be free and voluntary.[40]

In the usual case, the issue of plaintiff's knowledge and appreciation of the risk will be a question for the jury, and a subjective standard will be applied geared to the particular plaintiff and his or her situation. There are situations, however, where the danger is so patent or well known that, as a matter of law, a plaintiff assumes the risk.[41]

The key to the issue whether the plaintiff's decision to incur the known risk was free and voluntary focuses on the word "voluntary."[42] A plaintiff cannot be held to have voluntarily assumed a known risk where the defendant's tortious conduct has forced upon the plaintiff a choice of two courses of conduct, which leaves plaintiff with no reasonable alternative to taking his or her chances.[43]

Because plaintiff elects to proceed in the face of a known danger, the plaintiff is regarded as having consciously relieved the defendant of any duty which he or she otherwise would have owed to the plaintiff.[44] For this reason, the District of Columbia courts have recognized that the doctrine of assumption of risk may bar recovery even when contributory negligence does not.[45] Thus, assumption of risk by the injured party, if established, is a complete bar to recovery in a strict liability action. In such an action, to establish an assumption of risk, the defendant must show that the plaintiff knew of the specific defect in the product and was aware of the danger arising from it, but nevertheless voluntarily and unreasonably proceeded to use the product.[46] Unlike contributory negligence, the assumption of risk analysis focuses on the plaintiff's actual knowledge; the plaintiff must subjectively know of the existence of the risk and appreciate its unreasonable character.[47]

G. RES IPSA LOQUITUR AND INHERENTLY DANGEROUS ACTIVITIES

1. *Res Ipsa Loquitur*

The doctrine of *res ipsa loquitur* permits the jury to infer a lack of due care from the mere occurrence of an accident.[48] It should be applied with caution in a negligence action so that the mere happening of an accident will not permit the inference of a defendant's liability.[49] *Res ipsa loquitur* may only be invoked where the plaintiff demonstrates that (1) the occurrence is of the kind which ordinarily does not occur in the absence of negligence; (2) it must be caused by an agency or instrumentality within the control (exclusive or joint) of the defendant(s); and (3) it must not have been due to any voluntary action or contribution on the part of the plaintiff.[50]

If a clear distinction is to be preserved between *res ipsa loquitur* and strict liability, the elements of *res ipsa loquitur* must be established with some precision; it will not do to invoke inferences to establish the elements of *res ipsa loquitur* so that a further inference of unproven negligence can be invoked.[51] Thus, it may be invoked only where a lay person can infer negligence as a matter of common knowledge, or where expert testimony is presented that such accidents do not occur in the absence of negligence. Given the power of *res ipsa loquitur* to satisfy without further proof the element of negligence and the caution with which it should be applied, where the plaintiff relies upon common knowledge to invoke the doctrine, the fact that such events ordinarily do not occur in the absence of negligence must be based on a widespread consensus of common understanding.[52]

2. Inherently Dangerous Activities

In the District of Columbia, the general rule is that when someone hires another to do certain work, reserving no control over the work or the workmen, a contractual rather than employment relationship exists, and the contractee is not liable for injuries to a third party resulting from the work of the independent contractor. Where the work performed by the independent contractor is inherently dangerous, however, the duty to use due care becomes non-delegable, and the contractee is subject to liability for harm caused to others by the contractor's failure to take reasonable precautions against the danger.[53]

"Inherently dangerous" work is not limited to work that is intrinsically hazardous.[54] Work that may be safe in some contexts can be inherently dangerous where the contractee has special reason to contemplate a risk of harm under the particular circumstances under which the work is to be done.[55] Whether a particular kind of work is inherently dangerous is essentially a relative determination based upon the facts of the particular case, and the existence of a danger and knowledge of it by the contractee are normally questions of fact for the jury.[56]

H. NEGLIGENCE *PER SE*

To prevail on a negligence *per se* theory, the plaintiff may, in certain circumstances and under specified conditions, rely on a statute or regulation as proof of the applicable standard of care. Proof of an unexplained violation of that standard renders the defendant negligent as a matter of law, so long as the violation was the proximate cause of the injuries and the alleged injuries were of the type which the statute was designed to prevent. If the defendant submits evidence excusing the violation, however, the violation may be considered evidence of negligence rather than negligence *per se*.[57]

The decision to adopt a statute or regulation as a standard of care to be applied in determining common law negligence is a judicial one for the court to make.[58] At a minimum, the statute or regulation relied upon must promote public safety and have been enacted to protect persons in the plaintiff's position or to prevent the type of accident that occurred.[59] The statute or regulation also must impose some specific duties or obligations on the defendant.[60] Moreover, a statute or regulation must not merely repeat the common law duty of reasonable care, but must set forth specific guidelines to govern behavior.[61]

Before admitting statutes and regulations offered for negligence *per se* purposes, a trial judge must examine each law to determine first, whether it in fact established a standard of care, and if so, whether it could be reasonably understood by the jury without expert testimony or guidance by the court. Complex or technical statutes may not be used for negligence *per se* purposes without expert testimony or guidance from the court to assist the jury's understanding.[62] In addition, it is not enough to simply prove a standard of care based on statutes or regulations; where they are beyond the lay juror's ordinary experience, expert testimony is needed to prove a violation of those statutes and regulations.[63]

I. JOINT AND SEVERAL LIABILITY

When two or more tortfeasors jointly contribute to the harm to a plaintiff, the plaintiff may sue each one for the entire harm and hold defendants severally liable, but between themselves, they share equally (*pro rata*) in satisfaction of the judgment through the principle of contribution.[64] In this jurisdiction, the law pertaining to the right of contribution among joint tortfeasors has been established by case precedent rather than by statute.[65]

The District of Columbia long ago abandoned the common law requirement that the defendants have engaged in concerted action to be liable as joint tortfeasors.[66] To be joint tortfeasors, it is sufficient that their independent acts combined to cause a single injury.[67] In cases of successive tortfeasors, where each tortfeasor causes a separate and distinct injury to the same plaintiff, there is no basis for allowing one to recoup a proportionate share from the other for harm to which he or she did not contribute.[68]

When one defendant settles with the plaintiff, and the claim proceeds to verdict against a non-settling defendant, if the settling defendant is judicially determined to be a joint tortfeasor the non-settling defendant is entitled to a *pro rata* credit against the verdict.[69] When the plaintiff has settled with a party whose culpability has not been determined, or with a party whom the finder of fact later finds not to be liable, the court awards the non-settling defendants a credit against the verdict in the amount of the settlement (*pro tanto*).[70]

J. INDEMNITY

In the District of Columbia, indemnity is a form of restitution that involves the shifting of the entire loss from one who has paid it to another who would be unjustly enriched at the indemnitee's expense by the indemnitee's discharge of the obligation.[71] Although the right to indemnity may arise in contract, the courts have recognized that the obligation may be implied in fact, on an implied contract theory; or implied in law, in order to achieve an equitable result.[72] When based upon equitable principles, the application of indemnity to prevent unjust enrichment is limited to situations where the indemnitee's conduct is not as blameworthy as that of the indemnitor.[73] Even a joint tortfeasor may be entitled to indemnity where equity and justice so require, as in situations where the aggravation of an initial injury by negligent failure to treat it results in a much more serious injury.[74] Similarly, where a breach of warranty exposes a retailer to liability in circumstances where its fault lay only in failing to discover and correct a defect created by the manufacturer, upon whose skill and expertise the retailer reasonably relied, it is equitable to shift the burden of loss entirely to the manufacturer.[75]

A prerequisite to an equitable indemnity claim is that the party seeking it must have discharged the liability for the party against whom it is sought.[76] Whether the indemnitee has discharged the liability of the indemnitor turns on (1) whether the settlement is made and accepted as full satisfaction or merely as the best obtainable compromise for the settler's liability, and (2) whether the release was intended to release only the party named in the release or all others.[77]

K. BAR OF WORKERS' COMPENSATION STATUTE

It is undisputed that when an employee is injured or killed in the course of employment, the workers' compensation remedy is the exclusive remedy available to the employee.[78] The workers' compensation bar is, however, limited to actions at law for damages, and does not bar actions by an employee seeking injunctive relief to enforce the provisions of his or her employment contract.[79]

L. PREMISES LIABILITY

Under District of Columbia law, a property owner has a duty to keep his or her property in a reasonably safe condition, and to inspect the land and warn of any obvious dangers. Nevertheless, a landowner is not an insurer for the safety of others, and one who enters upon property also has a duty to exercise ordinary care for his or her own safety.[80]

The District of Columbia does not recognize varying standards of care depending upon the relationship of the parties but always requires reasonable care to be exercised under all the circumstances by an owner or occupier of land to those lawfully upon the premises.[81] Thus, the distinctions between the duties owed to licensees, social guests and business invitees have been eliminated in favor of one standard, that of reasonable care under all the circumstances.[82] A landlord is liable for dangerous conditions that are discoverable in the exercise of ordinary care, and the exercise of ordinary care may encompass a duty to conduct an inspection that would uncover a defect. Whether an inspection is required in a given case is a question of fact; appropriate considerations on which the jury should be instructed include the nature of the danger involved, and the foreseeability of the harm.[83]

The common law rule as to trespassers remains the law in the District of Columbia. A trespasser cannot hold the landowner to liability based on negligence in failing to make the premises safe. Recovery is only allowed for intentional, wanton or willful injury or the maintenance of a hidden engine of destruction.[84] The district recognizes the attractive nuisance doctrine as an exception to the general rule of landowner liability to trespassers, and the courts have adopted the formulation found in the Restatement (Second) of Torts, § 339.[85]

M. DRAM SHOP LIABILITY

The District of Columbia has no Dram Shop Act, nor does it recognize the "social host" doctrine.[86] In 1973, the United States Court of Appeals for the District of Columbia Circuit held, on a negligence *per se* theory, that the District's laws governing the sale of alcoholic beverages support an implied cause of action against a tavern-keeper who violates those laws, which among other things prohibits the sale of alcoholic beverages to intoxicated persons.[87] In 1978, a District of Columbia Superior Court held that the federal Court of Appeals misperceived the legislative purpose of the statute, and found that rather than being intended to ensure public safety, the statute (first enacted in the years immediately following the repeal of Prohibition) was meant as a licensing regulation aimed at promoting public morality.[88] Although the latter view was adopted by the federal Court of Appeals in 1986,[89] in the following year the District of Columbia Court of Appeals rejected that approach.[90] Most recently, the District of Columbia Court of Appeals held that "the Alcoholic Beverage Control Act has a public safety purpose, and that its unexcused violation therefore constitutes negligence *per se, i.e.,* breach of the duty of care that tavern keepers owe to the public. Thus, when members of the public allege . . . that the tavern keeper's negligence was the legal cause of their injuries, they state a cause of action under District of Columbia law."[91] So long as the injury suffered by the plaintiff is of the general type that the statute was intended to prevent, it is immaterial whether the plaintiff is the intoxicated patron or a third party injured by an intoxicated patron.[92]

N. ECONOMIC LOSS

The economic loss rule prohibits the plaintiff from recovering *in tort* for purely economic losses, *i.e.*, losses that involve neither a clear danger of physical injury or death and there is no damage to other property.[93] The District of Columbia has not expressly adopted or rejected the economic loss doctrine. While the courts may bar third parties from recovering purely economic losses in the absence of contractual privity under certain circumstances, such determinations are made on a case-by-case basis.

In cases involving negligent performance of a contract, the district courts hold that lack of contractual privity bars recovery of purely economic losses.[94] The liability to third parties that suffer only economic loss as a result of negligence depends on whether or not the defendant owed a duty or reasonable care to the plaintiff.[95] If there was no duty owed, the lack of contractual privity normally bars recovery.[96]

O. FRAUD AND MISREPRESENTATION

To prove fraud, a plaintiff must show by clear and convincing evidence that there is a false representation of material fact which is knowingly made with the intent to deceive, and action is taken in reliance on the misrepresentation.[97] To be actionable the false representation must be material.[98]

P. CONSUMER FRAUD STATUTES

The District of Columbia Consumer Protection Procedures Act[99] is intended to assure that a just mechanism exists to remedy all improper trade practices; to promote through effective enforcement fair business practices throughout the community; and to educate consumers to demand high standards and seek proper redress of grievances.[100] It is a comprehensive statute with an extensive regulatory framework, intended to protect consumers against an extensive list of specifically enumerated unlawful trade practices,[101] as well as practices prohibited by other statutes and common law.[102] The Act empowers agency investigation and regulation of businesses,[103] establishes consumer complaint procedures,[104] and allows for civil actions for multiple damages and fees.[105] Because statutes in derogation of the common law are interpreted strictly, however, a claim under the Act for an enumerated offense that also is a common law tort carries the same burden of proof as at common law. Thus, since at common law a clear and convincing standard is required to prove intentional misrepresentation, pursuing such a claim under the Act does not mean that a lower burden of proof applies.[106]

Q. PUNITIVE DAMAGES

In the District, punitive damages generally are recoverable, but are disfavored.[107] In order to recover, "the defendant must commit a tortious act accompanied by fraud, ill will, recklessness, wantonness, oppressiveness, willful disregard of the plaintiff's right, or other circumstances tending to aggravate the injury . . . the plaintiff must prove, by a preponderance of the evidence, that the defendant committed a tortious act, and by clear and convincing evidence, that the act was accompanied by conduct and a state of mind evincing malice or its equivalent."[108]

An award of punitive damages must be accompanied by an award of compensatory damages.[109]

Punitive damages will not be awarded for breach of contract, even if the breach is proven to be willful, wanton or malicious.[110] The only recognized narrow exception to this rule in the District is "where the alleged breach of contract merges with, and assumes the character of a willful tort."[111]

R. WRONGFUL DEATH AND SURVIVORSHIP ACTIONS

The Wrongful Death Act provides for a separate cause of action for the sole benefit of the spouse and the next of kin of the deceased person to recover compensable losses as a result of the decedent's death.[112] The injury causing the death must have occurred in the District of Columbia.[113]

The Wrongful Death Act allows for recovery of (1) pecuniary losses, calculated as the annual share of decedent's dependents in the decedent's earnings, multiplied by the decedent's work life expectancy, and discounted to present value, and; (2) compensation for the value of the services lost to the family as a result of the decedent's death.[114] The Wrongful Death Act does not allow for recovery for grief, loss of consortium or mental suffering.

On the death of a person in whose favor or against whom a right of action has accrued for any cause prior to his death, the right of action, for all such cases, survives in favor of or against the legal representative of the deceased.[115] Damages for the decedent's pain and suffering are recoverable, pursuant to the 1978 amendment to the statute. A claim of loss of consortium is not encompassed by the Survival Act.[116] Recovery under the Survival Act is limited to that which the deceased would have recovered had he lived.[117]

Robert N. Kelly
JACKSON & CAMPBELL, P.C.
1120 20th Street N.W.
Suite 300-South
Washington, D.C. 20036
(202) 457-1647
Fax (202) 457-1678
rkelly@jackscamp.com
www.jackscamp.com

ENDNOTES – DISTRICT OF COLUMBIA

1. D.C. Code Ann. §§ 12-301, 311 (1995 Repl. Vol.), § 5-521.03 (2001).

2. D.C. Code Ann. § 12-301 (2001).

3. D.C. Code Ann. § 28:2-725 (2001).

4. D.C. Code Ann. § 12-301 (2001).

5. D.C. Code Ann. § 12-310 (2001).

6. *Bussineau v. President & Dirs. of Georgetown College*, 518 A.2d 423, 425 (D.C. 1986).

7. *Mullin v. Washington Free Weekly, Inc.*, 2001 WL 1402029 (Nov. 8, 2001); *Ray v. Queen*, 747 A.2d 1137, 1141 (D.C. App. 2000).

8. *Morton v. National Medical Enterprises, Inc.*, 725 A.2d 462, 468 (D.C. 1999).

9. *Id.*

10. *Id.*

11. D.C. Code §§ 35-2401, *et seq.* (2001).

12. D.C. Code § 35-2404 (2001).

13. *Id.*

14. D.C. Code § 35-2405 (2001).

15. *State Farm Mutual Ins. Co. v. Hoang*, 682 A.2d 202, 207 (D.C. 1996).

16. *Haynesworth v. D.H. Stevens Co.*, 645 A.2d 1095, 1098 (D.C. 1994).

17. *Meek v. Shepard*, 484 A.2d 579 (D.C. 1984).

18. *District of Columbia v. Arnold & Porter*, 756 A.2d 427 (D.C. App. 2000); *see Plummer v. District of Columbia Bd. of Funeral Dirs.*, 730 A.2d 159 (D.C. 1999); *Phillips v. District of Columbia*, 714 A.2d 768 (D.C. 1998).

19. *See White v. United States*, 692 A.2d 1365 (D.C. 1997); Standard Civil Jury Instructions for the District of Columbia, No. 5-7 (Revised ed. 1998).

20. *See Sebastian v. District of Columbia*, 636 A.2d 958, 962 (D.C. 1993).

21. *McKethean v. Washington Metropolitan Transit Authority*, 588 A.2d 708, 716 (D.C. 1991), quoting *S.S. Kresge Co. v. Kenney*, 86 F.2d 651 (D.C. Cir. 1936), which itself was quoting *Goodlander Mill Co. v. Standard Oil Co.*, 63 F. 400 (7th Cir. 1894).

22. *Lacy v. District of Columbia*, 424 A.2d 317, 323 (D.C. 1980). An "intervening" act which breaks the chain of causation is what the Restatement (Second) of Torts § 440 calls a "superceding cause." *McKethean v. Washington Metropolitan Transit Authority*, 588 A.2d 708, 716 n.9 (D.C. 1991).

23. *Id.*, quoting *Lacy v. District of Columbia*, 424 A.2d 317, 321 (D.C. 1980).

24. *McKethean v. Washington Metropolitan Transit Authority*, 588 A.2d 708, 716-17 (D.C. 1991).

25. *Id.* at 717; *see also Cook v. Safeway Stores, Inc.*, 354 A.2d 507, 509-10 (D.C. 1976).

26. *Ferrell v. Rosenbaum*, 691 A.2d 641, 650 (D.C. 1997).

27. *Id.*

28. *Wingfield v. People's Drug Store*, 379 A.2d 685, 687 (D.C. 1977).

29. *Scoggins v. Jude*, 419 A.2d 999, 1004 (D.C. 1980).

30. *Washington Metro. Area Transit Auth. v. Johnson*, 726 A.2d 172 (D.C. 1999); *District of Columbia v. Huysman*, 650 A.2d 1323, 1326 (D.C. 1994).

31. *District of Columbia v. Huysman*, 650 A.2d 1323, 1326 (D.C. 1994).

32. *Id.*

33. *Washington Metro. Area Transit Auth. v. Johnson*, 726 A.2d 172 (D.C. 1999).

34. *Jarrett v. Woodward Bros.*, 751 A.2d 972 (D.C. App. 2000); *East Penn Mfg. Co. v. Pineda*, 578 A.2d 1113, 1118 (D.C. 1990); *Warner Fruehauf Trailer Co. v. Boston*, 654 A.2d 1272, 1274-75 (D.C. 1995).

35. *McNeil Pharmaceutical v. Hawkins*, 686 A.2d 567, 578 (D.C. 1996), *cert. denied*, 118 S. Ct. 63 (1997).

36. *Washington Metro. Area Transit Auth. v. Johnson*, 726 A.2d 172 (D.C. 1999).

37. *Hill v. McDonald*, 442 A.2d 133, 137 (D.C. 1982).

38. *Remeikis v. Boss & Phelps*, 419 A.2d 986, 992 n. 4 (D.C. 1980).

39. *Id.*

40. *Breheny v. The Catholic University of America*, 1989 U.S. Dist. LEXIS 14029 (Nov. 22, 1989).

41. *Id.*

42. *Id.*

43. *Kanelos v. Kettler*, 406 F.2d 951, 955 (D.C. Cir. 1968).

44. *Sinai v. Polinger Co.*, 498 A.2d 520, 524 (D.C. 1985).

45. *Washington Metro. Area Transit Auth. v. Johnson*, 726 A.2d 172, 175 (D.C. 1999).

46. *Warner Fruehauf Trailer Co. v. Boston*, 654 A.2d 1272, 1274-75 (D.C. 1995).

47. *Jarrett v. Woodward Bros.*, 751 A.2d 972 (D.C. App. 2000); *Sinai v. Polinger Co.*, 498 A.2d 520, 524 (D.C. 1985); *Payne v. Soft Sheen Products, Inc.*, 486 A.2d 712, 721-22 n.9 (D.C. 1985).

48. *Otis Elevator Co. v. Henderson*, 514 A.2d 784 (D.C. 1986).

49. *Washington Sheraton Corp. v. Keeter*, 239 A.2d 620 (D.C. 1968).

50. *Otis Elevator Co. v. Tuerr*, 616 A.2d 1254, 1258 (D.C. 1992).

51. *Hailey v. Otis Elevator Co.*, 636 A.2d 426, 429 (D.C. 1994).

52. *Id.* at 428.

53. *W. M. Schlosser Co., Inc. v. Maryland Drywall Co., Inc.*, 673 A.2d 647, 651 (D.C. 1996).

54. *District of Columbia v. Howell*, 607 A.2d 501, 505 (D.C. 1992).

55. *Levy v. Currier*, 587 A.2d 205, 209 (D.C. 1991), *quoting* Restatement (Second) of Torts § 427, comment b (1965).

56. *Fry v. Diamond Construction, Inc.*, 659 A.2d 241, 249 (D.C. 1995).

57. *McNeil Pharmaceutical v. Hawkins*, 686 A.2d 567 (D.C. 1996).

58. *Rong Yao Zhou v. Jennifer Mall Restaurant, Inc.*, 534 A.2d 1268 (D.C. 1987); *Lewis v. Washington Metro. Area Transit Auth.*, 463 A.2d 666 (D.C. 1983).

59. *Joy v. Bell Helicopter Textron, Inc.*, 999 F.2d 549 (D.C. Cir. 1993).

60. *District of Columbia v. White*, 442 A.2d 159 (D.C. 1982).

61. *See, e.g., Chadbourne v. Kappaz*, 779 A.2d 293, 296 (D.C. 2001); *Thoma v. Kettler Bros.*, 632 A.2d 725 (D.C. 1993).

62. *McNeil Pharmaceutical v. Hawkins*, 686 A.2d 567 (D.C. 1996).

63. *Id.*

64. *National Health Laboratories, Inc. v. Ahmadi*, 596 A.2d 555, 557 (D.C. 1991); *Leiken v. Wilson*, 445 A.2d 993, 999 (D.C. 1982).

65. *District of Columbia v. Washington Hospital Center*, 722 A.2d 332 (D.C. 1998).

66. *Hill v. McDonald*, 442 A.2d 133 (D.C. 1982).

67. *District of Columbia v. Washington Hospital Center*, 722 A.2d 332 (D.C. 1998).

68. *Id.*

69. *Berg v. Footer*, 673 A.2d 1244 (D.C. 1996); *see also Logan v. Providence Hospital, Inc.*, 778 A.2d 275 (2001); *Paul v. Bier*, 758 A.2d 40 (D.C. App. 2000).

70. *Id.*

71. *R. & G. Orthopedic Appliances v. Curtin*, 596 A.2d 530 (D.C. 1991).

72. *Id.*

73. *District of Columbia v. Washington Hospital Center*, 722 A.2d 332 (D.C. 1998). Earlier cases relied upon the "active/passive" or "primary/secondary" dichotomy, where if one tortfeasor's negligence is secondary or passive, the passive tortfeasor is entitled to indemnification from the active tortfeasor. *See Williams v. Steuart Motor Co.*, 494 F.2d 1074 (1974). More recent decisions have criticized the "active/passive" standard as indefinite and hence less than meaningful guideposts in the award of equitable indemnification. *East Penn Manufacturing Co. v. Pineda*, 578 A.2d 1113, 1127 n.20 (D.C. 1990).

74. *Id.*

75. *East Penn Manufacturing Co. v. Pineda*, 578 A.2d 1113, 1126-27 (D.C. 1990).

76. *Cokas v. Perkins*, 252 F. Supp. 563 (D.D.C. 1966).

77. *Lamphier v. Washington Hosp. Ctr.*, 524 A.2d 729 (D.C. 1987).

78. D.C. Code § 32-1504 (2001); *Hicks v. Allegheny East Conference Association of Seventh-Day Adventists, Inc.*, 712 A.2d 1021, 1022 (D.C. 1999).

79. *Id.*

80. *Breheny v. The Catholic University of America*, 1989 U.S. Dist. LEXIS 14029 (Nov. 22, 1989).

81. *Holland v. Baltimore & Ohio R.R. Co.*, 431 A.2d 597, 599 (D.C. 1981)(*en banc*).

82. *Sandoe v. Lefta Associates*, 559 A.2d 732, 742 (D.C. 1988).

83. *Id.* at 743.

84. *Lacy v. Sutton Place Condominium Association, Inc.*, 684 A.2d 390, 393 (D.C. 1996).

85. *Holland v. Baltimore & Ohio R.R. Co.*, 431 A.2d 597, 601-02 (D.C. 1981)(*en banc*).

86. *See Cartwright v. Hyatt Corp.*, 460 F. Supp. 80 (D.D.C. 1978).

87. *Marusa v. District of Columbia*, 484 F.2d 828 (D.C. Cir. 1973).

88. *Clevenger v. District of Columbia*, Civil No. 2969-76, 106 Daily Wash. Law Rptr. 1561 (1978).

89. *Norwood v. Marrocco*, 780 F.2d 110 (D.C. Cir. 1986).

90. *Zhou v. Jennifer Mall Restaurant, Inc.*, 534 A.2d 1268 (D.C. 1987).

91. *Wadley v. Aspillaga*, 163 F. Supp. 2d 1, 9-10 (D.D.C. 2001); *Jarrett v. Woodward Bros., Inc.*, 751 A.2d 972, 978 (D.C. 2000).

92. Compare *Zhou*, *supra* note 90, and *Jarrett*, *supra* note 91.

93. *See, e.g., Morris v. Osmose Wood Preserving*, 667 A.2d 624, 631 (Md. 1995).

94. *Aronoff v. Lenkin Co.*, 618 A.2d 669, 685 (D.C. 1992).

95. *Id.* at 685.

96. *Id.; see also Bowler v. Stewart-Warner Corp.*, 563 A.2d 344, 355 (D.C. 1989) (the court declined to rule, recognizing that the states are split whether the economic losses are recoverable under strict tort liability).

97. *Lund v. Watergate Investors Limited Partnership*, 728 A.2d 77, 86 (D.C. 1999); *Pyne v. Jamaice Nutrition Holdings, Ltd.*, 497 A.2d 118, 131 (D.C. 1985).

98. *Howard v. Riggs Nat'l Bank*, 432 A.2d 701, 706-07 (D.C. 1981).

99. D.C. Code §§ 28-3901 *et seq.* (2001).

100. D.C. Code § 28-3901(b) (2001).

101. D.C. Code § 28-3904 (2001).

102. *Atwater v. District of Columbia Dep't of Consumer & Regulatory Affairs*, 566 A.2d 462 (D.C. 1989).

103. D.C. Code §§ 28-3902, 3903 (2001).

104. D.C. Code § 28-3905 (2001).

105. D.C. Code § 28-3905(k)(1) (2001).

106. *Osbourne v. Capital City Mortgage Corp.*, 727 A.2d 322 (D.C. 1999).

107. *Jonathan Woodner Co. v. Breden*, 665 A.2d 929, 938 (D.C. 1995), *cert. denied*, 117 S. Ct. 1080 (1997).

108. *Id.*

109. *Bernstein v. Fernandez*, 649 A.2d 1064, 1073 (D.C. 1991).

110. *Id.; see also Sere v. Group Hospitalization, Inc.*, 443 A.2d 33, 37 (D.C. 1982), *cert. denied*, 459 U.S. 912 (1982).

111. *Id.*

112. D.C. Code § 16-2701 (1997 Repl. Vol.).

113. *Perry v. Criss Bros. Iron Works, Inc.*, 741 F. Supp. 985, 986 (D.D.C. 1990).

114. *Doe v. Binker*, 492 A.2d 857, 863 (D.C. 1985).

115. D.C. Code § 12-101 (1995 Repl. Vol.).

116. *Bonan v. Washington Hosp. Center*, 119 Daily Wash. L. Rep. 1685, 1992 (D.C. Super. Ct. Aug. 9, 1991).

117. *Graves v. United States*, 517 F. Supp. 95, 99 (D.D.C. 1981).

FLORIDA

A. STATUTES OF LIMITATION

A legal or equitable action on a contract, obligation or liability founded on a written instrument must be commenced within five years.[1] Causes of action founded on negligent, intentional, or tortious conduct causing personal injuries or property damage must be brought within four years.[2] Causes of action founded on a statutory liability,[3] those based on fraud,[4] and those based on a contract, obligation or liability not founded on a written instrument, including an action for the sale and delivery of nonconforming goods and merchandise under the Uniform Commercial Code,[5] must also be commenced within four years.

An action for injury to a person founded on the design, manufacture, distribution, or sale of personal property that is not permanently incorporated in an improvement to real property, including fixtures, must be commenced within four years of the accrual of the cause of action.[6]

Claims for injury or damage brought against the State of Florida, its agencies and its subdivisions, including counties and municipalities, must be commenced within four years after such claim accrues, unless based upon medical malpractice, which must be commenced within two years.[7] As a condition precedent to suit against the state, its agencies and subdivisions, notice of the claim must first be presented in writing to the appropriate agency and, in cases against a municipality, to the Florida Department of Insurance within three years after the claim accrues.[8]

Causes of action for wrongful death[9] and for libel and slander[10] must be brought within two years of the incident giving rise to the cause of action. Causes of action brought by those in privity based upon professional negligence, other than medical or dental malpractice, must be brought within two years from the time the cause of action is discovered or should have been discovered in the exercise of due diligence.[11] A nearly identical statute of limitations applies to actions against nursing homes for alleged abuse or neglect of residents.[12]

Actions involving medical or dental malpractice by those in privity must generally be brought within two years from the time the incident giving rise to the action occurred or within two years from the time the incident is or should have been discovered, but in no event later than four years from the date of the incident or occurrence out of which the cause of action accrued.[13] However, if the claimant demonstrates that the defendant's fraud, concealment, or intentional misrepresentation of fact prevented the discovery of the injury, then the period of limitations is extended for two additional years, but in no event to exceed a total of seven years from the date the incident giving rise to the injury occurred.[14]

The limitations periods provided for by statute run from the time "the cause of action accrues."[15] A cause of action is generally deemed to "accrue" when the last element constituting the cause of action occurs.[16] Generally, a cause of action for negligence is not deemed to accrue until the existence of a redressable harm or injury has been established and the injured party knows or should know of either the injury or the negligent act.[17] Absent a statutory provision to the contrary, the Florida courts will apply the "delayed discovery doctrine" in determining when a cause of action accrues for purposes of the limitations period.[18]

In an action for fraud, while it is necessary that all elements of the cause of action must exist before the cause of action accrues, the four-year limitations period will commence to run when the plaintiff has notice of a possible invasion of his or her legal rights, and it is not necessary that plaintiff have notice of all elements of the cause of action.[19] A 12-year statute of repose applies to actions based upon fraud, calculated from the date of the commission of the alleged fraud, regardless of the date the fraud was or should have been discovered.[20]

The "continuing repairs," "continuous treatment," and "continuing negotiations" doctrines have been found not to "toll" the running of the statute of limitations in most circumstances.[21] The limitations period may, however, be "tolled" in certain circumstances which are specifically delineated by statute,[22] including absence from the state of the person to be sued,[23] concealment in the state by the person to be sued,[24] use by the person to be sued of a false name unknown to the plaintiff,[25] payment of any part of the principal or interest of any obligation or liability founded on a written instrument,[26] and the pendency of any arbitral proceeding pertaining to a dispute that is the subject of the action.[27]

In 1975, Florida enacted a twelve year products liability statute of repose, which was later repealed in 1986.[28] However, it has been held that if twelve years elapsed from the date of the delivery of the product to its initial purchaser during the period of time that the statute of repose was still in force and effect, then the manufacturer gained a vested right not to be sued, even if an accident occurred following the repeal of the repose statute.[29]

In 1999, a new twelve-year products liability statute of repose was enacted, with the repose period being calculated from the date the product was delivered to the initial end user or lessee.[30] The statute conclusively presumes that most products have an expected useful life of ten years or less.[31] However, if the manufacturer, through express representation or labeling, specifically warranted the product to have an expected useful life in excess of ten years, then the repose period is extended to be commensurate with the period of the representation or warranty, or twelve years, whichever is later.[32] The new statute of repose does not apply if the claimant was exposed to or used the product within the repose period, but an injury caused by such exposure or use did not manifest itself until after expiration of the repose period.[33]

A 15-year statute of repose applies to actions arising out of the design, planning, or construction of improvements to real property, calculated from the latest of the date of the owner's actual possession of the property, the issuance of a certificate of occupancy for the improvement, or the abandonment of the project if not completed.[34]

B. TORT REFORM

During its 1999 session, Florida's legislature enacted a broad range of laws containing significant changes in the State's existing statutory and common law tort system. The new laws became effective on October 1, 1999 and should for the most part create a much more favorable business atmosphere in Florida for defendants in general and especially for commercial enterprises such as product manufacturers, employers, and rental car companies doing business in this state.[35]

The existing statute governing comparative fault and joint and several liability was completely rewritten to limit even further the applicability of the doctrine of joint and several liability.[36] The existing statutes governing the assessment of punitive damages in civil cases have been amended in several significant ways, including raising the standard of proof to "clear and convincing evidence," placing lowered maximum caps upon punitive damage awards, and the inclusion of the "one time punishment rule."[37]

In the area of products liability, the 1999 legislation re-enacted in different form a previously repealed 12-year products liability statute of repose.[38] A new statute was enacted which creates rebuttable presumptions based upon compliance or lack of compliance with governmental safety standards in effect at the time of a product's manufacture.[39] The legislature also enacted a statute which provides for a "state of the art" defense in cases involving alleged design defects in products.[40]

A significant change was also wrought by the 1999 legislature in the area of vicarious liability under the common law dangerous instrumentality doctrine.[41] Under the new law, dangerous instrumentality vicarious liability imposed upon lessors and natural persons has been limited to $100,000 per person and $300,000 per accident, provided that the vehicle operator has at least $500,000 in liability coverage.[42] The limitations on the extent of the owner's liability are not, however, applicable to vehicles that are used for commercial activity in the owner's ordinary course of business.[43]

The 1999 reforms included enactment of a new statute which provides for a presumption against negligent hiring when it is shown that the employer followed a five-step screening process specified in the new statute.[44] The legislature also amended the existing statute to broaden the qualified immunity granted to employers who disclose information to others concerning past or existing employees.[45]

The 1999 reforms additionally included enactment of a new statute which creates a presumption against liability in favor of convenience stores in situations involving harm to invitees caused by criminal acts on their premises if the convenience store has implemented certain security measures.[46] Another enactment limited the common law liability of owners and possessors of real property to discovered and undiscovered trespassers.[47]

In 2001, the legislature overhauled the statutes governing the operation of nursing homes in this state on two fronts.[48] First, the legislature adopted many new administrative requirements, standards, and enforcement provisions aimed at improving the level of care to residents. Secondly, the legislature tried to address a "nursing home litigation crisis" by adopting provisions aimed at discouraging frivolous lawsuits and restricting unbridled punitive damage verdicts.[49]

C. "NO FAULT" LIMITATIONS

The Florida Motor Vehicle No-Fault Law[50] ("No-Fault Law") controls the method of compensation for injuries resulting from motor vehicle accidents. The No Fault Law mandates that owners and operators of motor vehicles maintain a specified minimal level of Personal Injury Protection (PIP) insurance. In exchange for carrying the required minimum level of PIP insurance, the motor vehicle owner, operator, and anyone else legally responsible for the operator's negligence are granted a limited tort immunity.[51]

An integral part of Florida's no-fault concept is the so-called "tort threshold." In any action brought against the owner, registered operator, or occupant of a motor vehicle insured under the No-Fault Law, or against any person or organization legally responsible for the acts or omissions of such person, the plaintiff may recover tort damages for pain, suffering, mental anguish, and inconvenience *only if* the injury involves: (a) significant and permanent loss of an important bodily function; (b) permanent injury within a reasonable degree of medical probability, other than scarring or disfigurement; (c) significant and permanent scarring or disfigurement; or (d) death.[52] Although not specifically mentioned in the statute, the limited tort immunity under the No Fault Law has been extended to preclude the recovery of generalized, non-economic damages for disability, disfigurement, and loss of capacity for the enjoyment of life.[53]

Permanency must be established by expert medical testimony.[54] Even if the defendant presents no directly contrary medical testimony, the jury is not required to accept the medical testimony presented by the plaintiff if the evidence otherwise places the credibility of the plaintiff or the plaintiff's expert's opinions in issue.[55] In a few isolated cases, however, it has been found that a directed verdict in favor of the plaintiff on the permanency issue was appropriate.[56]

A claimant who does not reach the tort threshold is nonetheless still entitled to recover from the tortfeasor the 20 percent of past medical expenses and the 40 percent of lost income that is not payable under the PIP coverage.[57]

The tortfeasor is also responsible for past medical expenses and lost wages that exceed the statutory $10,000 PIP limits.[58] Lastly, the tortfeasor can in appropriate cases be held liable for future medical expenses and loss of earnings even without a finding that the plaintiff sustained a permanent injury.[59]

D. THE STANDARD FOR NEGLIGENCE

The elements necessary to establish a cause of action based upon negligence are: (1) the existence of a duty, or obligation, recognized by law, requiring the defendant to conform to a certain standard of conduct for the protection of others against foreseeable and unreasonable risks of harm; (2) a failure on the defendant's part to conform to that standard; (3) the defendant's breach of duty was both an actual and a proximate cause of the plaintiff's injury; and (4) the plaintiff suffered legally cognizable damages as a result of the actor's breach of duty.[60]

The initial question of whether the defendant owed a duty to the plaintiff to conform to a certain standard of conduct for the plaintiff's benefit is a question of law for the court to decide.[61] In general, where a defendant's conduct creates a foreseeable zone of risk, the courts will recognize a duty placed upon the defendant to either lessen the risk or see that sufficient precautions are taken to protect others from the type of harm that the risk poses.[62]

The existence of a duty owed by the defendant to the plaintiff has been found to exist by the Florida courts: (1) as a result of a legislative enactment or administrative regulation;[63] (2) as a result of the existence of a special relationship between the plaintiff and the defendant or between the defendant and the tortfeasor;[64] (3) as a result of a voluntary undertaking by the defendant;[65] (4) as a result of the defendant being engaged in an activity which by its nature presents a foreseeable and unreasonable risk of harm to the public at large if not performed in a careful fashion;[66] and (5) as a result of the defendant performing a "professional service" which, if not performed with due care, the defendant reasonably knew or should have known would likely result in foreseeable injury or economic damage to the person or entity for whose ultimate benefit the service was being performed.[67]

While no general duty of care is imposed upon the defendant to prevent misconduct by third parties which endangers the plaintiff,[68] the rule is otherwise if certain conditions are met.[69] A duty to exercise reasonable care to control the conduct of third parties will be found to exist where: (1) the defendant has the right or the ability to control either the conduct of the third party;[70] the instrumentality utilized by the third party in committing the tort,[71] or the premises upon which the tort is committed;[72] and (2) the defendant has actual or constructive knowledge that a failure to exercise such control presents a foreseeable risk of harm to individuals such as the plaintiff.[73]

A child under six years of age is conclusively presumed to be incapable of committing contributory negligence.[74] A child of age six and above, however, is subject to the general rules of negligence, with the child's conduct being judged by that standard of care which should reasonably be expected of a child of like age, mental capacity, intelligence, training and experience.[75] If a child of six years of age or older is engaged in an activity which is typically considered to be an "adult" activity such as the operation of a motor scooter or automobile, then the child will likely be held to an "adult" standard of care.[76]

A breach of duty occurs when the defendant fails to exercise reasonable care, that is, the defendant either does something that a reasonably careful person would not do under like circumstances or fails to do something that a reasonably careful person would do under like circumstances.[77] The standard of care which the defendant owed to the plaintiff will be formulated and defined in the context of the defendant's status and relationship to the plaintiff with respect to the accident at issue (*i.e.*, an ordinary person, a physician, a professional, etc.).[78] The jury will not ordinarily be instructed that one is presumed to have exercised reasonable care for his own safety or for the safety of others.[79]

Whether the defendant has breached the applicable legal duty is almost always a question for the jury to decide.[80]

E. CAUSATION

Florida follows the general rule that to establish the element of "causation" the plaintiff bears the burden of proving that the defendant's act or omission was both a "cause-in-fact" and a "proximate cause" of injury or damage to the plaintiff.[81] As to the former, the plaintiff must establish at a minimum that "but for" the defendant's act or omission, no injury or damage would have been sustained.[82]

In situations involving multiple causes combining either at the same time or in succession to cause an accident, the defendant remains responsible so long as his or her act or omission is found to be a "substantial contributing cause" of the ultimate outcome, and the other concurring or intervening causes were "reasonably foreseeable" in a broad sense.[83] In order for an accident or an injury to be a "foreseeable consequence" of the defendant's act or omission, it is not necessary, however, that the defendant be able to foresee the exact nature and extent of the injuries or the precise manner in which the injuries occur. Rather, all that is necessary for liability to arise is that the tortfeasor be able to foresee that *some injury* will likely result in *some manner* as a consequence of his or her act or omission.[84]

Although issues of causation are for the jury to determine in the vast majority of cases, Florida courts have on occasion refused to attach tort liability for results which, although caused-in-fact by the defendant's negligent acts or omissions, were deemed in hindsight to be highly unusual, extraordinary, bizarre, or, stated differently, seem to be beyond the scope of any fair assessment of the danger created by the defendant.[85]

F. CONTRIBUTORY NEGLIGENCE, COMPARATIVE NEGLIGENCE, AND ASSUMPTION OF RISK

1. Contributory Negligence

By both case law[86] and later by statute,[87] the defense of contributory negligence is no longer an absolute bar to claims based upon theories of negligence, strict liability, products liability, professional malpractice whether couched in terms of contract or tort, or breach of warranty and like theories.[88] A defendant may still argue, however, that the plaintiff's contributory negligence was the *sole* proximate cause of the injury or damages.[89]

2. Comparative Negligence

Florida follows a "pure comparative fault" system under which any contributory fault chargeable to the claimant diminishes proportionately the amount awarded as economic and noneconomic damages for an injury attributable to the claimant's contributory fault, but does not bar recovery.[90] A claimant's failure to wear an available and operational seatbelt is a species of comparative negligence that will reduce recovery.[91] A defendant accused of committing an intentional tort cannot assert the claimant's comparative negligence as a defense.[92]

3. Assumption of Risk

The common law defense of implied assumption of risk is no longer available to bar an action, but instead has merged into Florida's comparative negligence scheme and is to be treated merely as one form of comparative negligence.[93] On the other hand, the defense of express assumption of risk is still an available defense in limited circumstances to bar an action, including cases involving express contractual waivers and situations where the claimant is participating in certain sports events or similar activities *and* is shown to have knowingly and voluntarily assumed the risk of injury arising from specific dangers and risks associated with that activity.[94]

For the defense to apply, it must be demonstrated that the claimant knew of the existence of the danger complained of; realized and appreciated the possibility of injury as a result of such danger; and, having a reasonable opportunity to avoid it, voluntarily and deliberately exposed himself or herself to the danger complained of.[95] This is usually a jury question.[96]

G. *RES IPSA LOQUITUR* AND INHERENTLY DANGEROUS ACTIVITIES

1. *Res Ipsa Loquitur*

The common law doctrine of *res ipsa loquitur* applies only in rare instances in Florida. In order to be entitled to the benefit of the doctrine, the plaintiff bears the burden of submitting proof which reasonably establishes: (1) that the instrumentality causing the injury was in the exclusive control of the defendant; and (2) that the event causing the injury is of the kind that would not, in the ordinary course of human experience, have occurred without negligence on the part of the one in control of the instrumentality.[97]

The plaintiff is not required to eliminate with certainty all other possible explanations, causes or inferences.[98] All that is required is evidence from which reasonable persons can say that on the whole it is more likely that there was negligence associated with the cause of the event than that there was not.[99]

The court makes the initial determination of whether the proof adduced satisfies this minimal threshold showing.[100] If the court determines that the threshold has been satisfied, then the jury is instructed that it may infer that the defendant was negligent unless, taking into consideration all of the evidence in the case, it concludes that the occurrence was not due to any negligence on the part of the defendant.[101]

2. Inherently Dangerous Activities

The concept of "inherently dangerous activities" typically arises in the context of cases involving the issue of whether, contrary to the general rule, a principal will be held responsible to third parties for injuries or damage caused by the negligence of an independent contractor.[102] In Florida, an activity is inherently dangerous where the danger inheres in the performance of the work; and it is sufficient if there is a recognizable and substantial danger inherent in the work, even though a major hazard is not involved.[103] Inherently dangerous activity is of such a nature that in the ordinary course of events its performance would probably, and not merely possibly, cause injury if proper precautions are not taken.[104]

As a general rule, the question of whether an activity is an "inherently dangerous activity" is a fact question for the jury.[105] Where, however, a statute declares the activity inherently dangerous or where undisputed facts are presented to the court regarding the presence or absence of inherent danger in the activity at issue, the question may be decided as a matter of law.[106]

H. NEGLIGENCE *PER SE*

In Florida, evidence of a person's violation of a statute, ordinance or administrative regulation can have one of three effects in a civil suit, depending upon how the statute, ordinance or administrative regulation is classified by the court. The courts classify such statutes, ordinances and regulations into three categories: (1) strict liability; (2) negligence *per se*; and (3) mere evidence of negligence.[107]

Strict liability statutes, ordinances or regulations are those which the court determines are designed to protect a particular class of persons from their inability to protect themselves, such as those prohibiting the sale of firearms to minors and child-labor laws.[108] The strict liability classification is a narrow one, limited to unusual and exceptional laws, and in such cases, the defendant is precluded from raising causation and comparative negligence arguments.[109]

The second category involves statutes, ordinances and regulations which establish a duty to take precautions to protect a particular class of persons from a particular type of injury.[110] In order to establish actionable negligence based upon such laws, the plaintiff must show: (1) that he or she is of the class the statute was intended to protect; (2) that he or she suffered injury of the type the statute was designed to prevent; and (3) that the violation of the statute was the proximate cause of his or her injury.[111]

Evidence of violations falling in this category establishes, as a matter of law, the duty and breach of duty element of the plaintiff's cause of action, that is, the jury is instructed that it is not at liberty to determine that the violation of the law is not negligence.[112] The only issues remaining for submission to the jury are whether the violation was a legal cause of the plaintiff's injury, whether and to what extent the plaintiff was comparatively negligent in causing his or her damages and whether and to what extent other individuals or entities were at fault in causing the plaintiff's damages.[113]

Violation of any other type of statute, ordinance or regulation, including violations of general traffic regulations, may be considered only as *prima facie* evidence of negligence.[114] In cases involving these types of laws, the jury is instructed that the defendant's violation is some evidence, but not conclusive evidence, of the defendant's negligence and that it should consider the fact of the violation together with all of the other facts and circumstances in the case in determining whether the defendant was negligent.[115]

I. JOINT AND SEVERAL LIABILITY

Under Florida common law, when defendants acted in concert, or performed separate and independent acts which combined to produce a single accident or an indivisible injury, each of the defendants was held individually and collectively responsible for the entire consequence of their acts.[116] Joint and several liability was imposed on such "joint" tortfeasors, even where an individual caused only a part of the damages or where the individual's act, if it had occurred alone, might not have caused the ultimate result.[117]

"Successive" or "distinct and independent" tortfeasors, however, are not considered to be "joint" tortfeasors, at least for purposes of seeking contribution under Florida's Uniform Contribution Among Tortfeasors Act.[118] Nevertheless, if a jury is unable to apportion the causes of the plaintiff's various injuries between successive, independent tortfeasors, then the plaintiff will be permitted to proceed against either the initial or the successive tortfeasor and obtain full recovery for the entire resulting indivisible injury or condition.[119]

In 1986, Florida partially abrogated the common law doctrine of joint and several liability with the enactment of its Comparative Fault Act.[120] In 1999, the legislature amended the Act to provide for a more extensive abrogation of the joint and several liability doctrine.[121] Under both the 1986 and 1999 versions, the Act applies to "negligence" cases, which are defined to include claims based upon theories of negligence, strict liability, products liability, professional malpractice whether couched in terms of contract or tort, or breach of warranty and like theories.[122] Causes of action based upon intentional torts,[123] claims to recover actual damages caused by pollution, and certain statutory causes of action are excluded from the provisions of the Act, and the common law doctrine of joint and several liability will still apply in these circumstances.[124]

The 1986 version of the Act provides that if the total damages awarded do not exceed $25,000, then joint and several liability principles apply to both economic and noneconomic damages.[125] If the total damages awarded exceed $25,000, then, as to *economic damages*, joint and several liability principles apply to a defendant whose percentage of fault equals or exceeds that of a particular claimant,[126] and, as to *noneconomic damages*, several liability only will apply, with the court entering judgment against the defendant for these damages based upon such party's percentage of fault.[127]

The 1999 version of the Comparative Fault Act further limited joint and several liability in Florida. As with the 1986 version, a defendant's liability for *non-economic damages* continues, under the 1999 version, to be coextensive with the percentage of fault the jury assesses against that defendant.[128] However, a defendant's joint and several liability for *economic damages* is, under the 1999 version, determined in accordance with a specific layered schedule which provides greater relief as the defendant's fault decreases.[129] This layered schedule is keyed to the amount of economic damages awarded, the percentage of fault attributed to the defendant, and the percentage of fault attributed to the plaintiff by the jury.[130]

Under both the 1986 and the 1999 versions of the Act, the apportionment of damages is based upon the percentage of "fault" which the jury attributes to each party who contributed to causing the accident or injuries upon which the suit is based.[131] The term "party", as used in the statute, has been broadly defined so as to include in the apportionment calculation not only a true "party" to the litigation, but also "nonparties" to the litigation, irrespective of the fact that the non-party is beyond the jurisdiction of the court or may be immune to suit due to an immunity.[132]

Apportionment of fault amongst "joint tortfeasors"[133] under the Act is an affirmative defense which must be pled in the defendant's answer, and the identity of nonparties must be provided as soon as reasonably practical.[134] In order for a nonparty to be included on the verdict form for purposes of apportionment of fault, the defendant shoulders the burden of proving, by a preponderance of the evidence, the fault of the nonparty in causing the plaintiff's injuries.[135]

By statute, a plaintiff's settlement with, and release of, one tortfeasor does not discharge other tortfeasors unless the release so provides.[136] Instead, the settlement and release reduces the amount of damages recoverable from the non-settling tortfeasors to the extent of the consideration paid to obtain the settlement and release.[137] However, the non-settling defendant is not entitled to the benefit of the statutory set-off with respect to any damages awarded by the jury for noneconomic damages, since there exists no joint and several liability under the Comparative Fault Act for this category of damage.[138] The fact of the settlement or that a defendant has been dismissed from the action shall not be made known to the jury.[139]

J. INDEMNITY

In Florida, implied common law indemnity (as opposed to contractual indemnity) is only available to one who is wholly without fault.[140] Concepts of "active" versus "passive" negligence have been discarded.[141] In order to state a viable claim for common law indemnity it must be alleged and proven: (1) that an injured party has asserted a claim or filed a lawsuit against the indemnitee based upon some legally viable vicarious, constructive, derivative, or technical liability; (2) that the indemnitee was wholly without any fault in causing the injured party's damages; and (3) that the indemnitor was negligent or otherwise at fault in causing the injured party's damages.[142]

If the indemnitee made payments to settle a claim or lawsuit without legally being subject to some vicarious, constructive, derivative, or technical liability to the injured party, then the payments will been deemed "voluntary", and no indemnification will be allowed.[143] In such circumstances, recovery may, however, occasionally be permitted under a theory of equitable subrogation.[144]

Contractual indemnity will be permitted provided that the parties' agreement clearly and unequivocally expresses the necessary intent.[145] Thus, in cases involving injuries or damage caused by the *joint fault* of the contracting parties or the *sole* fault of the indemnitee, the indemnity provision in the parties' contract must expressly and sufficiently state the indemnitor's intent to indemnify the indemnitee for damages caused under the particular circumstances giving rise to the claim for contractual indemnity.[146] Broad, generalized language which does not sufficiently express an intent to indemnify the indemnitee for damages caused by its own fault will usually be deemed insufficient to express the required "clear and unequivocal" intent necessary to shift the loss from one party to another.[147]

When the case involves an agreement relating to the alteration, repair, construction or demolition of a building, structure, appurtenance, or appliance, then not only must the necessary intent be expressed in the contract, but the indemnitee must also allege and prove that the indemnification clause in the contract either contains a specific monetary limitation on the extent of the indemnification or is supported by the exchange of a separate, additional consideration between the parties.[148]

K. BAR OF WORKERS' COMPENSATION STATUTE

Under the Florida Workers' Compensation Act,[149] the employee is barred from suing the employer who has paid workers' compensation benefits for the employee's work-related injuries.[150] With only limited exceptions,[151] the workers' compensation benefits are payable by the employer regardless of fault, so long as the injury occurred within the course and scope of the worker's employment.[152]

The tort immunity provided by the Act is commensurate with the employer's statutory responsibility for securing worker's compensation coverage for the particular injured employee.[153] If no obligation is imposed upon the defendant under the Act to secure coverage for the particular injured employee, then no immunity is granted by the statute.

In accordance with this controlling principle of "liability for compensation benefits equals immunity," employees of subcontractors typically cannot sue up the contractual chain leading to the general contractor.[154] In contrast, an employee of one subcontractor can sue other subcontractors laterally,[155] an employee of the general contractor, a subcontractor, a sub-subcontractor, and an independent contractor can sue the premises owner,[156] an employee of an independent contractor[157] can generally sue everyone involved in a project,[158] and an employee of a wholly-owned subsidiary may sue the parent corporation.[159]

The payment of compensation benefits is the employee's exclusive remedy against the employer.[160] If the employer fails to secure the compensation coverage required by the Act, then the employee can elect to either claim compensation benefits according to the Act or file a common law action against the employer for damages.[161]

The acceptance of compensation benefits does not preclude the employee from pursuing a tort action against third parties.[162] The employer is immune from liability for contribution to the third party,[163] but may in rare instances be subject to a claim for contractual or common law indemnification brought by the third party.[164] Where the employee has collected worker's compensation benefits from an employer and then proceeds to sue a third party for the same incident, the employer is subrogated to the rights of the employee as against the third party to the extent of the compensation benefits paid or payable.[165]

The employer's statutory lien is generally for the full amount of the benefits paid or payable, less a pro rata share of the costs and attorneys' fees incurred by the employee in prosecuting the action.[166] If, however, the employee can demonstrate that he/she "did not recover the full value of damages sustained," then the extent of the lien is proportionately reduced.[167] If the parties cannot resolve the extent of the employer's lien rights, then the court will make the determination upon motion and hearing.[168]

Co-employees are immunized from tort liability unless the act which caused the injury to the fellow employee was committed with willful and wanton disregard or unprovoked physical aggression or with gross negligence or unless the co-employees are assigned primarily to "unrelated works" at the time of the injury-causing event.[169]

A narrow exception to the employer's broad immunity under the Act has been recognized where the employee can demonstrate that the injury was caused by the employer's commission of an intentional tort.[170] The test applied in determining whether an intentional tort has been committed is an objective test which focuses upon whether the employer exhibited either a deliberate intent to injure the employee or engaged in conduct that was substantially certain to result in injury or death.[171]

L. PREMISES LIABILITY

The extent of a landowner or possessor's liability for injuries sustained on the premises depends primarily upon the nature of the condition causing the harm and the status of the injured party while on the property.[172] If the harm is caused by the "active" conduct or operations of the landowner or possessor (including independent contractors hired by them), then the duty of care owed is to exercise reasonable care to prevent harm to those third parties on the property who the landowner or possessor should know may foreseeably be endangered by the activities being carried out on the property.[173]

In contrast, when it is alleged that the injury was caused by a dangerous condition which the landowner either created or allowed to exist on the premises, then the status of the injured party determines the nature of the landowner's duty.[174] In cases involving dangerous conditions existing on the property, Florida first classifies those who are injured by the condition into one of three categories. The particular duty, and consequent standard of care, owed by the landowner or possessor to the injured party is then determined by that party's status or classification.[175]

The duty owed by a landowner to a business or social invitee (which includes an invited licensee) is to keep the property in a reasonably safe condition *and* to warn the invitee of concealed dangers which are known or should be known to the landowner, but which are unknown to the invitee and cannot be discovered by the exercise of due care by the invitee.[176]

A person is considered to be an invitee when the person enters the premises at the express or implied invitation of the landowner.[177] A person will lose invitee status when he or she ceases to use the premises in the customary or expected manner or ventures into an area where he or she was not invited, permitted, or reasonably expected to be.[178] In most cases the courts will grant invitee status,[179] although in a few cases the courts have determined that a jury issue was presented as to whether the invitee had exceeded the scope of the landowner's invitation at the time of the injury, with the result that the duty owed by the landowner will be reduced to coincide with the changed status.[180]

A landowner is not an insurer of the safety of invitees on the premises, and in order for the landowner to be held liable, the injured party must in most circumstances show that the landowner had actual or constructive knowledge[181] of the existence of the danger on the premises[182] *and* that the landowner had the ability to eliminate, lessen, or otherwise protect the invitee from the danger.[183] The duty owed to invitees may require the landowner to provide adequate security or supervision on the premises to protect the invitee from dangers posed by the negligent or intentional acts committed by third parties on the premises.[184]

At common law, the duty owed by the landowner to uninvited licensees and trespassers whose presence on the premises is known or reasonably foreseeable is to avoid intentionally harming them *and* to warn them of dangerous conditions on the premises of which the landowner has actual knowledge.[185] A statute enacted in 1999 now provides that to avoid liability to discovered trespassers, the premises owner or possessor must refrain from gross negligence or intentional misconduct *and* must warn the discovered trespasser of dangerous conditions that are known to the owner or possessor but that are not readily observable by others.[186]

At common law, the duty owed by the landowner to trespassers whose presence on the premises is unknown is to avoid willful and wanton harm to them, and upon discovery of their presence, to warn them of known dangerous conditions or hidden traps not open to ordinary observation.[187] A statute enacted in 1999 now provides that to avoid liability to undiscovered trespassers, the premises owner or possessor must refrain from intentional misconduct, but owes no duty to warn unless the actual physical presence of the trespasser was detected at least 24 hours before the accident.[188]

The respective knowledge possessed by the landowner and the injured party concerning the existence and nature of the condition which caused the harm may also have a bearing on the extent of the landowner's liability.[189] Where the landowner is being charged with negligence in *failing to maintain* the premises in a reasonably safe condition, the invitee's actual or constructive knowledge of the injury-causing condition will be considered as comparative negligence reducing the damages recoverable.[190] However, where the landowner is being charged with negligence in *failing to warn* the invitee, there may be no liability if the invitee was aware of the existence of the condition or if the condition was open and obvious.[191]

M. DRAM SHOP LIABILITY

The liability of commercial vendors of alcoholic beverages to individuals who injure themselves or others due to their intoxication is restricted by statute.[192] The statute generally exempts such vendors from liability for injuries caused by their patrons, with two specific exceptions.

First, liability may be imposed upon one who willfully and unlawfully sells or furnishes alcoholic beverages to a person who was not of lawful drinking age and who thereafter causes injury or damage due to his or her intoxication.[193] The statute requires that the sale be both "unlawful," that is, to one under the age of twenty-one,[194] and that it be "willful," that is, that the sale is made under circumstances demonstrating that the vendor's employee either knew that the purchaser was not of lawful drinking age or acted with a reckless disregard of whether the purchaser was, in fact, of lawful drinking age.[195]

No liability attaches under this first exception where the vendor's employee sold an alcoholic beverage in good faith to a person who was not, in fact, of lawful drinking age, provided that: (1) the underage purchaser reasonably appeared to have been of lawful drinking age; and (2) the vendor's employee carefully examined at least one of the statutorily approved forms of identification presented by the underage purchaser prior to making the sale.[196]

Secondly, liability may be imposed under an exception to the statute where the vendor knowingly serves a person "habitually addicted" to the use of alcoholic beverages who causes injury or damage due to his or her intoxication.[197] This "habitual drunkard" exception does not encompass retail establishments which merely sell alcoholic beverages in closed containers to adults for consumption off the premises, such as package and convenience stores.[198]

With respect to this second exception to the statute's general tort immunity, the claimant may show the vendor's knowledge that the patron is "habitually addicted to the use of alcoholic beverages" through circumstantial evidence alone, including mere self-serving admissions of the intoxicated tortfeasor or members of his family, as well as the opinions of so-called "substance abuse" experts.[199] Some court decisions applying this "habitually addicted" exception to the general tort immunity set out in the statute have viewed the exception rather expansively, especially in situations involving an employer's furnishing of alcoholic beverages to employees during arguably work-related social functions.[200]

Individuals hosting private social events at their homes where alcoholic beverages are furnished to those in attendance, even if they are visibly intoxicated, have not been subjected to civil liability under the statute, as long as the intoxicated guest who caused the injury or damage was of lawful drinking age.[201] However, potential civil liability may be imposed upon adults who, in violation of an "open house party" criminal statute,[202] fail to exercise reasonable care to prohibit the consumption of alcoholic beverage by minors attending parties held on their premises.[203]

N. ECONOMIC LOSS

Although once broadly applied to preclude many types of tort causes of action seeking damages solely of an economic nature,[204] the so-called "economic loss rule" currently find its primary application in Florida in the context of products liability claims arising out of a product's deficient performance or its malfunction which causes damage solely to itself or another product into which it is incorporated.[205] Under the current view in Florida, the economic loss rule will not be applied so as to bar claims seeking purely economic losses in those situations where the plaintiff's claim is predicated upon a statutory cause of action[206] or upon theories of conversion,[207] civil theft[208] and other such "intentional misconduct" torts.[209]

The rule has also been held to be inapplicable to claims for economic losses sustained as a result of negligence committed by a "professional" with whom the claimant has no contractual relationship or as a result of information negligently supplied by the defendant for the guidance of others.[210]

The applicability of the rule in the context of cases where a contract exists between the parties is less clear.[211] It presently appears that the applicability of the economic loss rule in these situations will depend upon whether the plaintiff is able to allege and prove that the defendant committed a tort which is separate from, and independent of, a breach of the parties' contract.[212]

This so-called "independent tort" exception has been applied in cases involving causes of action based upon allegations of fraud in the inducement,[213] extra-contractual fraud and negligent misrepresentation,[214] and breach of fiduciary duty.[215] Where the facts alleged to constitute the "independent tort" are the same as, or are clearly intertwined with, the facts regarding the defendant's lack of performance under the parties' contract, however, some courts have determined that the tort alleged does not truly constitute an "independent tort" of the sort which can avoid the application of the economic loss rule.[216]

O. FRAUD AND MISREPRESENTATION

The Florida Rules of Civil Procedure require that a cause of action for fraud be pleaded with particularity.[217]

The standard of proof in cases involving fraudulent or negligent misrepresentation is "the greater weight of the evidence" standard, not the traditional "clear and convincing evidence" standard.[218] The required elements of a cause of action based upon fraud, deceit or intentional misrepresentation are: (1) a false statement concerning a material fact; (2) knowledge by the person making the statement that the representation is false; (3) the intent by the person making the statement that the representation will induce another to act on it; and (4) reliance on the representation to the injury of the other party.[219]

The elements of a cause of action for negligent misrepresentation are: (1) a misrepresentation of a material fact; (2) the one making the representation must either know of the misrepresentation, must make the representation without knowledge as to its truth or falsity, or must make the representation under circumstances in which he or she ought to have known of its falsity; (3) the representor must intend that the representation induce another to act on it; and (4) injury must result to the party acting in justifiable reliance on the misrepresentation.[220]

The primary distinction between the two torts is that the fraud cause of action requires proof that the representor had knowledge of the falsity of the representation, while the negligent misrepresentation cause of action only requires proof that the representation was made under circumstances in which its falsity should have been known.[221] A recipient may rely on the truth of a representation, even though its falsity could have been ascertained had an investigation been performed, unless the recipient knows the representation to be false or its falsity is obvious.[222] Nevertheless, the principles of comparative negligence have been found to be applicable in cases involving negligent misrepresentation claims which are pursued under the Restatement of Torts (Second), Section 552.[223]

There must be actual damage sustained by the recipient for recovery to be permitted under either theory.[224] Proof of fraud sufficient to support an award of compensatory damages is deemed necessarily sufficient to create a jury question regarding punitive damages.[225]

P. CONSUMER FRAUD STATUTES

Florida's Deceptive and Unfair Trade Practices Act (DUTPA) protects consumers from unfair methods of competition and deceptive acts and practices in the conduct of any trade or commerce.[226] Its purpose is to protect the consuming public and legitimate business enterprises from those who engage in unfair methods of competition, or unconscionable, deceptive, or unfair acts or practices in the conduct of any trade or commerce and to make Florida's consumer protection and enforcement consistent with established policies of federal law relating to consumer protection.[227]

While the DUTPA's coverage is broad, it does not apply to sales of real estate or homes, which are not considered to be "consumer transactions" within the scope of the Act.[228] The DUTPA also specifically exempts claims by consumers for personal injury or death or for damage to property other than the property that was the subject of the consumer transaction at issue.[229]

The DUTPA provides that the State Department of Legal Affairs and the Office of the Attorney General, through the local states attorneys, are empowered to investigate violations of the Act and to enforce its provisions by issuing cease and desist orders, imposing fines and penalties, and seeking injunctive, declaratory and monetary relief on behalf of consumers in both administrative and judicial proceedings.[230] Private civil actions may also be brought by "consumers" under the Act for declaratory and injunctive relief, "actual" damages, attorneys' fees and costs.[231] In suits between business competitors, injunctive relief is available to restrain violations of the Act, but the recovery of damages has not been allowed.[232]

Special or consequential damages are generally not recoverable in a private civil action brought by a consumer, with the scope of damages usually being limited to "actual damages," the difference in value between what the consumer bargained for and what was actually received in the transaction.[233] Absent proof of a separate and independent tort, punitive damages are also not recoverable under the Act.[234] Proof of misrepresentation or deceit as would constitute a fraud is not a necessary element in all private causes of action brought under the DUTPA.[235] A four-year statute of limitations is applicable to a private civil action brought by a consumer under the Act.[236]

Q. PUNITIVE DAMAGES

Claims for punitive damages in civil actions are controlled by statute in Florida.[237] Before a claim for punitive damages may be included in a pleading, the claimant must first show from evidence in the record or by proffer of additional evidence a reasonable basis for the recovery of such damages.[238] No discovery of the defendant's net worth is permitted until the court has first entered an order permitting the punitive damages pleading.[239]

Punitive damages are not recoverable in a civil action absent a showing, by "clear and convincing evidence,"[240] that the defendant was personally guilty of "intentional misconduct" or "gross negligence."[241] The general common law rule in Florida is that punitive damages are not recoverable in a breach of contract action, irrespective of the subjective motive of the defendant or the flagrant nature of the breach.[242] Before the recovery of punitive damages would be allowed, it had to be shown that the breach was attended by some additional intentional wrong, insult, abuse, or gross negligence which is sufficient to support a cause of action for a "separate and independent tort."[243]

"Intentional misconduct" is defined to mean that the defendant had actual knowledge of the wrongfulness of the conduct and the high probability that injury or damage to the claimant would result and, despite that knowledge, intentionally pursued that course of conduct, resulting in injury.[244] "Gross negligence" is defined to mean that the defendant's conduct was so reckless or wanting in care that it constituted a conscious disregard or indifference to the life, liberty, or rights of persons exposed to such conduct.[245]

In cases involving employers, principals, corporations or other such legal entities as defendants or co-defendants, punitive damages may be awarded against such entities on either a "direct" or a "vicarious" basis.[246] Punitive damages may be awarded against a corporation or other employer or principal on a theory of "direct liability" if it is shown that a managing agent, primary owner, or other officer or director personally engaged in conduct which would warrant the imposition of punitive damages.[247]

Punitive damages may also be awarded against a corporation or other employer or principal on a theory of "vicarious liability" if it is shown: (1) that the conduct of the entity's employee or agent rises to the level that punitive damages are warranted; *and* (2) the employer, principal, corporation or other such legal entity actively and knowingly participated in such conduct; or (b) the officers, directors, or managers of the employer, principal, corporation or other such legal entity knowingly condoned, ratified, or consented to such conduct; or (c) the employer, principal, corporation or other such legal entity engaged in conduct that constituted gross negligence and contributed to the loss, damages, or injury suffered by the claimant.[248]

Punishment and deterrence are the dual policies underlying punitive damage awards.[249] An award of compensatory damages is not a condition precedent to the award of punitive damages.[250] An award of punitive damages should exact from the defendant's pocketbook a sum of money which, according to the financial ability demonstrated, will hurt, but not bankrupt the defendant.[251]

In claims based on negligence, strict liability, products liability, misconduct in commercial transactions, professional liability, and breach of warranty which involve willful, wanton or gross misconduct occurring prior to October 1, 1999, the judgment for punitive damages may not exceed three times the amount of compensatory damages awarded to each claimant, unless the claimant demonstrates to the court by clear and convincing evidence that the greater award from the jury is not excessive in light of the facts and circumstances presented to it at trial.[252]

In 1999, additional limitations on punitive damage awards were enacted.[253] The new statute increases the cap on punitive damages to four times the compensatory damages awarded or $2 million, whichever is greater, in cases involving a showing of corporate knowledge and a motive of unreasonable financial gain.[254] Also, there is no cap on punitive damages where it is shown that the defendant had a specific intent to harm the claimant.[255] Finally, the new statute prohibits, in most circumstances, multiple awards of punitive damages against the defendant when based upon the same act or a single course of conduct.[256]

When presented with a timely motion, trial courts should bifurcate the jury's determination of the amount of punitive damages from the remaining issues at trial.[257]

R. WRONGFUL DEATH AND SURVIVORSHIP ACTIONS

Under Florida's common law, there was no cause of action permitting recovery for a decedent's personal injuries or wrongful death.[258] By statute, however, the recovery of certain elements of damages by a specified class of individuals is permitted under Florida's Wrongful Death Act.[259] The Act creates a cause of action for the recovery of certain specified damages when the death of a person is caused by the wrongful act, negligence, default, or breach of contract or warranty committed by another person or entity.[260] When a personal injury to the decedent results in death, no action for the decedent's personal injury damages shall survive the death, and any such action pending at the time of death shall abate.[261]

Actions under Florida's Wrongful Death Act must be brought within two years of the date of death by the decedent's personal representative, who is entitled to recover on behalf of the decedent's estate and on behalf of the decedent's statutory "survivors" those particular elements of damage delineated in the Act.[262] The Act defines "survivors" as including the decedent's spouse, children, parents, and, if partly or wholly dependent on the decedent for support or services, any blood relatives and adoptive brothers and sisters.[263] The particular elements of damage recoverable by each of these "survivors" differs depending upon their age, their relationship to the decedent, and the circumstances existing at the time of the decedent's death.[264]

Under the Act, the decedent's estate is entitled to recover as damages the loss of earnings of the deceased from the date of injury to the date of death, less the amount awarded to survivors for the loss of the decedent's support between the date of injury and the date of death.[265] The decedent's estate is also entitled to recover the medical or funeral expenses that have become a charge against the estate.[266] The decedent's estate may also recover the loss of the decedent's prospective net accumulations, reduced to present money value, in two circumstances: (1) when the decedent's survivors include a surviving spouse or lineal descendents; or (2) when the decedent is not a "minor child"[267] and leaves only a surviving parent who is not entitled to recover lost support and services under the Act.[268]

The extent of the recovery of the decedent's statutory "survivors" depends upon the status of the particular survivor.[269] Everyone who generally qualifies as a "survivor" under the Act may recover: (1) the value of the lost support and services from the date of the injury to the date of death, with interest, as well as any future loss of support and services, reduced to present money value;[270] and (2) the decedent's medical and funeral expenses due to the injury or death which are actually paid by the survivor.[271]

A surviving spouse may additionally recover for loss of the decedent's companionship and protection and for mental pain and suffering calculated from the date of the decedent's injury.[272] Surviving minor children may recover for lost parental companionship, instruction, and guidance and for mental pain and suffering from the date of the decedent's injury.[273] Each survivor who is a parent of a deceased minor child may recover for mental pain and suffering from the date of the minor child's injury.[274] Each survivor who is a parent of a deceased adult child may recover for mental pain and suffering from the date of the adult child's injury, but only if there are no other statutory survivors.[275]

A defense that would bar or reduce a particular survivor's recovery if he or she were the plaintiff, such as contributory or comparative negligence, may be asserted by the tortfeasor so as to bar or diminish that particular survivor's recovery, but will not affect the extent of recovery of any of the other survivors.[276]

G. William Bissett
HARDY & BISSETT, P.A.
13205 S.W. 137 Avenue, Suite 127
Miami, Florida 33186
(305) 969-3990
Fax (305) 969-3558
HardyBissettPA@aol.com

ENDNOTES - FLORIDA

1. Section 95.11(2)(b), Fla. Stat. (1997). The statute commences to run when the breach occurs, regardless of whether the injured party is aware of any damages resulting from the breach, *i.e.*, no "delayed discovery rule" applies. *See Federal Insurance Co. v. Southwest Florida Retirement Center, Inc.*, 707 So. 2d 1119 (Fla. 1998); *Abbott Laboratories, Inc. v. General Electric Capital*, 765 So. 2d 737 (Fla. 5th DCA 2000); *Beck v. Lazard Freres & Co., LLC*, 175 F.3d 913 (11th Cir. 1999) (applying Florida law).

2. Section 95.11(3)(a) and Section 95.11(3)(o), Fla. Stat. (1997).

3. Section 95.11(3)(f), Fla. Stat. (1997).

4. Section 95.11(3)(j), Fla. Stat. (1997).

5. Section 95.11(3)(k), Fla. Stat. (1997).

6. Section 95.11(3)(e), Fla. Stat. (1997).

7. Section 768.28(13) and Section 95.11(4)(b), Fla. Stat. (1998 Supp.).

8. Section 768.28(6), Fla. Stat. (1998 Supp.).

9. Section 95.11(4)(d), Fla. Stat. (1997).

10. Section 95.11(4)(g), Fla. Stat. (1997).

11. Section 95.11(4)(a), Fla. Stat. (1997).

12. Section 400.0236, Fla. Stat. (2001).

13. Section 95.11(4)(b), Fla. Stat. (1997).

14. *Id.*

15. Section 95.031, Fla. Stat. (1998 Supp.).

16. *Id. See Hearndon v. Graham*, 767 So. 2d 1179, 1184-85 (Fla. 2000); *State Farm Mut. Auto. Ins. Co. v. Lee*, 678 So. 2d 818, 821 (Fla. 1996).

17. *See Barron v. Shapiro*, 565 So. 2d 1319, 1320-22 (Fla. 1990); *Peat, Marwick, Mitchell & Co. v. Lane*, 565 So. 2d 1323, 1325 (Fla. 1990); *Ambrose v. Catholic Social Services, Inc.*, 736 So. 2d 146, 150 (Fla. 5th DCA 1999); *D. B. v. CCH – GP, Inc.*, 664 So. 2d 1094, 1095 (Fla. 2d DCA 1995); *Keller v. Reed*, 603 So. 2d 717, 719 (Fla. 2d DCA 1992).

18. *See Carter v. Brown & Williamson Tobacco Corp.*, 778 So. 2d 932, 936-39 (Fla. 2000); *Hearndon v. Graham*, 767 So. 2d 1179, 1184-85 (Fla. 2000); *Allapatah Services, Inc. v. Exxon Corp.*, 157 F. Supp. 2d 1291, 1309-11 (S.D. Fla. 2001) (applying Florida law).

19. *See Steinmetz v. G. D. Parker Sod, Inc.*, 673 So. 2d 968 (Fla. 5th DCA 1996); *Breitz v. Lykes-Pasco Packing Co.*, 561 So. 2d 1204 (Fla. 2d DCA 1990), *rev. denied*, 576 So. 2d 285 (Fla. 1990); *Korman v. Iglesias*, 825 F. Supp. 1010 (S.D. Fla. 1993), *aff'd*, 43 F.3d 678 (11th Cir. 1994) (applying Florida law).

20. Section 95.031(2)(a), Fla. Stat. (1999). *See Puchner v. Bache Halsey Stuart, Inc.*, 553 So. 2d 216, 218 (Fla. 3d DCA 1989). However, in cases involving allegations of an ongoing and continuing conspiracy to commit fraud, the critical date for statute of repose purposes is the date of the last act done in furtherance of the conspiracy. *Laschke v. Brown & Williamson Tobacco Corp.*, 766 So. 2d 1076, 1078-79 (Fla. 2d DCA 2000); *McLeod v. Barber*, 764 So. 2d 790 (Fla. 5th DCA 2000).

21. *See Kelley v. School Board of Seminole County*, 435 So. 2d 804 (Fla. 1983); *Mercedes Benz of North America, Inc. v. Kling*, 549 So. 2d 795 (Fla. 5th DCA 1989); *Dubin v. Dow Corning Corp.*, 478 So. 2d 71 (Fla. 2d DCA 1985); *Brogan v. Mullins*, 452 So. 2d 940 (Fla. 5th DCA 1984); *Bernard Schoninger Shopping Centers, Ltd. v. J. P. S. Elastomerics, Corp.*, 102 F.3d 1173, 1178-79 (11th Cir. 1997) (applying Florida law). To be distinguished is the "delayed discovery doctrine," whose viability was recently reaffirmed in Florida. *See Hearndon v. Graham*, 767 So. 2d 1179 (Fla. 2000). Additionally, it has been held that the doctrine of "equitable estoppel" may be applied in certain egregious circumstances so as to preclude a defendant from relying upon the expiration of the statute of limitations. *See Major League Baseball v. Morsani*, 790 So. 2d 1071 (Fla. 2001).

22. Section 95.051, Fla. Stat. (1997). Based on the Florida Supreme Court's recent decision in *Hearndon v. Graham*, 767 So. 2d 1179 (Fla. 2000), circumstances which are not specifically delineated in Section 95.051, such as fraudulent concealment of the cause of action or of the defendant's identity, will not be deemed to "toll" the running of the limitations period but may likely be judicially deemed to "delay" the "accrual of the cause of action," and therefore the running of the statute of limitations. *See Federal Insurance Co. v. Southwest Florida Retirement Center, Inc.*, 707 So. 2d 1119 (Fla. 1998). Similarly, the doctrine of "equitable estoppel" may be applied in certain egregious circumstances so as to preclude a defendant from relying upon the expiration of the statute of limitations. *See Major League Baseball v. Morsani*, 790 So. 2d 1071 (Fla. 2001).

23. Section 95.051(1)(a), Fla. Stat. (1997).

24. Section 95.051(1)(c), Fla. Stat. (1997).

25. Section 95.051(1)(b), Fla. Stat. (1997).

26. Section 95.051(1)(f), Fla. Stat. (1997).

27. Section 95.051(1)(g), Fla. Stat. (1997).

28. Section 95.031(2), Fla. Stat. (1975), repealed by Laws 1986, c. 86-272, § 2. The statute was upheld against various constitutional challenges in *Pullum v. Cincinnati, Inc.*, 476 So. 2d 657 (Fla. 1985). The statute will not be applied, however, to extinguish a cause of action if the injuries involved are latent and undiscoverable within the repose period. *Pulmosan Safety Equipment Corp. v. Barnes*, 752 So. 2d 556 (Fla. 2000).

29. *Firestone Tire & Rubber Co. v. Acosta*, 612 So. 2d 1361 (Fla. 1993).

30. Section 95.031(2)(b), Fla. Stat. (1999). The running of this new statute of repose is tolled if it is shown that affirmative steps were taken by the manufacturer to conceal the fact of its actual knowledge of the defect alleged by the claimant. Section 95.031(2)(d), Fla. Stat. (1999). The new statute is generally intended to be applicable to actions filed on or after July 1, 1999, regardless of when the cause of action accrued. Laws 1999, c. 99-225, § 12(1). There is, however, a "savings" clause which may apply under limited special circumstances. *Id.*

31. Section 95.031(2)(b), Fla. Stat. (1999). Commercial aircraft, vessels of more than 100 gross tons and commercial railroad equipment are not subject to the twelve year repose period. Section 95.031(2)(b)1., Fla. Stat. (1999). Instead, the repose period is extended to twenty years or for the term of any express representation or warranty, whichever is longer. Section 95.031(2)(b)3., Fla. Stat. (1999).

32. Section 95.031(2)(b)2., Fla. Stat. (1999).

33. Section 95.031(2)(c), Fla. Stat. (1999).

34. Section 95(3)(c), Fla. Stat. (1997).

35. It should be noted that this so-called Florida Tort Reform Act of 1999 has been declared unconstitutional by a trial court based on Florida's "single subject" rule regarding bills passed by the legislature. *See Florida Consumer Action Network v. Bush*, Case No. 99-6689 (Fla. Leon County Cir. Ct. Feb. 9, 2001). Florida's Supreme Court has not yet reviewed the matter.

36. *See* Section 768.81(3), Fla. Stat. (1999). As amended, this statute now provides a specific layered schedule to be used in determining a defendant's joint and several liability for *economic damages*, unless it is found that the defendant's percentage of fault is less than the plaintiff's percentage of

fault, in which case the doctrine of joint and several liability will not apply to economic damages. As to *noneconomic damages*, a defendant's liability is always coextensive with the percentage of fault the jury assesses against that defendant. Section 768.81(3)(a)-(c), Fla. Stat. (1999).

37. *See* Sections 768.725, 768.72, and 768.73, Fla. Stat. (1999).

38. *See* Section 95.031(2), Fla. Stat. (1999).

39. *See* Section 768.1256, Fla. Stat. (1999). Under the new statute, a rebuttable presumption exists that a product *is not* defective if its design, manufacture or labeling complied with applicable governmental standards in effect at the pertinent time. Conversely, a rebuttable presumption exists that a product *is* defective if its design, manufacture or labeling did not comply with applicable governmental standards in effect at the pertinent time.

40. *See* Section 768.1257, Fla. Stat. (1999). This new statute states that in actions brought against manufacturers based upon alleged defective design, the finder of fact shall consider the state of the art of scientific and technical knowledge and the other circumstances that existed at the time of the product's manufacture, as opposed to those in existence at the time of the loss or injury.

41. *See* Section 324.021, Fla. Stat. (1999).

42. *See* Section 324.021, Fla. Stat. (1999). If the operator does not carry at least $500,000 in liability insurance, then the owner of the vehicle can be held liable for an additional $500,000 in economic damages. *Id.*

43. *See* Section 324.021, Fla. Stat. (1999).

44. *See* Section 768.096, Fla. Stat. (1999). The five-step process includes a criminal background check, driver's license check if relevant to the job sought, reasonable efforts to contact references and former employers, completion of a written job application containing questions relating to criminal history, and conducting an interview of the applicant.

45. *See* Section 768.095, Fla. Stat. (1999). Under the amended statute, an employer who discloses information about a former or current employee to a prospective employer upon the request of the prospective employer or the prospective employee is immune from liability unless it is shown by clear and convincing evidence that the information disclosed by the employer was knowingly false or that the disclosure violated any civil right of the employee. *Id.*

46. Section 768.0705, Fla. Stat. (1999).

47. Section 768.075, Fla. Stat. (1999).

48. Florida Statutes, Section 400, *et seq.*

49. *See* Sections 400.023–400.0238, Fla. Stat. (2001).

50. Section 627.736-737, Fla. Stat. (1997).

51. Section 627.737, Fla. Stat (1997).

52. Section 627.737(2), Fla. Stat (1997); Fla. Std. J. Instr. (Civ.) 6.2(d).

53. *See Gill v. McGuire,* 806 So. 2d 629 (Fla. 4th DCA 2002); *Smiley v. Nelson,* 805 So. 2d 870 (Fla. 2d DCA 2001).

54. *See City of Tampa v. Long,* 638 So. 2d 35 (Fla. 1994); *Tolivert v. Estate of Scherer,* 715 So. 2d 358 (Fla. 5th DCA 1998); *Morey v. Harper,* 541 So. 2d 1285 (1st DCA 1989), review denied, 551 So. 2d 461 (Fla. 1989).

55. *See Weygant v. Fort Myers Lincoln Mercury, Inc.,* 640 So. 2d 1092 (Fla. 1994); *Easkold v. Rhodes,* 614 So. 2d 495 (Fla. 1993); *Interamerican Car Rental, Inc. v. Gonzales,* 638 So. 2d 89 (Fla. 3d DCA 1994). *But see Allstate Insurance Co. v. Thomas,* 637 So. 2d 1008 (Fla. 4th DCA 1994) (affirming directed verdict for plaintiff on permanency issue where the conflicts between the plaintiff's expert witness testimony and the lay witness testimony were minor, indirect, and immaterial).

56. *See Rose v. Dwin,* 762 So. 2d 532 (Fla. 4th DCA 2000); *Holmes v. State Farm Mut. Auto. Ins. Co.,* 624 So. 2d 824 (Fla. 2d DCA 1993).

57. *See Chapman v. Dillon,* 415 So. 2d 12 (Fla. 1982); Fla. Std. J. Instr. (Civ.) 6.2(d).

58. *See Bennett v. Florida Farm Bureau Casualty Insurance Co.,* 477 So. 2d 608 (Fla. 5th DCA 1985); Fla. Std. J. Instr. (Civ.) 6.2(d).

59. *See Auto-Owners Insurance Co. v. Tompkins,* 651 So. 2d 89 (Fla. 1995); *Metrolimo, Inc. v. Lamm,* 666 So. 2d 552 (Fla. 3d DCA 1995); *Hamilton v. Melbourne Sand Transport, Inc.,* 687 So. 2d 27 (Fla. 5th DCA 1997); Fla. Std. J. Instr. (Civ.) 6.2(d). These future economic damages must, however, be established with reasonable certainty, both as to their nature and as to their duration. *See Owen v. Morrisey,* 793 So. 2d 1018 (Fla. 4th DCA 2001); *Garriga v. Guerra,* 753 So. 2d 146 (Fla. 3d DCA 2000).

60. *See Humphreys v. General Motors Corp.,* 839 F. Supp. 822, 829 (N.D. Fla. 1993), *aff'd,* 47 F.3d 430 (11th Cir. 1994) (applying Florida law); *Paterson v. Deeb,* 472 So. 2d 1210, 1214 (Fla. 1st DCA 1985), rev. denied, 484 So. 2d 8 (Fla. 1986); *Florida Power & Light Company v. Lively,* 465 So. 2d 1270, 1273 (Fla. 3d DCA 1985) (en banc); *Simon v. Tampa Elec. Co.,* 202 So. 2d 209, 213 (Fla. 2d DCA 1967).

61. *See Florida Power & Light Company v. Periera*, 705 So. 2d 1359, 1361 (Fla. 1998); *McCain v. Florida Power Corp.*, 593 So. 2d 500, 502-3 (Fla. 1992); *Martinez v. Florida Power & Light Company*, 785 So. 2d 1251, 1252 (Fla. 3d DCA 2001); *Lipsky v. Padgett*, 730 So. 2d 818, 818 (Fla. 5th DCA 1999); *Glazer v. Florida Power & Light Company*, 689 So. 2d 308, 312 (Fla. 3d DCA 1997).

62. *See Kitchen v. K-Mart Corp.*, 697 So. 2d 1200 (Fla. 1997); *McCain v. Florida Power & Light Company*, 593 So. 2d 500, 502-3 (Fla. 1992); *Shurben v. Dollar Rent-A-Car*, 676 So. 2d 467, 468 (Fla. 3d DCA 1996). Mere foreseeability of harm alone, however, will not always give rise to the existence of a duty owed by the defendant for the plaintiff's benefit. *See Vic Potamkin Chevrolet, Inc. v. Horne*, 505 So. 2d 560 (Fla. 3d DCA 1987) (*en banc*), *approved*, 533 So. 2d 261 (Fla. 1988); *First American Title Ins. Co. v. First Title Service Co. of the Florida Keys, Inc.*, 457 So. 2d 467 (Fla. 1984). The concept of foreseeability is also relevant to the proximate cause element of a negligence action. *See* Section E, *infra*.

63. *See deJesus v. Seaboard Coast Line Railroad Co.*, 281 So. 2d 198 (Fla 1973); *Eckelbarger v. Frank*, 732 So. 2d 433 (Fla. 2d DCA 1999); *Newsome v. Haffner*, 710 So. 2d 184 (Fla. 1st DCA 1998), *rev. denied*, 722 So. 2d 193 (Fla. 1998); *Richardson v. Fountain*, 154 So. 2d 709, 711 (Fla. 2d DCA 1963), *cert. denied*, 157 So. 2d 818 (Fla. 1963); Fla. Std. J. Instr. (Civ.) 4.9, 4.11.

64. *See Nova University, Inc. v. Wagner*, 491 So. 2d 1116 (Fla. 1986) (relationship between defendant and tortfeasor); *Snow v. Nelson*, 450 So. 2d 269 (Fla. 3d DCA 1984), *approved*, 475 So. 2d 225 (Fla. 1985) (relationship between defendant and tortfeasor); *Premier Ins. Co. v. Adams*, 632 So. 2d 1054, 1056-57 (Fla. 5th DCA 1994) (relationship between defendant and tortfeasor); *Shurben v. Dollar Rent-A-Car*, 676 So. 2d 467, 468 (Fla. 3d DCA 1996) (relationship between defendant and plaintiff); *Carlisle v. Ulysses Line*, 475 So. 2d 248 (Fla. 3d DCA 1985) (relationship between defendant and plaintiff).

65. *See Union Park Memorial Chapel v. Hutt*, 670 So. 2d 64 (Fla. 1994); *Mininson v. Allright Miami, Inc.*, 732 So. 2d 389 (Fla. 3d DCA 1999); *Kowkabany v. Home Depot, Inc.*, 606 So. 2d 716 (Fla.1st DCA 1992). The voluntary undertaking to do an act which, if not accomplished with due care might increase the risk of harm to others or might result in harm to others due to their reliance upon the defendant's undertaking, confers a duty upon the defendant to exercise reasonable care in performing the task voluntarily assumed. *Union Park Memorial Chapel v. Hutt*, 670 So. 2d at 66-7; *Mininson v. Allright Miami, Inc.*, 732 So. 2d at 389-91.

66. *See City of Pinellas Park v. Brown*, 604 So. 2d 1222, 1225-26 (Fla. 1992).

67. *See Moransais v. Heathman*, 744 So. 2d 973 (Fla. 1999); *Hewett-Kier Construction, Inc. v. Lemuel Ramos and Assoc., Inc.*, 775 So. 2d 373 (Fla. 4th DCA 2001); *Ragsdale v. Mount Sinai Medical Center of Miami*, 770 So. 2d 167, 168-69 (Fla. 3d DCA 2001).

68. *See Vic Potamkin Chevrolet, Inc. v. Horne*, 505 So. 2d 560, 562 (Fla. 3d DCA 1987) (*en banc*), *approved*, 533 So. 2d 261 (Fla. 1988); *Trianon Park Condominium Ass'n. v. Hialeah*, 468 So. 2d 912, 918 (Fla. 1985); *Daly v. Denny's, Inc.*, 694 So. 2d 775 (Fla. 4th DCA 1997); *Lighthouse Mission of Orlando, Inc. v. Estate of McGowen*, 683 So. 2d 1086, 1088 (Fla. 5th DCA 1996).

69. *See Vic Potamkin Chevrolet, Inc. v. Horne*, 505 So. 2d 560, 562 (Fla. 3d DCA 1987) (*en banc*), *approved*, 533 So. 2d 261 (Fla. 1988); *Daly v. Denny's, Inc.*, 694 So. 2d 775 (Fla. 4th DCA 1997).

70. *See Nova University, Inc. v. Wagner*, 491 So. 2d 1116 (Fla. 1986); *Garrison Retirement Home Corp. v. Hancock*, 484 So. 2d 1257 (Fla. 4th DCA 1985). Implicit in this exception to the general rule of non-liability is the proposition that the defendant is shown to have the right or ability to control the third party tortfeasor's conduct. *See Lighthouse Mission of Orlando, Inc. v. Estate of McGowen*, 683 So. 2d 1086, 1088 (Fla. 5th DCA 1996); *Palmer v. Shearson Lehman Hutton, Inc.*, 622 So. 2d 1085, 1089 (Fla. 1st DCA 1993).

71. *See Kitchen v. K-Mart Corp.*, 697 So. 2d 1200 (Fla. 1997); *Susco Car Rental Sys. v. Leonard*, 112 So. 2d 832 (Fla. 1959); *Avis Rent-A-Car Sys. v. Garmas*, 440 So. 2d 1311 (Fla. 3d DCA 1983), *rev. denied*, 451 So. 2d 848 (Fla. 1984).

72. *See Allen v. Babrab, Inc.*, 438 So. 2d 356 (Fla. 1983); *Wal-Mart Stores, Inc. v. McDonald*, 676 So. 2d 12, 14-15 (Fla. 1st DCA 1996); *Slawson v. Fast Food Enterprises*, 671 So. 2d 255, 257-58 (Fla. 4th DCA 1996), *rev. dismissed*, 679 So. 2d 773 (Fla. 1996); *Bovis v. 7-Eleven, Inc.*, 505 So. 2d 661, 663-64 (Fla. 5th DCA 1987); *Holley v. Mt. Zion Terrace Apts., Inc.*, 382 So. 2d 98, 99-100 (Fla. 3d DCA 1980). In most instances, this duty will not be extended so as to require the defendant to protect the plaintiff from criminal attacks occurring on adjacent property. *Compare Daly v. Denny's, Inc.*, 694 So. 2d 775 (Fla. 4th DCA 1997), *with Holiday Inns, Inc. v. Shelburne*, 576 So. 2d 322 (Fla. 4th DCA 1991), *appeal dismissed*, 589 So. 2d 291 (Fla. 1991).

73. *See Stevens v. Jefferson*, 436 So. 2d 33, 34-35 (Fla. 1983); *Reichenbach v. Days Inn, Inc.*, 401 So. 2d 1366, 1367 (Fla. 5th DCA 1981).

74. *See Swindell v. Hellkamp*, 242 So. 2d 708, 710 (Fla. 1971). However, in *Reed v. Bowen*, 512 So. 2d 198 (Fla. 1987), it was held that the *Swindell* presumption did not defeat, as a matter of law, the statutory defense raised by the owner of a dog who was sued by the parents of a four-year old boy who was bitten by a dog which the owner claimed had been "mischievously or carelessly provoked or aggravated" by the minor child.

75. *See Thornton v. Elliott*, 288 So. 2d 254 (Fla. 1974); *McGregor v. Marini*, 256 So. 2d 542, 543 (Fla. 4th DCA 1972). However, if the action is brought under the doctrine of attractive nuisance, then these general principles of comparative negligence do not apply because an essential element of such a cause of action is that the child does not "realize the risk of intermeddling

with the dangerous condition." *See Martinello v. B & P USA, Inc.,* 566 So. 2d 761, 763 (Fla. 1990).

76. *See Medina v. McAllister,* 196 So. 2d 773 (Fla. 3d DCA 1967).

77. *See* Fla. Std. J. Instr. (Civ.) 4.1.

78. *See* Fla. Std. J. Instr. (Civ.) 4.2(a) and 4.2(c).

79. *See* Fla. Std. J. Instr. (Civ.) 4.1, comment 3, and Fla. Std. J. Instr. (Civ.) 4.7.

80. *See Florida Power & Light Company v. Periera,* 705 So. 2d 1359, 1361-62 (Fla. 1998); *McCain v. Florida Power Corp.,* 593 So. 2d 500, 503-4 (Fla. 1992); *Napoli v. Buchbinder,* 685 So. 2d 46 (Fla. 4th DCA 1997); *Kowkabany v. Home Depot, Inc.,* 606 So. 2d 716 (Fla.1st DCA 1992).

81. *See McCain v. Florida Power Corp.,* 593 So. 2d 500, 503-504 (Fla. 1992); *Department of Transportation v. Anglin,* 502 So. 2d 896, 898-900 (Fla. 1987); *Stahl v. Metropolitan Dade County,* 438 So. 2d 14, 17-21 (Fla. 3d DCA 1983).

82. *See Stahl v. Metropolitan Dade County,* 438 So. 2d 14, 17-19 (Fla. 3d DCA 1983); Fla. Std. J. Instr. (Civ.) 5.1(a). In certain cases, factual causation must be established by expert testimony, and such testimony must establish such causation by probabilities, not possibilities. *See Gooding v. University Hospital Building, Inc.,* 445 So. 2d 1015, 1018 (Fla. 1984) (medical malpractice); *Elder v. Farulla,* 768 So. 2d 1152, 1152-55 (Fla. 2d DCA 2000) (medical malpractice); *Rodriguez v. Feinstein,* 793 So. 2d 1057 (Fla. 3d DCA 2001) (medical malpractice); *Wong v. Crown Equipment Corp.,* 676 So. 2d 981 (Fla. 3d DCA 1996) (products liability).

83. *See McCain v. Florida Power Corp.,* 593 So. 2d 500, 503-4 (Fla. 1992); *Cruz v. Plasencia,* 778 So. 2d 458 (Fla. 3d DCA 2001); *Bennett M. Lifter, Inc. v. Varnado,* 480 So. 2d 1336, 1338-40 (Fla. 3d DCA 1985); *K-Mart Enterprises of Florida, Inc. v. Keller,* 439 So. 2d 283, 285-87 (Fla. 3d DCA 1983); *Stahl v. Metropolitan Dade County,* 438 So. 2d 14, 17-21 (Fla. 3d DCA 1983); Fla. Std. J. Instr. (Civ.) 5.1(b) and (c).

84. *See McCain v. Florida Power Corp.,* 593 So. 2d 500, 503 (Fla. 1992); *Bennett M. Lifter, Inc. v. Varnado,* 480 So. 2d 1336, 1340 (Fla. 3d DCA 1985); *K-Mart Enterprises of Florida, Inc. v. Keller,* 439 So. 2d 283, 286 (Fla. 3d DCA 1983); *Crislip v. Holland,* 401 So. 2d 1115, 1117 (Fla. 4th DCA 1981), *rev. denied sub. nom., City of Fort Pierce v. Crislip,* 411 So. 2d 380 (Fla. 1981).

85. *See Department of Transportation v. Anglin,* 502 So. 2d 896, 899-900 (Fla. 1987); *Barnes v. Gulf Power Corp.,* 517 So. 2d 717 (Fla. 1st DCA 1987); *Derrer v. Georgia Electric Co.,* 537 So. 2d 593 (Fla. 3d DCA 1988), *rev. denied,* 545 So. 2d 1366 (Fla. 1989); *Gomez v. Plasencia,* 522 So. 2d 423 (Fla. 3d DCA 1988);

Watson v. Lucerne Machinery & Equipment, Inc., 347 So. 2d 459 (Fla. 2d DCA 1977); *Goulah v. Ford Motor Co.*, 118 F.3d 1478, 1485-86 (11th Cir. 1997) (applying Florida law); *Kroon v. Beech Aircraft Corporation*, 628 F.2d 891 (5th Cir. 1980) (applying Florida law).

86. *See Hoffman v. Jones*, 280 So. 2d 431 (Fla. 1973).

87. *See* Section 768.81(2), Fla. Stat. (1997).

88. *See* Sections 768.81(2) and 768.81(4)(a), Fla. Stat. (1997).

89. *See Derrer v. Georgia Electric Co.*, 537 So. 2d 593 (Fla. 3d DCA 1989); *Gomez v. Plasencia*, 522 So. 2d 423 (Fla. 3d DCA 1988); *Watson v. Lucerne Machinery & Equipment, Inc.*, 347 So. 2d 459 (Fla. 2d DCA 1977); *Goulah v. Ford Motor Co.*, 118 F.3d 1478, 1485-86 (11th Cir. 1997) (applying Florida law); *Kroon v. Beech Aircraft Corporation*, 628 F.2d 891 (5th Cir. 1980) (applying Florida law).

90. Section 768.81(2), Fla. Stat. (1997). *See Hoffman v. Jones*, 280 So. 2d 431 (Fla. 1973); Fla. Std. J. Instr. (Civ.) 3.8(a). In the products liability context, Florida courts have held that the "open and obvious danger" doctrine is not a bar to liability, but is instead treated as an aspect of the plaintiff's comparative negligence. *Jones v. Auburn Machine Works*, 366 So. 2d 1167 (Fla. 1979); *Ford v. Highlands Ins. Co.*, 369 So. 2d 77 (Fla. 1st DCA 1979), *cert. denied*, (Fla. 1979). Indeed, it has been held that the plaintiff's knowing, unforseeable misuse of a product is only a form of comparative negligence and not a bar to liability for a design defect. *See Standard Havens Products, Inc. v. Benitez*, 648 So. 2d 1192 (Fla. 1995).

91. *See Ridley v. Safety Kleen Corp.*, 693 So. 2d 934 (Fla. 1996).

92. Section 768.81(4)(b), Fla. Stat.(1997). *See Island City Flying Service v. General Electric Credit Corp.*, 585 So. 2d 274 (Fla. 1991); *Deane v. Johnston*, 104 So. 2d 3 (Fla. 1958).

93. *See Kendrick v. Ed's Beach Service, Inc.*, 577 So. 2d 936 (Fla. 1991); *Mazzeo v. City of Sebastian*, 550 So. 2d 1113 (Fla. 1989); *Blackburn v. Dorta*, 436 So. 2d 78 (Fla. 1983).

94. *See Ashcroft v. Calder Race Course, Inc.*, 492 So. 2d 1309 (Fla. 1986) (participation in professional horse racing); *Raveson v. Walt Disney World Company*, 793 So. 2d 1171 (Fla. 5th DCA 2001) (release signed by horse rider enforceable to bar tort claim); *Keuhner v. Green*, 436 So. 2d 78 (Fla. 1983) (participation in karate exhibition); *VanTuyn v. Zurich American Insurance Co.*, 447 So. 2d 318 (Fla. 4th DCA 1984) (riding a "mechanical bull"); Fla. Std. J. Instr. (Civ.) 3.8. *Cf., Dilallo v. Riding Safely, Inc.*, 687 So. 2d 353, 356 (Fla. 4th DCA 1997) (release of stable operating horseback riding concession would have been enforceable had it not been signed by minor).

95. *See* Fla. Std. J. Instr. (Civ.) 3.8.

96. *See Ashcroft v. Calder Race Course, Inc.*, 492 So. 2d 1309 (Fla. 1986) (participation in professional horse racing event did not, as a matter of law, assume the risk of danger arising from negligently placed exit gap in railing).

97. *See McDougald v. Perry*, 716 So. 2d 783, 785-86 (Fla. 1998); *Marrero v. Goldsmith*, 486 So. 2d 530, 531-33 (Fla. 1986); *City of New Smyrna Beach Utilities Comm. v. McWhorter*, 418 So. 2d 261, 262-64 (Fla. 1982); *Goodyear Tire & Rubber Co. v. Hughes Supply, Inc.*, 358 So. 2d 1339, 1341-44 (Fla. 1978); Fla. Std. J. Instr. (Civ.) 4.6. The plaintiff must usually demonstrate as well that no direct evidence of specific negligent acts or omissions of the defendant is reasonably available. *See McDougald*, 716 So. 2d at 786-87; *Marrero*, 486 So. 2d at 531-33; *McWhorter*, 418 So. 2d at 263; *Goodyear*, 358 So. 2d at 1342. A witness's mere "speculation" that the defendant was negligent will not render the doctrine unavailable. *See Strahan v. Gauldin*, 756 So. 2d 158, 160 (Fla. 4th DCA 2000).

98. *See McDougald v. Perry*, 716 So. 2d 783, 786 (Fla. 1998).

99. *Id. See Strahan v. Gauldin*, 756 So. 2d 158, 160 (Fla. 4th DCA 2000).

100. *See McWhorter*, 418 So. 2d 261, 262-64 (Fla. 1982); *Goodyear*, 358 So. 2d at 1342-43; *Otis Elevator Company v. Chambliss*, 511 So. 2d 412 (Fla. 1st DCA 1987); *Bardy v. Sears, Roebuck & Co.*, 443 So. 2d 212 (Fla. 2d DCA 1983).

101. *See* Fla. Std. J. Instr. (Civ.) 4.6.

102. *See Florida Power and Light Co. v. Price*, 159 So. 2d 654 (Fla. 2d DCA), *rev'd*, 170 So. 2d 293 (Fla. 1964); *McCall v. Alabama Bruno's, Inc.*, 647 So. 2d 175 (Fla. 1st DCA 1994); *Florida Freight Terminals, Inc. v. Cabanis*, 354 So. 2d 1222 (Fla. 3d DCA 1978); *Atlantic Coast Development v. Napolean Steel*, 385 So. 2d 676 (Fla. 3d DCA 1980); Fla. Std. J. Instr. (Civ.) 3.3(c). The doctrine applies to protect third parties, as opposed to employees involved in the inherently dangerous or ultrahazardous activity or the party who contracted to have the activity performed. *See Gordon v. Sanders*, 692 So. 2d 939 (Fla. 3d DCA 1997); *Baxley v. Dixie Land & Timber Co.*, 521 So. 2d 170 (Fla. 1st DCA 1988). This doctrine also does not extend to encompass one who is merely the supplier of a non-defective instrumentality, such as a crane, which is thereafter utilized by another engaged in an inherently dangerous activity. *See Northern Trust Bank of Florida, N.A. v. Construction Equipment Int'l., Inc.*, 587 So. 2d 502 (Fla. 3d DCA 1991).

103. *See Madison v. Midyette*, 541 So. 2d 1315, 1317-18 (Fla. 1st DCA 1989), *approved*, 559 So. 2d 1126 (Fla. 1990); *Doak v. Green*, 677 So. 2d 301, 302 (Fla. 1st DCA 1996).

104. *See Doak v. Green*, 677 So. 2d 301, 302 (Fla. 1st DCA 1996); *Florida Power and Light Co. v. Price*, 170 So. 2d 293, 295 (Fla. 1964). *Cf.*, Fla. Std. J. Instr. (Civ.) 3.3(c) (the "performance of work is ultrahazardous if there is a real and substantial danger inherent in the work itself and if the work is of such a nature that, in the ordinary course of events, performance of the work will probably cause injury if proper precautions are not taken").

105. *See Doak v. Green*, 677 So. 2d 301, 302 (Fla. 1st DCA 1996); *Hill v. Walker's Cay Air Terminal, Inc.*, 405 So. 2d 198 (Fla. 4th DCA 1981), *rev. denied*, 412 So. 2d 471 (Fla. 1982).

106. *See Doak v. Green*, 677 So. 2d 301, 302 (Fla. 1st DCA 1996); *McCall v. Alabama Bruno's, Inc.*, 647 So. 2d 175 (Fla. 1st DCA 1994); *Florida Freight Terminals, Inc. v. Cabanis*, 354 So. 2d 1222 (Fla. 3d DCA 1978); *Atlantic Coast Development v. Napolean Steel*, 385 So. 2d 676 (Fla. 3d DCA 1980).

107. *See deJesus v. Seaboard Coast Line R.R.*, 281 So. 2d 198 (Fla. 1973).

108. *See Sloan v. Coit Int'l., Inc.*, 292 So. 2d 15 (Fla. 1974) (state penal statute prohibiting sale of firearms to minors); *Tamiami Gun Shop v. Klein*, 116 So. 2d 421 (Fla. 1959) (same); *Tampa Shipbuilding & Engineering v. Adams*, 132 Fla. 419, 181 So. 403 (1938) (state penal statute prohibiting certain child labor practices).

109. *See Tamiami Gun Shop v. Klein*, 116 So. 2d 421, 423 (Fla. 1959); *deJesus v. Seaboard Coast Line R.R.*, 281 So. 2d 198, 200 (Fla. 1973).

110. *See deJesus v. Seaboard Coast Line R.R.*, 281 So. 2d 198 (Fla. 1973) (state penal statute requiring trains blocking highways at night to post lighted warning devices); *Golden Shoreline Limited Partnership v. McGowan*, 787 So. 2d 109 (Fla. 2d DCA 2001) (non-penal statute imposing duty on elevator owner to be responsible for its operation and maintenance); *Eckelbarger v. Frank*, 732 So. 2d 433 (Fla. 2d DCA 1999) (non-penal county ordinance requiring self-closing, self-latching gate around swimming pools); *Newsome v. Haffner*, 710 So. 2d 184 (Fla. 1st DCA), *rev. denied*, 722 So. 2d 193 (Fla. 1998) (state penal statute prohibiting owners of residential dwellings from allowing minors to consume alcohol or use drugs at open house parties); *Bennett M. Lifter, Inc. v. Varnado*, 480 So. 2d 1336, 1338-39 (Fla. 3d DCA 1985) (non-penal county ordinance requiring landlord to provide and maintain running hot water system in tenant's residence); *K-Mart Enterprises of Florida, Inc. v. Keller*, 439 So. 2d 283, 285-87 (Fla. 3d DCA 1983) (federal penal statute requiring background checks and prohibiting sale of firearms to certain specified individuals); *H. K. Corporation v. Estate of Miller*, 405 So. 2d 218, 219 (Fla. 3d DCA 1981) (non-penal state administrative regulation establishing standards for minimum water depth underneath diving boards in pools); *Florida Freight Terminals, Inc. v. Cabanas*, 354 So. 2d 1222, 1224-25

(Fla. 3d DCA 1978) (non-penal federal FAA safety regulation requiring securing of cargo to prevent its shifting during flight).

111. *See deJesus v. Seaboard Coast Line R.R.*, 281 So. 2d 198, 201 (Fla. 1973); *Golden Shoreline Limited Partnership v. McGowan*, 787 So. 2d 109, 111 (Fla. 2d DCA 2001).

112. *See Florida Freight Terminals, Inc. v. Cabanas*, 354 So. 2d 1222, 1224-25 (Fla. 3d DCA 1978); *Richardson v. Fountain*, 154 So. 2d 709 (Fla. 2d DCA 1963); Fla. Std. J. Instr. (Civ.) 4.9 and Comment. It should be noted, however, that in order to be entitled to the giving of the negligence *per se* jury instruction, the plaintiff must present some competent evidence that the statute applies under the facts to impose a duty on the defendant and that the defendant actually violated the statute, ordinance or regulation *See Szilagyi v. North Florida Hotel Corp.*, 610 So. 2d 1319 (Fla. 1st DCA 1992) (no evidence of violation of non-penal statute); *R. D. Jackson v. Harsco Corp.*, 364 So. 2d 808, 809-10 (Fla. 3d DCA 1978) (non-penal administrative regulation not applicable to defendant).

113. *See deJesus v. Seaboard Coast Line R.R.*, 281 So. 2d 198, 201 (Fla. 1973); Section 769.81, Fla. Stat. (1997); Fla. Std. J. Instr. (Civ.) 4.9 and Comment.

114. Fla. Std. J. Instr. (Civ.) 4.11. *See Ridley v. Safety Kleen Corp.*, 693 So. 2d 934 (Fla. 1996) (state motor vehicle statute requiring use of seatbelts); *Baggett v. Davis*, 124 Fla. 701, 169 So. 372 (1936) (state motor vehicle statute establishing safe operation requirements); *Allen v. Hooper*, 126 Fla. 458, 171 So. 513 (1937) (same); *Clark v. Summer*, 72 So. 2d 375 (Fla.1954) (same); *Chevron U.S.A., Inc. v. Forbes*, 783 So. 2d 1215, 1217-20 (Fla. 4th DCA 2001) (non-penal state statute requiring self-service gas stations to have attendant on duty to control dispensing of flammable liquids); *Grand Union Co. v. Rocker*, 454 So. 2d 14 (Fla. 3d DCA 1984) (non-penal state statute establishing minimum building code standards).

115. *See* Fla. Std. J. Instr. (Civ.) 4.11. It should be noted, however, that the plaintiff must also present some competent evidence that the defendant's violation of the traffic regulation had some causal relationship to the plaintiff's injury in order to be entitled to the giving of such a jury instruction. *See Brackin v. Boles*, 452 So. 2d 540, 544-45 (Fla. 1984).

116. *See Smith v. Department of Ins.*, 507 So. 2d 1080, 1091 (Fla. 1987); *Feinstone v. Allison Hospital, Inc.*, 106 Fla. 302, 143 So. 251, 252-53 (1932).

117. *See Stuart v. Hertz Corp.*, 351 So. 2d 703, 705 (Fla. 1977); *Letzter v. Cephas*, 792 So. 2d 481 (Fla. 4th DCA 2001), *review granted*, 796 So. 2d 535 (Fla. 2001).

118. Section 768.31, Fla. Stat. (1997) (requiring the existence of a "common liability" owed to injured party arising out of the same transaction or series

of transactions in order for a right to contribution to arise). *See Stuart v. Hertz Corp.*, 351 So. 2d 703, 705 (Fla. 1977); *Letzter v. Cephas*, 792 So. 2d 481 (Fla. 4th DCA 2001), *review granted*, 796 So. 2d 535 (Fla. 2001); *Peoples Gas System v. Acme Gas Corp.*, 689 So. 2d 292, 299 (Fla. 3d DCA 1997); *Albertson's, Inc. v. Adams*, 473 So. 2d 231, 233 (Fla. 2d DCA 1985); *Touche Ross & Co. v. Sun Bank of Riverside*, 366 So. 2d 465 (Fla. 3d DCA 1979). An equitable subrogation action by an initial tortfeasor may, however, be permitted against a successive tortfeasor who aggravates or increases the nature or extent of the claimant's initial injury. *See Underwriters at Lloyds v. City of Lauderdale Lakes*, 382 So. 2d 702 (Fla. 1980); *Caccauella v. Silverman*, 2002 WL 530557 (Fla. 4th DCA 2002).

119. *See D'Amario v. Ford Motor Co.*, 2001 WL 1472600 (Fla. 2001); *Gross v. Lyons*, 763 So. 2d 276 (Fla. 2000); *Caccauella v. Silverman*, 2002 WL 530557 (Fla. 4th DCA 2002); *Letzter v. Cephas*, 792 So. 2d 481 (Fla. 4th DCA 2001), *review granted*, 796 So. 2d 535 (Fla. 2001); *Association for Retarded Citizens-Volusia, Inc. v. Fletcher*, 741 So. 2d 520 (5th DCA 1999), *rev. denied*, 744 So. 2d 452 (Fla. 1999).

120. Codified as Section 768.81(3), Fla. Stat.

121. *See* Laws 1999, c. 99-225, § 27. The 1999 amendments "shall take effect on October 1, 1999." *Id.* Whether the significant changes made to the Act in 1999 will apply to cases pending as of the amendment's effective date is currently an open question. *See* Hal B. Anderson, *Understanding And Applying Florida's New Limits On Joint And Several Liability*, Florida Defense Lawyers Assoc. Trial Advocate Quarterly Vol. 19, No. 4, Pp. 37-38 (Fall 2000).

122. Section 768.81(4)(a), Fla. Stat. (1997).

123. Section 768.81(4)(b), Fla. Stat. (1997). *See Merrill Crossings Associates v. McDonald*, 705 So. 2d 560 (Fla. 1997) (landowner charged with negligence in failing to employ reasonable security precautions on premises not entitled to reduce liability for entire damage award by trying to shift a portion of responsibility to a nonparty tortfeasor whose intentional criminal conduct was a foreseeable result of the landowner's negligence). *But see D'Amario v. Ford Motor Co.*, 806 So. 2d 424 (Fla. 2002); (holding that driving while intoxicated is not an "intentional tort" for purposes of apportionment of fault under the Act).

124. Section 768.81(4)(b), Fla. Stat. (1997). Included among those statutory causes of action expressly exempted from the Act are those involving certain land sales practices, sales of securities, combinations in restraint of trade or commerce, and offenses concerning racketeering and illegal debts.

125. Section 768.81(5), Fla. Stat (1997). *See Schultz v. Wilkes*, 689 So. 2d 435 (Fla. 5th DCA 1997).

126. Section 768.81(3), Fla. Stat (1997). If the defendant's percentage of fault is less than the plaintiff's percentage of fault, then the doctrine of joint and several liability will not apply to even the economic damages awarded. Section 768.81(3)(c), Fla. Stat. (1997).

127. Section 768.81(3). Fla. Stat. (1997). *See Olson v. N. Cole Construction Co.*, 681 So. 2d 799 (Fla. 2d DCA 1996); *Dewitt Excavating, Inc. v. Walters*, 642 So. 2d 833 (Fla. 5th DCA 1994).

128. Section 768.81(3), Fla. Stat. (1999). *See D'Amario v. Ford Motor Co.*, 806 So. 2d 424 (Fla. 2002); *Gouty v. Schnepel*, 795 So. 2d 959 (Fla. 2001); *Anderson v. Ewing*, 768 So. 2d 1161 (Fla. 4th DCA 2000).

129. Section 768.81(3)(a) - (b), Fla. Stat. (1999). As with the 1986 version, if it is found that the defendant's percentage of fault is less than the plaintiff's percentage of fault, the doctrine of joint and several liability will not apply to any extent to the economic damages awarded. Section 768.81(3)(c).

130. Section 768.81(3)(a) - (b), Fla. Stat. (1999).

131. Section 768.81(3), Fla. Stat. (1999).

132. Under the 1986 version, it was not clear from the statutory language whether "nonparties" should be included in the apportionment assessment. In *Fabre v. Marin*, 623 So. 2d 1182 (Fla. 1993), Florida's supreme court ruled that they should, even if the non-party could not be sued directly due to the existence of an immunity, such as the interspousal immunity involved in that case. *See Allied Signal v. Fox*, 623 So. 2d 1180 (1993) (contributing fault of immune employer who was not a party to suit should be considered by jury in apportioning damages in employee's lawsuit); *Y. H. Investments, Inc. v. Godales*, 690 So. 2d 1273 (Fla. 1997) (contributing fault of immune father who was not a party to suit should be considered by jury in apportioning damages in lawsuit brought on behalf of father's minor son). In contrast, the statutory language of the 1999 version expressly contemplates the inclusion of nonparties in the apportionment assessment. *See* Section 768.81(3)(d) -(e), Fla. Stat. (1999).

133. Apportionment of damages under the Act can only occur between "joint" tortfeasors. *See Anderson v. Ewing*, 768 So. 2d 1161 (Fla. 4th DCA 2000) (one defendant not entitled to have judgment entered against him based upon the specific percentage of fault the jury attributed to him in its verdict because the trial court ultimately entered JNOV for the other defendant to whom the jury had also attributed a percentage of fault). Additionally, if the tortfeasors are deemed to be "successive" tortfeasors or if they caused "separate" and "divisible" damages, then the Act will not apply to permit an apportionment of fault under the Act. *See D'Amario v. Ford Motor Co.*, 806 So. 2d 424 (Fla. 2002); *Gross v. Lyons*, 763 So. 2d 276 (Fla. 2000); *Letzter v. Cephas*, 792 So. 2d 481 (Fla. 4th DCA 2001), *rev. granted*, 796 So. 2d 535 (Fla.

2001); *Gordon v. Marvin M. Rosenberg, D.D.S., P. A.*, 654 So. 2d 643 (Fla. 4th DCA 1995).

134. Section 768.81(3)(d), Fla. Stat. (1999). *See Nash v. Wells Fargo Guard Service*, 678 So. 2d 1262, 1263 (Fla. 1996) (reading the same requirement into the 1986 version of the Act).

135. Section 768.81(3)(e), Fla. Stat. (1999). *See Clark v. Polk County*, 753 So. 2d 138 (Fla. 2d DCA 2000); *Snoozy v. U.S. Gypsum Co.*, 695 So. 2d 767, 769 (Fla. 3d DCA 1997); *W. R. Grace & Company-Conn. v. Dougherty*, 636 So. 2d 746, 747-48 (Fla. 2d DCA), *rev. denied*, 645 So. 2d 454 (Fla. 1994).

136. Sections 46.015(2), 768.041(1)-(2), and 768.31(5), Fla. Stat. (1997). *See J. R. Brooks & Son, Inc. v. Quiroz*, 707 So. 2d 861 (Fla. 3d DCA 1998); *Baudo v. Bon Secours Hospital/Villa Maria Nursing Center*, 684 So. 2d 211 (Fla. 3d DCA 1996).

137. Sections 46.015(2), 768.041(2), and 768.31(5), Fla. Stat. (1997). In order for a non-settling defendant to be entitled to the statutory setoff for economic damages, however, the settling party must be deemed to be a potential "joint tortfeasor" with the non-settling party. *See D'Amario v. Ford Motor Co.*, 806 So. 2d 424 (Fla. 2002); *Gross v. Lyons*, 763 So. 2d 276 (Fla. 2000); *Caccauella v. Silverman*, 2002 WL 530557 (Fla. 4th DCA 2002); *Letzter v. Cephas*, 792 So. 2d 481 (Fla. 4th DCA 2001), *rev. granted*, 796 So. 2d 535 (Fla. 2001); *Gordon v. Marvin M. Rosenberg, D.D.S., P.A.*, 654 So. 2d 643 (Fla. 4th DCA 1995). If the settling party is at least a "potential" joint tortfeasor, but the jury ultimately concludes that the settling party was not a tortfeasor (*i.e.*, not guilty of any "fault"), then the set-off will not be permitted. *See Schnepel v. Gouty*, 795 So. 2d 959 (Fla. 2001).

138. Section 768.81(3), Fla. Stat. (1997). *See Wells v. Tallahassee Mem. Med. Center*, 659 So. 2d 249, 253 (Fla. 1995). In determining the extent of the set-off to which the non-settling defendant is entitled, the court will apportion the settlement proceeds between economic and noneconomic damages in the same proportion as that found by the jury in its verdict. *Id.* at 254. In addition, a private settlement agreement under which several plaintiffs unilaterally decide how to allocate the settlement funds among themselves is not binding upon either the court or the non-settling defendant(s). *See Dionese v. City of West Palm Beach*, 500 So. 2d 1347 (Fla. 1987); *Anderson v. Ewing*, 768 So. 2d 1161, 1165-66 (Fla. 4th DCA 2000).

139. Section 768.041(3), Fla. Stat. (1997).

140. *See Houdaille Industries, Inc. v. Edwards*, 374 So. 2d 490 (Fla. 1979).

141. *Id.* at 493.

142. *See Dade County School Board v. Radio Station WQBA*, 731 So. 2d 638, 642 (Fla. 1999); *Houdaille Industries, Inc. v. Edwards*, 374 So. 2d 490, 492-94 (Fla. 1979); *Paul N. Howard Co. v. Affholder, Inc.*, 701 So. 2d 402, 403-4 (Fla. 5th DCA 1997); *Walter Taft Bradshaw & Associates, P.A. v. Bedsole*, 374 So. 2d 644 (Fla. 4th DCA 1979).

143. *See Dominion of Canada v. State Farm Fire and Casualty Co.*, 754 So. 2d 852, 855 (Fla. 2d DCA 2000); *Paul N. Howard Co. v. Affholder, Inc.*, 701 So. 2d 402 (Fla. 5th DCA 1997); *Transport International Pool, Inc. v. Pat Salmon & Sons of Florida, Inc.*, 609 So. 2d 658, 660-61 (Fla. 4th DCA 1993); *Scott & Jobalia Construction Co., Inc. v. Halifax Paving, Inc.*, 538 So. 2d 76, 79-82 (Fla. 5th DCA 1989), *approved*, 565 So. 2d 1346 (Fla. 1990); *Kala Investments. Inc. v. Sklar*, 538 So. 2d 909, 916-17 (Fla. 3d DCA 1989).

144. *See Dade County School Board v. Radio Station WQBA*, 731 So. 2d 638, 644-47 (Fla. 1999); *Dominion of Canada v. State Farm Fire and Casualty Co.*, 754 So. 2d 852, 855-57 (Fla. 2d DCA 2000); *Transport International Pool, Inc. v. Pat Salmon & Sons of Florida, Inc.*, 609 So. 2d 658, 661-64 (Fla. 4th DCA 1993); *Kala Investments, Inc. v. Sklar*, 538 So. 2d 909, 917-19 (Fla. 3d DCA 1989).

145. *See Cox Cable Corp. v. Gulf Power Co.*, 591 So. 2d 627 (Fla. 1992); *Charles Poe Masonry, Inc. v. Spring Lock Scaffolding Rental Equipment Co.*, 374 So. 2d 487 (Fla. 1979); *University Plaza Shopping Center v. Stewart*, 272 So. 2d 507 (Fla. 1973).

146. *See Winn Dixie Stores, Inc., v. D & J Construction Co.*, 633 So. 2d 65 (Fla. 4th DCA 1994); *Transport International Pool, Inc. v. Pat Salmon & Sons of Florida, Inc.*, 609 So. 2d 658, 660-61 (Fla. 4th DCA 1993); *Etiole International, N.V. v. Miami Elevator Company, Inc.*, 573 So. 2d 921 (Fla. 3d DCA 1991); *Snowhite Dust Control Services, Inc. v. Becker*, 568 So. 2d 110 (Fla. 4th DCA 1990); *Ryder Truck Rental, Inc. v. Coastline Distributing of Tampa, Inc.*, 512 So. 2d 1093 (Fla. 2d DCA 1987); *Walter Taft Bradshaw & Associates, P.A. v. Bedsole*, 374 So. 2d 644, 646-47 (Fla. 4th DCA 1979); *Joseph L. Rozier Machinery Co. v. Nilo Barge Line, Inc.*, 318 So. 2d 557 (Fla. 2d DCA 1975), *cert. denied*, 328 So. 2d 843 (Fla. 1976).

147. *See Cox Cable Corp. v. Gulf Power Co.*, 591 So. 2d 627 (Fla. 1992); *Charles Poe Masonry, Inc. v. Spring Lock Scaffolding Rental Equipment Co.*, 374 So. 2d 487 (Fla. 1979); *University Plaza Shopping Center v. Stewart*, 272 So. 2d 507 (Fla. 1973); *Ryder Truck Rental, Inc. v. Coastline Distributing of Tampa, Inc.*, 512 So. 2d 1093 (Fla. 2d DCA 1987); *Walter Taft Bradshaw & Associates, P.A. v. Bedsole*, 374 So. 2d 644 (Fla. 4th DCA 1979).

148. Section 725.06, Fla. Stat. (1997). *See Peoples Gas System, Inc. v. RSH Constructors, Inc.*, 563 So. 2d 107 (Fla. 1st DCA 1990). It should be noted that this statute has undergone substantive changes both in the year 2000 and in 2001. If the construction contract at issue was entered into prior to July 1, 2000, then the 1997 version of the statute should be consulted. If the

contract was entered into between July 1, 2000 and July 1, 2001, then the 2000 version of the statute should be consulted. As to construction contracts entered into after July 1, 2001, the 2001 version of the statute will apply.

149. Section 440, Fla. Stat. (1997).

150. Section 440.11(1), Fla. Stat. (1997).

151. *See* Sections 440.09 and 440.092, Fla. Stat. (1997).

152. *See* Sections 440.09 - 440.11, Fla. Stat. (1997).

153. *See Deen v. Quantum Resources, Inc.*, 750 So. 2d 616 (Fla. 1999); *Mandico v. Taos Construction, Inc.*, 605 So. 2d 850 (Fla. 1992); *Employers Insurance of Wassau v. Abernathy*, 442 So. 2d 953 (Fla. 1983); *Motchkavitz v. L. C. Boggs Industries, Inc.*, 407 So. 2d 910 (Fla. 1981); *Jones v. Florida Power Corp.*, 72 So. 2d 285 (Fla. 1954).

154. Section 440.10(1)(b), Fla. Stat. (1997). *See Gator Freightways, Inc. v. Roberts*, 550 So. 2d 1117 (Fla. 1989); *Motchkavitz v. L. C. Boggs Industries, Inc.*, 407 So. 2d 910 (Fla. 1981); *Brickley v. Gulf Coast Construction Co.*, 153 Fla. 216, 14 So. 2d 265 (1943); *Pinnacle Const., Inc. v. Alderman*, 639 So. 2d 1061 (Fla. 3d DCA 1994); *Walker v. United Steel Works, Inc.*, 606 So. 2d 1243 (Fla. 2d DCA 1992).

155. Section 440.10(1)(e), Fla. Stat. (1997).

156. *See Ramos v. Univision Holdings, Inc.*, 655 So. 2d 89 (Fla. 1995); *Batmasian v. Ballachino*, 755 So. 2d 157 (Fla. 4th DCA 2000); *Proctor & Gamble Cellulose Company*, 667 So. 2d 338 (Fla. 1st DCA 1995); *Perkins v. Scott*, 554 So. 2d 1220 (Fla. 2d DCA 1990).

157. Under the Act, the term "employee" does not include "independent contractors" who meet certain statutory criteria. *See* Sections 440.02(13)(d) and 440.02(13)(d)1.a.-(13)(d)1.i., Fla. Stat. (1997).

158. *See Sotomayor v. Huntington Broward Associates, L. P., Ltd.*, 697 So. 2d 1006 (Fla. 4th DCA 1997); *Proctor & Gamble Cellulose Company*, 667 So. 2d 338 (Fla. 1st DCA 1995).

159. *See Gulfstream Land & Development Corp. v. Wilkerson*, 420 So. 2d 587 (Fla. 1982).

160. *See United Parcel Service v. Welsh*, 659 So. 2d 1234 (Fla. 5th DCA 1995); *Delta Air Lines, Inc. v. Cunningham*, 658 So. 2d 556 (Fla. 3d DCA 1995), *rev. denied*, 668 So. 2d 602 (Fla. 1996).

161. *See Pearson v. Harris*, 449 So. 2d 339 (Fla. 1st DCA 1984); *Hume v. Thomason*, 440 So. 2d 441 (Fla. 1st DCA 1983); *Chorak v. Naughton*, 409 So. 2d 35 (Fla. 2d DCA 1982); *Matthews v. G.S.P. Corp.*, 354 So. 2d 1243 (Fla. 1st DCA 1978).

162. Section 440.39(1), Fla. Stat. (1997).

163. *See Seaboard Coast Line Railroad Co. v. Smith*, 359 So. 2d 427 (Fla. 1978); *Hyster Co. v. David*, 612 So. 2d 678 (Fla. 1st DCA 1993); *United Gas Pipeline Co. v. Gulf Power Co.*, 334 So. 2d 310 (Fla. 1st DCA 1976), *cert. denied*, 341 So. 2d 1086 (Fla. 1976).

164. *See Sunspan Engineering & Construction Co. v. Springlock Scaffolding Co.*, 310 So. 2d 4 (Fla. 1975) (holding Act unconstitutional to the extent it attempted to bar a cause of action for indemnity by third party sued by employee); *Houdaille Industries, Inc. v. Edwards*, 374 So. 2d 490 (Fla. 1979) (recognizing that third party had right to sue employer for common law indemnity, but holding that common law indemnity claim was not viable under facts); *City of Clearwater v. L. M. Duncan & Sons, Inc.*, 466 So. 2d 1116 (Fla. 2d DCA 1985), *aff'd*, 478 So. 2d 816 (Fla. 1985) (permitting third party's claim for contractual indemnity from employer); *Miami International Merchandise Mart v. Gene Somers & Associates, Inc.*, 506 So. 2d 54 (Fla. 3d DCA 1987) (holding that exclusive remedy provision of Act was unconstitutional to the extent that it attempted to immunize an employer from liability based upon contractual indemnity).

165. Section 440.39(2) and (3), Fla. Stat. (1997). If the injured employee or his representatives do not bring a suit against the third party within one year after the cause of action accrued, then the employer or the insurance carrier may proceed to file the suit for its own benefit and for the benefit of the injured employee and dependents. Section 440.39(4).

166. Section 440.39(3), Fla. Stat. (1997).

167. *Id*.

168. *Id*.

169. Section 440.11(1), Fla. Stat. (1997). *See Eller v. Shova*, 630 So. 2d 537 (Fla. 1993) (co-employees willful, wanton, gross negligence exception to immunity); *Cox v. Simeon, Inc.*, 668 So. 2d 706 (Fla. 5th DCA 1996) (same); *Holmes County School Board v. Duffell*, 651 So. 2d 1176 (Fla. 1995) (co-employee unrelated works exception).

170. *See Fisher v. Shenandoah General Construction Co.*, 498 So. 2d 882 (Fla. 1987) and *Lawton v. Alpine Engineered Products, Inc.*, 498 So. 2d 879 (Fla. 1987), both affirmed in part and receded from in part by *Turner v. PCR, Inc.*, 754 So. 2d

683 (Fla. 2000); *Pachecho v. Florida Power & Light Company*, 784 So. 2d 1159, 1163 (Fla. 3d DCA 2001); *Splaine v. City of West Palm Beach*, 768 So. 2d 1183 (Fla. 4th DCA 2000).

171. *See Turner v. PCR, Inc.*, 754 So. 2d 683 (Fla. 2000); *Inservices, Inc. v. Aguilera*, 2001 WL 1335817 (Fla. 3d DCA 2001); *Splaine v. City of West Palm Beach*, 768 So. 2d 1183 (Fla. 4th DCA 2000); *Myrick v. Luhrs Corp.*, 689 So. 2d 416 (Fla. 5th DCA 1997); *Connelly v. Arrow Air, Inc.*, 568 So. 2d 448 (Fla. 3d DCA 1990), *rev. denied*, 581 So. 2d 1307 (Fla. 1991).

172. *See Wood v. Camp*, 284 So. 2d 691 (Fla. 1973); *Gorin v. City of St. Augustine*, 595 So. 2d 1062 (Fla. 5th DCA 1992).

173. *See Maldonado v. Jack M. Berry Grove Corp.*, 351 So. 2d 967, 968-69 (Fla. 1977); *Hix v. Billen*, 284 So. 2d 209, 210 (Fla. 1973); *Seaboard System Railroad, Inc. v. Mells*, 528 So. 2d 934 (Fla. 1st DCA 1988).

174. *See Wood v. Camp*, 284 So. 2d 691 (Fla. 1973).

175. *Id.* In Florida, more than one party may owe a duty to persons who enter the premises, and the fact that one party fails to perform its duty is not a defense to a claim against another party who also owes a duty with respect to the safety of those on the premises. *See Worth v. Eugene Gentile Builders*, 697 So. 2d 945, 947 (Fla. 4th DCA 1997). Thus, it is not ownership of the property which determines the duty of care, but rather, the failure of a person who is in actual possession and control (be it the owner, an agent, a lessee, a construction contractor, or other possessor with authority or control), to use due care that gives rise to liability caused by dangerous operations, activities or conditions. *Id. See Link v. Gonzalez*, 699 So. 2d 266, 267 (Fla. 3d DCA 1997).

176. *See Owens v. Publix Supermarkets, Inc.*, 802 So. 2d 315 (Fla. 2001); *Yuniter v. A & A Edgewater of Florida, Inc.*, 707 So. 2d 763, 764 (Fla. 2d DCA 1998); *Cooper Hotel Services, Inc. v. MacFarland*, 662 So. 2d 710, 712 (Fla. 2d DCA 1995); *Arauz v. Truesdell*, 698 So. 2d 872, 874 (Fla. 3d DCA 1997); *La Villarena, Inc. v. Acosta*, 597 So. 2d 336, 337 (Fla. 3d DCA 1992); *Miller v. Wallace*, 591 So. 2d 971, 973 (Fla. 5th DCA 1991); *Spaulding v. City of Melbourne*, 473 So. 2d 226, 227 (Fla. 5th DCA 1985); *Pittman v. Volusia County*, 380 So. 2d 1192, 1193 (Fla. 5th DCA 1980); Fla. Std. J. Instr. (Civ.) 3.5(f).

177. *See Wood v. Camp*, 284 So. 2d 691 (Fla. 1973) (social invitee); *Post v. Lunney*, 261 So. 2d 146 (Fla. 1972) (business invitee); Fla. Std. J. Instr. (Civ.) 3.2(a).

178. *See Community Christian Center Ministries, Inc. v. Plante*, 719 So. 2d 368 (Fla. 4th DCA 1998); *Cardaman v. Sportatorium, Inc.*, 505 So. 2d 31 (Fla. 4th DCA 1987); *IRE Florida Income Partners, Ltd. v. Scott*, 381 So. 2d 1114, 1117 (Fla. 1st DCA 1979), *cert. denied*, 388 So. 2d 1118 (Fla. 1980); Fla. Std. J. Instr. (Civ.) 3.2(a). The invitee may also lose such status by engaging in an acti-

vity for which the premises were not held open. *See Doughtery v. Hernando County*, 419 So. 2d 679 (Fla. 5th DCA 1982) (although plaintiff was an invitee while a pedestrian on a bridge's walkway, he lost that status when he climbed onto the bridge's guardrail and used it as a diving platform).

179. *See Golfview Club at Fountainbleau Park Condominium, No. 1, Inc. v. Parker*, 549 So. 2d 1130 (Fla. 3d DCA 1989) (building resident's friend who died after falling into garbage chute whose top was located on building roof was an invitee as a matter of law since maintenance man had allegedly directed girl to rooftop to sing and play guitar).

180. *See Sonn v. Swindal-Powell Co.*, 88 So. 2d 319 (Fla. 1956); *Community Christian Center Ministries, Inc. v. Plante*, 719 So. 2d 368 (Fla. 4th DCA 1998); *Cardaman v. Sportatorium, Inc.*, 505 So. 2d 31 (Fla. 4th DCA 1987).

181. In those cases where this element is required, the possessor's "constructive knowledge" may be established by circumstantial evidence showing that (1) the dangerous condition existed for such a length of time that in the exercise of ordinary care, the possessor should have known of the condition; or (2) the condition occurred with regularity and was therefore foreseeable. *See Owens v. Publix Supermarkets, Inc.*, 802 So. 2d 315 (Fla. 2001). Liability has also been found in a few cases where, even without proof of constructive knowledge, the frequent existence of the particular condition at issue was shown to be generally foreseeable as a result of the particular nature of the defendant's enterprise and/or its usual method of operation. *Id.* Lastly, the element of constructive knowledge has now been totally eliminated from the liability analysis in cases involving slip and falls on transitory foreign substances at business premises like grocery stores. *Id.* Under the new liability standard, once it is shown that the customer slipped and fell as a result of a foreign transitory substance, a rebuttable presumption of negligence arises, which shifts the burden to the defendant to show it exercised reasonable care in the maintenance of the premises. *Id.*

182. *See Wal-Mart Stores, Inc. v. Reggie*, 714 So. 2d 601 (Fla. 4th DCA 1998); Metropolitan *Dade County v. Ivanov*, 689 So. 2d 1267 (Fla. 3d DCA 1997); *Carbonell v. BellSouth Telcoms.*, 675 So. 2d 705 (Fla. 3d DCA 1996); *Hamideh v. K-Mart Corp.*, 648 So. 2d 824 (Fla. 3d DCA 1995); *Schaap v. Publix Supermarkets, Inc.*, 579 So. 2d 831 (Fla. 1st DCA 1991); *Bennett v. Mattison*, 382 So. 2d 873 (Fla. 1st DCA 1980).

183. *See Crown Liquors of Broward, Inc. v. Evenrud*, 436 So. 2d 927, 930-31 (Fla. 2d DCA 1983) (on rehearing); *Reichenbach v. Days Inn, Inc.*, 401 So. 2d 1366 (Fla. 5th DCA 1981).

184. *See Orlando Executive Park, Inc. v. Robbins*, 433 So. 2d 491 (Fla. 1983); *Stevens v. Jefferson*, 436 So. 2d 33 (Fla. 1983); *Benton Inv. Co., Inc. v. Wal-Mart Stores, Inc.*, 704 So. 2d 130 (Fla. 1st DCA 1997); *Foster v. Po Folks, Inc.*, 674 So. 2d 843 (Fla. 4th DCA 1996); *U. S. Security Services Corp. v. Ramada Inn*, 665 So.

2d 268 (Fla. 3d DCA 1995); *Holiday Inns, Inc. v. Shelburne*, 576 So. 2d 322 (Fla. 4th DCA 1991), *appeal dism.*, 589 So. 2d 291 (Fla. 1991); *Holley v. Mt. Zion Terrace Apts., Inc.*, 382 So. 2d 98 (Fla. 3d DCA 1980). In 1999, the Florida legislature enacted a law which provides for a presumption against liability in favor of a convenience store operator for injuries caused by criminal acts of third parties if the operator implemented certain specified security measures. Section 768.0705, Fla. Stat. (1999).

185. *See Wood v. Camp*, 284 So. 2d 691, 693-94 (Fla. 1973); *Link v. Gonzalez*, 699 So. 2d 266 (Fla. 3d DCA 1997); *Dyals v. Hodges*, 659 So. 2d 482, 483-86 (Fla. 1st DCA 1995); Marks v. Delcastillo, 386 So. 2d 1259 (Fla. 3d DCA 1980), *rev. denied*, 397 So. 2d 778 (Fla. 1981); *Libby v. West Coast Rock Co.*, 308 So. 2d 602 (Fla. 2d DCA 1975), *cert. denied*, 325 So. 2d 6 (Fla. 1975); Fla. Std. J. Instr. (Civ.) 3.2 (c).

186. Section 768.075(2) and (3)(b), Fla. Stat. (1999).

187. *See Wood v. Camp*, 284 So. 2d 691, 693-94 (Fla. 1973); *Dyals v. Hodges*, 659 So. 2d 482, 483-86 (Fla. 1st DCA 1995); *Bovino v. Metropolitan Dade County*, 378 So. 2d 50 (Fla. 3d DCA 1979).

188. Section 768.075(2) and (3)(b), Fla. Stat. (1999).

189. *See Kersul v. Boca Raton Community Hospital, Inc.*, 711 So. 2d 234 (Fla. 4th DCA 1998); *Yuniter v. A & A Edgewater of Florida, Inc.*, 707 So. 2d 763 (Fla. 2d DCA 1998); *Arauz v. Truesdell*, 698 So. 2d 872 (Fla. 3d DCA 1997); *Gorin v. City of St. Augustine*, 595 So. 2d 1062 (Fla. 5th DCA 1992).

190. *See Kersul v. Boca Raton Community Hospital, Inc.*, 711 So. 2d 234 (Fla. 4th DCA 1998); *Yuniter v. A & A Edgewater of Florida, Inc.*, 707 So. 2d 763, 764 (Fla. 2d DCA 1998); *Lotto v. Point East Two Condominium Corporation*, 702 So. 2d 1361, 1362 (Fla. 3d DCA 1997); *Spaulding v. City of Melbourne*, 473 So. 2d 226, 227 (Fla. 5th DCA 1985); *Pittman v. Volusia County*, 380 So. 2d 1192, 1193 (Fla. 5th DCA 1980).

191. *See Lotto v. Point East Two Condominium Corporation*, 702 So2d 1361, 1362 (Fla. 3d DCA 1997); *Circle K Convenience Stores, Inc. v. Ferguson*, 556 So. 2d 1207, 1208 (Fla. 5th DCA 1990); *Spaulding v. City of Melbourne*, 473 So. 2d 226, 227 (Fla. 5th DCA 1985); *Pittman v. Volusia County*, 380 So. 2d 1192, 1193 (Fla. 5th DCA 1980).

192. Section 768.125, Fla. Stat. (1997).

193. *Id. See Sipes v. Albertson's, Inc.*, 728 So. 2d 1243 (Fla. 5th DCA 1999); *Tuttle v. Miami Dolphins, Ltd.*, 551 So. 2d 477 (Fla. 3d DCA 1988), *rev. denied*, 563 So. 2d 635 (Fla. 1990); *McCarthy v. Danny's West, Inc.*, 421 So. 2d 756 (Fla. 4th DCA 1982).

194. Section 562.11, Fla. Stat. (1997).

195. *See Publix Supermarkets, Inc. v. Austin*, 658 So. 2d 1064 (Fla. 5th DCA), *rev. denied*, 666 So. 2d 146 (Fla. 1995); *Armstrong v. Munford, Inc.*, 439 So. 2d 1009 (Fla. 2d DCA 1983), *aff'd*, 451 So. 2d (Fla. 1984).

196. Section 562.11(1)(b), Fla. Stat. (1997). *See Tobias v. Osorio*, 681 So. 2d 905 (Fla. 4th DCA 1996).

197. Section 768.125, Fla. Stat. (1997). *See Ellis v. N.G.N. of Tampa, Inc.*, 586 So. 2d 1042 (Fla. 1991); *Fleuridor v. Surf Café*, 775 So. 2d 411 (Fla. 4th DCA 2001); *Russo v. Plant City Moose Lodge No. 1668*, 656 So. 2d 957 (Fla. 2d DCA 1995); *Roster v. Moulton*, 602 So. 2d 975 (Fla. 4th DCA 1992); *Sabo v. Shamrock Communications, Inc.*, 566 So. 2d 267 (Fla. 5th DCA 1990).

198. *See Persen v. Southland Corp.*, 656 So. 2d 453 (Fla. 1995).

199. *See Ellis v. N.G.N. of Tampa, Inc.*, 586 So. 2d 1042 (Fla. 1991); *Sabo v. Shamrock Communications, Inc.*, 566 So. 2d 267 (Fla. 5th DCA 1990); *Roster v. Moulton*, 602 So. 2d 975 (Fla. 4th DCA 1992).

200. *See Bardy v. Walt Disney World Company*, 643 So. 2d 46 (Fla. 5th DCA 1994); *Carroll Air Systems, Inc. v. Greenbaum*, 629 So. 2d 914 (Fla. 4th DCA 1994).

201. *Dowell v. Gracewood Fruit Co.*, 559 So. 2d 217 (Fla. 1990); *Bankston v. Brennan*, 507 So. 2d 1385 (Fla. 1987).

202. Section 856.015, Fla. Stat. (1997).

203. *See Trainor v. Estate of Hansen*, 740 So. 2d 1201 (2d DCA 1999), *rev. denied*, 753 So. 2d 564 (Fla. 2000); *Newsome v. Haffner*, 710 So. 2d 184 (Fla. 1st DCA), *rev. denied*, 722 So. 2d 193 (Fla. 1998).

204. *See* Nancy C. Wear, *Planning Ahead: Some Tips For The Complaint Drafter Dealing With The Economic Loss Rule*, 73 Fla. B. J. 57 (May 1999).

205. *See Airport Rent-A-Car, Inc. v. Prevost Car, Inc.*, 660 So. 2d 628 (Fla. 1995); *Casa Clara Condominium Ass'n. v. Charley Toppino & Sons, Inc.*, 620 So. 2d 1244 (Fla. 1993); *Florida Power & Light Co. v. Westinghouse Elec. Corp.*, 510 So. 2d 899 (Fla. 1987).

206. *See Stallings v. Kennedy Electric, Inc.*, 710 So. 2d 195 (Fla. 5th DCA 1998), *approved sub nom., Comptech International, Inc. v. Milam Commerce Park, Ltd.*, 753 So. 2d 1219 (Fla. 1999) (violations of the state building code); *Invo Florida, Inc. v. Somerset Venturer, Inc.*, 751 So. 2d 1263 (Fla. 3d DCA 2000) (violation of Uniform Fraudulent Transfer Act); *Samuels v. King Motor Company*, 782 So. 2d 489, 499-500 (Fla. 4th DCA 2001) (violations of Deceptive

and Unfair Trade Practices Act); *Rubio v. State Farm Fire & Casualty Co.*, 662 So. 2d 956 (Fla. 3d DCA 1995) (violations of state insurance code).

207. See *Lajos v. duPont Publishing, Inc.*, 888 F. Supp. 143, 145-46 (M.D. Fla. 1995) (applying Florida law); *Pershing Industries, Inc. v. Estate of Sanz*, 740 So. 2d 1246 (Fla. 3d DCA 1999); *Slex Hofrichter, P.A. v. Zuckerman & Venditti, P.A.*, 710 So. 2d 127 (Fla. 3d DCA 1998); *Burke v. Napieracz*, 674 So. 2d 756 (Fla. 1st DCA 1996); *Ishii v. Welty*, 1998 WL 1064846 (M. D. Fla. 1998) (applying Florida law).

208. See *Pershing Industries, Inc. v. Estate of Sanz*, 740 So. 2d 1246 (Fla. 3d DCA 1999); *Slex Hofrichter, P.A. v. Zuckerman & Venditti, P.A.*, 710 So. 2d 127 (Fla. 3d DCA 1998); *Burke v. Napieracz*, 674 So. 2d 756 (Fla. 1st DCA 1996); *Ishii v. Welty*, 1998 WL 1064846 (M. D. Fla. 1998) (applying Florida law).

209. See *McLeod v. Barber*, 764 So. 2d 790 (Fla. 5th DCA 2000) (fraud); *Facchina v. Mutual Benefits Corp.*, 735 So. 2d 499 (Fla. 4th DCA 1998) (defamation and invasion of privacy); *Bankers Risk Management Services, Inc. v. Av-Med Managed Care*, 697 So. 2d 158 (Fla. 2d DCA 1997) (tortious interference with contractual relationship).

210. See *Moransais v. Heathman*, 744 So. 2d 973 (Fla. 1999); *Hewitt-Kier Constr., Inc. v. Lemuel Ramos and Associates, Inc.*, 775 So. 2d 373 (Fla. 4th DCA 2001); *Russell v. Sherwin Williams Company*, 767 So. 2d 592 (Fla. 4th DCA 2000); *Stone's Throw Condominium Assoc., Inc. v. Sand Cove Apartments, Inc.*, 749 So. 2d 520 (Fla. 2d DCA 1999).

211. See the discussion of the continuing refinement of Florida's economic loss rule in the bar journal articles, Paul J. Schwiep, *Fraudulent Inducement Claims Should Always Be Immune From Economic Loss Rule Attack*, 75 Fla. B. J. (April 2001); Susan E. Trench, *The Economic Loss Rule and Fraudulent Inducement Claims*, 74 Fla. B. J. 14 (Dec. 2000); and Nancy C. Wear, *Planning Ahead: Some Tips For The Complaint Drafter Dealing With The Economic Loss Rule*, 73 Fla. B. J. 57 (May 1999).

212. See, *HTP v. Lineas Aereas Costarricanses, S. A.*, 685 So. 2d 1238 (Fla. 1996); *Woodson v. Martin*, 685 So. 2d 140 (Fla. 1996); *Samuels v. King Motor Company*, 782 So. 2d 489, 497-98 (Fla. 4th DCA 2001) *Stone's Throw Condominium Assoc., Inc. v. Sand Cove Apartments, Inc.*, 749 So. 2d 520 (Fla. 2d DCA 1999); *Pershing Industries, Inc. v. Estate of Sanz*, 740 So. 2d 1246 (Fla. 3d DCA 1999); *Performance Paint Yacht Refinishing, Inc. v. Haines*, 190 F.R.D. 699 (S. D. Fla. 1999) (applying Florida law). Oral representations which are directly contradicted by or specifically addressed in the contract ultimately executed by the parties will not usually support a fraudulent inducement claim. See *Straub Capital Corp. v. L. Frank Chopin, P.A.*, 724 So. 2d 577 (Fla. 4th DCA 1999); *Pressman v. Wolf*, 732 So. 2d 356 (3d DCA 1999), *rev. denied*, 744 So. 2d 459 (Fla. 1999); *Hotels of Key Largo, Inc. v. RHI Hotels, Inc.*, 694 So. 2d 74 (3d

DCA 1997), *rev. denied*, 700 So. 2d 685 (Fla. 1997); *Eye Care International, Inc. v. Underhill*, 92 F. Supp. 2d 1310, 1314-15 (M.D. Fla. 2000) (applying Florida law).

213. *See HTP v. Lineas Aereas Costarricanses, S. A.*, 685 So. 2d 1238 (Fla. 1996); *Woodson v. Martin*, 685 So. 2d 140 (Fla. 1996); *Samuels v. King Motor Company*, 782 So. 2d 489, 499-500 (Fla. 4th DCA 2001); *Bankers Mutual Capital Corp. v. U.S.F. & G.*, 784 So. 2d 485 (Fla. 4th DCA 2001); *Allen v. Stephan Co.*, 784 So. 2d 456 (Fla. 4th DCA 2001); *Azam v. M/I Schottenstein Homes, Inc.* 761 So. 2d 1195 (Fla. 4th DCA 2000); *McLeod v. Barber*, 764 So. 2d 790 (Fla. 5th DCA 2000); *Pershing Industries, Inc. v. Estate of Sanz*, 740 So. 2d 1246 (Fla. 3d DCA 1999); *La Pesca Grande Charters, Inc. v. Moran*, 704 So. 2d 710 (Fla. 5th DCA 1998); *Bradley Factor, Inc. v. United States*, 86 F. Supp. 2d 1140, 1145 (M.D. Fla. 2000) (applying Florida law).

214. *See Bankers Mutual Capital Corp. v. U.S.F. & G.*, 784 So. 2d 485 (Fla. 4th DCA 2001); *Allen v. Stephan Co.*, 784 So. 2d 456 (Fla. 4th DCA 2001); *McLeod v. Barber*, 764 So. 2d 790 (Fla. 5th DCA 2000); *Stone's Throw Condominium Assoc., Inc. v. Sand Cove Apartments, Inc.*, 749 So. 2d 520 (Fla. 2d DCA 1999); *Nerbonne, N.V. v. Lake Bryan Properties*, 689 S0.2d 322 (Fla. 5th DCA 1997).

215. *See Invo Florida, Inc. v. Somerset Venturer, Inc.*, 751 So. 2d 1263 (Fla. 3d DCA 2000); *Crowell v. Morgan Stanley Dean Witter Services, Inc.*, 87 F. Supp. 2d 1287, 1292-94 (S.D. Fla. 2000) (applying Florida law); *Performance Paint Yacht Refinishing, Inc. v. Haines*, 190 F.R.D. 699 (S. D. Fla. 1999) (applying Florida law).

216. *See Samuels v. King Motor Company*, 782 So. 2d 489, 499-500 (Fla. 4th DCA 2001); *Allen v. Stephan Co.*, 784 So. 2d 456 (Fla. 4th DCA 2000); *Straub Capital Corp. v. L. Frank Chopin, P.A.*, 724 So. 2d 577 (Fla. 4th DCA 1999); *Hotels of Key Largo, Inc. v. RHI Hotels, Inc.*, 694 So. 2d 74 (3d DCA 1997), *rev. denied*, 700 So. 2d 685 (Fla. 1997); *Bankers Risk Management Services, Inc. v. Av-Med Managed Care*, 697 So. 2d 158, 161 (Fla. 2d DCA 1997); *Wilson v. De Angelis*, 156 F. Supp. 2d 1335, 1340 (S.D. Fla. 2001) (applying Florida law); *Eye Care International, Inc. v. Underhill*, 92 F. Supp. 2d 1310, 1314-15 (M.D. Fla. 2000) (applying Florida law); *Florida College of Osteopathic Medicine, Inc. v. Dean Witter Reynolds, Inc.*, 12 F. Supp. 2d 1306, 1310 (M. D. Fla. 1998) (applying Florida law); *Dantzler Lumber & Export Co. v. Bullington Lumber Co., Inc.*, 968 F. Supp. 1543, 1545-49 (M. D. Fla. 1997) (applying Florida law); *Serina v. Albertson's, Inc.*, 744 F. Supp. 1113, 1117-18 (M. D. Fla. 1990) (applying Florida law).

217. Rule 1.120(b), Fla. R. Civ. Pro. *See Reina v. Gingerale Corp.*, 472 So. 2d 530 (Fla. 3d DCA 1985).

218. *See Wieczoreck v. H & H Builders, Inc.*, 475 So. 2d 227, 228 (Fla. 1985) *Passaat v. Bettis*, 654 So. 2d 980, 981 (Fla. 4th DCA 1995); *Powerhouse, Inc. v. Walton*, 557 So. 2d 186, 187 (Fla. 1st DCA 1990); Fla. Std. J. Instr. (Civ.) MI(e).

219. *See First Interstate Development Corp. v. Ablanedo*, 511 So. 2d 536, 539 (Fla. 1987); *Johnson v. Davis*, 480 So. 2d 625, 627 (Fla. 1985); *Lance v. Wade*, 457 So. 2d 1008, 1011 (Fla. 1984); *Samuels v. King Motor Company*, 782 So. 2d 489, 499-500 (Fla. 4th DCA 2001); *Palm Beach Roamer, Inc. v. McClure*, 727 So. 2d 1005, 1007 (Fla. 5th DCA 1999); *La Pesca Grande Charters, Inc. v. Moran*, 704 So. 2d 710, 713 (Fla. 5th DCA 1998); *Eastern Cement v. Halliburton Company*, 600 So. 2d 469, 470-71 (Fla. 4th DCA 1992); Fla. Std. J. Instr. (Civ.) MI 8(a).

220. *See Wallerstein v. Hospital Corporation of America*, 573 So. 2d 9, 10 (Fla. 4th DCA 1991); *Atlantic Nat'l. Bank of Florida v. Vest*, 480 So. 2d 1328, 1331 (Fla. 2d DCA 1985), *rev. denied*, 491 So. 2d 281 (Fla. 1986) and 508 So. 2d 16 (Fla. 1987); Fla. Std. J. Instr. (Civ.) MI 8(c).

221. *See Wallerstein v. Hospital Corporation of America*, 573 So. 2d 9, 10 (Fla. 4th DCA 1991).

222. *See Johnson v. Davis*, 480 So. 2d 625, 627-28 (Fla. 1985); *Besett v. Basnett*, 389 So. 2d 995, 998 (Fla. 1980); *Camena Investments and Property Management Corp. v. Cross*, 791 So. 2d 595, 597-98 (Fla. 3d DCA 2001).

223. *See Gilchrist Timber Company v. ITT Rayonier, Inc.*, 696 So. 2d 334, 338-39 (Fla. 1997).

224. *See Casey v. Welch*, 50 So. 2d 124, 125 (Fla. 1951); *National Aircraft Services, Inc. v. Aeroserv International, Inc.*, 544 So. 2d 1063, 1065 (Fla. 3d DCA 1989); *National Equipment Rental, Ltd. V. Little Italy Restaurant & Delicatessen, Inc.*, 362 So. 2d 338, 339 (Fla. 4th DCA 1978).

225. *See First Interstate Development Corp. v. Ablanedo*, 511 So. 2d 536, 538-39 (Fla. 1987).

226. Sections 501.201-213, Fla. Stat. (1997). *See Beacon Property Management, Inc. v. PNR, Inc.*, 785 So. 2d 564, 567-68 (Fla. 4th DCA 2001).

227. Section 501.202, Fla. Stat. (1997). The DUTPA's consistency with federal law relating to consumer protection is furthered by defining a "violation" of the Act as including the violation of any rule promulgated pursuant to the Federal Trade Commission Act or the standards of unfairness and deception set forth and interpreted by the Federal Trade Commission or the federal courts. Sections 501.203(3)(a) and (b), 501.204(2), and 501.205(2), Fla. Stat. (1997). *See Samuels v. King Motor Company of Fort Lauderdale*, 782 So. 2d 489, 498-99 (Fla. 4th DCA 2001).

228. *See Kingswharf, Ltd. v. Kranz,* 545 So. 2d 276 (Fla. 3d DCA), *rev. denied,* 553 So. 2d 1165 (Fla. 1989); *Larry Kent Homes, Inc. v. Empire of America FSA,* 474 So. 2d 868 (Fla. 5th DCA 1985), *rev. denied,* 484 So. 2d 7 (Fla. 1986).

229. Section 501.212(3), Fla. Stat. (1997).

230. Sections 501.206, 501.207, 501.2075, 501.2077, and 501.208, Fla. Stat. (1997).

231. Sections 501.2105 and 501.211, Fla. Stat. (1997). The word "consumers" has been interpreted as applying only to those engaged in the purchase of goods or services. *See N.G.L. Travel Associates v. Celebrity Cruises, Inc.,* 764 So. 2d 672, 673-74 (Fla. 3d DCA 2000); *Burger King Corp. v. Ashland Equities, Inc.,* 161 F. Supp. 2d 1331, 1338 (S.D. Fla. 2001) (applying Florida law); *Shibata v. Lim,* 133 F. Supp. 2d 1311, 1320-21 (M.D. Fla. 2000) (applying Florida law).

232. *See Babbitt Electronics, Inc. v. Dynascan Corp.,* 38 F.3d 1161, 1182 (11th Cir. 1994) (applying Florida law); *M.G.B. Homes, Inc. v. Ameron Homes, Inc.,* 903 F.2d 1486, 1494 (11th Cir. 1990) (applying Florida law); *Nassau v. Unimotorcyclists Society of America, Inc.,* 59 F. Supp. 2d 1233, 1243 (M.D. Fla. 1999) (applying Florida law); *Big Tomato v. Tasty Concepts, Inc.,* 972 F. Supp. 662 (S.D. Fla. 1997) (applying Florida law). The damage remedy is only available to one who qualifies as a "consumer" engaged in a transaction to purchase goods or services. *See N.G.L. Travel Associates v. Celebrity Cruises, Inc.,* 764 So. 2d 672, 673-74 (Fla. 3d DCA 2000); *Burger King Corp. v. Ashland Equities, Inc.,* 161 F. Supp. 2d 1331, 1338 (S.D. Fla. 2001) (applying Florida law).

233. *See National Alcoholism Programs/Cooper City, Inc. v. Palm Springs Hosp. Employee Benefit Plan,* 825 F. Supp. 299 (S.D. Fla. 1993) (applying Florida law); *General Motors Acceptance Corp. v. Laesser,* 718 So. 2d 276 (Fla. 4th DCA 1998); *Fort Lauderdale Lincoln Mercury, Inc.,* 715 So. 2d 311 (Fla. 4th DCA 1998); *Urling v. Helms Exterminators, Inc.,* 468 So. 2d 451 (Fla. 1st DCA 1985).

234. *See Rollins, Inc. v. Heller,* 454 So. 2d 580 (Fla. 3d DCA 1984), *rev. denied,* 461 So. 2d 114 (Fla. 1985).

235. *See W.S. Babcock Corp. v. Myers,* 696 So. 2d 776, 779 (Fla. 1st DCA 1997); *Urling v. Helms Exterminators, Inc.,* 468 So. 2d 451, 453 (Fla. 1st DCA 1985); *Rollins, Inc. v. Heller,* 454 So. 2d 580, 584 (Fla. 3d DCA 1984), *review denied,* 461 So. 2d 114 (Fla. 1985); *Donald Frederick Evans and Associates, Inc. v. Continental Homes, Inc.,* 785 F.2d 897, 915-16 (11th Cir. 1986) (applying Florida law).

236. Section 95.11(3)(f), Fla. Stat. (1997).

237. *See* Sections 768.72–.736, Fla. Stat. (1999). While the 1999 version of the statutes cited herein only apply to causes of action arising after October 1, 1999 [Section 768.72(4), Fla. Stat. (1999)], the law stated in most of the statutes either mirrors the existing common law precedent in Florida or is an amended version of similar statutes that were first enacted in 1986. Laws 1986, c. 86-160, §§ 51-52. There are, however, some substantive differences between the legal standard applied to causes of action accruing before October 1, 1999 and those accruing after that date. These differences are identified in the Florida Standard Jury Instructions approved for publication in 2001 by Florida's Supreme Court. *See In re Standard Jury Instructions—Civil Cases*, 797 So. 2d 1199 (Fla. 2001) (approving publication of new Fla. Std. J. Instr. (Civ.) PD 1 and PD 2).

238. Section 768.72(1), Fla. Stat. (1999). This pleading requirement has been found to be inapplicable to Florida law claims asserted in diversity cases brought in federal court. *See Cohen v. Office Depot, Inc.*, 184 F.3d 1292, 1296-99 (11th Cir. 2000), *vacated on other grounds*, 204 F.3d 1069 (11th Cir. 2000).

239. *Id.*

240. The "clear and convincing" burden of proof applies to the determination of entitlement to punitive damages, while the "greater weight of the evidence" burden of proof applies to the determination of the amount of damages. Section 768.725, Fla. Stat. (1999). *See* Fla. Std. J. Instr. (Civ.) PD 1 and PD 2 (2001).

241. Section 768.72(2), Fla. Stat. (1999). *But see* Fla. Std. J. Instr. (Civ.) PD 1 (2)(a) and PD 2 (2)(a) (2001) (reflecting that if the cause of action accrued before October 1, 1999, then the standard to be applied is whether: (1) the conduct was so gross and flagrant as to show a reckless disregard of human life or of the safety of persons exposed to the effects of such conduct; or (2) the conduct showed such an entire lack of care that the defendant must have been consciously indifferent to the consequences; or (3) the conduct showed such an entire lack of care that the defendant must have wantonly or recklessly disregarded the safety and welfare of the public; or (4) the conduct showed such reckless indifference to the rights of others as to be equivalent to an intentional violation of those rights).

242. *See Ferguson Transportation, Inc. v. North American Van Lines, Inc.*, 687 So. 2d 821, 822-23 (Fla. 1997). Whether the statutory references to "any civil action based on ... misconduct in commercial transactions ... and involving willful, wanton, or gross misconduct" was intended to change this common law rule remains an open question. *Cf., Chemplex Florida v. Norelli*, 790 So. 2d 547 (Fla. 4th DCA 2001) (refusing to construe Sections 768.72 and 768.73 as permitting recovery of punitive damages in shareholder derivative action); *McGuire, Woods, Battle & Boothe, LLP v. Hollfelder*, 771 So. 2d 585, 586-87 (Fla. 1st DCA 2000) (same).

243. *Id.*

244. Section 768.72(2)(a), Fla. Stat. (1999). If the cause of action accrued prior to October 1, 1999, a slightly different standard will be applied. *See* n. 241, *supra*.

245. Section 768.72(2)(b), Fla. Stat. (1999). If the cause of action accrued prior to October 1, 1999, a slightly different standard will be applied. *See* n. 241, *supra*.

246. *See Schropp v. Crown Eurocars, Inc.*, 654 So. 2d 1158 (Fla. 1995) and Section 768.72(3), Fla.Stat. (1999).

247. *See* Section 768.72(3), Fla. Stat. (1999); Fla. Std. J. Instr. (Civ.) PD 1a.(3) (2001); *Schropp v. Crown Eurocars, Inc.*, 654 So. 2d 1158 (Fla. 1995); *Bankers Multiple Line Ins. Co. v. Farish*, 464 So. 2d 530 (Fla. 1985); *Winn-Dixie Stores, Inc. v. Robinson*, 472 So. 2d 722, 724 (Fla. 1985).

248. *See* Section 768.72(3), Fla. Stat. (1999); Fla. Std. J. Instr. (Civ.) PD 1a.(4)(b) (2001). If the cause of action accrued prior to October 1, 1999, then the plaintiff had to show: (1) that the employee or agent acted in such a manner as to warrant punitive damages; *and* (2) that the employer or principal itself committed negligence which was independent of the conduct of the employee or agent and that such independent negligence contributed to the plaintiff's loss or damages. Fla. Std. J. Instr. (Civ.) PD 1a.(4)(a) (2001). *See Mercury Motors Express, Inc. v. Smith*, 393 So. 2d 545 (Fla. 1981); *Partington v. Metallic Engineering Co., Inc.*, 792 So. 2d 498 (Fla. 4th DCA 2001).

249. *See W.R. Grace & Company-Conn. v. Waters*, 638 So. 2d 502, 504 (Fla. 1994); *St. Regis Paper Co. v. Watson*, 428 So. 2d 243, 247-48 (Fla. 1983).

250. *See Ault v. Lohr*, 538 So. 2d 454 (Fla. 1989); *Russin v. Richard F. Greminger, P.A.*, 563 So2d 1089 (Fla. 4th DCA 1990); *Platte v. Whitney Realty Company, Inc.*, 538 So. 2d 1358, 1360 (Fla. 1st DCA 1989). However, since there must be actual damages sustained by the plaintiff suing for fraud in order for a cause of action to exist (*see* n. 224, *supra*), it has been held that the plaintiff's inability to prove actual damages in a fraud claim prevents recovery of punitive damages as well. *See National Aircraft Services, Inc. v. Aeroserv International, Inc.*, 544 So. 2d 1063 (Fla. 3d DCA 1989).

251. *See Bould v. Touchette*, 349 So. 2d 1181, 1186-87 (Fla. 1977); *Atlas Properties, Inc. v. Didich*, 226 So. 2d 684, 689-90 (Fla. 1969). Evidence of the defendant's net worth is admissible, but is not required, unless the defendant seeks to challenge the award as being excessive. *See Turner v. Fitzsimmons*, 673 So. 2d 532 (Fla. 1st DCA 1996).

252. Section 768.73, Fla. Stat. (1997). Compare *Owens-Corning Fiberglass Corp. v. Ballard*, 749 So. 2d 483 (Fla. 1999) with *Sun International Bahamas, Ltd. v. Wagner*, 758 So. 2d 1190 (Fla. 3d DCA 2000).

253. Laws 1999, c. 99-225, § 23.

254. Section 768.73(1)(b), Fla. Stat. (1999).

255. Section 768.73(1)(c), Fla. Stat. (1999).

256. Section 768.73(2), Fla. Stat. (1999). This new section effectively overrules the decision in *W.R. Grace & Company-Conn. v. Waters*, 638 So. 2d 502 (Fla. 1994) on this point.

257. *See W.R. Grace & Company-Conn. v. Waters*, 638 So. 2d 502, 506 (Fla. 1994); Fla. Std. J. Instr. (Civ.) PD 1 (Note 1 of "Notes on Use of PD 1").

258. *See Chamberlain v. Florida Power Corp.*, 144 Fla. 719, 198 So. 486 (1940); *Nolan v. Moore*, 81 Fla. 594, 600, 88 So. 601 (1921).

259. Sections 768.16-768.27, Fla. Stat. (1997).

260. Section 768.19, Fla. Stat. (1997).

261. Section 768.20, Fla. Stat. (1997).

262. Sections 768.20- 768.21, Fla. Stat. (1997).

263. Section 768.18(1), Fla. Stat. (1997). The term "survivor" includes the child born out of wedlock of a mother, but does not include the child born out of wedlock of the father unless the father has recognized a responsibility for the child's support. *Id.* Under the Act, "support" is defined to include contributions in kind as well as money. Section 768.18(3), Fla. Stat. (1997). The term "services" is defined to mean tasks, usually of a household nature, regularly performed by the decedent that will be a necessary expense to the survivors of the decedent. Section 768.18(4), Fla. Stat. (1997). In order to be considered "dependent on the decedent," one must establish an actual need and expectation of such support from the decedent, as opposed to simply showing that the decedent voluntarily supplied money, food, and lodging which permitted a healthy and able relative to live without working. *See Thompson v. State Farm Mutual Auto. Ins. Co.*, 670 So. 2d 1070 (Fla. 3d DCA 1996); *Cinghina v. Racik*, 647 So. 2d 289 (Fla. 4th DCA 1994).

264. Section 768.21, Fla. Stat. (1997). In order for an adult blood relative who is not the parent, spouse, or child of the decedent to be considered a "survivor" under the Act, that person must establish financial dependency on

the decedent. *See Thompson v. State Farm Mutual Auto. Ins. Co.*, 670 So. 2d 1070, 1071 (Fla. 3d DCA 1996) (adult sister of decedent).

265. Section 768.21(6)(a), Fla. Stat. (1997).

266. Section 768.21(6)(b), Fla. Stat. (1997). If the medical or funeral expenses were paid by or on behalf of the decedent by someone other than the estate, then the estate is still entitled to recover this element, unless the amounts were paid by a statutory survivor, in which case the survivor is entitled to recover the amount he or she paid. *Id.*; Section 768.21(5), Fla. Stat. (1997).

267. The Act defines "minor children" to mean children under 25 years of age, notwithstanding the legal age of majority. Section 768.18(2), Fla. Stat. (1997).

268. Section 768.21(6)(a), Fla. Stat. (1997). "Net accumulations" is defined to mean the part of the decedent's expected net business or salary income, including pension benefits, that the decedent probably would have retained as savings and left as part of her or his estate if the decedent had lived her or his normal life expectancy. Section 768.18(5), Fla. Stat. (1997). "Net business or salary income" is that part of the decedent's probable gross income after taxes, excluding income from investments continuing beyond death, that remains after deducting the decedent's personal expenses and monetary support of his or her survivors. *Id.* Net accumulations are not recoverable by the estate of a minor child. *See* Section 768.21(6)(a)2, Fla. Stat. (1997). And, it has been held that the parents of a deceased minor child are not entitled to recover lost support and services, because the cost of raising the child to maturity would likely exceed the value of any support and services provided. *See Grayson v. United States*, 748 F. Supp. 854, 862 (S.D. Fla. 1990).

269. In every instance, however, the death of the survivor before final judgment in the wrongful death action shall limit the extent of the survivor's recovery under the Act to lost support and services to the date of the survivor's death. Section 768.24, Fla. Stat. (1997).

270. Section 768.21(1), Fla. Stat. (1997). In computing the duration of the future loss of support and services, the jury should consider the joint life expectancies of the decedent and the particular survivor, and in the case of healthy minor children, the period of their minority. *Id.*

271. Section 768.21(5), Fla. Stat. (1997).

272. Section 768.21(2), Fla. Stat. (1997).

273. Section 768.21(3), Fla. Stat. (1997). If there is no surviving spouse, all surviving children of the decedent may recover for lost parental companion-

ship, instruction, and guidance and for mental pain and suffering from the date of the decedent's injury. *Id.* If there is a surviving spouse, then the surviving adult children may not recover these intangible damages. Section 768.21(8), Fla. Stat. (1997).

274. Section 768.21(4), Fla. Stat. (1997).

275. *Id.* If the claim is based upon medical malpractice, the surviving parent of the adult child who left no other survivors may not recover these intangible damages. Section 768.21(8), Fla. Stat. (1997).

276. Section 768.20, Fla. Stat. (1997). *See Frazier v. Metropolitan Dade Co.*, 701 So. 2d 418 (Fla. 3d DCA 1997) (father's recovery as "survivor" of deceased minor child could not be reduced due to contributing negligence of mother found by jury); *Hudson v. Moss*, 653 So. 2d 1071 (Fla. 3d DCA 1995), *rev. denied*, 673 So. 2d 29 (Fla. 1996) (mother's recovery as "survivor" of deceased minor child could not be reduced due to contributing negligence of father found by jury).

GEORGIA

A. STATUTES OF LIMITATION

Causes of action based on negligent or intentional misconduct resulting in personal injuries or wrongful death must be brought within two years.[1] The "discovery rule" applies to personal injury claims but not wrongful death claims.[2] Claims for loss of consortium must be brought within four years.[3]

Causes of action for damage to personalty and realty must be brought within four years.[4] The "discovery rule" does not apply to property damage cases in general.[5]

Causes of action for injuries to reputation, including defamatory acts, must be brought within one year.[6]

The statute of limitations for tortious interference with business relations is four years.[7]

Causes of action for alleged breach of warranty under the Uniform Commercial Code must be brought within four years from the date of sale, including recovery for personal injuries, death, or property damage.[8]

Actions under the Georgia Fair Business Practices Act have a two-year statute of limitations.[9]

The omnibus "catch all" statute of limitations in Georgia is 20 years after the right of action accrues, and this has been held to apply to a claim for contribution among joint tortfeasors in Georgia.[10]

While the two-year personal injury or wrongful death statute of limitations applies to medical malpractice cases, these claims are subject to further statutes of repose.[11] In addition, Georgia has a ten-year statute of repose for product liability claims[12] and eight years for deficiencies in improvements to real estate.[13]

Causes of action against local governments in Georgia, where permitted, are generally subject to a six-month *ante litem* notice requirement.[14]

B. TORT REFORM

In the Tort Reform Act of 1987, the Georgia General Assembly undertook to change tort litigation to, *inter alia*, permit the disclosure of collateral sources at trial,[15] make substantial changes regarding punitive damages,[16] narrow damages for injury to "peace, happiness, or feelings,"[17] permit remittitur of jury verdicts[18] and modify the joint and several liability rule in some circumstances.[19]

For a further discussion of punitive damages, *see* Section Q, *infra*.

C. "NO-FAULT" INSURANCE

The Georgia Motor Vehicle Accident Reparations Act (No-Fault Act), O.C.G.A. §§ 33-34-1, *et seq.*, was repealed in October 1991.[20]

D. THE STANDARD FOR NEGLIGENCE

To succeed in a cause of action for negligence, the plaintiff must establish: (1) the defendant had a legal duty to exercise ordinary diligence or conform to a standard of conduct for the protection of others; (2) the defendant breached that standard of conduct; (3) a causal connection between the breach and the resulting injury; and (4) the plaintiff suffered a loss or damage as a result of the breach.[21]

Ordinary diligence is that degree of care exercised by "ordinarily prudent persons under the same or similar circumstances."[22]

Medical professionals are held to a general standard of care, rather than a local standard of care, regardless of specialty.[23]

In Georgia, infancy is not a defense to a tort action if the defendant has reached age 13, which is the age of discretion for criminal offenses.[24] Thus, children under age 13 are immune from actions in tort.[25] A child over age 13 is held to the standard of care that his mental and physical capacities enabled him to exercise in the *actual* circumstances under investigation.[26]

E. CAUSATION

To establish a *prima facie* case of negligence in Georgia, the plaintiff must demonstrate that the defendant's negligence was the proximate or legal cause of plaintiff's injury[27] and also that the defendant's negligence was the cause-in-fact of the plaintiff's injury.[28]

The plaintiff demonstrates proximate cause by tracing his injury directly to the defendant's negligence and showing that the injury would not have occurred but for the defendant's negligence.[29]

F. CONTRIBUTORY NEGLIGENCE, COMPARATIVE NEGLIGENCE, AND ASSUMPTION OF RISK

1. Contributory Negligence

In Georgia, the plaintiff is completely barred from recovering if he failed to exercise ordinary care to avoid injury to himself.[30]

2. Comparative Negligence

Georgia has a modified comparative negligence rule. Even if a plaintiff is negligent, he will still recover if his negligence was less than the defendant's and was not due to a failure to avoid the consequences of the defendant's negligence.[31]

3. Assumption of Risk

Assumption of risk is an affirmative defense barring recovery by the plaintiff. The defendant must show that the plaintiff (1) had actual knowledge of the danger; (2) understood and appreciated the risks associated with the danger; and (3) voluntarily encountered the danger.[32]

G. RES IPSA LOQUITUR AND INHERENTLY DANGEROUS ACTIVITIES

1. Res Ipsa Loquitur

Under the doctrine of *res ipsa loquitur*, the plaintiff must show that: (1) the injury-causing event is one that normally does not occur unless someone is negligent; (2) the injury-causing instrumentality was under the defendant's exclusive control; and (3) the plaintiff did not voluntarily act or contribute to his injury.[33] *Res ipsa loquitur* allows a jury to infer negligence by the defendant.[34] The plaintiff still must prove causation and damages.

2. Inherently Dangerous Activities

The degree of ordinary care varies with the amount of danger involved in the activity.[35] A person or entity engaged in inherently dangerous activities is held strictly liable for the damages resulting from such activities.[36]

H. NEGLIGENCE *PER SE*

Where a Georgia statute has been adopted as a standard of conduct, its violation constitutes negligence *per se*.[37] A plaintiff must establish that: (1) he is within the class of persons the statute was intended to protect; and (2) the injury from which he suffers is the type of harm the statute was intended to guard against.[38] Negligence *per se* provides only the duty and breach of duty elements of a tort.[39] The plaintiff still must prove causation and damages.[40]

I. JOINT AND SEVERAL LIABILITY

Georgia law defines joint tortfeasors as individuals whose separate and distinct acts of negligence come together to proximately cause an injury.[41] A plaintiff may recover damages for the greatest injury caused by any of the defendants against all of the defendants.[42] However, if the jury exercises its right to allocate particular damages to each defendant, then the judgment will be entered severally.[43]

J. INDEMNITY

Georgia follows an active-passive theory of indemnity. A passive tortfeasor may seek indemnity from an active tortfeasor whose conduct is the alleged proximate cause of the plaintiff's injury.[44] Whether a defendant's negligence is passive or active is a question for the jury.[45]

K. BAR OF WORKERS' COMPENSATION STATUTE

The Georgia Workers' Compensation Act[46] is intended to be the exclusive system for the resolution of disputes between employers and employees over employees' accidents and injuries arising out of, and in the course of, their employment.[47] The terms "employer" and "employee" are defined by the Act.[48] Under the Act, an employer is liable for an employee's injury without regard to fault or negligence.[49]

An injured employee may sue a third-party tortfeasor, other than a fellow employee, for damages arising out of his injury.[50] However, if the employer has paid workers' compensation benefits to the employee, the employer will have a subrogation lien against any recovery from a third party and may intervene in the action to protect its lien.[51]

If the injured employee does not bring an action against the third-party tortfeasor within the one-year statute of limitation, the employer or its insurer may assert the employee's tort action, either on its own or on the employee's behalf.[52] However, the employee may bring an action in the second year against the tortfeasor if the employer has not done so first. The employee also may intervene in the employer's action.[53]

L. PREMISES LIABILITY

The legal duty owed by the owner or occupier of the premises to a visitor is dependent on whether the visitor is a licensee or an invitee. An invitee is one whose presence on the premises benefits the owner or occupier,[54] and the owner or occupier owes an invitee the duty to exercise ordinary care in maintaining the premises.[55]

A licensee is one whose presence on the premises is for his own benefit or the benefit of someone other than the owner or occupier.[56] The owner or occupier is liable to a licensee only for willful and wanton injury.[57] The superior knowledge of the premises owner/occupier may be established constructively, but the owner/occupier can rebut constructive knowledge by a regular inspection procedure.[58]

M. DRAM SHOP LIABILITY

A person who "willfully, knowingly, and unlawfully" provides alcoholic beverages to someone who is not of legal drinking age or is noticeably intoxicated, knowing that such person will be driving soon, may be liable for injuries or property damage caused by the intoxicated driver, if providing the alcohol is the proximate cause of the injuries or damage.[59]

N. ECONOMIC LOSS

The Georgia "economic loss" rule precludes a plaintiff from recovering damages, in tort, when a defective product has resulted in the loss of the value or use of the product but the plaintiff has suffered no personal or physical injury.[60]

O. FRAUD AND MISREPRESENTATION

A plaintiff has an action for fraud if he proves that: (1) the defendant made representations; (2) that at the time he knew were false; (3) with the intent to deceive the plaintiff; (4) that plaintiff reasonably relied on; and (5) that caused the plaintiff to sustain a loss and damage as a proximate result.[61] The misrepresentation must be willful and about a material fact; mere concealment of a material fact is not enough.[62]

In 1983, the Georgia Supreme Court adopted the Restatement (Second) of Torts rule for negligent misrepresentation.[63] Under this rule, a person who supplies information during the course of his business or employment, or for pecuniary gain, has a duty of reasonable care to persons who rely on the information.[64] The supplier of information must be aware of the use to which the information is being put, and his liability is limited to foreseeable persons for whom the information is intended.[65]

P. CONSUMER FRAUD STATUTES

The Fair Business Practices Act of 1975 allows consumers to recover for injuries or damages resulting from "consumer acts or practices."[66]

Q. PUNITIVE DAMAGES

In Georgia, a jury may award punitive damages to a plaintiff who proves by clear and convincing evidence that the defendant's actions were willful, malicious, fraudulent, wanton, oppressive, or entirely without want of care.[67] Punitive damages are awarded "solely to punish, penalize, or deter a defendant."[68]

In product liability cases, there is no limit to the amount of punitive damages that may be awarded. However, 75 percent of the damages awarded, less a portion of litigation costs, goes to the state treasury.[69] The Georgia Supreme Court has held that this provision is constitutional.[70]

In intentional tort cases not arising from product liability, there is no limit to the amount of punitive damages that may be awarded.[71]

In all other tort cases, except those involving injury solely to the plaintiff's peace, happiness, and feelings, punitive damage awards are limited to $250,000.[72] The Georgia Supreme Court has held that this provision also is constitutional.[73]

Punitive damages are not recoverable when the plaintiff's entire injury is to his "peace, happiness, and feelings."[74] However, Georgia law allows a plaintiff to recover "vindictive damages" for such an injury, even in the absence of physical injury. The award is based on the enlightened consciences of impartial jurors.[75]

Punitive damages are counted in the amount in controversy for diversity jurisdiction.[76]

R. WRONGFUL DEATH AND SURVIVORSHIP ACTIONS

Wrongful death actions in Georgia arise out of statutory law, not common law.[77] The Georgia Wrongful Death Act[78] entitles only specific survivors[79] to recover for the wrongful death of a spouse or parent,[80] or a child.[81] Moreover, the provision of the Act that allows the personal representative of the decedent's estate to recover *ante mortem* expenses is a survival statute rather than a wrongful death statute.[82] In addition, causes of action under the wrongful death and survival statutes are separate and distinct.[83]

Recovery under the wrongful death statute is measured by the "full value of the life of the decedent."[84] Recovery under the survival statute is limited to medical and other necessary expenses resulting from the decedent's death-causing injury.[85] However, if there is evidence of conscious pain and suffering, the estate could recover for this damage and also for punitive damages.[86]

Alfred B. Adams III
Donna L. Johnson
HOLLAND & KNIGHT L.L.P.
2000 One Atlantic Center
1201 West Peachtree Street, N.E.
Atlanta, Georgia 30309-3400
(404) 817-8500
Fax (404) 881-0470
aadams@hklaw.com
www.hklaw.com

ENDNOTES - GEORGIA

1. O.C.G.A. § 9-3-33 (1982).

2. *Everhardt v. Rich's, Inc.*, 229 Ga. 798, 802, 194 S.E.2d 425 (1972); *Miles v. Ashland Chemical Co.*, 261 Ga. 726, 410 S.E.2d 290 (1991).

3. O.C.G.A. § 9-3-33 (1982).

4. O.C.G.A. §§ 9-3-32 & 9-3-30 (1982).

5. *Corporation of Mercer Univ. v. Nat'l Gypsum Co.*, 258 Ga. 365, 366, 368 S.E.2d 732 (1988).

6. O.C.G.A. § 9-3-33 (1982).

7. *Hill v. Crabb*, 166 Ga. App. 387, 304 S.E.2d 510 (1983).

8. O.C.G.A. § 11-2-725 (1994).

9. O.C.G.A. § 10-1-401 (1994).

10. O.C.G.A. § 9-3-22 (1982); *Krasaeath v. Parker*, 212 Ga. App. 525, 441 S.E.2d 868 (1994).

11. O.C.G.A. § 9-3-71 (Supp. 1999).

12. O.C.G.A. § 51-1-11 (Supp. 1999); ten years from the first sale of item or use or consumption, subject to certain exceptions.

13. O.C.G.A. § 9-3-51(a) (1982), subject to certain exceptions for injuries occurring in the seventh or eighth year following substantial completion of the improvements (O.C.G.A. § 9-3-51(b)) (1982), but not later than ten years following substantial completion. *See R. L. Sanders Roofing Co. v. Miller*, 153 Ga. App. 225, 264 S.E.2d 731 (1980).

14. O.C.G.A. § 36-33-5 (1993).

15. O.C.G.A. § 51-12-1(b) (Supp. 1999). But this was declared unconstitutional in *Denton v. Con-Way Southern Exp., Inc.*, 261 Ga. 41, 402 S.E.2d 269 (1991).

16. O.C.G.A. § 51-12-5.1 (Supp. 1999).

17. O.C.G.A. § 51-12-6 (Supp. 1999).

18. O.C.G.A. § 51-12-12(b) (Supp. 1999).

19. O.C.G.A. § 51-12-33(a) (Supp. 1999) now permits apportionment among joint tortfeasors *where the plaintiff is negligent or culpable.*

20. *Walker v. Willis,* 210 Ga. App. 139, 435 S.E.2d 621 (1993).

21. O.C.G.A. § 51-1-2 (1982); *Wilson v. Mallard Creek Holdings,* 238 Ga. App. 746, 519 S.E.2d 925 (1999).

22. O.C.G.A. § 51-1-2 (1982).

23. O.C.G.A. § 51-1-27 (1982); *McDaniel v. Hendrix,* 260 Ga. 857, 401 S.E.2d 260 (1991).

24. O.C.G.A. § 51-11-6 (1982). *See also* O.C.G.A. § 16-3-1.

25. *Horton v. Hinely,* 261 Ga. 863, 413 S.E.2d 199 (1992).

26. O.C.G.A. § 51-1-5 (1982).

27. *Williams v. EMRO Marketing Co.,* 229 Ga. App. 468, 494 S.E.2d 218 (1997).

28. *Id.*

29. *Pettigrew v. Citizens Trust Bank,* 229 B.R. 39 (1998).

30. O.C.G.A. § 51-11-7 (1982).

31. *Allen v. State,* 150 Ga. App. 109, 257 S.E.2d 5 (1979).

32. *Clayton v. Travis,* 109 F.3d 669 (11th Cir. 1997).

33. *Harlan by Harlan v. Six Flags over Georgia,* 699 F.2d 521 (11th Cir. 1983).

34. *Kicklighter v. Nails by Jannee, Inc.,* 616 F.2d 734 (5th Cir. 1980).

35. *See Aretz v. United States,* 604 F.2d 417, 429 (5th Cir. 1979).

36. *Combustion Chemical, Inc. v. Spires,* 209 Ga. App. 240, 433 S.E.2d 60 (1993), *cert. denied,* 209 Ga. App. 913, 433 S.E.2d 60 (1993).

37. *Central Anesthesia Assoc., P.C. v. Worthy,* 173 Ga. App. 150, 325 S.E.2d 819 (1984), *aff'd,* 254 Ga. 728, 333 S.E.2d 829 (1985).

38. *Id.*

39. *Central Anesthesia Assoc., P.C. v. Worthy*, 254 Ga. App. 728, 333 S.E.2d 829 (1985).

40. *Id.*

41. *St. Paul Fire and Marine Insurance Co. v. MAG Mutual Insurance Co.*, 209 Ga. App. 184, 433 S.E.2d 112 (1993).

42. O.C.G.A. § 51-12-31 (Supp. 1999).

43. *Id.*

44. *Lova/Daniel/Busby, Inc. v. B&W Mechanical Contractors, Inc.*, 167 Ga. App. 551, 307 S.E.2d 97 (1983).

45. *Id.*

46. O.C.G.A. §§ 34-9-1, *et seq.* (1998).

47. O.C.G.A. §§ 34-9-11 & 34-9-23 (1998).

48. O.C.G.A. § 34-9-1 (1998).

49. *Gay v. Greene*, 91 Ga. App. 78, 84 S.E.2d 847 (1952).

50. O.C.G.A. § 34-9-11 (1998).

51. O.C.G.A. § 34-9-11.1(b).

52. O.C.G.A. § 34-9-11.1(c).

53. *Id.*

54. *Burkhead v. American Legion Post No. 51, Inc.*, 175 Ga. App. 56, 332 S.E.2d 311 (1985).

55. O.C.G.A. § 51-3-1 (1982).

56. *Burkhead, supra.*

57. O.C.G.A. § 51-3-2 (1982).

58. *Straughter v. J.H. Harvey Co.*, 232 Ga. App. 29, 30(i), 500 S.E.2d 353 (1998); *Barge v. Melvin Carmichael Enterprises, Inc.*, —Ga. App. —, 556 S.E.2d 906 (2001).

59. O.C.G.A. § 51-1-40 (Supp. 1999).

60. *Bates & Assoc., Inc. v. Romei*, 207 Ga. App. 81, 426 S.E.2d 919 (1993).

61. O.C.G.A. § 51-6-1 (1982); *Eckerd's Columbia, Inc. v. Moore*, 155 Ga. App. 4, 270 S.E.2d 249 (1980).

62. O.C.G.A. § 51-6-2 (1982).

63. *Robert & Co., Assoc. v. Rhodes-Haverty Partnership*, 250 Ga. 680, 300 S.E.2d 503 (1983). *See also Williams v. Fallaize Ins. Agency, Inc.*, 220 Ga. App. 411, 469 S.E.2d 752 (1996).

64. *Robert & Co., Assoc., supra.*

65. *Id.*

66. O.C.G.A. § 10-1-399(a) (Supp. 1999).

67. O.C.G.A. § 51-12-5.1(b) (Supp. 1999).

68. O.C.G.A. § 51-12-5.1(c) (Supp. 1999).

69. O.C.G.A. § 51-12-5.1(e)(2) (Supp. 1999).

70. *State v. Moseley*, 263 Ga. 280, 436 S.E.2d 632 (1993), *cert. denied*, 511 U.S. 1107, 114 S. Ct. 2101, 128 L. Ed.2d 663 (1994).

71. O.C.G.A. § 51-12-5.1(f) (Supp. 1999).

72. O.C.G.A. § 51-12-5.1(g) (Supp. 1999).

73. *Bagley v. Shortt*, 261 Ga. 762, 410 S.E.2d 738 (1991).

74. O.C.G.A. § 51-12-6 (Supp. 1999).

75. *Id.*

76. *Turpeau v. Fidelity Financial Services, Inc.*, 936 F. Supp. 975 (N.D. Ga. 1996), *aff'd*, 112 F.3d 1173 (11th Cir. 1997).

77. *Dowling v. Lopez*, 211 Ga. App. 578, 440 S.E.2d 205 (1993); *cert. denied*, 211 Ga. App. 903, 440 S.E.2d 205 (1993).

78. O.C.G.A. §§ 51-4-1 *et seq.* (1982).

79. O.C.G.A. §§ 51-4-2 (Supp. 1999) & 51-4-4 (1982).

80. O.C.G.A. § 51-4-2 (Supp. 1999).

81. O.C.G.A. § 51-4-4 (1982).

82. O.C.G.A. § 51-4-5(b) (Supp. 1999); *Gay v. Piggly Wiggly Stores, Inc.*, 183 Ga. App. 175, 358 S.E.2d 468, *cert. denied*, 183 Ga. App. 906, 358 S.E.2d 468 (1987).

83. *Smith v. Memorial Medical Ctr., Inc.*, 208 Ga. App. 26, 430 S.E.2d 57 (1993).

84. O.C.G.A. § 51-4-1(a) (1982).

85. *Gay, supra.*

86. *Mark v. Dial*, 212 Ga. App. 362, 441 S.E.2d 857 (1994).

HAWAII

A. STATUTE OF LIMITATIONS

The statute of limitations is a defense that may be used to bar a plaintiff's claim. This defense, however, is a personal privilege that may only be exercised or waived by the defendant.[1] The relevant limitations period is based on the nature of the claim or right.[2] Generally, under current Hawaii law, the statute of limitations for the types of claims listed below are as follows:

1. **Damage to Persons or Property**

    Actions for the recovery of compensation for damage or injury to persons or property, such as products liability, negligence, malpractice, or wrongful death, must be instituted within two years after the cause of action accrued, unless the plaintiff is deemed incompetent.[3]

2. **Medical Torts**

    Medical tort claim must be brought within two years after the plaintiff discovers or should have discovered the injury, but not more than six years after the alleged act or omission causing the injury. However, with respect to minors, medical tort claims must commence on the later of either six years from the date of the alleged act or omission causing the injury or, if the minor is under ten years of age, six years from the minor's tenth birthday.[4]

3. **Libel and Slander**

    Actions for libel and slander must commence within two years after the cause of action accrues.[5] A claim for defamation accrues when the defamee discovers or reasonably should have discovered the publication of the defamation.[6]

4. **Taking of Personal Property**

    Actions for taking or detaining any goods, including actions of replevin, must commence within six years.[7]

5. **Debt**

    Actions for the recovery of any debt based on a contract, obligation, or liability, including legal malpractice,[8] must be commenced within six years of the breach of contract.[9]

6. **Catch-all**

    Personal actions of any nature that are not specifically covered by the laws of the state of Hawaii shall commence within six years.[10] Among other claims, this catch-all provision governs the limitation of actions for negligent representations, fraudulent representations, breach of implied covenant of good faith and fair dealing, constitutional causes of action, federal civil rights actions (civil rights actions under 42 U.S.C. § 1983), and securities law claims (federal and state).

7. Claims Brought Against the State

All tort claims must be brought against the state within two years after the claim accrues, except in the case of medical tort claims.[11]

8. Claims Brought by the State

Unless expressly stated in the statute, any actions brought by or on behalf of the state or its agencies shall not be barred by any statute of limitation.[12]

B. TORT REFORM

The Hawaii Legislature has considered a number of "civil justice reform" laws, but to date has not passed any sweeping legislation. Recently, the legislature considered a bill that would cap noneconomic damages in lawsuits at $500,000, and limit punitive damage awards to three times the amount of compensatory damages, and another bill that would extend a law giving the state and counties immunity from liability for accidents at public beach parks. With the majority of legislators currently focused on economic issues, Civil Justice Reform is considered to be a top priority in 2002.

C. "NO FAULT" LIMITATIONS

Under Hawaii's no-fault, or "personal injury protection" law, motorists are only permitted to bring suit against an owner, operator or user of an insured motor vehicle as a result of an automobile accident if: (1) death occurs to the person in such a motor vehicle accident;[13] (2) injury occurs to the person that consists, in whole or in part, in a significant permanent loss of use of a part or function of the body;[14] (3) injury occurs to the person that consists of a permanent and serious disfigurement that results in subjection of the injured person to mental or emotional suffering;[15] or (4) injury occurs to the person in a motor vehicle accident and as a result of such injury that the personal injury protection benefits incurred by such person equal or exceed $5,000.[16] Additionally, Hawaii law provides for a "covered loss deductible." This requires that whenever a person effects a recovery for bodily injury, whether by suit, arbitration, or settlement, and it is determined that the person is entitled to recover damages, the judgment, settlement, or award shall be reduced by $5,000 or the amount of personal injury protection benefits incurred, whichever is greater, up to the maximum limit.[17]

D. THE STANDARD FOR NEGLIGENCE

The Hawaii Supreme Court has defined actionable negligence "as the failure to do what a reasonable and prudent person would ordinarily have done under the circumstances of the situation, or doing what such person would not have done."[18] It is incumbent on the plaintiff to show the existence of a duty of care owed by the defendant to the plaintiff, "requiring the defendant to conform to a certain standard of conduct for the protection of others against unreasonable risks."[19] Whether such duty exists is entirely a question of law that involves weighing of the nature of the risk, the magnitude of the burden of guarding against the risk, and the public interest in the proposed solution.[20] However, what is reasonable and unreasonable and whether the defendant's conduct was reasonable under the circumstances are for the trier of fact to decide.[21]

The general rule is that a person does not have an affirmative duty to protect another person from harm.[22] The fact that a person realizes or should realize that action on his or her part is necessary for another's protection does not of itself impose a duty to take such action.[23] The exceptions to this general rule arise when a "special relationship" exists between the defendant and the plaintiff.[24] However, Hawaii courts have been reluctant to liberally apply the "special relationship" exception to negligence claims.[25]

The Hawaii Supreme Court has adopted the rule that a minor/child is "required to exercise care appropriate to his [or her] age, experience and mental capacity."[26] Children less than six years of age are conclusively presumed incapable of negligence.[27]

E. CAUSATION

Hawaii follows the general rule that, in order to prove negligence, the plaintiff must demonstrate a reasonably close causal connection between the defendant's negligence and the plaintiff's injury.[28] It rejects the more traditional "proximate cause" and "but for" approaches to legal causation because these tests fail to adequately account for circumstances involving plural or concurring causes.[29] Instead, Hawaii applies the substantial factor test. Under this framework, legal cause exists when the defendant's conduct is a substantial factor in bringing about harm to the plaintiff and there is no law relieving the defendant from liability.[30] This is the same test articulated by the Restatement (Second) of Torts and is the touchstone of any causation analysis.[31]

F. CONTRIBUTORY NEGLIGENCE, COMPARATIVE NEGLIGENCE, AND ASSUMPTION OF RISK

1. Contributory Negligence

Hawaii statutory law has abolished the common law defense of contributory negligence as a complete bar to recovery of damages for negligence resulting in death or in injury to person or property when the defendant's negligence is greater than the plaintiff's.[32] Hawaii's modified comparative negligence statute[33] has similarly made the doctrine of last clear chance obsolete.[34]

2. Comparative Negligence

Hawaii's modified comparative negligence statute applies to actions for death, personal injury, or injury to property.[35] When plaintiff's negligence does not exceed the aggregate of defendants' negligence, plaintiff may recover damages, which are reduced by the plaintiff's proportion of fault.[36] However, pure comparative negligence, rather than modified comparative negligence, applies to reduce a plaintiff's recovery in strict products liability cases.[37] In strict products liability cases, plaintiff's award will be reduced by his or her percentage of negligence, irrespective of whether it exceeds that of the defendants' proportion of negligence.[38]

3. Assumption of Risk

Assumption of risk remains available in Hawaii as an affirmative defense in negligence actions.[39] Where comparative negligence principles apply, assumption of risk that is a form of contributory negligence reduces, rather than bars, plaintiff's recoveries.[40] Hawaii recognizes express assumption of risk and primary and secondary implied assumption of risk.[41]

Express assumption of risk, in the sense of an express contract, is available as a defense that may bar plaintiff's recovery in tort and warranty strict products liability actions.[42] However, in implied warranty and strict products liability actions, primary implied assumption of risk is abolished, and secondary implied assumption of risk is retained solely as a form of contributory negligence to be compared against defendant's fault.[43]

G. *RES IPSA LOQUITUR* AND INHERENTLY DANGEROUS INSTRUMENTALITIES AND ACTIVITIES

1. *Res Ipsa Loquitur*

The doctrine of *res ipsa loquitur* makes it permissible to draw an inference of negligence from a set of facts but does not establish a presumption of negligence or shift the burden of proof.[44] There are three elements to the doctrine: (1) the event must be one that ordinarily does not occur in absence of someone's negligence; (2) the event must be caused by agency or instrumentality within defendant's exclusive control; and (3) the event must not have been caused by any voluntary action or contribution on plaintiff's part.[45]

Hawaii is in line with the majority of American jurisdictions that treat the doctrine of *res ipsa loquitur* as purely a procedural or evidentiary rule, rather than a substantive rule.[46] A court's instruction covering *res ipsa loquitur* should permit, but not compel, an inference of negligence;[47] it is merely a rebuttable inference that enables a plaintiff to put his case before the jury.[48]

2. Inherently Dangerous Activities and Instrumentalities

Liability for negligence with respect to a dangerous instrumentality or activity arises from failure to use due care.[49] The care exercised must be in proportion to the danger.[50] In addition, a person who controls an instrumentality that he knows or should know to be dangerous and the danger is not obvious has the duty to warn others of the danger.[51]

H. NEGLIGENCE *PER SE*

Negligence *per se* occurs where an act or omission is contrary to a statutory duty, or is so opposed to the dictates of common prudence that it can be said without hesitation or doubt that no careful person would have committed it.[52] Thus, the duty in a negligence action may be defined by a statute that lays down requirements of conduct, and provides expressly or by implication that a violation shall entail civil liability in tort.[53] Put differently, when a statute provides that under certain circumstances particular acts shall or shall not be done, it may be interpreted as fixing a standard from which it is negligence to deviate.[54] Even if a statute contains no express provision that its violation shall result in tort liability, and no implication to that effect, a court may, and in certain types of cases customarily will, adopt the requirements of the enactment as the standard of conduct necessary to avoid liability for negligence.[55] Courts may adopt the requirements of a statute as the standard of care when the purpose of the statute is to protect a class of persons that includes the one whose interest is invaded,[56] and the duty extends only to those persons for whose protection or benefit the statute was enacted for injuries of a character it was designed to protect against.[57] Where the statute does not provide that it must be given any effect in a civil suit, such as a criminal statute, courts are under no compulsion to accept it as defining the standard of care for purposes of a tort action.[58] Furthermore, even when courts accept a statute as defining the standard of care in a tort action, compliance with the statutory standard is not necessarily conclusive on the issue of negligence.[59]

I. JOINT AND SEVERAL LIABILITY

Under the Hawaii Uniform Contribution Among Tortfeasors Act (Contribution Act), joint tortfeasors are defined as "two or more persons jointly or severally liable in tort for the same injury to persons or property, whether or not a judgment has been recovered against all or some of them."[60] Joint tortfeasors are defendants who, acting together, commit the wrong or whose independent acts unite causing a single injury.[61] Status as a joint tortfeasor under the Contribution Act is based on liability for the alleged tort, and not on the basis of liability or the relationship among those liable for the tort.[62] Thus an employer who is vicariously liable for his employee's torts would be a joint tortfeasor with the employee under the Contribution Act.[63]

Effective June 28, 2001, Hawaii adopted a new procedure for the release of joint tortfeasors.[64] The newly adopted procedure applies to any release, dismissal with or without prejudice, or a covenant not to sue (hereinafter "release").[65] So long as the release is obtained in good faith as to one or more joint tortfeasors, then the release does not discharge the other tortfeasors unless the release so provides, but the release reduces the claims against the non-released party in the amount stipulated by the release, or by the amount of consideration paid for it, whichever is greater.[66] The release results in discharge of the released party from all liability for any contribution to any other party.[67] The settling parties are required to petition the court for a hearing on the issue of the good faith of the release, and must serve notice upon all other known joint tortfeasors by certified mail, return receipt requested.[68] A non-settling joint tortfeasor must file an objection within 25 days of mailing the notice to contest the good faith of the settlement, otherwise the court may approve the settlement without a hearing.[69] A determination by the court, either with or without a hearing, that a settlement is made in good faith, bars any other joint tortfeasor from further claims against the settling tortfeasor for equitable contribution, or comparative indemnity, negligence or fault.[70]

The right to contribution among joint tortfeasors accrues once a joint tortfeasor has either discharged the common liability or paid more than his *pro rata* share; but if the joint tortfeasor seeking contribution has settled with the plaintiff, he can only seek contribution if his settlement extinguished that other joint tortfeasor's liability to the plaintiff.[71]

Joint and several liability for government entities has been abolished, and government entities are only liable for their proportionate share of the damages.[72] In addition, general joint and several liability has been abolished, with several far-reaching exceptions.[73] Joint and several liability still applies to the recovery of economic damages in actions involving injury or death to persons.[74] In addition, joint and several liability applies to both economic and noneconomic damages in six categories of torts: (1) intentional torts; (2) environmental pollution torts; (3) toxic and asbestos related torts; (4) aircraft accident torts; (5) strict and product liability torts; and (6) motor vehicle accident torts (with one exception related to maintenance and design of highways).[75] Finally, for those torts that do not fit into the six above categories, joint and several liability for noneconomic damages still applies, if the action involves injury or death, as to those tortfeasors whose individual degree of negligence exceeds 25 percent or more.[76] For those whose negligence is less than 25 percent, their liability for noneconomic damages is in direct proportion to their degree of negligence.[77]

J. INDEMNITY

Indemnity generally means a right to claim reimbursement for any loss, damage, or tort liability from a person who has a duty to do so.[78] Further, indemnity is a "right of a party who is secondarily liable to recover from the party who is primarily liable for reimbursement of expenditures paid to a third party for injuries resulting from a violation of a common-law duty."[79]

The duty to indemnify may be based on an express or implied contract. In the case of an express indemnity contract, the Hawaii courts have strictly construed the language of such indemnification contract when the party claiming indemnity is seeking to be indemnified against that party's own act of negligence.[80] Even if there is no express indemnity contract, it is fairer to shift the burden of loss from one party to another to avoid such inequitable liability. In that case, courts may imply a contract of indemnity when there is a special legal relationship between the indemnitor and the indemnitee, such as an employer-employee relationship.[81] An indemnity contract can be implied from the terms of an existing contract or from a legal relationship between the parties.[82]

K. BAR OF WORKERS' COMPENSATION STATUTES

Under the Hawaii Workers' Compensation Act,[83] an employee is barred from suing an employer who has paid workers' compensation benefits for a work-related injury or disease.[84] The workers' compensation statutes were enacted to provide compensation to employees who suffer an injury or disease "arising out of and in the course of employment."[85] No compensation is allowed for injuries that result from the employee's willful intention to injure himself or another or by the employee's intoxication.[86] Workers' compensation benefits are also excluded for claims of mental distress resulting solely from disciplinary action taken in good faith by the employer, unless the collective bargaining agreement or employment agreement sets forth a different standard for disciplinary actions.[87]

Workers' compensation is designed to act as an employee's exclusive remedy for work-related injuries or diseases.[88] However, there are two exceptions to this principle: (1) victims of sexual harassment are permitted to seek tort damages for emotional distress or invasion of privacy related to the harassment in addition to the workers' compensation benefits;[89] and (2) a claim for workers' compensation does not prohibit an action for intentional infliction of emotional distress caused by discrimination.[90]

The receipt of benefits under the Hawaii Workers' Compensation Act does not bar an employee from seeking damages from a third party.[91] If the employee commences an action against a third party, he must timely notify the employer and the employer may, at any time prior to the commencement of trial on the matter, join as a party plaintiff.[92] If, within nine months after the injury was sustained, the employee has not commenced an action against such third person, the employer, having paid or being liable for workers' compensation benefits, shall be subrogated to the rights of the injured employee.[93] Whether the action is brought by the employee, the employer, or both, the employer or his insurer may be reimbursed for the previously paid workers' compensation benefits from any judgment or settlement, reduced proportionately by the costs of litigation and reasonable attorney's fees.[94] A release or settlement of a claim or action must be approved by both the employer and employee.[95]

L. PREMISES LIABILITY

Under Hawaii law, a landowner must use reasonable care to assure the safety of all persons reasonably anticipated to be on premises, regardless of legal status.[96] The possessor of land, who knows or should have known of the unreasonable risk of harm posed to persons using the land, owes the users a duty to take reasonable steps to eliminate the unreasonable risk of harm, or warn the users against it.[97] Distinctions with regard to status of users of land remain important when determining whether there is an exception to the general negligence rule that it is unreasonable to impose on landowners a duty to anticipate and control actions of third parties.[98]

A private landowner has substantial immunity from actions in tort by those who come onto his land for recreational purposes without a fee. Hawaii's recreational use statute precludes liability for negligence on the part of private landowners who allow persons onto their property for recreational purposes.[99]

M. DRAM SHOP LIABILITY

While Hawaii does not have dram shop legislation, the courts have imposed common law dram shop liability based on violations of Hawaii's liquor control law,[100] which prohibits serving alcohol to visibly intoxicated persons.[101] Licensed liquor suppliers who negligently sell or serve alcohol to an intoxicated person may be held liable in tort by a third party who was subsequently injured by the intoxicated person.[102] Similar liability has not been imposed on a social host, or unlicensed liquor supplier, who serves alcohol to an intoxicated guest who subsequently injures a third party.[103] A licenced liquor supplier will *not* be held liable for injuries to the first-party consumer of the liquor, based on the grounds that the consumer is not within the class of persons whom the statute was intended to protect.[104] Similarly, a minor consumer of liquor cannot recover for his or her own injuries caused by the prohibited sale of liquor to that minor, based on the same rationale.[105] However, based on the statute prohibiting sales of liquor to a minor,[106] a liquor supplier who sells liquor to a minor is liable to innocent third parties who are injured, even where the third party is injured by an intoxicated minor other than the minor to whom the liquor was sold in violation of the statute.[107]

Before liability can be found, it must be established that notice or knowledge on the part of the defendant that the person who was supplied the liquor was under the influence of liquor at the time he or she was served alcohol,[108] and that providing the alcohol to that person was the proximate cause of the third party's injuries.[109] However, as a matter of law, a tavern's sale or service of alcohol to an intoxicated automobile driver may be the proximate cause of injuries inflicted on a third party by the inebriated driver, in light of the fact that universal use of automobiles and the increasing frequency of accidents involving drunk drivers are foreseeable to a tavern owner.[110]

N. ECONOMIC LOSS

The economic loss doctrine is adopted in Hawaii insofar as it applies to claims for relief based on a product liability or negligent design and/or manufacture theory and acts to bar recovery of pure economic loss in actions based on these theories.[111] The economic loss rule, however, does not bar actions based on negligent misrepresentation or fraud.[112]

In the context of construction litigation, where a party is in privity of contract with a design professional, economic loss damages are limited to contractual remedies, and a negligence action may not be maintained.[113] The economic loss rule marks the fundamental boundary between the law of contracts, which is designed to enforce expectations created by agreement, and the law of torts, which is designed to protect citizens and their property by imposing a duty of reasonable care on others.[114] The economic loss rule was designed to prevent disproportionate liability and allow parties to allocate risk by contract.[115]

O. FRAUD AND MISREPRESENTATION

The Hawaii Rules of Civil Procedure require that a cause of action for fraud be stated with particularity.[116] A plaintiff must state the circumstances constituting fraud with particularity and specify the representations made.[117]

Each of the following elements are required for a cause of action based on fraud or deceit: (1) false representations made by the defendant; (2) with knowledge of their falsity (or without knowledge of their truth or falsity); (3) in contemplation of plaintiff's reliance on these false representations; and (4) plaintiff's detrimental reliance.[118]

Under Hawaii law, proof of fraud requires a heightened standard of proof. The party claiming fraud must establish the above elements by clear and convincing evidence.[119] To be actionable, the alleged false representation must relate to a past or existing material fact and not the occurrence of a future event.[120]

Hawaii courts apply the Restatement (Second) of Torts to claims for negligent misrepresentation.[121] The material elements of the tort of negligent misrepresentation are as follows:

> One who, in the course of his business, profession or employment, or in any other transaction in which he has a pecuniary interest, supplies false information for the guidance of others in their business transactions, is subject to liability for pecuniary loss caused by them by their justifiable reliance upon the information, if he fails to exercise reasonable care or competence in obtaining or communicating the information.[122]

P. CONSUMER FRAUD STATUTE

Hawaii's consumer protection law is designed to protect consumers from unfair and deceptive trade practices and unfair methods of competition.[123] A practice is considered unfair when it offends public policy and when the practice is immoral, unethical, oppressive, unscrupulous, or substantially injurious to consumers.[124] A practice whereby a seller uses false or misleading statements as to the nature of his product, for example, can be considered conduct that is unfair to both consumers and competitors.[125]

Hawaii limits standing to assert a statutory claim for deceptive trade practices and unfair competition to consumers, the state Attorney General and the director of the Office of Consumer Protection.[126] Thus, a private right of action does exist against those engaging in unfair and deceptive trade practices.[127] In order to be considered a "consumer" for purposes of standing, the plaintiff must be "a natural person who, primarily for personal, family, or household purposes, purchases, attempts to purchase, or is solicited to purchase goods or services or who commits money, property, or services in a personal investment."[128] A commercial enterprise lacks standing to bring a private action for unfair and deceptive trade practices.[129] It will have standing, however, to bring a statutory cause of action for unfair competition.[130]

If a plaintiff prevails on a claim for deceptive trade practices and/or unfair competition, he may be entitled to relief in the form of an injunction and/or monetary relief, including treble damages, attorney's fees, and costs.[131]

Q. PUNITIVE DAMAGES

Hawaii generally follows the Restatement (Second) of Torts Section 908 (1979) to determine if punitive damages should be awarded.[132] In order to recover punitive damages, a plaintiff must prove by clear and convincing evidence that the defendant has acted wantonly or oppressively or with such malice as implies a spirit of mischief or criminal indifference to civil obligations, or where there has been some willful misconduct or that entire want of care that would raise the presumption of a conscious indifference to consequences.[133] The fundamental purpose underlying an award of exemplary or punitive damages is to punish the wrongdoer and to deter the wrongdoer and others from committing similar wrongs and offenses in the future.[134]

In general, punitive damages can be based on nominal damages only.[135] For example, where actual damage is not an essential element of the cause of action, if the necessary culpability on the defendant's part is established, then a verdict for punitive damages is proper, even though the award of other damages is nominal or absent entirely.[136] However, where actual damage is an element of a cause of action, a finding of actual damages is a prerequisite to any punitive damages award.[137]

In determining whether an award of punitive damages is appropriate, the inquiry focuses primarily on the defendant's mental state and, to a lesser degree, the nature of his or her conduct.[138] To justify an award of punitive damages, a positive element of conscious wrongdoing is always required.[139] Conduct supporting an award of punitive damages should be treated as an intentional tort.[140] Thus, punitive damages are not awarded for mere inadvertence, mistake, or errors of judgment.[141] Something more than the mere commission of a tort is always required for punitive damages.[142]

Under Hawaii law, the proper measurement of punitive damages is the degree of malice, oppression, or gross negligence that forms the basis for the award and the amount of money required to punish the defendant.[143] In the past, the Supreme Court of Hawaii has acknowledged a rule that, while punitive damages must bear some relation to the injury inflicted and the cause thereof, they need not bear any relation to the damages allowed by way of the compensation.[144] However, that particular rule might no longer be valid because the United States Supreme Court has subsequently held that a comparison between the compensatory damages award and the punitive damages award is significant in determining whether a punitive damages award is grossly excessive under the United States Constitution.[145] The Due Process Clause of the Fourteenth Amendment prohibits a state from imposing a grossly excessive punishment on a tortfeasor.[146] Punitive damages pose an acute danger of arbitrary deprivation of property.[147] A grossly excessive punitive damages award amounts to an arbitrary deprivation of property without due process of law.[148] Elementary notions of fairness enshrined in constitutional jurisprudence dictate that a person receive fair notice not only of the conduct that will subject him to punishment, but also of the severity of the penalty that a state may impose.[149] Thus, the United States Supreme Court has established the following three "guideposts" for determining whether a civil punitive damages award is grossly excessive: (1) the degree of reprehensibility of the conduct; (2) the disparity between the harm or potential harm suffered by the plaintiff and his or her punitive damages award; and (3) the difference between this remedy and the civil or criminal penalties authorized or imposed in comparable cases.[150]

A plaintiff may recover punitive damages in a products liability action that is based on strict liability as long as the plaintiff proves the requisite aggravating conduct on the part of the defendant.[151] However, a plaintiff may not recover punitive damages in a breach of contract action in the absence of conduct that: (1) violates a duty that is independently recognized by principles of tort law, and (2) transcends the breach of the contract.[152] Furthermore, attorney's fees cannot be awarded in addition to punitive damages; rather, they must constitute the whole of the punitive damage award or be accounted for as a portion of the total punitive damage award.[153]

R. **WRONGFUL DEATH AND SURVIVORSHIP ACTIONS**

Hawaii provides statutory recovery for wrongful death[154] and a right of action for a decedent's personal injuries[155] — both of which exist as two separate and distinct causes of action.[156] In addition, Hawaii also recognizes a common law cause of action for death by a wrongful act.[157]

Hawaii's wrongful death statute limits recovery for death by wrongful act to the decedent's surviving spouse, reciprocal beneficiary, children, father, mother, and by any person dependent on the decedent.[158] These persons may recover for pecuniary injuries and for the loss of love and affection caused by the wrongful death of the deceased.[159]

The "surviving" cause of action for a decedent's personal injuries, such as pain and suffering,[160] provided for by Hawaii's survivor statute, resides in the legal representative of the decedent.[161] Damages, including future earnings of the decedent for the period of time the decedent would have likely lived,[162] that are recovered fall to the decedent's estate.[163]

William C. McCorriston
Darolyn H. Lendio
Lisa M. Ginoza
MCCORRISTON MILLER MUKAI MACKINNON
Five Waterfront Plaza, Suite 400
500 Ala Moana Boulevard
Honolulu, Hawaii 96813
(808) 529-7300
Fax (808) 524-8293
mccorriston@m4law.com
www.m4law.com

ENDNOTES - HAWAII

1. *See City Collectors, Ltd. v. Moku*, 50 Haw. 273, 439 P.2d 217 (1968).

2. *See Au v. Au*, 63 Haw. 210, 626 P.2d 173 (1981).

3. Haw. Rev. Stat. § 657-7 (2000).

4. Haw. Rev. Stat. § 657-7.3 (2000).

5. Haw. Rev. Stat. § 657-4 (2000).

6. *See Hoke v. Paul*, 65 Haw. 478, 653 P.2d 1155 (1982).

7. Haw. Rev. Stat. § 657-1 (2000).

8. *See Higa v. Mirikitani*, 55 Haw. 167, 517 P.2d 1 (1973).

9. Haw. Rev. Stat. § 657-1 (2000). *See Schimmelfennig v. Grove Farm Co.*, 41 Haw. 124 (1955) (finding that a right of action under this section accrues as of the breach, regardless of when the damage results).

10. Haw. Rev. Stat. § 657-1 (2000).

11. Haw. Rev. Stat. § 662-4 (2000).

12. Haw. Rev. Stat. § 657-1.5 (2000).

13. Haw. Rev. Stat. § 431:10C-306(b)(1) (2000).

14. Haw. Rev. Stat. § 431:10C-306(b)(2) (2000).

15. Haw. Rev. Stat. § 431:10C-306(b)(3) (2000).

16. Haw. Rev. Stat. § 431:10C-306(b)(4) (2000).

17. Haw. Rev. Stat. § 431:10C-301.5 (2000).

18. *Ward v. Inter-Island Stream Navigation Co.*, 22 Haw. 66, 69 (1914).

19. *Lee v. Corregedore*, 83 Haw. 154, 158, 925 P.2d 324, 328 (1996) (citations omitted).

20. *See Johnston v. KFC Nat'l Management Co.*, 71 Haw. 229, 232, 788 P.2d 159, 161 (1990).

21. *See Knodle v. Waikiki Gateway Hotel*, 69 Haw. 376, 387, 742 P.2d 377, 384 (1987).

22. *See Lee v. Corregedore*, 83 Haw. 154, 159, 925 P.2d 324, 329 (1996).

23. *See Lee v. Corregedore*, 83 Haw. 154, 159, 925 P.2d 324, 329 (1996) (citing Restatement (Second) of Torts § 314 (1965)).

24. *See Lee v. Corregedore*, 83 Haw. 154, 159, 925 P.2d 324, 329 (1996) (citing to Restatement (Second) of Torts § 314A (1965)).

25. *See Touchette v. Ganal*, 82 Haw. 293, 922 P.2d 347 (1996) (holding that a marital relationship alone was not a "special relationship"); *Moody v. Cawdrey and Associates, Inc.*, 68 Haw. 527, 721 P.2d 707 (1986) (holding that the landlord-tenant relationship was not a "special relationship"); *Wolsk v. State of Hawaii*, 68 Haw. 527, 711 P.2d 1300 (1986); *King v. Illikai Properties, Inc.*, 2 Haw. App. 359, 632 P.2d 657 (1981). *Contra Knodle v. Waikiki Gateway Hotel*, 69 Haw. 376, 742 P.2d 377 (1987) (holding that a "special relationship" existed between a hotel and its guest).

26. *Sherry v. Asing*, 56 Haw. 135, 154, 531 P.2d 648, 661 (1975) (citations omitted).

27. *See Ellis v. Mutual Telephone Co.*, 29 Haw. 604, 624, (1927) (holding that a five-year-old child was incapable of contributory negligence).

28. *Knodle v. Waikiki Gateway Hotel, Inc.*, 69 Haw. 376, 742 P.2d 377 (1987) (citing W. P. Keeton, Prosser and Keeton on the Law of Torts § 30, at 164–65 (5th ed. 1984)).

29. *Id.*

30. *Id.* (following the definition of legal causation set forth in Restatement (Second) of Torts § 431 (1965)). *See also Mitchell v. Branch*, 45 Haw. 128, 132, 363 P.2d 969, 973 (1961) (noting that the Restatement provides "[t]he best definition and the most workable test of proximate cause or legal cause so far suggested").

31. *See Knodle*, 69 Haw. at 390, 742 P.2d at 386.

32. *See* Haw. Rev. Stat. § 663-31 (LEXIS current through 2000 reg. sess.); *Ozaki v. Ass'n of Apt. Owners of Discovery Bay*, 87 Haw. 265, 954 P.2d 644 (1998).

33. *See* Haw. Rev. Stat. § 663-31.

34. *See Rapoza v. Parnell*, 83 Haw. 78, 83, 924 P.2d 572, 577 (Ct. App. 1996).

35. *See* Haw. Rev. Stat. § 663-31.

36. *See* Haw. Rev. Stat. § 663-31; *Wagatsuma v. Patch*, 10 Haw. App. 547, 582, 884 P.2d 574, 590 (1994).

37. *See Armstrong v. Cione*, 69 Haw. 176, 182–83, 738 P.2d 79, 83 (1987).

38. *See Armstrong v. Cione*, 69 Haw. 176, 182–83, 738 P.2d 79, 83 (1987).

39. *See Craft v. Peebles*, 78 Haw. 287, 303, 893 P.2d 138, 154 (1995); Haw. R. Civ. Proc. 8(c) (West 1999).

40. *See Larsen v. Pacesetter Sys.*, 74 Haw. 1, 33, 837 P.2d 1273 (1992).

41. *See Tancredi v. Dive Makai Charters*, 823 F. Supp. 778, 788 (D. Haw. 1993), *overruling in part on other grounds recognized by McClenahan v. Paradise Cruises, Ltd.*, 888 F. Supp. 120 (D. Haw. 1995); *Larsen v. Pacesetter Sys.*, 74 Haw. 1, 35–36, 837 P.2d 1273 (1992).

42. *See Larsen v. Pacesetter Sys.*, 74 Haw. 1, 35–36, 837 P.2d 1273 (1992).

43. *See Larsen v. Pacesetter Sys.*, 74 Haw. 1, 38–39, 837 P.2d 1273 (1992).

44. *See Wilson v. United States*, 645 F.2d 728, 730 (9th Cir. 1981); *see also Agee v. Kahului Trucking & Storage Inc.*, 67 Haw. 365, 688 P.2d 256 (1984); *Carlos v. MTL, Inc.*, 77 Haw. 269, 883 P.2d 691 (Haw. Ct. App. 1981).

45. *See Carlos v. MTL, Inc.*, 77 Haw. 269, 277–78, 883 P.2d 691 (Haw. Ct. App. 1981); *see also Akiona v. United States*, 938 F.2d 158 (9th Cir. 1991), *cert. denied*, 503 U.S. 962, 112 S. Ct. 1567, 118 L. Ed. 2d 212 (1992); *Winter v. Scherman*, 57 Haw. 279, 281–82, 554 P.2d 1137 (1976).

46. *See Carlos v. MTL, Inc.*, 77 Haw. 269, 883 P.2d 691 (Haw. Ct. App. 1981).

47. *See Cozine v. Hawaiian Catamaran, Ltd.*, 49 Haw. 77, 87, 412 P.2d 669, 678 (1966); *Turner v. Willis*, 59 Haw. 319, 324, 582 P.2d 710 (1978).

48. *See Winter v. Scherman*, 57 Haw. 279, 282, 554 P.2d 1137 (1976); *Turner v. Willis*, 59 Haw. 319, 324, 582 P.2d 710 (1978).

49. *See Kajiya v. Dept. of Water Supply*, 2 Haw. App. 221, 225, 629 P.2d 635 (Haw. Ct. App. 1981); *see also Nofoa v. U.S.*, 132 F.3d 39 (9th Cir. 1997).

50. *Id.*

51. *Id.*

52. *Bloudell v. Wailuku Sugar Co.*, 4 Haw. App. 498, 502 n.7, 669 P.2d 163, 168 n.7 (Ct. App. 1983).

53. *Lee v. Corregedore*, 83 Haw. 154, 172, 925 P.2d 324, 342 (1996) (citing Restatement (Second) of Torts § 285 comment b (1965)).

54. *Id.* (citing W. L. Prosser, Prosser & Keeton on the Law of Torts § 36 at 220 (5th ed. 1984)).

55. *Id.*, 83 Haw. at 173, 925 P.2d at 343 (1996) (citing Restatement (Second) of Torts § 285 comment c (1965)).

56. *Id.* (citing Restatement (Second) of Torts § 286(a) (1965)).

57. *Namauu v. City and County of Honolulu*, 62 Haw. 358, 362, 614 P.2d 943, 946 (1980) (citing W. L. Prosser, Prosser & Keeton on the Law of Torts § 36 (4th ed. 1971) and Restatement (Second) of Torts § 286 (1965)).

58. *Lee v. Corregedore*, 83 Haw. at 173, 925 P.2d at 343 (1996) (citing Restatement (Second) of Torts § 286 comment d (1965)).

59. *Pickering v. State*, 57 Haw. 405, 408, 557 P.2d 125, 127 (1976) (citing Restatement of Torts (Second) § 288C (1965)), *Potter v. Battle Creek Gas Co.*, 185 N.W.2d 37 (1970); *Grand Trunk Ry. Co. v. Ives*, 144 U.S. 408 (1892)).

60. Haw. Rev. Stat. § 663-11 (LEXIS current through 1999 reg. sess.).

61. *Karasawa v. TIG Insurance Co.*, 88 Haw. 77, 80–81, 961 P.2d 1171, 1174–75 (1998).

62. *Saranillio v. Silva*, 78 Haw. 1, 10, 889 P.2d 685, 694, *recon. denied*, 78 Haw. 421, 895 P.2d 172 (1995).

63. *Saranillio v. Silva*, 78 Haw. 1, 13, 889 P.2d 685, 697, *recon. denied*, 78 Haw. 421, 895 P.2d 172 (1995).

64. Haw. Rev. Stat. § 663-15.5 (Michie 2001 Supp.). Haw. Rev. Stat. §§ 663-14 and 663-15, *repealed*, effective June 28, 2001. *See* 2001 Haw. Sess. Laws, Act 300, §§ 3 and 4.

65. Haw. Rev. Stat. § 663-15.5 (a) (Michie 2001 Supp.).

66. Haw. Rev. Stat. § 663-15.5 (a) (1) & (2) (Michie 2001 Supp.).

67. Haw. Rev. Stat. § 663-15.5 (a) (3) (Michie 2001 Supp.).

68. Haw. Rev. Stat. § 663-15.5 (b) (Michie 2001 Supp.).

69. *Id.*

70. Haw. Rev. Stat. § 663-15.5 (d) (Michie 2001 Supp.).

71. Haw. Rev. Stat. § 663-12 (LEXIS current through 1999 reg. sess.).

72. Haw. Rev. Stat. § 663-10.5 (LEXIS current through 1999 reg. sess.).

73. Haw. Rev. Stat. § 663-10.9 (LEXIS current through 1999 reg. sess.).

74. *Id.*

75. *Id.*

76. *Id.*

77. *Id.*

78. Black's Law Dictionary (7th ed. 1999).

79. *Id.*

80. *See Kamali v. Hawaiian Electric Co., et al.,* 54 Haw. 153, 504 P.2d 861 (1972); *Straub Clinic and Hospital, Inc., et al. v. Chicago Insurance Co., et al.,* 4 Haw. App. 268, 665 P. 2d 176 (1983); *Ruth v. Fleming,* 2 Haw. App. 585, 637 P. 2d 784 (1981).

81. *See Sveldlund v. Pepsi Cola Bottling Co. of Hawaii, Ltd.,* 172 F. Supp. 597 (D. Haw. 1959); *Messier v. Association of Apartment Owners of Mt. Terrace, et al.,* 6 Haw. App. 525, 735 P.2d 939 (1987); *Kamali v. Hawaiian Electric Co.,* 54 Haw. 153, 504 P.2d 861 (1972).

82. *Id.*

83. Chapter 386, Haw. Rev. Stat. (LEXIS current through 2000 spec. sess.).

84. Haw. Rev. Stat. § 386-3(a) (1999) (LEXIS current through 2000 spec. sess.).

85. *Id.*

86. Haw. Rev. Stat. § 386-3(b) (1999) (LEXIS current through 2000 spec. sess.).

87. Haw. Rev. Stat. § 386-3(c) (1999) (LEXIS current through 2000 spec. sess.).

88. Haw. Rev. Stat. § 386-5 (1999) (LEXIS current through 2000 spec. sess.).

89. *Id.*

90. *Furakawa v. Honolulu Zoological Society,* 85 Haw. 7, 936 P.2d 643 (1997) (holding that the exclusivity provision of the Hawaii Workers' Compensation Act does not prohibit an employee from bringing an action against the employer for intentional infliction of emotional distress caused by discrimination); *Takaki v.*

Allied Machinery Corp., 87 Haw. 57, 951 P.2d 507 (1998) (holding that an employee may bring an action against employer for intentional infliction of emotional distress caused by discrimination in violation of the Hawaii Employment Practices Act and such an action is not barred by the exclusivity provision of the workers' compensation statutes).

91. Haw. Rev. Stat. § 386-8 (1999) (LEXIS current through 2000 spec. sess.).

92. *Id.*

93. *Id.*

94. *Id.*

95. *Id.*

96. *See Covington v. United States*, 916 F. Supp. 1511, 1520 (D. Haw. 1996), *aff'd*, 119 F.3d 612 (9th Cir. 1997); *see also Kaczmarczyk v. City and County of Honolulu*, 65 Haw. 612, 615, 656 P.2d 89 (1982); *Freidrich v. Dept. of Transp.*, 60 Haw. 32, 35, 586 P.2d 1037 (1978).

97. *See Richardson v. Sport Shinko*, 76 Haw. 494, 503, 880 P.2d 169 (1994); *see also Poston v. United States*, 396 F.2d 103, 108 (9th Cir. 1968) *cert. denied*, 393 U.S. 946, 89 S. Ct. 322, 21 L. Ed. 2d 285, *reh'g denied*, 393 U.S. 1072, 89 S. Ct. 724, 21 L. Ed. 2d 717 (1969); *Crichfield v. Grand Wailea Co.*, 93 Haw. 477, 489 P.3d 349 (2000).

98. *See Doe v. Grosvenor Properties (Hawaii) Ltd.*, 73 Haw. 158, 163, 829 P.2d 512 (1992); *see also Cuba v. Fernandez*, 71 Haw. 627, 631–32, 801 P.2d 1208 (1990).

99. Haw. Rev. Stat §§ 520-1 *et seq.* (LEXIS current through 2000 spec. sess.); *Covington v. United States*, 916 F. Supp. 1511, 1520, *aff'd*, 119 F.3d 5 (D. Haw. 1996), *aff'd*, 119 F.3d 612 (9th Cir. 1997).

100. *Ono v. Applegate*, 62 Haw. 131, 612 P.2d 533 (1980).

101. Haw. Rev. Stat. § 281-78(b)(1)(B) (LEXIS current through 1999 reg. sess.).

102. *Ono v. Applegate*, 62 Haw. 131, 612 P.2d 533 (1980).

103. *Johnston v. KFC National Management Co.*, 71 Haw. 229, 788 P.2d 159 (1990); *Faulk v. Suzuki Motors Co., Ltd.*, 9 Haw. App. 490, 493, 851 P.2d 332, 334 (1993).

104. *Bertelmann v. TAAS Associates*, 69 Haw. 95, 99–102, 735 P.2d 930, 933–34 (1987); *Feliciano v. Waikiki Deep Water Inc.*, 69 Haw. 605, 752 P.2d 1076 (1988).

105. *Winters v. Silver Fox Bar*, 71 Haw. 524, 797 P.2d 51 (1990).

106. Haw. Rev. Stat. § 281-78(b)(1)(A) (LEXIS current through 1999 reg. sess.), *see also* Haw. Rev. Stat. § 281-785 (Michie 1995 and 2001 Supp.).

107. *Delos Reyes v. Kuboyama*, 76 Haw. 137, 141–47, 870 P.2d 1281, 1285–91 (1994).

108. *Ono v. Applegate*, 62 Haw. 131, 138, 612 P.2d 533, 539 (1980).

109. *Ono*, 62 Haw. 131, 140–41, 612 P.2d 533, 540–41 (1980).

110. *Ono*, 62 Haw. 131, 612 P.2d 533 (1980).

111. *See State ex rel. Bronster v. United States Steel*, 82 Haw. 32, 40, 919 P.2d 294, 302 (1996).

112. *See Bronster*, 82 Haw. at 45, 919 P.2d at 307.

113. *City Express, Inc. v. Express Partners*, 87 Haw. 466, 469, 959 P.2d 836, 839 (1998).

114. *City Express*, 87 Haw. at 469, 959 Haw. at 839 (quoting *Berschauer/Philips Construction Co. v. Seattle School District*, 124 Wash. 2d 816, 881 P.2d 986 (1994)).

115. *Id*.

116. Haw. R. Civ. P. 9(b) (West 2001).

117. *Larsen v. Pacesetter Systems, Inc.*, 74 Haw. 1, 30, 837 P.2d 1273, 1288 (1992) (citing *Ellis v. Crockett*, 51 Haw. 45, 59, 451 P.2d 814, 823 (1969)).

118. *Larsen*, 74 Haw. at 30, 837 P.2d at 1288. *Hawaii's Thousand Friends v. Anderson*, 70 Haw. 276, 286, 768 P.2d 1293, 1301 (1989) (citing *Kang v. Harrington*, 59 Haw. 652, 656, 587 P.2d 285, 289 (1978)).

119. *Anderson*, 70 Haw. at 286, 768 P.2d at 1301 (citing *Dobison v. Bank of Hawaii*, 60 Haw. 225, 226, 587 P.2d 1234, 1235 (1978)).

120. *Stahl v. Balsara*, 60 Haw. 144, 149, 587 P.2d 1210, 1214 (1978).

121. *UCSF-Stanford Health Care v. Hawaii Management Alliance Benefits & Services, Inc.*, 58 F. Supp. 2d 1162, 1169 (D. Haw. 1999); *Shaffer v. Earl Thacker Co., Ltd.*, 6 Haw. App. 188, 191, 716 P.2d 163, 165 (1986).

122. *Hawaii Management*, 58 F. Supp. 2d at 1169; *Shaffer*, 6 Haw. App. at 191, 716 P.2d at 165 (citing Restatement (Second) of Torts § 552 (1977)).

123. Haw. Rev. Stat. § 480-2 (LEXIS current through 2000 spec. sess.).

124. *Robert's Waikiki U-Drive, Inc. v. Budget Rent-A-Car Sys.*, 491 F. Supp. 1199 (D. Haw. 1980), *aff'd*, 732 F.2d 1403 (9th Cir. 1984); *T.W. Elec. Serv., Inc. v. Pacific Elec. Contractors Ass'n*, 809 F.2d 626 (9th Cir. 1987).

125. *Kukui Nuts of Haw., Inc. v. R. Baird & Co.*, 7 Haw. App. 598, 789 P.2d 50, *cert. denied*, 71 Haw. 668, 833 P.2d 900 (1990).

126. *Lui Ciro, Inc. v. Ciro, Inc.*, 895 F. Supp. 1365 (D. Haw. 1995).

127. Haw. Rev. Stat. § 480-13 (LEXIS current through 2000 spec. sess.).

128. Haw. Rev. Stat. § 480-1 (LEXIS current through 1999 reg. sess.).

129. *See Paulson Inc. v. Bromar, Inc.*, 808 F. Supp. 736, 743 (D. Haw. 1992) ("the statute was amended to bar suit by a business for deceptive practices in 1987"); *GWC Restaurants, Inc. v. Hawaiian Flour Mills, Inc.*, 691 F. Supp. 247, 249 (D. Haw. 1988) ("Haw. Rev. Stat. § 480-2 [was] amended to preclude the bringing of unfair and deceptive trade practices by businessmen and merchants between themselves").

130. *Lui Ciro, Inc.*, 895 F. Supp. at 1388.

131. Haw. Rev. Stat. § 480-13 (current through 2000).

132. *Masaki v. General Motors Corp.*, 71 Haw. 1, 6, 780 P.2d 566, 570 (1989).

133. *Masaki v. General Motors Corp.*, 71 Haw. 1, 16–17, 780 P.2d 566, 575 (1989) (citing *Bright v. Quinn*, 20 Haw. 504, 512 (1911)).

134. *Masaki v. General Motors Corp.*, 71 Haw. 1, 16, 780 P.2d 566, 575 (1989).

135. *Weinberg v. Mauch*, 78 Haw. 40, 51, 890 P.2d 277, 288 (1995).

136. *Howell v. Associated Hotels, Ltd.*, 40 Haw. 492, 499 (1954).

137. *Weinberg v. Mauch*, 78 Haw. 40, 51, 890 P.2d 277, 288 (1995).

138. *Masaki v. General Motors Corp.*, 71 Haw. 1, 7, 780 P.2d 566, 570 (1989) (citing D. Dobbs, Handbook on the Law of Remedies, § 3.9, at 205 (1973)).

139. *Id.* (citing C. McCormick, Handbook on the Law of Damages § 77, at 280 (1935)).

140. *Iddings v. Mee-Lee*, 82 Haw. 1, 9, 919 P.2d 263, 271 (1996) (quoting *Pleasant v. Johnson*, 325 S.E.2d 244, 249 (N.C. 1985)).

141. *Masaki v. General Motors Corp.*, 71 Haw. 1, 7, 780 P.2d 566, 571 (1989) (citing Restatement (Second) of Torts § 908 comment b (1979), and W. P. Keeton, Prosser & Keeton on the Law of Torts § 2, at 10 (5th ed. 1984)).

142. *Id.* (citing W. P. Keeton, Prosser & Keeton on the Law of Torts § 2, at 9 (5th ed. 1984)).

143. *Kang v. Harrington*, 59 Haw. 652, 663, 587 P.2d 285, 291 (1978).

144. *Howell v. Associated Hotels, Ltd.*, 40 Haw. 492, 500–01 (1954).

145. *BMW of North America, Inc. v. Gore*, 517 U.S. 559, 581 (1996).

146. *BMW of North America, Inc. v. Gore*, 517 U.S. 559, 562 (1996) (citing *TXO Production Corp. v. Alliance Resources Corp.*, 509 U.S. 443, 454 (1993)).

147. *Honda Motor Co., Ltd. v. Oberg*, 512 U.S. 415, 432 (1994).

148. *TXO Production v. Alliance Resources*, 509 U.S. 443, 454 (1993) (quoting *Waters-Pierce Oil Co. v. Texas* (No. 1), 212 U.S. 86, 111 (1909)).

149. *BMW of North America, Inc. v. Gore*, 517 U.S. 559, 574 (1996).

150. *BMW of North America, Inc.*, 517 U.S. 559, 574–75 (1996).

151. *Masaki v. General Motors Corp.*, 71 Haw. 1, 11, 780 P.2d 566, 572–73 (1989).

152. *Francis v. Lee Enterprises, Inc.*, 89 Haw. 234, 244, 971 P.2d 707, 717 (1999).

153. *Lee v. Aiu*, 85 Haw. 19, 35, 936 P.2d 655, 672 (1997).

154. *See* Haw. Rev. Stat. § 663-3 (LEXIS current through 2000 reg. sess.).

155. *See* Haw. Rev. Stat. § 663-7 (LEXIS current through 2000 reg. sess.).

156. *See In re: Hawaii Federal Asbestos Cases, Iida v. Allied Signal, Inc.*, 854 F. Supp. 702, 712 (D. Haw. 1994).

157. *See Rohlfing v. Moses Akiona, Ltd.*, 45 Haw. 373, 383–84, 369 P.2d 96, 102 (1961), *overruled by on other grounds, Greene v. Texeira*, 54 Haw. 231, 505 P.2d 1169 (1973); *Kamanu v. E.E. Black, Ltd.*, 41 Haw. 442, 444–45 (1956); *Kake v. Horton*, 2 Haw. 209, 211–12 (1860).

158. *See* Haw. Rev. Stat. § 663-3.

159. *See* Haw. Rev. Stat. § 663-3; *Lealaimatafao v. Woodward-Clyde Consultants*, 75 Haw. 544, 552, 867 P.2d 220, 224 (1994).

160. *See Tancredi v. Dive Makai Charters*, 823 F. Supp. 778 (D. Haw. 1993), *overruling on other grounds recognized by, McClenahan v. Paradise Cruises, Ltd.*, 888 F. Supp. 120 (D. Haw. 1995).

161. *See* Haw. Rev. Stat. § 663-7.

162. *See* Haw. Rev. Stat. § 663-8; *Tancredi v. Dive Makai Charters*, 823 F. Supp. 778 (D. Haw. 1993), *overruling on other grounds recognized by, McClenahan v. Paradise Cruises, Ltd.*, 888 F. Supp. 120 (D. Haw. 1995).

163. *See* Haw. Rev. Stat. § 663-7.

IDAHO[*]

A. STATUTES OF LIMITATION

A two-year statute of limitations applies to claims for professional malpractice, for breach of an implied warranty or covenant, or that are based on negligent, intentional, or otherwise tortious conduct that gives rise to personal injuries or death.[1] The beginning of the limitation period, with two exceptions, is when some harm is objectively ascertainable.[2] The exceptions involve claims for the inadvertent leaving of a foreign object in the human body through the malpractice of a health-care professional or institution and claims where the fact of harm has been fraudulently concealed from the plaintiff by a wrongdoer that has a professional or commercial relationship to the plaintiff.[3] The limitation period for such claims begins to run at the time the plaintiff knows of the harm or should reasonably have been put on inquiry thereof, and suit must be brought within the later of one year after this time or two years after the occurrence of the underlying tortious conduct.[4] Outside of these limited exceptions, the "discovery" rule generally does not apply under Idaho law.[5]

However, another area in which a form of the "discovery" rule does apply is with respect to claims for fraud or mistake.[6] Such claims are subject to a three-year statute of limitations that begins to run when the claimant knew or reasonably should have known of the facts constituting the fraud or mistake.[7]

Claims for product liability, defamation, assault, battery, and false imprisonment are subject to a two-year statute of limitations,[8] as are claims under the Idaho Consumer Protection Act.[9]

Claims for trespass on real property, or for taking, detaining, or injuring personal property, are subject to a three-year statute of limitations.[10]

Claims against the state of Idaho or its political subdivisions must be asserted administratively within 180 days after they arose or reasonably should have been discovered by the claimant.[11] If the governmental entity does not approve a claim within 90 days of its assertion, the claimant may file suit at any time within two years after the claim arose or reasonably should have been discovered.[12]

A "catch-all" provision subjects all claims that are not subject to a specific statute of limitations to a four-year limitation period.[13]

Statutes of limitation are tolled under certain circumstances if the defendant departs Idaho after committing the wrongful act of which the plaintiff complains and the plaintiff cannot, through reasonably diligent efforts, locate and serve the defendant outside the state.[14] Where a defendant's civil wrong also results in his incarceration, the statute of limitations for a civil action by the victim of the crime against the defendant is tolled until one year after the defendant has been released from incarceration in full satisfaction of the sentence imposed.[15]

A limited type of statute of repose is applicable to product liability claims.[16] Where a product causes harm more than ten years after its delivery, a presumption arises that the product has outlived its useful safe life.[17] The claimant must rebut the presumption by clear and convincing evidence in order to maintain the claim.[18] The period of repose is extended to equal the period of any warranty that exceeds ten years.[19] The statute of repose does not apply if the seller intentionally misrepresents characteristics of the product so as to cause the harm complained of, or if the harm was caused by prolonged exposure to a defective product, or if the harmful aspect of the product would not have been discovered by a reasonably prudent person within the period of repose, or if the harm was caused within the period of repose but did not manifest itself within that period.[20]

B. TORT REFORM

The Idaho legislature has enacted several tort reform measures within the past 30 years, including measures that impose certain limitations on awards of damages and measures that require claimants to overcome additional hurdles before asserting their claims in court.

The first of these measures, enacted in 1976, requires submission of claims for medical malpractice to a prelitigation screening panel as a mandatory condition precedent to filing a lawsuit.[21] The four-member panels consist of one physician licensed by the state of Idaho, one hospital administrator of an Idaho hospital, one lawyer licensed by the Idaho State Bar, and one layperson chosen by the other panelists.[22] The panel's decision as to the merits of the claim is advisory only.[23] The limitations period is tolled during the proceedings and for 30 days thereafter, during which time no litigation may take place.[24] The measure also requires that the standard of practice and the alleged breach of the standard of practice be proved by an opinion given with reasonable medical certainty by an expert familiar with the applicable standard of practice (described in Section D herein).[25] The applicable standard of practice is determined in a manner that is protective particularly of health-care providers practicing in rural areas. Causation need not, however, be proved by expert testimony, but instead may be inferred by the trier of fact in appropriate circumstances.[26]

In 1980, the Idaho legislature limited product liability claims to the period of a product's useful safe life.[27] The seller bears the burden of proving, by a preponderance of the evidence, that the harm complained of was caused outside the product's useful safe life.[28] As discussed more fully in Section A herein, product liability claims are also subject to a limited statute of repose, whereby a product's useful safe life is ordinarily rebuttably presumed to end ten years after the time of its delivery.[29] These reforms were part of the Idaho Product Liability Reform Act, which also, among other things, limits the liability of sellers other than the manufacturer and restricts the admission of certain evidence of defective design or inadequate warnings that came into existence only after the product was first sold to a consumer.[30]

In 1987, the Idaho legislature enacted a cap on noneconomic damages awardable in claims for personal injuries or death.[31] The cap was initially set at $400,000, but is indexed to rise or fall in accordance with wage levels.[32] This indexing method has caused the cap to increase to $680,906, effective as of July 1, 2002.[33] If there are multiple wrongdoers, their collective liability is limited to the amount of the cap.[34] The jury is not to be informed about the existence or application of the cap.[35] The cap does not apply if the claim is based on reckless or willful conduct or on conduct that the trier of fact determines beyond a reasonable doubt constitutes a felony under state or federal law.[36] The constitutionality of the cap has been affirmed by the Idaho Supreme Court.[37]

As discussed more fully in Section Q herein, the Idaho legislature enacted a statute in 1987 that creates a significant procedural barrier to requests for punitive damages.[38]

In 1990, the Idaho legislature enacted a statutory prohibition, known as the "collateral source" rule, on double recoveries in actions for personal injuries or property damage.[39] The statute requires the court to reduce any award of damages to the claimant by any amounts the claimant received from other sources as compensation for the personal injuries or property damages that are the subject of the action, except for any amounts the claimant received as benefits: (1) under a federal program that must by law seek subrogation; (2) for death covered by a life-insurance policy; (3) from a health-care service corporation organized under Chapter 34 of Title 41 of the Idaho Code; or (4) that are recoverable by subrogation under a contract or under Idaho law.[40]

Finally, in 2000 the Idaho legislature enacted a statute giving a defendant employer the right to a pretrial hearing on a claim for vicarious liability based on an employee's conduct, in which the plaintiff must establish a reasonable likelihood of proving facts at trial sufficient to support a finding of vicarious liability.[41]

C. "NO FAULT" LIMITATIONS

Idaho does not have a "no fault" law applicable to automobile accidents.

D. THE STANDARD FOR NEGLIGENCE

A claim for negligence requires proof of the following elements: (1) a duty recognized by law that requires the defendant to conform to a certain standard of conduct; (2) a breach of the duty; (3) a causal connection between the breach and the harm of which the plaintiff complains; and (4) actual harm to the plaintiff.[42] In general, every person owes a duty to every other person in society to use reasonable care to avoid harm to the other person in any situation in which it could reasonably be anticipated or foreseen that a failure to use such care might result in harm to the other person.[43] Harm is "foreseeable" if it is likely enough to occur in the setting of modern life that a reasonably prudent person would take it into account in guiding his reasonable conduct.[44]

An actor has no duty to control the conduct of a third party to prevent him from causing harm to another person, unless a "special relationship" exists between the actor and the third party that imposes a duty on the actor to control the third party's conduct.[45]

The standard of care owed by a defendant health-care provider under Idaho law is determined solely with reference to the standard of practice by health-care providers of the same class and who practice in the same community in which the defendant practices, except that if no other providers of the same class practice in the same community, the standard of care is determined with reference to the standard of practice of providers of the same class who practice in similar Idaho communities.[46] To properly support a claim for medical malpractice, one qualified as an expert witness must familiarize himself with the community standard of care for the relevant class of providers, testify as to how he became familiar with the standard of care, and then describe the standard of care and how it was breached.[47] Acquaintance with the national standard of care is insufficient in itself to demonstrate familiarity with the community standard of care.[48] At a minimum, one acquainted with the national standard of care must inquire of a local provider to determine whether the community standard of care deviates from the national standard of care.[49]

Idaho does not have a system of bright-line rules whereby the capacity or incapacity of a child for negligence is presumed based on his age. Instead, a child is held to the standard of care expected of an ordinary child of the same age, experience, knowledge, and discretion.[50]

Idaho has retained the common law presumption that one who was killed or incapacitated exercised due care for his own safety at the time of the injury.[51]

E. **CAUSATION**

To establish a *prima facie* case of negligence, the plaintiff must demonstrate that the defendant's negligence was a proximate cause, including both the cause in fact and the legal cause, of the plaintiff's harm.[52] Where there is evidence of multiple possible causes of the plaintiff's harm, proximate cause is shown if the defendant's negligence was a substantial factor in causing the harm.[53] However, where there is evidence of only one possible cause of the plaintiff's harm, proximate cause is shown only if the defendant's negligence was the "but for" cause of the harm.[54]

F. **CONTRIBUTORY NEGLIGENCE, COMPARATIVE NEGLIGENCE, AND ASSUMPTION OF RISK**

1. **Contributory Negligence**

    In 1971, the Idaho legislature abolished contributory negligence as an absolute defense to claims for negligence, gross negligence, or comparative responsibility seeking recovery for death, personal injury, or injury to property, except where the plaintiff's negligence is equal to or greater than that of the particular defendant from whom recovery is sought.[55]

2. **Comparative Negligence**

    In an action for death, personal injury, or injury to property, the plaintiff may not recover damages against a particular defendant if the plaintiff's comparative responsibility is equal to or greater than that of the particular defendant.[56] If the plaintiff is entitled to recover, the plaintiff's recovery is reduced based on the plaintiff's comparative responsibility.[57]

3. **Assumption of Risk**

Assumption of risk is a viable affirmative defense only in cases involving an express assumption of risk, whether oral or written.[58] Because the defense in such cases sounds in contract and not in tort, the term "assumption of risk" has been abandoned in favor of terms, such as "consent," that are commonly thought to denote concepts of the law of contracts, as opposed to the law of torts.[59]

G. *RES IPSA LOQUITUR* AND INHERENTLY DANGEROUS ACTIVITIES

1. *Res Ipsa Loquitur*

The doctrine of *res ipsa loquitur* permits an inference that the defendant caused the plaintiff's injury if: (1) the agency or instrumentality that caused the injury was under the control and management of the defendant; and (2) the circumstances were such that common knowledge and experience would justify the inference that the accident would not have happened in the absence of negligence.[60] The doctrine does not shift the burden of proof from the plaintiff to the defendant; instead, it merely permits the finder of fact to infer negligence in the absence of direct evidence.[61]

Because *res ipsa loquitur* applies only to cases within the common knowledge and experience of an average layperson, it does not apply in actions for medical malpractice, which must be proved by expert testimony.[62]

2. **Inherently Dangerous Activities**

The precautions taken by a person responsible for a dangerous instrumentality must be commensurate with the dangers presented and sufficient under ordinary circumstances to prevent accidents and injuries.[63] Thus, the duty to anticipate injury and take protective action expands as the seriousness of the danger increases.[64]

H. NEGLIGENCE *PER SE*

A defendant is negligent *per se* if he fails to comply with a duty placed on him by a statute or other regulation, provided that the following four requirements are met: (1) the statute or regulation clearly defines the required standard of conduct; (2) the statute or regulation was intended to prevent the type of harm caused by the defendant; (3) the plaintiff is a member of the class of persons the statute or regulation was designed to protect; and (4) the defendant's violation of the statute or regulation proximately caused the plaintiff's harm.[65]

I. JOINT AND SEVERAL LIABILITY

Idaho has, in most circumstances, statutorily abolished the common law doctrine of joint and several liability.[66] The doctrine continues to apply only in the following circumstances: (1) where one defendant was acting as the agent or servant of another defendant, or where the defendants were pursuing a common plan or design that results in the commission of an intentional or reckless tortious act; (2) where the claim arises from a violation of state or federal law regarding hazardous wastes or solid waste disposal sites; and (3) where the claim arises from the manufacture of any medical device or pharmaceutical product.[67]

Joint tortfeasors are "two or more persons jointly or severally liable in tort for the same injury to person or property . . . "[68] A release by the plaintiff of one joint tortfeasor does not discharge other tortfeasors who are jointly and severally liable unless the release so provides, but the release reduces the claim against the other tortfeasors in the amount of the consideration paid for the release.[69] In contrast, a release by the plaintiff of one joint tortfeasor does not discharge other tortfeasors who are not jointly and severally liable, nor does the release reduce the claim against the other tortfeasors.[70]

The right of contribution among joint tortfeasors matures only if one joint tortfeasor has paid the common liability or has paid more than his *pro rata* share of it.[71] Contribution may only be obtained from those who would have been liable to the original plaintiff; thus, the party seeking contribution must show that the party from whom contribution is sought was comparatively more responsible than the original plaintiff for the original plaintiff's harm.[72]

J. INDEMNITY

Through the right of indemnity, a party compelled to pay damages to the plaintiff may shift the entire loss to the party responsible for the harm to the plaintiff.[73] Of course, a right of indemnity may be provided by contract. In addition, the common law right of indemnity is available in at least the following situations: (1) where the indemnitee's liability was based on passive neglect, while the indemnitor was reckless; (2) where the indemnitee owed only a secondary duty to the plaintiff, while the indemnitor owed a primary duty; and (3) where the indemnitee is only vicariously liable for the acts of the indemnitor, as in a master-servant relationship.[74]

K. BAR OF WORKERS' COMPENSATION STATUTE

Under the Idaho workers' compensation statute, an employee is barred, subject to certain limited exceptions described below, from suing an employer who has paid workers' compensation benefits for the employee's work-related injuries.[75] Workers' compensation is an exclusive remedy, and the employer assumes responsibility regardless of fault.[76] The receipt of benefits does not bar an employee from seeking damages from certain third parties.[77]

Where an employee has collected workers' compensation benefits from an employer and then sues a third party for the same incident, the employer is subrogated to the rights of the employee as against the third party, to the extent of the employer's workers' compensation liability.[78] If the employee successfully sues the third party, the employer or his insurer may be reimbursed for previously paid workers' compensation benefits, ordinarily reduced proportionately by the employer's share of the employee's costs and attorney's fees.[79]

An employer may initiate such an action against a third party in the event that the employee declines to do so, or the employer may join with the employee to initiate an action in the employee's name.[80]

The immunity from liability given to an employer by the workers' compensation statute extends to agents of the employer, including coemployees of the injured employee.[81] Thus, an employee may not sue a coemployee for injuries caused by the coemployee during the course of employment.[82]

Despite the general bar of suits against employers or coemployees, an employee may maintain a claim against his employer for workplace injuries or death caused by "the willful or unprovoked aggression of the employer . . ."[83] To make the required showing of aggression, the employee must demonstrate that the employer engaged in some offensive action or hostile attack.[84]

L. PREMISES LIABILITY

A landowner's liability for injuries sustained on the premises depends on the plaintiff's common law status as either a trespasser, invitee, or licensee.[85] An "invitee" is one who enters on the premises of the landowner for a purpose connected with the business conducted on the land or who enters in a situation in which it can reasonably be said that the visit may confer a tangible benefit on the landowner; a landowner's duty to an invitee is to warn of hidden or concealed dangers and to keep the land in a reasonably safe condition.[86] A "trespasser" is one who enters on the premises of the landowner without permission, invitation, or lawful authority; a landowner's duty to a trespasser is to refrain from willful or wanton acts that might cause injury.[87] A "licensee" is a visitor who enters on the premises of the landowner with the consent of the landowner in pursuit of the visitor's purpose; a landowner's duty to a licensee is to share with the licensee knowledge of dangerous conditions or activities on the land.[88]

M. DRAM SHOP LIABILITY

In 1986, the Idaho legislature passed a dram shop act in order to define and limit the liability of those who sell or otherwise furnish alcohol to persons who ultimately injure others as a result of their intoxication.[89] The act limits such liability to situations in which (1) the seller or other furnisher knew or should have known that the intoxicated person was younger than the legal drinking age, or (2) the seller or other furnisher knew or should have known that the intoxicated person was obviously intoxicated at the time it sold or otherwise furnished alcohol to him.[90] Liability extends to social hosts in the same fashion it extends to alcohol sellers.[91]

Further, the act limits the persons on whose behalf actions may be maintained to exclude (1) the intoxicated person or his estate or representatives, and (2) a passenger in an automobile driven by the intoxicated person or the estate or representatives of the passenger.[92] Finally, the act requires potential plaintiffs, as a condition precedent to bringing suit, to provide notice that suit will be brought to potential defendants by certified mail within 180 days after the claim accrued.[93]

N. ECONOMIC LOSS

Idaho adheres to the general rule that purely economic losses ordinarily cannot be recovered in tort actions.[94] Three exceptions to the general rule exist: (1) where the economic loss is parasitic to an injury to person or property; (2) where the occurrence of a unique circumstance requires a different allocation of risk; and (3) where a "special relationship" exists between the plaintiff and the defendant such that it would be equitable to impose a duty on the defendant to avoid the economic loss to the plaintiff.[95]

O. FRAUD AND MISREPRESENTATION

The Idaho Rules of Civil Procedure require that a claim for fraud be pleaded with particularity.[96]

A *prima facie* case of fraud consists of the following nine elements: (1) the defendant made a representation; (2) the representation was false; (3) the representation was material; (4) the defendant knew of the representation's falsity; (5) the defendant intended that the representation would be relied on by the plaintiff; (6) the plaintiff was ignorant of the representation's falsity; (7) the plaintiff relied on the representation's truth; (8) the plaintiff's reliance was justifiable; and (9) the plaintiff's reliance proximately caused the harm of which he complains.[97] To prevail on a claim for fraud, the plaintiff must prove these elements by clear and convincing evidence.[98] However, to defeat the defendant's motion for summary judgment, the plaintiff is not held to a heightened standard of proof.[99]

Idaho does not recognize the tort of negligent misrepresentation, except in the narrow confines of a professional relationship involving an accountant.[100]

P. CONSUMER FRAUD STATUTES

The Idaho Consumer Protection Act (ICPA) protects consumers against unfair methods of competition and unfair or deceptive acts or practices in the conduct of trade or commerce.[101] A broad array of specific types of practices is declared to violate ICPA, as is simply engaging in any practice likely to mislead or deceive consumers.[102] ICPA provides that the Idaho Attorney General may bring actions to enforce its provisions.[103] Private actions may also be brought under ICPA, but monetary relief is limited to the greater of the actual damages or $1,000, plus restitution and punitive damages.[104] However, the usual standard for awarding punitive damages under Idaho law, discussed in Section Q herein, is not applicable under ICPA; instead, the plaintiff must show repeated or flagrant violations of ICPA by the defendant.[105]

ICPA does not apply to actions or transactions permitted under laws administered by the Idaho Public Utilities Commission or other regulatory bodies or officers acting pursuant to statutory authority of Idaho or of the United States.[106] It also does not apply to publication or dissemination in good faith by the media or by retailers of advertisements based on information supplied by others.[107] Finally, ICPA has no application to the business of insurance, which is regulated by Chapter 13 of Title 41 of the Idaho Code.[108]

Q. PUNITIVE DAMAGES

Idaho law does not allow a party to include a request for punitive damages in his initial pleading.[109] The proper procedure for seeking punitive damages is instead to file a motion to amend the initial pleading to add a request for punitive damages, on which the court shall conduct a hearing and which the court shall grant if the moving party establishes a reasonable likelihood of proving facts at trial sufficient to support an award of punitive damages.[110] This procedure has been held to apply in federal, as well as state, courts.[111] The applicable limitations period for requesting punitive damages is tolled by the filing of the initial pleading.[112]

Punitive damages are disfavored under Idaho law and are awarded only in the most unusual and compelling circumstances.[113] A party seeking punitive damages must prove by a preponderance of the evidence that the conduct of the party against whom the damages are sought was an extreme deviation from reasonable standards of conduct and was engaged in with an understanding of or disregard for its likely consequences.[114] The *mens rea* component of this standard requires that the party against whom punitive damages are sought acted with an extremely harmful state of mind, whether that state of mind amounts to malice, oppression, fraud, gross negligence, wantonness, or willfulness.[115]

Punitive damages are exempt from Idaho's statutory limitation on noneconomic damages.[116]

An award of punitive damages need not bear any particular mathematical relationship to the amount of compensatory damages awarded, but must be reasonable in light of the interests furthered by the award.[117] Factors to be considered are the wealth or income of the party against whom the damages are to be awarded, the seriousness of the underlying conduct, and the nature and extent of the harm to the claimant.[118]

R. WRONGFUL DEATH AND SURVIVORSHIP ACTIONS

The right of recovery for wrongful death under Idaho law is created by Idaho's wrongful death statute.[119] This right extends to the following persons: (1) the "heirs" of the decedent, as that term is defined in the Uniform Probate Code;[120] (2) irrespective of whether they qualify as "heirs," the decedent's spouse, children, stepchildren, parents, and certain others who were dependent on the decedent; and (3) the decendent's putative spouse, provided that he or she was dependent on the decedent, irrespective of whether he or she falls into either of the preceding two categories.[121] However, recovery is subject to Idaho's comparative-responsibility statute, discussed more fully in Section F herein. The decedent's comparative responsibility for his own death is attributable to those pursuing a claim for his wrongful death.[122]

S. BAD FAITH IN INSURANCE CONTRACTS

Idaho recognizes a tort of bad faith in insurance contracts, which renders insurers liable in tort for intentionally and unreasonably denying or delaying benefits under an insurance contract.[123] Such claims are only available to first-party insureds.[124] The tort of bad faith is premised on the nature of the relationship between the insurer and the insured, in that insurance contracts are typically adhesionary and the insured is vulnerable to overreaching by the insurer.[125] Thus, in addition to contract remedies, the insured may seek the types of damages normally recoverable in a tort case, including damages for emotional distress.[126] Moreover, although damages for emotional distress may arise from conduct of the same sort as gives rise to a claim for punitive damages, both damages for emotional distress and punitive damages may be awarded in favor of the insured.[127] This is because of the distinction in purposes of the respective awards—the former is to compensate the insured and the latter is to punish the insurer for its bad-faith conduct.[128]

Ronald E. Bush
Jason D. Scott
HAWLEY TROXELL ENNIS & HAWLEY L.L.P.
333 South Main Street
P.O. Box 100
Pocatello, Idaho 83204-0100
(208) 233-0845
Fax (208) 233-1304
reb@hteh.com
jds@hteh.com
www.hteh.com

Boise, Idaho office:
HAWLEY TROXELL ENNIS & HAWLEY L.L.P.
877 West Main Street, Suite 1000
P.O. Box 1617
Boise, Idaho 83701-1617
(208) 344-6000
Fax (208) 342-3829

Ketchum, Idaho office:
HAWLEY TROXELL ENNIS & HAWLEY L.L.P.
540 Second Avenue North
P.O. Box 297
Ketchum, Idaho 83340-0297
(208) 726-1700
Fax (208) 726-9743

ENDNOTES - IDAHO

* This outline has been prepared by Hawley Troxell Ennis & Hawley L.L.P. for informational purposes only and is not intended as legal advice. Further, this outline is not intended to create, and receipt of it does not constitute, an attorney-client relationship. Use of this outline is not a substitute for consultation with legal counsel.

1. Idaho Code § 5-219(4) (1998).

2. *See, e.g., Hawley v. Green*, 117 Idaho 498, 502, 788 P.2d 1321, 1325 (1990); *Brennan v. Owens-Corning Fiberglas Corp.*, 134 Idaho 800, 801, 10 P.3d 749, 750 (2000).

3. Idaho Code § 5-219(4) (1998).

4. *Id.*

5. *See, e.g., Cosgrove v. Merrell Dow Pharmaceuticals, Inc.*, 117 Idaho 470, 475, 788 P.2d 1293, 1298 (1989).

6. Idaho Code § 5-218(4) (1998).

7. *Id.; see also Jones v. Runft, Leroy, Coffin & Matthews, Chartered*, 125 Idaho 607, 615, 873 P.2d 861, 869 (1994).

8. Product liability claims are subject to the statute of limitations set forth in Idaho Code § 6-1403(3), which references Idaho Code § 5-219 for the determination of when the limitation period begins. The other listed claims are directly subject to subsection (5) of section 219.

9. Idaho Code § 48-619 (1997).

10. Idaho Code §§ 5-218(2)–(3) (1998).

11. Idaho Code §§ 6-905–906 (1998).

12. Idaho Code §§ 6-909–911 (1998).

13. Idaho Code § 5-224 (1998).

14. Idaho Code § 5-229 (1998); *see also Lipe v. Javelin Tire Co.*, 96 Idaho 723, 536 P.2d 291 (1975).

15. Idaho Code § 5-248 (Supp. 2001).

16. Idaho Code § 6-1403(2) (1998).

17. Idaho Code § 6-1403(2)(a) (1998).

18. *Id.*

19. Idaho Code § 6-1403(2)(b)(1) (1998).

20. Idaho Code §§ 6-1403(2)(b)(2)–(2)(b)(4) (1998).

21. Idaho Code § 6-1001 (1998).

22. Idaho Code § 6-1002 (1998).

23. Idaho Code § 6-1004 (1998).

24. Idaho Code §§ 6-1005–1006 (1998).

25. Idaho Code § 6-1013 (1998).

26. *See Sheridan v. St. Luke's Regional Medical Ctr.*, 135 Idaho 775, 785-86, 25 P.3d 88, 98-99 (2001).

27. Idaho Code § 6-1403(1) (1998).

28. *Id.*

29. Idaho Code § 6-1403(2) (1998).

30. The Idaho Product Liability Reform Act is codified at Idaho Code §§ 6-1401–1410 (1998). The referenced measures are set forth in Sections 1406 and 1407 of the Act. Additionally, the Act generally does not apply to the provision of services, to sales of used products, or to the provision of financing that facilitates the lease of products. Idaho Code §§ 6-1402(1)(a)–(c) (1998).

31. Idaho Code § 6-1603(1) (1998).

32. *Id.*

33. Based on the language of Idaho Code § 6-1603(1), the starting point for the calculation of the cap is the average annual wage for 1987. The average annual wage for 2002, the most recent year for which the average annual wage has been determined, is more than 70 percent greater than the average annual wage was for 1987. On July 1 of each year after 1987, the cap is increased or decreased by the same percentage as the average annual wage has increased or decreased. By multiplying $400,000 by the 2002 average annual wage and then dividing the product by the 1987 average annual wage, the current cap is calculated at $680,906.

34. Idaho Code § 6-1603(2) (1998).

35. Idaho Code § 6-1603(3) (1998).

36. Idaho Code § 6-1603(4) (1998).

37. *Kirkland v. Blaine County Medical Ctr.*, 134 Idaho 464, 4 P.3d 1115 (2000).

38. Idaho Code § 6-1604(2) (1998).

39. Idaho Code § 6-1606 (1998).

40. *Id.*

41. Idaho Code § 6-1607 (Supp. 2001).

42. *See, e.g., West v. Sonke*, 132 Idaho 133, 142, 968 P.2d 228, 237 (1998); *Heath v. Honker's Mini-Mart, Inc.*, 134 Idaho 711, 713, 8 P.3d 1254, 1256 (Ct. App. 2000).

43. *See, e.g., Doe v. Garcia*, 131 Idaho 578, 581, 961 P.2d 1181, 1184 (1998).

44. *See, e.g., id.*

45. *See Litchfield v. Nelson*, 122 Idaho 416, 420, 835 P.2d 651, 655 (Ct. App. 1992).

46. Idaho Code § 6-1012 (1998).

47. *See Kolln v. St. Luke's Regional Medical Ctr.*, 130 Idaho 323, 331, 940 P.2d 1142, 1150 (1997).

48. *See, e.g., Strode v. Lenzi*, 116 Idaho 214, 775 P.2d 106 (1989).

49. *See, e.g., id.* at 216, 775 P.2d at 108.

50. *See, e.g., Goodfellow v. Coggburn*, 98 Idaho 202, 203, 560 P.2d 873, 874 (1977).

51. *See, e.g., Smith v. Angell*, 122 Idaho 25, 36 n.8, 830 P.2d 1164, 1174 n.8 (1992).

52. *See, e.g., Marias v. Marano*, 120 Idaho 11, 13, 813 P.2d 350, 352 (1991).

53. *See, e.g., LeGall v. Lewis County*, 128 Idaho 182, 186–87, 923 P.2d 427, 431–32 (1996).

54. *See, e.g., id.*

55. Idaho Code § 6-801 (1998).

56. *Id.*

57. *Id.*; Idaho Code § 6-802 (1998).

58. *See, e.g., Salinas v. Vierstra*, 107 Idaho 984, 989–90, 695 P.2d 369, 374–75 (1985).

59. *See id.*

60. *See, e.g., Kolln*, 130 Idaho at 333–34, 940 P.2d at 1152–53.

61. *See, e.g., id.*

62. *See id.*

63. *See Smith v. State*, 93 Idaho 795, 806, 473 P.2d 937, 948 (1970).

64. *See id.*

65. *See, e.g., Sanchez v. Galey*, 112 Idaho 609, 617, 733 P.2d 1234, 1242 (1986); *Orthman v. Idaho Power Co.*, 134 Idaho 598, 601, 7 P.3d 207, 210 (2000).

66. Idaho Code § 6-803 (1998).

67. Idaho Code § 6-803(3), (5)–(7) (1998).

68. Idaho Code § 6-803(4) (1998).

69. Idaho Code § 6-805(1) (1998).

70. Idaho Code § 6-805(2) (1998).

71. Idaho Code § 6-803(1) (1998).

72. *See Hydraulic Air & Equip. Co. v. Mobil Oil Corp.*, 117 Idaho 130, 785 P.2d 947 (1989).

73. *See, e.g., Chenery v. Agri-Lines Corp.*, 115 Idaho 281, 284, 766 P.2d 751, 754 (1988).

74. *See May Trucking Co. v. International Harvester Co.*, 97 Idaho 319, 321, 543 P.2d 1159, 1161 (1975).

75. Idaho Code § 72-201 (1999).

76. Idaho Code §§ 72-201, 211 (1999).

77. Idaho Code § 72-223 (1999 & Supp. 2001).

78. Idaho Code § 72-223(3) (1999 & Supp. 2001).

79. Idaho Code § 72-223(3)–(4) (1999 & Supp. 2001).

80. Idaho Code § 72-223(2) (1999 & Supp. 2001).

81. Idaho Code § 72-209(3) (1999).

82. *See, e.g., Wilder v. Redd*, 111 Idaho 141, 721 P.2d 1240 (1986).

83. Idaho Code § 72-209(3) (1999).

84. *See, e.g., Kearney v. Denker*, 114 Idaho 755, 757, 760 P.2d 1171, 1173 (1988).

85. *See, e.g., Peterson v. Romine*, 131 Idaho 537, 540, 960 P.2d 1266, 1269 (1998).

86. *See, e.g., id.*

87. *See, e.g., id.*

88. *See, e.g., Holzheimer v. Johannesen*, 125 Idaho 397, 399, 871 P.2d 814, 816 (1994).

89. Idaho Code § 23-808(1) (2001); *see also Slade v. Smith's Management Corp.*, 119 Idaho 482, 489, 808 P.2d 401, 408 (1991).

90. Idaho Code § 23-808(2)–(3) (2001).

91. *Id.*

92. Idaho Code § 23-808(4) (2001).

93. Idaho Code § 23-808(5) (2001).

94. *See, e.g., Duffin v. Idaho Crop Improvement Ass'n*, 126 Idaho 1002, 1007, 895 P.2d 1195, 1200 (1995).

95. *See, e.g., id.* at 1007–08, 895 P.2d at 1200–01.

96. Idaho R. Civ. P. 9(b) (2001).

97. *See, e.g., Hines v. Hines*, 129 Idaho 847, 851, 934 P.2d 20, 24 (1997); *Samuel v. Hepworth, Nungester & Lezamiz, Inc.*, 134 Idaho 84, 89, 996 P.2d 303, 308 (2000).

98. *See, e.g., Walston v. Monumental Life Ins. Co.*, 129 Idaho 211, 216, 923 P.2d 456, 461 (1996); *Sowards v. Rathburn*, 134 Idaho 702, 706, 8 P.3d 1245, 1249 (2000).

99. *See, e.g., Hines*, 129 Idaho at 852, 934 P.2d at 25.

100. *See, e.g., Duffin*, 126 Idaho at 1010, 895 P.2d at 1203.

101. ICPA is codified at Idaho Code §§ 48-601–609 (1997 & Supp. 2001).

102. Idaho Code §§ 48-603–603E (1997 & Supp. 2001).

103. Idaho Code § 48-606 (Supp. 2001).

104. Idaho Code § 48-608 (1997).

105. *See Mac Tools, Inc. v. Griffin*, 126 Idaho 193, 198, 879 P.2d 1126, 1131 (1994).

106. Idaho Code § 48-605(1) (1997).

107. Idaho Code § 48-605(2) (1997).

108. Idaho Code § 48-605(3) (1997).

109. Idaho Code § 6-1604(2) (1998).

110. *Id.*

111. *See, e.g., Windsor v. Guaranty Trust Life Ins. Co.*, 684 F. Supp. 630, 633 (D. Idaho 1988).

112. Idaho Code § 6-1604(2) (1998).

113. *See, e.g., Walston*, 129 Idaho at 221, 923 P.2d 456 at 466.

114. *See, e.g., Manning v. Twin Falls Clinic & Hospital*, 122 Idaho 47, 52, 830 P.2d 1185, 1190 (1992).

115. *See, e.g., id.*; Idaho Code § 6-1604(1) (1998).

116. Idaho Code § 6-1604(3) (1998).

117. *See Walston*, 129 Idaho at 223, 923 P.2d at 468.

118. *See id.* at 210–11, 923 P.2d at 467–68.

119. Idaho Code § 5-311 (1998).

120. The Uniform Probate Code, as enacted in Idaho, is codified at Idaho Code §§ 15-1-101–15-7-502 (2001).

121. Idaho Code § 5-311(2) (1998).

122. *See, e.g., Bevan v. Vassar Farms, Inc.*, 117 Idaho 1038, 793 P.2d 711 (1990).

123. *See, e.g., Walston*, 129 Idaho at 219, 923 P.2d at 464.

124. *See Idaho State Ins. Fund v. Van Tine*, 132 Idaho 902, 908, 980 P.2d 566, 572 (1999).

125. *See, e.g., id.*

126. *See id.* at 219–20, 923 P.2d at 464–65.

127. *See id.* at 220, 923 P.2d at 465.

128. *See id.*

ILLINOIS

A. STATUTES OF LIMITATION

Actions for damages for personal injuries, false imprisonment, or malicious prosecution must be brought within two years.[1] The personal representative of a deceased person must bring an action for wrongful death within two years of the death of the person.[2] Causes of action for an injury done to real or personal property, or to recover the possession of personal property, or for the detention or conversion of property shall be commenced within five years.[3] Actions for damages for injury or death against a physician, dentist, registered nurse, or hospital arising out of patient care vary from those previously indicated.[4]

Actions stemming from a breach of contract for sale must be brought within five years after the cause of action accrued if the contract was oral and ten years if the contract was written.[5] However, if the contract for sale arises under the Uniform Commercial Code, there is a four-year limitations period.[6]

Defamation and invasion of privacy must be commenced within one year after the cause of action accrued.[7]

Actions under the Consumer Fraud and Deceptive Business Practices Act will be barred unless commenced within three years after the cause of action accrued.[8] However, when the Attorney General or a State's Attorney initiates the action, the running of the statute of limitations, with respect to a private right of action for damages based in whole or part on a matter complained of by the Attorney General or the State's Attorney, is suspended during the pendency of that action and for one year thereafter.[9]

A four-year statute of limitations and a ten-year statute of repose applies to claims involving design, planning, supervision, observation, construction of, or improvements to real property.[10] A 12-year statute of repose governs product liability actions.[11]

A "catch-all" provision for actions that are neither subject to another limitation provision nor excluded from the application of a limitation period provides for a five-year statute of limitations.[12]

For many of the causes of action, if the person entitled to bring the action is under the age of 18 or is under a legal disability at the time the action accrues, he or she may bring the action within two years after the person attains the age of 18 or the disability is removed.[13]

If a person liable for an action fraudulently conceals the cause of such action from the person entitled to bring the action, the action may be commenced at any time within five years after the person entitled to sue discovers the cause of action.[14]

Computation of any time limitation excludes the first day and includes the last.[15] However, the last day should be excluded if it is a Saturday, Sunday, or holiday (as defined by statute).[16]

B. TORT REFORM

In 1997, the Supreme Court of Illinois struck down in its entirety the 1995 Tort Reform Act.[17] The court found certain "core provisions" of the Act unconstitutional.[18] In addition, the court held the remainder of the Act void on the grounds of severability.[19] However, the court invited the Illinois legislature to reenact any provisions struck down solely on the grounds of severability that it deemed "desirable or appropriate."[20]

C. "NO FAULT" LIMITATIONS

The section of the Illinois Motor Vehicle Code requiring proof of financial responsibility delineates the minimum amounts of damages that a person must be able to pay if that person, while operating a motor vehicle, caused the death or injury of another.[21]

D. THE STANDARD FOR NEGLIGENCE

There can be no negligence unless there is a duty owed by one party to another party.[22] Whether a duty exists is a question of law.[23] That question is shaped by public policy because the court must decide whether the defendant and plaintiff stand in such a relationship to one another that the law imposes on the defendant an obligation of reasonable conduct for the benefit of the plaintiff.[24] In determining if a duty exists a court will consider not only the reasonable (1) foreseeability and (2) likelihood of injury, but also (3) the magnitude of the burden on defendant in guarding against injury and (4) the consequences of placing that burden on defendant.[25]

If a duty exists, the basic standard of care is that of the "ordinarily careful person" or "reasonably prudent" person.[26] The basic formulation of the standard is objective, however, if it is subjective to a degree in order to make proper allowance for the actor's capacity to meet the risk apparent to him and the circumstances under which he must act.[27] Therefore, the basic reasonable person standard allows for and incorporates the physical characteristics of the defendants.[28] In addition, while children engaged in adult activities are held to an adult standard, generally children are held to a standard of care of a child of the actor's age, intelligence, capacity, and experience.[29] Furthermore, in Illinois, children under seven are considered incapable of being negligent; children between the ages of seven and fourteen are presumed incapable of negligence, but that presumption can be rebutted.[30]

Illinois recognizes a special standard of care for professionals. They must use the same degree of knowledge, skill, and ability as an ordinarily careful professional would exercise under similar circumstances.[31] However, unlike negligence actions in general, the plaintiff bears a burden to establish the standard of care through expert witness testimony.[32]

Generally, there is no duty to individuals injured by third persons.[33] However, a duty can arise if there is a special relationship either between the third person causing the injury and the party to be held liable or between the victim and the party to be held liable.[34]

E. CAUSATION

In order to state a cause of action in negligence, the plaintiff must establish proximate cause.[35] Proximate cause consists of two distinct elements: cause in fact and legal cause.[36] A defendant's conduct is a cause in fact of the plaintiff's injury if the conduct was a material element and substantial factor in bringing about the injury.[37] Legal cause turns on foreseeability because negligent conduct is deemed a proximate cause of an injury if a reasonable person would foresee the injury as a likely result of the conduct.[38]

F. CONTRIBUTORY NEGLIGENCE, COMPARATIVE NEGLIGENCE, AND ASSUMPTION OF RISK

1. Contributory Negligence

In 1981 the Supreme Court of Illinois abolished contributory negligence as a defense and adopted a pure comparative negligence regime.[39]

2. Comparative Negligence

By statute, the Illinois Legislature modified the pure comparative negligence regime that had been adopted by the Illinois courts. Under the statute, in actions on account of death, bodily injury, or physical damage to property in which recovery is predicated on fault, Illinois plaintiffs who are more than 50 percent at fault are barred from recovery; Illinois plaintiffs who are not more than 50 percent at fault have their recovery diminished in the proportion to the amount of their fault.[40] It is the defendant's burden to establish plaintiff's negligence.[41] Where defendant's actions are willful and wanton such that they can be considered intentional, plaintiff's negligence is not relevant and it will not reduce or bar plaintiff's recovery.[42]

3. Assumption of Risk

Assumption of risk remains a viable defense in Illinois.[43] However, unlike traditional assumption of risk, a finding that the plaintiff assumed the risk will not necessarily completely bar plaintiff's recovery. Instead, assumption of the risk is treated as a type of comparative fault.[44]

G. *RES IPSA LOQUITUR* AND INHERENTLY DANGEROUS ACTIVITIES

1. *Res Ipsa Loquitur*

As a general rule, a plaintiff must affirmatively prove negligence; it is not presumed.[45] The doctrine of *res ipsa loquitur* is an exception to this general rule.[46] *Res ipsa loquitur* permits an inference that a defendant was negligent if the plaintiff demonstrates that he was injured (1) in an occurrence that normally does not occur in the absence of negligence; (2) by an agency or instrumentality within the defendant's exclusive control; and (3) under circumstances not involving plaintiff's contributory negligence.[47] The purpose of *res ipsa loquitur* is to allow a plaintiff to prove negligence by circumstantial evidence if defendant has primary control over direct evidence regarding the cause of plaintiff's injury.[48]

2. Inherently Dangerous Activities

Illinois courts refer to an "inherently dangerous activity" as one where danger is inherent as opposed to simply a mere consequence of negligence.[49] In other words, an instrumentality or activity is inherently dangerous if it is dangerous in its normal, nondefective state.[50] Although all factors need not be present, courts consider six factors to determine whether an activity is inherently dangerous: (1) whether there is a high degree of risk of some harm to a person, land, or chattel; (2) the likelihood that any resulting harm will be great; (3) the ability to eliminate the risk by exercise of reasonable care; (4) the extent to which the activity is common; (5) the inappropriateness of the activity to the location on which it occurs; and (6) the extent to which the dangerous attributes outweigh the activity's value to the community.[51]

A defendant who performs an inherently dangerous activity is strictly liable for any harm to a person, land, or chattels of another that results from the activity.[52]

H. NEGLIGENCE *PER SE*

A violation of a statute or ordinance designed for the protection of human life or property is *prima facie* evidence of negligence.[53] However, a violation does not constitute negligence *per se* because the inference of negligence may be rebutted by proof that the party acted reasonably under the circumstances, despite the violation.[54]

I. JOINT AND SEVERAL LIABILITY

In 1997, the Illinois Supreme Court[55] held that several provisions of the Illinois Civil Justice Reform Amendments of 1995, including the amended Section 2-1117,[56] violated the Illinois Constitution of 1970. The Court concluded that those provisions were nonseverable and, thus, the entire Act was unconstitutional. The following are the relevant statutory provisions as they existed before the 1995 Act:

Limitation on Recovery in Tort Actions (735 ILCS 5/2-1116)

In all actions on account of bodily injury or death or physical damage to property, based on negligence, or product liability based on strict tort liability, the plaintiff shall be barred from recovering damages if the trier of fact finds that the contributory fault on the part of the plaintiff is *more than 50% of the proximate cause of the injury or damage for which recovery is sought*. The plaintiff shall not be barred from recovering damages if the trier of fact finds that the contributory fault on the part of the plaintiff is not more than 50% of the proximate cause of the injury or damage for which recovery is sought, but any damages allowed shall be diminished in the proportion to the amount of fault attributable to the plaintiff. . . .

Joint Liability (735 ILCS 5/2-1117)

Except as provided in Section 2-1118, in actions on account of bodily injury or death or physical damage to property, based on negligence, or product liability based on strict tort liability, all defendants found liable are jointly and severally liable for plaintiff's past and future medical and medically related expenses. Any defendant whose fault, as determined by the trier of fact, is less than 25% of *the total fault attributable to the plaintiff, the defendants sued by the plaintiff, and any third party defendant who could have been sued by the plaintiff*, shall be severally liable for all other damages. Any defendant whose fault, as determined by the trier of fact, is 25% or greater of *the total fault attributable to the plaintiff, the defendants sued by the plaintiff, and any third party defendants who could have been sued by the plaintiff*, shall be jointly and severally liable for all other damages.

Where two or more parties are liable for a person's injury or death, the Joint Tortfeasor Contribution Act provides a right of contribution among them even though judgment has not been entered against any or all of them.[57] The Act applies only when the plaintiff collects judgment in a manner inconsistent with the jury's determination of respective responsibility.[58] However, when the plaintiff and one of the defendants enter in good faith into a settlement agreement, that defendant is released from liability for any contribution to any other tortfeasor.[59]

J. INDEMNITY

Indemnity allows one tortfeasor to shift the entire loss to another tortfeasor.[60] The indemnitor has the obligation to make good a loss or damage the indemnitee has suffered.[61] The right to be indemnified by another may be express (contractual) or it may be implied. Implied indemnity arises in situations in which a promise to indemnify can be inferred from the relationship between the tortfeasors.[62] The cause of action finds its roots in principles of restitution; a contract to indemnify is implied in law based on the legal obligation of the indemnitee to satisfy liability caused by actions of its indemnitor.[63] However, where a purported indemnitee is negligent or otherwise at fault, indemnity does not lie.[64]

K. BAR OF WORKERS' COMPENSATION STATUTE

The Workers' Compensation Act bars employees from suing their employer for accidental injuries that arise out of and occur in the course of employment.[65] Under the so-called exclusivity clause, workers' compensation is an employee's sole remedy. However, the courts have created some exceptions. One exception permits an employee to sue his employer if the employee is able to show the employer had a specific intent to injure the employee.[66]

An employer's dual capacity may also avoid the exclusivity clause.[67] When the employer's conduct in the second capacity generates obligations unrelated to those flowing from its role as an employer, the employee is not limited to the Workers' Compensation Act.[68] For example, where a hospital acts both as employer and treating medical provider, it occupies a dual capacity and, thus, relinquishes its right to claim that workers' compensation is the employee's exclusive remedy.[69]

Although the Workers' Compensation Act typically prevents an employee from suing his employer, an employee can seek damages from a third party that may be liable for the employee's injuries.[70] The Joint Tortfeasor Contribution Act authorizes the third party to seek recovery from the employer for the employer's portion of fault.[71] However, the Illinois Supreme Court has limited the employer's liability to the amount of the workers' compensation lien.[72]

L. PREMISES LIABILITY

Pursuant to the Premises Liability Act, the standard of care with which a landowner must comply depends on whether the entrant is either lawfully or unlawfully on the premises.[73] At common law, Illinois distinguished between an entrant's status as either a trespasser (who is unlawfully on the premises) and a licensee or an invitee (who are lawfully on the premises).[74]

After eradicating the distinction between licensees and invitees, Illinois now requires a landowner to exercise toward entrants lawfully on the premises the duty of reasonable care.[75] To an entrant unlawfully on the premises, a landowner owes only the duty to refrain from willful and wanton conduct that may endanger the trespassing entrant's safety.[76]

M. DRAM SHOP LIABILITY

The Liquor Control Act of 1934[77] imposes liability on persons licensed to sell alcohol, who sell or give alcohol that causes the intoxication of a person who injuries another.[78] The Act imposes a form of "no-fault" liability.[79] However, an intoxicated person's tortious act must cause the injury[80] and the dramshop must cause the intoxication by furnishing more than a negligible amount of alcohol to the person.[81] Liability may be imposed when the dramshop operator has actual or constructive knowledge that a particular person will be consuming the alcohol unless the dramshop, by its method of distributing alcohol, essentially does not have the opportunity to refuse service to anyone.[82] The Act has preempted the entire field of alcohol-related liability in Illinois and provides the exclusive remedy for alcohol-induced injuries.[83]

The amount of damages are limited under the Act and there is a one-year statute of limitations.[84] Intoxicated persons whose conduct leads to their own injuries cannot recover under the Act.[85] Under the "complicity doctrine," an injured party must be free from fault in order to recover.[86]

Social hosts who serve alcohol to their guests are not liable under the Act.[87]

N. ECONOMIC LOSS

Illinois has adopted the economic loss rule; a products liability plaintiff cannot recover solely economic loss under the theories of strict liability, negligence, and innocent misrepresentation.[88] Economic losses are damages for inadequate value, costs of repair and replacement of the defective product, or consequent loss of profits—without any claim of personal injury or damage to other property.[89] There are three recognized exceptions to the economic loss rule: (1) where the plaintiff sustained damage (i.e., personal injury or property damage, resulting from a sudden or dangerous occurrence); (2) where the plaintiff's damages are proximately caused by a defendant's intentional, false representation (i.e., fraud) and (3) where the plaintiff's damages are proximately caused by a negligent misrepresentation by a defendant in the business of supplying information for the guidance of others in their business transactions.[90]

O. FRAUD AND MISREPRESENTATION

The elements of common law fraud are: (1) a false statement of material fact; (2) defendant's knowledge that the statement was false; (3) defendant's intent that the statement induce the plaintiff to act; (4) plaintiff's reliance on the truth of the statement; and (5) plaintiff's damages resulting from reliance on the statement.[91] A successful common law fraud complaint must allege, with specificity and particularity, facts from which fraud is the necessary or probable inference, including what misrepresentations were made, when they were made, who made the misrepresentations, and to whom they were made.[92]

The elements of negligent misrepresentation are: (1) a false statement of material fact; (2) carelessness or negligence in ascertaining the truth of the statement by the defendant; (3) an intention to induce the other party to act; (4) action by the other party in reliance on the truth of the statements; (5) damage to the other party resulting from such reliance; and (6) a duty owed by the defendant to the plaintiff to communicate accurate information.[93] Unlike fraud, then, to prove negligent misrepresentation the plaintiff need not show that the defendant knew the statement was false, only that the defendant was careless or negligent in ascertaining the statement's truth.[94] However, the plaintiff must show that the defendant owes her a duty to communicate accurate information, which is not required to prove fraud.[95]

P. CONSUMER FRAUD STATUTES

Illinois's Consumer Fraud and Deceptive Business Practices Act was enacted to create broad protective coverage of consumers from the many types of deceptive or unfair selling and advertising techniques, and to give consumers broader protection than a common law fraud action.[96] To state a claim under the Act, a plaintiff must allege: (1) the commission of a deceptive act or practice; (2) intent on defendant's part that plaintiff rely on the deception; and (3) that the deception occurred in the course of conduct involving trade or commerce.[97] In addition, a private party must show damages that were proximately caused by the defendant's actions. A party stating a claim under the Act is not required to establish all the elements of common law fraud, because the Act prohibits the making of any deceptive or false promises, including innocent misrepresentations.[98] In addition, the Act does not require that the complaining party prove actual reliance.[99]

The Act allows for suits by individuals other than consumers. The Attorney General or a State's Attorney may sue under the Act and seek (1) injunctive relief if she has reason to believe prohibited acts are occurring or are about to occur; (2) restitution and/or; (3) civil penalties.[100] A business that is not a "consumer" may bring an action under the Act if the alleged conduct involves trade practices addressed to the market generally or otherwise implicates consumer protection concerns.[101]

Q. PUNITIVE DAMAGES

A plaintiff may recover punitive damages if the defendant acted willfully or with such gross negligence as to indicate a wanton disregard for others' rights.[102] However, a plaintiff may not request punitive damages in the original complaint.[103] If, at a pretrial hearing, plaintiff demonstrates a reasonable likelihood of proving facts at trial sufficient to support an award of punitive damages, the court may permit plaintiff to amend the complaint to include a prayer for punitive damages.[104] Evidence of other accidents involving the product is, by itself, an insufficient basis for punitive damages.[105] A plaintiff may recover punitive damages in warranty actions only if the breach amounts to an independent, willful tort.[106]

R. WRONGFUL DEATH AND SURVIVORSHIP ACTIONS

At common law there was no action for wrongful death.[107] However, Illinois, by legislative decree, created a cause of action for wrongful death and expanded the survivorship actions.[108] A survival action addresses injuries personally suffered by the victim prior to death and allows for damages sustained up to the time of death; a wrongful death action covers the time after death and addresses injuries suffered by next of kin because of the death.[109]

The Wrongful Death Act was enacted to provide a means of recovery for a surviving spouse and next of kin.[110] However, if the deceased has no surviving spouse or kin, then individuals furnishing medical treatment to the deceased for the "last illness or injury of the deceased" as well as the decedent's personal representative may be entitled to a limited recovery under the Act.[111]

To maintain a claim under the Act, a plaintiff must demonstrate that: (1) the defendant owed a duty to decedent; (2) the defendant breached that duty; (3) the breach of duty proximately caused decedent's death; and (4) pecuniary damages arose therefrom to persons designated under the Act.[112]

Generally, a cause of action for wrongful death must be brought within two years of the death.[113]

Frances E. Prell
Thomas R. Woodrow
HOLLAND & KNIGHT
55 West Monroe Street
Suite 800
Chicago, Illinois 60603
(312) 263-3600
Fax (312) 578-6666
fprell@hklaw.com
www.hklaw.com

ENDNOTES - ILLINOIS

1. 735 ILCS 5/13-202 (1999).

2. 740 ILCS 180/2 (1999).

3. 735 ILCS 5/13-205 (1999).

4. 735 ILCS 5/13-212 (1999).

5. 735 ILCS 5/13-205 (1999).

6. 810 ILCS 5/2-725 (1999).

7. 735 ILCS 5/13-201 (1999).

8. 815 ILCS 505/10a (1999).

9. *Id.*

10. 735 ILCS 5/13-214 (1999).

11. 735 ILCS 5/13-213 (1999).

12. 735 ILCS 5/13-205 (1999).

13. 735 ILCS 5/13-211 (1999).

14. 735 ILCS 5/13-215 (1999).

15. 5 ILCS 70/1.11 (1999).

16. *Id.*

17. *Best v. Taylor Mach. Works,* 179 Ill. 2d 367, 689 N.E.2d 1057 (1997).

18. *Id.*

19. *Id.*

20. *Id.*

21. 625 ILCS 5/1-164.5 (1999) (requiring a person to show proof of ability to pay (1) $20,000 for any one person injured or killed in any one accident; (2) $40,000 for any two or more persons injured or killed in any one

accident; and (3) $15,000 for any property damage resulting from any one accident).

22. *Lafever v. Kemlite Co., a Division of Dyrotech Industries, Inc.*, 185 Ill. 2d 380, 706 N.E.2d 441 (1998) (citing *American National Bank & Trust Co. v. National Advertising Co.*, 149 Ill. 2d 14, 26, 594 N.E.2d 313 (1992)).

23. *Id.* (citing *Ward v. K-Mart Corp.*, 136 Ill. 2d 132, 140, 554 N.E.2d 223 (1990)).

24. *Id.* (citing *Ward*; *Kirk v. Michael Reese Hospital & Medical Center*, 117 Ill. 2d 507, 513 N.E.2d 387 (1987)).

25. *Id.* (citing *Ward*).

26. *Advincula v. United Blood Servs.*, 176 Ill. 2d 1, 678 N.E.2d 1009 (1996) (citing *Cunis v. Brennan*, 56 Ill. 2d 372, 308 N.E.2d 617 (1974)).

27. *Id.* (citing W. Keeton, Prosser & Keeton on Torts § 32, at 173 (6th ed. 1995)).

28. *Id.*

29. *Id.* (citing *Lewis v. Northern Illinois Gas Co.*, 97 Ill. App. 3d 227, 422 N.E.2d 889 (1981)); *Chu v. Bowers*, 275 Ill. App. 3d 861, 656 N.E.2d 436 (Ill. App. Ct. 1995).

30. *Chu*; *Cates v. Kinnard*, 255 Ill. App. 3d 952, 626 N.E.2d 770 (Ill. App. Ct. 1994).

31. *Id.* (citing *Taake v. WHGK, Inc.*, 228 Ill. App. 3d 692, 592 N.E.2d 1159 (Ill. App. Ct. 1992); *Eaves v. Hyster Co.*, 244 Ill. App. 3d 260, 614 N.E.2d 214 (Ill. App. Ct. 1993)).

32. *Id.*

33. *Doe v. Goff*, 306 Ill. App. 3d 1131, 716 N.E.2d 323 (Ill. App. Ct. 1999); *Abraham v. Wayside Cross Rescue Mission*, 289 Ill. App. 3d 1048, 682 N.E.2d 1240 (Ill. App. Ct. 1997).

34. *Doe*; *Abraham*.

35. *Vaughn v. City of West Frankfort*, 166 Ill. 2d 155, 651 N.E.2d 1115 (1995).

36. *First Springfield Band & Trust v. Galman*, 720 N.E.2d 1068, 1072 (1999) (citing *Lee v. Chicago Transit Auth.*, 152 Ill. 2d 432, 455, 605 N.E.2d 493 (1992)).

37. *Id.*

38. *Id.* at 456.

39. *Alvis v. Ribar*, 85 Ill. 2d 1, 421 N.E.2d 886 (1981).

40. 735 ILCS 5/2-1116 (1999).

41. *Zook v. Norfolgk & Western Ry Co.*, 268 Ill. App. 3d 157, 169, 642 N.E.2d 1348, 57 (Ill. App. Ct. 1994) (citing *Casey v. Baseden*, 111 Ill. 2d 341, 490 N.E.2d 4 (Ill. App. Ct. 1986)).

42. *Poole v. City of Rolling Meadows*, 167 Ill. 2d 41, 656 N.E.2d 768 (1995).

43. *Gratzle v. Sears, Roebuck & Co.*, 245 Ill. App. 3d 292, 613 N.E.2d 802 (Ill. App. Ct. 1993).

44. *Id.*

45. *See, e.g., Gatlin v. Ruder*, 137 Ill. 2d 284, 560 N.E.2d 586 (1990) (The doctrine of *res ipsa loquitur* is a rule of evidence. It is not to be invoked to overcome evidence, but is to be applied in its absence.).

46. *Id.* at 589.

47. *Spidle v. Steward*, 79 Ill. 2d 1, 402 N.E.2d 216 (1980).

48. *Metz v. Central Illinois Elec. & Gas Co.*, 32 Ill. 2d 446, 207 N.E.2d 305 (1965).

49. *See, e.g., In re Chicago Flood Litig.*, 176 Ill. 2d 179, 680 N.E.2d 265 (1997).

50. *Id.*

51. *Id.* at 280 (stating that a court should determine whether an activity is inherently dangerous because the issue is a question of law) (citing Restatement (Second) of Torts § 520, Comment *l*) (1977)).

52. *Id.* at 279 (citing Restatement (Second) of Torts § 519 (1977)).

53. *Leaks v. City of Chicago*, 238 Ill. App. 3d 12, 18, 606 N.E.2d 156 (Ill. App. Ct. 1992).

54. *Id.*

55. *Best v. Taylor Machine Works*, 179 Ill. 2d 367, 689 N.E.2d 1057 (1997).

56. 735 ILCS 5/2-1117 (1999).

57. 740 ILCS 100/2 (1999).

58. *Id.*

59. *Id.*

60. *Dixon v. Chicago and North Western Transp. Co.*, 151 Ill. 2d 108, 601 N.E.2d 704 (1992) (citing *Van Slambrouck v. Economy Baler Co.*, 105 Ill. 2d 462, 475 N.E.2d 867 (1985)).

61. *Id.* (citing 41 Am. Jur. 2d Indemnity § 1, at 687 (1968)).

62. *Id.* (citing *Frazer v. A. F. Munsterman, Inc.*, 123 Ill. 2d 245, 527 N.E.2d 1248 (1988)).

63. *Id.*

64. *Richardson v. Chapman*, 175 Ill. 2d 98, 118, 676 N.E.2d 621, 30 (1997) (citing *Frazer; Thatcher v. Commonwealth Edison Co.*, 123 Ill. 2d 275, 527 N.E.2d 1261 (1988)).

65. 820 ILCS 310/5(a) (1999).

66. *See, e.g., Limanowski v. Ashland Oil Co., Inc.*, 275 Ill. App. 3d 115, 655 N.E.2d 1049 (Ill. App. Ct. 1995); *Hartline v. Celotex Corp.*, 272 Ill. App. 3d 952, 651 N.E.2d 582 (Ill. App. Ct. 1995); *Copass v. Illinois Power Co.*, 211 Ill. App. 3d 205, 569 N.E.2d 1211 (Ill. App. Ct. 1991).

67. *McCormick v. Caterpillar Tractor Co.*, 85 Ill. 2d 352, 423 N.E.2d 876 (1981).

68. *Id.* at 878.

69. *Dalton v. Community General Hosp.*, 275 Ill. App. 3d 73, 655 N.E.2d 462 (Ill. App. Ct. 1995).

70. 820 ILCS 310/5(b) (1999).

71. 740 ILCS 100 *et seq.* (1999).

72. *Kotecki v. Cyclops Welding Corp.*, 146 Ill. 2d 155, 585 N.E.2d 1–23 (1991).

73. 740 ILCS 130/1 *et seq.* (1999). *See also Rhodes v. Illinois Cent. Gulf R.R.*, 172 Ill. 2d 213, 665 N.E.2d 1260 (1996); *Mt. Zion State Bank & Trust v. Consolidated Communications, Inc.*, 169 Ill. 2d 110, 660 N.E.2d 863, 214 Ill. Dec. 156 (1995).

74. 740 ILCS 130/2 (1999).

75. *Id.*

76. 740 ILCS 130/3 (1999).

77. 235 ILCS 5/1-1, *et seq.* (1999).

78. 235 ILCS 5/6-21 (1999).

79. *Charles v. Seigfried*, 165 Ill. 2d 482, 487, 651 N.E.2d 154 (1995).

80. *McDonald v. Risch*, 41 Ill. 2d 242, 244, 242 N.E.2d 245 (1968).

81. *Mohr v. Jilg*, 223 Ill. App. 3d 217, 221–22, 586 N.E.2d 807 (Ill. App. Ct. 1992); *Hartness v. Ruzich*, 155 Ill. App. 3d 878, 881, 508 N.E.2d 1071 (Ill. App. Ct. 1987).

82. *Welch v. Convenient Food Mart #550*, 106 Ill. App. 3d 131, 133–34, 435 N.E.2d 894 (Ill. App. Ct. 1982).

83. *Charles*, 165 Ill. 2d at 488–89.

84. 235 ILCS 5/6-21 (1999).

85. *Id.*; *Walter v. Carriage House Hotels, Ltd.*, 164 Ill. 2d 80, 93, 646 N.E.2d 599 (1995).

86. *Walter*, 164 Ill. 2d at 86–87.

87. *Charles*, 165 Ill. 2d at 487.

88. *Moorman Manufacturing Co. v. National Tank Co.*, 91 Ill. 2d 69, 91, 435 N.E.2d 443 (1982).

89. *Id.* at 82.

90. *In re Chicago Flood Litig.*, 176 Ill. 2d 179, 199, 680 N.E.2d 265 (1997) (citing *Moorman*).

91. *Connick v. Suzuki Motor Co., Ltd.*, 174 Ill. 2d 482, 496, 675 N.E.2d 584 (1997) (citing *Board of Educ. v. A.C. and S, Inc.*, 131 Ill. 2d 428, 52, 546 N.E.2d 580 (1989)).

92. *Id.* at 496–97 (citing *Board of Educ. v. A. C. and S, Inc.*, 131 Ill. 2d 428, 57, 546 N.E.2d 580 (1989)).

93. *Weisblatt v. Chicago Bar Ass'n*, 292 Ill. App. 3d 48, 684 N.E.2d 984 (Ill. App. Ct. 1997).

94. *Neptuno Treuhand-Und Verwaltungsgesellschaft MBH v. Arbor*, 295 Ill. App. 3d 567, 692 N.E.2d 812 (Ill. App. Ct. 1998).

95. *Brogan v. Mitchell Int'l, Inc.*, 181 Ill. 2d 178, 692 N.E.2d 276 (1998); *City of Chicago v. Michigan Beach Hous. Coop.*, 297 Ill. App. 3d 317, 696 N.E.2d 804 (Ill. App. Ct. 1998).

96. *Hartmann Co. v. Capital Bank and Trust Co.*, 296 Ill. App. 3d 593, 694 N.E.2d 1108 (Ill. App. Ct. 1998) (citing *Duhl v. Nash Realty Inc.*, 102 Ill. App. 3d 483, 429 N.E.2d 1267 (Ill. App. Ct. 1981)).

97. *Zekman v. Direct Am. Marketers, Inc.*, 182 Ill. 2d 359, 695 N.E.2d 853 (1998) (citing *Connick v. Suzuki Motor Co.*, 174 Ill. 2d 482, 675 N.E.2d 584 (1996)); *Hartmann* (citing *Siegel v. Levy Organization Development Co.*, 153 Ill. 2d 534, 607 N.E.2d 194 (1992)).

98. *Id.* (citing *Century Universal Enters., Inc. v. Triana Dev. Corp.*, 158 Ill. App. 3d 182, 510 N.E.2d 1260 (Ill. App. Ct. 1987); *Duhl v. Nash Realty, Inc.*, 102 Ill. App. 3d 483, 429 N.E.2d 1267 (Ill. App. Ct. 1981)).

99. *Id.* (citing *Siegel v. Levy Organization Development Co.*, 153 Ill. 2d 534, 607 N.E.2d 194 (1992)).

100. 815 ILCS 505/6.1 (1999).

101. *Id.* (citing *Lake County Grading Co. of Libertyville, Inc. v. Advance Mechanical Contractors, Inc.*, 275 Ill. App. 3d 452, 654 N.E.2d 1109 (Ill. App. Ct. 1995)).

102. *J. I. Case Co. v. McCartin-McAuliffe Plumbing & Heating, Inc.*, 118 Ill. 2d 447, 516 N.E.2d 260, 114 Ill. Dec. 105 (1987). *See also Proctor v. Davis*, 291 Ill. App. 3d 265, 682 N.E.2d 1203, 225 Ill. Dec. 26 (1997).

103. 735 ILCS 5/2-604.1 (1999).

104. *Id.*

105. *Loitz v. Remington Arms Co.*, 138 Ill. 2d 404, 563 N.E.2d 397, 150 Ill. Dec. 510 (1990).

106. *McGrady v. Chrysler Motors Corp.*, 46 Ill. App. 3d 136, 360 N.E.2d 818, 4 Ill. Dec. 705 (1977).

107. *LiPetri v. Turner Constr. Co.*, 36 Ill. 2d 597, 224 N.E.2d 841 (1967) (citing *Hall v. Gillins*, 13 Ill. 2d 26, 147 N.E.2d 352 (1958)).

108. 740 ILCS 180/0.01 *et seq.* (1999); 755 ILCS 5/27-6 (1999).

109. *Kaufman v. Cserny*, 856 F. Supp. 1307 (S.D. Ill. 1994).

110. *Kessinger v. Grefco, Inc.*, 251 Ill. App. 3d 980, 623 N.E.2d 946 (Ill. App. Ct. 1993).

111. 740 ILCS 180/2 (1999).

112. *Leavitt v. Farwell Tower Ltd. Partnership*, 252 Ill. App. 3d, 260, 625 N.E.2d 48 (Ill. App. Ct. 1993) (citing *Old Second Nat'l Bank of Aurora v. Aurora Township*, 156 Ill. App. 3d 62, 509 N.E.2d 692 (Ill. App. Ct. 1987)).

113. 740 ILCS 180/2 (1999).

INDIANA

A. STATUTES OF LIMITATION

Pursuant to Indiana Trial Rule 8(C), statutes of limitation are affirmative defenses that must be affirmatively set forth in a responsive pleading and which the party asserting has the burden of proving. Pursuant to Trial Rule 13(J), a statute of limitation will not bar a claim, asserted as a counterclaim, to the extent that it defeats or diminishes the opposing party's claim, if the claim arises out of the same transaction or occurrence that is the subject matter of the opposing party's claim, or if the claim could have been asserted as a counterclaim to the opposing party's claim before the counterclaim was barred. The Indiana Supreme Court recently held that the complaint, filing fee, and summons must all be filed in order to toll the running of the statute of limitations.[1]

A number, but not all, of Indiana's statutes of limitation are codified in Indiana Code Title 34-11. Most tort actions[2] are governed by a two-year statute of limitations. This includes actions based on injury to person or character, or personal property, which must be commenced within two years after the cause of action accrues.[3] Ordinarily, a discovery rule applies in tort cases and the cause of action in such cases accrues at the time the alleged negligence is or, in the exercise of reasonable or ordinary diligence, could have been discovered.[4] A two-year limitation period also generally applies to wrongful death actions,[5] and to employment related actions, except those based on written contract.[6]

The Medical Malpractice Act specifically indicates that, subject to certain limited exceptions, an action must be filed within two years from the date of the act, omission, or neglect complained of.[7] Thus, the discovery rule historically was not applied to extend the limitation period. However, the Indiana Supreme Court has recently indicated that, as a general rule, the two-year statute of limitations cannot be constitutionally applied to preclude a plaintiff from filing an action before the plaintiff either knows of the malpractice and resulting injury or discovers facts that should, in the course of reasonable diligence, result in discovering such information.[8] In such cases, the plaintiff has two years in which to bring an action.[9] The limitation period may also be extended under the continued wrong doctrine.[10] The Medical Malpractice Act, Indiana Code 34-18, precludes pursuit of an action, in most instances, before the claimant's proposed complaint has been presented to a medical review panel and an opinion is given by the panel.[11] The filing of a proposed complaint tolls the statute of limitations for 90 days following the receipt of the medical review panel's opinion.[12]

A two-year statute of limitations governs products liability actions, whether based on negligence or strict liability.[13] There is also a ten-year period of repose that generally applies and runs from the date of the delivery of the product to the initial user or consumer.[14] Certain causes of action based on asbestos-related injuries, including death, and damages to property, are covered by a separate two-year statute of limitations.[15] There are specific statutory provisions governing the accrual of such causes of action, but case law should also be consulted.[16]

A two-year statute of limitations applies to causes of action for violation of Indiana's Deceptive Practices Act, applicable to consumer sales.[17] However, as discussed more fully below, there are much shorter notice requirements under the Act that apply in some instances.[18]

Actions for injuries to real property, actions based on contracts not in writing, and actions for injuries based on fraud, actual or constructive, are governed by a six-year statute of limitations.[19]

There is a ten-year catch-all statute of limitations for actions not limited by any other statute.[20]

As a general rule, the statute of limitation period is extended if a person is under a legal disability when the cause of action accrues, and an action may be commenced within two years of the date the disability ceases.[21] However, there may be exceptions that apply.[22]

The limitation period may be affected by the death of a person who is subject to suit, if the statute of limitations has not yet expired. There are restrictions in the Probate Code with regard to claims against a decedent's estate.[23] As a general rule, claims must be filed against a decedent's estate within the earliest of five months after the date of the first notice to creditors or one year after the death of the decedent.[24] If the statute of limitations has not run at the time of the decedent's death, the limitations period may be extended by death.[25] The Probate Code does not affect or prevent the enforcement of a claim against the estate of a deceased tortfeasor if brought for injury to person or damage to property arising out of negligence within the applicable statute of limitations, but recovery may be limited to available insurance proceeds.[26]

The limitation period may also be affected by the death of the claimant. In such cases, generally a cause of action may be brought by the decedent's representative within 18 months after the date of death, even though the statute of limitations has expired.[27]

Indiana has a statute of repose applicable to causes of action to recover damages, whether based on contract, tort, nuisance, or otherwise, for deficiencies "in the design, planning, supervision, construction, or observation of construction of an improvement to real property."[28] Such an action must generally be brought within the earlier of ten years from the date of substantial completion of the improvement or twelve years after the completion and submission of the plans and specifications to the owner if the action is for deficiency in design.[29] This statute does not expand the statute of limitations otherwise applicable.[30] The period of repose may be extended for up to an additional two years in cases of personal injury or wrongful death occurring in the ninth and tenth year following completion of the improvement.[31] The statute of repose cannot be asserted by way of defense by a person in actual possession or control of the real property.[32]

Subject to certain exceptions, under the Indiana Tort Claims Act, causes of action against the state are barred unless an appropriate written notice is filed with the Attorney General or the state agency involved within 270 days after the loss.[33] Claims against political subdivisions are barred unless an appropriate notice is filed with the governing body of the political subdivision *and* the Indiana political subdivision risk management commission (if the political subdivision was a member at the time the alleged act or omission occurred), within 180 days after the loss occurs.[34] The notice period may be tolled during a period of incapacity and a claimant must then file the notice within 180 days after the incapacity is removed.[35]

B. TORT REFORM

To date, the Indiana Legislature has passed a number of tort reform statutes, which have modified substantive rights and the procedures that are applicable in the area of tort litigation. These statutes are incorporated in these materials. Legislative update services should be consulted regarding new developments.

C. "NO FAULT" LIMITATIONS/FINANCIAL RESPONSIBILITY LAWS

Indiana's Financial Responsibility Law provides that a vehicle cannot be operated on the public highways unless financial responsibility is in place "with respect to the motor vehicle."[36] The financial responsibility requirement may be met by either the owner of a vehicle or a nonowner operator.[37] Financial responsibility can be met through insurance, a bond, or with an appropriate certificate of self-insurance.[38] Certain minimum amounts of insurance are statutorily required to cover bodily injury or death and property damage.[39] Indiana has not adopted no-fault automobile insurance provisions.

D. THE STANDARD FOR NEGLIGENCE

The tort of negligence requires proof of three elements: (1) the existence of a duty on the part of the defendant to conform his conduct to a standard of care arising out of the defendant's relationship with the plaintiff; (2) a breach of that duty by a defendant; and (3) an injury to the plaintiff proximately caused by the defendant's breach of duty.[40] In the absence of a duty, there can be no negligence. The determination of whether a duty exists requires consideration of the relationship between the parties, the reasonable foreseeability of harm, and any public policy concerns.[41] Indiana does not generally recognize degrees of negligence.[42] Rather, what is required is that a person exercise the degree of care that an ordinary and reasonable person would exercise under the same or similar circumstances.[43]

Indiana recognizes a professional standard of care. A professional must exercise the degree of care, skill, and proficiency exercised by reasonably careful, skillful, and prudent practitioners in the same class acting under the same or similar circumstances.[44]

Children are generally not held to the same standard of care as adults. A child younger than seven years of age is conclusively presumed to be incapable of being guilty of contributory negligence.[45] A child between seven and fourteen years of age is generally required to exercise the same degree of care as would ordinarily be exercised by a child of similar age, experience, and knowledge.[46] An exception exists, however, where a child causes harm while engaged in an activity for which adult qualifications are required.[47] Absent proof of special circumstances, a child older than 14 years of age is charged with exercising the same standard of care as an adult.[48]

E. CAUSATION

Causation is an essential element in a cause of action based on negligence, and the claimant bears the burden of proof.[49] The legal requirement of causation also applies to claims of contributory fault.[50] An injury or loss is proximately caused by a party's action if it is the natural and probable consequence of such action and should have been reasonably foreseen and anticipated in light of all the circumstances.[51] Proof of proximate cause requires, at a minimum, that the plaintiff show that the harm sustained would not have occurred "but for" the defendant's conduct.[52] An intervening or superseding cause, which relieves the original wrongdoer from responsibility, occurs when the harm results from a subsequent intervening act that could not have been reasonably foreseen by the original wrongdoer.[53]

F. CONTRIBUTORY NEGLIGENCE, COMPARATIVE NEGLIGENCE/FAULT, AND ASSUMPTION OF RISK

Indiana's Comparative Fault Act[54] governs actions based on fault[55] that are brought to recover damages for personal injury or death or harm to property, except for medical malpractice actions under Indiana Code Title 34-18 and actions against governmental entities or public employees.[56] Defenses such as contributory negligence and other common law defenses no longer provide a complete defense in cases governed by the Comparative Fault Act.[57] However, such defenses remain viable in actions against governmental entities, and will bar recovery except where the defendant's conduct is willful and wanton.[58] Contributory negligence or fault by the plaintiff is governed by the same rules that apply to a defendant's negligence.[59]

Under Indiana law, "assumed risk" is a separate affirmative defense based on contract, whereas "incurred risk" is used when the plaintiff has voluntarily and knowingly placed himself in a position or undertakes activities that result in injury.[60] Incurred risk no longer exists as a complete defense to a negligence claim and it is subsumed within the concept of fault under the

Comparative Fault Act.[61] Where the defense is asserted, the defendant must show more than a general awareness of potential harm; he must demonstrate the plaintiff's appreciation of the specific risk involved and voluntary acceptance of that risk.[62]

Indiana continues to recognize the sudden-emergency doctrine as an affirmative defense.[63] A party will be denied the benefits of the sudden-emergency doctrine if the party's own conduct contributed to the creation of the emergency.[64]

In an action based on fault, a claimant may not recover if the fault attributable to him is greater than the fault of all persons whose fault proximately contributed to the claimant's damages.[65] If a claimant's fault is not more than 50 percent, the claimant's contributory fault is used to diminish the damages proportionately.[66] There are specific statutory provisions governing the instructions to be given to a jury in a comparative fault action, subject to an agreement of the parties otherwise.[67] Among other things, a jury is not to be advised of any immunity defense that is available to a nonparty.[68]

A defendant is generally liable only for its own portion of fault under the Comparative Fault Act.[69] An exception exists in cases of certain intentional torts. A claimant is entitled to recover 100 percent of his damages for an intentional tort from a defendant who was convicted after a prosecution based on the same evidence.[70]

As a result of the provisions of the Comparative Fault Act, the release of one tortfeasor generally no longer serves to release all tortfeasors in comparative fault actions.[71]

In an action based on fault, the party against whom a claim is made may assert as a defense a claim that the claimant's damages were caused, in whole or in part, by a nonparty.[72] The "nonparty defense" must be affirmatively pled by the defendant, who also bears the burden of proof in connection with the defense.[73] There are various time limitations that apply in connection with the nonparty defense.[74] A party that pleads a nonparty defense must specifically name the nonparty.[75] If the nonparty defense is not specially pleaded, allocation of fault should be limited to the parties to the action.[76] The statutes governing the nonparty defense do not change the claimant's burden of proving that the defendant's fault caused the claimant's damages, in whole or in part.[77]

The adoption of the Comparative Fault Act did not change Indiana's rule that the original tortfeasor remains responsible for the acts of a negligent health care provider.[78]

G. *RES IPSA LOQUITUR* AND INHERENTLY DANGEROUS ACTIVITIES

1. Res Ipsa Loquitur

Under the doctrine of *res ipsa loquitur,* Indiana law allows an inference of negligence if the plaintiff can show: (1) the injury is one which ordinarily would not occur in the absence of negligence; (2) the injury was caused by an instrumentality over which the defendant had exclusive control; and (3) the injury was not due to any voluntary act of the plaintiff.[79]

2. Inherently Dangerous Activities

Conduct that is inherently dangerous or ultrahazardous or abnormally dangerous may result in the imposition of strict liability.[80] The dangerous propensity of an activity or product is not determinative.[81] The decision as to whether strict liability should be imposed must be based on consideration of "the defendant's activity as a whole."[82] If reasonable care could have avoided the incident, strict liability is generally inapplicable.[83]

The dangerous instrumentality doctrine "imposes a duty to use reasonable care upon one who maintains something dangerous to children and adults alike and so exposed that there is a likelihood of their coming in contact with and being injured by it, notwithstanding they may be trespassers."[84]

H. NEGLIGENCE *PER SE*

An unexcused or unjustified violation of a statutory duty is negligence *per se*.[85] However, the rule of negligence *per se* is applied only when the plaintiff is among the class of persons intended to be protected by a statute and the statute was intended to protect against the risk of harm of the type that has been sustained as a result of a violation.[86] The same rule applies to municipal ordinances.[87]

Negligence *per se* does not necessarily result in liability. The plaintiff still must show that the statutory violation was a proximate cause of the injury sustained.[88]

I. JOINT AND SEVERAL LIABILITY

Where persons are jointly bound to perform a duty, they may be jointly and severally liable for the harm caused by negligently discharging their respective duties.[89] In addition, where the separate, independent acts of two or more persons combine to cause a single injury and the circumstances are such that it is not possible to determine in what proportion each contributed, any one person or all may be held responsible for the injury.[90] However, under the Comparative Fault Act, generally fault must be apportioned between defendants (and in certain circumstances nonparties), and a verdict is entered separately "against each defendant (and such other defendants as are liable with the defendant by reason of their relationship to defendant)" for an amount equal to the defendant's proportional share of the damages.[91]

The law is well settled in Indiana that there is no right to contribution among tortfeasors.[92]

J. INDEMNITY

The right to indemnify under Indiana law generally arises from an express or implied contract or statutory obligation.[93] In the absence of such an obligation, an indemnity action will lie only if the party seeking indemnity is without fault and has been compelled to pay damages as a result of another's wrongful conduct for which he is constructively liable.[94] The right to indemnification lies only against the party whose wrongful act has resulted in the imposition of liability on another.[95] Thus, indemnity in tort actions is generally recognized only when liability has been imposed as a result of a party's vicarious or derivative liability for the acts of another.[96] Indiana law generally allows contracts providing for indemnification of a party's own negligence if they are knowingly and willingly made.[97] However, exceptions exist if the parties have unequal bargaining power, the contract is unconscionable, or it affects the public interest, such as utilities and carriers.[98] A party seeking to enforce such an exculpatory provision has the burden of proving that the provision was "explained to the other party and came to his knowledge and there was in fact a real and voluntary meeting of the minds and not merely an objective meeting."[99] Moreover, indemnification provisions covering a party's own negligence are strictly construed.[100]

K. BAR OF WORKERS' COMPENSATION STATUTE

Under the Indiana Workers' Compensation Act, workers' compensation benefits are the exclusive remedy for a personal injury or death "by accident" arising out of and in the course of employment.[101] There is no intentional tort exception to the Act, but an injury occurs "by accident" "only when it is intended by neither the employee nor the employer."[102] Thus an employer's intentional tort is not included within the Act's coverage and an employee may sue.[103] In order to avoid the exclusivity of the Workers' Compensation Act, the employee has the burden of showing deliberate intent to inflict injury or death, or actual knowledge that injury or death is certain to occur.[104] Tortious intent is imputed to an employer that is a legal entity or artificial person if "either (1) the corporation is the tortfeasor's alter ego or (2) the corporation has substituted its will for that of the individual who committed the tortious acts."[105] An injured employee is barred from recovery for "an injury or death due to the employee's knowingly self inflicted injury, his intoxication, his commission of an offense, his knowing failure to use a safety appliance, his knowing failure to obey a reasonable written or printed rule of the employer which has been posted in a conspicuous position in the place of work, or his knowing failure to perform any statutory duty."[106]

An employee who has collected workers' compensation benefits from an employer is not barred from seeking damages from a person other than the employer and "not in the same employ."[107] If a coworker contributes to an injury or death and was not acting in the course of his employment at the time, then the coworker is not deemed to be "in the same employ" as the injured employee, who may be entitled to bring suit against the coworker in addition to collecting workers' compensation benefits.[108]

Under the Workers' Compensation Act, the employer is subrogated to the rights of the employee against a third party.[109] The statutory provisions allow only two ways of settling a claim against a third party: (1) receipt of the employer's written consent; or (2) full indemnification of the employer or protection by court order.[110] The procedural rights and responsibilities of both the employee and the employer are specifically described in the Act, which provides for a lien in favor of the employer on any settlement award or judgment out of which the employee's rights are compensated by a third party.[111]

L. PREMISES LIABILITY

A landowner's responsibility for injuries sustained on his property depends on the claimant's status as a trespasser, licensee, or invitee.[112] A landowner's only obligation to a trespasser is to refrain from willfully or wantonly injuring him.[113] A landowner owes the same duty to a licensee, but also must refrain from acting in a manner to increase his peril.[114] This latter duty includes a duty to warn of any latent danger on the premises of which the landowner has knowledge.[115] A landowner owes a duty to invitees of exercising reasonable care under the circumstances.[116] This includes a duty to protect invitees from criminal acts that are foreseeable based on the totality of the circumstances.[117] A landowner's duty of care may extend to those who, while outside the property, suffer harm from natural conditions on the property.[118]

M. DRAM SHOP LIABILITY

Indiana's dram shop statutes provide for civil liability in certain situations where a party furnishes alcohol to another who then causes an injury as a result of his intoxication.[119] In order to establish liability, a plaintiff must show: (1) that the person who furnished the alcohol had actual knowledge that they were furnishing alcohol to an intoxicated person; and (2) that the intoxication of the person to whom the alcohol was provided was a proximate cause of the death, injury, or damage claimed.[120] Actual knowledge of intoxication can be shown by indirect or circumstantial evidence and a subjective standard is used.[121] An intoxicated person is not necessarily barred from seeking recovery for his own injuries resulting from the negligent provision of alcohol,[122] but the intoxicated person's conduct is compared with the defendant's conduct as simple negligence.[123]

N. ECONOMIC LOSS

Economic loss is defined under Indiana law as "the diminution in the value of a product and consequent loss of profits because the product is inferior in quality and does not work for the general purposes for which it was manufactured and sold."[124] Lost profits, rental expense, and lost time are examples of economic loss.[125] Under Indiana law, when a negligence action is based on a product's failure to perform as expected, "economic losses are not recoverable unless such failure also causes personal injury or physical harm to property other than to the product itself."[126] Similarly, loss that is solely economic in nature is not recoverable under Indiana's Strict Products Liability Act, in the absence of damages to other property or person.[127] While personal injury or damage to other property from a defective product are actionable under the Act, their presence does not create a claim for damage to the product itself.[128]

O. FRAUD AND MISREPRESENTATION

Under Indiana law, fraud may be actual or constructive. To show actual fraud, a party must prove: (1) there was a material misrepresentation of past or existing fact; (2) the representation was false; (3) the representation was made with the knowledge or reckless ignorance of its falsity; (4) the complaining party relied on the representation; and (5) the complaining party's injury was proximately caused by such representation and reliance.[129] Constructive fraud is recognized in situations in which there is conduct that, if sanctioned by law, would result in an unconscionable advantage, regardless of an actual intent to defraud.[130] To sustain a cause of action for constructive fraud, the plaintiff must prove: (1) a duty that existed because of the parties' relationship; (2) representations or omissions that violated that duty; (3) reliance by the complaining party; (4) injury proximately caused thereby; and (5) an unfair advantage gained at the expense of the complaining party.[131]

A representation with regard to future conduct or expectations generally cannot support a cause of action for actual fraud, but it can under some circumstances support an action for constructive fraud.[132] Expressions of opinion are not actionable as either actual or constructive fraud.[133]

P. CONSUMER FRAUD STATUTES

Indiana has a number of consumer protection and trade statutes. The Deceptive Practices Act[134] provides a cause of action to consumers, individually or as a class, for deceptive acts in consumer sales.[135] The Act allows a consumer to recover actual damages and attorney's fees.[136] Persons 65 years or older may be awarded treble damages if appropriate.[137] The Attorney General may seek injunctive relief, seek a fine of not more than $500 for an incurable deceptive act, and take other action, including seeking civil penalties up to $15,000 for violations of an injunction.[138] While there is a two-year limitation period on claims that accrue at the time of the deceptive act, there are much shorter notice requirements that apply in cases in which the deceptive act is curable.[139] They are specifically set forth in the statute and must be followed.[140] The two-year limitation period may be extended in cases of fraudulent concealment, but the plaintiff must bring such an action within a reasonable time after the fraudulent concealment is discovered.[141]

Title 24 of the Indiana Code includes extensive additional statutes governing trade and consumer sales and credit. Examples include provisions relating to restraints of trade,[142] trademarks,[143] trade secrets,[144] consumer credit,[145] and promotional gifts and contests.[146] A detailed review of Title 24 should be made to determine what provisions may be applicable in such cases.

Q. PUNITIVE DAMAGES

Indiana statutes allow an award of punitive damages in civil actions arising out of tortious conduct if the defendant has acted with malice, fraud, gross negligence, or oppressiveness.[147] Punitive damages are not, however, recoverable in a wrongful death action.[148] The purpose of punitive damages is to punish the wrongdoer and thereby deter others from engaging in such conduct.[149] In order to be entitled to recover punitive damages, a party must show, by clear and convincing evidence, all of the facts relied on to support the claim for such damages.[150] Punitive damages cannot be awarded in the absence of compensatory damages.[151]

A punitive damage award may not be more than three times the amount of compensatory damages awarded or $50,000, whichever is greater.[152] If a jury's award exceeds these limits, the court is required to reduce the punitive damage award accordingly.[153] Awards of punitive damages must be paid to the clerk of court, who in turn pays 25 percent of the award to the party to whom the punitive damages were awarded, with the remaining 75 percent going to the state treasurer for deposit into the violent crime victims' compensation fund.[154] Statutory provisions specifically preclude advising the jury of the limitation on the amount of punitive damages or of the allocation of the money between the party and the state.[155]

If a person suffers a pecuniary loss as a result of certain criminal violations, the person is entitled to bring a civil action to recover up to three times the actual damages suffered by the person, various costs, and attorney's fees.[156]

R. WRONGFUL DEATH AND SURVIVAL ACTIONS

When an adult's death is caused by the wrongful act or omission of another, the personal representative of the decedent may bring an action for wrongful death.[157] An estate must be opened and a personal representative appointed for the decedent as a prerequisite to filing a wrongful death action.[158] The Wrongful Death Act creates a new cause of action to compensate the survivors for the losses caused by the decedent's death. It is separate and apart from any right of action the decedent might have had.

The damages recoverable and appropriate allocation of any amounts recovered are governed by statutory provisions, and depends on whether the decedent had dependents.[159] Effective January 1, 2000, there is a right of action as the result of the death of an unmarried individual who is not a child and who does not have any dependents.[160] The new provision allows recovery for the loss of the adult person's care and companionship subject to certain damage caps.[161]

A cause of action for the death of, and injuries to, a child is also recognized, but is governed by a separate statute.[162] The action may be brought by: (1) a child's parents jointly or by either parent, naming the other parent as a codefendant, to allow the other parent to protect his or her own interests; (2) in the case of divorce, the person to whom custody was awarded; and (3) a guardian of a protected person.[163] The damages recoverable are specifically defined by statute and include recovery for the loss of the child's love and companionship.[164] Damages for loss of love and companionship are recoverable from the time of the death of the child until the death of the child's last surviving parent.[165] The remedy provided by the child statute and the adult wrongful death statute are mutually exclusive; recovery under both is not allowed.[166] However, a party may simultaneously pursue a cause of action for wrongful death and a survival action, as long as a double recovery is prevented.[167]

Survival actions are governed by Indiana Code §§ 34-9-3-1 *et seq*. If a person who is entitled to sue or may be liable in a cause of action dies, the cause of action survives and may be brought by or against the decedent's representative, except for causes of action for libel, slander, malicious prosecution, false imprisonment, invasion of privacy, and personal injuries to the decedent.[168] The causes of action excepted from the general provisions for survival of actions survive only to the extent specifically provided in the statutes.[169] If a person receives personal injuries caused by the fault of another and subsequently dies from causes other than those personal injuries, the personal representative of the decedent may bring an action to recover all damages resulting before the date of death that the decedent would have been entitled to recover if the decedent had lived.[170] If a person obtains a judgment for personal injuries that is reversed on an appeal, the cause of action survives the plaintiff's death.[171]

Pamela J. Hermes
GAMBS MUCKER & BAUMAN
10 North Fourth Street, P.O. Box 1608
Lafayette, Indiana 47902
(765) 423-1001
Fax (765) 742-4535
PamH@gmbslaw.com

ENDNOTES - INDIANA

1. *Ray-Hayes v. Heinamann*, 760 N.E.2d 172 (Ind. 2002); *Fort Wayne Int'l Airport v. Wilburn*, 723 N.E.2d 967, 968 (Ind. App. 2000), *transfer denied; see* Ind. Trial Rule 3 (providing that a civil action is commenced "by filing a complaint payment of the filing fee, and furnishing the clerk with the required number of summons), effective April, 2002.

2. *See Wells v. Stone City Bank*, 691 N.E.2d 1246, 1249 (Ind. App. 1998) *transfer denied*, 706 N.E.2d 166 (Ind. 1998) (noting that a tort is a legal wrong committed on person or property, independent of contract), *called into doubt on other grounds; Spolnik v. Guardian Life Ins. Co.*, 94 F. Supp. 2d 998 (S.D. Ind. 2000).

3. Ind. Code § 34-11-2-4 (1998). This two-year statute applies to most professional negligence actions, *see, e.g., Morgan v. Benner*, 712 N.E.2d 500, 503 (Ind. App. 1999) *transfer denied* (legal malpractice), except those covered by the Medical Malpractice Act, which contains its own two-year statute of limitations, Ind. Code § 34-18-7-1(b) (1998). *See also* Ind. Code § 34-11-2-3 (1998) (setting forth a two-year statute of limitations for actions, whether brought in tort or contract, based on professional medical conduct).

4. *See INS Investigations Bureau, Inc. v. Lee*, 709 N.E.2d 736, 743 (Ind. App. 1999) *transfer denied*. The cause of action accrues when some ascertainable damage has occurred; it is not necessary that the claimant be aware of the full extent of the damages. *Morgan v. Benner*, 712 N.E.2d 500, 503 (Ind. App. 1999). A mere suspicion or speculation as to the cause of injuries is insufficient to trigger the statute of limitations. *DeGussa Corp. v. Mullens*, 744 N.E.2d 407, 411 (Ind. 2001).

5. *See* Ind. Code § 34-23-1-1 (1998) (requiring commencement of the cause of action by the personal representative of the decedent within two years of death); *Martin v. Rinck*, 491 N.E.2d 556, 559 (Ind. App. 1986) (indicating that the two-year period provided for in the wrongful death statute is not a statute of limitations but a condition precedent of the existence of a claim); *GMC v. Arnett*, 418 N.E.2d 546, 548 (Ind. App. 1981) (same).

6. Ind. Code § 34-11-2-1 (1998).

7. Ind. Code § 34-18-7-1(b) (1998). *See also* Ind. Code § 34-11-2-3 (1998); *Jordan v. Deery*, 609 N.E.2d 1104, 1107 (Ind. 1993) (applying prior similar law).

8. In *Martin v. Richey*, 711 N.E.2d 1273 (Ind. 1999), the Indiana Supreme Court held that the two-year limitation period applicable to malpractice was unconstitutional as applied to the plaintiff under Article 1, Sections 12 and 23

of the Indiana Constitution (the open court and privileges and immunities clauses), because it would have foreclosed the plaintiff from bringing her medical malpractice action before she had a meaningful opportunity to know of the malpractice and the resulting injury. *See also Harris v. Raymond*, 715 N.E.2d 388, 395–96 (Ind. 1999) *rehg. denied*; *Van Dusen v. Stotts*, 712 N.E.2d 491, 496 (Ind. 1999). The two-year statute of limitations in the Medical Malpractice Act can be applied to bar a claim discovered months before the limitations period expired without violating the Indiana Constitution. *Boggs v. Tri-State Radiology, Inc.*, 730 N.E.2d 692, 694 (Ind. 2000).

9. *Van Dusen v. Stotts*, 712 N.E.2d 491, 497 (Ind. 1999). In *Van Dusen*, the Supreme Court summarized the principles to be applied in determining what constitutes "discovery" of alleged malpractice, stating that as a general rule "a plaintiff's lay suspicion that there may have been malpractice is not sufficient to trigger the two-year period." *Id.* at 499. However, the Court has also made it clear that a plaintiff does not have to know with certainty that malpractice caused the injury in order for the limitation period to be triggered. *Id.*

10. *See Smith v. Washington*, 716 N.E.2d 607, 615-16 (Ind. App. 1999), *aff'd in part, vacated in part on other grounds*, 734 N.E.2d 548 (Ind. 2000).

11. The Act indicates that, except on agreement of all parties or in cases involving damages under $15,000, an action cannot be commenced before the proposed complaint has been presented to the medical review panel established under Indiana Code § 34-18-10. Ind. Code §§ 34-18-8-4 to 34-18-8-6 (1998). However, effective July 1, 1999, a plaintiff may commence an action at the same time as the proposed complaint is being considered by the Medical Review Panel, if the complaint filed with the court contains no information to allow identification of the defendants, and no action is taken. Ind. Code § 34-18-8-7 (1998).

12. Ind. Code § 34-18-7-3 (1998).

13. Ind. Code §§ 34-11-2-4 (1998) and 34-20-3-1 (1998).

14. *Id. See McIntosh v. Melroe Co., A Division of Clark*, 729 N.E.2d 972 (Ind. 2000) (upholding the statute of repose against constitutional challenges). *But see Jurich v. Garlock, Inc.*, 759 N.E.2d 1066 (Ind. App. 2001) (holding that the statute of repose was unconstitutional as applied to a plaintiff whose claim existed prior to the statute's enactment). The repose period may be extended under limited circumstances provided for in the statute.

15. Ind. Code §§ 34-20-3-1 and 34-20-3-2 (1998). The statutes provide an exception to the ten-year statute of repose generally applicable to products liability actions. However, the exception may not apply to sellers of as-

bestos-containing products, which are distinguished from commercial asbestos. *Jurich*, 759 N.E.2d at 1070-71.

16. *Holmes v. Acands, Inc.*, 709 N.E.2d 36, 44 (Ind. App. 1999), *affirmed on rehearing in part*, 711 N.E.2d 1289, *transfer denied* (interpreting the wrongful death and asbestos statutes and holding that a cause of action for wrongful death as a result of exposure to asbestos does not accrue until the decedent's death and is not barred if filed less than two years after the decedent's death).

17. Ind. Code § 24-5-0.5-5 (1996). The Deceptive Sales Act specifically requires an action to be commenced within two years "after the occurrence of the deceptive act." *Id.* However, as a general rule statutes of limitation are subject to the doctrine of fraudulent concealment, the application of which might estop a defendant from asserting the benefit of the limitations period. *See* Ind. Code § 34-11-5-1 (1998); *Southerland v. Hammond*, 693 N.E.2d 74, 78 (Ind. App. 1998).

18. Ind. Code § 24-5-0.5-5(a) (1996).

19. Ind. Code § 34-11-2-7 (1998). *See also Wells v. Stone City Bank*, 691 N.E.2d 1246 (Ind. App. 1998) (applying the six-year statute of limitations to claims for alleged damages resulting from a bank's failure to honor checks based on a contract not in writing and constructive fraud).

20. Ind. Code § 34-11-1-2 (1998).

21. Ind. Code § 34-11-6-1 (1998).

22. *See, e.g.*, Ind. Code § 34-18-7-2 (1998) (indicating that the generally applicable two-year statute of limitations in medical malpractice cases applies to claims by minors or those under legal disability); Ind. Code § 34-13-3-9 (1998) (indicating that the notice period for claims against governmental entities is extended for 180 days after incapacity is removed).

23. Ind. Code § 29-1-14-1 (Supp. 2001).

24. *Id.* Ind. Code § 29-1-14-1(d) (Supp. 2001).

25. *See* Ind. Code § 29-1-14-1(c) (Supp. 2001) (indicating that no claim shall be barred by the statute of limitations that was not barred at the time of the decedent's death if it is filed within five months after the first published notice to creditors); Ind. Code § 34-11-7-1 (1998) (indicating that if a liable party dies before the expiration of the time limit for an action against the party, the cause of action survives against the person's representatives and may be brought after the expiration of the limitations period within 18 months after death). The interplay between these two sections is not clear.

26. Ind. Code § 29-1-14-1(f) (Supp. 2001). Section 29-1-14-1(f) goes on to say: "A tort claim against the estate of the tort feasor may be opened or reopened and suit filed against the special representative of the estate within the period of the statute of limitations of the tort. Any recovery against the tort feasor's estate shall not affect any interest in the assets of the estate unless the suit was filed within the time allowed for filing claims against the estate."

27. Ind. Code § 34-11-7-1 (1998).

28. Ind. Code § 32-15-1-2 (Supp. 2001).

29. *Id. See also* Ind. Code § 32-15-1-1(4) (Supp. 1999) (defining the "date of substantial completion").

30. *See Berns Const. Co. v. Miller*, 491 N.E.2d 565, 572 (Ind. App. 1986), *aff'd*, 516 N.E.2d 1053 (Ind. 1987) (applying the two-year personal injury statute of limitation).

31. Ind. Code § 32-15-1-3 (Supp. 2001).

32. Ind. Code § 32-15-1-4 (Supp. 2001).

33. Ind. Code § 34-13-3-6 (1998). Substantial compliance with the statutory notice requirements may suffice. *Porter v. Ft. Wayne Community Schools*, 743 N.E.2d 341 (Ind. App. 2001), *transfer denied*.

34. Ind. Code § 34-13-3-8 (1998).

35. Ind. Code § 34-13-3-9 (1998).

36. Ind. Code § 9-25-4-1 (1997).

37. *See Allstate Ins. Co. v. United Farm Bureau Mutual Ins. Co.*, 618 N.E.2d 31, 34 (Ind. App. 1993).

38. Ind. Code § 9-25-4-4 (1997).

39. Ind. Code § 9-25-4-5 (1997).

40. *See Harris v. Raymond*, 715 N.E.2d 388, 393 (Ind. 1999) *reh'g denied*; *Delta Tau Delta v. Johnson*, 712 N.E.2d 968, 970–71 (Ind. 1999). Indiana recognizes a cause of action for an increased risk of harm. *Alexander v. Scheid*, 726 N.E.2d 272, 281 (Ind. 2000). Damages in such cases are measured by an award in proportion to the increased risk attributable to the defendant's negligence. *Smith v. Washington*, 734 N.E.2d 548, 551 (Ind. 2000).

41. *Harris*, 715 N.E.2d at 393.

42. *Prior v. GTE North Inc.*, 681 N.E.2d 768, 771 n.2 (Ind. App. 1997), *transfer denied*, 690 N.E.2d 1189.

43. *E.g., Osterman v. Baber*, 714 N.E.2d 735, 738 n.5 (Ind. App. 1999), *transfer denied*. As a general rule, no exception is made for a person with mental disabilities, but under certain circumstances no duty of care may exist. *Creasy v. Rusk*, 730 N.E.2d 659 (Ind. 2000) (patient with Alzheimer's disease owed no duty of care to nursing assistant in residential care facility).

44. *Harris v. Raymond*, 715 N.E.2d 388, 393–94 (Ind. 1999), *reh'g denied*.

45. *Creasy*, 730 N.E.2d at 662.

46. *Baller v. Corle*, 490 N.E.2d 382, 385 (Ind. App. 1986), *reh'g denied, transfer denied*.

47. *Bixenman v. Hall*, 242 N.E.2d 837, 840 (Ind. 1968).

48. *Creasy*, 730 N.E.2d at 662.

49. *Best Homes, Inc. v. Rainwater*, 714 N.E.2d 702, 706 (Ind. App. 1999); Ind. Code § 34-51-2-3 (1998).

50. Ind. Code § 34-51-2-3 (1998).

51. *Control Techniques, Inc. v. Johnson*, 762 N.E.2d 104, 108 (Ind. 2002); *Basicker v. Denny's, Inc.*, 704 N.E.2d 1077, 1080 (Ind. App. 1999), *reh'g denied, transfer denied*.

52. *Roberson v. Hicks*, 694 N.E.2d 1161, 1163 (Ind. App. 1998), *transfer denied*.

53. *Vernon v. Kroger Co.*, 712 N.E.2d 976, 981 (Ind. 1999). *See also Control Techniques*, 762 N.E.2d at 108.

54. Ind. Code § 34-51-2-1 *et seq.*

55. Ind. Code § 34-6-2-45(b) (1998) defines "fault" as including "any act or omission that is negligent, willful, wanton, reckless, or intentional toward the person or property of others. The term also includes unreasonable assumption of risk not constituting an enforceable express consent, incurred risk, and unreasonable failure to avoid an injury or to mitigate damage." *See also* Ind. Code § 34-20-8-1 (Supp. 2001) (applying comparative fault principles to product liability actions but allowing consideration of all causal fault regardless of whether a person could have been named as a party).

56. Ind. Code §§ 34-51-2-1 (1998) & 34-51-2-2 (1998).

57. Ind. Code §§ 34-51-2-5 (1998), 34-51-2-6 (1998), & 34-6-2-45(b) (1998). *See generally Hopper v. Carey*, 716 N.E.2d 566, 575–77 (Ind. App. 1999), *transfer denied, Hopper v. Scott County Hwy. Dept.*, 735 N.E.2d 227 (Ind. 2000).

58. *See Blackburn v. City of Rochester*, 640 N.E.2d 1068, 1070 (Ind. App. 1994). Thus, a plaintiff's contributory negligence will bar recovery regardless of the defendant's negligence, as long as it proximately contributed to his injuries. *Hapner v. State*, 699 N.E.2d 1200, 1205 (Ind. App. 1998); *Nesvig v. Town of Porter*, 668 N.E.2d 1276, 1280 (Ind. App. 1996).

59. *Hopper v. Carey*, 716 N.E.2d 566, 575–77 (Ind. App. 1999), *transfer denied*.

60. *E.g., Rouch v. Bisig*, 258 N.E.2d 883, 888 (Ind. App. 1970).

61. Ind. Code § 34-6-2-45(b) (1998); *Mark v. Moser*, 746 N.E.2d 410, 414 (Ind. App. 2001).

62. *Ooms v. USX Corp.*, 661 N.E.2d 1250, 1255 (Ind. App. 1996), *transfer denied*. It should be noted, however, that the Court of Appeals has held that "voluntary participants in sports activities assume the inherent foreseeable dangers of the activity and cannot recover for injury unless it can be established that the other participant either intentionally caused injury or engaged in conduct so reckless as to be totally outside the range of ordinary activity involved in the sport." *Mark v. Moser*, 746 N.E.2d 410, 420 (Ind. App. 2001).

63. *See Compton v. Pletch*, 580 N.E.2d 664, 664 (Ind. 1991).

64. *Cartwright v. Harris*, 400 N.E.2d 1192, 1195 (Ind. App. 1980).

65. Ind. Code § 34-51-2-6 (1998). *See Smith v. Beaty*, 639 N.E.2d 1029, 1035 (Ind. App. 1994).

66. Ind. Code § 34-51-2-7 (1998).

67. *Id*.

68. *Id*.

69. Ind. Code § 34-51-2-12 (1998); *see Control Techniques*, 762 N.E.2d at 109; *City of Vincennes v. Reuhl*, 672 N.E.2d 495, 498 (Ind. App. 1996) *reh'g denied, transfer denied*, 690 N.E.2d 1187 (Ind. 1997); *Indianapolis Power & Light Co. v. Brad Snodgrass, Inc.*, 578 N.E.2d 669, 673 (Ind. 1991). However, the Act does not affect indemnity rights. Ind. Code § 34-51-2-12. It should be noted that a defendant against whom a judgment is rendered is not entitled to a credit for money paid by a settling co-defendant who has not been added back into consideration under the third-party provisions of the Comparative Fault Act. *Mendenhall v. Skinner*, 728 N.E.2d 140, 145 (Ind. 2000).

70. Ind. Code § 34-51-2-10 (1998).

71. *See Huffman v. Monroe County Community School Corp.*, 588 N.E.2d 1264, 1267 (Ind. 1992). It should be noted, however, that a settlement and release of a responsible third party where there has been a work-related injury may preclude the filing of a claim for workers' compensation benefits. *Waldridge v. Futurex Industries, Inc.*, 714 N.E.2d 783, 787 (Ind. App. 1999), *reh'g denied, transfer denied.*

72. Ind. Code § 34-51-2-14 (1998). A nonparty is defined as "a person who caused or contributed to cause the alleged injury, death, or damage to property but who has not been joined in the action as a defendant." Ind. Code § 34-6-2-88 (1998). It should be noted, however, that an employer may be named as a non-party in an employee's tort action, allowing a percentage of the fault to be attributed to the employer. Ind. Code § 34-6-2-88 (1998); *Estate of Robinson v. C&I Leasing, Inc.*, 691 N.E.2d 474, 476 (Ind. App. 1998), *transfer denied.*

73. Ind. Code § 34-51-2-15 (1998).

74. Ind. Code § 34-51-2-16 (1998).

75. *See Cornell Harbison Excavating, Inc. v. May*, 546 N.E.2d 1186, 1187 (Ind. 1989).

76. *See Indianapolis Power & Light Co.*, 578 N.E.2d at 672; *Walters v. Dean*, 497 N.E.2d 247, 253 (Ind. App. 1986).

77. Ind. Code § 34-51-2-15 (1998).

78. *See Edwards v. Sisler*, 691 N.E.2d 1252, 1254–55 (Ind. App. 1998).

79. *See Narducci v. Tedrow*, 736 N.E.2d 1288, 1292-93 (Ind. App. 2000); *Slease v. Hughbanks*, 684 N.E.2d 496, 499 (Ind. App. 1997). *See also Gold v. Ishak*, 720 N.E.2d 1175, 1181 (Ind. App. 1999), *transfer denied* (discussing the element of "exclusive control").

80. *Inland Steel v. Pequignot*, 608 N.E.2d 1378, 1384–85 (Ind. App. 1993), *transfer denied* (citing the Restatement of Torts 2d §§ 519 & 520).

81. *Erbrich Products Co. v. Wills*, 509 N.E.2d 850, 856 (Ind. App. 1987), *reh'g denied, transfer denied.*

82. *Id.*

83. *Id.* at 857.

84. *Kelly v. Ladywood Apts.*, 622 N.E.2d 1044, 1048 n.1 (Ind. App. 1993), *reh'g denied, transfer denied* (citing Restatement of Torts (Second) § 342).

85. *Duneland School Corp. v. Bailey*, 701 N.E.2d 878, 881 (Ind. App. 1998).

86. *Carroll v. Jobe*, 638 N.E.2d 467, 469 (Ind. App. 1994), *reh'g denied, transfer denied*.

87. *Lever Bros. Co. v. Langdoc*, 655 N.E.2d 577, 580 (Ind. App. 1995).

88. *First Nat'l Bank v. City of Portage*, 590 N.E.2d 1110, 1112 n.3 (Ind. App. 1992), *transfer denied*.

89. *Indian Trucking v. Harber*, 752 N.E.2d 168, 172-73 (Ind. App. 2001); *National R.R. Passenger Corp. v. Everton*, 655 N.E.2d 360, 366 (Ind. App. 1995), *transfer denied*.

90. *E.Z. Gas, Inc. v. Hydrocarbon Transp., Inc.*, 471 N.E.2d 316, 321 (Ind. App. 1984).

91. Ind. Code §§ 34-51-2-8 (1998) & 34-51-2-9 (1998).

92. *Mullen v. Cogdell*, 643 N.E.2d 390, 400 (Ind. App. 1994), *reh'g denied, transfer denied* (there is no contribution among joint tortfeasors and no exceptions to the rule that there can be no indemnity if the party seeking indemnification is guilty of actual negligence); Ind. Code § 34-51-2-12 (1998). However, the Comparative Fault Act does not affect indemnity rights. Ind. Code § 34-51-2-12.

93. *R.N. Thompson & Assocs. v. Wickes Lumber Co.*, 687 N.E.2d 617, 619 (Ind. App. 1997), *transfer denied*, 698 N.E.2d 1188 (Ind. 1998).

94. *Rotec v. Murray Equipment, Inc.*, 626 N.E.2d 533, 535 (Ind. App. 1993), *reh'g denied*.

95. *Mullen*, 643 N.E.2d at 400.

96. *See Huber v. Henley*, 669 F. Supp. 1474, 1481 (S.D. Ind. 1987).

97. *Plan-Tec, Inc. v. Wiggins*, 443 N.E.2d 1212, 1221 (Ind. App. 1983). *But see* Ind. Code § 26-2-5-1 (1999) (clauses in construction and design contracts purporting to indemnify the promisee from his own negligence or willful conduct are against public policy and are unenforceable).

98. *See General Bargain Center v. American Alarm Co.*, 430 N.E.2d 407, 411–12 (Ind. App. 1982); *Weaver v. American Oil Co.*, 276 N.E.2d 144, 148 (Ind. 1971).

99. *Weaver*, 276 N.E.2d at 148.

100. *Hagerman Constr., Inc. v. Long Electric Co.*, 741 N.E.2d 390 (Ind. App. 2000), *transfer denied*; *Plan-Tec*, 443 N.E.2d at 1221.

101. Ind. Code § 22-3-2-6 (1997). The Workers' Compensation Act does not apply to an employee's actions against his employer for intentional infliction of emotional distress if the employee is not seeking damages for physical injuries. *See Perry v. Stitzer Buick GMC, Inc.*, 637 N.E.2d 1282, 1288–89 (Ind. 1994), *reh'g denied*.

102. *Baker v. Westinghouse Elec. Corp.*, 637 N.E.2d 1271, 1273 (Ind. 1994).

103. *Id.* at 1274; *Branham v. Celadon Trucking Services, Inc.*, 744 N.E.2d 514, 520 (Ind. App. 2001), *transfer denied*.

104. *Id.* at 1275.

105. *Perry v. Stitzer Buick GMC, Inc.*, 637 N.E.2d 1282, 1287 (Ind. 1994).

106. Ind. Code § 22-3-2-8 (Supp. 2001).

107. Ind. Code § 22-3-2-13 (Supp. 2001).

108. *Win-Settergren v. Lamey*, 716 N.E.2d 381, 387 (Ind. 1999); *Lutz v. DeMars*, 559 N.E.2d 1194, 1996-97 (Ind. App. 1990), *transfer denied*.

109. Ind. Code § 22-3-2-13 (Supp. 2001).

110. *Koval v. Simon Telelect, Inc.*, 693 N.E.2d 1299, 1309 (Ind. 1998). A settlement and release of a responsible third party may preclude the filing of a workers' compensation claim for a work-related injury. *Waldridge*, 714 N.E.2d at 787.

111. Ind. Code § 22-3-2-13 (Supp. 2001).

112. *Taylor v. Duke*, 713 N.E.2d 877, 881 (Ind. App. 1999). An invitee may be a public invitee, business visitor or social guest. *Id.* The required standard of care applicable to invitees is higher than that applied to licensees and trespassers, who are defined as those who enter the land of another for their own convenience, curiosity, or entertainment and take the premises as they find them. *Id.*

113. *Id.* Willful or wanton conduct is conduct that is so grossly deviant from everyday standards that a trespasser or licensee cannot be expected to anticipate it. *Id.* at 882.

114. *Id. at 881.*

115. *Id.*

116. *Id.*

117. *See Vernon v. Kroger Co.*, 712 N.E.2d 976, 980 (Ind. 1999); *Delta Tau Delta v. Johnson*, 712 N.E.2d 968, 973 (Ind. 1999). *But see Ellis v. Luxbury Hotels, Inc.*, 716 N.E.2d 359, 361 (Ind. 1999) (holding that there was no duty because the criminal act in question was not foreseeable); *L.W. v. Western Golf Ass'n*, 712 N.E.2d 983, 985 (Ind. 1999) (same).

118. *Miles v. Christensen*, 724 N.E.2d 643, 646 (Ind. App. 2000), *transfer denied*. However, there is generally no duty arising as a result of conditions on adjacent property. *Ward v. First Indiana Plaza Joint Venture*, 725 N.E.2d 134 (Ind. App. 2000), *transfer denied*; *Sizemore v. Templeton Oil Co.*, 724 N.E.2d 647, 653 (Ind. App. 2000).

119. Ind. Code § 7.1-5-10-15 (Supp. 2001). *See generally Delta Tau Delta*, 712 N.E.2d at 974. Liability may be imposed on family members, friends, and other individuals who furnished alcohol, as well as on establishments with liquor licenses. *Vanderhoek v. Willy*, 728 N.E.2d 213, 218 (Ind. App. 2000).

120. Ind. Code § 7.1-5-10-15.5 (1996); *Ward v. D&A Enterprises of Clark County, Inc.*, 714 N.E.2d 728, 729 (Ind. App. 1999); *Delta Tau Delta*, 712 N.E.2d at 974. If there is a breach of duty but the injury was caused by unforeseen intervening cause, the one who furnished alcohol is not liable. *See Fast Eddie's v. Hall*, 688 N.E.2d 1270, 1274–75 (Ind. App. 1997), *reh'g denied, transfer denied*.

121. *Ward*, 714 N.E.2d at 729–30; *Delta Tau Delta*, 712 N.E.2d at 974.

122. *See Booker, Inc. v. Morrill*, 639 N.E.2d 358, 361 (Ind. App. 1996) (holding that a dram shop action for the wrongful death of the intoxicated person was not barred and affirming a jury verdict in favor of the decedent's estate).

123. Ind. Code § 34-6-2-45 (1998); *Booker*, 639 N.E.2d at 361–62.

124. *Prairie Productions, Inc. v. Agchem Div.-Pennwalt Corp.*, 514 N.E.2d 1299, 1304 (Ind. 1987), *reh'g denied, quoted in Reed v. Central Soya Co.*, 621 N.E.2d 1069, 1074 (Ind. 1993), *modified on other grounds*, 644 N.E.2d 84 (Ind. 1994).

125. *Reed*, 621 N.E.2d at 1074.

126. *Bamberger & Feibleman v. Indianapolis Power & Light Co.*, 665 N.E.2d 933, 938 (Ind. App. 1996).

127. *Reed*, 621 N.E.2d at 1074–75.

128. *Fleetwood Enterprises, Inc. v. Progressive Northern Ins. Co.*, 749 N.E.2d 492 (Ind. 2001).

129. *Wells v. Stone City Bank*, 691 N.E.2d 1246, 1250 (Ind. App. 1998), *transfer denied*, 706 N.E.2d 166 (Ind. 1998), *called into doubt on other grounds; Solnik v. Guardian Life Ins. Co.*, 94 F. Supp. 2d 998 (S.D. Ind. 2000).

130. *Id.* at 1250.

131. *Id.* at 1250–51. In order to establish constructive fraud, the complaining party must have a right to reasonably rely on the representations made or omitted. *Marathon Oil Co. v. Collins*, 744 N.E.2d 474, 481 (Ind. App. 2001).

132. *Wells*, 691 N.E.2d at 1250; *Gable v. Curtis*, 673 N.E.2d 805, 811 (Ind. App. 1996).

133. *Darst v. Illinois Farmers Ins. Co.*, 716 N.E.2d 579, 581 (Ind. App. 1999), *transfer denied*.

134. Ind. Code §§ 24-5-0.5-1–24-5-0.5-10 (1996 & Supp. 2001).

135. Ind. Code § 24-5-0.5-4 (1996). *See also* Ind. Code §§ 24-5-0.5-3 (Supp. 2001) and 24-5-0.5-10 (Supp. 2001) (specifying acts constituting deceptive acts).

136. Ind. Code § 24-5-0.5-4 (1996).

137. Ind. Code §§ 24-5-0.5-4(h) (1996) & 24-5-0.5-2(10) (Supp. 2001).

138. Ind. Code §§ 24-5-0.5-4(c) (1996) & 24-5-0.5-8 (1996).

139. *See* Ind. Code § 24-5-0.5-5(a) (1996).

140. *Id. See also A.B.C. Home & Real Estate Inspection, Inc. v. Plummer*, 500 N.E.2d 1257 (Ind. App. 1996), *reh'g denied*.

141. *See Southerland v. Hammond*, 693 N.E.2d 74, 78 (Ind. App. 1998).

142. Ind. Code § 24-1 (1996).

143. Ind. Code §§ 24-2-1-1 *et seq.* (1996)

144. Ind. Code §§ 24-2-3-1 *et seq.* (1996)

145. Ind. Code § 24-4.5 (1996 & Supp. 2001).

146. Ind. Code § 24-8 (1996).

147. *See* Ind. Code § 34-51-3-2 (1998); *see Foster v. Evergreen Health Care Inc.*, 716 N.E.2d 19, 24 (Ind. App. 1999), *transfer denied; Northern Indiana Public Service Co. v. G.V.K. Corp.*, 713 N.E.2d 842, 849 (Ind. App. 1999), *reh'g denied, transfer denied.*

148. *Durham v. U-Haul Int'l*, 745 N.E.2d 755, 763 (Ind. 2001), *reh'g denied.*

149. *Foster v. Evergreen Healthcare, Inc.*, 716 N.E.2d 19, 24 (Ind. App. 1999), *transfer denied*, 725 N.E.2d 223.

150. Ind. Code § 34-51-3-2 (1998).

151. *See Erie Ins. Co. v. Hickman*, 622 N.E.2d 515, 523 (Ind. 1993).

152. Ind. Code § 34-51-3-5 (1998).

153. Ind. Code § 34-51-3-6 (1998).

154. *Id.* However, in *Cheathan v. Pohle*, 764 N.E.2d 272 (Ind. App. 2002), the Court of Appeals recently held that the statute was unconstitutional to the extent it allowed the state to recover 75 percent of the punitive damages without any obligation to pay attorney's fees.

155. Ind. Code § 34-51-3-3 (1998).

156. Ind. Code § 34-24-3-1 (1998). Recovery may be allowed from a defendant whose negligence significantly increases the probability of death. *Cahoon v. Cummings*, 734 N.E.2d 535, 539-40 (Ind. 2000).

157. Ind. Code § 34-23-1-1 (1998).

158. *Hosler v. Caterpillar, Inc.*, 710 N.E.2d 193, 196–97 (Ind. App. 1999), *transfer denied.*

159. Ind. Code §§ 34-23-1-1 (1998) & 34-23-1-2 (Supp. 2001). Loss of consortium damages are recoverable under the Act if the defendant's negligence caused or accelerated the other spouse's death. *Durham*, 745 N.E.2d at 766, *overruling Burk v. Anderson*, 109 N.E.2d 407, 408-09 (Ind. 1952).

160. Ind. Code § 34-23-1-2 (Supp. 1999).

161. *Id.*

162. Ind. Code § 34-23-2-1 (1998). A child is defined as an unmarried individual without dependents who is less than 20 years old or less than 23 years old and enrolled in an institution of higher education or vocational studies. *Id. See City of Terre Haute v. Simpson*, 746 N.E.2d 359, 366 (Ind. App 2001),

transfer denied (21 year old enrolled in school was a child within the meaning of the Act); *Ledbetter v. Ball Memorial Hosp.*, 724 N.E.2d 1113, 1117 (Ind. App. 2000), *transfer denied* (noting that in order to fall within the definition of a "child," a person over the age of twenty and under the age of twenty-three must actually be enrolled in school).

163. Ind. Code § 34-23-2-1. *See Elkhart Community School v. Yoder*, 696 N.E.2d 409 (Ind. App. 1998). Failure to join both parents makes an action subject to dismissal, but a defendant's failure to raise the issue of nonjoinder results in waiver of that issue. *City of Terre Haute v. Simpson*, 746 N.E.2d 359, 364-65 (Ind. App. 2001).

164. Ind. Code § 34-23-2-1. Where there is no evidence of any pecuniary loss to one parent, the other parent may receive 100 percent of the damages. *Hardiman v. Adkins*, 738 N.E.2d 693, 695 (Ind. App. 2000).

165. *Robinson v. Wroblewski*, 704 N.E.2d 467, 476 (Ind. 1998).

166. *City of Indianapolis v. Taylor*, 707 N.E.2d 1047, 1060–62 (Ind. App. 1999), *transfer denied*, 726 N.E.2d 309 (Ind. App. 1999).

167. *Cahoon v. Cummings*, 734 N.E.2d at 543.

168. Ind. Code § 34-9-3-1 (1998). *See Cahoon*, 734 N.E.2d at 542-43, and *Estate of Sears v. Griffin*, 752 N.E.2d 210, 216 (Ind. App. 2001) (indicating that a claim for personal injury does not survive death unless the death resulted from causes other than those alleged to have caused the personal injury claim).

169. *Id.*

170. Ind. Code § 34-9-3-4 (1998).

171. Ind. Code § 34-9-3-5 (1998).

IOWA

A. STATUTES OF LIMITATION

Causes of action founded on injuries to the person or reputation based upon either contract or tort must be brought within two years after accrual.[1] Iowa has adopted the "discovery rule" to apply to all personal injury causes of action.[2] Causes of action founded on injuries to property, unwritten contracts, and fraud must be brought within five years.[3] Causes of action founded on written contracts must be brought within ten years.[4] Professional malpractice causes of action, including those against physicians and dentists, must be brought within two years.[5] However, actions brought against attorneys are governed by a 5-year statute of limitations.[6] The discovery rule is also applicable to professional malpractice cases.[7]

Causes of action against the state of Iowa must be brought by filing a claim with the State Appeal Board within two years after the claim accrues.[8]

Consumer Credit Code violations must be brought within one year from the date of occurrence of the violation.[9]

A "catch-all" provision for causes of action not specifically covered by another limitation section provides for a five-year statute of limitations.[10]

B. TORT REFORM

There is currently pending House File 114, which proposes certain changes to tort law in Iowa. The heart of the bill involves legislation that would regulate the admissibility of expert testimony. The pending legislation would also serve to abolish joint and several liability among joint tortfeasors. House File 693, passed in 1997, provided the following changes to tort law in Iowa: (1) the interest rate on all judgments now accrues at the treasury bill rate plus 2 percent; (2) a plaintiff's comparative fault now applies to his or her spouse's loss of consortium claim; and (3) Iowa courts must now adjust all future damage awards to reflect present value.

C. "NO FAULT" LIMITATIONS

Current Iowa motor vehicle laws do not provide "no fault" insurance for motor vehicle accidents. Further, the Iowa Legislature has not provided for a "limited tort option" or a "full tort option" for individuals involved in motor vehicle accidents.

D. THE STANDARD FOR NEGLIGENCE

Iowa negligence law provides that the plaintiff must first show the defendant had a legal duty to conform to a standard of conduct that existed between the plaintiff and defendant at the time of the incident.[11] In deciding whether a legal duty exists, three factors govern a court's analysis: (1) the relationship of the parties; (2) the reasonable foreseeability of harm to the injured person; and (3) public policy considerations.[12] Once the plaintiff shows that a duty existed, the plaintiff must then show that the defendant breached that duty or failed to conform to the requisite standard of conduct.[13]

A legal duty or certain standard of conduct of a reasonable person may also be established by legislative enactment or by judicial decision.[14]

When a "professional" is involved thereby creating a special relationship between the parties, a professional standard of care is recognized that imposes a higher standard of care on the professional.[15]

Generally, a person does not have a duty to aid or protect another, or to control the conduct of a third person to prevent that person from causing harm to another.[16] However, exceptions to the foregoing rule exist when a special relationship exists between the parties that imposes a duty on the actor to control the third person's conduct, or when the special relationship is such between the actor and the other that a duty to provide protection exists.[17]

Iowa has abolished any presumptions regarding the capacity of children for negligence.[18] The question of capacity is an issue of fact to be determined subjectively on the basis of evidence of the child's age, intelligence, and experience.[19] Assuming the child has capable capacity, the standard of care is the objective test of a child of similar capacity under similar circumstances.[20] However, when a child is engaging in adult activities, Iowa law does not take age into account.[21]

Pursuant to Iowa law, everyone is presumed to have discharged his or her duty in a non-negligent fashion until the contrary is made to appear.[22] Further, mere occurrence of an injury does not give rise to an inference of negligence.[23]

E. **CAUSATION**

In order for a plaintiff to recover under a negligence cause of action, the plaintiff must prove both the negligence of the defendant and that the negligence was the proximate causey of the injury.[24] Causation has two components: (1) defendant's conduct must have in fact caused plaintiff's damages; and (2) a policy of law must require that the defendant be held legally responsible.[25] Under Iowa law, the causation requirement is satisfied when the harm would not have occurred "but for" the negligence of the defendant, and the negligence of the defendant was a "substantial factor" in bringing about the plaintiff's harm.[26]

F. **CONTRIBUTORY NEGLIGENCE, COMPARATIVE FAULT, ASSUMPTION OF RISK, AND OTHER RELATED DEFENSES**

1. **Contributory Negligence**

The adoption of the Iowa Comparative Fault Act[27] subsumed all cases in which contributory negligence was previously a defense, thereby abolishing contributory negligence as an absolute bar to recovery and establishing comparative fault as the governing principle in Iowa tort cases.[28]

2. **Comparative "Fault"**[29]

The Iowa Comparative Fault Act covers any "party"[30] and applies to tortious conduct that is negligent or reckless or subjects a person to strict tort liability or breach of warranty.[31] Pursuant to the Iowa Comparative Fault Act, a claimant's comparative fault reduces recovery in proportion to the fault percentage attributable to the claimant.[32] However, if the claimant bears a greater percentage of fault than the combined total attributed to the defendant(s), third-party defendant(s), and/or released person(s), then the claimant is barred from any recovery.[33] In other words, if the claimant is assigned more than 50 percent fault, the claim is barred.

3. **Assumption of Risk, Unreasonable Failure to Mitigate Damages, Avoidable Consequences, and Last Clear Chance**

The assumption of risk and failure to mitigate damages defenses are now subsumed within the Iowa Comparative Fault Act's definition of "fault."[34] Iowa also recognizes the avoidable consequences doctrine as a defense that states that a party cannot recover damages that result from consequences that the party could reasonably have avoided by his or her conduct after the defendant's prior negligent act.[35] The enactment of the Iowa Comparative Fault Act has also resulted in the abolition of the last clear chance doctrine as a separate defense.[36]

G. *RES IPSA LOQUITUR* AND INHERENTLY DANGEROUS ACTIVITIES

1. *Res Ipsa Loquitur*

In Iowa, the doctrine of *res ipsa loquitur* permits an inference of negligence based on the happening of an incident.[37] The doctrine of *res ipsa loquitur* applies if the plaintiff has shown both of the following: (1) the injury is caused by an instrumentality under the exclusive control of the defendant; and (2) the occurrence is such as in the ordinary course of things would not happen if reasonable care had been used.[38] The doctrine of *res ipsa loquitur* does not relieve a plaintiff of his or her burden to prove negligence; rather, it permits, but does not compel, a factfinder to infer negligence from the occurrence of an injury.[39]

2. **Inherently Dangerous Activities**

Pursuant to Iowa law, if an activity or instrumentality is deemed to be abnormally or inherently dangerous or ultrahazardous, then strict liability, not negligence, principles and standards apply.[40]

H. NEGLIGENCE *PER SE*

According to Iowa law, a party is *per se* negligent if: (1) a statute or regulation provides for a rule of conduct specifically designed for the safety and protection of a certain class of persons, (2) and a person within that class receives injuries as a proximate result of the violation of the statute or regulation, (3) and the harm incurred is the type or kind that the statute or regulation was intended to prevent.[41]

I. JOINT AND SEVERAL LIABILITY

Pursuant to Iowa law, if one act of negligence concurs or combines with another, and if each meets the proximate cause test, then resulting concurrent liability renders each act jointly and severally liable to the claimant for the resulting injury.[42] However, the foregoing rule is modified by the Iowa Comparative Fault Act, which provides that a defendant found to bear less than 50 percent of the total fault is responsible only for that amount of fault allocated to him or her thereby removing the burden of joint and several liability from defendants bearing less than 50 percent fault.[43] Correspondingly, a defendant found to bear 50 percent or more of the total fault amount is jointly and severally liable for the total damages awarded to the claimant.[44]

J. CONTRIBUTION AND INDEMNITY

The Iowa Comparative Fault Act also provides guidelines and procedures for contribution by and among joint tortfeasors.[45] Pursuant to Iowa law, contribution is available when two or more persons are liable to the claimant for an indivisible claim arising out of the same harm.[46] A party may bring a contribution claim either in the original action or in a separate action so long as the separate action is commenced within one year following final judgment in the original action.[47]

Under certain circumstances, the Iowa Comparative Fault Act provides for a right to contribution to a party who settles with the claimant.[48] The Iowa Comparative Fault Act also allows the claimant to release a liable party and insulate that party from liability for contribution without discharging other liable parties based on the same claim, but any claim by the released party against others is reduced by the amount of the released party's equitable share of fault.[49]

Indemnity is a form of restitution founded on equitable principles that is allowed where one person has discharged an obligation that another should bear thereby laying the final responsibility where equity would lay the ultimate burden.[50] However, indemnity is limited to the following circumstances: (1) express contract; (2) vicarious liability; or (3) breach of an independent duty of an indemnitor to an indemnitee.[51] The doctrine of indemnity based on active-passive negligence has been abandoned in Iowa.[52]

K. BAR OF WORKERS' COMPENSATION STATUTE

Pursuant to the Iowa Workers' Compensation Act,[53] an employer's liability to its employee is governed by the Act and is not dependent on a finding of negligence.[54] Workers' compensation law states that the employer provides, secures, or pays compensation for any and all injuries sustained by an employee arising out of and in the course of employment, and, by doing so, the employer is relieved from any other or further liability for the personal injury.[55] The Iowa Workers' Compensation Act bars traditional common law tort recovery by an employee from the employer for injuries sustained in the course of employment.[56] As such, the Act is the employee's exclusive remedy against the employer.[57] Workers' compensation actions must be brought within two years from the date of injury unless, the injured worker received weekly compensation benefits for the injury, then the statute of limitations is 3 years from the date of the last weekly compensation benefit.[58]

If an injured employee fails to bring an action against a third-party tortfeasor, then the employer or the employer's workers' compensation insurer has a right of subrogation and may maintain an action against the third-party tortfeasor.[59] Also, Iowa workers' compensation law provides an employer or the employer's insurer a statutory right to be indemnified and to have a lien on any recovery or judgment entered in an action against a third-party tortfeasor.[60] However, a workers' compensation insurance carrier who fails to timely file notice of a lien against a claimant's/employee's recovery loses its lien.[61]

L. PREMISES LIABILITY

Iowa law recently abolished the legal distinction between invitees and licensees in premises liability cases.[62] Iowa law has adopted the Restatement with regard to premises liability and also recognizes that owners and occupiers of land are not insurers of their premises.[63] Rather, the duty placed on owners and occupiers of land is to exercise reasonable care in the maintenance of their premises for the protection of lawful visitors with a variety of factors to be considered in evaluating whether an owner or occupier has exercised reasonable care.[64]

Iowa law is currently unsettled as to whether the distinction between trespassers and invitees or licensees still exists.[65] Assuming trespassers are subject to the traditional standard of care owed by land owners or occupiers pursuant to Iowa law, then the only duty owed to trespassers is to not willfully or wantonly injure them.[66]

M. DRAM SHOP LIABILITY

Iowa's Dram Shop Act[67] provides exclusive liability for a licensee or permitee in the service of alcohol to an intoxicated person.[68] It has been held that a plaintiff must prove that the defendant or one of the defendant's agents knew of the patron's intoxication at the time of service or that a readily observant person under the same or similar circumstances would have known that the patron was intoxicated.[69]

While provisions of the Iowa Comparative Fault Act[70] are not available to defendants in dram shop actions,[71] both lack of proximate cause[72] and assumption of risk[73] are viable defenses. The Dram Shop Act also expressly overrides social host liability.[74] However, an individual, other than a licensee or permittee, could be held liable to a third party for damages if they knowingly gave or otherwise supplied alcohol to a minor who, due to their intoxication, causes damages to another.[75] Also, a minor may be able to recover against another for injuries sustained due to their own intoxication, but any recovery by the minor would be subject to the Iowa Comparative Fault Act, which could bar or at least reduce the minor's recovery.[76]

N. **ECONOMIC LOSS**

Iowa law generally prohibits tort recovery for purely economic losses.[77] Further, purely economic losses without accompanying physical injury to the person or person's property is likewise prohibited in strict products liability cases.[78]

O. **FRAUD AND MISREPRESENTATION**

In order to prove fraud pursuant to Iowa law a plaintiff must show each of the following elements by clear and convincing evidence: (1) misrepresentation or failure to disclose when under a legal duty to do so; (2) materiality; (3) scienter; (4) intent to deceive; (5) justifiable reliance; and (6) resulting injury or damage.[79]

Iowa also recognizes a negligent misrepresentation cause of action in the business transaction context when the plaintiff proves the following elements: (1) the defendant in the course of his or her business, profession, or in a transaction in which he has pecuniary interest; (2) supplies false information for the guidance of others in their business transactions; and (3) supplies the information without exercising reasonable care or competence in obtaining or communicating the information.[80] If the plaintiff proves the foregoing, then the defendant subjects him- or herself to liability to the plaintiff for pecuniary loss suffered by justifiable reliance on information supplied by the defendant.[81]

The Iowa Comparative Fault Act does not apply to fraud actions.[82]

P. **CONSUMER FRAUD STATUTES**

The Iowa Consumer Credit Code[83] provides protection to consumers[84] against unfair practices by suppliers, solicitors, or collectors of consumer credit.[85] The Iowa Consumer Credit Code provides rights and remedies as well as limitations on both consumers[86] and creditors in their transactions.[87]

The Iowa Consumer Credit Code also regulates all debt collection practices[88] between debtors[89] and creditors.[90]

As previously noted, actions pursuant to the Iowa Consumer Credit Code have a one-year statute of limitations.[91]

Q. **PUNITIVE DAMAGES**

Iowa Code § 668A[92] codifies Iowa punitive damages law. The purpose of a punitive damage award is to punish a defendant for willful or malicious conduct and also to deter others from engaging in similar behavior.[93] Some actual damages must be present to support an award for punitive damages.[94] Iowa law requires a finding that the defendant acted with willful and wanton disregard for the rights or safety of the plaintiff.[95]

In determining the reasonableness of a punitive damages award, the court considers the following factors: (1) degree of reprehensibility of the defendant's conduct; (2) the ratio or relationship between the actual harm inflicted and the punitive damages award; and (3) civil penalties authorized or imposed for comparable misconduct.[96] Iowa courts have also allowed the financial condition of the defendant to be examined as well a consideration as to whether the case was an isolated incident in reviewing the appropriateness of a punitive damages award.[97]

However, punitive damages are not available in an action against the state of Iowa,[98] nor does "fault" pursuant to the Iowa Comparative Fault Act apply to reduce or bar a claimant's punitive damage claim.[99]

R. WRONGFUL DEATH AND SURVIVORSHIP ACTIONS

In Iowa, there is no common law action for wrongful death.[100] Rather, wrongful death recovery is governed strictly by statute.[101] The statute is seen as a combination of wrongful death and survival causes of action.[102]

In a wrongful death case, the general measure of damages due the estate is the present value of the estate that the decedent would have reasonably been expected to accumulate had the decedent lived to his or her normal life expectancy.[103] Punitive damages are also available to the estate,[104] as are pain and suffering damages if the death was not instantaneous.[105]

Iowa law provides by statute a cause of action to parents for the death of or injury to their minor child.[106]

Iowa law also provides for the following loss of consortium damages: (1) spousal claims;[107] (2) parent-child claims;[108] and (3) child-parent claims.[109]

Brent B. Green
Bradley C. Obermeier
DUNCAN, GREEN, BROWN, LANGENESS & ECKLEY, P.C.
400 Locust Street, Suite 380
Des Moines, Iowa 50309
(515) 288-6440
Fax (515) 288-6448
bgreen@duncangreenlaw.com
bobermeier@duncangreenlaw.com

ENDNOTES - IOWA

1. Iowa Code § 614.1(2) (1999).

2. *Chrischilles v. Griswald,* 260 Iowa 453, 150 N.W.2d 94, 100 (Iowa 1967); *see also Franzen v. Deere & Co.,* 377 N.W.2d 660, 662 (Iowa 1985) (stating that knowledge of the facts that would support a cause of action is all that is necessary to commence the statute of limitations; knowledge that the facts are actionable is unnecessary).

3. Iowa Code § 614.1(4) (1999).

4. Iowa Code § 614.1(5) (1999).

5. Iowa Code § 614.1(9) (1999).

6. *Bernard v. Winter,* 524 N.W.2d 163, 166 (Iowa 1994).

7. *See id.* (stating that in no event shall any action be brought more than six years after the date on which the act or omission occurred unless the cause of injury or death was by a foreign object unintentionally left in the body).

8. Iowa Code § 669.13 (1999).

9. Iowa Code § 537.5203(6) (1999).

10. Iowa Code § 614.1(4) (1999).

11. *Aetna Cas. and Sur. Co. v. Leo A. Daly Co.,* 870 F. Supp 925, 935 (S.D. Iowa 1994); *Godar v. Edwards,* 588 N.W.2d 701, 707 (Iowa 1999); *Rieger v. Jacque,* 584 N.W.2d 247, 250 (Iowa 1998).

12. *J.A.H. ex rel. R.M.H v. Wadle & Associates, P.C.,* 589 N.W.2d 256, 258 (Iowa 1999); *see also Lovik v. Wilrich,* 588 N.W.2d 688, 695 (Iowa 1999) (stating that the scope and parameters of the duty of care can vary depending on special circumstances faced by the defendant); *Reiger v. Jacque,* 584 N.W.2d 247, 250 (Iowa 1988) (whether a duty arises out of the parties' relationship is always a matter of law for the court).

13. *Ries v. Steffensmeier,* 570 N.W.2d 111, 114 (Iowa 1987); *see also Marcus v. Young,* 538 N.W.2d 285, 288 (Iowa 1995) (negligence defined as conduct falling below the standard established by law for the protection of others against unreasonable risk of harm).

14. *Engstrom v. State*, 461 N.W.2d 309, 315 (Iowa 1990); *Seeman v. Liberty Mut. Ins. Co.*, 322 N.W.2d 35, 37 (Iowa 1982).

15. *See Kurtenbach v. Tekippe*, 260 N.W.2d 53, 56 (Iowa 1977) (attorney has the duty to exercise ordinary care in the handling of a client's work, which duty obligates him or her to use the knowledge, skill, and ability ordinarily possessed and exercised by members of the legal profession in similar circumstances); *Bray v. Hill*, 517 N.W.2d 223, 226 (Iowa App. 1994) (doctors held to duty of reasonable care and skill, as that exercised by ordinary physician of good standing under like circumstances).

16. *Pierce v. Staley*, 587 N.W.2d 484, 487 (Iowa 1998); *Fiala v. Rains*, 519 N.W.2d 386, 389 (Iowa 1994); *Davis v. Kwik-Shop, Inc.*, 504 N.W.2d 877, 878 (Iowa 1993); *see also Husker News Co. v. South Ottumwa Sav. Bank*, 482 N.W.2d 404, 407 (Iowa 1992) (stating that there is no good-samaritan obligation to prevent the perpetration of a tort by a third party).

17. *Morgan v. Perlowski*, 508 N.W.2d 724, 726–27 (Iowa 1993); *Leonard v. State*, 491 N.W.2d 508, 510–11 (Iowa 1992).

18. *Peterson v. Taylor*, 316 N.W.2d 869, 873 (Iowa 1982).

19. *Id.*

20. *Id.*

21. *Christensen v. Kelley*, 135 N.W.2d 510, 513 (Iowa 1965).

22. *See Edwards v. City of Des Moines*, 349 N.W.2d 786, 789 (Iowa App. 1984) (citing with approval *Baker v. Beal*, 225 N.W.2d 106, 110 (Iowa 1975)).

23. *Citicorp of North America, Inc. v. Lifestyle Communications Corp.*, 836 F. Supp. 644, 665 (S.D. Iowa 1993); *Perin v. Hayne*, 210 N.W.2d 609, 613 (Iowa 1973).

24. *Pessagno v. United States*, 751 F. Supp. 149, 151–52 (S.D. Iowa 1990); *Crookham v. Riley*, 584 N.W.2d 258, 265 (Iowa 1998); *Gerst v. Marshall*, 549 N.W.2d 810, 813 (Iowa 1996); *see also Blackhawk Bldg. Systems, Ltd. v. Law Firm of Aspelmeier, Fisch, Power, Warner & Engberg*, 428 N.W.2d 288, 290 (Iowa 1988) (stating that proximate cause must be determined separately and does not necessarily follow a negligence finding).

25. *Gerst v. Marshall*, 549 N.W.2d 810, 815 (Iowa 1996); *Hagen v. Texaco Refining and Marketing, Inc.*, 526 N.W.2d 531, 537 (Iowa 1995).

26. *Rieger v. Jacque*, 584 N.W.2d 247, 251 (Iowa 1998); *Hayward v. P.D.A., Inc.*, 573 N.W.2d 29, 31–32 (Iowa 1997); *Huber v. Watson*, 568 N.W.2d 787, 790 (Iowa 1997); *see also Johnson v. Interstate Power Co.*, 481 N.W.2d 310, 323

(Iowa 1992) (there can be more than one proximate cause of injury or damages).

27. Iowa Code Chapter 668 *et seq.* (1999).

28. *Goetzman v. Wichern,* 327 N.W.2d 742, 754 (Iowa 1982); *see Slager v. HWA Corp.,* 435 N.W.2d 349, 350 (Iowa 1989) (stating *Goetzman* was superseded by enactment of Iowa Code Chapter 668 *et seq.*).

29. *See* Iowa Code § 668.1(1) (1999):

> "Fault" means one or more acts or omissions that are in any measure negligent or reckless toward the person or property of the actor or others, or that subject a person to strict tort liability. The term also includes breach of warranty, unreasonable assumption of risk not constituting an enforceable expressed consent, misuse of a product for which the defendant otherwise would be liable, and unreasonable failure to avoid an injury or to mitigate damages.

Id.

30. Iowa Code § 668.2 (1999) ("Party" means any of the following: 1) a claimant; 2) a person named as defendant; 3) a person who has been released pursuant to § 668.7; or, 4) a third-party defendant).

31. *Kelly v. State Farm Mut. Auto. Ins. Co.,* 764 F. Supp. 1337, 1340 (S.D. Iowa 1991).

32. Iowa Code § 668.3(1)(a) (1999).

33. Iowa Code § 668.3(1)(b) (1999).

34. Iowa Code § 668.1(1) (1999).

35. *See Coker v. Abell-Howe Co.,* 491 N.W.2d 143, 149 (Iowa 1992) (stating that the doctrine of unavoidable consequences is concerned with a plaintiff's conduct after the defendant's negligence but before injury results).

36. *Bokhoven v. Klinker,* 474 N.W.2d 553, 557 (Iowa 1991).

37. *Fosselman v. Waterloo Community School Dist. and Black Hawk County,* 229 N.W.2d 280, 283 (Iowa 1975); *see also Kulish v. Ellsworth,* 566 N.W.2d 885, 892 (Iowa 1987) (*res ispa loquitur* is a rule of evidence rather than one of pleading or substantive law); *Perin v. Hayne,* 210 N.W.2d 609, 615 (Iowa 1973) (rarity of occurrence is not a sufficient predicate for application of *res ipsa loquitur*).

38. *Koppinger v. Cullen-Schlitz and Associates,* 513 F.2d 901, 906 (8th Cir. 1975); *Brewster v. United States,* 860 F. Supp. 1377, 1387 (S.D. Iowa 1994); *see also*

Brewster v. United States, 542 N.W.2d 524, 530 (Iowa 1996) (plaintiff is not required to eliminate with certainty all the possible causes or inferences for *res ipsa loquitur* to apply).

39. *Wick v. Henderson*, 485 N.W.2d 645, 648–49 (Iowa 1992); *Wiles v. Myerly*, 210 N.W.2d 619, 624 (Iowa 1973).

40. *See Hagen v. Texaco Refining and Marketing, Inc.*, 526 N.W.2d 531, 539 (Iowa 1995) (factors to be considered in deciding whether activity is abnormally dangerous include the existence of a high risk of harm, the likelihood that such harm will be great, the inability to eliminate the risks of activity by exercise of reasonable care, the extent to which the activity is uncommon, whether the activity is inappropriate in the place where it is conducted, and the extent to which the activity's value to the community outweighs its dangerous attributes); *O'Tool v. Hathaway*, 461 N.W.2d 161, 164 (Iowa 1990).

41. *Wiersgalla v. Garrett*, 486 N.W.2d 290, 292–93 (Iowa 1992); *see also Griglione v. Martin*, 525 N.W.2d 810, 812 (Iowa 1994) (stating that rules of conduct that establish the absolute standards of care must be ordained by the state legislative body or an administrative agency regulating on a state-wide basis under the authority of the legislature).

42. *See Grinnell Mut. Reinsurance Co. v. Employer's Mut. Cas. Co.*, 494 N.W.2d 690, 693 (Iowa 1993) (citing with approval *Davis v. Crook*, 261 N.W.2d 500, 506 (Iowa 1978)).

43. Iowa Code § 668.4 (1999).

44. *Id.*

45. Iowa Code § 668.5 (1999).

46. *Chicago Cent. & Pacific R. Co. v. Union Pacific R. Co.*, 558 N.W.2d 711, 715 (Iowa 1997); *see also Allied Mut. Ins. Co. v. State*, 473 N.W.2d 24, 27 (Iowa 1991) (stating that it is not necessary for contribution that the common liability between the parties rest on the same legal theory).

47. Iowa Code § 668.6 (1999); *see also Interstate Power Co. v. Kansas City Power and Light Co.*, 909 F. Supp. 1224, 1238 (N.D. Iowa 1991); *Iowa Nat. Mut. Ins. Co. v. Granneman*, 438 N.W.2d 840, 843 (Iowa 1989).

48. *See* Iowa Code § 668.5(2) (1999) ("contribution is available to a person who enters into a settlement with the claimant *only if* the liability of a person against whom contribution is sought has been extinguished and *only to* the extent that the amount paid in settlement was reasonable") (emphasis added).

49. Iowa Code § 668.7 (1999).

50. *Tralon Court v. Cedarapids, Inc.*, 966 F. Supp. 812, 830 (N.D. Iowa 1997).

51. *See State ex rel Miller v. Phillip Morris, Inc.*, 577 N.W.2d 401, 406 (Iowa 1998) (citing with approval *Daniels v. Hi-Way Truck Equip., Inc.*, 505 N.W.2d 485, 490 (Iowa 1993)); *see also Howell v. River Products Company*, 379 N.W.2d 919, 921 (Iowa 1986) (stating that the right of an indemnitee is essentially equitable in nature and generally the measure of relief is the actual amount the person who is secondarily liable has been compelled to pay as a natural consequence of the indemnitor's negligence or other wrong).

52. *American Trust and Sav. Bank v. U.S. Fidelity & Guar. Co.*, 439 N.W.2d 188, 190 (Iowa 1989).

53. Iowa Code Chapter 85 *et seq.* (1999).

54. Iowa Code § 85.20 (1999); *Larimer v. Raque Mfg. Co., Inc.*, 498 F. Supp. 37, 38 (S.D. Iowa 1980); *Williams v. Weiler and Co.*, 498 F. Supp. 917, 919 (S.D. Iowa 1979).

55. Iowa Code § 85.3 (1999); *Sourbier v. State*, 498 N.W.2d 720, 723 (Iowa 1993).

56. Iowa Code § 85.20 (1999); *Swanson v. White Consol. Industries, Inc.*, 30 F.3d 971, 972 (8th Cir. 1994).

57. Iowa Code § 85.20 (1999); *Smith v. CRST Intern., Inc.*, 553 N.W.2d 890, 895 (1996); *White v. Northwestern Bell Telephone Co.*, 514 N.W.2d 70, 74 (Iowa 1994); *Suckow v. NEOWA FS, Inc.*, 445 N.W.2d 776, 780 (Iowa 1989).

58. Iowa Code § 85.26(1) (1999).

59. Iowa Code § 85.22(2) (1999); *Bride v. Heckart*, 556 N.W.2d 449, 454 (Iowa 1996); *Daniels v. Hi-Way Truck Equipment, Inc.*, 505 N.W.2d 485, 487 (Iowa 1993).

60. Iowa Code § 85.22(1) (1999); *Bride v. Heckart*, 556 N.W.2d 449, 454 (Iowa 1996); *Daniels v. Hi-Way Truck Equipment, Inc.*, 505 N.W.2d 485, 487 (Iowa 1993).

61. Iowa Code § 85.22(1) (1999); *Firstar Bank of Burlington, Iowa v. Hawkeye Paving Corp.*, 558 N.W.2d 423, 426 (Iowa 1997).

62. *Sheets v. Ritt, Ritt & Ritt, Inc.*, 581 N.W.2d 602, 606 (Iowa 1998).

63. *Id.*

64. *See id.* (listing the factors to consider as the following: (1) the foreseeability or possibility of harm; (2) the purpose for which the entrant entered the

premises; (3) the time, manner, and circumstances under which the entrant entered the premises; (4) the use to which the premises are put or are expected to be put; (5) the reasonableness of the inspection, repair, or warning; (6) the opportunity and ease of repair or correction or the giving of a warning; and (7) the burden on the land occupier and/or the community in terms of convenience or costs in providing adequate protection).

65. *Id.*

66. *Champlin v. Walker*, 249 N.W.2d 839, 842 (Iowa 1977).

67. *See* Iowa Code § 123.92 (1999), stating in pertinent part the following:

> Any person who is injured in person or property or means of support by an intoxicated person, or resulting from the intoxication of that person, has a right of action for all damages actually sustained, severally or jointly, against any licensee or permitee, . . . who sold and served any beer, wine, or intoxicating liquor to the intoxicated person when the licensee or permitee knew or should have known the person was intoxicated, or who sold to and served the person to a point where the licensee or permitee knew or should have known the person would become intoxicated. If the injury was caused by the intoxicated person, a permitee or licensee may establish as an affirmative defense that the intoxication did not contribute to the injurious action of the person.

Id.

68. *Nutting v. Zeiser*, 482 N.W.2d 424, 425 (Iowa 1992); *see also Paul v. Ron Moore Oil Co.*, 487 N.W.2d 337, 338 (Iowa 1992) (stating that the Act requires "service" of alcohol to the intoxicated person, meaning establishments that do not sell alcohol for on-premises consumption of alcohol are not liable under the Act).

69. *Hobbiebrunken v. GNS Enterprises, Inc.*, 470 N.W.2d 19, 21 (Iowa 1991).

70. Iowa Code §§ 668 *et seq.* (Iowa 1999).

71. *Slager v. HWA Corp.*, 435 N.W.2d 349, 352 (Iowa 1989).

72. *See Gremmel v. Junnie's Lounge*, 397 N.W.2d 717, 721 (Iowa 1986) (stating that a defendant can assert as a viable defense that the plaintiff would have been injured regardless of the intoxication of the person served by the dram shop).

73. *Id.*

74. Iowa Code § 123.49 (1999).

75. *Bauer v. Cole*, 467 N.W.2d 221, 223 (Iowa 1991).

76. *Sage v. Johnson*, 437 N.W.2d 582, 584–85 (Iowa 1989).

77. *American Fire & Cas. Co. v. Ford Motor Co.*, 588 N.W.2d 437, 439 (Iowa 1999); *Richards v. Midland Brick Sales Co., Inc.*, 551 N.W.2d 649, 650–51 (Iowa App. 1996).

78. *Bruce v. ICI Americas, Inc.*, 933 F. Supp. 781, 788 (S.D. Iowa 1996); *American Fire & Cas. Co. v. Ford Motor Co.*, 588 N.W.2d 437, 439 (Iowa 1999); *Nelson v. Todd's Ltd.*, 426 N.W.2d 120, 122–23 (Iowa 1988); *Richards v. Midland Brick Sales Co., Inc.*, 551 N.W.2d 649, 650–51 (Iowa App. 1996).

79. *Tralon Corp. v. Cedarapids, Inc.*, 966 F. Supp. 812, 827 (N.D. Iowa 1997); *In re Marriage of Cutler*, 588 N.W.2d 425, 430 (Iowa 1999); *Midwest Home Distributor, Inc. v. Domco Industries, Ltd.*, 585 N.W.2d 735, 738 (Iowa 1998); *Plymouth Farmers Mut. Ins. Assn. v. Armour*, 584 N.W.2d 289, 291 (Iowa 1998); *Clark v. McDaniel*, 546 N.W.2d 590, 592 (Iowa 1996); *Garren v. First Realty, Ltd.*, 481 N.W.2d 335, 338 (Iowa 1992).

80. *See Beeck v. Kapalis*, 302 N.W.2d 90, 96–97 (Iowa 1981) (citing with approval the Restatement (Second) of Torts § 552 (1977)).

81. *See id.* (limiting the liability of the defendant to the loss suffered by the person or one of a limited group of persons for whose benefit and guidance the defendant intended to supply the information or knows who the recipient intends to supply it and the defendant intends the information to influence the transaction based on the recipient's reliance).

82. *See Tratchel v. Essex Group, Inc.*, 452 N.W.2d 171 (Iowa 1990) (citing with approval *Slager v. HWA Corp.*, 435 N.W.2d 349, 352–53 (Iowa 1989)).

83. Iowa Code §§ 537.1101 *et seq.* (1999).

84. *Id.*

85. *See* Iowa Code § 537.1301(11) (1999) ("consumer credit transaction" means a consumer credit sale or consumer loan, or a refinancing or consolidation thereof, or a consumer lease, or a consumer rental purchase agreement).

86. Iowa Code §§ 537.5201, .5202 & .5203 (1999); *see also* Iowa Code §§ 537.5301 & .5302 (1999) (outlining criminal penalties for violations).

87. Iowa Code §§ 537.501–.5115 (1999).

88. Iowa Code §§ 537.701–.7103 (1999).

89. *See* Iowa Code § 537.7102(6) (1999) ("debtor" means the person obligated).

90. *See* Iowa Code § 537.7102(2) (1999) ("creditor" means the person to whom a debtor is obligated, either directly or indirectly, on a debt).

91. Iowa Code § 537.5203(6) (1999).

92. *See* Iowa Code § 668A (1999), which states as follows:

Punitive or exemplary damages

1. In a trial of a claim involving the request for punitive or exemplary damages, the court shall instruct the jury to answer special interrogatories or, if there is no jury, shall make findings, indicating all of the following:

    a. Whether, by a preponderance of clear, convincing, and satisfactory evidence, the conduct of the defendant from which the claim arose constituted willful and wanton disregard for the rights or safety of another.

    b. Whether the conduct of the defendant was directed specifically at the claimant, or at the person from which the claimant's claim is derived.

2. An award for punitive or exemplary damages shall not be made unless the answer or finding pursuant to subsection 1, paragraph "a", is affirmative. If such answer or finding is affirmative, the jury, or court if there is no jury, shall fix the amount of punitive or exemplary damages to be awarded, and such damages shall be ordered paid as follows:

    a. If the answer or finding pursuant to subsection 1, paragraph "b," is affirmative, the full amount of the punitive or exemplary damages awarded shall be paid to the claimant.

    b. If the answer or finding pursuant to subsection 1, paragraph "b," is negative, after payment of all applicable costs and fees, an amount not to exceed 25 percent of the punitive or exemplary damages awarded may be ordered paid to the claimant, with the remainder of the award to be ordered paid into a civil reparations trust fund administered by the state court administrator. Funds placed in the civil reparations trust shall be under the control and supervision of the executive counsel, and shall be disbursed only for purposes of indigent civil litigation programs or insurance assistance programs.

3. The mere allegation or assertion of a claim for punitive damages shall not form the basis for discovery of the wealth or ability to respond in damages on behalf of the party from whom punitive damages are claimed until such time as the claimant has established

that sufficient admissible evidence exists to support a prima facie case establishing the requirements of subsection 1, paragraph "a."

Id.

93. *Sisneros v. Nix*, 884 F. Supp. 1313, 1345 (S.D. Iowa 1995); *Midwest Home Distributor, Inc. v. Domco Industries, Ltd.*, 585 N.W.2d 735, 743 (Iowa 1998); *Nassen v. National States Ins. Co.*, 494 N.W.2d 231, 238 (Iowa 1992).

94. *Grand Laboratories, Inc. v. Midcon Labs of Iowa*, 32 F.3d 1277, 1286 (8th Cir. 1994); *Schlegel v. Ottumwa Courier, a Div. of Lee Enterprises, Inc.*, 585 N.W.2d 217, 226 (Iowa 1998); *Sundholm v. City of Bettendorf*, 389 N.W.2d 849, 853 (Iowa 1986).

95. Iowa Code § 668A(1)(a) (1999); *Watkins v. Lundell*, 169 F.3d 540, 544 (8th Cir. 1999); *Berglund v. State Farm Mut. Auto Ins. Co.*, 121 F.3d 1225, 1228 (8th Cir. 1997); *see also Jackson v. Travelers Ins. Company*, 26 F. Supp.2d 1153, 1169 (S.D. Iowa 1998) (stating that merely objectionable conduct is insufficient to support a punitive damages award under Iowa law); *Lovick v. Wil-Rich*, 588 N.W.2d 688, 699 (Iowa 1999); *Schultz v. Security Nat. Bank*, 583 N.W.2d 886, 888 (Iowa 1998).

96. *Kim v. Nash Finch Co.*, 123 F.3d 1046, 1067 (8th Cir. 1997).

97. *See Midwest Home Distributor, Inc. v. Domco Industries, Ltd.*, 585 N.W.2d 735, 743 (Iowa 1998) (citing with approval *Wilson v. IBP, Inc.*, 558 N.W.2d 132, 148 (Iowa 1996)).

98. Iowa Code § 669.4 (1999).

99. *Godbersen v. Miller*, 439 N.W.2d 206, 209 (Iowa 1989).

100. *Miller v. Wellman Dynamics Corp.*, 419 N.W.2d 380, 383 (Iowa 1988); *Trester v. Sisters of Mercy Health Corp.*, 328 N.W.2d 308, 312 (Iowa 1982); *Egan v. Naylor*, 208 N.W.2d 915, 917 (Iowa 1973).

101. *See* Iowa Code § 611.20 (1999) ("All causes of action shall survive and may be brought notwithstanding the death of the person entitled or liable to the same").

102. *Berenger v. Frink*, 314 N.W.2d 388, 390 (Iowa 1982).

103. *Iowa-Des Moines Nat'l Bank v. Schwerman Trucking Co.*, 288 N.W.2d 198, 201 (Iowa 1980); *Haumersen v. Ford Motor Company*, 257 N.W.2d 7, 16–17 (Iowa 1977); *Hardy v. Britt-Tech Corp.*, 378 N.W.2d 307, 310–11 (Iowa App. 1985).

104. *Koppinger v. Cullen-Schiltz & Associates*, 513 F.2d 901, 909 (8th Cir. 1975); *Berenger v. Frink*, 314 N.W.2d 388, 391-93 (Iowa 1982).

105. *Chester v. Mustang Mfg. Co., Inc.*, 998 F. Supp. 1039, 1043 (N.D. Iowa 1998); *Lang v. City of Des Moines*, 294 N.W.2d 557, 562 (Iowa 1980); *Schlichte v. Franklin Troy Trucks*, 265 N.W.2d 725, 727 (Iowa 1978).

106. *See* I.R.C.P. 8 (1999) ("A parent, or the parents, may sue for the expense and actual loss of services, companionship and society resulting from injury to or death of a minor child"); *see also Haumersen v. Ford Motor Company*, 257 N.W.2d 7, 17 (Iowa 1977) (damages pursuant to Rule 8 include the loss of services which is measured as the present value of what the decedent minor child would have earned during minority less than the present value of the costs and support and maintenance during that period).

107. *Madison v. Colby*, 348 N.W.2d 202, 209 (Iowa 1984).

108. *Id.*

109. *Id.*

KANSAS

A. STATUTES OF LIMITATION

The following actions must be brought within two years: (1) trespass on real estate, (2) torts against personal property, (3) fraud (cause of action does not accrue until discovery), (4) wrongful death, (6) actions to recover damages for ionizing radiation, and (7) actions for medical malpractice.[1]

Routine negligence actions are governed by the two-year statute of limitations.

Kansas has adopted the discovery rule for tort actions, limited by a ten-year statute of repose.[2] This statute encompasses actions for injuries to minors.[3] The statute of repose for actions against health care providers is four years.[4] The statute of repose for negligence causes of action by a corporation or association against its officers or directors is five years.[5]

Actions based on contract must be brought within five years if the contract is written[6] or within three years otherwise.[7] Serious intentional tort actions, such as for assault, battery, malicious prosecution, false imprisonment, defamation, or for statutory penalty or forfeiture must be brought within one year.[8] An advance or partial payment by a liability insurer to an injured person or to others on his behalf predicated on possible tort liability will serve to recommence the running of the statute from the date of last payment.[9]

B. TORT REFORM

Kansas has adopted a products liability act.[10] This act limits the useful safe life of products to 10 years,[11] restricts a manufacturer's and seller's duty to warn,[12] and provides a presumption of non-defectiveness if the manufacturer complies with regulatory standards.[13]

The availability of punitive damages has been circumscribed by the Kansas legislature. Statute dictates the amount of allowable punitive damages and the circumstances under which they may be awarded.[14]

Several Kansas tort reform initiative in the area of medical malpractice, collateral source rule reform and limitations on overall damages have been held unconstitutional.[15] The Kansas Supreme Court has expressed mixed reactions to the following new provisions of the Restatement (Third) of Torts: Products Liability, rejecting the availability of a defective design claim in spite of an adequate warning under comment *l* to section 2,[16] but citing with approval Restatement (Third) of Torts: Apportionment of Liability § 24(b) on apportionment of liability among intentional tortfeasors[17] and Restatement (Third) of Torts: Products Liability rejecting liability in tort by a component manufacturer to the end product owner for purely economic losses.[18]

No significant initiatives are pending in 2002, although some groups have attempted unsuccessfully to alter the exclusivity of workers' compensation as a remedy and are likely to continue this pursuit with poor prospects anticipated.

C. "NO FAULT" LIMITATIONS

In motor vehicle cases, pain and suffering damages are recoverable only if the value of reasonable and necessary medical treatment exceeds two thousand dollars or if there is permanent injury, fracture of a weight-bearing bone or permanent disfigurement.[19] The no-fault insurer is subrogated to the extent of its payments (less a reasonable attorney fee), reduced by the insured plaintiff's percentage of fault. This right of subrogation is conditioned upon a full recovery so that PIP benefits paid are duplicative of tort damages.[20]

D. THE STANDARD FOR NEGLIGENCE

The elements for negligence include (1) a duty to conform to a standard of care so as not to subject others to unreasonable risks of harm; (2) a breach of that duty; (3) a proximate causal relationship between the breach of duty and harm suffered by the plaintiff; and (4) actual damage to the plaintiff.[21]

Generally, the reasonable prudent person standard of care is applicable.[22] However, professional persons must conform to the standard of skill, knowledge and ability of members of their professions in good standing and in the same or a similar location.[23] Geographic proximity is merely one factor in determining the local standard of care for medical professionals.[24]

There is no affirmative duty to act in order to protect or assist another; although, certain special types of relationships may create such a duty. Examples of special relationships include parent/child, employer/employee, common carrier/passenger, innkeeper/guest, and real estate premises relationships.[25] An actor who stands in a special relationship to a third person has a duty to act with reasonable care to protect potential plaintiffs from intentional and negligent acts of the third person.[26]

Children are subject to the standard of care for children of similar age, intelligence and maturity.[27] Kansas has recognized an exception to the child standard of care when the child engages in an activity normally undertaken only by adults for which adult qualifications are required.[28]

E. CAUSATION

A *prima facie* showing of causation requires a showing of cause in fact and proximate cause.[29] An act or omission is a cause in fact of a harm if the harm would not have occurred but for the act or omission.[30] When a wrongful act or omission combines with another act in order to produce a single harm, the act or omission is a cause of the harm if it was a substantial factor in producing the harm.[31] An extension of the substantial factor test allows a cause of action for loss of chance of survival by a patient who dies because of a physician's malpractice.[32] Under standard jury instructions, the extent to which a defendant's act caused the plaintiff's injury may be considered along with the defendant's negligence in assessing fault.[33]

Proximate cause is a question of tort policy and is therefore decided by the judge.[34] The general rule is that the defendant is liable only for those harms that were foreseeable or natural and probable results of his negligent acts.[35] Where an intervening cause breaks the chain of events set in motion by a prior actor's negligence, the intervening cause is a superseding cause if it alone would have caused the injury in question and if it was not foreseeable to the prior actor.[36] A superseding cause extinguishes the liability of the prior actor.

F. CONTRIBUTORY NEGLIGENCE, COMPARATIVE NEGLIGENCE, AND ASSUMPTION OF RISK

1. Contributory Negligence

Kansas abolished its contributory negligence scheme when it adopted a modified form of comparative negligence in 1974.[37]

2. Comparative Negligence

In Kansas the plaintiff may recover a percentage of his damages only if the plaintiff's fault is less than the fault of the defendants.[38] The plaintiff is entitled to a jury instruction explaining the legal effect of the above rule.[39] Since 1987, comparative negligence applies to actions purely for economic loss, as well as for bodily injury and property damage.[40] Plaintiff's comparative negligence does not reduce his recovery where the defendant committed an intentional tort.[41]

The comparative negligence statute is applicable to claims based on liability theories other than common law negligence.[42] In any situation where contributory negligence would have been a defense, comparative negligence now applies.[43]

3. Assumption of Risk

Notwithstanding the enactment of the comparative negligence statute, assumption of risk remains a complete bar to recovery.[44] Kansas recognizes two forms of assumption of risk, express and implied. Express assumption of risk arises from a contractual arrangement.[45] Implied assumption of risk occurs when a plaintiff has knowledge and full appreciation of the risk caused by defendant's conduct.[46]

G. *RES IPSA LOQUITUR* AND INHERENTLY DANGEROUS ACTIVIES

1. *Res Ipsa Loquitur*

The doctrine of *res ipsa loquitur* allows evidence of an accident's occurrence, without direct evidence of negligence, to form the basis of a *prima facie* case of negligence.[47] There are three elements to this doctrine: (1) the accident must have been one that would not ordinarily occur without negligence, (2) the instrumentality causing the accident must have been under the exclusive control of the defendant, and (3) the plaintiff must have been without contributory negligence.[48]

2. Inherently Dangerous Activities

In Kansas one who carries on an abnormally dangerous activity is strictly liable for harm to person, land or chattels of another resulting from the activity, regardless of the reasonableness of care exercised.[49] The court determines as a matter of law whether a given activity is abnormally dangerous for purposes of strict liability.[50] Operation of an oil refinery has been held not to be an "abnormally dangerous activity."[51]

H. NEGLIGENCE *PER SE*

The court may adopt for use in a negligence action the standard of care provided by a statute.[52] However, negligence *per se* is applicable only under the following circumstances: (1) the statute must have been designed to protect a particular class of persons of which the plaintiff is a member; (2) the statute must have been designed to prevent the type do harm that plaintiff suffered; and (3) the violation must have been the proximate cause of plaintiff's injury.[53] Conversely, a defendant's compliance with a statute is not conclusive as a matter of law, but is treated only as evidence of reasonable care.[54]

I. JOINT AND SEVERAL LIABILITY

The comparative fault statutory scheme has abolished joint and several liability only in comparative fault cases.[55] The comparative fault statute has done nothing to alter other common law rules of joint and several liability.[56]

A release of one or more negligent tortfeasors generally has no effect on the claimant's right to recover from the tortfeasors not released from the action.[57] In such situations the unreleased tortfeasor is responsible for his apportioned percentage of damages but not damages apportioned to other tortfeasors not in privity. However, release of an employee or individual otherwise primarily liable will serve to bar any action against the employer or vicariously liable party in the absence of a condition or limitation to the contrary.[58] When two or more intentional tortfeasors are involved, as in a defamation case, the amounts paid by one in settlement may be credited against the actual, but not punitive, liability of the other.[59]

J. INDEMNITY

Implied indemnity occurs as a matter of law where the parties' legal relationship allows one party's liability to be imputed to another.[60]

Kansas has adopted the rule of comparative implied indemnity, although it is seldom applied because comparative fault is normally relied upon as a basis for defense. This rule provides that, where settlement of a plaintiff's entire damages has been made with one tortfeasor during the pendency of an action, and release of all liability has been given by the plaintiff to all who may have contributed to the damages, an apportionment action can be pursued by the settling tortfeasor.[61] In order to be entitled to indemnity, however, the settling defendant must show that there was a reasonable basis for settlement.[62]

K. BAR OF WORKERS' COMPENSATION STATUTE

Where workers' compensation benefits are payable (even if not actually paid), no civil action is permitted against the employer. This rule also protects statutory employers of subcontractors' employees and fellow employees.[63] Agricultural pursuits and very small enterprises (payroll below $20,000 per annum) are exempted from the Act unless an election for coverage is made.[64] The Kansas Supreme Court has held that a person may not maintain a civil damage action against a fellow employee for any injury for which compensation is recoverable under the Workmen's Compensation Act.[65]

An employer and its insurer are subrogated to the extent of the benefits paid, less reasonable attorney's fees, in an action against third parties.[66]

L. PREMISES LIABILITY

In order for a defendant to be liable for failing to maintain land in a reasonably safe condition, the defendant must be the owner, occupier or possessor of the land.[67] A possessor of land is one who is in occupation of the land with the intent to control it.[68]

A possessor of land has a duty to avoid injury to persons outside the land from unreasonably dangerous conditions occurring on the land that are not indigenous to the land.[69] Storage of inherently dangerous firearms is subject to a duty of "the highest standard of care."[70]

The duty of a possessor of land extending to those persons on the land depends upon the status of those persons on the land. In Kansas, a possessor of land is required to avoid injury to discovered trespassers only when the potential injury would result from willful, wanton or reckless conduct.[71] Kansas has adopted the attractive nuisance doctrine for child trespassers.[72] Kansas has abolished the distinction between licensees and invitees for purposes of premises liability.[73] "Slight defects," such as small sidewalk imperfections, are not subject to liability by both public and private property owners.[74]

M. DRAM SHOP LIABILITY

At common law, no redress exists against persons selling, giving or furnishing intoxicating beverages for resulting injuries or damages due to the acts of persons who consume the beverages. Because Kansas does not have a dram shop act, the common-law rule prevails.[75] Violations of regulatory liquor statutes does not give rise to actions for negligence.[76]

N. ECONOMIC LOSS

As a component of allowable personal injury damages, the plaintiff may be awarded damages for economic loss, including expected loss of time or income by reason of disability.[77] Generally, actions for pure economic damages by a product owner against a component manufacturer sound in contract or warranty, not in tort.[78]

Kansas does, however, recognize various business tort actions, which are based exclusively upon the loss of economic advantage.

O. FRAUD AND MISREPRESENTATION

The Kansas Code of Civil Procedure requires that fraud be pled with particularity.[79] Fraud requires proof of the following: (1) a representation of a material fact by the defendant with knowledge or belief that the representation was false or was lacking sufficient basis in truth; (2) defendant's intent to induce the plaintiff to act or refrain from acting in reliance upon the representation; and (3) damages sustained by plaintiff in reasonable reliance upon the representation.[80] Actionable fraud may be based upon silence.[81]

Kansas follows Section 552 of the Restatement (Second) of Torts in defining negligent misrepresentation.[82] In order for there to be negligent misrepresentation, the representation must have been made during the course of a transaction involving potential pecuniary gain for defendant, and defendant must have failed to exercise reasonable care or competence in obtaining or communicating the information upon which the plaintiff reasonably relied.[83]

P. CONSUMER FRAUD STATUTE

The Kansas Consumer Protection Act (KCPA) protects consumers of property or services from deceptive and unconscionable practices.[84] The KCPA provides a cause of action for the attorney general or county district attorneys.[85] It also provides private remedies for consumers, including injunctive relief, damages or civil penalties.[86] Unlike many acts of its kind, the KCPA provides extensive protection against unconscionable practices that occur before, during and after the consumer transaction in question.[87]

The KCPA also protects consumers from unbargained-for warranty disclaimers,[88] and it provides a three-day cancellation period for door-to-door sales.[89]

Q. PUNITIVE DAMAGES

Punitive, or exemplary, damages are awarded as punishment and deterrence of aggravated tortious conduct.[90] Plaintiff must recover actual damages in order to be awarded punitive damages; however, punitive damages may be awarded where equitable relief is ordered in lieu of actual damages.[91] Punitive damages are not required, even if the necessary conditions have been proven.[92]

Generally, in order for punitive damages to be recoverable, the defendant's conduct must be aggravated or outrageous. It must be provoked by willful or wanton conduct, malice, spite, fraud or some other evil motive.[93] In Kansas, punitive liability may not be assessed against a principal or employer for the acts of his agents or employees unless the acts were authorized or ratified by the principal or employer.[94]

Under the Punitive Damages Act, the jury determines whether punitive damages should be awarded under a clear and convincing standard. The trial judge assesses the amount of damages during a separate hearing.[95]

R. WRONGFUL DEATH AND SURVIVAL CLAIMS

The wrongful death cause of action is a creature of statute; it did not exist at common law.[96] Kansas's wrongful death statute provides that an action may be maintained for damages resulting from an act or omission of another that causes the death, if the action would have been actionable had the decedent lived.[97] A wrongful death action may be maintained by any one of the heirs at law of the decedent who has sustained loss by reason of the death.[98] The proceeds must be apportioned among the heirs by the court.[99] Noneconomic damages are limited to $250,000,[100] but economic damages are unlimited and are liberally construed.

The wrongful death action is for the exclusive benefit of the heirs. It allows the heirs to recover damages accruing after death for such things as mental anguish, loss of support, companionship, parental care and training.[101] In contrast, Kansas's survival cause of action allows the personal representative to recover, for the benefit of the decedent's estate, damages accrued by the injured party between the time of injury and the time of death.[102] Punitive damages are not permitted in actions solely for wrongful death but are available in survivorship cases.[103]

S. CONSORTIUM

The right of a spouse to collect damages for loss of consortium vests in the spouse sustaining the actual bodily injury.[104] As such, the non-injured spouse is not a party to a damage action. Minor children do not have a right to claim loss of parental consortium;[105] however, such damages are recoverable by heirs at law in a wrongful death action.[106] Because of the inherently nebulous nature of consortium claims, a jury may ignore uncontradicted evidence by plaintiffs and deny any damages, and to do so is not reversible error.[107]

T. CIVIL PROCEDURE

Kansas's Code of Civil Procedure is modeled upon the Federal Rules of Civil Procedure and follows those rules closely.[108] All federal courts in Kansas are comprised of a single judicial district, the District of Kansas. Removal actions to federal court must comply with mandatory guidelines for removal location (U.S. Dist. Ct. Rules for Kansas, 81.1(b)).[109]

Darrell L. Warta
Stephen M. Kerwick
FOULSTON & SIEFKIN, L.L.P.
Bank of America Center
100 N. Broadway, Suite 700
Wichita, Kansas 67202
(316) 267-6371
Fax (316) 267-6345
skerwick@foulston.com
www.foulston.com

ENDNOTES – KANSAS

1. Kan. Stat. Ann. § 60-513(a)(1)-(7) (1994 & Supp. 2000).

2. Kan. Stat. Ann. § 60-513(b) (1994 & Supp. 2000).

3. *Ripley v. Tolbert*, 260 Kan. 491, 921 P.2d 1210 (1996).

4. Kan. Stat. Ann. § 60-513(c) (1994 & Supp. 2000).

5. Kan. Stat. Ann. § 60-513(d) (1994 & Supp. 2000).

6. Kan. Stat. Ann. § 60-511 (1994 & Supp. 2000).

7. Kan. Stat. Ann. § 60-512 (1994 & Supp. 2000).

8. Kan. Stat. Ann. § 60-514 (1994 & Supp. 2000).

9. Kan. Stat. Ann. § 40-275; *Mast v. Kinnard*, ___ Kan. App. 2d ___, 25 P.3d 158 (2001).

10. Kan. Stat. Ann. § 60-3301, *et seq.* (1994 & Supp. 2000).

11. Kan. Stat. Ann. § 60-3303 (1994 & Supp. 2000).

12. Kan. Stat. Ann. § 3305 (1994 & Supp. 2000).

13. Kan. Stat. Ann. § 60-3304 (1994 & Supp. 2000).

14. Kan. Stat. Ann. § 60-3701 (1994 & Supp. 2000).

15. *Thompson v. KFB Ins. Co.*, 252 Kan. 1010, 850, P.2d 773 (1993); *Kansas Malpractice Victims Coalition v. Bell*, 243 Kan. 333, 757 P.2d 251 (1988).

16. *Delaney v. Deere & Co.*, 268 Kan. 769, 999 P.2d 930 (2000).

17. *Wright v. Bachmurski*, ___ Kan. App. 2d ___, 29 P.3d 979 (2001).

18. *Northwest Arkansas Masonry, Inc. v. Summit Specialty Prods.*, ___ Kan. App. 2d ___, 31 P.3d 982 (2001) and *Koss Constr. v. Caterpillar, Inc.* 25 Kan. App. 2d 200, 960 P.2d 255 (1998).

19. Kan. Stat. Ann. § 40-3117 (2000).

20. *State Farm v. Kroeker*, 234 Kan. 636, 676 P.2d 66 (1984).

21. *Hesler v. Osawatomie State Hosp.*, 971 P.2d 1169 (1999); *Jackson v. City of Kansas City*, 263 Kan. 143, 947 P.2d 31 (1997); *Cochrane v. Schneider Nat'l Carriers, Inc.*, 980 F. Supp. 371 (D. Kan. 1997).

22. *McDermott v. Midland Management, Inc.*, 997 F.2d 768 (1993); *Ettus v. Orkin Exterminating Co.*, 233 Kan. 555, 665 P.2d 730 (1983); *Hickert v. Wright*, 182 Kan.100, 319 P.2d 152 (1957).

23. *Roesch v. Clarke*, 861 F. Supp. 986 (D. Kan. 1994); *Rios v. Bigler*, 847 F. Supp. 1538 (D. Kan. 1994); *Sharples v. Roberts*, 249 Kan. 286, 816 P.2d 390 (1991); *Chandler v. Neosho Memorial Hosp.*, 223 Kan. 1, 574 P.2d 136 (1977).

24. *Chandler v. Neosho Memorial Hosp.*, 223 Kan. 1, 4, 574 P.2d 136, 138 (1977).

25. *State v. Hunter*, 22 Kan. App. 2d 103, 911 P.2d 1121 (1996).

26. *Melvin v. U.S.*, 963 F. Supp. 1052 (D. Kan. 1997); *Nero v. Kansas State University*, 253 Kan. 567, 861 P.2d 768 (1993).

27. *Honeycutt v. City of Wichita*, 247 Kan. 250, 264, 796 P.2d 549, 559 (1990).

28. *Williams v. Esaw*, 214 Kan. 658, 668, 522 P.2d 950, 959 (1974).

29. *McDermott v. Midland Management, Inc.*, 997 F.2d 768 (10th Cir. 1993); *Hoard v. Shawnee Mission Med. Ctr.*, 233 Kan. 267, 662 P.2d 1214 (1983); *Mills v. State Auto. Ins. Ass'n*, 183 Kan. 268, 326 P.2d 254 (1958).

30. *McDermott v. Midland Management, Inc.*, 997 F.2d 768 (10th Cir. 1993); *Cullip ex rel. Pitts v. Domann ex rel. Domann*, 266 Kan. 550, 972 P.2d 776 (1999); *Davey v. Hedden*, 260 Kan. 413, 920 P.2d 420 (1996).

31. *Comeau v. Rupp*, 810 F. Supp. 1127 (D. Kan. 1992).

32. *Delaney v. Cade*, 255 Kan. 199, 218, 873 P.2d 175 (1994).

33. Pattern Instructions Kansas—Civil (3d) (PIK) 105.01, citing *Miles v. West*, 224 Kan. 284, 287, 580 P.2d 876 (1978).

34. *Cullip ex rel. Pitts v. Domann ex rel. Domann*, 266 Kan. 550, 555, 972 P.2d 776, 782 (1999); *Schenck v. Thompson*, 201 Kan. 608, 617, 443 P.2d 298 (1968).

35. *Aguirre ex rel. Aguirre v. Adams*, 15 Kan. App. 2d 470, 472, 809 P.2d 8, 10 (Kan. Ct. App. 1991); *Davey v. Hedden*, 260 Kan. 413, 920 P.2d 420 (1996).

36. *Tinkler v. United States by F.A.A.*, 982 F.2d 1456, 1467 (10th Cir. 1992).

37. Kan. Stat. Ann. § 60-258a (1994 and Supp. 2000).

38. Kan. Stat. Ann. § 60-258a(a) (1994 and Supp. 2000).

39. *Nail v. Doctor's Bldg., Inc.*, 238 Kan. 65, 68, 708 P.2d 186, 189 (1985).

40. Kan. Stat. Ann. § 60-258a (1994 and Supp. 2000).

41. *York v. Intrust Bank, N.A.*, 265 Kan. 271, 310, 962 P.2d 405, 431 (1998); *Sieben v. Sieben*, 231 Kan. 372, 378, 646 P.2d 1036 (1982).

42. *Kennedy v. City of Sawyer*, 228 Kan. 439, 450, 618 P.2d 788 (1980); *Wilson v. Probst*, 224 Kan. 459, 581 P.2d 380 (1978).

43. *Sandifer Motors, Inc. v. City of Roeland Park*, 6 Kan. App. 2d 308, 628 P.2d 239 (1981).

44. *Tuley v. Kansas City Power & Light Co.*, 252 Kan. 205, Syl. ¶¶ 1-7, 843 P.2d 248 (1992).

45. *See, e.g., Anderson v. Union Pacific R.R. Co.*, 14 Kan. App. 2d 342, 344, 790 P.2d 438, 440 (1990).

46. *See, e.g., Calvert v. Garvey Elevators, Inc.*, 236 Kan. 570, 574, 694 P.2d 433, 437 (1985).

47. *Chandler v. Anchor Serum Co.*, 198 Kan. 571, 575, 426 P.2d 82, 85 (1967).

48. *Harmon v. Koch*, 24 Kan. App. 2d 149, 153, 942 P.2d 669, 673 (1997); *Savina v. Sterling Drug Inc.*, 247 Kan. 105, 130, 795 P.2d 915, 933 (1990).

49. *Williams v. Amoco Production Co.*, 241 Kan. 102, 102-03, ¶¶ 7, 8, 734 P.2d 1113 (1987), citing Restatement (Second) Torts § 519 (1976); *Helms v. Eastern Kansas Oil Co.*, 102 Kan. 164, 169, 169 P. 208 (1917).

50. *Falls v. Scott*, 249 Kan. 54, 54, ¶ 3, 815 P.2d 1104 (1991).

51. *Anderson v. Farmland Industries, Inc.*, 136 F. Supp. 2d 1192 (D. Kan. 2001).

52. *OMI Holdings, Inc. v. Howell*, 260 Kan. 305, 339, 918 P.2d 1274, 1296 (1996).

53. *Dietz v. Atchison, Topeka and Santa Fe Ry. Co.*, 16 Kan. App. 2d 342, 345, 823 P.2d 810, 814 (Kan. Ct. App. 1992); *Kansas State Bank & Trust Co. v. Specialized Transportation Serv., Inc.*, 249 Kan. 348, 371, 819 P.2d 587, 603 (1991).

54. *Miller v. Lee Apparel Co.*, 19 Kan. App. 2d 1015, 1028, 881 P.2d 567, 586 (1994).

55. *Kennedy v. City of Sawyer*, 228 Kan. 439, 618 P.2d 788 (1980); *Miles v. West*, 224 Kan. 284, 580 P.2d 876 (1978).

56. *Sieben v. Sieben*, 231 Kan. 372, 379-380, 646 P.2d 1036 (1982).

57. *Glenn v. Fleming*, 240 Kan. 724, 732 P.2d 750 (1987); *Geier v. Wikel*, 4 Kan. App. 2d 188, 603 P.2d 1028 (1979).

58. *Atkinson v. Wichita Clinic, P.A.*, 243 Kan. 705, 763 P.2d 1085 (1988).

59. *Wright v. Bachmurski*, ___ Kan. App. 2d ___, 29 P.3d 979 (2001).

60. *St. Paul Fire and Marine Ins. Co. v. Tyler*, 26 Kan. App. 2d 9, 14-15, 974 P.2d 611, 616 (1999).

61. *Kennedy v. City of Sawyer*, 228 Kan. 439, 618 P.2d 788 (1980).

62. *Id.*

63. Kan. Stat. Ann. § 44-501(b), § 44-503 (1993 & Supp. 1999). *Robinett v. The Haskell Co.*, 270 Kan. 95, 12 P.3d 411 (2000); *Price v. Western Resources, Inc.*, 232 F.3d 779 (10th Cir. 2000).

64. Kan. Stat. Ann. § 44-505(a) (2000).

65. *Rajala v. Doresky*, 233 Kan. 440, 661 P.2d 1251 (1983) (bar applies to battery action between fellow co-workers).

66. Kan. Stat. Ann. § 44-504 (2000).

67. *Gragg v. Wichita State University*, 261 Kan. 1037, 934 P.2d 121 (1997); *Miller v. Zep Mfg. Co.*, 249 Kan. 34, 815 P.2d 506 (1991).

68. *Gragg v. Wichita State University*, 261 Kan. 1037, 934 P.2d 121 (1997).

69. *State Highway Com. v. Empire Oil & Refining Co.*, 141 Kan. 161, 40 P.2d 355 (1935); *Jones v. Hittle Serv., Inc.*, 219 Kan. 627, 549 P.2d 1383 (1976).

70. *Wood v. Groh*, 269 Kan. 420, 7 P.3d 1163 (2000).

71. *Frazee v. St. Louis San Francisco Ry. Co.*, 219 Kan. 661, 549 P.2d 561 (1976); *Montague v. Burgerhoff*, 150 Kan. 217, 223, 92 P.2d 98 (1939), *rehearing denied*; *Riddle Quarries, Inc. v. Thompson*, 177 Kan. 307, 311, 279 P.2d 266 (1955).

72. *Carter v. Skelly Oil Co.*, 191 Kan. 474, 382 P.2d 277 (1963); *Brittain v. Cubbon*, 190 Kan. 641, 378 P.2d 141 (1963).

73. *Jones v. Hansen*, 254 Kan. 499, 867 P.2d 303 (1994).

74. *Barnett-Holdgraf v. Mutual Life Insurance Co. of New York,* 27 Kan. App. 2d 267, 3 P.3d 89 (2000).

75. *Mills v. City of Overland Park,* 251 Kan. 434, 837 P.2d 370 (1992).

76. *Ling v. Jan's Liquors,* 237 Kan. 629, 703 P.2d 731 (1985).

77. Kan. Stat. Ann. § 60-249a, § 60-1901, *et seq.,* and § 60-3406 (1994 & Supp. 2000).

78. *Plains Resources, Inc. v. Gable,* 235 Kan. 580, 682 P.2d 653, 664 (1984); *Northwest Arkansas Masonry, Inc. v. Summit Specialty Prods.,* ___ Kan. App. 2d ___, 31 P.3d 982 (2001) and *Koss Constr. v. Caterpillar, Inc.* 25 Kan. App. 2d 200, 960 P.2d 255 (1998).

79. Kan. Stat. Ann. § 60-209(b) (1994 & Supp. 2000).

80. *Broberg v. Boling,* 183 Kan. 627, 331 P.2d 570 (1958); *Sipes v. Crum,* 204 Kan. 591, 464 P.2d 1 (1970); *Minnesota Ave., Inc. v. Automatic Packagers, Inc.,* 211 Kan. 461, 507 P.2d 268 (1973).

81. *DuShane v. Union Nat'l Bank,* 223 Kan. 755, 576 P.2d 674 (1978).

82. *Mahler v. Keenan Real Estate, Inc.,* 255 Kan. 593, 605, 876 P.2d 609 (1994).

83. *Id.*

84. Kan. Stat. Ann. § 50-623, *et seq.* (1994 & Supp. 2000).

85. Kan. Stat. Ann. § 50-632 (1994 & Supp. 2000).

86. Kan. Stat. Ann. § 50-634 (1994 & Supp. 2000).

87. Kan. Stat. Ann. § 50-627(a) (1994 & Supp. 2000).

88. Kan. Stat. Ann. § 50-639 (1994 & Supp. 2000).

89. Kan. Stat. Ann. § 50-640 (1994 & Supp. 2000).

90. *York v. Intrust Bank, N.A.,* 265 Kan. 271, 307, 962 P.2d 405 (1998).

91. *Golconda Screw, Inc. v. West Bottoms Ltd.,* 20 Kan. App. 2d 1002, 1008, 894 P.2d 260, 266 (1995).

92. *Nordstrom v. Miller,* 227 Kan. 59, 605 P.2d 545 (1980).

93. *See, e.g., Will v. Hughes,* 172 Kan. 45, 238 P.2d 478 (1951); *Hammargren v. Montgomery Ward & Co.,* 172 Kan. 484, 241 P.2d 1192 (1952); *Newton v. Hornblower, Inc.,* 224 Kan. 506, 524, 582 P.2d 1136 (1978).

94. Kan. Stat. Ann. § 60-3701(d)(1) (1994 & Supp. 2000).

95. Kan. Stat. Ann. § 60-3701 (1994 & Supp. 2000).

96. *Goodyear v. Davis*, 114 Kan. 557, 220 P. 282 (1923).

97. Kan. Stat. Ann. § 60-1901 (1994 & Supp. 2000).

98. Kan. Stat. Ann. 60-1902 (1994 & Supp. 2000).

99. Kan. Stat. Ann. § 60-1905 (1994 & Supp. 2000).

100. Kan. Stat. Ann. § 60-1903 (1994 & Supp. 2000).

101. Kan. Stat. Ann. § 60-1904 (1994 & Supp. 2000).

102. *Mason v. Gerin Corp.*, 231 Kan. 718, 647 P.2d 1340 (1982).

103. *Smith v. Printup*, 254 Kan. 315, 335, 866 P.2d 985, 1000 (1993).

104. Kan. Stat. Ann. § 23-205 (1995 & Supp. 2000).

105. *Klaus v. Fox Valley Systems*, 259 Kan. 522, 912 P.2d 703 (1996).

106. Kan. Stat. Ann. § 60-1904(a) (1994 & Supp. 2000).

107. *Tice v. Ebeling*, 238 Kan. 704, 715 P.2d 397 (1986).

108. Kan. Stat. Ann. § 60-201, *et seq.* (1994 & Supp. 2000).

109. 28 U.S.C. § 96 (1986 & Supp. 2000).

KENTUCKY

A. **STATUTES OF LIMITATION**

Any action for personal injury sounding in negligence or strict liability must be bought within one year after the cause of action accrues.[1] The cause of action does not accrue until the plaintiff discovered, or in the exercise of due diligence should have discovered, that he has been injured and that his injury may have been caused by the defendant.[2] The statute of limitations for personal injury arising from a motor vehicle accident is two years.[3] The two-year period of limitations commences on either the date of the injury or the last payment of basic or added reparation benefits, whichever later occurs.[4]

If a personal representative is appointed to represent the estate of a decedent before the one-year statute of limitations for filing a claim for personal injuries expires, a wrongful death action must be filed within one year after the date that the personal representative is appointed.[5] If the personal representative is not appointed within one year after death, the personal representative has one additional year from the one year anniversary of the date of death to file the wrongful death action.[6]

Property damage claims must be brought within five years.[7] The Kentucky courts have not applied the discovery rule to property damage claims.[8]

Causes of action for breach of contract and fraud must be filed within five years.[9] However, breach of express or implied warranty claims involving personal injury must be brought within four years.[10] Libel and slander actions must be brought within one year.[11]

Any particular action that is neither specifically addressed by a statutory provision or excluded from the application of a limitation period must be brought within ten years.[12] Claims involving deficiencies in the construction of any improvement to real property must be brought within seven years following the substantial completion of the improvement.[13] Actions for personal injuries suffered by any person against a builder of a home or other improvements to real property must be filed within five years.[14]

B. **TORT REFORM**

The Kentucky Legislature has not passed any tort reform laws other than legislation addressing punitive damages. To support a claim for punitive damages, the legislature required a finding of subjective awareness by the defendant that the conduct would cause injury.[15] The Kentucky Supreme Court held that this requirement was unconstitutional.[16]

C. "NO-FAULT" LIMITATIONS

The Kentucky Motor Vehicle Reparations Act (MVRA) was adopted, in part, to provide prompt payment to victims of motor vehicle accidents without regard to fault.[17] As a general rule, tort liability with respect to motor vehicle accidents in Kentucky is abolished for personal injuries to the extent basic reparations benefits are paid or are payable to the injured person under the MVRA.[18] Basic reparations benefits are available to any person injured in the Commonwealth of Kentucky while occupying, entering into or alighting from a motor vehicle.[19]

The type of loss covered by basic reparation benefits include medical expenses, wage loss, and replacement services but does not include pain and suffering.[20] A person who seeks basic reparations benefits relinquishes the right to pursue tort claims unless the person meets certain thresholds delineated by statute.[21] If these thresholds are not met, the injured person cannot pursue a tort claim. Even if the thresholds are met, the injured party cannot recover from the tortfeasor any amounts paid or payable as basic reparations benefits.[22] However, the injured party's insurer may pursue the tortfeasor's insurer to recover "no fault" payments paid to the injured person.[23] "No fault" benefits may not be aggregated.[24]

D. THE STANDARD FOR NEGLIGENCE

Every negligence action requires: (1) a duty owed by the defendant; (2) breach of that duty; and (3) a causal connection between the breach and the injury suffered.[25] Every person owes a duty to every other person to exercise ordinary or reasonable care to prevent foreseeable injury.[26] Ordinary care is that degree of care which an ordinarily prudent person would exercise under the same or similar circumstances.[27] Negligence may be found from a failure to act when a reasonable person would act under the circumstances.[28]

E. CAUSATION

Kentucky has adopted the Restatement (Second) of Torts § 431 approach to causation in tort, the cornerstone of which is the concept of "substantial factor."[29] The actors negligent conduct is a legal cause of harm if the conduct is a substantial factor in bringing about the harm. It is incumbent upon the plaintiff to convince the jury that the defendant's conduct was a proximate cause, or legal cause, of the injury.[30] Although causation may be established by circumstantial evidence, the evidence must support a reasonable inference that the conduct was the probable, as opposed to possible, cause of harm.[31]

F. CONTRIBUTORY NEGLIGENCE, COMPARATIVE NEGLIGENCE, AND ASSUMPTION OF RISK

1. Contributory Negligence

The Kentucky Supreme Court struck down the common law doctrine of contributory negligence and adopted a comparative negligence system to apportion fault among plaintiffs and defendants.[32] Under the comparative fault standard, the plaintiff's contributory negligence does not bar plaintiff's recovery completely but it proportionately reduces the amount of fault to be allocated to other parties to the lawsuit in direct correlation with the percentage of fault assigned to the plaintiff.[33] The comparative fault statute negated the contributory negligence provision in Kentucky's products liability act.[34]

2. **Comparative Negligence**

Kentucky has adopted a pure comparative negligence standard for allocating fault in all tort actions, including products liability.[35] Kentucky court's apply the "fundamental fairness doctrine" in tort cases and liability is to be imposed on all parties in direct proportion to fault.[36] The percentage of fault attributable to a party must be predicated upon the party's actual fault, no more and no less.[37] For purposes of allocation of fault, parties include those who actively assert claims, offensively or defensively, as parties in the litigation or who have settled by release or agreement.[38]

3. **Assumption of Risk**

As noted above, the plaintiff's negligent conduct does not completely bar plaintiff's recovery under Kentucky's pure comparative fault system. The assumption of risk doctrine is not a valid defense to tort claims in Kentucky.[39]

G. *RES IPSA LOQUITUR* AND INHERENTLY DANGEROUS ACTIVITIES

1. *Res Ipsa Loquitur*

Res ipsa loquitur is an evidentiary doctrine which permits the jury to infer negligence.[40] In order to rely upon the doctrine, plaintiff must show the following: (1) defendant had full control of the instrumentality which caused the injury; (2) the accident could not have happened if those having control had not been negligent; and (3) plaintiff's injury resulted from the accident.[41] The doctrine cannot be applied unless the nature of the accident excludes all other inferences that it might have been due to one or more causes for which the defendant is not responsible.[42]

2. **Inherently Dangerous Activities**

Persons who own or operate extra hazardous instrumentalities owe a duty to use extreme care.[43]

H. NEGLIGENCE *PER SE*

The violation of a statute or regulation constitutes negligence *per se*.[44] Negligence *per se* is merely a negligence claim with a statutory standard of care substituted for the common law standard of care.[45] Not all statutory violations result in damages for that violation.[46] The statute must specifically intend to prevent the type of occurrence that has taken place and the violation must be a substantial factor in causing the plaintiff's injury.[47]

I. JOINT AND SEVERAL LIABILITY

Kentucky has adopted a pure comparative negligence standard for allocating fault in all tort actions.[48] Liability among joint tortfeasors is no longer joint and several but is several only.[49] Consistent with the concept of fundamental fairness, the Supreme Court recognized that it was fundamentally unfair to require one joint tortfeasor who was only 5 percent at fault to bear the entire loss when another tortfeasor actually caused 95 percent of the loss.[50]

J. INDEMNITY

A cause of action for indemnity arises where one of two parties does an act or creates a hazard that exposes the other party to liability.[51] Common law indemnity is generally available if one party's liability is secondary because it arose from the negligence of the other party.[52] Kentucky continues to recognize the viability of common law indemnity despite the judicial imposition of comparative negligence,[53] later codified in Ky. Rev. Stat. Ann. § 411.182.[54] The statute of limitations on an indemnity claim does not begin to run until some payment is made to the plaintiff by the party claiming indemnity.

K. BAR OF WORKERS' COMPENSATION STATUTE

Under Kentucky's Workers' Compensation Act, an injured employee's exclusive remedy against the employer is a proceeding under the workers' compensation provisions. The exemption from liability extends to the employer's carrier and to all employees, officers or directors of the employer.[55] The receipt of workers' compensation benefits from the employee does not preclude an employee from seeking damages from a third party.[56] However, an injured employee cannot obtain a double recovery from both the compensation carrier and a third party tortfeasor for the same injury.[57]

If the employee has been compensated by the employer under the workers' compensation statute and proceeds to exercise the right to sue a third party arising from the same incident, the employer or its carrier may intervene to recover the amount paid by the employer to the injured employee, less the employee's legal fees and expenses.[58]

L. PREMISES LIABILITY

A landowner is not liable for injuries sustained by a trespasser unless the injuries were intentionally inflicted by the landowner or another on his behalf.[59] The required conduct includes willful, wanton, or reckless acts.[60]

A landowner owes a licensee the duty to warn of dangerous conditions which are already known.[61]

A landowner owes an invitee the duty to exercise ordinary care to keep the premises in a reasonably safe condition.[62] This duty includes using reasonable diligence to discover, remedy or warn of conditions which involve an unreasonable risk to invitees.[63]

An owner of land who makes it available for recreational purposes without payment of fees owes no duty of care to keep the premises safe[64] unless the landowner willfully or maliciously fails to guard against or warn of a dangerous condition.[65] Willful or malicious conduct does not require an intentional act, but may be based upon a finding of great indifference to the safety of others.[66]

M. DRAM SHOP LIABILITY

A licensed seller of alcoholic beverages may not be held liable for injuries or property damage suffered off the premises unless a reasonable person should know that the adult patron was already intoxicated when served.[67] Even so, the Kentucky Legislature declared that the consumption of alcoholic beverages, rather than their sale, is the proximate cause of an injury inflicted by the patron on himself or others.[68] While the seller may be held secondarily liable, the seller can seek indemnity from the patron who caused the injury.[69]

An underaged patron cannot bring a claim against a licensed seller for self-inflicted injuries arising out of his voluntary intoxication.[70]

N. ECONOMIC LOSS

The Supreme Court of Kentucky has not adopted or rejected the economic loss doctrine.[71] However, other courts have held that the "economic loss doctrine" bars tort claims seeking to recover for damages to the actual product purchased by the plaintiff.[72] While the economic loss doctrine prevents recovery for purely economic losses in a product liability action based on negligence or strict liability, the doctrine does not preclude recovery for damage to other property allegedly caused by a defect in the product.[73]

O. FRAUD AND MISREPRESENTATION

The Kentucky Rules of Civil Procedure require that the circumstances constituting fraud be pleaded with particularity.[74]

Once properly plead, the following elements of actionable fraud must be proved by clear and convincing evidence:[75] (1) a false statement; (2) about a material fact; (3) made recklessly or with knowledge of its falsity; (4) with the intent to deceive; (5) plaintiff's reliance on the deception; and (6) injury.[76]

A failure to disclose information is not actionable absent a duty to disclose.[77] A duty to disclose may arise from a fiduciary relationship, from partial disclosure, or from circumstances where one of the parties has superior knowledge and is relied upon to disclose fully.[78]

P. **CONSUMER FRAUD STATUTES**

Kentucky's Consumer Protection Act[79] protects consumers from unfair, false, misleading, or deceptive acts or practices in the conduct of any trade or commerce.[80] The state attorney general, with assistance of local county attorneys, may investigate and impose civil and criminal penalties for any violations.[81] Consumers may also pursue civil claims in the circuit court where the seller has its principal place of business, where the transaction occurred, or in the county where the purchaser resides.[82] The court is authorized to award actual damages and other equitable relief at the court's discretion.[83] Civil actions for violation of the Consumer Protection Act must be filed within one year after any action by the attorney general has been terminated or within two years after the violation occurs, whichever is later.[84]

Q. **PUNITIVE DAMAGES**

The Kentucky Supreme Court[85] struck down the statutory requirement of subjective awareness that the conduct would cause harm. Consequently, punitive damages are awarded in negligence actions when the defendant's negligence is aggravated by wanton or reckless disregard for the safety or property of others.[86]

The courts require more than a finding of simple negligence although intentional conduct is not required.[87] Proof of the misconduct must be by clear and convincing evidence.[88]

An award of punitive damages need not bear a reasonable relation to the actual damages sustained as long as the character of the act is sufficient to support the award.[89] In determining the amount of punitive damages, the jury must consider: (1) the likelihood that serious harm would result from the misconduct;[90] (2) the degree of defendant's awareness;[91] (3) the profitability of the misconduct to the defendant;[92] (4) the duration of the misconduct and any concealment;[93] and (5) any action by defendant to remedy the misconduct.[94]

A principal or employer may not be liable for punitive damages for the acts of an agent or employee unless the principal or employer authorized, ratified or should have anticipated the conduct.[95]

R. **WRONGFUL DEATH AND SURVIVORSHIP ACTIONS**

A cause of action for wrongful death did not exist under Kentucky common law.[96] However, wrongful death and survivorship claims are authorized by the Kentucky Constitution and Kentucky statute.[97] The personal representative of the decedent may join the wrongful death and most personal injury claims which the decedent had prior to death in the same lawsuit.[98] A limited number of personal injury claims do not survive the death of the plaintiff.[99] The measure of damages in an action for wrongful death is the permanent reduction of the decedent's power to earn money.[100]

Charles M. Pritchett, Jr.
Steven M. Crawford
FROST BROWN TODD, LLC
400 Market Street
32nd Floor
Louisville, Kentucky 40202-3363
(502) 589-5400
Fax (502) 581-1087
cpritchett@fbtlaw.com
scrawford@fbtlaw.com
www.frostbrowntodd.com

ENDNOTES - KENTUCKY

1. Ky. Rev. Stat. Ann. § 413.140(1)(a).

2. *Wiseman v. Alliant Hospitals, Inc.*, 2000 Ky. Lexis 142 (Nov. 22, 2000); *Hazel v. GMC*, 863 F. Supp. 435 (W.D. Ky. 1994).

3. Ky. Rev. Stat. Ann. § 304.39.230(6); *Troxell v. Trammel*, 730 S.W.2d 525 (Ky. 1987).

4. *Lawson v. Helton Sanitation, Inc.*, 2000 Ky. Lexis 133 (Oct. 26, 2000).

5. Ky. Rev. Stat. Ann. § 413.180; *Ford v. Hill*, 874 F. Supp. 149 (E.D. Ky. 1995).

6. Ky. Rev. Stat. Ann. § 413.180(2); *Conner v. George W. Whitesides Co.*, 834 S.W.2d 652 (Ky. 1992).

7. Ky. Rev. Stat. Ann. § 413.120.

8. *G&K Dairy v. Princeton Electric Plant Bd.*, 781 F. Supp. 485 (W.D. Ky. 1991).

9. Ky. Rev. Stat. Ann. § 413.120.

10. Ky. Rev. Stat. Ann. § 355.2-725; *Williams v. Fulmer*, 695 S.W.2d 411 (Ky. 1985).

11. Ky. Rev. Stat. Ann. § 413.140(1)(d).

12. Ky. Rev. Stat. Ann. § 413.160; *Conner v. George W. Whitesides Co.*, 834 S.W.2d 652 (Ky. 1992).

13. Ky. Rev. Stat. Ann. § 413.135.

14. Ky. Rev. Stat. Ann. § 413.120(13).

15. Ky. Rev. Stat. Ann. § 411.184(1)(c).

16. *Williams v. Wilson*, 972 S.W. 2d 260 (Ky. 1998).

17. Ky. Rev. Stat. Ann. § 304.39-010(2)-(3).

18. Ky. Rev. Stat. Ann. § 304.30-060(2); Ky. Rev. Stat. Ann. § 304.39-030; *Stuart v. Capital Enterprise Ins. Co.*, 743 S.W.2d 856 (Ky. Ct. App. 1987).

19. Ky. Rev. Stat. Ann. § 304.39-020(6).

20. Ky. Rev. Stat. Ann. § 304.39-020(5).

21. Ky. Rev. Stat. Ann. § 304.39-060(2)(b).

22. *Carta v. Dale*, 718 S.W.2d 126 (Ky. 1986).

23. Ky. Rev. Stat. Ann. § 304.39-070; *Ohio Sec. Ins. Co. v. Drury*, 582 S.W.2d 64 (Ky. Ct. App. 1979); *Safeco Ins. Co. of America v. Brown*, 887 F. Supp. 974 (W.D. Ky. 1995).

24. *State Farm Mut. Auto. Ins. Co. v. Mattox*, 862 S.W.2d 325 (Ky. 1993).

25. *Mullins v. Commonwealth Life Ins. Co.*, 839 S.W. 2d 245, 247 (Ky. 1992).

26. *M&T Chemicals, Inc. v. Westrick*, 525 S.W. 2d 740, 741 (Ky. 1974).

27. *Smith v. Collins*, 277 S.W. 2d 38, 42 (Ky. 1955).

28. *Commonwealth, Dept. of Highways v. Begley*, 376 S.W. 2d 295, 297 (Ky. 1964).

29. *Morales v. American Honda Motor Co.*, 71 F.3d 531 (6th Cir. 1995); *Tennyson v. Brower*, 823 F. Supp. 421, 423 (E.D. Ky. 1993); *Deutsch v. Shein*, 597 S.W.2d 141, 143-144 (Ky. 1980); *But see Miller v. Marymount Med. Ctr. Inc.*, 2001 Ky. App. Lexis 76 (Ky. Ct. App. June 29, 2001); Restatement (Second) of Torts § 431 (1965).

30. *Perkins v. Trailco Mfg. & Sales Co.*, 613 S.W.2d 855, 857-58 (Ky. 1981); *Morales v. American Honda Motor Co.*, 71 F.3d 531 (6th Cir. 1995).

31. *Id.*

32. *Destock #14, Inc. v. Logsdon*, 993 S.W.2d 952, 958 (Ky. 1999); *Hilen v. Hays*, 673 S.W.2d 713 (Ky. 1984); *Caterpillar, Inc. v. Brock*, 915 S.W.2d 751 (Ky. 1996).

33. *Destock #14, Inc. v. Logsdon*, 993 S.W.2d 952, 958 (Ky. 1999); *Hilen v. Hays*, 673 S.W.2d 713 (Ky. 1984); *USF&G Co. v. Preston*, 26 S.W.3d 145, 148 (Ky. 2000).

34. Ky. Rev. Stat. Ann. § 411.182 ; *Caterpillar, Inc. v. Brock*, 915 S.W.2d 751 (Ky. 1996); Ky. Rev. Stat. Ann. § 411.320(1).

35. Ky. Rev. Stat. Ann. § 411.182.

36. *Hilen v. Hays*, 673 S.W.2d 713, 718 (Ky. 1984).

37. *Stratton v. Parker*, 793 S.W.2d 817, 820 (Ky. 1990); *Stanley v. Aeroquip Corp.*, 1999 U.S. App. Lexis 8034 (6th Cir. Apr. 22, 1999).

38. *Baker v. Webb*, 883 S.W.2d 898, 900 (Ky. Ct. App. 1994); *Floyd v. Carlisle Construction Co., Inc.*, 758 S.W.2d 430 (Ky. 1988).

39. *Wallingford v. Kroger Co.*, 761 S.W.2d 761 (Ky. Ct. App. 1988); *Parker v. Redden*, 421 S.W.2d 586 (Ky. 1967); *Hilen v. Hays*, 673 S.W.2d 713, 716 n.2 (Ky. 1984).

40. *Frank Fehr Brewing Co. v. Corley*, 96 S.W. 2d 860, 864 (Ky. 1936).

41. *Barber v. City of* Louisville, 777 S.W.2d 919, 921 (Ky. 1989);*Vernon v. Gentry*, 334 S.W. 2d 266, 268 (Ky. 1960); *Sadr v. Hager Beauty School, Inc.*, 723 S.W. 2d 886, 887 (Ky. App. 1987).

42. *Schroerlucke v. McDaniel Funeral Home, Inc.*, 291 S.W. 2d 6, 9 (Ky. 1956).

43. *Carr v. Kentucky Utilities Company*, 301 S.W. 2d 894, 898 (Ky. 1957); *Spivey v. Sheeler*, 514 S.W. 2d 667, 670 (Ky. 1974).

44. *Isaacs v. Smith*, 5 S.W.3d 500, 502 (Ky. 1999); *Britton v. Wooten*, 817 S.W.2d 443 (Ky. 1991).

45. *Real Estate Marketing v. Franz*, 885 S.W.2d 921, 927 (Ky. 1994).

46. *Estate of Wheeler v. Veal Realtors and Auctioneers*, 997 S.W.2d 497, 498 (Ky. Ct. App. 1999); *Peak v. Barlow Homes, Inc.*, 765 S.W.2d 577, 578 (Ky. Ct. App. 1988).

47. *Isaacs v. Smith*, 5 S.W.3d 500, 502 (Ky. 1999); *McGrew v. Stone*, 998 S.W.2d 5, 12 (Ky. 1999).

48. Ky. Rev. Stat. Ann. § 411.182(1); *Dix & Associates Pipeline Contractors, Inc. v. Key*, 799 S.W.2d 24, 27 (Ky. 1990).

49. *Dix* at 27.

50. *Hilen v. Hays*, 675 S.W.2d 713 (Ky. 1984); *Dix & Associates Pipeline Contractors, Inc. v. Key.*, 799 S.W.2d 24, 27 (Ky. 1990); *Radcliff Homes, Inc. v. Jackson*, 766 S.W.2d 63 (Ky. Ct. App. 1989).

51. *ARA Services, Inv. v. Pineville Community Hospital*, 2 S.W.3d 104, 106 (Ky. Ct. App. 1999); *Nally v. Boop*, 428 S.W.2d 607 (Ky. 1968).

52. *Brown Hotel Co. v. Pittsburgh Fuel Co.*, 224 S.W.2d 165 (Ky. 1949).

53. *Degener v. Hall Contracting Corp.*, 2000 Ky. Lexis 63 (May 18, 2000); *ARA Services, Inc. v. Pineville Community Hospital*, 2 S.W.3d 104, 106 (Ky. Ct. App. 1999); *Hilen v. Hays*, 675 S.W.2d 713 (Ky. 1984).

54. *Crime Fighters Patrol v. Hiles*, 740 S.W.2d 936, 938 (Ky. 1987); *see Destock #14, Inc. v. Logsden*, 993 S.W.2d 952, 957-958 (Ky. 1999).

55. Ky. Rev. Stat. Ann. § 342.690.

56. Ky. Rev. Stat. Ann. § 342.700.

57. *Old Republic Ins. Co. v. Ashley*, 722 S.W.2d 55 (Ky. Ct. App. 1986).

58. Ky. Rev. Stat. Ann. § 342.700(1); *Mastin v. Liberal Mkts.*, 674 S.W.2d 7 (Ky. 1984); *United States Fid. & Guar. Co. v. Fox*, 872 S.W.2d 91 (Ky. Ct. App. 1993).

59. Ky. Rev. Stat. Ann. § 381. 232.

60. *Kirschner v. Louisville Gas & Elec. Co.*, 743 S.W. 2d 840, 842 (Ky. 1988).

61. *Lloyd v. Lloyd*, 479 S.W. 2d 626 (Ky. 1972).

62. *McDonald v. Talbott*, 447 S.W. 2d 84, 86 (Ky. 1969).

63. *Ferrell v. Hellems*, 408 S.W. 2d 459, 463 (Ky. 1966); *Standard Oil Co. v. Manis*, 433 S.W. 2d 856, 857 (Ky. 1968).

64. Ky. Rev. Stat. Ann. § 411.190(3).

65. Ky. Rev. Stat. Ann. § 411.190(6)(a).

66. *Huddleston By And Through Lynch v. Hughes*, 843 S.W. 2d 901, 906 (Ky. App. 1992).

67. Ky. Rev. Stat. Ann. § 413.241(2).

68. Ky. Rev. Stat. Ann. § 413.241(1).

69. *Destock No. 14, Inc. v. Logsdon*, 993 S.W.2d 952, 958 (Ky. 1999).

70. *Dubord v. GMRI, Inc.*, 52 F. Supp. 2d 779 (W.D. Ky. 1999). Note that plaintiff did not raise whether seller should have recognized plaintiff was intoxicated when served. *But see Colvin v. Sixth-Eight Liquors, Inc.*, 48 K.L.S. 10, p. 31 (Sept. 21, 2001), motion for discretionary review pending.

71. *Gooch v. E.I. Dupont de NeMours & Co.*, 40 F. Supp. 2d 863 (W.D. Ky. 1999).

72. *Id.; Miller's Bottled Gas, Inc. v. Borg-Warner Corp.*, 955 F.2d 1043, 1050 (6th Cir. 1992).

73. *Falcon Coal Co. v. Clark Equip. Co.*, 802 S.W.2d 947, 948-949 (Ky. Ct. App. 1990).

74. Ky. R. Civ. P. 9.02.

75. *Sanford Construction Company v. S&H Contractors, Inc.*, 443 S.W. 2d 227, 235 (Ky. 1969).

76. *United Parcel Service Company v. Rickert*, 996 S.W.2d 464, 468 (Ky. 1999); *Wahba v. Don Corlett Motors, Inc.*, 573 S.W. 2d 357, 359 (Ky. App. 1978); *Cresent Grocery Co. v. Vick*, 240 S.W. 388, 389 (Ky. 1922).

77. *Hall v. Carter*, 324 S.W. 2d 410, 412 (Ky. 1959).

78. *Smith v. General Motors Corp.*, 979 S.W. 2d 127, 129 (Ky. App. 1998).

79. Ky. Rev. Stat. Ann. § 367.110-367.300.

80. Ky. Rev. Stat. Ann. § 367.170(1).

81. Ky. Rev. Stat. Ann. § 367.300; Ky. Rev. Stat. Ann. § 367.990.

82. Ky. Rev. Stat. Ann. § 367.220(1); *Gooch v. E.I. DuPont de Nemours & Co.*, 40 F. Supp. 2d 857, 861-862 (W.D. Ky. 1998).

83. Ky. Rev. Stat. Ann. § 367.220(1).

84. Ky. Rev. Stat. Ann. § 367.220(5).

85. Ky. Rev. Stat. Ann. § 411.184(1)(c); *Williams v. Wilson*, 972 S.W. 2d 260, 269 (Ky. 1998).

86. *Horton v. Union Light, Heat & Power Co.*, 690 S.W. 2d 382, 389 (Ky. 1985).

87. *Williams* at 264.

88. Ky. Rev. Stat. Ann. § 411.184(2).

89. *Fowler v. Mantooth*, 683 S.W. 2d 250, 253 (Ky. 1984).

90. Ky. Rev. Stat. Ann. § 411.186(2)(a).

91. Ky. Rev. Stat. Ann. § 411.186(2)(b).

92. Ky. Rev. Stat. Ann. § 411.186(2)(c).

93. Ky. Rev. Stat. Ann. § 411.186(2)(d).

94. Ky. Rev. Stat. Ann. § 411.186(2)(e).

95. Ky. Rev. Stat. Ann. § 411.184(3).

96. *Smith's Adm'r v. National Coal & Iron Co.*, 117 S.W. 280 (1909).

97. Ky. Const. Sect. 14, 54, 141; Ky. Rev. Stat. Ann. §§ 411.130, 411.133, 411.135, 411.140, 411.145.

98. Ky. Rev. Stat. Ann. § 411.133; *Conner v. George W. Whitesides, Co.*, 834 S.W.2d 652 (Ky. 1992).

99. Ky. Rev. Stat. Ann. § 411.140.

100. *Luttrell v. Wood*, 902 S.W.2d 817 (Ky. 1995); *But see Boarman v. Commonwealth*, 37 S.W.3d 759 (Ky. 2001).

LOUISIANA

A. STATUTES OF LIMITATION (PRESCRIPTION)

Delictual actions are subject to a liberative prescription of one year. This prescription commences to run from the day injury or damage is sustained. It does not run against minors or interdicts in actions involving permanent disability and brought pursuant to the Louisiana Products Liability Act or state law governing product liability actions in effect at the time of the injury or damage.[1]

A legal malpractice act must be filed within one year from the alleged act or within one year from the date that the alleged act, omission, or neglect is discovered or should have been discovered. There is also a three-year preemptive period from the alleged act, omission, or neglect.[2]

An action against a contractor or an architect on account of defects of construction, renovation, or repair of buildings and other works is subject to a liberative prescription of ten years.[3]

A medical malpractice action shall be filed within one year from the date of the discovery of the alleged act of neglect or omission.[4] A claim filed with the Commissioner of Insurance suspends the prescriptive period until 90 days after notification of the Medical Review Panel's decision.[5]

The right to recover damages under a survival and wrongful death action survives for a period of one year from the death of the deceased in favor of the designated beneficiaries.[6]

B. TORT REFORM

As referenced herein, tort reform abolished most forms of strict liability and changed the comparative fault scheme and the liability of joint tortfeasors. Louisiana's legislature has also passed the following reforms:

"Damages" under Louisiana's Civil Code does "not include cost for future medical treatment, services, surveillance, or procedures of any kind unless such treatment, services, surveillance, or procedures are directly related to a manifest physical or mental injury or disease."[7]

Louisiana's Code of Civil Procedure now provides that either side may make a motion for offer of judgment. If the offeree does not accept and a judgment is forthcoming that is 25 percent off the mark of the offer, the offeree shall pay court cost incurred subsequent to the offer.[8]

Louisiana's Code of Civil Procedure was amended to provide that courts *shall* grant a well-founded Motion for Summary Judgment. The mechanics for preparing a Motion for Summary Judgment, or defending against, have not changed.[9]

C. "NO FAULT" LIMITATIONS

No fault limitations are not recognized in Louisiana, except in divorce proceedings.

D. THE STANDARD OF NEGLIGENCE

A party's standard of care varies according to the conduct in which the party is engaged.[10] Louisiana jurisprudence has adopted a duty-risk analysis in determining "negligence." This analysis takes into account the conduct of each individual party and the peculiar circumstances of each case. The relevant inquires are: (1) was the conduct of which the plaintiff complains a cause-in-fact of the resulting harm; (2) what, if any, duties were owed by the respective parties; (3) whether the requisites duties were breached; (4) was the risk, and harm caused, within the scope of protection afforded by the duty breached; (5) were actual damages sustained?[11]

A six-year-old child is not capable of fault.[12]

Various parties and entities are immune from liability for negligent acts and a higher burden of proof is required to impose liability.[13]

E. CAUSATION

Under the duty-risk approach in determining tort liability, the defendant's conduct must be a cause-in-fact of the plaintiff's damages. This determination is usually a "but for" inquiry that tests whether the damages would not have occurred but for defendant's conduct. The "substantial factor" inquiry is also useful to determine cause-in-fact when the conduct of each of two or more persons actually contributes to the plaintiff's harm even though the harm would have occurred without the interaction of one.[14]

F. COMPARATIVE NEGLIGENCE

Louisiana's Civil Code requires that the percentage of fault of all persons causing or contributing to the injury, death, or loss be determined regardless of whether the person is a party to the action or a nonparty, and regardless of the person's insolvency, ability to pay, immunity by statute, including the workers' compensation statute, or that the other person's identity is not known or reasonably ascertainable.[15]

In assessing the nature of the conduct of the parties, various factors may influence the degree of fault assigned, including: (1) whether the conduct resulted from inadvertence or involved an awareness of the danger; (2) how great a risk was created by the conduct; (3) the significance of what was sought by the conduct; (4) the capacities of the actors, whether it is superior or inferior; and (5) any extenuating circumstances that might require the actor to proceed in haste, without proper thought.[16]

The concept of comparative fault does not apply when plaintiffs' fault is intentional in nature.[17]

G. RES IPSA LOQUITUR AND INHERENTLY DANGEROUS ACTIVITIES

1. Res Ipsa Loquitur

Res ipsa loquitur is a rule of circumstantial evidence that allows a court to infer negligence on the part of a defendant when the facts indicate the defendant's negligence, more probably than not, caused the injury.[18] However, the application of this doctrine is defeated if an inference that the plaintiff's injuries were due to a cause other than the defendant's negligence can be drawn as reasonably as the one that they were due to such negligence.[19]

2. Inherently Dangerous Activities

A party's standard of care varies according to the conduct in which the party is engaged.[20]

The duty of extraordinary care is placed on those who own or control a dangerous instrumentality, such as a firearm.[21]

Louisiana courts have imposed absolute liability (i.e., liability without proof of negligence or fault) when harm results from the risks inherent in the nature of certain activities that can cause injury even when conducted with the greatest prudence and care. The courts have generally adopted a three-prong test for determining the existence of an ultrahazardous activity: (1) the activity must relate to land or some other immovable; (2) the activity itself must cause the injury and the defendant must be engaged directly in the injury-producing activity; and (3) the activity must not require substandard conduct to cause injury.[22] Such activities have included pile driving, storage of toxic gas, blasting with explosives, and crop dusting with airplanes.[23]

H. NEGLIGENCE *PER SE*

The Doctrine of Negligence *Per Se* has been rejected in Louisiana, but statutory violations provide guidelines for civil liability.[24]

I. JOINT AND SEVERAL LIABILITY

Louisiana's Legislature revoked solidarity for nonconspiratorial acts and expresses defendant's liability as a joint and divisible obligation and therefore a joint tortfeasor cannot be liable for more than its degree of fault.[25] To recover under a theory of civil conspiracy, plaintiff must establish that there was an agreement to commit an illegal or tortious act that resulted in plaintiff's injury.[26]

When a plaintiff settles with and releases one of several joint tortfeasors, he thereby deprives the remaining obligors of their right to contribution against the released obligor. Accordingly, settlement of one solidary obligor reduces his recovery against the remaining obligor by the percentage of the proportion of fault of the released obligor.[27]

J. INDEMNITY

Indemnity shifts the entire loss from one defendant to another to pay damages occasioned by the negligence of another. The obligation to indemnify may be express, as in a contractual provision, or may be implied in law, even in the absence of an indemnity agreement.

An implied contract of indemnity arises only where the liability of the person seeking indemnification is solely constructive or derivative and only against one who, because of his act, has caused such constructive liability to be imposed.[28]

The general rules governing interpretation of contracts apply to indemnity agreements. A contract of indemnity whereby the indemnitee is indemnified against the consequences of his own negligence will be strictly construed, and such a contract will not be construed to indemnify an indemnitee against losses resulting to him through his own negligent acts unless such an intention is expressed in unequivocal terms.[29]

An action for indemnity is a separate substantive cause of action, independent of the underlying wrong, and distinct from an action for attorney's fees.[30]

K. BAR OF WORKERS' COMPENSATION STATUTE

Louisiana workers' compensation law limits an employee's claim to compensation benefits when a coemployee or his employer has negligently caused him to be injured.[31] The "intentional act" exception to this exclusivity provision has been narrowly interpreted and requires the defendant either to consciously desire to bring about the physical result of his act or believe that the result was substantially certain to follow his conduct.[32] An employee or his dependents may also file a negligence suit against a "third party" who is legally liable for the injury. The law also recognizes the right of the employer who has paid workers' compensation benefits (or who may become liable for workers' compensation benefits) to seek reimbursements from such a third person for benefits the employer has paid or may be required to pay in the future.[33] Should judgment be rendered against the third person and damages be recovered, the damage will be apportioned so that the employer will recover first from the award of the payments of worker's compensation benefits and medical benefits paid on behalf of the worker or his dependents. If the award is sufficient to satisfy the employer's lien, then the remainder of the award will be assessed in favor of the injured worker or his dependents, and when payments of this judgment is made to the employee or his dependents, the liability of the employer for compensation will cease until such time that the benefits that may be due exceed the amount of the excess judgment.[34]

L. PREMISES LIABILITY

The owner or operator of a facility has the duty of exercising reasonable care for the safety of persons on his premises and the duty of not exposing such persons to unreasonable risks of injury or harm.[35] This includes the duty to discover any unreasonably dangerous conditions and either correct the condition or warn of its existence.[36] When considering the duty owed by a landowner to keep property in a reasonably safe condition, the status of the injured person as an invitee or trespasser is relevant but not determinative.[37] Merchants, as defined by statute, have the same duty as a landowner but have a heightened standard of care,[38] which is reflected in the degree of risk posed by any foreign object on a floor and the reasonableness of the methods used to remove the risk.[39]

Businesses are not the insurers of their patron's safety and generally have no duty to protect others from the criminal activities of third persons.[40] This duty only arises under limited circumstances when a criminal act in question was reasonably foreseeable to the owner of the business. The foreseeability of the crime risk on the defendant's property and the gravity of the risk determine the existence and the extent of the defendant's duty. The greater the forseeability and gravity of the harm, the greater the duty of care that will be imposed on the business. The foreseeability and gravity of the harm are to be determined by the facts and circumstances of each case.[41]

M. DRAM SHOP LIABILITY

Louisiana's Dram Shop Statute provides that the consumption of alcohol, not the sale or the serving of the alcohol, is the proximate cause of any injury occurring off the premises. This applies to injuries to either the consumer who is over the age for the lawful purchase of alcohol or to any third person injured by the consumer due to the effects of alcohol. The statute does not relieve the seller or the furnisher of alcohol to minors or to third persons injured by minors due to the effects of alcohol.[42]

Louisiana statute makes it unlawful for any adult to purchase on behalf of a minor any alcoholic beverage. Although the statute does not directly impose civil responsibility, it serves as a guideline for the determination of an adult's civil duty to refrain from purchasing alcoholic beverages for use by a minor.[43]

N. ECONOMIC LOSS

Economic loss is recoverable under Louisiana's law.[44]

O. FRAUD AND MISREPRESENTATION

Louisiana's Code of Civil Procedure requires that causes of action for fraud be pleaded with particularity.[45]

Louisiana's Civil Code defines fraud as a misrepresentation or a suppression of the truth made with the intention either to obtain an unjust advantage for one party or to cause a loss of convenience to the other. Fraud may also result from silence or inaction.[46] The two necessary elements to prove fraud are an intention of fraud and an actual or potential loss of damages.[47]

The tort doctrine of negligent misrepresentation has been integrated into the duty/risk analysis. For the cause of action to arise, whether plaintiff is a third party or a party to a contract or transaction, there must be a legal duty on the part of the defendant to supply correct information, there must be a breach of that duty, and the breach must have caused plaintiff's damage.[48]

P. CONSUMER FRAUD STATUTES

Louisiana's Unfair Trade and Consumer Protection Law (UTCP) protects consumers and competitors from unfair methods of competition, and unfair or deceptive acts or practices and conduct of any trade or commerce.[49]

Either the Director of the Governor's Consumer Protection Division or Attorney General may impose penalties for any violation.[50] Private actions may also be brought under the UTCP,[51] in which case, the plaintiff must establish a causal connection between the unlawful practice and his ascertainable loss.[52]

Actions under the UTCP have a one-year prescriptive period from the time of the transaction or act that gives rise to the right of action.[53]

Q. PUNITIVE DAMAGES

Punitive damages are contrary to Louisiana's legal philosophy and are only permitted where specifically provided for by statute.[54] Louisiana's Civil Code does provide that exemplary damages may be awarded on proof that the injuries on which the action is based were caused by a wanton or reckless disregard for the rights and safety of others by a defendant whose intoxication while operating a motor vehicle was a cause-in-fact of the resulting injury and the operator is found more than 25 percent negligent as a result of his blood-alcohol concentration.[55] There is a presumption that a person is under the influence of alcoholic beverages if at that time 0.10 percent or more by weight of alcohol is in his blood.[56]

On April 16, 1996, La. Civ. Code Ann. Art. 2315.3, allowing for punitive damages for the wanton and reckless disregard for public safety in the storage, handling, or transportation of hazardous or toxic substances, was repealed. The legislative change is to be applied propectively only.

R. WRONGFUL DEATH AND SURVIVORSHIP ACTIONS

Louisiana's Civil Code provides for separate and distinct survival and wrongful death actions.[57] The survival action comes into existence simultaneously with the existence of the tort and is transmitted to beneficiaries on the victim's death and permits recovery only for the damages suffered by the victim from the time of injury to the moment of death.[58] A beneficiaries wrongful death action, by definition, comes into existence on the tort victim's death and serves to compensate a legislatively created class of persons for the loss occasioned by the wrongful killing of the decedent. The beneficiaries action encompasses their damages suffered from the moment of the tort victim's death and thereafter and compensates them for their own personal losses, both economical and emotional, suffered as a result of the tort victim's death.[59]

William J. Hamlin
William C. Ellison
BORDELON, HAMLIN & THERIOT
701 South Peters Street, Suite 100
New Orleans, Louisiana 70130
(504) 524-5328
Fax (504) 523-1071
whamlin@bh-t.com
wcellison@bh-t.com

ENDNOTES - LOUISIANA

1. La. Civ. Code Ann. art. 3492. *See also Crump v. Sabine River Authority*, 737 So. 2d 720 (La. 1999) and La. Civ. Code Ann. art. 3462 *et seq.*, art. 3467 *et seq.*, and art. 3503 concerning the interruption and suspension of prescription.

2. La. Rev. Stat. Ann. § 5605. *See also Boykin v. Coregis Insurance Co.*, 800 So. 2d 926 (La. App. 5th Cir. 2001).

3. La. Civ. Code Ann. art. 3500. *See also,* La. Rev. Stat. Ann. 9:2772.

4. La. Rev. Stat. Ann. § 9:5628.

5. La. Rev. Stat. Ann. § 40:1299.47(A)(2)(a).

6. La. Civ. Code Ann. arts. 2315.1, 2315.2.

7. La. Civ. Code Ann. art. 2315.

8. La. Civ. Code Proc. Ann. art. 920.

9. La. Civ. Code Proc. Ann. art. 966(c).

10. *Vendetto v. Sonat Offshore Drilling*, 725 So. 2d 474 (La. 1999). *See also* Frank L. Marars & Thomas C. Gallagan, Louisiana Tort Law § 39-2 (1996).

11. *Pitre v. Louisiana Tech University*, 673 So. 2d 585 (La. 1996); *Socorro v. City of New Orleans*, 579 So. 2d 931 (La. 1991).

    Effective June 1996, the Louisiana Legislature repealed La. Civ. Code Ann. art. 2317 and changed the requirement for liability under the article from strict liability to negligence. The Legislature also repealed arts. 660, 667, 2321 & 2322 to establish negligence standards. However, Civ. Code Ann. art. 667 retains its strict liability character for the ultrahazardous activities of pile driving and blasting with explosives and Civ. Code Ann. art. 2321 retains the rule of strict liability for damage caused by a dog.

12. *Jones v. Hawkins*, 708 So. 2d 749 (La. App. 2d Cir. 1998); *Moore v. State Farm*, 499 So. 2d 146 (La. App. 2d Cir. 1996).

13. La. Rev. Stat. Ann. §§ 9:2791–9:2800.10.

14. *Edwards v. Horstman*, 687 So. 2d 1007 (La. 1997) *reh'g denied*; *Saden v. Kirby*, 660 So. 2d 423 (La. 1995); *Boykin v. Louisiana Transit Co., Inc.*, 707 So. 2d 1225 (La. 1998), *reh'g denied*.

15. La. Civ. Code Ann. art. 2323.

16. *Watson v. State Farm & Cas. Ins.*, 469 So. 2d 967 (La. 1985).

17. La. Civ. Code Ann. Art 2323C. *See also Clark v. Burchard*, 2001 WL 1450742 (La. App. 4th Cir. Nov. 14, 2001).

18. *Spott v. Otis Elevator Company*, 601 So. 2d 1355 (La. 1992).

19. *Cross v. State, DOTD*, 670 So. 2d 1324 (La. App. 5th Cir. 1996); *Lexington Insurance v. Rheem/Ruud Manufacturing Co.*, 610 So. 2d 232 (La. App. 3d Cir. 1992).

20. *Vandetto v. Sonat Offshore Drilling Co.*, 725 So. 2d 424 (La. 1999).

21. *Saurage v. Palermo*, 672 So. 2d 351 (La. App. 1st Cir. 1996). *See also* La. Rev. Stat. Ann. § 9:2800.60 concerning liability for manufacturers and sellers of firearms.

22. *Bartlett v. Browning-Ferris Industries*, 683 So. 2d 1319 (La. App. 3d Cir. 1996).

23. *Id.*, citing *Langlois v. Allied Chemical Corp.*, 249 So. 2d 133 (La. 1971).

24. *Galloway v. State, DOTD*, 654 So. 2d 1345 (La. 1995).

25. La. Civ. Code Ann. art. 1804, 2323, 2324. *Aucoin v. State, DOTD*, 712 So. 2d 62 (La. 1998) held that the amendment to Civ. Code Ann. art. 2324 was not retroactive.

26. *Butz v. Lynch*, 710 So. 2d 1171 (La. App. 1st Cir. 1998).

27. La. Civ. Code Ann. art. 1803, 1804; *Taylor v. USF&G*, 630 So. 2d 237 (La. 1993); *Buckbee v. Aweco, Inc.*, 614 So. 2d 1233 (La. 1993); *Oxley v. Sabine River Authority*, 663 So. 2d 497 (La. App. 3d Cir. 1995).

28. *Nassif v. Sunrise Homes, Inc.*, 739 So. 2d 183 (La. 1999); *Housing Authority v. Standard Paint and Varnish*, 612 So. 2d 916 (La. App. 4th Cir. 1992).

29. *Perkins v. Rubicon, Inc.*, 563 So. 2d 258 (La. 1990).

30. *Nassif v. Sunrise Homes, Inc.*, 739 So. 2d 183 (La. 1999).

31. La. Rev. Stat. Ann. §§ 23:1021, *et seq.*

32. *Brown v. Diversified Hospitality Group*, 600 So. 2d (La. App. 4th Cir. 1992); *Bazley v. Tortorich*, 397 So. 2d 475 (La. 1981).

33. La. Rev. Stat. Ann. § 23:1101.

34. La. Rev. Stat. Ann. § 23:1103.

35. *Peterson v. Gibralter Savings & Loan*, 733 So. 2d (La. 1999); *Duke v. Weber's IGA Store*, 800 So. 2d 1002 (La. App. 5th Cir. 2001).

36. *Pitre v. Louisiana Tech University*, 673 So. 2d 585 (La. 1996).

37. *Fontenot v. Fontenot*, 688 So. 2d 1054 (La. App. 3d Cir. 1996), *writ denied*, 679 So. 2d 1347 (La. 1996); *Wiggins v. Ledet*, 643 So. 2d 797 (La. App. 4th Cir. 1994).

38. The rationale for imposing such a high degree of care on store merchants is because self-service grocery systems require customers to focus their attention on the shelves and to handle merchandise. The system increases the risk of harm from objects dropped on the floor by customers and, correspondingly, the duty to minimize the risk by frequent inspections and clean-ups. *Lachico v. First National Bank Sharer's, Inc.*, 673 So. 2d 305 (La. App. 1st Cir. 1996); citing *Gonzales v. Winn Dixie*, 326 So. 2d 486, 498 (La. 1996).

39. La. Rev. Stat. Ann. § 9:2800.6; *Lachico v. First National Bank Sharer's Inc.*, 673 So. 2d 305 (La. App. 1st Cir. 1996).

40. *Goins v. Wal-Mart Stores, Inc.*, 800 So. 2d 783 (La. 2001); *Posecai v. Wal-Mart Stores, Inc.*, 752 So.2d 762 (La. 1999); *Harris v. Pizza-Hut of Louisiana, Inc.*, 455 So. 2d 1364 (La. 1984). *See also Williams v. State*, 786 So. 2d 927 (La. App. 2d Cir. 2001), on applying the duty to a university dormitory.

41. *Posecai v. Wal-Mart Stores, Inc.*, 99-C-1222 (La. Nov. 30, 1999).

42. La. Rev. Stat. Ann. § 9:2800.1; *Spears v. Bradford*, 652 So. 2d 628 (La. App. 1st Cir. 1995). *But see Bery v. Zummo*, 786 So. 2d 708 (La. 2001).

43. La. Rev. Stat. Ann. § 14:91.3; *Spears v. Bradford*, 652 So. 2d 628 (La. App. 1st Cir. 1995).

44. *Steptoe v. Lallie Kemp Hospital*, 634 So. 2d 331 (La. 1994); *Folse v. Fakouri*, 371 So. 2d 1120 (La. 1979); *Marcel v. Becknel*, 691 So. 2d 1344 (La. App. 1st Cir. 1997). *See also* La. Civ. Code Ann. art. 2520, *et seq.*

45. *See* La. Code Civ. Proc. Ann. art. 856.

46. La. Civ. Code Ann. art. 1953.

47. *Williamson v. Haynes Best Western*, 688 So. 2d 1201 (La. App. 4th Cir. 1997); *Transworld Drilling Co. v. Texas General Resources, Inc.*, 604 So. 2d 586, 590 (La. App. 4th Cir. 1992).

48. *Barrie v. VP Exterminators, Inc.*, 625 So. 2d 1007 (La. 1993).

49. La. Rev. Stat. Ann. §§ 51:1401 *et seq.*

50. La. Rev. Stat. Ann. § 51:1407.

51. La. Rev. Stat. Ann. § 51:1409.

52. La. Rev. Stat. Ann. § 51:1409(a).

53. La. Rev. Stat. Ann. § 51:1409(e).

54. *Fairley v. Ocean Drilling and Exploration Co.*, 689 So. 2d 736 (La. App. 4th Cir. 1997); La. Civ. Code Ann. art. 3546.

55. La. Civ. Code Ann. art. 2315.4; La. Rev. Stat. Ann. § 9:2798.4; *Bourque v. Bailey*, 643 So. 2d 236 (La. App. 3d Cir. 1994).

56. La. Rev. Stat. Ann. § 32:662; *Parker v. Krogers, Inc.*, 394 So. 2d 1178 (La. 1981).

57. La. Civ. Code Ann. arts. 2350.1, 2350.2, respectively.

58. *Taylor v. Giddens*, 618 So. 2d 834, 840 (La. 1993).

59. *Brown v. Drillers, Inc.*, 630 So. 2d 741 (La. 1994).

MAINE

A. STATUTE OF LIMITATIONS

The statute of limitations for all claims in torts is six years except where the state law specifically provides for a different time period.[1] Notable exceptions to the six-year statute of limitations are a two-year statute of limitations for claims of assault and battery, false imprisonment, slander, libel,[2] wrongful death,[3] and for all causes of action against a ski area owner or operator.[4] In addition, the statute of limitations for malpractice or professional negligence against architects or engineers is four years after the discovery of such malpractice or negligence but no more than ten years after "substantial completion" of the project or services provided.[5] Similarly, all actions for professional negligence against land surveyors must be commenced within four years after the negligence is discovered, but no more than 20 years after the completion of the plan or services provided.[6]

A cause of action for professional malpractice against an attorney must be filed within six years of the act or omission giving rise to the injury.[7] The discovery rule applies only if the attorney negligently prepared a title opinion, providing that such suit is filed within 20 years after the act or omission took place.[8] In addition, the discovery rule applies to alleged professional negligence in the drafting of a last will and testament, with no limitation on when such action can be brought.[9]

A medical malpractice claim has a three-year statute of limitations that begins to run on the date of the act or omission giving rise to the injury, except when the malpractice involves the leaving of a foreign object in the patient's body. In such case, the statute of limitations accrues when the plaintiff discovers or reasonably should have discovered the harm.[10] Foreign objects do not include chemical compounds or devises intentionally implanted or permitted to remain in the patient's body as a part of the health care treatment.[11]

Claims against government entities or employees of the State of Maine, a category that includes municipalities, have a two-year statute of limitations.[12] A notice of a claim must be filed within 180 days of accrual of the cause of action.[13] Otherwise the claim will be dismissed, unless good cause can be shown for why notice was not timely filed.[14] Good cause has been interpreted to require a showing that the plaintiff was unable to file a claim or was meaningfully prevented from learning of the information forming the basis for his or her complaint.[15]

Tort claims are generally tolled during the period of a plaintiff's incompetence by reason of age, mental illness, or imprisonment,[16] except where specifically modified by statute. For example, a minor's claim against a medical professional must be commenced within six years after the cause of action first accrues or within three years after the minor reaches the age of majority, which ever occurs first.[17] In addition, the period of a defendant's absence from a state tolls the statute of limitations.[18]

Maine has no statue of limitations for claims based on a sexual act against a minor.[19]

B. THE STANDARD FOR NEGLIGENCE

To prove negligence under Maine law, a plaintiff must show that the defendant owed him a duty, that he breached that duty, and that the plaintiff's injuries were proximately caused by the breach.[20]

The standard of care in a negligence action is the level of care that an ordinary prudent and reasonable person would exercise when conducting his own affairs under similar circumstances.[21] "The duty is always the same-to conform to the legal standard of reasonable conduct in the light of the apparent risk."[22] A child "is judged in accordance with the standard of what might be expected of an ordinary careful [child] of like age, capacity and experience."[23] This subjective standard does not apply when the child's actions are adult in nature, such as driving an automobile. The Maine Supreme Judicial Court has rejected the doctrine of imputed parental negligence, and the negligence of the parent may not be imputed to the child.[24]

Professionals must adhere to a standard of care consistent with the skill, care and diligence exercised by the average and reasonably competent member of that same profession.[25] Establishing this standard ordinarily requires the testimony of an expert.[26]

Violating a statute or state or private regulation is not *per se* negligent, but it may be evidence of negligence.[27]

Duty is a question of law in Maine.[28] When a court is asked to determine whether a duty exists between a plaintiff and a defendant it weighs several factors, which includes the foreseeability of the injury to the plaintiff and policy considerations, such as society's social mores and values and the goal of limiting the scope of liability for a defendant's malfeasance in an appropriate manner.[29]

In a negligence case, causation is generally a question of fact for the jury.[30] However, "[t]he mere possibility of such causation is not enough; and when the matter remains one of pure speculation or conjecture, or the probabilities are at best evenly balanced, it becomes the duty of the court to direct a verdict for the defendant."[31] The Maine Supreme Judicial Court has cautioned courts against using jury instructions that invoke "but for" causation as the standard.[32] The Maine Supreme Judicial Court has also identified foreseeability as an important factor in determining whether an injury was proximately caused by the defendant's acts, finding that if an injury is "reasonably foreseeable," proximate cause exists.[33]

C. COMPARATIVE NEGLIGENCE AND ASSUMPTION OF RISK

1. Comparative Negligence

By statute, Maine is a comparative-fault state. The defendant's fault must be greater than the fault of the plaintiff in order for the plaintiff to recover.[34] The amount of a plaintiff's recovery, however, is determined by his relative blameworthiness. If the jury determines that the plaintiff's fault does not exceed that of the defendant, then it is asked to assess damages based on the relative blameworthiness of the parties.[35]

2. Assumption of Risk

The doctrine of the voluntary assumption of risk for the most part has been abolished by the Maine comparative negligence statute, since voluntary assumption of risk is a form of contributory negligence.[36] The defense of contractual assumption of risk, however, is still available in limited circumstances, such as when an employee contractually assumes the risk of an "open and obvious risk[ ] incident to [his] work," or "such dangers that are normally and necessarily incident to the occupation."[37]

D. *RES IPSA LOQUITUR* AND INHERENT DANGEROUS ACTIVITIES, AND PRODUCTS

1. *Res Ipsa Loquitur*

Under Maine law, the doctrine of *res ipsa loquitur* allows the plaintiff to shift the burden of proof in a negligence case to the defendant by proving that: (1) there has been an unexplained accident; (2) the instrument that caused the injury was under the management and control of the defendant; and in the ordinary course of events the accident would not have happened absent negligence on the part of the defendant.[38]

Unlike some other jurisdictions, in Maine there is no requirement that the instrument be within the "exclusive control" of the defendant for the jury to find liability under the doctrine of *res ipsa loquitur*.[39]

2. Inherent Dangerous Activity

There is no special standard of negligence for an activity that is considered inherently or extremely dangerous, but the standard of care in a negligence suit involving such instrumentality is an ordinary or reasonable level of care under the circumstances.[40] Courts have held that the circumstantial element of this duty requires that the exercise of care be in proportion to the danger involved.[41] Therefore, a higher duty of care exists when the risks attendant to an activity are great.[42]

In *Albison v. Robbins & White, Inc.*,[43] for example, the Maine Supreme Judicial Court was asked to determine the liability of a company whose blasting had caused significant damage to several homes near the blasting site. The court held that this was a negligence case, but that the defendant was required to exercise a high degree of care when blasting because blasting is an extremely dangerous activity.[44]

3. **Inherently Dangerous Product**

By statute, Maine has codified the essence of Section 402A of the Restatement of Torts.[45] Under Maine law, "one who sells any goods or products in a defective condition unreasonably dangerous to the user or consumer or his property is strictly liable for the physical harm thereby caused to a person whom the manufacturer, seller or supplier might reasonably have expected to use, consume or be affected by the goods, or to his property."[46] A product can be defective by means of an error in the manufacturing process, an error in the design process, or a failure to warn.[47] In determining whether a design is "unreasonably dangerous," Maine follows a "danger utility test," examining the utility of the product's design, the risk of the design and the feasibility of safer alternatives.[48] Evidence of modification of the product after an accident is not admissible to prove a defective product, design, or need for a warning when such modification is made by the manufacturer, but is admissible as evidence of the same when made by a third party.[49] A manufacturer's compliance with federal safety standards is relevant, but may not be outcome determinative, depending on whether the federal statute was intended to preempt state standards.[50]

Similarly Maine follows Comment j of the Restatement (Second) of Torts, Section 402A and recognizes that even where a product is faultlessly made, it may be deemed "defective" under the Maine Strict liability statute, if it is unreasonably dangerous to place the product in the hands of a user without a suitable warning and the product is supplied without such warning.[51] In Maine, an action for failure to warn requires a three-part analysis. (1) whether the defendant had a duty to warn the plaintiff; (2) whether the actual warning on the product, if any, was inadequate; and (3) whether the inadequate warning proximately caused the plaintiff's injury.[52]

E. **JOINT AND SEVERAL LIABILITY**

In order for there to be joint and several liability among two or more parties, the negligence of each party must be the proximate cause of the same injury.[53] An action in contribution may be brought as a cross-claim against a codefendant or it may be brought in a subsequent case. In a case with multiple defendants, any defendant has the right to ask the fact finder to determine the percentage of fault of any other defendant.[54] Such action for contribution can be brought even when the other joint tortfeasor is not legally liable to the injured person because his fault was not greater than that of the injured person.[55] If a joint tortfeasor is not a defendant in the initial action, claims for indemnity or contribution accrue against that party when one of the defendants pays an amount to the plaintiff that represents a percentage of the total damages that is greater than that defendant's percentage of fault.[56]

In 1999, the Maine comparative negligence statute was modified for the express purpose of allowing Pierringer releases.[57] Under the statute as amended, if a defendant is released by the plaintiff under an agreement that precludes the plaintiff from collecting against the remaining parties that portion of any damages attributable to the released defendant's share of responsibility, then the following rules apply:

- The released defendant is entitled to dismissal with prejudice from the case. The dismissal bars all related claims for contribution assertable by remaining parties against the released defendant.[58]

- The trial court must preserve for the remaining parties a fair opportunity to adjudicate the liability of the released and dismissed defendant. Remaining parties may conduct discovery against a released and dismissed defendant and invoke evidentiary rules at trial as if the released and dismissed defendant were still a party.[59]

- To apportion responsibility in the pending action for claims that were included in the settlement and presented at trial, a finding on the issue of the released and dismissed defendant's liability binds all parties to the suit, but such a finding has no binding effect in other actions relating to other damage claims.[60]

Any settlement between the plaintiff and any joint tortfeasor, is deducted from the amount of the plaintiff's final recovery.[61]

F. INDEMNITY

In Maine, indemnity is available under three different circumstances: (1) indemnity may be agreed to expressly; (2) a contractual right of indemnification may be implied from the nature of the relationship of the parties; and (3) a tort-based right to indemnity may be found where there is a great disparity in the fault of the parties.[62] There must be loss, not merely liability, before indemnity is due; no money judgment may be rendered for indemnity until the party seeking indemnity has suffered an actual loss.[63]

No Maine court has specifically defined the circumstances under which the relationship between the parties creates an implied contractual right to indemnity.

The concept of tort-based indemnity has never been fully embraced by the Maine Supreme Judicial Court. The court has, however, held that actions for both contribution and indemnity require a showing that both the defendant and the third-party defendant committed negligence that was the proximate cause of the plaintiff's injury.[64] The Maine Supreme Court has also held that a party is responsible in indemnity when it induces the commission of the tort.[65]

G. BAR OF WORKERS' COMPENSATION

Under Maine's Workers' Compensation Act,[66] an employee is barred from suiting a qualified employer.[67] Workers' compensation is the employee's sole means of redress.[68] Maine has not adopted the intentional tort exception to workers' compensation coverage that exists in a number of jurisdictions, but instead has taken the position that in the absence of legislative changes in the Act, the exclusivity and immunity in provisions of the Workers' Compensation Act should be construed broadly.[69]

If a party other than the covered employer is held liable for the employee's injury, the employee has two options. He may seek recovery from either the employer or from the third party. If the employee elects to recover from his employer, he may thereafter sue the third party, but the employer is entitled to a lien against any recovery for compensation, less legal and other compensation fees.[70] If the employee does not subsequently sue the third party, the employer may pursue the claim on 30-days' written notice to the employee.[71]

Finally, a third party is prohibited from recovering from an employer covered by the Workers' Compensation Act for indemnity or contribution.[72]

H. PREMISES LIABILITY

Under Maine common law, a landowner owes a duty to use reasonable care under the circumstances to any person that is lawfully on his property.[73] This common law duty has been modified by the Maine Recreational Use Statute, which grants property owners broad immunity from liability for failing to keep premises safe or failing to warn of hazardous conditions when the property is used for recreational or harvesting purposes.[74]

Those unlawfully on the property of another are disfavored plaintiffs under Maine law. A landowner is generally liable for a trespasser's injuries only if he wantonly or willfully injures the trespasser.[75]

In terms of children, the Maine Supreme Judicial Court has suggested an owner or an occupier of a business premise can be found negligent for failing to protect against reasonably recognizable dangers resulting from foreseeable misuse of the premise by children.[76] Parental supervision is deemed only one circumstance bearing on the premise owner's duty to exercise reasonable care.[77] In addition, the Maine Supreme Judicial Court has incorporated the attractive nuisance doctrine into Maine law by adopting Restatement (Second) of Torts, Section 339-Artificial Conditions Highly Dangerous to Trespassing Children, applying a strict interpretation of the Restatement criteria in determining whether a possessor of land should be subject to liability, including that the child's presence on the property must be reasonably foreseeable and allowing recovery only for dangerous conditions that involved a serious risk of harm.[78] No recovery is available where the child appreciates the risk.[79]

I. DRAM SHOP ACT

The Maine Liquor Liability Act[80] makes a person liable for injuries that result from his negligent or reckless service of alcohol to a minor or an individual whom a reasonably prudent person would conclude was intoxicated.[81] The statute specifically provides that the person who consumed the alcohol may not recover under the statute unless he is under the age of 18.[82] Under this law, liability for damages, other than those related to medical care, are limited to $250,000.[83]

J. ECONOMIC LOSS DOCTRINE

Under Maine law, there is no recovery in tort for economic loss caused by a defective product's damage to itself instead. The Maine Supreme Judicial Court has held that economic loss for damages flowing from the failure of a product to meet a customer's expectations are properly recovered in contract under a breach of warranty theory.[84]

K. FRAUD AND MISREPRESENTATION

A defendant is liable for fraud or misrepresentation when: (1) he makes a false and misleading statement; (2) of material fact; (3) with knowledge of its falsity or in reckless disregard of its truth or its falsity; (4) for the purposes of including another to act or to refrain from acting in reliance on the statement; and (5) the plaintiff justifiably relies on the statement as true and suffers an injury as a result.[85] These elements must be pled with particularity[86] and proven by clear and convincing evidence at trial.[87]

Similarly, the Maine Supreme Judicial Court has set forth a specific test for a claim for negligent misrepresentation:

> One who, in the course of his business, profession or employment, or in any other transaction in which he has a pecuniary interest, supplies false information for the guidance of others in their business transactions, is subject to liability for pecuniary losses caused to them by their justifiable reliance upon the information, if he fails to exercise reasonable care or competence in obtaining or communicating information.[88]

L. CONSUMER FRAUD

Maine's Unfair Trade Practices Act (UTPA) protects consumers from unfair methods of competition and deceptive acts in trade or commerce.[89] The statute specifically provides that it should be interpreted in a manner consistent with the Federal Trade Commission Act.[90]

Violations of the UTPA fall within Maine's six-year statue of limitations.[91]

M. PUNITIVE DAMAGES

The Maine Supreme Court's decision in *Tuttle v. Raymond*[92] sets the standard for when punitive damages may be awarded. The court held that in order to recover punitive damages, a plaintiff must prove that the defendant acted with malice. Gross negligence or reckless disregard for the circumstances are insufficient.[93] Plaintiff may prove malice either by showing that defendant's actions were motivated by actual ill will, or by proving that his actions were so outrageous that malice can be interred.[94] The malice standard must be met with "clear and convincing" evidence. The Maine Supreme Court has specifically rejected the preponderance-of-the-evidence standard under these circumstances.[95]

Facts to be considered by the fact finder in determining whether punitive damages should be imposed include the egregiousness of the defendant's conduct, the ability of the defendant to pay such award, and any criminal punishment imposed for the conduct in question such that would indicate that an award of punitive damages would serve a deterrent function beneficial to society.[96]

Punitive damages are not available in strict product liability claims in the absence of personal injury or damage to property other than the defective product.[97]

N. WRONGFUL DEATH AND SURVIVORSHIP

The right to recover for wrongful death is statutory in Maine.[98] The statute allows specific dependents to recover.[99] The statute specifically delineates how recovery is divided among those entitled to recover.[100] It also limits damages for the "loss of comfort, society, and companionship" of the deceased to $400,000[101] and punitive damages to $75,000.[102] A plaintiff may also recover pecuniary damages, and damages for medical and funeral reimbursement.[103] No recovery can be made under the statute for the benefit of the estate, creditors, or distributees.[104]

Peter W. Culley
Teresa A. Curtin
PIERCE ATWOOD
One Monument Square
Portland, Maine 04101
(207) 791-1100
Fax (207) 791-1350
www.pierceatwood.com

ENDNOTES - MAINE

1. Me. Rev. Stat. Ann. tit. 14 § 752 (1980 & Supp. 2001).

2. Me. Rev. Stat. Ann. tit. 14 § 753 (Supp. 2001).

3. Me. Rev. Stat. Ann. tit. 18-A § 2-804(b) (Supp. 2001).

4. Me. Rev. Stat. Ann. tit. 14 § 752 (1980 & Supp. 2001).

5. Me. Rev. Stat. Ann. tit. 14 § 752-A (1980 & Supp. 2001).

6. Me. Rev. Stat. Ann. tit. 14 § 752-D (Supp. 2001).

7. Me. Rev. Stat. Ann. tit. 14 § 453-B(1) (Supp. 2001) (replacing Me. Rev. Stat. Ann. tit. 14 § 753-A (repealed 2001)).

8. Me. Rev. Stat. Ann. tit. 14 § 753-B(2) (Supp. 2001) (replacing Me. Rev. Stat. Ann. tit. 14 § 753-A (repealed 2001)).

9. Me. Rev. Stat. Ann. tit. 14 § 753-B(3) (Supp. 2001) (replacing Me. Rev. Stat. Ann. tit. 14 § 753-A (repealed 2001)).

10. *Id.*

11. Me. Rev. Stat. Ann. tit. 24 § 2902 (2000).

12. Me. Rev. Stat. Ann. tit. 14 § 8110 (Supp. 2001).

13. Me. Rev. Stat. Ann. tit. 14 § 8107 (Supp. 2001).

14. *Cushman v. Tilton*, 652 A.2d 650, 651 (Me. 1995) (failure to comply with the notice provision bars claim); *Smith v. Voisine*, 650 A.2d 1350, 1351 (Me. 1994) (upholding summary judgment for failure to file timely notice of claim when party could not show good cause for failure to do so).

15. *Beaucage v. City of Rockland*, 760 A.2d 1054, 1056-57 (Me. 2000).

16. Me. Rev. Stat. Ann. tit. 14 § 853 (Supp. 2001).

17. Me. Rev. Stat. Ann. tit. 24 § 2902 (2000).

18. Me. Rev. Stat. Ann. tit. 14 § 853, 866 (1980 & Supp. 2001).

19. Me. Rev. Stat. Ann. tit. 14 § 752-C (Supp. 2001).

20. *See, e.g., Stanton v. University of Maine System*, 773 A.2d 1045, 1049 (Me. 2001); *Gayer v. Bath Iron Works Corp.*, 687 A.2d 617, 621 (Me. 1996); *Parker v. Harriman*, 516 A.2d 549, 550 (Me. 1986); *Wing v. Morse*, 300 A.2d 491, 495-96 (Me. 1973). *See also Aliberti, LaRochelle & Hodson Eng'g Corp. v. FDIC*, 844 F. Supp. 832, 844 (D. Me. 1994) (summarizing Maine negligence law).

21. *See Carter v. Bangor Hydro-Elec. Co.*, 598 A.2d 739, 742 (Me. 1991); *Raymond v. Portland Railroad Co.*, 62 A. 602, 604-05 (Me. 1905).

22. *Searles v. Trustees of St. Joesph's College*, 695 A.2d 1206, 1210 (Me. 1997) (citing *Trusiani v. Cumberland & York Distribs., Inc.*, 538 A.2d 258, 261 (Me.1988) (quoting W.P. Keeton, Prosser and Keeton on Torts § 53 at 359 (5th ed. 1984)).

23. *Orr v. First Nat'l Stores, Inc.*, 280 A.2d 785, 796 (Me. 1971) (citing cases).

24. *LaBier v. Pelletier*, 665 A.2d 1013, 1014-1016 (Me. 1995).

25. *See, e.g., Fisherman's Wharf Associates II v. Verrill & Dana*, 645 A.2d 1133, 1136 (Me. 1994) ("One who undertakes to render services in the practice of a profession owes a duty to exercise that degree of skill, care and diligence exercised by members of that same profession."); *Downer v. Veilleux*, 322 A.2d 82, 87 (Me. 1974) (standard of care ordinarily exercised by the average and reasonably competent physician in specific branch of medicine).

26. *See, e.g., Johnson v. Carleton*, 765 A.2d 571, 576 (Me. 2001) (expert testimony required to establish standard for legal malpractice); *Pitt v. Frawley*, 722 A.2d 358, 360 (Me. 1999) (same); *Searles v. Trustees of St. Joseph's College*, 695 A.2d 1206, 1210 (Me. 1997) (same for athletic trainer); But see *Seider v. Board of Examiners of Psychologists*, 754 A.2d 986, 992 (Me. 2000) (while ordinarily a plaintiff can discharge his burden of proof for a claim of negligent medical care only by expert medical testimony; this court has "long recognized that expert testimony may not be necessary 'where the negligence and harmful results are sufficiently obvious as to lie within common knowledge...'") (citing *Cyr v. Giesen*, 108 A.2d 316, 318 (Me. 1954)); *Downer v. Veilleux*, 322 A.2d 82, 87 (Me. 1974) (same); *Mitchell & Davis, P.A. v. Jackson*, 627 A.2d 1014, 1017 (Me. 1993) (adopting same exception in legal malpractice case).

27. *Binette v. Dyer Library Ass'n*, 688 A.2d 898, 904-05 (Me. 1996); *Trusiani v. Cumberland & York Distrib., Inc.*, 538 A.2d 258, 262-63 (Me. 1988); *Allen v. Hunter*, 505 A.2d 486, 487 (Me. 1986).

28. *Stanton v. University of Maine System*, 773 A.2d 1045, 1049 (Me. 2001); *Morrill v. Morrill*, 616 A.2d 1272, 1274 (Me. 1992).

29. *Decker v. New England Public Warehouse, Inc.*, 749 A.2d 762, 765 (Me. 2000);

Cameron v. Pepin, 610 A.2d 279, 282-83 (Me. 1992) (citing *Trusiani v. Cumberland & York Distributors, Inc.*, 538 A.2d 258, 261 (Me. 1988)).

30. *Webb v. Hass*, 728 A.2d 1261, 1267 (Me. 1999) (citing *Perron v. Peterson*, 593 A.2d 1057, 1058 (Me. 1991)); *Klingerman v. SOL Corp. of Maine*, 505 A.2d 474, 478 (Me. 1986).

31. *Webb v. Haas*, 728 A.2d 1261, 1267 (Me. 1999) (quoting *Champagne v. Mid-Maine Medical Center*, 711 A.2d 842, 845 (Me. 1998) (quoting Restatement (Second) of Torts § 433B cmt. a, at 442 (1965)).

32. *Wheeler v. White*, 714 A.2d 125, 127-28 (Me. 1998).

33. *Colvin v. A.R. Cable Services-Me., Inc.*, 697 A.2d 1289, 1290-91 (Me. 1997); *Fournier v. Rochambeau Club*, 611 A.2d 578, 579 (Me. 1992).

34. Me. Rev. Stat. Ann. tit. 14 § 156 (Supp. 2001).

35. *Walter v. Wal-Mart Stores, Inc.*, 748 A.2d 961, 971 n.7 (Me. 2000); *Wing v. Morse*, 300 A.2d 491, 500-01 (Me. 1973).

36. *Merrill v. Sugarloaf Mountain Corp.*, 745 A.2d 378, 383 n.3 (Me. 2000); *Wilson v. Gordon*, 354 A.2d 398, 401-02 (Me. 1976).

37. *Wilson v. Gordon*, 354 A.2d 398, 401-02 (Me. 1976).

38. *Ricci v. Alternative Energy, Inc.*, 211 F.3d 157, 161 (1st Cir. 2000); *Wellington Assocs., Inc. v. Capital Fire Protection Co., Inc.*, 594 A.2d 1089, 1092 (Me. 1991).

39. *Ginn v. Penobscot Co.*, 334 A.2d 874, 879 (Me. 1975).

40. *Coffin v. Lariat Assoc.*, 766 A.2d 1018, 1020 (Me. 2001); *Smith v. Drinkwater*, 185 A.2d 312, 314 (Me. 1962); *Albison v. Robbins & White*, 116 A.2d 608, 612 (Me. 1955).

41. *Albison v. Robbins & White*, 116 A.2d 608, 612 (Me. 1955).

42. *Id.*

43. *Id.*

44. *Id.* at 612-13.

45. *Adams v. Buffalo Forge Co.*, 443 A.2d 932, 940 (Me. 1982). *See also Lorfano v. Dura Stone Steps, Inc.*, 569 A.2d 195, 196 (Me. 1990); *Bernier v. Raymark*

Indus. Inc., 516 A.2d 534, 538 (Me. 1986); *Austin v. Raybestos-Manhattan, Inc.*, 471 A.2d 280, 286 n.8 (Me. 1984).

46. Me. Rev. Stat. Ann. tit. 14 § 221 (1980 & Supp. 2001).

47. *Bernier v. Raymark Indus., Inc.*, 516 A.2d 534, 537 n.3 (Me. 1986).

48. *St. Germain v. Husqvarna Corp.*, 544 A.2d 1283, 1285-86 (Me. 1988) (alleged defective chainsaw design); *Stanley v. Schiavi Mobile Homes, Inc.*, 462 A.2d 1144, 1148 (Me. 1983) (fall in mobile home); *Walker v. General Elec. Co.*, 968 F.2d 116, 119 (1st Cir. 1992) (fire caused by allegedly defective toaster).

49. *See* Me. R. Evid. 407 (1998) (modified to confirm to 1997 amendment to Fed. R. Evid. 407); *Espeaignnette v. Gene Tierney Company*, 43 F.3d 1, 10 (Me. 1994).

50. *Wilson v. Bradlees of New England, Inc.*, 96 F.3d 552, 556-559 (1st Cir. 1996), cert. denied, 519 U.S. 1149 (1997); *Johnston v. Deere & Co.*, 967 F. Supp. 574, 577-78 (D. Me. 1997).

51. *Varano v. Jabar*, 197 F.3d 1, 3-4 (1st Cir. 1999); *Pottle v. Up-Right, Inc.*, 628 A.2d 672, 675 (Me. 1993); *Lorfano v. Dura Stone Steps, Inc.*, 569 A.2d 195, 196 (Me. 1990); *Bernier v. Raymark Indust., Inc.*, 516 A.2d 534, 537 n.3 (Me. 1986).

52. *Bouchard v. American Orthodontics*, 661 A.2d 1143, 1145 (Me. 1995).

53. *Roberts v. American Chain & Cable Co.*, 259 A.2d 43, 50 (Me. 1969).

54. Me. Rev. Stat. Ann. tit. 14 § 156 (Supp. 2001).

55. *Otis Elevator Co. v. F.W. Cunningham & Son*, 454 A.2d 335, 340 (Me. 1983).

56. *Packard v. Whitten*, 274 A.2d 169, 174 (Me. 1971).

57. *See* P.L. 1999, ch. 633 titled "An Act To Validate Pierringer Releases In Multiparty Lawsuits."

58. Me. Rev. Stat. Ann. tit. 14 § 156(1) (Supp. 2001).

59. Me. Rev. Stat. Ann. tit. 14 § 156(2) (Supp. 2001).

60. Me. Rev. Stat. Ann. tit. 14 § 156(3) (Supp. 2001).

61. Me. Rev. Stat. Ann. tit. 14 § 163 (Supp. 2001); *Hoitt v. Hall*, 661 A.2d 669, 673 (Me. 1995).

62. *Emery v. Hussey Seating Co.*, 697 A.2d 1284, 1287 (Me. 1969).

63. *Peerless Div. v. United States Special Hydraulic Cylinders Corp.*, 742 A.2d 906, 910 (Me. 1999).

64. *Roberts v. American Chain & Cable Co.*, 259 A.2d 43, 50 (Me. 1969).

65. *Northern Bank of Lewiston & Auburn v. Murphy*, 512 A.2d 344, 350-51 (Me. 1986).

66. Me. Rev. Stat. Ann. tit. 39-A §§ 102 *et seq.* (2001 & Supp. 2001).

67. Me. Rev. Stat. Ann. tit. 39-A § 104, 408 (2001); *See, e.g., Gordan v. Cummings*, 756 A.2d 942, 945 (Me. 2000) (employee's intentional infliction of emotional distress claim barred by Workers' Compensation Act); *Searway v. Rainey*, 709 A.2d 735, 736 (Me. 1998) (employee's suit alleging physical and emotional damages, as well as loss of earnings resulting from intentional assault by employer, barred by Workers' Compensation Act); *Bond Builders, Inc. v. Commercial Union Insurance Co.*, 670 A.2d 1388, 1390 (Me. 1996) (Workers' Compensation carrier had no duty to defend against employee's common law and tort claims since such claims were barred by Worker's Compensation Act); *Li v. C.N. Brown Co.*, 645 A.2d 606, 607 (Me. 1994) (exclusivity and immunity provisions of the Workers' Compensation Act bar employee from pursing civil litigation against employer for the employer's intentional torts); *Fanion v. McNeal*, 577 A.2d 2, 3 (Me. 1990) (Workers' Compensation Act is to be construed broadly; refusing to create an exception from the exclusivity and immunity provisions beyond that provided in the Act for illegally employed minors injured in the course of employment); *Samson v. DiConzo*, 669 A.2d 760, 762 (Me. 1996) (Employee's action based on negligence barred by exclusivity provision of Workers' Compensation Act); *Beverage v. Cumberland Farms Northern, Inc.*, 502 A.2d 486, 489 (Me. 1985) (Employee's tort action against her employer related to rape on work premises barred by exclusivity provisions of Workers' Compensation); *Reed v. Avian Farms, Inc.* 941 F. Supp. 10, 13-14 (D. Me. 1996) (common-law tort claims such as intentional infliction of emotional distress fall within exclusivity and immunity provisions of the Maine Workers' Compensation Act).

68. *Id.*

69. *Li v. C.N. Brown Co.*, 645 A.2d 606, 608 (Me. 1994).

70. Me. Rev. Stat. Ann. tit. 39-A § 107 (2001).

71. *Id.*

72. *Roberts v. American Chain & Cable Co.*, 259 A.2d 43, 50 (Me. 1969); *Gagne v. Carl Bauer Schraubenfabrick, GmbH*, 595 F. Supp. 1081, 1084 (Me. 1979).

73. *Poulin v. Colby College*, 402 A.2d 846, 850-851 (Me. 1979).

74. Me. Rev. Stat. Ann. tit. 14 § 159-A (2001).

75. *Poulin v. Colby College*, 402 A.2d 846, 851 n.5 (Me. 1969); *Kapernaros v. Boston & Maine R.R.*, 99 A.2d 441, 442 (Me. 1916).

76. *Orr v. First Nat'l Stores*, 280 A.2d 785, 792 (Me. 1971).

77. *Id.* at 796.

78. *Merrill v. Central Maine Power Co.*, 628 A.2d 1062, 1063 (Me. 1993); *Jones v. Billing*, 289 A.2d 39, 42-43 (Me. 1972).

79. *Merrill v. Central Maine Power Co.*, 628 A.2d 1062, 1063-1964 (Me. 1993).

80. Me. Rev. Stat. Ann. tit. 28-A §§ 2501 *et seq.* (1988 & Supp. 2001).

81. Me. Rev. Stat. Ann. tit. 28-A § 2506, 2507 (1988 & Supp. 2001).

82. Me. Rev. Stat. Ann. tit. 28-A § 2504 (1988).

83. Me. Rev. Stat. Ann. tit. 28-A § 2509 (1988).

84. *Oceanside at Pine Point Condominium Owner's Association v. Peachtree Doors, Inc.*, 659 A.2d 267, 270-271 (Me. 1995).

85. *Letellier v. Small*, 400 A.2d 371, 376 (Me. 1979).

86. Me. R. Civ. P. 9(b).

87. *Mariello v. Giguere*, 667 A.2d 588, 590 (Me. 1999); *Arbour v. Hazelton*, 534 A.2d 1303, 1305 (Me. 1987).

88. *Brae Asset Fund, L.P. v. Adam*, 661 A.2d 1137, 1140 (Me. 1995) (citing *Chapman v. Rideout*, 568 A.2d 829, 830 (Me. 1990)).

89. Me. Rev. Stat. Ann. tit. 5 §§205-A *et seq.* (1989 & Supp. 2001).

90. Me. Rev. Stat. Ann. tit. 5 § 207 (1989).

91. *Campbell v. Machias Sav. Bank*, 865 F. Supp. 26, 33 (D. Me. 1994).

92. 494 A.2d 1353 (Me. 1985).

93. *Id.* at 1354.

94. *Grover v. Minete-Mills, Inc.*, 638 A.2d 712, 717-18 (Me. 1994).

95. *Id.*

96. *See, e.g., Baker v. Manter*, 765 A.2d 583, 586 n.4 (Me. 2001) (citing *Tuttle v. Raymond*, 494 A.2d 1353, 1359 (Me. 1985)); *Harris v. Soley*, 756 A.2d 499, 510 (Me. 2000); *Caron v. Caron*, 577 A.2d 1178, 1180 (Me. 1990).

97. *See Oceanside at Pine Point Condominium Owner's Association v. Peachtree Doors, Inc.*, 659 A.2d 267, 270 (Me. 1995) (tort theory not available in product liability action absent a showing of personal injury or damage to property other than the defective product); *Hanlin v. International Minerals & Chem. Corp.*, 759 F. Supp. 925, 938 (D. Me. 1990) (punitive damages not allowed on strict liability claim based hazardous waste release into river because no finding of malice).

98. Me. Rev. Stat. Ann. tit. 18-A § 2-804 (1998 & Supp. 2001).

99. Me. Rev. Stat. Ann. tit. 18-A § 2-804(b) (Supp. 2001).

100. *Id.*

101. Me. Rev. Stat. Ann. tit. 18-A § 2-804(b) (Supp. 2001).

102. *Id.*

103. *Id.*

104. Me. Rev. Stat. Ann. tit. 18-A § 2-804(c) (1998); *see also Danforth v. Emmons*, 126 A.2d 821, 822 (Me. 1924).

MARYLAND

A. STATUTES OF LIMITATIONS

In Maryland, a civil action at law must be brought within three years unless statutory law provides a different period of time within which an action may be commenced.[1] The statute of limitations begins to run on the date the civil action accrues.[2] Maryland generally applies the discovery rule, which provides that the cause of action "accrues" when a person knows or reasonably should have known of the wrong.[3] Similarly, if knowledge of a cause of action is kept from a party by the fraud of an adverse party, the cause of action does not accrue until the party discovered, or should have discovered by exercising ordinary diligence, that the fraud occurred.[4] An action based on strict liability in tort is governed by the general three-year limitations period.[5] The three-year period also governs a claim for intentional infliction of emotional distress.[6]

When a cause of action accrues in favor of a minor or mental incompetent, the person must file the action, within the lesser of three years, or the applicable period of limitations, after the date the disability is removed.[7] This provision does not apply if the limitations period has more than three years to run when the disability is removed.[8]

An action for the breach of a contract for sale must commence within four years after the action has accrued.[9] Unlike general civil actions at law, a cause of action for the breach of a contract of sale accrues when the breach occurs, regardless of the aggrieved party's lack of knowledge.[10] Tender of goods, whether conforming or non-conforming, will trigger the statute of limitations in warranty cases not involving explicit agreements to extend future performance.[11] In such an instance, the cause of action accrues when the breach is, or should have been, discovered.[12]

An action on a judgment must be filed within 12 years after the cause of action accrues.[13]

Unlike other civil actions, an action for assault, libel, or slander must be filed within one year from the date on which it accrues.[14] False light cases, however, concerning publications that unreasonably present a plaintiff to the public in a false light, are governed by the three-year limitations period.[15]

No cause of action for damages for wrongful death, personal injury, or injury to real or personal property resulting from the defective and unsafe condition of an improvement to real property may be brought more than 20 years after the entire improvement becomes available for its intended use.[16]

Actions for damages for injuries arising out of the rendering or failure to render professional services by a health care provider shall be filed within the earlier of five years after the time the injury occurred or three years after the date the injury was discovered.[17]

An action for unliquidated damages may not be brought against a local government or its employees unless notice of the claim, in the form and manner required by statute, is given within 180 days after the injury.[18]

B. TORT REFORM

The most significant piece of legislation passed by the Maryland Legislature that falls within this category is the Maryland Cap Statute.[19] Prior to that time there was no cap on noneconomic damages in either personal injury cases or wrongful death cases. Beginning on July 1, 1986, there was a $350,000 cap on noneconomic damages in personal injury cases but *no* cap in wrongful death cases. Effective October 1, 1994, the cap on noneconomic damages in personal injury cases was raised to $500,000 and the cap was also amended to apply to wrongful death cases. On or after October 1, 1994, in wrongful death cases the cap is $500,000 for one claimant or $750,000 for two or more claimants.

The cap has increased $15,000 per year each year beginning on October 1, 1995. The effective date for the Maryland Cap Statute is when a cause of action arises. A cause of action arises when the facts to support each element of the cause of action exist and not when the cause of action is discovered. The burden of proof to show that the statutory cap is not applicable rests with the plaintiff.[20] The cap is not applicable to intentional torts.[21] The cap is not applicable to punitive damages.[22]

C. "NO FAULT" LIMITATIONS

Maryland has not passed any true "no fault" legislation; however, personal injury protection coverage is mandated.[23]

D. THE STANDARD FOR NEGLIGENCE

A sufficient claim for negligence in Maryland requires four elements: that the defendant had a duty to protect the plaintiff from injury, that the defendant breached that duty, that the plaintiff suffered real injury or loss, and that the injury or loss proximately resulted from the breach.[24] Although negligence is ordinarily a question of fact, and meager evidence of negligence will create a jury question,[25] the evidence must establish more than mere speculation or conjecture.[26]

The requirement that a duty exist arises from the responsibility each person bears to exercise due care to avoid an unreasonable risk of harm to others.[27] Foreseeability of harm is a factor Maryland utilizes to determine the existence of a duty.[28] In the absence of either a statute or special relationship that creates a duty, a private person is under no duty to protect a third person from criminal acts.[29]

A claim for professional malpractice first requires the plaintiff to establish a duty owed by the professional.[30] Once the duty has been established, a claim for negligence must allege that the professional, whether an accountant, physician, lawyer, architect, or other professional, breached the standard of care applicable to other like professionals similarly situated, and that such breach caused the injury at issue.[31]

The standard Maryland uses to determine the negligence, or not, of a child is the care ordinarily exercised by reasonable children of the same age, capacity, discretion, and experience under similar circumstances.[32] As a matter of law, children under the age of five may not be contributorily negligent.[33] Children five years of age or over, however, may be contributorily negligent.[34] In an action on behalf of a child, negligence on the part of the parents may not be imputed to the child, [35] except in extraordinary situations wherein the parents' negligence is the intervening and superseding cause of the injury.[36]

E. CAUSATION

Negligence in Maryland is not actionable unless it is the proximate cause of the injury or damage alleged.[37] The proximate cause element is satisfied if the defendant's negligence is the cause in fact of the injury and the legally cognizable cause thereof.[38] There must be a reasonable connection between the defendant's alleged negligence and the plaintiff's injury.[39] When the injury suffered by the plaintiff would not have happened "but for" the defendant's negligence, proximate cause exists.[40] If it is alleged that the negligence of multiple parties caused the plaintiff's injury, Maryland employs the substantial factor test to determine which defendant(s) proximately caused the injury.[41]

F. CONTRIBUTORY NEGLIGENCE AND ASSUMPTION OF RISK

1. Contributory Negligence

Contributory negligence is the neglect of the duty imposed upon all individuals to observe reasonable care for their own safety, which includes both the doing of something that a person of ordinary prudence would not do and the failure to do something that a person of ordinary prudence would do, under the circumstances presented.[42] Contributory negligence occurs when a plaintiff's failure to observe reasonable care for his or her own safety combines with a defendant's negligence to cause the harm or injury to the plaintiff.[43] In Maryland, a finding of contributory negligence ordinarily bars the plaintiff from any recovery.[44]

The last clear chance doctrine, an exception to this rule, allows the plaintiff to recover despite his or her contributory negligence. The last clear chance doctrine assumes primary negligence by the defendant, contributory negligence by the plaintiff, and a showing of something new and independent that afforded the defendant a fresh opportunity, which was not utilized, to avoid the consequences of his original negligence.[45]

Contributory negligence is not a defense to strict liability claims.[46]

2. Assumption of Risk

The defense of assumption of risk, if established by the defendant, completely bars recovery by the plaintiff because it is a previous abandonment of the right to complain if the accident occurs.[47] In order to establish the defense of assumption of risk, the defendant must prove that the plaintiff: (1) had knowledge of the risk of danger, (2) appreciated the risk, and (3) voluntarily confronted the risk of danger.[48] The determination whether a plaintiff has knowledge and appreciation of the risk is made objectively, and the test is whether a person of normal intelligence in the position of the plaintiff would have understood the danger.[49] Although the defenses of contributory negligence and assumption of risk are distinct, they are closely related and often overlap.[50]

G. *RES IPSA LOQUITUR* AND ABNORMALLY DANGEROUS ACTIVITIES

1. *Res Ipsa Loquitur*

An inference that the defendant's negligence caused the harm complained of is permissible under the doctrine of *res ipsa loquitur* if the casualty: (1) is a kind that does not ordinarily happen in the absence of negligence, (2) is caused by an instrumentality exclusively within the defendant's control, and (3) is not caused by an act or omission of the plaintiff.[51] The purpose of *res ipsa loquitur* is to afford the plaintiff an opportunity to present a *prima facie* case of negligence where direct evidence of the specific cause of the accident is unavailable or in the hands of the defendant.[52]

2. Abnormally Dangerous Activity

Strict liability is imposed on a person who engages in an abnormally dangerous activity, which is determined by the following factors: (1) the existence of a high degree of risk to person, land, or chattels of others, (2) the likelihood that harm resulting from the activity will be great, (3) the inability to remove the risk through the exercise of reasonable care, (4) the extent to which the activity is not a common usage, (5) the inappropriateness of the activity for the place in which it occurs, and (6) the extent to which the value of the activity to the community is outweighed by its danger.[53]

H. NEGLIGENCE *PER SE*

Under Maryland law, a violation of a statute or regulation does not constitute negligence *per se*, and only may provide evidence of negligence under certain circumstances.[54] The alleged violation may provide evidence of negligence if the person alleging the negligence is within the class of persons sought to be protected and the harm suffered is the kind which the statute or regulation intended to prevent.[55] Evidence of a violation of either a statute or regulation does not preclude consideration of the defenses of contributory negligence and assumption of risk.[56]

I. JOINT AND SEVERAL LIABILITY

Under the Maryland Uniform Contribution Among Joint Tortfeasors Act,[57] joint tortfeasors are defined as "two or more persons jointly and severally liable in tort for the same injury to person or property," whether or not judgment has been recovered from all or some of them.[58] If a party's liability does not rest in tort, he or she may not be deemed a joint tortfeasor.[59]

In Maryland, recovery of a judgment by an injured person from one joint tortfeasor does not discharge the other joint tortfeasors.[60] Nor does a release of one joint tortfeasor by the injured person discharge the other joint tortfeasors unless the release so provides.[61] The release, however, does reduce the injured person's claim against the other joint tortfeasors by the amount of consideration that is paid for the release, or by any amount or proportion that the release designates, provided that the amount or proportion is greater than the amount of consideration paid.[62] The release of one joint tortfeasor by the injured person does not relieve that joint tortfeasor from the liability to make contribution to another joint tortfeasor unless the release: (1) is given before the right of the other joint tortfeasor to secure a money judgment for contribution has accrued, and (2) provides for a reduction, to the extent of the *pro rata* share of the released tortfeasor, of the injured person's damages recoverable against all other joint tortfeasors.[63]

The right of contribution exists among joint tortfeasors.[64] A joint tortfeasor, however, is not entitled to a money judgment for contribution unless he has discharged the common liability or paid more than his *pro rata* share of liability.[65] If a joint tortfeasor enters a settlement with the injured person, he cannot get contribution from another joint tortfeasor whose liability to the injured person is not extinguished by the settlement.[66] If one of the joint tortfeasors pays more than his *pro rata* share of the judgment, the court may enter judgment for contribution even though no cross-claims have been filed.[67]

The joint tortfeasor statute does not impair any right of indemnity.[68]

J. INDEMNITY

Maryland law defines indemnity as an agreement to reimburse a person held liable for a loss.[69] The right of indemnity may rise from an express agreement or by implication.[70] Notwithstanding the parties' joint and several liability, the right to indemnity may lie when there is considerable difference in degree of fault among wrongdoers.[71]

K. WORKERS COMPENSATION

The Maryland Workers' Compensation Act[72] provides that an employer must provide a covered employee[73] with compensation in accordance with the Act for a claim based on an accidental injury sustained by the employee and occurring within seven years after the date of the injury.[74] An employer also may have to provide compensation to a covered employee for a disability resulting from an occupational disease.[75]

The liability of an employer is exclusive.[76] The compensation provided to a covered employee under the Workers' Compensation Act is in place of any right of action against any person.[77] If the employer fails to secure compensation, the covered employee who is injured may (1) bring a claim for compensation under the statute, or (2) bring an action for damages.[78] Where a person other than an employee is liable for the injury of a covered employee, the injured employee may either (1) file a claim against the employer for compensation under the Act, or (2) bring an action for damages against the person(s) liable for the injury.[79]

If a claim was filed and compensation was awarded, a self-insured employer, the Subsequent Injury Fund, or the Uninsured Employers' Fund may bring an action for damages against the third party liable for the injury.[80] If none of those parties bring an action within two months after the Workers' Compensation Commission issues an award, the covered employee may bring an action against a third party.[81]

L. PREMISES LIABILITY

The extent of the duty a possessor of property owes to a person who comes in contact with the property depends on the person's status while on the property.[82] Maryland recognizes four classifications of entrants to property: invitee, licensee by invitation, bare licensee, and trespasser.[83]

An invitee is a person permitted or invited to enter property for purposes connected with the owner's business, and such status may be proven by a showing of mutual benefit or proof of an implied invitation.[84] A possessor of property must use reasonable and ordinary care to keep the premises safe for an invitee and to protect the invitee from any unreasonable risk which the invitee could not discover through the exercise of ordinary care for his own safety.[85]

A licensee by invitation is a social guest to whom the possessor of property owes a duty to exercise reasonable care to warn the guest of a dangerous condition known to the possessor but not easily discoverable.[86] A licensee, or bare licensee, is a person who enters property with the knowledge and consent of the owner but for the licensee's own purpose and interest.[87] The possessor of property owes no duty to a licensee except to refrain from willfully or wantonly injuring the licensee and from creating new and undisclosed sources of danger without warning the licensee.[88] A trespasser is one who intentionally and without consent or privilege enters another's property.[89] No duty is owed to a trespasser, even one of tender years, except that a possessor of land may not willfully or wantonly injure or entrap the trespasser.[90]

The attractive nuisance doctrine has not been adopted in Maryland with respect to children who are licensees or trespassers.[91]

M. DRAM SHOP LIABILITY

Due to the absence in Maryland of a dram shop statute authorizing an action for damages, no cause of action in tort lies against a tavern owner for injuries to third persons caused by an intoxicated person.[92] Furthermore, there is no social host liability to a party injured as the direct or indirect result of the host having served alcohol to the tortfeasor.[93] Maryland courts have suggested in their opinions that it would be beneficial for the legislature to revisit this issue.[94]

N. ECONOMIC LOSS

Tort recovery for purely economic loss is not ordinarily allowed in Maryland.[95] In cases where a plaintiff seeks recovery for a defective product, the loss or value of the product itself, and the cost to fix or replace the product, are usually viewed as economic losses.[96] A plaintiff suffering only economic loss because of a defective product is normally limited to contractual causes of action, including breach of warranty and, in the case of fraud, an action for deceit.[97] If recovery for a defective product is based purely on economic loss, a plaintiff may recover in tort if the defect creates a substantial or unreasonable risk of death or personal injury.[98]

O. FRAUD AND MISREPRESENTATION

In Maryland, to state a cause of action for fraud or deceit, the plaintiff must allege facts demonstrating that: (1) the defendant made a false representation to the plaintiff, (2) the falsity of the representation was either known to the defendant or the representation was made with reckless indifference to the truth, (3) the representation was made for the purpose of defrauding the plaintiff, (4) the plaintiff relied on the representation and had a right to rely on it, and (5) the plaintiff suffered compensable injury resulting from reliance on the representation.[99] The elements of fraud must be established by clear and convincing evidence.[100]

Maryland also recognizes constructive fraud for certain purposes.[101] Constructive fraud is the breach of a legal or equitable duty that, irrespective of the moral guilt of the defendant, is fraudulent because of its likelihood to deceive others, to violate public or private confidence, or to injure the public interest.[102]

The elements of a negligent misrepresentation claim in Maryland include: (1) the defendant, who owes a duty of care to the plaintiff, asserts a false statement; (2) the defendant intends that the plaintiff will rely on his statement; (3) the defendant has knowledge that the plaintiff will probably rely on the statement which, if erroneous, will cause loss or injury; (4) the plaintiff justifiably takes action in reliance on the statement; and (5) the plaintiff suffers damage proximately caused by the defendant's negligence.[103] A cause of action will not exist unless the defendant owes the plaintiff a duty of care.[104]

P. CONSUMER PROTECTION

The purpose of the Maryland Consumer Protection Act[105] is to set certain minimum statewide standards for merchants offering goods, services, realty and credit in order to protect consumers by preventing unlawful consumer practices and assisting consumers in obtaining relief from such practices.[106] The Division of Consumer Protection in the Office of the Attorney General administers the Act.[107] The Division receives and investigates complaints, initiates its own investigations of deceptive or unfair trade practices, and suspends or revokes licenses of offending merchants.[108]

A consumer may file a complaint with the Division, but the Consumer Protection Act does not prevent a consumer from seeking remedies through other agencies or the courts.[109]

Q. PUNITIVE DAMAGES

For both intentional and nonintentional torts, an award of punitive damages in Maryland must be based on actual malice in the sense of conscious and deliberate wrongdoing, evil or wrongful motive, intent to injure, ill will, or fraud.[110] Punitive damages are not recoverable based on any theory of implied malice.[111] A plaintiff must prove the requisite knowledge of the defendant by clear and convincing evidence.[112]

In a product liability action, the plaintiff must demonstrate the following to recover punitive damages: (1) that the defendant actually knew of the defect and danger of the product at the time it left the defendant's possession, and (2) that the defendant consciously or deliberately disregarded the potential harm to consumers.[113]

Punitive damages, which are reviewable for excessiveness, should not be disproportionate to the gravity of the defendant's wrong.[114]

R. WRONGFUL DEATH AND SURVIVAL ACTIONS

Maryland's wrongful death statute[115] and survival statute[116] provide two separate causes of action.[117] Damages in a wrongful death action measure the harm to others caused by the death of the victim, and a survival action measures the harm to the victim after the injury and prior to the death.[118]

In a wrongful death action the beneficiaries may recover, in addition to pecuniary loss, damages for mental anguish, emotional pain and suffering, loss of society, companionship, comfort, protection, marital care, parental care, filial care, attention, advice, counsel, training, guidance or education where applicable.[119] The statutory cap on noneconomic damages applies to wrongful death actions.[120]

A personal representative may bring a survival action, on behalf of the victim, that the victim might have commenced or prosecuted in the absence of death.[121] Damages for loss of future earnings are not recoverable in a survival action but are recoverable in a wrongful death suit.[122] The victim's estate may recover pre-impact fright damages in a survival action because the victim would be entitled to recover such damages had he or she survived.[123]

Sidney G. Leech
Carlos A. Braxton
GOODELL, DEVRIES, LEECH & DANN, LLP
One South Street, 20th Floor
Baltimore, Maryland 21202
(410) 783-4000
Fax (410) 783-4040
sgl@gdldlaw.com
cab@gdldlaw.com

ENDNOTES - MARYLAND

1. Md. Code Ann., Cts. & Jud. Proc. § 5-101 (1998).

2. *See id.* "However, the statute of limitations does not begin to run on an insured's claim that the insurer breached its duty to defend the insured in a tort suit brought by a third party until final judgment is entered, because while the action is continuing, the insurer can always step in and cure its breach." *Vigilant Ins. Co. v. Luppino*, 723 A.2d 14, 18-19 (Md. 1999).

3. *See Martin Marietta Corp. v. Gould, Inc.*, 70 F.3d 768, 771 (4th Cir. 1995); *Pennwalt Corp. v. Nasios*, 550 A.2d 1155, 1163 (Md. 1988); *Poffenberger v. Risser*, 431 A.2d 677, 680 (Md. 1981); *Shah v. HealthPlus, Inc.*, 696 A.2d 473, 478 (Md. App.), *cert. denied*, 702 A.2d 291 (Md. 1997).

4. Cts. & Jud. Proc. § 5-203 (1998).

5. *See Phipps v. General Motors Corp.*, 363 A.2d 955, 962 (Md. 1976).

6. *See Robinson v. Vitro Corp.*, 620 F. Supp. 1066, 1072 (D. Md. 1985).

7. Cts. & Jud. Proc. § 5-201(a) (1998).

8. *See id.* at § 5-201(b).

9. Md. Code Ann., Com. Law I § 2-725(1) (1997). The parties, by agreement, may reduce the limitations period to not less than one year, but the limitations period may not be extended. *See id.* If suit for the breach of a contract of sale is initiated within the four-year limitation period and subsequently terminated, another action for the same breach may commence after the expiration of the four-year period and within six months after termination, unless the termination results from voluntary discontinuance or a failure to prosecute. *See id.* at § 2-725(3); *Hanscome v. Perry*, 542 A.2d 421, 425 (Md. 1988).

10. Com. Law I at § 2-725(2).

11. *See id.*; *Freightliner, Inc. v. Shantytown Pier, Inc.*, 719 A.2d 541, 546 (Md. 1998). Where a warranty explicitly extends to future performance, an action for breach must be filed within four years after the earlier of either discovery of the breach or expiration of the breach or expiration of the warranty period. *Joswick v. Chesapeake Mobile Homes, Inc.*, 765 A.2d 90, 97 (Md. 2001).

12. *See id.*

13. Md. Code Ann., Cts. & Jud. Proc. § 5-102(a)(3) (1998).

14. *See id.* at § 5-105.

15. *See Allen v. Bethlehem Steel Corp.*, 547 A.2d 1105, 1108 (Md. App.), *cert. denied*, 550 A.2d 1168 (Md. 1988).

16. Cts. & Jud. Proc. § 5-108(a) (1998). This statute applies to subcontractors and contractors. *Hartford Ins. Co. v. American Automatic Sprinkler System*, 23 F. Supp. 2d 623, 628-29 (D. Md. 1998), *aff'd*, 201 F.3d 538 (4th Cir. 2000). The limitations period for an action against an architect, professional engineer, or contractor is ten years after the entire improvement becomes available for its intended use. *See id.* at § 5-108(b).

17. *See id.* at § 5-109(a). A claimant has the responsibility to perform a diligent investigation and has notice once he is aware of circumstances that ought to put a person of reasonable prudence on notice. *Jacobs v. Flynn*, 749 A.2d 174, 187 (Md. App. 2000). The commencement of the limitations period in this section may be delayed when the claimant is under the age of sixteen. *See id.* at § 5-109(b),(c).

18. *See id.* at § 5-304(a) (1998). The limitations clock begins to run at the moment the plaintiff is able to bring a claim. *Heron v. Strader*, 761 A.2d 56, 59 (Md. 2000).

19. This statement first became effective on July 1, 1986. Cts. & Jud. Proc. § 11-108(b) (1995 Repl. Vol.).

20. *Owens-Corning v. Walatka*, 725 A.2d 579, 583-86 (Md. App.), *cert. denied*, 731 A.2d 971 (Md. 1999). For an opinion discussing the sufficiency of proof, *see Porter Hayden Company v. Wyche*, 738 A.2d 326 (Md. App. 1999), *cert. denied*, 743 A.2d 246 (Md. 2000).

21. There is no separate cap for consortium which is a "derivative" claim. *Oaks v. Connor*, 660 A.2d 423, 428-29 (Md. 1995). The cap applies to all plaintiffs not each plaintiff in a wrongful death action. *See id.* at 430. Where there are two or more claimants, the award may not exceed 150 percent of the individual amount. *See id.; see also* Cts. & Jud. Proc. § 11-108(b)(3)(i). *Cole v. Sullivan*, 676 A.2d 85, 91-92 (Md. App. 1996).

22. Cts. & Jud. Proc. § 11-108(b)(3)(ii). *Id.* at § 11-108(a)(2)(ii). *See Dutta v. State Farm Ins. Co.*, 769 A.2d 948, 952 (Md. 2001).

23. However, personal injury protection coverage can be waived. MD. Code Ann., Ins. §§ 19-505, 19-506 (1997 Repl. Vol.); *Maryland Auto Ins. Fund v. Perry*, 741 A.2d 1114, 1119 (Md. 1999). Uninsured motorist coverage is mandated. *See id.* at §19-509; *Wright v. Allstate Ins. Co.*, 740 A.2d 50, 51 (Md. 1999).

24. *See Brown v. Derner*, 744 A.2d 47, 54 (Md. 2000); *Baltimore Gas & Elec. Co. v. Flippo*, 705 A.2d 1144, 1153-54 (Md. 1998).

25. *See McSlarrow v. Walker*, 467 A.2d 196, 200 (Md. App. 1983), *cert. denied*, 472 A.2d 1000 (Md. 1984).

26. *See Smith v. Warbasse*, 526 A.2d 991, 992 (Md. App. 1987).

27. *See Flippo*, 705 A.2d at 1154.

28. *See id.*

29. *See Valentine v. On Target, Inc.*, 727 A.2d 947, 950 (Md. 1999).

30. *See Shofer v. Stuart Hack Co.*, 723 A.2d 481, 487 (Md. App.), *cert. denied*, 731 A.2d 440 (Md. 1999).

31. *See id.*

32. *See Potomac Elec. Power Co. v. Smith*, 558 A.2d 768, 796 (Md. App.), *cert. denied*, 564 A.2d 407 (Md. 1989), *overruled on other grounds, United States v. Streidel*, 620 A.2d 905, 907 (Md. 1993).

33. *See State ex. rel. Taylor v. Barlly*, 140 A.2d 173, 176 (Md. 1958); *cf. Brown v. Rogers*, 313 A.2d 547, 550 (Md. 1974) (holding that a ten-year-old may be contributorily negligent as a matter of law).

34. *See Barlly*, 140 A.2d at 177.

35. Md. Code Ann., Cts. & Jud. Proc. § 10-910 (1998).

36. *See Caroline v. Reicher*, 304 A.2d 831, 834 (Md. 1973).

37. *See Stone v. Chicago Title Ins. Co.*, 624 A.2d 496, 500 (Md. 1993).

38. *See Yonce v. SmithKline Clinical Labs., Inc.*, 680 A.2d 569, 575 (Md. App.), *cert. denied*, 685 A.2d 452 (1996); *Wankel v. A & B Contractors, Inc.*, 732 A.2d 333, 349 (Md. App. 1999), *cert. denied*, 740 A.2d 614 (1999).

39. *See Taylor v. Feissner*, 653 A.2d 947, 952 (Md. App.), *cert. denied*, 663 A.2d 73 (Md. 1995); *see also Wankel*, 732 A.2d at 349.

40. *See id.*

41. *See Casey v. Grossman*, 720 A.2d 959, 964 (Md. App.), *cert. denied*, 725 A.2d 1068 (Md. 1998); *Pittman v. Atlantic Realty Co.*; 754 A.2d 1030, 1034 n.4 (Md. 2000).

42. *See Baltimore Gas & Elec. Co. v. Flippo*, 705 A.2d 1144, 1155 (Md. 1998); *Union Memorial Hosp. v. Dorsey*, 724 A.2d 1272, 1275 (Md. App. 1999).

43. *See Board of County Commr's v. Bell Atlantic-Maryland, Inc.*, 695 A.2d 171, 181 (Md. 1997).

44. *See id*. Before the defense may be successfully invoked, the defendant must demonstrate that the injured party acted, or failed to act, with actual or constructive knowledge of the danger his conduct involved. *See Leakas v. Columbia Country Club*, 831 F. Supp. 1231, 1235-36 (D. Md. 1993); *Menish v. Pollinger Co.*, 356 A.2d 233, 237 (Md. 1976).

45. *See Cohen v. Rubin*, 460 A.2d 1046, 1051 (Md. App.), *cert. denied*, 297 Md. 311 (Md. 1983).

46. *See Montgomery County v. Valk Mfg. Co.*, 562 A.2d 1246, 1247 (Md. 1989).

47. *See ADM Partnership v. Martin*, 702 A.2d 730, 734 (Md. 1997); *Saponari v. CSX Transp., Inc.*, 727 A.2d 396, 399 (Md. App. 1999).

48. *See Martin*, 702 A.2d at 734; *Schroyer v. McNeal*, 592 A.2d 1119, 1123 (Md. 1991).

49. *See Leakas*, 831 F. Supp. at 1236; *Martin*, 702 A.2d at 734.

50. *See Baltimore Gas & Elec. Co. v. Flippo*, 705 A.2d 1144, 1156 (Md. 1998).

51. *See Holzhauer v. Saks & Co.*, 697 A.2d 89, 92-93 (Md. 1997); *Cogan Kibler, Inc. v. Vito*, 695 A.2d 191, 195 (Md. 1997).

52. *See Dover Elevator Co. v. Swann*, 638 A.2d 762, 765 (Md. 1994).

53. *See Rosenblatt v. Exxon Co., U.S.A.*, 642 A.2d 180, 185-88 (Md. 1994).

54. *See Sheridan v. United States*, 969 F.2d 72, 75 (4th Cir. 1992); *Moura v. Randall*, 705 A.2d 334, 342 (Md. App.), *cert. denied*, 709 A.2d 140 (Md. 1998). This is a rule of evidence, not a rule of law implying a cause of action. *Bentley v. Carroll*, 734 A.2d 697, 705 n.8 (Md. 1999).

55. *See Atlantic Mut. Ins. Co. v. Kenney*, 591 A.2d 507, 510-11 (Md. 1991); *Moura*, 705 A.2d at 342.

56. *See Brady v. Ralph M. Parsons Co.*, 609 A.2d 297, 306 (Md. 1992).

57. Md. Code Ann., Cts. & Jud. Proc. §§ 3-1401 to 3-1409 (1998).

58. *See id*. at 3-1401(c). An agent and his principal, whose liability is solely vicarious, are not joint tortfeasors under Maryland's version of the Uni-

form Contribution Among Tort-Feasors Act. *Anne Arundel Medical Ctr., Inc. v. Condon*, 649 A.2d 1189, 1193 (1994). Third-party contribution actions may proceed in spite of the expiration of the limitations period with respect to plaintiff's direct claim against the third-party defendant. *Jacobs v. Flynn*, 749 A.2d 174, 189-91 (Md. App. 2000).

59. *See Baker, Watts & Co. v. Miles & Stockbridge*, 620 A.2d 356, 377 (Md. 1993). Contribution, however, is not limited to tort cases and may be applied to contractual obligations not arising out of tort liability. *See Hartford Accident & Indem. Co. v. Scarlett Harbor Assocs.*, 674 A.2d 106, 137 (Md. App. 1996), *aff'd*, 695 A.2d 153 (Md. 1997).

60. Cts. & Jud. Proc. § 3-1403.

61. *See id.* at § 3-1404.

62. *See id.*

63. *See id.* at § 3-1405.

64. *See id.* at § 3-1402(a).

65. *See id.* at § 3-1402(b).

66. *See id.* at § 3-1402(c). When a jury award against a non-settling tortfeasor is less than a settlement payment by a settling joint tortfeasor, judgment should not be entered for the non-settling defendant, but rather, the judgment for plaintiff is reduced and satisfied. *Hill v. Scartascini*, 758 A.2d 1087, 1090 (Md. 2000).

67. *See Lerman v. Heemann*, 701 A.2d 426, 430 (Md. 1997).

68. Cts. & Jud. Proc. at § 3-1406.

69. *See Strong v. Prince George's County*, 549 A.2d 1142, 1144 (Md. App.), *cert. denied*, 554 A.2d 393 (Md. 1988).

70. *See Haupt v. State*, 667 A.2d 179, 186 (Md. 1995). When former counsel is sued by the former client for professional malpractice, former counsel may implead the former client's successor counsel, for contributions or indemnification, where it is alleged that successor counsel's negligence contributed to the injury suffered by the common client. *Parler & Wobber v. Miles & Stockbridge, P.C.*, 756 A.2d 526, 531 (MD. 2000).

71. *See Hartford Accident & Indem. Co. v. Scarlett Harbor Assocs.*, 674 A.2d 106, 135 (Md. App. 1996), *aff'd*, 695 A.2d 153 (Md. 1997).

72. Md. Code Ann., Lab. & Empl. §§ 9-101 to 9-1201 (1999).

73. An individual is a covered employee while in the service of an employer under either an express or implied contract of apprenticeship or hire. *See id.* at § 9-202(a). A minor may be covered even if employed unlawfully. *See id. at §9-202(b).*

74. *See id.* at § 9-501(a). An accidental personal injury is an accidental injury (1) arising out of and in the course of employment, or (2) caused by a willful or negligent act of a third person directed against a covered employee in the course of the employee's employment. *See id.* at § 9-501(b). It also includes a disease or infection that naturally results from an accidental injury arising out of and in the course of employment. *See id.*

75. *See id.* at § 9-502(c), (d). Compensation is required if the occupational disease (1) is due to the nature of employment in which the hazards of the occupational disease exist and the employee was employed before the date of disablement, or (2) has manifestations consistent with those known to result from exposure to a biological, chemical, or physical agent attributable to the general type of employment, and it may reasonably be concluded that the occupational disease was incurred as a result of the employment. *See id.*

76. *See id.* at § 9-509(a).

77. *See id.* at § 9-509(b).

78. *See id.* at § 9-509(c).

79. *See id.* at § 9-901.

80. *See id.* at § 9-902(a).

81. *See id.* at 9-902(c). Any damages recovered in the action first must be distributed to reimburse the party that paid for the compensation. *See id.* at 9-902(e).

82. *See Baltimore Gas & Elec. Co. v. Flippo*, 705 A.2d 1144, 1148 (Md. 1998).

83. *See id.*

84. *See Bass v. Hardee's Food Systems, Inc.*, 982 F. Supp. 1041, 1044 (D. Md. 1997), *aff'd*, 229 F.3d 1141 (4th Cir. 2000).

85. *See id.* at 1043; *Shields v. Wagman*, 714 A.2d 881, 884 (Md. 1998).

86. *See Flippo*, 705 A.2d at 1148.

87. *See Flippo*, 705 A.2d at 1148; *Wells v. Polland*, 708 A.2d 34, 40 (Md. App. 1998).

88. *See Flippo,* 705 A.2d at 1148.

89. *See Flippo,* 705 A.2d at 1148; *Wagner v. Doehring,* 553 A.2d 684, 687 (Md. 1989).

90. *See id.*

91. *See Valentine v. On Target, Inc.,* 686 A.2d 636, 641 (Md. App.), *aff'd,* 727 A.2d 947 (Md. 1999).

92. *See Felder v. Butler,* 438 A.2d 494, 499-500 (Md. 1981) *Wright v. Sue & Charles, Inc.,* 749 A.2d 241, 244 (Md. App. 2000); *Moran v. Foodmaker, Inc.,* 594 A.2d 587, 589-91 (Md. App.), *cert. denied,* 599 A.2d 90 (Md. 1991).

93. *See Wright,* 749 A.2d 241, 246 (Md. App. 2000).

94. *See Moran,* 594 A.2d at 590-91; *Wright,* 749 A.2d at 245-46.

95. *See United States Gypsum Co. v. Mayor & City Council,* 647 A.2d 405, 410 (Md. 1994).

96. *See id.; Decoster v. Westinghouse Corp.,* 634 A.2d 1330, 1332-33 (Md. 1994).

97. *See United States Gypsum Co.,* 647 A.2d at 410; *Decoster,* 634 A.2d at 1332.

98. *See United States Gypsum Co.,* 647 A.2d at 410; *Council of Co-Owners v. Whiting-Turner,* 517 A.2d 336, 345 (Md. 1986).

99. *See Alleco Inc. v. Harry & Jeanette Weinberg Foundation, Inc.,* 665 A.2d 1038, 1047 (Md. 1995); *Ellerin v. Fairfax Savings,* 652 A.2d 1117, 1123 (Md. 1995). Under Maryland law, a plaintiff may hold a defendant liable for a fraudulent representation made to a third person. *See Maryland Nat'l Bank v. Resolution Trust Corp.,* 895 F. Supp. 762, 772 (D. Md. 1995).

100. *See VF Corp. v. Wrexham Aviation Corp.,* 715 A.2d 188, 193 (Md. 1998).

101. *See Ellerin,* 652 A.2d at 1126.

102. *See id.* at 1126 n.11.

103. *See Foster v. American Home Prods. Corp.,* 29 F.3d 165, 171 (4th Cir. 1994); *Hannon v. Exxon Co., U.S.A.,* 54 F. Supp. 2d 485, 497 (D. Md. 1999).

104. *See id.*

105. Md. Code Ann., Comm. Law II §§ 13-101 to 13-501 (1990 & 1999 Supp.).

106. *See id.* at § 13-102(b).

107. *See id.* at § 13-201.

108. *See id.* at § 13-204.

109. *See id.* at § 13-401.

110. *Bowden v. Caldor, Inc.*, 710 A.2d 267, 276 (Md. 1998); *Scott v. Jenkins*, 690 A.2d 1000, 1006 (Md. 1997).

111. *See Bowden*, 710 A.2d at 276; *United States Gypsum Co. v. Mayor & City Council*, 647 A.2d 405, 426 (Md. 1994).

112. *See Le Marc's Management Corp. v. Valentin*, 709 A.2d 1222, 1226 (Md. 1998).

113. *See Bowden*, 710 A.2d at 276-77; *AcandS, Inc. v. Asner*, 686 A.2d 250, 264-65 (Md. 1996).

114. *See Bowden*, 710 A.2d at 275, 277. For a discussion of the factors utilized in Maryland to determine the reasonableness of a punitive damages award, *see id.* at 277-85.

115. Md. Code Ann., Cts. & Jud. Proc. §§ 3-901 to 3-904 (1998).

116. Md. Code Ann., Est. & Trusts § 7-401 (1991 Repl. Vol. & 1999 Supp.).

117. *See Globe American Cas. Co. v. Chung*, 547 A.2d 654, 659-61 (Md. App. 1988), *vacated on other grounds*, 589 A.2d 956 (Md. 1991).

118. *See ACandS, Inc. v. Asner*, 657 A.2d 379, 397-98 (Md. App. 1995), *rev'd on other grounds and remanded*, 686 A.2d 250 (Md. 1996).

119. Cts. & Jud. Proc. § 3-904(d).

120. *See Anchor Packing Co. v. Grimshaw*, 692 A.2d 5, 13-14 (Md. App. 1997), *vacated on other grounds and remanded*, 713 A.2d 962 (Md. 1998).

121. Est. & Trusts § 7-401(y) (1999 Supp.).

122. *See Jones v. Flood*, 702 A.2d 440, 442-43 (Md. App. 1997), *aff'd*, 716 A.2d 285 (Md. 1998).

123. *See generally Benyon v. Montgomery Cablevision Ltd. Partnership*, 718 A.2d 1161 (Md. 1998).

MASSACHUSETTS

A. **STATUTES OF LIMITATION**

Causes of action founded on negligent, intentional, or tortious conduct for personal injury, death, or property damage have a three-year statute of limitation.[1] The "discovery" rule applies.[2] A six-year statute of repose is applicable to claims involving improvements to real property.[3] The statute of repose does not apply to actions for personal injury.[4]

Actions on contracts, except as noted below, and actions on judgments rendered by foreign courts have six-year statutes of limitation.[5]

Actions in contract to recover for personal injury,[6] actions for breach of warranty,[7] and claims against the Commonwealth[8] have three-year statutes of limitation.

Actions for breach of a contract for sale under Article 2 of the U.C.C.[9] and actions under the Massachusetts Consumer Protection Act[10] have four-year statutes of limitation.[11]

Actions against trustees on their contracts,[12] actions to recover the value of property taken by eminent domain,[13] and actions for deficiency judgment after real property mortgage foreclosure[14] have two-year statutes of limitation.

Actions on contracts under seal,[15] actions on notes issued by banks,[16] actions on court judgments,[17] and actions for the recovery of real property[18] have 20-year statutes of limitation.

The statute of limitation for foreclosure of mortgages is 50 years.[19]

A defense that a claim is barred by a statute of limitation must be pled as an affirmative defense.[20] The clock on the statute begins to run when the claim for relief accrues.[21] The limitation period is tolled if the defendant leaves the state after the claim accrues and before the limitation period ends.[22] If the claimant is a minor,[23] insane, or imprisoned at the time the claim accrues, the limitation period is tolled until the disability is removed.[24]

B. **TORT REFORM**

The Massachusetts Legislature has not passed any tort reform bills to date.

C. **"NO-FAULT" LIMITATIONS**

Massachusetts has a no-fault motor vehicle insurance statute,[25] enacted to reduce the number of small automobile tort cases filed and to help reduce the high cost of automobile insurance in the Commonwealth.[26] Under the statute, there are three types of personal injury protection benefits available as part of a single policy: (1) medical-related expenses, (2) lost wages (75 percent), and (3) replacement services.[27] Coverage is compulsory and a prerequisite to obtaining a Massachusetts vehicle registration certificate.[28] An injured party may recover a maximum of $8,000 under the statute.[29] Where an injured party is entitled to benefits under the statute, the tortfeasor is exempt from tort liability to the extent that the injured party is compensated by the statute.[30]

Although injured parties generally may not recover for pain and suffering under "no-fault" coverage, such damages are available if the injured party has at least $500 in medical or funeral expenses and: (1) dies, (2) loses a body party, (3) is permanently and seriously disfigured, (4) loses hearing or sight, or (5) suffers a fractured bone.[31]

D. THE STANDARD FOR NEGLIGENCE

Plaintiff must show duty and breach.[32] The relationship between the parties determines the existence and scope of the duty.[33] A relationship between two parties may also establish a duty to a third party.[34] A party breaches a duty of care where the party fails to conform its conduct to the applicable standard of care.[35] Reasonable or ordinary care is care that a person of ordinary prudence, sense, and capacity would use in the circumstances.[36]

Massachusetts recognizes a professional standard of care. Professionals must possess the learning, skill, and experience possessed by other members of the profession.[37] Doctors must possess the learning, skill, and experience of other doctors "in the community," which now consists of the entire profession.[38] A special relationship, such as one that creates a fiduciary duty, may impose a higher standard of duty.[39] The professional standard applies to accountants and attorneys as well as doctors.[40] Generally, a plaintiff must introduce expert testimony to establish the standard of care and a breach thereof unless the standard and breach are of the type that can be easily understood by a layperson.[41]

Generally, a party has no duty to control the actions of a third party, but if there is a special relationship between the defendant and either an intended victim or the plaintiff, the defendant could have a duty to control the third party.[42] Massachusetts recognizes the "good Samaritan" principles of the Restatement (Second) Torts, which provide that one who voluntarily undertakes the rescue of another or of another's property is liable for failure to exercise reasonable care in the execution of the rescue.[43]

A child is expected to exercise the care of a child of like age, intelligence and experience under the circumstances.[44] There is no definite age at which a child is too young to be found negligent. However, it has been held that a child as young as four could be found negligent.[45] A parent has a duty to exercise reasonable care to prevent a minor child from intentionally or negligently inflicting harm on another if the parent knows or should know of the child's propensity for a particular type of harmful conduct and has the opportunity to take reasonable corrective measures.[46]

By statute, the Legislature has abolished the presumption that a deceased plaintiff exercised due care at the time of injury.[47]

E. **CAUSATION**

In order to recover in negligence, a plaintiff must establish both proximate cause,[48] or legal cause,[49] and cause in fact, or "but for" causation.[50] Proximate cause is defined as the "active efficient cause that sets in motion a train of events which brings about a result without the intervention of any force started and working actively from a new and independent source . . . ."[51] Plaintiffs in medical malpractice cases involving death from a pre-existing condition need not prove that the physician's negligence caused death, but rather only that it was "more probably than not a cause of the loss of a substantial chance to survive."[52]

F. **CONTRIBUTORY NEGLIGENCE, COMPARATIVE NEGLIGENCE, AND ASSUMPTION OF RISK**

1. **Contributory Negligence**

In 1971, the Massachusetts Legislature abolished contributory negligence as a defense in all actions seeking recovery for wrongful death, personal injury, or injury to property.[53]

2. **Comparative Negligence**

Massachusetts is a partial comparative negligence state. The Massachusetts Comparative Negligence Act[54] applies to actions to recover damages for negligence resulting in death or injury to person or property.[55] A plaintiff is not barred from recovery except where the plaintiff's negligence exceeds the total negligence that is attributed to the defendant or defendants against whom recovery is sought.[56] Plaintiff's recovery is then reduced by the proportion of plaintiff's fault.[57] Where the defense applies, it must be pled affirmatively by the defendant.[58] Comparative negligence does not apply to strict liability actions;[59] actions based on the defendant's willful, wanton, or reckless conduct;[60] or to actions for breach of warranty, even if they sound in tort.[61]

3. **Assumption of Risk**

The legislature abolished assumption of risk as a defense to most actions arising after January 1, 1974.[62] Where the defense applies, it must be pled with affirmatively.[63] Assumption of risk may be a defense to trespass.[64]

In actions for personal injury or wrongful death based on breach of warranty, a defendant may avoid liability if the defendant shows that the plaintiff unreasonably used a product which the plaintiff knew to be defective and dangerous.[65]

G. *RES IPSA LOQUITUR* AND INHERENTLY DANGEROUS ACTIVITIES

1. *Res Ipsa Loquitur*

The doctrine of *res ipsa loquitur*[66] permits the jury to find negligence on the part of the defendant where the plaintiff meets four conditions. First, the plaintiff must show, independent of any *res ipsa loquitur* assistance, the specific act that caused the injury.[67] Second, the act that caused the plaintiff's injury must be of the type that does not normally occur in the absence of negligence.[68] Third, the instrumentality that caused plaintiff's injury must be in the exclusive control of the defendant.[69] The plaintiff bears the burden of proving that the negligence of intermediate handlers of the instrumentality did not cause the plaintiff's injury.[70] Fourth, the plaintiff must show that the plaintiff's handling of the instrument was not related to the accident.[71] Where these conditions are met, the jury may, but need not, find negligence.[72]

2. Inherently Dangerous Activities

Massachusetts imposes strict liability on one whose abnormally dangerous activity causes harm to another.[73] No type of activity is *per se* "abnormally dangerous;" rather, an activity must be considered in light of surrounding circumstances.[74] Where a plaintiff establishes a *prima facie* case of liability for an abnormally dangerous activity, the defendant can escape liability only by showing that the harm was caused by either an "act of God" or an intervening and unlawful act of a third person.[75]

H. NEGLIGENCE *PER SE*

Massachusetts does not recognize the doctrine of negligence *per se*. Rather, violation of a statute, ordinance, or regulation is evidence of negligence on the part of a violator as to all consequences that the statute, ordinance, or regulation was intended to prevent.[76] A party may introduce a statute, ordinance, or regulation at trial as evidence of the relevant standard of care.[77]

I. JOINT AND SEVERAL LIABILITY

Joint tortfeasors are "two or more wrongdoers [who] negligently contribute to the personal injury of another by their several acts."[78] All joint tortfeasors must be independently at fault for the wrongful act.[79] The relative degree of fault of the joint tortfeasors is not considered in apportioning liability.[80]

A defendant is jointly liable to a plaintiff if the defendant's conduct is the proximate cause of the plaintiff's injury and the defendant is one of two or more whose joint or concurrent acts of negligence caused the injury.[81] Further, a tortfeasor is liable "for the foreseeable intervening conduct of a third party whether the conduct is negligent or not,"[82] but a party whose negligence occurs after the first injury is responsible only for his own negligence.[83] In many cases it will be a question of fact for the jury as to whether the liability is "joint" or "independent."[84] A defendant may always defend by proving that the plaintiff's injury was caused entirely by others.[85]

Under the Massachusetts Contribution Among Joint Tortfeasors Act,[86] a release by the plaintiff of one of several joint tortfeasors does not discharge other tortfeasors unless the release so provides.[87] Even where the release discharges "all other persons, firms or corporations" from liability, a tortfeasor not specifically named in the release is not released from liability.[88] A tortfeasor who is not released has a right to have the amount of any judgment entered against him offset by the court for the amount, if any, paid by the released tortfeasor.[89] If the settlement is in good faith, the released tortfeasor has no liability for contribution to any tortfeasor who has not been so released.[90]

A tortfeasor who pays more than his *pro rata* share of the common liability is entitled to contribution from all other tortfeasors not released by the plaintiff.[91] The action to recover contribution may be enforced in the original action or in a separate action.[92] If there has been a judgment entered against the party seeking contribution, any separate action seeking contribution must be commenced within one year after the judgment becomes final.[93]

J. INDEMNITY

The law of indemnity in Massachusetts is complex and, unfortunately, sometimes confusing. Indemnity allows a party who is not at fault but compelled to defend itself against the wrongful act of another, to recover from the wrongdoer the entire amount of the loss, including attorney's fees.[94] There are three sets of circumstances giving rise to a right of indemnification under Massachusetts law.[95] First, indemnification is proper where expressly contracted for by the parties.[96] (By statute, contractual indemnity provisions in construction contracts are void if the provision requires a subcontractor to indemnify any party for personal injury or property damage not caused by the subcontractor, its employees, agents, or subcontractors.[97]) Second, indemnification may be implied by a contract between the parties.[98] An implied right of indemnification exists if either (1) "there are unique special factors demonstrating that the parties intended that the putative indemnitor bear the ultimate responsibility,"[99] or (2) "there is a generally recognized special relationship between the parties."[100] Third, indemnification may be proper at common law if the party seeking indemnification was not negligent but was vicariously exposed to liability for the wrongful act of another.[101] Common law indemnity is generally not permitted between negligent parties.[102]

Notice to a putative indemnitor is not a precondition to a subsequent indemnity action.[103] Failure to give notice does, however, impose on the putative indemnitee the burden of proving the indemnitor's liability to the original plaintiff and the facts giving rise to the right of indemnity.[104] Failure to give notice also precludes a binding effect of the original judgment or settlement on the subsequent indemnity action.[105]

Where two parties are each active tortfeasors there can be no indemnity between them,[106] although the tortfeasors may have a statutory right to contribution from each other.[107] By statute, there can be no right of contribution available to an indemnitor.[108]

K. BAR OF WORKERS' COMPENSATION STATUTE

The Massachusetts Workers' Compensation Act[109] prevents an employee from recovering for personal injuries from an employer who has paid workers' compensation benefits for an employee's work-related injuries.[110] Workers' compensation is an exclusive remedy and the employer assumes responsibility regardless of fault.[111] The Act does not preclude an injured worker from bringing a common law tort suit against third parties.[112]

Actions in tort by the employee against the employer are barred where the plaintiff is or was an employee, the plaintiff sustained a personal injury within the meaning of the Act, and the injury arose out of the employment.[113] If benefits are available, an employee injured by the negligence of a co-worker acting in the course of his employment may not recover in tort against the negligent co-worker.[114]

Where the employee's injury was caused by a third party, either the employee or insurer may bring a claim against the third party for the damages incurred.[115] The amount recovered is for the benefit of the insurer, unless the amount recovered is greater than what was paid by the insurer to the employee, in which case the excess is retained or paid to the employee.[116] Attorney's fees are divided proportionally between the parties.[117] Any settlement with a third party must have the approval of the court or Workers' Compensation Board.[118]

Section 15 of the workers' compensation statute gives an insurer standing to challenge the allocation of a settlement award paid by a third party to an injured worker and the worker's spouse even if the insurer is not a party to the action.[119] The insurer may attach a statutory lien to an award of damages and attorney fees in an injured worker's tort action against a third party to recover compensation paid by the insurer.[120]

Generally, injuries arising from intentional torts are compensable under the Act and common law actions for such claims are barred.[121] However, the Act does not preclude actions for libel, malicious prosecution, false imprisonment, invasion of privacy, alienation of affection, seduction, false arrest and other "kindred tortious acts," because these actions are not compensable under the Act.[122]

L. PREMISES LIABILITY

A landowner owes *all* lawful visitors the ordinary standard of care.[123] Massachusetts has abolished the distinction between licensees and invitees[124] and also the distinction between undiscovered and discovered trespassers.[125] Generally, no duty is owed a trespasser; the landowner need only refrain from willful, wanton, or reckless conduct,[126] although a landowner does have a duty of ordinary care to prevent injury where the landowner knows a trespasser is in a position of peril.[127] Although a landowner generally has no duty to warn of open and obvious dangers,[128] a landowner must use reasonable care to protect child trespassers from danger from artificial conditions on the landowner's property.[129] The Comparative Negligence Act applies to child trespassers.[130]

M. DRAM SHOP LIABILITY

Massachusetts' Dram Shop Act[131] prohibits the sale of alcohol to intoxicated persons on the premises of any place licensed by the Act.[132] The Act does not apply to social hosts, but social hosts may be liable under negligence theories.[133] Dram shop liability may also be imposed where adult customers at a liquor serving establishment provide alcohol to minors and the management or employees make no attempt to prevent or monitor consumption by minors.[134]

There are eight elements that a plaintiff must prove to establish "dram shop" liability.[135] The two most important and difficult elements to prove are (i) that the server knew that the defendant was intoxicated when the defendant was served[136] and (ii) that the defendant was the proximate cause of the plaintiff's injury.[137] A patron injured because of his own intoxication may also recover under the Act.[138]

N. ECONOMIC LOSS

The "economic loss" doctrine prevents recovery for purely economic loss in actions for negligence where the plaintiff cannot allege personal injury or damage to property.[139] The rule does not apply to claims of negligence against a fiduciary.[140] Massachusetts follows the traditional rule that in an action for negligent interference with a contract or economic opportunity, the economic loss doctrine bars recovery where there is no damage to property or personal injury.[141] The doctrine does not bar recovery for economic losses due to negligent misrepresentation.[142]

O. FRAUD AND MISREPRESENTATION

A cause of action for deceit must be pled with particularity.[143]

A plaintiff alleging deceit or intentional misrepresentation must prove (1) that the defendant made a misrepresentation of a material fact;[144] (2) knowledge of the falsity of the misrepresentation;[145] (3) intent that the plaintiff would rely on the misrepresentation;[146] (4) reasonable reliance by the plaintiff;[147] and (5) resulting damages from the reliance.[148] Knowledge of the falsity is not required where accurate facts were reasonably available to the speaker.[149]

Where a party fails to exercise reasonable care in obtaining or furnishing information for the guidance of others in their business transactions about which the party has a pecuniary interest, the party is liable for negligent misrepresentation.[150] Negligence in failing to discover the falsity of a representation is not grounds for a claim of deceit, but is sufficient for a claim of negligent misrepresentation.[151]

P. CONSUMER PROTECTION

The Massachusetts Consumer Protection Act[152] creates public and private rights of action for those injured because of "unfair methods of competition and unfair or deceptive acts or practices in the conduct of any trade or commerce."[153] These remedies are in addition to traditional tort and contract remedies.[154] The Attorney General may bring 93A enforcement actions on behalf of all members of the Commonwealth.[155] Private actions may also be brought under the Act. Actions by business persons are governed by Section 11 of the Act;[156] actions by consumers are governed by Section 9.[157] Double or treble damages may be imposed for knowing and willful violations; attorney's fees are required where the defendant has engaged in unfair trade practices.[158]

The defendant has a complete defense where the allegedly unfair conduct is specifically permitted under the laws and regulations of the United States or the Commonwealth.[159]

Business transactions that are completely private and not undertaken in the course of any regular business practice are not covered by the Act.[160] In making this determination courts "assess the nature of the transaction, the character of the parties involved, and the activities engaged in by the parties."[161] Examples of conduct outside the protections of the Act include: private real estate transactions;[162] claims by employees against employers regarding the employment relationship;[163] disputes regarding private actions of trustees;[164] disputes between parties to the same venture[165] or between members of the same legal entity;[166] and conduct engaged in prior to the March 26, 1968, effective date of the Act.[167] Although originally outside the coverage of the Act, securities transactions are now covered by 93A.[168]

When the plaintiff pleads both common law and 93A counts based on substantially the same facts, the trial court has the choice of letting the jury find facts on both counts, deciding itself all aspects of the unfair trade practices claim, or asking the jury for nonbinding, advisory findings as to the unfair trade practices claim.[169]

The statute of limitation for Consumer Protection actions is four years.[170]

Q. PUNITIVE DAMAGES

In Massachusetts, punitive damages are recoverable only where specifically authorized by statute.[171] In wrongful death actions, the plaintiff may recover compensatory damages and punitive damages where the wrongful death was caused "by the malicious, willful, wanton, or reckless conduct of the defendant or by the gross negligence of the defendant."[172] A plaintiff in a civil rights or discrimination action may recover punitive damages.[173] The Consumer Protection Act provides for damages in the form of double or treble damages for a "willful or knowing violation" of the Act or where the defendant failed to grant relief upon demand despite knowledge that the complained of practice violated the Act.[174] A plaintiff in a defamation action who alleges special damages may recover special, but not punitive, damages.[175]

R. WRONGFUL DEATH AND SURVIVORSHIP ACTIONS

Although in Massachusetts wrongful death actions are of common law origin,[176] the right to recover for wrongful death is now controlled by statute.[177] Parties may recover under the statute for any tortious conduct—negligent or intentional—resulting in death.[178] The defendant in a wrongful death action is liable for "the fair monetary value of the decedent to the persons entitled to recover [and] the reasonable funeral and burial expenses of the decedent."[179] Punitive damages are available where the defendant's conduct was "willful, wanton, or reckless [or] gross[ly] negligent."[180] Punitive damages must be in the amount of at least $5,000.[181] The action must be brought by the deceased's executor or administrator,[182] but the distribution of damages is determined by statute.[183] A tortfeasor who causes one to suffer before dying is liable for the suffering.[184] Recovery for suffering of the decedent is distributed through the estate and not through the statute.[185]

By statute and at common law, certain actions survive the death of a party. By statute, the legislature has provided for the survival of actions of replevin; tort actions for assault, battery, imprisonment or other damages to the person; tort actions for consequential damages arising out of personal injury; actions for conversion or for damage to property; and actions against sheriffs or their deputies for misconduct or negligence,[186] and actions for wrongful death.[187] Common law provides for the survival of actions founded on negligence,[188] and actions for interference with contractual relations.[189] Where an action survives, it may be brought by the decedent's executor or administrator.[190]

Francis H. Fox
Paul M. Robertson
James P. Lucking
BINGHAM DANA, LLP
150 Federal Street
Boston, Massachusetts
(617) 951-8000
Fax (617) 951-8736
www.bingham.com

ENDNOTES - MASSACHUSETTS

1. *See* Mass. Gen. Laws ch. 260, §§ 2A, 4 (1999).

2. *See Riley v. Presnell*, 409 Mass. 239, 243, 565 N.E.2d 780 (1991).

3. *See* Mass. Gen. Laws ch. 260, § 2B.

4. *See id.*

5. *See* Mass. Gen. Laws ch. 260, § 2.

6. *See* Mass. Gen. Laws ch. 260, § 2A.

7. *See* Mass. Gen. Laws ch. 106, § 2-318.

8. *See* Mass. Gen. Laws ch. 258, § 4.

9. *See* Mass. Gen. Laws ch. 106, § 2-275.

10. *See* Mass. Gen. Laws ch. 93A.

11. *See* Mass. Gen. Laws ch. 260, § 5A.

12. *See* Mass. Gen. Laws ch. 260, § 11.

13. *See* Mass. Gen. Laws ch. 244, § 13A.

14. *See id.*

15. *See* Mass. Gen. Laws ch. 260, § 1.

16. *See id.*

17. *See id.* There is a rebuttable presumption of payment of a judgment after 20 years. *See* Mass. Gen. Laws ch. 260, § 20.

18. *See* Mass. Gen. Laws ch. 260, §§ 21-23.

19. *See* Mass. Gen. Laws ch. 260, § 33.

20. *See* Mass. R. Civ. P. 8(c) (1999).

21. *See, e.g., Joseph A. Fortin Constr., Inc. v. Massachusetts Hous. Fin. Agency,* 392 Mass. 440, 442, 466 N.E.2d 514 (1984); *Cannon v. Sears, Roebuck & Co.,* 374 Mass. 739, 741, 374 N.E.2d 582 (1978).

22. *See* Mass. Gen. Laws ch. 260, § 9.

23. A plaintiff's disability does not toll the limitations period for medical malpractice claims. Where a plaintiff is a minor and the medical malpractice claim accrues before a minor reaches age six, a minor has until age nine to bring suit. All medical malpractice claims, however, must be brought within seven years of the negligent act or omission. *See* Mass. Gen. Laws ch. 231, § 60D. The SJC has found this statute to be constitutional. *See Harlfinger v. Martin,* 435 Mass. 38, 754 N.E.2d 63 (2001). This statute acts as a statute of repose, not one of limitation.

24. *See* Mass. Gen. Laws ch. 260, § 7.

25. *See* Mass. Gen. Laws ch. 90, §§ 34A, 34M, 34N & 34O.

26. *See Flanagan v. Liberty Mut. Ins. Co.,* 383 Mass. 195, 198, 417 N.E.2d 1216 (1981).

27. *See* Mass. Gen. Laws ch. 90, § 34M. Replacement services are "payments to someone outside of the household who has been hired to perform ordinary and necessary services that 'the injured person would have performed not for income but for the benefit of . . . his household.'" *Creswell v. Medical West Community Health Plan, Inc.,* 419 Mass. 327, 329, 644 N.E.2d 970 (1995).

28. *See* Mass. Gen. Laws ch. 90, § 34M.

29. *See id.*

30. *See id.*

31. *See* Mass. Gen. Laws ch. 231, § 6D.

32. *See Santos v. Kim,* 429 Mass. 130, 135-36, 706 N.E.2d 658 (1999); *O'Sullivan v. Hemisphere Broad. Corp.,* 402 Mass. 76, 78, 520 N.E.2d 1301 (1988); *Slaven v. City of Salem,* 386 Mass. 885, 887, 438 N.E.2d 348 (1982).

33. *See, e.g., Irwin v. Ware,* 392 Mass. 745, 754, 467 N.E.2d 1292 (1984); *Mounsey v. Ellard,* 363 Mass. 693, 695-97, 297 N.E.2d 43 (1973); *Ortiz v. County of Hampden,* 16 Mass. App. Ct. 138, 139, 449 N.E.2d 1227 (1983).

34. *See, e.g., Caldwell v. Zaher,* 344 Mass. 590, 592-93, 183 N.E.2d 706 (1962).

35. *See O'Sullivan, supra* note 32, 402 Mass. at 78; *Mason v. Geddes*, 258 Mass. 40, 44-45, 154 N.E. 519 (1926).

36. *See Bennett v. Eagle Brook Country Store, Inc.*, 408 Mass. 355, 358, 557 N.E.2d 1166 (1990).

37. *See Delaney v. Rosenthall*, 347 Mass. 143, 146-47, 196 N.E.2d 878 (1964).

38. *See Brune v. Belinkoff*, 354 Mass. 102, 104-109, 235 N.E.2d 793 (1968).

39. *See Webster's of Hudson v. David Shoe Co.*, 1993 WL 818567, *2 n.5 (Mass. Super. Ct. 1993).

40. *See Atlas Tack Corp. v. Donabed*, 47 Mass. App. Ct. 221, 226, 712 N.E.2d 617 (1999); *Comins v. Sharkansky*, 38 Mass. App. Ct. 37, 41 (1995).

41. *See Pongonis v. Saab*, 396 Mass. 1005, 1005, 486 N.E.2d 28 (1985); *Atlas Tack, supra* note 40, 47 Mass. App. Ct. at 41.

42. *See A. L. v. Commonwealth*, 402 Mass. 234, 521 N.E.2d 1017 (1988); *see also* Restatement (Second) Torts, § 315.

43. *See Davis v. Westwood*, 420 Mass. 739, 746 & n.12, 652 N.E.2d 567 (1995); *Thorson v. Mandell*, 402 Mass. 744, 748, 525 N.E.2d 375 (1988); *Mullins v. Pine Manor College*, 389 Mass. 47, 52, 449 N.E.2d 331 (1983); *see also* Restatement (Second) Torts, § 323.

44. *See Mathis v. Massachusetts Elec. Co.*, 409 Mass. 256, 263, 565 N.E.2d 1180 (1991); *Mann v. Cook*, 346 Mass. 174, 178, 190 N.E.2d 676 (1963); *Dennehy v. Jordan Marsh Co.*, 321 Mass. 78, 80, 71 N.E.2d 758 (1947).

45. *Compare McDonough v. Vozzela*, 247 Mass. 552, 556, 142 N.E. 831 (1924) (child of four capable of negligence) *with Coldiron v. Worcester Consolidated Street Rwy. Co.*, 253 Mass. 462, 463, 149 N.E. 141 (1925) (child of three years, 10 months not capable of negligence).

46. *See Alioto v. Marnell*, 402 Mass. 36, 38, 520 N.E.2d 1284 (1988); *Caldwell v. Zaher*, 344 Mass. 590, 592, 183 N.E.2d 706 (1962).

47. *See* Mass. Gen. Laws ch. 231, § 85.

48. *See McCann v. Davis, Malm, & D'Agostine*, 423 Mass. 558, 559-60, 669 N.E.2d 1077 (1996).

49. *See Tritsch v. Boston Edison Co.*, 363 Mass. 179, 182, 293 N.E.2d 264 (1973).

50. *See Jorgensen v. Massachusetts Port Auth.*, 905 F.2d 515, 522-23 (1st Cir. 1990) (construing Massachusetts law); *McKenna v. Andreassi*, 292 Mass. 213, 218,

197 N.E. 879 (1935); *Depina v. Ribeiro*, 1999 WL 46910, *3 (Mass. App. Ct. 1999).

51. *Lynn Gas & Elec. Co. v. Meriden Fire Ins. Co.*, 158 Mass. 570, 575, 33 N.E. 690 (1893); *see also Wallace v. Ludwig*, 292 Mass. 251, 254, 198 N.E. 159 (1935) ("proximate cause is that which in a continuous sequence, unbroken by any new cause, produces an event and without which the event would not have occurred").

52. *Bradford v. Baystate Medical Ctr.*, 415 Mass. 202, 208-209 (1993); *see also Keppler v. Tufts*, 38 Mass. App. Ct. 587, 590 (1995).

53. *See* Mass. Gen. Laws ch. 231, § 85.

54. *See id.*

55. *See id.*

56. *See id.*; *Graci v. Damon*, 376 Mass. 931, 383 N.E.2d 842 (1978).

57. *See* Mass. Gen. Laws ch. 231, § 85.

58. *See* Mass. R. Civ. P. 8(c).

59. *See id.*

60. *See id*; *Banks v. Braman*, 188 Mass. 367, 369-70, 74 N.E. 594 (1905) (negligence materially different from willful, wanton, or reckless conduct).

61. *Colter v. Barber-Greene Co.*, 403 Mass. 50, 60-65, 525 N.E.2d 1305 (1988).

62. *See* Mass. Gen. Laws ch. 231, § 85.

63. *See* Mass. R. Civ. P. 8(c).

64. *See Haley v. Moyen Constr. Corp.*, 381 Mass. 239, 243-44, 408 N.E.2d 864 (1980).

65. *See Correia v. Firestone Tire & Rubber Co.*, 388 Mass. 342, 355, 446 N.E.2d 1033 (1983). Actions for personal injury or wrongful death based on warranty liability are the Massachusetts equivalent of strict liability for products. *See id.*

66. Massachusetts courts have avoided use of the term even while applying the principles. *See Evangelio v. Metropolitan Bottling Co.*, 339 Mass. 177, 179-80, 158 N.E.2d 342 (1975).

67. *See Fitchburg Gas & Elec. Co. v. Samuel Evans Constr. Co.*, 338 Mass. 752, 754, 157 N.E.2d 529 (1959).

68. *See Graham v. Badger*, 164 Mass. 42, 48, 41 N.E. 61 (1895) (Holmes, J.).

69. *See Rafferty v. Hull Brewing Co.*, 350 Mass. 359, 362, 215 N.E.2d 85 (1966).

70. *See Charles v. American Stores Co.*, 1995 WL 389693, *2 (Mass. App. Div.).

71. *See Coyne v. John S. Tilley Co.*, 368 Mass. 230, 240, 331 N.E.2d 541 (1975).

72. *See McFarlane v. McCourt*, 295 Mass. 85, 87-88, 2 N.E.2d 1017 (1936).

73. *See Clark-Aiken Co. v. Cromwell-Wright Co.*, 367 Mass. 70, 73, 323 N.E.2d 876 (1975); *Ball v. Nye*, 99 Mass. 582 (1868) (adopting strict liability rule of *Rylands v. Fletcher*, L.R. 3 H.L. 330, 339-340 (1868)). Massachusetts uses the term "abnormally dangerous" rather that "inherently dangerous." *See id.*

74. *See id.* at 89-90. Massachusetts follows generally the Restatement (Second) Torts. *See id.* at 89.

75. *See id.* at 90 n.21; *Bratton v. Rudnick*, 283 Mass. 556, 560-61, 186 N.E. 669 (1933); *Gorham v. Gross*, 125 Mass. 232, 238 (1878).

76. *Guinan v. Famous Players-Laskey Corp.*, 267 Mass. 501, 506, 167 N.E. 235 (1929); *Resendes v. Boston Edison Co.*, 38 Mass. App. Ct. 344, 358, 648 N.E.2d 757 (1995).

77. *See Herson v. New Boston Garden Corp.*, 40 Mass. App. Ct. 779, 793, 667 N.E.2d 907, *rev. denied*, 423 Mass. 1108, 671 N.E.2d 951 (1996).

78. *See Elias v. Unisys Corp.*, 410 Mass. 479, 480-81, 573 N.E.2d 946 (1991) (quoting *O'Connor v. Raymark Indus., Inc.*, 401 Mass. 586, 591, 518 N.E.2d 510 (1988)).

79. *See Elias, supra* note 78, at 481.

80. *See Zeller v. Cantu*, 395 Mass. 76, 79, 478 N.E.2d 930 (1985).

81. *See Eckstein v. Scoffi*, 299 Mass. 573, 576, 13 N.E.2d 436 (1938); *Proctor v. Dillon*, 235 Mass. 538, 549, 129 N.E. 265 (1920).

82. *Correia v. Firestone Tire & Rubber Co.*, 388 Mass. 342, 352 n.10, 446 N.E.2d 1033 (1983) (quoting *Wilborg v. Denzell*, 359 Mass. 279, 285, 268 N.E.2d 855 (1971).

83. *See Cormier v. Bodkin*, 300 Mass. 357, 361, 15 N.E.2d 457 (1938).

84. *See, e.g., Chase v. Roy*, 363 Mass. 402, 294 N.E.2d 336 (1973); *Delfino v. Torosian*, 354 Mass. 395, 237 N.E.2d 694 (1968).

85. *See Correia, supra* note 82, 388 Mass. 352.

86. *See* Mass. Gen. Laws ch. 231B, §§ 1-4.

87. See Mass. Gen. Laws ch. 231B, § 4(a); *Cram v. Town of Northbridge*, 410 Mass. 800, 801, 575 N.E.2d 747 (1991); *Grace v. Buckley*, 13 Mass. App. Ct. 1081, 1082, 435 N.E.2d 655 (1982); *Robertson v. McCarte*, 13 Mass. App. Ct. 441, 442-444, 433 N.E.2d 1262 (1982).

88. *Cram, supra* note 87, 410 Mass. at 801.

89. *See* Mass. Gen. Laws ch. 231B, § 4(a); *Grace, supra* note 87, 13 Mass. App. Ct. at 1082.

90. *See* Mass. Gen. Laws ch. 231B, § 4(b); *Grace, supra* note 87, 13 Mass. App. Ct. at 1082.

91. *See* Mass. Gen. Laws ch. 231B, § 1(b); *Bishop v. Klein*, 380 Mass. 285, 294-295, 402 N.E.2d 1365 (1980).

92. *See* Mass. Gen. Laws ch. 231B, § 3(b); *Eck v. Mocalkins*, 43 Mass. App. Dec. 195, 197 (1969).

93. *See* Mass. Gen. Laws ch. 231B, § 3(c).

94. *See Elias v. Unisys Corp.*, 410 Mass. 479, 482, 573 N.E.2d 946 (1991); *Santos v. Chrysler Corp.*, 430 Mass. 198, 217, 715 N.E.2d 47 (1999).

95. *See Araujo v. Woods Hole, Martha's Vineyard*, 693 F.2d 1, 2 (1st Cir. 1982); *Samos Imex Corp. v. Nextel Communications, Inc.*, 20 F. Supp. 2d 248, 251 (D. Mass. 1998); *Leasetec Corp. v. Inhabitants of County of Cumberland*, 896 F. Supp. 35, 38 (D. Me. 1995) (construing Massachusetts law).

96. *See Shea v. Bay State Gas Co.*, 383 Mass. 218, 221, 418 N.E.2d 597 (1981). Courts construe contracts for indemnity as they would any other type of contract. *See id.* at 222-223.

97. *See* Mass. Gen. Laws ch. 149, § 29C.

98. *See Fireside Nissan, Inc. v. Nissan Motors Corp.*, 395 Mass. 366, 375-376, 479 N.E.2d 1386 (1985); *Decker v. Black & Decker Mfg. Co.*, 389 Mass. 35, 38, 449 N.E.2d 641 (1983).

99. *Id.*

100. *Fireside Nissan, supra* note 98, 395 Mass. at 395 (quoting *Araujo, supra* note 95, 693 F.2d at 2-3; *see also Liberty Mut. Ins. Co. v. Westerlind*, 374 Mass. 524, 527, 373 N.E.2d 957 (1978).

101. *See Rathbun v. Western Mass. Elec. Co.*, 395 Mass. 361, 364, 479 N.E.2d 1383 (1985). "The distinction between 'active' and 'passive' negligence, like the distinction between misfeasance and nonfeasance, is not favored in Massachusetts law." *Hamel v. Factory Mut. Eng'g Ass'n*, 409 Mass. 33, 36, 564 N.E.2d 395 (1990); *see also Narine v. Powers*, 400 Mass. 343, 346, 509 N.E.2d 905 (1987); *Whitney v. Worcester*, 373 Mass. 208, 221, 366 N.E.2d 1210 (1977).

102. *See Samos Imex Corp. v. Nextel Communications, Inc.*, 20 F. Supp. 2d 248, 252 (D. Mass. 1998).

103. *See Fireside Nissan, supra* note 98, 395 Mass. at 371.

104. *See id.; Monadock Display Fireworks, Inc. v. Andover*, 388 Mass. 153, 157-158 n.1, 445 N.E.2d 1053 (1983).

105. *See Fireside Nissan, supra* note 98, 395 Mass. at 372.

106. *See Decker v. Black & Decker Mfg. Co.*, 389 Mass. 35, 40, 449 N.E.2d 641 (1983); *Stewart v. Roy Bros.*, 358 Mass. 446, 459, 265 N.E.2d 357 (1970).

107. *See* Mass. Gen. Laws ch. 231B, § 1.

108. *See* Mass. Gen. Laws ch. 231B, § 1.

109. *See* Mass. Gen. Laws ch. 152.

110. *See* Mass. Gen. Laws ch. 152, § 1.

111. *See French v. United Parcel Service, Inc.*, 2 F. Supp. 2d 128, 132 (D. Mass. 1998); *Doe v. Purity Supreme, Inc.*, 422 Mass. 563, 565, 664 N.E.2d 815 (1996).

112. *See* Mass. Gen. Laws ch. 152, § 15.

113. *See Purity Supreme, supra* note 111, 422 Mass. at 565-566; *Green v. Wyman-Gordon Co.*, 422 Mass. 551, 553, 664 N.E.2d 808 (1996); *Foley v. Polaroid Corp.*, 381 Mass. 545, 548, 413 N.E.2d 711 (1980).

114. *See Mulford v. Mangano*, 418 Mass. 407, 410, 636 N.E.2d 272 (1994); *Saharceski v. Marcure*, 373 Mass. 304, 306, 366 N.E.2d 1245 (1977).

115. *See* Mass. Gen. Laws ch. 152, § 15.

116. *See id.*

117. *See id.*

118. *See* Mass. Gen. Laws ch. 152, § 15.

119. *See Corbett v. Related Companies Northeast, Inc.*, 424 Mass. 714, 717, 677 N.E.2d 1153 (1997); Mass. Gen. Laws ch. 152, § 15.

120. *See* Mass. Gen. Laws ch. 152, § 15; *Giolito v. Dow Corning Corp.*, 788 F. Supp. 102, 104 (D. Mass. 1992).

121. *See Doe v. Purity Supreme, Inc.*, 422 Mass. 563, 565, 664 N.E.2d 815 (1996).

122. *See Sarocco v. General Elec. Co.*, 879 F. Supp. 156, 160 (D. Mass. 1995); *Hamilton v. Baystate Med. Educ. & Research Foundation, Inc.*, 866 F. Supp. 51, 56 (D. Mass. 1994); *Foley v. Polaroid Corp.*, 381 Mass. 545, 552-553, 413 N.E.2d 711 (1980).

123. *See Mounsey v. Ellard*, 363 Mass. 693, 707, 297 N.E.2d 43 (1973).

124. *See id.*

125. *See Pridgen v. Boston Hous. Auth.*, 364 Mass. 696, 706-707, 308 N.E.2d 467 (1974).

126. *See Schofield v. Merrill*, 386 Mass. 244, 246, 253, 435 N.E.2d 339 (1982); *see also Commonwealth v. Welansky*, 316 Mass. 383, 396-401, 55 N.E.2d 902 (1944) (elements of willful, wanton, and reckless conduct).

127. *See Stamboulis v. Stamboulis*, 401 Mass. 762, 770, 519 N.E.2d 1299 (1988); *Schofield, supra* note 126, 386 Mass. at 246; *Pridgen, supra* note 125, 364 Mass. at 711.

128. *See O'Sullivan v. Shaw*, 431 Mass. 201, 205 (2000) (Comparative Negligence Act did not implicitly overrule the "open and obvious danger" rule).

129. *See* Mass. Gen. Laws ch. 231, § 85Q; *Soule v. Massachusetts Elec. Co.*, 378 Mass. 177, 182-84, 390 N.E.2d 716 (1979) (common law duty).

130. *See* Mass. Gen. Laws ch. 231, § 85; *Mathis v. Massachusetts Elec. Co.*, 409 Mass. 256, 261, 565 N.E.2d 1180 (1991).

131. *See* Mass. Gen. Laws ch. 138, § 69.

132. *See id.*

133. *See, e.g., McGuiggan v. New England Tel. & Tel. Co.*, 398 Mass. 152, 160, 496 N.E.2d 141 (1986); *Pollard v. Powers*, 50 Mass. App. Ct. 515, 518, 738 N.E.2d 1144 (2000).

134. *See Tobin v. Norwood Country Club*, 422 Mass. 126, 129, 661 N.E.2d 627 (1996).

135. *See Cimino v. Milford Keg, Inc.*, 385 Mass. 323, 331-32 n.9, 431 N.E.2d 920 (1982).

136. *See id.* at 327-28.

137. *See Michnik-Zilberman v. Gordon's Liquor, Inc.*, 390 Mass. 6, 11, 453 N.E.2d 430 (1983).

138. *See O'Hanley v. Ninety-Nine, Inc.*, 12 Mass. App. Ct. 64, 66, 421 N.E.2d 1217 (1981).

139. *See Garweth Corp. v. Boston Edison Co.*, 415 Mass. 303, 305, 613 N.E.2d 92 (1993); *Bay State-Spray & Provincetown S.S., Inc. v. Caterpillar Tractor Co.*, 404 Mass. 103, 107, 533 N.E.2d 1350 (1989); *Stop & Shop Cos. v. Fisher*, 387 Mass. 889, 893-94, 444 N.E.2d 368 (1983).

140. *See Clark v. Rowe*, 428 Mass. 339, 342, 701 N.E.2d 624 (1998).

141. *See Stop & Shop, supra* note 139, 387 Mass. at 893-94. *But see Craig v. Everett M. Brooks Co.*, 351 Mass. 497, 499, 222 N.E.2d 752 (1967) (allowing recovery for solely economic injury for claim of negligent misrepresentation).

142. *See Craig v. Everett M. Brooks Co.*, 351 Mass. 497, 499-501, 222 N.E.2d 752 (1967).

143. *See* Mass. R. Civ. P. 9(b).

144. *See Danca v. Taunton Sav. Bank*, 385 Mass. 1, 8, 429 N.E.2d 1129 (1982); *Powell v. Rasmussen*, 355 Mass. 117, 118-19, 243 N.E.2d 167 (1969).

145. *See id.*

146. *See id.*

147. *See Saxon Theatre Corp. v. Sage*, 347 Mass. 662, 666-667, 200 N.E.2d 241 (1964); *Warren H. Bennett, Inc. v. Charlestown Sav. Bank*, 3 Mass. App. Ct. 753 (1975).

148. *See Danca, supra* note 144, 385 Mass. at 8; *Powell, supra* note 144, 355 Mass. at 119.

149. *See Powell, supra* note 144, 355 Mass. at 118 (quoting *Chatham Furnace Co. v. Moffatt*, 147 Mass. 403, 406, 18 N.E. 168 (1888).

150. *See Lawton v. Dracousis*, 14 Mass. App. Ct. 164, 171, 437 N.E.2d 543, *app. denied*, 387 Mass. 1103, 440 N.E.2d 1177 (1982) (quoting Restatement (Second) Torts, § 552(1)).

151. *See Craig, supra* note 142, 351 Mass. at 499.

152. *See* Mass. Gen. Laws ch. 93A.

153. Mass. Gen. Laws ch. 93A, § 2(A).

154. *See* Mass. Gen. Laws ch. 93A; *McGrath v. Mishara*, 386 Mass. 74, 85, 434 N.E.2d 1215 (1982).

155. *See* Mass. Gen. Laws ch. 93A, § 4; *Commonwealth v. DeCotis*, 366 Mass. 234, 245-46, 316 N.E.2d 748 (1974).

156. *See* Mass. Gen. Laws ch. 93A, § 11.

157. *See* Mass. Gen. Laws ch. 93A, § 9.

158. *See* Mass. Gen. Laws ch. 93A, § 2; *Kapp v. Arbella Mut. Ins. Co.*, 426 Mass. 683, 686, 689 N.E.2d 1347 (1998); *Service Publs., Inc. v. Goverman*, 396 Mass. 567, 578 n.13, 487 N.E.2d 520 (1986).

159. *See* Mass. Gen. Laws ch. 93A, § 3 ("Nothing in this chapter shall apply to transactions or actions otherwise permitted under laws as administered by any regulatory board or officer acting under statutory authority of the commonwealth or of the United States.").

160. *See* Mass. Gen. Laws ch. 93A; *Linkage Corp. v. Trustees of Boston Univ.*, 425 Mass 1, 23, 679 N.E.2d 191 (1997).

161. *Begelfer v. Najarian*, 381 Mass. 177, 191, 409 N.E.2d 167 (1980).

162. *See Lantner v. Carson*, 374 Mass. 606, 611, 373 N.E.2d 973 (1978).

163. *See Manning v. Zuckerman*, 388 Mass. 8, 11-15, 444 N.E.2d 1262 (1983); *Weeks v. Harbor Natl. Bank*, 388 Mass. 141, 144, 445 N.E.2d 605 (1983); *Dorfman v. TDA Indus., Inc.*, 16 Mass. App. Ct. 714, 720-721, 455 N.E.2d 457 (1983).

164. *See Edinburg v. Cavers*, 22 Mass. App. Ct. 212, 229, 492 NE.2d 1171 (1986).

165. *See Szalla v. Locke*, 421 Mass. 448, 451-452, 657 N.E.2d 1267 (1995).

166. *See Doiron v. Castonguay*, 401 Mass. 705, 707, 519 N.E.2d 260 (1988).

167. *See Lewis v. Ariens Co.*, 49 Mass. App. Ct. 301, 307, 729 N.E.2d 323 (2000).

168. *See* Mass. Gen. Laws ch. 93A § 1(b), *overruling Cabot Corp. v. Baddour*, 394 Mass. 720, 477 N.E.2d 399 (1985).

169. *See W. Oliver Tripp Co. v. American Hoechst Corp.*, 34 Mass. App. Ct. 744, 753, 616 N.E.2d 118 (1993).

170. *See* Mass. Gen. Laws ch. 260, § 5A.

171. *See Flesner v. Technical Communications Group*, 410 Mass. 805, 813, 575 N.E.2d 1107 (1991).

172. Mass. Gen. Laws ch. 229, § 2.

173. *See* Mass. Gen. Laws ch. 151B; Mass. Gen. Laws ch. 11I.

174. *See* Mass. Gen. Laws ch. 93A, § 9; *see also Muchnick v. Post Publishing Co.*, 332 Mass. 304, 125 N.E.2d 137 (1955) (regarding special damages).

175. *See Stone v. Essex County Newspapers, Inc.*, 367 Mass. 849, 860, 330 N.E.2d 161 (1975).

176. *See Gaudette v. Webb*, 362 Mass. 60, 71, 284 N.E.2d 222 (1972).

177. *See* Mass. Gen. Laws ch. 229, § 2.

178. *See id.*

179. *Id.*

180. *Id.; Santos v. Lumbermens Mut. Cas. Co.*, 408 Mass. 70, 76-77, 556 N.E.2d 983 (1990).

181. *See id.*

182. *See id.*

183. *See* Mass. Gen. Laws ch. 229, § 1.

184. *See* Mass. Gen. Laws ch. 229, § 6.

185. *See* Mass. Gen. Laws ch. 229, § 6B.

186. *See* Mass. Gen. Laws ch. 228, § 1.

187. *See* Mass. Gen. Laws ch. 229, § 5A.

188. *See Gaudette v. Webb*, 362 Mass. 60, 71, 284 N.E.2d 222 (1972).

189. *See Bethlehem Fabricators v. H. D. Watts Co.*, 286 Mass. 556, 565-568, 190 N.E. 828 (1934).

190. *See* Mass. Gen. Laws ch. 228, § 4.

MICHIGAN

A. STATUTES OF LIMITATION

Causes of action based on assault, battery, false imprisonment, malicious prosecution, professional malpractice, and misconduct or neglect of office by a sheriff or sheriff's deputies must be brought within two years.[1]

An action alleging negligence or misconduct by a constable shall be brought within two years after the expiration of the year for which the constable was elected.[2]

Libel and slander actions must be brought within one year.[3]

A products liability action must be brought within three years.[4]

Actions arising out of the defective and unsafe condition of an improvement to real property accruing after March 31, 1986, against an architect, professional engineer, or contractor must be brought within six years after occupancy, use, or acceptance of the improvement or one year after the defect is discovered or should have been discovered but no later than ten years after occupancy, use, or acceptance of the improvement.[5] Actions to recover damages against a land surveyor in the preparation of a survey or report must be brought within six years of the delivery of the survey or report.[6]

All other actions to recover for injury to a person or property or for the death of a person must be brought within three years of the injury or death.[7]

The "discovery rule" may apply to determine when a claim accrues and the statute of limitations begins to run for products liability claims.[8]

A claim for medical malpractice must be brought within two years after the alleged act or omission. A person shall not commence a medical malpractice action, however, unless the person has given the health professional or health facility a *notice of intent* at least 182 days before the action is commenced.

If a person dies before or within 30 days after the period of limitations has run, an action may be commenced within two years after the letters of authority are issued, but no later than three years after the period of limitations has run.[9]

In actions based on tort or another legal theory seeking damages for personal injury, property damage, or wrongful death, filed on or after March 28, 1996, a party may file a notice identifying a nonparty who may be at fault. A cause of action against a nonparty at fault identified in a notice and added as a defendant is not barred by a period of limitation unless the cause of action would have been barred at the time of the filing of the original action.[10]

Dram shop actions involving the unlawful selling, giving, or furnishing of liquor to minors or visibly intoxicated persons must be brought within two years after the injury or death.[11]

B. TORT REFORM

On March 28, 1996, two Michigan "tort reform" statutes took effect that have had far-reaching implications in product liability actions filed in Michigan after the date. Those laws, which relate to, among other matters, venue, joint and several liability, fault allocation, comparative negligence, damage cap, alteration and misuse, warning, seller's liability, presumptions, and admissibility of expert opinion, have made Michigan a less hostile jurisdiction for manufacturers and sellers.

Venue

Previously, the Michigan statute applicable to venue in a product liability action provided for the commencement of an action in a county where "all or part of the cause of action arose" and the defendant resides or conducts business or the plaintiff resides or conducts business. This statute led to attempts to establish venue in a county other than the one in which the accident or original injury occurred. The Tort Reform Statute recasts the phrase "a county in which all or part of the cause of action arose" as "the county in which the original injury occurred."[12]

Joint and Several Liability

Joint and several liability has been eliminated in those tort cases subject to Michigan's tort reform statute. For example, in product liability actions, the liability of each defendant is "several only and not joint."[13]

Certain exceptions are recognized, however, where an action includes a medical malpractice claim or where the injuries, damages, or death are caused by criminal conduct involving gross negligence or the use of drugs or alcohol.[14]

Allocation of Fault to Nonparties

Liability may be allocated among all responsible persons, "regardless of whether the person is, or could have been, named as a party to the action."[15]

Comparative Negligence, Impaired Ability

In a product liability action, if the plaintiff's percentage of fault is greater than the aggregate percentage of fault attributable to all other persons, plaintiff's economic damages are reduced by the percentage of the comparative fault, and noneconomic damages (e.g., pain and suffering) shall not be awarded.[16] An absolute defense is recognized where the person injured or killed had an impaired ability due to alcohol or controlled substances and, due to that impairment, was 50 percent or more at fault.[17]

Damage Caps

A base limitation of $280,000 is established for noneconomic losses, with a higher cap of $500,000 set in the event of death or permanent loss of a vital bodily function.[18] The statute provides for adjustment of the caps annually based on changes in the Consumer Price Index.[19] Exceptions to the limit for death or permanent loss of vital bodily functions are established in the event of gross negligence or if the court determines that at the time of manufacture or distribution the defendant had actual knowledge the product was defective and that there was a substantial likelihood the defect would cause the injury that was the basis of the action, and defendant willfully disregarded that knowledge.[20]

Expert Witnesses

One of the potentially most significant provisions in PA 249 is a Michigan codification of a "gate keeper" responsibility on the part of the trial court similar to that recognized by the United States Supreme Court in *Daubert v. Merrill Dow Pharmaceuticals*, 509 U.S. 579, 125 L. Ed. 2d 469, 113 S. Ct. 2786 (1993). The Act sets forth seven factors that the trial court "shall consider" in determining whether expert testimony will be admissible. The Act requires a specific determination by the court that the proffered opinion will be reliable and will assist the trier of fact. Significant among the seven factors is the last one: "Whether the opinion or methodology is relied upon by experts outside the context of litigation."[21]

C. "NO FAULT" LIMITATIONS

The no-fault provisions of the Michigan Insurance Code[22] abolished tort liability arising from the ownership, maintenance, or use of a motor vehicle except as to (1) intentionally caused harm,[23] (2) damages for noneconomic loss if the injured person has suffered death, serious impairment of a body function, or a permanent disfigurement;[24] and (3) damages for allowable expenses, work loss, and survivor's loss in excess of the daily, monthly, and specified time limitations contained within the Act.[25]

The primary focus of litigation under the No-Fault Act involves noneconomic damages. In order to recover noneconomic damages, a plaintiff need establish serious impairment of a body function. The No-Fault Act provides that this determination is a question of law for the court if either there is no factual dispute concerning the nature and extent of the person's injuries or there is a factual dispute concerning the nature and extent of the person's injuries, but that dispute is not material to the determination as to whether the person has suffered a serious impairment of a body function or permanent serious disfigurement.[26] In the case of a closed head injury, however, a question of fact for the jury can exist if a licensed specialist who regularly diagnoses or treats closed head injuries testifies under oath that there may be a serious neurological injury.[27]

D. THE STANDARD FOR NEGLIGENCE

To establish negligence, a plaintiff must show: (1) duty; (2) breach of that duty; (3) proximate cause between the breach and damages; and (4) damages.[28] There can be no actionable negligence in the absence of a duty between the plaintiff and defendant.[29] The standard of care is that which a reasonably prudent person would exercise under the circumstances.[30]

E. CAUSATION

To establish causation, the plaintiff must show both cause in fact and legal cause.[31] To establish cause in fact, the plaintiff must show that it is more likely than not that the injuries would not have occurred, but for the defendant's conduct.[32] To prove legal cause, the plaintiff must show that it was foreseeable that the defendant's conduct could create a risk of harm and that the result of that conduct and intervening causes were foreseeable.[33]

F. CONTRIBUTORY NEGLIGENCE, COMPARATIVE NEGLIGENCE, AND ASSUMPTION OF RISK

Comparative negligence applies in all tort actions in Michigan regardless of theory.[34] Since the adoption of comparative negligence in the late 1970s and before Tort Reform, Michigan had been a "pure" comparative negligence state. There was no limit on the amount of plaintiff's comparative negligence—a plaintiff could be literally 99 percent at fault and still collect 1 percent of his or her damages from a liable defendant. Tort Reform in 1996, however, changed that. Now, if the plaintiff's percentage of fault is greater than the aggregate percentage of fault attributable to all other persons, plaintiff's economic damages are reduced by the percentage of comparative fault, and noneconomic damages (e.g., pain and suffering) shall not be awarded.[35] An absolute defense is recognized where the person injured or deceased has an impaired ability due to alcohol or controlled substances and, due to that impairment, was 50 percent or more at fault.[36] There are exceptions, however, to these limitations.

The adoption of comparative negligence also required Michigan courts to examine whether assumption of the risk should continue as an absolute defense. The doctrine is still recognized and enforced if statutory.[37] Although it has narrowed the scope, Michigan courts also continue to recognize the doctrine in work that involves fire protection, police, or security work.[38]

G. *RES IPSA LOQUITUR* AND INHERENTLY DANGEROUS ACTIVITIES

1. *Res Ipsa Loquitur*

The Michigan version of *res ipsa loquitur* entitles a plaintiff to a permissible inference of negligence from circumstantial evidence, if the plaintiff, in the case in chief, meets the following conditions for the doctrine to apply: (1) the event must be of a kind that ordinarily does not occur in the absence of someone's negligence; (2) the event must be caused by an agency or instrumentality within the exclusive control of the defendant; (3) the event must not have been due to any voluntary action or contribution on the part of the plaintiff; and (4) evidence of the true explanation for the event must be more readily accessible to the defendant than to the plaintiff.[39]

2. Inherently Dangerous Activities

In assessing negligence, the standard is reasonable care under the circumstances, but a higher degree of care is required when dealing with a dangerous instrumentality than in the ordinary affairs of life or business.[40] In the main, Michigan's law on "inherently dangerous" or "extrahazardous" activity has focused on blasting, the collection of water in a dangerous location, storage of flammable liquids, and like activities.[41] The inherently dangerous activity doctrine is also used in Michigan as an exception to the general rule that an employer of an independent contractor is not liable for the negligence of the contractor or his employees. If the circumstances under which the work is to be done creates a risk, recognizable in advance, of physical harm to others, then the employer may be liable if the contractor does not exercise reasonable care.[42]

H. NEGLIGENCE *PER SE*

Michigan does not subscribe to the doctrine of negligence *per se*.[43] Rather, Michigan subscribes to the minority view that a violation of a statute creates a rebuttable presumption of negligence, while the violation of an ordinance or administrative regulation constitutes evidence of negligence.[44] As a result, if the plaintiff establishes that the defendant violated a statute, the plaintiff has established negligent conduct on the part of the defendant.[45] It is then, however, the trier of fact who weighs this negligent conduct to determine if it constitutes a breach of the applicable standard of care.[46]

I. JOINT AND SEVERAL LIABILITY

For tort actions other than medical malpractice, liability is several and not joint, but employers can still be vicariously liable for the actions of an employee.[47] A tort defendant is jointly and severally liable if the action giving rise to the tort is a crime for which the defendant is convicted and (1) which contains an element of gross negligence, or (2) involves the use of alcohol or a controlled substance and which is a violation of certain provisions of Michigan law.[48]

In medical malpractice actions, liability is joint and several if the plaintiff is determined to be without fault.[49] If a medical malpractice plaintiff is determined to be at fault, upon a motion no later than six months after final judgment has been entered, the court shall determine whether any party's portion of the judgment is uncollectible from that party and shall reallocate the uncollectible amount among the other parties (except for governmental agencies that are not hospitals or medical care facilities) according to each party's percentage of fault.[50]

J. INDEMNITY

Indemnity permits an innocent party who was held liable to a plaintiff to shift the loss to the one who was actually guilty of the wrong.[51] Indemnity can arise from the common law, an implied contract, or an express contract.[52] Common law indemnity and implied contractual indemnity are only available to one free from active or causal negligence, which is determined by examining the allegations of the primary plaintiff's complaint.[53]

K. BAR OF WORKERS' COMPENSATION STATUTE

Under the Michigan Workers' Disability Compensation Act, the recovery of benefits as provided in the Act is the employee's exclusive remedy against the employer for personal injury or occupational disease.[54] The statute itself provides the only exception to the exclusive remedy scheme—intentional torts. An intentional tort exists only when an employee is injured as a result of a deliberate act of the employer and the employer specifically intended an injury. As defined in the statute, an employer shall be deemed to have intended to injure if the employer had actual knowledge that an injury was certain to occur and willfully disregarded that knowledge.[55] This is obviously a very difficult standard for a plaintiff to overcome. Acting recklessly is not enough to meet the threshold standard.[56] The issue of whether an act was an intentional tort for purposes of avoiding the exclusive-remedy bar is a question of law for the court.[57]

The phrase "deliberate act" of the employer has been interpreted to include situations in which the employer consciously fails to act.[58] And construction of the language "specifically intended an injury" means that in acting or failing to act, the employer must have determined to injure the employee; the employer must have had the particular purpose of inflicting injury on the employee.[59] It is not enough that a risk of injury existed or that someone, but not necessarily the plaintiff, was certain to suffer an injury. A plaintiff must show that the employer knew of a specific danger that was certain to result in an injury, and that the employer required the worker to proceed in the face of that danger.

If an employer has ordered or expressly authorized an assault on an employee, the resulting injury to the employee is not an accident, and the employer is liable in a civil action for intentional tort regardless of the exclusivity of workers' compensation.[60]

An employee is not barred from seeking damages in a civil action from third-party tortfeasors.[61] Any recovery against the third party, after deducting the expenses of recovery, are to first reimburse the employer or its carrier for any amounts paid or payable under the Act, although employers are often asked to waive or compromise that reimbursement.[62]

L. PREMISES LIABILITY

Premises liability is premised on the prerequisite of both possession of and control over the land or premises in question and requires actual exercise of domain and control over the property.[63] To establish premises liability in Michigan, the plaintiff must prove: (1) the landowner or possessor knew or, by the exercise of reasonable care, would have discovered the complained-of condition, and should have realized that it involved an unreasonable risk of harm to its customers, guests, or invitees; (2) should have expected that its customers, guests, or invitees would not discover or realize the danger, or would fail to protect themselves against it; and (3) failed to take reasonable steps to rectify the allegedly unsafe condition.[64]

Michigan landowners or possessors are not obligated to keep their premises in safe condition for trespassers.[65] They are, however, subject to liability for failing to take reasonable measures to protect their invitees from foreseeable harm caused by the criminal acts of third parties under certain circumstances.[66]

M. DRAM SHOP LIABILITY

Michigan's Dram Shop Act,[67] contained within the State's Liquor Control Code of 1998,[68] provides a cause of action for individuals who suffer damage or a personal injury by minors or visibly intoxicated persons as a result of the unlawful selling, giving, or furnishing of alcohol beverages to a minor or visibly intoxicated person if the provision of alcohol is established to have been a proximate cause of the harm.[69] The Act provides the exclusive remedy for damages against a licensee arising out of the sale or furnishing of liquor.[70] To succeed in a dram shop action, a plaintiff must establish that: (1) he was injured by an intoxicated person's wrongful or tortious conduct; (2) the principal defendant's intoxication was the sole or contributing cause of the injuries; and (3) the licensee sold to a visibly intoxicated person liquor that caused or contributed to the intoxication.[71]

The Act does not limit remedies against nonlicensees.[72] Therefore, while a social host is not expressly subject to the Act, a civil cause of action based in negligence does exist for damages caused by the furnishing of alcoholic beverages to persons under 21 years of age.[73]

N. ECONOMIC LOSS

Michigan courts have adopted the economic loss doctrine, which bars actions in tort for purely economic losses, such as lost profits, when the dispute arises out of a transaction involving the sale of goods between two commercial parties. The doctrine, as set forth by the Michigan Supreme Court, provides that the UCC is the sole remedy in cases involving economic loss arising from the purchase of goods.[74] The doctrine, however, does not hinder an individual consumer's cause of action in tort.[75]

O. FRAUD AND MISREPRESENTATION

The Michigan Rules of Civil Procedure require that a cause of action for fraud be pleaded with particularity.[76]

Each of the following elements for fraud must be proved by clear and convincing evidence: (1) the defendant made a material representation; (2) that was false; (3) that when he made it he knew that it was false, or made it recklessly, without any knowledge of its truth and as a positive assertion; (4) that he made it with the intention that it should be acted on by plaintiff; (5) that the plaintiff acted in reliance on it; and (6) that he thereby suffered injury.[77] In addition, the alleged fraud or misrepresentation must relate to a pre-existing or present fact. A promise to do an act in the future is not fraud.[78] Finally, statements of opinion cannot be relied on to support a fraud claim.[79]

Michigan courts also recognize the doctrine of innocent misrepresentation, which provides that a party can recover for misrepresentations made by one party to another, where: (1) in a transaction between them; (2) a representation was made that was false in fact; (3) the representation actually deceived the other; (4) the representation was relied on by him to his damage; and (5) the loss of the party deceived inures to the benefit of the other.[80] The innocent misrepresentation doctrine lacks the requirement that the misrepresentation be made with the intent that it should be acted on by the victim, and it applies irrespective of whether the party making the misrepresentation acted in good faith.[81]

Finally, Michigan courts also recognize the doctrine of silent fraud. This doctrine requires a party to a business transaction to exercise reasonable care to disclose to the other party, before the transaction is completed, any subsequently acquired information that the party recognizes as rendering untrue, or misleading, previous representations that, when made, were true or believed to be true.[82]

P. CONSUMER FRAUD STATUTES

The Michigan Consumer Protection Act (MCPA)[83] protects consumers from unfair methods of competition and deceptive acts and practices in any trade or commerce.[84] The MCPA entrusts the enforcement of the MCPA to both the Attorney General and the district attorney's office, who may institute actions for violations, including requests for injunctive relief to enjoin the prohibited conduct.[85] Private actions may also be brought under the MCPA.[86] Where a private plaintiff seeks monetary redress as a result of the violation, a causal connection between the violation and plaintiff's loss must be established.[87]

Actions under the MCPA are generally subject to a six-year statute of limitations.[88]

Q. PUNITIVE DAMAGES

Michigan law does not allow imposition of damages designed solely to punish or make an example of a defendant.[89] It does, however, recognize exemplary damages but only to compensate a plaintiff for humiliation, sense of outrage, and indignity resulting from injuries maliciously, willfully, and wantonly inflicted by a defendant.[90]

R. **WRONGFUL DEATH AND SURVIVORSHIP ACTIONS**

Wrongful death recoveries in Michigan derive solely from the Wrongful Death Act.[91] In wrongful death actions, the court or jury may award damages as the court or jury shall consider fair and equitable, under all the circumstances including reasonable medical, hospital, funeral, and burial expenses for which the estate is liable; reasonable compensation for pain and suffering, while conscious, undergone by the deceased person during the period intervening between the time of the injury and death; and damages for the loss of financial support and the loss of the society and companionship of the deceased.[92] Moreover, all actions and claims in Michigan survive death.[93] If an action is pending at the time of death, the claims may be amended to bring it under Michigan's Wrongful Death Statute. A failure to do so amounts to a waiver of the claim for additional damages resulting from death.[94]

BUTZEL LONG
150 W. Jefferson Ave., Suite 900
Detroit, Michigan 48226
(313) 225-7000
Fax (313) 225-7080
www.butzel.com

James J. Boutrous, II
(313) 225-7010
boutrous@butzel.com

Herbert C. Donovan
(313) 983-7439
donovan@butzel.com

Phillip C. Korovesis
(313) 983-7458
korovesi@butzel.com

Edward M. Kronk
(313) 225-7017
kronk@butzel.com

Daniel P. Malone
(313) 225-7032
malone@butzel.com

Donald B. Miller
(313) 225-7020
miller@butzel.com

Steven M. Ribiat
(313) 983-7484
ribiat@butzel.com

Christina Gill Roseman
(313) 225-7022
roseman@butzel.com

Lynn A. Sheehy
(313) 225-7078
sheehy@butzel.com

Michael G. Latiff
(313) 225-7052
latiff@butzel.com

ENDNOTES - MICHIGAN

1. Mich. Comp. Laws § 600.5805; Mich. Stat. Ann. § 27A.5805.

2. Mich. Comp. Laws § 600.5805(6); Mich. Stat. Ann. § 27A.5805(6).

3. Mich. Comp. Laws § 600.5805(7); Mich. Stat. Ann. § 27A.5805(7).

4. Mich. Comp. Laws § 600.5805(9); Mich. Stat. Ann. § 27A.5805(9).

5. Mich. Comp. Laws § 600.5839; Mich. Stat. Ann. § 27A.5839.

6. Mich. Comp. Laws § 600.5839(2); Mich. Stat. Ann. § 27A.5839(2).

7. Mich. Comp. Laws § 600.5805(8); Mich. Stat. Ann. § 27A.5805(8).

8. *Moll v. Abbott*, 444 Mich. 1, 506 N.W.2d 816 (1993).

9. Mich. Comp. Laws § 600.5852; Mich. Stat. Ann. § 27A.5852.

10. Mich. Comp. Laws § 600.2957(2); Mich. Stat. Ann. § 27A.2957(2).

11. Mich. Comp. Laws § 436.1801(4); Mich. Stat. Ann. § 18.1175(801)(4).

12. Mich. Comp. Laws § 600.1629.

13. Mich. Comp. Laws § 600.6304(4); Mich. Comp. Laws § 600.2956.

14. Mich. Comp. Laws § 600.6304(6); Mich. Comp. Laws § 600.6312.

15. Mich. Comp. Laws § 600.2957; Mich. Comp. Laws § 600.6304.

16. Mich. Comp. Laws § 600.2959.

17. Mich. Comp. Laws § 600.2955a.

18. Mich. Comp. Laws § 600.2946a.

19. Mich. Comp. Laws § 600.2946a(1).

20. Mich. Comp. Laws § 2946a(3).

21. Mich. Comp. Laws § 600.2955(1).

22. Mich. Comp. Laws § 500.3135; Mich. Stat. Ann. § 24.3135.

23. Mich. Comp. Laws § 500.3135(3)(a); Mich. Stat. Ann. § 24.3135(3)(a).

24. Mich. Comp. Laws § 500.3135(3)(b); Mich. Stat. Ann. § 24.3135(3)(b).

25. Mich. Comp. Laws § 500.3135(3)(c); Mich. Stat. Ann. § 24.3135(3)(c).

26. Mich. Comp. Laws § 500.3135(2)(a); Mich. Stat. Ann. § 24.3135(2)(a).

27. Mich. Comp. Laws § 500.3135(2)(a)(ii); Mich. Stat. Ann. § 24.3135(2)(a)(ii).

28. *Krass v. Tri-County Security*, 233 Mich. App. 661 (1999).

29. *Oja v. Kin*, 229 Mich. App. 184, 187 (1998).

30. *Antcliff v. State Employees Credit Union*, 414 Mich. 624, 327 N.W.2d 814 (1982).

31. *Skinner v. Square D Co*, 445 Mich. 153, 516 N.W.2d 475 (1994).

32. *Weymers v. Khera*, 454 Mich. 639, 563 N.W.2d 647 (1997).

33. *Moning v. Alfono*, 400 Mich. 425, 254 N.W.2d 759 (1977).

34. *Placek v. City of Sterling Heights*, 405 Mich. 638 (1979).

35. Mich. Comp. Laws § 600.2959.

36. Mich. Comp. Laws § 600.6304.

37. *See, e.g., Bar v. Mt. Brighton, Inc.*, 546 N.W.2d 273 (1996) (state skiing statute recognizes "obvious and necessary dangers").

38. *See, e.g., Marlis v. Fleur, Inc.*, 208 Mich. App. 631, 528 N.W.2d 218 (1995) (off-duty police officer does not assume risk that former arrestee will assault him in a bar).

39. *Jones v. Porretta*, 428 Mich. 132, 150–51 (1987). This opinion also mentions in a footnote another requirement, from the Restatement (Second) of Torts, namely, that other responsible causes, including the conduct of the plaintiff and third persons, are sufficiently eliminated by the evidence. *See also Hasselbach v. TG Canton, Inc.*, 209 Mich. App. 475; 531 N.W.2d 715 (1994); *Cloverleaf Car Co. v. Phillips Petroleum Co.*, 213 Mich. App. 186, 194; 540 N.W.2d 297 (1995).

40. *Young v. Lee*, 310 Mich. 42, 47 (1944); *St. Paul Fire & Marine Ins. Co. v. Michigan Consolidated Gas Co.*, 4 Mich. App. 56, 63 (1966).

41. *Avemco Ins. Co. v. Rooto Corp.*, 967 F.2d 1105, 1109 (6th Cir. 1992).

42. *Bosak v. Hutchinson*, 422 Mich. 712; 375 N.W.2d 333 (1985), *reh'g denied*, 424 Mich. 1201 (1985); *Samhoun v. Greenfield Co.*, 163 Mich. App. 34, 42–44 (1987).

43. *See Zeni v. Anderson*, 397 Mich. 117, 128–29; 243 N.W.2d 270 (1976); *Candelaria v. B.C. General Contractors, Inc.*, 236 Mich. App. 67, 82; 600 N.W.2d 348 (1999).

44. *Candelaria, supra*, 236 Mich. App. at 82 n.15, citing *Johnson v. Bobbie's Party Store*, 189 Mich. App. 652, 661; 473 N.W.2d 796 (1991).

45. *See Zeni, supra*, 397 Mich. at 128–29.

46. *Id.*

47. Mich. Comp. Laws § 600.2956; Mich. Stat. Ann. § 27A.2956.

48. Mich. Comp. Laws § 600.6312; Mich. Stat. Ann. § 27A.6312. The provisions of Michigan law that, combined with a crime involving the use of alcohol or a controlled substance, are as follows:

   (1) Section 14 of the Explosives Act of 1970, Mich. Comp. Laws § 29.54; Mich. Stat. Ann. § 4.559(54).
   (2) Section 111 of the Michigan Code of Military Justice of 1980, Mich. Comp. Laws § 32.1111; Mich. Stat. Ann. § 4.686(311).
   (3) Section 625 of the Michigan Vehicle Code, Mich. Comp. Laws § 257.625; Mich. Stat. Ann. § 9.2325.
   (4) Section 185 of the Aeronautics Code of the State of Michigan, Mich. Comp. Laws § 259.185; Mich. Stat. Ann. § 102.85.
   (5) Section 80176 of part 801 (marine safety), 81143 of part 811 (off-road recreation vehicles), or 82127 of part 821 (snowmobiles) of the Natural Resources and Environmental Protection Act, Mich. Comp. Laws § 324.80176; Mich. Stat. Ann. § 13A.80176, Mich. Comp. Laws § 324.81143; Mich. Stat. Ann. § 13A.81143 and Mich. Comp. Laws § 324.82127; Mich. Stat. Ann. § 13A.82127.
   (6) Section 353 of the Railroad Code of 1993, Mich. Comp. Laws § 462.353; Mich. Stat. Ann. § 22.1263(353).
   (7) Section 237 of the Michigan Penal Code, Mich. Comp. Laws § 750.237; Mich. Stat. Ann. § 28.434.

49. Mich. Comp. Laws § 600.6304(6)(a); Mich. Stat. Ann. § 27A.6304(6)(a).

50. Mich. Comp. Laws § 600.6304(6)(b); Mich. Stat. Ann. § 27A.6304(6)(b) and Mich. Comp. Laws § 600.6304(7); Mich. Stat. Ann. § 27A.6304(7).

51. *Peeples v. Detroit*, 99 Mich. App. 285, 292; 297 N.W.2d 839 (1980).

52. *Hartman v. Century Truss*, 132 Mich. App. 661, 664; 347 N.W.2d 777 (1984).

53. *Johnson v. Bundy*, 129 Mich. App. 393, 399; 342 N.W.2d 567 (1983).

54. Mich. Comp. Laws § 418.131.

55. *Id*.

56. *Oaks v. Twin City Foods, Inc.*, 198 Mich. App. 296; 497 N.W.2d 196 (1992), *appeal denied*, 444 Mich. 914; 512 N.W.2d 844 (1993).

57. Mich. Comp. Laws § 418.131.

58. *Travis v. Dreis and Krump Mfg. Co.*, 453 Mich. 149; 551 N.W.2d 132 (1996), *reh'g denied*, 453 Mich. 1205; 554 N.W.2d 11 (1996).

59. *Id*.

60. *Beauchamp v. Dow Chemical Co.*, 427 Mich. 1; 398 N.W.2d 882 (1986).

61. Mich. Comp. Laws § 418.827.

62. *Id*.

63. *Merritt v. Nickelson*, 407 Mich. 544, 552; 287 N.W.2d 178 (1978).

64. *Quinlivan v. Great Atlantic and Pacific Tea Co.*, 395 Mich. 244, 259; 235 N.W.2d 732 (1975).

65. *Blakely v. White Star Line*, 154 Mich. 635, 637; 118 N.W.2d 482 (1908).

66. *Mason v. Royal Dequindre*, 455 Mich. 391, 393; 566 N.W.2d 199 (1997).

67. Mich. Comp. Laws § 436.1801; Mich. Stat. Ann. § 18.1175(801).

68. Mich. Comp. Laws § 436.1101; Mich. Stat. Ann. § 18.1175(101).

69. Mich. Comp. Laws § 436.1801(3); Mich. Stat. Ann. § 18.1175(801)(3).

70. Mich. Comp. Laws § 436.1801(10); Mich. Stat. Ann. § 18.1175(801)(10).

71. *McKnight v. Carter*, 144 Mich. App. 623; 376 N.W.2d 190 (1985).

72. *Id*.

73. *Longstreth v. Gensel*, 423 Mich. 675; 377 N.W.2d 804 (1985).

74. *Niebarger v. Universal Cooperatives*, 439 Mich. 512, 520, 486 N.W.2d 612 (Mich. 1992).

75. *Id.*

76. MCR 2.112(B)(1).

77. *Hi-Way Motor Co. v. International Harvester Co.*, 398 Mich. 330, 336, 247 N.W.2d 813 (Mich. 1976).

78. *Id.; see also Kirk v. Vaccaro*, 344 Mich. 226, 232, 73 N.W.2d 871 (Mich. 1955); *Roy Annett, Inc. v. Kerezsy*, 336 Mich. 169, 172, 57 N.W.2d 483 (Mich. 1953); *Howard v. Reaume*, 310 Mich. 119, 126, 16 N.W.2d 686 (Mich. 1944); *Boston Piano & Music Co. v. Pontiac Clothing Co.*, 199 Mich. 141, 147, 165 N.W. 856 (Mich. 1917).

79. *Hayes Construction Co. v. Silverhorn*, 343 Mich. 421, 426, 72 N.W.2d 190 (Mich. 1955).

80. *U.S. Fidelity and Guaranty Co. v. Black*, 412 Mich. 99, 116, 313 N.W.2d 77 (Mich. 1981).

81. *Id.*

82. *Id.* at 127.

83. Mich. Comp. Laws § 445.901, *et seq.*

84. Mich. Comp. Laws § 445.903.

85. Mich. Comp. Laws § 445.905 & Mich. Comp. Laws § 445.915.

86. Mich. Comp. Laws § 445.911.

87. Mich. Comp. Laws § 445.911(2). *See also, Mayhall v. A. H. Pond Co., Inc.*, 129 Mich. App. 178; 341 N.W.2d 268 (1983).

88. Mich. Comp. Laws § 445.911(7).

89. *McAuley v. General Motors Corp.*, 578 N.W.2d 282, 457 Mich. 513 (1998).

90. *See, e.g., Morganroth & Morganroth v. DeLorean*, 123 F.3d 374, *reh'g denied, cert. denied*, 118 S. Ct. 1561 (1997).

91. Mich. Comp. Laws § 600.2922.

92. *Id.*

93. *See, e.g., In Re: Matter of Thornton*, 481 N.W.2d 828, 192 Mich. App. 709 (1992).

94. Mich. Comp. Laws § 600.2922.

MINNESOTA

A. STATUTES OF LIMITATION

In Minnesota, a claim generally accrues and the statutory period begins running at the time damage occurs.[1] Even nominal damages may be sufficient to start the statute of limitations running.[2] With a breach of contract claim, the claim accrues at the time of breach.[3] Claims for indemnity and contribution, however, do not accrue at the time the tort is committed, but, rather, at the time the underlying claim is paid.[4]

Typically, ignorance of a claim does not prevent the statute from running.[5] Minnesota has not adopted the discovery rule. When a claim involves fraud, however, the limitations period begins when the fraud is discovered, or, in the exercise of reasonable diligence, should have been discovered.[6] A limitations period may also be extended if a disability is present or if the plaintiff is under 18 years of age.[7] Furthermore, the statute does not generally run when the defendant is out of state and, while out of state, is not subject to process or cannot be found.[8]

One Year

A one-year limitation period applies to claims asserted under the Minnesota Human Rights Act.[9]

Two Year

Minnesota's statutory provisions[10] governing limitations periods provide for a two-year period for the following torts: "libel, slander, assault, battery, false imprisonment, or other tort, resulting in personal injury, and all actions against veterinarians...." Minnesota courts have also applied the two-year limitations period to certain torts[11] that are (1) considered intentional or strict liability torts;[12] (2) involve an injury to a person (other than a bodily injury),[13] rather than a property or contract claim; or (3) involve an action or injury that can usually be the basis of criminal prosecution.[14] A two-year statute of limitations further applies to claims of wrongful interference with business relationships (by means of defamation, misrepresentation, or intentional infliction of emotional distress),[15] malicious prosecution claims[16] and actions for intentional infliction of emotional distress.[17] For actions based on services or construction to improve real property, no action can be brought more than two years after discovery of the defective improvements, and not, in any event, more than ten years after substantial completion of the construction.[18]

Four Year

Minnesota's Uniform Commercial Code contains a four-year statute of limitations.[19] Medical malpractice claims are also subject to a four-year statute of limitations, with no discovery rule.[20]

Six Year

A six-year limitation period applies for most negligence-based claims,[21] including typical negligence, products liability, failure to warn actions, and attorney malpractice claims.[22] The six-year period also applies to breach of contract claims,[23] fraud and misrepresentation claims,[24] underinsured motorist insurer's subrogation claims,[25] Section 1983 claims,[26] claims under Minnesota's consumer fraud statutes,[27] conversion claims,[28] and common-law nuisance, trespass, waste, environmental claims,[29] and personal injury claims based on domestic abuse.[30]

B. **TORT REFORM**

Minnesota has not enacted any tort reform in recent years, although there have been unsuccessful efforts in the Minnesota legislature to modify the joint and several liability provisions of Minn. Stat. § 604.02.

C. **"NO FAULT" LIMITATIONS**

The Minnesota No-Fault Automobile Insurance Act was adopted to accomplish two distinct purposes: (1) provide prompt payments of basic economic losses for automobile accident victims regardless of fault; and (2) reduce litigation and noneconomic recoveries for minor accidents.[31] In other words, "as a quid pro quo for the right to receive Basic Economic Loss Benefits regardless of fault, injured parties covered by the Act are limited in their right to recover general damages in Tort."[32]

Thus, under the No-Fault Act, accident victims cannot assert a claim for noneconomic damages[33] unless they meet one of the statutory "tort thresholds": (1) an injury resulting in death; (2) a permanent injury or disfigurement; (3) a disability for 60 days or more; or (4) over $4,000 in medical expenses.[34]

Economic loss claims are not subject to the tort thresholds, however.[35] Moreover, the No-Fault Act limits the application of the thresholds only to those negligence claims "accruing as a result of injury arising out of the operation, ownership, maintenance or use of a motor vehicle with respect to which security has been provided as required" by the Minnesota No-Fault Automobile Insurance Act.[36]

D. **THE STANDARD FOR NEGLIGENCE**

In Minnesota, the elements of a negligence claim are: (1) an applicable duty of care; (2) a breach of that duty; (3) an injury; and (4) the breach is the proximate cause of the injury.[37]

Generally, negligence is the failure of a person "to exercise such care as persons of ordinary prudence usually exercise under such circumstances."[38]

Thus, a professional has a duty to exercise the "care, skill, and diligence" that members of the profession ordinarily exercise under like circumstances.[39] In determining whether there has been a negligent breach of the duty of care, the defendant's conduct is viewed from an objective, rather than subjective, standard.[40] An omission, however, constitutes negligence only where there is an affirmative duty to act.[41]

The observance or failure to observe a relevant custom "does not necessarily amount to due care or the lack of it," but it is admissible "to show what a reasonably prudent person would do under the same or similar circumstances."[42] Under some circumstances, however, the custom itself may be negligent.[43]

E. CAUSATION

To establish causation in Minnesota, the defendant's negligence must be the proximate or direct cause of the injury.[44] A mere possibility of causation is not enough.[45] Causation exists if the defendant's tortious conduct was a substantial factor in bringing about the injury.[46]

The test to determine the extent of a defendant's liability "is in causation and not in probability or foreseeability."[47] In this regard, Minnesota follows the majority rule in that if an actor's conduct "has been a substantial factor" in causing harm, it is immaterial that the harm is brought about in a manner that could not be foreseen.[48]

A negligent actor may, however, avoid liability where an "intervening act" constitutes a "superseding intervening cause."[49] A superseding intervening cause is one that satisfies four elements: (1) its harmful effects must have occurred after the original negligence; (2) it must not have been brought about by the original negligence; (3) it must have actively worked to bring about a result that would not otherwise have followed from the original negligence; and (4) it must not have been reasonably foreseeable by the original wrongdoer.[50] A superseding intervening cause will not relieve an original wrongdoer who owed the injured plaintiff a continuing duty.[51]

F. CONTRIBUTORY NEGLIGENCE, COMPARATIVE NEGLIGENCE, AND ASSUMPTION OF RISK

1. Contributory Negligence

In Minnesota, contributory negligence is one form of contributory fault under Minnesota's Comparative Fault Act.[52] Plaintiffs are subject to the same negligence standard as defendants. Contributory negligence generally consists of a failure by the plaintiff to use reasonable care for his or her own safety. It can also arise from an unreasonable failure to avoid an injury or to mitigate damages.[53]

2. Comparative Fault

Under Minnesota law, the defense of comparative fault is available to apportion, reduce, and bar the recovery of damages.[54] Minnesota's

Comparative Fault Act expressly recognizes several kinds of comparative "fault" including: (1) acts or omissions that are negligent or reckless; (2) acts or omissions that subject a person to strict tort liability; (3) breach of warranty; (4) unreasonable assumption of risk not constituting an express consent or primary assumption of risk; (5) misuse of a product and unreasonable failure to avoid an injury or to mitigate damages; and (6) the defense of complicity.[55] The Minnesota Supreme Court has held, however, that "principles of comparative negligence do not apply to an intentional tort."[56]

Under the Minnesota Comparative Fault Act,[57] contributory fault will only completely bar a plaintiff from recovery if the plaintiff's fault is greater than that of the defendant. Where the plaintiff's fault is less than or equal to the defendant's fault, the plaintiff's recovery must be diminished in proportion to the percentage of fault assigned to the plaintiff. In multiple-party litigation, the plaintiff's negligence generally must be compared to the individual negligence of each defendant to determine if that defendant is liable to the plaintiff. The fault of multiple defendants, however, may be aggregated for comparison with the plaintiff's fault if defendants acted together in a joint venture or otherwise had a joint duty.[58]

The Comparative Fault Act further provides that "[w]hen two or more persons are jointly liable, contributions to awards shall be in proportion to the percentage of fault attributable to each, except that each is jointly and severally liable for the whole award."[59] If, however, a jury finds any of the defendants to be 15 percent or less at fault, the Act limits the plaintiff's recovery from that defendant to "no greater than four times the percentage of [that defendant's] fault."[60]

3. **Assumption of Risk**

Minnesota law recognizes two types of assumption of risk—primary and secondary.[61] The elements of both are the same: Primary and secondary assumption of risk arise when "a person had (1) knowledge of the risk; (2) an appreciation of the risk; and (3) a choice to avoid the risk but voluntarily chose to chance the risk."[62] The manifestations of acceptance and consent to assume the risk dictate whether primary or secondary assumption of risk is applicable in a given case.[63]

Primary assumption of the risk acts as a complete bar to the claims against a defendant where an individual has consented to relieve the defendant of a duty of care by voluntarily encountering a known and appreciated risk.[64] On the other hand, secondary assumption of the risk is a type of contributory negligence that exists when a party has voluntarily encountered a known and appreciated risk without consenting, implicitly or explicitly, to relieve the defendant of his or her duty of care.[65] Thus, secondary assumption of risk will be apportioned as comparative fault by a fact finder pursuant to the Comparative Fault Act, and will reduce the plaintiff's recovery accordingly.

G. *RES IPSA LOQUITUR* AND INHERENTLY DANGEROUS ACTIVITIES

Where the cause of an accident is unknown,[66] *res ipsa loquitur* permits an inference under Minnesota law that the defendant caused the plaintiff's injury.[67] Three elements must exist: (1) the injury must not ordinarily occur in the absence of negligence;[68] (2) the cause of the injury must have been in the exclusive control of the defendant;[69] and (3) the injury must not be due to the plaintiff's conduct.

When all three elements exist, the court will provide a *res ipsa loquitur* instruction and then the jury must determine if these elements have been proven by a preponderance of the evidence.[70] A Minnesota court, however, may still provide a jury instruction that the mere happening of an accident does not necessarily mean that someone was negligent.[71] The plaintiff always bears the burden of persuasion.[72]

As the hazard from the use of a dangerous instrumentality increases, the responsibility of the person employing the instrumentality becomes stricter and may even amount to insurance of safety.[73] When a contractor engages in an ultrahazardous or inherently dangerous activity, he is not protected by the doctrine of sovereign immunity even though he follows the specifications and directions of the sovereign.[74]

H. NEGLIGENCE *PER SE*

A statute can provide the applicable duty of care where an injury is of the type the statute was enacted to prevent and the plaintiff is a member of the class protected by the statute.[75] When these two requirements are met, the prohibited conduct is generally negligence *per se*.[76] Compliance with a statutory standard is evidence of due care,[77] but a person "may still be negligent if there is a failure in special circumstances to take additional precautions."[78]

Negligence *per se* is not liability *per se*.[79] A defendant may still invoke defenses such as assumption of risk, contributory negligence, and proximate cause.[80]

A few "exceptional statutes" do impose absolute liability, however, where the purpose of the statute "is to protect a limited class of persons from their own inexperience, lack of judgment, inability to protect themselves or to resist pressure, or tendency toward negligence."[81] The legislative purpose is determined by looking at the character of the statute, the background of the social problem sought to be remedied, and the hazard to which the statute is directed.[82]

I. JOINT AND SEVERAL LIABILITY

Minnesota Statute Section 604.02 establishes standards for allocating liability among multiple defendants. Generally, liability for damages is in proportion to the percentage of fault attributed to each defendant by the fact finder. However, under Minnesota's joint and several statutory provision,[83] a plaintiff can seek to collect the entire judgment from any liable defendant.[84] Joint and several liability among defendants applies in all cases where there is (1) liability for a tort[85] and (2) more than one defendant, whether the defendants acted in concert, merely concurrently or even successively in time.[86] There is no requirement that there is a conspiracy or joint action between the defendants.[87]

A defendant who is jointly and severally liable is still entitled to contribution from codefendants in accordance with the jury's apportionment of fault.[88] However, where there have been independent consecutive acts of negligence and it is reasonably possible to determine which injuries were caused by which act, the "single, divisible injury" rule applies and a defendant may limit his or her liability to the damages caused by him or her.[89]

If a defendant's allocated share of a judgment has been found by the court to be uncollectible,[90] the joint and several liability statute requires that the share be reallocated to other litigants, including the plaintiff, according to their respective percentages of fault.[91] Thus, each defendant is, as necessary, responsible for the whole tort, although an injured party cannot have more than full satisfaction (except with punitive damages[92] or a *Pierringer*[93] or joint tortfeasor release). Notwithstanding this general rule, liability is capped for a defendant who is responsible for only a small portion of an injury.[94]

J. INDEMNITY

Indemnity and contribution are both equitable remedies[95] used by Minnesota courts to give restitution to one who has paid more than his or her fair share of a liability.[96] Indemnity and contribution differ in the kind and measure of relief provided.[97] Contribution is appropriate when common liability exists among the parties, and, therefore, the parties must share the liability or burden.[98] Indemnity, however, is appropriate when one party without personal fault is liable for the whole burden because a contractual relationship, either express or implied by law, requires that party to reimburse the other entirely.[99]

Minnesota courts have recognized four situations where indemnity is appropriate: (1) where the one seeking indemnity has only derivative or vicarious liability for damage caused by the one sought to be charged; (2) where the one seeking indemnity has incurred liability by action done at the direction, in the interest of, and in reliance on, the one sought to be charged; (3) where the one seeking indemnity has incurred liability because of a breach of duty owed to him by the one sought to be charged; and (4) where there is an express contract between the parties containing an explicit undertaking to reimburse for liability of the character involved.[100] A party may also be able to contract for indemnification for its own negligence.[101]

K. BAR OF WORKERS' COMPENSATION STATUTE

The Minnesota Workers' Compensation Act[102] is designed to provide a comprehensive system for compensating injured employees, regardless of fault or negligence.[103] Every employer must carry workers' compensation insurance or seek a written exemption permitting self-insurance.[104]

By design, the Act gives both employees and employers some benefits they did not have under the common law and, in return, both surrender certain common law advantages.[105] While payment of an employee's bona fide claim is guaranteed, and the employer will be strictly liable,[106] the employee's recovery is limited to a fixed schedule.[107] Moreover, an employee's right to sue for damages over and above medical and health care benefits and wage loss benefits is, to a certain degree, limited. On the other hand, the employer's right to raise common law defenses such as lack of negligence or contributory negligence is curtailed.[108]

The Act does not, however, destroy common law actions for injuries to employees against third parties.[109] An injured employee may sue a third-party tortfeasor for damages notwithstanding the receipt of workers' compensation from the plaintiff's employer, where the third party is not associated with the employer or covered by the Act.[110] Given such a situation, an employer who has compensated an employee under the Act has a right of subrogation and may intervene as a matter of right in an action between the injured employee and a third party.[111] The employer's subrogation action should be limited to recovery of common law damages for past and future wage loss, loss of earning capacity, and similar items of damage.[112] Common law damages not recoverable under workers' compensation include pain and suffering, general disability, embarrassment, disfigurement, and mental anguish.[113] The right of subrogation applies regardless of whether the employee's recovery against the third party would fully compensate the employee's losses.[114]

Minnesota is one of the few states that allows a third party tortfeasor to assert a claim for contribution against the plaintiff's employer. This doctrine was established by the Minnesota Supreme Court in 1977.[115] Typical claims include failure of the employer to properly train, instruct, or supervise the plaintiff, failure to establish and enforce safety rules, and failure to provide a safe workplace. The employer's liability in contribution is limited to the amount of workers' compensation benefits paid or payable.

The traditional principle of indemnity, which provides a right of recovery only where an identical duty owed by one is discharged by another, is not applicable when determining the rights and obligations established under the Act.[116]

L. PREMISES LIABILITY

Under Minnesota law, a landowner owes a duty of reasonable care for the safety of all persons invited on its premises, regardless of their status as invitees or licensees.[117] Traditionally, however, a landowner's duty of care shifted, depending on whether the plaintiff was classified as a trespasser, licensee, or invitee. As recently as 1997, the Minnesota Supreme Court still addressed the issue of what a landowner's duty was to a plaintiff "as a business invitee."[118] The continued use of the distinctions (such as "invitee") in modern premise liability cases dictates that practitioners should still be aware of the range of duties under traditional Minnesota tort law.

At one end of the spectrum is the trespasser to whom a landowner owes no general duty.[119] In Minnesota, a landowner is liable to a trespasser only for failure to warn of an artificial condition if: (1) the artificial condition is likely to cause death or serious bodily harm; (2) the landowner has actual knowledge of that danger; and (3) the danger is concealed or hidden from the trespasser.[120] Minnesota courts have recognized a narrow exception giving a landowner a duty of care for trespassing children when the landowner knows or has reason to know that children are likely to trespass.[121]

On the other hand, an invitee, as someone who is asked to come on the premises for the benefit of the landowner,[122] is entitled to expect that the landowner will take reasonable care to discover the actual condition of the premises and either make them safe or warn the invitee of dangerous conditions.[123] If the harm is caused by a known and obvious danger, the landowner is generally not liable unless the landowner "should anticipate the harm despite such knowledge or obviousness."[124] In the middle is the gratuitous licensee, who must take the premises as he or she finds them.[125] The landowner still owes the licensee the duty of not knowingly exposing him or her to hidden dangers and honestly disclosing the known dangers,[126] but the licensee must prove that the landowner had actual or constructive knowledge of a dangerous condition in order to establish liability.[127]

M. DRAM SHOP LIABILITY

Minnesota's Dram Shop Act imposes liability for illegal sales of alcoholic beverages when an intoxicated person who consumed the beverages causes injury or a loss of means of support to innocent third parties.[128] Actionable "illegal" sales under the Act include: (1) liquor sales by clubs to nonmembers; (2) sales during prohibited hours or days; (3) sales to minors; and (4) sales to obviously intoxicated persons.[129] By imposing absolute liability on the dealer for damages caused by an intoxicated person, the Act gives vendors "an extremely effective incentive" to avoid making illegal sales.[130] The Act does not apply to social hosts, even to those who charge a fee for the provision of alcohol;[131] however, it does permit common law tort claims against any adult who knowingly provides or furnishes alcohol to a minor.[132]

Actions under the Dram Shop Act must be commenced within two years after the injury.[133] The minority tolling provisions of Minn. Stat. § 541.15(a)(1) do not apply to actions brought under the Dram Shop Act.[134] Plaintiffs are required to give detailed written notice to the vendor within certain statutory time periods or their claim is barred.[135] In a claim for damages, the plaintiff's attorney must serve the written notice within 240 days after the date of entering the attorney-client relationship with the plaintiff regarding the claim.[136] In a claim for contribution or indemnity, the notice must be served within 120 days after the initial injury occurs or within 60 days after receiving written notice of a claim for contribution or indemnity, whichever is applicable.[137] An innocent third party plaintiff may have his or her own award against a dram shop reduced only to the extent that his or her own negligence contributed to the loss.[138] The negligence of the intoxicated person is not imputed to the innocent plaintiffs.[139] A dram shop may be allowed to bring a contribution action against the intoxicated driver.[140]

N. ECONOMIC LOSS

Minnesota's Economic Loss Doctrine was first articulated in the common law,[141] refined in subsequent case law,[142] and then codified by statute.[143] Essentially, Minnesota's courts have protected the exclusivity of the Uniform Commercial Code (Code) by holding that the Code preempts any tort theories of recovery for certain economic losses that arise from the commercial sale of goods.[144] In such cases, the purchaser is limited to the available contract and warranty remedies under the Code.[145] Thus, the Code has generally provided the exclusive remedy for damages arising out of the sale of goods when the sale fits the Code definition of "commercial transaction."[146]

The only exceptions to the exclusivity of the Code for actions arising from the sale of goods have been in: (1) cases involving personal injury; or (2) cases involving damage to "other property," that is, property other than the allegedly defective good that was the subject of the sale.[147] The economic loss that is recoverable in tort in a noncommercial transaction does not include damage to the goods themselves.[148] Further, a subpurchaser is also subject to preemption and limited to the UCC remedy under Minnesota case law.[149]

On April 20, 2000, Minnesota enacted a new economic loss statute, Minnesota Stat. § 604.101, in an effort to correct problems that had arisen under the existing statute and case law and to simplify the doctrine. The new statute limits "product defect claims" and "common law misrepresentation claims," and applies regardless of whether the goods are sold or leased, whether the parties are merchants, and whether the transaction is a consumer or commercial transaction. Under the new statute, a "buyer" is barred from bringing a "product defect" claim unless he or she alleges that the defect in the goods caused damage to "other" property, and even then the buyer's remedies are limited by the statute. The statute further clarifies that a "buyer may not bring a common law misrepresentation claim against a seller" unless "the misrepresentation was made intentionally or recklessly." The new statute is not retroactive; rather, it will only apply to a "sale or lease" that occurs on or after August 1, 2000.[150]

O. FRAUD AND MISREPRESENTATION

Minnesota's Rules of Civil Procedure require that a cause of action for fraud shall be pleaded with particularity.[151] The required elements of a fraud action are: (1) there must be a false representation of a past or existing material fact susceptible of knowledge; (2) the statement was made with knowledge of the falsity or made as of the parties' own knowledge without knowing whether it was true or false; (3) the statement was made with the intention to induce another to act in reliance thereon; (4) the representation caused the other party to act in reliance thereon; and (5) pecuniary damage was suffered as a result of the reliance.[152] Nondisclosure may constitute fraud, but there must be a suppression of facts that one party is under a legal or equitable obligation to communicate to the other.[153] Contributory negligence is not a defense in an intentional misrepresentation or fraud case.[154]

A negligent misrepresentation occurs when: (1) a person in the course of his or her business, or during a transaction in which he or she has a financial interest, supplies false information to guide another person in that person's own business transactions; (2) the person supplying information fails to use reasonable care in obtaining the information or communicating it; (3) the other person relies on the information; (4) the other person was justified in so relying; and (5) the other person was financially harmed by their reliance.[155]

P. CONSUMER FRAUD STATUTES

Minnesota has four different statutes that are often referred to collectively as Minnesota's consumer protection statutes.[156] These statutes were enacted to protect Minnesota consumers from unlawful, deceptive, misleading, and fraudulent business practices made in connection with the sale of any merchandise.[157] Because the statutes are remedial in purpose, they are broadly construed to protect the consuming public.[158] The acts apply to all consumers, not just individuals.[159]

Generally, private actions for damages for violations of three of the consumer protection statutes must be brought under Minnesota's Private Attorney General Statute, which authorizes persons "injured by" such a violation to recover damages, costs, investigation expenses, and attorney's fees.[160] Only injunctive relief, not damages, is available under the Minnesota Deceptive Trade Practices Act.[161]

To state a claim for damages under the consumer protection statutes, a plaintiff "need only plead that the defendant engaged in conduct prohibited by the statutes and that the plaintiff was damaged thereby."[162] To receive injunctive relief, however, no proof of damages or reliance is necessary.[163]

Q. PUNITIVE DAMAGES

Punitive damages are governed by Minnesota Statute Section 549.20 and are "allowed . . . only upon clear and convincing evidence that the acts of the defendant show deliberate disregard for the rights or safety of others."[164] "Deliberate disregard" arises where the defendant has knowledge of facts or intentionally disregards facts that create a high probability of injury to the rights or safety of others, and deliberately proceeds to act in either "conscious or intentional disregard" or "with indifference to the high probability of injury to the rights or safety of others."[165] Punitive damages are not recoverable where the conduct is merely negligent,[166] and even gross negligence is not sufficient.

Factors considered in measuring an award are provided by statute, and include, among other things, "the seriousness of hazard," the profitability, duration and concealment of the misconduct, the defendant's awareness of the hazard, "the attitude and conduct of the defendant upon discovery of the misconduct, the financial condition of the defendant," and the deterrent effect of such an award on others.[167]

A plaintiff in Minnesota may not seek punitive damages on commencement of an action.[168] Instead, "[a]fter filing the suit, a party may make a motion to amend the pleadings to claim punitive damages."[169] Prima facie evidence supporting a punitive damage award must exist for the court to grant leave to amend.[170]

Punitive damages cannot be awarded in product liability actions "where a plaintiff suffers only property damage."[171] A plaintiff may "seek punitive damages in an action for intentional damage to property where the only damage is to property, subject to the limitations of Minnesota Statute Section 549.20."[172]

R. WRONGFUL DEATH AND SURVIVORSHIP ACTIONS

Under the common law, a claim for personal injuries died with the victim.[173] Thus, in Minnesota, actions for wrongful death are prohibited except as provided for by statute.[174] An appointed trustee may bring an action "if the decedent might have maintained the action, had the decedent lived, for an injury caused by the wrongful act or omission."[175] The jury decides the amount of recovery for pecuniary loss, and the recovery shall be for the exclusive benefit of the surviving spouse and next of kin.[176] In considering the amount of pecuniary loss, the jury can consider a variety of factors and determine an award that will compensate the plaintiff for the losses suffered as a result of the decedent's death.[177] "Next of kin" is defined as those blood relatives who are "members of a class from which beneficiaries are chosen under the inheritance statute."[178] A surviving spouse or next of kin cannot legally assign their cause of action under the statute.[179]

An action for a death caused by an intentional act constituting murder can be commenced at any time.[180] An action to recover damages for a death caused by medical malpractice must be commenced within two years.[181] Any other type of action for wrongful death must be commenced within three years after the date of death, provided that the action is commenced within six years after the act or omission.[182]

William L. Killion
Erik T. Salveson
Kacy F. Kleinhans
GRAY, PLANT, MOOTY, MOOTY
& BENNETT, P.A.
3400 City Center
33 South Sixth Street
Minneapolis, Minnesota 55402
(612) 343-2800
Fax (612) 333-0066
www.gpmlaw.com

ENDNOTES - MINNESOTA

1. *Bonhiver v. Graff,* 248 N.W.2d 291, 296 (Minn. 1976) (stating that "action accrues at such time as it could be brought in a court of law without dismissal for failure to state a claim").

2. *Herrman v. McMenomy & Severson,* 590 N.W.2d 641, 642 (Minn. 1999) (statute began running when accountant provided negligent advice, even though full substantial damages were not incurred until later, since negligent advice created tax liability at time of advice).

3. *Zagaros v. Erickson,* 558 N.W.2d 516 (Minn. Ct. App. 1997).

4. *Metropolitan Property & Cas. Ins. Co. v. Metropolitan Transit Com'n,* 538 N.W.2d. 692 (Minn. 1995); *Hermeling v. Minnesota Fire & Cas. Co.,* 548 N.W.2d 270, 274 (Minn. 1996) ("a claim for contribution does not accrue until the person entitled to the contribution has sustained damage by paying more than his fair share of the obligation"). A claim for uninsured motorist benefits, however, accrues upon the date of settlement with or judgment against the uninsured motorist. *Danes v. Allstate Ins. Co.,* 617 N.W.2d 401, 406 (Minn. 2000).

5. *Herrman v. McMenomy & Severson,* 583 N.W.2d 283 (Minn. Ct. App. 1988), *rev'd on other grounds,* 590 N.W.2d 641 (Minn. 1999).

6. *Mackereth v. G.D. Searle & Co.,* 674 N.E.2d 936 (Ill. App. 1 1996) (applying Minnesota law); and *Haberle v. Buchwald,* 480 N.W.2d 351 (Minn. Ct. App. 1992).

7. *See* Minn. Stat. § 41.15 (providing that the limitations period does not run for various disabilities, for example, infancy, insanity, defendant's imprisonment for criminal charges, etc.); *Talley by Talley v. Portland Residence Inc.,* 582 N.W.2d 590 (Minn. Ct. App. 1998) (holding that limitations period was extended by reason of plaintiff's mental retardation).

8. Minn. Stat. § 541.13 (1999).

9. *Vaughn v. Northwest Airlines, Inc.,* 558 N.W.2d 736 (Minn. 1997); Minn. Stat. § 363.06, subd. 3; and *Bougie v. Sibley Manor, Inc.,* 504 N.W.2d 493 (Minn. Ct. App. 1993) (stating that the "continuing violations" doctrine may toll the human rights statute when acts that occurred prior to the one-year limitation period combine with acts within the limitation period and constitute a pattern sufficient to form a single act).

10. Minn. Stat. § 541.07 (1999).

11. *See, e.g., Larson v. New Richland Care Center*, 538 N.W.2d 915, 920 (Minn. Ct. App. 1995) (stating that "[a] tort is a civil wrong or breach of a legal duty that is not contractual").

12. *Wild v. Rarig*, 234 N.W.2d 775, 797 (Minn. 1975) (stating that assault, battery and false imprisonment are in the nature of intentional torts and that libel and slander are in the nature of strict liability torts as long as the defamer intends to publish statements to a third person), *cert. denied*, 424 U.S. 902 (1976).

13. *Id.* at 791 (Minn. 1975) (stating that personal injury should, here, be construed as equivalent to personal wrong, and not bodily injury), *cert. denied*, 424 U.S. 902 (1976).

14. *Larson v. New Richland Care Center*, 538 N.W.2d 915 (Minn. Ct. App. 1995).

15. *Id.*

16. *Bryant v. Am. Sur. Co. of New York*, 71 N.W. 826 (Minn. 1897).

17. *Christenson v. Argonaut Ins. Cos.*, 380 N.W.2d 515 (Minn. Ct. App. 1986).

18. Minn. Stat. § 541.051 (1999).

19. Minn. Stat. § 336.2-725(i) (1999).

20. Minn. Stat. §541.076 (2000).

21. Minn. Stat. § 541.05 (1999).

22. *Fletcher v. Zellmer*, 909 F. Supp. 678 (D. Minn. 1995), *aff'd*, 105 F.3d 662 (8th Cir. 1997).

23. *Union Pacific R. Co. v. Reilly Indus., Inc.*, 4 F. Supp. 2d 860, 865 (D. Minn. 1998).

24. *Klempka v. G.D. Searle & Co.*, 963 F.2d 168 (8th Cir. 1992).

25. *James v. Allstate Ins. Co..*, 617 N.W.2d 401 (Minn. 2000).

26. *Egerdahl v. Hibbing Community College*, 72 F.3d 615 (8th Cir. 1995).

27. *Estate of Reidel by Mirick v. Life Care Retirement Communities, Inc.*, 505 N.W.2d 78 (Minn. Ct. App. 1993).

28. *Franklin Auto Body Co. v. Wicker*, 414 N.W.2d 509 (Minn. Ct. App. 1987).

29. *Union Pacific R. Co. v. Reilly Indus., Inc.*, 4 F. Supp. 2d 860 (D. Minn. 1998) (holding that claim under Minnesota Environmental Response and Liability Act by purchaser against previous owner whose creosoting operation resulted in contamination had a six-year limitation period).

30. Minn. Stat. § 541.05 (1999).

31. Minn. Stat. § 65B.42 (1)–(2) (2000). The statute provides that it was adopted "to relieve the severe economic distress of uncompensated victims of automobile accidents" by requiring that automobile insurance policies provide prompt payment of basic economic loss benefits to automobile accident victims "without regard to whose fault caused the accident," and to also "prevent the overcompensation of . . . automobile accident victims . . . by restricting the right to recover general damages to causes of serious injury." *Id.*

32. *Marose v. Hennameyer*, 347 N.W.2d 509, 511 (Minn. Ct. App. 1984) (citation omitted).

33. "Noneconomic" damages are defined as "all dignitary losses . . . including pain and suffering, loss of consortium, and inconvenience." Minn. Stat. § 65B.43, subd. 8 (2000).

34. Minn. Stat. § 65B.51, subd. 3(a)–(b) (2000).

35. *See* Michael L. Weiner, *No-Fault Tort Thresholds: The Plaintiff's Perspective*, 24 W. Mitchell L. Rev. 985, 989, citing Minn. Stat. § 65B.51, subd. 3(a)–(b).

36. Minn. Stat. § 65B.51, subd. 1 (2000).

37. *Lubbers v. Anderson*, 539 N.W.2d 398, 401 (Minn. 1995); *see also Johnson v. State*, 553 N.W.2d 40, 49 (Minn. 1996).

38. *Flom v. Flom*, 291 N.W.2d 914, 916 (Minn. 1980).

39. *City of Eveleth v. Ruble*, 225 N.W.2d 521, 524 (Minn. 1974) (design engineers). Ordinarily, expert testimony is required to establish the applicable standard of care and the consequences of the defendant's failure to meet it. *Id.* at 525.

40. *Olson v. Duluth, M. & I. R. Ry. Co.*, 5 N.W.2d 492, 496 (Minn. 1942) (rejecting the plaintiff's assertion that "the reasonableness of the speed at which he was driving [in a case where he drove into the defendant's train] should be determined by 'the condition of the highway *apparent* to' him") (emphasis in original). It is "immaterial that a person charged with negligence thought he was acting carefully or exercised his best judgment." *Id.*

41. *Ruberg v. Skelly Oil Co.*, 297 N.W.2d 746, 750 (Minn. 1980). An affirmative duty to act may arise where there is a "special relationship." *Delgado v. Lohmar*, 289 N.W.2d 479, 483 (Minn. 1979). "Such special relationships exist between parents and children, masters and servants, possessors of land and licensees, common carriers and their customers, or people who have custody of a person with dangerous propensities." *Id.* at 483–84.

42. *Schmidt v. Beninga*, 173 N.W.2d 401, 408 (Minn. 1970) (defendant's actions analyzed against customary practice at a grain elevator).

43. *Edgewater Motels, Inc. v. Gatzke*, 277 N.W.2d 11, 18 (Minn. 1979).

44. *Zinnel v. Berghuis Constr. Co.*, 274 N.W.2d 495, 498–99 (Minn. 1979).

45. *Id.*

46. *Gits v. Norwest Bank Minneapolis*, 390 N.W.2d 835, 837 (Minn. Ct. App. 1986) (citing *Flom v. Flom*, 291 N.W.2d 914, 917 (Minn. 1980)).

47. *Marlowe v. Gunderson*, 109 N.W.2d 323, 326 (Minn. 1961).

48. *Rieger v. Zackoski*, 321 N.W.2d 16, 21 (Minn. 1982) (citing Restatement (Second) of Torts, § 442B, comment 6 (1966)); *see also Henjum v. Bok*, 110 N.W.2d 461, 462 (Minn. 1961) ("[c]onsequences which follow in unbroken sequence, without an intervening efficient cause, from the original negligent act, are natural and proximate; and for such consequences the original wrongdoer is responsible, even though he could not have foreseen the particular results which did follow").

49. *Gibraltar Sav. v. Commonwealth Land Title Ins. Co.*, 907 F.2d 844, 848 (8th Cir. 1990) (citing *Pontiacs v. K.M.S. Invs.*, 331 N.W.2d 907, 915 (Minn. 1983)).

50. *Canada v. McCarthy*, 567 N.W.2d 496, 507 (Minn. 1997); *Wartnick v. Moss & Barnett*, 490 N.W.2d 108, 113 (Minn. 1992).

51. *Mikes v. Baumgartner*, 152 N.W.2d 732, 737 (Minn. 1967).

52. Minn. Stat. § 604.01, subd. 1(a) (1998).

53. *Peterson v. Bendix Home Sys., Inc.*, 318 N.W.2d 50, 55 (Minn. 1982).

54. Minn. Stat. § 604.01, subd. 1 (1999).

55. Minn. Stat. § 604.01 (1999) (defining fault as "acts or omissions that are in any measure negligent or reckless toward the person or property of the actor or others, or that subject a person to strict tort liability. The term also includes breach of warranty, unreasonable assumption of risk not consti-

tuting an express consent or primary assumption of risk, misuse of a product and unreasonable failure to avoid an injury or to mitigate damages, and the defense of complicity under section 340A.801. Legal requirements of causal relation apply both to fault as the basis for liability and to contributory fault. The doctrine of last clear chance is abolished.").

56. *Florenzano v. Olson*, 387 N.W.2d 168, 175 (Minn. 1986).

57. In its entirety, Minn. Stat. § 604.01, subd. 1 (1999) provides:

> Contributory fault does not bar recovery in an action by any person or the person's legal representative to recover damages for fault resulting in death, in injury to the person or property, or in economic loss, if the contributory fault was not greater than the fault of the person against whom recovery is sought, but any damages allowed must be diminished in proportion to the amount of fault attributable to the person recovering. The court may, and when requested by any party shall, direct the jury to find separate special verdicts determining the amount of damages and the percentage of fault attributable to each party and the court shall then reduce the amount of damages in proportion to the amount of fault attributable to the person recovering.

See also Alden Wells Veterinarian Clinics, Inc. v. Wood, 324 N.W.2d 181, 184 (Minn. 1982) (plaintiff cannot recover where plaintiff was 55 percent at fault and the defendant was 45 percent at fault).

58. *See Kowalske v. Armour & Co.*, 220 N.W.2d 268 (Minn. 1974) (*overruled on other grounds by Ruberg v. Skelly Oil Co.*, 297 N.W.2d 746, 752 (Minn. 1974).

59. Minn. Stat. § 604.02, subd. 1 (1998); *see also Ruberg*, 297 N.W.2d at 752 (1974) (holding that a plaintiff's comparative negligence is relevant only to determine whether individual defendants are liable to the plaintiff at all, but after liability is established all liable defendants may be jointly and severally liable for the entire award).

60. Minn. Stat. § 604.02, subd. 1 (1998). Also, if a state or municipality's fault is less than 35 percent, its liability is limited to twice the amount of fault. *Id.*

61. *Andren v. White-Rodgers Co.*, 465 N.W.2d 102, 104 (Minn. Ct. App. 1991).

62. *Id.* at 104–05. *See also Kraft v. Ingersoll-Rand Co.*, 136 F.3d 584, 586 (8th Cir. 1998) (citing *Andren*, 465 N.W.2d at 104).

63. *Andren*, 465 N.W.2d at 105 (citing *Armstrong v. Mailand*, 284 N.W.2d 343, 351 (Minn. 1979)).

64. *See Andren*, 465 N.W.2d at 104–05 (primary assumption of risk barred recovery where party expressed "voluntary acceptance of a known danger"

by lighting a cigarette in a gas-filled room). *See also Walk v. Starkey Mach., Inc.*, 180 F.3d 937, 939–40 (8th Cir. 1999) (primary assumption of risk barred claims where plaintiff, who was experienced with the subject auger, was injured when he placed his hand in the auger to clean it despite "knowing the auger was engaged and knowing that the moving blades posed a substantial risk of injury to him").

65. *Armstrong*, 284 N.W.2d at 349.

66. *Zitzow v. Wal-Mart Stores, Inc.*, 568 N.W.2d 549, 551 (Minn. Ct. App. 1997) (*res ipsa loquitur* was not applicable because no dispute existed that an unidentified customer was cause of accident); *Johnson v. West Fargo Mfg. Co.*, 95 N.W.2d 497, 502 (Minn. 1959).

67. *Gardner v. Coca Cola Bottling Co.*, 127 N.W.2d 557 (Minn. 1964).

68. *Hoven v. Rice Mem. Hosp.*, 396 N.W.2d 569, 572 (Minn. 1986) (*res ipsa loquitur* was not applicable because patient did not meet the burden of showing that the injury ordinarily would not have occurred absent negligence from the operating team); *Spannaus v. Otolaryngology Clinic*, 242 N.W.2d 594, 596 (Minn. 1976).

69. *Spinett, Inc. v. Peoples Natural Gas Co.*, 385 N.W.2d 834, 837 (Minn. Ct. App. 1986) ("exclusive control" existed when gas distributor had nondelegable responsibility because the distributor owned and solely maintained the lines and the plaintiff relied entirely on distributor to repair and inspect the lines); and *Mahowald v. Minnesota Gas Co.*, 344 N.W.2d 856, 862–63 (Minn. 1984). Also, the possibility that other persons or factors caused the accident does not preclude a *res ipsa loquitur* instruction if the evidence reasonably excludes those causes. *Id.*; *Rinkel v. Lee's Plumbing & Heating Co.*, 99 N.W.2d 779, 782 (Minn. 1959); *Heath v. Wolesky*, 233 N.W. 239, 240 (Minn. 1930) (*res ipsa loquitur* instruction conditioned on jury's repudiation of other causes is proper).

70. *Stearns*, 482 N.W.2d at 498; *Anderson v. Burdick Grain Co.*, 363 N.W.2d 797, 800 (Minn. Ct. App. 1985).

71. *Stearns v. Plucinski*, 482 N.W.2d 496, 498 (Minn. Ct. App. 1992).

72. *Gardner v. Coca Cola Bottling Co.*, 127 N.W.2d 557 (Minn. 1964) (*res ipsa loquitur* warrants but does not compel an inference of negligence; therefore, jury can reject inference). For example, where defendants acted collectively and all possible causes of injury were under their collective control, Minnesota courts still have refused to put the burden on the defendants to explain how the plaintiff's injury occurred. *See Hoven v. Rice Mem. Hosp.*, 396 N.W.2d 569, 573 (Minn. 1986) (Minnesota Supreme Court has not adopted theory of *Ybarra v. Spanguard*, 25 Cal. 2d 486, 154 P.2d 687 (1944),

because adoption of that analysis would put the burden on the defendant rather than on the plaintiff and would amount to absolute liability); *Hanzel v. Good Earth, Inc.,* 371 N.W.2d 72, 74–75 (Minn. Ct. App. 1985).

73. *Whittaker v. Stangvick,* 111 N.W. 295, 297 (Minn. 1907) (inherent dangers to landowners from irresponsible and reckless hunters with guns).

74. *Lowry Hill Properties, Inc. v. Ashbach Constr. Co.,* 194 N.W.2d 767, 772 (Minn. 1972) (pile driving by contractor is an inherently dangerous or ultra-hazardous activity).

75. *Alderman's Inc. v. Shanks,* 536 N.W.2d 4, 8 (Minn. 1995) (Uniform Fire Code). This rule also applies to ordinances. *Pacific Indem. Co., et al. v. Thompson-Yaeger, Inc.,* 260 N.W.2d 548, 558–59 (Minn. 1977) (city ordinance governing the installation of heating systems).

76. *Alderman's,* 536 N.W.2d at 9. The conduct is not negligent *per se,* however, where the statute makes the violation merely *prima facie* evidence of negligence. *Butler v. Engel,* 68 N.W.2d 226, 230 (Minn. 1954).

77. *Hellman v. Kolesar,* 399 N.W.2d 654, 655 (Minn. Ct. App. 1987).

78. *Id.* The existence of special circumstances will depend on the probability and foreseeability of injury to the plaintiff. *Id.*

79. *Seim v. Garavalia,* 306 N.W.2d 806, 810 (Minn. 1981).

80. *Id.*

81. *Zerby v. Warren,* 210 N.W.2d 58, 62 (Minn. 1973) (listing child labor statutes, statutes for the protection of intoxicated persons, and statutes prohibiting the sale of dangerous articles to minors as "exceptional statutes" that impose absolute liability).

82. *Id.*

83. Minn. Stat. § 604.02 subd. (2) (2000).

84. Subject to the liability limitations under Minn. Stat. § 604.02 subd. (1), discussed *infra* endnote 92.

85. *See Mike's Fixtures, Inc. v. Bombard's Access Floor Sys., Inc.,* 354 N.W.2d 837 (Minn. Ct. App. 1984) (definition of "fault" in the comparative fault statute does not generally apply to contract actions); and *Peterson v. Bendix Home Sys., Inc.,* 318 N.W.2d 50 (Minn. 1982) (while statute encompasses breach of warranty claims, those claims are narrowly defined).

86. *Tolbert v. Gerber Indus., Inc.,* 255 N.W.2d 362 (Minn. 1977).

87. *Pete v. Lampi*, 203 N.W. 447 (Minn. 1925).

88. *Maday v. Yellow Taxi Co. of Minneapolis*, 311 N.W.2d 849 (Minn. 1981).

89. *Jenson v. Eveleth Taconite Co.*, 130 F.3d 1287 (8th Cir. 1997), *cert. denied*, 118 S. Ct. 2370 (1998).

90. *See Hosley v. Pittsburgh Corning Corp.*, 401 N.W.2d 136 (Minn. Ct. App. 1987) (a defendant going through Chapter 11 bankruptcy is not deemed uncollectible until the bankruptcy proceedings are over, at which time the determination would be made). *See also Johnson v. American Family Mut. Ins. Co.*, 413 N.W.2d 172 (Minn. Ct. App. 1987) (stating that the judicial determination of uncollectibility generally is to be made within a year following entry of judgment), *aff'd in part, rev'd in part on other grounds*, 426 N.W.2d 419 (Minn. 1988).

91. Minn. Stat. § 604.02, subd. (2) (2000).

92. *Gronquist v. Olson*, 64 N.W.2d 159, 165 (Minn. 1954).

93. The elements of a *Pierringer* release are: (1) release of the settling defendants from the action and the discharge of the part of the action attributable to their negligence; (2) survival of the plaintiff's causes of action against the nonsettling defendants; and (3) the plaintiff agrees to indemnify the settling defendants from any claims of contribution made by the nonsettling parties and to satisfy any judgment obtained from the nonsettling defendants to the extent the settling defendants have been released. *Frey v. Snelgrove*, 269 N.W.2d 918, 921 n.1 (Minn. 1978) (citing *Pierringer v. Hoger*, 124 N.W.2d 106 (Wis. 1963)).

94. Minn. Stat. § 604.02 subd. (1) (capping liability for defendant with 15 percent or less fault at four times his or her percentage of fault); *see also Lahr v. American Family Mut. Ins. Co.*, 551 N.W.2d 732 (Minn. Ct. App. 1996); Minn. Stat. § 604.02 subd. (1) (providing that if a municipality or state is found jointly liable, and its fault is less than 35 percent, then the municipality's or state's liability is no more than twice its percentage of fault).

95. *Sorenson v. Safety Flate, Inc.*, 216 N.W.2d 859, 864 (Minn. 1974) ("a study of our decisions reveals that indemnity is an equitable doctrine which does not lend itself to hard-and-fast rules and must turn on the facts of each case"); *Shore v. Minneapolis Auto Auction, Inc.*, 410 N.W.2d 862, 866 (Minn. Ct. App. 1987) ("indemnification is a flexible, equitable remedy designed to accomplish a fair allocation of loss among parties").

96. *Hermeling v. Minnesota Fire & Cas. Co.*, 548 N.W.2d 270, 274 (Minn. 1996); *Blomgren v. Marshall Management Servs., Inc.*, 483 N.W.2d 504, 507 (Minn. Ct. App. 1992) ("a joint tortfeasor need not wait until it has made the actual

payment to bring a contribution or indemnification claim, but may institute a third party action in conjunction with the original claim.... [w]hen such a third party action is brought, the contribution/indemnity claim is considered contingent upon the outcome of the original action.").

97. *Hendrickson v. Minnesota Power & Light Co.*,104 N.W.2d 843, 846–47 (Minn. 1960).

98. *Id.*

99. *Hermeling v. Minnesota Fire & Cas. Co.*, 548 N.W.2d 270, 274 (Minn. 1996); *Hendrickson v. Minnesota Power & Light Co.*,104 N.W.2d 843, 846–47 (Minn. 1960); *Blomgren v. Marshall Management Servs.*, 483 N.W.2d 504, 506 (Minn. Ct. App. 1992).

100. *Engrall v. Soo Line R.R. Co.*, 632 N.W.2d 560, 571-72 (Minn. 2001) (explaining the five situations where a joint tortfeasor may generally recover indemnity).

101. *St. Paul Fire & Marine Ins. Co. v. Perl*, 415 N.W.2d 663, 666 (Minn. 1987) (a party to a contract may "properly bargain for indemnity against his own negligence where the latter is only an undesired possibility in the performance of the bargain, and the bargain does not intend to induce the act") quoted in *Lake Cable Partners v. Interstate Power Co.*, 563 N.W.2d 81, 85–86 (Minn. Ct. App. 1997).

102. Minn. Stat. §§ 176.001–.86 (1999).

103. *Silva v. Maplewood Care Center*, 582 N.W.2d 566 (Minn. 1998). *See Yeager v. Chapman*, 45 N.W.2d 776 (Minn. 1951) (stating that, generally, the Act reimburses an employee who has sustained a personal injury arising out of and in the course of employment on or about the premises where the services required the presence of the employee at the time of injury and during the hours of service of the employee).

104. *D. W. Hutt Consultants, Inc. v. Construction Maintenance Sys., Inc.*, 526 N.W.2d 62 (Minn. Ct. App. 1995). *See* Minn. Stat. § 176.181, subd. 2 (1999).

105. *Lunderberg v. Bierman*, 63 N.W.2d 355 (Minn. 1954).

106. *D. W. Hutt Consultants, Inc. v. Construction Maintenance Sys., Inc.*, 526 N.W.2d 62 (Minn. Ct. App. 1995).

107. *Silva*, 582 N.W.2d at 566.

108. Minn. Stat. § 176.001 (1999).

109. *McCourtie v. U.S. Steel Corp.*, 93 N.W.2d 552 (Minn. 1958).

110. *Kipka v. Chicago & N.W. Ry. Co.*, 289 F. Supp. 750 (D. Minn. 1968).

111. *Norman v. Refsland*, 383 N.W.2d 673 (Minn. 1986).

112. *Tyroll v. Private Label Chems., Inc.*, 505 N.W.2d 54 (Minn. 1993).

113. *Id.*

114. *Paine v. Water Works Supply Co.*, 269 N.W.2d 725 (Minn. 1978).

115. *Lambertson v. Cincinnati Corp.*, 257 N.W.2d 679, 689 (Minn. 1977) (holding that an employer must contribute "in an amount proportional to its percentage of negligence, but not to exceed its total workers' compensation liability to plaintiff").

116. *Allstate Ins. Co. v. Eagle-Picher Indus., Inc.*, 410 N.W.2d 324 (Minn. 1987). *But see Shore v. Minneapolis Auto Auction, Inc.*, 410 N.W.2d 862 (Minn. Ct. App. 1987) (defendant entitled to indemnification from third party).

117. *Peterson v. Balach*, 199 N.W.2d 639, 647 (Minn. 1972); *Louis v. Louis*, 2001 WL 1553997 (Minn. 2001).

118. *Sutherland v. Barton*, 570 N.W.2d 1, 7 (Minn. 1997).

119. *Croaker v. Mackenhausen*, 592 N.W.2d 857, 860 (Minn. 1999); *Sirec v. State*, 496 N.W.2d 807, 809–10 (Minn. 1993) (Minnesota follows Restatement (Second) of Torts § 335) quoted in *Lundstrom v. City of Apple Valley*, 587 N.W.2d 517, 520 (Minn. Ct. App. 1998).

120. *Sirec v. State*, 496 N.W.2d 807, 809–10 (Minn. 1993) (Minnesota follows Restatement (Second) of Torts § 335) quoted in *Lundstrom v. City of Apple Valley*, 587 N.W.2d 517, 520 (Minn. Ct. App. 1998).

121. *Gimmestad v. Rose Bros. Co.*, 261 N.W. 194 (Minn. 1935) (rejecting attractive nuisance doctrine) quoted in *Croaker v. Mackenhausen*, 592 N.W.2d 857, 860 (Minn. 1999) (applying Restatement of Torts § 339, which states that a possessor of land is subject to liability for physical harm to trespassing children if the possessor knows or has reason to know that children are likely to trespass, the condition is one that the possessor knows or has reason to know will cause serious bodily harm, the children do not discover the condition or realize the risk involved, the burden of eliminating the danger is slight compared with the risk to the children involved, and the possessor fails to exercise reasonable care to eliminate the danger or to protect the children).

122. *Mourning v. Interlachen Country Club*, 158 N.W.2d 244, 249 (Minn. 1968) (a business visitor is entitled to more than a gratuitous licensee); *Dean v.*

Weisbrod, 217 N.W.2d 739, 743 (Minn. 1974) (landowner's express invitation to plaintiff to come on the premises and help landowner with releasing an entangled flag atop the flagpole would have justified instructions that plaintiff was an invitee).

123. *Id.*

124. *Sutherland*, 570 N.W.2d at 7 (manufacturing plant had no duty to warn independent electrical contractor about known and obvious danger from exposed buss bars); *Richtsmeier v. Johnson*, 2000 WL 1664990 (Minn. Ct. App. 2000) (resort had no duty to warn invitee about slippery boat ramp when resort knew invitee was experienced boater and nothing prevented invitee from observing the condition of the ramp); *Baber v. Dill*, 531 N.W.2d 493, 496 (Minn. 1995) (landowner had no duty to warn invitee about danger when the invitee had assisted in creating the conditions that caused the danger and the conditions were known and obvious); *Betzold v. Sherwin*, 404 N.W.2d 286, 289 (Minn. Ct. App. 1987) (homeowner had duty to warn of open stairwell even when it was an obvious or known danger because the homeowner could anticipate that the dangerous condition will cause physical harm to a guest at night when condition is not visible); *Rinn v. Minnesota State Agricultural Society*, 611 N.W.2d 361, 364 (Minn. Ct. App. 2000) (affirming a landowner's duty to warn of even an obvious danger if the landowner should anticipate the harm suffered by an invitee).

125. *Mourning v. Interlachen Country Club*, 280 Minn. 94, 100, 158 N.W.2d 244, 249 (Minn. 1968) (a waitress at the country club was a gratuitous licensee and was entitled to expect nothing more than an honest disclosure of the dangers that are known to the possessor); *Dean v. Weisbrod*, 300 Minn. 37, 42, 217 N.W.2d 739, 743 (Minn. 1974) (affirmed the trial court's jury instructions on duty to a licensee).

126. *Id.*

127. *Otto v. City of St. Paul*, 460 N.W.2d 359, 362 (Minn. Ct. App. 1990) quoted in *Wells v. Minneapolis Metro. Airport Comm'n*, 1993 WL 140861 (Minn. Ct. App. 1993); *see also Banovetz v. King*, 2000 WL 1182797 (Minn. Ct. App. 2000).

128. Minn. Stat. § 340A.801, subd. 1 (1998); *Englund v. MN CA Partners/MN Joint Ventures*, 555 N.W.2d 328, 330 (Minn. Ct. App. 1996), *aff'd*, 565 N.W.2d 433 (Minn. 1997); *see also Skelly v. Mount*, 620 N.W.2d 566, 568-69 (Minn. Ct. App. 2000) (holding that the Dram Shop Act permits recovery by individuals who have no legal relationship to the intoxicated person).

129. *Englund*, 555 N.W.2d at 338 (licensee's sale of alcohol that was consumed off-premises constitutes an "illegal sale" for dram shop liability if the licensee failed to act as a reasonable vendor to sell alcohol for consumption on the licensed premises only).

130. *Line Constr. Benefit Fund v. Skeates,* 563 N.W.2d 757, 759 (Minn. Ct. App. 1997).

131. *Koehnen v. Dufuor,* 590 N.W.2d 107, 110 (Minn. 1999).

132. Minn. Stat. § 340A.801, subd. 6 (2000); *Vanwagner v. Mattison,* 533 N.W.2d 75 (holding that Minn. Stat. § 340A.801, subd. 6 allows an intoxicated minor to bring a claim for damages against his social hosts under a comparative fault common law standard).

133. Minn. Stat. § 340A.802, subd. 2 (2000).

134. *Whitener v. Dahl,* 612 N.W.2d 188, 190 (Minn. Ct. App. 2000), *aff'd,* 625 N.W.2d 827 (Minn. 2001).

135. Minn. Stat. § 340A.802, subd. 1 (1992) (written notice must be given to the shop stating: the time and date when the alcoholic beverage was sold or bartered, names and addresses of those who were injured, and the approximate time, date, and place where the injury occurred); *Oslund v. Johnson,* 578 N.W.2d 353, 356–57 (Minn. 1998) (notice to tavern was untimely when more than 120 days passed after the original accident giving rise to the claim for contribution or indemnity); *Schulte v. Corner Club Bar,* 544 N.W.2d 486, 488–89 (Minn. 1996) (compliance with the written notice requirement in Section 340A.802 is a condition precedent to a civil damage action and plaintiffs did not satisfy their burden of proving that the shop had actual notice of a possible dram-shop claim even if the shop knew that one of its customers had died in a snowmobile accident).

136. Minn. Stat. § 340A.802, subd. 2 (2001); *Schulte v. Corner Club Bar,* 544 N.W.2d 486, 488 n.1 (Minn. 1996). *Cf. Brua v. Olson,* 621 N.W.2d 2000 472, 475 (Minn. Ct. App. 2001) (holding that the two-year statute of limitations in the Dram Shop Act does not apply to a contribution and indemnity claim against a liquor vendor by a tortfeasor who has complied with the notice provision under M.S.A. § 340A.802, subd. 2).

137. Minn. Stat. § 340A.802, subd. 1 (1998); *Oslund v. Johnson,* 578 N.W.2d 353, 356–57 (Minn. 1998).

138. *Bushland v. Corner Pocket Billiard Lounge of Moorhead, Inc.,* 462 N.W.2d 615, 616–17 (Minn. Ct. App. 1990) (intoxicated motorist's son brought dram shop action against lounge and the court would not impute his father's negligence to him); *K.R. v. Sanford,* 588 N.W.2d 545, 549 (Minn. Ct. App. 1999), *aff'd,* 605 N.W.2d 387 (Minn. 1987) (holding that complicity is no longer a complete bar to recovery under Dram Shop Act since comparative fault statute applies to such actions).

139. *Sanford,* 588 N.W.2d at 549.

140. *Moose Club v. LaBounty,* 442 N.W.2d 334, 339 (Minn. Ct. App. 1989) (dram shop could bring an action against the drunk driver for contribution because, under common law, the drunk driver would be a co-tortfeasor).

141. *Superwood Corp. v. Siempelkamp Corp.,* 311 N.W.2d 159 (Minn. 1981).

142. *See, e.g., Hapka v. Paquin Farms,* 458 N.W.2d 683 (Minn. 1990), superseded by Minn. Stat. § 604.10.

143. *See* Minn. Stat. § 604.10 (1998) (entitled Economic Loss Arising from the Sale of Goods).

144. *See, e.g., Lloyd F. Smith Co., Inc. v. Den-Tal-Ez, Inc.,* 491 N.W.2d 11, 15 (Minn. 1992) (stating that "when there is a claim by a buyer with damage to the defective product itself (and this includes consequential damages), the Code remedy is exclusive and tort will not lie"). *See also* Minn. Stat. § 604.10 (stating that "economic loss that arises from a sale of goods between parties who are each merchants in goods of the kind is not recoverable in tort").

145. *Marvin Lumber and Cedar Co. v. PPG Indus., Inc.,* 34 F. Supp. 2d 738 (D. Minn. 1999), *affirmed in part and reversed in part by Marvin Lumber and Cedar Co. v. PPG Indus., Inc.,* 223 F.3d 873 (8th Cir. 2000)).

146. *Lloyd F. Smith Co., Inc. v. Den-Tal-Ez, Inc.,* 491 N.W.2d 11 (Minn. 1992) (stating that a commercial transaction is one in which parties to the sale are "merchants in goods of the kind" (Minn. Stat. § 336.2-104(1)).

147. *Hapka v. Paquin Farms,* 458 N.W.2d 683, 688 (Minn. 1990) (stating that "(t)he economic loss recoverable in tort under this section does not include economic loss due to damage to the goods themselves").

148. Minn. Stat. § 604.10 subd. (c).

149. *Lloyd F. Smith Co.,* 491 N.W.2d at 17.

150. Minnesota Statute Section 604.101 provides, in part, the following: "A buyer may not bring a product defect tort claim against a seller for compensatory damages unless a defect in the goods sold or leased caused harm to the buyer's tangible personal property other than the goods or to the buyer's real property.... A buyer may not bring a common law misrepresentation claim against a seller relating to the goods sold or leased unless the misrepresentation was made intentionally or recklessly." *See* Minn. Stat. § 604.101(1), subds. 3 and 4. The amendment also provides for a broad definition of buyers and sellers to include both sales and leases, and states that if a good is a component of a manufactured good, harm caused by the component good to the manufactured good is not considered harm to other property.

151. Minn. R. Civ. P. 9.02.

152. *Specialized Tours, Inc. v. Hagen*, 392 N.W.2d 520, 532 (Minn. 1986).

153. *See Richfield Bank & Trust Co. v. Sjogren*, 244 N.W.2d 648, 650 (Minn. 1976).

154. *Florenzano v. Olson*, 387 N.W.2d 168, 176 (Minn. 1986) (comparative fault does not apply to an action for a knowing misrepresentation; however, contributory negligence is a defense in cases where the defendant's misrepresentation is made negligently or without knowledge of whether it is true or false).

155. *See* Minnesota Jury Instruction Guides, CivJig 57.20, p. 452 (West 1999); *Bonhiver v. Graff*, 248 N.W.2d 291, 298–99 (Minn. 1976).

156. *See* the Prevention of Consumer Fraud Act, Minn. Stat. § 325 F.68-.70, the Unlawful Trade Practices Act, Minn. Stat. § 325 D.09-16; the Deceptive Trade Practices Act, Minn. Stat. § 325 D.43-.48, and the False Statement in Advertising Act, Minn. Stat. § 325 F.67.

157. *See State of Minnesota v. Philip Morris, Inc.*, 551 N.W.2d 409, 496 (Minn. 1996); *State by Humphrey v. Alpine Air Prods.*, 500 N.W.2d 788, 790 (Minn. 1993); *Church of the Nativity v. WatPro, Inc.*, 491 N.W.2d 1, 10 (Minn. 1992).

158. *Philip Morris, Inc.*, 551 N.W.2d at 496.

159. *Nativity*, 491 N.W.2d at 10 (church could maintain action under statutes); *Carlock v. Pillsbury Co.*, 719 F. Supp. 791, 850 (D. Minn. 1989) (group of Haagen-Dazs franchisees properly stated claim for relief under Minnesota Consumer Fraud Act); *Indep. Sch. Dist. No. 197 v. W. R. Grace & Co.*, 752 F. Supp. 286, 304 (D. Minn. 1990) (school district could sue under statutes).

160. Minn. Stat. § 8.31, subd. 1 and 3(a) (2000). The Minnesota Supreme Court recently held that an award of attorney fees is only appropriate if the plaintiff has demonstrated that the cause of action was of benefit to the public. *Ly v. Nystrom*, 615 N.W.2d 302, 314 (Minn. 2000).

161. *Johnny's, Inc. v. Njaka*, 450 N.W.2d 166, 168 (Minn. Ct. App. 1990).

162. *Group Health Plan, Inc. v. Philip Morris, Inc.*, 621 N.W.2d 2, 12 (Minn. 2001). The court further held that it is "necessary to prove reliance on [the alleged misrepresentations] to satisfy the causation requirement." *Id.* at 13. However, in certain cases "direct evidence of reliance by individual consumers" may not be necessary; rather the court held that the required "causal nexus and its reliance component may be established by other direct or circumstantial evidence." *Id.* at 14. Potential examples of such proof might include consumer surveys, consumer reaction tests, or market research.

163. *Thompson v. American Tobacco Co., Inc.*, 189 F.R.D. 544, 553 (D. Minn. 1999); *Alpine Air*, 500 N.W.2d at 790 (awarding injunctive relief, including civil penalties and restitution).

164. Minn. Stat. § 549.20, subd. 1(a) (2000); *Morrow v. Air Methods, Inc.*, 884 F. Supp. 1353, 1358 (D. Minn. 1995).

165. Minn. Stat. § 549.20, subd. 1(b)(1)–(2) (2000).

166. *Cobb v. Midwest Recovery Bureau Co.*, 295 N.W.2d 232, 237 (Minn. 1980); *Johns v. Harborage I, Ltd.*, 585 N.W.2d 853, 863 (Minn. Ct. App. 1998).

167. Minn. Stat. § 549.20, subd. 3 (2000).

168. Minn. Stat. § 549.191 (2000). "Upon commencement of a civil action, the complaint must not seek punitive damages." *Id.*

169. *Id.* "It is well-settled that '[i]n the Federal Courts of this District, the pleading of a punitive damage claim, under causes of action premised upon the laws of the state of Minnesota, must generally conform to the requisites of Minnesota Statutes Sections 549.191 and 549.20.'" *Backlund v. City of Duluth*, 176 F.R.D. 316, 320 n.3 (D. Minn. 1997).

170. Minn. Stat. § 549.191 (2000).

171. *Indep. School Dist. No. 622 v. Keene Corp.*, 511 N.W.2d 728, 732 (Minn. 1994) (reversing punitive damages award to school district against manufacturer of asbestos-containing fireproofing where damages were only to property). Limiting punitive damages to cases involving personal injury, according to the court, "reflects the greater importance society places on protecting people." *Id.* See also *Jensen v. Walsh*, 623 N.W.2d 247, 250-51 (Minn. 2001) (limiting *Keene* to products liability actions).

172. *Jensen*, 623 N.W.2d at 251.

173. *Ortiz v. Gavenda*, 590 N.W.2d 119, 121 (Minn. 1999).

174. *Id.; see* Minn. Stat. § 573.02 (1998).

175. Minn. Stat. § 573.02, subd. 1 (1998).

176. *Ortiz v. Gavenda*, 590 N.W.2d 119, 121 (Minn. 1999).

177. *See* Minnesota Jury Instruction Guides, CivJig 91.75 p. 335 (West 1999) (CivJig 91.75 on "Measure of Damages—Wrongful Death" asks the jury to exclude punitive damages, damages for grief or emotional distress of plaintiff, and damages for the pain and suffering of decedent before his or

her death. Instead, the jury should consider factors such as the decedent's contributions in the past, life expectancy at the time of death, health, age, habits, talents, and success, occupation, past earnings, likely future earning capacity and prospects of bettering himself or herself, personal living expenses, legal obligation to support the surviving spouse or next of kin and the likelihood that those obligations would have been fulfilled, all reasonable expenses incurred for a funeral and burial, all reasonable expenses for support due to his or her last sickness, and the counsel, guidance, and aid decedent would have given plaintiff).

178. *Wynkoop v. Carpenter*, 574 N.W.2d 422, 425 (Minn. 1998) (jury in wrongful death action should have been allowed to consider pecuniary loss that brother suffered as a result of decedent's death).

179. *Regie De L'Assurance Auto. Du Quebec v. Jensen*, 399 N.W.2d 85 (Minn. 1987) (policy reasons that prohibit assignment of a cause of action for personal injuries also prohibit assignment of surviving spouse's statutory rights for wrongful death action).

180. Minn. Stat. § 573.02, subd. 1 (1998).

181. Minn. Stat. § 573.02, subd. 1 (1998); Minn. Stat. § 541.07, subd. 1 (1998).

182. Minn. Stat. § 573.02, subd. 1 (1998); *Ortiz v. Gavenda*, 590 N.W.2d 119, 121 (Minn. 1999) (limitation provisions in a statutorily created cause of action are jurisdictional and require dismissal for failure to comply).

MISSISSIPPI

A. STATUTES OF LIMITATION

Causes of action founded on negligence, breach of contract, products liability, wrongful death, and property damage generally fall under Mississippi's "catch-all" statute, which provides for a three-year limitation period.[1] All suits falling within this catch-all statute must be filed within three years from the date that the cause of action occurs or accrues.[2] The "discovery" rule applies in order to determine when the cause of action occurs or accrues.[3]

A one-year limitations period applies to most intentional torts, including the intentional torts of libel, slander, assault, battery, maiming, false imprisonment, malicious arrest (prosecution), and to some claims related to the failure to employ and claims under 42 U.S.C. Section 1983.[4]

Causes of action arising out of alleged medical malpractice must be brought within two years after the alleged act, omission, or neglect was or should have been discovered, subject to certain savings provisions.[5]

When a cause of action arises out of a deficiency in the design, planning, supervision, or construction of an improvement to real property, the action must be brought within six years after acceptance or actual occupancy or use by the owner.[6]

Causes of action against a governmental entity must be filed within one year of the commission of the tortious act.[7] However, the claimant must give notice of the claim to the governmental entity 90 days prior to filing suit.[8]

Limitations periods will be tolled when the person entitled to sue is, at the time when the cause of action accrues, under the disability of infancy (not yet reached age 21) or the disability of unsound mind.[9] In no case will this savings provision extend more than 21 years.[10] In medical malpractice cases, disability of infancy shall be removed at age six.[11] In medical malpractice cases accruing on or after July 1, 1998, in no event will the savings provision extend more than seven years after the date of the alleged act, omission, or neglect occurred.[12]

B. TORT REFORM

Certain aspects of tort reform have been adopted in Mississippi. The section later in this chapter concerning joint and several liability is certainly demonstrative of "tort reform." Additionally, the adoption of Miss. Code Ann. Section 11-1-65, which applies to punitive damages, is also in the nature of "tort reform."

C. "NO FAULT" LIMITATIONS

Mississippi is not a "no fault" automobile insurance state.

D. THE STANDARD FOR NEGLIGENCE

A plaintiff must plead and prove the following elements in order to establish a case of negligence against a defendant: (1) the defendant owed a duty to the plaintiff; (2) the defendant breached that duty; and (3) the breach was a proximate cause of the injuries and/or damages sustained by the plaintiff.[13] Mississippi applies the "reasonably prudent person" test in order to determine if a defendant breached its duty.[14]

Under Mississippi law, professionals, such as doctors, lawyers, and accountants, have a duty to act as a reasonably prudent person in their respective profession would act under similar conditions and circumstances.[15] A "minimally competent" professional is one whose skills and knowledge are sufficient to meet licensure or certification requirements for the profession or specialty practiced.[16]

In Mississippi, a child under the age of seven is irrefutably presumed to be incapable of negligence. A child between the ages of seven and fourteen is presumed to be incapable of negligence, but the presumption may be rebutted by showing that the child in question had exceptional capacity.[17] Children over the age of fourteen are presumed to be capable of negligence, and within this class the duty is to do what a person of like age, intelligence, and experience would do under the same circumstances.[18] A child engaged in an adult activity such as driving a motor vehicle is held to an adult standard of care.[19]

E. CAUSATION

Mississippi follows general tort law in determining whether or not a negligent act was the "legal" or "proximate" cause of an injury, with the "foreseeability" test used most frequently. The Mississippi Supreme Court has used both the "but for" test and the "substantial factor" test to determine if a negligent act was a cause-in-fact of an injury.[20] To establish a *prima facie* case of negligence, the plaintiff must demonstrate that the defendant's negligence was both the proximate cause and the cause-in-fact of plaintiff's injury.

F. CONTRIBUTORY NEGLIGENCE, COMPARATIVE NEGLIGENCE, AND ASSUMPTION OF RISK

1. Contributory Negligence

Mississippi is a pure comparative negligence state.[21] Therefore, in actions involving personal injuries, death or injury to property, contributory negligence of or by the plaintiff does not bar recovery. A plaintiff's damages must be diminished in proportion to the amount of negligence attributable to the plaintiff.[22] The burden of establishing contributory negligence lies with the defendant.[23]

2. Comparative Negligence

See discussion under Contributory Negligence, above.

3. Assumption of Risk

The defense of assumption of the risk has been abolished as a complete defense in Mississippi and is now subsumed in the comparative fault doctrine.[24]

G. RES IPSA LOQUITUR AND INHERENTLY DANGEROUS ACTIVITIES

1. Res Ipsa Loquitur

Res ipsa loquitur permits an inference that the defendant caused the plaintiff's harm if three elements are present: (1) the instrumentality causing damage was under the defendant's exclusive control; (2) the occurrence was such as in the ordinary course of things would not happen if the person in control used proper care; and (3) the occurrence must not be due to any voluntary act on the part of plaintiff.[25]

Mississippi follows general tort law in its treatment of the doctrine of *res ipsa loquitur* as one form of circumstantial evidence by which negligence may be proven. If the jury determines that the elements to establish *res ipsa loquitur* have been met, then the jury may, but is not bound to, infer negligence. Even if the plaintiff raises the inference and the defendant puts on no proof, the jury may still reject the inference and return a verdict for the defendant.[26]

2. Inherently Dangerous Activities

Individuals involved in inherently dangerous activities, such as handlers of electricity, are under a duty to use the highest degree of care.[27]

H. NEGLIGENCE *PER SE*

Mississippi follows the general rule that violation of a statute is negligence *per se* if the following two requirements are met: (1) the plaintiff is in the class of persons that the statute was designed to protect; and (2) the harm was of the type that the statute was designed to prevent.[28] Further, it should be noted that while the violation of a statute may be negligence *per se*, the violator is still not liable unless the violation of the statute was a proximate cause of the injury.[29]

I. JOINT AND SEVERAL LIABILITY

In cases involving personal injury, death, and damage to property (including negligence, strict liability, malpractice, and failure-to-warn cases), the liability for damages caused by two or more persons is joint and several only to the extent necessary for the claimant to recover 50 percent of his or her total damages.[30] Thereafter, such liability will be several only and a joint tortfeasor will be liable only for the amount of damages allocated to him or her by the jury in direct proportion to his or her percentage of fault, which the trier of fact will also determine.[31]

The Mississippi Supreme Court recently ruled that the jury must consider the negligence "of all participants to a particular incident which gives rise to a lawsuit." Any defendant now has the right to present his or her allegations of fault on the part of another—even if that other person or entity is not a party to the lawsuit—and request that the jury assign a percentage of fault to that "nonparty" person or entity.[32]

Mississippi Code Ann. Section 85-5-7 provides for contribution among tortfeasors. Thus, a defendant will be responsible for contribution to other joint tortfeasors for the percentage of fault assessed to him by the jury.[33]

J. INDEMNITY

In general, where one party has been required to discharge a claim for which he is only secondarily or derivatively liable, he may compel indemnity from the person or entity primarily liable for the obligation. The actively negligent party may be found to owe indemnification to the passively negligent party.[34]

This is especially true and mandated by statute in product liability cases.[35] Where a manufacturer is "found liable" for a defective product, Miss. Code Ann. Section 11-1-63(g) requires that if a seller of such product gives notice within 30 days to the manufacturer, the manufacturer must indemnify the seller for litigation costs, attorney's fees, and any damages awarded. The seller will not be entitled to such indemnity if he had control of the design, packaging, testing, or manufacture of the product; if he altered the product in any way and the alteration was a substantial factor in causing the harm; or if he had actual knowledge of the defect or made a factual representation about some aspect of the product that caused the harm.[36]

Provisions in construction contracts to indemnify or hold another person harmless from that person's own negligence are unenforceable and void as against public policy.[37]

K. BAR OF WORKERS' COMPENSATION STATUTE

Under the Mississippi Workers' Compensation Statute, an employee is barred from suing an employer who has paid workers' compensation benefits for the employee's work-related injuries.[38] This Code section provides that the exclusive remedy for such an employee is workers' compensation.[39] The employer assumes responsibility regardless of fault. An exception to this rule exists where the employer's actions are willful or wanton and bring about the injury.[40] However, the receipt of benefits by the employee does not bar an employee from seeking damages from a third party.[41]

Where an employee has collected workers' compensation benefits from an employer and then proceeds to sue a third party for the same incident, the employer may be subrogated to the rights of the employee as against a third party.[42] If the employee successfully sues a third party, the employer or his insurer may be reimbursed for previously paid workers' compensation benefits.[43]

The employer's right of subrogation gives the employer standing to intervene pursuant to Miss. Code Ann. Section 71-3-71.

L. PREMISES LIABILITY

A landowner's liability for injury sustained on the premises depends on the individual's legal status as a trespasser, licensee, or invitee. The duty owed to a trespasser is to refrain from willfully or wantonly injuring the trespasser. A landowner has no duty to keep a lookout for trespassers, or to make the premises safe for trespassers, but does have a duty to exercise reasonable care once a trespasser has been discovered.[44]

The duty owed to a licensee is almost the same as the duty owed to a trespasser—not to willfully or wantonly injure the trespasser. When the landowner is involved in active operations and the licensee's presence is known to the landowner, then the landowner owes the licensee the duty to use reasonable care.[45]

The duty owed to an invitee is to use reasonable care and to warn the invitee of any dangerous conditions of which the landowner has actual or constructive knowledge.[46]

M. DRAM SHOP LIABILITY

Mississippi's dram shop statute provides that "the consumption of intoxicating beverages, rather than the sale or serving or furnishing of such beverages, is a proximate cause of any injury, including death and property damage, inflicted by an intoxicated person upon himself or upon another person."[47] This limitation of liability protects lawful sellers and servers of alcohol, as well as social hosts who serve alcohol, from liability for injuries caused by the person to whom they sell, serve, or furnish the alcohol, provided that the person had a legal right to buy or consume alcohol.[48] A major exception to this limitation of liability is in situations where licensed sellers of alcohol sell alcohol to a person who at the time of sale was visibly intoxicated.[49]

N. ECONOMIC LOSS

Mississippi does not allow recovery for economic losses in negligence or strict liability claims. However, economic losses are recoverable in contract and breach of warranty actions.[50]

O. FRAUD AND MISREPRESENTATION

The Mississippi Rules of Civil Procedure require that a cause of action for fraud be pleaded with particularity.[51]

To establish a cause of action for fraud or intentional misrepresentation under Mississippi law, a plaintiff must prove by clear and convincing evidence the following elements: (1) a representation; (2) its falsity; (3) its materiality; (4) a speaker's knowledge of its falsity or ignorance of its truth; (5) the speaker's intent that it should be acted on by the person and in the manner reasonably contemplated; (6) the hearer's ignorance of its falsity; (7) the hearer's reliance on its truth; (8) the hearer's right to rely thereon; and (9) his/her consequent and proximate injury.[52]

To establish a cause of action for negligent misrepresentation under Mississippi law, a plaintiff must prove by a preponderance of the evidence the following elements: (1) a misrepresentation or omission of fact; (2) its materiality; (3) the failure to exercise ordinary care; (4) reasonable reliance; and (5) injury or damage.[53]

P. CONSUMER FRAUD STATUTES

Mississippi Code Ann. Section 75-24-1, *et seq.* protects consumers from unfair methods of competition affecting commerce and unfair or deceptive trade practices in or affecting commerce by prohibiting same.[54] This consumer protection statute provides that "whenever the Attorney General has reason to believe that any person is using, has used, or is about to use any method, act or practice prohibited by Section 75-24-5, and that proceedings would be in the public interest, he may bring an action in the name of the state against such person to restrain by temporary or permanent injunction the use of such method, act or practice."[55] Further, the court may issue additional orders or judgments as may be necessary to compensate any person victimized by any practice prohibited by this law.[56] Additionally, private suits may be brought under this law provided that the plaintiff first makes a reasonable attempt to resolve the claim through an informal dispute settlement program approved by the Attorney General.[57]

Q. **PUNITIVE DAMAGES**

Mississippi Code Ann. Section 11-1-65 sets forth the applicable standards and procedures for awarding punitive damages in Mississippi. This statute provides that punitive damages may not be awarded unless the claimant proves by clear and convincing evidence that the defendant against whom punitive damages are sought acted with actual malice, gross negligence which evidences a willful, wanton, or reckless disregard for the safety of others, or committed actual fraud.[58] Further, this statute provides for a bifurcated hearing on the punitive damage issue and only after compensatory damages are first awarded.[59] The primary purpose of punitive damages is to punish the wrongdoer and deter similar misconduct in the future by the defendant and others.[60]

The statute further provides that before entering a judgment for an award of punitive damages, the trial court must ascertain that the award is reasonable and is in an amount rationally related to the purpose to punish what occurred, taking into account the following factors: (1) whether there is a reasonable relationship between the punitive damages award and the harm likely to result from the defendant's conduct, as well as the harm that actually occurred; (2) the degree of reprehensibility of the defendant's conduct, the duration of that conduct, the defendant's awareness, any concealment, and the existence and frequency of similar past conduct; (3) the financial condition and net worth of the defendant; and (4) in mitigation, the imposition of criminal sanctions on the defendant for its conduct and the existence of other civil awards against the defendant for the same conduct.[61]

Mississippi's punitive damage statute does not apply to causes of action based on contract, libel and slander, or asbestos.[62] These causes of action are still governed by common law. The primary difference between Mississippi common law and the punitive damage statute is that common law only requires that the conduct warranting punitive damages be shown to exist by a preponderance of the evidence and common law does not require a bifurcated hearing on punitive damages.

R. **WRONGFUL DEATH AND SURVIVORSHIP ACTIONS**

Mississippi Code Ann. Section 11-7-13 gives a decedent's heirs at law or estate a cause of action for recovery for wrongful death. This statute provides that the party suing for wrongful death shall recover "such damages . . . as a jury may determine to be just, taking into consideration all the damages of every kind to the decedent and all damages of every kind to any and all parties interested in the suit."[63]

Wrongful death damages specifically include property damages; funeral, medical, or other related expenses; loss of love, companionship, and society; pain and suffering of decedent between time of injury and time of death; present net cash value for decedent's life expectancy; loss of household services; and loss of gifts and remembrances.[64]

Where a party dies (from related or unrelated causes) during the pendency of a lawsuit, the action will "survive" to his or her executor or administrator, provided the suit was a "personal action."[65] Thus, actions for recovery of personal property, for the enforcement of a contract, or for damages for breach of contract, or for personal injury or injury to property will survive, as will claims for loss of consortium.

Where a plaintiff dies and the claim is one that survives, the defendant may file a suggestion of death with the court. If a motion for substitution is not made within 90 days thereafter, the action shall be dismissed with prejudice.[66]

George E. Abdo, III
DANIEL COKER HORTON & BELL, P.A.
4400 Old Canton Road, Fourth floor
Jackson, Mississippi 39211
(601) 969-7607
Fax (601) 969-1116
gabdo@danielcoker.com

ENDNOTES - MISSISSIPPI

1. Miss. Code Ann. § 15-1-49.

2. *Id.*

3. *Id.*

4. Miss. Code Ann. § 15-1-35.

5. Miss. Code Ann. § 15-1-36.

6. Miss. Code Ann. § 15-1-41.

7. Miss. Code Ann. § 11-46-11.

8. *Id.*

9. Miss. Code Ann. § 15-1-59.

10. *Id.*

11. Miss. Code Ann. § 15-1-36.

12. *Id.*

13. *Grisham v. John Q. Long, VFW Post No. 4057, Inc.*, 519 So. 2d 413 (Miss. 1988).

14. *Smith v. City of West Point*, 475 So. 2d 816 (Miss. 1985).

15. *Hall v. Hilbun*, 466 So. 2d 856 (Miss. 1985).

16. *McCarty v. Mladineo*, 636 So. 2d 377 (Miss. 1994).

17. *Still v. Holiday Inn*, 626 So. 2d 593, 598 (Miss. 1993).

18. *Id.*

19. *Davis v. Waterman*, 420 So. 2d 1063, 1066 (Miss. 1982).

20. *City of New Albany v. Barkley*, 510 So. 2d 805 (Miss. 1987).

21. Miss. Code Ann. § 11-7-15.

22. *Id.*

23. *Gulf & S.I.R. Co. v. Saucier*, 139 Miss. 497, 104 So. 180 (1925).

24. *Wilus v. American Tobacco Co.*, 680 So. 2d 839 (Miss. 1996).

25. *Read v. Southern Pine Elect. Power Ass'n*, 515 So. 2d 916 (Miss. 1987).

26. *Id.*

27. *Upton v. Magnolia Elect. Power Ass'n*, 511 So. 2d 939 (Miss. 1987).

28. *Berg v. McGill*, 478 So. 2d 302 (Miss. 1985).

29. *Id.*

30. Miss. Code Ann. § 85-5-7. If a defendant's share of fault is 50 percent or less, the statute limits the payment obligation to 50 percent of the total recoverable damages.

31. *Id.; see also Narkeeta Timber Co. v. Thelma Jenkins*, 777 So. 2d 39 (Miss. 2000); *DePriest v. Barber*, 798 So. 2d 456 (Miss. 2001) (holding that percentage of fault attributable to plaintiff cannot be utilized to reduce obligation of defendant against whom judgment has been rendered to pay less than 50 percent of the judgment).

32. *Estate of Hunter v. General Motors Corp.*, 729 So. 2d 1264 (Miss. 1999). However, a party immune from suit because of sovereign immunity is exempt from the allocation process except to the extent that it purchased liability insurance. *Mississippi Transportation Commission v. Jenkins*, 699 So. 2d 597 (Miss. 1997). Likewise, where an employer is immune from liability pursuant to the workers' compensation exclusivity rule, the employer's fault cannot be considered by the jury. *Accu-Fab and Construction, Inc. v. Ladner*, 778 So. 2d 766 (Miss. 2001).

33. Miss. Code Ann. § 85-5-7.

34. *Strickland v. Rossini*, 589 So. 2d 1268 (Miss. 1991); *Home Ins. Co. v. Atlas Tank Mfg. Co.*, 230 So. 2d 549 (Miss. 1970).

35. Miss. Code Ann. § 11-1-63.

36. *Id.*

37. Miss. Code Ann. § 31-5-41.

38. Miss. Code Ann. § 71-3-9.

39. *Id.*

40. *Griffen v. Futorian Corp.*, 533 So. 2d 461 (Miss. 1988).

41. Miss. Code Ann. § 71-3-71.

42. *Id.*

43. *Id.*

44. *Maxwell v. I.C.G.R.R.*, 513 So. 2d 901 (Miss. 1987).

45. *Holley v. International Paper Co.*, 497 So. 2d 819 (Miss. 1986).

46. *Clark v. Moore Memorial United Methodist Church*, 538 So. 2d 760 (Miss. 1989); *Waller v. Dixie Land Food Stores, Inc.*, 492 So. 2d 283 (Miss. 1986).

47. Miss. Code Ann. § 67-3-73.

48. *Id.*

49. *Id.*

50. *State Farm Mut. Auto. Ins. Co. v. Ford Motor Co.*, 736 So. 2d 384 (Miss. App. 1999).

51. Miss. R. Civ. P. 9(b).

52. *Allen v. Mac Tools, Inc.*, 671 So. 2d 636, 642 (Miss. 1996); *Boling v. A-1 Detective Patrol, Inc.*, 659 So. 2d 586, 590 (Miss. 1995).

53. *Clark v. St. Dominic—Jackson Memorial Hospital*, 660 So. 2d 970, 974 (Miss. 1995); *Stonecipher v. Kornhaus*, 623 So. 2d 955, 964 (Miss. 1993).

54. Miss. Code Ann. § 75-24-5.

55. Miss. Code Ann. § 75-24-9.

56. Miss. Code Ann. § 75-24-11.

57. Miss. Code Ann. § 75-24-15.

58. Miss. Code Ann. § 11-1-65(1)(a).

59. Miss. Code Ann. §§ 11-1-65(1)(b)–(d).

60. Miss. Code Ann. § 11-1-65(1)(e).

61. Miss. Code Ann. § 11-1-65(1)(f).

62. Miss. Code Ann. § 11-1-65(2).

63. Miss. Code Ann. § 11-7-13.

64. *Id.*

65. Miss. Code Ann. § 91-7-237.

66. Miss. R. Civ. P. 25.

MISSOURI

A. STATUTES OF LIMITATION

Causes of action brought by a prisoner against the Missouri Department of Corrections must be brought within one year.[1]

Causes of action based upon libel, slander, assault, battery, false imprisonment, criminal conversion, malicious prosecution, or failure to provide an appropriate "service letter," pursuant to Rev. Stat. Mo. § 290.140, must be brought within two years.[2] In addition, any action for medical malpractice generally must be commenced within two years of the date of the alleged act of negligence.[3]

Causes of action based upon the Missouri Wrongful Death provisions must be brought within three years.[4] Actions against a sheriff, coroner, or other public officer arising out of an official act or omission must also be commenced within three years.[5]

Any other action arising from the taking, detaining, or injuring of any goods or chattel or otherwise arising from any other injury to the person or rights of another must be commenced within five years.[6]

Similar to the "discovery" rule,[7] Missouri law generally provides that a cause of action "accrues" for statute of limitation purposes when the damage is sustained *and* capable of ascertainment;[8] however in actions involving medical malpractice claims, a different rule applies.[9]

B. TORT REFORM

Missouri became one of the numerous states to modify its existing tort law when the Legislature enacted the Tort Reform Act of 1987. These provisions brought about a variety of changes to Missouri tort law, both procedural and substantive. The major changes are discussed below.

The Act revised such procedural aspects as prejudgment interest, by creating a statutory procedure for such recovery.[10] It also modified the collateral-source rule to afford juries the opportunity to consider some evidence of "advance payments."[11] Finally, the Act codified the principles of remittitur and additur.[12]

Substantively, the Act modified the existing laws relating to product defect and toxic torts. It created a potential defense for product "sellers," when their liability derives solely from the sale of a product in the stream of commerce.[13] It also enacted a "state-of-the-art" defense for strict liability-failure to warn claims[14] and mandated the use of pure comparative fault, rather than the previously-used doctrine of comparative fault, in product defect claims.[15] For toxic torts, the Act set statutory limits on damage against individuals and/or entities involved in the cleanup of environmental hazards that were generated by third parties.[16]

However, perhaps one of the most significant changes that the Act brought about was the modification to joint and several liability. The Act modified the law by providing that any party may move to reallocate uncollectable portions of the judgment.[17] The court may, in its discretion, then reallocate uncollectable portions amongst the remaining parties.[18] However, where a defendant's fault is determined to be less than the plaintiff's fault, that defendant's fault is limited to a maximum of twice its equitable share.[19]

C. THE STANDARD OF NEGLIGENCE

Under Missouri law, there are four basic elements to a valid negligence claim. First, the plaintiff must establish that the defendant owed a duty of care to the plaintiff.[20] This duty is generally premised upon the relationships between the parties.[21] Second, the plaintiff must show that the defendant breached his or her duty of care.[22] The plaintiff may establish this element by demonstrating a deviation from the standard of care required under the circumstances.[23] This standard of care may vary, depending upon the nature of the relationship between parties.[24] Third, the plaintiff must prove a causal link between the defendant's conduct and the resulting injury.[25] Finally, the plaintiff must be able to demonstrate actual damage or injury.[26]

Missouri recognizes a "heightened" professional standard of care when the defendant has special skills, education, or knowledge.[27]

In Missouri, there are no presumptions based upon the age of the minor. Minor children are required to exercise the same degree of care that an ordinarily careful child of the same age, capacity, and experience would have used under the same or similar circumstances.[28] The exception to this rule is that minors engaged in ultra-hazardous and/or adult activities (including operation of a motor vehicle) are required to exercise the same level of care that is required of all individuals, regardless of age.[29]

D. CAUSATION

Missouri conforms to the general rule that the plaintiff must establish that the defendant's conduct was the actual cause (cause-in-fact)[30] as well as the proximate cause of the plaintiff's damages.[31] Although the Missouri courts frequently struggle in defining "proximate cause," this element is satisfied by demonstrating that the defendant's conduct was a "substantial factor" in causing plaintiff's damages.[32]

E. CONTRIBUTORY NEGLIGENCE, COMPARATIVE NEGLIGENCE, AND ASSUMPTION OF RISK

1. Contributory Negligence

In 1983, the Missouri Supreme Court abolished comparative negligence as an absolute defense when it issued its opinion in *Gustafson v.*

Benda.[33] That decision created a comprehensive system of comparative fault to be applied in all cases tried after January 31, 1984.[34]

2. **Comparative Negligence**

Under Missouri's current "pure" comparative fault approach, a plaintiff may recover from a defendant those damages attributable to that defendant, even if the plaintiff's proportional share of fault is greater than that of the defendant.[35] Since its adoption in 1983, the application of "pure" comparative negligence has been legislatively modified from this general rule in actions involving claims for medical malpractice[36] and product defect[37] as well as for claims involving insolvent defendants.[38]

3. **Assumption of the Risk**

Even though Missouri has adopted a comparative fault approach, "assumption of the risk" remains a viable defense in certain circumstances in Missouri.[39] The theory continues to act as a bar when the plaintiff voluntarily consents to accept danger of known and appreciated risks.[40] The plaintiff must know more than simply the general conditions creating the danger; a plaintiff must actually know the real danger and must voluntarily and knowingly consent to assume that risk.[41]

F. *RES IPSA LOQUITUR*

In Missouri, *res ipsa loquitur* is considered a rule of evidence that enables one to plead and prove negligence through circumstantial evidence.[42] In order to successfully establish a claim of negligence through *res ipsa loquitur*, a plaintiff must demonstrate that: (1) the occurrence resulting in injury would not normally occur in the absence of negligence; (2) the instrumentalities are within the sole management and control of the defendant; and (3) the defendant possesses superior knowledge of the occurrence.[43]

G. **NEGLIGENCE** *PER SE*

In Missouri, actions for negligence *per se* can be established by proving a violation of a duly enacted statute or ordinance.[44] Missouri distinguishes between penal statutes and non-penal statutes for the purposes of establishing a valid civil claim with negligence *per se*.

For a violation of a non-penal statute to constitute a valid civil claim, a plaintiff must demonstrate: (1) that a violation of a statute occurred; (2) that the plaintiff was a member of the class of individuals sought to be protected by the statute; (3) that the plaintiff's injuries were the type that the statute sought to protect; and (4) that the violation of the statute was the proximate cause of plaintiff's injuries.[45]

For a violation of a penal statute to constitute a valid civil claim, a plaintiff must demonstrate that one of the purposes of the statute was to create a civil cause of action.[46] The Legislative intent may be gleaned from either the express language or the clear implication.[47]

Even if the plaintiff cannot demonstrate that the penal statute was intended to create a civil cause of action, he or she may still use the statute as evidence of the requisite standard of care.[48]

H. JOINT AND SEVERAL LIABILITY

In Missouri, joint and several liability is the default rule in tort actions for damages.[49] If the plaintiff is found to be "fault free," then each defendant against whom judgment is entered is jointly and severally liable for the judgment.[50] However, if the trier of fact apportions a percentage of fault to the plaintiff, then the defendants, with one exception, are jointly and severally liable for the judgment less the plaintiff's proportional share.[51]

The exception to this rule arises when all or part of an "at-fault" party's proportional share is deemed "uncollectable" by the court.[52] If so, then the court must reallocate the uncollectable amount among the other parties, including an at-fault plaintiff, in accordance with their respective degrees of fault.[53] However, if a defendant's percentage of fault is less than the plaintiff's percentage, then the maximum amount for which the defendant may be responsible is twice his or her actual percentage of fault.[54]

I. INDEMNITY

Indemnity allows a defendant to shift the plaintiff's entire loss to another when that defendant completely discharges an identical duty owed to the plaintiff and, as between defendants, reimbursement is required either to prevent unjust enrichment or by contract.[55] Common law indemnity is generally available to those who are secondarily liable from those who are primarily liable.[56] If the party seeking indemnification is actively negligent and that party's actions are also a cause of the plaintiff's underlying injuries, common law indemnity is not available.[57]

J. BAR OF WORKERS' COMPENSATION STATUTE

In Missouri, compensation for injured workers is governed by a comprehensive statutory scheme.[58] Under these provisions, an employer is required to provide any employee that is injured while in the course and scope of his or her employment with such treatment "as may reasonably be required after the injury or disability, to cure and relieve from the effects of the injury."[59] In addition to the provision of necessary medical expenses, the statutory scheme also provides for various other remedies, including payment of lost wages and disability payments, where appropriate.[60]

In exchange for this obligation to provide treatment and compensation for employment-related injuries, the statutory scheme bestows complete immunity from civil suit upon the employer, its agents, and its insurers.[61] This immunity from suit applies not only to direct actions brought by the injured employee but also to related actions for indemnity or contribution.[62] It further prohibits the trier of fact from assessing the employer's alleged fault, regardless of whether the employer was named as a defendant to the action.[63]

K. PREMISES LIABILITY

An owner or occupier of land may have legal obligations to individuals entering their premises, with respect to latent conditions on the premises, depending upon the third party's status as an invitee, licensee, or trespasser.[64] An owner/occupier owes a duty to invitees to warn of or keep the premises free from those dangerous conditions or defects of which the owner knows or reasonably should know in the exercise of ordinary care.[65] An owner/occupier owes a duty to licensees to warn of or keep the premises free from dangerous conditions of which the owner knows.[66] Finally, an owner/occupier generally owes no affirmative duty, with respect to latent conditions of the property, to trespassers.[67]

L. DRAM SHOP LIABILITY

Missouri recently adopted one of the most expansive liability schemes for Dram Shops in the United States. Prior to a recent decision of the Missouri Supreme Court, Missouri severely limited the liability of social hosts and taverns. The general rule was one of no liability.[68] Exceptions to this general rule existed only for taverns, licensed to sell liquor by the drink, when they have been convicted of selling alcohol either to underage or obviously intoxicated patrons and that sale is the "proximate cause" of the injury or death.[69]

However, the Missouri Supreme Court drastically altered this paradigm in *Kilmer v. Mun.*[70] While the rule of no liability for social hosts is still the law, [71] taverns and bars are now subject to liability, regardless of whether there was a prior criminal conviction, where the shop's acts are the proximate cause of a plaintiff's injuries.[72] In *Kilmer*, the Court held that the conviction requirement violated the "open courts" provisions of the Missouri Constitution.[73] Accordingly, licensed drinking establishments may now be held fully responsible for injuries proximately flowing from the sale to either a minor or an "obviously-intoxicated" individual.[74]

M. FRAUD AND MISREPRESENTATION

The Missouri Supreme Court Rules require that a party plead his or her cause of action for fraud with particularity.[75]

In order to prevail on such a claim for fraud, deceit, or misrepresentation, the plaintiff must prove the following elements: (1) a representation; (2) made falsely; (3) that is material to the transaction; (4) with either knowledge of the falsity or reckless disregard to the truth of the representation; (5) an intent, on the speaker's part, that the representation be relied on; (6) justifiable reliance; and (7) proximately caused injury.[76] Although some more-recent appellate decisions have suggested a "clear-and-convincing" standard,[77] the Missouri Supreme Court continues to hold that a plaintiff need only demonstrate the fraud by a preponderance of the evidence.[78]

Similarly, in order to prevail on a claim for negligent misrepresentation, a plaintiff must prove: (1) that the defendant supplied information in the course of his or her business or to further a pecuniary interest; (2) that the representation was false; (3) that the defendant failed to exercise reasonable care in obtaining or communicating the information represented; (4) that the plaintiff justifiably relied upon the representation; and (5) that the plaintiff sustained a pecuniary loss.[79]

N. CONSUMER PROTECTION STATUTES

The Missouri Merchandising Practices Act protects consumers from unfair and/or deceptive practices in connection with the sale or advertisement of any merchandise in trade or commerce within the state of Missouri.[80]

Under the provisions of the Act, the Attorney General is authorized to investigate allegations of deceptive practices[81] and to impose civil penalties for violations.[82] In addition, the Attorney General as well as the circuit prosecuting attorneys retains the authority to bring criminal proceedings as well.[83]

As a supplement to these enforcement mechanisms, the Act creates a private civil action that inures to individual citizens who suffer an ascertainable loss due to an unlawful (as prescribed by the Act) act in connection with a sale or lease of goods.[84] Prior to commencing such a civil action, the claimant must serve specific written notice upon the Attorney General,[85] although this requirement is likely *not* jurisdictional.[86] While there is no express statute of limitations prescribed by the Act, Missouri courts have concluded that actions under the Act must be commenced within three years.[87]

O. PUNITIVE DAMAGES

Unlike actual damages, which are awarded to compensate an individual for actual injuries or losses, punitive damages are awarded to punish wrongdoers and deter similar conduct in the future.[88] Ordinarily, punitive damages are not recoverable in actions based upon simple negligence.[89] Instead, a defendant must know or have reason to know that there is a high probability that an act will cause injury to others and must consciously disregard that risk before an award of punitive damages is appropriate.[90] However, some acts, although properly characterized as negligent, may manifest such reckless indifference that the law will deem any resulting injury as having been intentionally inflicted.[91] A person is deemed to act with complete indifference to or conscious disregard for the safety of others when, under the circumstances, a reasonable person would realize that the conduct creates an unreasonable risk of serious harm to another and that it creates a high probability that the harm will result.[92]

Because punitive damages are an extraordinary and harsh remedy, a higher standard of proof is required.[93] In order to submit a damage claim to a jury, a plaintiff must establish his or her claim by "clear and convincing" evidence.[94]

P. WRONGFUL DEATH

In Missouri, claims for wrongful death are governed by statute.[95] The statutory provisions allow a specific and limited group of individuals to commence an action for wrongful death against the tortfeasor(s).[96] The rights and remedies afforded under the statutory framework are exclusive and are not a survival or transmitted right.[97]

Under the Missouri Wrongful Death Act, the plaintiff(s) may seek and recover the following: (1) pecuniary losses; (2) funeral expenses; (3) pain and suffering sustained by the decedent between the time of the injury and the time of the decedent's death; and (4) the reasonable value of the decedent's services, companionship, and other measures of consortium.[98] In addition, the trier of fact may consider the mitigating and/or aggravating circumstances attending the death and may award, if it so chooses, exemplary damages in accordance with the rules governing punitive damages.[99]

Q. MEDICAL MALPRACTICE CLAIMS

In Missouri, medical malpractice claims are governed largely by specific statutory provisions.[100] Actions based upon medical malpractice generally must be commenced within two years of the date of the occurrence,[101] except that minors have two years from the date of their eighteenth birthday in which to commence their action.[102] In addition, Missouri law provides that claims arising from the placement of foreign objects with an individual's body shall be commenced within two years from the date of discovery of the negligent act or from the date on which the individual should have discovered the negligent act, whichever occurs first.[103]

In addition to the unique rules governing the statute of limitation, the medical malpractice provisions also modify Missouri's general tort law in a number of other respects. First, medical malpractice claims are subject to non-economic damage caps, which are adjusted annually.[104] In addition, the standards for punitive damages have been codified in slightly different terms, although the linguistic differences have, to date, had little effect on the applicable standards.[105] Next, in an attempt to reduce the number of frivolous medical malpractice claims, the provisions require a plaintiff to file an affidavit with the court, within ninety days of the filing of the lawsuit, which states that he or she has obtained the written opinion of a legally qualified health care provider who believes that the defendant failed to meet the requisite standard of care.[106] If the plaintiff fails to satisfy this requirement, the trial court may dismiss the action without prejudice.[107]

Finally, the medical malpractice provisions create special rules relating to apportionment of fault, settlement, and joint-and-several liability.[108]

Robert A. Horn
Horn Aylward & Bandy, LLC
2600 Grand Boulevard, Suite 500
Kansas City, Missouri 64108
(816) 421-0700
Fax (816) 421-0899

K. Christopher Jayaram
Horn Aylward & Bandy, LLC
2600 Grand Boulevard, Suite 500
Kansas City, Missouri 64108
(816) 421-0700
Fax (816) 421-0899
cjayaram@hab-law.com

ENDNOTES - MISSOURI

1. Rev. Stat. Mo. § 516.145 (1994).

2. Rev. Stat. Mo. § 516.140 (1994).

3. Rev. Stat. Mo. § 516.105 (1994).

4. Rev. Stat. Mo. § 537.100 (1994).

5. Rev. Stat. Mo. § 516.130 (1994).

6. Rev. Stat. Mo. § 516.120(4) (1994).

7. Although extremely similar to the "discovery" rule, the Missouri Supreme Court distinguishes the Missouri rule by noting that damages are "capable of ascertainment" when they are "substantially complete." *See Jepson v. Stubbs*, 555 S.W.2d 307, 313 (Mo. banc. 1977); *but see Martin v. Crowley Wade & Milstead, Inc.*, 702 S.W.2d 57 (Mo. banc. 1985).

8. Rev. Stat. Mo. § 516.100 (1994).

9. Rev. Stat. Mo. § 516.105 (1994).

10. Rev. Stat. Mo. § 408.040 (1994).

11. Rev. Stat. Mo. §§ 490.710 to .715 (1994).

12. Rev. Stat. Mo. § 537.068 (1994).

13. Rev. Stat. Mo. § 537.762 (1994).

14. Rev. Stat. Mo. § 537.764 (1994).

15. Rev. Stat. Mo. § 537.765 (1994).

16. Rev. Stat. Mo. § 260.552 (1994).

17. Rev. Stat. Mo. § 537.067.2(1) (1994).

18. Rev. Stat. Mo. § 537.067.2(2) (1994).

19. Rev. Stat. Mo. § 537.067.2(4) (1994).

20. *Hoover's Dairy, Inc. v. Mid-America Dairymen, Inc./Special Products, Inc.*, 700 S.W.2d 426, 431 (Mo. 1985).

21. *Id.*

22. *Id.*

23. *Id.*

24. *Davidson v. Otis Elevator Co.*, 811 S.W.2d 802 (Mo. Ct. App. 1991).

25. *Hoover's Dairy, Inc. v. Mid-America Dairymen, Inc./Special Products, Inc.*, 700 S.W.2d 426, 431 (Mo. 1985).

26. *Id.*

27. *Williams v. Chaimberlain*, 316 S.W.2d 505 (Mo. 1958); *Silberstein v. Berwald*, 460 S.W.2d 707 (Mo. 1970).

28. *Lester v. Sayles*, 850 S.W.2d 858 (Mo. banc. 1993).

29. *Wilson v. Shumate*, 296 S.W.2d 72 (Mo. 1956); *Root v. Mudd*, 981 S.W.2d 651, 653-54 (Mo. Ct. App. 1998).

30. *Quinn v. Lenau*, 996 S.W.2d 564, 569 (Mo. Ct. App. 1999).

31. *Stanley v. City of Independence*, 995 S.W.2d 485, 489 (Mo. banc. 1999).

32. *Ricketts v. K.C. Stockyards Co. of Maine*, 484 S.W.2d 216 (Mo. 1972).

33. 661 S.W.2d 11 (Mo. banc. 1983).

34. *Id.* at 15-16.

35. *Id.*

36. Rev. Stat. Mo. § 538.230 (1994).

37. Rev. Stat. Mo. § 537.765 (1994).

38. Rev. Stat. Mo. § 537.067 (1994).

39. *Sheppard v. Midway R-1 Sch. Dst.*, 904 S.W.2d 257 (Mo. Ct. App. 1995).

40. *Eide v. Midstate Oil Co.*, 895 S.W.2d 35, 40 (Mo. Ct. App. 1995).

41. *Gamble v. Bost*, 901 S.W.2d 182 (Mo. Ct. App. 1995).

42. *City of Kennett v. Akers*, 564 S.W.2d 41 (Mo. 1978).

43. *Id.*

44. *Downing v. Dixon*, 313 S.W.2d 644 (Mo. 1958).

45. *Sayers v. Haushalter*, 493 S.W.2d 406 (Mo. Ct. App. 1973).

46. *Christy v. Petrus*, 295 S.W.2d 122 (Mo. banc. 1956).

47. *Id.*

48. *State ex. rel. Wells v. Mayfield*, 281 S.W.2d 9 (Mo. banc. 1955).

49. Mo. Rev. Stat. § 537.067 (1994).

50. Mo. Rev. Stat. § 537.067.1 (1994).

51. Mo. Rev. Stat. § 537.067.2 (1994).

52. Mo. Rev. Stat. § 537.067.2(2) (1994).

53. Mo. Rev. Stat. § 537.067.2(2) (1994). Notwithstanding the reallocation, the original tortfeasor remains liable for his or her percentage of fault, either directly to the claimant or through contribution. Mo. Rev. Stat. § 537.067.2(3) (1994).

54. Mo. Rev. Stat. § 537.067.2(4) (1994).

55. *Koeller by and through Koeller v. Unival, Inc.*, 906 S.W.2d 744 (Mo. Ct. App. 1995).

56. *Crouch v. Tourtelot*, 350 S.W.2d 799, 805 (Mo. banc. 1961).

57. *Purk v. Purk*, 817 S.W.2d 915 (Mo. Ct. App. 1991).

58. *See* Mo. Rev. Stat. §§ 287.010 to .855 (1994).

59. Mo. Rev. Stat. § 287.140.1 (1994).

60. Mo. Rev. Stat. § 287.160 (1994)(wages); Mo. Rev. Stat. § 287.170-250 (1994) (disability and death benefits).

61. Mo. Rev. Stat. § 287.120 (1994).

62. *State ex. rel. Maryland Heights Concrete Contractors, Inc. v. Ferriss*, 588 S.W. 2d 489 (Mo. banc. 1979).

63. *Id.; Sweet v. Herman Bros., Inc.,* 688 S.W. 2d 31, 32 (Mo. 1985).

64. *Carter v. Kinney,* 896 S.W.2d 926, 928 (Mo. 1995).

65. *Id.*

66. *Id.*

67. *Id.*

68. Mo. Rev. Stat. § 537.053 (1994).

69. Mo. Rev. Stat. § 537.053 (1994).

70. 17 S.W.3d 545 (Mo. banc 2000).

71. *Id.* at 553 note 22.

72. *Id.* at 554.

73. *Id.* at 549-554.

74. Mo. Rev. Stat. § 537.053(3) (2000); *Kilmer, supra* at 554.

75. Rule 55.15 (1999).

76. *Clark v. Olson,* 726 S.W.2d 718 (Mo. 1987); *Slone v. Purina Mills,* 927 S.W.2d 358 (Mo. Ct. App. 1996).

77. *Wion v. Carl I. Brown & Co.,* 808 S.W.2d 950 (Mo. Ct. App. 1991).

78. *Crawford v. Smith,* 470 S.W.2d 529 (Mo. 1971).

79. *Vickers v. Progressive Cas. Ins. Co.,* 979 S.W.2d 200 (Mo. Ct. App. 1998); *Colgan v. Wash. Realty Co.,* 879 S.W.2d 686 (Mo. Ct. App. 1994).

80. Mo. Rev. Stat. § 407.020 (1994).

81. Mo. Rev. Stat. § 407.040 (1994).

82. Mo. Rev. Stat. §§ 407.100–407.110 (1994).

83. Mo. Rev. Stat. § 407.020 (1994).

84. Mo. Rev. Stat. § 407.025 (1994).

85. Mo. Rev. Stat. § 407.025 (1994).

86. *Pointer v. Edward L. Kuhs Co.*, 678 S.W.2d 836 (Mo. Ct. App. 1984).

87. *State ex rel. Webster v. Meyers*, 779 S.W.2d 286 (Mo. Ct. App. 1989).

88. *Vaughn v. Taft Broadcasting Co.*, 708 S.W.2d 656, 660 (Mo. 1986).

89. *Hoover's Dairy, Inc. v. Mid-American Dairymen, Inc./Specialty Products, Inc.*, 700 S.W.2d 426, 435 (Mo. 1985).

90. *Id.* at 436; *Alack v. Vic Tanny Intern. of Mo., Inc.*, 923 S.W.2d 330 (Mo. 1996).

91. *Hoover's Dairy, Inc. v. Mid-American Dairymen, Inc./Specialty Products, Inc.*, 700 S.W.2d 426, 435 (Mo. 1985)(citing *Sharp v. Robberson*, 495 S.W.2d 394, 397 (Mo. 1973)).

92. *Joyce v. Nash*, 630 S.W.2d 219 (Mo. Ct. App. 1982).

93. *Rodriguez v. Suzuki Motor Corp.*, 936 S.W.2d 104, 111 (Mo. 1996).

94. *Id.*

95. Mo. Rev. Stat. §§ 537.080–537.100 (1994).

96. Mo. Rev. Stat. § 537.080.1(1) to (3) (1994).

97. *Sullivan v. Carlisle*, 851 S.W.2d 510, 516 (Mo. banc. 1993).

98. Mo. Rev. Stat. § 537.090 (1994).

99. Mo. Rev. Stat. § 537.090 (1994).

100. *See* Mo. Rev. Stat. §§ 516.105, 538.205–516.230 (1994).

101. Mo. Rev. Stat. § 516.105 (1994). Notwithstanding this provision, there is a well-recognized exception for continuing care, which tolls the statute of limitation until the allegedly negligent provider ceases his or her treatment of the patient. *See Adams v. Lowe*, 949 S.W.2d 109 (1997).

102. *Strahler v. St. Luke's Hospital*, 706 S.W.2d 7 (Mo. banc. 1986); *Gleitz v. St. John's Mercy Medical Center*, 927 S.W.2d 506 (Mo. Ct. App. 1996); *Hodges v. Southeast Missouri Hospital Ass'n*, 963 S.W.2d 354 (Mo. Ct. App. 1998).

103. Mo. Rev. Stat. § 516.105 (1994).

104. Mo. Rev. Stat. § 538.210 (1994).

105. Mo. Rev. Stat. § 538.210.5 (1994).

106. *Menaugh v. Resler Optometry, Inc.*, 799 S.W.2d 71 (Mo. 1990); *Schroeder v. Lester E. Cox Medical Center, Inc.*, 833 S.W.2d 411 (Mo. Ct. App. 1992).

107. Mo. Rev. Stat. § 538.225 (1994).

108. Mo. Rev. Stat. § 538.230 (1994).

MONTANA

A. STATUTES OF LIMITATION

Claims for personal injury, based on a negligent act, including wrongful death claims, must be brought within three years.[1] The beginning of the limitation period is either the time that the injury occurred[2] or when the facts constituting the claim were discovered.[3]

Medical malpractice claims must also be brought within three years, with a discovery exception.[4] A five-year period of repose protects health care practitioners (including veterinarians) from late-discovered claims, unless the defendant failed to disclose an "act, error, or omission" of which the defendant knew or should have known.[5]

Montana medical and chiropractic malpractice claims are subject to procedures that interact with the limitation period, and which are a condition precedent to filing a claim against a health care provider in district court: the medical legal panel and the chiropractic legal panel.[6] Claims must first be submitted to the panel, but the limitation period is tolled during the proceedings and does not begin to run again until 30 days after an order of dismissal is issued by the panel.[7]

Claims for various intentional acts, enumerated as libel, slander, assault, battery, false imprisonment, and seduction, must be brought within two years.[8]

Legal malpractice claims must be brought within three years from the date of the error or omission, or discovery (using reasonable diligence) of the error or omission, with a ten-year period of repose.[9]

In general, claims for negligent injury to property must be brought within the same three-year period as claims for personal injury.[10] Claims for damage to real property arising out of work on improvements or surveying must be brought within ten years from completion of the project.[11]

When a claim is based both in tort and contract, the longer period of limitation applies, which is the contract limitation period.[12] The limitation period for claims based on written instruments is eight years, and for claims based on a "contract, account, or promise" not in writing is five years.[13]

Claims based on fraud or mistake must be brought within two years, but the time period does not begin until the aggrieved party is aware of the facts constituting the fraud or mistake.[14]

An action for misappropriation of a trade secret must be brought within three years after the misappropriation was, or should have been, discovered.[15]

A private statutory claim (akin to a bad faith claim) may be brought against an insurance company for unfair trade practices.[16] If the plaintiff is an insured, the limitation period is two years from the time that the statute was violated, while if the plaintiff is a third-party claimant, the claim must be brought within one year from the date of the settlement or a judgment on the underlying claim.[17] A common law bad faith claim is subject to a three-year statute of limitation.[18]

Claims for childhood sexual abuse and ritual abuse of a minor are subject to a three-year limitation period.[19] The limitation period begins as of the time of the abuse or when the plaintiff discovers or reasonably should have discovered the connection between abuse and injury caused by the abuse.[20] The time of reasonable discovery is a fact question.[21]

Montana has two catch-all provisions: (1) a three-year period for claims based on an "obligation or liability" other than a contract, account or promise;[22] and (2) five years for any "action for relief not otherwise provided for."[23] The Montana Supreme Court consistently applies the longer of the two limitation periods if both have potential applicability.[24]

For injuries to children, the limitation period for nearly all claims is tolled until the child reaches 18 years of age, and then begins to run.[25] However, in malpractice cases, for injury or death to children under the age of four years, the tolling only occurs until the child's eighth birthday, and then the limitation period of three years begins to run.[26]

A person under a "mental illness" disability is also entitled to tolling of the limitation period, if that person was committed to an institution after a trial to establish the disability.[27] While a "minority" disability continues to toll until the child's eighteenth birthday (except in malpractice cases), the "mental illness" disability can only extend the limitation period by five years.[28]

Claims against the state or a political subdivision cannot be filed in district court until first presented to and denied by the department of administration.[29] The department is required to make a final decision within 120 days, during which time the limitation period is tolled.[30] Claims against a county must be brought within six months after the commissioners have rejected the claim.[31]

B. TORT REFORM

As discussed above, health care providers successfully lobbied the Legislature for a mandatory prefiling procedure in all claims asserting medical malpractice.[32] The medical legal panel procedure has been in place since 1977. In 1989, chiropractors were able to have the legislature create a similar procedure in legislation termed the Montana Chiropractic Legal Panel Act.[33]

1987 was the major year for attempted tort reform legislation, with eight of nine bills passing, in some form.[34] Since 1987, however, the Montana Supreme Court has impacted many of the statutes passed as tort reform.

Prior to 1987, insurance companies could be sued for common law bad faith.[35] The 1987 legislature created a statutory "independent cause of action" that was intended to replace the common law claim.[36] The statute provides reference to an enumeration of the type of conduct giving rise to a claim, and provides limitations and defenses.[37] However, the Montana Supreme Court has held that the common law claim of bad faith still exists.[38]

Common law claims for wrongful termination from employment were also replaced with a statutory framework in 1987.[39] As a result of that reform, the doctrine of "at will" employment no longer exists in Montana.[40] The statutes define the claim for wrongful discharge, limit the amount of damages, and provide for arbitration as an alternative to litigation.[41]

1987 also saw a change to the common law collateral source rule, which permitted a plaintiff to have a double recovery of certain elements of damages (e.g., payment of medical expenses).[42] Currently, in actions where the total award is greater than $50,000, and the plaintiff is fully compensated for his damages, the recovery is reduced by any amount paid from a collateral source unless there is a subrogation right.[43]

The statute regarding punitive damages was revised substantially in 1987.[44] As further discussed below, since 1987, punitive damages are available only when the defendant has been guilty of actual fraud or actual malice, which are defined.[45] In addition, the 1987 legislature created a bifurcated system, with a second proceeding for issues related to punitive damages.[46]

The tort doctrine most manipulated by tort reform measures (including in 1987) and by the Montana Supreme Court is comparative fault and joint and several liability. This topic is discussed more fully below.

Other special interest groups have passed tort reform allowing for greater protection from liability. For example, ski resort owners,[47] individuals engaged in equine activities,[48] hunter education instructors,[49] etc., have all attempted to provide some legislative insulation for their occupations from tort liability.

C. "NO FAULT" LIMITATIONS

The Montana legislature has not passed any "no fault" provisions for injuries resulting from motor vehicle accidents. Liability insurance is mandatory in Montana.[50] In addition, all liability policies are required to include uninsured motorist coverage, unless the named insured rejects such coverage.[51] Uninsured motorist coverage applies even if the insured is not occupying an insured vehicle.[52]

In practice, many automobile insurance policies issued in Montana contain additional forms of "no fault" coverages that are not required by law (e.g., medical payment and underinsured coverage).[53] "No fault" policies issued out of state will provide coverage when the accident occurs in Montana.[54]

D. THE STANDARD FOR NEGLIGENCE

Four elements comprise a negligence claim in Montana: (1) duty; (2) breach of duty; (3) causation; and (4) damages.[55] Duty is the first element of a negligence claim and is a question of law.[56] The existence of a duty is based on the relationship between the plaintiff and defendant.[57] It also depends on the foreseeability of the risk and on the weighing of policy considerations for and against imposition of liability.[58] Everyone is responsible not only for willful acts but also for injury occasioned to another by the want of ordinary care in the management of his property or person.[59] Negligence is the breach of a legal duty and involves the failure of the actor to use reasonable care under the circumstances.[60]

Courts in Montana, at one time, created a "no duty" rule for livestock owners in relation to motorists, as the result of a doctrine termed "open range."[61] In 2000, the Montana Supreme Court overruled prior case law and held that a duty of reasonable care is equally imposed on livestock owners and motorists.[62]

Montana recognizes a professional standard of care.[63] Expert testimony is usually required to establish the standard of care, and a deviation from that standard.[64] The standard may be a national one if the standard of care for the particular conduct at issue is the same in all communities, regardless of size, throughout the United States.[65]

When a special relationship exists between the plaintiff and defendant, a higher standard of care is required.[66] Contrary to the general rule that there is no duty to protect a particular individual,[67] where a special relationship exists between the defendant and either an intended victim or the plaintiff, the defendant could have a duty to take action to protect the plaintiff.[68]

Children under the age of seven cannot, as a matter of law, be negligent.[69] The standard of care expected of a child over seven and under fourteen is a highly personal and subjective standard, not based on ordinary children of the same age and understanding,[70] but instead requiring a "dual inquiry": (1) the *capacity* of the particular child in a given case to be negligent; and (2) the *establishment in fact* of the particular child's negligence under the circumstances of a given case.[71] The controlling element is the particular child's capacity to be negligent: his ability to appreciate the danger, either to himself or others, of the act alleged to be negligent.[72] Children who are 14 years and older are presumed, as a matter of law, to be capable of negligence.[73] A parent may be liable for failing to exercise reasonable care to prevent a child from intentionally harming others.[74]

There exists in Montana, by statute, a disputable presumption that all persons take ordinary care of the person's own concerns.[75]

E.   CAUSATION

Montana follows the general rule that to establish a *prima facie* case in negligence, the plaintiff must demonstrate that the defendant's negligence was the proximate cause of the plaintiff's injury.[76] In negligence cases that do not involve issues of intervening cause, proof of causation is satisfied by proof that a party's conduct was a cause-in-fact of an event if the event would not have occurred *but for* that conduct.[77] Conversely, a party's conduct is not the cause of an event if the event would have occurred without it.[78] As an uncommon alternative to the "but for" test, the "substantial factor" rule of causation deals with cases in which the acts of more than one party combined to produce the result (e.g., plaintiff alleged to be contributorily negligent or multiple defendants).[79] The "substantial factor" rule is necessary when two or more causes concur to bring about an event and application of the "but for" test would allow responsible parties to escape liability.[80]

F. CONTRIBUTORY NEGLIGENCE, COMPARATIVE NEGLIGENCE, AND ASSUMPTION OF RISK

1. Contributory Negligence

Montana has abolished contributory negligence as an absolute defense in tort actions seeking recovery for death, personal injury, or property damage.[81] A negligent plaintiff can now recover damages if the fault is 50/50 or if the defendant's (or defendants') fault is greater than the plaintiff's.[82] The burden of establishing contributory negligence lies with the defendant, and must be established by a preponderance of the evidence.[83]

2. Comparative Negligence

Under Montana's comparative negligence law, all forms of conduct amounting to negligence in any form, including, but not limited to, ordinary negligence, gross negligence, willful negligence, wanton misconduct, reckless conduct, and heedless conduct, are to be compared with any conduct that falls short of conduct intended to cause injury or damage.[84] If the plaintiff has been negligent (50 percent or less), he will still recover damages but the amount is reduced by the percentage of his negligence.[85] However, a plaintiff's contributory negligence is not to be used to reduce a punitive damage award,[86] or when the damages were caused by insurance fraud.[87] Recovery for loss of consortium by a spouse or child may not be reduced by the percentage of negligence attributable to the plaintiff.[88] However, if the plaintiff's negligence is greater than that of the defendant, there can be no recovery for loss of consortium.[89] Tort conduct is compared to tort conduct, but when the other conduct does not amount to a tort, but rather a breach of contract, the conduct cannot be offset.[90] A plaintiff's negligent conduct which precedes treatment by a physician does not constitute comparative negligence.[91]

3. Assumption of Risk

Assumption of risk is no longer available as a separate affirmative defense in negligence claims, and in those cases where the court allows such a defense, knowledge of the specific danger that caused the plaintiff's injury is required.[92] However, the doctrine remains viable in the context of strict liability for abnormally dangerous activities[93] and for products liability.[94] The assumption of risk defense is available in a strict liability case if the user or consumer of the product discovered the defect or the defect was open and obvious, *and* the user or consumer *unreasonably* made use of the product and was injured by it.[95] Assumption of risk is analyzed under a subjective standard rather than under the objective "reasonable person" standard (i.e., what the particular plaintiff sees, knows, understands, and appreciates).[96] Assumption of risk must be applied in accordance with the principles of comparative negligence set forth in Mont. Code Ann. § 27-1-702.[97]

G. *RES IPSA LOQUITUR* AND INHERENTLY DANGEROUS ACTIVITIES

1. *Res Ipsa Loquitur*

Res ipsa loquitur permits proof of what happened to be made by circumstantial evidence.[98] It allows an inference that the harm suffered by the plaintiff was caused by the negligence of the defendant when: (1) the event is of a kind that does not ordinarily occur in the absence of negligence; (2) other responsible causes, including the conduct of the plaintiff and third persons, are sufficiently eliminated by the evidence; and (3) the indicated negligence is within the scope of the defendant's duty to the plaintiff.[99] Exclusive control by the defendant over the situation is not a necessary element but does assist in establishing the probable cause of the accident.[100]

The court's function is to determine whether the inference *may* be reasonably drawn by the jury, or whether it *must* necessarily be drawn.[101] The jury's function is to determine whether the inference is to be drawn in any case where different conclusions could reasonably be reached.[102]

2. Inherently Dangerous Activities

A high degree of care applies to inherently dangerous activities.[103] Individuals engaged in certain "inherently dangerous" activities in Montana, as a business, have sought and obtained limited legislative protection from liability.[104] An employer in Montana may be vicariously liable for injuries to others caused by a subcontractor's failure to take precautions to reduce risks while engaged in an inherently dangerous activity.[105]

H. NEGLIGENCE *PER SE*

In an ordinary negligence action, the plaintiff must prove the existence of a legal duty and a breach of that duty.[106] Negligence *per se* is a separate theory of liability premised on the violation of a statute.[107] In a negligence *per se* claim, the plaintiff need not establish the existence of a duty and a breach of that duty.[108] A negligence *per se* claim requires proof that: (1) the defendant violated a particular statute; (2) the statute was enacted to protect a specific class of persons; (3) the plaintiff is a member of that class; (4) the plaintiff's injury is of the sort that the statute was enacted to prevent; and (5) the statute was intended to regulate members of the defendant's class.[109] Violation of a nonstatutory standard, such as an administrative regulation, safety code, or professional standard, may be used as evidence of negligence, but is not a basis to find the defendant negligent *per se*.[110] Involuntary violation of a statute in an emergency due to circumstances beyond the actor's control does not constitute negligence *per se*.[111]

I. JOINT AND SEVERAL LIABILITY

Multiple tortfeasors who are parties to an action are jointly and severally liable for the amount that may be awarded to the claimant, but each has the right of contribution from any other person whose negligence may have contributed as a proximate cause to the injury.[112] This rule is subject to multiple exceptions.[113] A party to the action whose negligence is determined to be 50 percent or less of the combined negligence of all persons whose negligence may be considered[114] is severally liable only and is responsible only for the percentage of negligence attributable to that party.[115] However, that party may be jointly liable for all damages caused by the negligence of another if both acted in concert or if one acted as an agent of the other in causing the claimant's damages.[116]

On the motion of a party against whom a negligence claim is asserted, any other person whose negligence may have contributed as a proximate cause to the injury may be joined as a party to the action.[117] For purposes of determining the percentage of liability attributable to each party whose action contributed to the claimant's injury, the trier of fact must consider the negligence of, and apportion the percentage of, negligence among the claimant, injured person, defendants, third-party defendants, and, subject to certain conditions,[118] persons who have settled with or been released by the claimant.[119] In apportioning liability, the trier of fact may not consider the fault of any person who is immune from liability, who is not subject to the court's jurisdiction, or who could have been but was not named as a third-party defendant.[120]

If for any reason all or part of the contribution from a party liable for contribution cannot be obtained, each of the other parties shall contribute a proportional part of the unpaid portion of the noncontributing party's share and may obtain a judgment against the noncontributing party in a pending or subsequent action.[121] However, a party found to be 50 percent or less negligent for the injury complained of is liable for contribution only to the extent negligence is attributed to that party.[122]

A release or covenant not to sue given to one of two or more persons liable in tort for the same injury does not discharge any other tortfeasor from liability for that tortfeasor's several *pro rata* share of liability for the injury unless the release or covenant not to sue provides otherwise.[123] The release or covenant not to sue reduces the aggregate claim against the other tortfeasors to the extent of any percentage of fault attributed by the trier of fact[124] to the tortfeasor to whom the release or covenant is given.[125] The release or covenant not to sue discharges the tortfeasor to whom it is given from all liability for contribution.[126]

Contribution is not available from a settling tortfeasor or releasee.[127] However, a defendant may assert as a defense that the claimant's damages were caused in full or in part by a settling tortfeasor or releasee[128] and the negligence of a settling tortfeasor or releasee may be considered in apportioning liability among the parties to the action.[129] The claimant is deemed to have assumed the liability apportioned to the settling tortfeasor or releasee, and the claimant's claim against other persons is reduced by the percentage of the settling tortfeasor's or releasee's "equitable share of the obligation."[130]

The defendant alleging that the claimant's damages were caused in full or in part by a settling tortfeasor or releasee must affirmatively plead the settlement or release as a defense in the answer or with reasonable promptness if the defendant gains actual knowledge of the settling tortfeasor or releasee after filing of the answer,[131] and bears the burden of proving negligence and causation with respect to apportionment of fault to a settling tortfeasor or releasee.[132] In addition, the defendant alleging that a settling tortfeasor or releasee is at fault must notify the settling tortfeasor or releasee[133] and the settled or released party must be provided an opportunity to intervene in the action and defend against the claims affirmatively asserted.[134]

The current statutory provisions regarding apportionment of liability among multiple defendants were enacted[135] in response to a decision of the Montana Supreme Court, which declared unconstitutional the previous version of the statute because, *inter alia*, it permitted apportionment of liability to a nonparty without providing an opportunity for the nonparty to defend, and because it required the plaintiff to act in a dual capacity by representing nonparties.[136]

The Montana Supreme Court has not addressed the constitutionality of the current statute. If all or part[137] of the current statute is invalidated or found unconstitutional by the Montana Supreme Court, contingent statutory provisions become effective.[138] The contingent provisions would abolish joint and several liability and provide only several liability for most tort actions,[139] resurrect the nonparty or "empty chair" defense in its entirety,[140] implement the percentage credit rule contained in the current statute,[141] replace comparative negligence with comparative fault,[142] and allow comparison of the claimant's negligence with the combined fault of the defendants and nonparties.[143]

J. INDEMNITY

Indemnity is defined in the contract section of the Montana Code as a contract by which one engages to save another from a legal consequence of the conduct of one of the parties or of some other person.[144] An agreement to indemnify a person against a future unlawful act is void; however, an agreement to indemnify a person against an act already done is valid, even though the act was known to be wrongful, unless it was a felony.[145] In interpreting a contract of indemnity, the courts will apply the specific rules set out in statute, unless a contrary intention appears.[146] However, the courts have also recognized indemnity as an equitable principle, based on the general theory that one compelled to pay for damages caused by another should be able to seek recovery from that party.[147] Indemnity shifts the entire loss from the one who has been required to pay it to the one who should bear the loss.[148]

K. BAR OF WORKERS' COMPENSATION STATUTE

The Montana Workers' Compensation Act[149] provides the exclusive remedy[150] for injuries[151] sustained by an employee[152] while in the employ of a covered employer.[153] The right to compensation is not affected if the injury is caused by a third party. In which case, the employee or personal representative has a cause of action against the third party in addition to compensation.[154] An insurer has a right to subrogation on a third-party claim,[155] but only after the employee is made whole.[156]

The exclusivity of the Act applies no matter how wanton the allegations of negligence.[157] However, the Act is not exclusive if the employee is intentionally injured by an intentional and deliberate act and the employer or a fellow employee, but the employer is not vicariously liable for the intentional and deliberate acts of an employee.[158] Further, the Act is not exclusive for uninsured employers,[159] in which case the employee may be entitled to compensation and bring any other claim allowed by law.

The Act is not the exclusive remedy for injuries that are not covered injuries, which may include spoliation of evidence,[160] post traumatic stress disorder[161] and other injuries with a mental stimulus and a mental or physical consequence.[162] However, the exclusive remedy provision of the Act does bar an emotional distress claim made by a third–party family member whose claim arises from an injury to an insured employee.[163]

Finally, the Act does not apply to an Indian business that operates exclusively within the exterior boundaries of the reservation.[164]

L. PREMISES LIABILITY

In Montana, the status of the injured party as an invitee, licensee, or trespasser does not affect a property owner's general duty of care.[165] The possessor of the premises has a duty to use ordinary care in maintaining the premises in a reasonably safe condition and to warn of any hidden or lurking dangers. What constitutes a reasonably safe premises is generally considered to be a question of fact. Whether a premises is reasonably safe depends to a large extent on what use the property is put to, its setting, location, and other physical characteristics; the type of person who would foreseeably visit, use, or occupy the premises; and the specific type of hazard or unsafe condition alleged. The possessor of the premises is not liable to persons foreseeably on the premises for physical harm caused to them by any activity or condition on the premises whose danger is known or obvious to them, unless the possessor should anticipate the harm despite such knowledge or obviousness.[166] The Montana Supreme Court recently held that a landowner was not required to have notice of the existence of a hazard (barbed wire in grassy area owned by City that was three-to-four feet from side of street) before it could be held liable for pedestrian's injuries sustained when she tripped and fell on the hazard.[167]

M. DRAM SHOP LIABILITY

In 1986, Montana enacted a statute entitled "Civil Liability for injuries involving alcohol consumption."[168] Notably, no distinction is made between commercial and social purveyors of alcoholic beverages.[169] The statute also precludes any "negligence *per se*" claims on the basis that the alcohol server violated any of Montana liquor control statutes.[170]

Purveyors of alcohol are liable for serving consumers under the legal drinking age and consumers who are visibly intoxicated.[171] A purveyor's liability extends to situations where the consumer is forced or coerced into consumption, or was told that the beverage contained no alcohol.[172]

Purveyors of alcohol are liable for damages caused by drunken conduct that result from an uninterrupted course of events.[173] Serving alcohol to a visibly intoxicated person creates a situation in which most consequences are reasonably foreseeable precisely because of the causal relationship between serving alcohol and the problems caused by drunken conduct.[174]

N. ECONOMIC LOSS

Aside from the statutory limit on tort claims against the state of Montana or a political subdivision of the state,[175] there is no limit on economic damages incurred as a result of a tort. Otherwise, economic damages or loss are allowed under tort law, including negligence[176] and misrepresentation.[177] Economic damages or loss may not be recovered if the amount of the loss is speculative or if the causation element between the loss and the tort is speculative.[178]

O. FRAUD AND MISREPRESENTATION

1. Actual Fraud

The nine elements of actual fraud are as follows: (1) a representation; (2) falsity of the representation; (3) materiality of the representation; (4) the speaker's knowledge of the falsity of the representation or ignorance of its truth; (5) the speaker's intent that the representation should be relied on; (6) the hearer's ignorance of the falsity of the representation; (7) the hearer's reliance on the representation; (8) the hearer's right to rely on the representation; and (9) consequent and proximate injury caused by the reliance on the representation.[179] The circumstances constituting fraud must be pled with particularity.[180]

2. Constructive Fraud

Constructive fraud is: (1) any breach of duty that, without an actually fraudulent intent, gains an advantage to the person in fault or by misleading another to his prejudice; or (2) any such act or omission as the law especially declares to be fraudulent, without respect to actual fraud.[181] The presence of a legal duty is an essential element of a claim for constructive fraud.[182] Whether or not a legal duty exists is a question of law for the court's determination.[183]

Although the legal duty that often exists in constructive fraud cases is a fiduciary one, the constructive fraud statute does not require that the plaintiff demonstrate a fiduciary relationship, but merely requires the establishment of a duty.[184] Under "special circumstances," neither a confidential nor a fiduciary relationship is necessary for a finding of constructive fraud.[185] Special circumstances may include a party's creation, by words or conduct, of a false impression concerning important matters and a subsequent failure to disclose the relevant facts.[186]

3. Negligent Misrepresentation

A cause of action for negligent misrepresentation arises where: (1) the defendant made a representation as to a past or existing material fact; (2) the representation was untrue; (3) regardless of defendant's actual belief, the defendant made the representation without any reasonable ground for believing it to be true; (4) the representation was made with the intent to induce the plaintiff to rely on it; (5) plaintiff was unaware of the falsity of the representation; (6) plaintiff acted in reliance on the truth of the representation; (7) plaintiff was justified in relying on the representation;

and (8) plaintiff, as a result of reliance on the representation, sustained damage.[187]

P. CONSUMER FRAUD STATUTES

1. Montana Unfair Trade Practices and Consumer Protection Act

The Montana Unfair Trade Practices and Consumer Protection Act[188] (UTPCPA) prohibits unfair methods of competition and unfair or deceptive practices in the conduct of any trade or commerce.[189] In construing the provisions of the UTPCPA, "due consideration and weight" must be given to the interpretations of the Federal Trade Commission and the federal courts relating to section 5(a)(1) of the Federal Trade Commission Act.[190] The UTPCPA does not apply to national advertising, and does not apply to certain advertising activities done without knowledge of the false, misleading, or deceptive character of the advertisement and by specified persons or entities who do not have a direct financial interest in the advertised product or service.[191]

The UTPCPA is administered and enforced by the Montana Department of Commerce.[192] The department is authorized to conduct investigations and obtain information, documents, and physical evidence.[193] The department may bring an action for injunctive relief to restrain an act unlawful under the UTPCPA.[194] The Attorney General or county attorneys may prosecute actions under the UTPCPA.[195] Private actions may also be brought under the UTPCPA.[196]

In an action under the UTPCPA, a court may grant relief necessary, including appointment of a receiver, to restore money or property acquired through a practice unlawful under the UTPCPA.[197] A court may revoke a license or certificate that allows the person to engage in business,[198] and is authorized to order the dissolution, suspension, or forfeiture of franchise of any corporation that violates the terms of an injunction issued under the UTPCPA.[199] The UTPCPA also provides for the imposition of civil fines for willful violations[200] and criminal penalties for fraudulent violations.[201]

A consumer[202] who suffers any ascertainable loss of money or property as the result of a method, act, or practice unlawful under the UTPCPA may bring an individual but not a class action to recover the greater of actual damages or $200.[203] The court may award treble damages and necessary or proper equitable relief,[204] and may award the prevailing party reasonable attorney's fees incurred in prosecuting or defending the action.[205]

2. UTPCPA—Personal Solicitation Sales

Personal solicitation sales involving consideration in excess of $25[206] are specifically subject to certain disclosure requirements and rights of cancellation.[207] A violation of the statutory provisions regarding personal solicitation sales is a violation of the UTPCPA.[208] The personal solicitation sales statutes apply to sellers who regularly engage in "transactions of the same kind" to sell goods or services that are primarily for personal, family, or household purposes, when the seller contacts the buyer by telephone or in person other than at the seller's place of business in an attempt to sell such goods or services.[209] The Montana Supreme Court has interpreted "transactions of the same kind" to include not merely sales of the same goods or services but also use of the same mode of contact with the consumer.[210] Therefore, a regular seller of certain goods who does not regularly engage in solicitations by telephone or at the buyer's residence was not subject to the Personal Solicitation Sales Act with respect to a particular solicitation by telephone or visit to the buyer's residence.[211] The personal solicitation sales statutes do not apply to buyers who personally know the identity of the seller, contacts initiated by the buyer, or sales of insurance policies.[212] Nonprofit organizations are exempt from the disclosure requirements.[213]

The seller must at the time of initial contact or communication with the potential buyer, and before any personal solicitation, clearly and expressly disclose the individual seller's name, the name of the business, firm, or organization represented, the identity or kinds of goods or services to be demonstrated or offered, and that the seller wishes to demonstrate or sell the identified goods or services.[214] When the initial contact is made in person, the seller must also show the potential buyer an identification card that clearly states the seller's name and the business or organization represented.[215] These required disclosures must be made before asking any questions or making any statements other than an initial greeting.[216]

A buyer may cancel a personal solicitation sale until midnight of the third business day after the day on which the buyer signed an agreement or offer to purchase, or, in the case of a telephone sale, at any time before signing an agreement or offer to purchase.[217] However, the seller must furnish the buyer a notice statement containing prescribed language regarding the buyer's right of cancellation,[218] and the buyer may cancel the personal solicitation sale until the seller has complied with the notice requirements.[219] The cancellation occurs when written notice of cancellation is given to the seller, or, if by mail, when deposited in the mail properly addressed and postage prepaid.[220] No particular form of cancellation is required and a cancellation is sufficient if it indicates the intention of the buyer not to be bound.[221] A personal solicitation sale may not be canceled if, in the case of goods, the goods cannot be returned in substantially the same condition as when received by the buyer.[222]

The seller must tender to the buyer any payments made and any note or other evidence of indebtedness within ten days after cancellation of the sale or revocation of an offer to purchase.[223] If the down payment includes traded-in goods the goods must be tendered in substantially as good condition as when received by the seller.[224] If the seller fails to so tender the goods, the buyer may elect to recover an amount equal to the trade-in allowance stated in the agreement.[225] If the seller refuses within the ten-day period after cancellation or revocation to return the cash down payment or goods tendered as down payment, the seller is liable to the buyer for the entire down payment, and if the buyer prevails in an action to recover the down payment, the court shall also award the buyer $100 plus reasonable attorney's fees and costs.[226]

Until the seller has complied with the requirements to tender payments and evidence of indebtedness to the buyer who has canceled or revoked, the buyer may retain possession of goods delivered by the seller and the buyer has a lien on the goods in his possession for any recovery to which the buyer may be entitled.[227] Otherwise, the buyer on demand must tender the goods to the seller within a reasonable time after cancellation or revocation.[228] Tender may be made at the buyer's place of residence.[229] If the seller fails to demand possession of the goods within a reasonable time after cancellation or revocation, the goods become the property of the buyer without obligation to pay for them.[230] For purposes of demand by the seller and tender by the buyer, 40 days is presumed to be a reasonable time.[231]

3. Other UTPCPA Protections

Montana law provides additional statutory consumer protection requirements, violation of which may constitute an unfair or deceptive trade practice under the UTPCPA or which may give rise to remedies similar to the remedies available under the UTPCPA. Such protections are provided in the Home Inspection Trade Practices Act,[232] the Plain Language in [Consumer] Contracts Act,[233] and the Montana Telemarketing Registration and Fraud Prevention Act.[234]

Q. PUNITIVE DAMAGES

A judge or jury may award punitive damages for the sake of example and for the purpose of punishing a defendant.[235] Generally, punitive damages may not be awarded in an action arising from contract or breach of contract.[236] This provision does not prohibit recovery of punitive damages in a products liability action or an action under the Unfair Claims Settlement Practices Act.[237] Further, if the conduct of the defendant is tortious, the fact that there is an underlying contract does not defeat an award of punitive damages.[238] The state and other governmental entities are immune from punitive damages.[239]

An insurance contract may provide for coverage of punitive damages if the contract expressly so provides.[240] Punitive damages may be insured against and insurance coverage of punitive damages does not violate public policy.[241]

Reasonable punitive damages may be awarded when the defendant has been found guilty of actual fraud or actual malice.[242] Punitive damages may be awarded where no monetary value has been assigned to the actual damages suffered.[243] The terms "actual fraud" and "actual malice" are separately and specifically defined for purposes of determining entitlement to punitive damages,[244] and the contract definitions of fraud[245] do not apply to proof of actual fraud for purposes of punitive damages.[246]

For purposes of punitive damages, defendant is guilty of actual fraud if the defendant makes a representation with knowledge of its falsity, or conceals a material fact with the purpose of depriving the plaintiff of property or legal rights or otherwise causing injury.[247] Actual fraud exists only when the plaintiff has a right to rely on the representation of the defendant and suffers injury as a result of that reliance.[248] A defendant is guilty of actual malice if the defendant has knowledge of facts or intentionally disregards facts that create a high probability of injury to the plaintiff and deliberately proceeds to act in conscious or intentional disregard of, or with indifference to, the high probability of injury to the plaintiff.[249]

Liability for punitive damages must be determined by the trier of fact, whether judge or jury.[250] All elements of the claim for punitive damages must be proved by clear and convincing evidence.[251] Evidence regarding a defendant's financial affairs, financial condition, and net worth is not admissible in a trial to determine whether a defendant is liable for punitive damages, but must be considered and determined in an immediate, separate proceeding following a determination of liability for punitive damages.[252]

A jury award of punitive damages must be reviewed by the judge.[253] When an award of punitive damages is made by the judge, or when the judge reviews a jury's award of punitive damages, the judge must consider each of nine factors specified in the punitive damages statute.[254] The judge may increase or decrease a jury award of punitive damages, and must clearly state the reasons for increasing, decreasing, or not increasing or decreasing the jury's punitive damage award.[255]

R. WRONGFUL DEATH AND SURVIVORSHIP ACTIONS

When a tortfeasor's conduct results in the death of a person, an action may be instituted for "wrongful death" under Montana law, due to the wrongful death statute.[256] If the decedent was a minor, an action may be maintained for his injuries.[257] If an injured person has a claim against the tortfeasor(s), and dies before beginning the lawsuit, or has brought an action and then dies, Montana's survival statute allows the claim to be brought or the case to continue.[258] Wrongful death and survivorship actions must be combined into one legal action.[259]

If the injured persons were Montana residents at the time of the accident, Montana law governs the action, regardless of where the injury occurred.[260]

An action under the wrongful death statute can only be brought by the personal representative of the decedent's estate.[261] For minor decedents, the action is to be brought by the parent or guardian.[262] A survival action is to be maintained by the decedent's "representatives or successors in interest."[263]

Damages for wrongful death are to be "just" under the circumstances of the case.[264] However, the damages are not unrestricted. Montana follows the "pecuniary loss" rule, although recovery is permitted for loss of society and companionship to the extent that such loss has a pecuniary value.[265] For minor decedents, the parent or guardian may recover damages for their sorrow, mental distress, and grief.[266] A survival action carries forward the claims that the injured party had before death.[267] Therefore, the recovery can include: lost earnings from the time of injury to death, present value of reasonable earnings during the decedent's life expectancy, medical and funeral expenses, reasonable compensation for the decedent's pain and suffering, and other special damages.[268]

Kristi Blazer
Gregory G. Gould
LUXAN & MURFITT, P.L.L.P.
24 West 6th Avenue
Montana Club Building, 4th Floor
Helena, Montana 59601
(406) 442-7450
Fax (406) 442-7361

ENDNOTES - MONTANA

1. Mont. Code Ann. § 27-2-204(1), (2). All citations to the Montana Code Annotated are to the most recent edition of the code unless noted by year in parenthesis. As of this printing, the most recent edition of the code is 2001.

2. *Cechovic v. Hardin & Associates, Inc.*, 273 Mont. 104, 902 P.2d 520 (1995). *See also* Mont. Code Ann. § 27-2-102(1)(a) (1987) (claim accrues when all elements of claim exist).

3. Mont. Code Ann. § 27-2-102(3). The usual rule in Montana is that the claim accrues at the time of the injury (or damages), which is the final element of a negligence claim to occur. *Carroll v. W. R. Grace & Co.*, 252 Mont. 485, 830 P.2d 1253 (1992). The discovery exception to that usual rule is limited in Montana to instances where due diligence has been used by the plaintiff; and either: (1) the facts are by their nature concealed or self-concealing; or (2) the defendant has taken some action to prevent the injured party from discovering the facts. *See McCormick v. Brevig*, 1999 MT 86, 294 Mont. 144, 980 P.2d 603 (1999).

4. Mont. Code Ann. § 27-2-205(1).

5. *Id.* The repose statute's tolling provision applies only where a health care worker learns, or through the use of reasonable diligence would have learned, that he or she committed an error but subsequently conceals or fails to disclose that error to the patient. *Blackburn v. Blue Mountain Women's Clinic*, 286 Mont. 60, 951 P.2d 1 (1998).

6. *See generally* Mont. Code Ann. §§ 27-6-101–704 (Medical Legal Panel Act enacted 1977) & Mont. Code Ann. §§ 27-12-101–703. Specifically, Mont. Code Ann. §§ 27-6-701 & 27-12-301 preclude the filing of any court case until the medical or chiropractic panel has rendered a decision. Each panel is composed of three physicians and three lawyers who hear evidence about the claim and make a confidential nonbinding decision essentially as to whether substantial evidence was presented that malpractice occurred. *E.g.*, Mont. Code Ann. §§ 27-6-401, 606, 703, 602 & 27-12-401, 606, 703, 602. The term "medical malpractice claim" is broadly defined and includes claims against medical doctors, osteopaths, dentists, hospitals, and podiatrists. Chiropractic malpractice claims are covered under the separate section of statutes. Apparently claims against other types of health care providers, such as optometrists, Christian Scientists, naturopaths, and acupuncturists need not go through a screening panel.

7. Mont. Code Ann. § 27-6-702.

8. Mont. Code Ann. § 27-2-204(3).

9. Mont. Code Ann. § 27-2-206.

10. *Ritland v. Rowe*, 260 Mont. 453, 861 P.2d 175 (1993). *But see* Mont. Code Ann. § 27-2-207 (provides two-year limitation period for "injuries involving property").

11. Mont. Code Ann. § 27-2-208. If the "injury" to the real property occurs during the tenth year after completion, the action is still timely filed if brought within one year of the injury.

12. *Billings Clinic v. Peat Marwick Main & Co.*, 244 Mont. 324, 797 P.2d 899 (1990). In *Billings Clinic*, the defendant accounting firm's duties were defined by the parties' contract and by the legal duty to meet its obligations in a professional manner.

13. Mont. Code Ann. §§ 27-2-202(1), (2).

14. Mont. Code Ann. § 27-2-203.

15. Mont. Code Ann. § 30-14-407.

16. Mont. Code Ann. § 33-18-242(1).

17. Mont. Code Ann. § 33-18-242(7).

18. *Brewington v. Employers Fire Ins. Co.*, 1999 MT 312, 297 Mont. 243, 992 P.2d 237 (1999).

19. Mont. Code Ann. §§ 27-2-216, 27-2-217.

20. Mont. Code Ann. §§ 27-2-216(1)(a) & (b), 27-2-217(1)(a) & (b).

21. *Werre v. David*, 275 Mont. 376, 913 P.2d 625 (1996).

22. Mont. Code Ann. § 27-2-202.

23. Mont. Code Ann. § 27-2-231.

24. *Ritland v. Rowe*, 260 Mont. 453, 861 P.2d 175 (1993).

25. Mont. Code Ann. §§ 27-2-401(1); *Smith v. Sturm, Ruger & Co.*, 198 Mont. 47, 643 P.2d 576 (1982).

26. Mont. Code Ann. § 27-2-205(2). The constitutionality of the limitation on minors' medical malpractice claims was upheld in *Estate of McCarthy v. Montana Second Judicial Court*, 1999 MT 309, 297 Mont. 212, 994 P.2d 1090 (2000).

27. Mont. Code Ann. § 27-2-401(1) (1997). The requirement for "commitment after trial" was added when the statute was amended in 1997. Before that amendment, a question of fact was created as to whether the "mental illness" disability was serious enough to toll the limitation period. *Bestwina v. The Village Bank*, 235 Mont. 329, 767 P.2d 338 (1989). It is unclear whether claims tolled by the

earlier statute (with no commitment requirement) might survive as tolled if brought since the 1997 amendment. *See also Murphy v. State,* 229 Mont. 342, 748 P.2d 907 (1987) (limitation period tolled until patient ceased to be minor *and* ceased to suffer from mental illness).

28. Mont. Code Ann. § 27-2-401(1).

29. Mont. Code Ann. § 2-9-301(2).

30. *Id.*

31. Mont. Code Ann. § 27-2-209(3).

32. *See generally* Mont. Code Ann. §§ 27-6-101–704. The screening panel device was specifically held to be constitutional in *Linder v. Smith,* 193 Mont. 20, 629 P.2d 1187 (1981).

33. *See generally* Mont. Code Ann. §§ 27-12-101 & 703.

34. The tort reform measure regarding "emotional distress" damages was relatively minor and the final bill only affected contract damages. The changes to the wrongful death statute are included in the discussion of that topic below.

35. *Klaudt v. Flink,* 202 Mont. 247, 658 P.2d 1065 (1983).

36. Mont. Code Ann. § 33-18-242 (1987).

37. *Id.,* Mont. Code Ann. § 33-18-201 (1977).

38. *Brewington v. Employers Fire Ins. Co.,* 1999 MT 312, 297 Mont. 243, 992 P.2d 237 (1999). Beginning in 1998, the Montana Supreme Court adopted a new citation format, requiring that its opinions be cited by calendar year, followed by the Montana U.S. Postal Code (MT), followed by consecutive number by order of issuance. This citation format is provided where applicable.

39. *See* Mont. Code Ann. §§ 39-2-901–915. Insofar as tort law is concerned, prior to this legislation, Montana courts had imposed on employers a duty of good faith and fair dealing. *Crenshaw v. Bozeman Deaconess Hospital,* 213 Mont. 488, 693 P.2d 487 (1984).

40. *See Whidden v. John S. Nerison, Inc.,* 1999 MT 110, 294 Mont. 346, 981 P.2d 271, 275 (1999).

41. Mont. Code Ann. §§ 39-2-901–915 (1987, amended 1993). If an offer to arbitrate is rejected, and the rejecting party loses, that party must pay the attorney's fees of the prevailing party.

42. *See* Mont. Code Ann. §§ 27-1-307 & 308 (1987).

43. Mont. Code Ann. § 27-1-308 (1987). The statute also allows a deduction beneficial to the plaintiff for certain premiums paid for insurance. The court, rather than the jury, is to make the deduction. For an analysis of the type of collateral source payments which may or may not be deducted, see *Schutt v. A.T. Klembus & Son*, 2000 MT 357, 303 Mont. 274, 16 P.3d 1002 (2000).

44. Mont. Code Ann. § 27-1-221 (1987).

45. Mont. Code Ann. §§ 27-1-221(1)–(4) (1987).

46. Mont. Code Ann. § 27-1-221(7) (1987).

47. Mont. Code Ann. §§ 23-2-702–736. Skiers to accept responsibility for all injuries and damages that result from risks inherent in the sport of skiing.

48. Mont. Code Ann. §§ 27-1-725–728. Equine professional is not liable for injury or death to participants if it resulted from a risk inherent in equine activities.

49. Mont. Code Ann. § 27-1-721. Instructor must be "grossly negligent" before liability attaches.

50. Mont. Code Ann. § 61-6-301 (1995).

51. Mont. Code Ann. § 33-23-201 (1997).

52. *Georgeson v. Fidelity & Guaranty Ins. Co.*, 48 F. Supp.2d 1262 (D. Mont. 1998).

53. Liability insurers must pay an injured party's medical expenses on presentment, and prior to any final settlement, when liability is reasonably clear. *Ridley v. Guaranty Nat'l Ins. Co.*, 286 Mont. 325, 951 P.2d 987 (1997).

54. *Kemp v. Allstate Insurance Co.*, 183 Mont. 526, 601 P.2d 20 (1979).

55. *Jackson v. State*, 1999 MT 46, 287 Mont. 473, 956 P.2d 35 (1998).

56. *Yager v. Deane*, 258 Mont. 453, 853 P.2d 1214 (1995). *See also Poole v. Poole*, 2000 MT 117, 299 Mont. 435, 1 P.3d 936 (2000).

57. *Krieg v. Massey*, 239 Mont. 469, 781 P.2d 277 (1989) (no duty to protect another from harm in absence of special relationship of custody or control).

58. *Maguire v. State*, 254 Mont. 178, 835 P.2d 755 (1992).

59. Mont. Code Ann. § 27-1-701 (1987). *See also* Mont. Code Ann. § 28-1-201 (general duty of care, even in absence of contract, to abstain from injuring the person or property of another or infringing on his rights).

60. *Starkenburg v. State*, 282 Mont. 1, 934 P.2d 1018 (1997). No ("heightened standard of care") instruction needs to be given when a motorist was operating a vehicle in an area where children are likely to be present. *Hanson v. Edwards*, 2000 MT 221, 301 Mont. 185, 7 P.3d 419 (2000).

61. *See e.g., Bartsch v. Irvine Co.*, 149 Mont. 405, 427 P.2d 302 (1967).

62. *Larson-Murphy v. Steiner*, 2000 MT 334, 303 Mont. 96, 15 P.3d 1205 (2000); *Indendi v. Workman*, 272 Mont. 64, 899 P.2d 1085 (1995).

63. *Yellowstone Basin Properties, Inc. v. Burgess*, 255 Mont. 341, 843 P.2d 341 (1992).

64. *Newville v. State Dep't of Family*, 267 Mont. 237, 883 P.2d 793 (1994). The only exception to the requirement of expert testimony is when the medical error could be easily known by even a layperson, such as leaving a sponge in after surgery. *Rudeck v. Wright*, 218 Mont. 41, 709 P.2d (1990).

65. *Burlingham v. Mintz*, 270 Mont. 277, 891 P.2d 527 (1995).

66. *Story v. City of Bozeman*, 242 Mont. 436, 791 P.2d 767 (1990).

67. *Kreig v. Massey*, 239 Mont. 469, 781 P.2d 277 (1989).

68. *Nelson v. Driscoll*, 1999 MT 193, 295 Mont. 363, 983 P.2d 972 (1999) (husband of motorist killed while walking on roadway stated claim against police officer who had voluntarily assumed duty to protect motorist when he ordered her to park car because she had been drinking and because of road conditions). *See also LaTray v. City of Havre*, 2000 MT 119, 299 Mont. 449, 999 P.2d 1010 (2000) (police officers entered into special relationship of custody with intoxicated female brought to hospital and, therefore, could be held liable for injuries to nurse at hospital).

69. *Gilligan v. City of Butte*, 118 Mont. 350, 166 P.2d 797 (1946). Most of the Montana cases on this issue discuss the issue in terms of contributory negligence. However, no different analysis should logically apply for determining the primary negligence of a child. *See* Mary B. Troland, The Contributory Negligence of Children, *Ranard v. O'Neil*, 37 Mont. L. Rev. 257 (1976).

70. *Ranard v. O'Neil*, 166 Mont. 177, 531 P.2d 1000 (1975). *Compare Lesage v. Largey Lumber Co.*, 99 Mont. 372, 43 P.2d 896 (1935) (objective standard employed).

71. *Graham v. Rolandson*, 150 Mont. 270, 435 P.2d 263 (1967).

72. *Ranard v. O'Neil*, 166 Mont. 177, 531 P.2d 1000 (1975).

73. *Sherris v. Northern Pacific Ry. Co.*, 55 Mont. 189, 175 P. 269 (1918).

74. *Crisafulli v. Bass*, 2001 MT 316, 2001 WL 1666701 (Mont. Dec. 31, 2001).

75. Mont. Code Ann. § 26-1-602. This statute lists 38 different disputable presumptions.

76. *Knowlton v. Sandaker*, 150 Mont. 438, 436 P.2d 98 (1968).

77. *Busta v. Columbus Hospital Corp.*, 276 Mont. 342, 916 P.2d 122 (1996).

78. *Id. Busta* reversed *Kitchen Krafters v. Eastside Bank of Montana*, 242 Mont. 155, 789 P.2d 567 (Mont. 1990), which had previously been the seminal case on causation in Montana. *Kitchen Krafters* used a two-tiered analysis of causation as it related to independent intervening causes. Under *Busta*, foreseeability is now a part of the duty analysis rather than proximate cause. *Lacock v. 4B's Restaurant, Inc.*, 277 Mont. 17, 919 P.2d 373 (1996), is another exception to the foreseeability analysis: The specific injury need not have been foreseen. *See also Estate of Strever v. Cline*, 278 Mont. 165, 924 P.2d 666 (1996), (owner who stored handgun and ammunition in unlocked vehicle breached duty to safely store his firearm. However, two intervening criminal acts and an intervening grossly negligent act were not reasonably foreseeable and cut off gun owner's liability).

79. *Young v. Flathead County*, 232 Mont. 274, 757 P.2d 772 (1988), *appeal after remand*, 241 Mont. 223, 786 P.2d 658 (1990).

80. *Rudeck v. Wright*, 218 Mont. 41, 709 P.2d 621 (1990).

81. Mont. Code Ann. § 27-1-702 (1975).

82. *Lackey v. Wilson*, 205 Mont. 476, 668 P.2d 1051 (1983) (plaintiff who was 50 percent negligent entitled to recover). Mont. Code Ann. § 27-1-702 (1997).

83. *Bolstad v. Groskurth*, 139 Mont. 64, 360 P.2d 101 (1961).

84. *Martel v. Montana Power Co.*, 231 Mont. 96, 752 P.2d 140 (1988).

85. *Cain v. Stevenson*, 218 Mont. 101, 706 P.2d 128 (1985).

86. *Shahrokhfar v. State Farm Mutual Ins. Co.*, 194 Mont. 76, 634 P.2d 653 (1981).

87. *Cartwright v. Equitable Life Assurance Soc'y*, 276 Mont. 1, 914 P.2d 976 (1996).

88. *Mickelson v. Montana Rail Link, Inc.*, 2000 MT 111, ¶¶ 119-22, 299 Mont. 348, 999 P.2d 985, 1003 (2000).

89. *Id.*

90. *Stephens v. Safeco Ins. Co.*, 258 Mont. 142, 852 P.2d 565 (1993).

91. *Harding v. Deiss*, 2000 MT 169, 300 Mont. 312, 3 P.3d 1286 (2000).

92. *Mead v. M.S.B., Inc.*, 264 Mont. 465, 477, 872 P.2d 782, 790 (1994), citing *Abernathy v. Eline Oil Field Services, Inc.*, 200 Mont. 205, 209, 650 P.2d 772, 775 (1982).

93. *Matkovic v. Shell Oil Co.*, 218 Mont. 156, 707 P.2d 2 (1985).

94. Mont. Code Ann. § 27-1-719(5) (contingent).

95. *Lutz v. National Crane Corp.*, 267 Mont. 368, 379, 884 P.2d 455, 461 (1994) citing Mont. Code Ann. § 27-1-719(5)(a).

96. *Lutz v. National Crane Corp.*, 267 Mont. 368, 378, 884 P.2d 455, 461 (1994).

97. *Zahrte v. Sturm, Ruger & Co., Inc.*, 203 Mont. 90, 94, 661 P.2d 17, 18–19 (1983).

98. *Dalton v. Kalispell Regional Hospital*, 256 Mont. 243, 846 P.2d 960 (1993).

99. *Thompkins v. Northwestern Union Trust Co.*, 198 Mont. 170, 645 P.2d 402 (1982).

100. *Id.*

101. *Brothers v. General Motors Corp.*, 202 Mont. 477, 658 P.2d 1108 (1983).

102. *Id.*

103. *Bourke v. Butte Electric & Power Co.*, 33 Mont. 267, 83 P. 470 (1905). There is a paucity of law in Montana on inherently dangerous activities.

104. *See* Section B, Tort Reform.

105. *Beckman v. Butte-Silver Bow County*, 2000 MT 112, 299 Mont. 389, 1 P.3d 348 (2000).

106. *Indendi v. Workman*, 272 Mont. 64, 73–74, 899 P.2d 1085, 1091 (1995) (Gray, J., concurring). *Indendi* set forth the elements of negligence *per se* and held that a violation of the state's legal fence statute gave rise to a negligence *per se* claim by a motorist injured in a collision with the landowner's livestock that escaped through a defective fence. In *Larson-Murphy v. Steiner*, 2000 MT 334, 303 Mont. 96, 15 P.3d 1205 (2000), the court overruled *Indendi* to the extent it held that a violation of the fence statute may serve as a basis for negligence *per se*.

107. *Id.*

108. *Id.*

109. *Harwood v. Glacier Elec. Co-op., Inc.*, 285 Mont. 481, 489, 949 P.2d 651, 656 (1997); *Patten v. Raddatz*, 271 Mont. 276, 283–84, 895 P.2d 633, 638 (1995); *Hislop v. Cady*, 261 Mont. 243, 247, 862 P.2d 388, 391 (1993).

110. *Harwood v. Glacier Elec. Co-op., Inc.*, 285 Mont. 481, 489, 949 P.2d 651, 656 (1997); *Thayer v. Hicks*, 243 Mont. 138, 150, 793 P.2d 784, 792 (1990).

111. *Cameron v. Mercer*, 1998 MT 619, 289 Mont. 172, 175–76, 960 P.2d 302, 305 (1998).

112. Mont. Code Ann. § 27-1-703(1) (temporary).

113. *Id.*

114. *See* Mont. Code Ann. § 27-1-703(4) (temporary).

115. Mont. Code Ann. § 27-1-703(2) (temporary).

116. Mont. Code Ann. § 27-1-703(3) (temporary).

117. Mont. Code Ann. § 27-1-703(4) (temporary).

118. Mont. Code Ann. § 27-1-703(6)(b) (temporary).

119. Mont. Code Ann. § 27-1-703(4) (temporary); *but see Plumb v. District Court*, 279 Mont. 363, 371–80, 927 P.2d 1011, 1016–21 (1996) (in absence of joinder of settling tortfeasor, apportionment of percentage of negligence to settling tortfeasor violates substantive due process); *see also State ex rel. Maffei v. Second Judicial District Court*, 282 Mont. 65, 67–68, 935 P.2d 266, 267 (1997) (absent joinder of a third party, admission of evidence of the third party's negligence may be otherwise admissible in the trial court's discretion for another purpose); *Weaselboy v. Ingersoll-Rand Co.*, No. CV 89-24-BLG-JFB (D. Mont. Apr. 10, 1991) (absent joinder of third party, evidence of the third party's negligence may be admissible for purpose of proving lack of causation); *Bell v. Glock, Inc.*, 92 F. Supp.2d 1067, 1070-71 (D. Mont. 2000) (evidence of conduct of third parties not joined as defendants admissible on issue of causation).

120. Mont. Code Ann § 27-1-703(6)(c) (temporary).

121. Mont. Code Ann. § 27-1-703(5) (temporary).

122. *Id.*

123. Mont. Code Ann. § 27-1-704(1).

124. *See* Mont. Code Ann. § 27-1-703(4) (temporary).

125. Mont. Code Ann. § 27-1-704(2).

126. Mont. Code Ann. § 27-1-704(3).

127. Mont. Code Ann § 27-1-703, 27-1-704(3) (temporary). *See Cusenbary v. Mortensen*, 1999 MT 2219, 296 Mont. 25, 987 P.2d 351, 361 (1999).

128. Mont. Code Ann § 27-1-703(6)(a) (temporary).

129. Mont. Code Ann § 27-1-703(6)(b) (temporary).

130. The "equitable share of the obligation" appears to refer to the percentage of negligence apportioned by the trier of fact to the settling tortfeasor or releasee pursuant to Mont. Code Ann. § 27-1-703(4) (temporary).

131. Mont. Code Ann § 27-1-703(6)(f) (temporary).

132. Mont. Code Ann § 27-1-703(6)(e) (temporary).

133. Mont. Code Ann § 27-1-703(6)(g) (temporary).

134. Mont. Code Ann § 27-1-703(6)(f)(ii) (temporary).

135. Ch. 293, L. 1997; Ch. 429, L. 1997 Mont. Laws, Ch. 293 and Ch. 429.

136. *Plumb v. District Court*, 279 Mont. 363, 371–80, 927 P.2d 1011, 1016–21(1996).

137. The bill enacting the current statutory provisions contains a nonseverability clause, so that if the Montana Supreme Court finds any part of the bill to be unconstitutional or invalid, the entire bill is invalid. *See* Section 5, Ch. 293, L. 1997.

138. Mont. Code. Ann § 27-1-703 (contingent).

139. Mont. Code. Ann § 27-1-705 (contingent).

140. Mont. Code. Ann § 27-1-703 (contingent).

141. Mont. Code. Ann § 27-1-705 (contingent).

142. Mont. Code. Ann § 27-1-702, 27-1-705 (contingent).

143. Mont. Code. Ann § 27-1-702 (contingent). For an in-depth discussion of the history and issues regarding multiple-defendant liability and the "empty chair" defense in Montana, *see* S. Neuhardt, Settlement or Release Under Montana's Multiple Defendant Statute, 59 Mont. L. Rev. 113 (Winter 1998).

144. Mont. Code Ann. § 28-11-301 (1999).

145. Mont. Code Ann §§ 28-11-302 & 28-11-303.

146. Mont. Code Ann. § 28-11-313.

147. *Durden v. Hydro Flame Corp.*, 1999 MT 186, 295 Mont. 318, 983 P.2d 943 (1999), citing *Poulsen v. Treasure State Industries*, 192 Mont. 69, 626 P.2d 822 (1981).

148. *Raisler v. Burlington Northern R.R.*, 219 Mont. 254, 258, 717 P.2d 535, 537 (1985).

149. Mont. Code Ann. §§ 39-71-101 *et seq.*

150. Mont. Code Ann. § 39-71-411.

151. Mont. Code Ann. § 39-71-119.

152. Mont. Code Ann. § 39-71-118.

153. Mont. Code Ann. § 39-71-117, *Papp v. Rocky Mtn. Oil and Minerals, Inc.*, 236 Mont. 330, 769 P.2d 1249 (1989).

154. Mont. Code Ann. § 39-71-412.

155. Mont. Code Ann. § 39-71-414.

156. Art. II, Sect. 16, Mont. Const., *Ness v. Anaconda Minerals Co.*, 279 Mont. 472, 929 P.2d 205 (1996).

157. *Schmidt v. State of Montana*, 286 Mont. 98, 951 P.2d 23 (Mont. 1997).

158. Mont. Code Ann. § 39-71-413 (2001), *Cf. Sherner v. Conoco, Inc.*, 2000 MT 50, 298 Mont. 401, 995 P.2d 990 (2000). The statute was amended in 2001 in response to *Sherner*, limiting the scope of this exception.)

159. Mont. Code Ann. § 39-71-508, *Buerkley v. Aspen Meadows Limited Partnership*, 1999 MT 97, 294 Mont. 263, 980 P.2d 1046 (1999).

160. *Oliver v. Stimson Lumber Co.*, 1999 MT 328, 297 Mont. 336, 993 P.2d 11 (1999).

161. *Stratemeyer v. Lincoln County*, 276 Mont. 76, 915 P.2d 175 (1996).

162. *Kleinhesselink v. Chevron, U.S.A., et al.*, 277 Mont. 158, 920 P.2d 108 (1996).

163. *Maney v. Louisiana Pacific Corp.*, 2000 MT 366, 303 Mont. 398, 15 P.3d 962 (2000).

164. *Zempel v. Uninsured Employers' Fund*, 282 Mont. 424, 938 P.2d 658 (1997).

165. *Limberhand v. Big Ditch Co.*, 218 Mont. 132, 706 P.2d 491 (1985).

166. *Richardson v. Corvallis Public School Dist. No. 1.*, 286 Mont. 309, 321, 950 P.2d 748, 756 (1997). The Montana Supreme Court held that *Richardson* is retroactive in application; that is, actions predating *Richardson* are controlled by the law set out therein. *Benson v. Heritage Inn, Inc.*, 1999 MT 330, 292 Mont. 268, 971 P.2d 1227 (1998).

167. *Dobrocke v. City of Columbia Falls*, 2000 MT 179, 300 Mont. 348, 8 P.3d 71 (2000) overruling *Buck v. State*, 222 Mont. 423, 723 P.2d 210 (1986).

168. Mont. Code Ann. § 27-1-710.

169. Mont. Code Ann. § 27-1-710(1). *See also* Scott Heard, The Liability of Purveyors of Alcoholic Beverages for Torts of Intoxicated Consumers, 47 Mont. L. Rev. 495, 511 (1986).

170. Mont. Code Ann. § 27-1-710 (1989). The legislature enacted this subsection in reaction to *Nehring v. LaCounte*, 219 Mont. 462, 712 P.2d 1329 (1986). *Nehring* abrogated the common law rule of nonliablity, reasoned on the basis of causation.

171. Mont. Code Ann. § 27-1-710(3).

172. *Id.*

173. *Cusenbary v. Mortensen d/b/a Town Tavern*, 1999 MT 221, 296 Mont. 25, 987 P.2d 351 (1999). This case demonstrates that the Montana Supreme Court will readily impose liability on alcohol purveyors. After an evening of drinking, a bar patron was taken to his vehicle in a wheel chair. This bar patron would lose control of his legs after consuming alcohol, due to a previous paralyzation. His friends assisted and placed the patron in the passenger side of a vehicle. While sitting in the vehicle, the patron apparently moved to the driver's side of the vehicle, started it and drove through the wall of the bar, injuring the plaintiff. A jury found the bar owner liable, and the Montana Supreme Court affirmed.

174. *Id.*

175. Mont. Code Ann. § 2-9-108.

176. *Jim's Excavating Service, Inc. v. HKM Associates*, 265 Mont. 494, 878 P.2d 248 (1994).

177. *Fillinger v. Northwestern Agency, Inc. of Great Falls*, 283 Mont. 71, 938 P.2d 1347 (1997).

178. *Olson v. Parchen*, 249 Mont. 342, 816 P.2d 423 (1991).

179. *Durbin v. Ross*, 276 Mont. 463, 469, 916 P.2d 758, 762 (1996).

180. Mont. R. Civ. P. 9(b); *State ex rel. State Compensation Mut. Ins. Fund v. Berg*, 279 Mont. 161, 176–78, 927 P.2d 975, 983 (1996).

181. Mont. Code Ann. § 28-2-406.

182. *Mattingly v. First Bank of Lincoln*, 285 Mont. 209, 218, 947 P.2d 66, 71 (1997).

183. *Simmons v. Jenkins*, 230 Mont. 429, 435, 750 P.2d 1067, 1071 (1988).

184. *McJunkin v. Kaufman & Broad Home Systems,* 229 Mont. 432, 439, 748 P.2d 910, 915 (1987).

185. *Drilcon, Inc. v. Roil Energy Corp.,* 230 Mont. 166, 172, 749 P.2d 1058, 1061 (1988).

186. *See McGregor v. Mommer,* 220 Mont. 98, 109, 714 P.2d 536, 543 (1986).

187. *Mattingly v. First Bank of Lincoln,* 285 Mont. 209, 216, 947 P.2d 66, 70 (1997), citing *Kitchen Krafters v. Eastside Bank of Montana,* 242 Mont. 155, 165, 789 P.2d 567, 573 (1990).

188. Mont. Code Ann. § 30-14-142.

189. Mont. Code Ann. § 30-14-103.

190. 15 U.S.C. § 45(a)(1), as amended; Mont. Code Ann. § 30-14-104(1).

191. Mont. Code Ann. § 30-14-105.

192. Mont. Code Ann. §§ 30-14-101(1), 30-14-111.

193. Mont. Code Ann. § 30-14-113.

194. Mont. Code Ann. § 30-14-111.

195. Mont. Code Ann. § 30-14-121.

196. Mont. Code Ann. § 30-14-133.

197. Mont. Code Ann. §§ 30-14-132, 30-14-133.

198. Mont. Code Ann. § 30-14-131.

199. Mont. Code Ann. § 30-14-141.

200. Mont. Code Ann.§ 30-14-142(2).

201. Mont. Code Ann. § 30-14-142(3).

202. Specifically, a person who purchases or leases goods or services primarily for personal, family, or household purposes. *See* Mont. Code Ann. § 30-14-133(1).

203. Mont. Code Ann. § 30-14-133(1).

204. *Id.*

205. Mont. Code Ann. § 30-14-133(3).

206. Mont. Code Ann. § 30-14-502(3).

207. Mont. Code Ann. §§ 30-14-501–508.

208. Mont. Code Ann. § 30-14-508.

209. Mont. Code Ann. § 30-14-502(2).

210. *Bradley v. North Country Auto & Marine,* 2000 MT 81, 299 Mont. 157, 999 P.2d 308 (2000).

211. *Id.*

212. *Id.*

213. Mont. Code Ann. § 30-14-503.

214. *Id.*

215. *Id.*

216. *Id.*

217. Mont. Code Ann. § 30-14-504(1).

218. Mont. Code Ann. § 30-14-505.

219. Mont. Code Ann. § 30-14-505(2).

220. Mont. Code Ann. §§ 30-14-504(2), 30-14-504(3).

221. Mont. Code Ann. § 30-14-504(4).

222. Mont. Code Ann. § 30-14-504(5).

223. Mont. Code Ann. § 30-14-506(1).

224. Mont. Code Ann. § 30-14-506(2).

225. *Id.*

226. Mont. Code Ann. § 30-14-506(3).

227. Mont. Code Ann. § 30-14-506(4).

228. Mont. Code Ann. § 30-14-507(1).

229. *Id.*

230. *Id.*

231. *Id.*

232. Mont. Code Ann. §§ 30-14-1001–1005.

233. Mont. Code Ann. §§ 30-14-1101–1113.

234. Mont. Code Ann. §§ 30-14-1401–1414.

235. Mont. Code Ann. § 27-1-220(1).

236. Mont. Code Ann. § 27-1-220(2).

237. Mont. Code Ann. § 27-1-220(2)(b). The Unfair Claims Settlement Practices Act is codified at Mont. Code Ann. §§ 33-18-201, *et seq.*

238. *Purcell v. Automatic Gas Distributors, Inc.*, 207 Mont. 223, 230, 673 P.2d 1246, 1250 (1983); *Lee v. Armstrong*, 244 Mont. 289, 296, 798 P.2d 84, 88 (1990).

239. Mont. Code Ann. § 2-9-105. *See also White v. State*, 203 Mont. 363, 370–72, 661 P.2d 1272, 1275–76 (1983) (state immunity from punitive damages liability does not violate equal protection).

240. Mont. Code Ann. § 33-15-317. The current statute was enacted in 1987, after the Montana Supreme Court held that the language in the insurance policy relied on by the company to deny the payment of punitive damages was ambiguous and should be construed against the company to allow payment of punitive damages. *See Fitzgerald v. W. Fire Ins. Co.*, 209 Mont. 213, 216–17, 679 P.2d 790, 792 (1984).

241. *First Bank of Billings v. Transamerica Ins. Co.*, 209 Mont. 93, 103, 679 P.2d 1217, 1223 (1984), followed in *Fitzgerald v. W. Fire Ins. Co.*, 209 Mont. 213, 216–17, 679 P.2d 790, 792 (1984).

242. Mont. Code Ann. § 27-1-221(1).

243. *Weinberg v. Farmers St. Bank of Worden*, 231 Mont. 10, 31, 752 P.2d 719, 732–33 (1988).

244. Mont. Code Ann. §§ 27-1-221(2), 27-1-221(3).

245. Title 28, chapter 2, Mont. Code Ann.

246. Mont. Code Ann. § 27-1-221(4).

247. Mont. Code Ann. § 27-1-221(3).

248. Mont. Code Ann. § 27-1-221(4).

249. Mont. Code Ann. § 27-1-221(2).

250. Mont. Code Ann. § 27-1-221(6).

251. Mont. Code Ann. § 27-1-221(5).

252. Mont. Code Ann. § 27-1-221(7).

253. *Id.*

254. Mont. Code Ann. §§ 27-1-221(7)(b) & (c).

255. Mont. Code Ann. § 27-1-221(7)(c). *See Dees v. Am. Nat'l Fire Ins. Co.*, 260 Mont. 431, 448–49, 861 P.2d 141, 151–52 (1993) (trial court's reduction in punitive damages upheld where court performed its duty of reviewing the damages and reducing them when it found passion and prejudice).

256. Mont. Code Ann. § 27-1-513.

257. Mont. Code Ann. § 27-1-512.

258. Mont. Code Ann. § 27-1-501 (1987). *See also* Mont. Code Ann. § 27-1-502 (survival of counterclaim).

259. Mont. Code Ann. § 27-1-501(2).

260. *Phillips v. General Motors Corp.*, 2000 MT 55, 298 Mont. 438, 995 P.2d 1002 (2000).

261. Mont. Code Ann. § 27-1-513.

262. Mont. Code Ann. § 27-1-512.

263. Mont. Code Ann. § 27-1-501.

264. Mont. Code. Ann. § 27-1-323.

265. *Mize v. Rocky Mountain Bell Telephone Co.*, 38 Mont. 521, 100 P. 971 (1909).

266. *Dawson v. Hill & Hill Truck Lines*, 206 Mont. 325, 671 P.2d 589 (1983).

267. Mont. Code Ann. § 27-1-501.

268. *Swanson v. Champion International Corp.*, 197 Mont. 509, 646 P.2d 1166 (1982).

NEBRASKA

A. STATUTES OF LIMITATION

In Nebraska, civil actions can only be commenced within the time prescribed after the cause of action accrued.[1] A cause of action accrues when the aggrieved party has the right to institute and maintain the suit.[2]

Causes of action alleged to have arisen from a breach of a written contract can only be brought within five years.[3] Causes of action alleged to have arisen from the breach of an oral contract can only be brought within four years.[4]

Actions for invasion of privacy,[5] libel,[6] and slander[7] must be brought within one year.

An action based on professional negligence must be brought within two years.[8] However, the action can be brought within one year of the date of the discovery of the professional negligence, if the cause of action is not discovered and could not reasonably be discovered during the original two-year period.[9] Furthermore, there is a ten-year period of repose (calculated from the date of the rendering or the failure to render the professional service which forms the basis of the claim) after which no action for professional negligence may be brought.[10]

Actions that can only be brought within four years include: an action for trespass upon real property, taking personal property, or an action based on fraud.[11] In the case of an action based on fraud, the cause of action does not generally accrue until the discovery of the fraud.[12] Actions based upon the tortious interference with a business relationship must be brought within four years.[13]

Product liability actions must also be brought within four years of the date that the death, damage, or injury complained of has occurred.[14] Nebraska, however, does impose a ten-year statute of repose on product liability actions that applies from the date that the product, when manufactured in Nebraska, was first sold or leased for consumption or use.[15] For products manufactured outside of Nebraska, the statute of repose for the state or country where product was manufactured is applicable, but in no event will the statute of repose be less than ten years.[15.1] A special rule applies to actions for damages from exposure to asbestos. Such actions shall be commenced within four years after the injured person was informed of the discovery of the injury by medical authorities or within four years after the discovery of facts which would reasonably lead to discovery of the injury.[16]

An action based upon an alleged discriminatory housing practice must be commenced within two years.[17] An action based upon the Nebraska Consumer Protection Statute must be brought within four years.[18]

Any action against the state must be brought within two years of the date the claim arose.[19] For an action brought under the Political Subdivisions Tort Claims Act, the claimant must make a claim in writing to the governing body within one year after the claim accrued and the suit must be brought within two years after the cause of action accrued.[20] A cause of action accrues, thereby starting the period of limitations, when the plaintiff discovers, or should have discovered, the political subdivision's negligence.[21]

Actions which are not specified must be brought within four years after the cause of action accrued.[22] The statute of limitations period applicable to a particular claim may be tolled by a specified disability.[23]

B. TORT REFORM

The Nebraska Legislature has not enacted any tort reform laws, although some tort reform bills have been introduced in the Unicameral.

C. "NO FAULT" LIMITATIONS

No applicable Nebraska law exists regarding no fault limitations for motor vehicle accidents.

D. THE STANDARD FOR NEGLIGENCE

In order to establish negligence, the plaintiff must show that there was a legal duty on the part of the defendant to protect the plaintiff from injury.[24] Whether a duty is owed to the plaintiff is a question of law dependent on the facts in a particular situation.[25] The plaintiff must also establish that the defendant failed to discharge the legal duty and that there was damage proximately resulting from the defendant's failure to discharge the duty.[26] The duty that applies in negligence cases is that the defendant must conform to the legal standard of reasonable conduct in light of the apparent risk.[27]

Nebraska also recognizes a professional standard of care. In professional negligence cases, the burden is on the plaintiff to demonstrate the generally recognized professional standard of care.[28] Generally, the plaintiff cannot establish a *prima facie* case of professional negligence without expert testimony.[29] Many of the procedures applicable to claims of malpractice against health care providers are governed by the Nebraska Hospital-Medical Liability Act.[30]

Absent a duty of care, no negligence action will lie.[31] The Nebraska Supreme Court has stated that a duty to warn or control another's conduct could be imposed where there is a special relationship between the defendant and the victim or the dangerous person.[32]

The standard of care expected of children in Nebraska is that the child must conform to the conduct of a reasonable person of like age, intelligence, and experience under similar circumstances.[33] Nebraska does not have any arbitrary presumptions as to negligence that are based upon the age of the child.[34]

E. CAUSATION

In order to prevail on a negligence claim, the plaintiff must prove by a preponderance of the evidence that the defendant's claimed negligence was a proximate cause of the plaintiff's damages or that it was a cause that proximately contributed to the plaintiff's damages.[35] The defendant's negligent conduct is the proximate cause of the plaintiff's injury where it was a substantial factor in bringing about the harm.[36] Proximate cause is also described as the cause which in the natural and continuous sequence, unbroken by an efficient intervening cause, produces the injury and without which the injury would not have occurred.[37]

F. CONTRIBUTORY NEGLIGENCE, COMPARATIVE NEGLIGENCE, AND ASSUMPTION OF RISK

1. Contributory Negligence

For causes of action accruing before February 8, 1992, contributory negligence still operates as an absolute defense where the negligence of the plaintiff was more than slight and the negligence of the defendant was less than gross.[38] For causes of action arising on or after February 8, 1992, contributory negligence operates as a complete bar to recovery when the negligence of the claimant is equal to or greater than the total negligence of all persons against whom recovery is sought.[39] In Nebraska, a plaintiff is contributorily negligent if (1) he or she fails to protect himself or herself from injury, (2) his or her conduct concurs and cooperates with the defendant's actionable negligence, and (3) his or her conduct contributes to his or her injury as a proximate cause.[40]

2. Comparative Negligence

Under the Nebraska statutory framework, comparative negligence is termed contributory negligence.[41] In actions that accrue on or after February 8, 1992, any contributory negligence chargeable to the claimant reduces proportionately the amount awarded as damages for an injury attributable to the claimant's contributory negligence, except that if the claimant's contributory negligence is equal to or greater than the negligence of all persons against whom recovery is sought the claimant is totally barred from recovery.[42]

In the event of a settlement with one or more of several potentially responsible parties, the "claim of the claimant . . . [is] reduced by the amount of the released person's share of the obligation as determined by the trier of fact."[43]

3. Assumption of Risk

Assumption of risk remains an affirmative defense in Nebraska.[44] Assumption of risk contains three essential elements: (1) that the person knew of and understood the specific danger, (2) the person voluntarily exposed himself or herself to the danger, and (3) the person's injury or death or the harm to property occurred as a result of his or her exposure to the danger.[45] The defendant has the burden to establish the elements of assumption of the risk before the defense, as a question of fact, may be submitted to the jury.[46]

G. *RES IPSA LOQUITUR* AND INHERENTLY DANGEROUS ACTIVITIES

1. *Res Ipsa Loquitur*

Res ipsa loquitur permits an inference of negligence to be drawn when: (1) the instrumentality causing the injury is under the exclusive control of the defendant; and (2) the injury is one that would not ordinarily occur in the absence of negligence. In addition, the defendant cannot have an explanation or defense which precludes liability.[47] A plaintiff may not allege both specific acts of negligence and *res ipsa loquitur*.[48]

2. Inherently Dangerous Activities

The issue of whether or not Nebraska has adopted the doctrine of strict liability for ultrahazardous or abnormally dangerous activities has not yet been decided.[49] However, it has been stated that the degree of care required varies with the circumstances and the degree of care required increases greatly when a person is dealing with a dangerous instrumentality.[50]

H. NEGLIGENCE *PER SE*

Ordinarily, in Nebraska, the violation of a statute is only evidence of negligence and not negligence *per se*.[51] However, the Nebraska Supreme Court has held that the violation of a specific statute pertaining to scaffolding does constitute negligence *per se*.[52] Additionally, there is some limited authority that the violation of a statute providing for the protection of individuals constitutes negligence *per se*.[53]

I. JOINT AND SEVERAL LIABILITY

Nebraska common law provides for joint and several liability for wrongdoers acting jointly or through the cooperation of several parties or in the case of contemporaneous acts not done in concert.[54] Under common law joint and several liability, any of the tortfeasors may be held liable for the entire amount of damage suffered by the plaintiff.[55]

Nebraska law on this subject, however, has been changed recently by statute.[56] Under current law, in cases where the joint tortfeasors did not act in a common enterprise or plan, the plaintiff can only recover non-economic damages from any one tortfeasor in proportion to that tortfeasor's percentage of negligence.[57] The plaintiff can still recover economic damages from any one of the defendants under joint and several liability.[58] Nebraska does not allow the allocation of damages to intentional tortfeasors under comparative negligence law.[59]

Nebraska law has not changed regarding joint and several liability in cases where the defendants acted as part of a common enterprise or plan or acted in concert to cause harm.[60] In that case, the plaintiff can still recover all damages from any one of the defendants regardless of their proportion of negligence.[61]

Under Nebraska law, a settlement with an agent or employee operates as a settlement with the principal who was vicariously liable for the actions of the employee, regardless of the intent of the parties to the settlement.[62] Additionally, the same result applies whether the agreement was reached through a release or a covenant not to sue.[63] Furthermore, the Nebraska Supreme Court has stated that in cases where the persons are not actively joint tortfeasors, but one person actually committed the tort and the other person is secondarily liable, the acceptance of satisfaction from one of the parties discharges the other party as well.[64]

J. INDEMNITY

Indemnity shifts the plaintiff's entire loss from one defendant to another.[65] Indemnity may be provided for in a contract.[66] In addition, a party whose negligence is merely passive neglect may have indemnity from any active wrongdoer.[67] In describing what is meant by passive neglect, the Nebraska Supreme Court has stated that it includes "technical," "constructive," "vicarious," or "passive" negligence and the difference between these terms is merely a question of semantics.[68] As a result, an employer is entitled to indemnification from a negligent employee because the employer's liability is merely derivative.[69] A claim for indemnity does not accrue at the time of the underlying transaction, but at the time the indemnity claimant suffers loss.[70]

K. BAR OF WORKERS' COMPENSATION STATUTE

Under the Nebraska Workers' Compensation Act,[71] if an employee files a claim under the act or accepts any payment from the employer under the act, then the action of the employee constitutes a release to the employer of all claims at law arising from the injury.[72] Under the Nebraska Act, the employee is permitted to recover for a personal injury arising out of the employment as long as the employee was not willfully negligent.[73]

An employee who is paid benefits under the Nebraska Act is not barred from seeking damages from a third party.[74] However, the employee's right to seek damages against a third party is subject to the employer's right of subrogation and an employer who has paid or is making payments to the employee shall be made a party to the suit.[75] Additionally, Nebraska law also allows the employer to bring an independent action against the third party.[76] In fact, the employer can recover any amount that the employee would have been entitled to recover, however, any recovery in excess of payments made to the employee shall be paid to the employee.[77]

L. PREMISES LIABILITY

Historically, Nebraska law defined the duty owed by landowners to entrants upon their land based upon the classification of the entrants as either licensees, invitees, or trespassers.[78] However, the distinction between licensees and invitees has recently been abrogated.[79] A standard of reasonable care now applies to all lawful visitors.[80] As to a trespasser, there is no duty of reasonable care owed to those not lawfully on the property; the landowner must only refrain from willfully and wantonly injuring the trespasser.[81]

M. DRAM SHOP LIABILITY

The Nebraska Supreme Court has refused to impose dram shop liability where the legislature repealed statutes that had previously established dram shop liability in the state.[82] Additionally, the Nebraska Supreme Court has not authorized a minor's claim for injuries sustained as the result of being served alcoholic liquors.[83] The court noted that it is a violation of statute to sell alcohol to minors, but that the sale of alcohol was not the proximate cause of any injuries the minor might suffer.[84]

N. ECONOMIC LOSS

A plaintiff cannot recover economic losses in tort based on negligent manufacture or strict liability in the absence of physical harm to persons or property caused by the defective product.[85] Nebraska does recognize the tort of intentional interference with a business relationship.[86]

O. FRAUD AND MISREPRESENTATION

The elements of fraud must be proved by clear and convincing evidence.[87] The plaintiff must prove that the defendant: (1) made a material representation; (2) the representation was false; (3) the representation was known to be false or there was a reckless disregard as to its truth or falsity; (4) the defendant intended for the plaintiff to rely on the statement; (5) the plaintiff justifiably relied upon the false statement; and (6) the plaintiff suffered damage as a result.[88]

Negligent misrepresentation, on the other hand, is defined as providing false information for the guidance of others where the other party justifiably relies upon the information, provided the defendant failed to exercise reasonable care in obtaining or communicating the information.[89] Thus, the defendant need not know that the information is untrue in order to be held liable.

Fraudulent concealment is also available as a theory of recovery in Nebraska and consists of six elements.[90] The plaintiff must prove that: (1) the defendant concealed or suppressed a material fact; (2) the defendant had knowledge of the material fact; (3) the material fact was not within the reasonably diligent attention, observation, and judgment of the plaintiff; (4) the defendant suppressed or concealed the fact with the intention that the plaintiff be misled; (5) the plaintiff reasonably was misled; and (6) the plaintiff suffered damage as a result.[91]

P. CONSUMER FRAUD STATUTES

The Nebraska Consumer Protection Act,[92] protects consumers from unfair or deceptive acts in the conduct of any trade or commerce.[93] The Attorney General may bring an action against any person to restrain prohibited unfair acts.[94] Any person injured in his business or property, by a violation specified in the act, may bring a civil action to enjoin further violations and to recover the actual damages sustained as a result of the violations, along with the costs of the suit, including a reasonable attorney's fee.[95] However, the Act does not apply to purely private wrongs that do not affect the public interest.[96] As previously mentioned, a cause of action under the Consumer Protection Act must be commenced within four years.

Q. **PUNITIVE DAMAGES**

Nebraska does not allow the recovery of punitive damages.[97] In Nebraska, the measure of recovery in all civil cases is limited to compensation for the actual injury sustained.[98]

R. **WRONGFUL DEATH AND SURVIVORSHIP ACTIONS**

Nebraska has authorized an action for wrongful death by statute.[99] The action must be commenced within two years of the death of the decedent.[100] However, if the death is the result of malpractice, the action must be brought within two years of the last date upon which professional services were rendered.[101] An action under the wrongful death statute is brought by and in the name of the personal representative for the exclusive benefit of the next of kin.[102] Recovery is limited to the pecuniary loss sustained by the next of kin,[103] but the loss of comfort, society and companionship has been adjudged to have pecuniary value.[104]

Nebraska does have a survival statute which expands upon the claims that survived at common law.[105] Claims, however, for libel, slander, malicious prosecution, assault or assault and battery, or for a nuisance abate by the death of the defendant.[106] In cases where the party died and the action survives, the court may allow the action to continue with the representative or successor in interest.[107]

Mark A. Christensen
CLINE, WILLIAMS, WRIGHT, JOHNSON & OLDFATHER, L.L.P.
1900 U.S. Bank Building
233 South 13th Street
Lincoln, Nebraska 68508-2095
(402) 474-6900
Fax (402) 474-5393
mchristensen@cline-law.com
www.cline-law.com

ENDNOTES - NEBRASKA

1. *See* Neb. Rev. Stat. § 25-201 (Supp. 2001).

2. *See Weiss v. Weiss*, 179 Neb. 714, 140 N.W.2d 15 (1966).

3. *See* Neb. Rev. Stat. § 25-205 (2000).

4. *See* Neb. Rev. Stat. § 25-206 (1995).

5. *See* Neb. Rev. Stat. § 20-211 (1995).

6. *See* Neb. Rev. Stat. § 25-208 (2000).

7. *See* Neb. Rev. Stat. § 25-208 (2000).

8. *See* Neb. Rev. Stat. § 25-222 (1995).

9. *See* Neb. Rev. Stat. § 25-222 (1995).

10. *See* Neb. Rev. Stat. § 25-222 (1995).

11. *See* Neb. Rev. Stat. § 25-207 (1995).

12. *See* Neb. Rev. Stat. § 25-207 (1995).

13. *See Hroch v. Farmland Industries, Inc.*, 4 Neb. App. 709, 714, 548 N.W.2d 367, 371 (1996) (utilizing Neb. Rev. Stat. § 25-207 (1995) to find the applicable statute of limitations).

14. *See* Neb. Rev. Stat. § 25-224(1) (Supp. 2001).

15. *See* Neb. Rev. Stat. § 25-224(2)(a)(i) (Supp. 2001).

15.1. *See* Neb. Rev. Stat. § 25-224(2)(a)(ii) (Supp. 2001).

16. *See* Neb. Rev. Stat. § 25-224(5) (Supp. 2001).

17. *See* Neb. Rev. Stat. § 20-342 (1997).

18. *See* Neb. Rev. Stat. § 59-1612 (1998).

19. *See* Neb. Rev. Stat. § 25-218 (1995).

20. *See* Neb. Rev. Stat. § 13-919(1) (1997).

21. *See Polinski v. Omaha Pub. Power Dist.*, 251 Neb. 14, 18, 554 N.W.2d 636, 639 (1996).

22. *See* Neb. Rev. Stat. § 25-212 (1995).

23. *See* Neb. Rev. Stat. § 25-213 (1995) (specifying that people with mental disorders, prisoners, and those within the age of twenty at the time a cause of action accrued can still bring the action within the specified time limits applicable to the action after the disability is removed).

24. *See Doe v. Gunny's Limited Partnership*, 256 Neb. 653, 658, 593 N.W.2d 284, 289 (1999).

25. *See id.* at 659, 593 N.W.2d at 289 (citing *Gans v. Parkview Plaza Partnership*, 253 Neb. 373, 571 N.W.2d 261 (1997)).

26. *See id.* at 658, 593 N.W.2d at 289.

27. *See id.* at 658, 593 N.W.2d at 289 (citing *Anderson/Couvillon v. Nebraska Dept. of Soc. Servs.*, 248 Neb. 651, 538 N.W.2d 732 (1995)).

28. *See Doe v. Zedek*, 255 Neb. 963, 587 N.W.2d 885 (1999).

29. *See Boyd v. Chakraborty*, 250 Neb. 575, 581, 550 N.W.2d 44, 48 (1996).

30. *See* Neb. Rev. Stat. §§ 44-2801 to 44-2855 (1998).

31. *See Popple v. Rose*, 254 Neb. 1, 6, 573 N.W.2d 765, 769 (1998).

32. *See id.* at 7, 573 N.W.2d at 770.

33. *See Camerlinck v. Thomas*, 209 Neb. 843, 858, 312 N.W.2d 260, 268 (1981) (citing Restatement (Second) of Torts § 283A (1965)).

34. *See id.* at 859, 312 N.W.2d at 268.

35. *See Doe v. Zedek*, 255 Neb. 963, 970, 587 N.W.2d 885, 891 (1999).

36. *See Travelers Indem. Co. v. Center Bank*, 202 Neb. 294, 299, 275 N.W.2d 73, 76 (1979).

37. *See id.*

38. *See* Neb. Rev. Stat. § 25-21,185 (1995).

39. *See* Neb. Rev. Stat. § 25-21,185.09 (1995).

40. *See Brandon v. County of Richardson*, 261 Neb. 636, 666, 624 N.W.2d 604, 626-27 (2001).

41. *See* Neb. Rev. Stat. § 25-21,185.09 (1995).

42. *See* Neb. Rev. Stat. § 25-21,185.09 (1995).

43. *See* Neb. Rev. Stat. § 25-21,185.11 (1995).

44. *See* Neb. Rev. Stat. § 25-21,185.12 (1995).

45. *See* Neb. Rev. Stat. § 25-21,185.12 (1995), *see also Pleiss v. Barnes*, 260 Neb. 770, 775, 619 N.W.2d 825, 829 (2000).

46. *See Everts v. Hardcopf-Bickley*, 257 Neb. 151, 155-56, 595 N.W.2d 911, 915 (1999).

47. *See Darrah v. Bryan Memorial Hosp.*, 253 Neb. 710, 714, 571 N.W.2d 783, 787 (1998).

48. *See Bargmann v. Soll Oil Co.*, 253 Neb. 1018, 1026, 574 N.W.2d 478, 485 (1998).

49. *See Anderson v. Nashua Corp.*, 246 Neb. 420, 519 N.W.2d 275 (1994).

50. *See Martinez v. Hoveling*, 184 Neb. 560, 562, 169 N.W.2d 428, 430 (1969).

51. *See Parrish v. Omaha Public Power Dist.*, 242 Neb. 783, 496 N.W.2d 902 (1993); *Vanek v. Prohaska*, 233 Neb. 848, 448 N.W.2d 573 (1989).

52. *See Oddo v. Speedway Scaffold Co.*, 233 Neb. 1, 10, 443 N.W.2d 596, 603 (1989) (finding that Neb. Rev. Stat. § 48-425 (1998) requires that scaffolding be erected and constructed in a safe, suitable, and proper manner and that the violation of the statute amounts to negligence *per se* and not mere evidence of negligence).

53. *See Walker v. Klopp*, 99 Neb. 794, 157 N.W. 962 (1916) (holding that it was negligence *per se* for the defendant to allow his son to operate the defendant's automobile when he was below the age required by statute to operate a motor vehicle).

54. *See Lackman v. Rousselle*, 257 Neb. 87, 95, 596 N.W.2d 15, 21 (1999).

55. *See id.*

56. *See* Neb. Rev. Stat. § 25-21,185.10 (1995).

57. *See, e.g., Lackman v. Rousselle*, 257 Neb. 87, 95, 596 N.W.2d 15, 21 (1991) (citing Neb. Rev. Stat. § 25-21,185.10 (1995)).

58. *See* Neb. Rev. Stat. § 25-21,185.10 (1995).

59. *See Brandon v. County of Richardson*, 261 Neb. 636, 656, 624 N.W.2d 604, 620 (2001).

60. *See* Neb. Rev. Stat. § 25-21,185.10 (1995).

61. *See* Neb. Rev. Stat. § 25-21,185.10 (1995).

62. *See McCurry v. School Dist. of Valley*, 242 Neb. 504, 521, 496 N.W.2d 433, 444 (1993).

63. *See id.*

64. *See Brown v. American Tel. & Tel. Co.*, 252 Neb. 95, 99, 560 N.W.2d 482, 486 (1997).

65. *See, e.g., Lackman v. Rousselle*, 7 Neb. App. 698, 712, 585 N.W.2d 469, 480 (1998), *aff'd*, 257 Neb. 87, 596 N.W.2d 15 (1999) (stating that indemnity means a shifting of the entire loss, while contribution means that the loss is shared).

66. *See, e.g., Warner v. Reagan Buick, Inc.*, 240 Neb. 668, 483 N.W.2d 764 (1992); *Oddo v. Speedway Scaffold Co.*, 233 Neb. 1, 443 N.W.2d 596 (1989).

67. *See Hiway 20 Terminal, Inc. v. Tri-County Agri-Supply, Inc.*, 232 Neb. 763, 770, 443 N.W.2d 872, 876 (1980).

68. *See id.*

69. *See Kocsis v. Harrison*, 249 Neb. 274, 280-81, 543 N.W.2d 164, 169 (1996).

70. *See Id.* at 281, 543 N.W.2d at 169.

71. *See* Neb. Rev. Stat. § 48-101 to 1,118 (1998).

72. *See* Neb. Rev. Stat. § 48-148 (1998).

73. *See* Neb. Rev. Stat. § 48-101 (1998).

74. *See* Neb. Rev. Stat. § 48-118 (2000).

75. *See* Neb. Rev. Stat. § 48-118 (2000).

76. *See* Neb. Rev. Stat. § 48-118 (2000).

77. *See* Neb. Rev. Stat. § 48-118 (2000).

78. *See Heins v. Webster County*, 250 Neb. 750, 753, 552 N.W.2d 51, 53 (1996).

79. *See id.* at 761, 552 N.W.2d at 57.

80. *See id.* (the standard of reasonable care applicable to lawful visitors was applied by the court to causes of action arising after the date of the decision).

81. *See, e.g., Terry v. Metzger,* 241 Neb. 795, 491 N.W.2d 50 (1992).

82. *See Arant v. G.H., Inc.,* 229 Neb. 729, 731, 428 N.W.2d 631, 632 (1988).

83. *See Pelzek v. American Legion,* 236 Neb. 608, 611, 463 N.W.2d 321, 324 (1990).

84. *See id.* at 610, 463 N.W.2d at 323.

85. *See National Crane Corp. v. Ohio Steel Tube Co.,* 213 Neb. 782, 790, 332 N.W.2d 39, 44 (1983).

86. *See, e.g., Koster v. P & P Enterprises, Inc.,* 248 Neb. 759, 539 N.W.2d 274 (1995) (allowing the plaintiff to recover over $125,000 in damages for stock, salary, and commissions not paid as a result of the defendant's conduct).

87. *See Fletcher v. Mathew,* 233 Neb. 853, 858-59, 448 N.W.2d 576, 581 (1989).

88. *See Gibb v. Citicorp Mortg., Inc.,* 246 Neb. 355, 360, 518 N.W.2d 910, 916 (1994).

89. *See id.* at 372, 518 N.W.2d at 922.

90. *See id.* at 361, 518 N.W.2d at 916.

91. *See id.* (citing *Nelson v. Cheney,* 224 Neb. 756, 401 N.W.2d 472 (1987)).

92. *See* Neb. Rev. Stat. §§ 59-1601 to 1623 (1998).

93. *See* Neb. Rev. Stat. § 59-1602 (1998).

94. *See* Neb. Rev. Stat. § 59-1608 (1998).

95. *See* Neb. Rev. Stat. § 59-1609 (1998).

96. *See Nelson v. Lusterstone Surfacing Co.,* 258 Neb. 678, 684, 605 N.W.2d 136, 143 (2000).

97. *See Abel v. Conover,* 170 Neb. 926, 929, 104 N.W.2d 684, 688 (1960).

98. *See id.*

99. *See* Neb. Rev. Stat. § 30-809 (1995).

100. *See* Neb. Rev. Stat. § 30-810 (1995).

101. *See Alegent Health Bergan Mercy Medical Center v. Haworth*, 260 Neb. 63, 72, 615 N.W.2d 460, 467-68 (2000).

102. *See* Neb. Rev. Stat. § 30-810 (1995).

103. *See, e.g., Nelson v. Dolan*, 230 Neb. 848, 434 N.W.2d 25 (1989).

104. *See, e.g., Selders v. Armentrout*, 190 Neb. 275, 207 N.W.2d 686 (1973).

105. *See* Neb. Rev. Stat. § 25-1401 (1995) (stating that actions for mesne profits, injury to real or personal estate, or any deceit or fraud survive).

106. *See* Neb. Rev. Stat. § 25-1402 (1995).

107. *See* Neb. Rev. Stat. § 25-322 (1995).

NEVADA

A. STATUTES OF LIMITATION

Civil actions may only be commenced within the periods proscribed in Nevada Revised Statute (NRS), Chapter 11, after the cause of action shall have accrued, except where a different limitation is prescribed by statute.[1] The "discovery" rule applies.[2]

The following actions have a six-year statute of limitations: (1) an action upon a judgment or decree of any court of the United States, or any state or territory within the United States, or the renewal thereof; and (2) an action upon a contract, obligation or liability founded upon an instrument in writing, except those for the recovery of possession of real property.[3]

A cause of action for personal injuries resulting from breach of warranty falls within the four or six-year statute of limitations (six years for an express promise in writing, four years for an implied warranty).[4]

The following actions have a four-year statute of limitations: (1) an action on an open account for goods, wares and merchandise sold and delivered; (2) an action for any article charged on an account in a store; and (3) an action upon a contract, obligation or liability not founded upon an instrument in writing.[5]

A three-year statute of limitations applies to the following actions: (1) an action upon a liability created by statute, other than a penalty or forfeiture; (2) an action for waste or trespass of real property; (3) an action for taking, detaining or injuring personal property, including actions for specific recovery thereof; and (d) an action for relief on the ground of fraud or mistake, but the cause of action in such a case shall be deemed to accrue upon the discovery by the aggrieved party of the facts constituting fraud of mistake.[6]

The following actions have a two-year statute of limitations: (1) an action against a sheriff, coroner or constable upon liability incurred by acting in his official capacity, or by the omission of an official duty; (2) an action upon a statute for penalty or forfeiture, where the action is given to a person or the state; (3) an action for libel, slander, assault, battery, false imprisonment or seduction; (4) an action against a sheriff or other officer for the escape of a prisoner arrested or imprisoned on civil process; and (5) an action to recover damages for injuries to a person or for the death of a person caused by the wrongful act or neglect of another.[7]

The following action has a one-year statute of limitations: an action against an officer, or officer de facto, to recover property seized in his official capacity, or to recover the value of property so seized, or for damages for the seizure, detention or sale of, or injury to personal property seized, or for damages done to any person or property in making the seizure.[8]

Nevada's statutes of repose, NRS §§ 11.203-11.205, bar actions for injury or wrongful death resulting from deficient construction after a certain number of years from the date construction was substantially completed. An action based on a known deficiency may not be commenced more than ten years after substantial completion;[9] an action based on a latent deficiency may not be commenced after eight years;[10] and an action based on a patent deficiency may not be commenced after six years.[11]

An action for injury or death against a provider of health care may not be commenced more than four years after the date of injury or two years after the plaintiff discovers or should have discovered the injury, for injury to or the wrongful death of a person based upon: (1) the alleged professional negligence of the provider; (2) the rendering of professional services without consent; or (3) the error or omission in practice by the provider.[12] This time limitation is tolled: (1) for any period during which the provider has concealed any act, error or omission upon which the action is based and which is known or should have been known to him; (2) from the date a claimant files a complaint for medical malpractice before the screening panel pursuant to NRS §§ 41A.003 to 41A.069 inclusive.[13]

B. TORT REFORM

To date, the Nevada Legislature has not passed any tort reform laws nor are any currently pending, although many have been introduced.

C. "NO FAULT" LIMITATIONS

Nevada's Motor Vehicle Insurance and Financial Responsibility Act[14] provides for a bond or insurance policy as security for any judgment against the motorist and guarantees protection to one who is injured by an automobile not covered by liability insurance.[15]

Every owner of a motor vehicle which is registered or required to be registered in this state shall continuously provide, while the motor vehicle is present or registered in this state, insurance: (1) in the amount of $15,000 for bodily injury to or death of one person in any one accident; (2) subject to the limit for one person, in the amount of $30,000 for bodily injury to or death of two or more persons in any one accident; and (3) in the amount of $10,000 for injury to or destruction of property of others in any one accident, for the payment of tort liabilities arising from the maintenance or use of the motor vehicle.[16]

The failure to maintain the minimal insurance for payment of tort liabilities will require the motorist to file security (or face suspension of his operator's license) with the drivers' license division of the Department of Motor Vehicles after any accident unless the motorist has been released from liability, has been finally adjudicated not to be liable, or has executed an acknowledged written agreement providing for the payment of an agreed amount in installments with respect to all claims for injuries or damages resulting from the accident.[17]

D. THE STANDARD FOR NEGLIGENCE

The plaintiff must show that defendant owed a duty of care to the plaintiff; that defendant breached the duty; that the breach was the legal cause of plaintiff's injury; and that plaintiff suffered damages.[18] A "duty" is defined as an obligation, to which the law will give recognition and effect, to comport to a particular standard of conduct toward another, and in negligence cases, the duty is invariably the same: one must conform to a legal standard of reasonable conduct in light of the apparent risk.[19] Foreseeability of harm is a predicate to establishing the element of duty for purposes of a negligence action.[20]

"Negligence" is the failure to exercise that degree of care in a given situation which a reasonable man under similar circumstances would exercise.[21] The standard of care to be exercised under a given situation so as to avoid a charge of negligence is that of the ordinary prudent man, not that of an extraordinary prudent man.[22] Nevada recognizes a professional standard of care.[23] Though under common law a person generally owes no duty to control the dangerous conduct of another or to warn those endangered by such conduct, an exception to that rule exists in cases where the defendant bears some special relationship to the dangerous person or to the potential victim.[24]

A child is not held to the same standard of care as an adult and is only required to exercise that degree of care which ordinarily would be exercised by children of the same age, intelligence and experience.[25] There is no precise age at which, as a matter of law, a child comes to be held accountable for his actions by the standard as applies to an adult.[26] The fact that a child was only six years of age did not establish that she was incapable of negligence as a matter of law.[27]

Persons with impaired faculties are obligated to use ordinary care for their protection, and to achieve the standard of ordinary care, they must use their non-impaired faculties to rise to that standard.[28]

E. CAUSATION

No liability attaches in a negligence action unless there is a causal connection between negligence and injury.[29] Causation consists of two components: actual cause and proximate cause.[30]

To satisfy the actual causation element the plaintiff must show that but for the defendant's negligence the plaintiff's injuries would not have occurred.[31] Proximate cause is any cause which in a natural and continuous sequence, unbroken by any efficient intervening cause, produces the injury complained of and without which the result would not have occurred.[32] Negligence is not actionable unless, without intervention of intervening cause, it proximately causes harm for which the complaint was made.[33]

"Intervening cause" means not concurrent and contributing cause, but superceding cause which is itself the natural and logical cause of the harm.[34] Where an unforeseeable supervening cause intervenes between the defendant's negligence and the plaintiff's injury, the defendant is relieved of liability.[35] While criminal or tortious third-party conduct typically severs the chain of proximate causation between the plaintiff and the defendant, the chain remains unbroken when the third party's intervening intentional act is reasonably foreseeable.[36]

Proximate cause, or legal cause, consists of cause in fact and foreseeability.[37] An actor's negligent conduct is the legal cause of the harm if the conduct is a substantial factor in bringing about the harm.[38] To meet the legal causation requirement, the defendant must be able to foresee that his negligent actions may result in harm of particular variety to a certain type of plaintiff.[39] The defendant need not foresee the extent of harm or manner in which it occurred.[40]

F. CONTRIBUTORY NEGLIGENCE, COMPARATIVE NEGLIGENCE, AND ASSUMPTION OF RISK

1. Contributory Negligence

The Nevada Comparative Negligence Statute[41] abolished contributory negligence as an absolute defense in actions seeking damages for death or injury to persons or for injury to property when the plaintiff's comparative negligence is not greater than the negligence of the parties to the action against whom recovery is sought. The burden of establishing contributory negligence lies with the defendant.[42] Contributing fault on the part of the plaintiff, though it could reduce recovery under the doctrine of comparative negligence, does not negate a finding that the defendant's negligence was a proximate cause of the plaintiff's injury.[43]

2. Comparative Negligence

The Nevada Comparative Negligence Statute applies to actions seeking damages for death or injury to persons or for injury to property.[44] In those cases, the judge shall instruct the jury that: (1) the plaintiff may not recover if his comparative negligence is greater than the negligence of the defendant or the combined negligence of multiple defendants; (2) if the jury determines the plaintiff is entitled to recover, it shall return: (a) by general verdict the total amount of damages the plaintiff would be entitled to recover without regard to his comparative negligence; and (b) a special verdict indicating the percentage of negligence attributable to each party remaining in the action.[45]

Each defendant is severally liable to the plaintiff only for that portion of the judgment which represents the percentage of negligence attributable to him.[46] If a defendant settles with the plaintiff before the entry of judgment, the comparative negligence of that defendant and the amount of the settlement must not thereafter be admitted into evidence nor considered by the jury.[47] The judge shall deduct the amount of the settlement from the net sum otherwise recoverable by the plaintiff pursuant to the general and special verdicts.[48]

The comparative negligence statute does not affect the joint and several liability, if any, of the defendants in an action based upon: (1) strict liability; (2) intentional tort; (3) the emission, disposal or spillage of a toxic or hazardous substance; (4) the concerted actions of the defendants; or (5) an injury to any person or property resulting from a product which is manufactured, distributed, sold or used in this state.[49]

The comparative negligence statute, which substituted several, proportionate liability based on fault and abolished joint and several liability among joint tortfeasors, does not limit liability of a sole defendant or group of defendants whose negligence was the proximate cause of an indivisible injury to the plaintiff, where recovery was not allowed against any other defendants or group of defendants.[50]

Comparative negligence does not apply when the defendant is guilty of willful and wanton misconduct or in strict products liability actions.[51]

3. **Assumption of Risk**

With the single exception of an express assumption of risk, the assumption of risk doctrine has been subsumed by the comparative negligence statute and is no longer a bar to negligence.[52] The defense of "assumption of risk" is based on an injured plaintiff's actual knowledge of the danger, his voluntary exposure to it and consent to assume it.[53] Assumption of risk is based on theory of consent.[54]

G. *RES IPSA LOQUITOR* AND INHERENTLY DANGEROUS ACTIVITIES

1. *Res Ipsa Loquitur*

Res ipsa loquitur is a balancing doctrine where the plaintiff need not show the exact cause of injury, however, he must show that it is more probable than not that the injury resulted from the defendant's breach of duty and if that is shown, the inference of negligence on the part of the defendant arises and it is then incumbent on the defendant to come forward with rebuttal evidence.[55] The doctrine does not apply unless the event is the kind which ordinarily does not occur in the absence of someone's negligence.[56]

To create the inference of negligence plaintiff must prove that the thing or event which caused injury to the plaintiff was under the exclusive control and management of the defendant, and that the occurrence was such as in the ordinary course of things would not happen if those who had its control or management had used proper care.[57] A *res ipsa loquitur* instruction is appropriate only when the specific acts that caused the injury are unknown to the plaintiff.[58] Note that if the plaintiff's comparative negligence contributed more to the accident than did the defendant's, plaintiff may not recover damages.[59]

2. **Inherently Dangerous Activities**

The *Rylands* doctrine of strict liability as articulated in Section 519 of the Restatement (Second) of Torts has been adopted providing that one who carries on abnormally dangerous activity is subject to liability for harm to person, land or chattels of another resulting from the activity, although he has exercised utmost care.[60] Six factors are relevant to the determination of whether an activity is abnormally dangerous subjecting one who carries on the activity to strict liability: (1) existence of high degree of risk of some harm to person, land or chattels of others; (2) likelihood that the harm that results from it will be great; (3) inability to eliminate risk by exercise of reasonable care; (4) extent to which the activity is not a matter of common usage; (5) inappropriateness of the activity in the place where it is carried on; and (6) extent to which its value to the community is outweighed by its dangerous attributes.[61]

H. NEGLIGENCE *PER SE*

When a defendant violates a statute that was designed to protect the class of persons, to which the plaintiff belongs, and thereby proximately causes injury to the plaintiff, such a violation constitutes negligence *per se*, unless the defendant can show that the violation was excused.[62] A violation of a statute establishes the duty and breach elements of a negligence action under the doctrine of negligence *per se* only if the injured party belongs to the class of persons the statute is intended to protect and the injury is of the type against which the statute is intended to protect.[63]

A violation of a statute does not constitute negligence when the violation is excused or when the violation might reasonably have been expected from a person of ordinary prudence in acting in similar circumstances.[64] In the absence of legislative intent to impose civil liability, the violation of a penal statute is not negligence *per se*.[65]

I. JOINT AND SEVERAL LIABILITY

1. The Rule

Where two or more causes proximately contribute to the injuries complained of, recovery may be had against either one or both of the joint tortfeasors.[66]

2. Effect of Settlement

When a release or a covenant not to sue or not to enforce judgment is given in good faith to one of two or more persons liable in tort for the same injury or the same wrongful death:

(1) it does not discharge any of the other tortfeasors from liability for the injury or wrongful death unless its terms so provide, but it reduces the claim against the others to the extent of any amount stipulated by the release, or in the amount of the consideration paid for it, whichever is greater; and

(2) it discharges the tortfeasor to whom it is given from all liability for contribution and for equitable indemnity to any other tortfeasor.[67]

Where the plaintiff settles with one of several defendants, the jury must not be informed as to either the fact of the settlement or the amount paid.[68]

3. Contribution

Where two or more persons become jointly or severally liable in tort for the same injury to person or property or for the same wrongful death, there is a right of contribution among them even though the judgment has not been recovered against all or any of them.[69]

The right of contribution exists only in favor of a tortfeasor who has paid more than his equitable share of the common liability, and his total recovery is limited to the amount paid by him in excess of his equitable share. No tortfeasor is compelled to make contribution beyond his own equitable share of the entire liability.[70]

A tortfeasor who enters into a settlement with a claimant is not entitled to recover contribution from another tortfeasor whose liability for the injury or wrongful death is not extinguished by the settlement nor in respect to any amount paid in a settlement which is in excess of what was reasonable.[71] There is no right to contribution in favor of any tortfeasor who has intentionally caused or contributed to the injury or wrongful death.[72]

J. INDEMNITY

Indemnity shifts the burden of the entire loss from the defendant tortfeasor to another who should bear it instead.[73] Indemnity is not available in a case involving joint or concurrent tortfeasors having no legal relation to another and where each owes a duty of care to the injured party.[74]

The common law right to indemnity rests upon the difference between primary (active) and secondary (passive) liability of two persons, each of whom is made responsible by law to the injured person.[75] The difference between primary and secondary liability depends on the difference in the character or kinds of wrongs that cause injury and in the nature of the legal obligation owed by each of the wrongdoers to the injured party.[76]

Where one tortfeasor is entitled to indemnity from another, the right of the indemnity obligee is for indemnity and not contribution, and the indemnity obligor is not entitled to contribution from the obligee for any portion of his indemnity obligation.[77] No contribution exists where indemnity exists.[78]

K. BAR OF WORKERS' COMPENSATION STATUTE

The rights and remedies provided in Nevada's Industrial Insurance Act,[79] for an employee on account of an injury by accident sustained arising out of and in the course of employment shall be exclusive, except as otherwise provided in those chapters, of all other rights and remedies of the employee, his personal or legal representatives, dependents or next of kin, at common law or otherwise, on account of such injury.[80]

The terms, conditions and provisions of the Act for the payment of compensation and the amount thereof for injuries sustained or death resulting from such injuries shall be conclusive, compulsory and obligatory upon both employers and employees coming within the provisions of those chapters.[81]

If an employee receives any compensation or accident benefits under the Act, the acceptance of such compensation or benefits shall be in lieu of any other compensation, award or recovery against his employer under the laws of any other state or jurisdiction, and such employee is barred from commencing any action or proceeding for the enforcement or collection of any benefits or awards under the laws of any other state or jurisdiction.[82]

Employers who accept the Industrial Insurance Act and provide and secure compensation for injuries by accidents sustained by an employee arising out of and in the course of employment are relieved from other liability for recovery of damages or other compensation for such personal injuries; exclusive remedy provision of Act is exclusive in sense that no other common law or statutory remedy under local law is possessed by employee against his employer.[83]

The exclusivity provision of Industrial Insurance Act not only insulates the employer from liability to employees, but also from liability by way of indemnity to third party who supplied the defective product found to have caused injury to employees.[84]

Where an employee has collected benefits under these chapters and then proceeds to sue a third party for the same incident, the insured may be subrogated to the rights of the employee as against a third party and if suit is successful, the amount of compensation the employee is entitled to pursuant to this Act, including any future compensation must be reduced by the amount of the damages recovered.[85]

The employee is not limited to recovery under the Act where the employer has committed an intentional tort against the employee; instead, the employee is entitled to pursue a common law action against the employer.[86]

L. PREMISES LIABILITY

A landowner or occupant of property is not an insurer of the safety of a person on the premises, and in the absence of negligence, no liability lies.[87] An accident occurring on the premises does not of itself establish negligence.[88] A landowner or occupant owes a duty to people on the land to act reasonably under the circumstances; consideration of the status of the injured person as trespasser, licensee, or invitee is no longer determinative on this issue, but rather, determinations of liability should primarily depend upon whether the owner or occupier of land acted reasonably under the circumstances.[89] An owner is under no duty to warn of obvious dangers, however, even where the danger is obvious, the defendant may be negligent in having created the peril or in subjecting the plaintiff to the peril.[90]

M. DRAM SHOP LIABILITY

In 1995, the Legislature passed a law stating unequivocally that dram shop actions will not lie against a purveyor of alcoholic beverages: No person who serves or sells alcoholic beverages is liable in a civil action based on the grounds that the service or sale was the proximate cause of injuries inflicted by an intoxicated person upon himself or another person.[91] In light of this legislature, the courts will not entertain dram shop actions brought against purveyors of alcoholic beverages.[92]

The violation of any statute, regulation, or ordinance which regulates the sale or service of alcoholic beverages to a minor or an intoxicated person does not constitute negligence *per se* in any action brought against the server or seller for injuries inflicted by an intoxicated person upon himself or another person.[93]

N. ECONOMIC LOSS

Absent privity of contract or injury to person or property, a plaintiff cannot recover in negligence for purely economic loss.[94] A plaintiff may not recover economic loss under theories of strict products liability or negligence.[95]

The economic loss rule does not apply to negligence claims in construction defect cases asserted by owners of newly constructed homes against subcontractors.[96] The homeowners did not receive the "benefit of their bargain" and these economic losses from a defective building are not properly addressed by tort law.[97]

O. FRAUD AND MISREPRESENTATION

The Nevada Rules of Civil Procedure require that a cause of action for fraud be pleaded with particularity.[98] The circumstances that must be detailed in the complaint alleging fraud include averments as to time, place, identity of the parties involved, and the nature of the fraud or mistake; malice, intent, knowledge and other conditions of the mind of a person may be averred generally.[99]

To establish fraud, deceit or intentional misrepresentation, the plaintiff has the burden of proving by clear and convincing evidence: (1) a false representation made by the defendant; (2) the defendant's knowledge or belief that its representation was false or that defendant had an insufficient basis of information for making the representation; (3) that defendant intended to induce the plaintiff to act or refrain from acting upon the misrepresentation; (4) that the plaintiff justifiably relied on the representation; and (5) damage to the plaintiff as a result of relying on the misrepresentation.[100]

Nevada has adopted the Restatement (Second) of Torts § 552 definition of the tort of negligent misrepresentation: One who, in the course of his business, profession or employment, or in any other action in which he has a pecuniary interest, supplies false information for the guidance of others in their business transactions, is subject to liability for pecuniary loss caused to them by their justifiable reliance upon the information, if he fails to exercise reasonable care or competence in obtaining or communicating the information.[101]

P. CONSUMER FRAUD STATUTES

Nevada's Unfair Trade Practice Act[102] protects consumers from deceptive trade practices committed by any person in the course of his business or occupation.[103] This law provides that if any person violates this chapter, a complaint may be brought by the Commissioner of Consumer Affairs, the Director of the Department of Business and Industry, the District Attorney of any county of the state or the Attorney General seeking a court order or injunction to stop the trade practices.[104]

If the injunction or court order is violated, the person shall forfeit and pay to the state general fund a civil penalty of not more than $10,000 for each violation.[105] If that person is found to have willfully engaged in a deceptive trade practice, a civil penalty not to exceed $2,500 can be imposed for each violation.[106] Any person, firm, or officer of any corporation or association who knowingly engages in a deceptive trade practice is guilty of a misdemeanor for a first offense, a gross misdemeanor for a second offense, and a category D felony for any subsequent offenses.[107] The failure to comply with any judgment or court order concerning a violation may result in the suspension of the person's privilege to conduct business within the state.[108]

An action may be brought for damages sustained by any person who is a victim of consumer fraud which will include any deceptive trade practice as defined in NRS §§ 598.0915 to 598.0925, inclusive.[109] Such an action is grounded in fraud and is not an action upon any contract underlying the original transaction.[110]

Q. PUNITIVE DAMAGES

Nevada's punitive damage statute, Nev. Rev. Stat § 42.005, allows for an award of punitive damages where the defendant has been guilty of oppression, fraud, or malice, express or implied.[111] The purpose behind punitive damages is to make an example of and punish the defendant.[112]

Punitive damages are proportional to the amount of compensatory damages awarded to the plaintiff except in actions brought for: (1) defective products; (2) bad faith breach of insurance obligations; (3) violation of law prohibiting discriminatory housing practices; (4) damages from emission, disposal or spilling of toxic, hazardous materials; and (5) defamation.[113] Evidence of the defendant's financial condition is not admissible for the determination of the amount of punitive damages.[114]

R. WRONGFUL DEATH AND SURVIVORSHIP ACTIONS

No cause of action is lost by reason of the death of any person, and the action may be maintained by his executor or administrator.[115] When a person who has a cause of action dies before judgment, the damages recoverable by his executor or administrator include all losses or damages which the decedent incurred or sustained before his death, including any penalties or punitive and exemplary damages which the decedent would have recovered if he had lived, and damages for pain, suffering, or disfigurement, and loss of probable support, companionship, society, comfort, and consortium.[116] NRS § 41.100 does not apply to the cause of action of a decedent brought by his personal representative for his wrongful death.[117]

If the person entitled to bring an action dies before the expiration of the time limited for the commencement thereof, and the cause of action survives, an action may be commenced by his representative, after the expiration of that time, and within one year from his death.[118]

When the death of any person, whether or not a minor, is caused by the wrongful act or neglect of another, the heirs of the decedent and the personal representative of the decedent may each maintain an action for damages against the person who caused the death, or if the wrongdoer is dead, against his personal representative, whether the wrongdoer died before or after the death of the person he injured.[119]

The heirs may prove their respective damages in the action, and the court or jury may award each person pecuniary damages for his grief or sorrow, loss of probable support, companionship, society, comfort, and consortium, and damages for pain, suffering, or disfigurement of the decedent.[120] The proceeds of any judgment for damages awarded pursuant to NRS § 41.085(4) are not liable for any debt of the decedent.[121]

The damages recoverable by the personal representative of a decedent on behalf of his estate include: (1) any special damages, such as medical expenses, which the decedent incurred or sustained before his death, and funeral expenses; and (2) any penalties, including, but not limited to, exemplary or punitive damages, that the decedent would have recovered if he had lived, but do not include damages for pain, suffering, or disfigurement of the decedent.[122] The proceeds of any judgment for damages awarded under NRS § 41.085(5) are liable for the debts of the decedent unless exempted by law.[123]

Albert F. Pagni
Molly D. Malone
JONES VARGAS
100 West Liberty Street
P. O. Box 281
Reno, Nevada 89504-0281
(775) 786-5000
Fax (775) 786-1177

Douglas M. Cohen
JONES VARGAS
3773 Howard Hughes Parkway
Las Vegas, Nevada 89109
(702) 734-2220
Fax (702) 737-7705
www.jonesvargas.com

ENDNOTES - NEVADA

1. Nev. Rev. Stat. § 11.010.

2. *See Nevada State Bank v. Jamison Partnership*, 106 Nev. 792, 801 P.2d 1377 (1990); *G and H Associates v. Ernest W. Hahn, Inc.*, 113 Nev. 265, 934 P.2d 229 (1997).

3. Nev. Rev. Stat. § 11.190.

4. Nev. Rev. Stat. § 11.190.

5. Nev. Rev. Stat. § 11.190.

6. Nev. Rev. Stat. § 11.190.

7. Nev. Rev. Stat. § 11.190.

8. Nev. Rev. Stat. § 11.190.

9. Nev. Rev. Stat. § 11.203(1).

10. Nev. Rev. Stat. § 11.204(1).

11. Nev. Rev. Stat. § 11.205(1).

12. Nev. Rev. Stat. § 41A.097.

13. *Id.*

14. Nev. Rev. Stat. §§ 485.010 to 485.420, inclusive (1949).

15. *Id.*

16. Nev. Rev. Stat. § 485.185.

17. Nev. Rev. Stat. § 485.190.

18. *See Joynt v. California Hotel & Casino*, 108 Nev. 539, 835 P.2d 799 (1992); *Wiley v. Redd*, 110 Nev. 1310, 885 P.2d 592 (1994); *Hammerstein v. Jean Development West*, 111 Nev. 1471, 907 P.2d 975 (1995); *Scialabba v. Brandise Const. Co., Inc.*, 112 Nev. 965, 921 P.2d 928 (1996).

19. *Merluzzi v. Larson*, 96 Nev. 409, 610 P.2d 739 (1980)(*overruled in part on other grounds by Smith v. Clough*, 106 Nev. 568, 796 P.2d 592 (1990)).

20. *Ashwood v. Clark County*, 113 Nev. 80, 930 P.2d 740 (1997) (*overruled in part by Vega v. Eastern Courtyard Assoc.*, 24 P.3d 219 (Nev. 2001)).

21. *Driscoll v. Errguible*, 87 Nev. 97, 482 P.2d 291 (1971).

22. *Id.*

23. *See Wickliffe v. Sunrise Hospital., Inc.*, 104 Nev. 777, 766 P.2d 1322 (1988).

24. *Mangeris v. Gordon*, 94 Nev. 400, 580 P.2d 481 (1978). *See also Scialabba v. Brandise Const. Co., Inc.*, 112 Nev. 965, 921 P.2d 928 (1996).

25. *Quillian v. Mathews*, 86 Nev. 200, 467 P.2d 111 (1970).

26. *Id.*

27. *Id.*

28. *Otterbeck v. Lamb*, 85 Nev. 456, 456 P.2d 855 (1969).

29. *Mahan v. Hafen*, 76 Nev. 220, 351 P.2d 617 (1960).

30. *Dow Chemical Co. v. Mahlum*, 114 Nev. 1468, 970 P.2d 98 (1998) (*disagreed with on other grounds by GES, Inc. v. Corbitt*, 21 P.3d 11 (Nev. 2001)).

31. *Sims v. General Telephone & Electronics*, 107 Nev. 516, 815 P.2d 151 (1991) (*overruled in part on other grounds by Tucker v. Action Equipment & Scaffold Co.*, 113 Nev. 1349, 951 P.2d 1027 (1997)).

32. *See Mahan* 76 Nev. 220, 351 P.2d 617 (1960); *Doud v. Las Vegas Hilton Corp.*, 109 Nev.1096, 864 P.2d 796 (1993); *Dow Chemical Co.*, 114 Nev. 1468, 970 P.2d 98 (1998).

33. *Thomas v. Bokelman*, 86 Nev. 10, 462 P.2d 1020 (1970).

34. *Id.*

35. *El Dorado Hotel, Inc. v. Brown*, 100 Nev. 622, 691 P.2d 436 (1984)(*overruled in part on other grounds by Vinci v. Las Vegas Sands, Inc.*, 984 P.2d 750 (1999)).

36. *Id. See also Price v. Blaine Kern Artista, Inc.*, 111 Nev. 515, 893 P.2d 376 (1995); *Doud*, 109 Nev.1096, 864 P.2d 796 (1993).

37. *See Doud*, 109 Nev. 1096, 864 P.2d 796 (1993); *Van Cleave v. Kietz-Mill Minit Mart*, 97 Nev. 414, 633 P.2d 1220 (1981).

38. *Arnesano v. State ex rel. Dept. of Transp.*, 113 Nev. 815, 942 P.2d 139 (1997).

39. *Sims*, 107 Nev. 516, 815 P.2d 151 (1991).

40. *Id. See also Hammerstein v. Jean Development West*, 111 Nev. 1471, 907 P.2d 975 (1995).

41. Nev. Rev. Stat. § 41.141 (1973).

42. *Worth v. Reed*, 79 Nev. 351, 384 P.2d 1017 (1963).

43. Nev. Rev. Stat. § 41.141. *See also Taylor v. Silva*, 96 Nev. 738, 615 P.2d 970 (1980).

44. Nev. Rev. Stat. § 41.141.

45. Nev. Rev. Stat. § 41.141.

46. Nev. Rev. Stat. § 41.141.

47. Nev. Rev. Stat. § 41.141.

48. Nev. Rev. Stat. § 41.141.

49. Nev. Rev. Stat. § 41.141.

50. *Warmbrodt v. Blanchard*, 100 Nev. 703, 692 P.2d 1282 (1984).

51. *Davies v. Butler*, 95 Nev. 763, 602 P.2d 605 (1979); *Young's Mach. Co. v. Long*, 100 Nev. 692, 692 P.2d 24 (1984).

52. *See Central Telephone Co. v. Fixtures Mfg. Corp.*, 103 Nev. 298, 738 P.2d 510 (1987); *Auckenthaler v. Grundmeyer*, 110 Nev. 682, 877 P.2d 1039 (1994).

53. *Drummond v. Mid-West Growers Co-op. Corp.*, 91 Nev. 698, 542 P.2d 198 (1975); *Truckee-Carson Irr. Dist. V. Wyatt*, 84 Nev. 662, 448 P.2d 46 (1968).

54. *Renaud v. 200 Convention Center Ltd.*, 102 Nev. 500, 728 P.2d 445 (1986); *Sierra Pac. Power Co. v. Anderson*, 77 Nev. 68, 358 P.2d 892 (1961).

55. *American Elevator Co. v. Briscoe*, 93 Nev. 665, 572 P.2d 534 (1977).

56. *Bialer v. St. Mary's Hospital*, 83 Nev. 241, 427 P.2d 957 (1967) (*overruled in part by Woosley v. State Farm Ins. Co.*, 18 P.3d 317 (Nev. 2001)); *Johnson v. Egtedar*, 112 Nev. 428, 915 P.2d 271 (1996).

57. *See Las Vegas Hospital Ass'n v. Gaffney*, 64 Nev. 225, 180 P.2d. 594 (1947); *Nyberg v. Kirby*, 65 Nev. 42, 188 P.2d 1006 (1948); *Garibaldi Bros. Trucking Co. v. Waldren*, 74 Nev. 42, 321 P.2d 248 (1958); *Otis Elevator Co. v. Reid*, 101 Nev. 515, 706 P.2d 1378 (1985).

58. *Sheeketski v. Bortoli*, 86 Nev. 704, 475 P.2d 675 (1970).

59. *Woosley v. State Farm Ins. Co.*, 18 P.3d 317 (Nev. 2001).

60. *Valentine v. Pioneer Chlor Alkali Co. Inc.*, 109 Nev. 1107, 864 P.2d 295 (1993).

61. *Id.*

62. *Barnes v. Delta Lines, Inc.*, 99 Nev. 688, 669 P.2d 709 (1983); *see also Vega v. Eastern Courtyard Assoc.*, 24 P.3d 219 (Nev. 2001).

63. *Ashwood v. Clark County*, 113 Nev. 80, 930 P.2d 740 (1997).

64. *Gordon v. Hurtado*, 96 Nev. 375, 609 P.2d 327 (1980).

65. *Hinegardner v. Marcor Resorts, L.P.V.*, 108 Nev. 1091, 844 P.2d 800 (1992).

66. *See Mahan*, 76 Nev. 220, 351 P.2d 617 (1960).

67. Nev. Rev. Stat. § 17.245.

68. *Moore v. Bannen*, 106 Nev. 679, 799 P.2d 564 (1990).

69. Nev. Rev. Stat. § 17.225(1).

70. Nev. Rev. Stat. § 17.225(2).

71. Nev. Rev. Stat. § 17.225(3).

72. Nev. Rev. Stat. § 17.255.

73. *Central Telephone Co. v. Fixtures Manufacturing Corp.*, 103 Nev. 298, 738 P.2d 510 (1987); *see also Silver v. Telerent Leasing Corp.*, 105 Nev. 30, 768 P.2d 879 (1989) (*overruled on other grounds by Hansen v. Eighth Judicial District Court*, 116 Nev. Advance Opinion 76, 6 P.3d 982 (2000)).

74. *Id.*

75. *Black & Decker (U.S.), Inc. v. Essex Group, Inc.*, 105 Nev. 344, 775 P.2d 698 (1989).

76. *Id.*

77. Nev. Rev. Stat. § 17.265.

78. *Van Cleave v. Gamboni Constr. Co.*, 101 Nev. 524, 706 P.2d 845 (1985).

79. Nev. Rev. Stat. § 616A to 616D, inclusive (1947).

80. Nev. Rev. Stat. § 616A.020(1).

81. Nev. Rev. Stat. § 616A.020(2).

82. Nev. Rev. Stat. § 616A.020(4).

83. *Outboard Marine Corp. v. Schupbach*, 93 Nev. 158, 561 P.2d 450 (1977).

84. *Id.*

85. Nev. Rev. Stat. § 616C.215.

86. *Barjesteh v. Faye's Pub, Inc.*, 116 Nev. 120, 787 P.2d 405 (1990).

87. *Sprague v. Lucky Stores, Inc.*, 109 Nev. 247, 849 P.2d 320 (1993).

88. *Id.*

89. *See Harry v. Smith*, 111 Nev. 528, 893 P.2d 372 (1995); *Rockwell v. Sun Harbor Budget Suites*, 112 Nev. 1217, 925 P.2d 1175 (1996); *Hall v. SSF, Inc.*, 112 Nev 1384, 930 P.2d 94 (1996).

90. *See Sierra Pacific Power Co. v. Rinehart*, 99 Nev. 557, 665 P.2d 270 (1983); *Harrington v. Syufy Enterprises*, 113 Nev. 246, 931 P.2d 1378 (1997).

91. Nev. Rev. Stat. § 41.1305 (1995).

92. *See Snyder v. Viani*, 112 Nev. 568, 916 P.2d 170 (1996).

93. Nev. Rev. Stat. § 41.1305.

94. *Charlie Brown Const. Co., Inc. v. City of Boulder City*, 106 Nev. 497, 797 P.2d 946 (1990) (*overruled on other grounds by Calloway v. City of Reno*, 116 Nev. Advance Opinion 24, 993 P.2d 1259 (2000)).

95. *Central Bit Supply, Inc. v. Waldrop Drilling & Pump, Inc.*, 102 Nev. 139, 717 P.2d 35 (1986).

96. *Calloway v. City of Reno*, 116 Nev. Advance Opinion 24, 993 P.2d 1259 (2000).

97. *Id.*

98. Nev. R. Civ. Proc. Rule 8(a) and 9(b).

99. *Brown v. Kellar*, 97 Nev. 582, 636 P.2d 874 (1981).

100. *See Hartford Acc. and Indem. Co. v. Rogers*, 96 Nev. 576, 613 P.2d 1025 (1980); *Epperson v. Roloff*, 102 Nev. 206, 719 P.2d 799 (1986); *Collins v. Burns*, 103 Nev. 394, 741 P.2d 819 (1987); *Blanchard v. Blanchard*, 108 Nev. 908, 839 P.2d 1320 (1992); *Barmettler v. Reno Air, Inc.*, 114 Nev. 441, 956 P.2d 1382 (1998).

101. *Barmettler v. Reno Air, Inc.,* 114 Nev. 441, 956 P.2d 1382 (1998).

102. Nev. Rev. Stat. Chapter 598 (1975).

103. Nev. Rev. Stat. § 598.0915.

104. Nev. Rev. Stat. § 598.0999.

105. Nev. Rev. Stat. § 598.0999.

106. Nev. Rev. Stat. § 598.0999.

107. Nev. Rev. Stat. § 598.0999.

108. Nev. Rev. Stat. § 598.0999.

109. Nev. Rev. Stat. § 41.600.

110. *Id.*

111. Nev. Rev. Stat. § 42.005.

112. Nev. Rev. Stat. § 42.005.

113. Nev. Rev. Stat. § 42.005.

114. Nev. Rev. Stat. § 42.005.

115. Nev. Rev. Stat. § 41.100 (1937).

116. *Id.*

117. *Id.*

118. Nev. Rev. Stat. § 11.310.

119. Nev. Rev. Stat. § 41.085.

120. Nev. Rev. Stat. § 41.085.

121. Nev. Rev. Stat. § 41.085.

122. Nev. Rev. Stat. § 41.085.

123. Nev. Rev. Stat. § 41.085.

NEW HAMPSHIRE

A. STATUTES OF LIMITATION

The limitation period for all personal actions, except where otherwise specified, is three years from the act or omission complained of.[1] The "discovery rule" applies to all such claims.[2] Personal actions for slander or libel may be brought only within three years from the time that the cause of action accrued.[3]

Actions for injuries resulting from the creation of improvements to real property must be brought within eight years after substantial completion of the improvement.[4] "This provision does not apply to persons having actual possession or control of an improvement as an owner or lawful possession thereof."

If a plaintiff fails in an action brought within the time limit therefor, but the right of action is not barred by the judgment in that action, a new action may be brought within one year after such judgment.[5]

B. TORT REFORM

The New Hampshire legislature passed comprehensive tort reform in the late 1980's, but many of the enactments, including statutes regarding medical malpractice claims and product liability claims, have been held unconstitutional.[6] Other tort reform provisions include statutes governing comparative fault, apportionment of damages, dram shop liability, and contribution among tortfeasors. Specific provisions are addressed herein.

C. "NO FAULT" LIMITATIONS

New Hampshire has not adopted "no fault" insurance limitations.

D. THE STANDARD FOR NEGLIGENCE

To recover in negligence, a plaintiff must show that the defendant owed the plaintiff some duty of care.[7] A duty may be created by common law or by statute and whether a duty exists is a question of law.[8] The existence of a duty is predicated on a relationship between the parties.[9]

The plaintiff must also show a breach of the duty owed or failure to use reasonable care.[10] Reasonable care is that degree of care which a reasonably careful person would use under the same or similar circumstances.[11]

The standard of conduct required of children is that which is reasonable to expect of children of like age, intelligence and experience under similar circumstances, unless they are engaging in adult activities such as operating a motor vehicle.[12] Those with a physical disability or impairment must act as a reasonable person with the same or similar disability or impairment under the same or similar circumstances.[13] Mental deficiency does not relieve a person from liability for conduct which does not conform to the standard of a reasonably careful person who has no mental deficiency under the same or similar circumstances.[14]

One who voluntarily renders services for another owes a duty to act with reasonable care.[15]

E. CAUSATION

To recover in negligence, a plaintiff must demonstrate that the defendant's negligence was the proximate cause of the plaintiff's injury, that is the legal cause and the cause in fact of the injury.[16] Legal cause is established if the defendant's conduct was a substantial factor in bringing about the plaintiff's harm.[17] Conduct is the "cause in fact" of injury if the injury would not have occurred "but for" the conduct.[18]

In medical malpractice actions, a plaintiff may recover for "lost opportunity" injury when the defendant's alleged negligence aggravates the plaintiff's pre-existing injury such that it deprives the plaintiff of a substantially better outcome.[19]

F. CONTRIBUTORY NEGLIGENCE, COMPARATIVE NEGLIGENCE, AND ASSUMPTION OF RISK

1. Contributory Negligence

"Contributory negligence" is not a complete bar to a plaintiff's claims in tort for death, personal injury or property damage.[20]

2. Comparative Negligence

New Hampshire's comparative fault rules allow recovery of damages when the plaintiff's negligence does not exceed the aggregate of the defendants' negligence.[21] The plaintiff's recovery is then reduced by the plaintiff's proportion of fault.[22]

3. Assumption of Risk

The New Hampshire Supreme Court has characterized the "assumption of the risk" doctrine as an alternative expression for the proposition that the defendant was not negligent, that there was no duty owed, or that there was no breach of the existing duty.[23] The court has also indicated that the doctrine has "little vitality" in light of modern comparative fault rules.[24]

G. *RES IPSA LOQUITUR* AND INHERENTLY DANGEROUS ACTIVITIES

1. *Res Ipsa Loquitur*

A jury may infer that a defendant was legally at fault where a plaintiff has proved that it is more likely than not that: (1) the accident was of a kind which ordinarily does not occur in the absence of someone's fault; (2) the accident was caused by an agency or instrumentality within the exclusive control of the defendant; and (3) other responsible causes are sufficiently eliminated by the evidence.[25]

2. Inherently Dangerous Activities

Strict liability is not allowed for damages from inherently dangerous activities on land, unless otherwise provided by law.[26]

H. NEGLIGENCE *PER SE*

When an action exists at common law, the standard of conduct to which a defendant will be held can be defined by statute as an alternative to the reasonable person standard.[27] This is so if the person injured was a member of a class intended to be protected by the statute and the harm was of a kind intended to be prevented.[28]

I. JOINT AND SEVERAL LIABILITY

Judgments are entered against parties pursuant to the rules of joint and several liability except that, if any party shall be less than 50 percent at fault, then that party's liability shall be several and not joint and that party shall only be liable for the damages attributable to it. There is an exception to this rule where parties have been found to have knowingly pursued and taken active part in a common plan or design.[29] Also, in contribution actions upon motion filed not later than 60 days after judgment, the court shall determine whether all or part of a defendant's proportionate share of the obligation is uncollectible and shall reallocate any uncollectible amount among the other defendants according to their proportionate shares.[30]

A right of contribution exists between or among two or more persons who are jointly and severally liable upon the same indivisible claim or otherwise liable for the same injury, death or harm, whether or not judgment has been recovered against all or any of them. Contribution is not available to a person who enters into a settlement with a claimant unless the settlement extinguishes the liability of the person from whom contribution is sought and then only to the extent that the amount paid is reasonable.[31]

A release given in good faith to two or more persons liable in tort for the same injury discharges that person in accordance with its terms and from all liability for contribution, but it does not discharge any other person liable upon the same claim unless its terms expressly so provide. Such a release, however, reduces the claim of the releasing person against other persons by the amount of the consideration paid for the release.[32]

J. INDEMNITY

One joint tortfeasor can obtain indemnification against another where the indemnitee's liability is derivative or imputed by law or where an express or implied duty to indemnify exists.[33] Indemnity agreements are rarely implied and always strictly construed.[34] New Hampshire has only implicitly recognized the doctrine of common law indemnity.[35] Implied indemnity exists in cases of service contracts and cases involving the sale of products if the indemnitee was free of fault, other than merely failing to discover the indemnitor's negligence.[36]

K. BAR OF WORKERS' COMPENSATION STATUTE

Employees are presumed to have accepted the provisions of the Workers' Compensation Act and waived all rights of action for work related injuries against the employer or the employer's insurance carrier, except in cases of intentional torts.[37] The receipt of workers' compensation benefits does not bar an employee from seeking damages from one with whom there were no employment relationship at the time of injury.[38]

If there is a third-party suit for the same incident in which the employee has collected workers' compensation benefits, the employer may be subrogated to the rights of the employee against the third party.[39] If the employee successfully sues a third party, the employer or his insurer may be reimbursed to the extent of compensation, medical, hospital or other remedial care already paid or agreed or awarded to be paid under the provisions of the Workers' Compensation Act, subject to approval by the Superior Court or Labor Commissioner and division of expenses and costs of the action, including attorneys' fees, between an employer and employee as justice may require.[40]

L. PREMISES LIABILITY

Owners and occupiers of land must use reasonable care in the maintenance or operation of their property.[41] The character of and circumstances surrounding the entry on the land in question is "relevant and important" in determining the standard of care applicable to the landowner.[42]

An owner or occupier of land who permits any person to use his land without charge for recreational purposes or as a spectator of a recreational activity is not liable for personal injury or property damage to any person unless the injury or damage was caused intentionally.[43]

An owner of land who allows another to gather the produce of the land under a "pick your own" or "cut your own" arrangement, provided that the person is not an employee of the landowner, is not liable for personal injury or property damage to any person in the absence of willful, wanton or reckless conduct.[44]

Ski area operators also have limited liability by statute.[45]

An owner or possessor of business premises who employs an independent contractor to maintain such premises is subject to liability for the independent contractor's negligence.[46]

M. DRAM SHOP LIABILITY

The New Hampshire Alcoholic Beverages Licensee Liability Act imposes duties on persons licensed or required to be licensed to sell alcoholic beverages.[47] Plaintiffs are separated into two classes: (1) persons damaged by the negligent service of alcoholic beverages as a result of the conduct of an intoxicated patron of a licensee; and (2) persons who become intoxicated from the service of alcoholic beverages. The former class can bring actions for negligence and the latter class can only bring actions for reckless service.[48]

The Act acknowledges the "responsible business practices defense."[49] New Hampshire has not addressed whether comparative fault is an available defense under the Act.

A plaintiff can maintain an action against a social host only if the service was reckless, regardless of whether the injured person was a third party or a guest.[50]

N. ECONOMIC LOSS

A plaintiff cannot recover for "economic loss" in a tort case.[51]

O. FRAUD AND MISREPRESENTATION

To prove fraud, a plaintiff must show that the defendant intentionally made materially false statement which the defendant knew to be false or which he or she had no knowledge or belief was true, for the purpose of causing and which does cause the plaintiff to reasonably rely to his detriment.[52]

P. CONSUMER FRAUD STATUTES

It is unlawful to use any unfair method of competition or any unfair receptive act or practice in conduct of any trade or commerce pursuant to the New Hampshire Consumer Protection Act.[53] Private and class actions are allowed and the Attorney General may impose penalties for violations.[54] Recovery can be for actual damages or $1,000, whichever is greater, and damages can be tripled if the violation was willful or knowing.[55] The Consumer Protection Act applies to both buyers and sellers.[56]

Q. PUNITIVE DAMAGES

Punitive damages are not allowed in any action unless provided by statute.[57] Enhanced compensatory damages, however, are allowed in cases of actual malice, that is, ill will, hatred, hostility or evil motive on the part of the defendant.[58]

R. WRONGFUL DEATH AND SURVIVORSHIP ACTIONS

New Hampshire has a combination wrongful death and survival statute which allows actions for personal injury to survive death and damages for wrongful death by an executor or administrator.[59]

Damages for wrongful death include losses sustained by the deceased on account of the harm suffered during his lifetime and the value, at the time of the death, of what would have been the net earnings of the deceased less living expenses during the life expectancy and pain and suffering of the deceased as a consequence of the injury, including hedonic damages and mental anguish in anticipation of an impending accident.[60] Effective January 1, 1998, damages for loss of spousal consortium in a wrongful death case are limited to $150,000.[61] Effective January 1, 1999, damages for loss of parental consortium in a wrongful death case are limited to $50,000 per claimant.[62]

Loss of consortium damages are diminished by the decedent's fault pursuant to the laws of comparative fault.[63]

When an administrator recovers damages in a wrongful death/survival action, the damages recovery, less the expenses of recovery, expenses of administration, taxes and other debts approved by the Probate Court, become part of the decedent's estate and are distributed in accordance with the applicable provisions of law. The recovery in such an action passes through the estate in accordance with the provisions of the decedent's will or the laws of certain distribution. The expenses of recovery which may deducted from the estate include attorneys' fees.[64]

John E. Friberg, Sr.
Todd J. Hathaway
WADLEIGH, STARR & PETERS, P.L.L.C.
95 Market Street
Manchester, New Hampshire 03101
(603) 669-4140
Fax (603) 669-6018
www.wadleighlaw.com

ENDNOTES - NEW HAMPSHIRE

1. N.H. Rev. Stat. Ann. § 508:4(I) (1997).

2. *Id.*

3. *Id.* § 508:4(II).

4. *Id.* § 508:4-b(I).

5. *Id.* § 508:10.

6. *See Carson v. Maurer*, 120 N.H. 925, 424 A.2d 825 (1980); *Heath v. Sears, Roebuck & Co.*, 123 N.H. 512, 464 A.2d 288 (1983).

7. *Manchenton v. Auto Leasing Corp.*, 135 N.H. 298, 304, 605 A.2d 208, 213 (1992).

8. *Walls v. Oxford Management Co.*, 137 N.H. 653, 656, 633 A.2d 103, 104 (1993).

9. *See Gauitarini v. MacAllen Co.*, 98 N.H. 118, 119, 95 A.2d 784, 785 (1953).

10. *Ronayne v. State*, 137 N.H. 281, 284, 632 A.2d 1210, 1212 (1993).

11. *Id.*

12. *Dorais v. Paquin*, 113 N.H. 187, 190, 304 A.2d 369, 371-72 (1973).

13. *Donato v. Boutin*, 114 N.H. 65, 67, 314 A.2d 677, 678 (1974).

14. *Filip v. Gagne*, 104 N.H. 14, 17, 177 A.2d 509, 511 (1962).

15. *Smith v. American Employers' Ins. Co.*, 102 N.H. 530, 533, 163 A.2d 564, 566 (1960).

16. *Bronson v. Hitchcock Clinic*, 140 N.H. 798, 801, 677 A.2d 665, 668 (1996).

17. *See Peterson v. Gray*, 137 N.H. 374, 378, 624 A.2d 244, 246 (1993).

18. *Bronson*, 140 N.H. at 801, 677 A.2d at 668.

19. *Lord v. Lovett*, 145 N.H. __, 770 A.2d 1103, 1106 (2001).

20. *See* N.H. Rev. Stat. Ann. § 507:7-d (1997).

21. *See id.*

22. *See id.*

23. *See Nutbrown v. Mt. Cranmore, Inc.,* 140 N.H. 675, 690, 671 A.2d 548, 551 (1996).

24. *England v. Tasker,* 129 N.H. 467, 470, 529 A.2d 938, 940 (1987).

25. *See Rowe v. Public Service Co. of N.H.,* 115 N.H. 397, 399, 342 A.2d 656, 658 (1975).

26. *See Moulton v. Groveton Papers Co.,* 112 N.H. 50, 54, 289 A.2d 68, 72 (1972).

27. *Marquay v. Eno,* 139 N.H. 708, 713, 667 A.2d 272, 277 (1995).

28. *Id.*

29. N.H. Rev. Stat. Ann. § 507:7-e(I)(b) (1997).

30. N.H. Rev. Stat. Ann. § 507:7-e(III) (1997).

31. *See id.* § 507:7-f(I) (1997).

32. *Id.* § 507:7-h.

33. *See Consolidated Utility Equip. Services, Inc. v. Emhart Mfg. Corp.,* 123 N.H. 258, 261, 459 A.2d 287, 289 (1983).

34. *See Dunn v. CLD Paving, Inc.,* 140 N.H. 120, 122, 663 A.2d 104, 106 (1995).

35. *See Baker v. Lord,* 119 N.H. 868, 870, 409 A.2d 789, 790 (1979).

36. *See Hamilton v. Volkswagen of America,* 125 N.H. 561, 564, 484, A.2d 1116, 1118 (1984).

37. *See* N.H. Rev. Stat. Ann. § 281-A:8 (1999).

38. *See id.*

39. *See id.* § 281-A:13.

40. *See id.*

41. *Ouellette v. Blanchard,* 116 N.H. 552, 561, 364 A.2d 631, 637 (1976).

42. *Ouellette,* 116 N.H. at 557-58, 364 A.2d at 634.

43. *See* N.H. Rev. Stat. Ann. § 508:14(I) (1997).

44. *See id.* § 508:14(II).

45. *See* N.H. Rev. Stat. Ann. § 225-A:24 (1989).

46. *Valenti v. NET Properties Management, Inc.*, 142 N.H. 633, 636, 710 A.2d 399, 401 (1998).

47. *See* N.H. Rev. Stat. Ann. §507-F:3 (1997).

48. *See id.* § 507-F:4 § 507-F:5.

49. *See id.* § 507-F:6.

50. *See Hickingbotham v. Burke,* 140 N.H. 28, 36, 662 A.2d 297, 302 (1995).

51. *Ellis v. Morriss,* 128 N.H. 358, 361 573 A.2d 951, 952 (1986).

52. *Caladonia, Inc. v. Trainor,* 123 N.H. 116, 124, 459 A.2d 613, 617-18 (1983).

53. *See* N.H. Rev. Stat. Ann. § 358-A:2 (1995).

54. *See id.* § 358-A:10.

55. *See id.*

56. *Milford Lumber Co., Inc. v. RCB Realty, Inc.,* 2001 WL 1141414, p.2 (2001).

57. *See* N.H. Rev. Stat. Ann. § 507:16 (1997).

58. *See Munson v. Raudonis,* 118 N.H. 474, 479, 387 A.2d 1174, 1177 (1978).

59. *See* N.H. Rev. Stat. Ann. § 556:1, *et seq.* (Supp. 1999).

60. *See id.* § 556:12(I).

61. *See id.* § 556:12(II).

62. *See id.* § 556:12(III).

63. *See id.* § 556:12(II).

64. *See id.* § 556:14.

NEW JERSEY

A. STATUTES OF LIMITATIONS

A cause of action for personal injuries must be brought within two years after the cause of action accrues.[1] New Jersey courts apply a rather liberal "discovery rule," which tolls the limitations period when a plaintiff was not, and reasonably could not have been, aware of the underlying factual basis for a cause of action.[2] The New Jersey Court Rules also provide a "fictitious party" procedure where the defendant's true name is unknown.[3] Under this provision, a plaintiff may name as a defendant a "John Doe" person or company and must provide an appropriate description of the fictitious party.[4] By doing so, the statute of limitations is tolled until such time as the plaintiff, exercising due diligence, learns the correct identity of the party.[5]

An action for libel or slander must be commenced within one year after the publication of the alleged libel or slander.[6] A cause of action under the New Jersey Wrongful Death Act must be commenced within two years after the death of the decedent, unless the death was caused by murder or manslaughter in which case there is no limitations period.[7] If the personal injury/survival action of the plaintiff's decedent is time-barred because no claim was instituted for personal injuries within two years of the accident, a wrongful death action may still be maintained if it is brought within two years of the death of the decedent.[8] The statute of limitations for tortious interference with contractual rights, tortious interference with prospective economic advantage, and professional malpractice is six years.[9]

A cause of action for breach of contract for the sale of goods or breach of warranty is four years and accrues at the time the product is delivered.[10] A cause of action for breach of contract (other than for the sale of goods), property damage, or any action that is not subject to another limitations period must be brought within six years.[11] Claims for injuries arising from improvements to real property have a ten year statute of repose.[12]

Pursuant to the New Jersey Tort Claims Act, a tort claim against a state or local public entity or public employee must be presented to the applicable public entity within ninety (90) days after accrual of the cause of action.[13] A claimant must wait six (6) months from the date notice of claim is received by the public entity before filing suit, but is barred from recovering if he or she does not bring suit within two (2) years after the accrual of the cause of action.[14]

B. TORT REFORM

On June 29, 1995, Governor Whitman signed into law a package of five tort reform bills:

1. The Joint-And-Several Liability Act was modified to provide that the recovering party may recover the full amount of the damages from any party who is sixty percent (60 percent) or more responsible, but only the percentage of the damages directly attributable to the negligence or fault of a party less than sixty percent (60 percent) responsible.[15]

2. The Retail-Sellers' Liability Act, as amended, provides that, in a products liability action against a product seller, the product seller, after exercising due diligence, may file an affidavit certifying the correct identity of the manufacturer.[16] Upon the filing of the affidavit, the product seller is relieved of all strict liability claims.[17]

3. The Punitive Damages Act establishes standards with regard to punitive damage awards in civil cases.[18] It also places a cap on the amount of punitive damages recoverable.[19] The cap is set at "five times the liability of the defendant for compensatory damages or $350,000, whichever is greater."[20]

4. The Health-Care Providers' Liability Bill limits the liability of a health care provider, under the New Jersey Products Liability Act, for the harm allegedly caused by a medical device that was manufactured or designed in a defective manner, where the health care provider did not design or control the design of the device and did not know, or could not have known, of the defect.[21]

5. The Affidavit of Merit Bill requires that, in certain professional malpractice or negligence actions, the plaintiff must provide each defendant-professional with an affidavit by an appropriate licensed person stating that there exists a reasonable probability that the care, skill or knowledge exercised or exhibited in the treatment, practice or work that is the subject of the complaint fell outside acceptable professional or occupational standards or treatment practices.[22]

C. "NO FAULT" LIMITATIONS

In an effort to combat the increasing costs of automobile insurance in New Jersey, the Automobile Insurance Cost Reduction Act was signed into law on May 19, 1998. Under this new legislation, insureds must chose between two types of insurance policies, a "standard automobile insurance policy" and a "basic automobile insurance policy," which contains no bodily injury liability coverage, no underinsured/uninsured motorist coverage and limited personal injury protection (PIP) benefits.[23]

Insureds purchasing the standard policy must select between two types of tort options regarding the right to recover noneconomic losses.[24] The first, the "verbal threshold," allows recovery for noneconomic losses only when the claimant has sustained a bodily injury which results in death, dismemberment, significant disfigurement or scarring, displaced fractures, loss of a fetus, or a permanent injury within a reasonable degree of medical probability other than scarring or disfigurement.[25] The alternative option is the traditional tort option, which allows unrestricted recovery of noneconomic damages, but at a higher premium.[26] An insured who makes no election is deemed to have chosen the verbal threshold.[27] Basic policyholders are automatically assigned the verbal threshold.[28]

D. THE STANDARD FOR NEGLIGENCE

The elements necessary for a cause of action in negligence are as follows: (1) a duty of care owed by defendant to plaintiff; (2) a breach of that duty by defendant; and (3) an injury to plaintiff proximately caused by defendant's breach.[29]

Whether a duty exists is a question of law to be decided by a court.[30] However, whether there is a breach of duty, foreseeability and proximate cause are issues "peculiarly within the competence of a jury."[31] The determination of whether a duty exists involves weighing several factors—the relationship of the parties, the nature of the attendant risk, the opportunity and ability to exercise care or avoid the risk and the fairness and public policy interest in the proposed solution.[32] A major consideration, however, is the foreseeability of the risk of injury.[33]

A person is required to act as a reasonably prudent person to avoid causing foreseeable harm to others.[34] One who undertakes to render services in the practice of a profession or trade is required to exercise the skill and knowledge normally possessed by members of that profession in good standing in similar communities.[35]

When a risk of harm was posed by a third person, the plaintiff may be required to prove that the defendant was in position to know or have reason to know, from past experience, that the third person was likely to endanger the safety of another.[36]

The required standard of care for a minor is that of a reasonable person of like age, intelligence and experience under like circumstances.[37] Among those circumstances is the nature of the activity in which the minor is engaged.[38] A child less than seven years old is rebuttably presumed to be incapable of negligence,[39] however, the issue may not be submitted to the jury unless there is evidence of training and experience from which the jury could infer that the child was capable of understanding and avoiding the danger involved in the circumstances of the case.[40]

E. CAUSATION

To constitute actionable negligence, there must be proof of injury or damage resulting from the disregard or violation of a duty.[41] The plaintiff must show that the resulting injury probably would not have occurred "but for" the negligent conduct of the defendant.[42] When there are concurrent causes of harm, the plaintiff must also prove that defendant's conduct was the proximate cause of the plaintiff's injury.[43] Proximate cause has been defined "as being any cause which in the natural and continuous sequence, unbroken by an efficient intervening cause, produces the result complained of and without which the result would not have occurred."[44] A tortfeasor will be held answerable if its negligent conduct was a substantial factor in bringing about the injuries, even where there are other intervening causes that were foreseeable or were normal incidents of the risk.[45]

F. CONTRIBUTORY NEGLIGENCE, COMPARATIVE NEGLIGENCE, AND ASSUMPTION OF RISK

The contributory negligence of the claimant bars recovery only if the claimant's negligence exceeds that of the person against whom recovery is sought.[46]

The Comparative Negligence Act provides that the plaintiff may recover damages in any case where his or her negligence is less than or equal to the combined negligence of multiple defendants, *i.e.*, the aggregate approach to comparative negligence.[47] The Act requires that any damages sustained by the plaintiff must be diminished by the percentage of negligence attributable to the plaintiff.[48] The plaintiff may recover the full amount of the damages from any party who is 60 percent or more responsible but only the percentage of the damages directly attributable to the negligence or fault of a party less than 60 percent responsible.[49] In order to apportion liability, the fact finder should compare the fault of all parties whose negligence was a proximate cause of the plaintiff's injuries.[50]

When the plaintiff has knowledge of a risk, or facts sufficient to put a reasonably prudent person on notice of risk, the plaintiff must exercise the degree of care that the risk requires, or be subject to the defense of assumption of the risk.[51] The terminology of assumption of the risk is used to distinguish between two types of comparative fault defenses, but is not used when instructing a jury.[52]

G. *RES IPSA LOQUITUR* AND INHERENTLY DANGEROUS ACTIVITIES

1. *Res ipsa loquitur*

Res ipsa loquitur, which in Latin means "the thing speaks for itself," is not a theory of liability, but is an evidentiary rule that governs the adequacy of evidence in some negligence cases.[53] The doctrine of *res ipsa loquitur* is a method of circumstantially proving the existence of negligence.[54] It does not, however, shift the burden of persuasion to the defendant; rather, it requires the defendant to provide an explanation.[55]

Specifically, the doctrine permits an inference of defendant's want of due care when the following three conditions have been met: (1) the accident which produced a person's injury was one that ordinarily does not happen unless someone was negligent; (2) the instrumentality or agent that caused the accident was under the exclusive control of the defendant; and (3) the circumstances indicated that the event was not caused or contributed to by any act or neglect on the part of the injured person.[56]

2. Inherently Dangerous Activity

The "abnormally-dangerous activity" doctrine imposes strict liability, despite the social utility of the activity, on those who, for their own benefit, introduce an extraordinary risk of harm into the community.[57] New Jersey follows the six factors set forth in the Restatement (Second) of Torts, Section 520, to determine whether an activity is abnormally dangerous.[58]

H. NEGLIGENCE *PER SE*

A determination that a party violated a statutory duty of care is not conclusive on the issue of negligence unless the statute specifically incorporates the common-law standard of care.[59] The violation of a legislated standard of conduct may, however, be regarded as evidence of negligence if the plaintiff was a member of the class for whose benefit the standard was established.[60]

I. JOINT AND SEVERAL LIABILITY

Under the Comparative Negligence Act, a party may seek recovery of the entire verdict from any party who is found to be 60 percent or more responsible for the total damages.[61] A defendant will be required to pay only his proportionate share of the verdict if he or she is found to be less than 60 percent at fault.[62] Any party who is compelled to pay more than his or her percentage share may seek contribution from the other joint tortfeasors.[63]

The New Jersey Joint Tortfeasors Contribution Act applies to two or more persons who are jointly or severally liable in tort for the same injury to person or property.[64] A tortfeasor does not have a viable claim for contribution against a joint tortfeasor unless the plaintiff recovers an actual judgment.[65] A nonsettling defendant does not have a viable crossclaim against a settling defendant,[66] but has the right to have a settling tortfeasor's liability apportioned by the jury and is entitled to a credit reflecting the settler's share of the amount of the verdict.[67] The defendant is not entitled to a credit, however, if the plaintiff settles with a party who is found not to be a tortfeasor.[68]

J. INDEMNITY

A person who, without personal fault, becomes subject to tort liability for the unauthorized and wrongful conduct of another, is entitled to indemnity from the other for expenditures properly made in the discharge of such liability.[69] A right of indemnity may be created either by contract or by implication by the court as an equitable remedy.[70] If there is no express contractual indemnity agreement, a party may recover from another under common law indemnity if the indemnitee's negligence is merely "constructive" or "vicarious."[71] The party seeking common law indemnification must show that it is completely without fault in order to succeed with such an indemnity claim.[72]

New Jersey law recognizes the doctrine of "parental immunity" and only permits a defendant-tortfeasor to obtain contribution and indemnification from the parents of an injured child for failure to properly supervise the child if the parents' conduct was "willful and wanton."[73]

K. BAR OF WORKERS' COMPENSATION STATUTE

By statute, employers and fellow employees are generally immune from suit by an injured employee.[74] Employees may only file common law tort claims against an employer pursuant to the "intentional wrong" exception to the Workers' Compensation exclusivity rule.[75] The dual capacity doctrine, where an employer may be liable to his or her employee if the employer holds a second capacity that imposes a duty independent from the employment relationship, has not found favor in New Jersey.[76] The statute does not preclude an employer from assuming a contractual duty to indemnify a third party through an express agreement. To obtain such indemnification, the third party must be without fault unless a contrary intention is expressed in "unequivocal terms."[77]

L. PREMISES LIABILITY

At common law, the courts defined the extent of a landowner's tort liability toward a party injured due to a dangerous condition on the property based on the status of the injured party as a business invitee, licensee, or trespasser.[78] An owner or possessor of property owes a higher degree of care to the business invitee because that person has been invited on the premises for the commercial or business purposes of the owner.[79] An owner owes a duty to an invitee to make reasonable inspection of his or her premises to discover hazardous conditions and must take reasonable steps to correct defects or give a sufficient warning to invitees.[80] A lesser degree of care is owed to a social guest or licensee, whose purposes for being on the land may be personal as well as for the owner's benefit.[81] An owner is only required to warn social guests or licensees of dangerous conditions actually known to the host and unknown to the guest.[82] The owner owes a minimal degree of care to a trespasser and need only warn trespassers of known artificial conditions that pose a risk of death or serious bodily harm.[83]

New Jersey follows Section 339 of the Restatement of Torts, known as the infant-trespasser rule, which imposes liability on a possessor of land for bodily injury sustained by an infant trespasser where: (1) the infant's trespass was foreseeable; (2) an artificial condition existed on defendant's property; and (3) the condition posed an unreasonable risk of death or serious bodily injury.[84]

In some instances, the New Jersey courts have moved away from the common law analysis of landowner liability and not relied exclusively on the status of the injured party. Rather, the courts have analyzed the actual relationship between the parties under the surrounding circumstances to determine whether the imposition of a duty on the landowner is "fair and just."[85]

Business owners and landowners have a duty to protect patrons and tenants from foreseeable criminal acts of employees or third parties occurring on their premises.[86] However, to determine whether a criminal act was foreseeable to the landowner, New Jersey has rejected the prior similar incident rule in favor of the totality of circumstances rule.[87] Whether the proprietor's awareness of danger to the customer is such that it will subject him or her to liability is a question of fact.[88] All that is required is sufficient information to apprise the proprietor of the existence of danger and enough time to act on behalf of the patron's safety.[89] Expert testimony is not necessarily required to establish that a defendant's security procedures, or lack thereof, were inadequate.[90]

New Jersey has a "charitable immunity" statute which immunizes certain nonprofit corporations organized exclusively for religious, charitable, educational or hospital purposes from negligence claims asserted by "beneficiaries" of the charity's works, subject to certain exceptions.[91] There is also a $250,000 cap on damage awards recoverable from a nonprofit corporation, society or association organized exclusively for hospital purposes.[92]

M. LIQUOR LIABILITY

1. Dram Shop

The New Jersey Licensed Alcoholic Beverage Server Fair Liability Act provides the exclusive civil remedy for personal injury or property damage resulting from the negligent service of alcoholic beverages by a licensed alcoholic beverage server.[93] To recover, the plaintiff must prove: (1) negligent service as defined in N.J.S.A. 2A:22A-5(b);[94] (2) a nexus between the negligent service and the injury; and (3) that the type of injury was a foreseeable consequence of the negligent service.[95] The jury is to apportion fault between the patron and the tavern based upon the extent to which each party's negligence contributed to plaintiff's injuries.[96] Violation of the statute does not amount to negligence *per se*.[97]

2. Social Host

New Jersey also provides a statutory remedy for damages against a social host for an accident involving a vehicle caused by a guest to whom the host serves alcohol when the host knows the guest is intoxicated.[98]

N. ECONOMIC LOSS

Economic loss damages are recoverable despite lack of physical damages if suffered by individuals whom the defendant knows or has reason to know are likely to suffer.[99] However, a consumer cannot maintain a cause of action sounding in negligence to recover damages solely for the economic loss resulting from a defect in a product.[100]

O. **FRAUD AND MISREPRESENTATION**

The New Jersey Court Rules require that allegations of fraud or misrepresentation be plead with particularity.[101]

The elements of common law fraud are: (1) material misrepresentation of presently existing or past fact; (2) knowledge or belief by defendant of its falsity; (3) intention that other person rely on representation; (4) reasonable reliance thereon by other person; and (5) resulting damages.[102]

A plaintiff seeking only equitable relief such as contract rescission, rather than damages, needs only to establish the elements of equitable fraud, not legal fraud.[103] In order to prove equitable fraud, a plaintiff must demonstrate a material misrepresentation made with the intent that it be relied on, coupled with actual detrimental reliance.[104] Elements of scienter, that is, knowledge and intention to obtain an undue advantage therefrom, are not essential to prove equitable fraud.[105]

A cause of action for negligent misrepresentation exists when: (1) a party negligently provides false information; (2) the aggrieved party is a reasonably foreseeable recipient of the representation for its proper business purpose; (3) the aggrieved party relies on the misrepresentation; and (4) the misrepresentation is the proximate cause of the aggrieved party's damages.[106] Damages for negligent misrepresentation are limited to recovery for actual loss due to reliance on misstatements.[107]

P. **CONSUMER FRAUD STATUTE**

The New Jersey Legislature intended to create "one of the strongest consumer protection laws in the nation," when it amended the Consumer Fraud Act, which declares certain business practices to be unlawful in order to discourage deceptive sales and advertising practices "designed to induce consumers to purchase merchandise or real estate."[108] The Act provides the Attorney General with the power to investigate consumer fraud complaints and promulgate rules and regulations to enforce the Act.[109] The Act also provides for a private cause of action, with an award of treble damages, attorneys' fees and costs.[110] In order to prevail in a cause of action under the Act, a plaintiff must prove not only that the defendant committed an unlawful practice but also that he or she suffered an "ascertainable loss of moneys or property."[111] The Act creates two categories of unlawful practices: affirmative misrepresentations and acts of omissions (the suppression, concealment or omission of any material fact).[112] Under the first category, any misrepresentation, even done innocently, could state a viable Consumer Fraud Act claim. Under the second category, a plaintiff must establish that the act of "omission" was done knowingly ("the knowing, concealment, suppression, or omission of any material fact with intent that others rely upon such concealment, suppression or omission . . .").[113] Under the Act, a consumer need not show reliance on the defendant's misrepresentation.[114]

The six-year statute of limitations applies to claims based on the Consumer Fraud Act.[115]

Q. PUNITIVE DAMAGES

Punitive damages may be awarded in any case where the plaintiff proves by "clear and convincing evidence" that the harm suffered was the result of the defendant's acts or omissions actuated by actual malice or accompanied by a wanton and willful disregard of persons who foreseeably might be harmed by those acts or omissions.[116] This burden of proof may not be satisfied by proof of any degree of negligence including gross negligence. "Clear and convincing evidence" means "the trier of fact [has] a firm belief or conviction as to the truth of the allegations sought to be established."[117]

This standard of proof was codified by the New Jersey Legislature in a statute known as the Punitive Damages Act which applies to all punitive damage claims filed after October 27, 1995.[118] The Act sets forth the various factors that a fact finder should consider in determining whether punitive damages should be awarded.[119] Under the Act, once the fact finder determines that an award of punitive damages is appropriate, the fact finder must consider certain delineated factors in determining the amount of the award.[120] The Act also limits punitive damage awards to five times the liability of that defendant for compensatory damages or $350,000, whichever is greater.[121] Once the fact finder awards punitive damages, however, the Act mandates judicial review of the amount.[122]

An important issue addressed by the Act is severance of the liability and damage portions of the trial. The Act reserves to either party the right to request a bifurcated proceeding in which the trier of fact first determines liability, if any, for compensatory or nominal damages.[123] Evidence that is only relevant to punitive damage issues is not admissible in the first proceeding.[124] If the fact finder awards *compensatory* (not nominal) damages, only then must the punitive damage issues be resolved in the second proceeding.[125] Prior to the Act's passage, a defendant could only obtain separate trials of liability and punitive damages by filing a motion pursuant to N.J. Ct. R. 4:38-2(a).[126]

R. WRONGFUL DEATH AND SURVIVORSHIP ACTIONS

When an injured person dies as a result of an accident, his or her cause of action for injuries passes to his or her estate under the Survival Act.[127] The estate may recover any loss to the decedent that accrued between injury and death that the decedent would have been able to recover if he or she were living.[128]

A new and separate cause of action for wrongful death arises in favor of a limited group of beneficiaries defined by the Wrongful Death Statute to compensate them for the pecuniary injuries resulting from the death, together with the hospital, medical and funeral expenses incurred for the deceased.[129] Pecuniary loss is measured by the decedent's earnings, loss of service, including companionship and advice, having a pecuniary value that the decedent, had he or she lived, might have rendered.[130]

Edward A. Greenberg
Daniel M. Young
DALLER GREENBERG & DIETRICH, L.L.P.
457 Haddonfield Road, Suite 120
Cherry Hill, New Jersey 08002
(856) 488-0173
Fax (856) 488-5645
egreenberg@dallergreenberg.com
www.dallergreenberg.com

ENDNOTES - NEW JERSEY

1. N.J.S.A. 2A:14-2.

2. *See, e.g., Baird v. American Med. Optics*, 155 N.J. 54, 713 A.2d 1019 (1998); *Tevis v. Tevis*, 79 N.J. 422, 400 A.2d 1189 (1979).

3. N.J. Ct. R. 4:26-4.

4. *Id.*

5. *Cf. Stegmeier v. St. Elizabeth Hosp.*, 239 N.J. Super. 475, 571 A.2d 1006 (App. Div. 1990); *Mears v. Sandoz Pharm., Inc.*, 300 N.J. Super. 622, 693 A.2d 558 (App. Div. 1997).

6. N.J.S.A. 2A:14-3.

7. N.J.S.A. 2A:31-3; *Negron v. Llarena*, 156 N.J. 296, 716 A.2d 1158 (1998). The statute was amended effective November 17, 2000, to eliminate the limitations period in any wrongful death action where the death resulted from murder or manslaughter. *See* 2000 New Jersey Assembly Bill No. 1934.

8. N.J.S.A. 2A:31-3; *Silverman v. Lathrop*, 168 N.J. Super. 333, 403 A.2d 18 (App. Div. 1979). *Miller v. Estate of Sperling*, 166 N.J. 370, 766 A.2d 738 (2001).

9. *Fraser v. Bovino*, 317 N.J. Super. 23, 721 A.2d 20 (App. Div. 1998), *cert. denied*, 160 N.J. 476, 734 A.2d 791 (1999).

10. N.J.S.A. 12A:2-725; *Deluxe Sales & Serv., Inc. v. Hyundai Eng'g & Constr. Co., Ltd.*, 254 N.J. Super. 370, 603 A.2d 552 (App. Div. 1992); *Biocraft Lab., Inc. v. USM Corp.*, 163 N.J. Super. 570, 395 A.2d 521 (App. Div. 1978).

11. N.J.S.A. 2A:14-1 to -2.

12. N.J.S.A. 2A:14-1.1; *Hein v. GM Constr. Co., Inc.*, 330 N.J. Super. 282, 749 A.2d 422 (2000).

13. N.J.S.A. 59:8-8.

14. N.J.S.A. 59:8-8.

15. N.J.S.A. 2A:15-5.2 to -5.3.

16. N.J.S.A. 2A:58C-8 to -9.

17. N.J.S.A. 2A:58C-8 to -9.

18. N.J.S.A. 2A:15-5.9 to -5.17.

19. N.J.S.A. 2A:15-5.9 to -5.17.

20. N.J.S.A. 2A:15-5.14b.

21. N.J.S.A. 2A:58C-10 to –11.

22. N.J.S.A. 2A:53A-27. *Burns v. Belafsky*, 166 N.J. 466, 766 A.2d 1095 (2001); *Hubbard v. Reed*, 168 N.J. 387, 774 A.2d 495 (2001).

23. N.J.S.A. 39:6A-3; 39:6A-3.1.

24. N.J.S.A. 39:6A-8.

25. N.J.S.A. 39:6A-8(a). Under this section, "[a]n injury shall be considered permanent when the body part or organ, or both, has not healed to function normally and will not heal to function normally with further medical treatment." *Id.* To satisfy the verbal threshold, within 60 days following the date of the answer to plaintiff's complaint, the plaintiff must provide the defendant with a certification by a licensed treating physician or a board-certified licensed physician which states that the plaintiff has suffered one of the described injuries. *Id.* It is a fourth degree crime if someone makes or causes to be made a false or misleading statement in, or material omission from, such a certification. *Id.*

26. N.J.S.A. 39:6A-8(b).

27. N.J.S.A. 39:6A-8.1(b); *Oswin v. Shaw*, 129 N.J. 290, 609 A.2d 415 (1992).

28. N.J.S.A. 39:6A-3.1(c).

29. *Weinberg v. Dinger*, 106 N.J. 469, 524 A.2d 366 (1987); *Endre v. Arnold*, 300 N.J. Super. 136, 692 A.2d 97 (App. Div. 1997); *Anderson v. Sammy Redd & Assoc.*, 278 N.J. Super. 50, 650 A.2d 376 (App. Div. 1994).

30. *Wang v. Allstate Ins. Co.*, 125 N.J. 2, 592 A.2d 527 (1991); *Anderson*, 278 N.J. Super. at 55.

31. *Anderson*, 278 N.J. Super. at 55.

32. *Alloway v. Bradlees, Inc.*, 157 N.J. 221, 723 A.2d 960 (1999); *Hopkins v. Fox & Lazo Realtors*, 132 N.J. 426, 625 A.2d 1110 (1993); *Weinberg*, 106 N.J. at 484.

33. *J.S. v. R.T.H.*, 155 N.J. 330, 714 A.2d 924 (1998); *Carey v. Lovett*, 132 N.J. 44, 57, 622 A.2d 1279 (1993); *Weinberg*, 106 N.J. at 484-85.

34. *Weinberg*, 106 N.J. at 484-85.

35. *Ziegelheim v. Apollo*, 128 N.J. 250, 607 A.2d 1298 (1992); *Levine v. Wiss & Co.*, 97 N.J. 242, 246, 478 A.2d 397 (1984).

36. *J.S.*, 155 N.J. at 338; *Clohesy v. Food Circus Supermarkets, Inc.*, 149 N.J. 496, 694 A.2d 1017 (1997); *Blunt v. Klapproth*, 309 N.J. Super. 493, 707 A.2d 1021 (App. Div. 1998).

37. *Goss v. Allen*, 70 N.J. 442, 360 A.2d 388 (1976) (citing Restatement (Second) of Torts § 283A at 14 (1965)); *Schomp v. Wilkens*, 206 N.J. Super. 95, 501 A.2d 1036 (App. Div. 1985); *Zuckerbrod v. Burch*, 88 N.J. Super. 1, 210 A.2d 425 (App. Div. 1965).

38. *Goss*, 70 N.J. at 448.

39. *DeRobertis v. Randazzo*, 94 N.J. 144, 462 A.2d 1260 (1983); *Bush v. New Jersey & N.Y. Transit Co., Inc.*, 30 N.J. 345, 153 A.2d 28 (1959); *Zuckerbrod*, 88 N.J. Super. at 6.

40. *See Bush, supra*, 30 N.J. 345.

41. *Endre*, 300 N.J. Super. at 142.

42. *Conklin v. Hannoch Weisman, P.C.*, 145 N.J. 395, 678 A.2d 1060 (1996); *Camp v. Jiffy Lube No. 114*, 309 N.J. Super. 305, 706 A.2d 1193 (App. Div. 1998).

43. *Id.*

44. *Conklin*, 145 N.J. at 418 (citation omitted).

45. *Conklin*, 145 N.J. at 420; *Rappaport v. Nichols*, 31 N.J. 188, 203, 156 A.2d 1 (1959); *Camp v. Jiffy Lube No. 114*, 309 N.J. Super. 305, 706 A.2d 1193 (App. Div. 1998).

46. N.J.S.A. 2A:15-5.1 to -5.4; *Schwarze v. Mulrooney*, 291 N.J. Super. 530, 677 A.2d 1144 (App. Div. 1996).

47. N.J.S.A. 2A:15-5.1 to –5.4.

48. N.J.S.A. 2A:15-5.1.

49. N.J.S.A. 2A:15-5.2 to -5.3.

50. N.J.S.A. 2A:15-5.2; *Campione v. Soden*, 150 N.J. 163, 695 A.2d 1364 (1997).

51. *Lewis v. American Cyanamid Co.*, 155 N.J. 544, 715 A.2d 967 (1998); *Del Tufo v. Township of Old Bridge*, 147 N.J. 90, 685 A.2d 1287 (1996).

52. *Del Tufo*, 147 N.J. at 113.

53. *Myrlak v. Port Auth. of New York and New Jersey*, 157 N.J. 84, 723 A.2d 45 (1999); *Eaton v. Eaton*, 119 N.J. 628, 575 A.2d 858 (1990); *Brown v. Racquet Club of Bricktown*, 95 N.J. 280, 471 A.2d 25 (1984).

54. *Myrlak*, 157 N.J. at 95; *Tierney v. St. Michael's Med. Ctr.*, 214 N.J. Super. 27, 518 A.2d 242 (App. Div.1986).

55. *Myrlak*, 157 N.J. at 95; *Eaton*, 119 N.J. at 638.

56. *Eaton*, 119 N.J. at 638; *Bornstein v. Metropolitan Bottling Co.*, 26 N.J. 263, 139 A.2d 404 (1958); *Bahrle v. Exxon Corp.*, 279 N.J. Super. 5, 652 A.2d 178 (App. Div. 1995), *aff'd*, 145 N.J. 144, 678 A.2d 225 (1996).

57. *T & E Indus., Inc. v. Safety Light Corp.*, 123 N.J. 371, 587 A.2d 1249 (1991).

58. *Bahrle*, 279 N.J. Super. at 37. The factors include: (a) existence of a high degree of risk of some harm to the person, land or chattels of another; (b) likelihood that the harm that results from it will be great; (c) inability to eliminate the risk by the exercise of reasonable care; (d) extent to which the activity is not a matter of common usage; (e) inappropriateness of the activity to the place where it is carried on; and (f) extent to which its value to the community is outweighed by its dangerous attributes. Restatement (Second) of Torts § 520 (1976).

59. *Eaton*, 119 N.J. at 642-43.

60. *Alloway*, 157 N.J. at 236; *J.S.*, 155 N.J. at 348.

61. N.J.S.A. 2A:15-5.3(a).

62. N.J.S.A. 2A:15-5.3(c).

63. N.J.S.A. 2A:15-5.3(e); N.J.S.A. 2A:53A-1 to –3.

64. N.J.S.A. 2A:53A-1 to –3.

65. N.J.S.A. 2A:53A-3; *Gangemi v. National Health Lab., Inc.*, 305 N.J. Super. 97, 701 A.2d 965 (App. Div. 1997). Thus, a settling tortfeasor may not obtain contribution from a non-settling tortfeasor unless a consent *judgment*, rather than a stipulation of dismissal, is entered. *Gangemi*, 305 N.J. Super. at 103, 701 A.2d at 968.

66. *Tefft v. Tefft*, 192 N.J. Super. 561, 471 A.2d 790 (App. Div. 1983).

67. *Young v. Latta*, 123 N.J. 584, 589 A.2d 1020 (1991); *Mort v. Bess*, 287 N.J. Super. 423, 431, 671 A.2d 189, 194 (App. Div. 1996); *Tefft*, 192 N.J. Super. at 570.

68. *Johnson v. American Homestead Mortgage Corp.*, 306 N.J. Super. 429, 703 A.2d 984 (App. Div. 1997).

69. *Adler's Quality Bakery, Inc. v. Gaseteria, Inc.*, 32 N.J. 55, 159 A.2d 97 (1960).

70. *George Brewster & Son v. Catalytic Constr. Co.*, 17 N.J. 20, 109 A.2d 805 (1954); *New Milford Bd. of Educ. v. Juliano*, 219 N.J. Super. 182, 530 A.2d 43 (App. Div. 1987).

71. *Promaulayko v. Johns Manville Sales Corp.*, 116 N.J. 505, 562 A.2d 202 (1989) (citing Prosser & Keeton on the Law of Torts § 51 at 341 (5th ed. 1984)); *Central Motor Parts Corp. v. E.I. duPont deNemours & Co., Inc.*, 251 N.J. Super. 5, 596 A.2d 759 (App. Div. 1991); *Public Serv. Elec. & Gas Co. v. Waldroup*, 38 N.J. Super. 419, 119 A.2d 172 (App. Div. 1955).

72. *Id.*

73. *Foldi v. Jeffries*, 93 N.J. 533, 461 A.2d 1145 (1983).

74. N.J.S.A. 34:15-1; N.J.S.A. 34:15-8; *Bergen v. Miller*, 104 N.J. Super. 350, 250 A.2d 49 (App. Div. 1969); *Madaras v. Chinigo*, 131 N.J. Super. 314, 329 A.2d 592 (Law Div. 1974); *Kristiansen v. Morgan*, 153 N.J. 298, 708 A.2d 1173 (1998), *modified*, 158 N.J. 681, 730 A.2d 1289 (1999); *Volb v. G.E. Capital Corp.*, 139 N.J. 110, 651 A.2d 1002 (1995);

75. N.J.S.A. 34:15-8; *Kristiansen*, 153 N.J. at 312; *Mabee v. Borden, Inc.*, 316 N.J. Super. 218, 720 A.2d 342 (App. Div. 1998).

76. *Hawksby v. DePietro*, 319 N.J. Super. 89, 724 A.2d 881 (App. Div. 1999), *aff'd*, 165 N.J. 58, 754 A.2d 1168 (2000); *DeFigueiredo v. U.S. Metals Refining Co.*, 235 N.J. Super. 407, 563 A.2d 50 (App. Div. 1989); *Doe v. St. Michael's Med. Ctr.*, 184 N.J. Super. 1, 445 A.2d 40 (App. Div. 1982).

77. *Ramos v. Browning Ferris Indus. of S. Jersey, Inc.*, 103 N.J 177, 510 A.2d 1152 (1986); *Kane v. Hartz Mountain Indus., Inc.*, 278 N.J. Super. 129, 650 A.2d 808 (App. Div. 1994), *aff'd*, 143 N.J. 141, 669 A.2d 816 (1994).

78. *Hopkins*, 132 N.J. at 433.

79. *Id.*

80. *Berrios v. United Parcel Serv.*, 265 N.J. Super. 436, 627 A.2d 701 (Law Div. 1992), *aff'd*, 265 N.J. Super. 368, 627 A.2d 665 (App. Div. 1993); *Ridenour v. Bat Em Out*, 309 N.J. Super. 634, 707 A.2d 1093 (App. Div. 1998).

81. *Hopkins*, 132 N.J. at 433.

82. *Endre*, 300 N.J. Super. at 142; *Hopkins*, 132 N.J. at 434.

83. *Hopkins*, 132 N.J. at 434; *Diglio v. Jersey Cent. Power & Light Co.*, 39 N.J. Super. 140, 120 A.2d 650 (App. Div. 1956); *Imre v. Riegel Paper Corp.*, 24 N.J. 438, 132 A.2d 505 (1957).

84. *Vega by Muniz v. Piedilato*, 154 N.J. 496, 713 A.2d 442 (1998); *Mancuso v. Klose*, 322 N.J. Super. 289, 730 A.2d 911 (App. Div. 1999).

85. *Kuzmicz v. Ivy Hill Park Apartments, Inc.*, 147 N.J. 510, 688 A.2d 1018 (1997); *Hopkins*, 132 N.J. at 438.

86. *Clohesy*, 149 N.J. at 514; *Ventresco v. Gokvlesb Convenience, Inc.*, 318 N.J. Super. 473, 723 A.2d 1250 (App. Div. 1999); *Gaita v. Laurel Grove Cemetery Co.*, 323 N.J. Super. 89, 731 A.2d 1245 (Law Div. 1998); *Butler v. Acme Markets, Inc.*, 89 N.J. 270, 445 A.2d 1141 (1982).

87. *Id.*

88. *Ventresco*, 318 N.J. Super. at 478.

89. *Id.*

90. *Cf. Mann v. Menlo Park Mall*, A-4853-98T1 (App. Div. June 12, 2000) (unreported).

91. N.J.S.A. 2A:53A-7. *Cf. Brown v. St. Venantius Sch.*, 111 N.J. 325, 544 A.2d 842 (1988); *Loder v. St. Thomas Greek Orthodox Church*, 295 N.J. Super. 297, 685 A.2d 20 (App. Div. 1996); *Bieker v. Community House of Moorestown*, 169 N.J. 167, 777 A.2d 37 (2001).

92. N.J.S.A. 2A:53A-8.

93. N.J.S.A. 2A:22A-4.

94. N.J.S.A. 2A:22A- 5(b): "A licensed alcoholic beverage server shall be deemed to have been negligent only when the server served a visibly intoxicated person, or served a minor, under circumstances where the server knew, or reasonably should have known, that the person served was a minor."

95. N.J.S.A. 2A:22A-5; *Showalter v. Barilari, Inc.*, 312 N.J. Super. 494, 712 A.2d 244 (App. Div. 1998).

96. N.J.S.A. 2A:22A-6; *Steele v. Kerrigan*, 148 N.J. 1, 689 A.2d 685 (1997); *Lee v. Kiku Restaurant*, 127 N.J. 170, 603 A.2d 503 (1992).

97. *Fisch v. Bellshot*, 135 N.J. 374, 640 A.2d 801 (1994).

98. N.J.S.A. 2A:15-5.6 and -5.8; *Steele*, 148 N.J. at 24.

99. *People Express Airlines, Inc. v. Consolidated Rail Corp.*, 100 N.J. 246, 495 A.2d 107 (1985); *Bahrle*, 279 N.J. Super. at 38.

100. *Easling v. Glen-Gery Corp.*, 804 F. Supp. 585 (D.N.J. 1992); *Alloway v. General Marine Indust., L.P.*, 149 N.J. 620, 695 A.2d 264 (1997); *Spring Motors Distributors, Inc.*, 98 N.J. 555, 489 A.2d 660 (1985); *Goldson v. Carver Boat Corp.*, 309 N.J. Super. 384, 700 A.2d 193 (App. Div. 1998).

101. N.J. Ct. R. 4:5-8, 4:5-4.

102. *Gennari v. Weichert Co. Realtors*, 148 N.J. 582, 691 A.2d 350 (1997); *Bell Atlantic Network Serv., Inc. v. P.M. Video Corp.*, 322 N.J. Super. 74, 730 A.2d 406 (App. Div.), *cert. denied*, 162 N.J. 130, 741 A.2d 98 (1999).

103. *Nolan by Nolan v. Lee Ho*, 120 N.J. 465, 577 A.2d 143 (1990); *see also Frank Stamato & Co. v. Borough of Lodi*, 4 N.J. 14, 71 A.2d 336 (1950) (non-breaching party is relieved of its obligations under the agreement because of breach of material term by other party).

104. *Jewish Ctr. of Sussex County v. Whale*, 86 N.J. 619, 625, 432 A.2d 521 (1981).

105. *Id.*

106. *Karu v. Feldman*, 119 N.J. 135, 574 A.2d 420 (1990); *H. Rosenblum, Inc. v. Adler*, 93 N.J. 324, 461 A.2d 138 (1983); *Kuhnel v. CNA Ins. Companies*, 322 N.J. Super. 568, 731 A.2d 564 (App. Div. 1999).

107. *Karu*, 119 N.J. at 146.

108. N.J.S.A. 56:8-2 *et seq.*; *Hampton Hosp. v. Bresan*, 288 N.J. Super. 372, 672 A.2d 725 (App. Div. 1996); *Cox v. Sears Roebuck & Co.*, 138 N.J. 2, 647 A.2d 454 (1994).

109. N.J.S.A. 56:8-3.

110. N.J.S.A. 56:8-19; *Gennari v. Weichert Co. Realtors, supra*; *Cox, supra*.

111. N.J.S.A. 56:8-19.

112. *Chattin v. Cape May Greene, Inc.*, 243 N.J. Super. 590, 581 A.2d 91 (App. Div. 1990); *Fenwick v. Kay Am. Jeep, Inc.*, 72 N.J. 372, 371 A.2d 13 (1977); *D'Ercole Sales, Inc. v. Fruehauf Corp.*, 206 N.J. Super. 11, 501 A.2d 990 (App. Div. 1985).

113. *Id.*

114. *Gennari*, 148 N.J. at 607.

115. N.J.S.A. 2A:14-1; *D'Angelo v. Miller Yacht Sales*, 261 N.J. Super. 683, 619 A.2d 689 (App. Div. 1993).

116. N.J.S.A. 2A:15-5.12.

117. *In re Boardwalk Regency Casino License Application*, 180 N.J. Super. 324, 339 (App. Div. 1981).

118. N.J.S.A. 2A:15-5.9 *et seq.* The Act is applicable to federal courts sitting in diversity. *Cf. Inter Med. Supplies Ltd. v. EBI Med. Sys., Inc.*, 975 F. Supp. 681 (D.N.J. 1997).

119. The factors include, but are not limited to: (1) the likelihood, at the relevant time, that serious harm would arise from the defendant's conduct; (2) the defendant's awareness or reckless disregard of the likelihood that the serious harm at issue would arise from the defendant's conduct; (3) the conduct of the defendant upon learning that its initial conduct would likely cause harm; and (4) the duration of the conduct or any concealment of it by the defendant. N.J.S.A. 2A:15-5.12(b).

120. These factors include (1) all relevant evidence relating to the factors set forth in N.J.S.A. 2A:15-5.12(b); (2) the profitability of the misconduct to the defendant; (3) when the misconduct was terminated; and (4) the financial condition of the defendant. N.J.S.A. 2A:15-5.12(c).

121. N.J.S.A. 2A:15-5.14(b).

122. N.J.S.A. 2A:15-5.14(a).

123. N.J.S.A. 2A:15-5.13(b).

124. *Id.*

125. N.J.S.A. 2A:15-5.13(d).

126. N.J. Ct. R. 4:38-2(a) allows the court to conduct separate trials on any claim, cross-claim, counterclaim, third-party claim, or separate issue "for the convenience of the parties or to avoid prejudice."

127. N.J.S.A. 2A:15-3.

128. N.J.S.A. 2A:15-3; *Smith v. Whitaker*, 313 N.J. Super. 165, 713 A.2d 20 (App. Div. 1998), *aff'd*, 160 N.J. 221, 734 A.2d 243 (1998).

129. N.J.S.A. 2A:31-1, 4, 5; *Carey*, 132 N.J. at 67; *Smith*, 313 N.J. Super. at 174.

130. *Green v. Bittner*, 85 N.J. 1, 424 A.2d 210 (1980); *Thalman v. Owens-Corning Fiberglass Corp.*, 290 N.J. Super. 676, 676 A.2d 611 (App. Div. 1996).

NEW MEXICO

A. STATUTES OF LIMITATION

Causes of action for wrongful death must be brought within three years.[1] The limitations period begins to run on the date of death.[2]

Causes of action for injuries to person or reputation must be brought within three years, except as otherwise discussed below.[3] The personal injury statute of limitations applies if the essence of the claim is for personal injury, even if the stated theory of recovery is based on contract.[4] The limitations period generally begins to run at the time the cause of action accrues.

For personal injury claims based on medical malpractice by a qualified health care provider as defined in New Mexico's Medical Malpractice Act,[5] the cause of action accrues on the date of malpractice.[6] The Medical Malpractice Act statute of limitations applies to a claim of malpractice resulting in wrongful death.[7] In medical malpractice actions where the health care provider is not qualified under the Medical Malpractice Act, the cause of action accrues when the plaintiff knows or with reasonable diligence should have known of the injury and its cause.[8]

Personal injury suits based on childhood sexual abuse must be filed before the latest of "(1) the first instant of the person's twenty-fourth birthday; or (2) three years from the date of the time that a person knew or had reason to know of the childhood sexual abuse and that the childhood sexual abuse resulted in an injury to the person, as established by competent medical or psychological testimony."[9]

Suits against a governmental entity or public employee must be brought within two years.[10] A suit against the state or a public body for personal injury is barred, even if filed within the two-year limitations period, unless notice was given to the government entity within 90 days of the occurrence giving rise to the cause of action, unless the governmental entity had actual notice of the occurrence.[11] The 90 days does not include any time during which the injured person is incapacitated from giving the required notice by the injury.[12] If the claim against the governmental entity is for wrongful death, the required notice must be given within six months of the injury causing death, unless notice was given that would have been sufficient had the decedent survived the injury.[13]

Causes of action based on fraud, unwritten contracts, conversion or injuries to property must be filed within four years.[14] Actions based on fraud or mistake, and actions for injuries to, or conversion of, property do not accrue until the complaining party discovers the fraud, mistake, injury, or conversion.[15]

Causes of action based on breach of a written contract have a six-year statute of limitations.[16]

In general, the limitations period is expanded for minors and others under a legal incapacity and expires one year after the expiration of the incapacity.[17] However, the New Mexico Tort Claims Act statute of limitations applies regardless of minority or incapacity, except that minors not yet seven years old have until their ninth birthday to file suit.[18] Similarly, the Medical Malpractice Act statute of repose applies to all persons regardless of incapacity, except that minors not yet six years old have until their ninth birthday to file suit.[19]

Suits for personal injury or property damages arising out of defective or unsafe conditions of improvements to real property, including actions for contribution and indemnity, must be filed not later than ten years after the date of substantial completion of the improvement.[20] This limitation period does not apply to claims based on contract, warranty, or guarantee.[21]

A "catch-all" provision for actions not subject to a specified limitation period sets forth a four-year limitation period.[22]

B. TORT REFORM

New Mexico's Tort Claims Act,[23] governing tort claims against governmental entities, includes a cap on damages. A plaintiff may not recover more than the sum of the following in any tort action against a governmental entity or public employee: $100,000 for property damage, plus $300,000 for past and future medical expenses, plus either (1) $400,000 to any one person for all damages other than property damage and medical expenses, or (2) $750,000 for any number of claims for all damages other than property damage and medical expenses.[24] The Tort Claims Act also prohibits an award of punitive damages or prejudgment interest against a governmental entity or public employee.[25]

The New Mexico Supreme Court held the Tort Claims Act damages cap unconstitutional in an unusual case that applied intermediate scrutiny while holding that a rational basis standard of review would apply to future constitutional challenges to the same cap.[26]

The Medical Malpractice Act[27] also includes a damages cap. Recovery by all persons may not exceed the aggregate amount of $600,000 per occurrence, exclusive of punitive damages and future medical expenses.[28] A qualified health care provider's personal liability is capped at $200,000, with the remainder to be paid from the patient's compensation fund.[29]

New Mexico also has a damages cap in its Dramshop Act.[30] However, the New Mexico Supreme Court, applying intermediate scrutiny, held the cap unconstitutional.[31]

C. "NO FAULT" LIMITATIONS

To date, the New Mexico Legislature has not passed any "no fault" laws applicable in tort cases.

D. THE STANDARD FOR NEGLIGENCE

The elements necessary to establish negligence are duty, breach, harm, and proximate cause.[32] Duty is a question of law.[33] "A duty to an individual is closely intertwined with the foreseeability of injury to that individual resulting from an activity conducted with less than reasonable care by the alleged tort-feasor."[34] "A plaintiff must show that defendant's actions constituted a wrong against him, not merely that defendant acted beneath a required standard of care and that plaintiff was injured thereby. He must show that a relationship existed by which defendant was legally obliged to protect the interest of plaintiff. This concept limits liability for negligent conduct—a potential plaintiff must be reasonably foreseeable to the defendant because of defendant's actions."[35]

A child under age seven is conclusively presumed to be incapable of negligence.[36] A minor between seven and eighteen is not held to the same standard as an adult, but must exercise the degree of care that a reasonably careful minor of the same age, mental capacity, and experience as the defendant minor would use under similar circumstances.[37]

E. CAUSATION

In order to recover on a claim of negligence, a plaintiff must prove that the defendant's negligence was a proximate cause of the plaintiff's injury.[38] A proximate cause is one that produces the injury and without which the injury would not have occurred.[39] A proximate cause need not be the only cause, the last cause, nor the nearest cause, and may occur with some other cause acting at the same time where the combination causes the injury.[40]

F. CONTRIBUTORY NEGLIGENCE, COMPARATIVE NEGLIGENCE, AND ASSUMPTION OF RISK

1. Contributory Negligence

In 1981, the New Mexico Supreme Court abolished contributory negligence as a complete bar to recovery and substituted comparative negligence in its place.[41]

2. Comparative Negligence

The New Mexico Supreme Court adopted pure comparative negligence in 1981, replacing the prior common law rule that barred a plaintiff's recovery if the plaintiff was contributorily negligent.[42] With pure comparative negligence, a jury apportions fault, regardless of degrees of fault, between the plaintiff and the defendant.[43] The jury may also consider and apportion fault to a nonparty tortfeasor.[44]

The adoption of comparative negligence and the demise of contributory negligence has affected associated doctrines: Sudden emergency, unavoidable accident, last clear chance, and open and obvious danger have been abolished as affirmative defenses.[45]

3. **Assumption of Risk**

The New Mexico Supreme Court abolished assumption of risk as an affirmative defense to negligence actions in 1971.[46]

G. *RES IPSA LOQUITUR* AND INHERENTLY DANGEROUS ACTIVITIES

1. *Res Ipsa Loquitur*

Res ipsa loquitur permits, but does not require, a jury to infer that a defendant was negligent if a plaintiff proves each of the following elements: (1) that the plaintiff's injury was caused by an instrumentality or occurrence under the exclusive control and management of the defendant; and (2) that the event causing the injury was of a kind that does not ordinarily occur in the absence of negligence on the part of the person in control of the instrumentality or occurrence.[47] The foundation for application of *res ipsa loquitur* may be provided by expert testimony.[48]

2. **Inherently Dangerous Activities**

In New Mexico, whether work is inherently dangerous is a question of law, though fact-finding may be necessary initially.[49] If the court determines that the work is inherently dangerous, the jury must determine from the evidence:"(1) what precautions would be deemed reasonably necessary by one to whom knowledge of all the circumstances is attributed, and (2) whether the absence of a necessary precaution was a proximate cause of injury."[50] Liability for inherently dangerous activities is distinguished from absolute liability for abnormally dangerous or ultrahazardous activities.[51]

Although an employer generally is not liable for the negligence of an independent contractor, where work is inherently dangerous, the employer has a nondelegable duty and can be held liable for an independent contractor's negligence.[52] The employer has a nondelegable duty to ensure that reasonable precautions are taken.[53]

Where an employer has a nondelegable duty as a result of inherently dangerous work, the employer will be held jointly and severally liable for harm apportioned to its independent contractor for failure to take precautions reasonably necessary to protect third parties from injury arising from the work.[54]

H. NEGLIGENCE *PER SE*

Negligence *per se* is a method of proving negligence where a cause of action already exists.[55] A plaintiff can show negligence as a matter of law, negligence *per se*, by proving the following elements: "(1) there must be a statute which prescribes certain actions or defines a standard of conduct, either explicitly or implicitly, (2) the defendant must violate the statute, (3) the plaintiff must be in the class of persons sought to be protected by the statute, and (4) the harm or injury to the plaintiff must generally be of the type the legislature through the statute sought to prevent."[56]

I. **NEGLIGENT INFLICTION OF EMOTIONAL DISTRESS**

New Mexico recognizes a cause of action for negligent infliction of emotional distress (NIED), but it "is an extremely narrow tort that compensates a bystander who has suffered severe emotional shock as a result of witnessing a sudden, traumatic event that causes serious injury or death to a family member."[57] Plaintiffs have the burden of proving the following elements to establish a claim for NIED: "(1) the plaintiff and the victim enjoyed a marital or intimate family relationship, (2) the plaintiff suffered severe shock from the contemporaneous sensory perception of the accident, and (3) the accident caused physical injury or death to the victim."[58] In order to demonstrate contemporaneous sensory perception, plaintiffs "must (1) observe a sudden, traumatic, injury-producing event at the time of its occurrence or soon after, but before the arrival of emergency medical professionals and (2) be aware at the time that the injury-producing event is causing injury to the victim."[59]

J. **LOSS OF CHANCE**

The New Mexico Court of Appeals recognized a cause of action based on loss of chance in 1999[60] and the New Mexico Supreme Court concurred a few months later in a different case.[61] Lost chance cases generally involve a patient who presents to a health care provider with an existing medical condition.[62] Because the patient already has a condition that is causing, or may cause, injury or death, the health care provider cannot be deemed liable for the entire injury or death.[63] If the patient receives negligent care, he has lost the chance of a better outcome that would have existed with appropriate care.[64] "The injury is the lost opportunity of a better result, not the harm caused by the presenting problem."[65]

Traditional elements of negligence apply to loss of chance suits: duty, breach, damage, and causation.[66] "Loss of chance differs from other medical malpractice actions only in the nature of the harm for which relief is sought."[67] Damages for loss of chance are a proportional percentage of total damages based on the percentage reduction in chance of a better outcome.[68]

K. **LOSS OF CONSORTIUM**

In 1994, New Mexico became the last state in the United States to recognize a cause of action for loss of a spouse's consortium.[69] Loss of consortium is "the emotional distress suffered by one spouse who loses the normal company of his or her mate when the mate is physically injured due to the tortious conduct of another."[70] A spouse's loss of consortium action is derivative of the physically injured spouse's underlying action and the damages sought are consequential or special damages.[71] Thus, where a fact finder determines that a defendant is not liable for the physical injuries of an individual, the individual's spouse may not recover for loss of consortium.[72] Similarly, the New Mexico Workers' Compensation Act, which provides an exclusive remedy for workers injured on the job if the employer provides for workers' compensation insurance, bars spousal claims for loss of consortium.[73]

Less than five years after recognizing a cause of action for loss of spousal consortium, New Mexico became the first state to recognize a cause of action for loss of consortium on behalf of grandparents.[74] Where the victim of injury or death is a minor, the plaintiff is "a familial care-taker . . . who lived with and cared for the child for a significant period of time prior to the injury or death," and the plaintiff suffers emotional injury from losing the child's companionship, the plaintiff has a viable claim for loss of consortium.[75]

L. JOINT AND SEVERAL LIABILITY

New Mexico has abolished joint and several liability except under certain circumstances; several liability is the norm for any cause of action in which comparative fault applies.[76] Joint and several liability applies to the following situations: (1) to any person or persons who acted with the intention of inflicting injury or damage; (2) to any persons whose relationship to each other would make one person vicariously liable for the acts of the other, but only to that portion of the total liability attributed to those persons; (3) to any persons strictly liable for the manufacture and sale of a defective product, but only to that portion of the total liability attributed to those persons; or (4) to situations not covered by any of the foregoing and having a sound basis in public policy.[77]

The New Mexico Supreme Court has determined that nondelegable duties arising from inherently dangerous activities fall within the public policy exception to several liability.[78] Where the court determines, as a matter of law, that an employer has a nondelegable duty as a result of inherently dangerous work, the employer will be held jointly and severally liable for harm apportioned to its independent contractor for failure to take precautions reasonably necessary to protect third parties from injury arising from the work.[79]

New Mexico's Uniform Contribution Among Tortfeasors Act[80] defines joint tortfeasors as "two or more persons jointly or severally liable in tort for the same injury to person or property, whether or not judgment has been recovered against all or some of them."[81] The right of contribution exists among joint tortfeasors.[82] A joint tortfeasor is not entitled to a money judgment for contribution until he has, by payment, discharged the common liability or has paid more than his *pro rata* share thereof.[83] A joint tortfeasor who enters into a settlement with the injured person is not entitled to recover contribution from another joint tortfeasor whose liability to the injured person is not extinguished by the settlement.[84]

A release by the injured person of one joint tortfeasor does not discharge the other tortfeasors unless the release so provides; but, rather, it reduces the claim against the other tortfeasors in the amount of the consideration paid for the release, or in any amount or proportion by which the release provides that the total claim shall be reduced, if greater than the consideration paid.[85] A release by the injured person of one joint tortfeasor does not relieve him from liability to make contribution to another joint tortfeasor unless the release is given before the right of the other tortfeasor to secure a money judgment for contribution has accrued, and provides for a reduction, to the extent of the *pro rata* share of the released tortfeasor, of the injured person's damages recoverable against all the other tortfeasors.[86]

M. INDEMNITY

Traditional indemnification is a judicially created common law right that grants to one who is held liable an all-or-nothing right of recovery from a third party.[87] The right to indemnification may arise from contract or " 'by operation of law to prevent a result which is regarded as unjust or unsatisfactory.' "[88] New Mexico has adopted proportional indemnification as a means of equitably adjusting liability between concurrent tortfeasors where contribution or some other form of apportionment of fault among tortfeasors is not available.[89]

N. BAR OF WORKERS' COMPENSATION STATUTE

Under New Mexico's Workers' Compensation Act,[90] a worker may not sue his employer if the employer complied with the Act's provisions regarding workers' compensation insurance, the employee was within the course and scope of employment at the time of the accident, and the injury or death arising from such accident is not intentionally self-inflicted.[91] Workers' compensation is an exclusive remedy between the employee and employer.[92] However, a worker may sue a third-party tortfeasor.[93] If the worker sues a third party and recovers damages for injuries arising from an accident for which the worker received workers' compensation benefits, the employer has an interest in any recovery from the third party to the extent of compensation benefits paid.[94] The amount of a recovery from a third party to which the employer is entitled is reduced by the employer's proportional share of the attorney's fees[95] and the employer's proportional share of fault, if any.[96] The employer's share of any recovery is also limited to duplicative recovery and does not include any portion of the worker's recovery for such things as pain and suffering.[97]

An employer must have intended to injure a worker before the employer can be held liable to the worker outside the Act.[98] The New Mexico Supreme Court clarified the test for intent to injure in 2001. "[W]illfulness renders a worker's injury non-accidental, and therefore outside the scope of the Workers' Compensation Act, when: (1) the worker or employer engages in an intentional act or omission, without just cause or excuse, that is reasonably expected to result in the injury suffered by the worker; (2) the worker or employer expects the intentional act or omission to result in the injury, or has utterly disregarded the consequences; and (3) the intentional act or omission proximately causes the injury."[99]

O. PREMISES LIABILITY

A landowner's liability for injuries sustained on the premises depends on the individual's status as a trespasser or visitor.[100] A landowner has no liability to a trespasser injured on his land from a natural condition of that land.[101] If a landowner creates or maintains an artificial condition on the land, he has a duty to use ordinary care to warn the trespasser of the condition and risk involved if the condition involves an unreasonable risk of death or bodily harm, he knows or reasonably should know that there are constant intrusions into the dangerous area, or there are persons on the land dangerously close to the artificial condition and he has reason to believe the trespasser will not discover the condition or realize the risk involved.[102] A landowner engaged in activities on his land has a duty to use ordinary care to avoid injury to a trespasser under the same circumstances.[103] The landowner has no duty to make his land safe for a trespasser unless he knows or reasonably should know that the trespasser is on his land.[104] The "attractive nuisance" doctrine applies when the trespasser is a child.[105]

A landowner must use ordinary care to keep the premises safe for visitors, even as to open and obvious dangers.[106] Ordinary principles of negligence govern a landowner's conduct as to a visitor.[107] A landowner has a duty to exercise ordinary care to protect a visitor against harm resulting from the foreseeable conduct of a third person.[108] The landowner's fault is to be compared with the third person's fault and the landowner is liable only for his proportionate share of responsibility.[109]

A landowner may be held strictly liable for injuries resulting from the landowner's use of explosives.[110]

P. DRAM SHOP LIABILITY

New Mexico's dramshop act[111] provides private remedies for violation of state liquor license laws. If the holder of a liquor license sells or serves alcohol to a person when it was reasonably apparent to the licensee or the licensee knew from circumstances that the person was intoxicated, the licensee may be subject to civil liability.[112] The intoxicated person may not collect damages or obtain relief from the licensee unless the licensee was grossly negligent or acted with reckless disregard for the safety of the intoxicated person.[113] A licensee is not to be charged "with knowledge of previous acts by which a person becomes intoxicated at other locations unknown to the licensee."[114]

A licensee may also be civilly liable for violating liquor license laws requirements prohibiting service or sale of alcohol to a minor.[115] If the licensee knew or should have known that the person was a minor and the licensee's provision of alcohol to the minor was a proximate cause of a plaintiff's injury, death, or property damage, the licensee is liable for damages to the plaintiff.[116]

A social host is not liable for damages for personal injury, death, or property damage arising from the intoxication of the guest unless the host was reckless in serving alcohol to the guest.[117]

Q. ECONOMIC LOSS

New Mexico law prohibits recovery for economic loss between parties in a commercial setting, when there is no large disparity in bargaining power; loss arising from a product injuring itself cannot be recovered in a tort action for either strict products liability or negligence in New Mexico.[118] Such damages are recoverable only in contract actions.[119]

R. FRAUD AND MISREPRESENTATION

A cause of action for fraud must be pleaded with particularity.[120]

A plaintiff seeking to recover on a theory of fraud or fraudulent misrepresentation has the burden of proving the following elements: (1) the defendant made an untrue statement; (2) the defendant made the statement recklessly or with knowledge that it was false; (3) the defendant made the statement intending to deceive the plaintiff; and (4) that the plaintiff relied on the untrue statement to his detriment.[121] The plaintiff must prove each of these elements by clear and convincing evidence.[122]

The elements of negligent misrepresentation are as follows: (1) the defendant made a false or misleading representation of fact; (2) the defendant did not exercise ordinary care in obtaining or communicating the fact; (3) the defendant should reasonably have foreseen that the plaintiff would be harmed if the information conveyed was incorrect or misleading; and (4) the plaintiff justifiably relied on the representation.[123]

S. CONSUMER FRAUD STATUTES

New Mexico has two consumer fraud statutes: a general Unfair Practices Act (UPA)[124] and an Unfair Insurance Practices Act (UIPA).[125] The UPA protects consumers from unfair or deceptive trade practices in any trade or commerce.[126] The UPA expressly allows any person damaged or likely to be damaged by an unfair or deceptive trade practice or an unconscionable trade practice to sue.[127] Proof of monetary damage is not required where a party seeks an injunction against an unfair practice likely to damage that party.[128] If a person has been damaged, suffering loss of money or property, the person may sue for the greater of actual damages or $100.[129] If the trier of fact determines that the defendant willfully engaged in the unfair trade practice, the plaintiff may be awarded treble damages.[130] A prevailing plaintiff is entitled to attorney's fees and costs.[131] If the defendant prevails, it may recover attorney's fees and costs if the action was groundless.[132]

The UIPA governs unfair practices by insurers. Any person who has suffered damages as a result of a violation of the UIPA may sue the insurer to recover actual damages.[133] The prevailing party is entitled to costs.[134] If the plaintiff brought an action he knew to be groundless and the defendant prevails, the defendant may recover attorney's fees; if the defendant is found to have willfully violated the UIPA, the plaintiff may recover attorney's fees.[135]

T. HEDONIC DAMAGES

Hedonic damages are damages for the loss of enjoyment of life.[136] In 1994, the New Mexico Supreme Court held that such damages are recoverable in wrongful death actions.[137] Approximately one year later, the court of appeals held that hedonic damages are also recoverable in personal injury actions.[138] An economist properly qualified as an expert witness may offer an opinion as to the economic value of the plaintiff's lost enjoyment of life.[139]

U. PUNITIVE DAMAGES

Punitive damages may only be awarded if compensatory or nominal damages are awarded.[140] Punitive damages are available in both tort and contract cases.

A jury may be instructed to award punitive damages if it finds the acts of a defendant were "malicious, willful, reckless, wanton, fraudulent or in bad faith."[141] The limited purpose of punitive damages is "to punish and deter persons from conduct manifesting a 'culpable mental state.'"[142]

Punitive damage awards in New Mexico do not have to be in reasonable proportion to the actual damages but "must not be so unrelated to the injury and actual damages proven as to plainly manifest passion and prejudice rather than reason and justice."[143]

An employer cannot be vicariously liable for punitive damages simply because an employee commits a tortious act while acting within the scope of his or her employment. A plaintiff is foreclosed from recovering punitive damages from an employer based on the acts of its employee unless the plaintiff can establish that the employer ratified, authorized, or participated in the wrongful conduct, or that the employee engaging in the wrongful acts was in a managerial capacity.[144]

V. WRONGFUL DEATH AND SURVIVORSHIP ACTIONS

New Mexico's Wrongful Death Act is in derogation of the common law.[145] Wrongful death actions must be brought by, and in the name of, a personal representative of the decedent.[146] The Act allows the personal representative to collect any damages deemed by the fact finder to be fair and just, including medical and funeral expenses for the deceased, pain and suffering of the deceased between injury and death, lost earnings and lost earning capacity of the deceased, loss of household services of the deceased, the value of the deceased's life apart from earning capacity, emotional distress to the spouse of the deceased, loss of guidance and counseling to the deceased's minor children, and the loss to beneficiaries of other benefits that have a monetary value.[147] The fact finder may also consider and award damages for "mitigating or aggravating circumstances attending the wrongful act, neglect or default."[148] Any recovery under the Wrongful Death Act passes to beneficiaries identified in the statute in the order specified.[149] An attorney handling a wrongful death case owes a duty to the statutory beneficiaries to protect their interests in receiving any proceeds obtained.[150]

W. Robert Lasater, Jr.
Deborah E. Mann
RODEY, DICKASON, SLOAN, AKIN & ROBB, P.A.
P.O. Box 1888
201 3rd Street N.W., Suite 2200
Albuquerque, New Mexico 87103
(505) 765-5900
Fax (505) 768-7395
rlasater@rodey.com
demann@rodey.com
www.rodey.com

ENDNOTES - NEW MEXICO

1. N.M. Stat. Ann. 1978, § 41-2-2 (1961).

2. *Id.*

3. N.M. Stat. Ann. 1978, § 37-1-8 (1976).

4. *Chavez v. Kitsch*, 70 N.M. 439, 374 P.2d 497 (1962); *Mantz v. Follingstad*, 84 N.M. 473, 505 P.2d 68 (Ct. App. 1972).

5. N.M. Stat. Ann. 1978, §§ 41-5-1–29 (1976), as amended.

6. N.M. Stat. Ann. 1978, § 41-5-13 (1976). The triggering event is determined by the occurrence rule. This event is unrelated to the accrual date of the cause of action, and does not entail whether the injury has even been discovered. In this sense, if, four years after the occurrence of medical malpractice, a patient learns she has been injured, her claim is forever barred because this section functions as a statute of repose. *Cummings v. X-Ray Assocs.*, 1996-NMSC-035, 121 N.M. 821, 918 P.2d 1321.

7. *Armijo v. Tandysh*, 98 N.M. 181, 646 P.2d 1245 (Ct. App. 1981), *overruled on other grounds by Roberts v. Southwest Community Health Servs.*, 114 N.M. 248, 837 P.2d 442 (1992); *Mackey v. Burke*, 102 N.M. 294, 694 P.2d 1359 (Ct. App. 1984), *overruled on other grounds by Chavez v. Regents of Univ. of N.M.*, 103 N.M. 606, 711 P.2d 883 (1985).

8. *Roberts v. Southwest Community Health Servs.*, 114 N.M. 248, 837 P.2d 442 (1992).

9. N.M. Stat. Ann. 1978, § 37-1-30 (1995).

10. N.M. Stat. Ann. 1978, § 41-4-15 (1977).

11. N.M. Stat. Ann. 1978, § 41-4-16 (1977).

12. *Id.*

13. *Id.*

14. N.M. Stat. Ann. 1978, § 37-1-4 (1880).

15. N.M. Stat. Ann. 1978, § 37-1-7 (1880).

16. N.M. Stat. Ann. 1978, § 37-1-3 (1975).

17. N.M. Stat. Ann. 1978, § 37-1-10 (1975).

18. N.M. Stat. Ann. 1978, § 41-4-15 (1977).

19. N.M. Stat. Ann. 1978, § 41-5-13 (1976).

20. N.M. Stat. Ann. 1978, § 37-1-27 (1967).

21. Id.

22. N.M. Stat. Ann. 1978, § 37-1-4 (1880).

23. N.M. Stat. Ann. 1978, §§ 41-4-1–29 (1976), as amended.

24. N.M. Stat. Ann. 1978, § 41-4-19 (1991).

25. Id.

26. *Trujillo v. City of Albuquerque*, 1998-NMSC-031, 125 N.M. 721, 965 P.2d 305.

27. N.M. Stat. Ann. 1978, §§ 41-5-1–29 (1976), as amended.

28. N.M. Stat. Ann. 1978, § 41-5-6 (1992). The aggregate limit of $600,000 for all persons applies to claims where malpractice occurred on or after April 1, 1995. *Id.*

29. Id.

30. N.M. Stat. Ann. 1978, § 41-11-1 (1986).

31. *Richardson v. Carnegie Library Rest., Inc.*, 107 N.M. 688, 763 P.2d 1153 (1988), *overruled on other grounds by Trujillo v. City of Albuquerque*, 1998-NMSC-031, 125 N.M. 721, 965 P.2d 305. Although *Trujillo* overruled the intermediate scrutiny analysis employed in *Richardson*, mandating that future constitutional challenges to the dram shop damages cap be analyzed under the rational basis standard of review, dicta in the *Trujillo* opinion notes "that the damage cap at issue in *Richardson* would be held unconstitutional under the standard" adopted in *Trujillo*. 1998-NMSC-031, ¶ 32.

32. *Tafoya v. Seay Bros. Corp.*, 119 N.M. 350, 352, 890 P.2d 803, 805 (1995); *see also Goffe v. Pharmaseal Labs., Inc.*, 90 N.M. 764, 568 P.2d 600 (Ct. App. 1976), *rev'd in part on other grounds*, 90 N.M. 753, 568 P.2d 589 (1977).

> The elements necessary to . . . a [negligence] cause of action are:
>
> 1. A duty, or obligation, recognized by the law, requiring the actor to conform to a certain standard of conduct, for the protection of others against unreasonable risks.

2. A failure on his part to conform to the standard required. These two elements go to make up what the courts usually have called negligence; but the term quite frequently is applied to the second alone. Thus it may be said that the defendant was negligent, but is not liable because he was under no duty to the plaintiff not to be.
   3. A reasonably close causal connection between the conduct and the resulting injury. This is what is commonly known as "legal cause," or "proximate cause."
   4. Actual loss or damage resulting to the interests of another.

   90 N.M. at 767, 568 P.2d at 603 (quoting William L. Prosser, Handbook of the Law of Torts, § 30, at 143 (4th ed. 1971)).

33. *Calkins v. Cox Estates*, 110 N.M. 59, 61, 792 P.2d 36, 38 (1990).

34. *Fernandez v. Walgreen Hastings Co.*, 1998-NMSC-039, ¶ 29, 126 N.M. 263, 968 P.2d 774.

35. *Calkins*, 110 N.M. at 62, 792 P.2d at 39 (citing *Palsgraf v. Long Island R.R.*, 162 N.E. 99 (N.Y. 1928)).

36. UJI 13-1606 NMRA 2000.

37. UJI 13-1605 NMRA 2000.

38. *E.g., Fitzgerald v. Valdez*, 77 N.M. 769, 427 P.2d 655 (1967); *Martin v. Gomez*, 69 N.M. 1, 363 P.2d 365 (1961).

39. UJI 13-305 NMRA 2000.

40. *Id.*

41. *Scott v. Rizzo*, 96 N.M. 682, 634 P.2d 1234 (1981).

42. *Id.*

43. *Torres v. El Paso Elec. Co.*, 1999-NMSC-029, ¶ 13, 127 N.M. 129, 987 P.2d 386 (citing *Scott*, 96 N.M. at 689–90, 634 P.2d at 1241–42).

44. *Bartlett v. New Mexico Welding Supply, Inc.*, 98 N.M. 152, 159, 646 P.2d 579, 586 (Ct. App. 1982).

45. *Torres*, 1999-NMSC-029, ¶ 13. The *Torres* court held that a jury instruction on independent, intervening cause is no longer appropriate in cases involving multiple acts of negligence, *id.* ¶ 2, and does not apply to a plaintiff's comparative negligence, *id.* ¶ 18.

46. *Williamson v. Smith*, 83 N.M. 336, 491 P.2d 1147 (1971); *see also Yount v. Johnson*, 1996-NMCA-046, ¶¶ 18-20, 121 N.M. 585, 915 P.2d 341 (acknowledging

merging of assumption of risk into contributory negligence by *Williamson*—and later into comparative negligence—and noting that "so-called primary assumption of risk . . . [is] shorthand for a judicial declaration of no duty of ordinary care, or no breach of that duty, depending on the circumstances of a particular relationship between the parties").

47. UJI 13-1623 NMRA 2000.

48. *Mireles v. Broderick*, 117 N.M. 445, 872 P.2d 863 (1994).

49. *Saiz v. Belen Sch. Dist.*, 113 N.M. 387, 827 P.2d 102 (1992).

50. *Id.* at 396, 827 P.2d at 111.

51. *Id.*

52. *Id.* at 395, 827 P.2d at 110.

53. *Id.*

54. *Id.* at 400, 827 P.2d at 115.

55. *Garcia v. Rodey, Dickason, Sloan, Akin & Robb, P.A.*, 106 N.M. 757, 750 P.2d 118 (1988).

56. *Archibeque v. Homrich*, 88 N.M. 527, 532, 543 P.2d 820, 825 (1975).

57. *Fernandez v. Walgreen Hastings Co.*, 1998-NMSC-039, ¶ 6, 126 N.M. 263, 968 P.2d 774.

58. *Id.* ¶ 7 (footnote, internal quotation marks and citation omitted).

59. *Id.* ¶ 12.

60. *Baer v. Regents of Univ. of Cal.*, 1999-NMCA-005, 126 N.M. 508, 972 P.2d 9.

61. *Alberts v. Schultz*, 1999-NMSC-015, 126 N.M. 807, 975 P.2d 1279.

62. *Id.*

63. *Id.*

64. *Id.*

65. *Id.* ¶ 21.

66. *Id.*

67. *Id.* ¶ 17 (emphasis omitted).

68. *Id.* For example, if a patient had a 50 percent chance of survival based on the presenting condition and negligence reduced that chance to 20 percent, the loss of chance damages would be 30 percent of the value of the patient's life. *Id.* ¶ 32.

69. *Romero v. Byers*, 117 N.M. 422, 872 P.2d 840 (1994).

70. *Id.* at 425, 872 P.2d at 843.

71. *Archer v. Roadrunner Trucking, Inc.*, 1997-NMSC-003, 122 N.M. 703, 930 P.2d 1155.

72. *Turpie v. Southwest Cardiology Assocs., P.A.*, 1998-NMCA-042, 124 N.M. 787, 955 P.2d 716. However, the uninjured spouse may file suit seeking damages for loss of consortium even if the injured spouse elects not to pursue a claim against the tortfeasor. *Id.*

73. *Archer v. Roadrunner Trucking, Inc.*, 1997-NMSC-003, 122 N.M. 703, 930 P.2d 1155.

74. *Fernandez v. Walgreen Hastings Co.*, 1998-NMSC-039, 126 N.M. 263, 968 P.2d 774.

75. *Id.* ¶ 30.

76. N.M. Stat. Ann. 1978, § 41-3A-1 (1987).

77. *Id.*

78. *Saiz v. Belen Sch. Dist.*, 113 N.M. 387, 827 P.2d 102 (1992).

79. *Id.* at 400, 827 P.2d at 115; *see also Enriquez v. Cochran*, 1998-NMCA-157, 126 N.M. 196, 967 P.2d 1136.

80. N.M. Stat. Ann. 1978, §§ 41-3-1–8 (1947), as amended.

81. N.M. Stat. Ann. 1978, § 41-3-1 (1947).

82. N.M. Stat. Ann. 1978, § 41-3-2 (1987).

83. *Id.*

84. *Id.*

85. N.M. Stat. Ann. 1978, § 41-3-4 (1947).

86. N.M. Stat. Ann. 1978, § 41-3-5 (1947).

87. *Amrep Southwest, Inc. v. Shollenbarger Wood Treating, Inc. (In re Consol. Vista Hills Retaining Wall Litig.)*, 119 N.M. 542, 893 P.2d 438 (1995).

88. *Id.* at 546, 893 P.2d at 442 (quoting W. Page Keeton et al., Prosser and Keeton on the Law of Torts § 51, at 341 (5th ed. 1984)).

89. *Id.* at 552–53, 893 P.2d at 448–49; *Otero v. Jordan Rest. Enters.*, 1996-NMSC-047, 122 N.M. 187, 922 P.2d 569.

90. N.M. Stat. Ann. 1978, §§ 52-1-1–70 (1929), as amended.

91. N.M. Stat. Ann. 1978, § 52-1-9 (1973).

92. *Id.*

93. N.M. Stat. Ann. 1978, §§ 52-1-6(E) (1990), 52-5-17 (1990).

94. N.M. Stat. Ann. 1978, § 52-5-17 (1990).

95. *Trujillo v. Sonic Drive-In/Merritt*, 1996-NMCA-106, 122 N.M. 359, 924 P.2d 1371.

96. N.M. Stat. Ann. 1978, § 52-1-10.1 (1987).

97. *Gutierrez v. City of Albuquerque*, 1998-NMSC-027, 125 N.M. 643, 964 P.2d 807.

98. *Maestas v. El Paso Natural Gas Co.*, 110 N.M. 609, 798 P.2d 210 (Ct. App. 1990).

99. *Delgado v. Phelps Dodge Chino, Inc.*, 2001-NMSC-034, ¶ 26, ___ N.M. ___, 34 P.3d 1148 (2001).

100. *Ford v. Board of County Comm'rs*, 118 N.M. 134, 879 P.2d 766 (1994); *see also* UJI 13-1301–13-1320 NMRA 2000 (uniform jury instructions regarding tort liability for owners and occupiers of land). New Mexico has abolished the distinction between licensees and invitees, while retaining the separate classification of trespasser. *Ford*, 118 N.M. at 139, 879 P.2d at 771.

101. UJI 13-1307 NMRA 2000; *Ford v. Board of County Comm'rs*, 118 N.M. 134, 879 P.2d 766 (1994).

102. UJI 13-1305 NMRA 2000; *Ford v. Board of County Comm'rs*, 118 N.M. 134, 879 P.2d 766 (1994).

103. UJI 13-1306 NMRA 2000; *Ford v. Board of County Comm'rs*, 118 N.M. 134, 879 P.2d 766 (1994).

104. UJI 13-1305 NMRA 2000; *Ford v. Board of County Comm'rs*, 118 N.M. 134, 879 P.2d 766 (1994).

105. UJI 13-1312 NMRA 2000.

106. UJI 13-1309 NMRA 2000; *Ford v. Board of County Comm'rs*, 118 N.M. 134, 879 P.2d 766 (1994).

107. *Ford v. Board of County Comm'rs*, 118 N.M. 134, 879 P.2d 766 (1994).

108. UJI 13-1320 NMRA 2000; *Reichert v. Atler*, 117 N.M. 623, 875 P.2d 379 (1994).

109. *Id.*

110. *Ruiz v. Southern Pac. Transp. Co.*, 97 N.M. 194, 638 P.2d 406 (Ct. App. 1981).

111. N.M. Stat. Ann. 1978, § 41-11-1 (1986).

112. *Id.*

113. *Id.*

114. *Id.*

115. *Id.*

116. *Id.*

117. *Id.*

118. *Utah Int'l, Inc. v. Caterpillar Tractor Co.*, 108 N.M. 539, 775 P.2d 741 (Ct. App. 1989).

119. *Id.*

120. Rule 1-009(B) NMRA 2000.

121. *Eckhardt v. Charter Hosp. of Albuquerque*, 1998-NMCA-017, 124 N.M. 549, 953 P.2d 722; *see also Eoff v. Forrest*, 109 N.M. 695, 699, 789 P.2d 1262, 1266 (1990); *Sierra Blanca Sales Co. v. Newco Indus., Inc.*, 84 N.M. 524, 536, 505 P.2d 867, 879 (Ct. App. 1972); UJI 13-1633 NMRA 2000.

122. *Id.*

123. UJI 13-1632 NMRA 2000.

124. N.M. Stat. Ann. 1978, §§ 57-12-1–22 (1967), as amended.

125. N.M. Stat. Ann. 1978, §§ 59A-16-1–30 (1984), as amended.

126. *Id.*

127. N.M. Stat. Ann. 1978, § 57-12-10 (1987).

128. *Id.*

129. *Id.*

130. *Id.*

131. *Id.*

132. *Id.*

133. N.M. Stat. Ann. 1978, § 59A-16-30 (1990).

134. *Id.*

135. *Id.*

136. *Sena v. New Mexico State Police*, 119 N.M. 471, 892 P.2d 604 (Ct. App. 1995).

137. *Romero v. Byers*, 117 N.M. 422, 872 P.2d 840 (1994).

138. *Sena v. New Mexico State Police*, 119 N.M. 471, 892 P.2d 604 (Ct. App. 1995).

139. *Id.*

140. UJI 13-1827 NMRA 2000.

141. UJI 13-1827 NMRA 2000; *see also Green Tree Acceptance, Inc. v. Layton*, 108 N.M. 171, 174, 769 P.2d 84, 87 (1989); *Hood v. Fulkerson*, 102 N.M. 677, 680, 699 P.2d 608, 611 (1985).

142. *Paiz v. State Farm Fire & Cas. Co.*, 118 N.M. 203, 211, 880 P.2d 300, 308 (1994).

143. *Faubion v. Tucker*, 58 N.M. 303, 307, 270 P.2d 713, 716 (1954).

144. *Albuquerque Concrete Coring Co. v. Pan Am World Servs., Inc.*, 118 N.M. 140, 879 P.2d 772 (1994); UJI 13-1827 NMRA 2000.

145. *Cain v. Bowlby*, 114 F.2d 519 (10th Cir. 1940).

146. N.M. Stat. Ann. 1978, § 41-2-3 (1939).

147. *See* UJI 13-1830 NMRA 2000.

148. *Id.*

149. *Id.*

150. *Leyba v. Whitley*, 120 N.M. 768, 907 P.2d 172 (1995).

NEW YORK

A. STATUTES OF LIMITATIONS

Causes of action to recover damages for injury to property, personal injury, or malpractice,[1] other than medical, dental, or podiatric malpractice, must be brought within three years.[2] Causes of action to recover damages for medical, dental, or podiatric malpractice must be brought within two years and six months.[3] Causes of action based on a theory of strict products liability are also subject to the three-year statute of limitations as they sound in tort rather than contract.[4] However, where personal injuries are attributed to a breach of warranty, the action is subject to the four-year limitation period applicable to breaches of sale contracts under the Uniform Commercial Code.[5] The statute of limitations for tortious interference with a contract[6] and misappropriation of a business opportunity is also three years.[7]

A six-year statute of limitations period is applicable to claims of fraud.[8] The time period for a fraud claim runs from the time the plaintiff discovered the fraud or "with reasonable diligence," should have discovered the fraud.[9] New York also allows a plaintiff two extra years to bring an action after discovery or imputed discovery of the facts if the statute of limitations has run.[10] It is important to note that the discovery rule only applies to cases of actual fraud.[11] A cause of action based on constructive fraud must be commenced within six years from the date of the commission of the fraud.[12]

Except where the statute of limitations incorporates a discovery rule,[13] the limitations period begins to run at the time the cause of action accrued.[14]

Claims involving intentional torts, such as assault, battery, false imprisonment, malicious prosecution, libel, slander, false words causing special damages, and violations of privacy rights, are subject to a one-year limitations period.[15]

New York has a six-year "catch-all" limitations period for actions that are not subject to another statute of limitations or have been excluded from the scope of other statutes.[16]

If a cause of action accrues outside of New York in favor of a nonresident plaintiff, under its "borrowing statute," New York will apply the shorter of the New York statute of limitations or the statute of limitations of the state in which the cause of action accrued to bar the action.[17]

B. TORT REFORM

To date, the New York legislature has not passed any tort reform legislation although many bills have been introduced. However, New York did recently adopt rules that mirror the federal multi-distinct system allowing mass tort cases to be handled by a single judge for pretrial purposes. Under the new rules, a four-judge panel is being established to decide which lawsuits should be assigned to one or more judges where those cases present common facts and parties.[17.1]

C. "NO FAULT" LIMITATIONS

The purpose of New York's no-fault insurance law, the Comprehensive Motor Vehicle Insurance Reparations Act, is to compensate victims of vehicular accidents in an efficient way so the victim can avoid the costly and time-consuming process of litigation.[18] "[T]he legislative intent underlying this law was to weed out frivolous claims and limit recovery to significant injuries."[19]

The statutory scheme provides for prompt payment for basic economic losses incurred by the insured up to $50,000.[20] The bulk of the basic economic loss includes medical expenses and lost wages.[21]

Actions for basic economic loss or for noneconomic loss are barred, except in the case of serious injury.[22] The statute defines what constitutes a "serious injury."[23] The court decides whether the claimant has a serious injury before the case may be submitted to the jury.[24]

D. THE STANDARD FOR NEGLIGENCE

To recover for negligence, a plaintiff must show that the defendant owed the plaintiff a cognizable duty of care.[25] The existence of a duty to exercise due care is predicated on and varies with the relation of the parties.[26] Once the plaintiff establishes the existence of a duty, the plaintiff must demonstrate that the defendant "breached" or failed to discharge that duty because the defendant omitted to do something that should have been done or did something that should not have been done.[27]

Generally, the standard of care a defendant must observe is ordinary or reasonable care as measured by what a reasonably prudent and careful person would have done under the same circumstances.[28] However, the law demands that a greater level of care be provided to those unable to care for themselves, such as children (who are generally expected to act on instinct and impulse).[29]

The standard of care expected of a child is measured by comparing his or her conduct to the conduct of a reasonable minor of like age, experience, intelligence, and degree of development and capacity under the same circumstances.[30] When a child engages in activity normally undertaken only by adults, the child may be held to the standard of an adult without allowance for the child's immaturity.[31] While there is no fixed age at which a child becomes responsible for adhering to a duty of care, a child less than four years old is considered incapable of contributory negligence.[32] Parents may be liable for the negligent acts of their children under a negligent entrustment theory where the parents fail to prevent, or at least properly supervise, their children's improvident use or operation of dangerous instruments.[33]

E. CAUSATION

New York follows the general rule that no cause of action will lie unless the plaintiff can demonstrate that the defendant's negligence was the proximate or legal cause of the plaintiff's injury.[34] Negligent conduct is considered the legal or proximate cause of harm to another if the conduct is a substantial factor in causing the injury.[35]

F. CONTRIBUTORY NEGLIGENCE, COMPARATIVE NEGLIGENCE, AND ASSUMPTION OF RISK

1. Contributory Negligence

Prior to New York's enactment of the comparative negligence statute,[36] any finding that a plaintiff was contributorily negligent, even to a slight degree, barred recovery, irrespective of the defendant's own negligence.[37] Currently, contributory negligence on the plaintiff's part will only diminish damages owed by the defendant in proportion to the plaintiff's own culpable conduct.[38] Contributory negligence is an affirmative defense that must be pleaded and proved by the defendant.[39]

2. Comparative Negligence

The New York comparative negligence statute applies to actions for personal injury, injury to property, or wrongful death.[40] Under that statute, the culpable conduct of the plaintiff or the decedent, including contributory negligence or assumption of risk, is not a bar to recovery, but instead proportionately diminishes the amount of damages recoverable by the claimant's percentage of fault.[41] The burden of establishing culpable conduct by the claimant lies with the party asserting the defense.[42] Punitive damages are not subject to apportionment under the comparative negligence statute.[43]

3. Assumption of Risk

The New York comparative negligence statute also includes assumption of risk in its definition of culpable conduct, which, once established, proportionately diminishes the damages recoverable by a claimant.[44] Under the statute, assumption of risk is no longer a complete bar to recovery.[45] A comparative causation analysis is applied when there is an implied assumption of risk.[46] Implied assumption of risk requires knowledge or an appreciation of the risk and acceptance of the consequences by continued participation in the activity.[47] However, there are exceptions to the general rule. Assumption of risk acts as a complete bar to recovery in cases involving express assumption of risk.[48] Express assumption of risk occurs when the claimant is expressly informed of the risk and undertakes the activity anyway.[49] Another exception involves "primary" assumption of risk, which is applicable in cases of sporting events.[50] Primary assumption of risk is based on "actual consent implied from the act of the electing to participate in the activity."[51] It is important to note that the above exceptions are not applicable when the risks are "unassumed, concealed or unreasonably increased."[52]

G. *RES IPSA LOQUITUR* AND DANGEROUS INSTRUMENTALITIES

1. *Res Ipsa Loquitur*

Res ipsa loquitur permits an inference of culpability for harm to the plaintiff where the plaintiff establishes that the event: (1) is of a kind that ordinarily does not occur in the absence of negligence; (2) was caused by an agency or instrumentality within the defendant's exclusive control; and (3) was not due to any voluntary action or contribution by the plaintiff.[53] However, even where the plaintiff has established a *prima facie* case of *res ipsa loquitur*, the inference of negligence is not a mandatory presumption, but rather a permissive inference.[54]

2. Dangerous Instrumentalities or Activities

As is generally true in all negligence cases, the standard of care in maintaining a dangerous instrumentality is commensurate with the risk of danger involved.[55] Strict liability may only result when the defendant engages in abnormally dangerous or ultrahazardous activities.[56]

H. NEGLIGENCE *PER SE*

Liability under the doctrine of negligence *per se* arises where there is an unexcused breach of a statutory duty.[57] However, to establish liability under this doctrine, the plaintiff must show that he or she is a member of the class intended to be protected by the statute and that the statutory violation was the proximate cause of the injury.[58] Violations of local ordinances or administrative rules may constitute negligence or evidence of negligence, but not negligence *per se*.[59]

I. JOINT AND SEVERAL LIABILITY

The general rule is that when two or more people commit negligent acts that combine to cause a single injury, these joint tortfeasors will be jointly and severally liable to the victim.[60] This means "that each party is individually liable to plaintiff for the whole of the damage."[61] Joint and several liability is imposed only when the tortfeasors act concurrently or in concert.[62] There is no joint and several liability among tortfeasors who commit separate and distinct tortious acts that create separate injuries.[63] Whether tortfeasors acted concurrently or in concert is a question of fact for the jury.[64]

While as a general rule, each tortfeasor is liable for the entire damage sustained by the plaintiff,[65] under Section 1601 of the Civil Practice Law and Rules, the liability of certain parties who are jointly liable to a claimant is limited under certain circumstances.[66] Section 1601 applies when a joint tortfeasor is found to be 50 percent or less liable in a personal injury case.[67] The defendant's liability to the claimant is limited to the tortfeasor's relative culpability for noneconomic loss.[68] There are certain exclusions that apply to the statute.[69] For example, the statute does not apply to intentional torts or cases where the defendant acts with reckless disregard in causing the injury to the claimant.[70] Breach of a non-delegable duty to a plaintiff does not preclude apportionment for non-economic damages among joint tortfeasors pursuant to Section 1601.[71]

When several parties are jointly liable and one party has paid more than its fair share to the claimant, that party will be entitled to contribution from the other tortfeasors.[72] By law, a tortfeasor has a right to contribution regardless of whether the victim has sued the other joint tortfeasors.[73] The tortfeasor is entitled to contribution in the amount paid to the injured party in excess of its equitable share, derived from the tortfeasor's relative culpability.[74] Relative culpability is determined by the trier of fact.[75]

A settlement with one tortfeasor will not affect the ability of the injured person to sue another nonsettling tortfeasor.[76] In a suit against the nonsettling tortfeasor, the verdict will be reduced to the highest of the amount stipulated in the release, the consideration paid for the release or the settling tortfeasor's equitable share.[77] New York encourages settlement. However, a nonsettling defendant is protected from paying more than its equitable share.[78]

J. INDEMNITY

Indemnity shifts an entire economic loss to a party who is supposed to bear that loss.[79] It differs from contribution in that it "springs from a contract, express or implied, and full, not partial, reimbursement is sought."[80] Indemnity can arise out of an express contractual provision in which there is a promise by the indemnitor to be responsible for any claims brought against the indemnitee by a third party.[81] However, indemnity can be imposed under a theory of implied contract or if there is a great disparity in fault between the tortfeasors.[82] Indemnity may also be imposed by statute.[83]

K. BAR OF WORKERS' COMPENSATION STATUTE

Under the New York Workers' Compensation Law,[84] workers' compensation is, with certain exceptions, the exclusive remedy against the employer for damages sustained from injury or death that arose out of and in the course of the employment.[85] The exclusive remedy doctrine applies not only to the employer and fellow employees, but also to the employer's insurance companies (not only the workers' compensation carrier), the insurance companies' employees, the employee's collective bargaining agents (the union), the union's employees, and even when an employee works independently at his employer's residence.[86]

An injured worker may sue a third party who may in turn implead the employer for contribution or indemnity.[87] The employer's liability for contribution or indemnity is limited to instances where the employee sustained a "grave" injury.[88] The statute contains a restrictive list of injuries that are considered "grave." The limitations to an impleader action extend to fellow employees as well as to the employer's insurance carrier and the employee's collective bargaining unit.[89] Other exceptions to the exclusive liability rule include the employer's failure to provide coverage by one of the methods required in the statute[90] or where the injury results from an intentional tort carried out or authorized by the employer.[91]

If a worker has collected workers' compensation and then sues a third party in connection with the same incident, the workers' compensation carrier may be subrogated to the rights of the employee against the third party.[92] If the employee successfully sues the third party, the insurer may be reimbursed for previously paid workers' compensation benefits.[93] The proceeds available for reimbursement are reduced by the amount of reasonable litigation costs, which are equitably apportioned between the employee and the carrier to the extent each was benefitted by the recovery.[94] The employer or the workers' compensation carrier must approve any settlement or further workers' compensation payments may be cut off.[95]

L. PREMISES LIABILITY

Under New York law, landowners are held to a single standard of reasonable care under the circumstances whereby forseeability is a measure of liability.[96] A landowner's liability for injuries sustained on the premises no longer depends on the plaintiff's status as a trespasser, licensee, or invitee.[97] Rather, the duty of a landowner to persons on the premises is to keep the premises in a reasonably safe condition, considering all of the circumstances including the likelihood of injury, the seriousness of the injury, the burden of avoiding the risk, and the purpose of the person's presence.[98]

M. DRAM SHOP LIABILITY

The New York Dram Shop Act establishes a cause of action on behalf of a person injured due to the intoxication of another.[99] Liability arises when a person has caused or contributed to another's intoxication by illegally selling or assisting in procuring liquor for the intoxicated person and the intoxicated person causes injury to another.[100] The injured plaintiff must demonstrate some reasonable or practical connection between the unlawful sale and the injury. Proximate causation does not have to be established.[101] The injured party has a right to recover actual and exemplary damages.[102] No special duties exist under the Act with respect to minors.[103]

Social hosts are generally not liable under the Dram Shop Act.[104] However, social hosts may be liable if they are engaged in commercial activity that includes the sale of liquor for a profit.[105]

N. ECONOMIC LOSS

New York does not recognize a cause of action based on strict liability and negligence where the suit seeks recovery of economic loss.[106] A limited exception is permitted for claims of negligent performance of contractual services.[107]

O. FRAUD AND MISREPRESENTATION

The New York Civil Practice Law and Rules require a cause of action for fraud to be pleaded with particularity.[108]

The elements of a claim for fraud, deceit, or intentional misrepresentation are: (1) a representation of fact; (2) falsity; (3) scienter (intent); (4) reliance; (5) injury; and (6) proximate causation.[109] All of the foregoing elements must be proved by clear and convincing evidence.[110]

A claim for negligent misrepresentation must allege: (1) carelessness in imparting words; (2) on which others were expected to rely; (3) on which they did justifiably rely; (4) to their detriment; and (5) the author expressed the words directly, with knowledge they be acted on, to one whom the author is bound by some special relation or duty of care.[111] A claim for negligent misrepresentation exists only where there is a special relationship of trust and confidence which imposes a duty on a person to impart correct information to another.[112] New York requires that negligent misrepresentation be proved by clear and convincing evidence.[113]

P. CONSUMER FRAUD STATUTES

Sections 349-350 of New York's General Business Law, referred to as Consumer Protection from Deceptive Acts and Practices, protects consumers from deceptive acts or practices in the conduct of any business, trade, or commerce or in the furnishing of any service in the state.[114] The Attorney General may bring an action relating to violations of these laws.[115] Private actions are also available under these statutes.[116] While the statutes are consumer oriented, a business may file a deceptive practices claim if it was injured while acting as a consumer.[117] Reasonable attorney's fees may be awarded to a prevailing plaintiff.[118]

In claims brought under Sections 349 or 350, the plaintiff must show that: (1) the alleged practice was misleading in a material respect; and (2) the plaintiff was injured.[119] There is no requirement that the defendant's actions be shown to be intentional, fraudulent, or even reckless.[120] With respect to claims arising under Section 349, the plaintiff does not have to prove reliance, although they must prove that the defendant's "material deceptive act" caused the injury.[121]

It appears that the courts will apply a three-year limitations period to actions alleging deceptive acts or practices pursuant to Section 349.[122] Plaintiffs suing under Section 349 will not be able to take advantage of any discovery rule extending the limitations period even if they did not discover the deception in time to sue.[123]

Q. PUNITIVE DAMAGES

New York permits punitive or exemplary damages to be awarded in order to punish a defendant for the wrong in a particular case, to protect the public from similar acts, and to deter the defendant and others from similar acts.[124] In negligence actions, punitive damages are awarded where the defendant is found to have engaged in misconduct involving malice, oppression, insult, wanton or reckless disregard of the plaintiff's rights, or other egregious circumstances.[125] Gross negligence can support an award of punitive damages in rare cases.[126] Punitive damages are recoverable in a wrongful death action.[127]

The amount awarded should bear some relationship to the actual damages.[128] The court has the power to reduce the jury's verdict if the award is based on prejudice or partiality, or if the amount awarded is so unreasonable as to "shock the judicial conscience."[129]

There is no separate cause of action for punitive damages.[130] To justify punitive damages, there must be a showing of actual injury that justifies an award of compensatory damages,[131] although punitive damages can be awarded in connection with nominal damages.[132]

Factors considered include the defendant's financial assets or wealth[133] as well as his or her conduct and state of mind.[134] Punitive damages are not recoverable for an ordinary tort.[135] They must be assessed against the actual tortfeasor; punitive damages may not be imposed where liability is vicarious.[136]

R.   **WRONGFUL DEATH AND SURVIVORSHIP ACTIONS**

Under New York common law, there is no recovery for wrongful death.[137] Instead, wrongful death actions are governed entirely by statute.[138] The law authorizes an action by a personal representative to recover damages on behalf of a decedent's beneficiaries for a "wrongful act, neglect or default" that caused the decedent's death.[139] It is important to note that the two-year statute of limitations accrues on the date of the decedent's death.[140]

Under New York common law, all actions automatically ended on the death of any party.[141] However, a New York statute now permits survival actions by or against decedents.[142] The law authorizes either the bringing or continuation of an action by a personal representative on behalf of a decedent's estate for personal injuries or property damage.[143]

Susan T. Dwyer
Stacy Kellner Rosenberg
HERRICK, FEINSTEIN, L.L.P.
2 Park Avenue
New York, New York 10016
(212) 592-1400
Fax (212) 592-1500
sdwye@herrick.com
www.herrick.com

ENDNOTES - NEW YORK

1. With respect to claims of professional malpractice, C.P.L.R. 214(6) provides a three-year statute of limitations regardless of whether the underlying theory is based in contract or tort. N.Y. C.P.L.R. 214(6) (Supp. 2001). This statute, which was amended in September 1996 to shorten the statute of limitations for nonmedical malpractice claims from six years to three, applies to causes of action that accrued before the amendment's effective date not yet interposed by that date. *See Brothers v. Florence*, 95 N.Y.2d 290, 739 N.E.2d 733, 716 N.Y.S.2d 367 (2000).

2. N.Y. C.P.L.R. 214(4), (5) & (6) (Supp. 2001).

3. N.Y. C.P.L.R. 214-a (1990). The cause of action accrues on the date of the last continuous treatment for the complained-of illness or injury, unless the action is based on the discovery of a foreign object in the body, in which case the discovery rule would apply. Although governed by the three-year limitation period in C.P.L.R. 214(b), attorney malpractice claims are also subject to an analogous tolling provision, the "continuous representation rule," which starts the statute of limitations for a legal malpractice action running at the end of an attorney-client relationship that is continuous, ongoing, developing and dependant. *See Aaron v. Roemer, Wallens & Mineaux, LLP*, 272 A.D.2d 752, 754, 707 N.Y.S.2d 711, 713-14 (3d Dep't 2000).

4. *Victorson v. Bock Laundry Mach. Co.*, 37 N.Y.2d 395, 373 N.Y.S.2d 39, 335 N.E.2d 275 (1975).

5. N.Y. U.C.C. § 2-725(1) (1993); *see also Heller v. U.S. Suzuki Motor Corp.*, 64 N.Y.2d 407, 488 N.Y.S.2d 132, 477 N.E.2d 434 (1985); *Calabria v. St. Regis Corp.*, 124 A.D.2d 514, 508 N.Y.S.2d 186 (1st Dep't 1986); N.Y. U.C.C. § 2-318 (1993) (providing that "[a] seller's warranty whether express or implied extends to any natural person if it is reasonable to expect that such person may use, consume or be affected by the goods and who is injured in person by breach of warranty").

6. *Edward B. Fitzpatrick, Jr. Constr. Corp. v. County of Suffolk*, 138 A.D.2d 446, 525 N.Y.S. 2d 863, 866 (2d Dep't 1988); *Van Dussen-Storto Motor Inn, Inc. v. Rochester Tel. Corp.*, 63 A.D.2d 244, 407 N.Y.S.2d 287, 292 (4th Dep't 1978).

7. *Powers Mercantile Corp. v. Feinberg*, 109 A.D.2d 117, 490 N.Y.S.2d 190, 193 (1st Dep't 1985), *aff'd*, 67 N.Y.2d 981, 502 N.Y.S.2d 1001, 494 N.E.2d 106 (1986).

8. N.Y. C.P.L.R. 213(8) (1990).

9. *See id.*; *Kaufman v. Kaufman*, 135 A.D.2d 786, 522 N.Y.S.2d 899, 900 (2d Dep't 1987); *Scally v. Simcona Elec. Corp.*, 135 A.D.2d 1086, 523 N.Y.S.2d 307, 308 (4th Dep't 1987); *see also Lefkowitz v. Appelbaum*, 258 A.D.2d 563, 685 N.Y.S.2d 460, 461 (2d Dep't 1999) (asserting that "[t]he burden of establishing that the fraud could not have been discovered before the two-year period prior to the commencement of the action rests on the plaintiff, who seeks the benefit of the exception").

10. N.Y. C.P.L.R. 203(g) (Supp. 2001). However, this provision is not applicable to Article 2 of the U.C.C. or N.Y. C.P.L.R. 214-a. *Id.*

11. *Quadrozzi Concrete Corp. v. Mastroianni*, 56 A.D.2d 353, 392 N.Y.S.2d 687, 688 (2d Dep't 1977).

12. *Id.*

13. Under the discovery rule referred to by C.P.L.R. 214, the tolling period for actions to recover damages for personal injury or injury to property caused by the "latent effects of exposure to any substance or combination of substances, in any form, upon or within the body or upon or within the property," begins to run from the earlier of the date of discovery of the injury or the date when through exercise of reasonable diligence, such injury should have been discovered. N.Y. C.P.L.R. § 214-c(2) (1990).

14. N.Y. C.P.L.R. 203(a) (Supp. 2001).

15. N.Y. C.P.L.R. 215 (1990).

16. N.Y. C.P.L.R. 213(1) (1990).

17. Where the action accrues in the state of which the plaintiff is a resident, the court will apply that state's statute of limitations. N.Y. C.P.L.R. 202 (1990).

17.1. *See* N.Y. L.L.S. Unif. Rules, Trial, Cts. 55202.69 (2002).

18. *Walton v. Lumbermens Mut. Cas. Co.*, 88 N.Y.2d 211, 214, 644 N.Y.S.2d 133, 135, 666 N.E.2d 1046 (1996).

19. *Dufel v. Green*, 84 N.Y.2d 795, 798, 622 N.Y.S.2d 900, 902, 647 N.E.2d 105, 107 (1995) (citing *Licari v. Elliott*, 57 N.Y.2d 230, 234–35, 455 N.Y.S.2d 570, 441 N.E.2d 1088 (1982)).

20. N.Y. Ins. Law § 5102 (2000).

21. *Id.*

22. N.Y. Ins. Law § 5104 (2000). This section allows recovery for basic noneconomic loss in case of serious injury or economic loss otherwise.

23. N.Y. Ins. Law § 5102. The definition includes personal injuries that result in death, dismemberment, or significant disfigurement.

24. *Licari*, 57 N.Y.2d at 237, 455 N.Y.S.2d at 573–74, 441 N.E.2d at 1091–92.

25. *See Palka v. Servicemaster Mgt. Servs. Corp.*, 83 N.Y.2d 579, 584–85, 611 N.Y.S.2d 817, 820, 634 N.E.2d 189 (1994).

26. *Di Ponzio v. Riordan*, 89 N.Y.2d 578, 583, 657 N.Y.S.2d 377, 379, 679 N.E.2d 646 (1994).

27. *See Morgan v. State*, 90 N.Y.2d 47, 662 N.Y.S.2d 421, 685 N.E.2d 202 (1997); *see also Schumacher v. Richards Shear Co.*, 59 N.Y.2d 239, 246–47, 464 N.Y.S.2d 437, 441, 451 N.E.2d 195 (1983) (liability can arise from failure to warn).

28. *Bethel v. New York City Transit Auth.*, 92 N.Y.2d 348, 353, 681 N.Y.S.2d 201, 203, 703 N.E.2d 1214 (1998). Common carriers are no longer required to exercise an extraordinary degree of care. *Id.* at 356, 681 N.Y.S.2d at 205.

29. *Willis v. Young Men's Christian Ass'n*, 28 N.Y.2d 375, 379, 321 N.Y.S.2d 895, 989 (1971); *Day v. Johnson*, 265 A.D. 383, 39 N.Y.S.2d 203 (4th Dept. 1943); *Gloria X. v. Gibbs*, 241 A.D.2d 579, 659 N.Y.S.2d 349, 351 (3d Dep't 1997).

30. *Gonzalez v. Medina*, 69 A.D.2d 14, 417 N.Y.S.2d 953, 956 (1st Dep't 1979).

31. *See Neumann v. Shlansky*, 58 Misc. 2d 128, 294 N.Y.S.2d 628 (Westchester County Ct. 1968) (where a minor golfer struck another golfer with a golf ball, the minor was held to the standard of the reasonable man on the golf course since golf can easily be determined to be an adult activity engaged in by children), *aff'd*, 63 Misc. 2d 587, 312 N.Y.S.2d 951 (App. Term 1970), *aff'd*, 36 A.D.2d 540, 318 N.Y.S.2d 925 (2d Dep't 1971).

32. *See, e.g., Figueroa v. Waldbaum's Inc.*, 160 Misc. 2d 379, 609 N.Y.S.2d 764, 766 (Nassau County Sup. Ct. 1994) (three-year-old incapable of contributory negligence as a matter of law).

33. *See Rios v. Smith*, 95 N.Y.2d 647, 744 N.E.2d 1156, 722 N.Y.S.2d 220 (2001) (parent owed a duty to protect third parties from harm that was clearly foreseeable from child's use of ATV vehicles that could attain speeds of 20 to 30 miles an hour).

34. *See Doundoulakis v. Town of Hempstead*, 42 N.Y.2d 440, 398 N.Y.S.2d 401, 368 N.E.2d 24 (1977) (stating that defendant's activity must have been the proximate cause of the harm in order to impose liability on a theory of strict

liability or negligence); *Cisse v. S.F.J. Realty Corp.*, 256 A.D.2d 257, 682 N.Y.S.2d 199, 201 (1st Dep't 1998); *see also Nieves v. Holmes Protection, Inc.*, 56 N.Y.2d 914, 453 N.Y.S.2d 430, 438 N.E.2d 1145 (1982).

35. *See Rodriguez v. Forest City Jay Assocs.*, 234 A.D.2d 68, 650 N.Y.S.2d 229, 230 (1st Dep't 1996); *Morgan*, 90 N.Y.2d at 485, 662 N.Y.S.2d at 427, 685 N.E.2d 202.

36. N.Y. C.P.L.R. 1411 (1997).

37. *Fitzpatrick v. Int'l Ry. Co.*, 252 N.Y. 127, 134, 169 N.E. 112, 115 (1929).

38. N.Y. C.P.L.R. 1411.

39. N.Y. C.P.L.R. 1412 (1997).

40. N.Y. C.P.L.R. 1411.

41. *Id.*

42. N.Y. C.P.L.R. 1412.

43. *Comeau v. Lucas*, 90 A.D.2d 674, 675, 455 N.Y.S.2d 871, 873 (4th Dep't 1982).

44. N.Y. C.P.L.R. 1411.

45. *Id.*

46. *See Cohen v. Heritage Motor Tours, Inc.*, 205 A.D.2d 105, 618 N.Y.S.2d 387 (2d Dep't 1994); *Mesick v. State*, 118 A.D.2d 214, 504 N.Y.S.2d 279 (3d Dep't 1986).

47. *See also Mesick*, 118 A.D.2d at 218–19, 504 N.Y.S.2d at 282.

48. *Arbegast v. Board of Educ.*, 65 N.Y.2d 161, 490 N.Y.S.2d 751, 480 N.E.2d 365 (1985) (dismissing the complaint based on plaintiff's admission that she was informed of the risk of injury and that participants acted at their own risk).

49. *See id.*

50. *See Benitez v. New York City Bd. of Educ.*, 73 N.Y.2d 650, 543 N.Y.S.2d 29, 541 N.E.2d 29 (1989); *Turcotte v. Fell*, 68 N.Y.2d 432, 510 N.Y.S.2d 49, 502 N.E.2d 964 (1986).

51. *Turcotte*, 68 N.Y.2d at 439, 510 N.Y.S.2d at 53, 502 N.E.2d at 968 (noting that sports participants can be deemed to have consented "to those injury-causing events which are known, apparent or reasonably foreseeable consequences of the participation").

52. *Benitez*, 73 N.Y.2d at 658, 543 N.Y.S.2d at 33, 541 N.E.2d 29. *See also Turcotte*, 68 N.Y.2d at 439, 510 N.Y.S.2d at 53, 502 N.E.2d at 968 (stating that "participants do not consent to acts which are reckless or intentional").

53. *Kambat v. St. Francis Hosp.*, 89 N.Y.2d 489, 494, 655 N.Y.S.2d 844, 846, 678 N.E.2d 456 (1997). The plaintiff does not need to conclusively eliminate all other possible causes of injury to rely on *res ipsa loquitur*. Rather, "[i]t is enough that the evidence supporting the three conditions afford a rational basis for concluding that 'it is more likely than not' that the injury was caused by defendant's negligence." *Id.* at 494, 655 N.Y.S.2d at 846, 678 N.E.2d at 458 (citing Restatement (Second) of Torts § 328D cmt. e).

54. *Id.*

55. *Bennett v. New York & Queens Elec. Light & Power Co.*, 294 N.Y. 334, 62 N.E.2d 219 (1945).

56. *Doundoulakis*, 42 N.Y.2d at 448, 398 N.Y.S.2d at 404, 368 N.E.2d at 27 (stating that the policy behind this rule is that "those who engage in activity of sufficiently high risk of harm to others, especially where there are reasonable even if more costly alternatives, should bear the cost of harm").

57. *Dance v. Town of Southampton*, 95 A.D.2d 442, 467 N.Y.S.2d 203 (2d Dep't 1983).

58. *Id.* at 445, 467 N.Y.S.2d at 206.

59. *See, e.g., See Elliot v. City of New York*, 95 N.Y.2d 730, 734, 747 N.E.2d 760, 762, 724 N.Y.S.2d 397, 399 (2001) ("violation of a municipal ordinance constitutes only evidence of negligence"); *Vega v. Molina*, 240 A.D.2d 399, 658 N.Y.S.2d 387, 388 (2d Dep't 1997) (violation of administrative agency regulation is merely evidence of negligence); *Barnes v. Stone-Quinn*, 195 A.D.2d 12, 606 N.Y.S.2d 485, 486–87 (4th Dep't 1993); *Permuy v. City of New York*, 156 A.D.2d 174, 548 N.Y.S.2d 219, 221 (1st Dep't 1989).

60. *Mazyck v. LIRR*, 896 F. Supp. 1330, 1333 (E.D.N.Y. 1995) (quoting Restatement (Second) of Torts § 433A (1965)).

61. *Hecht v. City of New York*, 60 N.Y.2d 57, 62, 467 N.Y.S.2d 187, 190, 454 N.E.2d 527, 530 (1983).

62. *Ravo v. Rogatnick*, 70 N.Y.2d 305, 309, 520 N.Y.S.2d 533, 535, 514 N.E.2d 1104, 1106 (1987).

63. *Suria v. Shiffman*, 67 N.Y.2d 87, 98, 499 N.Y.S.2d 913, 490 N.E.2d 832 (1986).

64. *See Ravo*, 70 N.Y.2d at 313, 520 N.Y.S.2d at 539, 514 N.E.2d at 1108–09; *Herman v. Wesgate*, 94 A.D.2d 938, 939, 464 N.Y.S.2d 315 (4th Dep't 1983).

65. *Ravo*, 70 N.Y.2d at 313, 520 N.Y.S.2d at 538, 514 N.E.2d at 1108–09; *Graphic Arts Mut. Ins. Co. v. Bakers Mut. Ins. Co.*, 45 N.Y.2d 551, 557, 410 N.Y.S.2d 571, 574, 382 N.E.2d 1347, 1350 (1978).

66. N.Y. C.P.L.R. 1601 (1997).

67. *Id.* The statute is not applicable to property damage or wrongful death claims.

68. N.Y. C.P.L.R. 1601. Noneconomic loss generally includes pain and suffering, mental anguish, and loss of consortium. N.Y. C.P.L.R. 1600 (1997).

69. N.Y. C.P.L.R. 1602 (1997).

70. *Id.* See the statute for a comprehensive list of all of the exclusions. There has been a recent split within the First Department as to whether an unintentional tortfeasor, whose actions set the stage for a joint, intentional tortfeasor's actions, can utilize Section 1601, and apportion liability with the non-party intentional tortfeasor. *Compare Chianese v. Meier*, 729 N.Y.S.2d 460, 467-68 (1st Dep't 2001)("apportionment of liability under CPLR Article 16 is not available with non-party intentional tortfeasors") *to Concepcion v. NYC Health and Hospitals Corp.*, 284 A.D.2d 37, 39, 729 N.Y.S.2d 478, 480 (1st Dep't 2001)("There is nothing in the exclusion that would indicate that it was intended to preclude a negligent tortfeasor from seeking apportionment from an intentional tortfeasor."); *Roseboro v. NYC Transit Auth.*, 729 N.Y.S.2d 472, 474 (1st Dep't 2001).

71. *See Rangolan v. The County of Nassau*, 96 N.Y.2d 42, 49, 749 N.E.2d 178, 184, 725 N.Y.S.2d 611, 617 (2001).

72. N.Y. C.P.L.R. 1402 (1997); *Garrett v. Holiday Inns*, 58 N.Y.2d 253, 258, 460 N.Y.S.2d 774, 777, 447 N.E.2d 717 (1983) (stating that "[p]rinciples allowing apportionment among tort-feasors reflect the important policy that responsibility for damages to an injured person should be borne by those parties responsible for the injury, in proportion to their respective degrees of fault") (citations omitted).

73. N.Y. C.P.L.R. 1401 (1997) (providing that "two or more persons who are subject to liability for damages for the same personal injury, injury to property or wrongful death, may claim contribution among them whether or not an action has been brought or a judgment has been rendered against the person from whom contribution is sought").

74. N.Y. C.P.L.R. 1402.

75. *Ravo*, 70 N.Y.2d at 313, 520 N.Y.S.2d at 538, 514 N.E.2d at 1108.

76. N.Y. Gen. Oblig. Law § 15-108 (2001).

77. *Id.*

78. *Williams by Williams v. Niske*, 81 N.Y.2d 437, 443, 599 N.Y.S.2d 519, 523, 615 N.E.2d 1003 (1993).

79. *Mas v. Two Bridges Assocs.*, 75 N.Y.2d 680, 690, 555 N.Y.S.2d 669, 674, 554 N.E.2d 1257, 1262 (1990); *Perno v. For-Med Med. Group*, 176 Misc. 2d 655, 658, 673 N.Y.S.2d 849, 851 (Sup. Ct.), *appeal dismissed*, 254 A.D.2d 845, 679 N.Y.S.2d 280 (1st Dep't 1998).

80. *McDermott v. City of New York*, 50 N.Y.2d 211, 216, 428 N.Y.S.2d 643, 646, 406 N.E.2d 460, 462 (1980) (quoting *McFall v. Compagnie Maritime Belge*, 304 N.Y. 314, 327–28, 107 N.E.2d 463, 470 (1952)).

81. *General Conference of Seventh Day Adventists v. AON Reinsurance Agency, Inc.*, 860 F. Supp. 983, 986 (S.D.N.Y. 1994), *aff'd*, 50 F.3d 2 (2d Cir. 1995).

82. *General Conference of Seventh Day Adventists*, 860 F. Supp. at 986; *see also Mas*, 75 N.Y.2d at 690, 555 N.Y.S.2d at 674, 554 N.E.2d at 1262 (recognizing "[t]hat the right to [indemnity] may be based upon an express contract, but more commonly the indemnity obligation is implied, . . . based upon the law's notion of what is fair and proper as between the parties").

83. *See e.g.*, N.Y. Gen. Mun. Law § 50-b (1999); N.Y. Gen. Mun. Law § 50-d (1999).

84. N.Y. Work. Comp. Law §§ 1 *et seq.* (1992 and Supp. 1999-2000).

85. N.Y. Work. Comp. Law § 11 (Supp. 2001).

86. *See* N.Y. Work. Comp. Law § 29(6) (Supp. 2001); *Macchirole v. Giambori*, 97 N.Y. 2d 147, 736 N.Y.2d 660 (2001).

87. This practice, first allowed by *Dole v. Dow Chem. Co.*, 30 N.Y.2d 143, 331 N.Y.S.2d 382, 282 N.E.2d 288 (1972), was limited by statute in 1996. *See* N.Y. Work. Comp. Law § 11. If the injured employee enters into a settlement agreement with his or her employer, then the employer can seek dismissal of third-party action under General Obligations Law § 15-108. *See Trzaska v. Cincinnati, Inc.*, 715 N.Y.S.2d 810, 810-11 (4th Dep't 2000).

88. *Id.*; N.Y. Work. Comp. Law § 11; *see Majewski v. BroadAlbin-Perth Cent. Sch. Dist.*, 91 N.Y.2d 577, 673 N.Y.S.2d 966, 699 N.E.2d 978 (1998).

89. N.Y. Work. Comp. Law § 29(6).

90. If the employer has failed to secure workers' compensation coverage for its employee, the injured employee has the choice of electing coverage under the

compensation laws or maintaining an action for damages against the employer. N.Y. Work. Comp. Law § 11. In damage actions filed under this exception, the employer may not use contributory negligence, assumption of risk, or the negligence of a fellow employee as a defense. If the employee elects to sue the employer, he may not sue fellow employees, their collective bargaining agent, or the employer's insurance company or its employees. N.Y. Work. Comp. Law § 29(6).

91. *Acevedo v. Consolidated Edison Co.*, 189 A.D.2d 497, 596 N.Y.S.2d 68 (1st Dep't 1993); *Orzechowski v. Warner-Lambert Co.*, 92 A.D.2d 110, 460 N.Y.S.2d 64 (2d Dep't 1983). To bring a case within the intentional injury exception, the employee must prove that the specific act showed a willful intent to harm the particular employee. *Id.*; *Blanchard v. Integrated Food Sys.*, 220 A.D.2d 895, 632 N.Y.S.2d 329 (3d Dep't 1995). The act must reflect more than gross negligence or reckless conduct against the employee. *Acevedo*, 189 A.D.2d 497, 596 N.Y.S.2d at 71; *Blanchard*, 220 A.D.2d 895, 632 N.Y.S.2d at 330.

92. N.Y. Work. Comp. Law § 29(1) (1993); *see also Burlew v. American Mut. Ins. Co.*, 99 A.D.2d 11, 471 N.Y.S.2d 908 (4th Dep't 1984), *aff'd*, 63 N.Y.2d 412, 482 N.Y.S.2d 720, 472 N.E.2d 682 (1984); *Lear v. New York Helicopter Corp.*, 190 A.D.2d 7, 597 N.Y.S.2d 411 (2d Dep't 1993).

93. N.Y. Work. Comp. Law. § 29(1) (1993); *Kelly v. State Ins. Fund*, 60 N.Y.2d 131, 139, 468 N.Y.S.2d 850, 853, 455 N.E.2d 485 (1983).

94. *Smith v. Spinoccia*, 119 A.D.2d 660, 501 N.Y.S.2d 99 (2d Dep't 1986) (noting that the power to determine the equitable apportionment of litigation expenses is discretionary).

95. *Parmelee v. International Paper Co.*, 157 A.D.2d 878, 550 N.Y.S.2d 150 (3d Dep't 1990).

96. *Basso v. Miller*, 40 N.Y.2d 233, 386 N.Y.S.2d 564, 352 N.E.2d 868 (1976); *Scurti v. City of New York*, 40 N.Y.2d 433, 387 N.Y.S.2d 55, 354 N.E.2d 794 (1976); *Malloy v. Delk Transmission, Inc.*, 191 A.D.2d 303, 594 N.Y.S.2d 772 (1st Dep't 1993).

97. *See Scurti*, 40 N.Y.2d at 437, 387 N.Y.S.2d at 56 (stating that liability of landowners should not be governed "by the ancient and antiquated distinctions between trespassers, licensees, and invitees decisive under common law").

98. *Kellman v. 45 Tiemann Assocs., Inc.*, 87 N.Y.2d 871, 638 N.Y.S.2d 937, 662 N.E.2d 255 (1995); *Macey v. Truman*, 70 N.Y.2d 918, 524 N.Y.S.2d 393, 519 N.E.2d 304 (1987); *Basso*, 40 N.Y.2d 233, 386 N.Y.S.2d 564, 352 N.E.2d 868.

99. N.Y. Gen. Oblig. Law § 11-101(1) (2001).

100. *See id.*

101. *Adamy v. Ziriakus*, 231 A.D.2d 80, 659 N.Y.S.2d 623, 627–28 (4th Dep't 1997), aff'd, 92 N.Y.2d 805, 668 N.Y.S.2d 560, 691 N.E.2d 632 (1998); *Bartkowiak v. St. Adalbert's Roman Catholic Church Soc'y*, 40 A.D.2d 306, 340 N.Y.S.2d 137, 142–43 (4th Dep't 1973).

102. N.Y. Gen. Oblig. Law § 11-101(1); *Ray v. Galloway's Café*, 221 A.D.2d 612, 634 N.Y.S.2d 495 (2d Dep't 1995) (actual damages); *McCauley v. Carmel Lanes Inc.*, 178 A.D.2d 835, 577 N.Y.S.2d 546 (3d Dep't 1991) (exemplary damages).

103. *See Sherman v. Robinson*, 80 N.Y.2d 483, 591 N.Y.S.2d 974, 606 N.E.2d 1365 (1992); *Jacobs v. Amodeo*, 208 A.D.2d 1171, 618 N.Y.S.2d 120 (3d Dep't 1994). However, liability could be imposed under a theory of negligent supervision on parents who have permitted alcohol to be served to under-age guests in their home. *See Comeau v. Lucas*, 90 A.D.2d 674, 455 N.Y.S.2d 871 (4th Dep't 1982).

104. *See Conigliaro v. Franco*, 122 A.D.2d 15, 504 N.Y.S.2d 186, 186 (2d Dep't 1986); *see also Gabrielle v. Craft*, 75 A.D.2d 939, 428 N.Y.S.2d 84, 86 (3d Dep't 1980) (stating that the Dram Shop Act should be narrowly construed in order to effectuate its purpose, which is to "impose liability upon commercial dispensers of alcoholic beverages").

105. *See Conigliaro*, 122 A.D.2d 15, 504 N.Y.S.2d 186 (granting summary judgment for defendant when plaintiff failed to allege an unlawful sale); *Kohler v. Wray*, 114 Misc. 2d 856, 452 N.Y.S.2d 831, 833 (Sup. Ct. 1982) (stating that the Act "has no application to a social host in a non-commercial setting").

106. *See 532 Madison Ave. Gourmet Foods, Inc. v. Finlandia Center, Inc.*, 96 N.Y.2d 280, 292, 750 N.E.2d 1097, 1103, 727 N.Y.S.2d 49, 55 (2001).

107. *MCI Telecommunications Corp. v. John Mezzalingua Assocs., Inc.*, 921 F. Supp. 936, 945 (N.D.N.Y. 1996).

108. N.Y. C.P.L.R. 3016(b) (1991).

109. *New York Univ. v. Continental Ins. Co.*, 87 N.Y.2d 308, 639 N.Y.S.2d 283, 662 N.E.2d 763 (1995); *Shea v. Hambros PLC*, 244 A.D.2d 39, 673 N.Y.S.2d 369 (1st Dep't 1998).

110. *Simcuscki v. Saeli*, 44 N.Y.2d 442, 406 N.Y.S.2d 259, 265, 377 N.E.2d 713 (1978); *Rudman v. Cowles Communications, Inc.*, 30 N.Y.2d 1, 330 N.Y.S.2d 33, 39, 280 N.E.2d 867 (1972).

111. *Allen v. Westpoint-Pepperell, Inc.*, 11 F. Supp. 2d 277 (S.D.N.Y. 1997); *Kimmell v. Schaffer*, 89 N.Y.2d 257, 652 N.Y.S.2d 715, 675 N.E.2d 450 (1996); *Ultramares Corp. v. Touche*, 255 N.Y. 170, 174 N.E. 441 (1931).

112. *Kimmell*, 89 N.Y.2d at 263, 652 N.Y.S.2d at 718–19; *United Safety of Am., Inc. v. Consolidated Edison Co.*, 213 A.D.2d 283, 623 N.Y.S.2d 591 (1st Dep't 1995).

113. *See Allen*, 11 F. Supp. 2d 284.

114. N.Y. Gen. Bus. Law §§ 349–350 (1988).

115. N.Y. Gen. Bus. Law §§ 349(b), 350-c.

116. N.Y. Gen. Bus. Law §§ 349(h); 350-d.

117. *Oswego Laborers' Local 214 Pension Fund v. Marine Midland Bank*, 85 N.Y.2d 20, 623 N.Y.S.2d 529, 532, 647 N.E.2d 741 (1995).

118. N.Y. Gen. Bus. Law §§ 349(h), 350-e.

119. *See Moses v. Citicorp Mortgage, Inc.*, 982 F. Supp. 897, 903 (E.D.N.Y. 1997); *Oxman v. Amoroso*, 172 Misc. 2d 773, 659 N.Y.S.2d 963, 968 (City Ct. 1997); *McDonald v. North Shore Yacht Sales, Inc.*, 134 Misc. 2d 910, 513 N.Y.S.2d 590, 593 (Sup. Ct. 1987).

120. *Oxman*, 172 Misc. 2d 773, 659 N.Y.S.2d at 968. If there is proof of scienter, the court can treble damages up to $1,000. *Oswego Laborers' Local 214*, 85 N.Y.2d at 26, 623 N.Y.S.2d at 533, 647 N.E.2d 741.

121. *Stutman v. Chemical Bank*, 95 N.Y.2d 24, 29, 709 N.Y.S.2d 892, 896, 731 N.E.2d 608, 612 (2000).

122. *See Cole v. Equitable Life Assurance Society of the United States*, 271 A.D.2d 271, 707 N.Y.S.2d 56 (1st Dep't 2000) (applying C.P.L.R. 214(2) to claims arising under N.Y. Gen. Bus. Law § 349; *Russo v. Massachusetts Mutual Life Ins. Co.*, 274 A.D.2d 878, 711 N.Y.S.2d 254 (3d Dep't 2000) (same), *appeal dismissed*, 2000 N.Y. LEXIS 3901 (N.Y. Dec. 21, 2000); *Morelli v. Weider Nutrition Group, Inc.*, 275 A.D.2d 607, 712 N.Y.S.2d 551 (1st Dep't 2000) (same); *Wender v. The Gilberg Agency*, 276 A.D.2d 311, 716 N.Y.S.2d 40 (1st Dep't 2000) (same), *appeal denied*, 2000 N.Y. App. Div. LEXIS 13764 (1st Dep't Oct. 12, 2000). Until these cases, the question of whether the six-year period applicable to fraud claims or the three-year period applicable to rights created by statute should be applied to claims arising under Section 349 had not been resolved. *See Dornberger v. Metropolitan Life Ins. Co.*, 961 F. Supp. 506, 548-49 (S.D.N.Y. 1997) (applying the six-year period applicable to fraud claims contained in C.P.L.R. 213(8) to a claim under Section 349). A consensus now seems to have emerged.

123. *See Wender*, 276 A.D.2d at 312, 716 N.Y.S.2d at 41; *Russo*, 274 A.D.2d at 879; 711 N.Y.S.2d at 255.

124. *Home Ins. Co. v. American Home Prods. Corp.*, 75 N.Y.2d 196, 551 N.Y.S.2d 481, 485, 550 N.E.2d 930 (1990).

125. *Home Ins.*, 75 N.Y.2d at 204, 551 N.Y.S.2d at 485–86, 550 N.E.2d 930; *Rahn v. Carkner*, 241 A.D.2d 585, 659 N.Y.S.2d 143 (3d Dep't 1997); *Doe v. Roe*, 190 A.D.2d 463, 595 N.Y.S.2d 350, 356 (4th Dep't 1993).

126. *See Karen S. v. Streitferdt*, 172 A.D.2d 440, 568 N.Y.S.2d 946, 947 (1st Dep't 1991) (stating that punitive damages should only be awarded in "cases involving an improper state of mind or malice or cases involving wrongdoing to the public"); *Rand & Paseka Mfg. Co. v. Holmes Protection, Inc.*, 130 A.D.2d 429, 431, 515 N.Y.S.2d 468, 470 (1st Dep't 1987).

127. *See* N.Y. E.P.T.L. § 5-4.1 (1999); *Rigano v. Coram Bus Serv. Inc.*, N.Y.L.J., Mar. 15, 1995, at 25.

128. *See, e.g., Manolas v. 303 West 42nd Street Enters., Inc.*, 173 A.D.2d 316, 569 N.Y.S.2d 701, 702 (1st Dep't 1991) (setting aside punitive damage award that was almost 80 times the amount awarded for compensatory damages).

129. *Vasbinder v. Scott*, 976 F.2d 118, 121 (2d Cir. 1992).

130. *See, e.g. Staudacher v. City of Buffalo*, 155 A.D.2d 956, 547 N.Y.S.2d 770, 771 (4th Dep't 1989); *Steinberg v. Monasch*, 85 A.D.2d 403, 406, 448 N.Y.S.2d 200, 202 (1st Dep't 1982); *Mulder v. Donaldson, Lufkin & Jenrette*, 161 Misc. 2d 698, 611 N.Y.S.2d 1019, 1021 (Sup. Ct. 1994), *aff'd*, 208 A.D.2d 301, 623 N.Y.S.2d 560 (1st Dep't 1995).

131. *Bryce v. Wilde*, 39 A.D.2d 291, 333 N.Y.S.2d 614, 616 (3d Dep't 1972), *aff'd*, 31 N.Y.2d 882, 340 N.Y.S.2d 185, 292 N.E.2d 320 (1972); *Action House, Inc. v. Koolik*, 54 F.3d 1009, 1013 (2d Cir. 1995).

132. *Chlystun v. Kent*, 185 A.D.2d 525, 586 N.Y.S.2d 410, 412 (3d Dep't 1992) (affirming punitive damages award of $15,000 for trespass where the compensatory damages were $1); *Bryce*, 39 A.D.2d 291, 333 N.Y.S.2d at 616. Punitive damages have been awarded where equitable relief was sought. *See I.H.P. Corp. v. 210 Central Park South Corp.*, 16 A.D.2d 461, 228 N.Y.S.2d 883 (1st Dep't 1962).

133. *Rupert v. Sellers*, 48 A.D.2d 265, 368 N.Y.S.2d 904 (4th Dep't 1975).

134. *Boguslavsky v. Kaplan*, 159 F.3d 715 (2d Cir. 1998).

135. *Liberman v. Riverside Mem'l Chapel, Inc.*, 225 A.D.2d 283, 650 N.Y.S.2d 194 (1st Dep't 1996).

136. *Commonwealth Assocs. v. Letsos,* 40 F. Supp. 2d 170 (S.D.N.Y. 1999); *Heights Assocs. v. Bautista,* 178 Misc. 2d 669, 683 N.Y.S.2d 372 (2d Dep't 1998), citing *Lakeshore & M.S.R. Co. v. Prentice,* 147 U.S. 101 (1892).

137. *Carrick v. Central Gen. Hosp.,* 51 N.Y.2d 242, 434 N.Y.S.2d 130, 134 n.2, 414 N.E.2d 632 (1980).

138. Article 5, part 4 of the New York Estates, Powers and Trusts Law covers wrongful death law. *See* N.Y. E.P.T.L. §§ 5-4.1 *et seq.* (1999).

139. N.Y. E.P.T.L. § 5-4.1.

140. *Id.* The decedent must have a cause of action on the date of death. If the statute of limitations has run on the decedent's personal injury cause of action before the commencement of the wrongful death action, the distributee can only sue for wrongful death, not personal injury. *See Marlowe v. E.I. Dupont de Nemours & Co.,* 112 A.D.2d 769, 492 N.Y.S.2d 268 (4th Dep't 1985).

141. *Antoine v. State,* 103 Misc. 2d 664, 426 N.Y.S.2d 917, 921 (Ct. Cl. 1980); *Corbett v. Corbett,* 100 Misc. 2d 270, 418 N.Y.S.2d 981, 985 (Queens County Fam. Ct. 1979).

142. Article 11, part 3 of the New York Estates, Powers and Trusts Law covers survival actions. *See* N.Y. E.P.T.L. §§ 11-3.1 *et seq.* (2001).

143. N.Y. E.P.T.L. § 11-3.2. Punitive damages are not recoverable against an estate under the statute. *See id.; see also Flaum v. Birnbaum,* 177 A.D.2d 170, 582 N.Y.S.2d 853 (4th Dep't 1992). However, it is important to remember that punitive damages are recoverable in a wrongful death action, so long as plaintiff has made the required evidentiary showing. *See Rigano v. Coran Bus Services,* 226 A.D.2d 274, 641 N.Y.S.2d 285 (1st Dep't 1996).

NORTH CAROLINA

A. STATUTES OF LIMITATION AND REPOSE

1. Statutes of Limitation

A *one-year* statute of limitations applies to any action for libel and slander,[1] and for recovery of damages for injuries arising from the sale of alcohol to minors.[2]

All actions against local units of government arising out of a contract,[3] and all wrongful death actions are subject to a *two-year* statute of limitations. Wrongful death actions accrue at the date of death.[4] However, if a decedent's claim would have been barred by a different limiting statute had the decedent lived, the time for filing a complaint is not extended by the wrongful death limitation period.[5]

A *three-year* statute of limitations applies to actions for assault, battery and false imprisonment[5.1] arising out of contract;[6] actions based on statutorily created liability;[7] actions for trespass upon real property;[8] actions for conversion or injury to chattels;[9] actions for criminal conversation, emotional distress, and other injury to the person or rights of another;[10] actions for fraud or mistake;[11] actions for misappropriation of trade secrets;[12] and actions for trespass by a public officer under color of office.[13]

Causes of action for personal injury or property damage (except damage to the product in a product liability action), whether brought under negligence or contract (breach of warranty), must be commenced within *three years*.[14] The cause of action accrues on the date the damage or injury becomes apparent, "or ought reasonably to have become apparent to the claimant."[15]

Contract or breach of warranty actions based on the sale of goods, in which damages are limited to the product itself, are subject to the *four-year* UCC statute of limitations, running from the date of sale or delivery, unless the date when the period begins is altered by contract.[16] The cause of action for breach of contract accrues at the time of breach, and the cause of action for breach of warranty occurs when tender of delivery is made, with a very limited application of the discovery rule.[17] The statute of limitations for an unfair trade practice claim is four years.[18]

The statute of limitations on a judgment of any court of the United States[19] or for damages or economic losses due to the negligence of a registered land surveyor[20] is *ten years*. The North Carolina "catch all" provision for actions not specifically limited by other sections, such as constructive trusts and constructive fraud in breach of a fiduciary duty, also establishes a *ten-year* limitation.[21]

The statute of limitations for malpractice in the performance of *professional services* (e.g., medicine,[22] law,[23] accounting[24]) is three years from the "last act of the defendant giving rise to the cause of action."[25] A one-year extension from the date of discovery is allowed for losses "not readily apparent to the claimant," and a repose provision prevents the commencement of any suit more than four years "from the last act of the defendant giving rise to the cause of action."[26]

Conversely, "where damages are sought by reason of a foreign object ... having been left in the body," an action may be commenced therefor within one year of discovery, but in no event more than ten years "from the last act of the defendant giving rise to the cause of action."[27] When the injury is disease, a cause of action grounded in negligence accrues when the disease is diagnosed.[28]

Sexual exploitation by a psychotherapist is subject to a three-year statute of limitations, with accrual at the later of the last act giving rise to the cause of action or the time when the patient discovers or should have discovered the exploitation.[29]

The North Carolina Rules of Civil Procedure allow for the extension of any statute of limitations for one year from the date of a dismissal without prejudice, so long as the initial action was not already barred by the same or separate statute of limitations.[30] If a person is convicted of a criminal offense and is ordered by the court to pay restitution to the victim, then any statute of limitations is tolled from the time of the court order until the full amount of restitution has been paid, with the proviso that no action may be commenced in such a situation more than ten years after the last act of the defendant giving rise to the action.[31]

2. **Statutes of Repose**

Statutes of repose have a substantial practical effect on litigation. Statutes of repose are substantive definitions of rights rather than merely procedural bars as are statutes of limitation.[32]

A product liability cause of action on any theory is barred more than *six years* after the date of "initial purchase for use or consumption."[33] Sale to an intermediary or distributor is not a sale for initial use or consumption for purposes of beginning the repose period.[34]

Suits involving improvements to real property are limited by a *six-year* statute of repose, with the triggering event being the later of the "specific last act or omission of the defendant" or "substantial completion of the improvement."[35] This limitation is not available as a defense by a person who had control over the improvement at the time of injury and knew or should have known of the unsafe condition,[36] or to a person guilty of fraud or willful negligence in connection with the unsafe condition.[37]

North Carolina also has a general statute of repose which provides "that no cause of action shall accrue more than ten years from the last act or omission of the defendant giving rise to the cause of action."[38] The limitation and repose periods are tolled by statute for minors and others with disabilities whose claims accrue before expiration of the repose period.[39]

B. **TORT REFORM**

North Carolina has enacted tort reform incrementally over the past twenty years. In 1977, a provision was enacted codifying the discovery rule in professional malpractice actions and establishing a four year statute of repose for such actions.[40] A 1979 law codified the discovery rule and a ten-year statute of repose for all torts.[41]

The Legislature first enacted a products liability statute in 1979.[42] That statute was amended by a provision governing claims based on defective design of firearms,[43] which became effective in 1988, and by sections governing strict liability,[44] breach of warranty,[45] and claims based on inadequate warning[46] and inadequate design,[47] all of which became effective in 1996. Punitive damages were the subject of a comprehensive statute which took effect in 1996.[48]

Other limited reforms have recently been enacted or are pending. 1999 N.C. Session Laws established limitations regarding potential liability of North Carolina businesses arising from Y2K problems[49] and provide certain parties an affirmative defense based on Y2K problems.[50] Currently pending, Senate Bill 24 would require insurers to provide policy information prior to litigation and would allow an insurer who provides such information the option of initiating mediation.

C. **"NO FAULT" LIMITATIONS**

North Carolina has not adopted a "no fault" insurance regime. Regulations mandating insurance coverage for injuries resulting from motor vehicle accidents are legislated by The Motor Vehicle Safety and Financial Responsibility Act of 1953.[51] This act, however, does not include a "no fault" provision.

D. **THE STANDARD FOR NEGLIGENCE**

In North Carolina, negligence is generally "the failure to exercise the degree of care that a reasonably prudent person would exercise in the same circumstances."[52] A plaintiff in a negligence action must prove: (1) that the defendant owed him a duty; (2) that the defendant breached that duty; and (3) that the defendant's breach of the duty was a proximate cause of the plaintiff's injury.[53] The jury is instructed that the standard of care is that of a reasonable and prudent person under the same or similar circumstances.[54] The degree of care required of the "reasonably prudent man ... varies with the exigencies of the occasion."[55]

North Carolina also recognizes the "sudden emergency" doctrine, which provides a less stringent standard of care where someone is confronted, through no fault of their own, with sudden and unexpected danger.[56] The courts apply a two-pronged test in which they must first decide whether a sudden emergency in fact existed, and if so, whether or not the emergency was caused by the negligence of the defendant.[57] The defendant must pass both prongs to benefit from application of the lower standard.[58]

North Carolina requires that a medical, dental, or health care professional perform "in accordance with the standards of practice among members of the same health care profession with similar training and experience situated in the same or similar communities at the time of the alleged act giving rise to the cause of action."[59] An expert witness "in the particular field of practice of the defendant heath care provider or . . . equally familiar and competent to testify as to that limited field of practice" must be called to establish the applicable standard of care and breach.[60] A Rule of Procedure requires that in medical malpractice actions, the pleadings must assert that the medical care has been reviewed by such a person.[61] However, this Rule of Procedure was recently declared unconstitutional by the North Carolina Court of Appeals,[61.1] but the decision is currently being reviewed by the North Carolina Supreme Court. The "common knowledge exception" allows a plaintiff to forego testimony by an expert witness where the physician's conduct is grossly negligent or of such a nature that common knowledge among lay persons would establish the standard of care.[62]

The standard of care for a child in North Carolina requires a comparison with how a child of similar "age, capacity, discretion, knowledge and experience would ordinarily have acted under similar circumstances."[63] Children under seven years of age are incapable of negligence as a matter of law.[64] Children between the ages of seven and fourteen are presumed incapable of negligence, but the presumption can be overcome by evidence of capacity.[65] When a child reaches the age of fourteen, he is presumed capable of negligence, which presumption may be "rebutted by clear proof of the absence of such discretion as is usual with infants of that age."[66]

E. **CAUSATION**

For a plaintiff to show a prima facie case of negligence, the plaintiff must establish that the defendant's breach of duty was both the actual and proximate cause of plaintiff's injuries.[67] Proximate cause is defined as "a cause without which the claimed injury would not have occurred, and one which under the same or similar circumstances a reasonably careful and prudent person could foresee would probably produce such injury."[68] The defendant's negligence does not have to be the only proximate cause of the plaintiff's injury, so long as it is one of the proximate causes of that injury.[69]

Intervening negligence may relieve a defendant of liability for an original negligent act where the intervening act and the resultant injury are such that they were not reasonably foreseeable by the defendant.[70] North Carolina has not adopted the rule that subsequent medical malpractice is foreseeable as a matter of law, and therefore the foreseeability of subsequent malpractice is a question for the jury.[71]

The plaintiff in a products liability case must present evidence showing that the product was defective when it left the manufacturer's control and that the chain of causation has not been significantly interrupted by the intervention of third parties.[72] A manufacturer may not be held liable for injury, death or damage caused by misuse, alteration or modification of the product done without allowance, instruction or express consent of the manufacturer.[73]

Neither negligence[74] nor proximate cause[75] may be presumed by the mere fact of accident or injury while using a product. *Res ipsa loquitur* may apply, however, in those cases in which the instrumentality is shown to be under the exclusive control of the defendant and the occurrence is one that does not occur in the ordinary course, under proper care.[76]

F. **CONTRIBUTORY NEGLIGENCE, COMPARATIVE NEGLIGENCE, AND ASSUMPTION OF RISK**

1. **Contributory Negligence**

North Carolina continues to recognize contributory negligence[77] as a complete defense to claims of negligence and product liability.[78] Where a plaintiff is aware of a known danger, has an opportunity to avoid the known danger, and fails to avoid the known danger, such failure is contributory negligence and is a complete bar to recovery.[79] A child can be contributorily negligent. (See Section D, *supra*.)[80]

Contributory negligence does not, however, bar damages based on an action solely for breach of contract,[81] nor is contributory negligence a valid defense to an unfair trade practices claim.[81.1] Contributory negligence also does not bar recovery where defendant's conduct is found to be wanton or willful.[82] Where a patient, under care of a psychiatric hospital for suicidal tendencies, actually commits suicide as a result of the hospital's negligence, the act of suicide may not be contributory negligence and may not insulate the hospital from liability.[83]

A defendant alleging contributory negligence as an affirmative defense has the burden of proving that the plaintiff was negligent and that this negligence was a proximate cause of the plaintiff's injuries.[84] Failure to properly plead contributory negligence as an affirmative defense ordinarily results in a waiver of the defense, but it may still be tried by implied consent where neither party objects to submission of the issue to the jury.[85]

The contributory negligence doctrine is ameliorated by the "last clear chance" doctrine so that "if defendant had the last clear chance to avoid injury to the plaintiff and failed to exercise it, then his negligence, and not the contributory negligence of the plaintiff is the proximate cause of the injury."[86] Last clear chance becomes an issue for the jury once the plaintiff establishes its five essential elements.[87]

2. **Comparative Negligence**

Neither comparative negligence nor any other form of apportionment of fault by the fact finder has been adopted in North Carolina by statute or by judicial decision. Contributory negligence therefore remains a complete bar to recovery.[88] Likewise, common law joint and several liability among defendants continues to apply. (See Section I, *infra*.)

3. **Assumption of Risk**

Assumption of risk is a complete defense to a negligence action in North Carolina if there is a contractual relationship between the parties.[89] Assumption of risk in a contract for services "extends only to those risks which are normally incident to the occupation in which the plaintiff engages" and does not include extraordinary risks or additional hazards caused by a contractor's negligence.[90] Contributory negligence, rather than assumption of risk, is frequently the more effective affirmative defense before triers of fact in North Carolina. The primary distinction between contributory negligence, arising out of tort, and assumption of risk, arising out of contract, is that assumption of risk is based upon the contracting plaintiff's actual or constructive knowledge of the risks to be encountered in the work to be done, and acceptance thereof, while contributory negligence implies an "imprudent act" or "dereliction of duty" by an injured party.[91]

Assumption of risk is a complete, statutory defense to claims of negligence or breach of implied warranty in products liability actions, if it can be proved that the plaintiff knew of a dangerous condition of a product which was inconsistent with its safe use, but unreasonably and voluntarily exposed himself to the danger and was injured as a result of the known condition.[92]

G. *RES IPSA LOQUITUR* AND INHERENTLY DANGEROUS ACTIVITIES

1. Res Ipsa Loquitur

Res ipsa loquitur allows an inference of negligence by the defendant in the absence of specific "circumstances pointing to the responsible human cause" where: (1) there is an injury; (2) the injury causing occurrence would not normally occur in the absence of negligence; and (3) "the instrumentality which caused the injury was under the exclusive control and management of the defendant."[93] Where *res ipsa loquitur* applies, it is sufficient to carry the issue of negligence to the jury, but it is for the jury to decide whether the inference of negligence is sufficiently strong to warrant a finding of negligence by the defendant.[94]

Res ipsa loquitur may apply in those cases in which the instrumentality is shown to be under the exclusive control of the defendant and the occurrence is one that does not occur in the ordinary course of business under proper care.[95] For *Res ipsa loquitur* to apply, the plaintiff must show that the defendant was the only probable tort-feasor.[96] North Carolina courts have expressly stated that *res ipsa loquitur* does not apply to slip and fall cases.[97] *Res ipsa loquitur* also does not apply in actions against municipalities for injuries to persons using its public streets or sidewalks.[98]

2. Inherently Dangerous Activities

"Ultrahazardous" activities are those that are so dangerous that even the exercise of reasonable care cannot eliminate the risk of serious harm.[99] An employer who engages in, or a party who conducts, an ultrahazardous activity may be held liable, but in North Carolina only blasting operations are considered ultrahazardous.[100]

"Inherently dangerous" activities are those that can be performed safely only when certain precautions are taken and which ordinarily cause injury to others when those precautions are not taken.[101] One may be liable for failing to take the necessary precautions to control the risks associated with the activity. Negligence standards apply.[102] Whether an activity is inherently dangerous is frequently decided as a matter of law,[103] but the question may be left to a jury.[104]

H. NEGLIGENCE *PER SE*

Violation of a regulatory or statutory safety standard is generally held to be negligence *per se* if (1) the purpose of the standard is to protect the class of persons and interests harmed, (2) against the type of harm alleged, (3) caused by the particular hazard addressed by the standard.[105] Such negligence may be excused if it results from a sudden emergency.[106]

Non-statutory safety codes are generally inadmissible,[107] but this is not a hard and fast rule.[108] Such non-statutory standards may be admissible as *evidence* of negligence when they are published by a source that is considered reliable by persons involved in the subject matter area or when the standards are adopted by the defendant.[109] Compliance with government standards is evidence of reasonableness of design.[110]

I. JOINT AND SEVERAL LIABILITY

North Carolina common law provides joint and several liability among tort-feasors for resulting injury[111] without apportionment of fault.[112] The distinction between joint liability and "joint and several" liability lies in the ties between the defendants, so that where defendants are "so closely tied that the judgment against each must be consistent," then joint liability applies.[113] Joint and several liability allows a plaintiff to demand payment from or sue one or more parties separately or collectively, at his option, in order to recover the whole amount of damages.[114] Parties are joint tort-feasors where their independent wrongful acts unite to produce a single indivisible injury,[115] but only if each actively participates in an act which causes the injury.[116]

The Uniform Contribution Among Tortfeasors Act (the "Contribution Act") applies in North Carolina.[117] Under the Contribution Act, a right of contribution exists when two or more persons are jointly and severally liable for the same injury to a person or to property.[118] The total recovery available in contribution is limited to the amount paid in excess of a tortfeasor's *pro rata* share of liability. Contribution is not available for a tortfeasor who has intentionally contributed to an injury.[119]

A release given to one joint tortfeasor does not release other joint tortfeasors unless such additional release is provided for in the agreement, but such release reduces claims against other joint tortfeasors by the amount in the release or by the amount of the consideration paid for the release, whichever is greater.[120] Such a release discharges the recipient of any liability for contribution to any other tortfeasor.[121] The North Carolina Supreme Court has held that the statutory provision governing releases applies to "master-servant vicarious liability" and that a release of an employee does not necessarily release a defendant employer from liability.[122]

Where an injury arises as a result of a conspiracy, all conspirators are jointly and severally liable for damages resulting from the acts of any one of them in furtherance of the conspiracy.[123]

J. INDEMNITY

Indemnity allows one defendant to recover from another the full amount of liability owed to a plaintiff when the plaintiff's loss is caused by the other's negligence.[124] North Carolina allows for indemnity by contract, and also under the common law where defendants are jointly and severally liable and a distinction can be made in the degree of fault between the defendants.[125] A defendant who is secondarily liable may recover from a defendant who is primarily liable only when there is joint and several liability, and either (1) the negligence of the secondarily liable defendant was only passive, and exposure to liability was caused by the active negligence of the primarily responsible defendant, or (2) the liability of the secondarily liable defendant is purely derivative, which can occur in an agency or employment relationship.[126]

Where a party seeks contractual indemnification for a judgment of negligence, "indemnity against negligence must be made unequivocally clear in the contract, particularly in a situation where the parties have presumably dealt at arm's length."[127]

K. BAR OF WORKERS' COMPENSATION STATUTE

Workers' compensation is the subject of a comprehensive North Carolina statute.[128] By statute, the rights and remedies afforded an employee by the Workers' Compensation Act are exclusive, and those rights and remedies preclude any other relief by or on behalf of an employee against an employer covered by the Act, regardless of the employer's negligence.[129] Primary jurisdiction for almost all disputes arising under the Workers' Compensation Act lies with the North Carolina Industrial Commission.[130]

Receipt of benefits is not affected by the fact that a third party may also be liable,[131] and receipt of benefits does not bar an injured employee from seeking damages from a third party,[132] though an employee may have only one recovery for damages caused.[133] Employers who are not a cause of the injury, and their subrogated carriers, may generally seek reimbursement for amounts paid to employees injured by the negligence of third parties.[134]

The Workers' Compensation Act "includes employment by the State and all political subdivisions thereof," as well as all private employers with three or more regular employees.[135] The Act covers "only injury by accident arising out of and in the course of the employment,"[136] and whether an injury arises out of and in the course of the employment is a mixed question of fact and law.[137] A statutory presumption exists that all employers and employees as defined by the Act have accepted the provisions of the Act and will pay and accept benefits for on the job injuries as set out in the statute.[138]

The North Carolina Supreme Court has created a narrow exception to the exclusive remedy provision where an employer's conduct is *intentional* and substantially certain to cause the injury or death (a "Woodson" claim).[139] An employee, or the employee's estate, may then pursue *both* a workers' compensation claim and a civil action against the employer, though there can be only one remedy.[140]

An employer's subrogated claim against a third party for injury to an employee may not be recovered if the employer's negligence was a concurrent cause of the injury, and the amount of any verdict against the third party is offset by the amount paid by the employer.[141] The third party defending must plead the negligence of the employer and serve the pleading on the employer. Though the employer need *not* be a named party to the suit, the employer has a right to appear and participate in trial if the employer's negligence is pleaded as a cause of the damages sought.[142]

Settlement by a third party of any claim involving a workers' compensation payment by an employer must be disbursed by order of the Industrial Commission.[143]

L. PREMISES LIABILITY

Until recently, North Carolina followed the traditional common law rule that a property owner's duty to a third party depended upon whether that person was a trespasser, licensee, or invitee.[144] A property owner in North Carolina traditionally had no duty to keep premises safe for use by a licensee. A licensee, a person who entered with permission but for his own purposes, assumed the risk of enjoying the use of the property "subject to its accompanying perils," and with no subsequent liability against the property owner for negligence.[145]

This traditional rule has been modified by the North Carolina Supreme Court so that "the distinction between licensees and invitees" is eliminated[146] and replaced with "a standard of reasonable care toward all lawful visitors."[147] The Supreme Court specifically retained the traditional rule regarding trespassers, so that as to them "a landowner need only refrain from the willful or wanton infliction of injury."[148]

M. DRAM SHOP LIABILITY

The North Carolina Dram Shop Act[149] allows a claim where a party can show that a seller (1) "negligently sold or furnished an alcoholic beverage to an underage person;" (2) that the consumption of the beverage contributed to the underage driver's impairment; and (3) that this impairment contributed to the underage driver's negligent operation of a vehicle that was a proximate cause of the injury alleged.[150] The Act limits recovery to "aggrieved parties," defined as those persons injured by an underage intoxicated person within the parameters of the Act, but not anyone "who aided or abetted in the sale or furnishing" of alcohol to the underage person.[151]

Additionally, the North Carolina Supreme Court has allowed common law negligence claims for negligent provision of alcohol by a social host and by a commercial vendor where the host or vendor provided alcohol to a guest and "knew or should have known that the guest was intoxicated and was going to drive a car shortly after consuming the alcohol."[152] Selling or providing alcoholic beverages to an underage person is not, standing alone, negligence *per se*.[153]

N. ECONOMIC LOSS

North Carolina has adopted the "economic loss rule," which states that purely economic loss is not recoverable in tort.[154] Losses from damage to the product itself are not recoverable in a product liability or other tort action, but must be sought in a contract/UCC claim.[155] "Where a defective product causes damage to property other than the product itself, losses attributable to the defective product are recoverable in tort rather than contract."[156]

O. FRAUD AND MISREPRESENTATION

The North Carolina Rules of Civil Procedure require that all fraud claims be pleaded with particularity.[157]

Fraud and intentional misrepresentation require pleading and proof of the following elements: (1) a false representation or concealment of material fact; (2) reasonably calculated to deceive; (3) made with intent to deceive; (4) upon which representation there is reasonable reliance and action; (5) which action results in damages to the injured party.[158] North Carolina requires *scienter*, which includes an intent to deceive and knowledge of the falsity of the representation, to prove the elements of fraud.[159] Reckless indifference to the truth or falsity of a representation is not sufficient to satisfy the knowledge requirement.[160]

The tort of negligent misrepresentation occurs when an individual, (1) while engaged in a course of business or other transaction in which he has a pecuniary interest, (2) supplies false information, (3) for the guidance of others in a business transaction, (4) without exercising reasonable care in obtaining or communicating the information, and (5) that the plaintiff is among those intended to receive the information and (6) justifiably relies on that information to plaintiff's detriment.[161] The primary distinction between fraud/intentional misrepresentation and negligent misrepresentation is that the former requires knowledge of falsity and intent to deceive by the defendant, whereas the latter is based on a lack of reasonable care.[162] Liability for negligent misrepresentation may be extended to third parties where the defendant knew or intended that the third party would rely on his opinion, and the third party did in fact justifiably rely on that opinion to his detriment.[163]

P. CONSUMER FRAUD STATUTES

North Carolina statutes provide that unfair methods of competition and unfair or deceptive acts or practices in or affecting commerce are unlawful.[164] Commerce is defined as all business activities, however defined, but not including professional services provided by a member of a learned profession.[165] A party claiming exemption from the statute has the burden of proving the exemption.[166]

A claim of unfair and deceptive trade practices must be founded upon evidence of (1) an unfair or deceptive act or practice or unfair method of competition, (2) in or affecting commerce, (3) proximately causing actual injury to plaintiff or his business.[167] Practices are deceptive if they have the tendency to deceive the average consumer, but proof of bad faith or actual deception is not required.[168]

North Carolina courts have also held that actions constitute unfair trade practices when they are "immoral, unethical, oppressive, unscrupulous, or substantially injurious to consumers" and when a party "engages in conduct which amounts to an inequitable assertion of its power or position."[169] Whether a particular act is unfair or deceptive depends on the facts surrounding the transaction and the transaction's impact on the marketplace, and the determination as to whether it is an unfair or deceptive practice is a question of law to be decided by the court.[170]

Nominal damages, and actual damages proved with a reasonable degree of certainty to have been caused by the violation of the Unfair and Deceptive Trade Practices Act, are recoverable.[171] Proof of unfair or deceptive trade practices requires the trial court, after verdict, to treble damages and award reasonable attorney fees and costs in a civil action.[172] A plaintiff may not recover both treble and punitive damages, but the election is allowed in the judgment after a verdict is rendered.[173]

Q. PUNITIVE DAMAGES

Punitive damages are the subject of a comprehensive statute which applies to all claims arising after January 1, 1996.[174] They are recoverable in negligence actions only where the plaintiff recovers compensatory damages and there is clear and convincing evidence of actual fraud, malice, or willful or wanton conduct related to the injury.[175] The conduct must be more than gross negligence.[176] A willful act is one done purposely and deliberately in violation of the law, and a wanton act is one done with "wicked purpose" or "with reckless indifference to the rights of others."[177]

Specificity is required in pleading[178] and only nine categories of evidence may be considered by the jury.[179] Vicarious liability cannot be the basis for punitive damages.[180]

Generally, the amount awarded is limited to the greater of three times compensatory damages, or $250,000.[181] The jury is not thus instructed.[182] The cap on punitive damages does not apply in actions where the defendant was operating an automobile while intoxicated.[183] Separate trial is required upon defendant's motion.[184] Attorneys' fees shall be awarded as penalty for frivolous pleading of punitive damages.[185] Punitive damages are not recoverable under breach of warranty or breach of contract.[186]

Claims for punitive damages arising *before* January 1, 1996, may rest upon gross negligence as well as willful or wanton misconduct, and those claims have no limits other than as provided by the U.S. Supreme Court.[187]

R. WRONGFUL DEATH AND SURVIVORSHIP ACTIONS

1. Wrongful Death

North Carolina provides recovery for wrongful death only in accord with the applicable statute.[188] The statute allows a decedent's personal representative to recover damages upon an action the decedent could have brought had the decedent lived.[189] The statute allows recovery for expenses incurred in treatment of the injury resulting in death up to the lesser of

$4,500 or 50 percent of the net recovery, and it provides that any recovery shall be applied by the estate first to any expenses incurred by the estate in pursuing the action, second to the payment of attorney's fees, and the remainder to be distributed according to the Intestate Succession Act.[190] Damages recoverable include only: (1) expenses for care incident to the injury causing death; (2) compensation for pain and suffering of the decedent; (3) reasonable funeral expenses; (4) present monetary value to the statutory beneficiaries of the reasonably expected (a) amount of the net income of the decedent, (b) services, protection and care from decedent, and (c) society and companionship from decedent; (5) punitive damages; and (6) nominal damages.[191] The statute deems admissible any evidence which reasonably tends to establish any of the allowed damages or the monetary value of the decedent to the persons entitled to recover.[192]

Settlement of all wrongful death claims in which a minor is a potential beneficiary must be approved by the court.[193]

North Carolina does not recognize either an action for "wrongful life" by a child, or an action for "wrongful birth" by a parent.[194]

2. **Survivorship**

The North Carolina survival statute allows actions for or against a deceased to survive death and pass to the personal representative,[195] excluding actions for libel, slander, false imprisonment, or any causes of action in which the relief sought could not be enjoyed after the decedent's death.[196] Under the statute, settlement offers in a lawsuit survive the death of the plaintiff and pass to the personal representative.[197] The rights of a viable fetus survive its death and pass to its personal representative, but are joined with the parents' action for personal injuries or wrongful death.[198] Damages for pecuniary loss, loss of services, and companionship of a fetus are not recoverable because of their speculative nature, but damages for adequately proved pain and suffering, funeral expenses, punitive and nominal damages are recoverable.[199]

William F. Womble, Jr.
Jack M. Strauch
WOMBLE CARLYLE SANDRIDGE & RICE, P.L.L.C.
P.O. Drawer 84
Winston-Salem, North Carlolina 27102
(336) 721-3600
Fax (336) 733-8318
bwomble@wcsr.com
jstrauch@wcsr.com
www.wcsr.com

ENDNOTES - NORTH CAROLINA

1. N.C. Gen. Stat. § 1-54(3); *Ward v. Lyall*, 125 N.C. App. 732, 482 S.E.2d 740, *rev. denied*, 346 N.C. 290, 487 S.E.2d 573, *app. dismissed*, 488 S.E.2d 791 (1997) (defamation) (holding that statute is tolled as long as action based on state substantive law and arising out of same set of facts is pending in federal court).

2. N.C. Gen. Stat. § 1-54(7a); *see also* N.C. Gen. Stat. §§ 18B-120 through 18B-129 (Chap. 18B: Regulation of Alcoholic Beverages; Art. 1A: Compensation for Injury Caused by Sales to Underage Persons").

3. N.C. Gen. Stat. § 1-53(1); *Cooke v. Town of Rich Square*, 65 N.C. App. 606, 310 S.E.2d 76 (1983), *rev. denied*, 311 N.C. 753, 321 S.E.2d 130 (1984).

4. N.C. Gen. Stat. § 1-53(4); *Friedland v. Gales*, 131 N.C. App. 802, 509 S.E.2d 793 (1998) (holding that defendant who deliberately conceals identity as tortfeasor in wrongful death action is equitably estopped from asserting statute of limitations as defense to suit resulting from tortious act).

5. *See id.* (where such action would have been barred by N.C. Gen. Stat. § 1-15(c), statute runs from accrual of action) or § 1-52(16) (discovery rule and ten-year repose provision)).

5.1. N.C. Gen. Stat. § 1-52(19) (eff. Oct. 1, 2001).

6. N.C. Gen. Stat. § 1-52(1) (unless governed by § 1-53(1)); *Thomas v. Thomas*, 102 N.C. App. 124, 401 S.E.2d 396 (1991) (holding that for continuous services under contract, the cause of action accrues as services are rendered, and recovery is limited to three years prior to filing of suit).

7. N.C. Gen. Stat. § 1-52(2) (unless the statute specifies another time); *Capital Outdoor Advertising, Inc. v. City of Raleigh*, 337 N.C. 150, 160, 446 S.E.2d 289, 295, *rev. denied*, 337 N.C. 807, 449 S.E.2d 566 (1994) (finding § 1-52 the appropriate North Carolina statute of limitations for claim under 42 U.S.C. § 1983).

8. N.C. Gen. Stat. § 1-52(3) (where trespass is continuing, the cause of action accrues, and the three-year period runs, from date of original trespass); *Robertson v. City of High Point*, 129 N.C. App. 88, 497 S.E.2d 300, *rev. denied*, 348 N.C. 500, 510 S.E.2d 654 (1998).

9. N.C. Gen. Stat. § 1-52(4).

10. N.C. Gen. Stat. § 1-52(5) (and "any other injury . . . not arising on contract and not hereinafter enumerated); *Jones v. Asheville Radiological Group, P.A.*, 134 N.C. App. 520, 518 S.E.2d 528, 532-33 (1999), *reversed in part on other grounds*, 351 N.C. 348, 524 S.E.2d 804 (2000).

11. N.C. Gen. Stat. § 1-52(9) (discovery rule applies); *Seigel v. Patel*, 132 N.C. App. 783, 513 S.E.2d 602 (1999).

12. N.C. Gen. Stat. § 66-157 (discovery rule applies).

13. N.C. Gen. Stat. § 1-52(13); *Staley*, supra note 1, at 517 S.E.2d 392.

14. N.C. Gen. Stat. § 1-52(1)-(5); *Hanover Ins. Co. v. Amana Refrigeration, Inc.*, 106 N.C. App. 79, 415 S.E.2d 99, 101, *rev. denied*, 332 N.C. 344, 421 S.E.2d 147 (1992) (property damage); *Bernick v. Jurden*, 306 N.C. 435, 293 S.E.2d 405 (1982) (personal injury, non-privity); *Smith v. Cessna Aircraft Co.*, 571 F. Supp. 433 (M.D.N.C. 1983) (personal injury).

15. N.C. Gen. Stat. § 1-52(16).

16. N.C. Gen. Stat. § 25-2-725(1); *Reece v. Homette Corp.*, 110 N.C. App. 462, 429 S.E.2d 768 (1993) (holding that product liability remedies are not available for damage to product; also, UCC limitation period runs from date of sale); *Bobbet v. Tannewitz*, 538 F. Supp. 654 (M.D.N.C. 1982); *Smith v. Cessna Aircraft*, supra note 14, at 571 F. Supp. 433.

17. N.C. Gen. Stat. § 25-2-725(2) (limited discovery rule applies only to breach of warranty; four year period for breach of contract runs regardless of knowledge of harm by aggrieved party).

18. N.C. Gen. Stat. § 75-16.2; *Seigel v. Patel*, 132 N.C. App. 783, 513 S.E.2d 602 (1999).

19. N.C. Gen. Stat. § 1-47(1); *Silvering v. Vito*, 107 N.C. App. 270, 419 S.E.2d 360 (1992) (recognizing that a judgment is still valid within ten years of entry even if judgment is for amount owed for more than ten years).

20. N.C. Gen. Stat. § 1-47(6).

21. N.C. Gen. Stat. § 1-56; *Barger v. McCoy Hilliard & Parks*, 120 N.C. App. 326, 335-36, 462 S.E.2d 252 (1995), *aff'd in part, rev'd in part on other grounds*, 346 N.C. 650, 488 S.E.2d 215 (1997); *Davis v. Wrenn*, 121 N.C. App. 156, 464 S.E.2d 708 (1995), *cert. denied*, 343 N.C. 305, 471 S.E.2d 69 (1996) (constructive trusts); *Guy v. Guy*, 104 N.C. App. 753, 411 S.E.2d 403 (1991) (constructive trusts); *Adams v. Moore*, 96 N.C. App. 359, 385 S.E.2d 799 (1989), *rev. denied*, 326 N.C. 46, 389 S.E.2d 83 (1990) (constructive fraud based on breach of fiduciary duty).

22. *Nelson v. Patrick*, 58 N.C. App. 546, 293 S.E.2d 829 (1982).

23. *Clodfelter v. Bates*, 44 N.C. App. 107, 260 S.E.2d 672 (1979), *rev. denied*, 299 N.C. 329, 265 S.E.2d 394 (1980).

24. *Barger*, supra note 21, at 462 S.E.2d 252.

25. N.C. Gen. Stat. § 1-15(c) and § 1-52(16); *Goins v. Puleo*, 130 N.C. App. 28, 502 S.E.2d 621 (1998), *rev'd on other grounds*, 350 N.C. 277, 512 S.E.2d 748 (1999) (also discussing "continuing course of treatment doctrine" which tolls applicable statute of limitations under very limited circumstances); *Trexler v. Pollock*, 135 N.C. App. 601, 602, 522 S.E.2d 84 (1999) (taking medication not "continuing course of treatment").

26. N.C. Gen. Stat. § 1-15(c); *Delta Environmental Consultants of North Carolina, Inc. v. Wysong & Miles Co.*, 132 N.C. App. 160, 510 S.E.2d 690, *rev. denied and dismissed*, 350 N.C. 379, 536 S.E.2d 70 (1999) (repose provision); *Teague v. Randolph Surgical Associates, P.A.*, 129 N.C. App. 766, 501 S.E.2d 382 (1998) (one-year extension from discovery).

27. N.C. Gen. Stat. § 1-15(c); *Hensell v. Winslow*, 106 N.C. App. 285, 416 S.E.2d 426, *rev. denied*, 332 N.C. 344, 421 S.E.2d 148 (1992).

28. *Dunn v. Pacific Employers Inc. Co.*, 332 N.C. 129, 132, 418 S.E.2d 645, 647 (1992); *Wilder v. Amatex Corp.*, 314 N.C. 550, 560-561, 336 S.E.2d 66, 72 (1985).

29. N.C. Gen. Stat. § 90-21.47 (including ten year statute of repose provision) (enacted 1998, became effective Jan. 1, 1999).

30. N.C. Gen. Stat. § 1A-1, Rule 41(a)(1)(1990); *Staley*, supra note 1, at 517 S.E.2d 392.

31. N.C. Gen. Stat. § 1-15.1; *Whitley v. Kennerly*, 132 N.C. App. 390, 512 S.E.2d 426, *rev. denied*, 350 N.C. 385, 536 S.E.2d 320 (1999) (statute is tolled even if court does not enter specific amount of restitution to be paid).

32. *Boudreau v. Baughman*, 322 N.C. 331, 368 S.E.2d 849, 857 (1988); *Tipton & Young Const. Co., Inc. v. Blue Ridge Structure Co.*, 116 N.C. App. 115, 117, 446 S.E.2d 603, 604 (1994), *aff'd*, 340 N.C. 257, 456 S.E.2d 308 (1995).

33. N.C. Gen. Stat. § 1-50(a)(6); *Vogl v. LVD Corp.*, 132 N.C. App. 797, 514 S.E.2d 113, 115 (1999) (evidence of later purchase of replacement parts is insufficient to overcome six-year bar); *Hyer v. Pittsburgh Corning Corp.*, 790 F.2d 30 (4th Cir. 1986).

34. *Chicopee, Inc. v. Sims Metal Works, Inc.*, 98 N.C. App. 423, 391 S.E.2d 211, *rev. denied*, 327 N.C. 426, 395 S.E.2d 674, *reconsid. den.*, 327 N.C. 632, 397 S.E.2d 76 (1990).

35. N.C. Gen. Stat. § 1-50(a)(5)a.; *Monson v. Paramount Homes, Inc.*, 133 N.C. App. 235, 515 S.E.2d 445, 450 (1999) (repairs "did not reset the running of the statute

of repose"); *Forsyth Mem. Hosp., Inc. v. Armstrong World Indus., Inc.*, 336 N.C. 438, 444 S.E.2d 423 (1994).

36. N.C. Gen. Stat. § 1-50(a)(5)d; *Cage v. Colonial Bldg. Co., Inc. of Raleigh*, 337 N.C. 682, 448 S.E.2d 115 (1994).

37. N.C. Gen. Stat. § 1-50(a)(5)e; *Forsyth Mem. Hosp.*, supra note 35, at 444 S.E.2d 423.

38. N.C. Gen. Stat. § 1-52(16); *Cage,* supra note 36, at 448 S.E.2d 115; *Jordan v. Foust Oil Co., Inc.*, 116 N.C. App. 155, 447 S.E.2d 491 (1994), *rev. denied*, 339 N.C. 613, 454 S.E.2d 252 (1995); *Doe v. Doe*, 973 F.2d 237 (4th Cir. 1992).

39. N.C. Gen. Stat. § 1-17; *Bryant v. Adams*, 116 N.C. App. 448, 448 S.E.2d 832 (1994), *rev. denied*, 339 N.C. 736, 454 S.E.2d 647 (1995).

40. N.C. Gen. Stat. § 1-15(c).

41. N.C. Gen. Stat. § 1-52(16).

42. N.C. Gen. Stat. §§ 99B-1 to 99B-11.

43. N.C. Gen. Stat. § 99B-11.

44. N.C. Gen. Stat. § 99B-1.1 (codifying the common law of no strict liability in tort in product liability actions).

45. N.C. Gen. Stat. § 99B-1.2.

46. N.C. Gen. Stat. § 99B-5.

47. N.C. Gen. Stat. § 99B-6.

48. N.C. Gen. Stat. Chapter 1D (applies to claims *arising* after January 1, 1996).

49. 1999 N.C. Sess. Laws 295 (codified at N.C. Gen. Stat. §§ 66-280 through 66-283).

50. 1999 N.C. Sess. Laws 308 (codified at N.C. Gen. Stat. §§ 1-539.25 through 1-539.26).

51. N.C. Gen. Stat. § 20-279.21.

52. *Sweat v. Brunswick Elec. Membership Corp.*, 133 N.C. App. 63, 514 S.E.2d 526 (1999); *see also* N.C. Pattern Jury Instructions—Civil 102.11.

53. *Davies ex rel. Hardy v. Lewis*, 133 N.C. App. 167, 514 S.E.2d 742, *rev. denied*, 350 N.C. 827, 537 S.E.2d 819 (1999); *see also* N.C. Pattern Jury Instructions—Civil 102.10, *et seq.*

54. *Bolkhir v. North Carolina State Univ.*, 321 N.C. 706, 365 S.E.2d 898 (1988); *City of Thomasville v. Lease-Afex, Inc.*, 300 N.C. 651, 268 S.E.2d 190 (1980); *Lorinovich v. Kmart Corp.*, 134 N.C. App. 158, 516 S.E.2d 643 (1999); *see also* N.C. Pattern Jury Instructions—Civil 102.11.

55. *Ziglar v. E. I. Du Pont De Nemours and Co.*, 53 N.C. App. 147, 153-55, 280 S.E.2d 510, 515-16 (1981), *rev. denied*, 304 N.C. 393, 285 S.E.2d 838 (1981) (sufficiency of warnings on "inherently dangerous" insecticide in a jug); *Greene v. Meredith*, 264 N.C. 178, 183, 141 S.E.2d 287, 291 (1965); *see also* N.C. Pattern Jury Instructions—Civil 102.14 (no duty to anticipate negligence of others).

56. *Holbrook v. Henley*, 118 N.C. App. 151, 454 S.E.2d 676 (1995); *see also* N.C. Pattern Jury Instructions—Civil 102.15.

57. *Keith v. Polier*, 109 N.C. App. 94, 425 S.E.2d 723 (1993); *Holbrook*, supra note 56, at 454 S.E.2d 676.

58. *Holbrook*, supra note 56, at 454 S.E.2d 676.

59. N.C. Gen. Stat. § 90-21.12; *Weatherford v. Glassman*, 129 N.C. App. 618, 500 S.E.2d 466 (1998); *see also* N.C. Pattern Jury Instructions—Civil 809.00 through 809.90 (instructions for claims of negligence by medical and legal professionals).

60. N.C. R. Evid. 702(b)-(d); *Heatherly v. Industrial Health Council*, 130 N.C. App. 616, 504 S.E.2d 102 (1998).

61. N.C. R. Civ. P. 9(j).

61.1. *Anderson v. Assimos*, 146 N.C. App. 339, 553 S.E. 2d 63 (2001).

62. *Weatherford*, supra note 59, at 500 S.E.2d 466.

63. *Welch v. Jenkins*, 271 N.C. 138, 155 S.E.2d 763 (1967); *see also* N.C. Pattern Jury Instructions—Civil 102.13.

64. *Allen v. Equity & Investors Management Corp.*, 56 N.C. App. 706, 289 S.E.2d 623 (1982).

65. *See id.*

66. *Welch*, supra note 63, at 155 S.E.2d 763.

67. *Lamm v. Bissette Realty*, 327 N.C. 412, 395 S.E.2d 112 (1990); *Carter v. Food Lion, Inc.*, 127 N.C. App. 271, 488 S.E.2d 617, *rev. denied*, 347 N.C. 396, 494 S.E.2d 408 (1997); *Smith v. Wal-Mart Stores, Inc.*, 128 N.C. App. 282, 495 S.E.2d 149 (1998); *see also* N.C. Pattern Jury Instructions—Civil 102.19 through 102.30.

68. *Lumley v. Capoferi*, 120 N.C. App. 578, 463 S.E.2d 264 (1995); *see also* N.C. Pattern Jury Instructions—Civil 102.19 and 102.20.

69. *Simmons v. North Carolina Dept. of Transp.*, 128 N.C. App. 402, 496 S.E.2d 790 (1998); *see also* N.C. Pattern Jury Instructions—Civil 102.19, 102.27 and 102.60.

70. *Adams v. Mills*, 312 N.C. 181, 322 S.E.2d 164 (1984); *Muse v. Charter Hospital of Winston-Salem*, 117 N.C. App. 468, 452 S.E.2d 589, *aff'd per curiam*, 342 N.C. 403, 464 S.E.2d 44 (1995); *see also* N.C. Pattern Jury Instructions—Civil 102.28.

71. *Barber v. Constien*, 130 N.C. App. 380, 502 S.E.2d 912, *rev. denied*, 349 N.C. 351, 515 S.E.2d 699 (1998).

72. *Goodman v. Wenco Foods, Inc.*, 333 N.C. 1, 26-27, 423 S.E.2d 444, 457 (1992); *see also* N.C. Pattern Jury Instructions—Civil 741.65 through 744.17 (elements of product liability actions).

73. N.C. Gen. Stat. § 99B-3(a); *Rich v. Shaw*, 98 N.C. App. 489, 391 S.E.2d 220, *rev. denied*, 327 N.C. 432, 395 S.E.2d 689 (1990); *see also* N.C. Pattern Jury Instructions—Civil 743.07 (pre-1996 cause of action) or 744.07.

74. *Kekelis v. Whitin Mach. Works*, 273 N.C. 439, 160 S.E.2d 320 (1968); *see also* N.C. Pattern Jury Instructions—Civil 102.35.

75. *Pack v. Auman*, 220 N.C. 704, 18 S.E.2d 247 (1942).

76. *Madden v. Carolina Door Controls*, 117 N.C. App. 56, 449 S.E.2d 769 (1994); *Schaffner v. Cumberland County Hosp. System, Inc.*, 77 N.C. App. 689, 336 S.E.2d 116 (1985), *rev. denied*, 316 N.C. 195, 341 S.E.2d 579 (1986).

77. N.C. Gen. Stat. § 99B-4(3); *Smith v. Fiber Controls*, 300 N.C. 669, 268 S.E.2d 504 (1980); *Nicholson v. American Safety Util. Corp.*, 346 N.C. 767, 488 S.E.2d 240 (1997); *see also* N.C. Pattern Jury Instructions—Civil 743.10 or 744.10 (contributory negligence may apply to claims of failure to warn, defective design, or defective manufacture).

78. *Nicholson*, supra note 77, at 488 S.E.2d 240; *see also Champs Convenience Stores, Inc. v. United Chem. Co.*, 329 N.C. 446, 406 S.E.2d 856 (1991) (defense applies to all product liability actions).

79. *Lenz v. Ridgewood Associates*, 55 N.C. App. 115, 284 S.E.2d 702 (1981), *rev. denied by*, 305 N.C. 300, 290 S.E.2d 702 (1982); *Davies ex rel. Hardy v. Lewis*, 133 N.C.

App. 167, 514 S.E.2d 742, *rev. denied*, 350 N.C. 827, 537 S.E.2d 819 (1999); *see also* N.C. Pattern Jury Instructions—Civil 104.10 and 104.50.

80. *Davies ex rel. Hardy*, supra note 53, at 514 S.E.2d 742 (using the language "nearly fifteen"); *Welch v. Jenkins*, 271 N.C. 138, 155 S.E.2d 763 (1967)("At ... age [fourteen], there is a rebuttable presumption that [a minor] possessed the capacity of an adult to protect himself and he is, therefore, presumptively chargeable with the same standard of care for his own safety as if he were an adult."); *see also* N.C. Pattern Jury Instructions—Civil 104.25.

81. *Steelcase, Inc. v. Lilly Co.*, 93 N.C. App. 697, 701, 379 S.E.2d 40, 43, *rev. denied*, 325 N.C. 276, 384 S.E.2d 530 (1989).

81.1. *Winston Realty Co., Inc. v. G.H.G. Inc.*, 314 N.C. 90, 331 S.E.2d 677 (1985).

82. *Jarvis v. Sanders*, 34 N.C. App. 283, 237 S.E.2d 865 (1977); *King v. Allred*, 76 N.C. App. 427, 333 S.E.2d 758, *rev. denied*, 315 N.C. 184, 337 S.E.2d 857 (1985); *Muse*, 452 S.E.2d 589; *see also* N.C. Pattern Jury Instructions—Civil 102.86.

83. *Muse*, supra note 70, at 452 S.E.2d 589.

84. *Adams*, supra note 70, at 322 S.E.2d 164; *see also* N.C. Pattern Jury Instructions—Civil 104.10.

85. N.C. R. Civ. P. 8(c); *Alston v. Monk*, 92 N.C. App. 59, 373 S.E.2d 463 (1988), *rev. denied*, 324 N.C. 246, 378 S.E.2d 420 (1989).

86. *Vernon v. Crist*, 291 N.C. 646, 231 S.E.2d 591 (1977); *see also* N.C. Pattern Jury Instructions—Civil 104.10 n.3, 104.25 n.8, 805.56 n.4, 805.72 n.3, and 805.74 n.2.

87. *Trantham v. Sorrells*, 121 N.C. App. 611, 468 S.E.2d 401, *rev. denied*, 343 N.C. 311, 471 S.E.2d 82 (1996); *Kenan v. Bass*, 132 N.C. App 30, 511 S.E.2d 6 (1999).

88. *Morrison v. Cornelius*, 63 N.C. 346 (1869); *Bosley v. Alexander*, 114 N.C. App. 470, 442 S.E.2d 82 (1994); *Bowden v. Bell*, 116 N.C. App. 64, 446 S.E.2d 816 (1994); *Jones (Griffin) v. Rochelle*, 125 N.C. App. 82, 479 S.E.2d 231, *rev. denied*, 346 N.C. 178, 486 S.E.2d 205 (1997).

89. *McWilliams v. Parham*, 269 N.C. 162, 152 S.E.2d 117 (1967).

90. *Id.*

91. *Cobia v. Atlantic Coast Line R. Co.*, 188 N.C. 487, 125 S.E. 18 (1924); *Horton v. Seaboard Air Line R.R.*, 175 N.C. 472, 95 S.E. 883 (1918), *appeal dismissed*, 251 U.S. 566, 40 S. Ct. 180, 64 L. Ed. 417 (1920).

92. N.C. Gen. Stat. § 99B-4(2); *Oates v. Jag, Inc.*, 66 N.C. App. 244, 311 S.E.2d 369 (N.C. Ct. App. 1984), *rev'd on other grounds*, 314 N.C. 276, 333 S.E.2d 222 (1985);

Nicholson, supra note 77, at 488 S.E.2d 240 (§ 99B-4 applies to actions for breach of implied warranty as well as negligence actions).

93. *Williams v. 100 Block Associates, Ltd. Partnership,* 132 N.C. App. 655, 513 S.E.2d 582 (1999); *see* N.C. Pattern Jury Instructions—Civil 809.03 and 809.05.

94. *Lea v. Light Co.,* 246 N.C. 287, 98 S.E.2d 9 (1957); *Kekelis,* supra note 74, at 160 S.E.2d 320; *Madden v. Carolina Door Controls,* 117 N.C. App. 56, 449 S.E.2d 769 (1994).

95. *See id.; see also Schaffner v. Cumberland Co. Hosp. System, Inc.,* 77 N.C. App. 689, 336 S.E.2d 116 (1985).

96. *100 Block Associates,* supra note 93, at 513 S.E.2d 582; *Bryan v. Elevator Co.,* 2 N.C. App. 593, 163 S.E.2d 534 (1968).

97. *Williamson v. Food Lion, Inc.,* 131 N.C. App. 365, 507 S.E.2d 313 (1998), *aff'd,* 350 N.C. 305, 513 S.E.2d 561 (1999).

98. *Smith v. Hickory,* 252 N.C. 316, 113 S.E.2d 557 (1960).

99. *Woodson v. Rowland,* 329 N.C. 330, 350, 407 S.E.2d 222, 234 (1991).

100. *See id.; see also Kinsey v. Spann,* 139 N.C. App. 370, 533 S.E.2d 487, 491 (2000); *Jones v. Willamette Industries, Inc.,* 120 N.C. App. 591, 463 S.E.2d 294 (1995), *rev. denied,* 342 N.C. 656, 467 S.E.2d 714 (1996); *Maybank v. S. S. Kresge Co.,* 46 N.C. App. 687, 266 S.E.2d 409 (1980), *aff'd as modified by on other grounds,* 302 N.C. 129, 273 S.E.2d 681 (1981).

101. *Kinsey,* supra note 100, at 533 S.E.2d 491; *Sweat v. Brunswick Elec. Membership Corp.,* 133 N.C. App. 63, 514 S.E.2d 526 (1999); *Haymore,* 116 N.C. App. 40, 446 S.E.2d 865 (1994); *McCollum v. Grove Mfg. Co.,* 58 N.C. App. 283, 293 S.E.2d 632 (N.C. Ct. App. 1982), *aff'd,* 307 N.C. 695, 300 S.E.2d 374 (1983); *see* N.C. Pattern Jury Instructions—Civil 744.12 (obvious risk of product) and 744.16 (inherent characteristic).

102. *Woodson,* supra note 99, at 407 S.E.2d 234; *Kinsey,* supra note 100, at 533 S.E.2d 491-92; *Sweat,* supra note 101, at 514 S.E.2d 528.

103. *McCollum,* supra note 101, at 293 S.E.2d 532; *Kinsey,* supra note 100, at 533 S.E.2d 492.

104. *Kinsey,* supra note 100, at 533 S.E.2d 492; *see* N.C. Pattern Jury Instructions—Civil 640.48.

105. *Williams v. City of Durham,* 123 N.C. App. 595, 473 S.E.2d 665 (1996); *Baldwin v. GTE South, Inc.,* 110 N.C. App. 54, 428 S.E.2d 857 (1993) (quoting Restatement (Second) of Torts § 286 (1965)), *rev'd on other grounds,* 335 N.C. 544, 439 S.E.2d 108 (1994); *see also* N.C. Pattern Jury Instructions—Civil 102.12 and 102.16.

106. *Ingram v. Smoky Mountain Stages, Inc.*, 225 N.C. 444, 450, 35 S.E.2d 337, 341 (1945); *see also* N.C. Pattern Jury Instructions—Civil 102.16.

107. *Sloan v. Carolina Power & Light Co.*, 248 N.C. 125, 102 S.E.2d 822 (1958).

108. *Manganello v. Permastone, Inc.*, 291 N.C. 666, 231 S.E.2d 678 (1977); *Slade v. New Hanover County Bd. of Educ.*, 10 N.C. App. 287, 178 S.E.2d 316 (1971), *cert. denied*, 278 N.C. 104, 179 S.E.2d 453 (1971).

109. *Stone v. Proctor*, 259 N.C. 633, 131 S.E.2d 297 (1963); *Bucham v. King*, 182 N.C. 171, 108 S.E. 635 (1921); *see also Horne v. Owens-Corning Fiberglas Corp.*, 4 F.3d 276 (4th Cir. 1993) (involving industry standards and state of the art evidence); *Edwards v. ATRO SpA*, 891 F. Supp. 1085 (E.D.N.C. 1995).

110. N.C. Gen. Stat. § 99B-6(b)(3).

111. *Young v. Baltimore & Ohio R. Co.*, 266 N.C. 458, 465, 146 S.E.2d 441, 445 (1966).

112. N.C. Gen Stat. § 1B-2(1) (relative degree of fault is not considered); *Hall v. Carroll*, 253 N.C. 220, 222, 116 S.E.2d 459, 461 (1960).

113. *Harlow v. Voyager Communications V*, 348 N.C. 568, 501 S.E.2d 72 (1998).

114. *See id.*; *Frow v. De La Vega*, 82 U.S. 552, 21 L. Ed. 60 (1872).

115. *Cox v. Robert C. Rhein Interest, Inc.*, 100 N.C. App. 584, 397 S.E.2d 358 (1990); *see also State Farm Mut. Auto. Ins. Co. v. Holland*, 324 N.C. 466, 380 S.E.2d 100 (1989); *see also* N.C. Pattern Jury Instructions—Civil 102.90.

116. *Sullivan v. Smith*, 56 N.C. App. 525, 289 S.E.2d 870, *rev. denied*, 306 N.C. 392, 294 S.E.2d 220, *reconsid. denied*, 294 S.E.2d 741 (1982); *Brown v. Louisburg*, 126 N.C. 701, 36 S.E. 166 (1900).

117. N.C. Gen. Stat. §§ 1B-1 to 1B-7.

118. N.C. Gen. Stat. § 1B-1(a); *Baity v. Brewer*, 122 N.C. App. 645, 470 S.E.2d 836 (1996).

119. N.C. Gen. Stat. §§ 1B-1(b)-(c).

120. N.C. Gen. Stat. § 1B-4.

121. *See id.*

122. *Yates v. New South Pizza, Ltd.*, 330 N.C. 790, 412 S.E.2d 666, *reh'g denied*, 331 N.C. 292, 417 S.E.2d 73 (1992) (recognizing that at common law the release of the servant also served to release the master, but holding that § 1B-4 broadens

the definition of tortfeasor so as to expose a vicariously liable master to liability if servant settles independently with injured party); *Wrenn v. Maria Parham Hosp., Inc.*, 135 N.C. App. 672, 522 S.E.2d 789, 793-794 (1999) (distinguishing *Yates* and holding that adjudication that servant is not liable removes all vicarious liability of master).

123. *State ex rel. Long v. Petree Stockton, L.L.P.*, 129 N.C. App. 432, 499 S.E.2d 790 (1998), *cert. dismissed*, 350 N.C. 57, 510 S.E.2d 374 (1999).

124. *Edwards v. Hamill*, 262 N.C. 528, 138 S.E.2d 151 (1964).

125. *Sullivan*, supra note 116, at 289 S.E.2d 870; *Hartrick Erectors, Inc. v. Maxson-Betts, Inc.*, 98 N.C. App. 120, 389 S.E.2d 607 (N.C. Ct. App. 1990), *rev. dismissed*, 328 N.C. 326, 410 S.E.2d 359 (1991).

126. *Sullivan*, supra note 116, at 289 S.E.2d 870 (citing *Hendricks v. Fay, Inc.*, 273 N.C. 59, 159 S.E.2d 362 (1968)); *Hartrick Erectors, Inc.*, supra note 125, at 389 S.E.2d 607 (citing *Ingram v. Smith*, 16 N.C. App. 147, 191 S.E.2d 390, *cert. denied*, 282 N.C. 304, 192 S.E.2d 195 (1972) (citing *Edwards v. Hamill*, 262 N.C. 528, 138 S.E.2d 151 (1964))).

127. *Hoisington v. ZT-Winston-Salem Associates*, 133 N.C. App. 485, 516 S.E.2d 176 (1999), *cert. dismissed*, 351 N.C. 342, 525 S.E.2d 173 (2000) (shopping center guard not liable under contract); *Holshouser v. Shaner Hotel Group Properties*, 134 N.C. App. 391, 518 S.E.2d 17, 23-24 (N.C. Ct. App. 1999) (involving a jury question regarding an ambiguous contract); *Candid Camera Video v. Mathews*, 76 N.C. App. 634, 636, 334 S.E.2d 94, 96 (1985), *rev. denied*, 315 N.C. 390, 338 S.E.2d 879 (1986).

128. N.C. Gen. Stat. §§ 97-1 to 97-200.

129. N.C. Gen. Stat. § 97-10.1; *Brown v. Motor Inns of North Carolina*, 47 N.C. App. 115, 266 S.E.2d 848, *rev. denied*, 301 N.C. 86 (1980).

130. N.C. Gen. Stat. § 97-91; *Johnson v. Southern Indus. Constructors, Inc.*, 347 N.C. 530, 495 S.E.2d 356 (1998).

131. N.C. Gen. Stat. § 97-10.2(a); *M.B. Haynes Corp. v. Strand Electro Controls, Inc.*, 127 N.C. App. 177, 487 S.E.2d 819 (1997).

132. N.C. Gen. Stat. § 97-10.2; *M.B. Haynes Corp.*, supra note 131, at 487 S.E.2d 819.

133. *Southern Indus. Constructors, Inc.*, supra note 130, at 495 S.E.2d 356; *Radzisz v. Harley Davidson of Metrolina, Inc.*, 346 N.C. 84, 484 S.E.2d 566 (1997).

134. *Southern Indus. Constructors, Inc.*, supra note 130, at 495 S.E.2d 356.

135. N.C. Gen. Stat. § 97-2(1); *Williams v. ARL, Inc.*, 133 N.C. App. 625, 516 S.E.2d 187 (1999).

136. N.C. Gen. Stat. § 97-2(6); *Roman v. Southland Transp. Co.*, 350 N.C. 549, 515 S.E.2d 214 (1999).

137. *See id.* at 515 S.E.2d 214.

138. N.C. Gen. Stat. § 97-3; *Poythress v. Libbey-Owens Ford Co.*, 67 N.C. App. 720, 313 S.E.2d 893, *rev. denied*, 311 N.C. 403, 319 S.E.2d 273 (1984).

139. *Woodson*, supra note 99, at 407 S.E.2d 222.

140. *See id.*

141. N.C. Gen. Stat. § 97-10.2(e).

142. *See id.*

143. N.C. Gen. Stat. § 97-10.2(f).

144. *Nelson v. Freeland*, 349 N.C. 615, 507 S.E.2d 882 (1998); *reh'g denied by*, 350 N.C. 108, 533 S.E.2d 467 (1999); *see also* N.C. Pattern Jury Instructions—Civil 805.50 through 805.74 (duties of landowners).

145. *Jenkins v. Lake Montonia Club, Inc.*, 125 N.C. App. 102, 479 S.E.2d 259 (1997); *Howard v. Jackson*, 120 N.C. App. 243, 461 S.E.2d 793 (1995).

146. *Nelson*, supra note 144, at 507 S.E.2d 882.

147. *100 Block Associates, Ltd. Partnership*, supra note 93, at 513 S.E.2d 582.

148. *Nelson*, supra note 144, at 507 S.E.2d 882.

149. N.C. Gen. Stat. § 18B-120 to 129.

150. N.C. Gen. Stat. § 18B-121; *Estate of Mullis by Dixon v. Monroe Oil Co., Inc.*, 349 N.C. 196, 505 S.E.2d 131 (1998).

151. N.C. Gen. Stat. § 18B-120; *Estate of Darby by Darby v. Monroe Oil Co., Inc.*, 127 N.C. App. 301, 488 S.E.2d 828, *rev. denied*, 347 N.C. 397, 494 S.E.2d 602 (1997).

152. *Estate of Mullis by Dixon*, supra note 150, at 505 S.E.2d 131 (commercial vendor); *Camalier v. Jeffries*, 340 N.C. 699, 460 S.E.2d 133 (1995) (social host); *Hart v. Ivey*, 332 N.C. 299, 420 S.E.2d 174 (1992) (social host).

153. *Hart*, supra note 152, at 420 S.E.2d 174.

154. *Moore v. Coachmen Industries, Inc.*, 129 N.C. App. 389, 499 S.E.2d 772 (1998); *Chicopee, Inc.*, supra note 34, at 391 S.E.2d 211 (adopting rule for product liability cases).

155. *Moore*, supra note 154, at 499 S.E.2d 772; *Reece*, supra note 16, at 429 S.E.2d 768.

156. *Moore*, supra note 154, at 499 S.E.2d 772; *Reece*, supra note 16, at 429 S.E.2d 768.

157. N.C. R. Civ. P. 9(b).

158. *Myers & Chapman, Inc. v. Thomas G. Evans, Inc.*, 323 N.C. 559, 374 S.E.2d 385 (1988), *reh'g denied*, 324 N.C. 117, 377 S.E.2d 235 (1989); *Ragsdale v. Kennedy*, 286 N.C. 130, 209 S.E.2d 494 (1974).

159. *Myers & Chapman, Inc.*, supra note 158, at 374 S.E.2d 385; *Malone v. Topsail Area Jaycees, Inc.*, 113 N.C. App. 498, 439 S.E.2d 192 (1994).

160. *See id.*

161. *Ausley v. Bishop*, 133 N.C. App. 210, 515 S.E.2d 72 (1999); *Fulton v. Vickery*, 73 N.C. App. 382, 326 S.E.2d 354, *rev. denied*, 313 N.C. 599, 332 S.E.2d 178 (1985); *Marcus Bros. Textiles, Inc. v. Price Waterhouse, LLP*, 350 N.C. 214, 513 S.E.2d 320 (1999) (citing *Raritan River Steel Co. v. Cherry, Bekaert & Holland*, 322 N.C. 200, 367 S.E.2d 609 (1988), *reversed*, 329 N.C. 646, 407 S.E.2d 178 (1991) (adopting Restatement (Second) of Torts § 552 as defining the elements of negligent misrepresentation)).

162. *Ausley*, supra note 161, at 515 S.E.2d 72.

163. *Marcus Bros. Textiles, Inc.*, supra note 161, at 513 S.E.2d 320.

164. N.C. Gen. Stat. § 75-1.1(a); *Marshall v. Miller*, 302 N.C. 539, 276 S.E.2d 397 (1981); *Johnson v. Insurance Co.*, 300 N.C. 247, 266 S.E.2d 610 (1980); *Market America, Inc. v. Christman-Orth*, 135 N.C. App. 143, 520 S.E.2d 570 (1999), *rev. denied*, 351 N.C. 358, 542 S.E.2d 213 (2000); *Hageman v. Twin City Chrysler-Plymouth, Inc.*, 681 F. Supp. 303, 306-309 (M.D.N.C. 1988); *see also* N.C. Pattern Jury Instructions—Civil 813.21.

165. N.C. Gen. Stat. § 75-1.1(b); *HAJMM Co. v. House of Raeford Farms, Inc.*, 328 N.C. 578, 594, 403 S.E.2d 483, 493 (1991); *see also* N.C. Pattern Jury Instructions—Civil 813.62.

166. N.C. Gen. Stat. § 75-1.1(d).

167. *Spartan Leasing Inc. v. Pollard*, 101 N.C. App. 450, 400 S.E.2d 476 (1991).

168. *See id.*

169. *Opsahl v. Pinehurst, Inc.*, 81 N.C. App. 56, 344 S.E.2d 68 (1986), *rev. dismissed*, 319 N.C. 222, 353 S.E.2d 400 (1987) (recognizing that statute makes "unfair and deceptive acts" unlawful without defining the nature of such acts thus making the facts of each case determinative).

170. *Martin Marietta Corp. v. Wake Stone Corp.*, 111 N.C. App. 269, 432 S.E.2d 428 (1993), *aff'd*, 339 N.C. 602, 453 S.E.2d 146 (1995).

171. N.C. Gen. Stat. § 75-1 *et seq.*; *Olivetti v. Ames Business Systems*, 319 N.C. 534, 546, 356 S.E.2d 578, 586 (1987); *see also* N.C. Pattern Jury Instructions—Civil 810.00 through 810.85, and 813.80.

172. N.C. Gen. Stat. §§ 75-16 and 75-16.1.

173. *United Laboratories, Inc. v. Kuykendall*, 335 N.C. 183, 437 S.E.2d 374 (1993); *Mapp v. Toyota World, Inc.*, 81 N.C. App. 421, 344 S.E.2d 297, *rev. denied*, 318 N.C. 283, 347 S.E.2d 464 (1986).

174. N.C. Gen. Stat. Chapter 1D; *see also* N.C. Pattern Jury Instructions—Civil 810.00 through 810.06.

175. N.C. Gen. Stat. §§ 1D-15(a)-(b); § 1D-5(4) (defining fraud).

176. *See id.; see also* N.C. Gen. Stat. §§ 1D-15(a), 1D-5(7).

177. *Muse*, supra note 70, at 452 S.E.2d 589; *see also King v. Allred*, 76 N.C. App. 427, 333 S.E.2d 758 (1985).

178. N.C. R. Civ. P. 9(k).

179. N.C. Gen. Stat. § 1D-35(2).

180. *See id.; see also* N.C. Gen. Stat. § 1D-15(c).

181. *See id.*; see also N.C. Gen. Stat. §§ 1D-25(b)-(c) (cap and jury instructions); see also N.C. Gen. Stat. § 1D-26 (exception for driving while impaired cases); *see also* N.C. Pattern Jury Instructions—Civil 810.05 and 810.06; *applied in Hutelmyer v. Cox*, 133 N.C. App. 364, 514 S.E.2d 554 (1999), *app. dismissed*, 351 N.C. 356, 542 S.E.2d 211 (2000) (alienation of affections).

182. *See id.*

183. N.C. Gen. Stat. § 1D-26.

184. *See id.; see also* N.C. Gen. Stat. § 1D-30.

185. *See id.; see also* N.C. Gen. Stat. § 1D-45.

186. *Stanback v. Stanback,* 297 N.C. 181, 254 S.E.2d 611 (1979); *Newton v. Standard Fire Ins. Co.,* 291 N.C. 105, 229 S.E.2d 297 (1976); *Miller v. Nationwide Mut. Ins. Co.,* 112 N.C. App. 295, 435 S.E.2d 537 (1993), *rev. denied,* 335 N.C. 770, 442 S.E.2d 519 (1994).

187. *BMW of North America, Inc. v. Gore,* 517 U.S. 559, 116 S.Ct. 1589, 134 L. Ed.2d 809 (1996), *reh'g denied,* 701 So.2d 507, 65 USLW 2800 (1997); *Cole v. Duke Power Co.,* 81 N.C. App. 213, 217, 344 S.E.2d 130, *rev. denied,* 318 N.C. 281, 347 S.E.2d 462 (1986); *Hinson v. Dawson,* 244 N.C. 23, 92 S.E.2d 393 (1956).

188. N.C. Gen. Stat. § 28A-18-2.

189. *Meachum v. Faw,* 112 N.C. App. 489, 436 S.E.2d 141 (1993); *see also* N.C. Pattern Jury Instructions—Civil 810.60.

190. N.C. Gen. Stat. § 28A-18-2(a).

191. *See id.; see also* N.C. Gen. Stat. § 28A-18-2(b); *Keys v. Duke University,* 112 N.C. App. 518, 435 S.E.2d 820 (1993); *see also* N.C. Pattern Jury Instructions—Civil 810.40 through 810.50, 810.54 and 810.56.

192. N.C. Gen. Stat. § 28A-18-2(c).

193. N.C. Gen. Stat. § 28A-13-3(23).

194. *Azzolino v. Dingfelder,* 315 N.C. 103, 337 S.E.2d 528 (1985), *cert. denied,* 479 U.S. 835, 107 S.Ct. 131 (1986), *reh'g denied,* 319 N.C. 227, 353 S.E.2d 401 (1987) (parent's claim that child born with Down's Syndrome would have been aborted but for negligence of physician in not properly advising parents of possibility of discovery by amniocentesis).

195. N.C. Gen. Stat. § 28A-18-1(a).

196. *See id.; see also* N.C. Gen. Stat. § 28A-18-1(b).

197. *McGowen v. Rental Tool Co.,* 109 N.C. App. 688, 428 S.E.2d 275 (1993).

198. *DiDonato v. Wortman,* 320 N.C. 423, 358 S.E.2d 489, *reh'g denied,* 320 N.C. 799, 361 S.E.2d 73 (1987); *Greer v. Parsons,* 331 N.C. 368, 416 S.E.2d 174 (1992).

199. *DiDonato,* supra note 197, at 358 S.E.2d 489.

NORTH DAKOTA

A. STATUTES OF LIMITATION

Causes of action founded on express or implied liability, personal injury that does not result in death, breach of contract, trespass, fraud, or negligent conduct must be brought within six years after the claim for relief has accrued.[1] The discovery rule applies.[2] Where there is perceptible personal injury caused by accident or trauma, the statute of limitations starts to run at the time of injury.[3]

An action against the state or its employees acting within the scope of their employment or office must be commenced within three years after the claim for relief has accrued.[4] A claim accrues at the time it is discovered or could have been discovered in the exercise of due diligence.[5] A person bringing a claim against the state or a state employee for an injury must present to the director of the office of management and budget within 180 days after the alleged injury is discovered, or reasonably should have been discovered, a written notice stating the time, place, and circumstances of the injury, the names of any state employees known to be involved, and the amount of compensation or other relief demanded.[6]

Causes of action founded on libel, slander, assault, battery, false imprisonment, malpractice, and personal injuries that result in death must be brought within two years after the claim for relief has accrued.[7] The discovery rule applies.[8] However, an action for malpractice against a physician or licensed hospital will not be extended beyond six years because of nondiscovery of the alleged malpractice unless discovery was prevented by fraudulent conduct.[9] A two-year statute of limitations period also applies to wrongful death actions.[10]

The statute of limitations for a continuing tort does not begin to run until the tortious acts cease.[11]

When a party against whom a claim for relief exists prevents the person in whose favor such claim exists from learning of the claim by fraud or fraudulent concealment, an action may be commenced within one year from the time the claim is discovered or might have been discovered with diligence.[12]

If at the time a claim for relief accrues the person who is entitled to bring the action is under the age of 18, insane, or imprisoned for a term less than for life, the time of such disability is not considered a part of the time limited for the commencement of the action.[13] However, the period within which the claim may be brought may not be extended by more than five years except for infancy, nor may it be extended longer than one year after the disability ceases.[14] In actions for professional malpractice, the extension of the limitation due to infancy is limited to 12 years.[15] When two or more disabilities coexist at the time the claim for relief accrues, the limitation does not attach until they are all removed.[16]

If a person who is entitled to bring an action dies before the expiration of the statute of limitations, an action may be commenced by his representatives after the expiration of that time and within one year from his death.[17] If a person against whom an action can be brought dies before the expiration the statute of limitations, an action may be commenced against his personal representative after the expiration of that time and within one year after the issuing of letters.[18] Only breach of promise, alienation of affections, libel, and slander abates at the death of a party or a person who might have been a party had death not occurred.[19]

If a person against whom a claim can be brought is out of state at the time the claim accrues, the statute of limitation does not run until the person returns to the state.[20]

For actions not otherwise provided for, a "catch-all" provision sets the statute of limitations at ten years after the claim for relief has accrued.[21]

There may be no recovery of damages in a products liability action unless the injury, death, or property damage occurs within ten years of the date of initial purchase for use or consumption, or within 11 years of the date of manufacture when the action is based on, or arises out of, breach of implied warranties, defects in design, inspection, testing, or manufacture, failure to warn, or failure to properly instruct in the use of the product.[22] The statute of limitation does not apply where a manufacturer, wholesaler, or retailer issues a recall, or becomes aware of a defect and fails to take reasonable steps to warn users of the product defect.[23] Actions based on exposure to asbestos must be commenced within three years after an injured person is informed of discovery of the injury, or within three years after discovery of facts that would reasonably lead to such discovery, whichever is less. [24]

B.   TORT REFORM

The North Dakota Legislative Assembly did not enact any new tort reform measures during the last session. Several existing provisions which fall under the heading "Tort Reform" are addressed herein.

C.   "NO FAULT" LIMITATIONS

A person injured in an automobile accident is covered only to the extent of basic no-fault benefits and optional excess no-fault benefits provided on the motor vehicle involved in the accident.[25] Basic no-fault benefits may not be stacked.[26] An injured person is not entitled to noneconomic loss unless the injury is a "serious injury."[27]

A basic no-fault insurer that has paid no-fault benefits can recover that amount from the insurer of a secured person if the injured person has sustained a serious injury or the injury results from an accident involving two or more vehicles, with at least one of those vehicles weighing in excess of 6,500 pounds.[28]

D. THE STANDARD FOR NEGLIGENCE

To recover for negligence, a claimant must establish: (1) a duty; (2) a breach of that duty; (3) causation; and (4) damages. [29] In determining whether a duty exists, courts balance the following factors: "(1) foreseeability of harm to plaintiff; (2) degree of certainty that plaintiff suffered injury; (3) closeness of connection between defendant's conduct and injury suffered; (4) moral blame attached to defendant's conduct; (5) policy of preventing future harm; (6) extent of burden to defendant and the consequences to the community of imposing a duty to exercise care with resulting liability for breach; and (7) availability, cost, and prevalence of insurance for the risk involved."[30] Whether a duty exists or not is generally a preliminary question of law for the court.[31]

The duty of care in negligence actions is to exercise reasonable care under the circumstances, which includes any specialized knowledge, facts, or skill on the part of the one charged with a duty.[32] There is no requirement in ordinary negligence cases for expert testimony to establish the standard of care and whether a defendant's conduct deviated from that standard.[33] Under the "sudden emergency" doctrine, a person confronted with an emergency not of his own making is required only to exercise a degree of care that an ordinarily prudent person would exercise under the same circumstances.[34]

E. CAUSATION

A plaintiff in a negligence action must affirmatively prove lack of due care and causation and cannot rest on presumption arising from occurrence of the accident.[35] To sustain an action for negligence, the defendant's negligent act must be a proximate cause of the damages incurred by the plaintiff.[36] Proximate cause is that cause that in natural and continuous sequence, unbroken by any controlling intervening cause, produces the injury, and without which the injury would not have occurred.[37] Negligence or other wrongful conduct of two or more persons may contribute concurrently as the proximate cause of an injury, and to be a proximate cause of an injury one's conduct need not be the last cause nor the sole cause of the injury.[38] In order to relieve a defendant of responsibility for the consequences of his negligence, an intervening cause must be one that severs the connection of cause and effect between the negligent act and the injury.[39] If an act of God and the negligence of the defendant combine to produce the injury, the defendant is still liable.[40]

F. CONTRIBUTORY NEGLIGENCE, COMPARATIVE NEGLIGENCE, AND ASSUMPTION OF RISK

1. Contributory Negligence

Contributory fault does not bar recovery of damages for death or injury to person or property unless the claimant's fault was as great as the combined fault of all others who contributed to the injury.[41] Contributory negligence can be present only when the negligence of a plaintiff combines with the negligence of a defendant to proximately cause injury to the plaintiff.[42]

2. **Comparative Fault**

North Dakota has adopted a modified comparative fault statute.[43] Contributory fault does not bar recovery for damages for death or injury to person or property unless the claimant's fault was as great as the combined fault of all other persons who contributed to the injury.[44] However, damages are diminished in proportion to the amount of contributing fault attributable to the claimant.[45]

3. **Assumption of Risk**

The legislature's adoption of the doctrine of comparative negligence abrogated the affirmative defense of assumption of risk.[46]

G. *RES IPSA LOQUITUR* AND INHERENTLY DANGEROUS ACTIVITIES

1. *Res Ipsa Loquitur*

As applied in North Dakota, "*res ipsa loquitur* allows the fact-finder to draw an inference that the defendant's conduct was negligent if the following foundational facts are proved: (1) the accident was one which does not ordinarily occur in the absence of negligence; (2) the instrumentality which caused the plaintiff's injury was in the exclusive control of the defendant; and (3) there was no voluntary action or contribution on the part of the plaintiff."[47] *Res ipsa loquitur*, as a form of circumstantial evidence, can be used to affirmatively prove negligence.[48] *Res ipsa loquitur* does not shift the burden of proof; application of the doctrine merely raises a permissible inference of negligence that the jury is free to accept or reject.[49]

2. **Inherently Dangerous Activities**

Those who engage in inherently dangerous activities are bound to use care and diligence proportional to the risk, and peculiar circumstances of the situation will be considered when determining the question of what amounted to reasonable care and diligence.[50]

H. NEGLIGENCE *PER SE*

Violation of a statute is not negligence *per se*, but it may evidence negligence if there is a showing of causal connection between violation of the statute and injury.[51] Compliance with a standard of care prescribed by a statute or ordinance is a minimum standard of care and does not preclude a finding that an actor was negligent in failing to take additional precautions.[52]

I. JOINT AND SEVERAL LIABILITY

When two or more parties are found to have contributed to an injury, the liability of each party is several only, and is not joint, and each party is liable only for the amount of damages attributable to the percentage of fault of that party, except that any persons who act in concert in committing a tortious act or aid or encourage the act, or ratify or adopt the act for their benefit, are jointly liable for all damages attributable to their combined percentage of fault.[53] The intent of the comparative fault statute is to replace joint and several liability with several allocation of damages among those who commit torts in proportion to the fault of those who contributed to an injury.[54]

J. INDEMNITY

A party is entitled to indemnity when he has only a derivative or vicarious liability for damage caused by the one sought to be charged.[55]

K. BAR OF WORKERS' COMPENSATION STATUTE

Employers who participate in North Dakota's workers' compensation program are not liable at common law for the injury or death of their employees.[56] However, employers are not relieved of common law liability for injuries to an employee of another employer, even though injury was incurred in the course of employment and both employers participate in the workers' compensation program.[57]

Employers also are not immune from damages for intentional injuries.[58] An employer is deemed to have intended to injure an employee if the employer had knowledge that injury was certain to occur and willfully disregarded that knowledge.[59] However, once an employee has received workers' compensation benefits, he is precluded from pursuing a common law action against his employer, even if the injuries were intentionally inflicted. [60]

An employee injured by a third party can claim benefits under the workers' compensation program and then proceed at law to recover damages from that third party, subject to the subrogation interest of the workers' compensation fund.[61] When an employer and a third party both negligently cause an employee's injuries, liability is imposed on the third party for the negligence of the third party and the employer without permitting the third party to get contribution from the employer.[62] However, a third party may enforce a contractual agreement for indemnification in such situations.[63]

The "dual capacity theory" is not recognized in North Dakota, so employees who receive an injury that is covered under the act cannot maintain an action against the employer for breach of warranty or products liability.[64]

L. PREMISES LIABILITY

Where property owners or occupiers conduct dangerous activities or permit dangerous instruments and conditions to exist on their premises, they must take reasonable measures to prevent injury to those whose presence on the property reasonably can be foreseen.[65] Before they owe a duty of care, however, it must be shown that they had control of the premises.[66]

Property owners and occupiers owe a general duty to lawful entrants to maintain their property in a reasonably safe manner and to consider the likelihood of injury, the potential seriousness of injury, and the burden of avoiding risk.[67] They owe no duty to trespassers other than to refrain from willfully or wantonly injuring them or causing injury to them through such gross negligence as is equivalent to willfulness or wantonness.[68] They owe no duty of care toward customers who have left their premises and are injured on an adjacent roadway by instrumentalities outside of their control.[69]

Property owners and occupiers are liable for physical harm to trespassing children caused by artificial conditions on the land if they know or have reason to know that children are likely to trespass, the condition is one that they know or have reason to know will involve unreasonable risk of death or serious bodily harm, the children do not discover the condition or realize the risk involved in coming within the area made dangerous by it, there is little utility to the owner or occupier to maintain the condition, the burden of eliminating the danger is slight as compared with the risk to children involved, and the owner or occupier fails to exercise reasonable care to eliminate the danger or otherwise protect the children.[70]

M. DRAM SHOP LIABILITY

North Dakota's dram shop statute creates a cause of action against any person who knowingly disposes, sells, barters, or gives away alcoholic beverages to someone who is under 21 years of age, an incompetent, or obviously intoxicated.[71] This claim for relief can be brought against all persons, not only professional merchants of alcohol, who knowingly commit the prohibited conduct, including those who act to promote business good will or supply alcohol as hospitality.[72] However, no claim under the dram shop statute may be brought by or on behalf of the intoxicated person or by or on behalf of any adult person travelling in the same vehicle as the intoxicated person.[73] Whether customers pay for their own drinks or take turns paying for each other's drinks is irrelevant.[74]

Liability under the dram shop statute is precluded where there is a superseding, intervening cause that breaks the causal link between the dram shop vendor's fault and the injuries.[75]

The dram shop statute does not supersede common law premises liability of bar owners.[76] Bar owners owe a duty to patrons to protect them from assault by other patrons when they have reasonable cause to anticipate conduct on the part of third persons that is likely to endanger safety of patrons.[77]

N. ECONOMIC LOSS

In North Dakota, juries may award economic or noneconomic damages in any civil action for wrongful death or injury to a person.[78] Economic damages are those "arising from medical expenses and medical care, rehabilitation services, custodial care, loss of earnings and earning capacity, loss of income or support, burial costs, cost of substitute domestic services, loss of employment or business or employment opportunities, and other monetary losses."[79] Noneconomic damages are those "arising from pain, suffering, inconvenience, physical impairment, disfigurement, mental anguish, emotional distress, fear of injury, loss or illness, loss of society and companionship, loss of consortium, injury to reputation, humiliation, and other nonpecuniary damage."[80]

Under the economic loss doctrine, economic loss resulting from damage to a defective product, as distinguished from damage to other property or persons, may be recovered in a cause of action for breach of warranty or contract, but not in a tort action.[81]

The party responsible for the payment of economic damages is entitled to a reduction of those damages to the extent that they are covered by payment from a collateral source.[82]

A plaintiff covered under a no-fault automobile insurance policy cannot recover in tort for economic loss unless he shows that his economic loss exceeds the basic no-fault benefits paid or payable to him.[83]

O. FRAUD AND MISREPRESENTATION

Fraud is either actual or constructive.[84] Actual fraud "consists in any of the following acts committed by a party to the contract, or with his connivance, with intent to deceive another party thereto or to induce him to enter into the contract: 1. The suggestion as a fact of that which is not true by one who does not believe it to be true; 2. The positive assertion, in a manner not warranted by the information of the person making it, of that which is not true though he believes it to be true; 3. The suppression of that which is true by one having knowledge or belief of the fact; 4. A promise made without any intention of performing it; or 5. Any other act fitted to deceive."[85] Constructive fraud consists of: "1. In any breach of duty which, without an actually fraudulent intent, gains an advantage to the person in fault or anyone claiming under him, by misleading another to his prejudice or to the prejudice of anyone claiming under him; or 2. In any such act or omission as the law specially declares to be fraudulent without respect to actual fraud."[86]

Fraud may be characterized as misrepresentation where an action intended or expected by the perpetrator to result in forbearance or inaction causes such result.[87]

Although the same conduct can be both deceitful and fraudulent, "fraud" technically applies to parties to contract, while "deceit" applies when there is no contract between parties.[88] Proof of actual damage proximately caused by a misrepresentation or nondisclosure is an essential element of a tort action for fraud and deceit.[89] Generally, expressions of mere opinion or predictions of future events are not actionable in fraud.[90]

Although no particular formal language is required when a claimant alleges fraud, a claimant must fairly apprise the other party of the factual basis for the claim, and the other party must receive enough information to prepare a response and a defense.[91]

Negligent misrepresentation made to induce a party to enter into contract is "actual fraud" under the statute defining actual fraud.[92]

Deceit is: "1. The suggestion as a fact of that which is not true by one who does not believe it to be true; 2. The assertion as a fact of that which is not true by one who has no reasonable ground for believing it to be true; 3. The suppression of a fact by one who is bound to disclose it, or who gives information of other facts which are likely to mislead for want of communication of that fact; or 4. A promise made without any intention of performing."[93]

P. CONSUMER FRAUD STATUTES

North Dakota's Unfair Trade Practices Law[94] and Consumer Fraud and Unlawful Credit Practices statute[95] protect consumers from unfair methods of competition and deceptive acts or practices in trade and commerce.

Q. PUNITIVE DAMAGES

A court or jury may give exemplary damages in addition to actual damages for the sake of example or to punish a defendant "when the defendant has been guilty by clear and convincing evidence of oppression, fraud, or actual malice."[96] Evidence of a defendant's financial position is not admissible to determine exemplary damages, and "the amount of exemplary damages may not exceed two times the amount of compensatory damages or two hundred fifty thousand dollars, whichever is greater; provided, however, that no award of exemplary damages may be made if the claimant is not entitled to compensatory damages."[97]

Before awarding exemplary damages, "the finder of fact must find by clear and convincing evidence that the amount of exemplary damages awarded is consistent with the following principles and factors: a. Whether there is a reasonable relationship between the exemplary damage award claimed and the harm likely to result from the defendant's conduct as well as the harm that actually has occurred; b. The degree of reprehensibility of the defendant's conduct and the duration of that conduct; and c. Any of the following factors as to which evidence is presented: (1) The defendant's awareness of, and any concealment of, the conduct; (2) The profitability to the defendant of the wrongful conduct and the desirability of removing that profit and of having the defendant also sustain a loss; and (3) Criminal sanctions imposed on the defendant for the same conduct that is the basis for the exemplary damage claim, these to be taken into account if offered in mitigation of the exemplary damage award."[98]

A manufacturer or seller cannot be charged with exemplary damages "if the product's manufacture, design, formulation, inspection, testing, packaging, labeling, and warning complied with: a. Federal statutes existing at the time the product was produced; b. Administrative regulations existing at the time the product was produced that were adopted by an agency of the federal government which had responsibility to regulate the safety of the product or to establish safety standards for the product pursuant to a federal statute; or c. Premarket approval or certification by an agency of the federal government."[99] However, a manufacturer or seller can be charged with exemplary damages "if the plaintiff proves by clear and convincing evidence that the product manufacturer or product seller: a. Knowingly and in violation of applicable agency regulations withheld or misrepresented information required to be submitted to the agency, which information was material and relevant to the harm in question; or b. Made an illegal payment to an official of the federal agency for the purpose of securing approval of the product."[100]

Exemplary damages may not be awarded against a principal because of an act by an agent unless the plaintiff proves by clear and convincing evidence that: "a. The principal or a managerial agent authorized the doing and manner of the act; b. The agent was unfit and the principal or a managerial agent was reckless in employing or retaining the agent; c. The agent was employed in a managerial capacity and was acting in the scope of employment; or d. The principal or managerial agent ratified or approved the doing and manner of the act."

Exemplary damages may be awarded in a civil action involving a motor vehicle accident resulting in bodily injury, if the plaintiff shows by clear and convincing evidence that the accident was caused by a driver who had been convicted of driving under the influence in the five years immediately preceding the accident and who was operating or was in physical control of a motor vehicle while under the influence of drugs or alcohol when the accident occurred.[101]

Minors and persons of unsound mind cannot be subjected to exemplary damages unless they were capable of knowing that the act was wrongful at the time that they committed it.[102]

R. WRONGFUL DEATH AND SURVIVORSHIP ACTIONS

An action for wrongful death may be brought whenever the death of a person is caused by a wrongful act, neglect, or default, and the decedent would have been able to maintain an action and recover damages for the wrongful act, neglect, or default.[103] Recovery for wrongful death passes to a limited group of beneficiaries defined by statute.[104] Substantial damages will be presumed, and they need not be established by proof of a specific amount.[105]

Damages for mental anguish may be recovered in a wrongful death action.[106] One may also recover damages for loss of society, comfort, and companionship in an action for the wrongful death of a child or a viable unborn child.[107]

H. Patrick Weir
VOGEL LAW FIRM
502 First Avenue North
P.O. Box 1389
Fargo, North Dakota 58107-1389
(701) 237-6983
Fax (701) 237-0847
vogellaw@vogellaw.com

ENDNOTES - NORTH DAKOTA

1. N.D. Cent. Code § 28-01-16. *See Lang v. Barrios*, 472 N.W.2d 464 (N.D. 1991).

2. *See Kuntz v. Muehler*, 1999 ND 215, 603 N.W.2d 43.

3. *See Erickson v. Scotsman, Inc.*, 456 N.W.2d 535 (N.D. 1990).

4. N.D. Cent. Code §§ 28-01-22.1, 28-01-17.

5. *Id.*

6. N.D. Cent. Code § 32-12.2-04(1).

7. N.D. Cent. Code § 28-01-18.

8. *See Wall v. Lewis*, 393 N.W.2d 758 (N.D. 1986).

9. N.D. Cent. Code § 28-01-18.

10. *See Braaten v. Deere & Co.*, 1997 ND 202, 569 N.W.2d 563.

11. *See Beavers v. Walters*, 537 N.W.2d 647 (N.D. 1995).

12. N.D. Cent. Code § 28-01-24.

13. N.D. Cent. Code § 28-01-25.

14. *Id.*

15. *Id.*

16. N.D. Cent. Code § 28-01-31.

17. N.D. Cent. Code § 28-01-26.

18. *Id.*

19. N.D. Cent. Code § 28-01-26.1.

20. N.D. Cent. Code § 28-01-32.

21. N.D. Cent. Code § 28-01-22.

22. N.D. Cent. Code § 28-01.3-08.

23. *Id.*

24. *Id.*

25. N.D. Cent. Code § 26.1-41-14.

26. *Id.*

27. N.D. Cent. Code § 26.1-41-08.

28. N.D. Cent. Code § 26.1-41-17.

29. *See Nelson v. Gilette*, 1997 ND 205, 571 N.W.2d 332.

30. *See Hurt v. Freeland*, 1999 ND 12, 589 N.W.2d 813.

31. *See Stanley v. Turtle Mountain Gas & Oil, Inc.*, 1997 ND 169, 567 N.W.2d 288.

32. *See Tom Beuchler Const., Inc. v. City of Williston*, 392 N.W.2d 403 (N.D. 1986).

33. *See Johansen v. Anderson*, 555 N.W.2d 588 (N.D. 1996).

34. *See Haider v. Finken*, 239 N.W.2d 508 (N.D. 1976); *Ebach v. Ralston*, 510 N.W.2d 604 (N.D. 1994).

35. *See Anderson v. Kroh*, 301 N.W.2d 359 (N.D. 1980).

36. *See Rued Ins., Inc. v. Blackburn, Nickels & Smith, Inc.*, 543 N.W.2d 770 (N.D. 1996).

37. *See id.*

38. *See id.*

39. *See Lang v. Wonnenberg*, 455 N.W.2d 832 (N.D. 1990).

40. *See North Shore, Inc. v. Wakefield*, 542 N.W.2d 725 (N.D. 1996).

41. N.D. Cent. Code § 32-03.2-02.

42. *See Gowin v. Trangsrud*, 1997 ND 226, 571 N.W.2d 824.

43. N.D. Cent. Code § 32-03.2-02.

44. *Id.*

45. *Id.*

46. *See First Trust Co. of North Dakota v. Scheels Hardware & Sports Shop, Inc.*, 429 N.W.2d 5 (N.D. 1988); *Feuerherm v. Ertelt*, 286 N.W.2d 509 (N.D. 1979); *Wentz v. Deseth*, 221 N.W.2d 101 (N.D. 1974).

47. *See Robert v. Aircraft Investment Co.*, 1998 ND 62, 575 N.W.2d 672.

48. *Id.*

49. *See Wasem v. Laskowski*, 274 N.W.2d 219 (N.D. 1979).

50. *See Krueger v. North American Creameries, Inc.*, 27 N.W.2d 240 (N.D. 1947).

51. *See Horstmeyer v. Golden Eagle Fireworks*, 532 N.W.2d 835 (N.D. 1995).

52. *See Keyes v. Amundson*, 391 N.W.2d 602 (N.D. 1986).

53. *See Reed v. University of North Dakota*, 1999 ND 25, 589 N.W.2d 880; N.D. Cent. Code § 32-03.2-02.

54. *See Hurt v. Freeland*, 1999 ND 12, 589 N.W.2d 551; *Kavadas v. Lorenzen*, 448 N.W.2d 219 (N.D. 1989).

55. *See Horejsi v. Anderson*, 353 N.W.2d 316 (N.D. 1984); *Nelson v. Johnson*, 1997 ND 203, 599 N.W.2d 246.

56. N.D. Cent. Code §§ 65-04-28, 65-05-06.

57. *See State ex rel. Workmen's Comp. Fund v. E. W. Wylie Co.*, 58 N.W.2d 76 (N.D. 1953).

58. *See Zimmerman v. Valdak Corp.*, 570 N.W.2d 204 (N.D. 1997).

59. *See id.*

60. *See Hulne v. International Harvester Co.*, 496 F. Supp. 849 (D.N.D. 1980).

61. N.D. Cent. Code § 65-01-09.

62. *See Barsness v. General Diesel & Equip. Co.*, 422 N.W.2d 819 (N.D. 1988).

63. *See id.*

64. *See Schlenk v. Aerial Contractors*, 268 N.W.2d 466 (N.D. 1978).

65. *See O'Leary v. Coenen*, 251 N.W.2d 746 (N.D. 1977).

66. *See Stanley v. Turtle Mountain Gas & Oil, Inc.*, 1997 ND 169, 567 N.W.2d 345.

67. *See Sternberger v. City of Williston*, 556 N.W.2d 288 (N.D. 1996); *O'Leary v. Coenen*, 251 N.W.2d 746 (N.D. 1977).

68. *See Hart v. Kern*, 268 N.W.2d 746 (N.D. 1977); *Sternburger v. City of Williston*, 556 N.W.2d 288 (N.D. 1996).

69. *See Holter v. Sheyenne*, 480 N.W.2d 736 (N.D. 1992).

70. *See Mikkelson v. Risovil*, 141 N.W.2d 150 (N.D. 1966).

71. N.D. Cent. Code § 5-01-06.1.

72. *See Born v. Mayers*, 514 N.W.2d 687 (N.D. 1994); *Stewart v. Ryan*, 520 N.W.2d 39 (N.D. 1994).

73. N.D. Cent. Code § 5-01-06.1.

74. *See Aanenson v. Bastien*, 438 N.W.2d 151 (N.D. 1989).

75. *See Stewart v. Ryan*, 520 N.W.2d 39 (N.D. 1994).

76. *See Zueger v. Carlson*, 542 N.W.2d 92 (N.D. 1996).

77. *See id.*

78. N.D. Cent. Code § 32-03.2-04.

79. *Id.*

80. *Id.*

81. *See Steiner v. Ford Motor Co.*, 2000 ND 31, 606 N.W.2d 881; *Cooperative Power Ass'n v. Westinghouse Elec. Corp.*, 493 N.W.2d ___ (N.D. 1992).

82. N.D. Cent. Code § 32-03.2-06.

83. *See Reisenauer v. Schaefer*, 515 N.W.2d 152 (N.D. 1994).

84. N.D. Cent. Code § 9-03-07.

85. N.D. Cent. Code § 9-03-08.

86. N.D. Cent. Code § 9-03-09.

87. *See In re Valeu*, 57 B.R. 488 (Bankr. D.N.D. 1986).

88. *See Delzer v. United Bank of Bismarck*, 527 N.W.2d 650 (N.D. 1995); *Bourgois v. Montana-Dakota Utils. Co.*, 466 N.W.2d 813 (N.D. 1991); N.D. Cent. Code § 9-03-08.

89. *See Eckmann v. Northwestern Federal Sav. & Loan Ass'n*, 436 N.W.2d 258 (N.D. 1989); *Olson v. Fraase*, 421 N.W.2d 820 (N.D. 1988).

90. *See Kary v. Prudential Ins. Co. of America*, 541 N.W.2d 703 (N.D. 1996).

91. *See* N.D. R. Civ. P. 9(b); *Matter of Estate of Ketterling*, 515 N.W.2d 158 (N.D. 1994).

92. *See Kaler v. Kraemer*, 574 N.W.2d 588 (N.D. 1998); *Bourgois v. Montana-Dakota Utils. Co.*, 466 N.W.2d 813 (N.D. 1991).

93. N.D. Cent. Code §§ 9-10-02; 9-10-03.

94. N.D. Cent. Code § 51-10.

95. N.D. Cent. Code § 51-15.

96. N.D. Cent. Code § 32-03.2-11.

97. *Id.*

98. *Id.*

99. *Id.*

100. *Id.*

101. *Id.*

102. N.D. Cent. Code § 32-03-08.

103. N.D. Cent. Code § 32-21-01.

104. N.D. Cent. Code § 32-21-03.

105. *See Hopkins v. McBane*, 427 N.W.2d 85 (N.D. 1988).

106. *See id.*

107. *See id.*

OHIO

A. STATUTES OF LIMITATION

Tort claims for recovery for bodily injury or damage to personal property are subject to a two-year statute of limitations.[1] Such actions generally accrue when the injury or loss to the person or property occurs,[2] although the discovery rule applies.[3] The discovery rule provides that when an injury does not manifest itself immediately, the cause of action does not arise until the plaintiff knows or, by the exercise of reasonable diligence should have known, that he had been injured by the conduct of the defendant.[4]

Claims for assault or battery must be brought within one year after the cause of action accrues.[5] A cause of action for assault or battery accrues on the date on which the assault or battery occurred.[6] The discovery rule applies if the identity of the tortfeasor is not known.[7]

Claims for wrongful death must be brought within two years.[8] The discovery rule applies to wrongful death claims.[9]

The statute of limitations for an employment intentional tort action is two years. The discovery rule applies.[10]

Trespass, conversion, and fraud claims must be brought within four years.[11] The discovery rule generally applies.[12]

Intentional infliction of emotional distress claims are subject to a four-year statute of limitations,[13] while negligent infliction of emotional distress claims are subject to a two-year statute.[14]

Actions for violation of the Consumer Sales Practices Act must be brought within two years.[15]

Actions for libel, slander, malicious prosecution, and false imprisonment are subject to a one-year statute of limitations.[16]

Claims for malpractice are subject to a one-year statute of limitations.[17]

A "catch-all" provision for actions that are not subject to another limitation section establishes a four-year limitation period.[18]

B. TORT REFORM

During the last decade, the Ohio Supreme Court has repeatedly invalidated legislative tort reform enactments as unconstitutional.[19] In August 1999, the Ohio Supreme Court struck down, in its entirety, Ohio's most recent comprehensive tort reform law on the ground that it usurped judicial power in violation of the Ohio constitutional doctrine of separation of powers.[20] The tort reform law would have amended, enacted, or repealed over 100 sections of the Ohio Revised Code.[21] Its more significant changes would have included caps on punitive and noneconomic damages, statutes of repose for product liability and malpractice claims, a certificate-of-merit requirement for malpractice claims, setoffs for collateral benefits received by plaintiff, and an altered summary judgment standard in toxic tort cases.[22]

C. "NO FAULT" LIMITATIONS

Ohio does not have a "no fault" automobile insurance law.

D. THE STANDARD FOR NEGLIGENCE

The plaintiff must show that: (1) the defendant had a legal duty to the plaintiff; (2) the defendant breached the duty; and (3) the breach proximately caused an injury.[23] The existence of a duty is a question of law that depends on the foreseeability of injury,[24] policy considerations, and the particular facts of the case.[25] Breach is shown when a plaintiff demonstrates that the defendant failed to exercise the degree of care that an ordinary reasonable person would exercise under similar circumstances.[26]

If a person has superior knowledge, skill, or intelligence, the law requires conduct consistent with the superior abilities.[27] A professional has a duty to exercise the professional standard of care: the skill and knowledge normally possessed by professionals in the particular field in similar communities.[28] There is no duty to control the actions of a third party unless a special relationship exists between the defendant and the third party or a person likely to be harmed by the third party.[29]

The standard of care applicable to a child is the degree of care ordinarily exercised by children of like age, capacity, knowledge, and experience under similar circumstances.[30] Children under the age of seven are conclusively presumed incapable of negligence.[31] Whether children older than seven years of age are negligent is ordinarily a question for the trier of fact based on the particular facts and circumstances of the case.[32]

E. CAUSATION

In order to recover on a negligence claim under Ohio law, a plaintiff must prove that the defendants' breach of duty proximately caused the plaintiff's injury.[33] The proximate cause of an injury is that which, in a natural and continued sequence, directly produces the injury and without which the injury would not have happened.[34] There can be more than one proximate cause of an injury.[35] A person is not responsible for an injury to another if his negligence is a remote cause and not a proximate cause.[36]

F. CONTRIBUTORY NEGLIGENCE, COMPARATIVE NEGLIGENCE, AND ASSUMPTION OF RISK

1. Contributory Negligence

Contributory negligence may be asserted as an affirmative defense to a negligence claim, but Ohio's enactment of a comparative negligence statute eliminated contributory negligence as a complete bar to recovering damages for negligence, unless the percentage of contributory negligence attributed to the plaintiff is greater than the total percentage of the negligence attributed to all parties to whom he seeks recovery.[37] Contributory negligence has been defined as want of ordinary care on the part of the person injured, which combined and concurred with the defendant's negligence and contributed to the injury as a proximate cause thereof, without which the injury would not have occurred.[38]

2. Comparative Negligence

The comparative negligence statute provides that the jury shall determine the percentage of negligence or implied assumption of the risk attributable to the plaintiff and the percentage of negligence attributable to each defendant;[39] damages are then reduced by an amount proportional to the plaintiff's percentage of fault.[40] If the percentage of fault attributed to the plaintiff is greater than that attributed to all of the defendants, the plaintiff is barred from recovery.[41]

When determining comparative negligence, three-fourths of the jury must agree as to the causal negligence of both parties, and only those jurors who so find may participate in the apportionment of negligence.[42]

3. Assumption of Risk

Implied assumption of the risk may be asserted as a defense to a negligence claim, but it is an element of comparative fault and will not operate as a complete bar unless the percentage of fault attributed to the plaintiff for his assumption of the risk is greater than the total percentage of the negligence attributed to all parties to whom he seeks recovery.[43] A plaintiff impliedly assumes the risk of injury if he had knowledge of a condition that was obviously dangerous and voluntarily exposed himself to that risk of injury.[44]

Primary assumption of the risk continues as a complete bar to negligence claims under Ohio law.[45] If the activity is one that is inherently dangerous and from which the risks cannot be eliminated, then a finding of primary assumption of the risk is appropriate.[46]

Express assumption of the risk also remains as a complete bar to recovery for negligence.[47] Express assumption of the risk will be found where the plaintiff has expressly agreed or contracted with the defendant not to sue for any future injuries which might be caused by the defendant's negligence.[48]

G. *RES IPSA LOQUITUR* AND INHERENTLY DANGEROUS ACTIVITIES

1. *Res Ipsa Loquitur*

The *res ipsa loquitur* doctrine is a rule of evidence that permits, but does not require, an inference of negligence where: (1) "the instrumentality causing the injury was, at the time of the injury, or at the time of the creation of the condition causing the injury, under the exclusive management and control of the defendant; and (2) that the injury occurred under such circumstances that in the ordinary course of events it would not have occurred if ordinary care had been observed."[49]

Res ipsa loquitur does not apply if the injury could have occurred even if defendant had exercised ordinary care.[50] Likewise, the doctrine does not apply if anyone other than defendant could have had control over the instrumentality that caused the injury.[51]

2. Inherently Dangerous Activities

Because the degree of care required by the general standard of ordinary or reasonable care varies with the particular circumstances and foreseeability of injury, a defendant engaged in inherently dangerous activities will be held to a higher degree of care.[52]

H. NEGLIGENCE *PER SE*

Negligence *per se* is based on the breach of a statutory duty and conclusively establishes both duty and breach.[53] A negligence *per se* claim requires that: (1) the statute or regulation must impose a duty for the safety or protection of others;[54] (2) the statute or regulation must impose a specific requirement, not an abstract or ambiguous duty;[55] (3) the defendant must violate the statute or regulation;[56] and (4) the violation of the statute or regulation must proximately cause the plaintiff's injury.[57] A negligence *per se* claim is subject to the defense of legal excuse, including, for example, a lack of notice of a property's defective condition.[58]

I. JOINT AND SEVERAL LIABILITY

Joint and several liability exists when an injury is caused by the joint or concurrent wrongful acts of two or more persons.[59] The criterion for joint and several liability is indivisibility of harm, not indivisibility of causation.[60] Multiple tortfeasors are jointly and severally liable unless the plaintiff's negligence contributes to the injury.[61] If the plaintiff's negligence contributes to his injury, the tortfeasors are jointly and severally liable only for the plaintiff's economic loss;[62] they are severally liable for their proportionate share of any noneconomic loss.[63]

A right of contribution exists in favor of a joint tortfeasor who has paid more than his proportionate share of the common liability, unless he has intentionally caused or contributed to an injury.[64] The right of contribution exists regardless of whether a judgment has been recovered against all or any of the tortfeasors.[65] A tortfeasor's right of contribution is limited to the amount paid by him in excess of his proportionate share.[66]

A plaintiff's release of one tortfeasor does not discharge others from liability unless the terms of the release so provides.[67] Rather, a release operates to reduce the claims against other tortfeasors in the amount stipulated by the release or in the amount of the consideration paid for it, whichever is greater.[68] The release also discharges the tortfeasor to whom it is given from all liability for contribution to any other tortfeasor.[69]

J. **INDEMNITY**

Indemnity is the right of a person who has been compelled to pay what another party should have paid to recover complete reimbursement from the other party.[70] Indemnity may be expressly provided by contract or may be implied by common law.[71] Indemnity is available to a related tortfeasor who, by virtue of a relationship to another, is compelled to pay damages for wrongdoing solely committed by the other party.[72] However, indemnity is available only to persons who are not actively negligent; it is not available to joint or concurrent tortfeasors who are chargeable with actual negligence.[73]

K. **BAR OF WORKERS' COMPENSATION STATUTE**

The Ohio Workers' Compensation Act bars an employee from suing an employer who has complied with the Act for the employee's work-related injuries.[74] Normally, workers' compensation is the injured employee's exclusive remedy.[75]

Until recently, the receipt of workers' compensation benefits creates an automatic right of subrogation in an employer who pays workers' compensation benefits against any third parties against whom the injured employee may have a right of recovery.[76] In June 2001, however, the Ohio Supreme Court held that the Workers' Compensation subrogation statute violated the Ohio Constitution's right to remedy, due process, and equal protection provisions.[77]

An employment intentional tort is an exception to the exclusive remedy of the Ohio Workers' Compensation Act.[78] To establish an intentional tort, a plaintiff must prove that the employer: (1) knew of a dangerous condition, instrumentality, or procedure in the workplace; (2) knew that if the employee was subjected to the danger, then harm to the employee would be a "substantial certainty"; and (3) despite such knowledge, required the employee to continue to perform the dangerous task.[79] The Ohio Supreme Court has struck down as unconstitutional in their entirety three different tort reform laws intended to limit the scope of employment intentional tort actions.[80]

L. **PREMISES LIABILITY**

Whether a landowner is liable for injuries incurred on the premises turns on the injured party's common law classification as a trespasser, invitee, or licensee.[81] The landowner is liable to a trespasser[82] only if the owner engages in willful, wanton, or reckless conduct that is likely to cause injury.[83] The landowner has the same duty to a licensee[84] as to a trespasser except that the owner must warn a licensee of hidden dangers.[85] Once the owner discovers that a trespasser or licensee is on the premises and is in danger, the owner has a duty to exercise ordinary care to prevent injury.[86] The owner's duty to an invitee[87] is to exercise ordinary care to maintain the premises in a reasonably safe condition so that invitees are not unreasonably exposed to dangers that they would not realize or anticipate.[88]

In 2001, Ohio adopted the attractive nuisance doctrine set forth in Section 339 of the Restatement of the Law 2d, Torts (1965). A landowner who knows or has reason to know that children are likely to trespass on a part of his property containing a dangerous condition has a duty of ordinary care to child trespassers.[89]

M. DRAM SHOP LIABILITY

Ohio's Dram Shop Act[90] enables a plaintiff injured by an intoxicated person to recover from the establishment that sold the person the intoxicating beverages. The elements an injured plaintiff must prove differ depending on where the plaintiff received his injuries. When the injuries occur on the defendant's premises, the plaintiff can recover if he proves that his injuries were proximately caused by the negligence of the defendant in providing alcohol to the intoxicated person.[91] If the injury occurs off of the defendant's premises, the plaintiff must prove that the intoxication proximately caused the plaintiff's injury and that the defendant knew that the intoxicated person: (1) was noticeably intoxicated; (2) habitually drinks to excess; (3) was placed on a prohibit-sale list by the Department of Liquor Control; or (4) was under 21. Actual knowledge by the defendant is not required.[92] Unless he is a minor, neither an intoxicated person nor his family may recover under these provisions.[93]

Another Ohio statute permits a plaintiff injured by an intoxicated person to recover against the entity that sold alcohol to the intoxicated person if an order of the Department of Liquor Control prohibited the sale to the person.[94]

As a general rule, a social host is not liable for injuries caused by a guest who becomes intoxicated.[95] However, if he provides alcohol to a minor, even a social host may be liable for injuries to third parties.[96]

N. ECONOMIC LOSS

A commercial party may not recover in tort for purely economic losses.[97] In such cases, the injured party must resort to any contract or Uniform Commercial Code claims it may have.[98] This rule, however, does not prohibit a plaintiff from recovering economic losses under tort theories when other, noneconomic damages are also alleged.[99] A noncommercial plaintiff may recover for purely economic damages under the common law theory of implied warranty in tort.[100]

O. FRAUD AND MISREPRESENTATION

Like its federal counterpart, Ohio Rule of Civil Procedure 9(b) requires that allegations of fraud be pled with particularity.[101]

A claim for fraud under Ohio law may be based on either a false representation or a knowing concealment.[102] The elements of a fraud claim are: (1) a representation or, when there is a duty to disclose, concealment of a fact; (2) that is material to the transaction at hand; (3) made falsely, with knowledge of its falsity, or with such utter disregard and recklessness as to whether it is true or false that knowledge may be inferred; (4) with the intent of misleading another into relying on it; (5) justifiable reliance on the representation or concealment; and (6) a resulting injury proximately caused by the reliance.[103]

The Ohio Supreme Court has recognized a claim for negligent misrepresentation in certain limited circumstances, following the Restatement (Second) of Torts

Section 552.[104] One who, in the course of his business, profession, or employment, or in any other transaction in which he has a pecuniary interest, supplies false information for the guidance of others in their business transactions, is subject to liability for pecuniary loss caused to them by their justifiable reliance on the information, if he fails to exercise reasonable care or competence in obtaining or communicating the information.[105]

In a civil action for money damages, the degree of proof necessary on a fraud claim is a preponderance of the evidence.[106] In certain cases (e.g., on contracts within the statute of frauds or to set aside a document for fraud), clear and convincing proof is required.[107]

P. CONSUMER FRAUD STATUTES

Ohio's Consumer Sales Practices Act (CSPA)[108] prohibits a broad variety of unfair, deceptive, or unconscionable practices in connection with consumer transactions.[109] The Ohio Attorney General has the authority to conduct investigations and hold evidentiary hearings into alleged violations of the CSPA.[110] The Attorney General may also bring an action under the CSPA for declaratory judgment, injunction, monetary damages, and civil penalties.[111]

A consumer may bring a private cause of action under the CSPA for declaratory judgment, injunction, rescission of the transaction, monetary damages and attorney's fees.[112] In order to recover monetary damages, a consumer must establish that the violation of the CSPA caused him to be injured.[113] Under certain circumstances, a consumer may recover statutory minimum damages ($200) without proof of actual damages.[114]

The CSPA does not apply to claims for personal injury or death.[115] The CSPA also does not apply to an act or practice required or specifically permitted by or under federal law or the Ohio Revised Code.[116]

As noted above, actions under the CSPA must be brought within two years of the occurrence of the violation or within one year after the termination of proceedings by the Attorney General with respect to the violation.[117]

Q. PUNITIVE DAMAGES

The purpose of a punitive damages award under Ohio law is not to compensate the plaintiff, but to punish the offender and deter others from offending in a likewise manner.[118] The Ohio Legislature has enacted Ohio Rev. Code Section 2315.21, which governs the recovery of punitive damages in tort actions. Under Ohio law, proof of actual damages on an underlying claim is a necessary predicate for an award of punitive damages.[119] A plaintiff must also establish that the conduct at the base of the punitive damages claim was the cause of the injury complained of in the underlying claim.[120] An award of punitive damages must bear a reasonable relationship to the injury sustained.[121]

A plaintiff who seeks punitive damages must show not only the elements of the underlying tort, but also that the wrongdoing was particularly gross or egregious.[122] Punitive damages awards require clear and convincing evidence of malice, aggravated or egregious fraud, oppression, or insult.[123]

R. WRONGFUL DEATH AND SURVIVORSHIP ACTIONS

Ohio's wrongful death statute affords a civil action for damages for the wrongful death of a person.[124] The Ohio survival statute provides that an action for personal injuries or injuries to property, or for deceit or fraud, survives the death of the person entitled to bring it.[125] Neither provision existed at common law.

The two causes of action are independent and the damages sought in a wrongful death action and a survival action are mutually exclusive.[126] The wrongful death action is designed to compensate a decedent's beneficiaries for any injuries they may have suffered by virtue of his untimely death; a survival action, on the other hand, is concerned with the wrong done to the injured person and is brought by the person's estate.[127]

Damages recovered in a wrongful death action include loss of support, loss of services, loss of society, loss of prospective inheritance, and mental anguish incurred by the decedent's beneficiaries. A wrongful death claim does not arise until the death of the injured person,[128] and must be brought within two years of the death.[129]

Mark A. Belasic
Dennis L. Murphy
JONES DAY REAVIS & POGUE
North Point
901 Lakeside Avenue
Cleveland, Ohio 44114
(216) 586-3939
Fax (216) 579-0212
mabelasic@jonesday.com
www.jonesday.com

ENDNOTES - OHIO

1. Ohio Rev. Code § 2305.10 (Anderson Supp. 2000).

2. *Id.*

3. *O'Stricker v. Jim Walter Corp.*, 4 Ohio St. 3d 84, 90, 447 N.E.2d 727, 732 (1983). The Ohio Legislature has expressly provided a discovery rule for exposures to: (1) asbestos or chromium; (2) chemical defoliants, herbicides, or similar agents; and (3) DES or similar compounds. Ohio Rev. Code § 2305.10.

4. *O'Stricker*, 4 Ohio St. 3d at 90, 447 N.E.2d at 732.

5. Ohio Rev. Code § 2305.111.

6. Ohio Rev. Code § 2305.111(A).

7. Ohio Rev. Code § 2305.111(B).

8. Ohio Rev. Code § 2125.02(D).

9. *Collins v. Sotka*, 81 Ohio St. 3d 506, 511, 692 N.E.2d 581, 584–85 (1998).

10. Ohio Rev. Code § 2305.10. *See Funk v. Rent-All Mart, Inc.*, 91 Ohio St. 3d 78, 81, 742 N.E.2d 127, 130 (2001).

11. Ohio Rev. Code § 2305.09.

12. *Id.* (discovery rule applies to fraud claims, conversion claims, and certain types of trespass claims).

13. *Yeager v. Local Union 20*, 6 Ohio St. 3d 369, 375, 453 N.E.2d 666, 672 (Ohio 1983) (holding that such claims are governed by the four-year statute of Ohio Rev. Code § 2305.09(D)).

14. *Lawyers Coop. Publishing Co. v. Muething*, 65 Ohio St. 3d 273, 280–81, 603 N.E.2d 969, 975 (Ohio 1992) (holding that such claims are governed by two-year statute of Ohio Rev. Code § 2305.10).

15. Ohio Rev. Code § 1345.10(C).

16. Ohio Rev. Code § 2305.11.

17. *Id.* (legal, medical); § 2305.113 (psychologist, social worker, counselor). If proper notice is provided within this one-year period, the time for filing an action may be extended. Ohio Rev. Code §§ 2305.11 (B)(1); 2305.113 (B).

18. Ohio Rev. Code § 2305.09(D).

19. In *State ex rel. Ohio Academy of Trial Lawyers v. Sheward*, 86 Ohio St. 3d 451, 457 n.5, 715 N.E.2d 1062, 1072 n.5 (1999), the Ohio Supreme Court listed more than a dozen decisions in which it struck down tort reform legislation as unconstitutional.

20. *Id.* at 475–94, 715 N.E.2d at 1085–97. The Ohio Supreme Court further held that the tort reform bill violated the "one-subject rule" of the Ohio constitution and was, therefore, unconstitutional in its entirety. *Id.* at 494–501, 715 N.E.2d at 1097–1102.

21. *Id.* at 458 n.6, 715 N.E.2d at 1073 n.6.

22. *Id.* at 475–91, 715 N.E.2d at 1085–96.

23. *Chambers v. St. Mary's School*, 82 Ohio St. 3d 563, 565, 697 N.E.2d 198, 200 (1998); *Mussivand v. David*, 45 Ohio St. 3d 314, 318, 544 N.E.2d 265, 269–70 (1989); *Jeffers v. Olexo*, 43 Ohio St. 3d 140, 142, 539 N.E.2d 614, 616 (1989).

24. "The test for foreseeability is whether a reasonably prudent person would have anticipated that an injury was likely to result from the performance or nonperformance of an act." *Morgan v. Fairfield Family Counseling Center*, 77 Ohio St. 3d 284, 293, 673 N.E.2d 1311, 1319 (1997).

25. *Morgan*, 77 Ohio St. 3d at 293, 297–98, 673 N.E.2d at 1319, 1322; *Mussivand*, 45 Ohio St. 3d at 318, 544 N.E.2d at 270; *Jeffers*, 43 Ohio St. 3d at 142, 539 N.E.2d at 616–17.

26. *Morgan*, 77 Ohio St. 3d at 293, 673 N.E.2d at 1319 ("reasonably prudent person"); *Mussivand*, 45 Ohio St. 3d at 318–19, 544 N.E.2d at 270 ("ordinarily reasonable and prudent person" will exercise "that care necessary to avoid injury to others"); *Jeffers*, 43 Ohio St. 3d at 144, 539 N.E.2d at 618 ("reasonably prudent and careful person, under the same or similar circumstances").

27. *Morgan*, 77 Ohio St. 3d at 293, 673 N.E.2d at 1319.

28. *See, e.g., Turner v. Sinha*, 65 Ohio App. 3d 30, 34–35, 582 N.E.2d 1018, 1021 (1989); *Richard v. Staehle*, 70 Ohio App. 2d 93, 98–99, 434 N.E.2d 1379, 1384 (1980).

29. *Morgan*, 77 Ohio St. 3d at 293–94, 673 N.E.2d at 1319–20 (citing Restatement (Second) of Torts (1965) §§ 314–19).

30. *Karr v. McNeil*, 92 Ohio App. 458, 462–63, 110 N.E.2d 714, 716–17 (1952); *Scott v. Marshall*, 90 Ohio App. 347, 349–50, 105 N.E.2d 281, 283–84 (1951).

31. *Hunter v. City of Cleveland*, 46 Ohio St. 2d 91, 92, 346 N.E.2d 303, 304 (1976); *DeLuca v. Bowden*, 42 Ohio St. 2d 392, 395–96, 329 N.E.2d 109, 112 (1975); *Holbrock v. Hamilton Distributing, Inc.*, 11 Ohio St. 2d 185, 189, 228 N.E.2d 628, 630 (1967).

32. *See Hunter*, 46 Ohio St. 2d at 92, 228 N.E.2d at 304 ("Had the plaintiff not been of such tender years [age six], this court would have been compelled to find that the injuries were the result of his own conduct."); *Deluca*, 42 Ohio St. 2d at 394, 329 N.E.2d at 394 (while holding that children under age seven are legally incapable of negligence, noting that children "gradually acquire the capacity to understand and appreciate the consequences of their acts" and act reasonably); *Scott*, 90 Ohio App. at 348–50, 105 N.E.2d at 283–84 (reversing judgment for plaintiff and entering judgment for defendant on grounds that, among other things, nine-year-old girl and her parents were contributorily negligent; noting that prior decisions held contributory negligence defense applied to children as young as eight years old); *Karr*, 92 Ohio App. at 462, 110 N.E.2d at 716 (holding that it is "generally recognized" that an "initial capacity for some negligence" occurs in "a child beyond babyhood or early infancy").

33. *E.g., Chambers*, 82 Ohio St. 3d at 563, 697 N.E.2d at 200.

34. *Garbe v. Halloran*, 150 Ohio St. 476, 481, 83 N.E.2d 217, 221 (1948); 70 Ohio Jur. 3d Negligence §§ 37, 39 (1986).

35. 1 Ohio Jury Instr. § 11.10.

36. *Osler v. Lorain*, 28 Ohio St. 3d 345, 347, 504 N.E.2d 19, 21 (1986); *Armour & Co. v. Ott*, 117 Ohio St. 252, 257, 158 N.E. 189, 191 (1927).

37. Ohio Rev. Code §§ 2315.19(A)(1), 2315.19(A)(2) & 2315.19(B).

38. *Brinkmoeller v. Wilson*, 41 Ohio St. 2d 223, 226, 325 N.E.2d 233, 235 (1975).

39. Ohio Rev. Code § 2315.19(B)(4).

40. Ohio Rev. Code § 2315.19(C).

41. *Id.*

42. *O'Connell v. Chesapeake & Ohio Ry. Co.*, 58 Ohio St. 3d 226, 236–37, 569 N.E.2d 889, 898 (1991).

43. Ohio Rev. Code § 2315.19(C).

44. *Anderson v. Ceccardi*, 6 Ohio St. 3d 110, 112, 451 N.E.2d 780, 782 (1983).

45. *Gallagher v. Cleveland Browns Football Co.*, 74 Ohio St. 3d 427, 431, 659 N.E.2d 1232, 1236 (1996).

46. *Gehri v. Capital Racing Club, Inc.*, No. 96APE10-1307, 1997 Ohio App. LEXIS 2527, *10 (Ohio Ct. App. June 12, 1997).

47. 1 Ohio Jury Instr. § 9.50; *Anderson*, 6 Ohio St. 3d at 114, 451 N.E.2d at 783.

48. *Anderson*, 6 Ohio St. 3d at 114, 451 N.E.2d at 783.

49. *Jennings Buick, Inc. v. City of Cincinnati*, 63 Ohio St. 2d 167, 170, 406 N.E.2d 1385, 1388 (1980) (quoting *Hake v. Wiedemann Brewing Co.*, 23 Ohio St. 2d 65, 66–67, 262 N.E.2d 703, 705 (1970)).

50. *Schmidt v. Univ. of Cincinnati Med. Ctr.*, 117 Ohio App. 3d 427, 431–32, 690 N.E.2d 946, 949 (1997) (rejecting application of doctrine in medical malpractice case, citing *Johnson v. Hammond*, 68 Ohio App. 3d 491, 493–94, 589 N.E.2d 65, 66–67 (1990)); *George v. Ottawa Lanes*, No. L-00-1241, 2001 Ohio App. LEXIS 1724, *9–*10 (Ohio Ct. App. Apr. 13, 2001) (rejecting application of doctrine for failure to establish lack of ordinary care).

51. *Kemper v. Builder's Square Inc.*, 109 Ohio App. 3d 127, 138, 671 N.E.2d 1104 (1996) (rejecting application of doctrine where customers or other third parties may have moved posts that fell on plaintiff); *Knox v. Bag-N-Save Foods*, No. 1998AP080100, 1999 Ohio App. LEXIS 1675, *6-*7 (Ohio Ct. App. Apr. 8, 1999) (rejecting application of doctrine where automatic door was not under store's exclusive control).

52. *Mussivand*, 45 Ohio St. 3d at 318–19, 594 N.E.2d at 269–70 (degree of care required depends on circumstances); *Jeffers*, 43 Ohio St. 3d at 142–43, 539 N.E.2d at 616 (scope of duty turns on foreseeability and probability of injury).

53. *E.g., Chambers*, 82 Ohio St. 3d at 565, 697 N.E.2d at 201; *Hurst v. Dep't of Rehab. & Correction*, 72 Ohio St. 3d 325, 327, 650 N.E.2d 104, 106 (1995); *Becker v. Shaul*, 62 Ohio St. 3d 480, 483, 584 N.E.2d 684, 686 (1992).

54. *E.g., Sikora v. Wenzel*, 88 Ohio St. 3d 493, 496-97, 727 N.E.2d 1277, 1280-81 (2000); *Chambers*, 82 Ohio St. 3d at 565, 697 N.E.2d at 201; *Hurst*, 72 Ohio St. 3d at 327, 650 N.E.2d at 106; *Becker*, 62 Ohio St. 3d at 483, 584 N.E.2d at 686.

55. *E.g., Chambers*, 82 Ohio St. 3d at 565, 697 N.E.2d at 201 (a "specific duty" and "positive and definite standard of care"); *Hurst*, 72 Ohio St. 3d at 327, 650 N.E.2d at 106 (a "specific act" rather than a duty defined "only in abstract or general terms").

56. *E.g., Hurst*, 72 Ohio St. 3d at 327, 650 N.E.2d at 106; *Becker*, 62 Ohio St. 3d at 483, 584 N.E.2d at 686.

57. *E.g., Chambers*, 82 Ohio St. 3d at 565, 697 N.E.2d at 201 (negligence *per se* "is not a finding of liability *per se* because the plaintiff will also have to prove proximate cause and damages"); *Wireman v. Keneco Distr., Inc.*, 75 Ohio St. 3d 103, 109, 661 N.E.2d 744, 749 (1996) (negligence *per se* claim rejected because plaintiff's injury was not caused by breach of regulation).

58. *Sikora*, 88 Ohio St. 3d at 496-97, 727 N.E.2d at 1280-81.

59. *Bowling v. Heil*, 31 Ohio St. 3d 277, 286, 511 N.E.2d 373, 380–81 (1987).

60. *Nichols v. Hanzel*, 110 Ohio App. 3d 591, 602, 674 N.E.2d 1237, 1244 (Ohio Ct. App. 1996) (citing *Pang v. Minch*, 53 Ohio St. 3d 186, 197, 559 N.E.2d 1313, 1323–24 (1990)).

61. *Abrahamsen v. Trans-State Express, Inc.*, 24 F.3d 804, 805 (6th Cir. 1994).

62. Ohio Rev. Code § 2315.19(D)(1)(c); *Abrahamsen*, 24 F.3d at 805. Economic loss includes lost wages or salary and all expenditures resulting from the injury. Ohio Rev. Code §§ 2315.19(E)(1)(a)–(c).

63. Ohio Rev. Code §§ 2315.19(D)(1)(a), (b); *Abrahamsen*, 24 F.3d at 805. Noneconomic loss consists of all nonpecuniary harm resulting from the injury and includes such damages as pain and suffering, mental anguish, loss of society or consortium, and other intangibles. Ohio Rev. Code § 2315.19(E)(3).

64. Ohio Rev. Code § 2307.31(A).

65. *Id.* Ohio Rev. Code § 2307.31(G).

66. Ohio Rev. Code § 2307.31(A); *National Mut. Ins. Co. v. Whitmer*, 70 Ohio St. 2d 149, 151–52, 435 N.E.2d 1121, 1123 (1982).

67. Ohio Rev. Code § 2307.32(F)(1).

68. *Id.*

69. Ohio Rev. Code § 2307.32(F)(2).

70. *Worth v. Aetna Casualty & Surety Co.*, 32 Ohio St. 3d 238, 240, 513 N.E.2d 253, 256 (1987); *Whitney v. Horrigan*, 112 Ohio App. 3d 511, 514–15, 679 N.E.2d 315, 317 (1996).

71. *Worth*, 32 Ohio St. 3d at 240, 513 N.E.2d at 256; *Whitney*, 112 Ohio App. 3d at 514–15, 679 N.E.2d at 317.

72. *Motorist Mutual Ins. Co. v. Huron Road Hospital*, 73 Ohio St. 3d 391, 394, 653 N.E.2d 235, 238–39 (1995) (overruling *Travelers Indemn. Co. v. Trowbridge*, 41

Ohio St. 2d 11, 321 N.E.2d 787 (1975) to the extent that it erroneously deemed a right to contribution among concurrent tortfeasors a right to indemnity); *Reynolds v. Physicians Ins. Co. of Ohio*, 68 Ohio St. 3d 14, 16, 623 N.E.2d 30 (1993).

73. *Motorist Mutual*, 73 Ohio St. 3d at 394, 653 N.E.2d at 238–39; *Reynolds*, 68 Ohio St. 3d at 16, 623 N.E.2d at 31–32; *Whitney*, 112 Ohio App. 3d at 515, 679 N.E.2d at 317. Joint or concurrent tortfeasors who have paid more than their proportionate share of damages have a statutory right to contribution under Ohio Rev. Code Ann. § 2307.31 rather than a common law right to indemnity. *Motorist Mutual*, 73 Ohio St. 3d at 395, 653 N.E.2d at 239.

74. Ohio Rev. Code § 4123.74.

75. *Waller v. Mayfield*, 37 Ohio St. 3d 118, 121, 524 N.E.2d 458, 461 (1988).

76. Ohio Rev. Code § 4123.931(A), (C).

77. *Holeton v. Crouse Cartage Co.*, 92 Ohio St. 3d 115, 121-33, 748 N.E.2d 1111, 1118-27 (2001).

78. See, e.g., *Van Fossen v. Babcock & Wilcox*, 36 Ohio St. 3d 100, 111–13, 522 N.E.2d 489, 499–501 (1988).

79. *Fyffe v. Jeno's, Inc.*, 59 Ohio St. 3d 115, 118, 570 N.E.2d 1108, 1112 (1991); *Sanek v. Duracote Corp.*, 43 Ohio St. 3d 169, 539 N.E.2d 1114, 1116 (1989); *Van Fossen*, 36 Ohio St. 3d at 116, 522 N.E.2d at 504. Proof beyond that required to establish negligence or recklessness is required. *Fyffe*, 59 Ohio St. 3d at 118, 570 N.E.2d at 1112; *Van Fossen*, 36 Ohio St. 3d at 117, 522 N.E.2d at 504. "[T]he mere knowledge and appreciation of a risk—something short of substantial certainty" is insufficient to establish an employment intentional tort. *Fyffe*, 59 Ohio St. 3d at 118, 570 N.E.2d at 1112; *Van Fossen*, 36 Ohio St. 3d at 117, 522 N.E.2d at 504.

80. *Johnson v. BP Chemicals, Inc.*, 85 Ohio St. 3d 298, 707 N.E.2d 1107 (1999) (Ohio Rev. Code § 2745.01 held unconstitutional); *State ex rel. Ohio AFL-CIO v. Voinovich*, 69 Ohio St. 3d 225, 631 N.E.2d 582, *clarified*, 69 Ohio St. 3d 1208, 632 N.E.2d 907 (1994) (workers' compensation reform law, which modified employment intentional tort requirements, held unconstitutional); *Brady v. Safety-Kleen Corp.*, 61 Ohio St. 3d 624, 576 N.E.2d 722 (1991) (Ohio Rev. Code § 4121.80 held unconstitutional).

81. *Gladon v. Greater Cleveland Regional Transit Authority*, 75 Ohio St. 3d 312, 315, 662 N.E.2d 287, 291 (1996); *Shump v. First Continental-Robinwood Ass'n*, 71 Ohio St. 3d 414, 417, 644 N.E.2d 291, 294 (1994); *Brown v. Central Trux & Parts, Inc.*, No. L-00-1278, 2001 Ohio App. LEXIS 1495, at *6-*8 (Ohio Ct. App. Mar. 30, 2001).

82. A trespasser is any person who comes on the premises without the express or implied authorization of the owner or is initially invited on the premises but without authorization enters an area of the premises beyond the scope of the invitation. *Gladon*, 75 Ohio St. 3d at 315–16, 662 N.E.2d at 291–92 (citing Restatement (Second) of Torts (1965) § 332, comment l); *Jeffers v. Olexo*, 43 Ohio St. 3d 140, 144, 539 N.E.2d 614, 619 (1989).

83. *Gladon*, 75 Ohio St. 3d at 317, 662 N.E.2d at 293; *Jeffers*, 43 Ohio St. 3d at 145–46, 539 N.E.2d at 619; *McKinney v. Hartz & Restle Realtors, Inc.*, 31 Ohio St. 3d 244, 246, 510 N.E.2d 386, 388 (1987). Under the dangerous instrumentalities exception, a landowner has a higher degree of care to a child trespasser if the landowner negligently operates hazardous machinery or other apparatus, the danger of which is not obvious to children, on or immediately adjacent to public property. *McKinney*, 31 Ohio St. 3d at 247, 510 N.E.2d at 389; *Richards v. Cincinnati W. Baptist Church*, 112 Ohio App. 3d 769, 771, 680 N.E.2d 191, 192 (1996).

84. "A licensee is a person who is privileged to enter or remain on land only by virtue of the possessor's consent." *Boydston v. Norfolk Southern Corp.*, 73 Ohio App. 3d 727, 730, 598 N.E.2d 171, 173 (1991) (quoting Restatement (Second) of Torts (1965) § 330). A licensee comes on the premises "by permission and acquiescence of the landowner for the licensee's own pleasure or convenience and not by invitation." *Qualchoice, Inc. v. Yost Constr. Co.*, No. 98CA007224, 2000 Ohio App. LEXIS 8, at *10–11 (Ohio Ct. App. Jan. 5, 2000) (citing *Hannan v. Ehrlich*, 102 Ohio St. 176, 185, 131 N.E. 504, 507 (1921)).

85. *See Gladon*, 75 Ohio St. 3d at 317, 662 N.E.2d at 293; *Qualchoice*, 2000 Ohio App. LEXIS at *12.

86. *Gladon*, 75 Ohio St. 3d at 318, 662 N.E.2d at 293; *Jeffers*, 43 Ohio St. 3d at 145–46, 539 N.E.2d at 619.

87. An invitee is a person who comes on the premises "by invitation, express or implied, for some purpose which is beneficial to the owner." *Gladon*, 75 Ohio St. 3d at 315, 662 N.E.2d at 291; *see also Light v. Ohio Univ.*, 28 Ohio St. 3d 66, 68, 502 N.E.2d 611, 613 (1986).

88. *Gladon*, 75 Ohio St. 3d at 317, 662 N.E.2d at 293; *Paschal v. Rite Aid Pharmacy, Inc.*, 18 Ohio St. 3d 203, 204, 480 N.E.2d 474 (1985); *Brown*, 2001 Ohio App. LEXIS 1495, at *6-*7.

89. *Bennett v. Stanley*, 92 Ohio St. 3d 35, 42-43, 748 N.E.2d 41, 47-49 (2001).

90. Ohio Rev. Code § 4399.18.

91. *Id.*

92. *Id.*; *Lesnau v. Andale Enterprises, Inc.*, 93 Ohio St. 3d 419, 423, 756 N.E.2d 97, 103 (2001).

93. *Klever v. Canton Sachsenheim, Inc.*, 86 Ohio St. 3d 419, 423, 715 N.E.2d 536, 540 (1999); *Smith v. The 10th Inning, Inc.*, 49 Ohio St. 3d 289, 291, 551 N.E.2d 1296, 1298 (1990).

94. Ohio Rev. Code § 4399.01.

95. *Settlemyer v. Wilmington Veterans Post No. 49*, 11 Ohio St. 3d 123, 127, 464 N.E.2d 521, 524 (1984).

96. *Mitseff v. Wheeler*, 38 Ohio St. 3d 112, 114, 526 N.E.2d 798, 800 (1988).

97. *Foster Wheeler Enviresponse, Inc. v. Franklin Cty. Conv. Fac. Auth.*, 78 Ohio St. 3d 353, 366–67, 678 N.E.2d 519, 529–30 (1997); *Sun Ref'g & Mkt'g Co. v. Crosby Valve & Gage Co.*, 68 Ohio St. 3d 397, 398–99, 627 N.E.2d 552, 554 (1994); *Chemtrol Adhesives, Inc. v. American Mfrs. Mut. Ins. Co.*, 42 Ohio St. 3d 40, 51, 537 N.E.2d 624, 635 (1989).

98. *Floor Craft Floor Covering, Inc. v. Parma Comm. Gen. Hosp. Assoc.*, 54 Ohio St. 3d 1, 8, 560 N.E.2d 206, 212 (1990); *Chemtrol Adhesives, Inc.*, 42 Ohio St. 3d at 51, 537 N.E.2d at 635.

99. *Sun Ref'g & Mkt'g Co.*, 68 Ohio St. 3d at 399, 627 N.E.2d at 555; *Lawyers Cooperative Pub. Co. v. Muething*, 65 Ohio St. 3d 273, 277, 603 N.E.2d 969, 972–73 (1992).

100. *LaPuma v. Collinwood Concrete*, 75 Ohio St. 3d 64, 67, 661 N.E.2d 714, 716 (1996); *Iacono v. Anderson Concrete Corp.*, 42 Ohio St. 2d 88, 93, 326 N.E.2d 267, 271 (1975).

101. Ohio R. Civ. P. 9(b) (West 1999).

102. *Williams v. Aetna Finance Co.*, 83 Ohio St. 3d 462, 475, 700 N.E.2d 859, 868 (1998); *Burr v. Board of County Comm'rs of Stark Cty.*, 23 Ohio St. 3d 69, 73, 491 N.E.2d 1101, 1105 (1986); *Miles v. McSwegin*, 58 Ohio St. 2d 97, 100, 388 N.E.2d 1367, 1369 (1979).

103. *Williams*, 83 Ohio St. 3d at 475, 700 N.E.2d at 868; *Burr*, 23 Ohio St. 3d at 73, 491 N.E.2d at 1105; *Glassner v. R.J. Reynolds Tobacco Co.*, 223 F.3d 343, 352 (6th Cir. 2000).

104. *Gutter v. Dow Jones, Inc.*, 22 Ohio St. 3d 286, 288–89, 490 N.E.2d 898, 900 (1986); *Hadden View Invest. Co. v. Coopers & Lybrand*, 70 Ohio St. 2d 154, 156–57 & n.1, 436 N.E.2d 212, 214–15 & n.1 (1982).

105. *Delman v. City of Cleveland Heights*, 41 Ohio St. 3d 1, 4, 534 N.E.2d 835, 838 (1989).

106. *Household Finance Corp. v. Altenberg*, 5 Ohio St. 2d 190, 193, 214 N.E.2d 667, 669–70 (1966).

107. *Cross v. Ledford*, 161 Ohio St. 469, 475, 120 N.E.2d 118, 122 (1954).

108. Ohio Rev. Code §§ 1345.01 *et seq.*

109. Ohio Rev. Code §§ 1345.02–1345.03. "Consumer transaction" is defined at Ohio Rev. Code § 1345.01.

110. Ohio Rev. Code §§ 1345.05(B)–1345.06.

111. Ohio Rev. Code §§ 1345.05–1345.07.

112. Ohio Rev. Code § 1345.09; *Parker v. I & F Insulation Co.*, 89 Ohio St. 3d 261 (2000) (attorney's fees and interest). The Ohio Attorney General may intervene in the private action. *Id.* at § 1345.09(E).

113. *See Brooks v. Hurst Buick-Pontiac-Olds-GMC Inc.*, 23 Ohio App. 3d 85, 90, 491 N.E.2d 345, 350 (1985) (noting that the legislative intent of the CSPA was "to assure that consumers will recover any damages caused by such acts and practices"); *Pasco v. McCoy*, No. OT-94-046, 1995 Ohio App. LEXIS 2730, at *36, *42–43 (Ohio Ct. App. June 30, 1995) (where loss of use of boat was caused by plaintiff's own negligence, plaintiff could not recover damages under either CSPA or negligence claims); *Eckert v. Tony LaRiche Chevrolet*, No. 60429, 1992 Ohio App. LEXIS 2587, at *6 (Ohio Ct. App. May 21, 1992) ("we agree that [plaintiff] was required to prove a relationship between the statutory violation and his injuries").

114. If the Ohio Attorney General has previously issued a rule declaring the act or practice to be deceptive or unconscionable, or if an Ohio state court has previously declared the act or practice to be deceptive or unconscionable and has made its decision available for public inspection, then the consumer may recover three times the amount of his actual damages or $200, whichever is higher. Ohio Rev. Code § 1345.09(B); *Shaver v. Standard Oil Co.*, 89 Ohio App. 3d 52, 63, 623 N.E.2d 602, 610 (1993) ("a consumer who is subjected to the same behavior which has already been declared to be unfair, deceptive or unconscionable can seek special statutory damages"); *Gaylan v. Dave Towell Cadillac, Inc.*, 15 Ohio Misc. 2d 1, 3, 473 N.E.2d 64, 66 (Ohio Muni. Ct. 1984) (failure to prove damages precluded award of actual damages but statutory minimum damages were available where defendant's act violated administrative regulation promulgated by Attorney General).

115. Ohio Rev. Code § 1345.12(C); *Pomianowski v. Merle Norman Cosmetics, Inc.*, 507 F. Supp. 435 (S.D. Ohio 1980).

116. Ohio Rev. Code § 1345.12(A). If the violation of the CSPA was an act required by FTC orders or federal courts' interpretations of the FTC Act, 15 U.S.C. § 41, the Ohio Attorney General may seek injunctive relief but the supplier is not subject to any liability or penalty in either the Attorney General action or a private action. Ohio Rev. Code Ann. § 1345.11(B).

117. Ohio Rev. Code § 1345.10(C).

118. *Williams v. Aetna Finance Co.*, 83 Ohio St. 3d 462, 480, 700 N.E.2d 859, 871 (1998); *Moran v. Johns-Manville Sales Corp.*, 691 F.2d 811 (6th Cir. 1982); 30 Ohio Jur. 3d Damages § 148 (1986).

119. Ohio Rev. Code § 2315.21(B); *Moskovitz v. Mount Sinai Med. Ctr.*, 69 Ohio St. 3d 638, 649, 635 N.E.2d 331, 342 (1994); *Richard v. Hunter*, 151 Ohio St. 185, 192, 85 N.E.2d 109, 112 (1949).

120. *Detling v. Chockley*, 70 Ohio St. 2d 134, 139–40, 436 N.E.2d 208, 211–12 (1982).

121. *Williams*, 83 Ohio St. 3d at 480, 700 N.E.2d at 871; *Alessio v. Hamilton Auto Body, Inc.*, 21 Ohio App. 3d 247, 248, 486 N.E.2d 1224, 1225 (Ohio Ct. App. 1985); 30 Ohio Jur. 3d Damages § 161 (1986).

122. *Logson v. Graham Ford Co.*, 54 Ohio St. 2d 336, 340 n.2, 376 N.E.2d 1333, 1336 n.2 (1978).

123. Ohio Rev. Code § 2315.21(B), (C); *Preston v. Murty*, 32 Ohio St. 3d 334, 346, 512 N.E.2d 1174, 1176 (1987).

124. Ohio Rev. Code § 2125.01.

125. Ohio Rev. Code § 2305.21.

126. *Thompson v. Wing*, 70 Ohio St. 3d 176, 183, 637 N.E.2d 917, 922 (1994).

127. *E.g., Thompson*, 70 Ohio St. 3d at 183, 637 N.E.2d at 922; *Jones v. Wittenberg Univ.*, 534 F.2d 1203, 1207 (1976).

128. Ohio Rev. Code § 2125.02(B); *Thompson*, 70 Ohio St. 3d at 183, 637 N.E.2d at 922.

129. Ohio Rev. Code § 2125.02(D).

OKLAHOMA

A. **STATUTES OF LIMITATION**

Causes of action for trespass, conversion, or tortious injury to personal or real property must be brought within two years after the cause of action arose. Actions for injury to persons or property, or injury to the rights of others, not otherwise noted below and not arising in contract must be brought within two years. An action for relief on the ground of fraud must also be brought within two years, but in such case the action shall not be deemed to have accrued until the discovery of the fraud.[1] The "discovery" rule is applicable to several classes of cases.[2]

Actions for libel, slander, assault, battery, malicious prosecution, or false imprisonment must be brought within one year.[3]

Causes of Action under written contracts have a five-year statute of limitations, while actions on implied or oral contracts have a three-year limitation.[4]

For any action not previously provided for, there is a "catch-all" provision that provides for a five-year statute of limitations.[5]

The statute of limitations may be tolled under several exceptions set out below. First, as noted above, the "discovery rule" may toll the statute until the plaintiff has knowledge or a reasonable opportunity to know the fact of injury. Second, there is an extension of the limitation during periods of disability. Third, there is an extension during the "absence or flight" of a defendant, under certain circumstances.[6]

Persons under a disability at the time the cause of action accrues (including minors) may bring an action within one year after removal of such disability.[7] There is an exception set out in the statute for medical negligence actions involving minors. An action for personal injury to a minor under the age of 12 arising from medical malpractice must be brought by the minor's parent or guardian within seven years of the infliction of the injury. A minor 12 years of age and older must bring the action within one year after attaining majority, but in no event less than two years from the date of infliction of the injury. An action for personal injury arising from medical negligence involving an incompetent person must be brought within seven years of the infliction of the injury, or within one year of the time the person is adjudicated competent, but in no event less than two years from the date of infliction of the injury.[8]

There is a ten-year statute of repose for claims involving improvements to real property, regardless of whether the claim involves injury to person or property.[9]

The Governmental Tort Claims Act[10] governs actions against state or local governments for personal injuries and provides detailed procedures and limitations.

The litigation must be commenced by filing a claim with the clerk of the political subdivision, within one year of the date of loss. The political subdivision then has 90 days within which to accept or deny the claim. Thereafter, the claimant may file his lawsuit within 180 days of the denial of the claim. No suit may be filed absent the filing of a claim against the political subdivision and its acceptance or denial.[11]

There is an Oklahoma "savings statute," which allows for the refiling of an action, within one year, which has "failed otherwise than on the merits."[12]

B. **TORT REFORM**

There has been no recent "tort reform" legislation in Oklahoma, although a number of attempts have been made. With the exception of the punitive damages statute addressed below, there are no "caps" on damages in Oklahoma. In addition to the "Rule 11" requirement, Oklahoma has long had a statute which allows for recovery of attorneys' fees to the prevailing party where a frivolous appeal is filed.[13]

C. **"NO FAULT" LIMITATIONS**

Oklahoma has no provisions for "no fault" in motor vehicle accidents. While an adjudication of liability is necessary for recovery in a motor vehicle accident case, Oklahoma has mandated the offer of uninsured or underinsured motorist coverage by insurers writing liability coverage in Oklahoma.[14]

D. **THE STANDARD FOR NEGLIGENCE**

In general, the four elements of actionable negligence are outlined as follows: (1) a duty upon the defendant; (2) breach of that duty by the defendant; (3) injury to the plaintiff; and (4) an injury which proximately results from the breach.[15]

The existence and scope of a duty is predicated on the relationship between the parties and the parties' status.[16] A breach of duty is established when the evidence shows defendant's conduct deviated from the standard of care expected under the circumstances.

The standard of care expected of a child depends upon the child's age, experience, and capacity.[17] As a matter of law, a child "of tender years" is incapable of negligence.[18] However, a child operating a motor vehicle is held to the same standard of care as an adult.[19]

Oklahoma recognizes a heightened standard of care for professionals. For the physician, the standard is determined by national standards, whether or not the physician is a "specialist."[20] The standard of care which applies to other professionals requires the degree of knowledge and ability ordinarily possessed by other members of the profession, as well as the exercise of ordinary care, diligence, and judgment.[21]

There is no presumption of due care as to any party, whether or not deceased or incapacitated.[22]

E. **CAUSATION**

One of the elements of a negligence case is the existence of causation. The term "proximate cause," has been replaced in Oklahoma by the term "direct cause." Direct cause is that cause which in a natural and continuous sequence produces injury, and without which the injury would not have happened. While the specific result of the act need not be foreseen, it is necessary that some injury to the person or property of someone in the plaintiff's situation be reasonably foreseeable.[23]

Where an injury is the result of the combined negligence of two or more persons, the conduct of each is considered a direct cause, regardless of the extent to which each contributes to the injury. It is only when an act interrupts or breaks the chain of causation that an act is said to be an "intervening cause," which relieves a party of liability. To be an intervening cause, the act must be independent of the other party's act or omission, adequate by itself to cause the injury, and not reasonably foreseeable by the party.[24]

F. **CONTRIBUTORY NEGLIGENCE, COMPARATIVE NEGLIGENCE, AND ASSUMPTION OF RISK**

1. **Contributory Negligence**

    The doctrine of contributory negligence was abolished in 1973 by the adoption of the Comparative Negligence Act. That statute was amended again in 1979. The statute abolished the common law doctrine which bars plaintiff from recovery if his negligence contributed to his injuries.[25]

2. **Comparative Negligence**

    The Doctrine of Comparative Negligence applies to all types of negligence actions, but does not apply to other "negligent-based" torts.[26] There is no "comparative fault" doctrine applicable to cases such as products liability in Oklahoma.[27] In a negligence case, the plaintiff may recover as long as his negligence is *50 percent or less* of the negligence causing the injuries.[28] Where the plaintiff is negligent, the liability of the defendants is "several" (i.e., it is limited to his or her proportionate share of damages, based upon the percentage assessed against the party.)[29] Where the plaintiff is "faultless," there is joint and several liability, and the plaintiff may recover all of his damages against any of the defendants found to be at fault.[30]

3. **Assumption of Risk**

    In a negligence case, Oklahoma recognizes a constitutionally protected doctrine of assumption of risk as a defense separate and distinct from contributory or comparative negligence.[31] While comparative or contributory negligence is not a defense in a product liability case, the voluntary assumption of risk of a known defect remains a viable defense.[32]

    Three types of assumption of risk are recognized in Oklahoma: express assumption of risk;[33] implied primary assumption of risk; and implied secondary assumption of risk. Each of these is to be distinguished from the defense of contributory negligence, in that each involves evidence that the plaintiff voluntarily exposed himself to injury with a knowledge and appreciation of the danger and risk involved.[34]

Implied primary assumption of risk involves those situations where the plaintiff is presumed to have consented to a release of the defendant because the plaintiff has participated in a particular activity or situation which involves inherent and well-known risks.[35] This type of risk assumption involves an objective element in that a jury could decide that the risks in question were inherent in the activity, and therefore, well known despite the fact that the plaintiff denies any knowledge of the risks.

Implied secondary assumption of risk involves those situations where the plaintiff implicitly assumes the risk created by the defendant's conduct and voluntarily chose to encounter that risk.[36]

G. *RES IPSA LOQUITUR* AND INHERENTLY DANGEROUS ACTIVITIES

1. *Res Ipsa Loquitur*

Res ipsa loquitur is an evidentiary doctrine, which permits, under certain situations, an inference of negligence from the mere fact that an accident occurred. The requirements for application of the doctrine are: (1) that the injury was caused by some instrumentality, act or omission which was under the exclusive control and management of the defendant; and, (2) that the event causing the injury to plaintiff was of a kind which ordinarily does not occur in the absence of negligence on the part of the person in control of the instrumentality or responsible for the act or omission.[37]

It is the court's duty to determine if there is evidence sufficient to submit the theory to the jury. If so, the jury is instructed to determine first whether each of the propositions is "more probably true than not true," and then *may, but is not required* to find negligence.[38]

2. **Inherently Dangerous Activities**

While Oklahoma has adopted a general rule that a person is required to use care to avoid injury to himself and others in proportion to the danger involved,[39] it has also fashioned a "strict liability" standard for what is termed "ultrahazardous activity." It is for the judge to determine, in the first instance, whether the particular activity involved is "ultrahazardous." The factors to be considered in making such determination are: the existence of a high degree of risk of some harm to person or property; the likelihood of harm; the inability to eliminate the risk with the exercise of reasonable care; the extent to which the activity is not a matter of common usage; the inappropriateness of the activity to the place where it is carried on; and the extent to which its value to the community is outweighed by its dangerous attributes.[40]

The most common type of ultrahazardous activity is the use of explosives, but the doctrine has been applied to the keeping of wild animals.[41]

H. NEGLIGENCE *PER SE*

The violation of a statute or ordinance constitutes negligence *per se* when three criteria are met: (1) the injury complained of must have been caused by the violation; (2) the injury must have been of the type intended to be prevented by the ordinance or statute; and (3) the injured party must have been in the class to be protected by the ordinance or statute. [42] If these requirements are met, the evidence establishes both the duty and the breach of duty required in a negligence case. Of course, the duty to comply with statutes or ordinances is in addition to the duty to exercise ordinary care, and compliance with those duties does not excuse one from the duty to exercise ordinary care.[43]

I. JOINT AND SEVERAL LIABILITY

Joint tortfeasors are two or more persons jointly or severally liable for the same injury to person or property. It is not necessary that all be liable under the same theory of recovery, only that multiple tortfeasors cause or contribute to the same injuries sustained by the plaintiff.[44]

In 1978, the Oklahoma Supreme Court abolished the joint and several liability rule in multiple tortfeasor situations, and adopted a rule of several liability only. Under this doctrine, each defendant's liability to the plaintiff is limited to that amount which his proportionate percentage of negligence bears to the plaintiff's total damages.[45] However, the court has subsequently made clear that where the plaintiff is "zero percent" at fault, the rule of joint and several liability continues in effect.[46] The abolition of the joint and several rule was intended only as to comparative negligence situations, and not other negligent torts.[47]

Prior to adoption in 1978 of a statute providing for contribution among joint tortfeasors, Oklahoma did not afford to any joint tortfeasor the right of recovery against another joint tortfeasor when the first joint tortfeasor was required to pay more than his *pro rata* share of plaintiff's damages.[48] With the advent of this statute, there is a right to recovery among joint tortfeasors, whether or not judgment has been recovered against all or any of them.

Under Oklahoma's statutory scheme, a tortfeasor who enters into a settlement with a claimant is not entitled to recover contribution from another tortfeasor whose liability is not extinguished by the settlement, nor to the extent the payment was not reasonable.[49]

When given in good faith, a release given to one of multiple tortfeasors does not release other tortfeasors unless specifically named, but does reduce the amount of the claim by the consideration paid or stipulated in the release. It also discharges the released party from any liability for contribution to any other tortfeasor.[50]

Oklahoma adheres to the "one satisfaction" rule.[51]

J. INDEMNITY

Indemnity is a right which inures to a person who has discharged a duty which was owed by him but which as between himself and another should have been discharged by another. Indemnity may be contractual or through "common law indemnity." Indemnity generally implies a primary liability in one person, although a second person is also liable to a third party.[52] Common law indemnity is generally available from a primarily liable tortfeasor to those whose liability is secondary.[53]

One of the situations in which common law indemnity is available, as a matter of law, in Oklahoma relates to a claim under manufacturers' products liability which in Oklahoma also applies to retailers, wholesalers, and suppliers.[54] Under Oklahoma's version of products liability, it is immaterial to the plaintiff's case that the defect in the product was not caused by the retailer or distributor. The liability of the manufacturer and the distributor or retailer is co-extensive. To avoid the potential for unfair treatment of a party who was not responsible for the defect, Oklahoma courts turn to the theory of indemnity.[55]

Of course, a party is clearly not entitled to indemnity if the party was a cause of the underlying injuries.[56]

K. BAR OF WORKERS' COMPENSATION STATUTE

Under the Oklahoma Workers' Compensation Act,[57] the employer is responsible for compensation to an employee injured on the job regardless of fault.[58] Neither an employee nor a third party may sue an employer whose employee is injured while "on the job" regardless of whether the employer is acting in a "dual capacity" or the injury is the result of the employer or co-employee's gross negligence.[59] Workers' compensation is the exclusive remedy against the employer (or a co-employee).[60]

An employee may sue a third party, but if compensation benefits have been paid, the employer is subrogated to the rights of the employee to the extent of those payments; with the employer paying its *pro rata* share of the attorney's fees.[61]

In an action against a third party, when the employer has paid compensation to an employee, the employer may intervene, as a matter or right, pursuant to the Oklahoma Rules of Civil Procedure, if the employer can show that disposition of the matter may impair or impede his ability to protect his subrogation interest.[62]

There is no exception to the exclusive remedy provision of the Workers' Compensation Act for gross negligence. However, there is an exception where the actions complained of are intentional or willful.[63] Recently, the Oklahoma Supreme Court has recognized the "dual persona" doctrine, in which an employer may be liable outside of the parameters of the workers' compensation statute if an additional injury or aggravation is caused by the employer acting in a different capacity.[64]

L. PREMISES LIABILITY

A landowner's liability for injuries sustained on the premises depends upon the individual's status as trespasser, licensee, or invitee.[65] A landowner is liable to a trespasser only if the landowner is guilty of wanton or willful negligence or misconduct.[66] Licensees are entitled to warning of dangerous conditions, which are known (actually or constructively) by the landowner.[67]

The duty a business owes to its customers is to exercise reasonable care to prevent injury to its customers.[68] There is no duty to reconstruct or alter its premises so as to remove or warn of open and obvious dangers, nor is the landowner liable for any injury to the plaintiff resulting from a danger which was obvious or should have been observed in the exercise of due care.[69]

M. DRAM SHOP LIABILITY

Oklahoma's "dram shop" legislation falls within the ambit of the Oklahoma Alcoholic Beverage Control Act.[70] The Act prohibits the sale of alcoholic beverages to persons under 21 years of age, or to an intoxicated or incompetent person.

The supplying of intoxicating beverages to an intoxicated person has been recognized as a breach of both common law and statutory duties.[71]

Violation of the Act is negligence *per se*.[72] However, the class of person intended to be protected is members of the "unsuspecting public."[73] Thus, although negligence *per se* will not extend to an adult who is injured by his own inability to drive due to his intoxication; because minors, as a class, are incompetent to deal responsibly with the effects of alcohol, they are within the class to be protected, and thus may rely on violation of the statute as negligence *per se*.[74] The liability of a vendor extends to both on-premises and off-premises consumption.[75]

The Oklahoma Supreme Court has recently declined to extend the duty to social hosts.[76]

N. ECONOMIC LOSS

Oklahoma makes no distinction in the area of tort law between "economic loss" and other types of compensable losses, except in the area of products liability. In products liability, recovery is available for damage to a product, but not for a solely economic loss arising from a product defect.[77]

O. FRAUD AND MISREPRESENTATION

Oklahoma's Rules of Civil Procedure, patterned after the Federal Rules, require a cause of action for fraud be plead with particularity.[78]

The elements of a cause of action for fraud, deceit or intentional misrepresentation require proof by clear and convincing evidence. Those elements are: (1) a material representation; (2) which is false; (3) made with knowledge of its falsity or as a positive assertion, recklessly, without knowledge of its truth; (4) made with the intention that it be relied upon; (5) reliance upon it; and (6) resulting injury.[79]

Although the Oklahoma Supreme Court has not specifically identified and adopted the theory of "negligent misrepresentation," the federal court sitting in Oklahoma has recognized the theory. The elements of the two theories differ only in that negligent misrepresentation requires only a failure to exercise ordinary care in making the representation.[80]

P. CONSUMER FRAUD STATUTES

The Oklahoma Consumer Protection Act[81] provides protection for the consumer against any false or misleading representation regarding the nature, origin or qualities of a product; and against false and misleading advertising of a product.

The Act creates a private cause of action for damages. Should the actions complained of be determined to have been unconscionable, a civil penalty not to exceed $2000.00 may be awarded. Should the consumer prevail, costs, and attorney's fees may be awarded.

An action for violations for the Act may be brought in small claims court.[82]

Q. PUNITIVE DAMAGES

In Oklahoma, punitive damages are allowed by statute[83] in any noncontractual action, where the defendant is guilty of fraud, oppression, malice, actual or presumed, or conduct evincing wanton or reckless disregard for the rights of another. Punitive damages are awarded "for the sake of example, and by way of punishing the defendant."[84]

The statute sets out multiple categories of conduct, setting statutory maximums for each category. Where the jury finds intentional and malicious conduct, there is no "cap" on the jury's award.[85]

The statute outlines the factors upon which the jury should base its award. These include: the seriousness of the hazard arising from the misconduct, its profitability, the duration of the misconduct, the degree of knowledge of the defendant, and the defendant's financial condition.[86] The ratio of actual damages to punitive damages is one factor to be considered in determining whether punitive damages are excessive[87] as is the amount in controversy.[88] Punitive damages are available only in cases in which the jury awards damages,[89] although nominal damages will support an award.[90]

R. WRONGFUL DEATH AND SURVIVORSHIP ACTIONS

The common law rule that actions for personal injury or death do not survive has been abrogated in Oklahoma by the adoption of the Wrongful Death and Survival statutes.[91] Only actions for libel, slander or malicious prosecution abate by reason of the death of either of the parties.[92]

Oklahoma has, by Constitutional provision, forbidden the abrogation of the right of action for wrongful death,[93] which is provided for by statute.[94] Under the Oklahoma statutes, all damages for personal injury resulting in wrongful death may be brought in one action, for the benefit of the estate and the next of kin.

The statute provides for recovery for the pain and suffering of the decedent, as well as recovery for pecuniary losses to the surviving spouse and dependants, medical and funeral expenses, and grief and loss of companionship to the children and parents. In proper cases, punitive damages are also available.

The personal representative or next of kin must bring the cause of action for wrongful death.[95]

Oklahoma has adopted a separate statute covering the wrongful death of a minor child.[96] The damages recoverable include loss of anticipated services and support, loss of companionship and love of the child, destruction of the parent-child relationship, and loss of monies expended by parents or guardian in support, maintenance, and education of the child.[97]

John C. Niemeyer
Linda G. Alexander
NIEMEYER, ALEXANDER, AUSTIN & PHILLIPS, P.C.
300 N. Walker
Oklahoma City, Oklahoma 73102-1822
(405) 232-2725
(405) 239-7185
johnniemeyer@niemeyerfirm.com
lindaalexander@niemeyerfirm.com

ENDNOTES - OKLAHOMA

1. 12 Okla. Stat. Ann. § 95 (2001). The two-year statute of limitations applies to the following legal theories: negligence, products liability, tortious interference with or breach of contract (to include breach of the covenant of good faith and fair dealing "bad faith" breach of an insurance contract).

2. For a discussion of the distinction between statutes of limitation and statutes of repose, *see Reynolds v. Porter*, 1988 OK 88, 760 P.2d 816, 820 (Okla. 1988). The "discovery rule" has been applied to medical malpractice claims, pollution cases, cases involving damage to realty, and negligent exposure to infectious disease with latent symptoms. *Reynolds*, at 823 nn. 31-35.

3. 12 Okla. Stat. Ann. § 95(4) (2001).

4. 12 Okla. Stat. Ann. § 95(1) and (2) (2001).

5. 12 Okla. Stat. Ann. § 95(10) (2001).

6. 12 Okla. Stat. Ann. § 98 (2001). The tolling provisions of this section are not available where substituted service, or service by publication is available.

7. 12 Okla. Stat. Ann. § 96 (2001).

8. 12 Okla. Stat. Ann. § 96 (2001). The portion of the statute dealing with the rights of minors and incompetents with medical malpractice claims has been declared unconstitutional, on the grounds that it is an unconstitutional "special law," by the Oklahoma Court of Appeals. *Mowles By and Through Mowles v. Hillcrest Health Center*, 1991 OK CIV APP 118, 832 P.2d 24 (Okla. 1991), *cert. denied*.

9. 12 Okla. Stat. Ann. § 109 (2001). The statute of repose is designed to provide protection for those involved in design and construction; the manufacturer of products used in construction is not included in the class of persons protected by the statute of repose. *Ball v. Harnischfeger Corp.*, 1994 OK 65, 877 P.2d 45 (Okla. 1994).

10. 51 Okla. Stat. Ann. § 151 *et seq.*

11. 51 Okla. Stat. Ann. § 156(e).

12. 12 Okla. Stat. Ann. § 100.

13. 12 Okla. Stat. Ann. § 2011 (2001); 12 Okla. Stat. Ann. § 995 (2001).

14. 36 Okla. Stat. Ann. § 3636 (2001).

15. *Bettis v. Brown*, 1991 OK CIV APP 93, 819 P.2d 1381 (Okla. 1991); *Wofford v. Eastern State Hosp.*, 1990 OK 77, 795 P.2d 516 (Okla. 1990); *Sloan v. Owen*, 1977 OK 239, 579 P.2d 812 (Okla. 1977); *Nicholson v. Tacker*, 1973 OK 75, 512 P.2d 156 (Okla. 1973).

16. *Brown v. C.H. Guernsey & Co.*, 1973 OK CIV APP 23, 533 P.2d 1009 (Okla. 1973); *Delbrel v. Doenges Bros. Ford, Inc.*, 1996 OK 36, 913 P.2d 1318 (Okla. 1996).

17. *Federer v. Davis*, 1967 OK 208, 434 P.2d 197 (Okla. 1967).

18. *See Connor v. Houtman*, 1960 OK 52, 350 P.2d 311 (Okla. 1960)(holding that an infant under the age of five years is incapable of negligence); *see also Strong v. Allen*, 1989 OK 17, 768 P.2d 369 (Okla. 1989)("a child under seven years of age is conclusively presumed to be incapable of any negligence." (*Opala, J. dissenting*)(emphasis in original).

19. *See Baxter v. Fugett*, 1967 OK 72, 425 P.2d 462 (Okla. 1967).

20. 76 Okla. Stat. Ann. § 20.1 (2001); *Spencer by and through Spencer v. Seikel*, 1987 OK 75, 742 P.2d 1126 (Okla. 1987); *see also Sisson By and Through Allen v. Elkins*, 1990 OK 123, 801 P.2d 722 (Okla. 1990).

21. *See Wabaunsee v. Harris*, 1980 OK 52, 610 P.2d 782 (Okla. 1980).

22. Although the Oklahoma Supreme Court has made passing reference to such presumption, it has never been specifically adopted. The Oklahoma Uniform Jury Instructions now direct that such an instruction not be given. *See Service Pipe Line Co. v. Donahue*, 1955 OK 28, 283 P.2d 844 (Okla. 1955); *Lowden v. Friddle*, 1941 OK 297, 189 Okla. 415, 117 P.2d 533 (Okla. 1941).

23. *Atherton v. Devine*, 1979 OK 132, 602 P.2d 634 (Okla. 1979).

24. *See Strong v. Allen*, 1989 OK 17, 768 P.2d 369 (Okla. 1989); *Thompson v. Presbyterian Hosp., Inc.*, 1982 OK 87, 652 P.2d 260 (Okla. 1982).

25. 23 Okla. Stat. Ann. § 13 (2001). The comparative negligence statute is a substitute for the concept of contributory negligence referred to in Okla. Const. art. § 6 (2001). It calls for a comparison of plaintiff's fault to that of the "other side," (*i.e.*, defendant or defendants). It does not call for comparison or apportionment of negligence among multiple defendants. The 1979 amendment to the statute provides for recovery by the plaintiff if his negligence is 50 percent or less of the negligence causing his injuries.

26. *See Boyles v. Oklahoma Natural Gas Co.*, 1980 OK 163, 619 P.2d 613 (Okla. 1980).

27. *Kirkland v. General Motors Corp.*, 1974 OK 52, 521 P.2d 1353 (Okla. 1974).

28. 23 Okla. Stat. Ann. § 13 (2001).

29. *See* 12 Okla. Stat. Ann. § 832; *Barringer v. Baptist Healthcare of Oklahoma*, 2001 OK 29, 22 P.3d 695 (Okla. 2001).

30. *See Berry v. Empire Indem. Ins. Co.*, 1981 OK 106, 634 P.2d 718 (Okla. 1981).

31. The Oklahoma Constitution provides that:

    the defense of contributory negligence or of assumption of risk shall, in all cases whatsoever, be a question of fact, and shall at all times be left to the jury.

32. *Kirkland v. General Motors Corp.*, 1974 OK 52, 521 P.2d 1353 (Okla. 1974).

33. *See Valeo v. Pocono Int'l Raceway, Inc.*, 500 A.2d 492 (Pa. Super. 1985). Such agreements may be found unenforceable as against public policy. *See Oklahoma Natural Gas Co. v. Appel*, 1953 OK 344, 266 P.2d 442 (Okla. 1953).

34. *Thomas v. Holliday By and Through Holliday*, 1988 OK 116, 764 P.2d 165 (Okla. 1988).

35. *Thomas* at 168, n.8.

36. *Id.*

37. *See Turney v. Anspaugh*, 1978 OK 101, 581 P.2d 1301 (Okla. 1978); *Flick v. Crouch*, 1976 OK 116, 555 P.2d 1274 (Okla. 1976); *Boxberger v. Martin*, 1976 OK 78, 552 P.2d 370 (Okla. 1976); *Sisson By and Through Allen v. Elkins*, 1990 OK 123, 801 P.2d 722 (Okla. 1990); 76 Okla. Stat. Ann. § 21 (2001).

38. For a discussion of the court's role in the application of *res ipsa loquitur*, *see Furr v. McGrath*, 1959 OK 34, 340 P.2d 243 (Okla. 1959).

39. *See Tulsa Stockyards Co. v. Moore*, 1938 OK 426, 184 Okla. 6, 84 P.2d 37 (Okla. 1938).

40. Restatement (Second) of Torts § 520, comment 1; *see also Wetsel v. Independent School Dist. I-1*, 1983 OK 85, 670 P.2d 986 (Okla. 1983).

41. *Id.*

42. *See Boyles v. Oklahoma Natural Gas Co.*, 1980 OK 163, 619 P.2d 613 (Okla. 1980).

43. *See Levi v. Ashland Oil & Refining Co.*, 1972 OK 63, 496 P.2d 370 (Okla. 1972).

44. *See In re Jones*, 1986 10CIR 289, 804 F.2d 1133 (10th Cir. 1986).

45. *See* 12 Okla. Stat. Ann. § 832; *Barringer v. Baptist Healthcare of Oklahoma*, 2001 OK 29, 22 P.3d 695 (Okla. 2001).

46. *See Boyles v. Oklahoma Natural Gas Co.*, 1980 OK 163, 619 P.2d 613 (Okla. 1980).

47. *Id.*

48. 12 Okla. Stat. Ann. § 832 (2001). The statute was most recently amended in 1995.

49. 12 Okla. Stat. Ann. § 832(D) (2001).

50. 12 Okla. Stat. Ann. § 832(H) (2001).

51. *See Allen v. Ouachita Marine and Indus. Corp.*, 1979 OK CIV APP 70, 606 P.2d 607 (Okla. 1979)

52. *State Insurance Fund v. Taron*, 1958 OK 282, 333 P.2d 508 (Okla. 1958).

53. *Id.*

54. *Moss v. Polyco*, 1974 OK 53, 522 P.2d 622 (Okla. 1974); *Gonser v. Decker*, 1991 OK CIV APP 64, 814 P.2d 1056 (Okla. Ct. App. 1991).

55. *Daugherty v. Farmers Co-op. Ass'n*, 1989 OK CIV APP 89, 790 P.2d 1118 (Okla. 1989).

56. *Booker v. Sears Roebuck & Co.*, 1989 OK 156, 785 P.2d 297 (Okla. 1989).

57. 85 Okla. Stat. Ann. § 1 *et seq.* (2001).

58. *Darco Transp. v. Dulen*, 1996 OK 50, 922 P.2d 591 (Okla. 1996).

59. *Rios v. Nicor Drilling Co.*, 1983 OK 74, 665 P.2d 1183 (Okla. 1983); *Love v. Flour Mills of America*, 1981 10CIR 134, 647 F.2d 1058 (10th Cir. 1981).

60. *Noyce v. Ratliff Drilling Co.*, 1989 OK CIV APP 99, 790 P.2d 1129 (Okla. Ct. App. 1989).

61. *Prettyman v. Halliburton Co.*, 1992 OK 63, 841 P.2d 573 (Okla. 1992).

62. 12 Okla. Stat. Ann. § 2024 (2001).

63. *Pursell v. Pizza Inn Inc.*, 1990 OK CIV APP 4, 786 P.2d 716 (Okla. Ct. App. 1990); *Thompson v. Madison Mach. Co., Inc.*, 1984 OK CIV APP 24, 684 P.2d 565 (Okla. Ct. App. 1984).

64. *Dyke v. St. Francis Hospital, Inc.*, 1993 OK 114, 861 P.2d 295 (Okla. 1993).

65. *Sutherland v. St. Francis Hospital, Inc.*, 1979 OK 18, 595 P.2d 780 (Okla. 1979).

66. *Good v. Wahn*, 1959 OK 5, 335 P.2d 911 (Okla. 1959).

67. *Id.*

68. *Taylor v. Hynson*, 1993 OK 93, 856 P.2d 278 (Okla.1993); *Nicholson v. Tacker*, 1973 OK 75, 512 P.2d 156 (Okla. 1973).

69. *See Safeway Stores, Inc. v. Saunders*, 1962 OK 162, 372 P.2d 1021 (Okla. 1962); *Safeway Stores, Inc. v. McCoy*, 1962 OK 194, 376 P.2d 285 (Okla. 1962); *Beatty v. Dixon*, 1965 OK 169, 408 P.2d 339 (Okla. 1965); *C.R. Anthony Co. v. Million*, 1967 OK 231, 435 P.2d 116 (Okla. 1967).

70. 37 Okla. Stat. Ann. § 502 *et seq.*

71. *Brigance v. Velvet Dove Restaurant, Inc.*, 1986 OK 41, 725 P.2d 300 (Okla. 1986).

72. *Busby v. Quail Creek Golf and Country Club*, 1994 OK 63, 885 P.2d 1326 (Okla. 1994).

73. *Ohio Casualty Ins. Co. v. Todd*, 1991 OK 54, 813 P.2d 508 (Okla. 1991).

74. *Busby v. Quail Creek Golf and Country Club*, 1994 OK 63, 885 P.2d 1326 (Okla. 1994).

75. *Tomlinson v. Love's Country Stores, Inc.*, 1993 OK 83, 854 P.2d 910 (Okla. 1993).

76. *McGee v. Alexander*, 2001 OK 10, 37 P.3d 900 (Okla. 2001).

77. *Waggoner v. Town & Country Mobile Homes, Inc.*, 1990 OK 139, 808 P.2d 649 (Okla. 1990).

78. 12 Okla. Stat. Ann. § 2009(B) (2001).

79. *D&H Co., Inc. v. Schultz*, 1978 OK 71, 579 P.2d 821 (Okla. 1978); *Steiger v. Commerce Acceptance of Okla.City, Inc.*, 1969 OK 78, 455 P.2d 81 (Okla. 1969).

80. *Ragland v. Shatuck Nat. Bank*, 1994 10CIR 1139 , 36 F.3d 983 (10th Cir. 1994); *see also Robertson v. Painewebber*, 2001 OK Civ. App. 17, 998 P.2d 190 (Okla. Civ. App. 2000).

81. 15 Okla. Stat. Ann. § 751 *et seq.* (2001).

82. *Patterson v. Beall*, 1997 OK CIV APP 64, 947 P.2d 617 (Okla. Ct. App. 1997).

83. 23 Okla. Stat. Ann. § 9.1 (2001).

84. 23 Okla. Stat. Ann. § 9.1(A) (2001).

85. 23 Okla. Stat. Ann. § 9.1(D) (2001).

86. 23 Okla. Stat. Ann. § 9.1(A) (2001).

87. *Capstick v. Allstate Inc. Co.*, 1993 10CIR 779, 998 F.2d 810 (10th Cir. 1993).

88. *Buzzard v. Farmers Ins. Co.*, 1991 OK 127, 824 P.2d 1105 (Okla. 1991).

89. *Phillips Mach Co. v. LeBlond, Inc.*, 494 F. Supp. 318 (N.D. Okla. 1980).

90. *Beavers v. Lamplighters Realty, Inc.*, 1976 OK CIV APP 48, 556 P.2d 1328 (Okla. Ct. App. 1976).

91. 12 Okla. Stat. Ann. §§ 1051 and 1053 (2001).

92. 12 Okla. Stat. Ann. § 1052 (2001).

93. Okla. Const. art. 23 § 7 (2001).

94. 12 Okla. Stat. Ann. § 1053 (2001).

95. 12 Okla. Stat. Ann. § 1054 (2001).

96. 12 Okla. Stat. Ann. § 1055 (2001).

97. *Currens v. Hampton*, 1997 OK 58, 939 P.2d 1138 (Okla. 1997).

OREGON

A. STATUTES OF LIMITATIONS

Causes of action for assault, battery, false imprisonment, or for any injury to the person or rights of another, not arising in contact, and not otherwise provided for by statute, must be brought within two years.[1] The beginning of the two-year period is the time the cause of action accrued.[2] A "discovery" rule applies to actions at law for fraud or deceit by statute,[3] to actions for medical malpractice by statute,[4] and on a case-by-case basis as engrafted by judicial decision.[5]

Wrongful death actions (other than those which are characterized as product liability civil actions)[6] must be brought within three years after the injury causing the death of the decedent is discovered or should have been discovered by the decedent, the personal representative, or the beneficiary.[7]

Causes of action for breach of a contract, express or implied, have a six-year statute of limitations.[8] Causes of action for breach of a contract of sale have a four-year statute of limitations, unless otherwise agreed upon by the parties.[9] The tort discovery rule does not apply to the statute of limitations on breach of warranty actions.[10]

"Product liability civil actions," which are defined as actions brought against a manufacturer, distributor, seller, or lessor of a product for damages for personal injury, death or property damage arising out of a design, manufacturing, or warning defect or failure to instruct on the use of a product,[11] are to be brought within two years of the date that the death, injury, or damage complained of occurs,[12] and the death, injury, or damage itself must occur within eight years of the date the product was first purchased for use or consumption.[13] The combined effect of the statue of limitations and statute of repose is that product liability civil actions must involve an injury within eight years, and the action must be commenced within two years thereafter.[14] The two-year limitation period can be and has been extended by statutory "discovery" rules;[15] the eight-year repose period generally has not been.[16]

An action for libel or slander must be brought within one year after the cause of action accrues.[17] Actions for damage to or interference with personal or real property have a six-year statute of limitations.[18] A ten-year statute of ultimate repose is applicable to claims involving negligent injury to person or property[19] and for construction, alteration and improvement of real property, running ten years from the date of substantial completion.[20]

Private actions for violation of the Unlawful Trade Practices Act must be commenced within one year of the unlawful method, act, or practice.[21]

A "catch-all" provision for actions that are neither subject to another limitation section nor excluded from the application of a limitation period provides for a ten-year limitation.[22]

Claims against public bodies and their officers, employees, or agents acting within the scope of their employment are covered by a two-year statute of limitations under the Oregon Tort Claims Act.[23] There is an additional 180-day notice requirement (one year for wrongful death) which must be satisfied.[24]

B. TORT REFORM

The Oregon Legislative Assembly has on several occasions engaged in tort reform. For example, in 1977, it codified portions of Restatement (Second) of Torts § 402A, together with certain defenses.[25] In 1987, the Legislative Assembly adopted the provisions of Fed. R. Civ. P. 11;[26] imposed standards for contingent fee agreements;[27] provided that punitive damages were to be shared with the state Criminal Injuries Compensation Account;[28] and for a cap (since found to be unconstitutional) on noneconomic damages.[29] In 1995, it converted many statutes providing for attorney fees to one party, but not both, into prevailing party fee statutes;[30] provided standards for the court to consider in awarding statutory attorney fees, and where the court has discretion in awarding such fees;[31] for enhanced prevailing party fees in cases where a party is entitled to "costs" only, and not attorney fees;[32] provided that a claim for punitive damages must be added by amendment,[33] and for other punitive damage reforms;[34] and made a number of changes to the rules governing joint and several liability.[35] Additional legislation is introduced nearly each session, which is held in odd-numbered years.

C. "NO FAULT" LIMITATIONS

Oregon is not a no-fault state. However, every "motor vehicle liability policy issued for delivery in this state that covers any private passenger motor vehicle shall provide personal injury protection benefits" to the insured, the insured's family, passengers, and pedestrians.[36] Personal injury protection (PIP) benefits consist of reasonable and necessary medical expenses incurred within one year from the date of the accident, up to $10,000 per person,[37] 70 percent of income loss for 52 weeks, subject to a monthly maximum,[38] benefits for persons not earning income,[39] and reasonable and necessary funeral expenses, up to a cap.[40] There is no provision for no-fault general damages. Disputes regarding PIP benefits may be resolved by arbitration.[41]

D. THE STANDARD FOR NEGLIGENCE

Negligence is proven when a person's conduct falls below the standard of conduct expected so as to protect others, or oneself, against unreasonable risks of harm.[42] In 1987, the Oregon Supreme Court restated the method of analysis to be used in negligence actions.[43] In common law negligence actions, the defendant's liability depends upon whether such conduct unreasonably created a foreseeable risk to a protected interest of the kind of harm that befell the plaintiff.[44] In common law negligence cases, it is generally not necessary for the plaintiff to plead or prove the existence of a duty. A claim that there is "no duty" generally is interpreted as a request by the court to limit the defendant's liability because (1) the harm was not foreseeable, or (2) because some rule or status disqualifies the plaintiff, individually or as a member of a class, from recovering damages.[45] When a negligence claim involves an obligation arising out of a special relationship, or a contract, statute or rule which creates an obligation or defines the standard of care, then "duty" remains an element of plaintiff's claim.[46]

Negligence is judged under all of the circumstances, including the existence of any emergency.[47] Because the existence of an emergency is simply one of the circumstances to be considered by the jury, special instruction on that topic is generally disapproved.[48]

Oregon recognizes a professional standard of care.[49] Further, when a special relationship exists, or there is a special status, the standard of care is defined by that relationship or status.[50] Whether a person is responsible for the conduct of a third party depends upon the existence of a foreseeable specific risk of harm to the plaintiff.[51]

The standard of care expected of a child requires a comparison of the individual child to minors of like age, intelligence and experience under like circumstances.[52] A limited exception has been recognized where the minor is engaged in an adult activity for which adult qualifications are required.[53]

Oregon follows the majority rule that a mental incompetent is responsible for his or her negligent conduct.[54] There is no presumption that any person —a decedent, or an incapacitated plaintiff or defendant—exercised due care at the time of the injury.[55]

Oregon recognizes both the doctrine of negligence *per se*, where the statute or regulation was violated, the plaintiff was within the class of persons intended to be protected, and the injury was of the type intended to be avoided,[56] and the rule that a statute or regulation can be considered as evidence of negligence.[57]

E. CAUSATION

Oregon follows the general rule that to establish a claim, plaintiff must show that the defendant's negligence was a substantial factor in causing plaintiff's injury.[58] The defendant's conduct need not be the only cause of the plaintiff's injury.[59] The existence of causation is a factual issue for the factfinder to resolve[60] unless the court can resolve it as a matter of law.[61]

F. CONTRIBUTORY NEGLIGENCE, COMPARATIVE NEGLIGENCE, AND ASSUMPTION OF RISK

1. Contributory Negligence

Contributory negligence is not a bar to recovery in an action for death or negligence if the fault attributable to the claimant is not greater than the combined fault of all of the persons whose conduct is to be compared.[62]

2. Comparative Negligence

The Oregon comparative negligence statute applies to actions for death, personal injury, or injury to property.[63] Under Oregon law, a plaintiff may recover damages when the plaintiff's negligence is not greater than the combined fault of all persons whose conduct is to be compared.[64] The trier of fact compares the plaintiff's fault with that of all persons against whom recovery is sought, the fault of third-party defendants who are liable to the claimant, and any person with whom the claimant has settled.[65] Except for persons who have settled, there is no comparison of fault with a person who is immune from liability, not subject to the jurisdiction of the court, or not subject to action because of a statute of limitations or statute of repose.[66] If plaintiff is entitled to recover, his or her proportion of fault reduces the recovery.[67] Comparative negligence does apply when defendant is said to be guilty of gross negligence[68] or strict liability.[69] It is an open question in Oregon whether statutory negligence and ordinary negligence can be compared.[70]

3. Assumption of Risk

The doctrine of implied assumption of risk has been abolished in Oregon.[71] Assumption of risk remains a viable affirmative defense in cases involving express assumption of risk. However, such conduct is compared with the conduct of the defendant under the comparative fault analysis.[72]

G. *RES IPSA LOQUITUR* AND INHERENTLY DANGEROUS ACTIVITIES

1. *Res Ipsa Loquitur*

Res ipsa loquitur is a rule of circumstantial evidence that permits an inference that the defendant was negligent, where it is not possible to identify the particular way in which the defendant was negligent.[73] A plaintiff relying upon the doctrine must plead and prove that (1) the injury occurred in circumstances that more probably than not would not have occurred in the absence of negligence, and (2) the negligence that caused the event was probably that of the defendant.[74] The doctrine does not specifically require that the defendant have exclusive control over the instrumentality, or that the plaintiff be free from fault.[75]

2. Inherently Dangerous Activities

Ordinarily, the likelihood of harm and the severity of the harm are simply two factors that are considered in determining whether the conduct was unreasonable.[76] The greater the danger, the greater the care which must be exercised.[77] However, some abnormally dangerous activities may result in strict liability.[78]

H. NEGLIGENCE *PER SE*

Negligence *per se* is based upon a violation of a statute or regulation.[79] In order for a statute or regulation to be considered as supporting a negligence *per se* claim (1) the injured person must be a member of the class intended by the legislature to be protected, and (2) the harm must be of the kind the statute or regulation was intended to prevent.[80] A finding that a statute will support a negligence *per se* claim shifts to the defendant the burden of showing that the conduct was nonetheless reasonable.[81] The Oregon Supreme Court has been inconsistent on the question of whether negligence *per se* eliminates any consideration of foreseeability.[82]

I. JOINT AND SEVERAL LIABILITY

In 1995, the Oregon Legislature provided that in causes of action arising on or after September 9, 1995, the liability of each defendant for damages is several only and not joint.[83] Accordingly, there is not much significance to the term "joint tortfeasor" in Oregon.[84]

Regardless of whether two or more tortfeasors are joint, the trier of fact must first determine the amount of damages that the injured party would be entitled to if he or she was not at fault.[85] The trier of fact must determine the percentage of fault of all parties against whom recovery is sought, the fault of third-party defendants who are liable in tort to the claimant,[86] and persons who have settled with the claimant.[87] The court must calculate each party's share of the damages by multiplying the percentage of fault by the total amount of damages, with no reduction for settlement or contribution.[88] The judgment must separately set out the several liability of each party for his or her share of the obligation.[89] The share of a defendant that proves to be uncollectible may be reallocated among the other parties, including the plaintiff, on motion of the claimant made within one year of the final judgment.[90]

A release by the plaintiff of one joint tortfeasor does not discharge the other tortfeasors unless the release so provides.[91] Under the contribution statute, the right of contribution exists among joint tortfeasors so long as two requirements are met: one joint tortfeasor has paid more than his or her proportional share of the common liability,[92] and the liability of the other joint tortfeasor to the plaintiff has been extinguished.[93]

When defendants that are joined are not joint tortfeasors,[94] their liability is similarly several only.[95] When requested by any party, a special verdict is to be submitted.[96]

Where several tortfeasors cause the plaintiff's injury, the plaintiff may recover only one satisfaction of the damages.[97]

J. INDEMNITY

Indemnity shifts the entire loss of the plaintiff from one defendant to another by reason of some legal obligation to pay damages occasioned by the negligence of another.[98] Of course, indemnity may be provided by contract.[99] Common law indemnity in Oregon is not based strictly on "active/passive" or "primary/secondary" principles. "[T]he duty to indemnify will be recognized in cases where community opinion would consider that in justice the responsibility should rest upon one rather than the other. This may be because of the relation of the parties to one another, and the consequent duty owed; or it may be because of a significant difference in the kind or quality of their conduct."[100]

K. BAR OF WORKERS' COMPENSATION STATUTE

Under the Oregon Workers' Compensation Law,[101] the Act provides the exclusive remedy to a subject worker and beneficiaries for compensable injuries, unless one of the exceptions applies. In lieu of damages for compensable injuries, the law establishes schedules for recovery of benefits and compensation.[102] Generally, the worker is permitted to bring a claim against any third party that is not the employer or a subject worker of the employer.[103]

The worker may elect to pursue a claim against a third party.[104] An election not to proceed against the noncomplying employer or the third party operates as an assignment of the claim to the paying agency (generally, the insurer).[105] If the worker is successful in pursuing the third party, the employer or its insurer is entitled to reimbursement.[106]

Oregon has a statutory exception to the exclusive remedy provisions where the employer with "deliberate intention" causes the worker's injury or death[107] or where the injury is "proximately caused by willful and unprovoked aggression by the person otherwise exempt.[108] There are additional exceptions where the employer is non-complying[109] and where the injury is caused by the failure of the employer to comply with a "red tag" notice.[110]

L. PREMISES LIABILITY

A landowner's liability for injuries sustained on the premises depends upon the individual's common law legal status as trespasser, licensee, or invitee.[111] A landowner is liable to a trespasser if the landowner is guilty of wanton or willful injury.[112] The landowner must exercise reasonable care to protect the licensee from activities on the land,[113] and must refrain from willful or wanton acts with respect to conditions on the land.[114] The landowner must warn a licensee of any pitfall or trap known to the occupier that might cause injury notwithstanding reasonable care.[115] A landowner must exercise reasonable care to protect invitees from both activities and conditions.[116]

M. DRAM SHOP LIABILITY

Oregon's liquor liability cases are primarily litigated on the issue of serving alcohol to visibly intoxicated persons. There are several bases of liability currently recognized: (1) a common law negligence claim without reference to any statute;[117] (2) a negligence claim proved as a matter of law by violation of Or. Rev. Stat. Chap. 471 as it relates to serving minors;[118] and (3) a statutory tort based upon Or. Rev. Stat. § 30.905, a statute prohibiting sales to visibly intoxicated persons.[119] Of the three bases, the second and third apply to Oregon Liquor Control Commission (OLCC) licensees. A common law negligence claim can be stated against a social host.[120]

In claims based upon Or. Rev. Stat. § 30.905, the plaintiff must show that by clear and convincing evidence that the patron or guest was served while visibly intoxicated.[121]

N. ECONOMIC LOSS

Recovery under tort law is permitted for personal injury or property damage.[122] Recovery solely for economic damages is prohibited in strict liability actions,[123] but the range of damages recoverable on claims other than strict liability is broader.[124] In "business torts," a full range of damages is recoverable, including economic loss, emotional distress, and punitive damages.[125]

O. FRAUD AND MISREPRESENTATION

The Oregon Rules of Civil Procedure do not require that a claim for fraud be pleaded with particularity.[126]

Each of the following elements for fraud, deceit or intentional misrepresentation must be proved by clear and convincing evidence:[127] (1) a representation (2) which is material to the transaction; (3) made falsely; (4) with the intent of misleading another into relying on it; (5) the recipient's justifiable reliance on the misrepresentation; and (6) the resulting injury was caused by the misrepresentation.[128]

In purely arms-length transactions, economic losses arising from negligent misrepresentation are not actionable in Oregon.[129] The tort of negligent misrepresentation requires that the allegedly negligent party owe to the injured party a duty "beyond the common law duty to exercise reasonable care to prevent foreseeable harm."[130]

P. CONSUMER FRAUD STATUTES

Oregon's Unlawful Trade Practices Act (UTPA) protects consumers from specified deceptive practices in certain transactions.[131] The UTPA provides that the Attorney General may impose penalties or obtain injunctions against the specified activities. Private actions for $200, or the amount of "ascertainable loss," together with any punitive damages, may also be pursued.[132]

Methods, acts, or practices must be declared unlawful by the express language of the statute.[133] There is no "catch all" provision.

As previously noted, actions under the UTPA have a one-year statute of limitations.[134]

Q. PUNITIVE DAMAGES

In Oregon, punitive damages are governed by statute and by common law principles.

An initial pleading in a civil action cannot request an award of punitive damages.[135] Such claims must be added by amendment after the initial filing, and are tested against the directed verdict standard.[136] Punitive damages are not recoverable in civil actions unless it is shown by clear and convincing evidence that the party against whom they would be awarded has acted with malice or has shown a reckless and outrageous indifference to a highly unreasonable risk of harm and has acted with a conscious indifference to the health, safety, and welfare of others.[137] In product liability civil actions, there are additional standards that must be met.[138] Following a jury award, punitives are subject to review to determine whether the award is within the range of damages that a rational juror would be entitled to award based upon the record as a whole, in light of the statutory and common law factors applicable to the specific claim.[139]

Punitive damages are not awarded for misconduct constituting ordinary negligence.[140] They can be awarded in wrongful death actions.[141] There are prohibitions against awards of punitive damages against health care providers[142] and drug manufacturers.[143] Punitive damages are not recoverable in defamation cases, having been held unconstitutional under the Oregon Constitution.[144]

As previously noted, awards of punitive damages must be shared with the Oregon Criminal Injuries Compensation Fund.[145]

R. WRONGFUL DEATH AND SURVIVORSHIP ACTIONS

Under common law, there was no recovery for wrongful death[146] nor provision for the survival of actions for a decedent's personal injuries.[147] However, recovery is allowed under the Wrongful Death Act[148] and provisions for the survival of actions,[149] two separate and distinct causes of action, whose remedies are cumulative and not alternative.[150]

Recovery under the Wrongful Death Act passes to a limited group of beneficiaries defined by statute[151] to compensate them for their loss.[152] Recovery under the survival statutes for personal injury passes to the decedent's estate.[153] A survival action is not a new cause of action, but simply a recognition that the decedent's claim is not abated by death.[154]

Bruce C. Hamlin
LANE POWELL SPEARS LUBERSKY, L.L.P.
601 SW Second Ave., Suite 2100
Portland, Oregon 97204
(503) 778-2100
Fax (503) 778-2200
hamlinb@lanepowell.com
www.lanepowell.com

ENDNOTES - OREGON

1. Or. Rev. Stat. § 12.110 (1).

2. Or. Rev. Stat. § 12.010.

3. Or. Rev. Stat. § 12.110 (1).

4. Or. Rev. Stat. § 12.110 (4).

5. 2 Torts (Oregon cle 1992) § 31.39. A "discovery" rule has not been implied for every statute of limitations. Generally, the "discovery" rule is to apply "to kinds of actions where the underlying wrong and its relationship to the injury are inherently resistant to prompt discovery." *Workman v. Rajneesh Foundation International*, 84 Or. App. 226, 231, 733 P.2d 908, *rev. denied*, 303 Or. 700, 740 P.2d 1213 (1987).

6. Because there is a specific two-year statute of limitations for death caused by a product, that statute controls over the more general three-year statute of limitations. *Gladhart v. Oregon Vineyard Supply Co.*, 332 Or. 226, 26 P.3d 817 (2001).

7. Or. Rev. Stat. § 30.020 (1). In no case can the wrongful death action be brought later than three years after the earliest of the death of the decedent or the expiration of the statute of ultimate repose. Or. Rev. Stat. § 30.020 (1).

8. Or. Rev. Stat. § 12.080 (1).

9. Or. Rev. Stat. § 72.7250 (1).

10. The statute of limitations for such claims begins to run when the goods are tendered, except when the warranty extends to future performance, in which case the statute runs from the date the breach. Or. Rev. Stat. § 72.7250 (2).

11. Or. Rev. Stat. § 30.900. The term "product liability civil action," as defined in this section, embraces all legal theories a plaintiff can state in an action for product defect. *Marinelli v. Ford Motor Co.*, 72 Or. App. 268, 696 P.2d 1, *rev. denied*, 299 Or. 251 (1985); *Bancorp Leasing and Financial Corp. v. Agusta Aviation Corp.*, 813 F.2d 272 (9th Cir. 1997).

12. Or. Rev. Stat. § 30.905 (2).

13. Or. Rev. Stat. § 30.905 (1).

14. *Baird v. Electro Mart Factory Direct*, 47 Or. App. 565, 615 P.2d 335 (1980).

15. *Gladhart, supra* at n.6. *But see Schiele v. Hobart Corporation*, 284 Or. 483, 490, 587 P.2d 1010 (1978).

16. The legislature enacted an exception to the eight-year statute of repose for breast implants, Or. Rev. Stat. § 30.908 (2), for asbestos-related diseases, Or. Rev. Stat. § 30.907, sidesaddle gas tank ruptures on pickup trucks, Or. Rev. Stat. § 12.278 (2), and for a period of time, IUD claims. *See* discussion in 2 Torts (Oregon CLE 1992) § 19.57.

17. Or. Rev. Stat. § 12.120 (2).

18. Or. Rev. Stat. § 12.080 (3), (4).

19. Or. Rev. Stat. § 12.115 (1).

20. Or. Rev. Stat. § 12.135.

21. Or. Rev. Stat. § 646.638 (6).

22. Or. Rev. Stat. § 12.140.

23. Or. Rev. Stat. § 30.275 (8).

24. Or. Rev. Stat. § 30.275 (2).

25. Or. Rev. Stat. §§ 30.900 – 30.920.

26. Oregon Rule of Civil Procedure (ORCP) 17.

27. Or. Rev. Stat. § 20.340.

28. Or. Rev. Stat. § 18.540.

29. Or. Rev. Stat. § 18.560 (1), which provided for a $500,000 cap on noneconomic damages.

30. *See, e.g.,* Or. Rev. Stat. § 20.094 (attorney fees in actions in which discharge in bankruptcy is asserted).

31. Or. Rev. Stat. § 20.075.

32. Or. Rev. Stat. § 20.190.

33. Or. Rev. Stat. § 18.535.

34. *See, e.g.*, Or. Rev. Stat. § 18.537 (requiring proof by "clear and convincing" evidence, and providing standards for review).

35. Or. Rev. Stat. § 18.485.

36. Or. Rev. Stat. § 742.520 (1).

37. Or. Rev. Stat. § 742.524 (1)(a).

38. Or. Rev. Stat. § 742.524 (1)(b).

39. Or. Rev. Stat. § 742.524 (1)(c).

40. Or. Rev. Stat. § 742.524 (1)(d).

41. Or. Rev. Stat. §§ 742.520 (6) and 742.522.

42. *Woolston v. Wells*, 297 Or. 548, 557, 687 P.2d 144 (1984).

43. *Fazzolari v. Portland School Dist. No. 1J*, 303 Or. 1, 734 P.2d 1326 (1987).

44. *Fazzolari v. Portland School Dist. No. 1J*, 303 Or. 1, 17, 734 P.2d 1326 (1987).

45. 1 Torts (Oregon CLE 1992) § 8.3.

46. 1 Torts (Oregon CLE 1992) § 8.6.

47. 1 Torts (Oregon CLE 1992) § 8.17.

48. *Scott v. Iverson*, 120 Or. App. 538, 853 P.2d 302, *rev. denied*, 317 Or. 486 (1993).

49. *Getchell v. Mansfield*, 260 Or. 174, 179, 489 P.2d 953 (1971).

50. Examples are landowner/trespasser, *Abbott v. West Extension Irrigation District*, 110 Or. App. 385, 822 P.2d 747 (1991) *rev. denied*, 313 Or. 299 (1992), landlord/tenant, *Park v. Hoffard*, 315 Or. 624, 847 P.2d 852 (1993), and *Budd v. American Savings & Loan*, 89 Or. App. 609, 750 P.2d 513 (1988) (employee must show existence of special duty to train arising out of employer/employee relationship).

51. *Compare Buchler v. Oregon Corrections Div.*, 316 Or. 499, 853 P.2d 798 (1993) (prisoner escaped in state van left with keys; because prisoner's criminal history involved only property crimes, state not liable) with *Hoke v. The May Department Stores Co.*, 133 Or. App. 410, 891 P.2d 686 (1995) (jury question whether defendant is responsible for failing to properly investigate an earlier sexual assault claim).

52. *Thomas v. Inman*, 282 Or. 279, 285, 578 P.2d 399 (1978). Oregon does not recognize any conclusive or rebuttable presumptions based upon the age of the child.

53. *Nielsen v. Brown*, 232 Or. 426, 445, 374 P.2d 896 (1962). So far, the rule has been limited to driving automobiles, and has not been extended to the use of firearms. *Thomas v. Inman, supra.*

54. *Schumann v. Crofoot*, 43 Or. App. 53, 55, 602 P.2d 298 (1979). A commentator has suggested that mental competency may be a factor for the jury to consider. 1 Torts (Oregon CLE 1992) § 8.16.

55. Oregon Rule of Evidence (ORE) 311 (presumptions). *Compare* Or. Rev. Stat. § 30.910 (it is a disputable presumption that a product as manufactured and sold or leased is not unreasonably dangerous for its intended use) and ORE 311 (1)(b) ("A person takes ordinary care of the person's own concerns.").

56. *Bob Godfrey Pontiac v. Roloff*, 291 Or. 318, 630 P.2d 840 (1981).

57. *Shahtout v. Emco Garbage Co.*, 298 Or. 598, 695 P.2d 897 (1985) (regulation that did not create negligence *per se* could be considered by the jury as some evidence of the standard of care).

58. *Brennen v. City of Eugene*, 285 Or. 401, 413, 591 P.2d 719 (1979).

59. *Ollison v. Weinberg Racing Assoc.*, 69 Or. App. 653, 688 P.2d 847 (1984).

60. *Babler Bros. v. Pac. Intermountain*, 244 Or. 459, 464, 415 P.2d 735 (1966).

61. In this regard, foreseeability and causation are intertwined. For example, in *Buchler v. Oregon Corrections Div.*, 316 Or. 499, 853 P.2d 798 (1993), there was a direct factual link between leaving the keys in the state-owned vehicle, the escape, and the subsequent crime. The court found that foreseeability was lacking.

62. Or. Rev. Stat. § 18.470.

63. Or. Rev. Stat. § 18.470 (1).

64. Or. Rev. Stat. § 18.470 (1).

65. Or. Rev. Stat. § 18.470 (2).

66. Or. Rev. Stat. § 18.470 (2).

67. Or. Rev. Stat. § 18.470 (1).

68. *Johnson v. Tilden*, 278 Or. 11, 562 P.2d 1188 (1977); *DeYoung v. Fallon*, 104 Or. App. 66, 798 P.2d 1114 (1990) *rev. denied*, 311 Or. 222 (1991).

69. *Baccelleri v. Hyster Co.*, 287 Or. 3, 597 P.2d 351 (1979). In the case of product liability, plaintiff's negligence can consist of ordinary negligence, except such fault that consists of unobservant, inattentive, ignorant, or awkward failure to discover or to guard against the defect that makes the product defective in the first place. *Sanford v. Chev. Div. Gen. Motors*, 292 Or. 590, 610, 642 P.2d 624 (1982).

70. 1 Torts (Oregon CLE 1992) § 9.6.

71. Or. Rev. Stat. § 18.475 (1).

72. *Blair v. Mt. Hood Meadows Development Corp.*, 291 Or. 293, 301, 630 P.2d 827 (1981).

73. *Watzig v. Tobin*, 292 Or. 645, 642 P.2d 651 (1982); *Kaufman v. Fisher*, 230 Or. 626, 635, 371 P.2d 948 (1962).

74. *Watzig v. Tobin*, 292 Or. 645, 642 P.2d 651 (1982); *McKee Electric Co. v. Carson Oil Co.*, 301 Or. 339, 348, 723 P.2d 288 (1986).

75. *Watzig v. Tobin*, 292 Or. 645, 650, 642 P.2d 651 (1982).

76. *Donaca v. Curry Co.*, 303 Or. 30, 37, 734 P.2d 1339 (1987) (risk of collisions at intersection and cost of clearing vegetation may be considered in judging reasonableness); *Little v. Wimmer*, 303 Or. 580, 739 P.2d 564 (1987) (existence and magnitude of risks and cost of eliminating the same can be considered in judging reasonableness of highway design).

77. 1 Torts (Oregon CLE 1992) § 8.17.

78. *Koos v. Roth*, 293 Or. 670, 676-682, 652 P.2d 1255 (1982) (test for determining an abnormally dangerous activity is based upon the magnitude of the potential harmful events, and their probability, despite all reasonable precautions). *See generally*, 1 Torts (Oregon cle 1992) §§ 18.3 to 18.9 (dealing with water, blasting and highly flammable substances, herbicidal spraying, product cases, fire, and radiation therapy).

79. *Chartrand v. Coos Bay Tavern*, 298 Or. 689, 696 P.2d 513 (1985) (plaintiff could state a negligence *per se* claim based upon a statute governing liquor licensees).

80. *Miller v. City of Portland*, 288 Or. 271, 276, 604 P.2d 1261 (1980), *abrogated on other grounds*, *Fulmer v. Timber Inn Rest. and Lounge, Inc.*, 330 Or. 413, 9 P.3d 710 (2000).

81. *Barnum v. Williams,* 264 Or. 71, 79, 504 P.2d 122 (1972).

82. 2 Torts (Oregon CLE 1992) § 32.22.

83. Or. Rev. Stat. § 18.485. *See generally,* 1 Torts (Oregon CLE 1992 & 1996 Supp.) § 15.4.

84. For a discussion of the different types of joint tortfeasors recognized by Oregon law, *see* 1 Torts (Oregon CLE 1992) §§ 15.5 to 15.16 (common plan or design, common duty, "hybrid" theories of joint liability, and independent actions concurring to cause harm).

85. Or. Rev. Stat. § 18.485 (1)(a).

86. The failure of the plaintiff to file a direct action against the third-party defendant does not affect the allocation of fault. Or. Rev. Stat. § 18.470 (2).

87. Or. Rev. Stat. §§ 18.470 (2), 18.480.

88. Or. Rev. Stat. § 18.485 (2).

89. Or. Rev. Stat. § 18.485 (2).

90. Or. Rev. Stat. § 18.485 (3). Reallocation is not available as to a defendant that is 25 percent or less at fault. Or. Rev. Stat. § 18.485 (4). In addition, there are detailed rules governing such reallocations. Or. Rev. Stat. § 18.485 (3), (4) and (5).

91. *Hicklin v. Anders,* 201 Or. 128, 253 P.2d 897, 269 P.2d 521 (1954) (dealing with a covenant not to sue); *Cranford v. McNiece,* 252 Or. 446, 450 P.2d 529 (1969) (dealing with a release).

92. Or. Rev. Stat. § 18.440 (2).

93. Or. Rev. Stat. § 18.440 (3).

94. ORCP 28A permits joinder of defendants "if there is asserted against them jointly, severally, or in the alternative, any right to relief" arising out of the same transaction, occurrence, or series of transactions or occurrences.

95. Or. Rev. Stat. § 18.485 (1).

96. Or. Rev. Stat. § 18.480. Nothing in that statute limits special verdicts to cases involving joint tortfeasors.

97. *Savelich v. Preston Mill Co.,* 265 Or. 456, 509 P.2d 1179 (1973).

98. *Piehl v. The Dalles General Hospital*, 280 Or. 613, 621, 571 P.2d 149 (1977). Contribution, on the other hand, represents a partial shifting of the liability. "[T]he total recovery of the tortfeasor is limited to the amount paid by the tortfeasor in excess of the proportional share." Or. Rev. Stat. § 18.440 (2).

99. 1 Torts (Oregon CLE 1992) §§ 16.2 to 16.5.

100. *Piehl v. The Dalles General Hospital*, 280 Or. 613, 621, 571 P.2d 149 (1977).

101. Or. Rev. Stat. Chap. 656.

102. Or. Rev. Stat. §§ 656.202 to 656.258.

103. Or. Rev. Stat. § 656.154.

104. Or. Rev. Stat. § 656.578.

105. Or. Rev. Stat. § 656.591 (1).

106. Or. Rev. Stat. § 656.593 (1)(a) and Oregon Administrative Rule (OAR) 435-15-095.

107. Or. Rev. Stat. § 656.156 (2).

108. Or. Rev. Stat. § 656.018 (3).

109. Or. Rev. Stat. § 656.017.

110. Or. Rev. Stat. § 656.018 (3)(c).

111. *Settle v. PGE*, 81 Or. App. 474, 726 P.2d 389, *rev. denied*, 302 Or. 460 (1986). Thus far, Oregon appellate courts have declined to eliminate the traditional common law distinctions. *Sargent v. Inger*, 274 Or. 811, 813, 548 P.2d 1303 (1976); *Ragnone v. Portland School Dist. No. 1J*, 291 Or. 617, 633 P.2d 1287 (1981); *Abbott v. West Extension Irrigation District*, 110 Or. App. 385, 822 P.2d 747 (1991), *rev. denied*, 313 Or. 299 (1922).

112. *Baker v. Lane County*, 28 Or. App. 53, 56, 558P.2d 1247 (1977).

113. *Ragnone v. Portland School Dist. No. 1J*, 291 Or. 617, 633 P.2d 1287 (1981).

114. *Elliott v. Rogers Construction*, 257 Or. 421, 431, 479 P.2d 753 (1971).

115. 1 Torts (Oregon CLE 1992) § 10.14.

116. *Woolston v. Wells*, 297 Or. 548, 557-558, 687 P.2d 144 (1984).

117. *Campbell v. Carpenter*, 279 Or. 237, 566 P.2d 893 (1977).

118. *Fulmer v. Timber Inn Restaurant ad Lounge, Inc.*, 330 Or. 413, 417-19, 9 P.3d 710 (2000)(also recognizing a first-party negligence claim by an intoxicated patron).

119. *Chartrand v. Coos Bay Tavern*, 298 Or. 689, 696 P.2d 513 (1985), referring to Or. Rev. Stat. § 30.905.

120. *Stein v. Beta Rho Alumni Ass'n*, 49 Or. App. 965, 621 P.2d 632 (1980).

121. Or. Rev. Stat. § 30.905 (2).

122. *Oksenholt v. Lederle Laboratories*, 294 Or. 213, 656 P.2d 293 (1982) (damages recoverable in action for intentional misrepresentation include losses suffered through injury to reputation, lost business and impairment of earning capacity, as well as punitive damages).

123. Restatement (Second) Torts, § 402A, codified at Or. Rev. Stat. § 30.920 (1).

124. 1 Torts (Oregon cle 1992) § 19.90, citing *Oksenholt v. Lederle Laboratories*, 294 Or. 213, 656 P.2d 293 (1982).

125. *Wampler v. Palmerton*, 250 Or. 65, 73, 439 P.2d 601 (1968) cited in 1 Torts (Oregon cle 1992) § 24.8.

126. ORCP 20, unlike its federal counterpart, does not require fraud to be pleaded with particularity. However, ORCP 18A requires all claims to include a "plain and concise statement of the ultimate facts constituting a claim for relief. . . ."

127. *Riley Hill General Contractor v. Tandy Corp.*, 303 Or. 390, 407-408, 737 P.2d 595 (1987).

128. *Musgrave v. Lucas*, 193 Or. 401, 410, 238 P.2d 780 (1951). In traditional formulations of the tort, nine elements are listed. They have been somewhat compressed here.

129. *Onita Pacific Corp. v. Trustees of Bronson*, 315 Or. 149, 160-161, 843 P.2d 890 (1992).

130. *Onita Pacific Corp. v. Trustees of Bronson*, 315 Or. 149, 159, 843 P.2d 890 (1992). Often what is required is a "special relationship." *Gebrayel v. Transamerica Title Ins. Co.* 132 Or. App. 271, 280 n.8, 888 P.2d 83, *rev. denied*, 321 Or. 47 (1995).

131. Or. Rev. Stat. §§ 646.605 to 646.656.

132. Or. Rev. Stat. § 646.638 (1).

133. Or. Rev. Stat. § 646.608.

134. Or. Rev. Stat. § 646.638 (6).

135. Or. Rev. Stat. § 18.535 (1).

136. Or. Rev. Stat. § 18.535 (2)-(4).

137. Or. Rev. Stat. § 18.537 (1).

138. Or. Rev. Stat. § 30.925.

139. Or. Rev. Stat. § 18.537 (2).

140. Or. Rev. Stat. § 18.537 (1).

141. Or. Rev. Stat. § 30.020 (2)(e).

142. Or. Rev. Stat. § 18.550.

143. Or. Rev. Stat. § 30.927.

144. *Wheeler v. Green*, 286 Or. 99, 593 P.2d 777 (1977).

145. Or. Rev. Stat. § 18.540.

146. *Ore-Ida Foods v. Indian Head*, 290 Or. 909, 627 P.2d 469 (1981).

147. 2 Torts (Oregon CLE 1992) § 29.15.

148. Or. Rev. Stat. §§ 30.020 to 30.070.

149. Or. Rev. Stat. §§ 115.305 to 115.325.

150. 2 Torts (Oregon CLE 1992) § 29.1.

151. Or. Rev. Stat. § 30.020 (1).

152. Or. Rev. Stat. § 30.020 (2).

153. Or. Rev. Stat. § 30.075 (1).

154. Or. Rev. Stat. § 30.075 (1).

PENNSYLVANIA

A. **STATUTES OF LIMITATION**

Causes of action founded on negligent, intentional, or tortious conduct for personal injuries, death, or property damage must be brought within two years.[1] The beginning of the tolling period is either the time the cause of action accrued[2] or in accordance with specific court rules.[3] Pennsylvania applies a liberal "discovery" rule.[4] The statute of limitations for tortious interference with business relations is two years.[5]

Causes of action alleged to have arisen from a breach of contract for sale and breach of warranty have a four-year statute of limitations, including recovery for personal injuries, death, or property damage.[6] The tort discovery rule does not apply to the statute of limitations on breach of warranty actions.[7]

Actions for libel, slander, defamation, invasion of privacy and actions upon a bond must be brought within one year.[8]

Actions under the Unfair Trade Practices and Consumer Protection Law[9] have a six-year statute of limitations.[10]

A "catch-all" provision for actions that are neither subject to another limitation section nor excluded from the application of a limitation period must be commenced within six years.[11]

A 12-year statute of repose is applicable to claims involving improvements to real property.[12]

Any person who is to commence any civil action or proceeding against the Commonwealth or government unit for damages to his person or property must file a statement of claim within six months from the accrual of the cause of action.[13]

B. **TORT REFORM**

There has been no recent "tort reform" legislation in Pennsylvania, although many bills have been introduced. Currently pending is Senate Bill 5, also known as the Lawsuit Abuse/Civil Justice Reform Act, which proposes to reduce frivolous lawsuits, abolish joint and several liability, adopt a 15-year statute of repose for most consumer products, institute an "innocent seller provision" for merchants who unknowingly sell defective products that injure plaintiffs and place a cap on punitive damages.

C. **"NO FAULT" LIMITATIONS**

The Pennsylvania Motor Vehicle Financial Responsibility Law[14] (MVFRL) legislates insurance compensation for injuries resulting from motor vehicle accidents.[15] The "limited tort option"[16] under the MVFRL provides for reduced insurance premiums, but limits recovery to economic damages, absent the suffering of a serious injury[17] from a vehicle accident.[18] In all but the clearest of cases, whether the injured suffered "a serious injury" is a question for the jury.[19] Without the reduced premium, the "full tort option"[20] allows recovery for both noneconomic[21] and economic damages.[22] In close or doubtful cases, the court will resolve the insurance policy in favor of the greatest possible coverage to the injured claimants.[23]

D. THE STANDARD FOR NEGLIGENCE

To establish negligence under Pennsylvania law, plaintiff must prove (1) a duty; (2) a breach of that duty; (3) a causal connection between the breach and the resulting injury; and (4) injury suffered by the plaintiffs.[24] Breach is shown when the plaintiff demonstrates that the defendant engaged in conduct that deviated from the general standard of care expected under the circumstances.[25]

Pennsylvania recognizes a professional standard of care.[26] When a special relationship exists between the plaintiff and defendant, a higher standard of care is required.[27] Contrary to the general rule that there is no duty to control the actions of a third party, when a special relationship exists between the defendant and either an intended victim or the plaintiff, the defendant could have a duty to control the third party.[28]

The standard of care expected of a child requires a comparison of the individual child to minors of like age, experience, capacity and development under similar circumstances.[29] Children less than seven years old are conclusively presumed incapable of negligence.[30] Children between the ages of seven and fourteen are presumed incapable of negligence, but the presumption may be rebutted and weakens as the child nears fourteen years.[31] Minors older than 14 are presumptively capable of negligence.[32]

Pennsylvania's Supreme Court has abolished the common law presumption that a deceased or incapacitated plaintiff[33] or defendant[34] exercised due care at the time of injury.

E. CAUSATION

Pennsylvania follows the general rule that to establish a *prima facie* case in negligence, the plaintiff must demonstrate that the defendant's negligence was the proximate cause, or legal cause, of plaintiff's injury[35] and the defendant's negligence was the cause-in-fact of plaintiff's injury.[36] Proximate cause is shown when the defendant's negligence was a substantial factor in causing the plaintiff's injury.[37]

Pennsylvania follows the Restatement (Second) of Torts § 447 to determine whether an intervening cause constitutes a superseding cause that relieves the original actor from liability.[38] In determining whether an intervening force is a superseding cause, the test is whether the intervening conduct was so extraordinary as not to have been reasonably foreseeable.[39]

F. CONTRIBUTORY NEGLIGENCE, COMPARATIVE NEGLIGENCE, AND ASSUMPTION OF RISK

1. Contributory Negligence

The Pennsylvania Comparative Negligence Act[40] abolished contributory negligence as an absolute defense in actions seeking recovery for death, personal injury, or injury to property when the defendant's negligence is greater than the plaintiff's negligence.[41] Contributory negligence is still an absolute defense in actions seeking recovery for financial loss.[42] The burden of establishing contributory negligence lies with the defendant.[43]

2. Comparative Negligence

The Pennsylvania Comparative Negligence Act applies to actions for death, personal injury, or injury to property.[44] Under the Act, the plaintiff may recover damages when plaintiff's negligence does not exceed the aggregate of the defendants' negligence.[45] Plaintiff's recovery is then reduced by plaintiff's proportion of fault.[46] Comparative negligence does not apply when defendant is guilty of willful or wanton misconduct.[47]

3. Assumption of Risk

Assumption of risk remains a viable affirmative defense in cases involving express assumption of risk, strict liability, or when assumption of risk is preserved by statute.[48] The essential elements of assumption of risk are the plaintiff's subjective understanding of the risk, voluntary choice to encounter the risk, and willingness to accept that risk.[49] In negligence actions, assumption of risk is a matter of law, incorporated into the analysis of whether defendant's duty of care to plaintiff is relieved because plaintiff voluntarily and knowingly assumed a risk.[50] If the court finds the defendant still owed the plaintiff a duty of care, then the case proceeds to the jury on a comparative negligence theory.[51]

G. *RES IPSA LOQUITUR* AND INHERENTLY DANGEROUS ACTIVITIES

1. *Res Ipsa Loquitur*

Res ipsa loquitur permits an inference that the defendant caused the plaintiff's harm if: (1) the event is of the kind that ordinarily does not occur in the absence of negligence; (2) other responsible causes, including the conduct of the plaintiff and third persons, are sufficiently eliminated; and (3) the negligence is within the scope of the defendant's duty to the plaintiff.[52]

The court's function is to determine whether the inference *may* reasonably be drawn by the jury, or whether it *must* necessarily be drawn.[53] The jury's function is to determine whether the inference is to be drawn in any case where different conclusions may reasonably be reached.[54]

2. **Inherently Dangerous Activities**

The standard of reasonable care applies, but the standard of care is proportionate to the danger involved.[55] The greater the danger, the greater the care which must be exercised.[56]

H. NEGLIGENCE *PER SE*

Negligence *per se* is based upon the breach by a party of a statutory duty[57] and establishes both duty and the required breach of duty elements of a negligence action.[58] A negligence *per se* claim must fulfill four requirements: (1) the purpose of the statute or regulation on which the plaintiff relies must be, at least in part, to protect the interests of a group of individuals, as opposed to the general public;[59] (2) the statute or regulations must clearly apply to the conduct of the defendant;[60] (3) the defendant must violate the statute or regulation;[61] and (4) violation of the statute or regulation must be the proximate cause of the plaintiff's injuries.[62]

Negligence *per se* is not liability *per se*. A defendant may still invoke defenses such as contributory negligence and proximate cause.[63]

I. JOINT AND SEVERAL LIABILITY

Under the Pennsylvania Uniform Contribution Among Joint Tortfeasors Act (the "Contribution Act"), joint tortfeasors are "two or more persons jointly or severally liable in tort for the same injury to persons or property. . . . "[64] Joint tortfeasors are defendants who acting together commit the wrong or whose independent acts unite in causing a single injury[65] which is incapable of apportionment between the defendants.[66] Whether the injury is capable of apportionment is a question of law for the court.[67]

Courts consider several factors to determine if the defendants are separate or joint tortfeasors: identity of a cause of action against each of two or more defendants; existence of a common duty; whether the same evidence will support an action against each defendant; the single, indivisible nature of the injury to the plaintiff; identity of the facts as to time, place, or result; and whether the injury is direct and immediate.[68]

A release by the plaintiff of one joint tortfeasor does not discharge the other tortfeasors unless the release so provides, but the release reduces the claim against the other tortfeasors in the amount of the consideration paid for the release.[69] Under the Contribution Act, the right of contribution exists among joint tortfeasors so long as two requirements are met: one joint tortfeasor has discharged the common liability or paid more than his *pro rata* share;[70] and the liability of the other joint tortfeasor to the plaintiff has been extinguished by the settlement.[71]

When defendants are held liable for plaintiff's injury, but not as joint tortfeasors, the jury determines apportionment in situations when sufficient evidence is presented for the jury to make a reasonable determination.[72]

Where several tortfeasors independently cause the plaintiff's injury, but not jointly, the plaintiff may bring a cause of action and recover a judgment against any or all of the tortfeasors, but the plaintiff only has "one satisfaction."[73]

J. INDEMNITY

Indemnity shifts the entire loss of the plaintiff from one defendant to another by reason of some legal obligation to pay damages occasioned by the negligence of another.[74] Of course, indemnity may be provided by contract. Common law indemnity is generally available to those who are secondarily liable from those who are primarily liable.[75] If the party seeking indemnification is actively negligent, and whose negligence also is a cause of underlying injuries, common law indemnity is not available as a matter of law.[76]

K. BAR OF WORKERS' COMPENSATION STATUTE

Under the Pennsylvania Workers' Compensation Act,[77] the employee is barred from suing the employer who has paid workers' compensation benefits for the employee's work-related injuries.[78] Workers' compensation is an exclusive remedy.[79]

A general contractor can be deemed a statutory employer and covered under the Workers' Compensation Act where: (1) an employer is under contract with an owner or one in the position of an owner; (2) the premises are occupied by or under the control of such employer; (3) a subcontract is made by such employer; (4) part of the employer's regular business is entrusted to such subcontractor; and (5) there is an employee of such subcontractor.[80] There need not be a direct contractual relationship between the general contractor and the employee. It is intended to cover employees who do work in furtherance of the employer's business.[81]

The receipt of benefits does not bar an employee from seeking damages from a third party.[82] Where an employee has collected workers' compensation benefits from an employer and then proceeds to sue a third party for the same incident, the employer may be subrogated to the rights of the employee as against a third party.[83] If the employee successfully sues the third party, the employer or his insurer may be reimbursed for previously paid workers' compensation benefits, reduced proportionately by the employer's share of the attorney's fees.[84]

The employer's right of subrogation gives the employer standing to intervene pursuant to Pennsylvania Rules of Civil Procedure 2327.[85] Standing, however, does not guarantee that the court will grant permission to intervene.[86]

Certain work-related injuries caused by the intentional conduct of the employer have been found to be covered by the Act, but not all intentional torts committed by an employer fall within this category.[87] In determining whether an intentional act will give rise to a cause of action against a coworker, Pennsylvania courts examine whether the alleged "intentional wrong" is one that is not normally expected to be present in the workplace and if the wrong is one that is not normally expected to be present in the workplace, an intentional tort is actionable.[88] An employee may maintain a cause of action against an employer for injuries sustained on the employer's premises from personal animosity,[89] fraudulent misrepresentation,[90] defamation,[91] or abuse of process.[92] Additionally, where an employee is claiming that his or her injuries were aggravated by the employer's intentional conduct, the employee can maintain a common law cause of action against the employer.[93]

L. PREMISES LIABILITY

A landowner's liability for injuries sustained on the premises depends upon the individual's common law legal status as trespasser, licensee, or invitee.[94] A landowner is liable to a trespasser if the landowner is guilty of wanton or willful negligence or misconduct.[95] The landowner must take care to warn licensees of actually or constructively known dangerous conditions.[96] A landowner must exercise reasonable care to protect invitees from any actually or constructively known dangerous conditions that the invitees will not realize or will fail to protect themselves against.[97]

A possessor of land is subject to liability for the criminal acts of third parties when he knows or has reason to know of the dangerous condition and fails to give a warning adequate to enable a visitor to the premises to avoid harm or otherwise take reasonable precautions to prevent the type of injuries plaintiff claims he suffered.[98]

M. DRAM SHOP LIABILITY

Pennsylvania's Dram Shop Act[99] is primarily litigated in the area of liability for serving alcohol to visibly intoxicated persons. The Act does not apply to social hosts who serve alcohol to adults, but there is some indication that it may apply when alcohol is served to a visibly intoxicated minor.[100]

While a violation of the Dram Shop Act is negligence *per se*,[101] liability for the violation will not attach absent proof that the patron served alcohol to a visibly intoxicated person[102] and that the patron's service of alcohol to that visibly intoxicated person was the proximate cause of the plaintiff's injury.[103]

N. ECONOMIC LOSS

Recovery under tort law is permitted only for personal injury or property damage.[104] Recovery solely for economic loss is prohibited in strict liability and negligence actions.[105] Although courts prohibit the recovery of economic loss in traditional tort cases, the application of this rule is unclear in the case of "business torts."[106] The better reasoning would not prohibit such recovery in "business torts."

O. FRAUD AND MISREPRESENTATION

The Pennsylvania Rules of Civil Procedure require that a cause of action for fraud be pleaded with particularity.[107]

Each of the following elements for fraud, deceit or intentional misrepresentation must be proved by clear and convincing evidence:[108] (1) a representation; (2) which is material to the transaction; (3) made falsely; (4) with the intent of misleading another into relying on it; (5) the recipient's justifiable reliance on the misrepresentation; and (6) the resulting injury was proximately caused by the reliance.[109]

The elements of negligent misrepresentation are as follows: (1) a misrepresentation of a material fact; (2) made under circumstances in which the misrepresenter ought to have known of its falsity; (3) with the intent to induce another to act on it; and (4) which results in injury to a party acting in justifiable reliance on the misrepresentation.[110] These elements differ from intentional misrepresentation in that the speaker need not know his/her words are untrue, but must have failed to make a reasonable investigation of the truth of the words.[111]

P. CONSUMER FRAUD STATUTES

Pennsylvania's Unfair Trade Practices and Consumer Protection Law[112] (the UTPCPL) protects consumers from unfair methods of competition and deceptive acts or practices in any trade or commerce.[113] The UTPCPL provides that Attorneys General or District Attorneys may impose penalties for any violations.[114] Private actions may also be brought under the UTPCPL,[115] in which case, the plaintiff must establish a causal connection between the unlawful practice and the plaintiff's loss.[116]

The "catch-all" section[117] of the UTPCPL is designed to cover generally all unfair and deceptive acts or practices in the conduct of trade or commerce.[118] Under the "catch-all" section, elements of common law fraud must be proved.[119] As previously noted, actions under the UTPCPL have a six-year statute of limitations.[120]

The Unfair Insurance Practices Act (UIPA) prohibits unfair methods of competition or unfair or deceptive act or practice in the business of insurance.[121]

Q. PUNITIVE DAMAGES

Pennsylvania follows the Restatement (Second) of Torts § 908 to determine if punitive damages should be awarded.[122] Punitive damages are awarded in negligence actions when the defendant acts with an evil motive,[123] or in reckless disregard for the rights of others.[124] The purposes behind punitive damages are to deter and punish the defendant's conduct.[125]

Compensatory and/or nominal damages are generally not a condition precedent to the award of punitive damages as long as the facts are sufficient to maintain the cause of action.[126] Punitive damages need not bear a reasonable relationship to the amount of compensatory or nominal damages awarded.[127] Finders of fact consider several factors, including the defendant's wealth, the seriousness of the act, and the nature and extent of the harm in assessing punitive damages.[128]

Punitive damages are not awarded for misconduct constituting ordinary negligence[129] or for wrongful death.[130]

R. WRONGFUL DEATH AND SURVIVORSHIP ACTIONS

Under common law, there is no recovery for wrongful death[131] or right of action for a decedent's personal injuries. However, recovery is allowed under the Pennsylvania Wrongful Death Statute[132] and the Pennsylvania Survival Act,[133] two separate and distinct causes of action, whose remedies are cumulative and not alternative.[134]

Recovery under the Wrongful Death Statute passes to a limited group of beneficiaries defined by statute[135] to compensate them for their loss.[136] Recovery under the Survival Act passes to the decedent's estate and is measured by the pecuniary loss to the decedent.[137] A survival action is not a new cause of action, but "'continues in the decedent's personal representatives the right of action which accrued to the deceased at common law because of the tort.'"[138]

Morton F. Daller
Brendan P. Burke
DALLER GREENBERG & DIETRICH, L.L.P.
Valley Green Corporate Center
7111 Valley Green Road
Fort Washington, Pennsylvania 19034
(215) 836-1100
Fax (215) 836-2845
mdaller@dallergreenberg.com
www.dallergreenberg.com

ENDNOTES - PENNSYLVANIA

1. 42 Pa. Cons. Stat. Ann. § 5524. Under Section 5524 the following actions have a two-year statute of limitations: (1) assault, battery, false imprisonment, false arrest, malicious prosecution, or malicious abuse of process; (2) to recover injuries to the person or death caused by another's wrongful acts; (3) taking, detaining, or injuring personal property; (4) waste or trespass of real property; (5) upon a statute for a civil penalty or forfeiture; (6) against any governmental officer or unity for the nonpayment of money or nondelivery of property collected upon an execution or otherwise in his possession.

2. *Id.* § 5502(a).

3. *Id.* § 5502(b).

4. *Bohus v. Beloff,* 950 F.2d 919 (3d Cir. 1991); *Tuman v. Genesis Assoc.,* 935 F. Supp. 1375, 1381 (E.D. Pa. 1996); *Dalrymple v. Brown,* 549 Pa. 217, 701 A.2d 164 (1997); *Hayward v. Medical Center of Beaver County,* 530 Pa. 320, 608 A.2d 1040 (1992); *Stauffer v. Ebersole, M.D.,* 385 Pa. Super. 306, 309, 560 A.2d 816, 817 (1989).

5. 42 Pa. Cons. Stat. Ann. § 5524(3); *Dellape v. Murray,* 651 A.2d 638, 640 (Pa. Cmwlth. 1994).

6. 42 Pa. Cons. Stat. Ann. § 5525; *Stransky v. American Isuzu Motors, Inc.,* 829 F. Supp. 788, 791 (E.D. Pa. 1993); *Northampton County Area Community College v. Dow Chem., U.S.A.,* 389 Pa. Super. 11, 27, 566 A.2d 591, 599 (1989).

7. *Brownstein v. Dow Corning Wright,* 678 F. Supp. 1151, 1155 (E.D. Pa. 1988); *Northampton County Area Community College v. Dow Chem., U.S.A.,* 389 Pa. Super. 11, 28, 566 A.2d 591, 599 (1989).

8. 42 Pa. Cons. Stat. Ann. § 5523.

9. 73 Pa. Cons. Stat. Ann. §§ 201-1 to 201-9.1.

10. *Woody v. State Farm Fire and Cas. Co.,* 965 F. Supp. 691, 695 (E.D. Pa. 1997); *Gabriel v. O'Hara,* 368 Pa. Super. 383, 398, 534 A.2d 488, 496 (1987); *see* 42 Pa. Cons. Stat. Ann. § 5527.

11. 42 Pa. Cons. Stat. Ann. § 5527.

12. 42 Pa. Cons. Stat. Ann. § 5536; *Vargo v. Koppers Co., Inc., Eng'g & Constr. Div.,* 552 Pa. 371, 374, 715 A.2d 423, 425 (1998); *Noll by Noll v. Harrisburg*

Area YMCA, 537 Pa. 274, 280, 643 A.2d 81, 84 (1994); *McCormick v. Columbus Conveyor Co.*, 522 Pa. 520, 524, 564 A.2d 907, 909 (1989).

13. 75 Pa. Cons. Stat. Ann. § 5522.

14. 75 Pa. Cons. Stat. Ann. §§ 1701 *et seq.*

15. 75 Pa. Cons. Stat. Ann. § 1701; *Huber v. Erie Ins. Exch.*, 402 Pa. Super. 443, 446, 587 A.2d 333, 334 (1991).

16. 75 Pa. Cons. Stat. Ann. § 1705(d).

17. The MVFRL defines "serious injury" as "a personal injury resulting in death, serious impairment of body function or permanent serious disfigurement." 75 Pa. Cons. Stat. Ann. § 1702.

18. *Id.*

19. *Washington v. Baxter*, 553 Pa. 434, 446-47, 719 A.2d 733, 740 (1998).

20. 75 Pa. Cons. Stat. Ann. § 1705(d).

21. 75 Pa. Cons. Stat. Ann. § 1702. The MVFRL defines "noneconomic loss" as "pain and suffering and other nonmonetary detriment." *Id.*

22. 75 Pa. Cons. Stat. Ann. § 1705(d).

23. *Ickes v. Burkes*, 713 A.2d 653, 656-57 (Pa. Super. 1998); *Panichelli v. Liberty Mut. Ins. Co.*, 435 Pa. Super. 290, 296, 645 A.2d 865, 868 (1994).

24. *Estate of Zimmerman v. Southeastern Pennsylvania Transp. Auth.*, 168 F.3d 680 (3d Cir. 1999); *Martin v. Evans*, 551 Pa. 496, 502, 711 A.2d 458, 461 (1998); *Swift v. Northeastern Hosp. of Philadelphia*, 456 Pa. Super. 330, 335, 690 A.2d 719, 722 (1997).

25. *See Martin*, 551 Pa. at 502, 711 A.2d at 461 (1998).

26. *Giorno v. Temple Univ. Hosp.*, 875 F. Supp. 267, 269 (E.D. Pa. 1995); *Wendy H. by and through Smith v. City of Philadelphia*, 849 F. Supp. 367, 372 (E.D. Pa. 1994).

27. *Emerich v. Philadelphia Ctr. for Human Dev., Inc.*, 554 Pa. 209, 216, 720 A.2d 1032, 1040 (1998).

28. *See id.*

29. *Kuhns v. Brugger*, 390 Pa. 331, 340, 135 A.2d 395, 401 (1957); *Smith v. Stribling*, 168 Pa. Cmwlth. 188, 196; 649 A.2d 1003, 1006 (1994).

30. *Kuhns*, 390 Pa. at 341, 135 A.2d at 401; *City of Philadelphia v. Duda by Duda*, 141 Pa. Cmwlth. 88, 97, 595 A.2d 206, 211 (1991).

31. *See id.*

32. *See id.*

33. *Marks v. Swayne*, 549 Pa. 336, 342, 701 A.2d 224, 226 (1997) (overruling *Waddle v. Nelkin*, 511 Pa. 641, 515 A.2d 909 (1986)).

34. *Rice v. Shuman*, 513 Pa. 204, 212, 519 A.2d 391, 396 (1986); *Bressler v. Dannon Yogurt*, 392 Pa. Super. 475, 487, 573 A.2d 562, 568 (1990).

35. *Skipworth by Williams v. Lead Industries Ass'n, Inc.*, 547 Pa. 224, 231, 690 A.2d 169, 172 (1997); *Hamil v. Bashline*, 481 Pa. 256, 265, 392 A.2d 1280, 1284 (1978); *First v. Zem Zem Temple*, 454 Pa. Super. 548, 553 n.2, 686 A.2d 18, 21 n.2 (1996); *Reilly v. Tiergarten Inc.*, 430 Pa. Super. 10, 15, 633 A.2d 208, 210 (1993).

36. *Zem Zem Temple*, 454 Pa. Super. at 553 n.2, 686 A.2d at 21 n.2; *Reilly*, 430 Pa. Super. at 15, 633 A.2d at 210; *McDonald v. Marriott Corp.*, 388 Pa. Super 121, 125, 564 A.2d 1296, 1298 (1989).

37. *Bashline*, 481 Pa. at 265, 392 A.2d at 1284; *Jeter v. Owens-Corning Fiberglas Corp.*, 716 A.2d 633, 636 (Pa. Super. 1998).

38. *Johnson v. Garden State Brickface and Stucco Co.*, 833 F. Supp. 524 (E.D. Pa. 1993); *Estate of Flickinger v. Ritsky*, 452 Pa. 69, 305 A.2d 40 (1973).

39. *Powell v. Drumheller*, 539 Pa. 484, 653 A.2d 619 (1995); *Huddleston v. Infertility Center of America*, 700 A.2d 453 (Pa. Super. 1997).

40. 42 Pa. Cons. Stat. Ann. § 7102.

41. *See id.*

42. *Commonwealth Fed. Sav. & Loan Ass'n v. Pettit*, 137 Pa. Commw. 523, 532, 586 A.2d 1021, 1026 (1991).

43. *Pascal v. Carter*, 436 Pa. Super. 40, 43, 647 A.2d 231, 233 (1994); *McCullough v. Monroeville Home Ass'n, Etc.*, 270 Pa. Super. 428, 431, 411 A.2d 794, 795 (1979).

44. 42 Pa. Cons. Stat. Ann. § 7102.

45. *See id.*

46. *See id.*

47. *Summit Fasteners, Inc. v. Harleysville Nat'l Bank & Trust Co., Inc.* 410 Pa. Super. 56, 63, 599 A.2d 203, 206 (1991); *Krivijanski v. Union R. Co.,* 357 Pa. Super. 196, 205, 515 A.2d 933, 936 (1986).

48. *Howell v. Clyde,* 533 Pa. 151, 162 n.10, 620 A.2d 1107, 1112-13 n.10 (1993).

49. *Barnes v. American Tobacco Co. Inc.,* 984 F. Supp. 842, 869 (E.D. Pa. 1997) (citing *Howell,* 533 Pa. at 162, 620 A.2d at 1112-13)).

50. *See id.; Barrett v. Fredavid Builders, Inc.,* 454 Pa. Super. 162, 166, 685 A.2d 129 130 (1996).

51. *Howell,* 533 Pa. at 162 n.10, 620 A.2d at 1112-13 n.10.

52. *D'Ardenne by D'Ardenne v. Strawbridge & Clothier, Inc.,* 712 A.2d 318, 321 (Pa. Super. 1998) (citing *Gilbert v. Korvette, Inc.,* 457 Pa. 602, 611-13, 327 A.2d 94, 100 (1974)). Note that *Gilbert v. Korvette, Inc.* abandoned the requirement that the defendant have "exclusive control" over the instrumentality of the injury. *See Gilbert,* 457 Pa. at 614, 327 A.2d at 101.

53. *D'Ardenne,* 712 A.2d at 321.

54. *Id.*

55. *Stewart v. Motts,* 539 Pa. 596, 601, 654 A.2d 535, 537 (1995).

56. *Id.*

57. *Alfred M. Lutheran Distrib., Inc. v. A.P. Weilersbacher,* 437 Pa. Super. 391, 406-08, 650 A.2d 83, 91 (1994).

58. *J.E.J. v. Tri-County Big Brothers/Big Sisters, Inc.,* 692 A.2d 582, 585 (Pa. Super. 1997).

59. *Tri-County,* 692 A.2d at 585; *Wagner v. Anzon, Inc.,* 453 Pa. Super. 619, 627, 684 A.2d 570, 574 (1996).

60. *Id.*

61. *Wagner,* 453 Pa. Super. at 627, 684 A.2d at 574.

62. *Id.*

63. *Reilly v. Tiergarten Inc.,* 430 Pa. Super. 10, 633 A.2d 208 (1993); *Herr v. Booten,* 398 Pa. Super. 166, 580 A.2d 1115 (1990).

64. 42 Pa. Cons. Stat. Ann. § 8322.

65. *Smith v. Pulcinella*, 440 Pa. Super. 525, 529, 656 A.2d 494, 497 (1995).

66. *Mattia v. Sears, Roebuck & Co.*, 366 Pa. Super. 504, 507, 531 A.2d 789, 791 (1987); *Harka v. Nabati*, 337 Pa. Super. 617, 622, 487 A.2d 432, 434 (1985).

67. *Harka*, 337 Pa. Super. at 622, 487 A.2d at 434.

68. *Carrasquilla v. Mazda Motor Corp.*, 963 F. Supp. 455, 459-60 (M.D. Pa. 1997); *Smith v. Pulcinella*, 440 Pa. Super. at 529-30, 656 A.2d at 496; *Harka*, 337 Pa. Super. at 622, 487 A.2d at 434.

69. 42 Pa. Cons. Stat. Ann. § 8326.

70. *Id.*

71. *Id.*

72. *Corbett v. Weisband*, 380 Pa. Super. 292, 332-33, 551 A.2d 1059, 1079 (1988).

73. *Brown v. City of Pittsburgh*, 409 Pa. 357, 363, 186 A.2d 399, 402 (1962); *Franklin Decorators, Inc. v. Kalson*, 330 Pa. Super. 140, 143, 479 A.2d 3, 4 (1984).

74. *Travelers Indem. Co. v. Stedman*, 895 F. Supp. 742, 748-49 (E.D. Pa. 1995).

75. *Globe Indem. Co. v. Agway, Inc.*, 456 F.2d 472, 475 (3d Cir. 1972); *Burbage v. Boiler Eng'g & Supply Co.*, 433 Pa. 319, 326, 249 A.2d 563, 567 (1969); *Kemper Nat'l P & C Co. v. Smith*, 419 Pa. Super. 295, 300, 615 A.2d 372, 375 (1992).

76. *Stedman*, 895 F. Supp. at 749.

77. 77 Pa. Cons. Stat. Ann. §§ 1 *et seq.*

78. 77 Pa. Cons. Stat. Ann. § 481; *see also* 77 Pa. Cons. Stat. Ann. § 22 for the definition of "employee" and 77 Pa. Cons. Stat. Ann. § 21 for the definition of "employer."

79. *Ducjai v. Dennis*, 540 Pa. 103, 109, 656 A.2d 102, 105 (1995); *Alston v. St. Paul Ins. Co.*, 531 Pa. 261, 267, 612 A.2d 421, 424 (1992); *Gertz v. Temple University-Commonwealth System of Higher Educ.*, 443 Pa. Super. 177, 181, 661 A.2d 13, 15 (1995); *Snyder v. Pocono Med. Ctr.*, 440 Pa. Super. 606, 611, 656 A.2d 535, 536 (1995), *aff'd*, 547 Pa. 415, 690 A.2d 1152 (1997).

80. 77 Pa. Cons. Stat. Ann. § 52 (an employer who permits the entry upon premises occupied by him or under his control of a laborer or an assistant hired by an employee or contractor, for the performance upon such premises of a part of the employer's regular business entrusted to such employee or contractor, shall be liable to such laborer or assistant in the same

manner and to the same extent as to his own employee); *McDonald v. Levinson Steel Co.*, 302 Pa. 287, 294, 153 A. 424, 426 (1930); *Emery v. Leavesly McCollum*, 725 A.2d 807 (Pa. Super. 1999).

81. *Qualp v. James Stewart Co.*, 266 Pa. 502, 109 A. 780 (1920); *Lascio v. Belcher Roofing Corp.*, 704 A.2d 644 (1997).

82. 77 Pa. Cons. Stat. Ann. § 481(b).

83. 77 Pa. Cons. Stat. Ann. § 671; *see also PMA Ins. Group v. Workmen's Compensation Appeal Bd.*, 665 A.2d 538, 543 (1995); *Reliance Ins. Co. v. Richmond Mach. Co.*, 309 Pa. Super. 430, 435, 455 A.2d 686, 689 (1983).

84. *Stalmaster v. W.C.A.B.*, 679 A.2d 293, 296 (Pa. Cmwlth. 1996); *Allegheny Beverage Corp. v. W.C.A.B.*, 166 Pa. Commw. 646, 650, 646 A.2d 762, 764 (1994); *Pendleton v. W.C.A.B.*, 155 Pa. Commw. 440, 445, 625 A.2d 187, 190 (1993).

85. *See* Pa. Cons. Stat. Ann. § 2327(3) and (4).

86. *McDaniel v. Rexnord, Inc.*, 371 Pa. Super. 32, 35, 537 A.2d 365, 367 (1988); *Maginley v. Robert J. Elliott, Inc.*, 345 Pa. Super. 582, 586, 498 A.2d 977, 980 (1985).

87. 77 Pa. Cons. Stat. Ann. § 72; *Urban v. Dollar Bank*, 725 A.2d 815 (Pa. Super. 1999).

88. *Holdampf v. Fidelity & Cas. Co. of New York*, 793 F. Supp. 111(W.D.Pa.1992), aff'd, 16 F.3d 403 (3d Cir. 1992); *Snyder v. Specialty Glass Products, Inc.*, 441 Pa. Super. 613, 658 A.2d 374 (1995).

89. *See Kohler v. McCrory Stores*, 532 Pa. 130, 137, 615 A.2d 27, 32 (1992) (holding "spirit and intent of the [Worker's Compensation] Act not violated by permitting an employee injured by a co-worker for personal reasons to maintain a negligence action against his employer for any associated negligence in maintaining a safe workplace"); *cf., Shaffer v. Procter & Gamble*, 412 Pa. Super. 630, 637, 604 A.2d 289, 292-93 (1992) (finding Workers' Compensation Act's exclusivity provision applicable to employee's lawsuit against employer because grievance was job related).

90. *See Martin v. Lancaster Battery Co., Inc.*, 530 Pa. 11, 18, 606 A.2d 444, 447-48 (1992); *Snyder v. Specialty Glass Prod., Inc.*, 441 Pa. Super. 613, 623, 658 A.2d 366, 371 (1995).

91. *See Urban v. Dollar Bank*, 725 A.2d 815, 819 (Pa. Super. 1999) (held defamation action designed to redress harm to employee's reputation, thus,

essence of action was not to compensate employee for "injury" as contemplated by Act).

92. *Id.* at 821 (held malicious abuse of process action designed to redress harm to employee's reputation and financial injury sustained as result, thus, essence of action was not to compensate employee for "injury" as contemplated by Act).

93. *Martin v. Lancaster Battery Co., Inc.*, 530 Pa. 11, 606 A.2d 444 (1992).

94. *See Updyke v. BP Oil Co.*, 717 A.2d 546, 549 (Pa. Super. 1998); *Swift v. Northeastern Hosp. of Philadelphia*, 456 Pa. Super. 330, 335, 690 A.2d 719, 722 (1997); *Palange v. Philadelphia Law Dept.*, 433 Pa. Super. 373, 375-77, 640 A.2d 1305, 1307 (1994). Pennsylvania follows the Restatement (Second) of Torts, defining trespasser as "'a person who enters or remains upon land in the possession of another without a privilege to do so created by the possessor's consent or otherwise. A licensee is a person who is privileged to enter or remain on the land only by virtue of the possessor's consent. An invitee is a person invited to enter or remain on land as a member of the public for a purpose for which the land is held open to the public, or for a purpose directly or indirectly connected with business dealings with the possessor of land.'" Restatement (Second) of Torts §§ 330-32; *Updyke*, 717 A.2d at 549 (citations omitted).

95. *See Zimmerman v. Southeastern Penn. Transp. Auth.*, 17 F. Supp. 2d 372, 380 (E.D. Pa. 1998); *Rossino v. Kovacs*, 553 Pa. 168, ___, 718 A.2d 755, 756 (1998).

96. *See Wiegand by Wiegand v. Mars Nat. Bank*, 308 Pa. Super. 218, 221, 454 A.2d 99, 101 (1982); *see also* Restatement (Second) of Torts §§ 341 and 342 (1965).

97. *See Swift*, 456 Pa. Super. at 335, 690 A.2d at 722; *Blackman v. Federal Realty Inv. Trust*, 444 Pa. Super. 411, 415, 64 A.2d 139, 142 (1995); *see also* Restatement (Second) of Torts §§ 341A and 343 (1965).

98. *Feld v. Merriam*, 506 Pa. 383, 485 A.2d 749 (1984); *Moran v. Valley Forge Drive-In Theater, Inc.*, 431 Pa. 432, 246 A.2d 875 (1968); *Kerns v. Methodist Hospital*, 393 Pa. Super. 533, 574 A.2d 1068 (1990).

99. 47 Pa. Cons. Stat. Ann. § 4-493.

100. *See Klein v. Raysinger*, 504 Pa. 141, 148, 470 A.2d 507, 510 (1983).

101. *See Fandozzi v. Kelly Hotel, Inc.*, 711 A.2d 524, 525 (Pa. Super. 1998); *Miller v. Brass Rail*, 702 A.2d 1072, 1078 (Pa. Super. 1997); *Holpp v. Fez, Inc.*, 440 Pa. Super. 512, 517, 656 A.2d 147, 149 (1995).

102. *Fandozzi*, 711 A.2d at 525; *Detwiler v. Brumbaugh*, 441 Pa. Super. 110, 115, 656 A.2d 944, 946 (1995); *Hiles v. Brandywine Club*, 443 Pa. Super. 462, 469, 662 A.2d 16, 19 (1995).

103. *Fandozzi*, 711 A.2d at 525; *Brass Rail Tavern*, 702 A.2d at 1078; *Holpp*, 440 Pa. Super. at 518, 656 A.2d at 150; *Reilly v. Tiergarten, Inc.*, 430 Pa. Super. 10, 15, 633 A.2d 208, 210 (1993).

104. *See Lucker Mfg. v. Milwaukee Steel Foundry, a Div. of Grede Foundries*, 777 F. Supp. 413, 415 (E.D. Pa. 1991); *New York State Elec., & Gas Corp. v. Westinghouse Elec. Corp.*, 387 Pa. Super. 537, 549, 564 A.2d 919, 925 (1989).

105. *See 2-J Corp. v. Tice*, 126 F.3d 539, 541 (3d Cir. 1997); *Jones v. General Motors Corp.*, 428 Pa. Super. 544, 546, 631 A.2d 665, 666 (citing *REM Coal Co., Inc. v. Clark Equipment Co.* 386 Pa. Super. 401, 412-13, 562 A.2d 128, 134 (1989)); *New York State Elec., & Gas Corp.*, 387 Pa. Super. at 539, 564 A.2d at 925; *Lower Lake Dock Co. v. Messinger Bearing Corp.* 395 Pa. Super. 456, 463, 577 A.2d 631, 635 (1990) (finding economic loss rule equally applicable to negligence actions sounding in tort as products liability action).

106. *See SHV Coal, Inc. v. Continental Grain Co.*, 376 Pa. Super. 241, 250, 545 A.2d 917, 921 (1988) (stating that an intentional interference with a current or prospective business relationship which results in economic loss is actionable); *but see Aikens v. Baltimore and Ohio R. Co.*, 348 Pa. Super. 17, 20, 501 A.2d 277, 278 (1985) (finding recovery for purely economic loss occasioned by tortious interference with contract or economic advantage is not available under negligence theory); *Valley Forge Convention & Visitors Bureau v. Visitor's Services, Inc.*, 28 F. Supp. 2d 947, 951 (E.D. Pa. 1998) (stating "[t]he economic loss doctrine precludes recovery in tort for economic losses arising from breach of contract").

107. Pa. R. Civ. P. Rule 1019(b).

108. *Gerfin v. Colonial Smelting & Ref. Co., Inc.*, 374 Pa. 66, 67, 97 A.2d 71, 72 (1953); *Sewak v. Lockhart*, 699 A.2d 755, 759 (Pa. Super. 1997); *Pittsburgh Live, Inc. v. Servov*, 419 Pa. Super. 423, 429, 615 A.2d 438, 441 (1992).

109. *Gibbs v. Ernst*, 538 Pa. 193, 207, 647 A.2d 882, 889 (1994); *Bortz v. Noon*, 556 Pa. 569, 729 A.2d 555, 560 (1999) (adopting Restatement (Second) of Torts § 525 (1977); *accord Sewak*, 699 A.2d at 759; *Servov*, 410 Pa. Super. at 429-30, 615 A.2d at 441.

110. *Gibbs*, 538 Pa. 210, 647 A.2d at 890; *Bortz*, 556 Pa. at ___, 729 A.3d at 561) (following Restatement (Second) of Torts § 552).

111. *See id.*

112. 73 Pa. Cons. Stat. Ann. §§ 201-1 to 201-9.1.

113. 73 Pa. Cons. Stat. Ann. § 201-1.

114. *Id.*

115. 73 Pa. Cons. Stat. Ann. § 201-9.2.

116. *DiLucido v. Terminix Int'l, Inc.*, 450 Pa. Super. 393, 401, 676 A.2d 1237, 1240-41 (1996).

117. "Engaging in any other fraudulent or deceptive conduct which creates a likelihood of confusion or of misunderstanding." 73 Pa. Cons. Stat. Ann. § 201-2(4)(xxi).

118. *Pirozzi v. Penske Olds-Cadillac-GMC*, 413 Pa. Super. 308, 313, 605 A.2d 373, 375 (1992) (citing *Com., by Creamer v. Monumental Properties, Inc.*, 459 Pa. 450, 329 A.2d 812 (1974)); *Hammer v. Nikol*, 659 A.2d 617, 619 (Pa. Comwlth. 1995).

119. *Prime Meats, Inc. v. Yochim*, 422 Pa. Super. 460, 469, 619 A.2d 769, 6773 (1993). *See supra* note 106 and accompanying text for the elements of common law fraud.

120. *Woody v. State Farm Fire and Cas. Co.*, 965 F. Supp. 691, 695 (E.D. Pa. 1997); *Gabriel v. O'Hara*, 368 Pa. Super. 383, 398, 534 A.2d 488, 496 (1987).

121. 40 Pa. Cons. Stat. Ann. §§ 1171.1 *et seq.*

122. *Kirkbride v. Lisbon Contractors, Inc.*, 521 Pa. 97, 102, 555 A.2d 800, 803 (1989); *Feld v. Merriam*, 506 Pa. 383, 395, 485 A.2d 742, 747 (1984); *Karpiak v. Russo*, 450 Pa. Super. 471, 480-81, 676 A.2d 270, 275 (1996); *Rhoads v. Heberling*, 306 Pa. Super. 35, 39, 451 A.2d 1378, 1380 (1982); *Focht v. Rabada*, 217 Pa. Super. 35, 38, 268 A.2d 157, 169 (1970).

123. *Logue v. Logano Trucking Co.*, 921 F. Supp. 1425, 1427 (E.D. Pa. 1996).

124. *Feld*, 506 Pa. at 395, 485 A.2d at 748; *Martin v. Johns-Manville Corp.*, 508 Pa. 154, 170, 494 A.2d 1088, 1097, (1985), *rev'd on other grounds by Martin v. Johns-Manville Corp.*, 551 Pa. 496, 711 A.2d 458 (1998); *Taylor v. Albert Einstein Medical Ctr.*, 723 A.2d 1027, 1037(Pa. Super. 1998); *Rhoads*, 306 Pa. Super. at 46, 451 A.2d at 1384.

125. *G.J.D. by G.J.D. v. Johnson*, 552 Pa. 169, 176, 713 A.2d 1127, 1131 (Pa. 1998) (citing *Kirkbride*, 521 Pa. at 104, 555 A.2d at 803).

126. *See Kirkbride v Lisbon Contractors, Inc.*, 521 Pa. 97, 102, 555 A.2d 800, 803 (1989); *Laniecki v. Polish Army Veterans Ass'n of Lucyan Chwalkowski*, 331 Pa. Super. 413, 426, 480 A.2d 1101, 1108 (1984); *Rhoads*, 306 Pa. Super. at 40-41, 451 A.2d at 1381; *but see Martin*, 508 Pa. at 173, 494 A.2d at 1098 (Hutchison, J. with four justices concurring in result) (held plaintiff must prove actual compensatory damages before recovering punitive damages in a products liability case); *Smith v. Grab*, 705 A.2d 894, 901 (Pa. Super. 1997 (citing *Schecter v. Watkins*, 395 Pa. Super. 363, 383, 577 A.2d 585, 595 (1990)).

127. *Kirkbride*, 521 Pa. at 103-04, 555 A.2d at 803; *but see Martin*, 508 Pa. at 174, 494 A.2d at 1098.

128. *Kirkbride*, 521 Pa. at 102, 555 A.2d at 803; *Feld v. Merriam*, 506 Pa. at 396, 485 A.2d at 748; *Sprague v. Walter*, 441 Pa. Super. 1, 61, 656 A.2d 890, 920 (1995).

129. *Logue*, 921 F. Supp. at 1427; *Martin*, 508 Pa. at 170, 494 A.2d at 1097; *McDaniel v. Merck, Sharp & Dohme*, 367 Pa. Super. 600, 623, 533 A.2d 436, 447 (1987).

130. *Harvey v. Hassinger*, 315 Pa. Super. 97, 100, 461 A.2d 814, 815 (1983).

131. *See Tulewicz v. Southeastern Pennsylvania Transp. Authority*, 529 Pa. 588, 596, 606 A.2d 427, 431, (1992); *Miller v. Preitz*, 422 Pa. 383, 221 A.2d 320 (1966), *overruled on other grounds*, *Kassab v. Central Soya*, 432 Pa. 217, 246 A.2d 848 (1968).

132. 42 Pa. Cons. Stat. Ann. § 8301.

133. 42 Pa. Cons. Stat. Ann. § 8302.

134. *See Tulewicz*, 529 Pa. at 597, 606 A.2d at 431; *Pezzulli v. D'Ambrosia*, 344 Pa. 643, 645, 26 A.2d 659, 661 (1942).

135. 42 Pa. Cons. Stat. Ann. § 8301(b).

136. *Tulewicz*, 529 Pa. at 596; 606 A.2d at 431; *Fisher v. Dye*, 386 Pa. 141, 145, 125 A.2d 472, 475 (1956).

137. *Id.*

138. *Tulewicz*, 529 Pa. at 597, 606 A.2d at 431 (citing *Pezzulli v. D'Ambrosia*, 344 Pa. at 647, 26 A.2d at 661).

RHODE ISLAND

A. STATUTE OF LIMITATIONS

A personal injury action must be brought within three years after the cause of action has accrued.[1] In the context of medical malpractice, Rhode Island has adopted the discovery rule whereby the statute of limitations does not begin to run until the plaintiff discovers or reasonably should have discovered the injury that forms the basis for the cause of action.[2] The three-year limitation is applicable to all personal injuries regardless of the nature of the cause of action.[3]

All civil actions involving product liability are subject to a ten-year statute of limitation commencing after the cause of action has accrued.[4] The cause of action accrues at the time the injury occurs.[5] Note, however, that where recovery for personal injuries is involved, the three-year statute of limitations as provided for in R.I. Gen. Laws Section 9-1-14 is applicable.[6]

In cases involving fraudulent concealment or fraudulent misrepresentation, the discovery rule applies, delaying the initiation date of the limitation period to the time when the person entitled to a potential recovery first discovers or reasonably should have first discovered the existence of the cause of action.[7]

Wrongful death actions are subject to a three-year statute of limitation, which begins to run at the time the wrongful act, neglect, or default is discovered or reasonably should have been discovered.[8]

Tort actions instituted against the state, a political subdivision, or a city or town in Rhode Island must be instituted within three years of the accrual of the claim.[9]

There is a ten-year statute of limitations for actions involving damage to real or personal property relating to architectural or professional engineering design, plan, or supervision of construction deficiencies.[10] Should such a cause of action involve damages for personal injuries, the three-year statute of limitations under R.I. Gen. Law Section 9-1-14 is applicable.[11]

Defamation actions involving slander are subject to a one-year statute of limitations.[12] Because the statutory language specifies one year for actions involving "words spoken," the limitation period for libel falls under the broader three-year limitation period as provided by Section 9-1-14(b).[13]

Actions involving contracts or liabilities under seal and actions on judgments or decrees of any court of record in the United States are subject to a 20-year statute of limitations.[14] However, contract actions not under seal are subject to a ten-year limitation period.[15]

Any civil causes of action not specifically provided for in the State Code are subject to a ten-year statute of limitation pursuant to the catch-all provision of R.I. Gen. Laws Section 9-1-13(a).

B. TORT REFORM

To date, the Rhode Island legislature has not passed any tort reform legislation. There are no tort reform bills currently pending.

C. MOTOR VEHICLE REPARATIONS ACT

Rhode Island requires motorists to be financially responsible for potential negligent acts.[16] Motor vehicle liability insurance, a financial security bond, a financial security deposit, or qualification as a self-insurer under either title 31 of the Rhode Island General Laws, or under the self-insurance provisions of laws in the jurisdiction of an out-of-state driver, satisfy this requirement.[17] Proof of financial responsibility is required whenever a motor vehicle is stopped by a police officer or is involved in an accident or a motor vehicle offense.[18]

The statutory minimum amount of policy or bond coverage needed to satisfy the financial responsibility requirement includes coverage of not less than $25,000 for bodily injury or death to one person in an accident, and not less than $50,000 for two individuals in one accident.[19] There is also a provision requiring coverage of not less than $25,000 for injury or destruction of property.[20] Although the insurer is required to provide uninsured motorist coverage, the named insured may sign an approved advisory notice acknowledging the hazard of uninsured/underinsured motorists and reject the uninsured provision if they are purchasing only the minimum required coverage.[21]

D. THE STANDARD FOR NEGLIGENCE

To establish a *prima facie* case for negligence under Rhode Island law, the plaintiff must prove that: (1) the defendant owed the plaintiff a legal duty to refrain from negligent activities; (2) that the defendant breached that duty; (3) the breach proximately caused harm to the plaintiff; and (4) that there was actual loss or damage resulting.[22] Unlike the federal rules, evidence of subsequent remedial measures is admissible.[23]

Legal Duty and Breach

A legal duty is a legal obligation requiring an individual to conform his/her actions to what is considered the ordinary standard of care in a given situation.[24] Ordinary care is the level of care a reasonably prudent person would exercise given the same set of circumstances.[25] The greater the level of risk, the higher the degree of care required to meet the standard.[26] For example, the ordinary duty of care to be exercised by a physician is the degree of care a physician in the same type of practice in a similar location would have exercised in the same situation.[27] Children of tender years are expected to exercise the same "degree of care as children of the same age, education, and experience would be expected to exercise in similar circumstances."[28]

To establish the existence of a legal duty between the plaintiff and the defendant, the court performs an ad hoc factual analysis. Among the factors taken into consideration are the relationship of the parties, the scope and burden of the obligation to be imposed on the defendant, public policy considerations, and the notion of fairness.[29] Because Rhode Island does not recognize more than one degree of negligence, allegations of negligence, gross negligence, and negligence *per se* are considered as one allegation.[30]

Rhode Island law requires the plaintiff to establish both the appropriate standard of care and that a deviation from that standard has occurred to proceed with the negligence inquiry.[31] A defendant cannot be found liable without a determination that a duty owed was breached.[32]

E. CAUSATION

To satisfy the causation requirement, Rhode Island law requires a showing that the breach of the duty owed is both the actual and the proximate cause.[33] In most cases, causation is established by showing that "but for the negligence of defendant the harm to plaintiff would not have occurred."[34] Proof of causation need not exclude all other possible causes as long as it is based on reasonable inferences derived from facts in evidence.[35]

F. CONTRIBUTORY NEGLIGENCE, COMPARATIVE NEGLIGENCE, ASSUMPTION OF THE RISK, AND LAST CLEAR CHANCE

1. Contributory Negligence

In Rhode Island, contributory negligence does not bar recovery in personal injury or injury to property actions.[36] The degree of contributory negligence is taken into consideration as an offset when calculating damages.[37] Contributory negligence does bar recovery under the Wrongful Death Act.[38]

2. Comparative Negligence

Actions involving personal injuries, death resulting from personal injuries, or injury to property are subject to the Rhode Island comparative negligence statute whereby contributory negligence shall reduce but not bar total recovery.[39] The rescue doctrine survived the adoption of the comparative negligence statute, making application of the statute appropriate only when the rescuer's actions are shown to have been rash or reckless.[40]

3. Assumption of the Risk

Assumption of the risk is available as an affirmative defense to bar or diminish a plaintiff's potential recovery.[41] A subjective standard is applied, requiring a determination that the plaintiff knew of and understood the extent of the risk he/she incurred and voluntarily exposed himself/herself to that risk based on what the plaintiff in fact saw, knew, understood, and appreciated.[42] Generally, a finding of assumed risk is to be made by the trier of fact and is not considered a question of law.[43]

4. **Last Clear Chance**

The Last Clear Chance Doctrine is recognized in Rhode Island.[44] To be applicable, "the plaintiff must have negligently placed himself or his property in a position of peril; that the defendant thereafter had become aware or in the exercise of due care ought to have become aware of plaintiff's peril and his lack of comprehension of it or apparent inability to extricate himself from it; that the defendant if he had been in the exercise of due care had a reasonable opportunity thereafter to avoid injuring the plaintiff; and that defendant failed to exercise such care."[45]

G. *RES IPSA LOQUITUR*

The doctrine of *res ipsa loquitur* permits a plaintiff to recover for defendant's negligence when circumstantial evidence provides a sufficient evidentiary basis for recovery.[46] Rhode Island has rejected the need to prove exclusive control of the instrumentality involved and adopted Restatement (Second) of Torts Section 328(D).[47] Therefore, the plaintiff bears the burden of providing evidence such that a reasonable man could say it was more likely than not that the defendant was negligent.[48]

H. **NEGLIGENCE** *PER SE*

Rhode Island does not recognize more than one degree of negligence.[49] Therefore, the applicable analysis for negligence *per se* is the same as that for negligence or gross negligence.[50]

I. **JOINT AND SEVERAL LIABILITY**

The Rhode Island Uniform Contribution Among Tortfeasors Act defines joint tortfeasors as "two (2) or more persons jointly or severally liable in tort for the same injury to person or property."[51] A party is liable in tort if he/she negligently contributed to another's injury.[52] Whether the parties contributed to the same injury requires consideration of "the time each party acted or failed to act and whether a party had the ability to guard against the negligence of the other."[53] For example, operators of two vehicles involved in the same automobile accident were found to be joint tortfeasors,[54] whereas the owner of a building where a plaintiff fell and the doctors who subsequently operated on her at distinctly separate times were not found to be joint tortfeasors.[55] By statute, individuals involved in a master-servant or principal-agent relationship are to be considered a single tortfeasor.[56]

The Act only addresses the relationship between defendant joint tortfeasors, not tortfeasor liability to an injured plaintiff.[57] A plaintiff may recover his/her total damages from one of the tortfeasors.[58] Pursuant to the Act, that tortfeasor may then seek contribution from a joint tortfeasor through a separate action or by impleading the tortfeasor,[59] provided his/her payment discharged the common liability or he/she paid more than his/her *pro rata* share.[60]

A release by the plaintiff of one tortfeasor does not discharge the remaining tortfeasors unless the release so provides, but the amount of consideration paid for the release reduces the claim against the remaining tortfeasors.[61] A settling joint tortfeasor who no longer has liability to any of the parties to a suit cannot be retained in the suit that was the basis for the release.[62]

J. INDEMNITY

Indemnity is an equitable right that arises "'where one person is exposed to liability by the wrongful acts of another in which he does not join' such that the indemnitor will be 'liable for the whole outlay and not just a pro rata share.'"[63] The right may be created expressly or impliedly by contract or it may arise as an equitable remedy to compel the primarily negligent party to pay damages assessed to a faultless individual.[64]

In Rhode Island, the right to indemnity has been statutorily preserved.[65] However, by statute, construction indemnity agreements in which a party seeks indemnification from another for the consequences of its own or its agent's negligence are invalid.[66] To bring a successful action for equitable indemnity three elements must be met: "First, the party seeking indemnity must be liable to a third party. Second, the prospective indemnitor must also be liable to the third party. Third, as between the prospective indemnitee and indemnitor, the obligation ought to be discharged by the indemnitor."[67]

K. BAR OF WORKERS' COMPENSATION STATUTE

Under the Rhode Island Workers' Compensation Act,[68] an injured employee who has received benefits under the Act is barred from pursuing any other right or remedy from the employer related to the covered injury.[69] An eligible employee is not required to show fault of another to receive benefits.[70] By statute, the defenses of employee negligence, coworker negligence, and assumption of the risk have been abrogated.[71]

Employees waive their common law rights to recovery from an employer subject to the Act, unless they provide written notice at the time of their contract of hire, specifically claiming that right, and then, within ten days, file a copy of that written notice with the Director of Labor.[72] Common law rights preserved by notice may subsequently be waived by the employee via written waiver notice to the employer or his/her agent.[73] The subsequent waiver will become effective five days after delivery of the written notice.[74]

An injured employee who has received or is receiving compensation benefits may still pursue recovery of damages from a legally liable third party.[75] The employee must have either agreed to reimburse his employer out of any such recovery or establish that his employer would not enter into such an agreement in order to exercise this right.[76] Should the employer refuse to enter into an agreement, the ultimate recovery from the tortfeasor should be reduced by the amount of the compensation benefits received.[77] Tortfeasor recovery that exceeds the amount paid in benefits is to be credited toward the employer's future compensation liability.[78]

L. PREMISES LIABILITY

A Rhode Island landowner has "a duty to exercise reasonable care toward persons reasonably expected to be on his or her premises."[79] Rhode Island law has officially rejected recognition of the common law categories of invitee and licensee.[80] With regard to trespassers, no duty of care other than to refrain from willful or wanton injury is owed.[81] To encourage public use of private lands, persons directly or indirectly invited or permitted to use private property for recreational use without charge are to be treated as trespassors.[82]

M. DRAM SHOP LIABILITY

Rhode Island's Liquor Liability Act[83] imposes liability for intoxication-related injuries on licensed alcoholic beverage servers and their agents, and those legally required to be licensed.[84] There is currently no policy holding social hosts accountable.[85]

Defendant liability arises for damages that occur when liquor is negligently served to a minor, is negligently served to a visibly intoxicated person, and when a reasonably prudent person in similar circumstances would know the individual being served is intoxicated or a minor.[86] A rebuttable presumption of negligence arises when there is proof of service of alcohol to a person under 21 without requesting identification.[87] Common law claims and defenses applicable to negligence based tort actions are not limited by the Act.[88] The police officer's rule is a viable affirmative defense.[89]

N. ECONOMIC LOSS

The economic loss doctrine is intended to bar recovery of purely economic losses through tort action when the basis of the loss arises from a breach of contract.[90] Rhode Island case law on the application of the doctrine is sparse. The most recent state Supreme Court opinion states that "if a defendant owes a duty of care to a third party that arises out of an existing contract, and the party to whom the duty is owed is injured, the injured party may bring a negligence action against the defendant even though the damages are purely economic."[91] Significantly, the court bars application of the doctrine to consumer transactions.[92]

O. FRAUD AND MISREPRESENTATION

The Rhode Island Superior Court Rules of Civil Procedure require assertions of fraud to be pled with particularity.[93] When used as a defense, fraud must be pled affirmatively or it is waived.[94] Fraud provides a sufficient basis for relief from judgment.[95]

To establish a prima facie case for fraud, deceit, or fraudulent misrepresentation, the plaintiff must show that: (1) there has been a fraudulent representation made; (2) with the intent to induce the plaintiff's reliance (or to deceive); and (3) that the plaintiff detrimentally relied on that misrepresentation.[96]

The elements required to prove negligent misrepresentation are: (1) that a material fact has been misrepresented; (2) that the person making the representation either knew it to be a misrepresentation, made the misrepresentation without knowledge of its truth or falsity, or made the representation under circumstances where he/she should have known of its falsity; (3) the representation must have been intended to induce another to act; and (4) an injury must have resulted from justifiable reliance on the misrepresentation.[97]

P. CONSUMER FRAUD STATUTES

Rhode Island's Deceptive Trade Practices Act[98] protects consumers from unfair methods of competition and unfair or deceptive acts or practices involving trade or commerce.[99] The Attorney General is empowered to bring an action for a temporary or permanent injunction with notice.[100] The court is empowered to grant injunctions and make any additional orders or judgments it deems necessary to "restore to any person in interest any moneys or property, real or personal, which may have been acquired by means of any practice . . . declared to be unlawful."[101] Private party actions are permitted under the Act.[102] All activities and businesses subject to state or federal regulatory monitoring are exempt from application of the Act.[103]

Q. PUNITIVE DAMAGES

Punitive damages are considered to be an extraordinary sanction available in only a narrowly defined set of circumstances.[104] To justify such an award, the moving party is required to produce "evidence of such willfulness, recklessness or wickedness, on the part of the party at fault, as amount[s] to criminality, which for the good of society and warning to the individual, ought to be punished."[105] There must be a showing of action having been taken with malice or in bad faith to warrant such punishment.[106]

Whether the moving party has met the requisite burden is a question of law for the court to decide.[107] If the burden has been met, plaintiff's entitlement to punitive damages is left to the trier of fact to decide.[108]

Because punitive damages are intended to punish malicious or intentional conduct and to deter the tortfeasor and others from similar conduct,[109] the tortfeasor's financial ability to pay is relevant for determining the appropriate amount of damages, but not for determining whether a punitive award is appropriate.[110]

Although the finder of fact determines the award, the trial justice may "set aside a punitive award if the award 'clearly appears to be excessive, or to represent the passion and prejudice of the jury rather than their unbiased judgment.'"[111] A new trial on damages may be ordered if the trial justice deems an award excessive, or the parties may agree to a remittitur.[112] Under no circumstances is a trial justice permitted to determine a damage award to be inadequate.[113]

R. WRONGFUL DEATH AND SURVIVORSHIP ACTIONS

Rhode Island's Wrongful Death Act,[114] in derogation of common law,[115] provides a means of recovery for the death of an individual in situations where the deceased would have been able to maintain a cause of action had he/she suffered an injury rather than loss of life.[116] Actions brought pursuant to the Act, other than for loss of consortium, must be brought by, and in the name of, the executor or administrator of the deceased. If there is no executor or administrator, or no action has been initiated within six months of the death, one or more of the beneficiaries may bring one action for the benefit of all the beneficiaries.[117] Action for loss of consortium must be brought by, and in the name of, the person or persons who suffered the loss.[118]

Causes of action under the Act survive the death of any person liable for damages.[119] Damages are to be measured by reducing the gross amount of the decedent's prospective income based on life expectancy by his/her estimated expenses.[120] That amount is then reduced to present value.[121] The statutory minimum recovery under the Wrongful Death Act Sections 10-7-1–10-7-4 is $150,000.[122] Distribution of recovered damages is statutorily prescribed.[123]

Mark O. Denehy
Linda A. Mayer
ADLER POLLOCK & SHEEHAN P.C.
2300 Financial Plaza
Providence, Rhode Island 02903
(401) 274-7200
Fax (401) 751-0604

ENDNOTES - RHODE ISLAND

1. R.I. Gen. Laws § 9-1-14(b) (1997).

2. *Wilkinson v. Harrington*, 243 A.2d 745, 753 (R.I. 1968).

3. *Pirri v. Toledo Scale Corp.*, 619 A.2d 429, 431 (R.I. 1993).

4. R.I. Gen. Laws § 9-1-13(a) (1997).

5. *Swift v. Ely Lilly & Co.*, 559 F. Supp. 621, 624 (D.R.I. 1982).

6. *Pirri*, 619 A.2d at 431.

7. R.I. Gen. Laws § 9-1-20 (1997).

8. R.I. Gen. Laws § 10-7-2 (Supp. 2001).

9. R.I. Gen. Laws § 9-1-25 (1997).

10. R.I. Gen. Laws § 9-1-29 (1997).

11. *Pirri*, 619 A.2d at 431.

12. R.I. Gen. Laws § 9-1-14(a) (1997).

13. *Mikaelin v. Drug Abuse Unit*, 501 A.2d 721, 723–24 (R.I. 1985).

14. R.I. Gen. Laws § 9-1-17 (1997).

15. R.I. Gen. Laws § 9-1-13(a) (1997).

16. R.I. Gen. Laws § 31-47-1(b) (2000).

17. R.I. Gen. Laws § 31-47-2(15) (2000). *See also* R.I. Gen. Laws § 31-47-12(d)(1)(4) (2002).

18. R.I. Gen. Laws § 31-47-12(e) (2000).

19. R.I. Gen. Laws § 31-31-7 (2000).

20. R.I. Gen. Laws § 27-7-2.1 (1998). *See also* R.I. Gen. Laws § 31-47-1.1(2) (2000).

21. R.I. Gen. Laws §§ 27-7-2.1(a) & (b) (1998).

22. *Liu v. Striuli*, 36 F. Supp. 2d 452 (D.R.I. 1999); *Munsill v. United States*, 14 F. Supp. 2d 214 (D.R.I. 1998); *Travelers Ins. Co. v. Priority Business Forms, Inc.*, 11 F. Supp. 2d 194 (D.R.I. 1998).

23. R.I. R. Evid. 407.

24. *Kuzniar v. Kuzniar*, 709 A.2d 1050, 1055 (R.I. 1998).

25. *Lawton v. Vadenais*, 122 A.2d 138, 141 (R.I. 1956).

26. *Welsh Mfg., Div. of Textron, Inc. v. Pinkerton's, Inc.*, 474 A.2d 436, 440 (R.I. 1984); *Lawton*, 122 A.2d at 141.

27. *Marshall v. Tomaselli*, 372 A.2d 1280, 1284 (R.I. 1977). *See also Benson v. New York, N.H. & H.R. Co.*, 49 A. 689, 692 (R.I. 1901) (standard of care is that of the average prudent man in the given profession or trade).

28. *Haddad v. First Nat'l Stores, Inc.*, 280 A.2d 93, 96 (R.I. 1971).

29. *Hennessey v. Pyne*, 694 A.2d 691, 697 (R.I. 1997). *See also Salmeron v. Nova*, 694 A.2d 709, 712–13 (R.I. 1997); *Kuzniar*, 709 A.2d at 1055.

30. *National Credit Union Admin. Bd. v. Regine*, 795 F. Supp. 59, 69 (D.R.I. 1992); *Wilson Auto Enterprises, Inc. v. Mobil Oil Corp.*, 778 F. Supp. 101, 104 (D.R.I. 1991).

31. *Bogosian v. Mercedes-Benz of North America*, 104 F.3d 472, 475 (1st Cir. 1997).

32. *Wilson Auto*, 778 F. Supp. at 104.

33. *Wells v. Uvex Winter Optical, Inc.*, 635 A.2d 1188, 1191 (R.I. 1994).

34. *Mullaney v. Goldman*, 398 A.2d 1133, 1136 (R.I. 1979). *See also Federal Express Corp. v. State of Rhode Island, Dep't of Transp.*, 664 F.2d 830, 837 (1st Cir. 1981); *Salk v. Alpine Ski Shop, Inc.*, 342 A.2d 622, 625 (R.I. 1975); *Evans v. Liguori*, 374 A.2d 774, 777 (R.I. 1977); *Schenck v. Roger Williams Gen. Hosp.*, 382 A.2d 514, 517 (R.I. 1977).

35. *Hill v. State*, 398 A.2d 1130, 1132 (R.I. 1979) (citations omitted).

36. R.I. Gen. Laws § 9-20-4 (1997).

37. *Raymond v. Jenard*, 390 A.2d 358, 360 (R.I. 1978).

38. *Commercial Union Ins. Co. v. Pelchat*, 727 A.2d 676, 681–82 (R.I. 1999); *Aetna Cas. & Sur. Co. v. Curley*, 585 A.2d 640, 642, 643 (R.I. 1991).

39. R.I. Gen. Laws § 9-20-4 (1997).

40. *Ouellette v. Carde*, 612 A.2d 687, 690 (R.I. 1992).

41. *Hennessey*, 694 A.2d at 699.

42. *Id.*; *Kennedy v. Providence Hockey Club, Inc.*, 376 A.2d 329, 332 (R.I. 1977).

43. *Hennessey*, 694 A.2d at 699 (citing *Labrie v. Pace Membership Warehouse, Inc.*, 678 A.2d 867, 872 (R.I. 1996)).

44. *Cinq-Mars v. Standard Cab Co.*, 235 A.2d 81, 84 (R.I. 1967); *Major v. Grieg*, 230 A.2d 846, 851 (R.I. 1967); *New England Pretzel Co. v. Palmer*, 67 A.2d 39, 42 (R.I. 1949).

45. *Cinq-Mars*, 235 A.2d at 84 (citing *New England Pretzel Co.*, 67 A.2d at 42). *See also Major*, 230 A.2d at 851–52.

46. *Parillo v. Giroux Co., Inc.*, 426 A.2d 1313, 1320 (R.I. 1981). *See also McLaughlin v. Moura*, 754 A.2d 95, 98 (R.I. 2000).

47. *Parillo*, 426 A.2d at 1320.

48. *Thomas v. Amway Corp.*, 488 A.2d 716, 722 (R.I. 1985).

49. *Wilson Auto*, 778 F. Supp. at 104.

50. *Id.*

51. R.I. Gen. Laws § 10-6-2 (1997).

52. *Lawrence v. Pokraka*, 606 A.2d 987, 988 (R.I. 1992) (citing *Wilson v. Krasnoff*, 560 A.2d 335, 340) (R.I. 1989).

53. *Id.*

54. *Hackett v. Hyson*, 48 A.2d 353 (R.I. 1946).

55. *Krasnoff*, 560 A.2d at 341.

56. R.I. Gen. Laws § 10-6-2 (1997).

57. *Krasnoff*, 560 A.2d at 340.

58. *Roberts-Robertson v. Lombardi*, 598 A.2d 1380, 1381 (R.I. 1991) (citation omitted).

59. *Id. See also* R.I. Gen. Laws §§ 10-6-3, -4 & -6 (1997).

60. R.I. Gen. Laws § 10-6-4 (1997).

61. R.I. Gen. Laws § 10-6-7 (1997).

62. *Cooney v. Molis*, 640 A.2d 527, 530 (R.I. 1994).

63. *Hawkins v. Gadoury*, 713 A.2d 799, 803 (R.I. 1998) (citing *Helgerson v. Mammoth Mart, Inc.*, 335 A.2d 339, 341 (R.I. 1975)).

64. *Helgerson*, 335 A.2d at 341.

65. R.I. Gen. Laws § 10-6-9 (1997).

66. R.I. Gen. Laws § 6-34-1 (2001).

67. *Fish v. Burns Bros. Donut Shop, Inc.*, 617 A.2d 874, 875 (R.I. 1992) (citing *Muldowney v. Weatherking Products, Inc.*, 509 A.2d 441, 443 (R.I. 1986)).

68. R.I. Gen. Laws §§ 28-29-1–38 (2000).

69. R.I. Gen. Laws § 28-29-20 (2000); *DiQuinzio v. Panciera Lease Co., Inc.*, 612 A.2d 40, 42 (R.I. 1992).

70. *DiQuinzio*, 612 A.2d at 42.

71. R.I. Gen. Laws § 28-29-3 (2000).

72. R.I. Gen. Laws § 28-29-17 (2000).

73. R.I. Gen. Laws § 28-29-19 (2000).

74. *Id.*

75. R.I. Gen. Laws § 28-35-58 (2000).

76. *Colarusso v. Mills*, 208 A.2d 381, 385 (R.I. 1965). *See also Commercial Union Cos. v. Graham*, 495 A.2d 243, 245 (R.I. 1985).

77. *Id.*

78. *Rison v. Air Filter Systems, Inc.*, 707 A.2d 675, 683 (R.I. 1998); R.I. Gen. Laws § 28-35-58 (1995).

79. *Ferreira v. Strack*, 636 A.2d 682, 685 (R.I. 1994).

80. *Tantimonico v. Allendale Mut. Ins. Co.*, 637 A.2d 1056, 1058 (R.I. 1994) (citing *Mariorenzi v. Joseph DiPonte, Inc.*, 333 A.2d 127, 133 (R.I. 1975) (rejecting all three common law categories)).

81. *Tantimonico*, 637 A.2d at 1060, 1061.

82. *Id.*; R.I. Gen. Laws § 32-6-3 (1994). *See generally* R.I. Gen. Laws §§ 32-6-1–6 (1994).

83. R.I. Gen. Laws §§ 3-14-1–14 (1998).

84. R.I. Gen Laws § 3-14-5 (1998).

85. *Ferreira v. Strack*, No. NC 890089, 1992 WL 813593, at *2 (R.I. Super. 1992).

86. R.I. Gen. Laws § 3-14-6 (1998).

87. R.I. Gen. Laws § 3-14-6(e) (1998).

88. R.I. Gen. Laws § 3-14-9 (1998). *See also Smith v. Tully*, 665 A.2d 1333, 1336 (R.I. 1995).

89. *Tully*, 665 A.2d at 1336.

90. *Gail Frances, Inc. v. Alaska Diesel Elec., Inc.*, 62 F. Supp. 2d 511, 518 (D.R.I. 1999).

91. *Rousseau v. K.N. Const., Inc.*, 727 A.2d 190, 192 (R.I. 1999).

92. *Id.* at 193.

93. R.I. Super. R. Civ. P. 9.

94. R.I. Super. R. Civ. P. 8(c). *See also Rhode Island Hosp. Trust Nat'l Bank v. DeBeru*, 553 A.2d 544, 547 (R.I. 1989).

95. R.I. Super. R. Civ. P. 60(b).

96. *Asermely v. Allstate Ins. Co.*, 728 A.2d 461, 464 (R.I. 1999); *Travers v. Spidell*, 682 A.2d 471, 473 (R.I. 1996); *Cliftex Clothing Co. v. DiSanto*, 148 A.2d 273, 275 (R.I. 1959).

97. *Mallette v. Children's Friend and Service*, 661 A.2d 67, 69 (R.I. 1995).

98. R.I. Gen. Laws §§ 6-13.1-1–27 (2001).

99. R.I. Gen. Laws §§ 6-13.1-1(4) & (5) (2001).

100. R.I. Gen. Laws § 6-13.1-5(a) (2001).

101. R.I. Gen. Laws § 6-13.1-5(c) (2001).

102. R.I. Gen. Laws § 6-13.1-5.2 (2001).

103. *Doyle v. Chihoski*, 443 A.2d 1243, 1244 (R.I. 1982); *State v. Piedmont Funding Corp.*, 382 A.2d 819, 822 (R.I. 1978).

104. *Palmisano v. Toth*, 624 A.2d 314, 318 (R.I. 1993); *Berberian v. New England Tel. & Tel. Co.*, 369 A.2d 1109, 1112 (R.I. 1977).

105. *Palmisano*, 624 A.2d at 318 (citations omitted); *Sherman v. McDermott*, 329 A.2d 195, 196 (R.I. 1974).

106. *Id.*

107. *Sherman*, 329 A.2d at 196.

108. *Id. See also Palmisano*, 624 A.2d at 318.

109. *Palmisano*, 624 A.2d at 317–18.

110. *Sherman*, 329 A.2d at 197.

111. *Palmisano*, 624 A.2d at 318 (citing *Zarrella v. Robinson*, 460 A.2d 415, 418–19 (R.I. 1983)).

112. *Palmisano*, 624 A.2d at 318.

113. *Id.*

114. R.I. Gen. Laws §§ 10-7-1–14 (1997).

115. *Pelchat*, 727 A.2d at 681.

116. R.I. Gen. Laws § 10-7-1 (1997).

117. R.I. Gen. Laws § 10-7-3 (1997).

118. R.I. Gen. Laws § 10-7-2 (Supp. 2001).

119. R.I. Gen. Laws §§ 10-7-4 & -8 (1997).

120. R.I. Gen. Laws § 10-7-1.1 (1997).

121. *Id.*

122. R.I. Gen. Laws § 10-7-2 (Supp. 2001).

123. *Id.*

SOUTH CAROLINA

A. STATUTES OF LIMITATION

Claims for personal injury, injury to property, wrongful death, assault and battery, and fraud must be brought within three years.[1] Claims for false imprisonment must be brought within two years.[2] The "discovery" rule applies to all cases concerning any personal injury or injury to the rights of another.[3] The beginning of the tolling period for the statutes of limitation is the time the cause of action accrued.[4]

Causes of action based upon a contract must be brought within three years. The "discovery" rule also applies to contract claims.[5]

Defamation actions must be brought within two years from the time of the statement,[6] while actions for invasion of privacy must be brought within three years.[7] Causes of action based on bonds which are secured by a mortgage of real property must be brought within 20 years.[8]

The Statute of limitations for actions based on sexual abuse or incest is six years from the time a person becomes 21 or within three years of discovering the injury and the causal relationship between the injury and the abuse or incest.[9] A lawsuit based on abuse or incest previously brought and barred by the statue of limitations may be brought within three years of the Act's effective date, which was August 8, 2001.[10]

Causes of action brought under the South Carolina Unfair Trade Practices Act[11] have a three-year statue of limitation.[12]

Actions involving improvements to real property are subject to a 13-year statute of repose.[13]

Causes of action against the state or local governments must be brought within two years.[14]

B. TORT REFORM

With the exception of capping damages recoverable from government entities, the South Carolina legislature has not passed any tort reform laws, as commonly understood.

C. "NO FAULT" LIMITATIONS

As of the current date, the South Carolina legislature has not passed any laws limiting insurance compensation for injuries resulting from motor vehicle accidents. South Carolina's version of the Motor Vehicle Financial Responsibility Law[15] provides for uninsured motorist coverage.[16]

D. THE STANDARD FOR NEGLIGENCE

In a suit for negligence in South Carolina, the plaintiff must show that the defendant owed the plaintiff a duty of due care, that the defendant breached this duty, and that this breach of duty proximately injured the plaintiff. The question of the existence of a duty is a legal question, to be decided by the court; however, there are no explicit criteria to be used in determining the existence of a duty.[17] A duty may arise from statute, contract, or by operation of law, based upon the relationship of the parties. In order to show a breach of the duty of due care, a plaintiff must demonstrate that the defendant failed to take reasonable precautions in response to a foreseeable risk.[18]

Where one has reason to foresee that a person may pose a threat of harm to another, there may be a duty to act to prevent the harm.[19]

In South Carolina, a person fourteen years old or older is held to an adult standard,[20] while a child below 14 years of age is held to the standard of a reasonable child of the same age.[21]

E. CAUSATION

In order to establish negligence in South Carolina, a plaintiff must prove that the defendant's breach of the duty of care was the cause-in-fact of the injury[22] and also that the breach was the proximate cause, often referred to as the legal cause, of the injury.[23] South Carolina follows the doctrine that negligent conduct proximately causes an injury if the injury is within the scope of foreseeable risks associated with the conduct.[24]

F. CONTRIBUTORY NEGLIGENCE, COMPARATIVE NEGLIGENCE, AND ASSUMPTION OF RISK

1. Contributory Negligence

South Carolina case law has abandoned the traditional common law doctrine of contributory negligence, in favor of the rule of comparative negligence. Under South Carolina's comparative negligence system, the plaintiff may recover unless he/she is more than 50 percent at fault.[25]

2. Comparative Negligence

Under South Carolina common law, the doctrine of comparative negligence applies to all negligence claims arising on or after July 1, 1991.[26] The plaintiff may recover damages if the plaintiff's negligence is not greater than that of the defendant. The plaintiff's recovery is reduced in proportion to the amount of the plaintiff's negligence. If the plaintiff's negligence is found, as a matter of law, to be greater than that of the defendant's, the defendant is entitled to judgment as a matter of law.[27] Comparative negligence likely does not apply where the defendant is guilty of recklessness or willful or wanton misconduct.[28] Also, comparative negligence might not apply to a strict liability claim. This question has not been specifically addressed, but the pre-comparative negligence common law rule was that contributory negligence did not apply to strict liability.[29]

3. **Assumption of Risk**

Under traditional South Carolina common law, a victim's assumption of risk served as a complete bar to suit for any injury resulting from this assumption.[30] For all claims arising after November 9, 1998, however, assumption of risk, will be considered as another factor in determining comparative negligence, rather than as an absolute bar to recovery.[31] Implied assumption of risk is an issue for a jury, unless the facts support only one inference.[32] An express assumption of risk, such as by contract, still acts as a complete bar to recovery.[33] In order to establish the defense of assumption of risk, a defendant must satisfy four requirements: (1) the plaintiff must have knowledge of the facts constituting a dangerous condition; (2) the plaintiff must know the condition is dangerous; (3) the plaintiff must appreciate the nature and extent of the danger; and (4) the plaintiff must voluntarily expose himself to the danger.[34]

G. *RES IPSA LOQUITUR* AND CIRCUMSTANTIAL EVIDENCE

South Carolina courts do not apply the doctrine of *res ipsa loquitur* in negligence cases.[35] However, negligence may be proved through the use of circumstantial evidence, in addition to direct evidence.[36] Circumstantial evidence must support a reasonable inference of the fact for which it is offered. [37]

H. NEGLIGENCE PER SE

South Carolina recognizes the doctrine of negligence *per se*; that is, violation of a statute or regulation is conclusive proof of negligence.[38] Four requirements must be shown in order for negligence *per se* to apply: (1) that a duty of due care existed;[39] (2) that the statute was breached;[40] (3) that the statute provided the applicable standard of care in that the injury was within the scope of that to be prevented by the statute or regulation, and that there was no legislative intent to exclude such use;[41] and (4) that there was no justification or excuse for violating the statute.[42]

I. JOINT AND SEVERAL LIABILITY, CONTRIBUTION

South Carolina courts follow the common law rule that joint tortfeasors are jointly and severally liable to a plaintiff.[43] Under the South Carolina Contribution Among Tortfeasors Act, ("Contribution Act"),[44] joint tortfeasors are "two or more persons [who] become jointly or severally liable in tort for the same injury to person or property . . . ."[45] The phrase "joint tortfeasor" is a term of art applying to persons who acted together and to persons who acted independently, but whose actions have "joined" to injure the plaintiff.[46] The plaintiff may elect to sue the defendants together in one suit, or individually in separate suits.[47]

South Carolina follows the view that a "release of one tortfeasor does not release others who wrongfully contributed to plaintiff's injuries unless this was the intention of the parties, or unless plaintiff has, in fact, received full compensation amounting to satisfaction."[48] While a non-settling defendant is not released, his/her liability is reduced by the amount of the settlement.[49] Under the Contribution Act, the right of contribution exists "only in favor of a tortfeasor who has paid more than his pro rata share of the common liability, and his total recovery is limited to the amount paid by him in excess of his pro rata share."[50]

Where a plaintiff initiates separate suits against multiple tortfeasors, the plaintiff is limited to only one full recovery for his injury.[51]

J. INDEMNITY

South Carolina recognizes the doctrine of indemnity.[52] Indemnification may arise from a contract, or in equity. Equitable indemnity requires that the party seeking indemnity be free of any fault. There is no right of indemnity between joint tortfeasors.[53] The South Carolina Contribution Act, as noted above, provides for allocating among defendants based on general pro rata principles.[54]

K. BAR OF WORKERS' COMPENSATION STATUTE

Under the South Carolina Workers' Compensation Act,[55] an employee who avails himself of the rights and remedies available under the Act is excluded from pursuing any other rights or remedies available against his employer.[56] However, the receipt of benefits does not prohibit an employee from suing a third party for damages.[57]

If a carrier has payed benefits to an employee under the Act, and that employee successfully sues a third party for damages, the carrier has a lien on the proceeds of any recovery from the third party, to the extent of the total amount of compensation, less expenses, including attorney's fees.[58] A carrier does not necessarily have the right to intervene in an action against a third party; however, if an employee settles for less than the amount paid in benefits, the carrier may pursue a separate action against the third party to recover the total compensation paid.[59]

South Carolina's Workers' Compensation Act serves as the exclusive remedy for personal injury to an employee arising from accidents in the course of employment.[60] However, this exclusivity does not apply to nonpersonal injuries, such as defamation,[61] or intentional harm to the employee, on the theory that these are not "accidental" injuries.[62]

L. PREMISES LIABILITY

South Carolina follows the traditional system that an owner or occupier of land owes varying degrees of care to different categories of persons.[63] If the person who comes on an owner's premises is an adult trespasser, the owner does not have to exercise due care, but must merely refrain from intentional injury or willful or wanton conduct.[64] An owner does not owe a licensee, or one who is on the premises with permission of the owner, a duty of due care, but does owe the licensee the duty to warn him of any concealed dangers which are known to the owner.[65] An owner owes an invitee a duty of due care to discover threats to the invitee and warn of or eliminate unreasonable risks.[66]

M. DRAM SHOP LIABILITY

South Carolina prohibits businesses with a license to sell alcohol from selling alcohol to a visibly intoxicated person, and allows third-party claims against tavern owners violating this prohibition.[67] However, South Carolina does not recognize "first party" actions against tavern owners by intoxicated persons.[68] While there is not a similar prohibition against social hosts, a social host may have a duty to use due care in the provision of alcohol to guests.[69]

N. ECONOMIC AND BUSINESS TORTS

South Carolina recognizes claims for tortious interference with contractual relations,[70] tortious interference with prospective contractual relations,[71] and civil conspiracy.[72]

O. FRAUD AND MISREPRESENTATION

The South Carolina Rules of Civil Procedure require that a plaintiff plead a claim for fraud with particularity.[73]

In order to state a claim for fraud, a plaintiff must allege the following elements, which must be proved by clear, cogent and convincing evidence: (1) a representation; (2) its falsity; (3) its materiality; (4) either knowledge of its falsity or a reckless disregard of its truth or falsity; (5) intent that the representation be acted upon; (6) the hearer's ignorance of its falsity; (7) the hearer's reliance on its truth; (8) the hearer's right to rely thereon; and (9) the hearer's consequent and proximate injury.[74]

In order to succeed in a cause of action for negligent misrepresentation, a plaintiff must establish the following elements: (1) the defendant made a false representation to the plaintiff; (2) the defendant had a pecuniary interest in making the statement; (3) the defendant owed a duty of care to see that he communicated truthful information to the plaintiff; (4) the defendant breached that duty by failing to exercise due care; (5) the plaintiff justifiably relied on the representation; and (6) the plaintiff suffered a pecuniary loss as the proximate result of his reliance upon the representation.[75]

Because the elements of negligent misrepresentation are similar to fraud, these elements likely must be plead with particularity.[76]

P. UNFAIR TRADE CLAIMS

The South Carolina Unfair Trade Practices Act (UTPA)[77] protects against unfair methods of competition and unfair or deceptive acts or practices in the conduct of trade or commerce.[78] The Act provides a private remedy, whereby an injured party may bring a civil action upon sustaining an ascertainable loss as a result of unfair or deceptive trade practices. The conduct must have an adverse impact upon the public, or be capable of repetition.[79]

Causes of action under UTPA must be brought within three years.[80]

Q. PUNITIVE DAMAGES

In South Carolina, punitive damages are awarded when the plaintiff proves, through clear and convincing evidence, that a defendant's conduct was reckless, willful, wanton, or malicious.[81] Punitive damages may not be based on simple negligence.

Before punitive damages may be awarded, there must be an award for either actual damages[82] or an award for nominal or presumed damages.[83] Punitive damages may be limited by statute.[84] Where punitive damages are not limited by statue, South Carolina courts follow an eight factor test to ensure that punitive damage awards comply with due process: (1) defendant's degree of culpability; (2) duration of the conduct; (3) defendant's awareness or concealment; (4) the existence of similar past conduct; (5) likelihood the award will deter the defendant or others from like conduct; (6) whether the award is reasonably related to the harm likely to result from such conduct; (7) defendant's ability to pay; and (8) other factors deemed appropriate.[85]

R. **WRONGFUL DEATH AND SURVIVAL ACTIONS**

South Carolina provides for recovery for wrongful death under the South Carolina Wrongful Death Act.[86] Recovery for the conscious pain and suffering of the decedent is available under the Survival statute. Because wrongful death and survival actions involve different and independent statutory claims, the two causes of action may not be joined into one cause of action.[87]

A wrongful death cause of action may be brought only by the legally appointed executor or administrator of the estate of the deceased, and is brought for the benefit of the statutory beneficiaries.[88] Any award passes to these statutory beneficiaries. Survival actions may be brought by the executor or administrator of the Estate, for injuries suffered by the decedent prior to death. Recovery in a survival action goes to the Estate.[89]

Val H. Stieglitz
NEXSEN PRUET JACOBS & POLLARD, L.L.P.
1441 Main Street, Suite 1500
Columbia, South Carolina 29201
(803) 771-8900
Fax (803) 253-8277
vstieglitz@npjp.com
www.npjp.com

ENDNOTES - SOUTH CAROLINA

1. S.C. Code Ann. § 15-3-530, 15-3-535 (Law. Co-op. Supp. 1996); 2001 S.C. Acts 102, § 1.

2. S.C. Code Ann. § 15-3-550 (Law. Co-op. 1976).

3. S.C. Code Ann. § 15-3-535 (Law. Co-op. Supp. 1996).

4. S.C. Code Ann. § 15-3-20 (Law. Co-op. Supp. 1976).

5. S.C. Code Ann. § 15-3-530 (Law. Co-op. Supp. 1996).

6. S.C. Code Ann. § 15-3-550 (Law. Co.-op. 1976); *Jones v. City of Folly Beach*, 326 S.C. 360, 483 S.E.2d 770 (Ct. App. 1997).

7. S.C. Code Ann. § 15-3-530 (Law. Co.-op. Supp. 1996).

8. S.C. Code Ann. § 15-3-520 (Law. Co.-op. 1976).

9. S.C. Code Ann. § 15-3-555 (Law. Co.-op. 2001); 2001 S.C. Acts 102, § 3.

10. 2001 S.C. Acts 102, § 4.

11. S.C. Code Ann. § 39-5-10 *et seq.* (Law. Co-op. 1976).

12. S.C. Code Ann. § 39-5-150 (Law. Co.-op. 1976).

13. S.C. Code Ann. § 15-3–640 (Law. Co.-op. 1976).

14. S.C. Code Ann. § 15-78-110 (Law. Co.-op. 1976).

15. S.C. Code Ann. § 38-77-150 (Law. Co.-op. Supp. 1997).

16. *Id.*

17. *Araujo v. Southern Bell Telephone and Telephone Co.*, 291 S.C. 54, 57-58, 351 S.E.2d 908 (Ct. App. 1986); *Arthurs v. Aiken County*, 338 S.C. 253, 525 S.E.2d 542 (Ct. App. 1999).

18. *See Bass v. Farr*, 315 S.C. 400, 434 S.E.2d 274 (1993).

19. *See Mickle v. Blackmon*, 252 S.C. 202, 166 S.E.2d 173 (1969), *appeal after remand*, 255 S.C. 136, 177 S.E.2d 548 (1970).

20. *McCormick v. Campbell*, 285 S.C. 272, 329 S.E.2d 752 (1985); *Dalon v. Golden Lanes, Inc.*, 320 S.C. 534, 466 S.E.2d 368 (Ct. App. 1996).

21. *Standard v. Shine*, 278 S.C. 337, 295 S.E.2d 786 (1982); *Brown v. Smalls*, 325 S.C. 547, 481 S.E.2d 449 (Ct. App. 1997).

22. *See Hughes v. Children's Clinic, P.A.*, 269 S.C. 389, 237 S.E.2d 753 (1977); *Accordini v. Security Cent., Inc.*, 283 S.C. 16, 320 S.E.2d 713 (Ct. App. 1984).

23. *See Bramlette v. Charter-Medical-Columbia*, 302 S.C. 68, 393 S.E.2d 914 (1990).

24. *See Young v. Tide Craft, Inc.*, 270 S.C. 453, 242 S.E.2d 671 (1978).

25. *Nelson v. Concrete Supply Co.*, 303 S.C. 243, 399 S.E.2d 783 (1991).

26. *Id.*

27. *Id.*

28. *See Orangeburg Sausage Co. v. Cincinnati Insurance Co.*, 316 S.C. 331, 450 S.E.2d 66 (Ct. App. 1994); *Cooper v. County of Florence*, 306 S.C. 408, 412 S.E.2d 417 (1991).

29. *See Wallace v. Owens-Illinois, Inc.*, 300 S.C. 518, 389 S.E.2d 155 (Ct. App. 1989).

30. *See Turner v. Sinclair Ref. Co.*, 254 S.C. 36, 173 S.E.2d 356 (1970).

31. *Davenport v. Cotton Hope Plantation Horizontal Property Regime*, 333 S.C. 71, 508 S.E.2d 565 (1998).

32. *See, e.g., Baxley v. Rosenblum*, 303 S.C. 340, 400 S.E.2d 502 (Ct. App. 1991).

33. *Id.*

34. *Id.*

35. *See, e.g., Legette v. Smith*, 265 S.C. 573, 220 S.E.2d 429 (1975); *Nguyen v. Uniflex Corp.*, 312 S.C. 417, 440 S.E.2d 887 (Ct. App. 1994).

36. *Chaney v. Burgess*, 246 S.C. 261, 143 S.E.2d 521 (1965).

37. *See, e.g., McQuillen v. Dobbs*, 262 S.C. 386, 204 S.E.2d 732 (1974).

38. *See, e.g., Wise v. Broadway*, 315 S.C. 273, 433 S.E.2d 857 (1993).

39. *See, e.g., Seals v. Winburn*, 314 S.C. 416, 445 S.E.2d 94 (Ct. App. 1994).

40. *See, e.g., Still v. Blake*, 255 S.C. 95, 177 S.E.2d 469 (1970).

41. *See, e.g., Coleman v. Shaw*, 281 S.C. 107, 314 S.E.2d 154 (Ct. App. 1984); *Smith v. Haynsworth, Marion, McKay & Guerard*, 322 S.C. 433, 472 S.E.2d 612 (1996).

42. *See, e.g., State v. Rochelle*, 310 S.C. 20, 425 S.E.2d 32 (1993).

43. *See, e.g., Christiansen v. Campbell*, 285 S.C. 164, 328 S.E.2d 351 (Ct. App. 1985) overruled on other grounds by *Tobias v. Sports Club, Inc.*, 332 S.C. 90, 504 S.E.2d 318 (1998).

44. S.C. Code Ann. § 15-38-10 *et seq.* (Law. Co.-op. Supp. 1996).

45. S.C. Code Ann. § 15-38-20 (Law. Co.-op. Supp. 1996).

46. *See, e.g., Pendleton v. Columbia Ry., Gas & Elec. Co.*, 133 S.C. 326, 131 S.E. 265 (1926).

47. *See supra* note 43.

48. *Bartholomew v. McCartha*, 255 S.C. 489, 492, 179 S.E.2d 912 (1971); *Trustees of Grace Episcopal Church v. Charleston Insurance Co.*, 868 F.Supp. 128 (D.S.C. 1994). *See also*, S.C. Code Ann. § 15-38-50(1) (Law. Co.-op. Supp. 1996).

49. *See, e.g., Scott v. Fruehauf Corp.*, 302 S.C. 364, 396 S.E.2d 354 (1990).

50. S.C. Code Ann. § 15-38-20(B) (Law. Co.-op. 1996).

51. *See E.A. Prince & Sons, Inc. v. Selective Insurance Co.*, 818 F. Supp. 910 (D.S.C. 1993).

52. *See* S.C. Code Ann. § 15-38-20(F) (Law. Co.-op. 1996).

53. *Atlantic Coast Line Railroad Co. v. Whetstone*, 243 S.C. 61, 132 S.E.2d 172 (1963); *See, e.g., Town of Winnsboro v. Weidman-Singleton, Inc.*, 307 S.C. 128, 414 S.E.2d 118 (1992).

54. S.C. Code Ann. § 15-38-20 (Law. Co.-op. 1976).

55. S.C. Code Ann. § 42-1-10 *et seq.* (Law. Co.-op. 1976).

56. S.C. Code Ann. § 42-1-540 (Law. Co.-op. 1976).

57. S.C. Code Ann. § 42-1-560 (Law. Co.-op. 1976).

58. S.C. Code Ann. § 42-1-560 (Law. Co.-op. 1976).

59. *Id.*

60. S.C. Code Ann. § 42-1-540 (Law. Co.-op. 1976).

61. *See, e.g., Loges v. Mack Trucks, Inc.*, 308 S.C. 134, 417 S.E.2d 538 (1992).

62. *See, e.g., McSwain v. SHEI*, 304 S.C. 25, 402 S.E.2d 890 (1991).

63. *See, e.g., Neil v. Byrum*, 288 S.C. 472, 343 S.E.2d 615 (1986).

64. *See, e.g., Nettles v. Your Ice Co.*, 191 S.C. 429, 4 S.E.2d 797 (1939).

65. *Neil v. Byrum*, 288 S.C. 472, 343 S.E.2d 615 (1986); *Miletic v. Wal-Mart Stores, Inc.*, 339 S.C. 327, 529 S.E.2d 68 (Ct. App. 2000).

66. *See, e.g., Shipes v. Piggly Wiggly St. Andrews, Inc.*, 269 S.C. 479, 238 S.E.2d 167 (1977).

67. S.C. Code Ann. § 61-4-580 (Law. Co.-op. Supp. 1997); *see Tobias v. Sports Club, Inc.*, 332 S.C. 90, 504 S.E.2d 318 (1998).

68. *Tobias v. Sports Club, Inc.*, 332 S.C. 90, 504 S.E.2d 318 (1998).

69. *See, e.g., Ballou v. Sigma Nu Gen. Fraternity*, 291 S.C. 140, 352 S.E.2d 488 (Ct. App. 1986).

70. *See First Union Mortgage Corp. v. Thomas*, 317 S.C. 63, 451 S.E.2d 907 (Ct. App. 1994).

71. *See Crandall Corp. v. Navistar International Transp. Corp.*, 302 S.C. 265, 395 S.E.2d 179 (1990).

72. *See Gynecology Clinic, Inc. v. Cloer*, 334 S.C. 555, 514 S.E.2d 592 (1999).

73. S.C. R. Civ. P. 9(b).

74. *Kahn Construction Co. v. South Carolina National Bank of Charleston*, 275 S.C. 381, 384, 271 S.E.2d 414 (1980).

75. *AMA Management Corp. v. Strasburger*, 309 S.C. 213, 222, 420 S.E.2d 868, 874 (Ct. App. 1992).

76. *See, e.g., Pitten v. Jacobs*, 903 F. Supp. 937 (D.S.C. 1995).

77. S.C. Code Ann. § 39-5-10 *et seq.* (Law Co.-op. 1976).

78. S.C. Code Ann. § 39-5-20 (Law. Co.-op. 1976).

79. *See NOACK Enterprises, Inc. v. Country Corner Interiors of Hilton Head, Inc.*, 290 S.C. 475, 351 S.E.2d 347 (1986).

80. S.C. Code Ann. § 39-5-150 (Law. Co.-op. 1976).

81. *See, e.g., Gilbert v. Duke Power Co.*, 255 S.C. 495, 179 S.E.2d 720 (1971).

82. *Prickett v. A&B Electrical Service, Inc.*, 280 S.C. 123, 311 S.E.2d 402 (1984).

83. *See O'Neal v. Carolina Farm Supply of Johnston, Inc.*, 279 S.C. 490, 309 S.E.2d 776 (Ct. App. 1983).

84. *See, e.g.,* S.C. Code Ann. § 39-5-140(a) (Law. Co.-op. 1976).

85. *Gamble v. Stevenson*, 305 S.C. 104, 111-112, 406 S.E.2d 350, 354 (1991).

86. S.C. Code Ann. § 15-51-10 *et seq.* (Law. Co.-op. 1976).

87. *Grainger v. Greenville, Spartanburg & Anderson Railway*, 101 S.C. 399, 85 S.E. 968 (1915).

88. S.C. Code Ann. § 15-51-20 (Law. Co.-op. 1976).

89. S.C. Code Ann. § 15-5-90 (Law. Co.-op. 1976).

SOUTH DAKOTA

A. **STATUTES OF LIMITATION**

The following is a list of causes of action and the time available to bring such a claim:

Cause of Action	Statute of Limitations
Personal injury	3 years[1]
Product liability	3 years[2]
General breach of contract	6 years[3]
Trespass	6 years[4]
Claim against sheriff or coroner	3 years[5]
Medical malpractice	2 years[6]
Legal and accountant malpractice	3 years[7]
Libel or Slander	2 years[8]
Assault, Battery, False Imprisonment	2 years[9]
Federal Civil Rights	3 years[10]
Breach of contract for sale of goods	4 years[11]

In South Dakota, the occurrence rule governs legal,[12] accounting,[13] and medical malpractice.[14] Continuous representation tolls the statute of limitations in professional malpractice cases.[15] The statute of limitations is also tolled in all cases for fraudulent concealment. In fraud cases the discovery rule applies.[16]

B. **TORT REFORM**

The lone piece of legislation concerning tort reform in South Dakota concerns general damages in medical malpractice cases. According to statute, general damages in a medical malpractice action are capped at $500,000, but there is no limitation on the amount of special damages that may be awarded.[17]

C. **MOTOR VEHICLE INSURANCE**

Under South Dakota's Financial Responsibility law, vehicles are required to have liability coverage limits of at least $25,000 for each person injured, up to an aggregate limit of $50,000 for each accident.[18] The same minimum coverage limits apply for uninsured[19] and underinsured[20] coverage. However, coverage required for underinsured and uninsured motorists may not exceed limits of $100,000 for injury or death to one person, and $300,000 for injury to two or more persons unless additional coverage is requested by the insured. Policies insuring government owned vehicles are not required to provide underinsured motorist coverage.[21]

Regardless of the number of vehicles involved, persons covered, or vehicles or premium shown on the policy, the limits of liability of uninsured and underinsured coverage for two or more vehicles insured under the same policy cannot be "stacked."[22] Physical contact is not a prerequisite for underinsured motorist or uninsured motorist coverage.[23]

South Dakota repealed its guest statute in1978, thereby permitting a passenger in a vehicle to sue a negligent driver. Household, or family, exclusion provisions of motor vehicle insurance policies are void only as to the minimum statutory requirements outlined above.[24]

D. THE STANDARD FOR NEGLIGENCE

A successful plaintiff in a negligence action must satisfy three elements: (1) a duty on the part of defendant; (2) failure to meet that duty; and (3) injury to plaintiff resulting from the failure to perform the duty.[25]

Foreseeability is a factor in determining both the duty and causation elements of a negligence claim.[26] Foreseeability in the duty context is to be viewed from the time the act or omission occurred and for causation from the time the damage was done.[27]

A duty is defined as an obligation "'to conform to a particular standard of conduct toward another.'"[28] South Dakota recognizes a professional standard of care.[29] Expert testimony is required to establish the standard.[30] The standard of care for children is subjective and involves consideration of the conduct of children of like age, intelligence, experience, and capacity.[31]

South Dakota abides by the "special relationship" or "special duty" rule which invokes a standard of care for situations in which normally a duty does not exist.[32]

Finally, a negligence claimant must establish that defendant's breach of duty caused injury or damage.[33] The harm or injury suffered must have been foreseeable to establish proximate cause.[34] The negligent act must "be a substantial factor in bringing about the harm."[35]

E. NEGLIGENCE DEFENSES

1. Contributory/Comparative Negligence

In actions for personal injury or damage to property caused by the negligence of another, the fact that the injured party was contributorily negligent does not operate as a bar on recovery if the contributory negligence was "slight" in comparison with the defendant's negligence. However, in such a case, damages shall be reduced in proportion to the amount of the plaintiff's contributory negligence.[36]

If, on the other hand, a plaintiff's contributory negligence is more than "slight" in relation to the negligence of defendant, plaintiff may not recover anything.[37] For purposes of this rule, "slight" means "small in quantum in comparison with the negligence of the defendant."[38] Whether plaintiff's negligence is slight is a question of fact that varies with each case.[39] Determination of the degree of plaintiff's negligence is determined without resort to use of percentages of fault in a special interrogatory.[40]

2. Assumption of Risk

Assumption of the risk is well recognized in South Dakota and is composed of three elements: (1) plaintiff must have actual or constructive knowledge of the risk; (2) plaintiff must appreciate the character of the risk; and (3) plaintiff must have "voluntarily accepted the risk, with the time, knowledge, and experience to make an intelligent choice."[41] Typically, knowledge and appreciation of the risk are questions for the jury.[42] Defendant bears the burden of showing all three elements.

Constructive knowledge of the risk will be imputed if the risk is so obvious "that anyone of competent faculties [could be] charged with knowledge of it."[43] Assumption of the risk involves attention to reasonable alternatives so that plaintiff had an opportunity to decide whether to subject himself to danger.[44]

F. RES IPSA LOQUITUR

South Dakota recognizes the theory of *res ipsa loquitur* and requires a successful plaintiff to demonstrate: (1) that the instrumentality causing injury was under control of defendant; (2) the accident causing injury would not have happened if defendant had not been negligent; and (3) injury to plaintiff resulted.[45] *Res ipsa loquitur* is invoked sparingly.[46]

G. NEGLIGENCE *PER SE*

Violation of a statute enacted to promote safety is negligence *per se*.[47] South Dakota has adopted the legal excuse doctrine and the party who is negligent *per se* bears the burden of establishing that the negligent conduct was in response to an emergency not of his own making.[48]

H. JOINT AND SEVERAL LIABILITY

Under the Uniform Contribution Among Tortfeasors Act, joint tortfeasors are defined as "two or more persons jointly or severally liable in tort for the same injury to person or property, whether or not judgment has been recovered against all or some of them."[49] In determining the apportionment of fault, the trier of fact is to consider the nature of the conduct of each party and the causal relationship between that conduct and the damages caused.[50] Several parties will be treated as one if their conduct proximately caused damage and it would be inequitable to distinguish between them.[51] However, the degree of fault of each party is considered in determining the *pro rata* share of liability.[52]

A release by plaintiff of one joint tortfeasor does not discharge the other tortfeasor unless so provided in the release.[53] The release reduces the amount plaintiff can claim against the other tortfeasor in the amount of consideration paid.[54] A release obtained by one tortfeasor does not extinguish the duty of contribution to another tortfeasor unless the release is obtained before the right of the other tortfeasor to secure a judgment for contribution has accrued and provides for a *pro rata* reduction of the released tortfeasor's share of damages reasonably calculable against all tortfeasors.[55]

I. INDEMNITY

Indemnification secures "the right of the first party to be reimbursed by the second party for the discharge of a liability which, as between the parties, should equitably be discharged by the second party."[56] It is properly utilized only when the party seeking indemnification demonstrates that the liability should be shifted to a second party.[57] Indemnity may be provided by contract and will be interpreted in accordance with statutory guidelines.[58]

J. BAR OF WORKERS COMPENSATION STATUTE

Under the South Dakota Workers' Compensation Act,[59] workers' compensation is the exclusive remedy an employee who is injured while working has against the employer.[60] However, if an employer's conduct is considered an intentional tort the exclusive remedy provision does not prohibit a common law cause of action against the employer.[61] In such cases, the employee must demonstrate that the employer "had 'actual knowledge of the exact danger which ultimately caused' injury."[62]

If an employer does not provide workers' compensation coverage an injured employee can maintain a negligence action or proceed under the workers' compensation laws, but not both. Recovery under the workers' compensation laws shall be doubled in such circumstances.[63]

When employment related injury is caused by a third party the employee may pursue damages against the third party, the employer, or both.[64] Any recovery from the third party will be an offset against workers' compensation benefits from the employer.[65] The employer has the right to pursue recovery from the third party either on its behalf or on behalf of the employee.[66] Any recovery in excess of the benefits paid under workers' compensation is owed to the employee, less the amount required to obtain the damages, not to exceed 35 percent of damages collected.[67]

K. PREMISES LIABILITY

The duty owed by landowners to those who enter their land is dependent upon the common law classifications of trespasser, licensee, and invitee.[68] In other words, the extent of the landowner's duty depends upon the classification of the entrant.

A trespasser is defined as one whom, having no title to the property or right to possess it, makes entry thereon or therein without the consent of the owner or the person lawfully entitled to possession.[69] An owner or occupant of the land is not under a duty to use ordinary care to ensure the premises are safe for a trespasser.[70] Rather, the occupant merely owes the trespasser the duty not to willfully or wantonly injure him after he has become aware or should have become aware of the entrant's presence.[71]

A licensee is a person who is on the premises, at the consent of the owner, for his own purposes and not for a purpose connected with the owner's business or other activities.[72] Generally, the landowner owes no duty to a licensee, except that he may not willfully injure or entrap.[73] However, once the landowner is aware of the presence of a licensee on the property or in the exercise of reasonable care ought to know of the licensee's presence, the landowner must exercise reasonable care to avoid causing injury to the licensee.[74]

An invitee is a person who is on the owner's property at the owner's request for a purpose connected with the owner's business or other activities.[75] The possessor of land owes an invitee the duty to exercise reasonable or ordinary care in ensuring the invitee's safety.[76]

L. DRAM SHOP LIABILITY

South Dakota adheres to the common law rule that "the consumption of alcoholic beverages, rather than the serving of alcoholic beverages, is the proximate cause of any injury inflicted upon another by an intoxicated person."[77] While it is a criminal offense for an establishment to serve alcohol to someone who is "obviously intoxicated" no civil liability attaches for violations of this rule.[78] The no liability rule extends to social hosts as well.[79]

M. ECONOMIC LOSS AND OTHER DAMAGES

South Dakota adheres to the general rule that tort recovery for economic loss alone is not permitted.[80] Damages for a breach of contract claim must be "clearly ascertainable."[81]

N. FRAUD AND MISREPRESENTATION

The South Dakota Rules of Civil Procedure generally track the Federal Rules of Civil Procedure and the requirement that fraud and mistake be plead with particularity is no exception.[82] The elements of a fraud claim are: (1) a false representation known to be untrue by the party making it, or recklessly made; (2) the representation was made with the intent to deceive and to induce action; and (3) the party to whom the representation was made relied upon it to act to his detriment.[83] Statutory deceit[84] and common law fraud are essentially the same in South Dakota.[85]

A party asserting negligent misrepresentation must show: (1) knowledge that information given is desired and material; (2) that the recipient of the knowledge intended to rely upon it; and (3) detriment to the party relying on the information.[86] In order for a negligent misrepresentation claim to stand, the relationship between the parties must be one in which the recipient of the information was relying on the superior knowledge of the other.[87]

O. CONSUMER FRAUD STATUTES

South Dakota's Deceptive Trade Practices and Consumer Protection Law protects any consumer, including businesses, corporations, etc., from deceptive trade practices.[88] The law provides for both criminal penalties[89] and civil relief.[90]

The statute of limitations for a deceptive trade practices claim is two years after occurrence or discovery.[91]

P. PUNITIVE DAMAGES

In determining if punitive damages should be awarded, and the amount, South Dakota follows Restatement (Second) of Torts § 908.[92] Punitive damages are appropriate in tort actions when the tortfeasor's conduct is willful and wanton.[93] Negligence alone is not enough to warrant punitive damages.[94]

To determine if the amount of punitive damages is excessive, courts are to consider: (1) the amount of compensatory damages awarded; (2) the nature and significance of the wrong; (3) the intent of the tortfeasor; (4) the tortfeasor's financial condition; and (5) the circumstances surrounding tortfeasor's conduct.[95] Punitive damages must "bear a reasonable relationship to the compensatory damages."[96] Prior to any discovery, or submission to the finder of fact, on the issue of punitive damages the court must find, following a hearing, that there is a reasonable basis for the assertion that the opposing party's conduct was willful, wanton or malicious.[97]

Q. WRONGFUL DEATH AND SURVIVORSHIP ACTIONS

Actions for wrongful death must be for the exclusive benefit of the surviving spouse and children of the deceased, or there being neither, for the benefit of the parents and next of kin.[98] The suit must be brought in the name of the executor or regular special administrator of the deceased.[99] The jury may give such damages as it may think proportionate to the pecuniary injury resulting from the death of the person for whose benefit the action is brought.[100] Loss of society, advice, assistance, and protection are proper elements of damages in a wrongful death action; however, loss of consortium, sorrow, mental distress and grief suffered, or any pain or suffering on the part of the decedent are not recoverable.[101] There is no limitation on the amount recoverable for wrongful death.

All causes of action survive the death of either the claimant or the defendant.[102] This means that such actions may be prosecuted by the personal representatives of deceased claimants and by claimants against the estate of deceased defendants.[103]

J. Crisman Palmer
David E. Lust
GUNDERSON, PALMER, GOODSELL & NELSON, L.L.P.
440 Mount Rushmore Road
P. O. Box 8045
Rapid City, South Dakota 57709-8045
(605) 342-1078
Fax (605) 342-9503
cpalmer@gpgnlaw.com
dlust@gpgnlaw.com

ENDNOTES - SOUTH DAKOTA

1. S.D. Codified Laws § 15-2-14(3) (1984).

2. S.D. Codified Laws § 15-2-12.2 (1985).

3. S.D. Codified Laws § 15-2-13(1) (1984).

4. S.D. Codified Laws § 15-2-13(3) (1984).

5. S.D. Codified Laws § 15-2-14(1) (1984).

6. S.D. Codified Laws § 15-2-14.1 (1984).

7. S.D. Codified Laws § 15-2-14.2 (legal); S.D. Codified Laws § 15-2-14.4 (1996) (accountant).

8. S.D. Codified Laws § 15-2-15(1) (1984).

9. *Id.*

10. S.D. Codified Laws § 15-2-15.2 (1986).

11. S.D. Codified Laws § 57A-2-725 (2001) (The statute of limitations begins when the sale occurred).

12. *Witte v. Goldey*, 590 N.W.2d 266, 268 (S.D. 1999); *Kurylas, Inc. v. Bradsky*, 452 N.W.2d 111, 113-14 (S.D. 1990).

13. *Witte*, 590 N.W.2d at 269.

14. *Beckel v. Gerber*, 578 N.W.2d 574, 576 (S.D. 1998).

15. *Witte*, 590 N.W.2d at 269 (legal and accounting malpractice); *Greene v. Morgan, Theeler, Cogley & Petersen*, 575 N.W.2d 457, 460 (S.D. 1998) (legal malpractice); *Beckel*, 578 N.W.2d at 576 (medical malpractice).

16. S.D. Codified Laws § 15-2-3 (1984); *Stassberg v. Citizens State Bank*, 581 N.W.2d 510, 515 (S.D. 1998) (discovery rule applies, however, the entire extent of damages and all underlying facts need not be known for accrual of cause of action).

17. S.D. Codified Laws § 21-3-11 (1997); *Matter of Certification of Questions of Law From U.S. Court of Appeals for Eighth Circuit, Pursuant to Provisions of S.D. Codified Laws 15-24-1*, 544 N.W.2d 183, 204 (S.D. 1996).

18. S.D. Codified Laws § 32-35-2 (1998).

19. S.D. Codified Laws § 58-11-9 (1997).

20. S.D. Codified Laws § 58-11-9.4 (1997).

21. S.D. Codified Laws § 58-11-9 (1997).

22. *Union Ins. Co. v. Stanage*, 454 N.W.2d 736, 738-39 (S.D. 1990) (citing *Cunningham v. Western Casualty Ins. Co.*, 243 N.W.2d, 172 (S.D. 1976)).

23. *Clark v. Regent*, 270 N.W.2d 26, 31 (S.D. 1978).

24. *Cimarron Ins. Co. v. Croyle*, 479 N.W.2d 881, 884-85 (S.D. 1992).

25. *Thompson v. Summers*, 567 N.W.2d 387, 394 (S.D. 1997) (citing *Stevens v. Wood Sawmill Inc.*, 426 N.W.2d, 13, 14 (S.D. 1988)).

26. *Peterson v. Spink Electric Cooperative, Inc.*, 578 N.W.2d 589, 592 (S.D. 1998).

27. *Id.*

28. *Tipton v. Town of Tabor*, 567 N.W.2d 351, 357 (S.D. 1997) (quoting *Prosser and Keeton on the Law of Torts* (Fifth ed. 1984) § 53 at 356).

29. *Magbuhat v. Kovarik*, 382 N.W.2d 43, 46 (S.D. 1986).

30. *Id.*

31. *Tipton*, 567 N.W.2d at 370 (citing *Alley v. Siepman*, 214 N.W.2d 7, 10 (S.D. 1974)).

32. *Id.* (recognizing the special relationship theory in conjunction with public duty doctrine and the rescue doctrine).

33. *Thompson*, 567 N.W.2d at 394.

34. *Id.* (quoting *Williams v. United States*, 450 F. Supp. 1040, 1046 (D. S.D. 1978)).

35. *Id.*

36. S.D. Codified Laws § 20-9-2 (1998).

37. *Id.*; see also *Chambers v. Dakota Charter, Inc.*, 488 N.W.2d 63, 68 (S.D. 1992).

38. *Estate of Largent v. United States*, 910 F.2d 497 (8th Cir. 1990).

39. *Id.*

40. S.D. Codified Laws § 20-9-2 (1998).

41. *Ray v. Downes*, 576 N.W.2d 896, 897 (S.D. 1998).

42. *Id.*

43. *Goepfert v. Filler*, 563 N.W.2d 140, 143 (S.D. 1997) (quoting *Westover v. East River Elec. Coop, Inc.*, 488 N.W.2d 892, 901 (S.D. 1992)).

44. *Id.* at 144 (citing *Berg v. Sukup Mfg. Co.*, 355 N.W.2d 833, 835 (S.D. 1984)).

45. *Wuest ex rel. Carver v. McKennan Hosp.*, 619 N.W.2d 682 (S.D. 2000) (citing *Fleege v. Cimpl*, 305 N.W.2d 409 (S.D. 1981)).

46. *Shipley*, 235 N.W.2d at 913.

47. *Hansen v. South Dakota Dept. of Trans.*, 584 N.W.2d 881, 894 (S.D. 1998).

48. *Dartt v. Berghorst*, 484 N.W.2d 891, 894 (S.D. 1992) (citing *Meyer v. Johnson*, 254 N.W.2d 107, 110 (S.D. 1977)).

49. S.D. Codified Laws § 15-8-11 (1984).

50. S.D. Codified Laws § 15-8-15.2 (1987).

51. *Id.*

52. S.D. Codified Laws § 15-8-15 (1984).

53. S.D. Codified Laws § 15-8-17 (1984).

54. *Id.*

55. S.D. Codified Laws § 15-8-18 (1984).

56. *Mark, Inc. v. Maguire Ins. Agency, Inc.*, 518 N.W.2d 227, 230 (S.D. 1994) (citing *Ebert v. Fort Pierre Moose Lodge #1813*, 312 N.W.2d 119, 122 (1981)).

57. *Id.* (citing *Manning v. First Federal Savings and Loan*, 441 N.W.2d 924, 926 (S.D. 1989)).

58. S.D. Codified Laws § 56-3-7 (2001) (noting that the rules set forth in S.D. Codified Laws §§ 15-3-8 to 15-3-15 are made applicable to contracts containing indemnity provisions unless contrary intentions are stated therein).

59. *See generally* S.D. Codified Laws title 62.

60. S.D. Codified Laws § 62-3-2 (1993).

61. *Id.*; *Harn v. Continental Lumber Co.*, 506 N.W.2d 91, 95 (S.D. 1993).

62. *Harn*, 506 N.W.2d at 99 (quoting *Sanek v. Duracote Corp.*, 539 N.E.2d 1114, 1117 (Ohio 1989)).

63. S.D. Codified Laws § 62-3-11 (1993); *Jackson v. Lee's Travelers' Lodge Inc.*, 563 N.W.2d 858, 860 (S.D. 1997).

64. S.D. Codified Laws § 62-4-38 (1994); *Liberty Mutual Ins. Co. v. Garry*, 574 N.W.2d 895, 896-97 (S.D. 1998) (noting that the employer is entitled to recover any amounts it has paid the employee from the employee's recovery from third party).

65. *Id.*

66. S.D. Codified Laws § 62-4-40 (1993).

67. *Id.*

68. *Musch v. H-D Elec. Co-op, Inc.*, 460 N.W.2d 149, 151-52 (S.D. 1992); *Underberg v. Cain*, 348 N.W.2d 145, 146 (S.D. 1990).

69. S.D. Civil Pattern Jury Instructions § 120-01 (2000).

70. *Id.* at § 120-02(2000) (citing *Underberg v. Cain*, 348 N.W.2d 145, 146 (S.D. 1984)).

71. *Id.*

72. *Id.* at § 120-03 (2000).

73. *Musch*, 460 N.W.2d at 152; *Underberg*, 348 N.W.2d at 145-46.

74. S.D. Civil Pattern Jury Instructions § 120-04 (2000).

75. S.D. Civil Pattern Jury Instructions at § 120.06 (1995).

76. *Jones v. Kartar Plaza Ltd.*, 488 N.W.2d 428, 429-30 (S.D. 1992) (citing *Stenholtz v. Modica*, 264 N.W.2d 514, 516-517 (S.D. 1978)); *Mitchell v. Ankney*, 396 N.W.2d 312, 314 (S.D. 1986).

77. S.D. Codified Laws § 35-11-1 (1999); *Wegleitner v. Sattler*, 582 N.W.2d 688, 690-91 (S.D. 1998) (tracking the common law and statutory history of dram shop liability in South Dakota).

78. S.D. Codified Laws § 35-4-78 (1999); *Weglietner*, 582 N.W.2d at 690.

79. S.D. Codified Laws § 35-11-2 (1999).

80. *Diamond Surface v. State Cement Plant Com'n*, 583 N.W.2d 155, 160-61 (S.D. 1998); *City of Lennox v. Mitek Indus., Inc.*, 519 N.W.2d 330, 333 (S.D. 1994).

81. S.D. Codified Laws § 21-2-1 (1987); *High Plains Genetics Research, Inc. v. JK Mill-Iron Ranch*, 535 N.W.2d 839, 844 (S.D. 1995) (prohibiting jury instruction on loss of business reputation because no specific date was provided in support of the claim).

82. S.D. Codified Laws § 15-6-9(b) (1984).

83. *Paint Brush Corp., Parts Brush Div. v. Neu*, 599 N.W.2d 384, 391 (S.D. 1999) (citing *Stene v. State Farm Insurance*, 583 N.W.2d 399, 404 (S.D. 1998)).

84. S.D. Codified Laws § 20-10-1 (1995).

85. *Stockmen's Livestock Mkt., Inc. v. Norwest Bank of Sioux City*, 135 F.3d 1236, 1243 (8th Cir. 1998).

86. *Littau v. Midwest Commmodities, Inc.*, 316 N.W.2d 639, 644 (S.D. 1982).

87. *Rumpza v. Larsen*, 551 N.W.2d 810, 814 (citing *Swanson v. Sioux Valley Empire Elec. Ass'n*, 535 N.W.2d 755, 757 (S.D. 1995)).

88. *See generally* S.D. Codified Laws Ch. 37-24; *Moss v. Guttormson*, 551 N.W.2d 14, 17 (S.D. 1996).

89. S.D. Codified Laws § 37-24-6 (2001) (setting forth acts deemed deceptive).

90. S.D. Codified Laws § 37-24-7 (2000) (indicating that civil relief is available but only for those practices which are unlawful as defined in S.D. Codified Laws § 37-24-6); S.D. Codified Laws § 37-24-31 (2000); *Moss v. Guttormson*, 551 N.W.2d 14, 18 (S.D. 1996).

91. S.D. Codified Laws § 37-24-33 (2000).

92. *Schaffer v. Edward D. Jones & Co.*, 521 N.W.2d 921, 927 (S.D. 1994).

93. *Dahl v. Sittner*, 474 N.W.2d 897, 900 (S.D. 1991).

94. *Vilhauer v. Horsemans' Sports Inc.*, 598 N.W.2d 525, 529 (S.D. 1999) (citing *Grynberg v. Citation Oil & Gas Corp.*, 573 N.W.2d 493, 506, n.10 (S.D. 1997)).

95. *Veeder v. Kennedy*, 589 N.W.2d 610, 621 (S.D. 1999).

96. *Id.* (citing *Grynberg*, 573 N.W.2d at 504).

97. S.D. Codified Laws § 21-1-4.1 (1987); *Kjerstad v. Ravellette Publications, Inc.*, 517 N.W.2d 419, 425 (S.D. 1994).

98. S.D. Codified Laws § 21-5-5 (1987).

99. *Id.*

100. S.D. Codified Laws § 21-5-7 (1987).

101. *Zoss v. Dakota Truck Underwriters*, 590 N.W.2d 911, 913-14 (S.D. 1999) (citing *Selchert v. Lien*, 371 N.W.2d 791, 794 (S.D. 1985)).

102. S.D. Codified Laws § 15-4-1 (1984).

103. *Id.*

TENNESSEE

A. **STATUTES OF LIMITATIONS**

Personal tort actions such as libel, false imprisonment, malicious prosecution, and personal injuries resulting from negligence, intentional torts, and wrongful death must be brought within one year after the cause of action accrues.[1] Similarly, a cause of action for personal injuries stemming from products liability must also be brought within a year from the date of injury.[2] A cause of action accrues on the date that the injury occurs or the date when the injury should have been discovered by a reasonable person.[3] The "Discovery Rule" applies only where the plaintiff does not discover and reasonably could not be expected to discover that he or she has a cause of action.[4]

Actions for property damage caused by most forms of tort have a three-year statute of limitations.[5] These include actions for injuries to personal or real property and actions for the detention or conversion of personal property.[6]

Actions for slander must be brought within six months after the words are uttered.[7]

Malpractice claims based on wrongful or tortious conduct are governed by a one-year statute of limitations, but if the injury is not discovered during the one-year period, the action accrues from the date of discovery.[8]

Actions arising under the Tennessee Consumer Protection Act have a one-year statute of limitations and a four-year statute of repose.[9]

A four-year statute of limitations is applicable to claims involving improvements to real property,[10] which are also governed by a five-year statute of repose.[11] Similarly, medical malpractice claims are subject to a three-year statute of repose,[12] and products liability actions are subject to a ten-year statute of repose.[13]

A defendant's fraudulent concealment of a cause of action will toll the statute of limitations.[14] The continuing tort doctrine also may toll the statute of limitations if the tortious conduct is continuous in nature; however, the Tennessee courts have expressed doubt as to the doctrine's continued viability in light of the discovery rule.[15]

Tennessee has a savings statute that allows a plaintiff to bring a new cause of action within one year after a judgment or decree has been entered against the plaintiff on a ground that ordinarily would not prevent relitigating the issues except for the running of the statute of limitations.[16] A special savings statute allows a plaintiff 90 days to amend his pleading to join third-party defendants once the plaintiff has received an answer that alleges comparative fault and identifies nonparty tort-feasors.[17]

B. TORT REFORM

The most current form of tort reform legislation is the Tennessee Governmental Tort Liability Act.[18] The Act grants governmental entities immunity from suit when an injury results from their tortious actions—except when immunity is expressly removed under the Act.[19] Immunity has been removed for certain injuries caused by governmental employees,[20] for injuries resulting from the negligent operation of a motor vehicle or other equipment,[21] injuries caused by unsafe streets and highways[22] and injuries caused by a dangerous or defective condition in a public structure.[23] Further, immunity from liability for intentional torts by government entities is limited to those intentional torts specifically enumerated in the Act.[24] There is a cap placed on liability under the Act. Damages may not exceed the minimum amounts of insurance coverage specified in Tenn. Code Ann. § 29-20-403, or the governmental entity's insurance limits.[25] Liability coverage under § 29-20-404 is limited to $130,000 per person and $350,000 per occurrence. The statute also allows governmental liability for injuries resulting from a high-speed chase by police.[26]

C. "NO FAULT" LIMITATIONS

The Tennessee legislature has not enacted a "no fault" statute, and the Tennessee Financial Responsibility Law (TFRL)[27] does not mandate liability insurance coverage for owners or operators of motor vehicles.

Under the TFRL, a party who sustains bodily injury or property damage in an automobile accident and who has not yet obtained a judgment may file a claim with the commissioner of safety against the owner or operator of the motor vehicle who caused the accident.[28] If the commissioner determines that a judgment against the owner or operator is reasonably possible, the license and all registrations of the owner, operator, or both will be revoked unless financial security sufficient to satisfy a potential judgment resulting from the accident is provided.[29] Acceptable proof of financial security is limited to written proof of liability insurance coverage, a cash deposit, a bond, or notarized releases executed by all parties who had previously filed claims with the commissioner as a result of the accident.[30]

D. THE STANDARD FOR NEGLIGENCE

In order for a negligence claim to succeed in Tennessee, a plaintiff must prove all of the following elements: (1) a duty of care owed by the defendant to the plaintiff; (2) conduct falling below the applicable standard of care amounting to a breach of that duty; (3) an injury or loss; (4) causation in fact; and (5) proximate or legal cause.[31] The existence of a duty is a question of law requiring the court to consider whether the defendant had the legal obligation to protect the plaintiff from an unreasonable risk of harm.[32] Once a duty is established, the standard of conduct to determine whether a duty is breached is that of reasonable care under all of the circumstances, based upon the foreseeability of the risk of injury and the dangers involved in the particular situation.[33]

Professionals in medical malpractice actions are held to a local standard of care and expert testimony is limited to doctors from Tennessee or a contiguous border state.[34] In a medical malpractice action based on a lack of informed consent, the standard is whether a reasonable person in the plaintiff's position would have consented if adequately informed of the risks.[35] However, if a medical professional is accused of fraudulent concealment for failing to disclose material facts related to medical treatment, expert proof is required.[36] A possessor of property owes a duty of reasonable care under all the circumstances,[37] and a landowner has no duty to certain recreational landusers.[38] In cases of negligent infliction of emotional distress, Tennessee does not require physical injury, but does require expert proof of serious emotional injury that a reasonable person under the circumstances would suffer.[39] This special proof requirement applies only to stand-alone claims for emotional distress.[40] Tennessee has rejected the "zone of danger" test in favor of a "foreseeability" test for emotional distress claims brought bystanders for injuries to third parties.[41] Further, Tennessee has a good samaritan law, which provides that anyone who voluntarily offers emergency assistance can only be held liable for gross negligence.[42]

E. CAUSATION

To establish a *prima facie* case of negligence in Tennessee, the plaintiff must prove by a preponderance of the evidence that the defendant's negligence was both the cause-in-fact, or "but for" cause, of the plaintiff's injury and the proximate cause of the harm alleged.[43] Proximate cause is shown where: (1) the tortfeasor's conduct was a substantial factor in causing the plaintiff's injury; (2) there is no rule or policy that should relieve the wrongdoer from liability; and (3) the injury could reasonably have been foreseen or anticipated by a person of ordinary intelligence or prudence.[44] The issue of proximate cause is usually a question to be decided by the jury.[45]

An independent intervening cause will break the chain of proximate causation and preclude recovery in a negligence action.[46] The intervening cause doctrine only applies when the intervening act: (1) was sufficient by itself to cause the injury; (2) was not reasonably foreseeable by the negligent actor; and (3) was not a normal response to the original negligent actor's conduct.[47]

F. CONTRIBUTORY NEGLIGENCE, COMPARATIVE FAULT, AND ASSUMPTION OF RISK

1. Contributory Negligence

In 1992, Tennessee joined the majority of jurisdictions in abolishing contributory negligence as an absolute defense.[48]

2. Comparative Fault

In *McIntyre v. Balentine*,[49] the Tennessee Supreme Court abolished contributory negligence and adopted a modified version of comparative fault in its place. A plaintiff in Tennessee may now recover damages only when the plaintiff's negligence is less than the combined fault of all the tortfeasors.[50] The plaintiff's recovery is reduced by the percentage of fault attributed to the plaintiff.[51]

In pleading the affirmative defense of comparative fault, the defendant must identify or describe other potential tortfeasors who should share fault.[52] The defendant's failure to identify these potential tortfeasors precludes the factfinder from assigning fault to them and leaves the defendant liable for all damages except those attributable to the plaintiff.[53] Where the defendant alleges that a nonparty caused or contributed to the injury or damage claimed by the plaintiff, the trial court must instruct the jury to assign to this nonparty a percentage of the fault, and this fault will be considered in determining whether the plaintiff is entitled to recover.[54] The plaintiff also has the right to add this nonparty as a defendant in the lawsuit. Where the statute of limitations against that person bars the plaintiff's claim, Tenn. Code Ann. § 20-1-119 gives the plaintiff the right, within 90 days of the first answer or amended answer alleging that person's fault, to either institute a separate action against that person by filing a summons and complaint, or to amend the existing complaint to add this person as a defendant and cause process to be issued.[55]

Although the Tennessee Supreme Court held in *Ridings v. Ralph M. Parsons Co.*[56] that fault could only be attributed to persons against whom the plaintiff had a cause of action, the court has retreated from this position in recent cases. Fault may be apportioned to parties who are immune from suit[57] and to parties who are not subject to liability because of a statute of repose.[58] The court has also held that fault may not be apportioned against unidentified (phantom) tortfeasors,[59] except in the uninsured motorist setting.[60] However, a jury cannot apportion fault to a nonparty employer who is immune because of the Workers' Compensation Law.[61]

With limited exceptions, the adoption of comparative fault by the Tennessee Supreme Court made obsolete the doctrines of remote contributory negligence, joint and several liability,[62] implied assumption of risk and last clear chance, which previously existed in Tennessee.[63] Additionally, the Contribution Among Tort-Feasors Act[64] no longer determines the apportionment of liability among codefendants, as this is now covered by comparative fault.[65]

3. **Assumption of Risk**

The defense of implied assumption of risk has been abolished in Tennessee and subsumed into the comparative fault analysis.[66] The plaintiff's conduct in confronting a known danger is now considered by the factfinder when apportioning fault.[67] An express release, waiver, or exculpatory words by which one party agrees to assume the risk of harm arising from another party's negligent conduct remains enforceable as long as it does not extend to liability for willful or gross negligence and does not otherwise offend public policy.[68]

G. *RES IPSA LOQUITUR* AND INHERENTLY DANGEROUS ACTIVITIES

1. *Res Ipsa Loquitur*

The doctrine of *res ipsa loquitur* allows an inference of negligence when the jury has a common knowledge or understanding that events that caused the plaintiff's injury do not ordinarily occur unless someone was negligent.[69] *Res ipsa loquitur* permits a reasonable inference, in the absence of an explanation by the defendant, that the defendant was negligent if the plaintiff shows: (1) that he or she was injured by an instrumentality that was within the defendant's exclusive control, and (2) that the injury would not ordinarily have occurred in the absence of negligence.[70]

The court's function is to determine whether the inference may be reasonably drawn by the jury and, if so, to instruct the jury that it may infer negligence from the occurrence of the accident.[71] The jury is permitted, but not compelled, to draw the inference of negligence in preference to other permissible or reasonable inferences and is free to determine the weight of the inference to be given.[72] A plaintiff may use *res ipsa loquitur* in medical malpractice actions to raise an inference of negligence in either of two ways: (1) by presenting proof such that the jury can reasonably infer from common knowledge and experience that the defendant was negligent, or (2) by utilizing expert testimony.[73]

2. Inherently Dangerous Activities

One who deals with an inherently dangerous or hazardous article owes a duty to all who may be endangered by it to exercise caution that is proportionate to the risk of danger involved.[74] To impose liability for an inherently dangerous activity, the thing must be dangerous according to common experience.[75] Although Tennessee has not expressly adopted the Restatement of Torts (Second) § 519 (1976), a federal court analyzed Tennessee law and concluded that strict or absolute liability for "non-natural, ultrahazardous and abnormally dangerous activities" under the Restatement would be recognized by the Tennessee courts.[76]

H. NEGLIGENCE *PER SE*

When a statute prescribes the standard of conduct expected of a reasonable person, a violation of that statute may constitute negligence *per se*.[77] Although a violation of a statute is negligence in and of itself, the imposition of liability based upon such a violation requires a showing that the violation was the proximate cause of the plaintiff's injury.[78]

The Tennessee courts require a plaintiff to show three elements to prove negligence *per se:* (1) the defendant violated a statute (or ordinance) that imposes a duty or prohibition for the benefit of a person or the public; (2) the injured party is within the class of persons intended to benefit from or be protected by the statute; and (3) the violation of the statute is the proximate cause of the injury.[79] If the statute at issue merely imposes an administrative requirement, instead of establishing a standard of care, a negligence *per se* claim cannot stand.[80]

Negligence *per se* is also applicable to regulations relating to public safety,[81] such as health regulations and rules of the road.[82] If a claim of negligence *per se* is based on a safety statute, the defendant's negligence may be excused if compliance with the statute was impossible under the circumstances or would have subjected him to imminent danger.[83]

I. **JOINT AND SEVERAL LIABILITY**

Tennessee's adoption of a modified version of comparative fault purported to completely abolish joint and several liability.[84] Nonetheless, the Tennessee Supreme Court has issued a series of opinions that apply joint and several liability in certain circumstances. For example, joint and several liability still applies in cases in which liability is premised upon the family purpose doctrine[85] or when *respondeat superior* allows vicarious liability arising out of an agency relationship.[86] The doctrine also is applicable to cases in which multiple defendants are part of a product's distribution chain and are liable under a theory of strict products liability.[87] Most recently, joint and several liability has been reinstated where an intentional and a negligent actor are both named defendants and the intentional misconduct was the result of a foreseeable risk created by the negligent defendant.[88]

Joint and several liability is also retained in cases in which tortfeasors act in concert to cause injury to another.[89] In *Resolution Trust*, officers, and directors of a corporation who were sued for their collective breach of fiduciary duty, negligence, and breach of contract were jointly and severally liable to the corporation.[90] The court relied on the historical underpinnings of joint and several liability, noting that it attached to actions by two or more people who owe a duty to another and, by their common neglect of that duty, injure the other. The court stated that defined this way, joint and several liability of tortfeasors who act in concert need not be affected by the adoption of comparative fault.[91]

1. **The Right of Contribution**

The right of contribution for defendants held jointly and severally liable has been limited by Tennessee's adoption of comparative fault. In *Bervoets v. Harde Ralls Pontiac-Olds, Inc.*,[92] the court explained that, although it abolished joint and several liability "to the extent that it allows a plaintiff to sue and obtain a full recovery against any one or more of several parties against whom liability could be established," it did not intend to abolish the remedy of contribution.[93]

Contribution is still viable in the following circumstances: (1) cases in which the cause of action arose prior to *McIntyre v. Balentine*, the suit was filed, and the parties made irrevocable litigation decisions based on pre-*McIntyre* law; (2) cases in which joint and several liability is still applicable (such as cases involving the family purpose doctrine, cases in which tortfeasors act in concert or collectively with one another, cases in which respondeat superior allows vicarious liability, or in the appropriate products liability case); and (3) cases in which fairness demands it.[94] The third circumstance is not a "catch-all" provision, but is only applicable when a failure to allow contribution would impose an injustice.[95] The *General Electric* decision explains the limited circumstances when the Uniform Contribution Among Tort-feasors Act, Tenn. Code Ann. § 29-11-101 *et seq.*, is applicable.[96]

Tortfeasors jointly and severally liable in tort for the same injury to person or property or for the same wrongful death have a right of contribution except when, because of immunity, a claimant is barred from bringing a tort action against the party from whom contribution is sought.[97] The right of contribution exists only for a tortfeasor who has paid more than his proportionate share of the shared liability and it is limited to the amount the tortfeasor paid in excess of his proportionate share.[98] A tortfeasor who enters into a settlement with a claimant may not recover contribution from another tortfeasor whose liability is not extinguished by the settlement and may not recover any amount paid in a settlement that is in "excess of what was reasonable."[99]

All actions for contribution are to be tried in accordance with the principles of comparative fault.[100] In determining the proportionate share of the defendant's shared liability, the jury is to compare the reasonable amount of the settlement and the relative degree of fault of the tortfeasors and the injured party or parties.[101] If the jury determines that the amount of the settlement is unreasonable, it will determine the proper amount of damages and attribute fault accordingly, and contribution will be ordered from a defendant commensurate with his percentage of fault.[102]

If a release, covenant not to sue, or covenant not to enforce a judgment is given in good faith to one of two or more persons liable in tort for the same injury or wrongful death, it does not discharge any of the other tortfeasors unless its terms so provide.[103] It does reduce the claim against the others by the amount so stipulated or the amount of consideration paid for it, whichever is greater.[104]

J. INDEMNITY

Indemnification is the complete shifting of liability for loss from one person to another. There are two types in Tennessee—express indemnity, which arises from the contracts between parties, and implied indemnity, which is imposed by law.[105] Contracts of indemnity are enforceable if the terms of the indemnity clause are clear and fully evidence the parties' intent to indemnify.[106] Implied indemnity will be imposed when the obligation is "a necessary element of the parties' relationship" or when "justice and fairness demand that the burden of paying for the loss be shifted to the party whose fault or responsibility is qualitatively different from the other parties."[107]

The general rule is that a person who, in whole or in part, discharges a legal obligation that should have been discharged by another is entitled to indemnity from the other person.[108] The right of action for indemnity arises when the party becomes obligated to pay. In Tennessee, a right of indemnification may exist between joint tortfeasors when one of the tortfeasors was actively negligent and the other merely passively negligent.[109] The common liability must exist at the time the plaintiff's claim arose.[110]

K. BAR OF WORKERS' COMPENSATION STATUTE

Tennessee's Workers' Compensation Law, originally enacted in 1919, precludes an employee, his personal representatives, dependents, or next of kin from seeking a common law tort remedy against his employer for injuries caused by the employer's negligence,[111] provided the type of employment is not exempt from the statute.[112] This law creates a *quid pro quo* in that workers relinquish their common law rights of action against their employers for a system of recovery that provides compensation for injury completely independent of employer fault.[113] The employee is limited to a specific recovery as set forth in the Workers' Compensation statutory schedule, but the employee is allowed to recover without proving fault. The employer may not plead common law defenses, but is protected from a potentially greater common law measure of damages.[114]

The Workers' Compensation Law provides the exclusive remedies available to an employee in a lawsuit against his employer for an injury by accident or occupational disease "arising out of and in the course of employment."[115] However, an employer may not use the Tennessee Workers' Compensation Law as a shield against an intentional tort action based on assault, battery, false imprisonment, deceit, defamation, and intentional infliction of emotional distress.[116] To maintain such an action, the employee must prove that the employer had actual intent to cause injury to the employee.[117]

In recent years, trial courts have been confronted with the question of whether a jury in a negligence action may assign fault to an employer who is immune from suit under the Workers' Compensation Law. For example, in a products liability case, there may be strong evidence of employer negligence that may constitute the proximate cause of the plaintiff's injuries. The Tennessee Supreme Court addressed this issue in *Snyder v. LTG. Lufttechnische GmbH*.[118] Plaintiff was employed as a textile factory worker and suffered injuries while working on a stalled cotton baller. He filed a lawsuit against the seller of the machine and the German manufacturer. These defendants sought to have fault assigned against the employer. The *Snyder* court made a policy decision to prohibit the assessment of fault against an "immune employer"[119] but held that products liability defendants "may introduce relevant evidence at trial that the plaintiff's employer's alteration, change, improper maintenance, or abnormal use of the defendant's product was a cause in fact of the plaintiff's injuries."[120]

L. PREMISES LIABILITY

In premises liability cases, Tennessee common law no longer classifies persons as "invitees" or "licensees" when assessing a landowner's duty of care.[121] Instead, a landowner must exercise reasonable care under all of the circumstances, so as not to cause injury to a person upon the subject premises.[122] When assessing liability, the duty of reasonable care is extended to all persons and the foreseeability of the injured person's presence and the likelihood of harm are principal factors considered.[123]

A premises liability claim based on negligence requires a plaintiff to prove: (1) a duty of care owed by the defendant to the plaintiff; (2) conduct by the defendant falling below the standard of care amounting to a breach of the duty; (3) an injury or loss; (4) causation in fact; and (5) proximate cause.[124]

In analyzing liability in a negligence claim, foreseeability is the key factor. If the injury is not reasonably foreseeable, a duty of care is not breached even if the defendant's act or omission caused the injury.[125]

The mere existence of a defective or dangerous condition is insufficient to establish liability.[126] A landowner does not have a duty to warn of an unanticipated or unreasonable risk of which she is not aware and could not have discovered by exercising reasonable care.[127] Thus, a premises owner must have either actual or constructive notice of a defective or dangerous condition and if a landowner knows or should have known of a defective or dangerous condition on the premises, that owner has a general duty to remove or warn of any such hazard by exercising reasonable diligence.[128]

Further, in regard to analyzing the duty of the landowner, the Tennessee Supreme Court has held that a defendant does not have an absolute duty to anticipate all potential harm to persons on his land. A court must weigh the foreseeability and gravity of the risk of harm to the injured plaintiff against the potential burden on the defendant of protecting the injured person from harm.[129]

M. DRAM SHOP LIABILITY

Tennessee's Dram Shop Act[130] only allows liability for selling alcohol to obviously intoxicated persons and to known minors.

The Act requires an extremely high standard of proof to find liability. The trier of fact must find beyond a reasonable doubt that the sale of the alcohol was the proximate cause of the injury, and that either: (1) the seller knew that the person to whom the alcohol was sold was under 21 and that "such person caused the personal injury or death as the direct result of the consumption of the alcoholic beverage or beer so sold"; or (2) the seller sold the alcohol to an obviously intoxicated person and that "such person caused the personal injury or death as the direct result of the consumption of the alcoholic beverage or beer so sold."[131] Tennessee courts require direct evidence of a sale of an alcoholic beverage or beer, and without such evidence there can be no liability on the part of the provider.[132] Further, the finding of liability for the sale of alcohol to a minor must be supported by evidence showing that the seller actually knew the buyer was a minor.[133]

N. ECONOMIC LOSS

The economic loss doctrine provides that there can be no recovery for economic loss without accompanying personal injuries or property damage.[134] Recovery under tort law has been allowed for personal injury and property damage,[135] loss of earning capacity,[136] lost profits[137] and expenses incurred because of negligence of a tort-feasor,[138] and no recovery is permitted solely for economic damages under strict liability.[139] However, Tennessee has adopted Section 552 of the

Restatement (Second) of Torts (1976) and allows suits for economic losses based upon negligent misrepresentation; this doctrine does not apply to products liability actions.[140]

O. FRAUD AND MISREPRESENTATION

The Tennessee Rules of Civil Procedure require a cause of action for fraud to be pleaded with particularity.[141] Fraud is never presumed; when it is alleged, the facts supporting it must be "clearly made out."[142] The only exception to this rule is when the parties are in a confidential relationship, in which case a presumption of fraud may arise.[143]

Tennessee courts purport to recognize two causes of action: (1) fraud and deceit; and (2) intentional misrepresentation, although some courts use the terms interchangeably,[144] and the elements of each are virtually identical. Elements of common law fraud and deceit are: (1) intentional misrepresentation of a past or existing material fact; (2) made with knowledge of its falsity and with fraudulent intent;[145] and (3) reasonable reliance by plaintiff to his injury.[146]

The elements of common law intentional misrepresentation are: (1) the defendant made a representation of fact; (2) the representation was false; (3) the representation related to a material fact; (4) the representation was made either knowingly, recklessly, or without belief of its truth; (5) the plaintiff reasonably relied on the representation; and (6) suffered damage as a result.[147]

The elements of negligent misrepresentation are: (1) the defendant acted in the course of his business or in a transaction in which he has a pecuniary interest; (2) the defendant supplied false information meant to guide others in their transaction; (3) the defendant failed to exercise reasonable care in obtaining or communicating the information; (4) plaintiff justifiably relied upon the information; and (5) suffered a pecuniary loss as a result.[148]

P. CONSUMER FRAUD STATUTES

The Tennessee Consumer Protection Act (TCPA) protects consumers from unfair and deceptive acts or practices in any trade or commerce.[149] Specific violations include falsely passing off goods or services as those of another and causing likelihood of confusion or misunderstanding as to the source of goods or services, although there are a variety of other types of misrepresentation included within the Act.[150] The TCPA provides for the imposition of civil penalties for violation of an agreement of voluntary compliance with the TCPA or for interfering with the division of consumer affairs's request for information.[151] Private actions may be brought under the TCPA for an ascertainable loss of money or property as a result of an unfair or deceptive act.[152] Violations of the Act are Class B misdemeanors.[153]

The TCPA gives the court discretion to award treble damages,[154] attorneys' fees and costs.[155] The Act enumerates many violations, but also contains a "catch-all" provision for "any other act or practice which is deceptive to the consumer or to any other person."[156] The TCPA contains a one-year statute of limitations and a four-year statute of repose.[157]

A corporation has standing to sue under the TCPA and, like other persons, may recover treble damages.[158]

Q. PUNITIVE DAMAGES

In the wake of the United States Supreme Court's observation that unfettered jury discretion in awarding punitive damages may produce "extreme results that jar one's constitutional sensibilities,"[159] the Tennessee Supreme Court established specific criteria and procedures to guide finders of fact in determining whether and in what amount punitive damages should be awarded.[160] In a case where punitive damages are sought, the court must bifurcate the trial upon motion of the defendant.[161] In the first phase of the trial, the factfinder determines liability for, and the amount of, compensatory damages and liability for punitive damages.[162] A defendant can be liable for punitive damages only if it is shown by clear and convincing evidence that the defendant has acted either (1) intentionally, (2) fraudulently, (3) maliciously, or (4) recklessly.[163] Generally, actual damage must be sustained by the plaintiff before punitive damages may be awarded.[164]

If the defendant is found to be liable to the plaintiff for punitive damages, the amount of the punitive damage award is set in the second phase of the trial.[165] Evidence of the defendant's wealth is admissible only in the second phase of the trial, and must be considered together with other factors in determining the amount of the award. These factors include the nature of the wrongdoing, the harm to the plaintiff and the defendant's awareness of the same, the duration of the misconduct and any effort by the defendant to conceal his wrongdoing, the expense plaintiff incurred in the attempt to recover the losses, any profit to the defendant as a result of the wrongdoing, whether and to what extent the defendant has been subject to punitive damage awards based on the same conduct, whether the defendant took remedial action or attempted to make amends, and any other circumstance bearing on the proper amount of the award.[166]

Any punitive damage award returned by a jury must be scrutinized by the trial judge, who is required to set forth his reasoning for decreasing or approving the punitive damage award in written findings of fact and conclusions of law.[167] When a plaintiff is entitled to both punitive damages arising out of a common-law claim and to multiple damages pursuant to a statutory remedy, the plaintiff must elect between the two remedies, but is entitled to a calculation of the amount of damages afforded under each remedy before making an election.[168]

The Tennessee Supreme Court has recently addressed the issue of whether a successor corporation can be held liable for punitive damages based on the predecessor's conduct in *Culbreath v. First Tennessee Bank Nat'l Assoc*, answering the question in the affirmative.[169]

R. WRONGFUL DEATH AND SURVIVORSHIP ACTIONS

The right of recovery in a wrongful death case is strictly a creation of statute and was unavailable at common law.[170] The applicable statutory scheme is a hybrid between survival and wrongful death statutes. The cause of action is the decedent's and is preserved by the passing of his right of action to a class of beneficiaries identified by statute.[171]

A beneficiary's right of recovery, however, is not limited to damages sustained by the decedent, but also includes compensation for the survivors' losses.[172] Recoverable damages sustained by the decedent include medical expenses, physical and mental pain and suffering, funeral expenses, lost wages, and loss of earning capacity.[173] Consortium damages are also recoverable in a wrongful death action.[174]

The surviving spouse maintains control of the right of action unless and until he or she waives that right.[175] Thus, if two wrongful death actions overlap, the surviving spouse has the superior rights to maintain the action.[176] There is authority that proceeds from a wrongful death action that are distributed as personal property.[177]

Robert L. Crawford
Scott B. Ostrow
WYATT, TARRANT & COMBS, L.L.P.
1715 Aaron Brenner Drive, Suite 800
Memphis, Tennessee 38120-4367
(901) 537-1000
Fax (901) 537-1010
lcrawford@wyattfirm.com
sostrow@wyattfirm.com
www.wyattfirm.com

ENDNOTES - TENNESSEE

1. *See* Tenn. Code Ann. § 28-3-104 (2000).

2. *See id.*

3. *See Huggins v. Fulton*, 505 F. Supp. 7 (M.D. Tenn. 1980).

4. *See id.*

5. *See* Tenn. Code Ann. § 28-3-105 (2000).

6. *See id.*

7. *See* Tenn. Code Ann. § 28-3-103 (2000).

8. *See* Tenn. Code Ann. § 29-26-116 (2000).

9. *See* Tenn. Code Ann. § 47-18-110 (1995).

10. *See* Tenn. Code Ann. § 28-3-202 (2000). This also includes personal injuries arising from a deficiency in construction. *See id.*

11. *See* Tenn. Code Ann. § 28-3-203 (2000).

12. *See* Tenn. Code Ann. § 29-26-116 (2000).

13. *See* Tenn. Code Ann. § 29-28-103 (2000). The action must be brought within ten years of when the product was first purchased for use or consumption or within one year of the anticipated life of the product, whichever is shorter. *See id.*

14. *See Willis v. Smith*, 683 S.W.2d 682 (Tenn. Ct. App. 1985).

15. *See, e.g., Housh v. Morris*, 818 S.W.2d 39 (Tenn. Ct. App. 1991).

16. *See* Tenn. Code Ann. § 28-1-105 (2000).

17. *See* Tenn. Code Ann. § 20-1-119 (1994).

18. *See* Tenn. Code Ann. §§ 29-20-101 *et seq.* (2000).

19. *See* Tenn. Code Ann. § 29-20-201 (2000).

20. *See* Tenn. Code Ann. § 29-20-205 (2000).

21. *See* Tenn. Code Ann. § 29-20-202 (2000).

22. *See* Tenn. Code Ann. § 29-20-203 (2000).

23. *See* Tenn. Code Ann. § 29-20-204 (2000).

24. *See Limbaugh v. Coffee Medical Center*, 59 S.W.3d 73 (Tenn. 2001).

25. *See* Tenn. Code Ann. § 29-20-311 (2000).

26. *See Haynes v. Hamilton County*, 883 S.W.2d 606 (Tenn. 1994).

27. *See* Tenn. Code Ann. §§ 55-12-101 -138 (1998 & Supp. 2000).

28. *See* Tenn. Code Ann. § 55-12-105(a) (1998).

29. *See id*. The maximum amount of security required is the lesser of the total amount of all damages suffered or $60,000. *See* Tenn. Code Ann. § 55-12-105(b) and 55-12-102(12)(C) (1998). To establish the amount of damages for determination of the security required, proof of damages may be in the form of an affidavit or accident report submitted to the commissioner. *See* Tenn. Code Ann. § 55-12-110 (1998).

30. *See* Tenn. Code Ann. § 55-12-105(b) (1998).

31. *See Coln v. City of Savannah*, 966 S.W.2d 34, 39 (Tenn. 1998); *McCall v. Wilder*, 913 S.W.2d 150, 153 (Tenn. 1995); *Bradshaw v. Daniel*, 854 S.W.2d 865, 869 (Tenn. 1993).

32. *See Coln*, 966 S.W.2d at 39.

33. *See id*.

34. *See* Tenn. Code Ann. § 29-26-115 (2000).

35. *See Ashe v. Radiation Oncology Assocs.*, 9 S.W.3d 119 (Tenn. 1999).

36. *See Green v. Sacks*, 56 S.W.3d 513 (Tenn. Ct. App. 2001).

37. *See Coln*, 966 S.W.2d at 40; *Hudson v. Gaitan*, 675 S.W.2d 699 (Tenn. 1984) (holding that there is no distinction between a licensee and an invitee) (overruled on other grounds).

38. *See* Tenn. Code Ann. § 70-7-101-105 (1995); *but see* Tenn. Code Ann. § 70-7-104 (1995), which provides that liability is not limited in certain circumstances.

39. *See Camper v. Minor*, 915 S.W.2d 437 (Tenn. 1996). Expert medical or scientific proof is not required for claims of intentional infliction of emotional distress. *See Miller v. Willbanks*, 8 S.W.3d 607 (Tenn. 1999).

40. *See Estate of Amos v. Vanderbilt University*, 62 S.W.3d 133 (Tenn. 2001).

41. *See Ramsey v. Beavers*, 931 S.W.2d 527 (Tenn. 1996).

42. *See* Tenn. Code Ann. § 63-6-218 (Supp. 2000).

43. *See Kilpatrick v. Bryant*, 868 S.W.2d 594, 598 (Tenn. 1993); *Doe v. Linder Constr. Co.*, 845 S.W.2d 173, 181 (Tenn. 1992) ("[p]roof of negligence without proof of causation is nothing") (citing *Drewry v. County of Obion*, 619 S.W.2d 397, 398 (Tenn. Ct. App. 1981)).

44. *See McClenahan v. Cooley*, 806 S.W.2d 767, 775 (Tenn. 1991).

45. *See id.* ("proximate causation is a jury question unless the uncontroverted facts and inferences to be drawn from them make it so clear that all reasonable persons must agree on the proper outcome.")

46. *See White v. Lawrence*, 975 S.W.2d 525 (Tenn. 1998).

47. *See Waste Management, Inc. of Tennessee v. South Central Bell Telephone Co.*, 15 S.W.3d 425 (Tenn. Ct. App. 1997).

48. *See McIntyre v. Balentine*, 833 S.W.2d 52 (Tenn. 1992).

49. *See id.*

50. *See id.* at 57-58.

51. *See id.* at 57.

52. *See George v. Alexander*, 931 S.W.2d 517, 520-22 (Tenn. 1996) (citing Tenn. R. Civ. P. 8.03 Advisory Commission Comment to 1993 Amendment).

53. *See Ridings v. Ralph M. Parsons, Co.*, 914 S.W.2d 79, 84 (Tenn. 1996).

54. See *McIntyre*, 833 S.W.2d at 58.

55. *See* Tenn. Code Ann. § 20-1-119 (1994).

56. 914 S.W.2d 79 (Tenn. 1996).

57. *See Carroll v. Whitney*, 29 S.W.2d 14 (Tenn. 2000) (holding that when a defendant raises the nonparty defense in a negligence action, the trier of fact may apportion fault to immune nonparties).

58. *See Dotson v. Blake*, 29 S.W.3d 26 (Tenn. 2000) (holding that a trier of fact in a negligence action may apportion fault to a tortfeasor protected from liability by a statute of repose).

59. *See Brown v. Wal-Mart Discount Cities*, 12 S.W.3d 785 (Tenn. 2000).

60. *See Breeding v. Edwards*, 62 S.W.3d 170 (Tenn. Ct. App. 2001).

61. *See Ridings*, 914 S.W.2d at 89.

62. *See*, Section I., *infra*, for situations where joint and several liability still applies.

63. *See McIntyre*, 833 S.W.2d at 57-58; *Perez v. McConkey*, 872 S.W.2d 897 (Tenn. 1994) (abolishing implied assumption of risk as a defense).

64. *See* Tenn. Code Ann. § 29-11-101 *et seq.* (1980 and Supp. 1999).

65. *McIntyre*, 833 S.W.2d at 58.

66. *Perez*, 872 S.W.2d at 905.

67. *See id.* at 906.

68. *See id.* at 904.

69. *See Seavers v. Methodist Medical Center of Oak Ridge*, 9 S.W.3d 86 (Tenn. 1999).

70. *See id.* at 91; *Sullivan v. Crabtree*, 258 S.W.2d 782, 783-84 (Tenn. 1953).

71. *See, e.g., Summit Hill Assocs. v. Knoxville Util. Bd.*, 667 S.W.2d 91, 95-96 (Tenn. Ct. App. 1983).

72. *See Sullivan*, 258 S.W.2d at 784-85.

73. *See Seavers*, 9 S.W.3d at 93 n.10, 94-95.

74. *See International Harvester Co. v. Sartain*, 222 S.W.2d 854, 867 (Tenn. Ct. App. 1948).

75. *See Rye v. City of Nashville*, 156 S.W.2d 460, 462 (Tenn. Ct. App. 1941).

76. *See Sterling v. Velsicol Chem. Corp.*, 647 F. Supp. 303 (W.D. Tenn. 1986) (*aff'd in part and rev'd in part*, 855 F.2d 1188 (6th Cir. 1988)).

77. *See Cook By and Through Uithoven v. Spinnaker's of Rivergate, Inc.*, 878 S.W.2d 934 (Tenn. 1994).

78. *See Tennessee Farmers Mut. Ins. Co. v. Hinson*, 651 S.W.2d 235 (Tenn. Ct. App. 1983).

79. *See Harden v. Danek Med., Inc.*, 985 S.W.2d 449 (Tenn. Ct. App. 1998).

80. *See King v. Danek Med., Inc.*, No. W1999-02651-COA-R3-CV, 2000 WL 311143 (Tenn. Ct. App. Mar. 28, 2000).

81. *See Wren v. Sullivan Elec., Inc.*, 797 F.2d 323 (6th Cir. 1986).

82. *See Scarborough v. Brown Group, Inc.*, 935 F.Supp. 954 (W.D. Tenn. 1995).

83. *See Standridge v. Godsey*, 226 S.W.2d 277 (Tenn. 1949).

84. *See Volz v. Ledes*, 895 S.W.2d 677 (Tenn. 1995). The Tennessee Supreme Court expressly rejected the Uniform Comparative Fault Act's approach of shifting a share of a judgment from an insolvent tortfeasor to a remaining solvent tortfeasor. *See id.*

85. *See Camper v. Minor*, 915 S.W.2d 437 (Tenn. 1996).

86. *See General Elec. Co. v. Process Control Co.*, 969 S.W.2d 914 (Tenn. 1998).

87. *See Owens v. Truckstops of Am.*, 915 S.W.2d 420 (Tenn. 1996). The court's reasoning in *Owens* was that because joint and several liability is essential to the theory of strict products liability, parties in a chain of distribution must be treated as a single unit for the purpose of determining and allocating fault. *See id.* at 432. The defendants are only jointly and severally liable for that percentage of the plaintiff's damages caused by the product. *See id.* at 433.

88. *See Limbaugh*, 59 S.W.3d at 87.

89. *See Resolution Trust Corp. v. Block*, 924 S.W.2d 354 (Tenn. 1996).

90. *See id.* at 355.

91. *See id.* at 356. A person acts in concert with another when he "acts *with another* to bring about some preconceived result." *Smith v. Methodist Hosp. of Memphis*, 995 S.W.2d 584 (Tenn. Ct. App. 1999).

92. 891 S.W.2d 905 (Tenn. 1994).

93. *Id.* at 907.

94. *See General Elec. Co.*, 969 S.W.2d at 916.

95. *See id.*

96. *See Smith*, 995 S.W.2d at 591.

97. *See* Tenn. Code Ann. § 29-11-102(a) (2000). The statute lists as exceptions "intrafamily immunity, immunity under the workers' compensation laws of the state of Tennessee, or like immunity." *Id.*

98. *See* Tenn. Code Ann. § 29-11-102(b) (2000).

99. Tenn. Code Ann. § 29-11-102(d) (2000).

100. *See Bervoets v. Harde Ralls Pontiac-Olds, Inc.*, 891 S.W.2d 905 (Tenn. 1994).

101. *See* Tenn. Code Ann. § 29-11-103(1) (2000).

102. *See Bervoets*, 891 S.W.2d at 908.

103. *See* Tenn. Code Ann. § 29-11-105(a)(1) (2000).

104. *See id.*

105. *See Winter v. Smith*, 914 S.W.2d 527 (Tenn. Ct. App. 1995).

106. *See Union Carbide Corp. v. Dunn Bros. Gen. Contractors*, 294 F. Supp. 704 (M.D. Tenn. 1986).

107. *See Winter*, 914 S.W.2d at 542 (stating that absent an express contract, indemnification will be implied only if the party from whom indemnification is sought breached a contract or committed a tortious act).

108. *See Southern Coal and Coke Co. v. Beech Grove Mining Co.*, 381 S.W.2d 299 (Tenn. Ct. App. 1963).

109. *See Starr Printing Co. v. Air Jamaica*, 45 F. Supp. 2d 625, 632 (W.D. Tenn. 1999).

110. *See City of Kingsport, Tennessee v. SCM Corp.*, 429 F. Supp. 96 (E.D. Tenn. 1976).

111. *See* Tenn. Code Ann. § 50-6-108 (1999); *see generally* Tenn. Code Ann. §§ 50-6-101 - 50-6-623 (1999).

112. *See* Tenn. Code Ann. § 50-6-106 (1999); Thomas A. Reynolds, Tennessee Workers' Compensation Practice and Procedure, §§ 2, 4 (1994).

113. *See Newman v. National Union Fire Ins. Co.*, 786 S.W.2d 932, 935 (Tenn. 1990); *Perry v. Transamerica Ins. Group*, 703 S.W.2d 151, 153 (Tenn. Ct. App. 1985).

114. *See Newman*, 786 S.W.2d at 935.

115. *See* Tenn. Code Ann. § 50-6-102(12) (1999); *see also* Tenn. Code Ann. § 50-6-301 for the definition of "occupational diseases." The phrase "arising out of and in the course of employment" is construed broadly and can include injuries that occur when the employee is off the clock. *See, e.g., McCormick v. Aabakus Inc.*, 2000 WL 1473915 (Tenn. Oct. 5, 2000) (not released for publication as of yet).

116. *See Cooper v. Queen*, 586 S.W.2d 830 (Tenn. Ct. App. 1979). The court explained that the theoretical basis for this rule was that an employer cannot allege an accident when he or she intentionally committed the act. *See id.* at 833. *See also Blair v. Allied Maintenance Corp.*, 756 S.W.2d 267 (Tenn. Ct. App. 1988).

117. *See King v. Ross Coal Co.*, 684 S.W.2d 617 (Tenn. Ct. App. 1984).

118. 955 S.W.2d 252 (Tenn. 1997).

119. *Id.* at 256.

120. *Id.* at 257 (reconciling the worker's compensation statute with Tenn. Code Ann. § 29-28-108 (2000)). The jury can only consider this evidence to determine whether the plaintiff has met his burden of establishing the elements of his claim. *See id.*

121. *See Rice v. Sabir*, 979 S.W.2d 305, 308 n.3 (Tenn. 1998).

122. *See Eaton v. McLain*, 891 S.W.2d 587, 593-94 (Tenn. 1994).

123. *See Goodman v. Memphis Park Comm'n*, 851 S.W.2d 165, 166 (Tenn. 1992).

124. *See Rice v. Sabir*, 979 S.W.2d at 308.

125. *See Doe v. Linder Const. Co.*, 845 S.W.2d 173, 178 (Tenn. 1992).

126. *See Hardesty v. Service Merchandise Co.*, 953 S.W.2d 678 (Tenn. Ct. App. 1997); *Paradiso v. Kroger Co.*, 499 S.W.2d 78, 79 (Tenn. Ct. App. 1973). In *Hardesty*, the court stated the rule as a plaintiff must establish either (1) that the defendant created the dangerous condition, or (2) that the defendant had actual or constructive knowledge of the condition prior to the plaintiff's injury. *See Hardesty*, 953 S.W.2d at 682.

127. *See Rice*, 979 S.W.2d at 308.

128. *See Eaton v. McLain*, 891 S.W.2d 587, 593 (Tenn. 1994).

129. *See McClung v. Delta Square Ltd. Partnership*, 937 S.W.2d 891, 902 (Tenn. 1996) (analyzing duty of business premises owner to protect customers from criminal acts of third parties).

130. *See* Tenn. Code Ann. §§ 57-10-101 - 102 (1989).

131. Tenn. Code Ann. § 57-10-102 (1989).

132. *See LaRue v. 1817 Lake, Inc.*, 966 S.W.2d 423, 426 (Tenn. Ct. App. 1998).

133. *See Worley v. Weigels, Inc.*, 919 S.W.2d 589, 593 (Tenn. 1996) (holding that there can be no "constructive knowledge" as to the age of the buyer).

134. *See United Textile Workers Of Am., AFL-CIO, CLC v. Lear Siegler Seating Corp.*, 825 S.W.2d 83 (Tenn. Ct. App. 1990).

135. *See id.; see also John Martin Co. v. Morse/Diesel, Inc.*, 819 S.W.2d 428 (stating that it is a general principle that recovery for purely economic losses absent privity with the defendant is prohibited).

136. *See Overstreet v. Shoney's, Inc.*, 4 S.W.3d 694 (Tenn. Ct. App. 1999); *see also Benson v. Tennessee Valley Elec. Co-op.*, 868 S.W.2d 630, 640 (Tenn. Ct. App. 1993).

137. *See, e.g., United States Brake Sys., Inc. v. American Envtl. Protection, Inc.*, 963 S.W.2d 749 (Tenn. Ct. App. 1997) (allowing recovery for lost profits in claim based on breach of contract and tort if lost profits can be proved with reasonable certainty and are not in fact remote or speculative); *see also Starnes v. First Am. Nat'l Bank*, 723 S.W.2d 113 (Tenn. Ct. App. 1986) (stating recovery for loss of profits is recognized depending on nature and extent of proof involved).

138. *See Brown v. Null*, 863 S.W.2d 425, 430 (Tenn. Ct. App. 1993).

139. *See First Nat'l Bank v. Brooks Farms*, 821 S.W.2d 925 (Tenn. 1991); *see also Corporate Air Fleet of Tennessee, Inc. v. Gate Learjet, Inc.*, 589 F. Supp. 1076, 1080 (M.D. Tenn. 1984); *Ritter v. Custom Chemicides, Inc.*, 912 S.W.2d 128 (Tenn. 1996).

140. *See John Martin Co. v. Morse/Diesel, Inc.*, 819 S.W.2d 428 (Tenn. 1991); *Bethlehem Steel Corp. v. Ernst & Whinney*, 822 S.W.2d 592 (Tenn. 1991).

141. *See* Tenn. R. Civ. P. 9.02; *City State Bank v. Dean Witter Reynolds, Inc.*, 948 S.W.2d 729, 738 (Tenn. Ct. App. 1996).

142. *Hiller v. Hailey*, 915 S.W.2d 800 (Tenn. Ct. App. 1995).

143. *See Piccadilly Square v. Intercontinental Const. Co.*, 782 S.W.2d 178 (Tenn. Ct. App. 1989).

144. *See Fairway Village Condominium Assoc., Inc. v. Connecticut Mut. Life Ins. Co.*, 934 S.W.2d 342, 347 (Tenn. Ct. App. 1996); *Tschira v. Willingham*, 135 F.3d 1077, 1087 (6th Cir. 1998) (applying Tennessee law); *see also City State Bank*, 948 S.W.2d at 738. Fraud can be an intentional misrepresentation of a known, material fact or it can be the concealment or nondisclosure of a known, material fact when there is a duty to do so. *See Justice v. Anderson Co.*, 955 S.W.2d 613, 616 (Tenn. Ct. App. 1997).

145. There is some authority that recklessness may satisfy the intent requirement. *See, e.g., Menuskin v. Williams*, 145 F.3d 755, 764 (6th Cir. 1998) (applying Tennessee law).

146. *See Holt v. American Progressive Life Ins Co.*, 731 S.W.2d 923, 927-28 (Tenn. Ct. App. 1987).

147. *See City State Bank,* 948 S.W.2d at 738; *Metropolitan Gov't of Nashville v. McKinney,* 852 S.W.2d 233, 237 (Tenn. Ct. App. 1992).

148. *See Medical Education Assistance Corp. v. State*, 19 S.W.3d 803, 816-17 (Tenn. Ct. App. 2000).

149. *See* Tenn. Code Ann. §§ 47-18-101 *et seq.* (1995 & Supp. 2000).

150. *See* Tenn. Code Ann. §§ 47-18-104(b) (Supp. 2000).

151. *See* Tenn. Code Ann. §§ 47-18-106(e) (1995); Tenn. Code Ann. § 47-18-107(f).

152. *See* Tenn. Code Ann. § 47-18-109(a)(1) (1995).

153. *See* Tenn. Code Ann. § 47-18-104(a) (1995).

154. *See* Tenn. Code Ann. § 47-18-109(a)(3) - (4) (1995) (court may award three times the actual damages if the violation is willful or knowing).

155. *See* Tenn. Code Ann. §§ 47-18-109(e)(1) (1995).

156. Tenn. Code Ann. § 47-18-104(b)(27) (Supp. 2000).

157. *See* Tenn. Code Ann. § 47-18-110 (1995).

158. *See ATS Southeast, Inc. v. Carrier Corp.*, 18 S.W.3d 626 (Tenn. 2000) (answering the question as certified from the United States District Court for the Middle District of Tennessee).

159. *Pacific Mut. Life Ins. Co. v. Haslip*, 499 U.S. 1 (1991).

160. *See Hodges v. S.C. Toof & Co.*, 833 S.W.2d 896, 900 - 901 (Tenn. 1992)

161. *See id.* at 901.

162. *See id.*

163. *See id.*

164. *See Whittington v. Grand Valley Lakes, Inc.*, 547 S.W. 2d 241, 243 (Tenn. 1977); *Oakley v. Simmons*, 799 S.W.2d 669, 672 (Tenn. Ct. App. 1990). In *Beaty v. McGraw*, 15 S.W.3d 819, 829 (Tenn. Ct. App. 1998), the court explained that this long-recognized rule is actually a roundabout way of saying there can be no action for punitive damages alone.

165. *See Hodges*, 833 S.W. 2d at 901.

166. *See Hodges*, 833 S.W.2d at 901-902.

167. *See id.* at 902.

168. *See Concrete Spaces, Inc. v. Sender*, 2 S.W.3d 901, 909 (Tenn. 1999).

169. *See Culbreath v. First Tennessee Bank Nat'l Assoc.*, 44 S.W.3d 518 (Tenn. 2001) (relying on the existence of a merger agreement in which the successor corporation had assumed all liabilities of its predecessor).

170. *See Jordan v. Baptist Three Rivers Hosp.*, 984 S.W. 2d 593, 597 (Tenn. 1999).

171. *See* Tenn. Code Ann. § 20-5-106 (Supp. 1999); *Jones v. Black*, 539 S.W. 2d 123 (Tenn. 1976).

172. *See* Tenn. Code Ann. § 20-5-113 (1994); *Jordan*, 984 S.W. 2d at 597.

173. *See Thrailkill v. Patterson*, 879 S.W. 2d 836, 840-41 (Tenn. 1994).

174. *See Jordan*, 984 S.W. 2d at 599 (overruling 96 years of prior case law); *Hancock v. Chattanooga-Hamilton County Hospital Authority*, 54 S.W.3d 234 (Tenn. 2001) (extending *Jordan* and holding that filial consortium damages are recoverable as part of the pecuniary value of the decedent's life).

175. *See Baker v. Maples*, 995 S.W.2d 114, 115 (Tenn. Ct. App. 1999).

176. *See id.*

177. *See Gilliam v. Calcott*, 2000 WL 336503 (Tenn. Ct. App. Mar. 30, 2000).

TEXAS

A. STATUTES OF LIMITATION

Causes of action founded on wrongful death, personal injury, and property damage, whether brought in strict liability or negligence, must be brought within two years after the cause of action accrues.[1] Statutes of limitation for most causes of action begin to run at the time of injury or when facts come into existence that authorize a claimant to seek a judicial remedy.[2] The general rule in Texas is that a cause of action accrues when the wrongful act effects an injury, regardless of when the plaintiff learned of such injury.[3] The discovery rule is an exception to the general rule that has been applied in certain, defined situations.[4] The cause of action for wrongful death accrues on the death of the injured person.[5] An individual's period of legal disability (e.g., under 18 years of age, or of unsound mind) is not counted in a limitations period.[6]

An action for malicious prosecution, libel, slander, or breach of promise of marriage must commence within one year after the day the cause of action accrues.[7]

An action under the Deceptive Trade Practices Act (DTPA) must commence within two years after the date on which the deceptive act or practice occurred, or within two years after the consumer discovered or should have discovered the deceptive act or practice.[8] A liberal discovery rule applies.[9]

An action for misappropriation of trade secrets must commence within three years after the claimant discovers or should have discovered the misappropriation.[10]

An action for fraud or breach of fiduciary duty must commence within four years after the date the cause of action accrues.[11]

An action for personal injury must commence within five years after the day the cause of action accrues if the injury arises out of a sexual assault.[12]

A ten-year statute of repose is applicable to claims arising out of improvements to real property.[13] The statute of repose includes actions for personal injury and wrongful death.[14] Likewise, an action for damages arising from an injury caused by an error in a survey conducted by a registered public surveyor or licensed state land surveyor must commence within ten years after the date of completion of the survey.[15]

A products liability action against a manufacturer or seller of manufacturing equipment (equipment and machinery used in the manufacturing, processing, or fabrication of tangible personal property, but not including agricultural equipment or machinery) must commence before the end of 15 years after the date of sale.[16]

A cause of action for breach of warranty under the Texas Uniform Commercial Code must be brought within four years of the date of original delivery of the product.[17]

B. **TORT REFORM**

In 1995 the Texas Legislature passed several tort reform bills in areas including venue, punitive damages, governmental liability, medical malpractice liability, proportionate responsibility of parties, property owner's liability for acts of independent contractors, and sanctions for frivolous pleadings and motions.

C. **"NO FAULT" LIMITATIONS**

The Texas legislature has not adopted a "no fault" regime.

D. **THE STANDARD FOR NEGLIGENCE**

Liability in negligence is premised on duty, a breach of which proximately causes injuries, and damages resulting from that breach.[18] Whether a legal duty exists is a threshold question of law for the court to decide from the facts surrounding the occurrence in question.[19] Duty is the threshold inquiry; it is the function of several interrelated factors, the dominant consideration being foreseeability of the risk.[20]

Contrary to the general rule that there is no duty to control the conduct of third persons, when a "special relationship" exists between the defendant and the third person, the defendant may have a duty to control the third person.[21]

A physician who holds himself out as a specialist is generally expected to possess a higher degree of skill and learning than a general practitioner.[22]

With respect to children, the general rule is that a minor child is required to use only the care that a child of the same age, intelligence, and experience would use.[23] Generally, a child who is beneath the age of five is incapable of negligence as a matter of law.[24] Where negligence of a child above the age of five is at issue, the child's negligence is to be judged by the standard of conduct applicable to a child of the same age.[25] If the child is under the age of 14, the standard of care applicable to children applies; if the child is over the age of 14, the adult standard of care applies (unless the child has a mental disability).[26] Where the minor child assumes to act as an adult, he/she may be judged by the adult standard of care.[27]

E. **CAUSATION**

In order to establish a *prima facie* case of negligence in Texas, the plaintiff must plead and prove that the defendant's negligence was the proximate cause of the plaintiff's injury.[28] Proximate cause consists of cause in fact and foreseeability.[29] Cause in fact is shown when the plaintiff proves the negligent act or omission was a substantial factor in bringing about the plaintiff's injury, without which the harm would not have occurred.[30] Foreseeability requires that a person of ordinary intelligence should have anticipated the danger created by the negligent act or omission.[31] However, it is not necessary that the defendant anticipate the exact injury that may grow out of a particular situation.[32] In Texas, the danger of injury is foreseeable if its general character might reasonably have been anticipated.[33]

Producing cause is required in strict liability actions. A "producing cause" is an efficient, exciting, or contributing cause that, in a natural sequence, produced the occurrence or injury. Foreseeability is not required. There may be more than one producing cause.[34]

F. CONTRIBUTORY NEGLIGENCE, COMPARATIVE NEGLIGENCE, AND ASSUMPTION OF RISK

1. Proportionate Responsibility

Texas uses a proportionate responsibility scheme to determine a claimant's recovery in tort actions.[35] In Texas, a claimant may not recover damages from a defendant if the claimant's percentage of responsibility is more than 50 percent.[36] If the trier of fact determines the claimant's percentage of responsibility to be 50 percent or less, the claimant's damages will be reduced by the percentage of the claimant's responsibility.[37]

2. Assumption of Risk

Assumption of risk, as a general rule, is not an affirmative defense to negligence actions in Texas.[38] Instead, a plaintiff's assumption of the risk is considered as a comparative responsibility factor.[39]

G. *RES IPSA LOQUITUR* AND INHERENTLY DANGEROUS ACTIVITIES

1. *Res Ipsa Loquitur*

Res ipsa loquitur is used in limited types of cases when the circumstances surrounding an accident constitute sufficient evidence of a defendant's negligence.[40] Additionally, *res ipsa loquitur* is a rule of evidence by which negligence may be inferred by the jury; it is not a separate cause of action from negligence.[41]

In Texas, the doctrine of *res ipsa loquitur* applies only when two factors are present: (1) the character of the accident is such that it would not ordinarily occur in the absence of negligence; and (2) the instrumentality causing the injury is shown to have been under the management and control of the defendant.[42] In order for *res ipsa loquitur* to be submitted to the jury, there must be evidence of both factors.[43]

2. Inherently Dangerous Activities

Texas does not recognize a strict liability cause of action for "ultra-hazardous" or inherently dangerous activities.[44] Therefore, in the absence of some other showing, such as negligence, there is no basis for recovery.[45]

H. NEGLIGENCE *PER SE*

Negligence *per se* is the theory of tort law by which courts adopt a legislatively imposed standard of conduct in place of the common law standard of a reasonably prudent person.[46] Any unexcused violation of this statutory duty constitutes negligence *per se* without regard to any common law duties.[47] In order to prevail under a negligence *per se* claim, Texas courts require a plaintiff prove three elements: (1) that the defendant committed an unexcused breach of the legislatively created duty;[48] (2) that plaintiff is a member of the class of persons that the statutory standard of care was designed to protect and that the injury was a type that the statute was designed to prevent;[49] and (3) that the defendant's violation of the statute proximately caused the plaintiff's damages.[50]

I. JOINT AND SEVERAL LIABILITY

The doctrine of joint and several liability maintains that, when the actions of two or more tortfeasors combine to cause an indivisible injury, each tortfeasor is jointly and severally liable to the injured party for the entire amount of his/her damages.[51] As a result, the injured party may obtain a full judgment against either of the culpable tortfeasors, jointly or individually.[52]

In 1995, the Texas Legislature enacted a system of proportionate responsibility for virtually all tort causes of action that accrued on or after September 1, 1995.[53] Pursuant to this system of proportionate responsibility, the trier of fact assigns a percentage of responsibility to: (1) each claimant; (2) each defendant; (3) each settling person; and (4) each responsible third party brought into the lawsuit, based on that party's "causing or contributing to cause in any way the harm for which recovery of damages is sought."[54] A culpable defendant will be liable to the claimant only for its respective percentage of responsibility.[55] However, if a culpable defendant's percentage of responsibility is greater than 50 percent, it is jointly and severally liable for all damages suffered by the claimant.[56] In cases involving toxic tort claims, however, a defendant is jointly and severally liable if the defendant's percentage of responsibility is 15 percent or greater.[57] A jointly and severally liable defendant, nevertheless, has a right of contribution for overpayment against other defendants to the extent that the other defendants have not contributed their respective percentage of responsibility.[58]

J. INDEMNITY

Indemnity is a legal concept in which one tortfeasor becomes liable for the acts or omissions of another tortfeasor based solely on some special relationship between the two tortfeasors.[59] Ordinarily, the right of indemnity may be implied by law or may arise under a contractual agreement.[60] A common law duty to indemnify exists in situations in which one party may be vicariously liable for the actions of another.[61] A common law duty to indemnify also exists in products liability cases to protect the "innocent retailer" in the chain of distribution.[62] Furthermore, Texas has adopted, by code, the "Manufacturer's Duty to Indemnify," which provides that a product manufacturer has a duty to "indemnify and hold harmless a seller against loss arising out of a products liability action except for any loss caused by the seller's negligence, intentional misconduct, or other act or omission. . . ."[63]

The duty to indemnify may also arise out of contract.[64] An indemnity agreement is a promise by the indemnitor to hold the indemnitee harmless from present or future loss liability.[65] Texas courts seek to construe such agreements in accord with the parties' intent as expressed by the four corners of the document.[66]

Contractual agreements that indemnify the indemnitee for his/her own negligence are wholly enforceable if the instrument gives the indemnitor "fair notice" of his duty to indemnify.[67] "Fair notice" means that the obligation to indemnify must be expressed clearly and unequivocally (the "express negligence doctrine") and that such provision be stated conspicuously within the contract.[68] The express negligence doctrine mandates that the party seeking indemnity for his/her own negligence express that intent in specific terms within the instrument.[69] In addition, the conspicuousness requirement specifies that the indemnity provision must "appear on the face of the [contract] to attract the attention of a reasonable person when he/she looks at it."[70] Examples of a "conspicuous" provision include printing in all capital letters and language in the body of the contract that is larger or in contrasting type or color.[71]

K. BAR OF WORKERS' COMPENSATION STATUTE

Under the Texas Workers' Compensation Act, an employee is barred from suing his/her employer who has paid workers' compensation benefits for the employee's work-related injuries.[72] Recovery of workers' compensation benefits is the exclusive remedy of an employee covered by workers' compensation insurance or a legal beneficiary against the employer for work-related injuries or death.[73] However, an injured worker, instead of receiving workers' compensation benefits, may elect to sue his/her employer for intentional torts committed by his/her employer.[74] Furthermore, beneficiaries of a deceased employee may recover punitive damages for the death of an employee that was caused by the intentional act or omission of the employer or that was caused by the employer's gross negligence.[75]

L. PREMISES LIABILITY

The occupier of the premises is the party in control of the premises.[76] The duty owed by a premises owner or occupant (possessor) is determined by the status of the complaining party at the time and place of injury.[77] A person who enters the property of another will normally be classified as an invitee, a licensee, or a trespasser.[78] An invitee is a person who enters the premises of another in answer to an express or implied invitation from the owner or occupier for their mutual benefit.[79] The occupier of the premises owes an invitee a duty of ordinary care to keep the premises in a reasonably safe condition, to inspect the premises to discover any latent defects, and to make safe any defect or give adequate warning of the defect.[80] A licensee is a person whose entrance on or use of the premises of another is permitted by the occupier under such circumstances that he/she is not a trespasser but is without any express or implied invitation.[81] Generally, the duty the occupier of the premises owes a licensee is not to injure the licensee through willful, wanton, or grossly negligent conduct.[82] However, an exception to the general rule is that if the occupier of the premises has knowledge of a dangerous condition and the licensee does not, the occupier has a duty either to warn the licensee or to make the condition reasonably safe.[83] A person is a trespasser where he/she enters on the property of another without any right, lawful authority, or express or implied invitation, permission or license, not in performance of any duties to the owner or person in charge or on any business of such person, but merely for his/her own purposes, pleasure, or convenience, or out of curiosity, and without any enticement, allurement, inducement, or express or implied assurance of safety from the owner or occupier of the premises.[84] The owner or occupier is under a duty not to injure the trespasser willfully, wantonly, or through gross negligence.[85]

M. DRAM SHOP LIABILITY

Texas's Dram Shop Act creates a cause of action against one who provides, sells, or serves an alcoholic beverage to a person obviously intoxicated such that he/she presents a danger to himself or others, and the intoxication of the recipient of the alcoholic beverage is a proximate cause of the damages suffered.[86] A third party, injured by an intoxicated consumer of alcohol, has a cause of action against the provider of the alcohol.[87] Additionally, an individual who is provided with alcohol in violation of this Act and injures himself may assert a cause of action against the provider.[88] In either case, comparative responsibility applies.[89]

The Texas Dram Shop Act is the exclusive remedy for injuries resulting from alcohol being provided to an obviously intoxicated person.[90] The Act precludes common law causes of action against the provider for negligence, negligence *per se*, and serving alcohol to a minor.[91] The scope of the Act creates a cause of action for providing an alcoholic beverage to a person 18 years of age or older.[92] The Act does not provide for a cause of action against a social host[93] and there is no common law duty for a social host to avoid making alcohol available to an intoxicated adult guest the host knows will be driving.[94]

N. ECONOMIC LOSS

When the injury is only economic loss to the subject of a contract itself, the action sounds in contract alone.[95] Such economic losses are not recoverable in actions for negligence[96] or strict liability.[97]

O. FRAUD AND MISREPRESENTATION

In Texas, the elements of common law fraud are: (1) a material representation was made; (2) the representation was false; (3) when the representation was made, the speaker knew it was false or made it recklessly without any knowledge of its truth and as a positive assertion; (4) the representation was made with the intent that it be acted on by the other party; (5) the other party acted in reliance on the representation; and (6) that party suffered injury.[98] Texas also recognizes a cause of action for constructive fraud.[99] Constructive fraud is the breach of a legal or equitable duty that the law declares fraudulent because it violates a fiduciary relationship.[100]

The elements of negligent misrepresentation are as follows: (1) the defendant made a representation in the course of its business or in a transaction in which it had a pecuniary interest; (2) the defendant supplied false information for guidance of others in their business; (3) the defendant did not exercise reasonable care or competence in obtaining or communicating information; and (4) the plaintiff suffered pecuniary loss by justifiably relying on the representation.[101]

Section 402B of the Restatement (Second) of Torts has been adopted in Texas.[102]

P. CONSUMER FRAUD STATUTES

The Texas Deceptive Trade Practices/Consumer Protection Act (DTPA) protects consumers from false, misleading, or deceptive acts or practices in trade and commerce.[103] The DTPA provides that the Consumer Protection Division of the Texas Attorney General's Office, or a district or county attorney, with prior written notice to the Consumer Protection Division, may prosecute actions seeking injunctive relief and civil penalties against a person or entity engaging in a deceptive trade practice.[104] Private actions may also be brought under the DTPA if the plaintiff meets the statutory definition of a "consumer."[105] A consumer/plaintiff may file suit if any of the following constitute a producing cause[106] of an actionable injury:

1. The use or employment by any person of a false, misleading, or deceptive act or practice that is specifically enumerated in the statute[107] and relied upon by a consumer to the consumer's detriment;

2. A breach of an express or implied warranty;

3. Any unconscionable action or course of action by any person; or

4. The use or employment by any person of an act or practice in violation of Article 21.21 of the Texas Insurance Code.[108]

A DTPA plaintiff is generally limited to his or her economic damages for DTPA violations.[109] "Economic damages" means compensatory damages for pecuniary loss, including the cost of repair and replacement, but does not include damages for personal injuries or exemplary damages.[110] However, if the jury finds that the defendant's conduct was committed "knowingly," the plaintiff may also recover mental anguish damages and up to three times the amount of economic damages.[111] If the defendant's conduct was committed "intentionally," the plaintiff may recover up to three times the amount of mental anguish and economic damages.[112] A plaintiff is also entitled to injunctive relief enjoining the deceptive acts, restitution, and any other relief that the court deems proper.[113] Additionally, each plaintiff who prevails in a DTPA suit shall be awarded court costs and reasonable and necessary attorney's fees.[114]

Q. PUNITIVE DAMAGES

Punitive damages, and all other exemplary damages, for most causes of action are governed by Chapter 41 of the Texas Civil Practice and Remedies Code.[115] To recover punitive damages, a plaintiff must prove by clear and convincing evidence that the defendant acted with fraud, malice, or, in a wrongful death action only, willfully or with gross neglect.[116] "Fraud" means fraud other than constructive fraud.[117] "Malice" requires either a specific intent to cause substantial injury or a conscious disregard of an extreme degree of risk.[118]

Punitive damages may not be awarded unless actual damages are awarded, or unless nominal damages are awarded and the jury finds that the defendant acted with malice.[119] The jury must separately determine the amount of economic damages and punitive damages to be awarded.[120] The amount of any punitive damage award is within the discretion of the jury, but state law sets a maximum limit on punitive damage judgments for most cases.[121] Generally, punitive damages are limited to the greater of: (1) two times the amount of economic damages, plus an amount equal to any noneconomic damages up to $75,000; or (2) $200,000.[122] However, this limit does not apply if the defendant's underlying conduct was a felony that was committed intentionally or knowingly,[123] or if the lawsuit was brought under the DTPA, discussed in the previous section.[124]

In determining a punitive damage award, the jury shall consider evidence relating to the following factors: (1) the nature of the wrong; (2) the character of the conduct involved; (3) the degree of culpability of the wrongdoer; (4) the situation and sensibilities of the parties concerned; (5) the extent to which such conduct offends a public sense of justice and propriety; and (6) the net worth of the defendant.[125] An appellate court reviewing a punitive damage award will not disturb the amount awarded unless it is unjust, unreasonable, and so excessive as to justify a conclusion that it was the result of passion, prejudice, or other improper motive rather than a review of the evidence listed above.[126]

On motion by a defendant, the court shall bifurcate a trial as to actual and punitive damages.[127] In any action involving more than one defendant, an award of punitive damages must be against a specific defendant, and each defendant is liable only for the amount of award made against it.[128]

C. Vernon Hartline, Jr., Esquire
Scott G. Edwards, Esquire
Hartline, Dacus, Dreyer & Kern, L.L.P.
6688 North Central Expressway, Suite 1000
Dallas, Texas 75206
(214) 369-2100
(214) 369-2118 (fax)
hartline@flash.net
sedwards@hddk.com
www.hddk.com

ENDNOTES - TEXAS

1. Tex. Civ. Prac. & Rem. Code Ann. § 16.003 (Vernon 2000).

2. *See Johnson & Higgins of Texas, Inc. v. Kennoco Energy, Inc.*, 962 S.W.2d 507, 514 (Tex. 1998). *See also Allgood v. R.J. Reynolds Tobacco Co.*, 80 F.3d 168 (5th Cir. 1996) (claim accrues generally at time of tortious act), *cert. denied*, 519 U.S. 930; *Snyder v. Eanes Indep. Sch. Dist.*, 860 S.W.2d 692, 699 (Tex. App.—Austin 1993) (in tort actions generally, limitations period begins to run at time duty owed to one person breached by wrongful act of another).

3. *Moreno v. Sterling Drug, Inc.*, 787 S.W.2d 348, 351 (Tex. 1990); *Robinson v. Weaver*, 550 S.W.2d 18, 19 (Tex. 1977).

4. *See Vaught v. Showa Denko K.K.*, 107 F.3d 1137 (5th Cir. 1997); *Childs v. Haussecker*, 974 S.W.2d 31 (Tex. 1998) (discovery rule applies in latent occupational exposure case); *Moreno v. Sterling Drug, Inc.*, 787 S.W.2d 348, 351 (Tex. 1990).

5. Tex. Civ. Prac. & Rem. Code Ann. § 16.003(b) (Vernon 2000); *see also Moreno v. Sterling Drug, Inc.*, 787 S.W.2d 348, 349 (Tex. 1990) (discovery rule does not apply to wrongful death action).

6. Tex. Civ. Prac. & Rem. Code Ann. § 16.001 (Vernon 2000).

7. Tex. Civ. Prac. & Rem. Code Ann. § 16.002(a) (Vernon 2000).

8. Tex. Bus. & Comm. Code Ann. § 17.565 (Vernon 2000).

9. *Id.*

10. Tex. Civ. Prac. & Rem. Code Ann. § 16.0010 (Vernon 2000).

11. Tex. Civ. Prac. & Rem. Code Ann. § 16.004(a) (Vernon 2000).

12. Tex. Civ. Prac. & Rem. Code Ann. § 16.0045 (Vernon 2000). The limitations period under this section is tolled where a petition is filed alleging that the identity of the defendant is unknown. *Id.*

13. Tex. Civ. Prac. & Rem. Code Ann. § 16.009 (Vernon 2000).

14. *Id.*

15. Tex. Civ. Prac. & Rem. Code Ann. § 16.011 (Vernon 2000).

16. Tex. Civ. Prac. & Rem. Code Ann. § 16.012 (Vernon 2000). If a manufacturer or seller expressly represents that the manufacturing equipment has a useful safe life greater than 15 years, the claimant must commence the products liability action before the end of the number of years represented after the date of sale by the seller. *Id.*

17. *American Tobacco Co. v. Grinnell*, 951 S.W.2d 420, 435 (Tex. 1997) (four-year statute of limitations on implied warranties began to run at time of delivery tobacco, not when plaintiff discovered cancer) (citing Tex. Bus. and Comm. Code Ann. § 2.725(b) (Vernon 1994)).

18. *Thapar v. Zezulka*, 994 S.W.2d 635, 637 (Tex. 1999).

19. *Id.*

20. *See El Chico Corp. v. Poole*, 732 S.W.2d 306, 311 (Tex. 1987). *See also e.g., Sedona Contracting v. Ford, Powell & Carson*, 995 S.W.2d 192, 197 (Tex. App.—San Antonio 1999) (plaintiff must establish privity or relationship between himself and defendant), *reh'g overruled,* and *rev. denied.*

21. *Greater Houston Transp. Co. v. Phillips*, 801 S.W.2d 523, 525 (Tex. 1990) (such relationships include employer-employee, parent-child, and independent contractor–contractee under special circumstances).

22. *King v. Flamm*, 442 S.W.2d 679, 681 (Tex. 1969).

23. *See Rudes v. Gottschalk*, 324 S.W.2d 201 (Tex. 1959); *City of Austin v. Hoffman*, 379 S.W.2d 103, 107 (Tex. App.—Austin 1964).

24. *See MacConnell v. Hill*, 569 S.W.2d 524, 526 (Tex. App.—Corpus Christi, 1978). *See also Thompson v. Wooten*, 650 S.W.2d 499, 500 (Tex. App.—Houston [14th Dist.], 1983).

25. *Id.*

26. *Hoffman*, 379 S.W.2d at 107.

27. *Id. See also Starr v. United States*, 393 F. Supp. 1359, 1366 (N.D. Tex. 1975).

28. *Leitch v. Hornsby*, 935 S.W.2d 114, 118 (Tex. 1996).

29. *Id.; Farley v. M. M. Cattle Co.*, 529 S.W.2d 751, 755 (Tex. 1975).

30. *Doe v. Boys Club of Greater Dallas*, 907 S.W.2d 472, 477 (Tex. 1995).

31. *Id.; Pifer v. Muse*, 984 S.W.2d 739, 743 (Tex. App.—Texarkana 1998, no writ).

32. *Brown v. Edwards Transfer Co.*, 764 S.W.2d 220, 223 (Tex. 1988).

33. *Nixon v. Mr. Property Mgmt. Co.*, 690 S.W.2d 546, 551 (Tex. 1985).

34. *See Union Pump Co. v. Allbritton*, 898 S.W.2d 773, 775 (Tex. 1995); *Rourke v. Garza*, 530 S.W.2d 794, 801 (Tex. 1975).

35. Tex. Civ. Prac. Rem. Code §§ 33.001–33.017 (Vernon 2000).

36. Tex. Civ. Prac. & Rem. Code § 33.001 (Vernon 2000).

37. Tex. Civ. Prac. & Rem. Code § 33.003 (Vernon 2000).

38. *See Farley v. M. M. Cattle Co.*, 529 S.W.2d 751, 758 (Tex. 1975); *Moore v. Phi Delta Theta Co.*, 976 S.W.2d 738, 741 (Tex. App.—Houston [1st Dist.] 1998), *petition denied*.

39. *Id.*

40. *See Haddock v. Arnspiger*, 793 S.W.2d 948, 950 (Tex. 1990); *Schorlemer v. Reyes*, 974 S.W.2d 141, 145 (Tex. App.—San Antonio 1998), *petition denied*.

41. *Id.*

42. *Id.*

43. *See Marathon Oil Co. v. Sterner*, 632 S.W.2d 571, 573–74 (Tex. 1982); *Schorlemer*, 974 S.W.2d at 145.

44. *Prather v. Brandt*, 981 S.W.2d 801, 804 (Tex. App.—Houston [1st Dist.] 1998), *petition denied*.

45. *Barras v. Monsanto Co.*, 831 S.W.2d 859, 865 (Tex. App.—Houston [14th Dist.] 1992), *writ denied*.

46. *See Hayes v. United States*, 899 F.2d 438 (5th Cir. 1990); *Nixon v. Mr. Property Mgmt. Co.*, 690 S.W.2d 546, 549 (Tex. 1985); *Carter v. William Sommerville & Son, Inc.*, 584 S.W.2d 274, 278 (Tex. 1979); *Moughon v. Wolf*, 576 S.W.2d 603, 604 (Tex. 1978); *Southern Pacific Co. v. Castro*, 493 S.W.2d 491 (Tex. 1973).

47. *Missouri Pac. R.R. Co. v. Austin American Statesman*, 552 S.W.2d 99, 102 (Tex. 1977).

48. *Id.*

49. *Moughon*, 576 S.W.2d at 604; *Perry v. S.N.*, 973 S.W.2d 301 (Tex. 1998).

50. *Nixon*, 690 S.W.2d at 549.

51. *See Riley v. Industrial Finance Service Co.*, 302 S.W.2d 652 (Tex. 1957); *Landers v. East Texas Salt Water Disposal Co.*, 248 S.W.2d 731 (Tex. 1952).

52. *See Hardy v. Gulf Oil Co.*, 949 F.2d 826 (5th Cir. 1992); *MacMillan Bloedel Ltd. v. Flintkote Co.*, 760 F.2d 580 (5th Cir. 1985); *Riley*, 302 S.W.2d at 652; *Landers*, 248 S.W.2d at 731; Tex. Civ. Prac. & Rem. Code § 33.013(b) & (c) (Vernon 2000).

53. Tex. Civ. Prac. & Rem. Code § 33.001 cmt. (Vernon 2000) (quoting section 3 of the 1995 amendatory act). Proportionate responsibility also applies to causes of action that accrued before September 1, 1995, but for which suit was filed on or after September 1, 1996. *See id.* The law immediately in effect prior to September 1, 1995, governs all causes of action that accrued before September 1, 1995, and for which suit was filed before September 1, 1996. *See id.*

54. *Id.* at § 33.003. Definitions of these terms can be found at Section 33.011 of the Texas Civil Practices & Remedies Code.

55. *Id.* at § 33.013(a).

56. *Id.* at § 33.013(b); *see also* Tex. Civ. Prac. & Rem. Code § 33.012(b).

57. *Id.* at § 33.013(c).

58. *Id.* at § 33.015(a).

59. *St. Anthony's Hosp. v. Whitfield*, 946 S.W.2d 174 (Tex. App.—Amarillo 1997), *writ denied*.

60. *Texas Constr. Assocs., Inc. v. Balli*, 558 S.W.2d 513 (Tex. Civ. App.—Corpus Christi 1977), *no writ*.

61. *Bonniwell v. Beech*, 663 S.W.2d 816, 819 (Tex. 1984).

62. *Id.*

63. Tex. Civ. Prac. & Rem. Code Ann. § 82.002(a) (Vernon 2000).

64. *H.M.R. Constr. Co. v. Wolco of Houston, Inc.*, 422 S.W.2d 214 (Tex. Civ. App.—Houston [14th Dist.] 1967), *writ ref'd n.r.e.*

65. *See Dresser Inds., Inc. v. Page Petroleum, Inc.*, 853 S.W.2d 505 (Tex. 1993) (citing *Russell v. Lemons*, 205 S.W.2d 629, 631 (Tex. Civ. App.— Amarillo 1947), *writ ref'd n.r.e.*).

66. *Ideal Lease Service v. Amoco Production Co.*, 662 S.W.2d 951, 953 (Tex. 1983).

67. *Leonard v. Aluminum Co. of America*, 767 F.2d 134 (5th Cir. 1985) *and on rehearing*, 800 F.2d 523 (5th Cir. 1986).

68. *See id.; Enserch Corp. v. Parker*, 794 S.W.2d 2, 8 (Tex. 1990).

69. *See Houston Lighting & Power Co. v. Atchison, Topeka, & Santa Fe Ry. Co.*, 890 S.W.2d 455 (Tex. 1994); *Dresser Inds., Inc. v. Page Petroleum, Inc.*, 853 S.W.2d 505 (Tex. 1993); *Enserch Corp. v. Parker*, 794 S.W.2d 2, 8 (Tex. 1990); *Ethyl Corp. v. Daniel Constr. Co.*, 725 S.W.2d 705, 707–08 (Tex. 1987).

70. *Dresser Inds., Inc.*, 853 S.W.2d at 505 (quoting *Ling & Co. v. Trinity Sav. & Loan Ass'n*, 482 S.W.2d 841, 843 (Tex. 1972)).

71. *Dresser Inds., Inc.*, 853 S.W.2d at 511 (quoting Tex. Bus. & Com. Code Ann. § 1.201(10)).

72. Tex. Lab. Code Ann. § 401.001 *et seq.* (Vernon 2000).

73. Tex. Lab. Code Ann. § 408.001(a) (Vernon 2000).

74. *See id.* at § 340.45; *Rodriguez v. Naylor Industries*, 763 S.W.2d 411, 412 (Tex. 1989).

75. Tex. Lab. Code Ann. §§ 408.001(b) & 340.44 (Vernon 2000).

76. *Wal-Mart Stores, Inc. v. Alexander*, 868 S.W.2d 322, 324 (Tex. 1993).

77. *See State v. Tennison*, 509 S.W.2d 560, 562 (Tex. 1974); *Graham v. Atlantic Richfield Co.*, 848 S.W.2d 747, 751 (Tex. App.—Corpus Christi 1993), *writ denied*.

78. *Rowland v. Corpus Christi*, 620 S.W.2d 930, 933 (Tex. Civ. App.—Corpus Christi 1981), *writ ref'd n.r.e.*

79. *Texas Power & Light Co. v. Holder*, 385 S.W.2d 873, 885 (Tex. Civ. App.—Tyler 1964) *writ ref'd n.r.e. per curiam*, 393 S.W.2d 821, 822 (Tex. 1965).

80. *See Carlisle v. J. Weingarten, Inc.*, 137 Tex. 220, 152 S.W.2d 1073, 1074 (1941); *Adam Dante Corp. v. Sharpe*, 483 S.W.2d 452 (Tex. 1972).

81. *Rowland v. City of Corpus Christi*, 620 S.W.2d 930, 933 (Tex. Civ. App.—Corpus Christi 1981), *writ ref'd n.r.e.*

82. *City of Grapevine v. Roberts*, 946 S.W.2d 841, 843 (Tex. 1997).

83. *Id.*

84. *Texas Power & Light Co. v. Holder*, 385 S.W.2d 873, 885 (Tex. Civ. App.—Tyler 1964) *writ ref'd n.r.e. per curiam*, 393 S.W.2d 821, 822 (Tex. 1965).

85. *Texas Utilities Elec. Co. v. Timmons*, 947 S.W.2d 191, 193 (Tex. 1997).

86. Tex. Alco. Bev. Code Ann. §§ 2.01 (Vernon 2000) *et seq.*

87. *El Chico Corp. v. Poole*, 732 S.W.2d 306 (Tex. 1987).

88. *Smith v. Sewell*, 858 S.W.2d 350, 355 (Tex. 1993).

89. *Id.* at 356.

90. *Sewell v. Smith*, 819 S.W.2d 565, 567 (Tex. App.—Dallas 1991), *aff'd*, 858 S.W.2d 350.

91. *Id.*

92. Tex. Alco. Bev. Code Ann. § 2.03 (Vernon 2000).

93. Tex. Alco. Bev. Code Ann. § 2.01(1) (Vernon 2000) (" 'Provider' means a person who sells or serves an alcoholic beverage under authority of a license or permit issued under the terms of this code or who otherwise sells an alcoholic beverage to an individual.").

94. *Graff v. Beard*, 858 S.W.2d 918, 919 (Tex. 1993).

95. *See Jim Walter Homes, Inc. v. Reed*, 711 S.W.2d 617, 618 (Tex. 1986); *Airborne Freight Corp. v. C. R. Lee Enterprises*, 847 S.W.2d 289, 293 (Tex. App—El Paso 1992), *writ denied*, citing *Southwestern Bell Telephone Co. v. Delanney*, 809 S.W.2d 493, 495 (Tex. 1991).

96. *Indelco, Inc. v. Hanson Indus. N.A.*, 967 S.W.2d 931 (Tex. App.—Houston [14th Dist.] 1998), *writ denied*.

97. *See Garcia v. Texas Instruments, Inc.*, 610 S.W.2d 456 (Tex. 1980); *Mid-Continent Aircraft Corp. v. Curry County Spraying Serv., Inc.*, 572 S.W.2d 308, 313 (Tex. 1978); *Nobility Homes of Texas, Inc. v. Shivers*, 557 S.W.2d 77, 80 (Tex. 1977); *Signal Oil & Gas Co. v. Universal Oil Prods.*, 572 S.W.2d 320, 325 (Tex. 1978) (allowing recovery for damage to product itself if collateral property damage has also occurred).

98. *See Eagle Properties, Ltd. v. Scharbauer*, 807 S.W.2d 714, 723 (Tex. 1990); *Trenholm v. Ratliff*, 646 S.W.2d 927, 930 (Tex. 1983).

99. *Archer v. Griffith*, 390 S.W.2d 735 (Tex. 1964).

100. *See id.*; *In re Estate of Herring*, 970 S.W.2d 583, 586 n.3 (Tex. App.—Corpus Christi 1998, n.p.h.); *Stephanz v. Laird*, 846 S.W.2d 895, 903 (Tex. App.—Houston [1st Dist.] 1993), *writ denied*.

101. *See Federal Land Bank Ass'n of Tyler v. Sloane*, 825 S.W.2d 439, 442 (Tex. 1991); *Abbott v. Polock*, 946 S.W.2d 513 (Tex. App.—Austin 1997), *writ denied*.

102. *Crocker v. Winthrop Labs.*, 514 S.W.2d 429, 431 (Tex. 1974).

103. Tex. Bus. & Com. Code Ann. § 17.46(a) (Vernon 2000).

104. Tex. Bus. & Com. Code Ann. §§ 17.47, 17.48 (Vernon 2000).

105. Tex. Bus. & Com. Code Ann.§ 17.50(a) (Vernon 2000). "Consumer" is defined as an "individual, partnership, corporation, this state, or a subdivision or agency of this state who seeks or acquires by purchase or lease, any goods or services, except that the term does not include a business consumer that has assets of $25 million or more, or that is owned or controlled by a corporation or entity with assets of $25 million or more." Tex. Bus. & Com. Code Ann. § 17.45(4) (Vernon 2000). Only a consumer may be a DTPA plaintiff. Tex. Bus. & Com. Code Ann. § 17.50(a) (Vernon 2000).

106. "Producing cause" means that the act or omission was a substantial factor in bringing about the injury, but, in a DTPA suit, the plaintiff need not establish that the harm was foreseeable. *Doe v. Boys Clubs of Greater Dallas, Inc.*, 907 S.W.2d 473, 481 (Tex. 1995) (citations omitted).

107. Tex. Bus. & Com. Code Ann. § 17.46(b) (Vernon 2000).

108. Tex. Bus. & Com. Code Ann. § 17.50(a) (Vernon 2000).

109. Tex. Bus. & Com. Code Ann. § 17.50(a) (Vernon 2000). The DTPA damage limitations apply only to causes of action arising from a DTPA violation. Several Texas statutes outside the DTPA give civil plaintiffs the right to bring a cause of action under the DTPA if they suffer harm from a violation that particular statute. In such a situation, the DTPA damage limitations do not apply. Tex. Bus. & Com. Code Ann. § 17.50(h) (Vernon Supp. 2000).

110. Tex. Bus. & Com. Code Ann. § 17.45(11) (Vernon 2000).

111. Tex. Bus. & Com. Code Ann. § 17.50(b)(1) (Vernon 2000).

112. *Id.*

113. Tex. Bus. & Com. Code Ann. §§ 17.50(b)(2)–(4) (Vernon 2000).

114. Tex. Bus. & Com. Code Ann. § 17.50(d) (Vernon 2000).

115. Tex. Civ. Prac. & Rem. Code § 41.002(a) (Vernon 2000).

116. Tex. Civ. Prac. & Rem. Code § 41.003 (Vernon 2000).

117. Tex. Civ. Prac. & Rem. Code § 41.001(6) (Vernon 2000).

118. *Universal Services Co., Inc. v. Ung,* 904 S.W.2d 638, 641 n.2 (Tex. 1995) (construing Tex. Civ. Prac. & Rem. Code § 41.001(7) (Vernon 1997)).

119. Tex. Civ. Prac. & Rem. Code § 41.004 (Vernon 2000).

120. Tex. Civ. Prac. & Rem. Code § 41.008(a) (Vernon 2000).

121. Tex. Civ. Prac. & Rem. Code §§ 41.010, 41.008(b) (Vernon 2000).

122. Tex. Civ. Prac. & Rem. Code § 41.008(b) (Vernon 2000).

123. Tex. Civ. Prac. & Rem. Code § 41.008(c) (Vernon 2000).

124. Tex. Civ. Prac. & Rem. Code § 41.002(d) (Vernon 2000); Tex. Bus. & Com. Code Ann. § 17.50(g) (Vernon 2000).

125. *Alamo National Bank v. Kraus,* 616 S.W.2d 908, 910 (Tex. 1981).

126. *Chasewood Const. Co. v. Rico,* 696 S.W.2d 439, 448 (Tex. App.—San Antonio 1985), *writ ref'd n.r.e.*

127. Tex. Civ. Prac. & Rem. Code § 41.009(a) (Vernon 2000).

128. Tex. Civ. Prac. & Rem. Code § 41.006 (Vernon 2000).

UTAH

A. STATUTES OF LIMITATION

Causes of action founded upon negligent, intentional, or tortious conduct for personal injuries, except death, must be brought within four years.[1] Claims for wrongful death must be brought within two years.[2] Claims for injury to personal or real property must be brought within three years.[3] Claims for breach of warranty seeking damages for personal injury or tortious injury to personal property are treated as tort claims and are subject to the applicable tort limitations period.[4]

Defamation actions must be brought within one year.[5]

In construction cases, injuries due to defective design or construction of improvements to real property must be brought within two years of the earlier of when the claim was discovered or should have been discovered through reasonable diligence.[6] Breach of warranty claims must be brought within six years of completion of the improvement, unless an express contract or warranty provides otherwise.[7] In the absence of fraud, express warranty, or intentional wrongdoing, no claims may be commenced more than 12 years after the improvement is completed.[8] Claims discovered in the eleventh or twelfth year of the 12-year period may be brought within two years of the discovery date.[9]

Under a "catch-all" provision, all actions that are neither subject to another, specific limitations period nor excluded from the application of a limitations period must be brought within four years.[10] Although the issue has not been decided by Utah courts, the statute of limitations for tortious interference with contractual or prospective economic relations is likely four years under the catch-all provision.

B. TORT REFORM

To date, the Utah legislature has not passed any tort reform laws.

C. "NO FAULT" LIMITATIONS

Under Utah law, a person injured in an automobile accident may not maintain a cause of action for general damages except where the person has sustained one or more of the following: (a) death, (b) dismemberment, (c) permanent disability or permanent impairment based upon objective findings, (d) permanent disfigurement, or (e) medical expenses in excess of $3,000.[11] This no-fault tort immunity does not apply to defendants who fail to carry the required liability insurance on their vehicles at the time of the accident.[12]

D. THE STANDARD FOR NEGLIGENCE

To prevail on a negligence claim, a plaintiff must show the defendant owed her a duty, which the defendant breached, and the breach was a proximate cause of the plaintiff's injury and there was, in fact an injury.[13] The duty of care is breached if the defendant's conduct falls below the level of ordinary, reasonable care appropriate under the particular circumstances.[14]

State or local governmental agencies owe only a general duty to the public, and have no duty of care toward an individual who may be harmed by the government's acts unless there is a special relationship between the government and the individual.[15] At least four circumstances may establish a special relationship: (1) a statute is in place which is intended to protect a class of persons, which the plaintiff belongs, from a particular type of harm; (2) a government agent undertakes to protect a specific person or property; (3) the government acts in a way which reasonably should induce reliance by a member of the public; (4) the government agency has actual custody of the plaintiff or of a third person who harms the plaintiff.[16]

A child must exercise the degree of care that a child of the same age, intelligence, and experience would ordinarily exercise under the circumstances.[17] The question of a child's negligence must go to the jury, unless the child is so old and mature the court may take notice that the child is responsible for her acts or so young and immature the court may take notice the child is not responsible for her acts.[18]

E. CAUSATION

A plaintiff cannot prevail on a negligence claim unless she shows the defendant's acts proximately caused her injuries.[19] Proximate cause is that cause which in natural, continual sequence—unbroken by an efficient intervening cause—produces the injury and without which the result would not have occurred.[20] It is the "efficient cause" which sets in motion the actions which ultimately injure the plaintiff.[21]

F. CONTRIBUTORY NEGLIGENCE, COMPARATIVE NEGLIGENCE, AND ASSUMPTION OF RISK

1. Comparative Negligence

Utah applies a statutory comparative fault scheme to all tort claims, including strict liability.[22] Fault by the plaintiff does not alone bar recovery. A plaintiff may recover the proportion of damages attributable to the percentage of fault of the defendants if the fault attributable to the plaintiff is less than 50 percent (prior to any post-verdict reallocation of fault by the trial court, as described below).[23] The fact finder may allocate fault to each person seeking recovery, to each defendant, and to any other person whether immune from suit or joined as a party or not.[24] No defendant may be held liable for more than that defendant's proportionate share of the plaintiff's damages attributable to that defendant's fault.[25] There are no actions for contribution among tortfeasors in Utah.[26]

If one or more of the defendants is immune from suit (i.e., an employer), and the total percentage of fault attributed to all defendants immune from suit is less then 40 percent, the trial court is required to reduce that percentage of fault to zero and reallocate that percentage of fault among the other parties in proportion to the percentage of fault initially attributed to each party by the fact finder.[27]

2. **Assumption of Risk**

Assumption of risk, meaning knowledge of the defect and awareness of the danger by the user or consumer who unreasonably proceeds to make use of the product, may be considered as fault by the plaintiff under the comparative fault scheme.[28]

G. RES IPSA LOQUITUR AND INHERENTLY DANGEROUS ACTIVITIES

1. *Res Ipsa Loquitur*

The doctrine of *res ipsa loquitur* is an evidentiary doctrine created to help a plaintiff establish a case of negligence when "human experience provides a reasonable basis for concluding that an injury probably would not have happened if due care had been exercised."[29] The doctrine does not relieve the plaintiff of the obligation of proving causation. "[R]ather, it permits him, in lieu of linking his injury to a specific act on the defendant's part, to causally connect it with an agency or instrumentality, under the exclusive control of the defendant, functioning in a manner which, under the circumstances would produce no injury absent negligence."[30]

Res ipsa loquitur requires the plaintiff to establish an evidentiary foundation which includes the following: (1) the accident was of a kind which in the ordinary course of events, would not have happened had the defendant(s) used due care; (2) the instrument or thing causing the injury was at the time of the accident under the management and control of the defendant(s); and (3) the accident happened irrespective of any participation at the time by the plaintiff.[31] Whether a plaintiff has established the requisite foundation for a *res ipsa loquitur* instruction is a question of law for the trial court to answer.[32]

2. **Inherently Dangerous Activities**

Utah has adopted § 520 of the Restatement (Second) of Torts with respect to liability for inherently dangerous activities. One who carried on an inherently or abnormally dangerous activity is strictly liable for harm resulting from the activity.[33] In determining whether a particular activity is inherently dangerous, the following factors are to be considered: (1) the existence of a high degree of risk of some harm to the third person, land or chattels of others; (2) likelihood that the harm that results from it will be great; (3) extent to which the activity is not a matter of common usage; (4) inability to eliminate the risk by the exercise of reasonable care; (5) inappropriateness of the activity to the place where it is carried on; and (6) extent to which its value to the community is outweighed by its dangerous attributes.[34]

H. NEGLIGENCE *PER SE*

Utah follows Section 286 of the Restatement (Second) of Torts for establishing when a statutory standard should be applied as the standard of conduct of a reasonable person.[35] Thus, a court may find a statute establishes the appropriate standard of care if the statute's purpose, in whole or part, is to: (1) protect a class of persons of which the plaintiff is a member; (2) protect the particular interest that was invaded; (3) protect the particular interest against the type of harm that occurred; (4) protect the particular interest from the particular danger that caused the harm.[36]

If the court finds a statute establishes the requisite standard of care, then it may instruct the jury that violation of that statute *may be prima facie* evidence of negligence.[37] Violation of a statute is not negligent if the violation was excusable under the circumstances.[38]

I. JOINT AND SEVERAL LIABILITY

Under Utah's statutory comparative fault scheme, which applies in product liability actions, joint and several liability is effectively abolished. The maximum amount for which a defendant may be liable is the percentage of the total damages equivalent to the percentage of fault attributed to that defendant,[39] after any reallocation of fault that may be applicable if some fault is attributed to persons immune from suit in a combined amount of less than forty percent.[40] No defendant may seek contribution from any other person.[41]

J. INDEMNITY

Utah applies the common law rule that one who has become liable in tort for another's wrongful, unauthorized conduct has a right to indemnity, even if there is no express contract between the parties.[42] In a product liability action, a seller or a distributor of a defective product who is free of active wrongdoing has a right to recover from the manufacturer any judgment the retailer is required to pay, as well as attorney fees, if the retailer has notified the manufacturer of its indemnity claim.[43] The retailer cannot recover attorney fees incurred for defending itself against allegations of its own active wrongdoing.[44]

The Utah Supreme Court recently held that while generally releases of liability for prospective negligence are enforceable, a parent may not release a minor's prospective claim for negligence.[45]

K. BAR OF WORKERS' COMPENSATION STATUTE

The right of an employee to recover under the Utah Workers' Compensation Act or Utah Occupational Disease Act is the exclusive remedy of the employee against the employer and against any officer, agent, or employee of the employer.[46]

L. PREMISES LIABILITY

The duty owed by a possessor of land to another person depends on whether that person is an invitee, a licensee, or a trespasser.[47] Utah law generally follows the duties and exceptions for premises liability set forth in Sections 329 to 343 of the Restatement (Second) of Torts.

With respect to invitees, including business visitors or business invitees, the landowner has a duty to exercise ordinary care to keep the premises in a condition reasonably safe for the invitee who is in reasonable pursuit of a purpose embraced within the invitation. The landowner has a duty to warn invitees of latent dangers if the landowner knows or reasonably should know of the danger from a reasonable inspection of the property. The landowner is not duty bound to discovery defects that a reasonable inspection would not disclose.[48]

With respect to licensees, who is a person who goes upon the property of another by express or implied permission, the landowner has a duty to exercise reasonable care in carrying on the activities on the land to avoid injury to the licensee. A landowner has a duty to warn a licensee of latent hazards on the land of which the landowner is aware (of both the hazard and that it involves an unreasonable risk to the plaintiff), but the landowner generally has no duty to inspect the land to discovery possible dangers or to prepare a safe place for the reception of the licensee.[49]

With respect to trespassers, who is a person on the land without invitation, privilege, or consent, the landowner generally owes no duty to the trespasser except to refrain from causing willful and wanton injury. However, a different rule applies when the trespasser is a child. The landowner owes a duty to exercise reasonable care to eliminate a danger or otherwise protect trespassing children from bodily injury caused by an artificial and uncommon condition that is attractive and alluring to children of immature judgment and discretion where the condition is inherently dangerous; the landowner knows or has reason to know of the condition and realizes or should realize that it involves an unreasonable risk of serious bodily harm to children; the child or children, because of their youth, do not discover the condition or do not realize the risk involved in going near it; and if it is practical to guard against the danger to children without serious inconvenience or great expense to the landowner.[50]

Utah has statutes limiting the liability of ski area operators and of other landowners whose property is used for recreational purposes.[51]

M. DRAM SHOP LIABILITY

Utah amended its Dramshop Act in 1997 to eliminate the distinction between alcoholic beverages (defined to include both beer and liquor) and liquor (defined to exclude beer, malt liquor, or any malted beverage with an alcohol content of less than 4 percent alcohol by volume)[52] and to limit the liability of those who are not in the business of providing or selling alcoholic beverages.[53] As amended, the Act imposes liability upon those who are in the business of selling, providing, or serving alcoholic beverages[54] (with an exception for general food stores)[55] and upon social hosts who serve alcoholic beverages to minors.[56] Although the issue has not yet been tested in a reported case, it appears that under the amended statute the liability of a social host is limited to circumstances in which the host serves or provides alcoholic beverages to anyone who the host knows or should know is under the age of 21 years and that individual becomes intoxicated causing a third person personal injury or property damage.

To recover under the Dramshop Act, a plaintiff must bring a cause of action within two years after the date of the injury.[57] For accidents occurring after January 1, 1998, damages are capped at $500,000 per person or $1,000,000 per occurrence.[58] However, "[n]othing in this chapter precludes any cause of action or additional recovery against the person causing the injury."[59] The Act gives the government immunity from dramshop liability.[60]

The Act also prohibits employers from terminating or sanctioning the employment of an employee of a restaurant, airport lounge, private club, on-premise beer retailer, or any other establishment serving alcoholic beverages as a result of an employee refusing to sell alcoholic beverages to anyone the employee considers to be under 21 years of age, under the influence of alcohol or drugs.[61]

N. ECONOMIC LOSS

Utah courts have recognized the economic loss doctrine, prohibiting recovery of purely economic losses in actions based on non-intentional torts.[62] The doctrine is not limited to product liability claims.[63] Economic loss is defined as damages for inadequate value, costs of repair and replacement of the defective product, or consequent loss of profits, without any claim of personal injury or damage to other property, as well as the diminution in the value of the product because it is inferior in quality and does not work for the general purposes for which it was sold.[64] Some question remains as to the viability of an earlier holding permitting recovery of economic loss in a case involving the "negligent manufacture" of a product.[65] Economic loss is recoverable in actions involving intentional torts.[66]

O. FRAUD AND MISREPRESENTATION

The Utah Rules of Civil Procedure require that the circumstances of fraud be pleaded with particularity.[67]

The elements of an action based on fraudulent misrepresentation are:

> "(1) a representation; (2) concerning a presently existing material fact; (3) which was false; (4) which the representor either (a) knew to be false, or (b) made recklessly, knowing that he had insufficient knowledge upon which to base such representation; (5) for the purpose of inducting the other party to act upon it; (6) that the other party, acting reasonably and in ignorance of its falisty; (7) did in fact rely upon it; (8) and was thereby induced to act; (9) to his injury and damage."[68]

An independent claim of negligent misrepresentation exists if a plaintiff is injured by reasonable reliance upon a defendant's careless or negligent misrepresentation of a material fact, when the defendant had a pecuniary interest in the transaction, was in a superior position to know the material facts, and should have reasonably foreseen that the injured party was likely to rely upon the misrepresented fact.[69]

Utah also recognizes a claim of fraudulent nondisclosure. To prevail, a plaintiff must show "(1) that the nondisclosed information is material, (2) that the nondisclosed information is known to the party failing to disclose, and (3) that there is a legal duty to communicate."[70]

P. PUNITIVE DAMAGES

Punitive damages may be awarded in Utah only if compensatory or general damages are awarded and it is established by clear and convincing evidence that the acts or omissions of the tortfeasor are the result of willful and malicious or intentionally fraudulent conduct, or conduct that manifests a knowing and reckless indifference toward, and a disregard of, the rights of others.[71]

An award of punitive damages may not be predicated solely upon a finding of simple negligence.[72] Although actual intent to cause injury need not be shown, Utah case law requires that the defendant must or ought to know (1) that a high degree of probability exists that the conduct would result in substantial harm; (2) that the conduct is "highly unreasonable or an extreme departure from ordinary care;" and (3) that a "high degree of danger is apparent."[73] Notice or knowledge of a dangerous condition and failure to act, absent more, do not support a claim for punitive damages.[74]

Before punitive damages may be awarded, the plaintiff must sustain compensatory damages.[75] Compensatory damages need not be recoverable.[76] The jury must consider the following factors in assessing the amount of punitive damages to be awarded: (1) the relative wealth of the defendant; (2) the nature of the alleged misconduct; (3) the facts and circumstances surrounding such conduct; (4) the effect thereof on the lives of the plaintiff and others; (5) the probability of future recurrence of the misconduct; (6) the relationship of the parties; and (7) the amount of actual damages awarded.[77] Failure on the part of the plaintiff to introduce evidence of the relative wealth of the defendant is not fatal to an award of punitive damages.[78]

In cases seeking punitive damages against an intoxicated driver, a specific statute eliminates the requirements that compensatory damages be awarded first and that the plaintiff prove by clear and convincing evidence that the tortfeasor's conduct rises to the willful, malicious, intentional, or reckless indifference standards.[79]

Q. WRONGFUL DEATH AND SURVIVORSHIP ACTIONS

An action for damages for the wrongful death of a person, other than a minor, may be brought by either the heirs or the personal representative for the benefit of the heirs of the decedent against the person causing the death.[80] If the decedent had a guardian at the time of death, then either the personal representative for the benefit of the heirs or the guardian may bring an action for damages for wrongful death, but only one such action may be maintained.[81]

An action for damages for the wrongful injury or death of a child may be brought by either a parent or guardian of the minor child. If a parent, stepparent, adoptive parent, or legal guardian is an alleged defendant, then a guardian ad litem may be appointed for the injured child or any other surviving children.[82]

A cause of action arising out of personal injury or death caused by the wrongful act or negligence of another does not abate upon the death of the wrongdoer or the injured person. The injured person or the personal representatives or heirs of the person who died have a cause of action against the wrongdoer or the personal representatives of the wrongdoer for special and general damages; provided, however, that if prior to a judgment or settlement the injured person dies as a result of a cause other than the injury received from the wrongdoer, the personal representatives or heirs of that person are entitled to receive no more than the out-of-pocket expenses incurred by or on behalf of that injured person as a result of his injury.[83]

Rick L. Rose
Melissa H. Bailey
Cheri K. Gochberg
Kristine M. Larsen
RAY, QUINNEY & NEBEKER
36 South State Street, Suite 1400
P.O. Box 45385
Salt Lake City, Utah 84111
(801) 532-1500
Fax (801) 532-7543
www.rqn.com

ENDNOTES - UTAH

1. Utah Code Ann. § 78-12-25(3) (1996).

2. *Id.* § 78-12-28(2) (2000 Supp.).

3. *Id.* § 78-12-26 (1996).

4. *Davidson Lumber Sales, Inc. v. Bonneville Inv., Inc.*, 794 P.2d 11 (Utah 1990); *McCollin v. Synthes, Inc.*, 50 F. Supp. 2d 1119, 1122 (D. Utah 1999).

5. Utah Code Ann. § 78-12-29 (1996).

6. *Id.* § 78-12-21.5(3)(b) (1999 Supp.).

7. *Id.* § 78-12-21.5(3)(a) (1999 Supp.).

8. *Id.* § 78-12-21.5(4) (1999 Supp.).

9. *Id.*

10. *Id.* § 78-12-25(3) (1996). *See Anderson v. Dean Witter Reynolds, Inc.*, 920 P.2d 575, 578 (Utah Ct. App. 1996) (in which the court applied the four-year residual statute of limitations to plaintiff's tortious interference claim); *but see Valley Colour, Inc. v. Beuchert Builders, Inc.*, 944 P.2d 361, 364 (Utah 1997) (in which the court applied the two-year statute for the underlying tort, slander of title, to plaintiff's tortious interference claim).

11. Utah Code Ann. § 31A-22-309(1) (1999 Supp.).

12. *Id.* § 41-12a-304 (1998).

13. *Jackson v. Righter*, 891 P.2d 1387, 1392 (Utah 1995).

14. *DeWeese v. J.C. Penney Co.*, 297 P.2d 898, 901 (Utah 1956).

15. *Day v. State*, 980 P.2d 1171, 1175 (Utah 1999).

16. *Nelson v. Salt Lake City*, 919 P.2d 568 (Utah 1996); *Rollins v. Petersen*, 813 P.2d 1156 (Utah 1991); *Ferree v. State*, 784 P.2d 149 (Utah 1989); *Little v. Division of Family Servs.*, 667 P.2d 49, 53-54 (Utah 1983).

17. *Rivas v. Pacific Finance Co.*, 397 P.2d 990, 991 (Utah 1964).

18. *Mann v. Fairbourn*, 366 P.2d 603, 606 (Utah 1961).

19. *Jackson*, 891 P.2d at 1392.

20. *Harline v. Barker*, 912 P.2d 433, 439 (Utah 1996).

21. *Id.*

22. *Mulherin v. Ingersoll-Rand Co.*, 628 P.2d 1301, 1303-04 (Utah 1981); Utah Code Ann. § 78-27-37(2) (1999 Supp.).

23. Utah Code Ann. § 78-27-38 (1999 Supp.); *Mulherin*, 628 P.2d at 1304.

24. Utah Code Ann. § 78-27-38(4)(a) (1999 Supp.).

25. *Id.* § 78-27-40(1) (1996).

26. *Id.* § 78-27-40(2) (1996).

27. *Id.* § 78-27-39(2) (1996).

28. *Id.* § 78-27-39(2) (1999 Supp.); *Jacobson Constr. Co. v. Structo-Lite Eng'g., Inc.*, 619 P.2d 306 (Utah 1980); *Ernest W. Hahn, Inc. v. Armco Steele Co.*, 601 P.2d 152, 158 (Utah 1979); Restatement (Second) of Torts § 402A.

29. *King v. Searle Pharm., Inc.*, 832 P.2d 858, 861 (Utah 1992); *see also Dalley v. Utah Valley Regional Med. Center*, 791 P.2d 193, 196 (Utah 1990).

30. *Anderton v. Montgomery*, 607 P.2d 828, 834 (Utah 1980).

31. *Id.; see also Nixdorf v. Hicken*, 612 P.2d 348, 352-53 (Utah 1980).

32. *Walker v. Parish Chem. Co.*, 914 P.2d 1157, 1160 (Utah Ct. App. 1996).

33. *Walker Drug Co., Inc. v. La Sal Oil Co.*, 902 P.2d 1229, 1233 (Utah 1995); *see also Branch v. Western Petroleum, Inc.*, 657 P.2d 267, 274-75 (Utah 1982).

34. *Copier v. Smith & Wesson Corp.*, 138 F.3d 833, 836 (10th Cir. 1998).

35. *Rollins*, 813 P.2d at 1163.

36. *Id.*

37. *Intermountain Farmers Ass'n v. Fitzgerald*, 574 P.2d 1162, 1164-65 (Utah 1978).

38. *Id.*

39. *Id.* § 78-27-40(1) (1996).

40. *See id.* § 78-27-39(2) (1999 Supp.).

41. *Id.* § 78-27-40(2) (1996).

42. *Hanover Ltd. v. Cessna Aircraft Co.*, 758 P.2d 443, 445 (Utah Ct. App. 1988).

43. *Id.* at 447.

44. *Id.* at 449.

45. *Hawkins v. Peart*, 433 Utah Adv. Rep. 19 (Utah Oct. 30, 2001).

46. Utah Code Ann. § 34A-2-105(1) (2001); *id.* § 34A-3-102 (2001).

47. *Whipple v. American Fork Irrig. Co.*, 910 P.2d 1218, 1220 (Utah 1996).

48. *Glenn v. Gibbons & Reed Co.*, 265 P.2d 1013 (Utah 1954); Model Utah Jury Instruction (MUJI) 11.3.

49. MUJI 11.4, 11.5, 11.6.

50. *Pratt v. Mitchell Hollow Irrig. Co.*, 813 P.2d 1169 (Utah 1991); *Weber v. Springville City*, 725 P.2d 1360 (Utah 1986); MUJI 11.1.

51. Utah Code Ann. § 78-27-51 to -54 (1996); *id.* § 57-14-1 *et seq.* (2001).

52. *Stephens v. Bonneville Travel, Inc.*, 935 P.2d 518, 519 (Utah 1997).

53. Utah Code Ann. § 32A-14a-101, *et seq.* (2001).

54. *Id.* § 32A-14a-102(1) (2001).

55. *Id.* § 32A-14a-102(9) (2001).

56. *Id.* § 32A-14a-102(2) (2001).

57. *Id.* § 32A-14a-102(7) (2001).

58. *Id.* § 32A-14a-102(6) (2001).

59. *Id.* § 32A-14a-102(8) (2001).

60. *Id.* § 32A-14a-104 (2001).

61. *Id.* § 32A-14a-103 (2001).

62. *American Towers Owners Ass'n, Inc. v. CCI Mechanical, Inc.*, 930 P.2d 1182, 1189-92 (Utah 1996); *Schafir v. Harrigan*, 879 P.2d 1384, 1388 (Utah Ct. App. 1994); *Maack v. Resource Design & Constr., Inc.*, 875 P.2d 570, 579-81 (Utah Ct. App. 1994).

63. *SME Indus., Inc. v. Thompson, Ventulett, Stainback and Assoc., Inc.*, 28 P.3d 669, 680 (Utah 2001). *But see Steiner Corp. v. Johnson & Higgins of Ca.*, 196 F.R.D. 653, 658 (D. Utah 2000) (applying Utah law, court held that economic loss doctrine "was primarily intended to limit actions in the product liability context, and its application should generally be limited to those contexts or situations where the policy considerations are substantially identical to those underlying the product liability-type analysis[,]" and therefore doctrine does not bar negligence claims against professionals) (citation omitted).

64. *Maack*, 875 P.2d at 580 (quoting *2314 Lincoln Park W. Condominium v. Mann, Gin, Ebel & Frazier, Ltd.*, 555 N.E.2d 346, 348 (Ill. 1990)).

65. *See W.R.H., Inc. v. Economy Builders Supply*, 633 P.2d 42, 43-44 (Utah 1981).

66. *American Towers Owners Ass'n*, 930 P.2d at 1190 n.11.

67. Utah R. Civ. P. 9(b) (2001).

68. *Maack*, 875 P.2d at 576.

69. *Id.* at 584 (quoting *Dugan v. Jones*, 615 P.2d 1239, 1246 (Utah 1980)).

70. *Mitchell v. Christensen*, 31 P.3d 572, 574 (Utah 2001).

71. Utah Code Ann. § 78-18-1(1) (1996).

72. *Boyette v. L.W. Looney & Son, Inc.*, 932 F. Supp. 1344, 1349 (D. Utah 1996) ("Simple negligence will never suffice as a basis upon which such damages may be awarded. 'Punitive damages are not awarded for mere inadvertence, mistake, errors of judgment and the like, which constitute negligence.'") (citations omitted).

73. *Behrens v. Raleigh Hills Hosp., Inc.*, 675 P.2d 1179, 1186-8 (Utah 1983); *Gleave v. Denver & Rio Grande Western R. Co.*, 749 P.2d 660, 670 (Utah Ct. App. 1988).

74. *Orr v. Brigham Young University*, 960 F. Supp. 1522, 1531 (D. Utah 1994).

75. *C.T.*, 977 P.2d at 482.

76. *Id.*

77. *Crookston v. Fire Ins. Exchange*, 817 P.2d 789, 808 (Utah 1991).

78. *Hall v. Wal-Mart Stores, Inc.*, 959 P.2d 109, 113 (Utah 1998).

79. *Id.* § 78-18-1(1)(b) (1996); *C.T. v. Johnson*, 977 P.2d 479, 482 (Utah 1999).

80. Utah Code Ann. § 78-11-7 (1996).

81. *Id.*

82. *Id.* § 78-11-6 (1996).

83. *Id.* § 78-11-12(1) (1996).

VERMONT

A. STATUTES OF LIMITATION

Under most statutes of limitations the period starts to run only when the plaintiff "discovers" the injury. The limitations period is a time to investigate. Plaintiff need not have an airtight case before the limitations period begins to run. Plaintiff must have information sufficient to put a reasonable person on notice that a particular defendant may be liable for the plaintiff's injuries.[1] Plaintiffs are ultimately chargeable with notice of all the facts that could have been obtained by the exercise of reasonable diligence in prosecuting the inquiry.[2]

Commencement of suit for purposes of the statute of limitations occurs on the date of filing, if suit is commenced by filing, or on the date of service if suit is commenced by service.[3] In practice it is accepted that an order granting an extension of time for service is effective for purposes of the statute of limitations only if the request therefor is made before the time expires.

The statute of limitations is an affirmative defense that is waived by failure to specify the specific statute of limitations upon which defendant relies.[4]

In Vermont the nature of harm done, rather than party's characterization of action as contract or tort, is the governing factor in determining which limitations period should apply.[5] Here are some specific rules:

General civil action, six years.[6]

Bodily injury, three years.[7]

Products liability, there is no specific statute of limitations. Generally, it is three years for injuries to the person or damage to personal property,[8] four years from "tender of delivery" for claims based on U.C.C. breach of warranty.[9]

Property damage, three years for personal property,[10] six years for real property.

Assault and Battery, three years.[11]

False imprisonment, three years.[12]

Slander and libel, three years.[13]

Medical malpractice, three years from incident or two years from discovery, whichever is later.[14]

Wrongful death, two years from discovery of death.[15]

Dram shop, two years.[16]

Injuries sustained downhill skiing, one year.[17]

Insurance direct action, one year.[18]

There is no statute of limitations specific to indemnify actions. The Court has applied the same limitation period to an indemnity action as would apply to the underlying of the action.[18.1] An indemnification claim arises or accrues when the plaintiff files the complaint in the original action because, under Rule 14, the third-party complaint may be filed.[18.2]

B. TORT REFORM

Vermont has not passed any tort reform laws.

C. "NO FAULT" LIMITATIONS

Vermont has not adopted any "no fault" laws.

D. THE STANDARD FOR NEGLIGENCE

Negligence is conduct which falls below the standard established by law for the protection of others against unreasonable risk.[19] The elements required for a cause of action in common law negligence are: (1) the defendant must owe a legal duty to conform to a certain standard of conduct so as to protect the plaintiff from an unreasonable risk of harm; (2) the defendant must have committed a breach of this duty by failing to conform to the standard of conduct required; (3) the defendant's conduct must be the proximate cause of the plaintiff's injury; and (4) the plaintiff must have suffered actual loss or damage.[20]

Duty means a legal obligation to do or not do some act, depending on the particular circumstances of the case. In most cases duty is assumed to exist simply on the basis of the actor's creation of an unreasonable risk of foreseeable harm resulting in injury. However, the existence of duty is primarily a question of law.[21] The inquiry involves a weighing of the relationship of the parties, the nature of the risk, and the public interest in the proposed solution.[22] The imposition of a duty is "'an expression of the sum total of those considerations of policy which lead the law to say that the plaintiff is entitled to protection.'"[23]

The Vermont Supreme Court, after weighing policy considerations, has held: A mortgagee bank has no duty of care to inform a third party who had been paying the mortgage of the cancellation of property insurance.[24] A ski area has no duty of care to assist an injured patron's litigation interest by pursuing and identifying the other skier involved in an accident.[25]

A licensed vendor of alcohol has a duty of care to a patron to guard against the risk of self-injury by excessive consumption.[26]

In determining whether a governmental body has undertaken a duty of care toward specified persons beyond its duty to the public at large, the Vermont Supreme Court considers: (1) whether an ordinance or statute sets forth mandatory acts clearly for the protection of a particular class of persons, rather than the public as a whole; (2) whether the government has actual knowledge of a condition dangerous to those persons; (3) whether there has been reliance by those persons on the government's representations and conduct; and (4) whether failure by the government to use due care would increase the risk of harm beyond its present potential by the person the State intends to isolate.[27]

Vermont agrees with the Restatement that there is no duty to control the conduct of a third person so as to prevent that person from causing harm to another. Vermont also agrees that there is an exception where "a special relation exists between the actor and the other which gives rise to the other a right to protection."[28]

Once duty is imposed, the standard of conduct is generally that of a reasonable person under like circumstances.[29] The test is what would a careful and prudent person have done under like circumstances, acting on his or her judgment then, and not on a judgment based on subsequent reflection.[30]

Vermont recognizes a professional standard of care, measured by the degree of care, skill, diligence, and knowledge commonly possessed and exercised by a reasonable, careful, and prudent professional practicing in Vermont.[31] The elements of medical malpractice and elements of a claim for lack of informed consent are statutory.[32] Ordinarily, expert testimony is required to show both standard of care and breach.[33] However, where a the lack of care is so apparent that only common knowledge and experience are needed to comprehend it, expert testimony is not required to prove professional negligence.[34]

There is no arbitrary age limit below which a child is deemed incapable of negligence. The standard of care of child plaintiff, generally stated, is that a child who has arrived at a sufficient age to be capable of some degree of caution for his or her own safety, must exercise the care reasonably to be expected of children of like age, capacity, education, and experience. A time when a child is capable of negligence is not a mere matter of age, but it depends on the circumstances shown, especially said child's mental development, previous training, previous experience, and knowledge of the dangers of the situation.[35]

Vermont has not addressed whether a dead or incapacitated person is presumed to have exercised due care at the time of the injury.

E. **CAUSATION**

Proximate cause is the law's method of keeping the scope of liability for a defendant's negligence from extending by ever-expanding causal links.[36] The term "proximate cause" has been considered misleading in that it is not necessarily predicated on nearness in time or distance.[37] Vermont trial courts may give a "three-prong" causation instruction, referring to "uninterrupted sequence," "substantial factor" and "but-for" causation.[38]

To prove that any negligence was a proximate cause of injury, three things must be shown. One, the negligence led to the injury in a natural and uninterrupted sequence of events.[39] Foreseeability is not a factor in this determination. Defendant is liable for the results that flow directly from its negligence whether they were to be reasonably anticipated or not.[40] Second, the negligence was a substantial factor in bringing about the injury.[41] And, third, the injury would not have happened if that defendant had not been negligent.[42]

There may be more than one proximate cause. Defendant's negligence need not be the only cause of the injury, and any defendant may be found liable if its negligence was a substantial factor, concurring with some other cause acting at the same time, in bringing about the harm.[43] The wrongful act of a third person generally is an intervening cause unless the negligence consists of the failure to anticipate the wrongful act.[44]

F. CONTRIBUTORY NEGLIGENCE, COMPARATIVE NEGLIGENCE, AND ASSUMPTION OF RISK

1. Contributory Negligence

Under the comparative negligence statute, contributory negligence is no longer and absolute defense "in an action by any plaintiff, or his legal representative, to recover damages for negligence resulting in death, personal injury or property damage."[45]

Contributory negligence is still a defense in other cases, but the court on its own may apply comparative principles.[46] Failure to wear a safety belt in violation of law "shall not constitute negligence or contributory negligence in any civil proceeding."[47] Contributory negligence is an affirmative defense which must be established by the one pleading it.[48]

2. Comparative Negligence

By statute, a plaintiff's negligence bars recovery only if it is "greater than the causal total negligence of the defendant or defendants" against whom a verdict is rendered.[49] Otherwise the plaintiff's damages are diminished in proportion to the amount of negligence attributed to plaintiff. For example, in a case against a single defendant, if the plaintiff is found to be 51 percent at fault or more, the plaintiff recovers nothing. If the plaintiff is 50 percent at fault or less, and the defendant is found to be 50 percent at fault or more, the plaintiff recovers the proportionate percentage of the compensatory damages. In a case against two defendants, if the defendants are each found 30 percent at fault and plaintiff is 40 percent at fault, the plaintiff recovers 60 percent of his or her damages.

3. Assumption of Risk

The defense of secondary assumption of risk is not charged separately from comparative negligence, although it is still often plead as a distinct defense.[50] Secondary assumption of risk involves knowledge of the existence of the risk, appreciation of the extent of the danger, and consent to assume it.[51]

G. *RES IPSA LOQUITUR* AND INHERENTLY DANGEROUS ACTIVITIES

1. *Res Ipsa Loquitur*

Res ipsa loquitur refers to a form of circumstantial evidence that allows plaintiff to escape a directed verdict without directly establishing negligence, and allows the jury to infer negligence from the circumstances of an injury.[52] Four elements must be satisfied to support a charge of *res ipsa loquitur:* (1) a legal duty owing from the defendant to exercise a certain degree of care in connection with a particular instrumentality to prevent the very occurrence that has happened; (2) the subject instrumentality at the time of the occurrence must have been under the defendant's control and management in such a way that there can be no serious question concerning the defendant's responsibility for the misadventure of the instrument; (3) the instrument for which the defendant was responsible must be the producing cause of the injury; and (4) the event which brought on the plaintiff's harm is such that would not ordinarily occur except for the want of requisite care on the part of the defendant as the person responsible for the injuring agency.[53]

The local federal court has concluded that, assuming the other elements of the doctrine have been satisfied, Vermont would apply *res ipsa loquitur* to medical malpractice actions either (1) where the common knowledge or experience of lay persons is sufficient to establish that an injury would not have occurred in the absence of negligence or (2) where expert testimony establishes that it is common knowledge among experts that an injury would not have happened in the absence of negligence.[54]

Satisfaction of an element of *res ipsa loquitur* requires only reasonably supportive evidence, not conclusive proof.[55] For example, in order for the fourth element to be applicable, the evidence need only permit a reasonable fact finder to conclude that the event probably would not have occurred if defendant had used requisite care.[56]

2. Inherently Dangerous Activities

Those who engage in a dangerous activity or who distribute a dangerous article owe a degree of protection to the public proportionate to and commensurate with the dangers involved, but they are not insurers.[57] However, absolute liability applies in cases involving the use of explosives: negligence need not be demonstrated, but only the use of explosives and resulting damage.[58]

H. NEGLIGENCE *PER SE*

The courts allow evidence of a safety regulation as evidence of a standard of care.[59] Safety rules are not hard and fast, nor absolute in application to all circumstances. They are guides to the main issue of whether the actor's conduct meets the standard required of a prudent man under the circumstances.[60]

Vermont has historically rejected the notion that violation of a safety statute is negligence *per se*.[61] Instead, the violation creates a *prima facie* case of negligence that helps plaintiff over the hurdle of defendant's motion for judgment as a matter of law. It gives rise to a rebuttable, rather than conclusive presumption of negligence.[62] Being a rebuttable presumption, when the defendant produces evidence fairly and reasonably tending to show that the real fact (*i.e.*, negligent conduct) is not as presumed, the office of the presumption is performed and disappears from the arena.[63] The case is submitted to the jury on the issue of negligence without reference to the presumption.[64] Where unrebutted, plaintiff is entitled to judgment as a matter of law on the issue of defendant's negligence.[65]

I. JOINT AND SEVERAL LIABILITY

1. Joint and Several Liability

In Vermont, liability is generally joint and several. A plaintiff may recover from any one of several tortfeasors for the full amount of the loss. This is true, for example, even when compared to the other tortfeasors, the tortfeasor from whom recovery is sought is only 1 percent responsible for the loss.

The rule against contribution among joint tortfeasors precludes a defendant from bringing other responsible parties into the suit solely on the basis that they are also liable to the plaintiff.

However, when plaintiff chooses to sue more than one defendant on a negligence theory, the comparative negligence statute applies, and liability is several, not joint and several. That is, whenever one defendant is found to have negligently caused plaintiff's injuries, and another defendant is also found to have negligently caused plaintiff's injuries, then each defendant's liability is limited to its proportionate share of liability.[66] This rule applies only to defendants against whom judgment is allowed.

In practice a plaintiff can maintain joint and several liability among defending parties by choosing to settle with one defendant prior to judgment. In such case the remaining defendant is liable for the full amount of the damages, less the amount of the settlement.[67]

J. INDEMNITY

Contribution is the right to shift a portion of a loss or liability to another responsible party. There is no right of contribution among joint tortfeasors in Vermont.[68] Vermont has not adopted the Uniform Contribution Among Joint Tortfeasors Act in any form. This means that a defendant may not sue anyone else who might also be liable to plaintiff merely on that basis.

Indemnification is the right to shift an entire loss or liability to another party.[69] Vermont law recognizes a right of indemnity, even among joint tortfeasors, if there is an express agreement by one party to indemnify another, or if the circumstances are such that the law will imply such an undertaking.[70] Generally, indemnity will be implied only when equitable considerations concerning the nature of the parties' obligations to one another or the significant difference in the kind or quality of their conduct demonstrate that it is fair to shift the entire loss occasioned by the injury from one party to another.[71] Thus, a right of implied indemnification accrues "to a party who, without active fault, has been compelled by some legal obligation, such as a finding of vicarious liability, to pay damages occasioned by the negligence of another.[72] Indemnification is also appropriate because of the indemnitee's failure to discover a dangerous condition caused by the act of the indemnitor, who is primarily responsible for the condition.[73]

K. BAR OF WORKERS' COMPENSATION STATUTE

The Vermont Workers' Compensation Act provides that "the rights and remedies granted by the [Act] to an employee on account of a personal injury for which he is entitled to compensation . . . shall exclude all other rights and remedies of the employee . . . at common law or otherwise on account of such injury."[74] The Act allows an injured worker to sue "some person other than the employer."[75]

"Employer" includes the owner or lessee of premises or other person who is virtually the proprietor or operator of the business there carried on, but who, by reason of there being an independent contractor or for any other reason, is not the direct employer of the workers there employed.[76]

Co-employees, including those acting in a supervisory capacity may be sued for negligence as "some person other than the employer."[77] But the Workers' Compensation Act permits a recovery from an officer or supervisor only when the officer or supervisor breaches a personal duty, as contrasted to a nondelegable duty owed by the employer such as the duty to provide a safe workplace.[78]

The Legislature has set a public policy favoring no-fault recovery in employment-related injuries, and the court has been reluctant to create exceptions to the exclusivity rule.[79] Allegation of "wanton and willful" acts and omissions of an employer leading to an employee's injury do not take the injury outside of the scope of this chapter so as to allow a suit against employer at common law.[80] Nothing short of a specific intent to injure falls outside the scope of the Act.[81]

The exclusive remedy provision does not protect employers from employement discrimination suits[81.1] nor employers who fail to obtain workers' compensation insurance. Where the employer fails to obtain insurance the worker may bring suit against the employer for full damages. The employer has the burden of proving that the injury did not result from the employer's negligence and that the employer's negligence was not the proximate cause of the injury. The employer may not raise comparative negligence or assumption of risk as defenses nor that the injury was caused by the negligence of a fellow employee.[82]

L. PREMISES LIABILITY

A landowner's liability for injuries sustained on premises traditionally depends on whether the individual's status as an "invitee," "licensee" or "trespasser." The Vermont Supreme Court has not been presented with a case requiring it to consider whether to abandon these distinctions in favor of a general duty of reasonable care.[83] Landowner liability is founded on negligence, and a landowner is not the guarantor of the safety of all patrons, nor is it liable for every injury patrons may suffer on the premises.[84]

In general, liability depends on control, rather than ownership.[85] In Vermont, a landowner generally owes no duty of care to a trespasser, except to avoid willful or wanton misconduct.[86] Vermont has not adopted the doctrine of attractive nuisance, so the absence of duty applies to both adult and child trespassers.[87] Also there is no duty to a person who has permission to enter land, but who becomes a trespasser by exceeding the scope of the invitation.[88]

The landowner is not liable to a gratuitous licensee for passive negligence, but may be liable for affirmative and active negligence.[89] There is no duty on the part of a social host to reconstruct or improve the premises for the purpose of making his or her house more convenient, or more safe, for the guest. However, the guest may recover where there is a hidden defect on the property that it amounts to a trap or pitfall, and which landowner did not warn the guest about.[90] By statute a landowner is not liable for property damage or personal injury sustained by a person who, without consideration, enters or goes upon the owner's land for a recreational use unless the damage or injury is the result of the willful or wanton misconduct of the owner.[91]

The Vermont business owner has a duty "of active care to make sure that its premises are in safe and suitable condition for its customers."[92] Plaintiff ordinarily must show that the dangerous condition of the premises was known to the defendant or existed for such time that it was his duty to know it.[93] The business owner has a duty to warn of hidden dangers, and the business invitee has a right to assume that the premises, aside from obvious dangers, are reasonably safe for the purpose for which he is upon them, and that proper precaution has been taken to make them so.[94]

M. DRAM SHOP LIABILITY

Vermont's Dram Shop statute provides that a licensee is strictly liable for injuries caused because of the intoxication of a person or by an intoxicated person where the licensee caused the intoxication by furnishing drink either to a minor, to a person apparently under the influence, to a person after legal serving hours, or to a person one would expect to be under the influence as a result of the amount of drink served.[95]

An intoxicated person who causes injury to himself has no right of recovery under the Act.[96] Relatives of a deceased or injured imbiber have an independent and direct right of recovery. A parent, an unmarried partner and the child of the unmarried partner are all within the potential class of claimants enumerated in the Act. Such third persons injured in consequence of the death or injury of an imbiber are entitled to recover only for their loss of means of support, if any, and not for loss of companionship nor for loss of parental training and guidance.[97]

The dram shop statute does not apply to social hosts.[98] Common law negligence liability may apply to social hosts. However landowners are not liable for injuries caused by the consumption of alcohol on their property where they were not present, did not furnish the alcohol, and did not control the alcohol consumed.[99]

N. ECONOMIC LOSS

The court has been careful to maintain a dividing line between contract and tort theories of recovery.[100] Negligence law does not generally recognize a duty to exercise reasonable care to avoid intangible economic loss to another unless one's conduct has inflicted some accompanying physical harm.[101] The rule against tort recovery for economic loss applies to commercial disputes generally,[102] as well as to claims asserting the theory of strict product liability.[103] On the other hand, certain tort theories are limited to economic loss, and recovery for consequential emotional distress is prohibited.[104]

O. FRAUD AND MISREPRESENTATION

The Vermont Rules of Civil Procedure require that the circumstances constituting fraud shall be stated with particularity.[105] In a suit for damages, each of the following elements of fraud must be proved by clear and convincing evidence:[106] (1) that defendant misrepresented an existing fact that affects the essence of the transaction; (2) that defendant did so intentionally; (3) that the misrepresentation was false when made and defendant knew it to be false at the time; (4) that the correct information was not available to plaintiff; and (5) that plaintiff relied on the misrepresentation to plaintiff's detriment.[107]

The misrepresentations must relate distinctly and directly to the contract, must affect its very essence and substance, and must be material to the contract. Representations are not material if they relate to other matters, or relate to the contract in a trivial and unimportant respect only, or are wholly collateral. A statement of the motives underlying a party's bargaining position is generally not deemed to be material.[108]

Liability for fraud may be premised on the failure to disclose material facts as well as on affirmative misrepresentations.[109] Where a duty to disclose is present, the failure to disclose a material fact coupled with an intention to mislead or defraud rises to the level of material misrepresentation.[110]

Vermont follows the Restatement (Second) of Torts in setting forth the elements of a claim of negligent misrepresentation.[111] "One who, in the course of his business, profession or employment, or in any other transaction in which he has a pecuniary interest, supplies false information for the guidance of others in their business transactions, is subject to liability for pecuniary loss caused to them by their justifiable reliance upon the information, if he fails to exercise reasonable care or competence in obtaining or communicating the information."[112] This liability is limited to losses suffered (a) by the person or one of a limited group of persons for whose benefit and guidance the actor intends to supply the information or knows that the recipient intends to supply it; and (b) through reliance upon it in a transaction that the actor intends the information to influence or knows that the recipient so intends.[113] A negligent misrepresentation claim does not require privity of contract, only "information negligently supplied for the guidance of others."[114]

The "justifiable reliance" element of the claim of negligent misrepresentation connotes an objective standard.[115] Plaintiffs may justifiably rely upon a representation when the representation is not obviously false and the truth of the representation is not within the knowledge of, or known by the plaintiffs.[116] The damages recoverable are those necessary to compensate the plaintiff for the pecuniary loss suffered, and not emotional distress.[117]

P. CONSUMER FRAUD STATUTES

The Vermont Consumer Fraud Act prohibits "unfair or deceptive acts or practices in commerce,"[118] and authorizes the consumer to recover damages caused by the violation, reasonable attorney's fees, and exemplary damages not exceeding three times the value of the consideration.[119] The Act provides "a much broader right than common law fraud."[120] Intent to deceive and bad faith are not elements under the Consumer Fraud Act.[121]

To establish a "deceptive act or practice" under the Act requires three elements: (1) there must be a representation, omission, or practice likely to mislead consumers; (2) the consumer must be interpreting the message reasonably under the circumstances; and (3) the misleading effects must be material, that is, likely to affect the consumer's conduct or decision regarding the product.[122] Deception is measured by an objective standard, looking to whether the representation or omission had the "capacity or tendency to deceive" a reasonable consumer; actual injury need not be shown.[123] Materiality is also generally measured by an objective standard, premised on what a reasonable person would regard as important in making a decision.[124]

Q. PUNITIVE DAMAGES

The purpose of punitive damages is not to compensate plaintiff, but to punish conduct that is morally culpable and to deter potential wrongdoers from repeating the conduct in the future.[125] No plaintiff has a right to punitive damages.[126]

Punitive damages may be awarded only where the defendant acted with malice.[127] Negligence alone will not support a finding of malice.[128] Even knowing, willful or intentional conduct is not malicious unless it is done with a bad motive.[129] Malice denotes hatred or ill will on the part of the defendant, or a desire to do harm for the mere satisfaction of doing it.[130]

The nature of defendant's conduct and the surrounding circumstances can establish motive and state of mind.[131] Malice may be shown by "conduct manifesting personal ill will or carried out under circumstances evidencing insult or oppression, or . . . a reckless or wanton disregard of one's rights."[132] In the last analysis, however, the evidence must support a finding of evil motive or malice.[133]

Punitive damages may not be imposed where the plaintiff is not entitled to actual damages.[134] Vermont law does not impose vicarious liability for punitive damages.[135] Because punitive damages "are never suffered to fall on a party innocent," they cannot be allowed against a corporation "unless such corporation, in some legal way, either authorizes, or subsequently approves of, the wrongful act or neglect."[136] The malicious act relied upon must be that of the governing officers of the corporation or one lawfully exercising their authority, or, if the act relied upon is that of a servant or agent of the corporation, it must be clearly shown that the governing officers either directed the act, participated in it, or subsequently ratified it.[137]

The amount assessed as punitive damages should be an amount that is reasonable and appropriate for the purpose to punish conduct that is morally culpable and to deter defendant and other potential wrongdoers from repeating the conduct in the future. Defendant's wealth is a factor,[138] however proof of a defendant's actual means or wealth is not essential to the recovery of punitive damages.[139] The jury may consider the cost of litigation, including attorney's fees as evidence of the overall harm done by the defendant.[140] Vermont has said that that the punitive award need bear no reasonable proportion to the compensatory damages awarded to the plaintiff,[141] however, Constitutional considerations require close judicial supervision of any award.[142]

R. **WRONGFUL DEATH AND SURVIVORSHIP ACTIONS**

At common law there is no recovery for wrongful death or right of action for a decedent's personal injuries.[143] However, recovery is allowed under the Vermont Wrongful Death Statute[144] and Vermont Survival Act,[145] two separate and distinct causes of action.

Recovery under the Wrongful Death Statute is measured by the pecuniary injuries to the spouse and next-of-kin.[146] "Pecuniary injury" now includes loss of comfort, society and companionship of the decedent resulting from the death.[147] Recovery under the Survival Act passes to the decedent's estate and is measured by the damages the decedent sustained at and after the injury and prior to death.[148]

Allan R. Keyes
RYAN SMITH & CARBINE, Ltd.
P.O. Box 310
Rutland, Vermont 05702-0313
(802) 786-1035
Fax (802) 786-1100
ark@rsclaw.com

ENDNOTES - VERMONT

1. *Rodrigue v. VALCO Enterprises, Inc.*, 169 Vt. 539, 726 A.2d 61 (1999).

2. *Galfetti v. Berg, Carmoli & Kent Real Estate Corp.*, 756 A.2d 1229 (Vt. 2000).

3. V.R.C.P. 3 (2000); 12 Vt. Stat. Ann. § 466 (1973).

4. *In re Estate of Peters*, 765 A.2d 468 (Vt. 2000).

5. *Fitzgerald v. Congleton*, 155 Vt. 283, 288, 583 A.2d 595, 598 (1990); *see Rennie v. State* (762 A.2d 1272) (Vt. 2000) (claim barred under the three-year statute of limitations even though economic losses alleged, where "gravamen or essence" of the claim was physical and emotional harm); *Bull v. Pinkham Engineering Assoc. Inc.*, 752 A.2d 26 (Vt. 2000) (six-year statute of limitations governs where the harm is economic loss and diminution of the value of real property rather than damage to personal property); *Politi v. Tyler*, 751 A.2d 788 (Vt. 2000) (suit barred under three-year statute as to emotional distress claim).

6. 12 Vt. Stat. Ann. § 511.

7. 12 Vt. Stat. Ann. § 512(4).

8. 12 Vt. Stat. Ann. § 512(4) and (5).

9. 9A Vt. Stat. Ann. § 2-725; *Aube v. O'Brien*, 140 Vt. 1, 433 A.2d 298 (1981); *Gus' Catering, Inc. v. Menusoft Systems*, 762 A.2d 804 (Vt. 2000) (software warranty claim was time barred four years after tender of delivery, notwithstanding argument that additional warranties arose during time when seller unsuccessfully attempted to fix problem).

10. 12 Vt. Stat. Ann. § 512(5) (1973).

11. 12 Vt. Stat. Ann. § 512(1) (1973).

12. 12 Vt. Stat. Ann. § 512(2) (1973).

13. 12 Vt. Stat. Ann. § 512(3) (1973).

14. 12 Vt. Stat. Ann. § 521 (Supp. 2000).

15. 14 Vt. Stat. Ann. § 1492 (Supp. 2000).

16. 7 Vt. Stat. Ann. § 501 (1999).

17. 12 Vt. Stat. Ann. § 513 (1973).

18. 8 Vt. Stat. Ann. § 4203(2) (1993); *Copeland & Sons v. Kansa General Insurance Co.,* 762 A.2d 471 (Vt. 2000).

18.1. *Investment Properties, Inc. v. Lyttle,* 169 Vt. 487, 739 A.2d 1222 (1995).

18.2. *Riblet Tramway Co. v. Marathon Electronics-Artek Drive Div.,* 159 Vt. 503, 506, 621 A.2d 1274, 1275 (1993).

19. *Lavallee v. Vermont Motor Inns, Inc.,* 153 Vt. 80, 569 A.2d 1073 (1989).

20. *Langle v. Kurkul,* 146 Vt. 513, 510 A.2d 1301 (1986); *Thurber v. Russ Smith, Inc.,* 128 Vt. 216, 260 A.2d 390, 392 (1969). Where there is no existing harm caused by defendant's breach of duty, there is no liability for failing to prevent foreseeable future damage. *Graham v. Town of Duxbury* (Vt. #2000-063, filed Nov. 5, 2001) (entry order).

21. *Denis Bail Bonds, Inc. v. State,* 159 Vt. 481, 487, 622 A.2d 495, 499 (1993).

22. *Langle v. Kurkul,* 146 Vt. 513, 510 A.2d 1301 (1986).

23. *O'Connell v. Killington, Ltd.,* 164 Vt. 73, 665 A.2d 39 (1995).

24. *McGee v. Vermont Fed. Bank,* 726 A.2d 42 (Vt. 1999).

25. *O'Connell v. Killington, Ltd.,* 164 Vt. 73, 665 A.2d 39 (1995).

26. *Estate Of Kelley v. Moguls, Inc.,* 160 Vt. 531, 632 A.2d 360 (1993).

27. *Sorge v. State,* 762 A.2d 816 (Vt. 2000); *Corbin v. Buchanan,* 163 Vt. 141, 657 A.2d 170 (1994) (individual plaintiff may not recover against a municipality for its failure to enforce an ordinance whose purpose is protection of the public as a whole).

28. Restatement § 315(b); *see Sorge v. State,* 762 A.2d 816 (Vt. 2000) (state has no duty to control juvenile in custody where the purpose in taking charge of the juvenile was not explicitly to control juvenile); *Sabia v. State,* 164 Vt. 293, 669 A.2d 1187 (1995) (state social workers had duty of care to children seeking protection from sexual abuse); *Poplaski v. Lamphere,* 152 Vt. 251, 256, 565 A.2d 1326, 1329 (1989) (employer never voluntarily "took charge" of intoxicated employee so as to trigger a duty of care to prevent him from leaving plant in own car); *Bradley v. H.A. Manosh Corp* 157 Vt. 477, 601 A.2d 978. (1991) (employer has a duty to act reasonably to control servant's actions on employer's premises to protect a third person from harm, if the employer has knowledge of (1) ability to control, (2) need to control, and (3) opportunity to control that employee); *Smith v. Day,* 148 Vt. 595, 597, 538 A.2d 157, 158 (1987) (university has no duty to control the volitional criminal acts of its students, despite fact that university may exercise a large degree of control over the activities of its students generally, where university had no reasonably foreseeable notice of criminal acts); *Peck v. Counseling Service of Addison County, Inc.,* 146 Vt. 61, 65, 499 A.2d 422,

425 (1985) (mental health professional has duty of reasonable care to protect third parties from patient).

29. *Zukatis v. Perry*, 165 Vt. 298, 682 A.2d 964 (1996); Restatement (Second) of Torts § 283 (1965).

30. *Garafano v. Neshobe Beach Club, Inc.*, 126 Vt. 566, 573, 238 A.2d 70, 76 (1967).

31. *Russo v. Griffin*, 147 Vt. 20, 24, 510 A.2d 436, 438 (1986) (legal malpractice); *see Irving v. Agency of Transportation*, 12 Vt. L.W. 47, 768 A.2d 1286 (2001) (entry order) (an inexperienced pilot is not held to a lesser standard of care because of that lack of experience).

32. The elements of medical malpractice are set out in 12 Vt. Stat. Ann. § 1908 (Supp. 2000). Under the statute, plaintiffs must prove: (1) the requisite standard of care; (2) that defendant failed to exercise the applicable degree of care; and (3) as a proximate result of (2), plaintiffs suffered damages. *Begin v. Richmond*, 150 Vt. 517, 520, 555 A.2d 363, 365 (1988).

33. *Mello v. Cohen*, 168 Vt. 639, 724 A.2d 471 (1998) (medical malpractice: court properly granted summary judgment to defendant, where medical issues were technical and obscure, and plaintiff failed to produce expert testimony to establish an informed consent claim.); *Tetreault v. Greenwood*, 165 Vt. 577, 578, 682 A.2d 949, 950 (1996) (mem.) (attorney malpractice); *Utzler v. Medical Ctr. Hosp. Of Vt.*, 149 Vt. 126, 540 A.2d 652 (1987) (medical malpractice); *Larson v. Candlish*, 144 Vt. 499, 502, 480 A.2d 417, 418 (1984) (dental malpractice); see *South Burlington School District. v. Calcagni*, 138 Vt. 33, 410 A.2d 1359 (1980) (architect malpractice: "the record is devoid of evidence as to what the 'reasonable roof designer' would have done in a similar situation").

34. *Bull v. Pinkham Engineering Assoc. Inc.*, 752 A.2d 26 (Vt. 2000) (surveyor); *Fleming v. Nicholson*, 168 Vt. 495, 497-98, 724 A.2d 1026, 1028 (1998) (attorney malpractice); *Mello v. Cohen*, 168 Vt. 639, 724 A.2d 471 (1998) (medical malpractice: expert testimony required because tongue lesion types and associated diagnostic procedures and treatments do not fall within the common knowledge of lay fact finders).

35. *Mitchell v. Amadon*, 128 Vt. 169, 260 A.2d 213 (1969) (5-year-old plaintiff negligent in running into street); *Beaucage v. Russell*, 127 Vt. 58, 238 A.2d 631 (1968) (evidence supported finding of contributory negligence where 8-year-old plaintiff on bicycle tried to cross directly in front of car); *Johnson's Admr. v. Rutland R. R. Co.*, 93 Vt. 132, 106 A. 682 (railroad crossing accident: capacity of 6-year-old was a question of fact to be submitted to the jury on the evidence); *Howe v. Central Vermont Ry. Co.*, 91 Vt. 485, 493, 101 A. 45 (1917) (the plaintiff, a child two years and seven months old, "was of such tender years, at the time of her injury, as to be incapable of exercising care").

36. *Roberts v. State*, 147 Vt. 160, 163, 514 A.2d 694, 695 (1986).

37. *Gilman v. Towmotor Corp.*, 160 Vt. 116, 621 A.2d 1260. (1992)

38. *Rooney v. Medical Center Hospital Of Vt.*, 162 Vt. 513, 649 A.2d 756 (1994) (malpractice case: court did not specifically approve of the "three-prong" instruction); *Gilman v. Towmotor Corp.*, 160 Vt. 116, 621 A.2d 1260 (1992) (products liability; same).

39. *Woodcock's Adm'r v. Hallock*, 98 Vt. 284, 290, 127 A. 380, 382 (1925) (once negligence is established, liability attaches to "all the injurious consequences that flow [therefrom] until . . . the force set in motion by the negligent act has so far spent itself as to be too small for the law's notice").

40. *Dodge v. McArthur*, 126 Vt. 81, 83, 223 A.2d 453 (1966) (long settled in this jurisdiction that proximate cause relates only to cause-in-fact, with no foreseeability required); *Perkins v. Vermont Hydro-Electric Corp.*, 106 Vt. 367, 177 A. 631. (1934) ("It is not necessary that injury in the precise form suffered should have been foreseen; it is only essential that, viewing the occurrence in retrospect, the consequences appear to flow in unbroken sequence from the negligence.").

41. *Lorrain v. Ryan*, 160 Vt. 202, 628 A.2d 543 (1993) (citing Restatement (Second) of Torts § 434 (jury's responsibility to determine whether defendant's conduct was a substantial factor in causing plaintiff's harm)).

42. *Town Of Bridport v. Sterling Clark Lurton Corp.*, 166 Vt. 304, 693 A.2d 701 (1997) (product liability "failure to warn" case: where the user did not read the actual warning given, plaintiff could show proximate cause only by showing that the warning should have been more conspicuous); *Wheeler v. Central Vt. Medical Ctr., Inc.*, 155 Vt. 85, 582 A.2d 165 (1989) (malpractice case: jury was cautioned not to consider physical or mental conditions that would have occurred irrespective of the actions or inactions of defendant); *Tufts v. Wyand*, 148 Vt. 528, 530, 536 A.2d 541, 542 (1987) (finding of proximate cause depends on showing that negligent act was cause-in-fact of injury).

43. *Rooney v. Medical Center Hospital Of Vt.*, 162 Vt. 513, 649 A.2d 756 (1994) (medical malpractice); *Tufts v. Wyand*, 148 Vt. 528 , 536 A.2d 541 (1987).

44. *Estate of Sumner v. Department of Social and Rehabilitation Services*, 162 Vt. 628, 649 A.2d 1034 (1994).

45. 12 Vt. Stat. Ann. § 1036 (Supp. 2000).

46. *Webb v. Navistar International 1994 Transportation Corp.*, 166 Vt. 119, 692 A.2d 343 (1996).

47. 23 Vt. Stat. Ann. § 1259(e); *Ulm v. Ford Motor Company*, 170 Vt. 281, 750 A.2d 981 (2000) (statute prohibits the introduction of evidence of a failure to wear a safety belt, not only on issue of comparative fault but also on issue of proximate cause); *see Smith v. Goodyear Tire & Rubber Co.*, 600 F. Supp. 1561, 1563-64

(D. Vt. 1985) (evidence of the failure to wear a seatbelt allowed on the issue of contributory or comparative negligence, or as a mitigating factor in determining the victim's damages).

48. *Campbell v. Beede,* 124 Vt. 434, 207 A.2d 236 (1965).

49. 12 Vt. Stat. Ann. § 1036 (Supp. 2000).

50. *Perkins v. Windsor Hospital Corp.*, 142 Vt. 305, 310, 455 A.2d 810, 814 (1982) (use of assumption of risk language reversible error because "parties were entitled to a jury free from irrelevancies and possible confusion"); *Sunday v. Stratton Corp.*, 136 Vt. 293, 390 A.2d 398 (1978) ("the doctrine is logically only a phase of contributory negligence and ... use of assumption of risk language is irrelevant and confusing in a jury instruction on comparative negligence").

51. *Sunday v. Stratton Corp.*, 136 Vt. 293, 390 A.2d 398 (1978).

52. *See Cyr v. Green Mountain Power Corp.*, 145 Vt. 231, 235, 485 A.2d 1265 (1984) (citing *Prosser and Keeton on the Law of Torts* § 40, at 257-58) (W. Keeton 5th ed. 1984).

53. *Cyr*, 145 Vt. at 235-36.

54. *Connors v. University Associates In Obstetrics And Gynecology, Inc.*, 769 F. Supp. 578 (D. Vt. 1991) (Billings, J.), *aff'd*, 4 F.3d 123 (2d Cir 1993).

55. *Cyr*, 145 Vt. at 236, 485 A.2d at 1269 (citing Prosser & Keeton, *supra,* at 250-51).

56. *Gentles v. Lanctot*, 145 Vt. 396, 491 A.2d 336 (1985).

57. *Mobbs v. Central Vt. Ry., Inc.*, 155 Vt. 210, 583 A.2d 566 (1990) (RR grade crossing); *Bosley v. Central Vt. Pub. Serv. Corp.*, 127 Vt. 581, 255 A.2d 671 (1969) (transmission of electricity); *Greenberg v. Giddings* 127 Vt. 242, 246 A.2d 832 (1968) (propane gas); *Lewis v. Vermont Gas Corp* 121 Vt. 168, 151 A.2d 297 (1959) (propane gas); *Humphrey v. Twin State Gas & Electric Co.*, 100 Vt. 414, 422, 139 A 440 (1927) (transmission of electricity).

58. *Malloy v. Lane Construction Corp.*, 123 Vt. 500, 194 A.2d 398 (1963).

59. *Marzec-Gerrior v. D.C.P. Industries, Inc.*, 164 Vt. 569, 674 A.2d 1248 (1995); *Ball v. Melsur Corp.*, 161 Vt. 35, 43-44, 633 A.2d 705, 712 (1993).

60. *Beaucage v. Russell*, 127 Vt. 58, 62, 238 A.2d 631, 634 (1968).

61. *See Landry v. Hubert*, 101 Vt. 111, 113, 141 A. 593, 594 (1928); *Gerrior v. D.C.P. Industries, Inc.*, 164 Vt. 569, 674 A.2d 1248 (1995) (Dooley, J. concurring).

62. *Landry v. Hubert*, 101 Vt. 111, 113, 141 A. 593, 594 (1928); *Gerrior v. D.C.P. Industries, Inc.*, 164 Vt. 569, 674 A.2d 1248 (1995) (Dooley, J. concurring).

63. *Larmay v. VanEtten*, 129 Vt. 368, 371, 278 A.2d 736, 738-39 (1971) (citations omitted). Vermont Rules of Evidence 301; *see Favreau v. Miller*, 156 Vt. 222, 233, 591 A.2d 68, 75 (1991).

64. *See* Vermont Rule of Evidence 301; *but see Gerrior v. D.C.P. Industries, Inc.*, 164 Vt. 569, 674 A.2d 1248 (1995) (Dooley, J. concurring).

65. *Brown v. Roadway Express, Inc.*, 169 Vt. 633, 740 A.2d 352 (1999) (trial court correctly granted judgment as a matter of law to Plaintiff on issue of defendant's drivers negligence where defendant crossed the center line in violation of statute and did not rebut the resulting presumption of negligence).

66. 12 Vt. Stat. Ann. § 1036.

67. *Slayton v. Ford Motor Co.*, 140 Vt. 27, 29, 435 A.2d 946, 947 (1981) (where there has been a liquidated settlement between one of several defendants and a plaintiff, the jury is not be informed of such fact, or the sum paid, but it is the function of the court following the verdict to find the amount by which the verdict should be reduced).

68. *Howard v. Spafford*, 132 Vt. 434, 321 A.2d 74 (1974).

69. *Peters v. Mindell*, 159 Vt. 424, 428, 620 A.2d 1268 (1992) (citing *Viens v. Anthony Co.*, 282 F. Supp. 983, 985, n.2 (D. Vt. 1968)).

70. *White v. Quechee Lakes Landowners' Assoc., Inc.*, 170 Vt. 25, 742 A.2d 734 (1999).

71. *Id.*

72. *Morris v. American Motors Corp.*, 142 Vt. 566, 576, 459 A.2d 968, 974 (1982).

73. Indemnification allowed: *Peters v. Mindell*, 159 Vt. 424, 427-28, 620 A.2d 1268 (1992) (engineering company that designed and built septic system liable to indemnify sellers found liable to buyers for a defective condition in the system); *Morris v. American Motors Corp.*, 142 Vt. 566, 576, 459 A.2d 968, 974 (1982) (manufacturer of defective automobile part required to indemnify automobile manufacturer with respect to injuries sustained as a result of defect); *Bardwell Motor Inn, Inc. v. Accavallo*, 135 Vt. 571, 381 A.2d 1061 (1977) (hotel operator entitled to indemnity when a patron was injured as a result of the negligence of individuals hired to make repairs on the premises); *Digregorio v. Champlain Valley Fruit Co.*, 127 Vt. 562, 566, 255 A.2d 183, 186 (1969) (wholesaler whose employee had inserted a glass thermometer into a banana was required to indemnify the owners of a market for liability to customer injured biting into the banana). Indemnity denied: *City of Burlington v. Arthur J. Gallagher & Co.*, 12 Vt. L.W. 325 (#2000-482, filed Oct. 29, 2001) (entry order) (insurance broker had

no implied duty to indemnify insurer because equity does not require shifting the loss from the party with insurance coverage obligations); *Knisely v. Central Vermont Hospital* 769 A.2d 5 (S. Ct. 2000) (contractor who tested anesthesia machines did not assume hospital's duty to provide safe place to work, and therefore had no duty to indemnify the hospital for its settlement with injured doctor); *White v. Quechee Lakes Landowners' Assoc., Inc.*, 170 Vt. 25, 742 A.2d 734 (1999) (indemnification denied where for twenty years third party plaintiff had acquiesced in the continuation of the dangerous condition in the sauna it now alleges was attributable to the manufacturer); *Hopper v. Kelz*, 166 Vt. 616, 617, 694 A.2d 415, 416 (1997) (homeowner not entitled to indemnification from employer for employee's injuries caused by the defective condition of the homeowners' basement steps); *Goulette v. Babock*, 153 Vt. 650, 651, 571 A.2d 74, 75 (1990) (architect of apartment complex containing a pond in which two children drowned was not required to indemnify the owner of the complex, who acquiesced in the obvious risk presented by the absence of a fence around the pond); *Hiltz v. John Deere Indus. Equip. Co.*, 146 Vt. 12, 15, 497 A.2d 748, 752 (1985) (the employer of employee injured while operating a defective side-boom counterweight used on a tractor was not required to indemnify the manufacturer of the defective equipment, notwithstanding the manufacturer's claim that the employer was aware of the defect).

74. 21 Vt. Stat. Ann. § 622 (Supp. 2000).

75. 21 Vt. Stat. Ann. § 624(a) (Supp. 2000).

76. 21 Vt. Stat. Ann. § 601(3) (1987).

77. *Libercent v. Aldrich*, 149 Vt. 76, 79, 539 A.2d 981 (1987).

78. *Gerrish v. Savard*, 169 Vt. 468, 739 A.2d 1195 (1999) (officer not liable for negligently rigged a crane, causing a cable to snap and a piece of granite to fall on plaintiff); *Dunham v. Chase*, 165 Vt. 543, 674 A.2d 1279 (1996) (principal stockholder and president could not be sued for negligent supervision of employee, in violation of company policy, drove a customer's car with its hood open into a service bay and hit plaintiff); *Garrity v. Manning*, 164 Vt. 507, 671 A.2d 808, 811 (1996) (president and majority stockholder could not be sued for negligent failure to sand parking lot).

79. *Bruley v. Fonda Group, Inc.*, 157 Vt. 1, 595 A.2d 269 (1991) (employment of minor).

80. *Kittell v. Vermont Weatherboard, Inc.*, 138 Vt. 439, 417 A.2d 926 (1980).

81. *Id.*; *Goodstein v. Bombardier Capital, Inc.*, 889 F. Supp. 760 (D. Vt. 1995) (employer may be sued for intentional infliction of emotional distress).

81.1. *Gallipo v. City of Rutland* (2000-217) (Vt. filed 21-Dec-2001).

82. 21 Vt. Stat. Ann. § 618 (Supp. 2000).

83. *Baisley v. Missisquoi Cemetery Ass'n*, 167 Vt. 473, 708 A.2d 924 (1998) (no-duty-to-trespassers rule does not apply to person impaled on a boundary fence; without considering whether to modify the landowner liability rules generally, Court holds that defendants owed plaintiff a duty of ordinary care to keep their property from becoming a source of danger to those on adjoining lands); *Zukatis v. Perry*, 165 Vt. 298, 305, 682 A.2d 964, 968 (1996) (Dooley, J., dissenting) ("our law on landowner liability is in serious need of reexamination"); *Buzzell v. Jones*, 151 Vt. 4, 7, 556 A.2d 106, 109 (1989) (noting that other jurisdictions have modified some or all of the traditional distinctions in the duties of care owed to persons entering land).

84. *Favreau v. Miller*, 156 Vt. 222, 224, 591 A.2d 68 (1991); *Smith v. Monmaney & Speno*, 127 Vt. 585, 588, 255 A.2d 674 (1969); *Doyle v. Exxon Corp.*, 592 F.2d 44, 46 (2d Cir. 1979).

85. *O'Brien v. Island Corp.*, 157 Vt. 135, 596 A.2d 1295 (1991); *see Gero v. J.W.J. Realty*, 757 A.2d 475 (Vt. 2000) (landowner with no supervisory control not liable to employee of contractor for dangerous condition on site arising from the contractor's methods); *Knight v. Rower*, 170 Vt. 96, 742 A.2d 1237 (Vt. 1999) (absent landowner not liable for injuries caused by the consumption of alcohol on their property where landowner did not furnish or control the alcohol consumed).

86. *Buzzell v. Jones*, 151 Vt. 4, 6, 556 A.2d 106, 108 (1989); *Hillier v. Noble*, 142 Vt. 552, 556, 458 A.2d 1101, 1103 (1983).

87. *See Zukatis v. Perry*, 165 Vt. 298, 300-01, 682 A.2d 964, 965-66 (1996).

88. *Hillier v. Noble*, 142 Vt. 552, 556, 458 A.2d 1101, 1103 (1983).

89. *Lucas v. Kelley*, 102 Vt. 173, 179, 147 A. 281(1929).

90. *Lomberg v. Renner*, 121 Vt. 311, 315, 157 A.2d 222 (1959).

91. 12 Vt. Stat. Ann. § 5793 (a) (Supp 2000).

92. *Debus v. Grand Union Stores*, 159 Vt. 537, 621 A.2d 1288 (1993) (store's practice of bringing pallets stacked with merchandise into the aisle for restocking purposes during business hours came within "business practice" exception to the notice requirement); *Forcier v. Grand Union Stores*, 128 Vt. 389, 264 A.2d 796 (1970) (store which sold produce in self-service bins had heightened duty to anticipate foreseeable accidents such as a customer slipping on a piece of banana).

93. *Wakefield v. Levin*, 118 Vt. 392, 397, 110 A.2d 712 (1955); *Dooley v. Economy Store, Inc.*, 109 Vt. 138, 142 194 A. 375 (1937); *Randall v. K-Mart Corp.*, 150 F.3d 210 (2d Cir. 1998).

94. *Garafano v. Neshobe Beach Club*, 126 Vt. 566, 572, 238 A.2d 70, 75 (1967).

95. 7 Vt. Stat. Ann. § 501 (1999).

96. *Langle v. Kurkul*, 146 Vt. 513, 515-16, 510 A.2d 1301, 1303 (1986).

97. *Thompson v. Dewey's South Royalton, Inc.*, 169 Vt. 274, 733 A.2d 65 (1999).

98. 7 Vt. Stat. Ann. § 501(g) (1999).

99. *Knight v. Rower*, 10 Vt.L.W. 315, 742 A.2d 1237 (1999).

100. *Howard v. Usiak*, 12 Vt. L.W. 134, 775 A.2d 909 (2001) (no showing of negligent misrepresentation in architectural malpractice case; there is a difference between a misrepresentation and a breach of promise); *Gus' Catering, Inc. v. Menusoft Systems*, 762 A.2d 804 (Vt. 2000) (computer software provider had no duty of care to avoid intangible economic losses); *Breslauer v. Fayston School District*, 163 Vt. 416, 659 A.2d 1129, 1132 (1995) (no tort liability for negative job reference that caused breach of contract and the loss of jobs); *Winey v. William E. Dailey, Inc.*, 161 Vt. 129, 136, 636 A.2d 744, 749 (1993) (under consumer fraud law, mere breach of contract does not raise presumption of fraud); *Favreau v. Miller*, 156 Vt. 222, 229, 591 A.2d 68, 73 (1991) (where personal injury is alleged, "concepts of tort and negligence law," rather than contract law, "provide the more straightforward way to describe the respective duties and liabilities of the parties"); *Bevins v. King*, 147 Vt. 203, 204, 514 A.2d 1044, 1045 (1986) (fraudulent nonperformance of contract is not a tort); *Lyon v. Bennington College Corp.*, 137 Vt. 135, 137, 400 A.2d 1010, 1012 (1979) (conversion action against college for taking of tenure of professor not maintainable because "contractual rights, which are personal and without marketability" are not goods that can be converted); *Lapoint v. Dumont Construction Co.*, 128 Vt. 8, 10, 258 A.2d 570, 571 (1969) (law of negligence inapplicable to breach of contract action).

101. *O'Connell v. Killington, Ltd.*, 164 Vt. 73, 665 A.2d 39 (1995) (absent a special relationship or undertaking, there is no duty to protect another's litigation interest, therefore defendant ski area had no duty to obtain the name of a skier who collided with plaintiff so plaintiff could sue that skier for her damages).

102. *Springfield Hydroelectric Co. v. Corp.*, 779 A.2d 67 (2001) (no recovery for purely economic losses absent breach of professional or other special duty).

103. *Paquette v. Deere & Co.*, 168 Vt. 258, 719 A.2d 410 (1998) (purchasers of allegedly defective motor home did not seek damages for any physical harm, but only for disappointed commercial expectations; claim was actionable only under warranty law).

104. *Pearson v. Simmonds Precision Prods., Inc.*, 160 Vt. 168, 624 A.2d 1134 (1993) (plaintiff may not recover damages for emotional distress on theories of negligent misrepresentation or negligent nondisclosure).

105. V.R.C.P. 9 (b) (2000).

106. *Poulin v. Ford Motor Co.*, 147 Vt. 120, 125, 513 A.2d 1168, 1172 (1986). However, a party seeking to rescind a fraudulently induced contract is not required to prove its case by clear and convincing evidence. *Sarvis v. Vermont State Colleges*, 12 Vt. L.W. 43, 772 A.2d 494 (2001).

107. *Silva v. Stevens*, 156 Vt. 94, 589 A.2d 852 (1991); *Union Bank v. Jones*, 138 Vt. 115, 121, 411 A.2d 1338, 1342 (1980).

108. *Goldman v. Town of Plainfield*, 762 A.2d 854 (Vt. 2000).

109. *Sugarline Assocs. v. Alpen Assocs* 155 Vt. 437, 586 A.2d 1115. (1990).

110. *White v. Pepin*, 151 Vt. 413, 416, 561 A.2d 94, 96 (1989); *Standard Packaging Corp. v. Julian Goodrich Architects, Inc.*, 136 Vt. 376, 381, 392 A.2d 402, 404 (1978).

111. *McGee v. Vermont Fed. Bank*, 169 Vt. 529, 726 A.2d 42 (1999); *Silva v. Stevens*, 156 Vt. 94, 589 A.2d 852, 860 (1991).

112. Restatement (Second) of Torts § 552(1) (1977).

113. *Id.* at § 552; *Behn v. Northeast Appraisal Co.*, 145 Vt. 101, 483 A.2d 604 (1984) (appraiser hired by bank had no duty of care to property owner where no evidence that the appraiser intended to supply the report to the property owner or knew the prospective purchaser would supply the report to the property owner); *Hughes v. Holt*, 140 Vt. 38, 435 A.2d 687 (1981) ("The appraisal report was for the exclusive use of the bank, and right or wrong in content, it was confidential. This being so, it certainly was not intended to, and could not, operate as any sort of representation to the buyers about the quality of the building to be purchased").

114. *Washington Elec. Coop. v. Massachusetts Municipal Wholesale Electric Co.*, 894 F. Supp. 777 (D. VT 1995) (suit against an attorney).

115. *Silva v. Stevens*, 156 Vt. 94, 109, 589 A.2d 852, 860 (1991).

116. *Id.* at 108, 589 A.2d at 860.

117. *Pearson v. Simmonds Precision Prods., Inc.* 160 Vt. 168, 624 A.2d 1134 (1993).

118. 9 Vt. Stat. Ann. § 2453 (a) (1993).

119. 9 Vt. Stat. Ann. § 2461(b) (1999).

120. *Poulin v. Ford Motor Co.*, 147 Vt. 120, 124, 513 A.2d 1168, 1171 (1986).

121. *Carter v. Gugliuzzi*, 168 Vt. 48, 716 A.2d 17 (1998).

122. *Peabody v. P.J.'s Auto Village, Inc.*, 153 Vt. 55, 57, 569 A.2d 460, 462 (1989).

123. *Bisson v. Ward*, 160 Vt. 343, 351, 628 A.2d 1256, 1261 (1993); *Peabody*, 153 Vt. at 57, 569 A.2d at 462.

124. *Carter v. Gugliuzzi*, 168 Vt. 48, 716 A.2d 17 (1998).

125. *Turcotte v. Estate Of LaRose*, 153 Vt. 196, 569 A.2d 1086 (1989); *Coty v. Ramsey Assocs.*, 149 Vt. 451, 467, 546 A.2d 196, 207 (1988).

126. *Pezzano v. Bonneau*, 133 Vt. 88, 329 A.2d 659 (1974).

127. *See Murphy v. Stowe Club Highlands*, 761 A.2d 688 (Vt. 2000) (in a breach of contract case malice alone is not sufficient to support an award of punitive damages; defendants' actions must also be akin to a willful and wanton, or fraudulent, tort).

128. *City of Burlington v. Arthur J. Gallagher & Co.*, 788 A.2d 18, 12 Vt. L.W. 325 (2001) (entry order) (simply engaging in wrongful conduct is insufficient to establish the element of malice necessary to successfully recover punitive damages); *Brueckner v. Norwich University*, 169 Vt. 118, 730 A.2d 1086 (1999) (negligence and indifference, however gross, are insufficient to support and award of punitive damages. Punitive damages may not awarded against a corporation on the basis of inaction or inattention of senior corporate officers, without evidence to support an inference that their inaction was infused with a bad motive that evinces the degree of malice required to support a punitive award.); *Ryan v. Herald Ass'n, Inc.*, 152 Vt. 275, 286, 566 A.2d 1316 (1989); *Leblanc v. UPS* 1996 U.S. Dist. LEXIS 5351 (D. Vt. 1996); *see also Parris v. St. Johnsbury Trucking Co.*, 395 F.2d 543 (2d Cir. 1968).

129. *State v. Riendeau*, 157 Vt. 615, 624-25, 603 A.2d 360 (1991); *Meadowbrook Condominium Ass'n. v. South Burlington Realty Corp.*, 152 Vt. 16, 28, 565 A.2d 238 (1989).

130. *See Vermont Microsystems, Inc. v. Autodesk, Inc.* 1994 U.S. Dist. LEXIS 18737 (D. Vt. 1994) quoting 23 Cal. Jur. 3d § 123, at 246-47 (1975).

131. *Chandler v. Bombardier Capital, Inc.* 1992 U.S. Dist. LEXIS 21802 (D. Vt. 1992); *Coty v. Ramsey Assoc., Inc.*, 149 Vt. 451, 464, 546 A.2d 196, *cert. denied*, 487 U.S. 1236 (1988)).

132. *Chandler v. Bombardier Capital, Inc.* 1992 U.S. Dist. LEXIS 21802 (D. Vt. 1992) (*quoting Coty v. Ramsey Assoc., Inc.*, 149 Vt. 451, 464, 546 A.2d 196 (citations omitted), *cert. denied*, 487 U.S. 1236 (1988)).

133. *Coty v. Ramsey Associates. Inc.*, 149 Vt. 451, 464, 546 A.2d 196 *cert. denied*, 487 U.S. 1236 (1988). *See Vermont Microsystems, Inc. v. Autodesk, Inc.*, 1994 U.S. Dist. LEXIS 18737 (D. Vt. 1994) (applying California law). That a defendant sought the advice of counsel before acting is relevant to defendant's intent, but does not necessarily preclude an award of punitive damages. *Cooper v. Cooper*, 783 A.2d 430 (Vt. 2001).

134. *Suburban Propane v. Proctor Gas, Inc.* 953 F.2d 780 (2d Cir. 1992); *McCormick v. McCormick*, 159 Vt. 472, 479, 621 A.2d 238 (1993); *Lent v. Huntoon*, 143 Vt. 539, 550, 470 A.2d 1162 (1983); *Allard v. Ford Motor Credit Corp.*, 139 Vt. 162, 164, 422 A.2d 940 (1980).

135. *See Jewett v. Pudlo*, 106 Vt. 249, 256-57, 172 A 423 (1934) ("To render a master liable in exemplary damages for the willful, malicious, or wanton act of the servant done within the scope of his employment, some misconduct of the master beyond that which the law implies from the mere relation of master and servant, must be shown.").

136. *Willett v. Village of St. Albans*, 69 Vt. 330, 337, 38 A. 72 (1897); *see also Shortle v. Central Vermont Public Service Corp.*, 137 Vt. 32, 33, 399 A.2d 517 (1979).

137. *Shortle v. Central Vermont Public Service Corp.*, 137 Vt. 32, 33, 399 A.2d 517, 518 (1979).

138. *Parker v. Hoefer* 118 Vt. 1, 100 A.2d 434 (1953).

139. *In re Estate of Peters* 765 A.2d 468 (Vt. 2000).

140. *Imported Car Ctr., Inc. v. Billings*, 163 Vt. 76, 653 A.2d 765 (1994).

141. *Pezzano v. Bonneau*, 133 Vt. 88, 329 A.2d 659 (1974).

142. *BMW of North America, Inc. v. Gore*, 517 U.S. 559, 575-85 (1996) (punitive damages award grossly excessive in light of (1) degree of reprehensibility of the defendant's conduct, (2) ratio between the plaintiff's compensatory damages and the amount of the punitive damages, and (3) the civil or criminal sanctions that could be imposed for comparable misconduct); *Pacific Mutual Life Insurance. Co. v. Haslip*, 499 U.S. 1, 21-22 (1991) (discussing relevant factors for ensuring that punitive damages are reasonable).

143. *Quesnel v. Town Of Middlebury*, 167 Vt. 252, 706 A.2d 436 (1997) (parents have no common law recovery for wrongful death of child).

144. 14 Vt. Stat. Ann. § 1492 (1999).

145. 14 Vt. Stat. Ann. §§ 1451-1453 (1999).

146. 14 Vt. Stat. Ann. § 1492(b); *Whitchurch v. Perry*, 137 Vt. 464, 408 A.2d 627 (1979) (a spouse or next-of-kin must exist if damages for wrongful death are to be recovered).

147. *Clymer v. Webster*, 156 Vt. 614, 596 A.2d 905 (1991).

148. *Clymer v. Webster*, 156 Vt. 614 596 A.2d 905 (1991) (damages for loss of decedent's future earnings not available under the Survival Statute).

VIRGINIA

A. **STATUTES OF LIMITATION**

Causes of action for personal injuries must be brought within two years regardless of whether the action alleges negligence or an intentional tort.[1] The discovery rule generally does not apply.[2] Nonphysical personal torts such as defamation, slander, libel, and fighting words have a one-year limitations period.[3] Fraud claims must be brought within two years of the fraud or in actions for malpractice against a health care provider involving fraud, concealment or intentional misrepresentation, one year from the date of discovery or the date the fraud reasonably should have been discovered up to a maximum of ten years from the time of injury.[4] Claims for damage to property have a five-year limitations period.[5] Claims for property damage for sales covered by the Uniform Commercial Code have a four-year statute of limitations as do claims for breach of contract for the sale of goods under the U.C.C.[6] Unlawful entry or detainer actions have a three-year statute of limitations.[7] The limitations period for wrongful death actions is two years from the death.[8] Suits on written contracts have a five-year limitations period[9] unless otherwise stated in the contract while those on oral contracts, whether express or implied, must be brought within three years.[10]

B. **TORT REFORM**

The most recent tort reform discussions in Virginia have centered around medical malpractice actions. Effective August 1, 1999, "the total amount recoverable for any injury to, or death of, a patient shall not exceed $1.5 million."[11] The maximum recovery limit will increase $50,000 per year until 2006.[12] In years 2007 and 2008, the final annual increases, the limit will increase $75,000 per year.[13]

Similarly, in actions accruing on or after July 1, 1988, including medical malpractice cases, "the total amount awarded for punitive damages against all defendants" shall not "exceed $350,000."[14]

C. **"NO-FAULT" LIMITATIONS**

No-fault auto insurance is defined as "[a]n agreement to indemnify for a loss due to personal injury or property damage arising from the use of an automobile, regardless of who caused the accident."[15] No-fault insurance does not exist in Virginia.

D. **THE STANDARD FOR NEGLIGENCE**

There can be no actionable negligence unless there is a legal duty flowing from the defendant to the plaintiff, a violation of that duty, and a consequent injury.[16] The legal duty may arise from statute, ordinance, or relation of the parties.[17]

In order to recover, the plaintiff must show not only that the defendant owed a legal duty to the plaintiff, but also that the defendant breached that duty.[18] Breach is shown when the plaintiff demonstrates that the defendant failed to use due care for the safety of others.[19]

Due care is that degree of care that an ordinarily prudent person would exercise under the same or similar circumstances to avoid injury to another.[20] Where the defendant has injured the plaintiff while engaged in a particular activity or occupation, the applicable standard is that of the ordinary prudent person engaged in that activity or occupation.[21]

In general, there is no duty to control the conduct of a third person so as to prevent that third person from harming another.[22] However, when a special relationship exists between the defendant and either the third party or the plaintiff, the defendant could have a duty to control the third party.[23]

Children are not measured by the adult standard of care.[24] Children under the age of seven years are conclusively presumed to be incapable of negligence.[25] When the child is over the age of seven years, the standard by which his or her conduct will be judged is that degree of care that would be exercised by a reasonable person of like age, intelligence, and experience under like circumstances.[26] Children between the ages of seven and fourteen are presumed to be incapable of negligence, but the presumption may be rebutted by sufficient proof to the contrary in the individual case.[27] Children over the age of 14 are presumed to be capable of negligence, but this presumption may also be rebutted by sufficient proof to the contrary in the individual case.[28]

E. CAUSATION

In Virginia, actionable negligence requires a direct causal connection between the prohibited conduct and the injury.[29]

The term "proximate cause" is traditionally used to describe the causal connection that must be present in order for the defendant to be liable for the plaintiff's injuries.

The proximate cause of an event is that act or omission that in natural and continuous sequence, unbroken by an intervening cause, produced the event, and without which that event would not have occurred.[30]

F. CONTRIBUTORY NEGLIGENCE, COMPARATIVE NEGLIGENCE, AND ASSUMPTION OF RISK

1. Contributory Negligence

Virginia is a contributory negligence state, following the legal principle that no person is entitled to recover from another for damages that have been occasioned by his own neglect.[31] In most actions in Virginia the contributory negligence of the plaintiff is an absolute bar to the plaintiff's recovery.[32] In such actions, negligence of a plaintiff, however slight, that is a proximate cause of the accident will bar a recovery.[33]

2. **Comparative Negligence**

Since Virginia follows the contributory negligence doctrine, the comparative negligence doctrine has historically had little applicability. There are many cases that state categorically that there is no doctrine of comparative negligence in Virginia and that negligence will not be apportioned in this state.[34]

There are a few instances in which comparative negligence principles are applied in Virginia. For example, cases involving railroad crossing accidents,[35] actions brought under the Federal Employer's Liability Act,[36] and admiralty cases[37] apply comparative negligence principles.

3. **Assumption of Risk**

Assumption of the risk, like contributory negligence, is a complete bar to a plaintiff's recovery.[38] The essential elements of assumption of risk are that the nature and extent of the risk must be fully understood and appreciated by the plaintiff and the plaintiff must voluntarily elect to incur the risk.[39]

Where the danger is "open and obvious," it may be assumed that the plaintiff knew of the risk.[40]

Assumption of the risk will bar a plaintiff's recovery only if the risk assumed is the proximate cause of the plaintiff's injury.[41]

G. *RES IPSA LOQUITUR* AND INHERENTLY DANGEROUS ACTIVITIES

1. *Res Ipsa Loquitur*

In Virginia, the doctrine of *res ipsa loquitur* has been limited and restricted to a great extent.[42] The doctrine applies in negligence cases where: (1) the instrumentality causing the damage is in the exclusive possession or under the exclusive management of the defendant; (2) the accident is of such a nature and character as does not ordinarily occur if due care is used; and (3) the evidence regarding the cause of the incident is accessible to the defendant and not accessible to the injured party.[43]

Res ipsa loquitur is an evidentiary presumption sometimes resorted to in the absence of evidence, but it is not to be applied when evidence is available.[44] It is not applicable in the case of an unexplained accident that may be attributable to one of events, some of which the defendant did not cause.[45]

2. **Inherently Dangerous Activities**

A product or activity is inherently dangerous when the danger of injury stems from the product or activity itself and not from any defect or negligence during the performance of the activity.[46] Those dealing with inherently dangerous products or activities are required to use a high degree of care commensurate with the danger involved so as to prevent injury to others.[47] Activities determined to be inherently dangerous in Virginia include blasting,[48] moving heavy earth across railroad tracks,[49] the operation of a truck by an inexperienced person,[50] and carrying an over-wide load on a dark rainy night.[51] The "dangerous instrumentality" rule has also been applied to the operation of high-voltage transmission lines.[52]

H. NEGLIGENCE *PER SE*[53]

In Virginia, the violation of a statute or ordinance may constitute negligence *per se*.[54] Negligence *per se* involves the use of a statutory standard to determine negligence. For example, the violation of motor vehicle or other traffic laws is often asserted to be negligence *per se*.[55] Negligence *per se* will not support recovery of damages unless the statutory violation was the proximate cause of the injury.[56] The doctrine of negligence *per se* does not create a cause of action where one did not exist at common law.[57]

In order for the violation of a statute to constitute negligence *per se*, the statute must have been enacted for the public safety;[58] and the plaintiff must belong to the class of persons for whose benefit the statute was enacted.[59] Moreover, the harm that occurred must be the type of harm against which the statute was designed to protect.[60]

Although negligence *per se* is a common law doctrine, the General Assembly of Virginia has codified it in Virginia Code Section 8.01-221, which states in part that "[a]ny person injured by the violation of any statute may recover from the offender such damages as he may sustain by reason of the violation. . . ."[61]

The doctrine of negligence *per se* applies to plaintiffs as well as to defendants; therefore, violation of a statute may constitute contributory negligence, barring a plaintiff's recovery.[62]

I. JOINT AND SEVERAL LIABILITY

Under Virginia law, where the wrongful acts of two of more persons produce a single injury, both tortfeasors may be held liable for the entire amount of the injured person's damages.[63] The law does not attempt to apportion the injury, and each joint tortfeasor is held liable for the whole of the damages.[64] The comparative degrees of negligence of the tortfeasors are not considered, and each is liable for the whole of the damages even though the others were equally culpable, or contributed in a greater or lesser degree to the injury.[65] Therefore, a defendant may not escape liability for his own negligence by showing that another was also negligent.[66]

The plaintiff may choose to sue one or more joint tortfeasors where two or more persons jointly participated in causing the wrong.[67] The plaintiff may dismiss his or her claim against one tortfeasor without releasing the other joint tortfeasors in the absence of satisfaction.[68] The plaintiff may bring separate actions against the tortfeasors and proceed to judgment in separate actions or in one action against all tortfeasors. A judgment against one tortfeasor does not affect the ability of the plaintiff to obtain judgments against the other tortfeasors *unless the judgment has been satisfied.*[69] The plaintiff may obtain successive judgments against several tortfeasors before deciding on which tortfeasor to pursue to satisfy the judgment. Where a plaintiff obtains a judgment against one or more joint tortfeasors, the complete satisfaction of that judgment shall operate to discharge all joint tortfeasors.[70]

When a release or covenant not to sue is given in good faith to one of two or more persons liable in tort for the same injury, it shall not discharge the liability of any of the other tortfeasors unless its terms so provide.[71] However, any amount recovered against the other tortfeasors or any one of them shall be reduced by any amount stipulated by the covenant or the release, or in the amount of the consideration paid for it, whichever is greater.[72] Such release or covenant not to sue shall discharge the tortfeasor to whom it is given from all liability for contribution to any other tortfeasor.[73] A tortfeasor who enters into a release or covenant not to sue with a claimant is not entitled to recover contribution from another tortfeasor whose liability is not extinguished by the release or covenant not to sue.[74] A contribution plaintiff cannot recover from a contribution defendant unless the injured party could have recovered against the contribution defendant.[75] Additionally, contribution among tortfeasors may be enforced when the wrong results from negligence and involves no moral turpitude.[76] The statute of limitations for contribution in Virginia is three years and begins to run on payment or discharge of an obligation.[77]

J. INDEMNITY

Indemnity shifts the entire loss of the plaintiff from one defendant to another by reason of some legal obligation to pay damages occasioned by the negligence of another.[78] A cause of action for indemnity can only be sustained if specifically provided for by contract, with one possible exception. This possible exception to this general rule can be found in a 1936 case[79] in which the Virginia Supreme Court seemed to indicate that a passively negligent party could recover indemnity from an actively negligent one.[80] Although some jurisdictions allow parties who are secondarily liable to be indemnified by parties who are primarily liable, Virginia does not.[81]

K. BAR OF WORKERS' COMPENSATION STATUTE

In Virginia, an employee's sole and exclusive remedy for an injury[82] or death arising out of and in the course of the employment is under the Virginia Workers' Compensation Act.[83] Every employer and employee are presumed to have accepted the provisions of the Act.[84]

The Act is in the nature of a compromise between the employer and employee[85] to settle their differences arising out of personal injuries.[86] Both employer and employee surrender former rights, but gain certain advantages.[87] For example, an employee surrenders his right to bring an action at law against his employer for damages and agrees to accept benefits under the Act. In exchange, the employee may receive benefits under the Act even if he was negligent.[88] Similarly, under the Act, the employer forfeits the common law defenses of contributory negligence and assumption of the risk, but is relieved from liability for damages to the employee for which he might otherwise be liable to a much greater extent in an action at law.[89]

The rights and remedies granted under the Act exclude all other rights and remedies the employee may have to recover for an injury received during the course of his employment.[90] However, if the employee's injury is caused by the negligent act of a third party who is a stranger to the trade, occupation, or business of his employer, the employee may maintain an action at law against the third party.[91] An employee injured by the negligence of a fellow employee, rather than a stranger, is limited to the compensation afforded by the Act, and cannot maintain a common law action.[92]

However, an employee who is injured in the course of employment by a stranger is not entitled to a double recovery.[93] In many instances, an employer will be subrogated to the rights of the employee.[94]

Victims of sexual assault in the workplace may have the right to elect their remedy. Assaulted employees who can identify the attacker may elect to pursue an action at law against the attacker, in lieu of benefits under the Act, even if the attacker is the assaulted employee's employer or coemployee.[95] However, when an action at law is elected, the assaulted employee must repay any benefits received under the Act.[96]

The Act also delineates the rights and responsibilities of owners, contractors, and subcontractors, a question that frequently arises in a construction setting.[97] All persons engaged in any work that is a part of the trade, business, or occupation of the original party who undertakes as owner, or contracts as contractor, to perform that work, fall within the coverage of the Act. Similarly, every owner, contractor, or subcontractor above an employee who is engaged in such work is liable to that employee.[98] Employers, then, may not escape the coverage of the Act by doing, through independent contractors, and subcontractors, what they normally would do through their own employees.[99]

L. PREMISES LIABILITY

In Virginia a premises owner/occupier's (hereinafter "occupant") duty to an individual depends on that person's status as an invitee (one who is lawfully on the premises at the express or implied invitation of the occupant[100]), a licensee (one who enters the premises of another for her own convenience, benefit, or pleasure with the knowledge and express or implied consent of the occupant, including a social guest[101]), or a trespasser (someone on the premises without any legal right or without invitation, authority, or consent of the premises' occupant or who intentionally fails to leave the premises after being requested to do so by the occupant[102]).

With regard to an invitee, a premises' occupant has the duty (1) to use ordinary care to have the premises in a reasonably safe condition for an invitee's use (consistent with the invitation), but does not guarantee an invitee's safety; and (2) to use ordinary care to warn an invitee of any unsafe condition about which the occupant has actual or constructive notice unless the unsafe condition is open and obvious to a person using ordinary care for her own safety.[103] The invitee, however, has a right to assume that the premises are reasonably safe for her visit, although the assumption does not apply if the invitee knows or should know of an unsafe condition or if the invitee exceeds the scope of the invitation.[104] The occupier's duty to an invitee does not normally include protection against third-party criminal acts against the invitee absent evidence that such attack was imminent and probable.[105]

With regard to a licensee, an occupant owes a duty to use ordinary care in her activities or conduct to avoid injury to the licensee.[106]

An undiscovered trespasser takes the premises as he finds them and has no right to expect that the landowner will keep the premises in a safe condition.[107] With regard to a discovered trespasser, the occupant has a duty to use reasonable care not to willfully or wantonly cause injury to a trespasser once the trespasser's presence is discovered.[108]

Most litigated cases relate to an occupier's duty to an invitee. The plaintiff bears the burden of proving that the defendant had actual or constructive knowledge of the defective condition on the premises in order to establish a *prima facie* case of negligence.[109] Absent evidence of actual notice on the part of the defendant, the plaintiff must establish that a dangerous condition existed for a sufficient length of time such that the defendant should have discovered it in the exercise of ordinary care.[110] If the plaintiff's evidence fails to show *when* a defect occurred, the plaintiff has not made out a *prima facie* case.[111]

There are two lines of constructive notice cases in Virginia, depending on whether the evidence establishes (1) passive negligence with regard to an unknown condition or (2) active negligence on the part of the defendant, where the evidence establishes that affirmative conduct of the defendant caused the condition to exist. Where there is evidence that a particular defect or dangerous condition that caused the plaintiff's accident existed due to the affirmative conduct or active negligence of the defendant, Virginia courts will apply a foreseeability standard and consider whether the defendant could have foreseen the risk of danger resulting from its own conduct.[112]

M. DRAM SHOP LIABILITY

Virginia does not recognize dram shop liability.[113] The Virginia common law considers the act of selling the intoxicating beverage as too remote to be a proximate cause of an injury resulting from the negligent conduct of the purchaser of the drink.

N. ECONOMIC LOSS

Recovery under tort law is available only for personal injury or property damage and not for the diminution in value or "economic loss" of a product or item of property.[114] Recovery for solely economic loss is prohibited in tort actions absent privity where negligent performance of a contract is alleged.[115]

O. FRAUD AND MISREPRESENTATION

Notice pleading is the general rule in Virginia,[116] but, as in federal practice, fraud must be pleaded with particularity.[117]

Actual or constructive fraud must be proven by clear and convincing evidence.[118] The elements of actual fraud are: (1) a false representation; (2) of a material fact; (3) made intentionally and knowingly; (4) with intent to mislead; (5) reliance by the party misled; and (6) resulting damage to the party misled.[119] The elements of constructive fraud are the same except that the false representation of material fact need only have been made innocently or negligently.[120] The essence of constructive fraud is negligent misrepresentation.[121]

P. CONSUMER FRAUD STATUTES

Virginia's Consumer Protection Act protects consumers from fraudulent acts or practices by sellers or lessors in the course of certain transactions.[122] Transactions covered by the Act include sales for the purpose of enabling an individual to start a business to be operated from home; sales or leases of goods or services for personal, family, or household purposes; sales related to an individual's finding or obtaining employment; and layaway agreements.[123] The Act generally prohibits misrepresentations in the course of such sales, leases, or advertisements therefor.[124]

The Attorney General and any attorney for the Commonwealth or for any city, county, or town is empowered to initiate civil investigations regarding suspected violations of the Act, file suits to enjoin violations, and seek civil penalties and attorney's fees for willful violations.[125]

Additionally, consumers can bring private actions for damages or penalties for violations of the Act.[126] Private recovery is limited in the case of nonwillful violations to actual damages or $500, whichever is greater.[127] For willful violations, private recovery is limited to three times the actual damages sustained or $1,000, whichever is greater.[128] A private plaintiff also may be awarded reasonable attorney's fees and court costs.[129]

The defendant is excused from liability for actual damages or penalties if it shows by a preponderance of the evidence that the alleged violation resulted from a bona fide error, notwithstanding the maintenance of procedures reasonably adopted to avoid a violation.[130] However, the plaintiff in such cases still may be awarded reasonable attorney's fees and court costs.[131]

The statute of limitations for a private action under the Act is two years from accrual of the action.[132] The action accrues on the date the injury is sustained by the plaintiff.[133]

Q. PUNITIVE DAMAGES

Punitive damages are not favored in Virginia courts[134] and the Virginia General Assembly has enacted a cap on the recovery of punitive damages fixed at $350,000.[135] An award of compensatory damages is a requirement for the award of punitive damages, except in actions for defamation,[136] and punitive damages should bear a reasonable relationship to compensatory damages.[137]

Punitive damages may be awarded in tort actions but cannot generally be recovered in actions for the breach of ordinary contracts.[138] A claim for punitive damages must be specifically pled in order to be awarded.[139] Punitive damages can only be awarded against one who has participated in the offense[140] and cannot be awarded against a deceased individual.[141] In order to recover, the plaintiff must prove "willful and wanton" negligence or malice.[142] The cases that have awarded punitive damages concentrate on the ill will, malevolence, spite, or wicked intention of the defendant.[143] "Actual malice" need not be proven to recover punitive damages.[144]

The determination of punitive damages in drunk driving cases is controlled by Virginia Code Section 8.01-44.5, which authorizes awards of punitive damages in personal injury or death cases where the defendant's conduct was "so willful and wanton as to show a conscious disregard for the rights of others." By statute, a defendant's conduct is deemed sufficiently willful and wanton as to merit an award of punitive damages if: (1) the evidence shows that the defendant had a blood alcohol concentration of 0.15 percent or more at the time of the injurious incident; (2) the defendant knew at the time he was drinking that he would be operating a vehicle; and (3) the defendant's intoxication was a proximate cause of the injury or death of the plaintiff. If the defendant refused a blood or breath alcohol test, the plaintiff need only prove that: (1) the defendant was intoxicated at the time of the events; (2) the defendant knew when he was drinking that he would be driving; and (3) there is a causal relation between the intoxication and the injury or death of the plaintiff.

R. WRONGFUL DEATH AND SURVIVORSHIP ACTIONS

In Virginia, no cause of action exists under common law against a person for the wrongful death of another, because a right of action for personal injuries does not survive the death of the injured.[145] The General Assembly, however, has created such a right by statute and included it in the portion of the Code of Virginia entitled "Death by Wrongful Act" (the "Wrongful Death Act").[146]

Under the Wrongful Death Act, if the decedent would have had a cause of action for personal injury against the tortfeasor if death had not ensued, the personal representative of the decedent (normally the executor or administrator of the estate) can maintain the cause of action in the personal representative's own name on behalf of the decedent's estate.[147] Generally, the personal representative must file suit within two years after the death of the decedent.[148]

Recovery under the Wrongful Death Act is limited to one of five statutorily defined classes of beneficiaries.[149] The primary class of beneficiaries consists of the decedent's surviving spouse, children (including adopted or stepchildren), and children of any deceased child of the decedent.[150] The particular class and the individuals within that class are established at the time a verdict is entered by a jury or judgment is rendered by a judge in a nonjury trial.[151]

The class beneficiaries are entitled to recovery for the following losses:

1. Sorrow, mental anguish, and solace, which may include society, companionship, comfort, guidance, kindly offices, and advice of the decedent;

2. Compensation for reasonably expected loss of (a) income of the decedent and (b) services, protection, care, and assistance provided by the decedent;

3. Expenses for the care, treatment, and hospitalization of the decedent incident to the injury resulting in death;

4. Reasonable funeral expenses; and

5. Punitive damages that may be recovered for willful or wanton conduct, or such recklessness as evinces a conscious disregard for the safety of others.[152]

The court is required to direct how any recovery is apportioned among the individual beneficiaries within the relevant class.[153] Any claim under the Wrongful Death Act that is compromised prior to entry of judgment must be approved by the circuit court where any action is pending, or, if suit has not been filed, any circuit court.[154]

Virginia's General Assembly has also enacted a statute, within the section of the Virginia Code entitled "Survival and Assignment of Causes of Action," to address the status of a cause of action if "the person against whom the cause of action is or may be asserted" and/or the "person in whose favor the cause of action existed" dies.[155] Under this statute, the cause of action survives, except that punitive damages cannot be awarded against a deceased defendant.[156] If the cause of action was for personal injuries that resulted in the subsequent death of the decedent, the claim then falls within the parameters of the Wrongful Death Act.[157]

William R. Rakes, Esquire
J. Scott Sexton, Esquire
Gentry Locke Rakes & Moore
P.O. Box 40013
Roanoke, Virginia 24022-0013
(540) 983-9300
(fax) (540) 983-9468
www.gentrylocke.com

ENDNOTES - VIRGINIA

1. Va. Code Ann. § 8.01-243(A) (Michie 1950), as amended.

2. *See id.* § 8.01-230 for when a right of action is deemed to accrue. Generally, rights of action for personal injury and injury to property accrue on the date the injury is sustained. For the time of accrual of specific personal actions, see *id.* § 8.01-2. For other exceptions, see *id.* §§ 8.01-233, 8.01-245, 8.01-250.

3. *Id.* § 8.01-247.1.

4. *Id.* §§ 8.01-243(A) & (C) & 8.01-249.

5. *Id.* § 8.01-243(B).

6. *Id.* § 8.2-725. The Uniform Commercial Code has been adopted in Virginia. *Id.* §§ 8.1-101–8.11-108

7. *Id.* § 8.01-236.

8. *Id.* § 8.01-244.

9. *Id.* § 8.01-246(3).

10. *Id.* § 8.01-246(4).

11. *Id.* § 8.01-581.15.

12. *Id.*

13. *Id.*

14. *Id.* § 8.01-38.1.

15. Black's Law Dictionary 806 (7th ed. 1999).

16. *Chesapeake & Potomac Tel. Co. v. Dowdy*, 235 Va. 55, 365 S.E.2d 751 (1988).

17. *Perlin v. Chappell*, 198 Va. 861, 96 S.E.2d 805 (1957).

18. *Trimyer v. Norfolk Tallow Company*, 192 Va. 776, 66 S.E.2d 441 (1951).

19. *Boggs v. Plybon*, 157 Va. 30, 160 S.E. 77 (1931).

20. *Wright v. Kelly*, 203 Va. 135, 122 S.E.2d 670 (1961).

21. *Doe v. Scott*, 221 Va. 997, 277 S.E.2d 159 (1981).

22. *Marshall v. Winston*, 239 Va. 315, 389 S.E.2d 902 (1990).

23. *Nasser v. Parker*, 249 Va. 172, 455 S.E.2d 502 (1995).

24. *Sullivan v. Sutherland*, 206 Va. 377, 143 S.E.2d 920 (1965).

25. *Grant v. Mays*, 204 Va. 41, 129 S.E.2d 10 (1963).

26. *Norfolk & Potomac Beltline R.R. v. Barker*, 221 Va. 924, 275 S.E.2d 613 (1981).

27. *Read v. Daniel*, 197 Va. 853, 91 S.E.2d 400 (1956).

28. *Reid v. Medley's Adm'r*, 118 Va. 462, 87 S.E. 616 (1916).

29. *Speer v. Kellam*, 204 Va. 893, 134 S.E.2d 300 (1964).

30. *Jenkins v. Payne*, 251 Va. 122, 465 S.E.2d 795 (1996).

31. *Baskett v. Banks*, 186 Va. 1022, 45 S.E.2d 173 (1947).

32. *Balderson v. Robertson*, 203 Va. 484, 125 S.E.2d 180 (1962).

33. *Litchford v. Hancock*, 232 Va. 496, 352 S.E.2d 335 (1987).

34. *Waynick v. Walrond*, 155 Va. 400, 154 S.E. 522 (1930); *Yeary v. Holbrook*, 171 Va. 266, 198 S.E. 441 (1938).

35. Va. Code Ann. § 56-416 (Michie 1950), as amended.

36. 45 U.S.C. §§ 51–60 (1999).

37. *Matthews v. Dept. of Transp.*, 253 Va. 180, 482 S.E.2d 810 (1997).

38. *Arndt v. Russillo*, 231 Va. 328, 343 S.E.2d 84 (1986).

39. *Greater Richmond Transit Co. v. Wilkerson*, 242 Va. 65, 406 S.E.2d 28 (1991).

40. *High v. Coleman*, 215 Va. 7, 205 S.E.2d 408 (1974).

41. *Major v. Hoppe*, 209 Va. 193, 163 S.E.2d 164 (1968).

42. *Lewis v. Carpenter Co.*, 252 Va. 296, 477 S.E.2d 492 (1996).

43. *Id.*

44. *Logan v. Montgomery Ward & Co.*, 216 Va. 425, 219 S.E.2d 685 (1975).

45. *Id.*

46. *See General Bronze Corp. v. Kostopulos*, 203 Va. 66, 122 S.E.2d 548 (1961).

47. *See Robbins v. Old Dominion Power Co., Inc.*, 204 Va. 390, 131 S.E.2d 274 (1963).

48. *M.W. Worley Constr. v. Hungerford, Inc.*, 215 Va. 377, 210 S.E.2d 161 (1974).

49. *T.E. Ritter Corp. v. Rose*, 200 Va. 736, 107 S.E.2d 479 (1959).

50. *Meek v. Graybeal*, 195 Va. 381, 78 S.E.2d 593 (1953).

51. *Atlantic Greyhound Corp. v. Shelton*, 184 Va. 684, 36 S.E.2d 625 (1946).

52. *Robbins v. Old Dominion Power Co., Inc.*, 204 Va. 390, 131 S.E.2d 274 (1963).

53. *See* Charles E. Friend, Personal Injury Law in Virginia, § 2.3.2 (2d ed. 1998).

54. *See, e.g., Smith v. New Dixie Lines*, 201 Va. 466, 111 S.E.2d 434 (1959).

55. *See, e.g., King v. Eccles*, 209 Va. 726, 167 S.E.2d 349 (1969).

56. *Baxley v. Fischer*, 204 Va. 792, 134 S.E.2d 291 (1964).

57. *Williamson v. Old Brogue, Inc.*, 232 Va. 350, 350 S.E.2d 621 (1986).

58. *Moore v. Virginia Transit Co.*, 188 Va. 493, 50 S.E.2d 268 (1948).

59. *Williamson v. Old Brogue, Inc.*, 232 Va. 350, 350 S.E.2d 621 (1986).

60. *Hamilton v. Glemming*, 187 Va. 309, 46 S.E.2d 438 (1948).

61. Va. Code Ann. § 8.01-221 (Michie 1950), as amended.

62. *White v. Doe*, 207 Va. 276, 148 S.E.2d 797 (1966).

63. *See, e.g., Freeman v. Sproles*, 204 Va. 353, 131 S.E.2d 410 (1963); *Schools v. Walker*, 187 Va. 619, 47 S.E.2d 418 (1948); *Richmond Coca-Cola Bottling Works v. Andrews*, 173 Va. 240, 3 S.E.2d 419 (1939).

64. *Southern Ry. v. Fitzpatrick*, 129 Va. 246, 105 S.E. 663 (1921).

65. *See Maroulis v. Elliott*, 207 Va. 503, 151 S.E.2d 339 (1966).

66. *See Von Roy v. Whitescarver*, 197 Va. 384, 89 S.E.2d 346 (1955).

67. *Lavenstein v. Maile*, 146 Va. 789, 132 S.E. 844 (1926); *Bowles v. City of Richmond*, 147 Va. 720, 129 S.E. 489 (1925).

68. *Dickenson v. Tabb*, 208 Va. 184, 194, 156 S.E.2d 795, 802–03 (1967).

69. Va. Code Ann. § 8.01-443 (Michie 1950), as amended.

70. *Id.*

71. *Id.*

72. *Id.*

73. *Id.*

74. *Id.*

75. *Pierce v. Martin, ex rel. Commercial Union Ins. Co.*, 230 Va. 94, 334 S.E.2d 576 (1985).

76. Va. Code Ann. § 8.01-34 (Michie 1950), as amended.

77. *Gemco-Ware, Inc. v. Rongene Mold & Plastics Corp.*, 234 Va. 54, 360 S.E.2d 342 (1987).

78. *Royal Indem. Co. v. Hook*, 155 Va. 956, 157 S.E. 414 (1931).

79. *McLaughlin v. Siegel*, 166 Va. 374, 185 S.E. 873 (1936).

80. *Id.* at 377.

81. *Sykes v. Stone & Webster Eng'g Corp.*, 186 Va. 116, 41 S.E.2d 469 (1947).

82. The term "injury" is defined in Va. Code Ann. § 65.2-101 (Michie 1950), as amended.

83. Va. Code Ann. §§ 65.2-100 to –1310 (Michie 1950), as amended.

84. *Id.* §§ 65.2-300(A).

85. The terms "employer" and "employee" are defined in Va. Code Ann. § 65.2-101 (Michie 1950), as amended.

86. *Humphrees v. Boxley Bros. Co.*, 146 Va. 91, 135 S.E. 890 (1926).

87. *Fauver v. Bell*, 192 Va. 518, 65 S.E.2d 575 (1951).

88. *Id.*

89. *Id.*

90. Va. Code Ann. § 65.2-307(A) (Michie 1950), as amended.

91. *Conlin v. Turner's Express, Inc.*, 229 Va. 557, 331 S.E.2d 453 (1985).

92. *Feitig v. Chalkley*, 185 Va. 96, 38 S.E.2d 73 (1946).

93. *Tomlin v. Vance Int'l, Inc.*, 22 Va. App. 448, 470 S.E.2d 599 (1996).

94. Va. Code Ann. § 65.2-309 (Michie 1950), as amended.

95. *Id.* § 65.2-301.

96. *Id.*

97. *Id.* §§ 65.2-302 to -304.

98. *Vess v. Davis Elec. Contractors, Inc.*, 613 F. Supp. 1047 (W.D. Va. 1985), *aff'd*, 818 F.2d 30 (4th Cir. 1987).

99. *Id.*

100. *Franconia Assoc. v. Clark*, 250 Va. 444, 463 S.E.2d 670 (1995).

101. *Pearson v. Canada Contracting Co.*, 232 Va. 177, 349 S.E.2d 106 (1986).

102. *Id.*

103. *Wynne v. Spainhour*, 215 Va. 16, 205 S.E.2d 634 (1974); *Grim v. Rahe, Inc.*, 246 Va. 239, 434 S.E. 888 (1993); *Ashby v. Faison & Assocs.*, 247 Va. 166, 440 S.E.2d 603 (1994).

104. *Franconia Assocs. v. Clark*, 250 Va. 444, 463 S.E.2d 670 (1995).

105. *Wright v. Webb*, 234 Va. 527, 362 S.E.2d 919 (1987); *Gupton v. Quicke*, 247 Va. 362, 442 S.E.2d 658 (1994); *Burns v. Johnson*, 250 Va. 41, 458 S.E.2d 448 (1995).

106. *Bradshaw v. Minter*, 206 Va. 450, 143 S.E.2d 827 (1965); *Reagan v. Perez*, 215 Va. 325, 209 S.E.2d 901 (1974).

107. *Thalhimer Bros. v. Casci*, 160 Va. 439, 168 S.E. 433 (1933).

108. *Norfolk Southern Ry. Co. v. Fincham*, 213 Va. 122, 189 S.E.2d 380 (1972).

109. *Roll'R'Way Rinks, Inc. v. Smith*, 218 Va. 321, 237 S.E.2d 157 (1977).

110. *Winn-Dixie Stores, Inc. v. Parker*, 240 Va. 180, 396 S.E.2d 649 (1990); *Colonial Stores, Inc. v. Pulley*, 203 Va. 535, 125 S.E.2d 188 (1962).

111. *Grim v. Rahe, Inc.*, 246 Va. 239, 242, 434 S.E.2d 888, 890 (1993) (emphasis in original).

112. *Memco Stores, Inc. v. Yeatman*, 232 Va. 50, 348 S.E.2d 228 (1986); *Austin v. Shoney's, Inc.*, 254 Va. 134, 486 S.E.2d 285 (1997); *O'Brien v. Everfast, Inc.*, 254 Va. 326, 491 S.E.2d 712 (1997). For an excellent opinion by the Chief Justice of the Virginia Supreme Court analyzing the differences between these two lines of cases, see *Ashby v. Faison & Assocs., Inc.*, 247 Va. 166, 440 S.E.2d 603 (1994).

113. *Corrigan v. United States*, 815 F.2d 954 (4th Cir. 1987); *Webb v. Blackie's House of Beef, Inc.*, 811 F.2d 840 (4th Cir. 1987).

114. See, e.g., *Ward v. Ernst & Young*, 246 Va. 317, 435 S.E.2d 628 (1993).

115. *Sensenbrenner v. Rust, Orling & Neale Architects, Inc.*, 236 Va. 419, 374 S.E.2d 55 (1988); *Blake Constr. Co. v. Alley*, 233 Va. 31, 353 S.E.2d 724 (1987); *Gerald M. Moore & Son, Inc. v. Drewry*, 251 Va. 277, 467 S.E.2d 811 (1996).

116. Rules of Supreme Ct. of Va. 1:4(d) & (j), Virginia Rules Ann. 8 (Michie 2000).

117. *Tuscarora, Inc. v. B.V.A. Credit Corp.*, 218 Va. 849, 241 S.E.2d 778 (1978); *Koch v. Seventh St. Realty Corp.*, 205 Va. 65, 135 S.E.2d 131 (1964).

118. *Prospect Dev. Co., Inc. v. Bershader*, 258 Va. 75, 515 S.E.2d 291 (1999).

119. *Bryant v. Peckinpaugh*, 241 Va. 172, 400 S.E.2d 201 (1991).

120. *Evaluation Research Corp. v. Alequin*, 247 Va. 143, 439 S.E.2d 387 (1994).

121. *Richmond Metro. Auth. v. McDevitt St. Bovis, Inc.*, 256 Va. 553, 507 S.E.2d 344 (1998).

122. Va. Code Ann. §§ 59.1-196 to 1-207 (Michie 1950), as amended.

123. *Id.* § 59.1-198.

124. *Id.* § 59.1-200.

125. *Id.* §§ 59.1-201 to -203 & 59.1-206.

126. *Id.* § 59.1-204.

127. *Id.*

128. *Id.*

129. *Id.*

130. *Id.* § 59.1-207.

131. *Id.*

132. *Id.* § 59.1-204.1.

133. *Id.* § 8.01-230.

134. *Owens-Corning Fiberglas Corp. v. Watson*, 243 Va. 128, 144, 413 S.E.2d 630, 639 (1992).

135. Va. Code Ann. § 8.01-38.1 (Michie 1950), as amended.

136. *Gasque v. Mooers Motor Car Co.*, 227 Va. 154, 159, 313 S.E.2d 384, 388 (1984).

137. *TXO Prod. Corp. v. Alliance Resources Corp.*, 509 U.S. 443 (1993); *Gazette, Inc. v. Harris*, 229 Va. 1, 51, 325 S.E.2d 713, 747 (1985).

138. *Wright v. Everett*, 197 Va. 608, 90 S.E.2d 855 (1956).

139. *Harrell v. Woodson*, 233 Va. 117, 122, 353 S.E.2d 770, 773 (1987).

140. *Dalton v. Johnson*, 204 Va. 102, 107, 129 S.E.2d 647, 650–51 (1963).

141. *Id.* at 107, 129 S.E.2d at 650–51.

142. *Owens-Corning Fiberglas Corp. v. Watson*, 243 Va. 128, 144, 413 S.E.2d 630, 640; *Thomas v. Snow*, 162 Va. 654, 664, 174 S.E. 837, 839 (1934).

143. *Wright v. Everett*, 197 Va. 608, 90 S.E.2d 860 (1956).

144. *Avocet Dev. Corp. v. McLean Bank*, 234 Va. 658, 666, 364 S.E.2d 757, 762 (1988).

145. *Wilson v. Whittaker*, 207 Va. 1032, 154 S.E.2d 124 (1967).

146. *See* Va. Code Ann. §§ 8.01-50 to -56 (Michie 1950), as amended.

147. *Id.* § 8.01-50.

148. *Id.* § 8.01-244.

149. *Id.* § 8.01-53(A).

150. *Id.*

151. *Id.* § 8.01-53(B).

152. *Id.* § 8.01-52.

153. *Id.* § 8.01-54.

154. *Id.* § 8.01-55.

155. *Id.* § 8.01-25.

156. *Id.*

157. *Id.* §§ 8.01-25 & § 8.01-56.

WASHINGTON

A. STATUTES OF LIMITATION

Washington's statutes of limitation are found in Wash. Rev. Code Sections 4.16 *et seq*, and the Washington Product Liability Act at Wash. Rev. Code Sections 7.72.060. Generally, the bar for intentional acts is two years, negligence claims is three years, contracts for the sale of goods under the Uniform Commercial Code (U.C.C.) is four years, and written contracts is six years.[1] The beginning of the tolling period is either the time the cause of action accrued[2] or in accordance with specific statutes and case law.[3] The discovery rule applies.[4]

Causes of action alleged to have arisen from a breach of contract for sale of goods have a four-year statute of limitation.[5] The four-year statute of limitation of the U.C.C. is not applicable to products liability cases even if the liability is alleged on implied warranty.[6] The tort discovery rule does not apply to the statute of limitation on breach of warranty actions because a cause of action under the U.C.C. accrues when the breach occurs, regardless of lack of knowledge of the breach.[7]

Libel, slander, assault, assault and battery, false imprisonment, and bond actions must be brought within two years.[8]

Actions under the Unfair Business Practices—Consumer Protection Act have a four-year statute of limitation.[9]

A "catch-all" provision for actions not otherwise identified in Wash. Rev. Code sections 4.16 provides for a two-year limitation after accrual of the cause of action.[10]

Washington has a six-year statute of repose for construction claims[11] and a 12-year rebuttable presumption of a useful safe life for product liability actions.[12] The statute of repose for construction claims bars claims that do not arise within six years of substantial completeness of the project.[13]

In causes of action against the state or local governments for personal injuries, plaintiff must present a notice of claim prior to suit and in accordance with governing statutes and be within the limitation period for the tort claimed.[14]

Statutes of limitation in Washington can be tolled by absence from the state, by personal disability, or by death.[15] For purposes of tolling a statute of limitation, an action in Washington is deemed commenced when the complaint is filed or summons is served, whichever occurs first.[16] The Supreme Court of Washington has ruled that service of process on one defendant tolled the statute of limitation as to unserved defendants.[17] The Court of Appeals has held that timely service of one tortfeasor tolled the statute of limitation as to a second tortfeasor, even though the action alleged separate causes of action against each tortfeasor and they were joined under the successive tortfeasor doctrine.[18]

B. TORT REFORM

Considerable tort reform in Washington occurred in the 1980s. In 1986, the Washington Legislature placed a limit on the noneconomic damages that a plaintiff could recover in actions for personal injury or wrongful death. The Washington Supreme Court deemed these caps on noneconomic damages unconstitutional.[19] Tort reform resulted in the Washington Product Liability Act, modification of joint and several liability, and adoption of the Comparative Fault Rule.[20] (See sections below for a more complete description.)

C. "NO FAULT" LIMITATION

Washington does not have "no fault" limitation for tort claims.

D. THE STANDARD FOR NEGLIGENCE

A plaintiff must establish four elements to prove negligence: (1) the existence of a duty owed; (2) breach of that duty; (3) injury resulting from that breach; and (4) a proximate cause between the breach and the injury.[21] Generally the standard for duty is one of ordinary care or "the care that a reasonably careful person would take under the circumstances."[22] The threshold determination of whether a duty exists is a question of law and "[t]he existence of a duty may be predicated upon statutory provisions or on common law principles."[23] "When no duty of care exists, a defendant cannot be subject to liability for negligent conduct."[24]

A duty can arise in three general situations: (1) where a defendant, in some manner, creates the risk that causes injury to the plaintiff or where the defendant does not give rise to the risk but induces justifiable reliance by the plaintiff that the defendant will use reasonable care to prevent injury to the plaintiff; (2) where a "special relationship" exists between the defendant and the plaintiff;[25] or (3) where a statute specifically imposes a duty to exercise care for another's safety.[26] A plaintiff must also show that a breach of the duty owed has occurred.[27] Breach is shown when the plaintiff demonstrates that the defendant acted or failed to act.[28]

Washington recognizes a professional standard of care.[29] Expert testimony is necessary to establish the standard of care in an action for professional negligence. Furthermore, the expert establishing the standard of care must practice in the same field.[30]

The issue of negligence for minors from six to sixteen years of age is generally a question for the trier of fact. Washington recognizes a special standard of care applicable to children of this age. The standard for a child's conduct is measured against the conduct of a reasonably careful child of the same age, intelligence, maturity, training, and experience.[31] Children less than six years old are conclusively presumed incapable of negligence.[32] Minors older than 16 are presumptively capable of negligence.[33]

Washington recognizes the presumption that a decedent, prior to death, used due care cannot be used to establish defendant's negligence as proximate cause of death merely because of an absence of evidence to the contrary.[34]

E. CAUSATION

Washington follows the general rule that to establish negligence, the plaintiff must demonstrate that the defendant's negligence was a proximate cause of plaintiff's injury.[35] Proximate cause consists of cause in fact and legal causation.[36] Cause in fact concerns "but for" causation and includes events the act produced in a direct unbroken sequence that would not have resulted had the act not occurred.[37] Legal causation, distinct from cause in fact, involves a determination of whether liability should attach as a matter of law given the existence of cause in fact.[38] Legal causation is intertwined with the existence of a duty, but "legal causation should not be assumed to exist every time a duty of care has been established."[39] "A determination of legal cause rests on matters of policy and common sense as to how far a defendant's responsibility for the consequences of its actions should extend."[40]

F. CONTRIBUTORY NEGLIGENCE, COMPARATIVE NEGLIGENCE, AND ASSUMPTION OF RISK

1. Contributory Negligence

In 1973, Washington abolished contributory negligence as a total bar in actions seeking recovery for death, personal injury, or injury to property.[41]

2. Comparative Negligence

Pure comparative negligence became the law in Washington in 1974 and applies to actions for death, personal injury, or injury to property.[42] Plaintiff's recovery is reduced by plaintiff's proportion of fault.[43] A plaintiff who is 99 percent at fault can still recover one percent of his or her damages.

3. Assumption of Risk

Assumption of risk remains a viable affirmative defense. The Washington Supreme Court has identified four separate classes of assumption of risk: (1) express; (2) implied primary; (3) implied reasonable; and (4) implied unreasonable.[44] The essential elements of assumption of risk are the plaintiff's subjective understanding of the risk, voluntary choice to encounter the risk, and willingness to accept that risk.[45] In negligence actions, assumption of risk is generally a question of fact.[46] If the court finds the defendant still owed the plaintiff a duty of care, then the case proceeds to the jury on a comparative negligence theory.[47]

4. Special Alcohol/Drug Rule

Wash. Rev. Code Section 5.40.060 provides:

> [I]t is a complete defense to an action for damages for personal injury or wrongful death that the person injured or killed was under the influence of intoxicating liquor or any drug at the time of the occurrence causing the injury or death and that such condition was a proximate cause of the

injury or death and the trier of fact finds such person to have *been more than fifty percent at fault.*

(Emphasis added.)

G. *RES IPSA LOQUITUR* AND INHERENTLY DANGEROUS ACTIVITIES

1. *Res Ipsa Loquitur*

Res ipsa loquitur permits an inference that the defendant caused plaintiff's harm and is a method of proof, not an additional form of negligence. Whether the doctrine applies is a question of law for the court to determine.[48] The doctrine applies "if three conditions are met: (1) the accident or occurrence producing the injury is of a kind that does not ordinarily happen in the absence of someone's negligence; (2) the injuries are caused by an agency or instrumentality within the exclusive control of the defendant; and (3) the injury-causing accident or occurrence is not due to any voluntary action or contribution on the part of the plaintiff."[49]

"The doctrine of *res ipsa loquitur* is applied in exceptional cases, when supported by the facts of the case and the demands of justice. A plaintiff that successfully establishes the elements of *res ipsa loquitur* is entitled to an inference of negligence. Because such a plaintiff is, in effect, spared the necessity of establishing a complete prima facie case of negligence against the defendant, the doctrine is to be used sparingly."[50]

2. Inherently Dangerous Activities

An ultrahazardous activity renders a party strictly liable for injuries arising therefrom due to the high risk inherent in the activity.[51] Whether an activity is abnormally dangerous is a question of law for the court to decide.[52] Washington generally looks to the Restatement (Second) of Torts for guidance in determining whether an activity is ultrahazardous.[53]

H. NEGLIGENCE *PER SE*

Negligence *per se* is no longer applied in Washington. Revised Code of Washington Section 5.40.050 is controlling on the issue and provides "[a] breach of a duty imposed by statute . . . shall not be considered negligence per se, but may be considered by the trier of fact as evidence of negligence." "Although violation of a statute/duty is no longer negligence per se under RCW 5.40.050, this does not mean RCW 5.40.050 necessarily bars a trial court from finding negligence as a matter of law."[54]

I. JOINT AND SEVERAL LIABILITY/ALLOCATION OF FAULT

The 1981 Tort Reform Act retained joint and several liability and established a right of contribution between or among two or more persons who are jointly and severally liable for the same harm.[55] This was amended by the 1986 Tort Reform Act, which eliminated joint and several liability except in certain situations (which are listed below).[56]

Revised Code of Washington Section 4.22.070 provides that in all actions involving the fault of more than one entity (including the plaintiff), the trier of fact is to determine the percentage of total fault attributable to every entity that causes plaintiff's damages, including the claimant, defendant, third-party defendants, entities released by claimant, and immune entities. Judgment is entered against the parties at fault for their proportionate share of the total damages.[57] In 1993, RCW 4.22.070 was amended to preclude an assignment of fault to the claimants' employer.

This liability is *several* and not joint, except in the following four circumstances: (1) where the plaintiff is not at fault; (2) the defendants were acting in concert; (3) a person acted as an agent or servant of a party; or (4) in certain other instances involving hazardous materials or substances.[58]

Where the plaintiff is not at fault, a modified form of joint and several liability applies, whereby joint and several liability is imposed on defendants against whom judgment is rendered for the *sum* of those defendants' fault. The modified form of joint and several liability does not include the fault of immune entities or released entities.[59]

A release by the plaintiff of one joint tortfeasor does not discharge the other tortfeasors unless the release so provides, but the release reduces the claim against the other tortfeasors in the amount of the consideration paid for the release or by the percentage of fault assigned to the settling defendant(s), depending on whether there is joint or joint and several liability.[60]

J. INDEMNITY

In 1981, the Washington legislature abolished active/passive indemnity.[61] Thereafter, only written indemnity contracts were deemed enforceable.[62] In 1997, the Washington Supreme Court created a new equitable indemnity theory arising from the U.C.C. implied warranty and a defective product.[63]

Indemnity shifts the entire loss of the plaintiff from one defendant to another by reason of some legal obligation to pay damages occasioned by the negligence of another.

K. BAR OF WORKERS' COMPENSATION STATUTE

Workers' compensation is largely run by the state through the Department of Labor & Industries.[64] Employers either pay premiums into a state fund or can elect to be self-insured.[65]

Washington state's Industrial Insurance Act bars an employee from bringing a civil action for nonintentional torts against his or her employer when the employee's claims arise while the employee is acting in the course of his or her employment.[66] Workers' compensation is an employee's exclusive remedy against the employer.[67] Under the Act, a self-insured employer assumes responsibility, assuming a third party does not share fault, regardless of fault of the employee.[68]

The receipt of workers' compensation benefits does not bar an employee from seeking damages from a third party.[69] Where an employee has collected workers' compensation benefits from an self-insured employer or the state fund and then proceeds to sue a third party for the same incident, the employer or state may be subrogated to the rights of the employee as against a third party.[70] If the employee successfully sues the third party, the state or the self-insured employer holds a lien on any recovery, which is reduced proportionately by the employer's share of the attorney's fees.[71]

Washington's industrial insurance does not limit actions by employees against employers for injuries sustained from intentional acts by the employer.[72] In recent cases, the court has relaxed the standard to prove intentional conduct.[73]

L. PREMISES LIABILITY

There are three common law legal classifications of an individual or an owner/occupier of land's premises: (1) trespasser; (2) licensee; or (3) invitee, which determine the liability of an owner/occupier for injuries sustained by that individual on the premises.[74] For a trespasser, liability of an owner/occupier differs for adult and child trespassers.[75] For an adult trespasser, the owner or occupier of land must refrain from wanton or willful negligence or misconduct.[76] For a child trespasser, the owner or occupier of land must protect against any attractive nuisances.[77] The second legal classification of licensee (or social guest) requires that the owner or occupier of land warn the licensee of a dangerous condition known to the owner or occupier that creates an unreasonable risk of harm to the licensee and also where the owner or occupier knows the licensee is unaware of the condition and is unlikely to discover it.[78] For the third legal classification of invitees, the owner or occupier owes an invitee a general duty to use reasonable and ordinary care in keeping the property reasonably safe for the benefit of the invitee. This general duty includes the duties owed to licensees plus an affirmative duty to make reasonable inspections to discover dangerous conditions and thereafter make them safe.[79]

M. CONSTRUCTION CLAIM

Washington does not recognize a cause of action for negligent construction on behalf of residential homeowners. Beyond the terms expressed in the contract of sale, the only recognized duty owing from a public vendor of a newly completed residence to its first purchaser is that embodied in the implied warranty of habitability.[80] Thus far, Washington's failure to recognize a negligent construction theory has applied to residences where there has been neither personal injury nor evidence of physical damage. If plaintiffs suffer only economic damage (the cost to repair deteriorated parts of the building), courts force the claimants to rely on their contract remedies and not a tort remedy.

In 1990, the Supreme Court of Washington created a new form of liability for contractors to workers on the job site. A general contractor has a duty to subcontractors' workers arising from the subcontractors' WSHA/OSHA violations.[81] Subsequently, this rationale was extended to upper-tier contractors and owner/developers.[82]

N. DRAM SHOP LIABILITY

The Supreme Court of Washington has long held that commercial vendors of alcohol have a duty to avoid serving an obviously intoxicated person.[83] As a result, a tavern or other commercial vendor is liable if it serves alcohol to an obviously intoxicated patron who injures and/or kills a third party.[84] Vendors, with few exception, are not liable for the intentional acts of an intoxicated person that cause injury to another.[85]

Washington does not recognize a cause of action in negligence for a third person injured by an intoxicated adult against the social host that served the person while in an obviously intoxicated state. The Supreme Court has also held that Wash. Rev. Code Section 66.44.270, the statute prohibiting the sale of alcohol to minors, does not protect third persons injured by an intoxicated minor, but, rather, is intended to protect minors from their own injuries as a result of their intoxication.[86] Therefore, a minor who is injured after consuming alcohol may have a cause of action against a social host.[87] Further, a social host who does not furnish alcohol to a minor, but who permits the minor to consume alcohol that the minor obtained someplace other than from the host on the host's premises, does not owe to the minor a common law duty of reasonable care.[88]

O. FRAUD AND MISREPRESENTATION

Washington's Rules of Civil Procedure require that the circumstances constituting fraud be pleaded with particularity.[89]

Each of the following elements of fraud must be proved by clear, cogent, and convincing evidence: (1) representation of an existing fact; (2) materiality of the representation; (3) falsity of the representation; (4) knowledge of the falsity or reckless disregard as to its truth; (5) intent to induce reliance on the representation; (6) ignorance of the falsity; (7) reliance on the truth of the representation; (8) justifiable reliance; and (9) damages.[90]

To establish negligent misrepresentation, a plaintiff must prove: (1) one who in the course of his or her business, profession, or employment; (2) supplies false information for the guidance of others in their business transactions; (3) that was justifiably relied on by plaintiff; and (4) to his or her pecuniary loss.[91]

P. CONSUMER FRAUD STATUTES

The Washington Consumer Protection Act (CPA) or Unfair Business Practices Act, Wash. Rev. Code Sections 19.86.010 *et seq.*, provides a comprehensive set of laws to foster fair and honest competition in Washington and to protect consumers from unfair methods of competition and deceptive acts or practices in trade or commerce.[92] The Attorney General may bring an action to enforce the statute.[93] Additionally, any person injured may also bring a private right of action to enforce the Act.[94]

To prove a violation of the CPA, a plaintiff must establish five elements: (1) an unfair or deceptive act or practice; (2) occurring in the conduct of trade or commerce; (3) affecting the public interest; (4) injuring the plaintiffs' business or property; and (5) causation between the act and the injury.[95]

Damages include actual damages and the cost of the suit, including reasonable attorney's fees. Additionally, the court may, at its discretion, award treble damages not greater than $10,000.[96]

Q. DAMAGES ALLOWED

Washington courts allow recovery for pain and suffering (both mental and physical), past and with reasonable probability to be experienced in the future; the reasonable value of necessary medical care (and that care with reasonable probability to be required in the future); the reasonable value of time, earnings, earning capacity, with the reasonable probability to be lost in the future.[97]

R. ECONOMIC LOSS

Recovery for economic loss is permitted. Washington limits the recovery of economic loss due to construction delays to the remedies provided by contract.[98] In a personal injury action based on fault where there is a verdict or award for future economic damages of at least $100,000, "the court or arbitrator shall, at the request of a party, enter a judgment which provides for the periodic payment in whole or in part of the future economic damages."[99]

Washington courts have adopted the "risk of harm" analysis to determine whether recovery can occur under tort theories, such as the Product Liability Act, or whether the claimant is relegated to warranty recovery under the U.C.C. The risk of harm analysis is conducted using either a "sudden and dangerous" or an "evaluative" task.[100] The goal in applying these tasks is to determine whether the safety insurance policy of tort law or the expectation bargain policy of warranty law are most applicable to the claim.

S. PUNITIVE DAMAGES

Washington courts consistently adhere to the rule that punitive damages are contrary to public policy and may not be awarded under Washington law in the absence of explicit statutory authorization.[101] Punitive damages are *unavailable* in (1) intentional tort cases;[102] and (2) negligence cases.[103] The Washington Legislature has never authorized open-ended punitive damage recoveries or the recovery generally of more than compensatory damages.[104]

The Legislature has authorized the recovery of more than compensatory damages only in limited kinds of cases.[105] Further, the Washington Supreme Court has made clear its disinclination to liberally construe even those statutes.[106]

T. WRONGFUL DEATH AND SURVIVORSHIP ACTIONS

The wrongful death statutes (Wash. Rev. Code Sections 4.20.010 & 4.20.020) authorize the personal representative of a decedent to seek damages from the person who caused the death to compensate the beneficiaries for the loss of economic and other benefits they would have otherwise received from the decedent.[107] The personal representative is a nominal plaintiff and brings the action for the benefit of statutorily designated beneficiaries, the decedent's spouse, children, and stepchildren, or, if none, then for the benefit of the decedent's financially dependent parents and siblings (who are residents of the United States).[108] The measure of damages is the "actual pecuniary loss" suffered by the beneficiaries. This includes monetary contributions the decedent would have made, as well as intangible losses, such as support, services, love, affection, care, companionship, and consortium.[109] It does not include mental anguish, grief, or sorrow of the beneficiaries, or the pain and suffering of the decedent.[110]

Under the general survival statute (Wash. Rev. Code Section 4.20.046), a cause of action held by a person at the time of the person's death may be the basis for a suit by the decedent's personal representative.[111] It is also the case that a cause of action against a person survives the person's death and may be brought against the personal representative. Unlike the wrongful death statutes, under this statute the decedent's personal representative may assert a claim for harm suffered by the decedent, which may or may not have been connected with the decedent's death and which could have been the basis for a suit by the decedent if death had not intervened. Damages include pecuniary loss, pain and suffering, emotional distress, and humiliation suffered by the decedent.[112] Lost earning capacity may be limited by the death if the death was the result of something other than the subject matter of the suit.[113]

The special death by personal injury survival statute (Wash. Rev. Code Section 4.20.060) provides that a decedent's own action for personal injuries may be prosecuted by the personal representative of the decedent's estate on behalf of certain statutorily designated beneficiaries if the personal injuries caused the death. This is a companion to the wrongful death statute. Unlike the general survival statute (Wash. Rev. Code Section 4.24.010), this statute only permits actions by the estate, not those against the estate. Like the wrongful death statute, recovery is for the decedent's spouse and children, or, if none, then for financially dependent parents and siblings.[114] Damages include pecuniary loss, pain and suffering, anxiety, emotional distress, and humiliation suffered by the decedent.[115]

Under the special wrongful death or injury to a minor survival statute, a parent can maintain a direct action—without the need for a personal representative—for the wrongful death or injury to a minor child or a child on whom they are financially dependent. Damages include medical, hospital, medication expenses, loss of services and support, loss of love and companionship, and injury to or destruction of the parent/child relationship.[116] Recovery is for the exclusive benefit of the beneficiaries.[117]

Douglas A. Hofmann, Esquire
S. Jay Terry, Esquire
Mary R. Knack, Esquire
Williams, Kastner & Gibbs P.L.L.C.
Two Union Square
601 Union Street, Suite 4100
P.O. Box 21926
Seattle, WA 98111-3926
(206) 628-6600
(fax) (206) 628-6611
dhofmann@wkg.com
jterry@wkg.com
mknack@wkg.com

ENDNOTES - WASHINGTON

1. Wash. Rev. Code § 4.16.100 (intentional acts), Wash. Rev. Code § 4.16.080–090 (waste, trespass, taking, detaining, or injuring personal property, on contract not in writing, and any other injury to person not otherwise enumerated). Wash. Rev. Code § 4.16.350 (actions for professional negligence "shall be commenced within three years of the act or omission alleged to have caused the injury or condition, or one year of the time the patient or his representative discovered or reasonably should have discovered that the injury or condition was caused by said act or omission, whichever period expires later, except that in no event shall an action be commenced more than eight years after said act or omission: PROVIDED, that the time for commencement of an action is tolled upon proof of fraud, intentional concealment, or the presence of a foreign body not intended to have a therapeutic or diagnostic purpose or effect, until the date the patient or the patient's representative has actual knowledge of the act of fraud or concealment, or of the presence of the foreign body; the patient or the patient's representative has one year from the date of the actual knowledge in which to commence a civil action for damages"). Wash. Rev. Code § 62A.2-725 (sale of goods under U.C.C.). Wash. Rev. Code § 4.16.040 (written contract).

2. *E.g., Ruth v. Dight*, 75 Wash. 2d 660, 453 P.2d 631 (1969).

3. *See* Wash. Rev. Code § 4.16.170, Wash. Rev. Code § 4.16.180, Wash. Rev. Code § 4.16.190, Wash. Rev. Code § 4.16.350 (professional negligence); *see also Augustson v. Graham*, 77 Wash. App. 921, 895 P.2d 20 (1995) (statute of limitation tolled after death of the tortfeasor until a personal representative is appointed because the probate nonclaim statute is incorporated into, and takes precedence over, the general three-year statute of limitation).

4. *Hibbard v. Gordon, Thomas, Honeywell, Malanca, Peterson and O'Hern*, 60 Wash. App. 252, 803 P.2d 1312 (1991). *See also* Wash. Rev. Code § 4.16.350 (professional negligence).

5. Wash. Rev. Code § 62A.2-725 (sale of goods).

6. *See* Wash. Rev. Code §§ 7.72.030(2)(b), (c); *see also Martin v. Patent Scaffolding*, 37 Wash. App. 37, 678 P.2d 362 (1984) (personal injury three-year statute held to be appropriate).

7. Wash. Rev. Code § 62A.2-725(2).

8. Wash. Rev. Code § 4.16.100.

9. Wash. Rev. Code § 19.86.120.

10. Wash. Rev. Code § 4.16.130.

11. Wash. Rev. Code § 4.16.310.

12. Wash. Rev. Code § 7.72.060.

13. This defense does not apply to manufacturers where contractors are deemed manufacturers. *See Washburn v. Beatt Equipment Co.*, 120 Wash. 2d 246, 840 P.2d 860 (1992).

14. Wash. Rev. Code §§ 4.92.100–110 & 4.96.

15. Wash. Rev. Code §§ 4.16.180, 4.16.190 & 4.16.200.

16. Wash. Rev. Code § 4.16.170.

17. *Sidis v. Brodie*, 117 Wash. 2d 325, 815 P.2d 718 (1991).

18. *Wakeman v. Lommers*, 67 Wash. App. 819, 840 P.2d 232 (1992).

19. *Sofie v. Fibreboard Corp.*, 112 Wash. 2d 636, 771 P.2d 711, *reconsideration denied, amended*, 112 Wash. 2d 636, 780 P.2d 260 (1989).

20. Wash. Rev. Code § 7.72 (products liability), Wash. Rev. Code §§ 4.22.030, 070 (joint and several liability), and Wash. Rev. Code §§ 4.22.050–020 (comparative fault). *See* Tort Reform Acts of 1981, 1986 and 1987.

21. *Tincani v. Inland Empire Zoological Soc'y*, 124 Wash. 2d 121, 127–28, 875 P.2d 621 (1994).

22. Comments to WPI 10.01, Negligence, Adult, Definition; *see also Baughn v. Malone*, 33 Wash. App. 592, 656 P.2d 1118 (1983).

23. *Degel v. Majestic Mobile Manor, Inc.*, 129 Wash. 2d 43, 48, 914 P.2d 728 (1996).

24. *Webstad v. Stortini*, 83 Wash. App. 857, 865, 924 P.2d 940 (1996).

25. Contrary to the general rule that there is no duty to control actions of a third party when a special relationship exists between the defendant and either an intended victim or the plaintiff, the defendant could have a duty to control the third party. *See, e.g., Nivens v. 7-11 Hoagy's Corner*, 133 Wash. 2d 192, 200, 943 P.2d 286 (1997); *C.J.C. v. Corporation of Catholic Bishop of Yakima*, 138 Wash. 2d 699, 985 P.2d 262 (1999).

26. *Howard v. Horn*, 61 Wash. App. 520, 810 P.2d 1387 (1991); *Doss v. ITT Rayonier, Inc.*, 60 Wash. App. 125, 803 P.2d 4 (1991).

27. *Tincani v. Inland Empire Zoologists Soc'y*, 124 Wash. 2d 121, 127–28, 875 P.2d 621 (1994).

28. "To prove breach a plaintiff must show (1) that the defendant is a member of the obligated class; (2) that the plaintiff is a member of the protected class; and (3) that the defendant violated the standard of care. Each of these questions is a question of fact for the jury, unless reasonable minds could not differ." *Schooley v. Pinch's Deli Market, Inc.*, 80 Wash. App. 862, 874, 912 P.2d 1044 (1996).

29. Wash. Rev. Code § 7.70.040(1) states that the plaintiff in an action for professional negligence must show the health care provider "failed to exercise that degree of care, skill, and learning expected of a reasonably prudent health care provider in the profession or class to which he belongs, in the state of Washington, acting in the same or similar circumstances." Wash. Rev. Code § 4.24.290 states, in relevant part, that a "plaintiff in order to prevail shall . . . prove by a preponderance of the evidence that the defendant failed to exercise that degree of skill, care, and learning possessed at that time by other persons in the same profession, and that as a proximate result of such failure the plaintiff suffered damages."

30. *See McKee v. American Home Products*, 113 Wash. 2d 701, 782 P.2d 1045 (1989) (the standard of care of a pharmacist practicing in Washington may not be established by an affidavit of an Arizona physician); *Young v. Key Pharmaceuticals, Inc.*, 112 Wash. 2d 216, 770 P.2d 182 (1989) (a pharmacist is not competent to testify to a physician's standard of care for treatment using medication).

31. *Scott v. Pacific West Mountain Resort*, 119 Wash. 2d 484, 583, 834 P.2d 6 (1992).

32. In Washington, there is a conclusive presumption that a child under six is incapable of negligence. *Price v. Kitsap Transit*, 125 Wash. 2d 456, 463, 886 P.2d 556 (1994).

33. *Bauman by Chapman v. Crawford*, 104 Wash. 2d 241, 704 P.2d 1181 (1985).

34. *NeSmith v. Bowden*, 17 Wash. App. 602, 609, 563 P.2d 1322 (1977), *citing Gardner v. Seymour*, 27 Wash. 2d 802, 180 P.2d 564 (1947); *see also Hutton v. Martin*, 41 Wash. 2d 780, 790, 252 P.2d 581 (1953) (the rule that no person is presumed to have been negligent until the party having the burden of proof establishes that fact by a preponderance of the evidence furnishes adequate protection to a deceased person as well as to a living person).

35. *Taggart v. State*, 118 Wash. 2d 195, 226, 822 P.2d 243 (1992).

36. *Id.* at 225–26; *Hartley v. State*, 103 Wash. 2d 768, 777, 698 P.2d 77 (1985).

37. *Hertog, ex rel. S.A.H. v. City of Seattle*, 138 Wash. 2d 265, 979 P.2d 400 (1999), citing *Taggart v. State*, 118 Wash. 2d 195, 226, 822 P.2d 243 (1992); *Hartley v. State*, 103 Wash. 2d 768, 778, 698 P.2d 77 (1985).

38. *Hartley v. State*, 103 Wash. 2d 768, 778, 698 P.2d 77 (1985).

39. *Schooley v. Pinch's Deli Market, Inc.*, 134 Wash. 2d 468, 480, 951 P.2d 749 (1998).

40. *Tyner v. State, Dep't of Social and Health Services, Child Protective Services*, 92 Wash. App. 504, 515, 963 P.2d 215 (1998), citing *Taggart v. State*, 118 Wash. 2d 195, 226, 822 P.2d 243 (1992).

41. Laws of 1973, 1st ex. sess., ch. 138, codified at Wash. Rev. Code §§ 4.22.005–015.

42. Wash. Rev. Code §§ 4.22.005–020.

43. Wash. Rev. Code §§ 4.22.005–015.

44. *Scott v. Pacific W. Mountain Resort*, 119 Wash. 2d 484, 500–01, 834 P.2d 6 (1992).

45. *Home v. North Kitsap School Dist.*, 92 Wash. App. 709, 720, 965 P.2d 1112 (1998) (plaintiff must "(1) [have] a full subjective understanding (2) of the presence and nature of the specific risk, and (3) voluntarily chose to encounter the risk").

46. *Scott v. Pacific W. Mountain Resort*, 119 Wash. 2d 484, 498 n.30, 834 P.2d 6 (1992). Note: Plaintiff's knowledge and voluntariness are questions of fact for jury, except when reasonable minds could not differ. *Home v. North Kitsap School Dist.*, 92 Wash. App. 709, 720, 965 P.2d 1112 (1998).

47. Implied reasonable and implied unreasonable "assumption of risk (which involve the plaintiff's voluntary choice to encounter a risk created by the defendant's negligence) retain no independent significance from contributory negligence after the adoption of comparative negligence." *Scott v. Pacific W. Mountain Resort*, 119 Wash. 2d 484, 500–01, 834 P.2d 6 (1992).

48. *Tinder v. Nordstrom, Inc.*, 84 Wash. App. 789–90, 929 P.2d 1209 (1997).

49. *Kimball v. Otis Elevator Co.*, 89 Wash. App. 169, 177, 947 P.2d 1275 (1997). Comparative fault renders the third element of little relevance. Therefore, it is usually merged into the second element. *Marshall v. Western Air Lines, Inc.*, 62 Wash. App. 251, 261, 813 P.2d 1269, *rev. denied*, 118 Wash. 2d 1002, 822 P.2d 287 (1991).

50. *Tinder v. Nordstrom, Inc.*, 84 Wash. App. 787, 789, 791–92, 929 P.2d 1209 (1997).

51. *Dorsch v. City of Tacoma*, 92 Wash. App. 131, 137, 960 P.2d 489 (1998) citing *New Meadows Holding Co. v. Washington Water Power Co.*, 102 Wash. 2d 495, 500, 687 P.2d 212 (1984).

52. *Langan v. Valicopters, Inc.*, 88 Wash. 2d 855, 861, 567 P.2d 218 (1977).

53. *Dorsch v. City of Tacoma*, 92 Wash. App. 131, 960 P.2d 489 (1998).

54. *Pudmaroff v. Allen*, 138 Wash. 2d 55, 977 P.2d 574, 580 (1999).

55. Laws of 1981, ch. 27.

56. Laws of 1986, ch. 305.

57. Wash. Rev. Code § 4.22.070.

58. Wash. Rev. Code §§ 4.22.070(1)(a), (b); *Sofie v. Fibreboard Corp.*, 112 Wash. 2d 636, 771 P.2d 711, *reconsideration denied, amended*, 112 Wash. 2d 636, 780 P.2d 260 (1989).

59. Wash. Rev. Code § 4.22.070.

60. *Id.*

61. Laws of 1981, ch. 27; Wash. Rev. Code § 4.22.040(3); *Stocker v. Shell Oil Co.*, 105 Wash. 2d 546, 716 P.2d 306 (1986) (indemnity agreements "are essentially agreements for contractual contribution, whereby one tort-feasor, against whom damages in favor of an injured party have been assessed, may look to another for reimbursement).

62. *Gilbert H. Moen Co. v. Island Steel Erectors, Inc.*, 75 Wash. App. 480, 878 P.2d 1246, *rev. granted*, 125 Wash. 2d 1020, 890 P.2d 464, *reversed*, 128 Wash. 2d 745, 912 P.2d 472 (1994).

63. *Central Wash. Refrigeration, Inc. v. Barbee*, 133 Wash. 2d 509, 516–18, 946 P.2d 760 (1997).

64. *See generally* Wash. Rev. Code §§ 51.04. *et seq.*, Wash. Rev. Code §§ 51.24. *et seq.*, Wash. Rev. Code §§ 51.32 *et seq.*

65. *See generally* Wash. Rev. Code §§ 51.16. *et seq.*

66. Wash. Rev. Code § 51.04.010 states in relevant part: "The state of Washington, therefore, exercising herein its police and sovereign power, declares that all phases of the premises are withdrawn from private controversy, and sure and certain relief for workers, injured in their work, and their families and dependents is hereby provided regardless of questions of fault and to the

exclusion of every other remedy, proceeding or compensation, except as otherwise provided in this title; and to that end all civil actions and civil causes of action for such personal injuries and all jurisdiction of the courts of the state over such causes are hereby abolished, except as in this title provided."

67. Wash. Rev. Code § 51.32.010; Wash. Rev. Code § 51.04.010.

68. *Id.* Note that a self-insured employer has a statutory right of contribution or to call for an assignment of a cause of action against a third party. Wash. Rev. Code § 51.24.030.

69. Wash. Rev. Code § 51.24.020; *Flanigan v. Department of Labor and Industries*, 123 Wash. 2d 418, 434, 869 P.2d 14 (1994) ("In its current form, the Act permits compensated workers or their beneficiaries to proceed against third parties without precluding the worker from receiving benefits.").

70. Wash. Rev. Code § 51.24.030.

71. *Id.*

72. Wash. Rev. Code § 51.24.020 provides: "If injury results to a worker from the deliberate intention of his or her employer to produce such injury, the worker or beneficiary of the worker shall have the privilege to take under this title and also have cause of action against the employer as if this title had not been enacted, for any damages in excess of compensation and benefits paid or payable under this title."

73. *Birklid v. Boeing Co.*, 127 Wash. 2d 853, 861–65, 904 P.2d 278 (1995) (concluding that courts' traditional interpretation of the exception to employer immunity was too narrow and that the phrase "deliberate intention" in Wash. Rev. Code § 51.24.020 could mean that an employer had actual knowledge an injury was certain to occur and willfully disregarded that knowledge).

74. *Younce v. Ferguson*, 106 Wash. 2d 658, 661–62, 724 P.2d 991 (1986).

75. *Ochamp v. Seattle*, 91 Wash. 2d 514, 588 P.2d 1351 (1979).

76. *Mail v. M. R. Smith Lumber & Shingle Co.*, 47 Wash. 2d 447, 449, 287 P.2d 877 (1955).

77. *Ochamp v. Seattle*, 91 Wash. 2d 514, 518, 588 P.2d 1351 (1979). Under the Washington "attractive nuisance" doctrine, a plaintiff must show the following: (1) the instrumentality of artificial condition must be attractive and alluring or enticing to young children; (2) the instrumentality or condition must have been left unguarded and exposed at a place to which children of tender years are accustomed to resort or where it is reasonable to expect they will resort, for play, amusement, or gratification of youthful curiosity; (3) the thing

must be "dangerous in itself" (i.e., likely to cause injury to children); (4) the child must have been incapable by reason of youth of comprehending the danger involved; (5) it must have been reasonably practicable and feasible either to prevent access or else to render the instrumentality of condition innocuous without obstructing any reasonable purpose for which it was intended. Id.

78. Ford v. Red Lion Inns, 67 Wash. App. 766, 770, 840 P.2d 198 (1992); Swanson v. McKain, 59 Wash. App. 303, 313–14, 796 P.2d 1291 (1990).

79. Egede-Nissen v. Crystal Mountain, Inc., 93 Wash. 2d 127, 606 P.2d 124 (1980).

80. Stuart v. Coldwell Banker, 109 Wash. 2d 408, 745 P.2d 1284 (1987).

81. Stute v. PBMC, Inc., 114 Wash. 2d 454, 788 P.2d 545 (1990).

82. Husfloen v. MTA Construction, 58 Wash. App. 686, 794 P.2d 859 (1990); Weinert v. Bronco National Co., 58 Wash. App. 692, 795 P.2d 1167 (1990).

83. Christen v. Lee, 113 Wash. 2d 479, 505, 780 P.2d 1307 (1989); see also Dickinson v. Edwards, 105 Wash. 2d 457, 471, 716 P.2d 814 (1986).

84. Dickinson v. Edwards, 105 Wash. 2d 457, 471, 716 P.2d 814 (1986).

85. Christen v. Lee, 113 Wash. 2d 479, 497, 780 P.2d 1307 (1989) ("The cases addressing the liability of a drinking establishment for a criminal assault by one of its patrons typically involve the establishment's duty to properly supervise its premises, rather than, or perhaps in addition to, its duty concerning the furnishing of intoxicating liquor.").

86. Reynolds v. Hicks, 134 Wash. 2d 491, 498, 951 P.2d 761 (1998).

87. Hansen v. Friend, 118 Wash. 2d 476, 482–83, 824 P.2d 483 (1992) ("If a social host breaches his or her duty not to furnish liquor to a minor, the trier of fact may consider the breach as evidence of negligence.").

88. In re Estate of Templeton, No. 23111-5 (January 7, 2000).

89. CR 9(b); Murphy v. Campbell Investment Co., 79 Wash. 2d 417, 486 P.2d 1280 (1971).

90. In re Patterson, 93 Wash. App. 579, 586, 969 P.2d 1106 (1999); Farrell v. Score, 67 Wash. 2d 957, 958–59, 411 P.2d 146 (1966).

91. ESCA Corp. v. KPMG Peat Marwick, 135 Wash. 2d 820, 959 P.2d 651 (1998); Janda v. Brier Realty, 97 Wash. App. 45, 984 P.2d 412 (1999).

92. *Lightfoot v. MacDonald*, 86 Wash. 2d 331, 332, 544 P.2d 88 (1976).

93. Wash. Rev. Code § 19.86.080.

94. Wash. Rev. Code § 19.86.090; *Quimby v. Fine*, 45 Wash. App. 175, 189–90, 724 P.2d 403 (1986).

95. *Hangman Ridge v. Safeco Title*, 105 Wash. 2d 778, 784–85, 719 P.2d 531 (1986); *Goodyear Tire v. Whiteman Tire*, 86 Wash. App. 732, 743, 935 P.2d 628 (1997).

96. Wash. Rev. Code § 19.86.090.

97. *See* WPI 30.

98. *Berschauer/Phillips Const. Co. v. Seattle School Dist. No. 1*, 124 Wash. 2d 816, 826, 881 P.2d 986 (1994).

99. Wash. Rev. Code § 4.56.260.

100. *Touchet Valley v. Opp & Siebold General Construction, Inc.*, 119 Wash. 2d 334, 831 P.2d 724 (1992); *WWP v. Graybar Electric Co.*, 112 Wash. 2d 847, 774 P.2d 1119 (1989).

101. *Spokane Truck & Dray Co. v. Hoefer*, 2 Wash. 45, 56, 25 P. 1072 (1891) (punitive damages are "unsound in principle, and unfair and dangerous in practice"); *Essig v. Keating*, 158 Wash. 443, 444, 291 P. 323 (1930); *Barr v. Interbay Citizens Bank of Tampa*, 96 Wash. 2d 692, 649 P.2d 827 (1981). *See also Fisher Properties v. Arden-Mayfair*, 106 Wash. 2d 826, 852, 726 P.2d 976 (1986) ("[Washington Supreme Court] has long held that punitive damages are not allowed unless expressly authorized by Legislature"); *Anderson v. Dalton*, 40 Wash. 2d 894, 898, 246 P.2d 853 (1952); *Johnson v. Steele*, 76 Wash. 2d 750, 751, 45 P.2d 887 (1969); *Stanard v. Bolin*, 88 Wash. 2d 614, 621, 565 P.2d 94 (1977).

102. *Hickman v. Desimone*, 188 Wash. 499, 501–03, 62 P.2d 1338 (1936).

103. *Taskett v. KING Broadcasting Co.*, 86 Wash. 2d 439, 447, 546 P.2d 81 (1976). It should be noted the Washington Product Liability Act "preempts tort-based common-law product liability remedies." *Washington Water Power Co. v. Graybar Elec. Co.*, 112 Wash. 2d 847, 853, 774 P.2d 1199. "Wash. Rev. Code § 7.72.010(4) includes misrepresentation among the common-law claims that can be brought as product liability claims." *Central Washington Refrigeration, Inc. v. Barbee*, 81 Wash. App. 212, 226, 913 P.2d 836 (1996).

104. The Legislature's unwillingness to change the state's general policy against punitive damages is chronicled in *Kammerer v. Western Gear Corp.*, 96 Wash. 2d 416, 428 n.3, 635 P.2d 708 (1981) (dissenting opinion of Justice Stafford). In 1961, the Washington Legislature enacted a law entitled "Civil Actions—Ex-

emplary Damages for Intentional Injury to Person or Character." Laws of 1961, ch. 97, p.1583. Less than three weeks later the same legislature reconsidered the wisdom of its acts and repealed the legislation. Laws of 1961, 1st Ex. Sess, ch. 27, § 6, p.2722. *Kammerer*, 96 Wash. 2d at 428 n.3 (dissenting opinion of Justice Stafford).

105. *See* Wash. Rev. Code § 19.86.090 (Consumer Protection Act provision for treble damages to maximum of $10,000); Wash. Rev. Code § 59.12.170 (landlord entitled to double the rent found due in unlawful detainer action); Wash. Rev. Code § 64.12.020 (treble damages for commissive waste by a tenant); and Wash. Rev. Code § 64.12.030 (treble damages for injury to trees, shrubs, timber).

106. *See Fisher Properties, Inc. v. Arden-Mayfair, Inc.*, 106 Wash. 2d 826, 852, 726 P.2d 8 (1986) (declining to construe Wash. Rev. Code § 64.12.020 as requiring treble damages for permissive, as opposed to commissive, waste).

107. *Huntington v. Samaritan Hosp.*, 101 Wash. 2d 466, 680 P.2d 58 (1984); *Wood v. Dunlop*, 83 Wash. 2d 719, 521 P.2d 1177 (1974).

108. Wash. Rev. Code § 4.20.020.

109. *Parrish v. Jones*, 44 Wash. App. 449, 722 P.2d 878 (1986).

110. *Pancratz v. Turon*, 3 Wash. App. 182, 473 P.2d 409 (1970).

111. *Criscuola v. Andrews*, 82 Wash. 2d 68, 507 P.2d 149 (1973).

112. Wash. Rev. Code § 4.20.046(1).

113. *See Zimny v. Lovric*, 59 Wash. App. 737, 801 P.2d 259 (1990), *review denied*, 116 Wash. 2d 1013, 807 P.2d 884 (1991).

114. *Higbee v. Shorewood Osteopathic Hospital*, 105 Wash. 2d 33, 711 P.2d 306 (1985).

115. *Walton v. Absher Construction Co., Inc.*, 101 Wash. 2d 238, 676 P.2d 1002 (1984).

116. Wash. Rev. Code § 4.24.010; WPI 31.06; *see also Hinzman v. Palmanteer*, 91 Wash. 2d 327, 501 P.2d 1228 (1972).

117. *Higbee v. Shorewood Osteopathic Hospital*, 105 Wash. 2d 33, 711 P.2d 306 (1985).

WEST VIRGINIA

A. STATUTE OF LIMITATIONS

In any given transaction or occurrence, more than one statute of limitations may apply, and the claimant may have a choice of two or more different statutory time periods.[1] There is a presumption favoring a longer limitation period when the complaint could be construed as either in tort or on contract.[2]

The specific statutes of limitations in tort are as follows:

1. Actions not surviving death, including libel, defamation, false arrest, false imprisonment, malicious prosecution, and intentional infliction of emotional distress have a one-year statute of limitations.[3]

2. Actions that survive death, including claims for injury to property, real or personal; injuries to the person not resulting in death, actions based on deceit or fraud; actions for retaliatory discharge; and actions for severe emotional distress, have a two-year statute of limitations.[4] Furthermore, claims against local government,[5] medical malpractice,[6] violation of a wage statute,[7] and actions under West Virginia Human Rights Act [8] have a two-year statute of limitations.

3. Generally, wrongful death actions have a two-year statute of limitations from the date of death.[9] However, the discovery rule applies to wrongful death actions "when the decedent's representative knows or by the exercise of reasonable diligence should know that . . . the death was a result of a wrongful act, neglect, or default; the identity of the person or entity who owed the decedent a duty . . . is known; and that the wrongful act, neglect or default of that person or entity has a casual relation to the decedent's death."[10]

4. Misappropriation of a trade secret has a three-year statute of limitations.[11]

5. Violation of an antitrust law has a four-year statute of limitations.[12]

6. Actions against a fiduciary for account[13] and actions for injuries resulting from planning, design, or supervision of construction[14] have a ten-year statute of limitations.

B. TORT REFORM

To date, the West Virginia state legislature has addressed the issue of tort reform in only one area, medical malpractice.

First, West Virginia placed a statutory cap on damages in medical malpractice actions, limiting recovery for non-economic losses to one million dollars.[15]

Second, the Medical Professional Liability Act, codified at West Virginia Code § 55-7B-1 to -11, was significantly amended during a special session of the legislature held in December 2001.[16] The changes affect all causes of action alleging medical professional liability filed on or after March 1, 2001.[17] From the effective date, all third-party bad faith claims against insurance companies will be prohibited;[18] a plaintiff who prevails against an insured tortfeasor will no longer have a cause of action against the tortfeasor's insurance company for bad faith settlement.[19] Additionally, a health care provider sued for malpractice will not be permitted to file a first-party bad faith claim against his insurer until the underlying lawsuit has been resolved.[20]

Another revision to Article 7B pertains to the prerequisites to filing a medical professional liability action. Prior to filing an action, a claimant must provide the healthcare provider with a notice of claim and an expert's opinion, called a "screening certificate of merit,"[21] to which the provider may respond with a demand for pre-litigation mediation.[22] A full-scale addition to the Act demands that medical records be provided on an expedited basis.[23] Within thirty days of the filing of the last answer to a complaint, the parties are obligated to provide one another with access to all reasonably related medical records in their control, and the plaintiff must provide releases for related records known to exist but not under his control.[24] Demand procedures for access to additional records are also provided.[25]

The Act is further expanded to expedite the resolution of medical professional liability cases,[26] including a status conference within 60 days,[27] trial within two years,[28] mandatory mediation,[29] and/or a summary jury trial proceeding by consent of the parties at the court's discretion.[30] The medical professional liability jury is expanded to 12 members, with the agreement of nine jurors sufficient to constitute a verdict.[31]

By contrast, the summary trial jury is composed of six jurors who hear a one-day trial with one-hour presentations from each side and are given abbreviated instructions.[32] The parties to a summary trial have 30 days to accept or reject the verdict.[33] "If a verdict is rendered upon the subsequent trial of the case which is not more than twenty percent more favorable to a party who rejected the summary trial verdict and indicated a desire to proceed to trial, the rejecting party is liable for the costs [and attorneys' fees] incurred by the other party or parties subsequent to the summary jury trial."[34]

C. "NO FAULT" LIMITATIONS

To date, West Virginia has not adopted any "no-fault" provisions.

D. THE STANDARD FOR NEGLIGENCE

The strong public policy of West Virginia is that persons injured by the negligence of another should be able to recover in tort.[35] In order to prove actionable negligence there must be shown a duty on the part of the person charged with negligence and a breach of such duty.[36] The elements of duty, breach, and injury are essential to actionable negligence and in the absence of any of them the action must fail.[37]

In West Virginia, the violation of a statute is *prima facie* negligence and not negligence *per se*.[38] Apart from the violation of a statute, breach of duty is determined by the various standards of care recognized in West Virginia and predicated on the relationship between the plaintiff and the defendant.[39] Ordinary care is that degree of care that a reasonably prudent and cautious person would take to avoid injury under like circumstances.[40] Common carriers owe the highest degree of care to their passengers in the operation of their vehicles.[41] West Virginia also recognizes various professional standards of care, including but not limited to attorneys [42] and health care providers.[43]

"The ultimate test of the existence of a duty to use care is found in the foreseeability that harm may result if it is not exercised."[44] "Beyond the question of foreseeability, the existence of duty also involves policy considerations underlying the core issues of the scope of the legal system's protection. Such considerations include the likelihood of injury, the magnitude of the burden of guarding against it, and the consequences of placing that burden on the defendant."[45]

In West Virginia, children under the age of seven are conclusively presumed to be incapable of negligence.[46] For children between ages seven and 14, a rebuttable presumption applies, and a party seeking to overcome the presumption has the burden of proving the child had the capacity for negligence. Alternatively, a child 14 years old or older is presumed to be capable of negligence.[47]

The Supreme Court of Appeals of West Virginia has repudiated the so-called attractive nuisance doctrine, but recognizes the fact that, where a dangerous instrumentality or condition exists at a place frequented by children who thereby suffer injury, the parties responsible for such dangerous condition may be held liable if they knew, or should have known, of the dangerous condition and that children frequented the dangerous premises.[48]

A person confronted with a sudden emergency, who acts according to his or her best judgment, or who because of insufficient time to form a judgment fails to act in the most judicious manner, will not be held responsible for the consequences of any act or omission if he or she exercised the care that would be exercised by a reasonable prudent person in like circumstances.[49] To rely on the sudden emergency doctrine, a defendant must not be in the position of having wholly or partly created the emergency.[50] The application of the sudden emergency doctrine ordinarily involves a judicial determination by the trier of fact of three factual propositions: (1) whether the defendant was confronted with a sudden emergency; (2) if so, whether the emergency was created by the defendant; and (3) whether in the circumstances of such emergency he acted as a reasonably prudent person would have acted in like circumstances.[51]

E. CAUSATION

In order to establish a *prima facie* case in negligence, the plaintiff must demonstrate by a preponderance of the evidence that the negligence charged was one of the efficient causes of the injury.[52] The negligence charged must be the "superior and controlling agency from which springs the harm, as distinguished from those causes that are merely incidental or subsidiary to such principle and controlling causes."[53] The plaintiff need not show the negligence charged was the sole cause of the injury.[54] A person is not liable for damages that result from an event that was not expected and could not reasonably have been anticipated by an ordinary prudent person.[55] Foreseeable injury is a requisite of proximate cause.[56]

"[A] tortfeasor whose negligence is a substantial factor in bringing about injury is not relieved from liability by the intervening acts of third persons if those acts were reasonably foreseeable by the original tortfeasor at the time of his negligent conduct."[57]

F. CONTRIBUTORY NEGLIGENCE, COMPARATIVE NEGLIGENCE, AND ASSUMPTION OF RISK

1. Contributory Negligence

Prior to 1979, West Virginia utilized the doctrine of contributory negligence,[58] however, since 1979 the state has adopted and followed the doctrine of comparative negligence.[59]

2. Comparative Negligence

The Supreme Court of Appeals of West Virginia adopted comparative negligence whereby "a party is not barred from recovering damages in a tort action so long as his negligence or fault does not equal or exceed the combined negligence or fault of the other parties involved."[60] The Court has stated that "the term 'comparative causation' as more accurate than 'comparative negligence' or even 'comparative fault' in that the concept is applicable not only to negligence actions, but also, under certain circumstances, actions involving strict liability."[61] As a result of adopting a comparative negligence standard, West Virginia no longer recognizes the last clear chance doctrine.[62] The Supreme Court of Appeals of West Virginia abolished the last clear chance doctrine in 1981 stating that the historical reasons for establishing the doctrine, namely to ameliorate the harshness of contributory negligence, no longer exist.[63]

3. Assumption of Risk

Assumption of the risk is a separate defense in the West Virginia scheme of comparative negligence.[64] However, "the plaintiff is not barred from recovery by the doctrine of assumption of risk unless his degree of fault . . . equals or exceeds the combined fault or negligence of the other parties."[65] Assumption of the risk only applies in products liability cases, however, where the plaintiff had actual knowledge of the defective or dangerous condition, fully appreciated the risk involved, and continued to use the product or participate in the activity.[66]

G. *RES IPSA LOQUITUR* AND INHERENTLY DANGEROUS ACTIVITIES

1. *Res Ipsa Loquitur*

In West Virginia, "*res ipsa loquitur* means that the facts of the occurrence warrant the inference of negligence."[67] "It may be inferred that harm suffered by the plaintiff is caused by the negligence of the defendant when: (a) the event is of a kind that ordinarily does not occur in the absence of negligence; (b) other responsible causes, including the conduct of the plaintiff and third persons, are sufficiently eliminated by the evidence; and (c) the indicated negligence is within the scope of the defendant's duty to the plaintiff."[68] "It is the function of the court to determine whether the inference may reasonably be drawn by the jury, or whether it must necessarily be drawn. It is the function of the jury to determine whether the inference is to be drawn in any case where different conclusions may reasonably be reached.[69] *Res ipsa loquitur* does not apply to medical malpractice actions.[70]

2. **Inherently Dangerous Activities**

A party operating or using an inherently dangerous instrumentality is strictly liable for injuries proximately caused by the instrumentality.[71] A party engaging in an inherently dangerous activity, such as maintaining electric lines or transmitting natural gas, must exercise a higher degree of care and diligence to prevent injury and other damages.[72]

H. NEGLIGENCE *PER SE*

"Any person injured by the violation of any statute may recover from the offender such damages as he may sustain by reason of the violation . . ."[73] However, the violation of a statute is only *prima facie* negligence, and not negligence *per se*.[74] In other words, violation of a statute raises only a rebuttable presumption of negligence.[75]

I. JOINT AND SEVERAL LIABILITY

"A plaintiff may elect to sue any or all of those responsible for his injuries and collect his damages from whomever is able to pay, irrespective of their percentage of fault."[76] Joint and several liability among joint tortfeasors is unaffected by the modified comparative negligence rule.[77]

J. INDEMNITY

Indemnity is the attempt by one party to shift an entire loss or liability to another party by agreement or statute (express indemnity) or by operation of law (implied indemnity). A party seeking implied indemnity must be without fault.[78]

A contract providing indemnification for the indemnitee's own negligence does not contravene public policy,[79] as long as the contract does not provide indemnification for the indemnitee's sole negligence.[80] If a contract provides for indemnification of an indemnitee's sole negligence, it is valid only if there is an appropriate insurance fund, bought pursuant to the underlying contract, for the express purpose of protecting all concerned.[81]

K. BAR OF WORKERS' COMPENSATORY STATUTE

Employers in good standing with the West Virginia Workers' Compensation Fund "shall not" be liable for the injury or death of any employee occurring in the course of and resulting from employment.[82] This immunity also applies to coemployees who act in furtherance of the employer's business and do not inflict injury with deliberate intention.[83]

In *Mandolidis v. Elkins Industries, Inc.*, the Supreme Court of Appeals of West Virginia interpreted the language "deliberate intent to produce such injury or death" from West Virginia Code § 23-4-2 (1969) and held the phrase to mean, "an employer loses immunity from common law actions where such employer's conduct constitutes an intentional tort or willful, wanton, and reckless misconduct."[84] In response to the *Mandolidis* decision, the legislature amended West Virginia Code § 23-4-2 in 1983 to allow an employee to recover damages in excess of workers' compensation benefits through a civil action "if injury or death results to any employee from the *deliberate intention* of his or her employer to produce such injury or death."[85] The plaintiff can prove "deliberate intention" in two ways: (1) specific intent[86] or (2) five-factor analysis.[87] Suggesting that negligent behavior is not enough to state a cause of action under the Act, the Supreme Court of Appeals of West Virginia subsequently stated, "The 'deliberate intention' exception to the Workers' Compensation system is meant to deter the malicious employer, not to punish the stupid one."[88]

The receipt of benefits under the Workers' Compensation Act does not bar an employee from seeking damages from a third party.[89] Notwithstanding the inapplicability of the "made whole" rule,[90] if the employee recovers from a third party, the Commissioner of Workers' Compensation and any self-insured employer has a right of subrogation with regard to medical benefits up to 50 percent of the amount received from the third party.[91]

L. PREMISES LIABILITY

West Virginia has abolished the common law distinction between licensees and invitees.[92] As such, a landowner or possessor's liability for injuries sustained on the premises depends on whether the entrant is a nontrespasser or a trespasser.

Landowners and possessors owe any nontrespassing entrant a duty of reasonable care under the circumstances.[93] In determining whether a defendant in a premises liability case met his or her burden of reasonable care under the circumstances to all nontrespassing entrants, the trier of fact must consider: (1) the foreseeability that an injury might occur; (2) the severity of injury; (3) the time, manner, and circumstances under which the injured party entered the premises; (4) the normal or expected use made of the premises; and (5) the magnitude of the burden placed on the defendant to guard against injury.[94]

A trespasser is one who goes on the property or premises of another without invitation, express or implied, and does so out of curiosity, or for his own purpose or convenience, and not in the performance of any duty to the owner.[95] As for a duty owed to a trespasser, a landowner or possessor need only refrain from willful or wanton injury.[96]

M. DRAM SHOP LIABILITY

West Virginia does not statutorily recognize dram shop or social host liability.[97] There are also no statutes specifically imposing liability on the owners of property on which alcoholic beverages are served.[98] Therefore, absent a basis under common law principles of negligence, there is generally no liability on the part of the social host who gratuitously furnishes alcohol to a guest when an injury to an innocent third party occurs as a result of the guest's intoxication.[99] Moreover, an employer who gratuitously furnishes alcohol to an employee will not be held liable to a third party where there is a lack of affirmative conduct creating an unreasonable risk of harm.[100]

Apart from the lack of statutory liability, the Supreme Court of Appeals of West Virginia has recognized that the illegal sale of alcohol to an intoxicated person may give rise to a negligence action against the vendor for personal injuries suffered by third persons as a result of such sale.[101] For example, the illegal sale of beer to a person less than 21 years of age in violation of a statute is *prima facie* evidence of negligence against the licensee-vendor in favor of a purchaser or a third party injured as a proximate result of the unlawful sale.[102] Such licensee-vendor may rebut this inference of negligence by demonstrating that the purchaser appeared to be of age and that the vendor used reasonable means of identification to ascertain his age.[103] Whether the licensee was negligent in making the sale is a question of fact that ordinarily must be resolved by a jury.[104]

In West Virginia, a motor vehicle passenger may also be found liable for injuries to a third party caused by an intoxicated driver, if the following conditions are met: (1) the driver was operating his vehicle under the influence of alcohol or drugs that proximately caused the accident resulting in the third party's injuries; and (2) the passenger's conduct substantially encouraged or assisted the driver's alcohol or drug impairment.[105]

N. ECONOMIC LOSS

West Virginia continues to recognize a distinction between tort and contract causes of action where the damages claimed are economic in nature.[106] Tort law traditionally has been concerned with compensating for physical injury to person or property.[107] As such, recovery solely for economic loss is generally prohibited in West Virginia under the theory of strict liability in tort.[108] West Virginia does not allow recovery solely for economic loss under a negligence theory unless the person claiming the loss can show there is a physical harm to his person or property, a contractual relationship exists, or that a special relationship exists between the alleged tortfeasor and the person claiming the loss, which is sufficient to establish that the alleged tortfeasor had a duty to the person claiming the loss and the injury was clearly foreseeable.[109]

In the context of strict liability in tort, there are two types of economic loss damages. First, there is "direct economic loss," which is damage to a defective product.[110] Second, there is "consequential economic loss," which is loss of profits.[111]

A strict liability in tort theory cannot be used to recover economic loss such as a decline in the intrinsic value of a product or lost profits.[112] Specifically, West Virginia does not permit the use of strict liability in tort to recover the difference between the value of the product received and the purchase price where there is no sudden calamitous event involved.[113] However, property damage to defective products that does result from a sudden calamitous event is recoverable under a strict liability in tort cause of action.[114]

O. FRAUD AND MISREPRESENTATION

In all averments of fraud or mistake, the circumstances constituting fraud or mistake must be stated with particularity.[115] In order to establish fraud, the circumstances must be clearly alleged and proved.[116]

In order to maintain an action for fraud, the essential elements are that: (1) the act claimed to be fraudulent was the act of the defendant or induced by him; (2) it was material and false; (3) the plaintiff relied on it innocently and was justified under the circumstances in relying on it; and (4) he was damaged because he relied on it.[117]

An action for false representation may be maintained against a party who makes a false representation of fact with knowledge of its falsity, to one who is ignorant of the falsity, with an intent that it should be acted on, where the person to whom it is made acts on it, and by doing so suffers injury.[118] However, "fraud does not require in all circumstances that its perpetrator have actual knowledge of the material falsity of a statement."[119] An action for fraud may lie when a defendant makes a statement, upon which the complaining party relies, without knowledge as to its truth or falsity or under circumstances such that he should have known of its falsity.[120]

P. CONSUMER FRAUD STATUTES

West Virginia Consumer Credit and Protection Act (WVCCPA) and the West Virginia Consumer Good Rental Protection Act contain comprehensive consumer protection provisions.[121] These acts apply primarily to consumer credit sales, consumer leases, consumer loans, and consumer goods under rent-to-own agreements. The WVCCPA declares unlawful any unfair methods of competition and unfair or deceptive acts or practices in the conduct of any trade or commerce.[122]

The Attorney General may bring a civil action to restrain a creditor or a person acting in his behalf from engaging in fraudulent or unconscionable conduct.[123] Any person who purchases or leases goods or services and thereby suffers any ascertainable loss of money or property by the unlawful fraudulent or unconscionable acts or practices of another may bring a civil action to recover actual damages or $200, whichever is greater.[124]

Q. PUNITIVE DAMAGES

Punitive damages are allowed in tort actions "where gross fraud, malice, oppression, or wanton, willful, or reckless conduct or criminal indifference to civil obligations affecting the rights of others appear, or where legislative enactment authorizes it."[125] Punitive damages based on gross, reckless, or wanton negligence are also allowed.[126] A finding of compensatory damages is an indispensable predicate to the finding of punitive damages,[127] and punitive damages must be reasonable in proportion to the compensatory damages awarded.[128]

When the trial court instructs the jury on punitive damages, the court should, at a minimum, carefully explain the factors to be considered in awarding punitive damages. These factors are as follows:

1. Punitive damages should bear a reasonable relationship to the harm that is likely to occur from the defendant's conduct as well as to the harm that actually has occurred. If the defendant's actions caused or would likely cause in a similar situation only slight harm, the damages should be relatively small. If the harm is grievous, the damages should be greater.

2. The jury may consider (although the court need not specifically instruct on each element if doing so would be unfairly prejudicial to the defendant) the reprehensibility of the defendant's conduct. The jury should take into account how long the defendant continued in his actions, whether he was aware his actions were causing or were likely to cause harm, whether he attempted to conceal or cover up his actions or the harm caused by them, whether/how often the defendant engaged in similar conduct in the past, and whether the defendant made reasonable efforts to make amends by offering fair and prompt settlement for the actual harm caused once his liability became clear to him.

3. If the defendant profited from his wrongful conduct, the punitive damages should remove the profit and should be in excess of the profit, so that the award discourages future bad acts by the defendant.

4. As a matter of fundamental fairness, punitive damages should bear a reasonable relationship to compensatory damages.

5. The financial position of the defendant is relevant.[129]

When the trial court reviews an award of punitive damages, the court should, at a minimum, consider the factors given to the jury as well as the following additional factors:

1. The costs of the litigation;

2. Any criminal sanctions imposed on the defendant for his conduct;

3. Any other civil actions against the same defendant, based on the same conduct; and

4. The appropriateness of punitive damages to encourage fair and reasonable settlements when a clear wrong has been committed. A factor that may justify punitive damages is the cost of litigation to the plaintiff.[130] Where recovery is obtained for intentional or reckless infliction of emotional distress, and the plaintiff has not provided substantial and concrete evidence of physical trauma or concomitant medical or psychiatric proof of emotional or mental trauma, a punitive damages award may constitute an impermissible double recovery.[131]

R. **WRONGFUL DEATH AND SURVIVORSHIP ACTIONS**

As no right of action for death by a wrongful act existed at common law, the right or cause of action for wrongful death exists under and by virtue of the provisions of the wrongful death statute of West Virginia.[132] Recovery under the Wrongful Death Act passes to a limited group of beneficiaries defined by statute.[133]

West Virginia also preserves the existence of a cause of action in the injured person during his lifetime and carries forward such action in favor of his personal representative.[134] The survival statute authorizes the decedent's beneficiaries to recover damages incurred by the decedent between the time of injury and death where an action for personal injuries was instituted prior to his death.[135]

S. MEDICAL MONITORING COSTS

A plaintiff may sue for medical monitoring costs in West Virginia if the expenses are necessary and reasonably certain to be incurred as a proximate result of the defendant's tortious conduct.[136] To succeed, the plaintiff must prove that: (1) he was significantly exposed; (2) to a substance proved to be hazardous; (3) due to the defendant's tortious conduct; (4) plaintiff has an increased risk of contracting a serious, latent disease in relation to the general population, which was a proximate result of the exposure; (5) the increased risk makes it reasonably necessary for the plaintiff to have periodic medical exams that would not have been prescribed prior to the exposure; and (6) monitoring procedures exist that make it possible to provide early detection of the disease.[137]

Stephen R. Crislip
Amber L. Hoback
JACKSON & KELLY P.L.L.C.
1600 Laidley Tower
P.O. Box 553
Charleston, West Virginia 25322
(304) 340-1000
Fax (304) 340-1050
scrislip@jacksonkelly.com
ahoback@jacksonkelly.com
www.jacksonkelly.com

ENDNOTES - WEST VIRGINIA

1. *See Harrison v. Casto*, 271 S.E.2d 774, 775-76 (W. Va. 1980).

2. *See Fuller v. Riffe*, 544 S.E.2d 911, 912 (W. Va. 2001); *Cochran v. Appalachian Power Co.*, 246 S.E.2d 624, 628 (W. Va. 1978).

3. *See* W. Va. Code § 55-2-12 (2000); *Duffy v. Ogden Newspapers, Inc.*, 294 S.E.2d 121, 122 (W. Va. 1982); *Cavendish v. Moffitt*, 253 S.E.2d 558, 559 (W. Va. 1979); *Snodgrass v. Sisson's Mobile Home Sales, Inc.*, 244 S.E.2d 321, 325 (W. Va. 1978). *See also Thompson v. Branches-Domestic Violence Shelter of Huntington, West Virginia, Inc.*, 534 S.E.2d 33, 39 (W. Va. 2000), *cert. denied*, 531 U.S. 1055 (2000) (holding that the tort of breach of confidentiality also is governed by a one-year statute of limitations).

4. *See* W. Va. Code §§ 55-2-12, 55-7-8a (2000). *See also Courtney v. Courtney*, 437 S.E.2d 436, 443 (W. Va. 1993); *Stanley v. Sewell Coal Co.*, 285 S.E.2d 679 (W. Va. 1981); *Snodgrass*, 244 S.E.2d at 324-25.

5. *See* W. Va. Code § 29-12A-6 (2001).

6. *See* W. Va. Code § 55-7B-4 (2000).

7. *See id.* at § 55-2-12.

8. *See* W. Va. Code §§ 5-11-1, 5-11-13 (1999); W. Va. Code § 55-2-12 (2000). *See also McCourt v. Oneida Coal Co.*, 425 S.E.2d 602, 606-09 (W. Va. 1992).

9. *See* W. Va. Code § 55-7-6 (2000).

10. *See Bradshaw v. Soulsby*, 558 S.E.2d 681, 683 (W. Va. 2000).

11. *See* W. Va. Code § 47-22-6 (1999).

12. *See id.* at § 47-18-11.

13. *See* W. Va. Code § 55-2-7 (2000).

14. *See id.* at § 55-2-6a.

15. *See id.* at § 55-7B-8.

16. *See* H.B. 601, 2001 Leg., 6th Spec. Sess. (W. Va. 2001) (enacted) (to be published at W. Va. Code §§ 55-7B-1 to -11).

17. *See id.* (to be published at § 55-7B-10(b)).

18. *See id.* (to be published at § 55-7B-5(b)).

19. Examples of third-party bad faith settlement cases decided by the Supreme Court of Appeals of West Virginia include *Doddrill v. Nationwide Mut. Ins. Co.*, 491 S.E.2d 721 (W. Va. 1994), *State ex rel. State Farm Fire & Cas. v. Madden*, 451 S.E.2d 721 (W.Va. 1994) and *Jenkins v. J.C. Penney Cas. Ins. Co.*, 280 S.E.2d 252 (W.Va. 1981). *See State ex rel. Allstate Ins. Co. v. Gaughan*, 508 S.E.2d 75, 87 n.16 (W. Va. 1998).

20. *See* H.B. 601, 2001 Leg., 6th Spec. Sess. (W. Va. 2001) (to be published at § 55-B-(c)).

21. *See id.* (to be published at § 55-7B-6(b)).

22. *See id.* (to be published at § 55-7B-6(f)).

23. *See id.* (to be published at § 55-7B-6a).

24. *See id.* (to be published at § 55-7B-6a(a)).

25. *See id.* (to be published at § 55-7B-6a(b)-(e)).

26. *See id.* (to be published at § 55-7B-6b).

27. *See id.* (to be published at § 55-7B-6b(a)).

28. *See id.* (to be published at § 55-7B-6b(c)).

29. *See id.* (to be published at § 55-7B-6b(b)).

30. *See id.* (to be published at § 55-7B-6b(d)).

31. *See id.* (to be published at § 55-7B-6(d)).

32. *See id.* (to be published at § 55-7B-6(a), (c), (e) & (g)).

33. *See id.* (to be published at § 55-7B-6(i)).

34. *Id.*

35. *See Mill v. Quality Supplier Trucking, Inc.*, 510 S.E.2d 280, 282 (W. Va. 1998).

36. *See Miller v. Whitworth*, 455 S.E.2d 821, 824 (W. Va. 1995); *Jack v. Fritts*, 457 S.E.2d 431, 434-35 (W. Va. 1995); *Atkinson v. Harman*, 158 S.E.2d 169, 173 (W. Va. 1967).

37. *See Atkinson*, 158 S.E.2d at 173.

38. *See Gillingham v. Stephenson*, 551 S.E.2d 663, 670 (W. Va. 2001); *Price v. Halstead*, 355 S.E.2d 380, 387 (W. Va. 1987); *Vandergrift v. Johnson*, 206 S.E.2d 515, 517 (W. Va. 1974); *Spurlin v. Nardo*, 114 S.E.2d 913, 918 (W. Va. 1960).

39. *See Robertson v. LeMaster*, 301 S.E.2d 563, 568-69 (W. Va. 1983). "A duty owing to everyone can never become the foundation of an action until some individual is placed in a position that gives him particular occasion to insist upon its performance." *Id.* at 567 (quoting Thomas Cooley, *Law of Torts* § 478 (4th ed. 1932)).

40. *See Honaker v. Mahon*, 552 S.E.2d 788, 793 (W. Va. 2001); *Koontz v. Whitney*, 153 S.E. 797, 798 (W. Va. 1930).

41. *See Abdulla v. Pittsburgh & Weirton Bus Co.*, 213 S.E.2d 810, Syl. Pt. 2 (W. Va. 1975).

42. *See* W. Va. Code § 30-2-11 (1998). *See also Keister v. Talbott*, 391 S.E.2d 895, 898 (W. Va. 1990).

43. *See* W. Va. Code § 55-7B-3 (2000) (providing the standard of care for health care providers). *See also Duling v. Bluefield Sanitarium, Inc.*, 142 S.E.2d 754, 764 (W. Va. 1965) (stating "[a] private hospital, conducted for profit, owes to its patients such reasonable care and attention for their safety as their mental and physical condition, if known, may require. The care to be exercised should be commensurate with the known inability of the patient to take care of himself.").

44. *Sewell v. Gregory*, 371 S.E.2d 82, Syl. Pt. 3 (W. Va. 1988). *See also E. Steel Constructors, Inc. v. City of Salem*, 549 S.E.2d 266, 271 (W. Va. 2001) (discussing the general rule precluding economic damages, in a cause of action where negligence is claimed in the absence of either physical injury, property damage, or a contract, an issue not reached in *Sewell*).

45. *Robertson v. LeMaster*, 301 S.E.2d 563, 568 (W. Va. 1983).

46. *See Pino v. Szuch*, 408 S.E.2d 55, 57 (W. Va. 1991).

47. *See Jordan v. Bero*, 210 S.E.2d 618, 625 (W. Va. 1974); *Sutton v. Monongahela Power Co.*, 158 S.E.2d 98, 106 (W. Va. 1967).

48. *See Sutton*, 158 S.E.2d at 104-05; *White v. Kanawha City Co.*, 34 S.E.2d 17, 19 (W. Va. 1945).

49. *See Moran v. Atha Trucking, Inc.*, 540 S.E.2d 903, 908 (W. Va. 1997).

50. *See id.; Lilly v. Taylor*, 155 S.E.2d 579, 588 (W. Va. 1967).

51. *See Moran*, 540 S.E.2d at 908; *Lilly*, 155 S.E.2d at 588-89; *Reilley v. Byard*, 119 S.E.2d 650, Syl. Pt. 3 (W. Va. 1961).

52. *See Long v. City of Weirton*, 214 S.E.2d 832, 846 (W. Va. 1975), *superseded in part by statute as stated in, Pritchard v. Arvon*, 413 S.E.2d 100, 103 (W. Va. 1991) (addressing the governmental immunity statute). *See also Antco, Inc., v. Dodge Fuel Corp.*, 550 S.E.2d 622, 634 (W.Va. 2001) (stating that a breach of duty is not actionable unless it is proven by a preponderance of the evidence that the negligence was the proximate cause of the injury suffered); *Louk v. Isuzu Motors, Inc.*, 479 S.E.2d 911, 923 (W. Va. 1996) (same); *Walton v. Given*, 215 S.E.2d 647, 651 (W. Va. 1975) (same).

53. *Lilly*, 155 S.E.2d at 589.

54. *See Long*, 214 S.E.2d at 845.

55. *See Doe v. Wal-Mart Stores, Inc.*, 479 S.E.2d 610, 617 (W. Va. 1996); *Anderson v. Moulder*, 394 S.E.2d 61, 72 (W. Va. 1990); *Haddox v. Suburban Lanes, Inc.*, 349 S.E.2d 910, 914 (W. Va. 1986).

56. *See Doe*, 479 S.E.2d at 617; *Anderson*, 394 S.E.2d at 72; *Haddox*, 349 S.E.2d at 914.

57. *Anderson*, 394 S.E.2d at 73.

58. *See Kidd v. Norfolk & W. Ry. Co.*, 192 S.E.2d 890 (W. Va. 1972), *overruled by, Bradley v. Appalachian Power Co.*, 256 S.E.2d 879, 885 (W. Va. 1979).

59. *See Bradley*, 256 S.E.2d at 885.

60. *Id.*

61. *Reager v. Anderson*, 371 S.E.2d 619, 625 n.1 (W. Va. 1988) (citing *Star Furniture v. Pulaski Furniture Co.*, 297 S.E.2d 854, 863 (W. Va. 1982)).

62. *See Ratlief v. Yokum*, 280 S.E.2d 584 (W. Va. 1981).

63. *See id.*

64. *See King v. Kayak Mfg. Corp.*, 387 S.E.2d 511, 517 (W. Va. 1989).

65. *Id.* at Syl. Pt. 2.

66. *See id.* at Syl. Pts. 1, 3.

67. *Holley v. Purity Baking Co.*, 37 S.E.2d 729, 732 (W. Va. 1946). *See also Lipscomb v. King Knob Coal Co.*, 300 S.E.2d 635, Syl. Pt. 2 (W.Va. 1983) (stating "[a]n in-

ference of negligence which may arise upon the application of the *res ipsa loquitur* doctrine may be rebutted.").

68. *Foster v. City of Keyser*, 501 S.E.2d 165, Syl. Pt. 4 (W. Va. 1997) (adopting the Restatement (Second) of Torts approach to the doctrine of *res ipsa loquitur*).

69. *Id.*

70. *See Hinkle v. Martin*, 256 S.E.2d 768 (W. Va. 1979).

71. *See Peneschi v. Nat'l Steel Corp.*, 295 S.E.2d 1, 10-11 (W. Va. 1982) (adopting the Restatement (Second) of Torts view on strict liability for abnormally dangerous activities).

72. *See Foster*, 501 S.E.2d at 175 (requiring a high standard of care in the transmission of natural gas); *Huffman v. Appalachian Power Co.*, 415 S.E.2d 145, 150-51 (W. Va. 1991) (noting a higher standard of care required of those who maintain and operate electrical wires).

73. W. Va. Code § 55-7-9 (2000).

74. *See Gillingham v. Stephenson*, 551 S.E.2d 663, 670 (W. Va. 2001); *Price v. Halstead*, 355 S.E.2d 380, Syl. Pt. 11 (W. Va. 1987); *Vandergrift v. Johnson*, 206 S.E.2d 515, 517 (W. Va. 1974); *Spurlin v. Nardo*, 114 S.E.2d 913, 918 (W. Va. 1960). *See also* text accompanying note 18, *supra*.

75. *See Flanagan v. Mott*, 114 S.E.2d 331, 335 (W. Va. 1960).

76. *Kodym v. Frazier*, 412 S.E.2d 219, Syl. Pt. 1 (W. Va. 1991); *Sitzes v. Anchor Motor Freight, Inc.*, 289 S.E.2d 679, 684 (W. Va. 1982).

77. *See Kodym*, 412 S.E.2d at Syl. Pt. 2; *Sitzes*, 289 S.E.2d at 684.

78. *Hager v. Marshall*, 505 S.E.2d 640, 649 (W. Va. 1998) (citing *Sydenstricker v. Unipunch Products, Inc.*, 288 S.E.2d 511, Syl. Pt. 2 (W. Va. 1982)).

79. *State ex rel. Vapor Corp. v. Narick*, 320 S.E.2d 345, 349 (W. Va. 1984) (citing *Sellers v. Owens-Illinois Glass Co.*, 191 S.E.2d 166, Syl. Pt. 1 (W. Va. 1972)).

80. *See* W. Va. Code § 55-8-14 (2000).

81. *See Dalton v. Childress Services Corp.*, 432 S.E.2d 98, 101 (W. Va. 1993).

82. W. Va. Code § 23-2-6 (1998). *See also Bell v. Vecellio & Grogan, Inc.*, 447 S.E.2d 269, 271 (W. Va. 1994); *Sias v. W-P Coal Co.*, 408 S.E.2d 321, 325-26 (W. Va. 1991). *But see Erie Ins. Property and Casualty Co. v. Stage Show Pizza, JTS, Inc.*, 553 S.E.2d 257, 266-67 (W. Va. 2001) (Albright, J. dissenting in part) (Maynard, J. dissenting in part) (interpreting exclusion in stop gap insurance coverage,

holding that the deliberate intention cause of action is not a purely statutory cause of action "arising under" the Workers' Compensation Act and that the Act only specifies what evidence is sufficient to extinguish an employer's immunity under the Act, exposing the employer to an obligation under the common law). *Cf. Bell*, 447 S.E.2d at Syl. Pt. 2 (deciding a choice of law question, concluding that the enactment of W. Va. Code § 23-4-2 represented a "wholesale abandonment of the common law tort concept of a deliberate intention cause of action . . ., to be replaced by a statutory direct cause of action . . . expressed within the workers' compensation system").

83. W. Va. Code § 23-3-6a (1998). *See also Henry v. Benyo*, 506 S.E.2d 615, 620 (W. Va. 1998); *Wisman v. Rhodes & Shamblin Stone, Inc.*, 447 S.E.2d 5, 8-9 (W. Va. 1994); *Henderson v. Meredith Lumber Co., Inc.*, 438 S.E.2d 324, 329-30 (W. Va. 1993); *Deller v. Naymick*, 342 S.E.2d 73, 78-81 (W. Va. 1985) (McGraw, J. dissenting).

84. *Mandolidis v. Elkins Indus., Inc.*, 246 S.E.2d 907, 914 (W. Va. 1978), *superceded by statute as stated in Handley v. Union Carbide Corp.*, 804 F.2d 265 (4th Cir. 1986).

85. W. Va. Code § 23-4-2(b) (effective May 8, 1983).

86. The plaintiff may prove that (1) a specific unsafe working condition existed in the work place that presented a high degree of risk and a strong probability of serious injury or death; (2) the employer had a subjective realization and an appreciation of element 1; (3) the specific unsafe working condition was a violation of a state or federal safety statute, rule, or regulation, whether cited or not, of a commonly accepted and well-known safety standard within the industry or business of such employer, which statute, rule, regulation, or standard was specifically applicable to the particular work and working condition involved, as contrasted with a statute, rule, regulation, or standard generally requiring safe work places, equipment, and working conditions; (4) notwithstanding the existence of the facts set forth in elements 1 through 3, above, the employer nevertheless thereafter exposed an employee to the specific unsafe working condition intentionally; and (5) the employee so exposed suffered serious injury or death as a direct and proximate result of the specific unsafe working condition. W. Va. Code § 23-4-2(c)(2)(ii) (1998); *see also Mayles v. Shoney's, Inc.*, 405 S.E.2d 15, Syl. Pt. 2 (W. Va. 1990). A plaintiff need only prove the five statutory elements. *Id.* at 24. "[W]hile a plaintiff may choose to introduce evidence of prior similar incidents or complaints to circumstantially establish that an employer has acted with deliberate intention, evidence of prior similar incidents or complaints is not mandated by W. Va. Code, 23-4-2(c)(2)(ii)." *Nutter v. Owens-Illinois, Inc.*, 550 S.E.2d 398, 403 (W. Va. 2001).

87. *See Helmick v. Potomac Edison Co.*, 406 S.E.2d 700, 705 (W. Va. 1991).

88. The plaintiff may prove that the person against whom liability is asserted acted with a consciously, subjectively and deliberately formed intention to produce

the specific result of injury or death to an employee. *Id.* at § 23-4-2(c)(2)(i) (1998); *see also Tolliver v. The Kroger Co.*, 498 S.E.2d 702, Syl. Pt. 9 (W. Va. 1998).

89. W. Va. Code § 23-2A-1(a) (1998).

90. *See Bush v. Richardson*, 484 S.E.2d 490, 492-93 (W. Va. 1997).

91. W. Va. Code § 23-2A-1(b) (1998).

92. *Stevens v. West Virginia Inst. of Tech.*, 532 S.E.2d 639, Syl. Pt. 4 (W. Va. 1999) (citing *Mallet v. Pickens*, 522 S.E.2d 436, Syl. Pt. 4, *in part* (W. Va. 1999)).

93. *Senkus v. Moore*, 535 S.E.2d 724, 727 (2000) (citing *Mallet*, 522 S.E.2d at Syl. Pt. 4, *in part*).

94. *Mallet*, 522 S.E.2d at Syl. Pt. 6.

95. *Mallet*, 522 S.E.2d at 439 (citing *Huffman v. Appalachian Power Co.*, 415 S.E.2d 145, Syl. Pt. 1 (W. Va. 1991)).

96. *Stevens*, 532 S.E.2d at 639 (citing *Mallet*, 522 S.E.2d at Syl. Pt. 4, *in part*).

97. *Overbaugh v. McCutcheon*, 396 S.E.2d 153, 155-56 (W. Va. 1990). "The first civil damage act in West Virginia was enacted by 1872-73 W. Va. Acts ch. 99, § 6. This provision was codified in the 1906 Code at ch. 32, § 26 and in the 1931 Code at 60-1-22. The provision was repealed by 1935 W. Va. Acts ch. 4." *Anderson v. Moulder*, 394 S.E.2d 61, 66 n.5 (W. Va. 1990).

98. *Farmers & Mechanics Mut. Fire Ins. Co. of West Virginia v. Hutzler*, 447 S.E.2d 22, 24 (W. Va. 1994).

99. *Overbaugh*, 396 S.E.2d at Syl. Pt. 2.

100. *Id.* at Syl. Pt. 3.

101. "W. Va. Code, 55-7-9 [1923], recognizing a cause of action in tort for the violation of a statute, and W. Va. Code, 60-7-12 [1986], making it illegal for a licensee to sell alcohol to intoxicated persons, read together, create a tort action against a licensee for personal injuries caused by the licensee's selling alcohol to anyone who is physically incapacitated by drinking." *Bailey v. Black*, 394 S.E.2d 58, Syl. Pt. 1 (W. Va. 1990).

102. *See Anderson*, 394 S.E.2d at Syl. Pts. 1 & 2.

103. *Id.* at Syl. Pt. 4, *in part*.

104. *Id.*

105. *Id.* at 71 (citing *Price v. Halstead*, 355 S.E.2d 380, Syl. Pt. 12 (W. Va. 1987)).

106. *National Steel Erection, Inc. v. J.A. Jones Constr. Co.*, 899 F. Supp. 268, 272 (N.D. W. Va. 1995) (citing *Basham v. General Shale*, 377 S.E.2d 830, 834 (W. Va. 1988) and *Star Furniture Co. v. Pulaski Furniture Co.*, 297 S.E.2d 854, 859 (W. Va. 1982)).

107. *Star Furniture Co.*, 297 S.E.2d at 859.

108. *See, e.g., Roxalana Hills, Ltd. v. Masonite Corp.*, 627 F. Supp. 1194, 1196 (S. D. W. Va. 1986) (citing *Star Furniture Co.*, 297 S.E.2d 854); *Basham*, 377 S.E.2d at 834 ("[W]hile a strict liability tort claim may arise when a defective product causes injury, a party who suffers mere economic loss as a result of a defective product must turn to the Uniform Commercial Code to seek relief.").

109. *Aikens v. Debow*, 541 S.E.2d 576, 589 (W. Va. 2000). *See, e.g., E. Steel Constructors, Inc.*, 549 S.E.2d 266, Syl. Pt. 6 (W. Va. 2001) (holding that a design professional owes a duty of care to a contractor who relies on the design professional's work in carrying out his obligations to the owner, notwithstanding the absence of a contract between the design professional and contractor, due to the special relationship that exists between the two).

110. *Star Furniture Co.*, 297 S.E.2d at 857.

111. *Id.* at 857-58.

112. *See Basham*, 377 S.E.2d at 834 (citing *Star Furniture Co.*, 297 S.E.2d at 859).

113. *See Star Furniture Co.*, 297 S.E.2d at 859.

114. *See Basham*, 377 S.E.2d at 830 (citing *Star Furniture Co.*, 297 S.E.2d at 859).

115. *Kessel v. Leavitt*, 511 S.E.2d 720 (W. Va. 1998) (relying on W. Va. R. Civ. P. 9(b); *Funeral Servs. ex rel. Gregory, Inc. v. Bluefield Cmty. Hosp.*, 413 S.E.2d 79 (W. Va. 1991), *overruled on other grounds by Courtney v. Courtney*, 437 S.E.2d 436 (W. Va. 1993); and *Hager v. Exxon Corp.*, 241 S.E.2d 920 (W. Va. 1978)).

116. *Funeral Servs. ex rel. Gregory, Inc.*, 413 S.E.2d at 85.

117. *Capitol Chrysler-Plymouth, Inc. v. Megginson*, 532 S.E.2d 43, Syl. Pt. 2 (W. Va. 2000); *Lengyel v. Lint*, 280 S.E.2d 66, Syl. Pt. 1 (W. Va. 1981)).

118. *Lengyel*, 280 S.E.2d at 69 (citing *Horton v. Tyree*, 139 S.E. 737, 738 (W. Va. 1927)).

119. *Cordial v. Ernst & Young*, 483 S.E.2d 248, 259 (W. Va. 1996) (quoting *Bowling v. Ansted Chrysler-Plymouth-Dodge*, 425 S.E.2d 144, Syl. Pt. 1 (W. Va. 1992); *Horton v. Tyree*, 139 S.E. 737, Syl. Pt. 1 (W. Va. 1927)).

120. *Lengyel*, 280 S.E.2d at 69 (citing *State v. Berkeley*, 23 S.E. 608 (W. Va. 1895)); *accord Darrisaw v. Old Colony Realty Company*, 501 S.E.2d 187, Syl. Pt. 4 (W. Va.

1997) (relying on *Teter v. Old Colony Co.*, 441 S.E.2d 728, Syl. Pt. 1 (W. Va. 1994)) (holding that real estate broker may be liable to purchaser for material misrepresentations made with regard to fitness or habitability of residential property or for failure to disclose defects or conditions in property that substantially affect value or habitability, of which broker is aware or reasonably should be aware and of which purchaser is not aware and would not discover by reasonably diligent inspection, with additional requirement that misrepresentation or concealment be a substantial factor in inducing the purchaser to buy the property"). *But see Powell v. Time Insurance Co.*, 382 S.E.2d 342, Syl. Pt. 4 (W. Va. 1989) (finding misrepresentations made by insured in application for insurance fraudulent only when material and knowingly made with intent to deceive insurer).

121. *See* W. Va. Code chs. 46A & 46B (1999).

122. W. Va. Code § 46A-6-104 (1999).

123. *See* W. Va. Code § 46A-7-109 (1999).

124. *See* W. Va. Code § 46A-6-106 (1999).

125. *Alkire v. First Nat'l Bank of Parsons*, 475 S.E.2d 122, 129 (W. Va. 1996) (citing *Mayer v. Frobe*, 22 S.E. 58, Syl. Pt. 4 (W. Va. 1895)).

126. *See Jarvis v. Modern Woodmen of America*, 406 S.E.2d 736, 742 (W. Va. 1991) (citing *Hensley v. Erie Ins. Co.*, 283 S.E.2d 227, 233 (W. Va. 1981)).

127. *LaPlaca v. Odeh*, 428 S.E.2d 322, Syl. (W. Va. 1993) (citing *Toler v. Cassinelli*, 41 S.E.2d 672, Syl. Pt. 3 (W. Va. 1946)).

128. *See Alkire*, 475 S.E.2d 122, 131 n.10 (W. Va. 1996) (citing *Garnes v. Fleming Landfill, Inc.*, 413 S.E.2d 897, Syl. Pt. 3 (W. Va. 1991)).

129. *Id.*

130. *Id.* (citing *Garnes*, 413 S.E.2d at Syl. Pt. 4).

131. *See Sheetz, Inc. v. Bowles, Rice, McDavid, Graff & Love*, 547 S.E.2d 256, 272-76 (2001) (discussing *Tudor v. Charleston Area Medical Center*, 506 S.E.2d 554, Syl. Pt. 14 (W. Va. 1997)).

132. *See* W. Va. Code §§ 55-7-5--55-7-8a (2000). *See also Farley v. Sartin*, 466 S.E.2d 522, 525-26 (W. Va. 1995); *Baldwin v. Butcher*, 184 S.E.2d 428, 431 (W. Va. 1971). Section 55-7-6 should be read in *pari materia* with Section 55-7-6. *Adams v. Grogg*, 166 S.E.2d 755, 756 (W. Va. 1969), *overruled on other grounds by Lee v. Comer*, 224 S.E.2d 721 (W. Va. 1976).

133. *See* W. Va. Code § 55-7-6(b) (2000).

134. *See* W. Va. Code § 55-7-8 (2000). *See also City of Wheeling v. American Cas. Co.*, 48 S.E.2d 404, 408 (W. Va. 1948).

135. *See* W. Va. Code § 55-7-7 (2000). *See also Estate of Helmick ex rel. Fox v. Martin*, 425 S.E.2d 235, Syl. Pt. 3 (W. Va. 1992).

136. *Bower v. Westinghouse Elec. Corp.*, 522 S.E.2d 424, Syl. Pt. 2 (W. Va. 1999).

137. *Id.* at Syl. Pt. 3

WISCONSIN

A. STATUTES OF LIMITATION

Wisconsin's statute of limitation for causes of action seeking damages to recover for "injuries to the person" is three years.[1] Wrongful death actions must also be brought within the three-year statute of limitation. The beginning of the tolling period is either the date when the cause of action accrues or as otherwise specified by law.[2] The "discovery" rule applies.[3] Wisconsin has carved out an exception in asbestos-related injuries, such that although the plaintiff previously discovered that he had a non-malignant asbestos-related disease, the subsequent discovery of a malignancy is a separate disease and starts the limitations period running anew for that malignancy.[4]

Causes of action based on contract, whether express or implied, must be brought within six years after the cause of action accrues.[5] A contract cause of action accrues at the time of the breach. The discovery rule is not applicable.[6]

Causes of action for damage to real or personal property must be brought within six years,[7] and the discovery rule applies.[8]

Libel, slander, and other intentional torts have a two-year statute of limitation.[9] The discovery rule applies.[10]

Actions for contribution or indemnification must be commenced within one year after the action accrues.[11]

There is a six-year "catch-all" provision for all causes of action created by statute where a specific statute of limitation is not delineated.[12] However, the "catch-all" provision does not apply to subrogation claims.[13]

Wisconsin has no statute of repose for products liability despite the Supreme Court's suggestion that such a statute is needed.[14]

Wisconsin has a ten-year statute of repose which is applicable to actions involving improvements to real property.[15] The statute protects architects, engineers, contractors, and materialmen in connection with real property improvements, however, it does not apply to manufacturers or suppliers of products or their components.[16]

Wisconsin has enacted several statutory requirements that must be met before a suit may be commenced against a governmental subdivision or its employees. Within 120 days of the event or occurrence giving rise to the injury, a plaintiff must file a notice of injury or circumstances with the governmental body.[17] If the notice of injury or circumstances is not filed, a suit may still be maintained if the governmental body had actual notice and a plaintiff can demonstrate that it was not prejudiced by the failure to file the notice.[18]

A second statutory requirement mandates that a plaintiff also file a notice of claim with the governmental body. The notice of claim must contain an itemized statement of the relief being sought.[19] The notice of claim is a separate and distinct instrument from the notice of injury or circumstances. After the notice of claim is filed, the governmental body has 120 days to evaluate and settle or disallow the notice of claim.[20] If no official written disallowance of the claim has been received by the plaintiff within 120 days of its filing, the claim is then deemed disallowed. Once the notice of claim is disallowed, the plaintiff must commence suit within six months or the suit is barred.[21] The notice of claim provisions, along with Wisconsin's tolling statute extend the initial three-year personal injury statute of limitations by 120 days for all claims subject to the notice requirement.[22]

If the occurrence that gives rise to an injury is a result of medical malpractice, a plaintiff must file a notice of injury or circumstances within 180 days after discovery of the injury.[23]

B. TORT REFORM

Wisconsin within the past several years has passed a number of "tort reform" statutes, including provisions dealing with joint and several liability, punitive damages (both discussed in their respective sections), insurance coverage, and medical malpractice. However, the Wisconsin Supreme Court has recently ruled that retroactive application of the joint and several liability changes is unconstitutional.[24]

A recently-enacted Wisconsin statute overturns case law which held that insurers could not prohibit the stacking of uninsured and under-insured motorists coverage. An insurer may now include anti-stacking clauses in its insurance policies.[25] Insurers may now also reduce coverages by the amount the insured receives from a legally-responsible party, a workers' compensation carrier, and/or a disability benefits policy.[26] Insurance policies also may now contain a "drive-other-car" exclusion which allows the policy to provide that it does not apply to loss resulting from use of a motor vehicle owned by the insured, or a relative living in the same household, when a vehicle is not described in the policy and is not covered under the terms of the policy as a newly-acquired or replacement motor vehicle.[27]

In the medical malpractice area, Wisconsin law now requires that future medical expenses in excess of $100,000 be paid into the Wisconsin Patients' Compensation Fund. The payments are to be made under a system to be developed by the insurance commissioner and continue until the account is exhausted or the patient dies.[28] Additionally, if liability for future payments is more than $1,000,000, the Patients' Compensation Fund is to pay no more than $500,000 per year after deducting costs of collection and full medical expenses.[29] The total noneconomic damages for each occurrence is limited to $350,000.[30] The amount of damages recoverable in a wrongful death cause of action due to medical malpractice is $500,000 in the case of a minor and $350,000 in the case of an adult.[31]

C. "NO FAULT" LIMITATIONS

Wisconsin has not passed any no fault insurance provisions.

D. THE STANDARD FOR NEGLIGENCE

The plaintiff must show the existence of a duty of care on the part of the defendant, a breach of that duty, a causal connection between the breach and the injury, and actual loss or damage to maintain a cause of action for negligence.[32] Unlike most jurisdictions, a plaintiff in Wisconsin need not demonstrate that he or she was owed a specific duty by a defendant. Wisconsin courts have stated that every person owes a duty of care to everyone else to refrain from conduct which may result in harm.[33] A person breaches this duty when he or she fails to exercise "ordinary care" which is defined as the degree of care that an ordinary person would exercise under similar circumstances.[34]

Wisconsin recognizes a professional standard of care.[35] Wisconsin has not adopted the rule that the existence of a special relationship creates a higher duty of care, however, if a special relationship exists, the court may find an exception to the general rule that there is no duty to control the actions of third parties or protect others from harm.[36]

The standard of care applied to the actions of children is that of an ordinary child of the same age, intelligence, and experience under the same circumstances.[37] Children less than seven years old are conclusively presumed incapable of negligence or contributory negligence.[38] Mentally disabled individuals are held to the same standard of care as a person who has normal mental capacity.[39]

The presumption that due care was exercised by a deceased person is used, however, the presumption is rebutttable and may be overcome by the presentation of contrary evidence.[40]

E. CAUSATION

A plaintiff must demonstrate that the defendant's negligence was a "substantial factor" in producing the harm or injury.[41] In Wisconsin, the doctrine of proximate cause, as used in its traditional sense, has been replaced by the substantial factor or legal cause test. As such, there may be several substantial factors contributing to the same harm or injury.[42]

F. CONTRIBUTORY NEGLIGENCE, COMPARATIVE NEGLIGENCE, AND ASSUMPTION OF RISK

1. Contributory Negligence

The Wisconsin legislature long ago abolished contributory negligence as an absolute bar to recovery for injuries, death, or property damage.[43]

The doctrine is now encompassed and governed by Wisconsin's Comparative Negligence Statute.

2. **Comparative Negligence**

Wisconsin's comparative negligence law applies to actions for death, personal injury, or property damage.[44] A plaintiff may recover damages when his or her negligence does not exceed the negligence attributed to any defendant. The negligence of each defendant is separately measured against any negligence attributed to the plaintiff (*see* Joint & Several Liability section). A court may grant summary judgment for the defendant when the plaintiff, as a matter of law, is at least 51 percent contributorily negligent.[45] The plaintiff's recovery is reduced in proportion to the percentage of negligence attributed to him or her.[46]

Comparative negligence principles will reduce the amount of damages recovered in a strict products liability action.[47] The amount of damages a plaintiff recovers will be reduced by the percentage of negligence attributed to him or her. However, the comparison is only made as between the plaintiff and the "product." Consequently, the comparison is not applied as to each individual defendant in the chain of commerce.[48]

Comparative negligence principles will not proportionateley reduce an award of punitive damages.[49] A plaintiff's ordinary negligence would still be compared to a defendant's negligence, even if the defendant's negligence would form the basis for the imposition of punitive damages.

3. **Assumption of Risk**

Express assumption of risk, for example by way of contract, remains a viable absolute defense in Wisconsin. However, implied assumption of risk is now framed in terms of comparative negligence principles.[50] Express assumption of risk, defined as express consent to exposure to a particular hazard, remains a viable defense.[51] The Wisconsin Court of Appeals has also held that where a plaintiff confronts an open and obvious danger, it is merely an element to be considered by the jury in apportioning negligence and will not bar plaintiff's recovery.[52]

G. *RES IPSA LOQUITUR* AND INHERENTLY DANGEROUS ACTIVITIES

1. *Res Ipsa Loquitur*

Wisconsin courts will permit a *res ipsa loquitur* inference, that the defendant caused the plaintiff's harm, if: (1) the accident is the kind which does not ordinarily occur absent someone's negligence; and (2) the event was caused by an agency or instrumentality within the exclusive control of the defendant.[53] The doctrine constitutes a permissive inference in Wisconsin.[54]

2. Inherently Dangerous Activities

The reasonable care standard applies, however, the standard of care increases as the amount of danger increases.[55]

H. NEGLIGENCE *PER SE*

Negligence *per se* results from a violation of a statute in which the legislature has established the proper standard of care.[56] If the fact-finder determines that the statute was violated, the duty and breach elements of a cause of action are conclusively determined to have been met. However, the plaintiff must still prove that the defendant's negligence was a substantial factor, and comparative negligence principles still apply.[57]

I. JOINT AND SEVERAL LIABILITY

Recent amendments to Wisconsin law have all but abolished joint and several liability. The negligence of the plaintiff is now measured separately against the negligence of each party found to be causally negligent. In addition, the liability of each causally negligent party is limited to its percentage of causal negligence if such causal negligence is less than 51 percent. If the causally negligent party is 51 percent or more causally at fault, then it is still jointly and severally liable to the plaintiff. Joint and several liability also is still allowed against parties acting with a common scheme or plan.[58]

A plaintiff may discharge one tort defendant through a release without discharging another—known as a Perringer release.[59] If this is done, the plaintiff agrees to satisfy the settling defendant's percentage of the ultimate judgment in the case based on the apportionment of negligence. This also discharges the released party from liability for contribution to nonsettling tortfeasors.[60] A release of an intentional tortfeasor also releases nonsettling, negligent tortfeasors from any claims by plaintiff because the nonsettling negligent tortfeasor has a right to indemnity from the intentional tortfeasor.[61] A release of a wholly-negligent joint venturer also releases other joint venturers.[62]

Contribution is allowed between joint tortfeasors, and it requires each party to pay their proportionate share of damages on a comparative fault basis.[63] A contribution claim must be brought within one year from when the party seeking contribution paid more than its share.[64]

J. INDEMNITY

Indemnity shifts an entire loss from one person who has been compelled to pay it to another, who on the basis of equitable principles, should bear the loss.[65] Indemnification may be provided for by contract, however, an indemnification agreement which purports to cover a party for his own negligent acts is valid only if it is explicitly stated in the agreement that such a result was clearly intended.[66]

K. BAR OF WORKERS' COMPENSATION STATUTE

Under Wisconsin's Workers' Compensation Act, an employee is barred from suing his employer for work-related injuries, and recovery under the Act is the employee's exclusive remedy as against the employer.[67] The employer assumes responsibility regardless of fault. The making of a claim for benefits for injury or death does not eliminate the right of the employee to make a claim against third parties for such injury or death.[68]

Where an employee who has received benefits sues a third party, the employer, or their insurer, is automatically subrogated to the rights of the employee for the amount of its payments. Any funds recovered are apportioned by the statutorily-imposed formula.[69] An employer or insurer does not have to participate in the action to recover for its payments,[70] and third-party tortfeasors may not sue the employer or insurer for contribution.[71]

The Workers' Compensation Act does not bar a suit against a coemployee for assault, negligent operation of a nonemployer owned or leased vehicle,[72] or for negligent supervision by a coemployee.[73]

L. PREMISES LIABILITY

A landowner owes invitees as well as licensees the same duty of care, that of ordinary care.[74] A landowner is not liable to a trespasser for damages resulting from a lack of ordinary care, but he or she has a duty to refrain from willful and intentional infliction of injury.[75] Wisconsin courts have acknowledged that there may be a duty to warn of highly dangerous conditions.[76] Wisconsin recognizes the doctrine of "attractive nuisance" which acts as an exception to the general doctrine for trespassers who are minors.[77]

Wisconsin has enacted a recreational activities statute which provides that no landowner or agent owes a person who enters property to engage in recreational activity (1) a duty to keep the property safe for recreational activity; (2) a duty to inspect the property; or (3) a duty to warn of an unsafe condition, use, or activity on the property.[78] The statute specifically deliniates certain examples of recreational activities, however, the definition of "recreational" as to activities not specifically listed is subjective.[79]

Wisconsin has also enacted a "Safe Place Statute" which requires a higher degree of care by landowners who provide a place of employment. The statute provides that an employer shall furnish a place of employment which shall be safe for the employees therein and frequenters, in that the property owner shall adopt and use methods and processes reasonably adequate to render such employment and places of employment safe.[80] Owners or employers may be imputed with constructive knowledge of a hazard, and thus found liable, if the defect existed for a sufficient period of time so that the employer or owner should have discovered and remedied the problem. However, when no evidence has been offered as to how long a hazard existed, a defendant will not be found liable for injuries resulting from the hazard.[81]

M. DRAM SHOP LIABILITY

Wisconsin has enacted a general statute of immunity which provides that a person is immune from civil liability arising out of the act of procuring, selling, dispensing, or giving away alcoholic beverages to another person.[82] The word "person" includes all partnerships, corporations, associations, or bodies politic, as well as natural persons.[83]

The grant of immunity does not apply if the person who is invoking it has provided or sold alcoholic beverages to a person who the provider knew, or should have known, was under the legal drinking age of 21, and the beverages were a substantial factor in causing injury to a third party. In determining whether the grant of immunity applies, the court must consider all of the facts and circumstances, and immunity will exist if the underaged person falsely represented their age, the underaged person supported the representation with documentation, the beverages were provided in good faith reliance on the representation, and the underaged person appeared to a reasonable person to be of legal drinking age.[84] However, the court may use any or all of the listed factors and determine that the grant of immunity should apply.[85] The sale of alcoholic beverages to a minor is negligence *per se*, but the fact-finder must still find that the sale was a substantial factor in causing injuries sustained by third party.[86] An underage claimant's participation in procuring alcohol will preclude him or her from asserting the exception for injured third parties.[87]

N. ECONOMIC LOSS

The economic loss doctrine traditionally precludes a commercial purchaser from recovering economic losses, including damage to the product itself, caused by a defective product.[88] The purchaser is limited to contractual damages. The doctrine does not preclude recovery of economic losses arising from damage to property other than the defective product itself,[89] however, it does preclude recovery when the defective product caused damage to a system into which the purchaser had integrated the product as a component part.[90]

Wisconsin has adopted an exception to the economic loss doctrine when the product at issue is inherently dangerous, such as asbestos.[91] This exception has been narrowly construed, and Wisconsin has not created a broader "public safety" exception for the sale of products that could have dangerous applications.[92] Wisconsin courts have recently expanded the doctrine to preclude recoveries for "consumer transactions"[93] even if the product was damaged under "sudden and calamitous" conditions.[94]

O. FRAUD AND MISREPRESENTATION

Wisconsin Rules of Civil Procedure require that a cause of action based upon fraud be plead with particularity.[95]

The elements for fraud or intentional misrepresentation must be proved by clear and convincing evidence.[96] These include: (1) a representation of fact;

(2) that the representation was untrue; (3) that the representation was made knowing that it was untrue or recklessly without caring whether it was true or false; (4) that the defendant made the representation with intent to deceive and induce the plaintiff to act upon it to the plaintiff's detriment; and (5) that the plaintiff believed the representation to be true and relied on it.[97]

The elements of negligent misrepresentation are: (1) that the defendant made a representation of fact; (2) that the representation of fact was untrue; (3) that the defendant was negligent in making the representation (negligence is used in its ordinary sense—failure to exercise ordinary care); and (4) that the plaintiff believed the representation to be true and relied thereon to his or her detriment.[98]

P. CONSUMER FRAUD STATUTES

Wisconsin law prohibits unfair methods of competition and trade practices.[99] The state may prosecute actions, or individual citizens may bring suit.[100] A citizen who successfully brings suit shall recover double damages plus reasonable actual attorneys' fees.[101]

Wisconsin law also prohibits fraudulent representations by sellers.[102] The state or private citizen may prosecute actions, and a private citizen recovers double damages plus reasonable actual attorneys' fees if successful. These causes of action fall under Wisconsin's six-year statute of limitations.[103]

Q. PUNITIVE DAMAGES

Wisconsin's Punitive Damage Statute, enacted in 1995, provides that a plaintiff may recover punitive damages if evidence is introduced showing that the defendant acted "maliciously toward the plaintiff or in an intentional disregard of the rights of the plaintiff."[104] The statute was intended to create a higher burden than prior case law which allowed punitive damages for conduct which demonstrated a "reckless indifference to, or disregard" of the rights of others.[105] If the plaintiff establishes a *prima facia* case for punitive damages, then the plaintiff may introduce evidence of the wealth of the defendant, and the judge must submit a special verdict regarding punitive damages to the jury. Joint and several liability does not apply to punitive damages.

Punitive damages are not awarded for wrongful death actions.[106] A party must recover compensatory damages in order to state a claim for punitive damages. Consequently, if a plaintiff is barred from receiving compensatory damages under Wisconsin's comparative negligence law, they are not entitled to punitive damages.[107] However, nominal damages may support a recovery.[108]

It is not against Wisconsin Public Policy to insure against punitive damages. Where the language of the policy does not specifically exclude coverage of punitive damages, the court will find in favor of coverage.[109]

R. **WRONGFUL DEATH AND SURVIVORSHIP ACTIONS**

The right to sue for wrongful death is strictly statutory, because no cause of action existed at common law.[110] Wisconsin statutes provide for a wrongful death cause of action which allows survivors, designated by statute, to sue for their own loss caused by the decedents's death.[111] Also, a decedent's estate may bring a survival action for pre-death medical expenses, lost wages, and pain/suffering damages.[112] The right of survivors to recover for wrongful death is limited to cases in which the decedent could have recovered damages if he or she had lived,[113] therefore, the decedent's negligence is automatically attributed to the survivor/plaintiff(s).[114]

Under Wisconsin's Wrongful Death Statute, any person entitled to recover may obtain all damages "for pecuniary injury from wrongful death."[115] "Pecuniary injury" means "a loss of any benefit which the beneficiary would have received from the decedent if the decedent had lived."[116] Damages for loss of society and companionship may be recovered by a spouse, children, parents, or siblings (who were minors at the time of the accident) of the decedent.[117] Recovery for loss of society and companionship damages is statutorily capped at $500,000 in the case of a deceased minor and $350,000 in the case of an deceased adult.[118] The statute does not limit recovery for pecuniary loss. Loss of society and companionship damages based on a claim against a governmental body, however, is limited to $50,000.[119] Punitive damages are not available in wrongful death claims, however, they may be awarded in survival actions upon evidence of the deceased pain and suffering prior to death.[120]

J. Ric Gass
Thomas Gonzalez
Kravit, Gass, Hovel & Leitner, S.C.
825 N. Jefferson, Suite 500
Milwaukee, Wisconsin 53202
(414) 271-7100
Fax (414) 271-8135
jrg@kravit-gass.com
tg@kravit-gass.com

ENDNOTES - WISCONSIN

1. Wis. Stat. § 893.54.

2. Wis. Stat. § 893.04.

3. *Hansen v. A.H. Robbins, Inc.*, 113 Wis. 2d 550, 335 N.W.2d 578 (1983).

4. *Sopha v. Owens-Corning Fiberglass Corp.*, 230 Wis. 2d 212, 601 N.W.2d 627 (1999).

5. Wis. Stat. § 893.43.

6. *CLL Assoc. v. Arrowhead Pacific*, 174 Wis. 2d 604, 497 N.W.2d 115 (1993).

7. Wis. Stat. § 893.52.

8. *Koplin v. Pioneer Power & Light*, 162 Wis. 2d 1, 469 N.W.2d 595 (1991).

9. Wis. Stat. § 893.57.

10. *Spitler v. Dean*, 148 Wis. 2d 630, 436 N.W.2d 308 (1989).

11. Wis. Stat. § 893.92.

12. Wis. Stat. § 893.93(1).

13. *Schwittay v. Sheboygan Falls Mutual Ins. Co.*, 2001 WI App. 140, 246 Wis. 2d 385, 630 N.W.2d 772.

14. *Sharp v. Case Corp.*, 227 Wis. 2d 1, 595 N.W. 2d 380 (1999).

15. Wis. Stat. § 893.89.

16. *Swanson Furniture Co. of Marshfield, Inc. v. Advance Transformer Co.*, 105 Wis. 2d 321, 313 N.W. 2d 840 (1982).

17. Wis. Stat. § 893.80(1g).

18. *Id.*

19. Wis. Stat. § 893.80(1)(b).

20. Wis. Stat. § 893.80(1g).

21. *Id.*

22. *Colby v. Columbia County,* 202 Wis. 2d 342, 550 N.W. 2d 124 (1996).

23. Wis. Stat. § 893.80(1)(m).

24. *Matthies v. The Positive Safety Manufacturing Co.,* 2001 WI 82, 244 Wis. 2d 720, 628 N.W.2d 842.

25. Wis. Stat. § 632.32(5).

26. Wis. Stat. § 632.32(5)(i).

27. Wis. Stat. § 632.32(5)(j).

28. Wis. Stat. § 655.01(5).

29. Wis. Stat. § 655.27(5)(d).

30. Wis. Stat. § 893.55(4)(d).

31. Wis. Stat. §§ 893.55(4)(f) and 895.04(4).

32. *Rockweit v. Senecal,* 197 Wis. 2d 409, 418, 541 N.W.2d 742 (1995).

33. *Peters v. Menard, Inc.,* 224 Wis. 2d 174, 589 N.W.2d 395 (1999).

34. *Osbourne v. Montgomery,* 203 Wis. 223, 234 N.W. 372 (1931).

35. *Nowatske v. Osterloh,* 198 Wis. 2d 419, 543 N.W.2d 265 (1996); *Duffy Law Office v. Tank Transport, Inc.,* 194 Wis. 2d 675, 535 N.W.2d 91 (1995); *Nelson v. Davidson,* 155 Wis. 2d 674, 680-82, 456 N.W.2d 343 (1990).

36. *DeBauche v. Knott,* 69 Wis. 2d 119, 122-23, 230 N.W.2d 158, 160-61 (1975); *Gritzner v. Michael R.,* 228 Wis. 2d 541, 598 N.W.2d 282 (Ct. App. 1999).

37. *Brice v. Milwaukee Auto Ins. Co.,* 272 Wis. 520, 76 N.W.2d 337 (1956).

38. Wis. Stat. § 891.44.

39. *Burch v. American Family Mut. Ins. Co.,* 198 Wis. 2d 465, 475, 543 N.W.2d 277 (1996).

40. *Fiedler v. Kapsa,* 255 Wis. 559, 39 N.W.2d 682 (1949).

41. *Pfeifer v. Standard Gateway Theatre, Inc.,* 262 Wis. 229, 236-38, 55 N.W.2d 29 (1952).

42. *Sampson v. Laskin*, 66 Wis. 2d 318, 325, 224 N.W.2d 594 (1975).

43. Wis. Stat. § 895.045(1).

44. *Id.*

45. *Jankee v. Clark County*, 2000 WI 64, 235 Wis. 2d 700, 612 N.W. 2d 297.

46. *Id.*

47. *Fuchsgruber v. Custom Accessories, Inc.* 2000 WI 81, 244 Wis. 2d 758, 628 N.W.2d 833.

48. *Id.*

49. *Tucker v. Marcus*, 142 Wis. 2d 425, 418 N.W.2d 818 (1988).

50. *Polsky v. Levine*, 73 Wis. 2d 547, 243 N.W.2d 503 (1974).

51. *Polsky v. Levine*, 73 Wis. 2d 547, 243 N.W.2d 503 (1976).

52. *Wagner v. Wisconsin Mun. Mut. Ins. Co.*, 230 Wis.2d 633, 601 N.W. 2d 856 (Ct. App. 1999).

53. *Freitag v. City of Montello*, 36 Wis. 2d 409, 153 N.W.2d 505 (1967).

54. *Millonig v. Bakken*, 112 Wis. 2d 445, 334 N.W.2d 80 (1983).

55. Wis. J.I.—Civ. 1020.

56. *D.L. v. Huebner*, 110 Wis. 2d 581, 329 N.W.2d 890 (1983) (*overruled on other grounds*).

57. *Id.*

58. Wis. Stat. § 895.045.

59. *Perringer v. Hoger*, 21 Wis. 2d 182, 124 N.W.2d 106 (1963).

60. *I-Mark Industries v. Arthur Young & Co.*, 148 Wis. 2d 605, 436 N.W.2d 311 (1989).

61. *Fleming v. Threshermen's Mut. Ins. Co.*, 131 Wis. 2d 123, 388 N.W.2d 908 (1986).

62. *Schroeder v. Pedersen*, 131 Wis. 2d 446, 388 N.W.2d 927 (1986).

63. *Swanigan v. State Farm Ins. Co.*, 99 Wis. 2d 179, 299 N.W.2d 234 (1980).

64. Wis. Stat. § 893.92.

65. *Kiellsen v. Stonecrest, Inc.*, 47 Wis. 2d 8, 12, 176 N.W.2d 321 (1970).

66. *Spivey v. Great Atlantic & Pacific Tea Co.*, 79 Wis. 2d 58, 63, 255 N.W.2d 469 (1977).

67. Wis. Stat. § 102.03(2).

68. Wis. Stat. § 102.29(1).

69. *Id.*

70. *Guyette v. West Bend Mut. Ins. Co.*, 102 Wis. 2d 496, 307 N.W.2d 311 (Ct. App. 1981).

71. *Mulder v. Acme-Cleveland Corp.*, 95 Wis. 2d 173, 290 N.W.2d 276 (1980).

72. Wis. Stat. § 102.29(2).

73. *Lampada v. State Sand & Gravel Co.*, 58 Wis. 2d 315, 206 N.W.2d 138 (1973).

74. *Antoniewicz v. Reszczynski*, 70 Wis. 2d 836, 856-57, 236 N.W.2d 1 (1975).

75. *Shannon v. Shannon*, 150 Wis.2d 434, 442 N.W.2d 25 (1989).

76. *Szafranski v. Radetzky*, 31 Wis. 2d 119, 126, 141 N.W.2d 902 (1966).

77. *McWilliams v. Guzinski*, 71 Wis. 2d 57, 61-62, 237 N.W.2d 437 (1975).

78. Wis. Stat. § 895.52(2).

79. *Auman v. Sch. Dis. of Stanley–Boyd*, 2001 WI 125, 635 N.W. 2d 762.

80. Wis. Stat. § 101.11(1).

81. *Low v. Siewert*, 54 Wis. 2d 251, 195 N.W.2d 451 (1972).

82. Wis. Stat. § 125.035(2).

83. Wis. Stat. § 990.01(26).

84. Wis. Stat. § 125.035(4)(b).

85. *Id.*

86. *Paskiet v. Quality State Oil Company, Inc.*, 164 Wis. 2d 800, 476 N.W.2d 871 (1991).

87. *Meier v. Champ's Sportsbar and Grill, Inc.* 2000 WI 20, 241 Wis. 2d 605, 623 N.W.2d 94.

88. *Sunnyslope Grading, Inc. v. Miller, Bradford & Risberg, Inc.*, 148 Wis. 2d 910, 437 N.W.2d 213 (1989).

89. *Northridge Co. v. W.R. Grace & Co.*, 162 Wis. 2d 918, 923, 471 N.W.2d 179 (1991).

90. *Midwhey Powder Co. v. Clayton Industries*, 157 Wis. 2d 585, 590-91, 460 N.W.2d 426 (Ct. App. 1990).

91. *Northridge Co. v. W.R. Grace & Co.*, 162 Wis. 2d 918, 471 N.W. 2d 179 (1991).

92. *Wausau Tile, Inc. v. County Concrete Corp.*, 226 Wis. 2d 235, 539 N.W. 2d 445 (1999).

93. *State Farm Mut. Auto. Ins. Co. v. Ford Motor Co.*, 225 Wis. 2d 305, 592 N.W.2d 201 (1999).

94. *General Casualty Co. of Wisconsin v. Ford Motor Co.*, 225 Wis. 2d 353, 592 N.W.2d 198 (1999).

95. Wis. Stat. § 802.03(2).

96. Wis. J.I.—Civ. 2401.

97. *Id.*

98. Wis. J.I.—Civ. 2403.

99. Wis. Stat. § 100.20(1).

100. Wis. Stat. §§ 100.20(4) and (5).

101. Wis. Stat. § 100.20(5).

102. Wis. Stat. § 100.18(1).

103. Wis. Stat. § 893.93(1).

104. Wis. Stat. § 895.85.

105. Wis. J.I.—Civ. 1707.01.

106. *Wangen v. Ford Motor Co.*, 97 Wis. 2d 260, 294 N.W.2d 437 (1980).

107. *Tucker v. Marcus*, 142 Wis. 2d 425, 418 N.W.2d 818 (1988).

108. *Jacque v. Steenberg Homes*, 209 Wis. 2d 605, 563 N.W.2d 154 (1997).

109. *Brown v. Maxey*, 124 Wis. 2d 426, 369 N.W. 2d 677 (1985).

110. *Krause v. Home Mutual Ins. Co.*, 14 Wis. 2d 666, 112 N.W.2d 144 (1961).

111. Wis. Stat. §§ 895.03 and 895.04.

112. Wis. Stat. § 895.01(1).

113. Wis .Stat. § 895.03; *Haase v. Employer's Mutual Liability Ins. Co.*, 250 Wis. 422, 433 27 N.W.2d 468 (1947).

114. Wis. Stat. § 895.04(7); *Delvaux v. Vanden Langenberg*, 130 Wis. 2d 464, 387 N.W.2d 751 (1986).

115. Wis. Stat. § 895.04(4).

116. *Estate of Holt v. State Farm Fire & Casualty Co.*, 151 Wis. 2d 455, 460, 444 N.W.2d 453 (Ct. App. 1989).

117. Wis. Stat. § 895.04(4).

118. *Id.*

119. Wis. Stat. § 893.80 (3).

120. *Wangen v. Ford Motor Co.*, 97 Wis. 2d 260, 294 N.W.2d 437 (1980).

WYOMING

A. STATUTES OF LIMITATION

Wyoming is a "discovery" state in which the statute of limitations is triggered when the plaintiff knows or has reason to know of the existence of a cause of action.[1]

No action may be brought against the state or governmental entity, unless the party first files a notice of claim within two years of the alleged act, error, or omission, regardless of the statute of limitations for the cause of action.[2] The plaintiff has one year from the date of filing the notice of claim to file suit.[3]

A negligence cause of action must be brought within four years after the cause of action accrues.[4]

A cause of action for intentional infliction of emotional distress must be brought within four years.[5]

A cause of action for strict liability must be brought within four years from the date of injury.[6]

A wrongful death cause of action must be brought within two years after the death of the decedent.[7]

The limitation period found in the wrongful death statute is a condition precedent, not a statute of limitations, and the discovery rule does not apply to a condition precedent.[8]

A ten-year statute of repose applies to actions involving improvements to real property.[9]

A legal malpractice cause of action must be brought within two years from the alleged act, error, or omission, or two years from the discovery of alleged act, error, or omission if not reasonably discoverable.[10]

If the alleged act, error, or omission is discovered during the second year of the two-year period, the period for commencing a lawsuit is extended by six months.[11]

For injury to a minor, suit must be brought by his/her eighth birthday or two years from discovery of the alleged act, error, or omission, whichever is longer.[12]

Wyoming has not adopted continuous representation doctrine to toll the statute of limitations on legal malpractice claims.[13]

A medical malpractice cause of action must be brought within two years from the alleged act, error, or omission or two years from the discovery of alleged act, error, or omission if not reasonably discoverable.[14]

If the alleged act, error, or omission is discovered during the second year of the two-year period, the period for commencing a lawsuit is extended by six months.[15]

For injury to a minor, suit must be brought by his/her eighth birthday or two years from discovery of the alleged act, error, or omission, whichever is longer.[16]

Act, error, or omission that starts the running of the statute of limitations in a medical malpractice cause of action is the termination of course of treatment for the same or related illness or injury.[17]

A cause of action for libel or slander must be brought within one year.[18]

An invasion of privacy claim must be brought within one year.[19]

No action may be brought under Wyoming's Consumer Protection Act, unless the consumer bringing the action gives written notice to the alleged violator of the Act within one year after the initial discovery of the unlawful deceptive trade practice or within two years following the consumer transaction, whichever occurs first. The consumer has one year from the date of furnishing written notice to file suit.[20]

A products liability or breach of warranty claim must be brought within four years from the date of delivery of the product.[21]

A workers' compensation claim for benefits involving an injury that is the result of a single brief occurrence must be filed within one year after the date the injury occurred, or for injuries not readily apparent, within one year after discovery of the injury by the employee.[22]

A "catch-all" provision for an injury to the rights of the plaintiff, not arising on contract and not enumerated elsewhere within the statutes, is four years.[23]

B. TORT REFORM

To date, the Wyoming legislature has not passed any tort reform laws.

C. "NO FAULT" LIMITATIONS

To date, the Wyoming legislature has not passed any statutes relating to "no fault" limitations.

D. THE STANDARD FOR NEGLIGENCE

To sustain a negligence claim, a plaintiff must establish that: (1) the defendant owed a duty to the plaintiff; (2) the defendant breached that duty; (3) the defendant's breach of his duty was the proximate cause of the plaintiff's injuries; and (4) the plaintiff was injured.[24]

1. Duty

A duty may arise by contract, statute, or common law, or when the relationship of the parties is such that the law imposes an obligation on the defendant to act reasonably for the protection of the plaintiff.[25]

2. Breach of Duty

Breach of duty is shown when the plaintiff demonstrates that the defendant engaged in conduct that deviates from the standard of care. The standard of care owed to another is that of a reasonable person in light of all the circumstances.[26]

Children

Children are held to a standard of care that may fairly and reasonably be expected from children of that age.[27]

Willful or Wanton Conduct

Willful misconduct is distinguished from ordinary negligence by the actor's state of mind. To prove that the actor has engaged in willful misconduct, one must demonstrate that he acted with a state of mind that approaches an intent to do harm.[28]

E. CAUSATION

Proximate cause means that the accident or injury was a natural and probable consequence of the act of negligence.[29]

1. Concurrent Cause

A concurrent cause involves acts of negligence of two or more people that, although not working in concert, combine to produce a single injury. Each concurrent cause that contributes directly to the accident or injury is a proximate cause.[30]

2. Intervening Cause

An intervening cause is one that occurs after a defendant's negligent act or omission. An intervening cause does not relieve the earlier actor of liability if it was reasonably foreseeable.[31]

3. Act of God

An act of God is any action that is due directly and exclusively to natural causes without human intervention and which could not have been prevented. To assert the act of God defense, the act of God must be the sole cause of the injury; there can be no combination of an act of God and fault of man.[32]

4. Damage

Damage is an essential element of plaintiff's *prima facie* case for negligence. This means actual harm or injury.[33]

F. COMPARATIVE FAULT

Contributory fault shall not bar a recovery in an action by any claimant to recover damages for wrongful death or injury to person or property, if the contributory fault of the claimant is not more than 50 percent of the total fault of all actors. Any damages allowed shall be diminished in proportion to the amount of fault attributed to the claimant.[34]

The comparative fault statute applies to claims for negligence, strict liability, products liability, and breach of warranty that accrue after July 1, 1994.[35]

The court shall reduce the amount of damages in proportion to the percentage of fault attributed to the claimant.[36]

Joint and several liability is abolished. Each defendant is liable only to the extent of that defendant's proportion of the total fault.[37]

G. *RES IPSA LOQUITUR* AND INHERENTLY DANGEROUS ACTIVITIES

1. *Res Ipsa Loquitur*

    The doctrine of *res ipsa loquitur* is limited to those situations where: (1) something causes injury without fault of the injured person; (2) that thing is under the exclusive control of the defendant; and (3) the injury is one that, in the ordinary course of things, does not occur if the one having such control uses proper care.[38]

    The doctrine of *res ipsa loquitur* cannot be applied when an inference that the injury was due to a cause other than defendant's negligence could be drawn as reasonably as one that it was due to his negligence.[39]

2. **Inherently Dangerous Activities**

    Wyoming does not impose strict liability on individuals engaging in inherently dangerous activities, but instead adheres to the principle that the standard of care is always ordinary or reasonable care under the circumstances.[40]

    Persons who knowingly engage in inherently dangerous activities must exercise care commensurate with the danger involved.[41]

H. **NEGLIGENCE** *PER SE*

The thrust of the negligence *per se* rule is that a legislative or administrative rule fixes a standard of conduct for all members of the community, which does not require a specific interpretation by the jury.[42]

The Wyoming Supreme Court has held, pursuant to Restatement (Second) of Torts Section 286 (1965), that a court may, under certain circumstances, adopt as the standard of conduct of a reasonable man the requirements of a legislative enactment. However, if such a standard is not adopted, the unexcused violation of the enactment may serve as evidence of negligence, but does not establish negligence per se.[43]

I. **JOINT AND SEVERAL LIABILITY**

Joint and several liability is abolished. Each defendant is liable only to the extent of that defendant's proportion of the total fault.[44]

Joint and several liability is abolished in all negligence cases, including those where the plaintiff was not comparatively at fault.[45]

J. INDEMNITY

Indemnity allows one who has discharged a common obligation to recover up to the entire amount that has been paid from the party primarily responsible.[46] A prerequisite to a claim for indemnity is the existence of an independent legal relationship under which the indemnitor owes a duty either in contract or tort to the indemnitee apart from the joint duty owed to the injured party.[47]

The Wyoming Supreme Court has recognized actions for express contractual indemnity, implied contractual indemnity, and equitable implied indemnity under various circumstances.[48]

Wyoming recognizes partial indemnity for indemnity actions premised on negligence that is consistent with the legislative acceptance of comparative fault outlined in Wyo. Stat. Section 1-1-109 (LEXIS 1999).

1. Express Contractual Indemnity

Express indemnity arises from specific language of a contract where one party expressly promises to indemnify the other for a particular kind of loss.[49]

2. Implied Contractual Indemnity

Implied contractual indemnity arises where a duty to indemnify may be implied from a contractual relationship between the party seeking indemnity and the party against whom indemnity is sought so that the latter owes an independent duty to the former.[50]

To state a cause of action for implied contractual indemnity, the indemnitee must allege: (1) an independent relationship with the indemnitor; (2) negligent breach by indemnitor of duty created by independent relationship; (3) under circumstances falling within situations addressed in Section 886B of Restatement (Second) of Torts; and (4) that breach of duty to indemnitee contributed to cause injuries and damage to original plaintiff.[51]

3. Equitable Implied Indemnity

Equitable implied indemnity arises in the absence of a contract or contractual relationship, but where there are equitable reasons under the circumstances allowing indemnity. Equitable implied indemnity actions may be premised on negligence, strict liability, or breach of warranty. The nature of the indemnity available will differ on the theory of liability claimed.[52]

To state a cause of action for equitable implied indemnity, the indemnitee must allege: (1) an independent relationship with the indemnitor; (2) negligent breach by indemnitor of duty created by independent relationship; (3) under circumstances falling within situations addressed in Section 886B of Restatement (Second) of Torts; and

(4) that breach of duty to indemnitee contributed to cause injuries and damage to original plaintiff.[53]

K. BAR OF WORKERS' COMPENSATION STATUTE

1. Exclusive Remedy

The Wyoming Workers' Safety and Compensation Act provides immunity to employers who contribute to the fund for employees injured while acting within the scope of their employment. Wyo. Stat. Section 27-14-104 (LEXIS 1999) provides:

> (a) The rights and remedies provided in this act for an employee including any joint employee, and his dependents for injuries incurred in extrahazardous employment are in lieu of all other rights and remedies against any employer and any joint employer making contributions required by this act, or their employees acting within the scope of their employment unless the employees intentionally act to cause physical harm or injury to the injured employee, but do not supercede any rights and remedies available to an employee and his dependents against any other person.

2. Coemployee Liability

The workers' compensation statute also provides immunity for acts done by coemployees, unless the coemployee intentionally acts to cause physical harm or injury.[54]

3. Third Parties

The workers' compensation statute does not provide immunity to third parties from suit by the injured employee or his dependents. However, as stated above, the third party may have an indemnity claim against the employer.[55]

4. Action Against Third Party or Coemployee

If the injured employee files suit against a third party or coemployee to the extent permitted by Wyo. Stat. Section 27-14-104(a), the employee is required by statute to serve a copy of the complaint with the director of the Department of Employment and with the Attorney General office.[56]

If the employee recovers from the third party or the coemployee in any manner including judgment, compromise, settlement, or release, the state is entitled to be reimbursed for all payments made, or to be made on behalf of the employee but not to exceed one-third of the total proceeds of the recovery.[57]

L. PREMISES LIABILITY

The distinction between tort claimants on the basis of status as licensee or invitee has been abandoned, and, except as to trespassers, a landowner's duty is reasonable care under the circumstances.[58]

A landowner is liable to a trespasser if the landowner is guilty of wanton or willful negligence.[59]

Attractive Nuisance

Attractive nuisance doctrine applies in Wyoming. A landowner is liable to child for physical harm caused by artificial condition if: (1) landowner knows or should know that children are likely to trespass; (2) condition poses unreasonable risk of death or serious bodily harm to trespassing child; (3) the child, because of its youth, does not discover the condition or realize the risk; and (4) the risk greatly outweighs the utility of the condition and the burden of eliminating the risk are slight compared with the risk.[60]

M. DRAM SHOP LIABILITY

No person who has legally provided alcoholic liquor or malt beverage to any other person is liable for damages caused by the intoxication of the other person.[61] This immunity covers both holders of alcoholic licenses and their employees and private individuals serving alcohol in their homes.

A vendor of liquor owes a duty to exercise the degree of care required of a reasonable person in light of all the circumstances. Wyo. Stat. §§ 12-5-301(a)(v) and 12-6-101(a), which prohibit the sale of alcoholic beverages to minors, were meant not only to protect minors but to protect the general public.[62]

Violation of Wyo. Stat. §§ 12-5-301(a)(v) and 12-6-101(a) is evidence of negligence and may be considered by the trier of fact together with other circumstances in determining the issue of negligence.[63]

If any court, parent, or guardian gives written notice to any licensee that his or her child or ward is under the age of 21 years, or any spouse or dependent gives written notice to a licensee that his or her spouse or person liable for the support of the dependent is an habitual drunkard and by reason of habitual drunkenness is neglecting to provide support for the spouse or defendant and the licensee or permitee so notified thereafter sells or gives any alcoholic liquor or malt beverage to the child, ward, or habitual drunkard, the person giving the notice may bring an action in district court, against the licensee and on proof of acts stated in the notice recover in the action the actual damages sustained, punitive damages, and costs.[64]

N. ECONOMIC LOSS

The economic loss rule bars recovery in tort when the plaintiff claims purely economic damages unaccompanied by physical injury to persons or property. The purpose of the economic loss rule is to maintain the distinction between those claims properly brought under contract theory and those that fall within tort principles.[65]

The Wyoming Supreme Court has adopted the economic loss rule in products liability based on negligence and strict liability.[66]

O. FRAUD AND MISREPRESENTATION

1. Intentional Misrepresentation — Fraud — Deceit

The Wyoming Rules of Civil Procedure require that a cause of action for intentional misrepresentation must be pled with particularity and proved by clear and convincing evidence.[67]

To establish a *prima facie* case of intentional misrepresentation, fraud, or deceit, the following elements must be proved: (1) misrepresentation made by the defendant; (2) guilty knowledge or scienter; (3) intent to deceive or cause someone to believe the falsehood; (4) reliance on the misrepresentation; (5) justifiable reliance by the plaintiff on the misrepresentation; and (6) injury or damage to the plaintiff.[68]

2. Negligent Misrepresentation

A cause of action for negligent misrepresentation must be proved by a preponderance of the evidence.[69]

To establish a *prima facie* case of negligent misrepresentation, the following elements must be proved: (1) false information supplied in the course of one's business for guidance of others in their business; (2) failure by the defendant to exercise reasonable care in obtaining or relating the information; and (3) pecuniary loss resulting from justifiable reliance thereon.[70]

Where a contract includes a disclaimer provision, stating that the buyer is not relying upon any representation of the seller or seller's agent, the buyer may not assert a claim for negligent misrepresentation.[71]

P. CONSUMER FRAUD STATUTES

Wyoming's Unfair Trade Practices Act[72] as well as Wyoming's Consumer Protection Act[73] protect consumers from unfair methods of competition and deceptive acts or practices in any trade or commerce. The enforcing authority of these Acts is the Attorney General of Wyoming.[74] Private actions may also be brought under Wyoming's Consumer Protection Act on any uncured unlawful deceptive trade practice; in which case, the plaintiff must establish a causal connection between the unlawful deceptive trade practice and the damages actually suffered.[75]

As previously noted, actions under Wyoming's Consumer Protection Act must be brought within one year after providing written notice to the alleged violator of the Act.[76]

Q. PUNITIVE DAMAGES

The purpose of punitive damages is to punish the tortfeasor and deter that person from repeating the wrongful act in the future.[77]

Absent compensatory damages, there can be no cause of action for punitive damages.[78]

Punitive damages are awarded in negligence actions when the defendant acts or fails to act in reckless disregard of the consequences, and under such circumstances and conditions that a reasonable person would know, or have reason to know, that such conduct would, in a high degree of probability, result in substantial harm to another.[79] Punitive damages are to be awarded only for conduct involving some element of outrage, similar to that usually found in crime.[80]

A claim for punitive damages cannot stand as a separate cause of action; it merely constitutes an element of recovery on the underlying cause of action.[81]

Relying on the United States Supreme Court decision in *BMW of North America, Inc. v. Gore*,[82] the Wyoming Supreme Court adopted the following factors that must be given to the jury to assist them in determining the appropriate amount of punitive damages:

(1) Punitive damages should bear a reasonable relationship to the harm that is likely to occur from the defendant's conduct as well as the harm that actually has occurred. If the actual or likely harm is slight, the damages should be relatively small. If grievous, the damages should be much greater.

(2) The degree of reprehensibility of the defendant's conduct should be considered. The duration of this conduct, the degree of the defendant's awareness of any hazard that his conduct has caused or is likely to cause, and any concealment or "cover-up" of that hazard, and the existence and frequency of similar past conduct, should all be relevant in determining this degree of reprehensibility.

(3) If the wrongful conduct was profitable to the defendant, the punitive damages should remove the profit and should be in excess of the profit, so that the defendant recognizes a loss.

(4) The financial position of the defendant would be relevant.

(5) All the costs of litigation should be included, so as to encourage plaintiffs to bring wrongdoers to trial.

(6) If criminal sanctions have been imposed on the defendant for his conduct, this should be taken into account in mitigation of the punitive damages award.

(7) If there have been other civil actions against the same defendant, based on the same conduct, this should be taken into account in mitigation of the punitive damages award.[83]

R. WRONGFUL DEATH AND SURVIVORSHIP ACTIONS

Under Wyoming's Wrongful Death statute, a wrongful death claim must be brought in the name of a personal representative appointed for that purpose.[84]

The class of plaintiffs who may bring a wrongful death action are defined by intestacy statute.[85]

Damages that may be recovered in a wrongful death claim include loss of probable future companionship, society, and comfort.[86] Under Wyoming law, a minor child may recover for loss of parental consortium; however, parents may not recover for loss of filial companionship.[87]

A wrongful death claim must be brought within two years after the death of the decedent.[88]

Wrongful death claims are derivative claims. Each person entitled to participate in a wrongful death claim must establish his or her damages.[89]

Wyoming recognizes a separate and distinct cause of action under its survival statute.[90] There can be a wrongful death action or a survival action, but not both.

The primary difference between survival and wrongful death statutes is that the survival statute merely continues a cause of action in existence and the injured party's claim after death is an asset of the estate, while the wrongful death statute creates a new cause of action for the benefit of designated persons who have suffered the loss of a loved one and provider.[91]

The survival statute protects the creditors of the estate; the wrongful death statute does not.[92]

Scott P. Klosterman, Esquire
Brown, Drew & Massey, L.L.P.
123 West First Street, Suite 800
Casper, Wyoming 82601
(307) 234-1000
(fax) (307) 265-8025
spk@browndrew.com

ENDNOTES - WYOMING

1. *James v. Montoya*, 963 P.2d 993 (Wyo. 1998).
2. Wyo. Stat. § 1-39-113 (LEXIS 1999).
3. Wyo. Stat. § 1-39-114 (LEXIS 1999).
4. Wyo. Stat. § 1-3-105(a)(iv)(C) (LEXIS 1999).
5. *Gustafson v. Bridger Coal Co.*, 834 F. Supp. 352 (D. Wyo. 1993).
6. *Ogle v. Caterpillar Tractor Co.*, 716 P.2d 334 (Wyo. 1986).
7. Wyo. Stat. § 1-38-102(d) (LEXIS 1999).
8. *Corkill v. Knowles*, 955 P.2d 438 (Wyo. 1998).
9. Wyo. Stat. § 1-3-111 (LEXIS 1999).
10. Wyo. Stat. § 1-3-107(a)(i) (LEXIS 1999).
11. Wyo. Stat. § 1-3-107(a)(iv) (LEXIS 1999).
12. Wyo. Stat. § 1-3-107(a)(ii) (LEXIS 1999).
13. *Connell v. Barrett*, 949 P.2d 871 (Wyo. 1997).
14. Wyo. Stat. § 1-3-107(a)(i) (LEXIS 1999).
15. Wyo. Stat. § 1-3-107(a)(iv) (LEXIS 1999).
16. Wyo. Stat. § 1-3-107(a)(ii) (LEXIS 1999).
17. *Metzger v. Kalke*, 709 P.2d 414 (Wyo. 1985).
18. Wyo. Stat. § 1-3-105(a)(v)(A) (LEXIS 1999).
19. Wyo. Stat. § 1-3-105(a)(v) (LEXIS 1999).
20. Wyo. Stat. § 40-12-109 (LEXIS 1999).
21. *McLaughlin v. Michelin*, 778 P.2d 59 (Wyo. 1989).
22. Wyo. Stat. § 27-14-503(a) (LEXIS 1999).
23. Wyo. Stat. § 1-3-105(a)(iv)(C) (LEXIS 1999).

24. *Anderson v. Duncan*, 968 P.2d 440 (Wyo. 1998).

25. *Hamilton v. Natrona County Educ. Ass'n*, 901 P.2d 381 (Wyo. 1995).

26. *Hill v. Park County by and through Bd. of County Comm'rs*, 856 P.2d 456 (Wyo. 1993).

27. *Smith v. United States*, 546 F.2d 872 (10th Cir. 1976).

28. *Krier v. Safeway Stores 46, Inc.*, 943 P.2d 405 (Wyo. 1997).

29. *Turcq v. Shanahan*, 950 P.2d 47 (Wyo. 1997).

30. *Natural Gas Processing Co. v. Hull*, 886 P.2d 1181 (Wyo. 1994).

31. *Bloomquist v. State*, 914 P.2d 812 (Wyo. 1996).

32. *Ely v. Kirk*, 707 P.2d 706 (Wyo. 1985).

33. *Bird v. Rozier*, 948 P.2d 888 (Wyo. 1997).

34. Wyo. Stat. § 1-1-109(b) (LEXIS 1999).

35. Wyo. Stat. § 1-1-109(a)(iv) (LEXIS 1999).

36. Wyo. Stat. § 1-1-109(d) (LEXIS 1999).

37. Wyo. Stat. § 1-1-109(e) (LEXIS 1999).

38. *Reese v. Board of Directors of Memorial Hosp. of Laramie County*, 955 P.2d 425 (Wyo. 1998).

39. *Id.*

40. *Wilson v. Amoco Corp.*, 33 F. Supp. 981 (D. Wyo. 1998).

41. *Case v. Goss*, 776 P.2d 188 (Wyo. 1989).

42. *Distad v. Cubin*, 633 P.2d 167 (Wyo. 1981).

43. *Pullman v. Outzen*, 924 P.2d 416 (Wyo. 1996).

44. Wyo. Stat. § 1-1-109(e); *see* Section F, Comparative Fault, *supra*.

45. *Anderson Highway Signs & Supply, Inc. v. Close*, 6 P.3d 123 (Wyo. 2000).

46. *Miller v. New York Oil Co.*, 243 P. 118 (Wyo. 1926).

47. *Schneider Nat'l, Inc. v. Holland Hitch Co.*, 843 P.2d 561 (Wyo. 1992).

48. *See, e.g., Diamond Surface, Inc. v. Cleveland,* 963 P.2d 996 (Wyo. 1998); *Northwinds of Wyoming, Inc. v. Phillips Petroleum Co.,* 779 P.2d 753 (Wyo. 1989); *Kemper Architects, P.C. v. McFall, Konkel & Kimball Consulting Engineers, Inc.,* 843 P.2d 1178 (Wyo. 1992); and *Schneider Nat'l, Inc. v. Holland Hitch Co.,* 843 P.2d 561 (Wyo. 1992).

49. *Schneider Nat'l, Inc.,* 843 P.2d at 573.

50. *Id.*

51. *Diamond Surface, Inc. v. Cleveland,* 963 P.2d 996 (Wyo. 1998).

52. *Schneider Nat'l, Inc.,* 843 P.2d at 576.

53. *Diamond Surface, Inc. v. Cleveland,* 963 P.2d 996 (Wyo. 1998).

54. Wyo. Stat. § 27-14-104 (LEXIS 1999).

55. *See* Section J, Indemnity, *supra.*

56. Wyo. Stat. § 27-14-105(b) (LEXIS 1999).

57. Wyo. Stat. § 27-14-105(a) (LEXIS 1999).

58. *Clarke v. Beckwith,* 858 P.2d 293 (Wyo. 1993).

59. *Id.*

60. *Thunder Hawk by and through Jensen v. Union Pacific R. Co.,* 844 P.2d 1045 (Wyo. 1992).

61. Wyo. Stat. § 12-8-301 (LEXIS 1999).

62. *McClellan v. Tottenhoff,* 666 P.2d 408 (Wyo. 1983).

63. *Id.*

64. Wyo. Stat. § 12-5-502 (LEXIS 1999).

65. *Rissler & McMurry Co. v. Sheridan Area Water Supply Joint Powers,* 929 P.2d 1228 (Wyo. 1996).

66. *Id.*

67. *Duffy v. Brown,* 708 P.2d 433 (Wyo. 1985).

68. *Jurkovich v. Tomlinson,* 905 P.2d 409 (Wyo. 1995).

69. *Verschoor v. Mountain West Farm Bureau Mutual Insurance Co.,* 907 P.2d 1293 (Wyo. 1995).

70. *Richey v. Patrick*, 904 P.2d 798 (Wyo. 1995) (citing Restatement (Second) of Torts § 552(1) (1977)).

71. *Sundown, Inc. v. Pearson Estate Co., Inc.*, 8 P.3d 324 (Wyo. 2000).

72. Wyo. Stat. §§ 26-13-101, *et seq.* (LEXIS 1999).

73. Wyo. Stat. §§ 40-12-101, *et seq.* (LEXIS 1999).

74. Wyo. Stat. § 40-12-102(a)(vii) (LEXIS 1999).

75. Wyo. Stat. § 40-12-108 (LEXIS 1999).

76. Wyo. Stat. § 40-12-109 (LEXIS 1999).

77. *Parker v. Artery*, 889 P.2d 520 (Wyo. 1995).

78. *Bird v. Rozier*, 948 P.2d 888 (Wyo. 1997).

79. *Danculovich v. Brown*, 593 P.2d 187 (Wyo. 1979).

80. *Weaver v. Mitchell*, 715 P.2d 1361 (Wyo. 1986).

81. *Errington v. Zolessi*, 9 P.3d 966 (Wyo. 2000).

82. 517 U.S. 559, 116 S. Ct. 1589, 134 L. Ed. 2d 809 (1996).

83. *Farmers Insurance Exchange v. Shirley*, 958 P.2d 1040 (Wyo. 1998).

84. Wyo. Stat. §§ 1-38-101, *et seq.* (LEXIS 1999).

85. Wyo. Stat. § 2-4-101 (LEXIS 1999).

86. Wyo. Stat. § 1-38-102(c) (LEXIS 1999).

87. *Gates v. Richardson*, 719 P.2d 193 (Wyo. 1986).

88. Wyo. Stat. § 1-38-102(d) (LEXIS 1999).

89. *Farmers Ins. Exchange v. Dahlheimer*, 3 P.3d 820 (Wyo. 2000).

90. Wyo. Stat. §§ 1-4-101, *et seq.* (LEXIS 1999).

91. *DeHerrera v. Herrera*, 565 P.2d 479 (Wyo. 1977).

92. *Id.*